Local Council
Administration

	HOUSE OF COMMONS LIBRARY
LOCATION	Pcc 352.14
AUTHOR	CLAYDEN
Acc DATE	0 9 JAN 2014

D1388314

BY AUTHOR

House of Commons Library

5405600124054

Also by Charles Arnold-Baker:

The Local Government Act 1972
The Local Government Planning and Land Act 1980
The Five Thousand and the Living Constitution
Practical Law for Arts Administrators
The Companion to British History (revised edn, 2001)

Local Council Administration

In English Parishes and Welsh Communities

Ninth Edition

CHARLES ARNOLD-BAKER OBE
of the Inner Temple, Barrister-at-law
and

PAUL CLAYDEN
Solicitor

Chief executives of the National Association of Local Councils respectively from 1953 to 1978 and from 1995 to 1998

 LexisNexis®

Members of the LexisNexis Group worldwide

United Kingdom	LexisNexis, a Division of Reed Elsevier (UK) Ltd, Halsbury House, 35 Chancery Lane, London WC2A 1EL, and London House, 20–22 East London Street, Edinburgh EH7 4BQ
Australia	LexisNexis Butterworths, Chatswood, New South Wales
Austria	LexisNexis Verlag ARD Orac GmbH & Co KG, Vienna
Benelux	LexisNexis Benelux, Amsterdam
Canada	LexisNexis Canada, Markham, Ontario
China	LexisNexis China, Beijing and Shanghai
France	LexisNexis SA, Paris
Germany	LexisNexis Deutschland GmbH, Munster
Hong Kong	LexisNexis Hong Kong, Hong Kong
India	LexisNexis India, New Delhi
Italy	Giuffrè Editore, Milan
Japan	LexisNexis Japan, Tokyo
Malaysia	Malayan Law Journal Sdn Bhd, Kuala Lumpur
New Zealand	LexisNexis NZ Ltd, Wellington
Poland	Wydawnictwo Prawnicze LexisNexis Sp, Warsaw
Singapore	LexisNexis Singapore, Singapore
South Africa	LexisNexis Butterworths, Durban
USA	LexisNexis, Dayton, Ohio

First published in 1975

© Reed Elsevier (UK) Ltd 2013

Published by LexisNexis

All rights reserved. No part of this publication may be reproduced in any material form (including photocopying or storing it in any medium by electronic means and whether or not transiently or incidentally to some other use of this publication) without the written permission of the copyright owner except in accordance with the provisions of the Copyright, Designs and Patents Act 1988 or under the terms of a licence issued by the Copyright Licensing Agency Ltd, Saffron House, 6–10 Kirby Street, London EC1N 8TS. Applications for the copyright owner's written permission to reproduce any part of this publication should be addressed to the publisher.
Warning: The doing of an unauthorised act in relation to a copyright work may result in both a civil claim for damages and criminal prosecution.

Crown copyright material is reproduced with the permission of the Controller of HMSO and the Queen's Printer for Scotland. Parliamentary copyright material is reproduced with the permission of the Controller of Her Majesty's Stationery Office on behalf of Parliament. Any European material in this work which has been reproduced from EUR-lex, the official European Communities legislation website, is European Communities copyright.
A CIP Catalogue record for this book is available from the British Library.

ISBN for this volume: ISBN 13: 9781405774055

Printed and bound by Hobbs the Printers Ltd, Totton, Hampshire

Visit LexisNexis at www.lexisnexis.co.uk

To the Knowledgeable Amateurs Without Whom Democracy is Impossible

Special textual expressions used in this book

To avoid wearisome repetition and constant qualification the following expedients have been used:

The expression 'local council' means 'parish and community council', and accordingly 'locality' means 'parish and community'.

'Electors' meeting' means 'parish and community meeting'.

The symbol 'T'

The symbol 'T' (standing for transfer): structural changes at principal area level resulted in the consequential transfer of functions from district to county or (in Wales) county borough councils, or in England, vice versa. Hence, in Wales, the word 'district' must after 1 April 1996 be read as 'county or county borough'. In England the structural changes were not all effective at the same time and the words 'district' and 'county' retained their previous meanings for some time; alternatively 'district' may be read as 'county' or 'county' as 'district', depending on the local outcome of the reviews. Thus, where functions are attributed to a district or county council, it must be born in mind that they may have been transferred. The relevant passages are marked 'T', but further changes of this type are not expected.

The symbol 'W'

The Government of Wales Act 1998 provided for the progressive transfer of ministerial functions to the National Assembly for Wales. Where this is known to have been done the relevant passages in Part I are marked 'W'.

Preface

The problems which faced me when I became Secretary of the National Association of Parish (now Local) Councils in 1953 were very different at the legal and geographical, let alone the social, level from those which existed when I left it 26 years later. In particular, though the Association had been providing its members with an, especially legal, advisory service, there was no modern book in which the necessary material could be found. The volume of requests and correspondence was vast and because of the absence of a reliable canon of information, consumed time which might, in those disturbing times, be put to better use. I resolved, as much for my own information as for my correspondents', to write such a book in the hope that the councils would acquire copies of it and so reduce their demands upon my then tiny office. The two first editions appeared under the name *Parish Administration*. The change to the present title came with the Association's change of name in 1972. Nominally this is the seventh edition, but really it is the ninth.

The problems have, of course, changed again and, on the legal side, have called for successive revisions of the book. On the social and geographical side every village in the land has been affected by the growing dependence upon the internal combustion engine, the invasion of the heavy goods vehicle and by migration. Less than 10 per cent of rural dwellers now live in the place where they were born. If village life is not to disintegrate altogether, there must be a more self-conscious mode of organising it than has hitherto existed.

The necessary reappraisal has been forced upon rural society cumulatively, as by the pressure of a rising tide. The changes will, I believe, continue. Word processing, and cable and facsimile and screen transmission may render large town offices unnecessary, for many who now work in them will be able to work at home and communicate face-to-face from their desks. This in its turn may cause a migration of shopping facilities and catering out of the urban centres. All this, the threatened abolition of a tier of local government and much more, will increase the social importance of the local council. The rising numbers of these councils perhaps indicate the shape of things to come. Well over a thousand have been created since 1974.

Meanwhile legislation continues. Local government has experienced the effects of the council tax, and there has been the controversy about restrictions on the official promotion of homosexuality, but to these parliamentary issues must now be added the incursion of legislation originating in Brussels. The interminably-named *Town and Country Planning (Assessment of Environmental Effects) Regulations 1988* were issued to comply with EEC Council Directive 85/337. An impartial observer may feel surprised that the Council of the then EEC should, or indeed lawfully could, concern itself with the procedural details of planning processes in its member states. Obviously its activities need to be closely watched not only by national governments and political bodies, but by the local authority associations and their international alliances.

This in turn draws attention to the acceleration and widening scope of law-making by departmental order. *Parish Administration*, published in 1958, needed only five pages for such orders. The reader may care to compare this with the Appendix of Statutory Instruments in this edition. Moreover the provisions of the older statutory instruments were mostly of minor effect. By contrast, s 119 of the Local Government Finance Act 1988 conferred power upon the Secretary of State to amend references to rates and rateable values in existing public and private Acts by substituting 'some factor other than the one connected with rating'. This enormous ministerial power is not more precisely defined. It affects many widely separated matters.

It is a commonplace that the life and shape of smaller settlements is changing rapidly, and with it, necessarily, the parochial and communal system which reflects them. There would be less paper, less distraction and probably less expense if our law on these things were more generalised and adaptable. Local councils should be empowered to do as they please and leave it to common sense and their own economics to do what is right. This is the principle of French and other European local systems, which are not, in consequence, half-throttled by legalism. The 'free resource' (or rather its predecessors, the 'free two pence' and the 'free fifth') was the fruit of foreign precedents, and probably saved the local councils during the dangerous time of the Redcliffe-Maude Commission. The international sharing of experience is vital to progress, even to survival.

At the other end of the spectrum, there are great changes of local practice and personnel. It is a far cry from the old ecclesiastical parish clerk who was supposed to be able to 'read and write, and, if possible, sing', to the well organised and versatile village administrator now, with his word processor and answer-phone and his Cheltenham qualification in local policy, who is increasingly in evidence; and, despite the rigidities in the law, local councils continue to show much enterprise and originality. As a result of forty-odd years of correspondence with them and the many who have kindly made suggestions for this book, its content is not exclusively legal nor confined solely to local councils.

Moreover, the work of local councils is obstructed by constant changes in the law. In the 1997 edition we expressed surprise at the number of changes since 1994, but substantially the layout of this work had remained the same since the first edition some fifty years ago. In 2002 we had to re-organise it. Users of previous editions will find that this is a very different work from the last. We do not apologise for this: we place the responsibility squarely upon restless governments and ambitious administrators.

Consistently with this, we must again draw attention to an important and, in our view, malign trend. The reforms of 1972 and later years have destroyed much of the elected content of our system. About seventeen-thousand elective seats have been abolished with the destruction of the municipal corporations, small districts and two-tier principal government. There are equivalents elsewhere: elected traffic commissioners, for example, have gone, and bodies for entertaining complaints against public services seem less than independent. It is becoming doubtful if the public is properly in control of its own affairs.

In principal councils, as too in the House of Commons, the members do not (save by accident) represent communities, but electoral aggregations designed for numerical similarity rather than human quality. These aggregations are mostly too large for their representatives to supervise in detail, while local councils, aided by advertising, increasingly focus opinion on branches of a system not their own. The local council is becoming important because of what it thinks of other authorities, and, in the words of the late Professor Brian Keith-Lucas, Chairman of the National Association of Local Councils, to the Redcliffe-Maude Commission, their increasingly important function is 'to raise hell'.

Like it or not, the local councillor is becoming the last democratic survivor.

Acknowledgment

I would like to have thanked Ann Rowen, MBE for her work in typing the manuscript of the 1981 edition. However, sadly, she died just before the previous one was published.

Charles Arnold-Baker

Temple

Note on the ninth edition

Since the publication of the eighth edition, the original author of this book, Charles Arnold-Baker OBE, has died. As secretary of the National Association of Local Councils from 1953 to 1978, he probably did more than any other individual to give local councils a proper voice in the national forum of local government. As a result, local councils today have more powers and influence than ever before. They have shown that they are competent and confident in taking the lead in local affairs.

Although only four years have passed since the eighth edition, a new edition is warranted to cover the many changes in the law since April 2009 with direct application to local councils. These include: (1) the Localism Act 2011, which applies only to England so far as it relates to local councils. The Act re-writes the legislation covering codes of conduct and the declaration of pecuniary interests, confers powers on "eligible" parish councils to adopt a general power of competence, introduces the concept of neighbourhood planning and confers a right on local communities to bid for community assets (e.g. recreational buildings) when the owners wish to dispose of them; parish councils can pay a key role in preparation of neighbourhood plans and in the acquisition of community assets; (2) revised accounts and audit regulations (the Accounts and Audit Regulations 2011) in England; (3) a consolidation of charity law into the Charities Act 2011; (4) the Equality Act 2010, which broadens the scope of the law against discrimination, and, in Wales only, the conferring on community councils the power to promote well-being. In Wales, the powers of the National Assembly to legislate on Welsh matters have been widened. The Local Government (Wales) Measure 2011 and the Welsh Language (Wales) Measure 2011 affect community councils. One effect of the widening of the legislative powers of the Assembly has been to increase the differences between the legal powers and constitutional arrangements of parish and community councils.

As well as the foregoing, many detailed changes to regulations and orders have been made.

The law is stated at 1 April 2013.

Paul Clayden

Henley-on-Thames

March 2013

Contents

References are to paragraph numbers.

Contents

Contents

Contents

Contents

Contents

Contents

Abbreviations used in this book

A	Act
AA	Allotments Act
ACA	Audit Commission Act
AMC	Association of Municipal Corporations
BA	Burial Act
CA	Charities Act
DEFRA	Department for Environment, Food and Rural Affairs
E	(see Appendix I)
F	Finance
FP	Financial Provisions
GDO	General Development Order
HA	Highways Act
LAMIT	Local Authorities Mutual Investment Trust
LG	Local Government
LG&HA	Local Government and Housing Act
LG&RA	Local Government and Rating Act
LGPS	Local Government Pensions Scheme
MP	Miscellaneous Provisions
NALC	National Association of Local Councils
ODPM	Office of the Deputy Prime Minister
OS	Open Spaces
P	(see Appendix I)

Abbreviations used in this book

PAWA	Public Audit (Wales) Act 2004
PC	Parish Councils
PH	Public Health
PLA	Poor Law Amendment
PSWC	Private Street Works Code
PWL	Public Works Loans
RP	Representation of the People
RT	Road Traffic
RV	Rating and Valuation
SH	Small Holdings
SLCC	Society of Local Council Clerks
T	(see previous page)
TCP	Town and Country Planning
W	(see previous page)

Table of Statutes

M

N

O

Table of Statutory Instruments

W

Table of European Legislation

Table of Cases

A

B

K

L

M

N

O

P

R

S

T

V

W

Part I

MATTERS COMMON TO ENGLAND AND WALES

Chapter 1
HISTORY

A ORIGINS

1.1 The origin of most English parishes and Welsh communities is the same as that of the manors which commonly formed their nucleus and with which they were often conterminous; in an era when money was seldom used and trade an abnormal activity, when agriculture was primitive, when the countryside was nearly empty of inhabitants and largely virgin, and when no effective central authority existed to enforce daily order, the manor was simultaneously a collective farm, a unit of local administration and police and a defensive organisation. Its inhabitants were the lord and his family, his retainers headed by the steward, and the free and unfree tenants, and they were bound to each other by a network of obligations and services. Naturally these varied from place to place but the way in which they were regulated was determined by committees or assemblies known as courts and held by the lord or the steward. The most important of these were the Court Baron for the free tenants and the Court Customary for the unfree. The lord was under an obligation to hold them regularly and the tenants were bound to attend. Their principal, and in a moneyless society, their all-important business was the management of the land, the rotation of agriculture and the regulation of agricultural jobs.

The commonest agricultural organisation consisted of an open field in which the tenants had their holdings, a waste or common in which each tenant was entitled to certain rights (such as pasture) and a demesne or 'home farm' belonging to the lord and upon which some tenants were bound to do a certain amount of work in each year. A tenant's holding was not consolidated, but was divided into strips scattered about the open field and intermingled with the holdings of the other tenants. After the harvest all the cattle were pastured upon the open field indiscriminately so that the holdings would benefit equally. Obviously such a system was likely to keep the Courts Baron and Customary well occupied settling disputes and services, and equally it was a system which required a simple administrative apparatus and a local criminal jurisdiction for its enforcement. Since officials could not be paid, officialdom was a duty rather than a profession: the constable, the hayward, the pinder and other officials were elected annually and laid down their offices with a sigh of relief. The criminal jurisdiction was vested in the Court Leet. Some manors had their own Leets but in many cases towards the later middle ages a Leet was held for a group of manors under one lordship. In some manors the functions of the Courts Leet and Baron were exercised by the same body.

Sometimes the priest came with the first settlers. More usually he arrived after the manor was established. Initially he came as the representative of his bishop and often as a missionary, but he could not live upon the manor unless he was given a holding, and he could not have a church unless the manor provided the labour and the materials with which to build it. At the beginning the lord was in a strong position and so the right to appoint the priest often passed into his hands, but the priest nevertheless kept a certain independence because he had the (sometimes very distant) support of the Church, which soon became more powerful than the greatest noble in the realm.

The lord's power rested originally on force restrained by local opinion which hardened first into custom and then into a local law which the King's new circuit courts would enforce. A custom is by definition inflexible and immovable, but agriculture moved steadily forward leaving the customs and the manor courts which enforced them behind. This process was accelerated by the improvement in communications, by increased trade in manufactured goods, by the circulation of money and the consequent commutation of labour services for cash, by ever-increasing external interference in manorial and parochial affairs, and by the Black Death and the social upheavals which followed it. When the first Tudor ascended the throne the manor courts had already ceased to be important, though they survived (mainly for conveyancing purposes) well into the twentieth century.

As the manor courts declined, the influence, wealth and responsibility of the Church increased. The chancel of the parish church was sacred, but the body of the building was the parish hall and the only sheltered public meeting place of the inhabitants. The Church as an organisation had recognised rights and also obligations of Christian charity. The parson was paid by means of the tithe, which was a local income tax levied in kind on the produce of land. He combined in his person the offices of schoolmaster, registrar and religious adviser. Attendance at church was normal and enforceable. At Easter everybody went.

It is, therefore, not surprising that the inhabitants began to meet together under the parson's direction for the social and administrative purposes of their religious life. Such meetings were often held in the vestry after which they came to be named. The old civil obligation of the lord of the manor to maintain his starving tenants was matched by the religious obligations of charity. Here again facts outran institutions. The Church and especially the monasteries came to administer the only generally recognised system of unemployment relief, and it was the parson's duty to enjoin almsgiving and the succour of the poor upon his flock. Charity, however, remained a virtue and its organisation local. It was essential that the burden should be evenly spread, and as early as the fourteenth century attempts were made to make vagrancy a crime. The dissolution of the monasteries and the improvement in communications made the voluntary system unworkable. It was accordingly quite natural for the legislators of 1601 to confer upon the vestries the power of levying a poor rate: in so doing they were merely strengthening machinery which existed already, and which was in their mind proper to the relief of poverty and the exercise of charity.

But meetings of inhabitants in an expanding population have an inherent disadvantage; they became unwieldily large and so, especially but by no means exclusively, in urban areas authority tended to slip into the hands of smaller committees called select vestries which claimed a separate existence by immemorial custom and which often were self-perpetuating. These bodies could be administratively more efficient than the open vestries and so their number was increased by public and private legislation, but in the absence of a powerful and impartial auditing system they became notoriously corrupt. By the Napoleonic Wars this latter characteristic had become important because the vestries were beginning to administer huge sums of money. By 1819 they were levying rates which in the aggregate exceeded £10 million a year—in real terms about a hundred times the total precepted in 1966–67; a reform was demanded and attempted: the Sturges Bourne Act enabled an open vestry, by adopting the Act, to create an annually elected committee (also called a select vestry) to administer poor relief.

Meanwhile the countryside was being transformed by inclosures. The manors had resembled islands of cultivation in a sea of common or unenclosed waste which was subject to public or quasi-public rights; the modernisation of agriculture ended the older collective methods of farming. Private ownership spread across the wastes, and the commoners of the manor were compensated for their extinguished rights with smallholdings and allotments for food, fuel, stone and recreation. Such allotments existed mainly for the relief of poverty, and it was as natural to place them under the control of the vestry as it had been to enable that same vestry to raise poor rates. The inclosure awards, in redistributing property, made extensive redistributions of public obligations and usually committed their supervision to the vestries. As a result the awards became, and in many places still are, the fundamental documents of parish or community administration.

The vestry was in origin an ecclesiastical institution and depended for its efficacy upon religious unity. The damage done to the reputation of the ancient parochial system by its amateurishness and occasional corruption was completed by the Methodist revival. In hundreds of parishes the representative of the established church had to preside over an assembly composed mainly or wholly of people who were actively hostile to that church. Over extensive areas the church rate ceased to be levied; it was abolished in 1868 and parish administration was reduced to the barest legal minimum. The critics who prized efficiency above democracy found unexpected allies in the democratic assemblies themselves and the glaring injustices inherent in the working of the Poor Law cried out for reform. From the third decade of the nineteenth century onwards public opinion turned, on the whole, against the parish. The Poor Law Act of 1834 withdrew much of the poor law administration from the parochial authorities, and as new administrative services were created to meet the increasing elaboration of society, they were committed as a rule to specialised bodies. The technique of organising these services on a comprehensive basis had not been learned. Local government, notorious in the 1820s for inefficiency and corruption, became notorious half a century later for inefficiency and complication. The confusion was spectacular and required twenty years of legislation and experiment to straighten out. The coping stone of the new edifice was the Local Government Act 1894. This took a year to pass and excited much controversy both in Parliament and outside; Gladstone's government had to deal with over 800 amendments; it was the proposal to create parish councils which caused the uproar.

In relation to parish affairs the Act of 1894 was based upon two apparently simple principles. First it created institutions having a civil origin, status and affiliations—the parish meeting and the parish council. Second, it transferred the civil functions of the older parish authorities to the new institutions. As a result the church was excluded from formal participation in local government, and the traditional functions of the parish, which had always had a 'Christian' complexion, were to be administered by laymen. This caused perturbation and acrimony at the time, and it was expected that the new parish councils would embark upon a stormy career. Events, however, belied expectations. Parish councils fell rapidly into an undeserved obscurity from which they began to emerge only 60 years later.

In 1894 the squire, the parson and sometimes the schoolmaster were the leaders of the village. Their influence depended upon their traditional prestige, their superior education and their relative wealth, and, in a hierarchical society, upon their social standing. The vestries had followed their lead, taken their advice or bowed to their power. The parish councils were regarded as an intrusion. Most of them began without the co-operation of the influential, and had even to face their active opposition. This, in an age when higher education was the privilege of a class, was a serious matter.

But their difficulties had only begun. In the 1870s agriculture entered upon the long decline which only ended with the Second World War. The squire maintained his state on industrial investments. The revenues of parish councils came mainly from rates on agricultural land. Within 18 months of their creation agricultural land was derated by 50 per cent without compensation. Until 1914 parish councils were locally opposed, often derided and poor. Nevertheless Parliament from time to time saw fit to increase their functions, and it was in this period that they acquired their modern powers in relation to allotments, postal facilities and open spaces. The inconsistent currents of government policy (of which these early events are examples) are mainly responsible for the peculiar history of twentieth-century parish administration: the tendency (it can scarcely be called a policy) to give new functions to parish councils whilst reducing their financial assets was exaggerated during the period of the wars. Their spending powers, already attenuated by inflation, were again reduced (as usual without compensation) by still further de-rating and by the new administrative methods introduced for collecting rates from nationalised industries. Until the 1970s financial legislation was mostly passed without regard to the interests of the localities.

In the meantime their position in English social life had altered. The sons of the Big House went away to the wars and were killed. Taxation uprooted the squires and impoverished the clergy, and educational policy began to drive the schoolmasters away from the villages. On the other hand the general standard both of living and of education rose and the commuter appeared. The old internal quarrels have died a natural death and new problems have had to be faced.

The characteristics of modern government are determined largely by the enormous growth and movement of population, and by the nature of the equipment proper to an industrial organisation. Facts have again outrun institutions and the powers which are needed for the administration of the new society have for the most part been conferred upon new ad hoc authorities or upon authorities exercising their functions over substantial areas. From a strictly administrative standpoint the parish councils remained the repositories of powers appropriate to an earlier stage in the development of society. This did not, of course, mean that parish councils were obsolete since these powers are still necessary now, but it did mean that parish councils, in common with all other types of local authority, had to consider how they as institutions could be squared with the requirements of the new age.

In local government perhaps the most significant single modern development was the creation of local authority associations whose principal function was to consider, formulate and represent policies on national administration from the standpoint of a particular class of authority. These associations were a characteristically modern reaction to the modern situation; the earliest, that of the municipal corporations, was formed in 1873; the latest, the National Association of Local (then Parish) Councils, in 1947. Individuals and individual bodies in the modern mass democracy have little chance of defending their peculiar interest unless they combine with others of like mind. It was largely due to the associations that local government retained its local character, and it is largely due to the fact that parish councils formed their own half a century later than the others that parish administration was still comparatively primitive. Until an organisation existed for the purpose it was not possible to rethink the relationship between the small community and modern society or to convert into effective action any conclusions which might have been reached.

The Second World War brought utopianism into many departments of life, and from 1942 onwards discussion raged about the future of government. Local authorities were not immune to these controversies, and the four then existing associations began discussions at the time. Accordingly the post-war government appointed the Local Government Boundary Commission because it was believed that the problems were geographical. The commission's preliminary findings soon disabused the government of that fallacy. It said that it could not properly perform its geographical task without power to reallocate functions and without some influence over finance. Aneurin Bevan, the responsible minister, took fright and dissolved the commission. What the politicians rejected, the technicians made the headstone of the corner. The associations tried again. They soon fell out, because the relationship between functions and finance on the one hand, and geography on the other, drove the champions into opposing camps. The Association of Municipal Corporations (AMC) and those who favoured efficiency and co-ordination held up the former county boroughs as their model, and proposed a reorganisation based upon a substantial number of areas organised like them. Those who remembered the great recent achievements of local government and represented authorities likely to be abolished by any such scheme doubted the need for such a drastic remedy. The County, Rural District and Urban District Councils Associations were of this opinion. They proposed a rearrangement of powers and geography based upon the existing principle of specialisation of powers.

During the war the then National Council of Social Service, encouraged by the Development Commission, began to speculate on ways of encouraging leadership and enterprise in the countryside, now reviving through the accidents of war from its long debility. One of the many proposals was an advisory service for parish councils which, for the most part, could not afford professional advice at their own expense. Their advisory committee soon attracted recruits, subscriptions and a demand for the creation of a parish councils association. By 1947 there were about 1,000 councils affiliated to the committee. A national association was launched which, by 1952, could speak for about half of the existing parish councils. This was better than no bread, and it was just in time.

The assumption upon which almost everyone approached reform was that authorities should be larger and that there should be fewer of them. This, of course, seemed to imply that whatever else the outcome, the extinction of the 7,000 parish councils was now certain. They had, after all, been abolished in Scotland in 1929.

The parish councils organisation did not, however, see the issues in this light. The controversies were primarily administrative and financial, but parish councils had not for some decades been primarily administrative authorities, nor could they be said to create a major financial problem. It could with equal force be argued that whatever administrative and financial solutions were reached, the continuance of parish councils could not prejudice them. Their prime function, it was said, was to 'focus village opinion', to represent such opinion to the outside world, as well as to carry out on a small scale those local tasks which would be uninteresting or uneconomic for the larger authorities.

It happened that in 1952 there was a final breach between the AMC and the other three associations. A Labour government might come to power, based upon the large urban electorates which the AMC also represented. The other three felt themselves in danger and sought alliance and help. It was in these circumstances that the National Association of Parish Councils (NAPC) was wooed as a potential supporter of the county and district councils and so found itself, rather breathless, in the main stream of the national discussions.

Though ready to support on general grounds of principle the proposals put forward by the three associations, the parish councils organisation never abdicated its right to speak with their opponents. This was proper in a political dispensation where changes of party government were the only certainty. It soon found that the AMC had never been hostile to the parish council concept. As could soon be gathered from the rival manifestoes, the continuance of the parish council turned out to be the only point upon which the two sides agreed.

The details of the negotiations and manoeuvres which led to the passing of the Local Government Act 1972 are not germane to the subject of this book, but certain features of the story are. The financial and human size of the issues between the factions were so great that little government time or civil service talent could be spared for the increasingly exasperating but admittedly small-scale problems of the parishes. The law which Parliament had made about them, before they had their own association, had been made speculatively and often without proper advice or knowledge. Legal confusion[1], accountancy traps[2], and obstruction[3] and even nonsensical rules abounded[4]. The NAPC therefore undertook, simultaneously with the reform negotiations, a programme of change through public and private members' bills in Parliament—for which the climate happened to be propitious. A clause on bus shelters in the Local Government (Miscellaneous Provisions) Act 1953 was the first fruit of this policy. The Parish Councils Act 1957 conferred some powers and abolished some of the more absurd controls. The Physical Training and

Recreation Act 1958 ironed out one particular anomaly, and three sections in the Town and Country Planning Act 1959 another. The Local Government (Miscellaneous Provisions) Act 1963 allowed parish councils to spend a minute sum at their discretion for the benefit of the parish. Modest though the scale of these various operations was, their cumulative effect not only on parish councils but on parliamentary and public attitudes was noticeable. The NAPC undertook a programme of continental research and discovered to everybody's surprise that the powers of the *communes* and *gemeinden* (the local equivalents of parishes) in France, some Swiss cantons and to a lesser degree in Austria were controlled not by enforceable legal definitions and *ultra vires* rules but only by the practical pressure of economics which, of course, varied both with the size, population and resources of each unit. This bore a very tender but significant fruit.

The Conservative Local Government Act 1958 did not so much reform the system as create a machine for doing so. It followed (with some variations) the policy proposed by the County Councils Association. Unfortunately the machine was heavily geared down by a procedural system which prevented movement above a snail's pace. By 1965, with Labour again in power, too little had been done. In particular, because parish geography was always the last in the queue for treatment; a thorough-going modern appraisal of parish boundaries was achieved, alone of all counties, in Shropshire where, also, the new and short-lived concept of the rural borough made its first appearance. These boroughs were small ancient boroughs converted into parish councils with ceremonial trappings, corporate property and a few special powers. Only Bishops Castle, Bridgnorth, Ludlow, Much Wenlock and Oswestry in Shropshire, Lostwithiel in Cornwall and South Molton in Devon ever saw the light of day.

In 1965 the Labour government decided to wind up the machinery of 1958, and set up the celebrated Royal Commission on Local Government under the Chairmanship of Lord Redcliffe-Maude. The commission was distinguished in its membership and allowed to listen to and recommend anything which did not touch finance. Its report, and the dissenting memorandum by Mr Derek Senior published in 1969, provided one of the few local government sensations of the twentieth century. They proposed a two-tier system in which the major or unitary authority wielded all the defined statutory powers possessed hitherto by county, borough and district councils, and in which, on the continental model, the minor or local council was to be empowered on a parochial scale to do what it pleased for its people. Endorsement of the small community principle from such a very distinguished quarter did much to raise it in public esteem. The government accepted the report but was promptly overthrown. It seems likely that its proposal to abolish the counties had some influence on the relevant general election, but the outcome did the small community council no harm.

When the Conservatives returned to power they inherited an undertaking to reform local government but not along the lines of the Redcliffe-Maude report. The undertaking referred mainly to the larger authorities, the improvement in the position of the local councils being taken for granted. Thus the issue was not whether they should be abolished, but the extent to which they should benefit. A comparison of the pre-1972 legislation with the Bill for the Act of

1972 revealed very important changes. Even more were made during the Bill's passage through Parliament. For these improvements their association was very largely responsible.

1 The general law on burials was contained in 17 Acts and parts of 61 others.
2 The method of calculating the limits on expenditure was based upon a penny rate product computed differently from any other penny rate product.
3 A parish council was not allowed to accumulate funds for a capital purpose.
4 The clerk of the rural district council paid for elections and claimed his outlay from the parish council. The parish council precepted upon the RDC for the money. The RDC paid the parish council. The parish council then paid the clerk of the RDC.

B   LOCAL COUNCILS AT AND AFTER 1974

1.2 The 'administrative' parish existed exclusively in the former rural districts. There were about 7,600 parish councils in England and Wales immediately before 1 April 1974, and 3,200 parishes without parish councils. Populations of parishes varied from 2 to 36,000 and penny rate products from £3 to £66,000; for parishes with parish councils the lowest population was 102 and the lowest penny rate product £90. There were about 63,000 parish councillors and total expenditure from the rates was about £4,500,000.

The principal feature of parish administration until that date was the strait waistcoat of controls under which it had to operate. Some functions could not be exercised at all without the consent of the parish meeting; their consent, as well as that of the government, had to be obtained to borrow money or dispose of property. Though there were certain cases (based on no known principle) where expenditure was not limited by law, outside these, aggregate expenditure in excess of a 1.7p rate required the consent of the meeting, and the Secretary of State's consent was needed for more than 3.3p. A controversial parish meeting might easily end up with an electors' poll three weeks later. As if this were not enough there were special limits, so to speak, inside the general limit on particular items. For example, not more than 0.6p could be spent on a war memorial, no matter who consented.

The psychological damage which these restrictions did was always serious. It was not merely that they might induce an unenterprising frame of mind; they could not be enforced save through a mass of technical and pettifogging rules whose main effect was to trap the innocent but unwary. It was quite extraordinary how many formalities accompanied some simple idea like acquiring a cemetery.

The practical damage was capable of being even more serious. The parish councils were prevented by law from acting on the promptings of foresight normal in private and business life. They could not, for example, establish depreciation funds or buy land in advance of a clearly defined requirement; nor could they appear at a planning or transport inquiry affecting all the village, unless they had a legal interest of their own to defend as a landowner[1].

Despite these absurdities, the useful work done by the parish councils increased steadily after the Second World War. Many of them refused to be deterred, and either found ways to circumvent the law or were able by persistence to get the necessary sanctions. There is no doubt that the legal and practical advisory service provided by their association played a part in this:

but the achievement of results only in particular instances resembled the slow erosion of an essentially Victorian system, when what was needed was radical reform. This was achieved, with limitations, only in 1972.

On 1 April 1974, as a result of the Local Government Act 1972, the English and Welsh localities began as institutions to drift apart, the English continuing with their original name, the Welsh becoming statutory communities with slightly altered attributes, while in both countries the councils became entitled, if they wished, to call themselves a town council and their chairman the town mayor. Not many did so. Their work and functions remained alike but a special review by a Welsh Local Government Boundary Commission established a definitive Welsh geography which in theory the district councils could alter if they pleased, while sporadic, often reluctant reviews by English district councils over the next eighteen years, created many, if haphazardly distributed, new councils. This English process came to a halt in 1992 when the power to review was transferred to a new English Local Government Commission designed to reduce the number of principal tiers in local government from two to one and which might deal with parishes only incidentally to this main purpose. In any case this commission's functions, save the power to alter the electoral cycle, were transferred back to the Electoral Commission in 2001. In 1993 a Bill was introduced to reorganise Welsh local government by abolishing the districts on 1 April 1996. The result in both countries was a practical moratorium on changes in the geography of the localities. In Wales the special review has reduced the importance of this, but in England it was plain that demographic changes, notably outward migration from the big cities, would in the end force a government to bring the moratorium to an end.

This happened sooner than might have been expected. The Local Government and Rating Act 1997 was passed to facilitate the creation of new parishes either after a review or on petition by parish electors. Almost incidentally it conferred some new powers concerned with public transport, traffic calming and crime prevention. It also empowered the Secretary of State to designate subjects upon which principal councils will be obliged to consult them. This brought the basic law almost into line with the law since 1994 in Wales where, however, the Government of Wales Act 1998 provided for the transfer to the new National Assembly of many functions of the Secretary of State; it imposed upon it an obligation to frame a local government scheme[2] and created a Partnership Council[3] composed of members of the Assembly and representatives of local authorities and their associations. The exact purpose of the scheme and the council is not stated in the Act. The first order made under the Act[4] transferred, as far as local government was concerned, mostly the minor provisions which had grown up since 1845 but not the wider elements of recent legislation such as the Local Government Act 1972.

In 1999, however, a danger sign appeared on the horizon. The Best Value schemes made under that year's Local Government Act and the Quality Parish Council Scheme of 2003, while offering inducements to larger local councils to adopt particular government ordained standards and to submit to their enforcement, effectively deprived them, once they had entered such a scheme, of their discretion and perhaps even their right to vote, on such matters. In these cases this reversed the hitherto accepted progress towards greater local freedom and variety based upon the NAPC (now the National Association of Local Councils) continental research.

In 2007 the Local Government and Public Involvement in Health Act of that year removed local councils from the ambit of the best value legislation, the change coming into force on 1 April 2008. The 2007 Act also extended the power to promote well-being, conferred on principal authorities by the Local Government Act 2000, to 'eligible' parish councils, ie those which met the criteria prescribed by the Secretary of State.

The coalition government established in May 2010 promised to devolve powers away from Whitehall to local authorities and local communities. The Localism Act 2011 provides the statutory basis for many changes to local council law and practice, relating almost exclusively to England. In Wales, the National Assembly has passed its own legislation which makes significant different provision for community councils. The divergence between the law relating to local councils in England and Wales, which began in 1974, has been greatly widened, and the trend is likely to continue.

[1] In one case a parish council had, successfully, to base its right to be heard at a Traffic Inquiry on a half share in a pond.
[2] Government of Wales Act 1998, s 113(1).
[3] Government of Wales Act 1998, s 113(2).
[4] National Assembly for Wales (Transfer of Functions) Order 1999, SI 1999/672.

Chapter 2

GENERAL DESCRIPTION OF THE SYSTEMS

A   TERMINOLOGY

2.1 Custom and statute have confused the technical language. Before 1 April 1974, there were three kinds of parishes, viz, the ecclesiastical parish which has a parochial church council and with which this book is only incidentally concerned; the urban parish which had no function save in the law of rating, and the rural parish which was an administrative unit with a parish council existing only in rural districts. After 31 March 1974, the ecclesiastical parish remained as before, parishes in Wales were replaced by communities, and in England the distinction between urban and rural parishes disappeared, all of them being styled simply parishes.

The word community has an unfortunate history. Used originally as a collective word for a group of settled human beings, it soon became the embodiment of an ideal to which service might be given. Consequently there arose voluntary organisations usually covering a county and called community or rural community councils. The Local Government Act 1972 terminated the legal existence of the Welsh parishes, urban districts and boroughs and converted them into statutory communities which closely resemble the English (civil) parishes, and whose councils are local authorities. The Local Government (Scotland) Act 1973 set up a different kind of community. This is a unit of parochial size with a community council which, though it exists by virtue of statute, is not a local authority at all, having neither powers nor access, as of right, to public funds. There are about 1,100 of them.

These changes induced the voluntary bodies above named to alter their designation, and since 1974 some have called themselves councils of voluntary organisations. The Local Government (Finance) Act 1988 and its earlier Scottish equivalent, however, abolished domestic rating and substituted a head tax. This was dignified with the title community charge, but here the word was not related to the statutory communities but (presumably) to the earlier service ideal. It was greeted with riots and, tax strikes having created vast arrears, it was replaced in 1993 by the compositely-based council tax.

In addition to the special textual expressions already explained, a local council can resolve to call itself a town council, in which case its area will in common parlance, if not in law, be called a town, and:

- 'parish' means an English civil parish;
- 'community' means a Welsh community created by the Local Government Act 1972;
- 'local authority' means any county, county borough, district, parish or Welsh community council, or any London borough council (see the Local Government Act 1972, s 270);
- 'principal council' means a county, county borough, or district council;
- 'non parochial place' means an English area outside London which is not a parish.

Finally there is the rural settlement. This is a place in or partly in an area designated as rural by the Secretary of State and appearing to the billing authority to have less than 3001 inhabitants on 31 December before the commencement of a financial year. Within it a general store selling food and household goods, and a post office, if, in either case there is only one, is entitled to considerable rate reductions if its rateable value does not exceed a prescribed amount. There is no requirement that the boundaries of such a settlement should coincide with those of a locality[1].

[1] Local Government Finance Act 1988, ss 42A, 43, 47, 48, 58, 148, representing amendments by the LGRA 1997.

B OFFICIAL BODIES AT THE CENTRE

2.2 In Wales the ministerial responsibility is exercised collectively in the National Assembly. The ministers particularly responsible for English local government to the Crown and Parliament are the Secretaries of State for Culture, Media and Sport, for Transport and for Communities and Local Government. The Home Office, the Departments for Business, Innovation and Skills, for Work and Pensions and for Environment, Food and Rural Affairs are also involved. The central direction, in so far as it relates to local government functions, is mainly indirect. The legislation of 1972, 1974 and 1980 abolished many of the 1,500 petty and less petty controls exercisable by government departments. They now influence local authorities through the grants system, tax capping, and the control of borrowing and capital investment, or less immediately, by the facility with which they can promote (or oppose) public legislation, or make statutory instruments, or, finally, by exhortation and advice contained in departmental circulars and guidance.

The departments' influence over the activities of the local authorities is exerted mainly through direct contact, but their oversight and influence on local authorities' constitutional structure has to be exerted through the respective Secretaries of State who consult their own Commissions.

The central machine contains or contained several other bodies of great interest to some, and often most, localities. The Rural Development Commission offered mainly small but useful grants to worthwhile projects which had local support. The Countryside Commission was concerned to protect rural amenities. These two bodies were combined into the Countryside Agency. The Agency has been split up again with its powers devolving the Commission for Rural Communities and Natural England (itself a successor to English Nature). The Forestry Commission grows timber, and controls the exploitation of woods by private developers. The Sports Council investigates and recommends development policies concerned with recreation. The Charity Commission controls the application of charitable trusts. The Public Works Loans Board acts as a reserve source of loan capital.

Details of addresses and websites of these bodies can be found in APPENDIX III.

C   UNOFFICIAL BODIES AT THE CENTRE

2.3 There are many professional and unofficial bodies with national status which matter to local government because they exert pressure or influence on the central official bodies, or because they provide specialist services and advice. A list of contacts appears in APPENDIX III below. The role of local authority associations has been mentioned in the previous chapter. Here it may be helpful to note some other organisations.

In the realm of amenities Civic Voice is interested in the appearance of towns, the Campaign to Protect Rural England and the Campaign for the Protection of Rural Wales in that of the countryside. The Society for the Protection of Ancient Buildings influentially supports the purposes which its name describes, and the National Trust preserves beautiful or interesting places and buildings by acquisition in the interests of the nation. In general it may be said that bodies of this kind deal with those parts of the government machine concerned, in a general sense, with the planning of land use. On the other hand the promotion of better standards of planning in general is the concern of the Town and Country Planning Association, while the Royal Town Planning Institute deals with the professional qualifications of planners.

Second, there are important organisations concerned with recreation. These include Fields in Trust (formerly known as the National Playing Fields Association), the Open Spaces Society, the Byways and Bridleways Trust, the Arboricultural Association, the Ramblers' Association, the Caravan Club, the Royal Yachting Association, the British Horse Society and the Amateur Swimming Association.

Third, social welfare has a great variety of interested bodies; these include the Citizens' Advice Bureaux, the National Council for Voluntary Organisations, which has a unit concerned with voluntary action in rural areas, Age Concern, ACRE (Action with Communities in Rural England), and the Welsh Council of Social Service.

Fourth, there are several organisations concerned with the promotion of the interests of small communities. Amongst these will be found the National Federation of Community Associations, the Association for Neighbourhood Democracy, and also the National Association of Local Councils.

Fifth, there are powerful women's organisations; the National Federation of Women's Institutes for the countryside, townswomen (the National Federation of Towns Women's Guilds) in urban areas.

Details of addresses and websites of these bodies can be found in APPENDIX III.

D   LOCAL GOVERNMENT BODIES

2.4 Wales is wholly divided into three types of area, namely counties, county boroughs and communities, and may have area committees. England outside London has five, and may have seven, namely counties, metropolitan and non-metropolitan districts, unitary county and unitary districts, parishes and non-parochial places. Communities and parishes differ legally, but for purposes of a general conspectus may be regarded as equivalents. The picture is further complicated because some districts are called boroughs, some communities and parishes have no councils, and parishes but not communities without councils have parish trustees, and some non-parochial places in districts which are not boroughs, have charter trustees. Finally, the councils of some parishes and communities are called town councils.

Most local authorities are constituted in the same way, with councillors elected by their local government electorate and a chairman who must be one of them. The chairman is called the mayor or lord mayor in a borough and the town mayor where there is a town council. In principle the period of office is four years, and local government elections were to take place on the same day, usually in May. Until the completion of the reforms and reviews, interim arrangements and the need to elect certain types of council by fractions created a transitional period, with some tenures of office varying from the norm. A few principal councils (currently 17) have mayors directly elected by local government electors.

Principal councils together exercise the same collection of functions, but the way in which those functions are divided between them differs as between England and Wales, and as between English metropolitan and non-metropolitan councils. In unitary English areas one council will exercise both sets of functions. These distinctions are important to local councils, who have to know to which principal authority suggestions, complaints or support should be addressed. The following table is intended to summarise the position. The entries in italics are cases where local councils themselves have powers:

(a)   non-metropolitan county and metropolitan district councils:
    (i)   education;
    (ii)   libraries;
    (iii)   personal social services;
    (iv)   youth development.
(b)   concurrent powers for all county and district councils:
    (i)   museums and art galleries;
    (ii)   town development;
    (iii)   derelict land;
    (iv)   country parks;
    (v)   conservation areas;
    (vi)   building preservation notices;
    (vii)   tree preservation;
    (viii)   acquisition of land for planning and development;
    (ix)   rights of way creation, diversion and extinguishment;
    (x)   rights of way protection;
    (xi)   'footway' lighting;
    (xii)   swimming baths;

       (xiii)   physical training and recreation;
       (xiv)   parks;
       (xv)   open spaces;
       (xvi)   airports;
(c)   other powers.

County councils	District councils

Housing—
    reserve powers
	Housing—
	    slum clearance
	    house and area improve-
	    ment

Planning—
    minerals and waste develop-
    ment schemes
    development control (national
    parks and 'county matters')
	Planning—
	    local development schemes
	
	    development control
	    (ordinary)
	    advertisement control
	    listed building control

Rights of way—
    surveys
    maintenance[1]
    signposting	

Transportation—
    transport planning
    highways[1]
    traffic
    parking
    public transport[2]
 	
    road safety
	Transportation—
	
	Off-street parking—
	    public transport
	    undertakings[3]

Highway lighting	

Environmental health—
    animal diseases
	Environmental health—
	    food hygiene
	    communicable disease
	    slaughterhouses

Offices, shops and railway premises
(fire precautions)—
 	
    refuse disposal
	Offices, shops and railway premises
	(fire precautions)—
	    factories
	    home safety
	    building regulations
	    refuse collection
	    clean air

Consumer protection—
    weights and measures
    trade descriptions	

County councils	District councils
explosives food and drugs	coast protection *cemeteries and crematoria* markets and fairs *byelaws*
Fire[4] Smallholdings	Allotments Local licensing

[1]   District councils may claim maintenance powers for footpaths, bridleways and such urban roads as are neither trunk roads nor classified.

[2]   Non-metropolitan county councils have only co-ordinating functions.

[3]   Those non-metropolitan district councils alone which have Local Act powers.

[4]   But some fire services are amalgamated over areas of several counties.

E   LOCAL STATUTORY BODIES OUTSIDE LOCAL GOVERNMENT

2.5 The number of statutory or quasi-statutory bodies which exercise local administrative functions outside the ambit of local government grows or changes (or both) continually so that any apparently exhaustive list would be out of date by the time that it was published. They share in varying degrees certain similar characteristics: in particular their functions are specialised and their activities are controlled by persons who, however sensitive to local opinion, are not directly (or sometimes even indirectly) responsible to the local populations. Some of these bodies have consultative committees or councils whose nominated membership is supposed to reflect the tastes and wishes of users. The effectiveness of these consultative organs varies from one service to another.

The reader who needs to know the particulars and addresses of such bodies is advised to consult the *Municipal Year Book*, or *Whitaker's Almanack*. The following is merely a selection.

---

1 Local or regional offices of government departments

Revenue & Customs	Health
Transport	Work and Pensions
Environment, Food and Rural Affairs	Land Registry

---

2 Local sub-managements of nationalised or privatised national industries

British Telecommunications	British Waterways
Electricity	Post Office
Gas	Network Rail

---

3 Specialised authorities, boards and councils	
Fire Authorities	if not the county council
Police and Crime Commissioners	
Valuation officers and panels	
Health authorities and trusts	
Sports councils	
Traffic commissioners	

Chapter 3

GENERAL DESCRIPTION OF THE LOCALITIES AS A SYSTEM

3.1 In 2013 England contained about 10,200 parishes (of which about 230 were in metropolitan districts) and a number of non-parochial places. Wales was wholly divided into communities, of which there were about 790. These geographical units varied widely in area, population and resources. English parish populations varied from single figures to nearly 49,000; areas from a few acres to nearly 100 square miles, and regular expenditure from a few pounds to £2,000,000. The variation in the Welsh communities was even greater because of the inclusion of great cities such as Cardiff and Swansea in the communities. Moreover, the boundaries were very often out of date, and sometimes very ancient, so that they had become more or less irrelevant to the modern pattern of settlement.

Every locality has a meeting consisting of all its electors. In England every parish meeting must meet annually, but there is no equivalent requirement in Wales. In practice many such meetings had seldom met, because of the smallness or the scattered nature of the populations, whilst in some localities full meetings are impracticable because there is no place big enough. Since 1 April 1974, the power (if not necessarily the influence) of electors' meetings has been very limited.

Some 9,000 parishes and 735 communities have, in addition to their electors' meeting, an elected council called a parish or community council, which is a corporation and whose powers are considerably greater than those of an electors' meeting. The number of such councils is somewhat less than the number of parishes and communities in which the full powers of the councils are exercised, for they are of two distinguishable kinds, viz, separate local councils each administering a single locality, and group or joint local councils each administering two or more parishes or communities.

In 2013 there were thought to be about 80,000 local councillors. Formerly a large minority of these were members of other authorities, but the wholesale abolition of district council seats and the substitution of unitary for district and county councils has reduced this form of cross-fertilisation.

The constitutional oversight of local councils in England is, subject to some exceptions, exercised by the district or (as the case may be) unitary councils, which can initiate the process (called a community governance review) whereby boundaries and electoral arrangements are altered or whereby, in addition, the parochial status of an area can be changed. It is also possible for a new parish to be created on the petition of a specified number or percentage of the electorate. Some 3,000 new local councils have come into existence since 1953. No parish councils can be created for the Scilly Isles. In Wales the first or initial review of communities was carried out by the Local Government Boundary Commission for Wales. Primary responsibility for reviews now rests with county and county borough councils.

The power to create and dissolve local councils in England is vested in the district or unitary council, but in Wales no discretion exists at all, the principal council being required to act at the lawful behest of the community meeting. The power to create or dissolve groups of parishes or communities can be exercised in both countries only at the request or with the consent of the electors' meeting.

There is, however, some institutional flexibility. All local authorities can arrange for most of their functions to be exercised by committees, or by their officers or by another local authority, and authorities can arrange to lend staff to each other. Moreover in England, district councils may confer any power of a parish council on a parish meeting where there is no separate parish council, and any such meeting may arrange to discharge its functions through a committee.

Parishes not represented on a parish council, and non-parochial places in districts which are not boroughs, have respectively a body of parish trustees, and of charter trustees. These are not local authorities. Their function is to own the relevant property, and in the case of charter trustees to manage it and to appoint a town mayor and other officers of dignity. These bodies do not exist in Wales, where the relevant property is generally vested in the county or county borough council in trust for the community.

Any local council may call itself a town council, and its chairman is then entitled to be called the town mayor. If there are officers of dignity, descended from a previously existing borough conterminous with the parish or community, the local council appoints them.

Chapter 4

CREATION, ALTERATION AND DISSOLUTION OF LOCALITIES AND THEIR ORGANISATION

4.1 There is a clear distinction between England and Wales relating to the processes which create, alter and extinguish a locality and those which lead to the formation, constitution and dissolution of a local council. In England, the responsibility for undertaking 'community governance reviews' (see section C below) lies solely with principal councils. In Wales, both principal councils and the Welsh Commission are involved[1] in changes to communities.

[1] Local Government and Public Involvement in Health Act 2007, Part 4, Chapter 3 (England); LGA 1972, s 58 (Wales).

A   THE DEFINITION OF A PARISH AND SURVIVAL OF ENGLISH PARISH COUNCILS

4.2 Originally parishes were ecclesiastical areas coinciding with manors. Neither parishes nor manors covered the whole of the country, and because many of them were very large, sub-divisions were recognised from the earliest times. It thus becomes necessary to notice, in addition to the parish, the sub-divisions known as chapelries and townships as well as the (old) extra-parochial place. Civil administration made use of the boundaries which the church had drawn; sometimes there was no boundary and parishes shared (and still share) lands in common. In undisputed cases the boundaries could, after 1849, be settled by inclosure award[1] but as the population increased or shifted, it tended on the one hand to ignore the distinction between parishes and extra-parochial places, and on the other to erect into civil parishes areas which from the church's point of view were only sub-divisions. The details of this ancient organisation can still be of local importance, since most inclosure awards and parochial charity deeds were drawn in relation to them.

The Poor Relief Act of 1601 enjoined the appointment of overseers and the levying of a poor rate in parishes and Foulness only[2]. As the word 'parish' was not defined, the Act was extended by judicial interpretation to a few areas which were reputed parishes at the passing of the Act; these were sometimes sub-divisions[3] and sometimes combinations[4] of ecclesiastical areas. In the following 60 years, however, it was realised that the Act was unworkable in the large parishes which were found everywhere but especially in Cheshire,

23

Derbyshire, Yorkshire and northwards. There were only 70 parishes in Lancashire in 1834[5]. In 1662 it became lawful for such appointments and levies to be made for townships and villages within the parishes[6]. A township was a place for which a constable was appointed[7]; a village was a group of more than two dwelling-houses which had a common name by reputation and in which it was inconvenient to execute the Act of 1601 without special provision[8]. The Act of 1662 made possible the creation of a class of civil parish which was visibly distinct from the ecclesiastical parish and which owed its existence solely to administrative convenience; and the process of sub-division which it initiated continued sporadically until 1844, when new appointments for townships and villages were forbidden[9]. Meanwhile extra-parochial places (of which 598 still survived in 1851)[5] had been left largely outside the system, but after 1857 it became possible either to appoint overseers and levy rates in them separately or to annex them to neighbouring parishes[10].

It had thus taken over two and a half centuries for the civil parochial system to be extended effectively over the whole country, but the ancient framework of boundaries had (save for the provisions relating to annexation) remained virtually untouched. Boundaries were sometimes inconvenient. In 1873, 1,296 ecclesiastical parishes and many more Poor Law parishes were divided into two or more parts[5] and so power to make adjustments was given to the proper government department[11] and the appointment of overseers for any new parishes so created was legalised notwithstanding the prohibition of 1844[12]. In 1882, isolated parts of parishes were amalgamated with the parish surrounding them[13].

Although these powers of boundary reorganisation were created over a century ago and had since devolved through county and district to unitary councils, the responsible authorities have been dilatory in exercising them. A number of intermingled parishes in Northumberland were not abolished until 1955.

In 1889, the word 'parish' in every Act passed after 1866 was statutorily defined as 'a place for which a separate poor rate is or can be made or for which a separate overseer is or can be appointed'[14] and this remained the ruling definition even though overseer and poor rate were both abolished in 1925, for it was then substantially re-enacted subject, however, to any alteration of area made on or after 1 April 1927[15].

Urban parishes, boroughs and urban districts were abolished as from 1 April 1974 but subject to certain locally limited provisions all rural parishes were continued as parishes, rural boroughs became and were continued as parishes, and previously existing boroughs and urban districts were to become and be continued as parishes if the English Commission so recommended and the Secretary of State so ordered by statutory instrument subject to negative resolution[16]. There was, in consequence, a residue of non-parochial areas.

A parish with a parish council on 1 April 1974 continued to have one, in five cases. These were first that apart from the 'Part IV cases' the parish was a rural parish with a parish council on the day before[17], or second that it was a rural borough on 26 October 1972[18], or third that on that day it was co-extensive with a rural district[19], or fourth that it was one of the 27 'Part IV cases' created by division or the eight 'Part IV cases' created by aggregation[20], or fifth that it was one of 299 borough or urban districts converted into successor parishes[21].

In addition, if a parish has no parish council the district council (T) must, or if it is grouped may, create one by order if the parish has 200 or more electors, or if it has between 151 and 199 electors and the parish meeting so resolves[22]. If the electorate is under 151 and the parish meeting so resolves, the district council (T) has a discretion in the matter[23].

Where the electorate is less than 151 the parish meeting may apply to the district council (T) to have its parish council dissolved. If such an application is refused, another may not be made for two years from the making of the previous application[24]. Parish councils can, of course, also be dissolved as part of a community governance review.

The above progression applied equally in England and Wales, save that no rural boroughs had been set up in Wales. The marked divergence of the Welsh rules from that day are described in CHAPTER 35.

The remainder of this chapter deals only with England. For the position in Wales, see CHAPTER 35.

[1]   Inclosure Act 1849, s 1.
[2]   Poor Relief Act 1601, ss 1 and 18.
[3]   *Nichols v Walter and Carter* (1635) Cro Car 394.
[4]   *Sharpley v Mablethorpe* (1854) 3 El & Bl 906.
[5]   See V D Lipman, *Local Government Areas 1934–1945*.
[6]   Poor Relief Act 1662, s 21.
[7]   Per Buller J in *R v Horton* (1786) 1 Term Rep 374.
[8]   *R v Leigh* (1790) 3 Term Rep 746.
[9]   Poor Law Amendment Act 1844, s 22.
[10] Extra-Parochial Places Act 1857, ss I and IV.
[11] Poor Law Amendment Act 1867, s 2 (Poor Law Board); Divided Parishes and Poor Law Amendment Act 1876, ss 1 and 2 (Local Government Board).
[12] Divided Parishes and Poor Law Amendment Act 1876, s 6.
[13] Divided Parishes and Poor Law Amendment Act 1882.
[14] Interpretation Act 1889, s 5 (repealed).
[15] Rating and Valuation Act 1925, s 68(1) and (4), s 69(1) and Sch 8.
[16] Local Government Act 1972, s 1 and Sch 1, Part V.
[17] This appears to be the effect of LGA 1972, s 1(6) and (10).
[18] LGA 1972, s 9(4)(a).
[19] LGA 1972, s 9(4)(b).
[20] LGA 1972, s 9(4)(c) and (d); and see Sch 1, Part IV and the New Parishes Order 1973, SI 1973/688, and Amendment Order, SI 1973/1466.
[21] LGA 1972, s 9(4); and see Sch 1, Part V and the Successor Orders SI 1973/1110, SI 1973/1538 and SI 1974/569.
[22] LGA 1972, s 9(6).
[23] LGA 1972, s 9(6).
[24] LGA 1972, s 10.

B   ALTERATIONS OF STATUS

4.3 In England the law is more complex than in Wales. Though most of the area of the country is parochial, some of it is not; but changes between the two categories can be made. A non-parochial area may be converted into parish territory in consequence of a community governance review (which could be initiated or amended by a community governance petition), either by its establishment as a parish, or by addition to an area which is already parochial[1]. Conversely a parish can likewise be abolished or have its area distributed among other parishes[2].

The procedure by petition was first enacted in 1997 and enabled urban populations to initiate a lawful procedure for establishing parishes and parish councils in unparished areas. The procedure was altered and extended to Greater London by the Local Government and Public Involvement in Health Act 2007.

[1]   Local Government and Public Involvement in Health Act 2007, s 87(2).
[2]   LGPIHA 2007, s 87(2).

C   COMMUNITY GOVERNANCE REVIEWS

4.4 Parishes are created, dissolved or altered (if at all) by a community governance review and the subsequent adoption (with or without amendment) of the recommendations made by the review. The review is the process of discovering all the facts and opinions required to draw up a recommendation on which changes can be implemented by way of a reorganisation order.

The review is conducted by the principal council, that is to say the district or unitary county or the London borough. The effect of the inclusion of the last-named enables a review to include a recommendation for the creation of parishes within London boroughs[1]. A district council must notify the county council for its area if it undertakes a review and supply details of the terms of the review[2].

[1]   LGPIHA 2007, Part 4, Chapter 3.
[2]   LGPIHA 2007, s 79(3).

Procedure

4.5 The principal council determines and must publicise the terms of reference of a review, and any modifications thereto (if any), and must specify the area concerned. Legislation does not prescribe publication requirements, but the Secretary of State has power to make regulations of general application which can address the matter[1].

The principal council is not now obliged to undertake a review unless it has received a community governance petition (see **4.6** below). The former power of the Secretary of State to direct a review has been abolished.

The procedure is a matter for the principal council to decide, subject to the following statutory duties:

(a)   to consult the local government electors for the area under review and any other person or body (including a local authority) which appears to have an interest in the review;

(b)   to have regard to the need to ensure that community governance in the review area reflects the identities and interests of the communities in that area and is effective and convenient;

(c)   to take into account any other arrangements (other than those relating to parishes) which have been or could be made for the purpose of community representation or community engagement in the review area;

(d)   to take into account any representations received in connection with the review;

(e)   as soon as practicable after making any recommendations to publish them and to take such steps as it considers sufficient to ensure that those persons who are likely to be interested in the review are informed of them;

(f)   to complete the review within 12 months[2].

[1]   LGPIHA 2007, s 97.
[2]   LGPIHA 2007, s 93.

Petitions

4.6 A community governance petition is a petition for a community governance review to be undertaken[1].

To be valid, it must:

(a)   be signed as follows:

    (i)   if the petition area has fewer than 500 local government electors, the petition must be signed by at least 50% of them;

    (ii)   between 500 and 2,500 such electors, by at least 250 of them;

    (iii)   has more than 2,500 such electors, by at least 10% of them;

(b)   define the area for review (whether by a map or otherwise); and

(c)   specify the recommendation(s) which the petitioners wish the review to consider making.

In practice, all concerned in these processes will find it convenient to negotiate on the relevant issues *beforehand*. In particular, this will avoid needless quarrels and improve drafting.

If the petition seeks the creation of a new parish, the area of the parish must be defined (whether by map or otherwise) and its name specified. In addition, the petition must say whether or not the new parish should have a council and, if so, whether or not the parish should have one of the alternative styles (see **4.15** below). If the petition seeks the establishment of a parish council or a parish meeting for an area which does not exist as a parish, the petition is to be treated as if it also seeks the establishment of a parish for that area (either by the constitution of a new parish or by the alteration of an existing parish)[2].

Where a council is not in the course of conducting a review and receives a petition, it must undertake a review encompassing the subject matter of the petition, unless it has carried out a review covering the area to which the petition relates within two years before the date on which the petition was received[3].

Where a council is conducting a review and receives a petition relating to an area wholly outside the area under review, it must exercise one of the following three options:

(a)   to modify the terms of its review to allow the petition to be considered;

(b)   to undertake a separate review for the petition area; or

(c)   to modify the terms of its review so as to enable both that review and a separate review relating to the petition are taken together and deal with the petition[4].

The two year moratorium also applies in this case[5].

Where a council receives a petition in any of the following cases, it may (but need not) either undertake a review or modify the terms of an existing review to accommodate the petition:

(a)   no review is being undertaken and a petition is received during the two year moratorium period; or

(b)   a review is being undertaken and a petition is received relating to an area wholly outside the review area within the two year moratorium period; or

(c)   a review is being undertaken of part of the council's area and a petition is received relating to an area not wholly outside the review area; or

(d)   a review is being undertaken of part of the council's area and a petition is received relating to the whole of the council's area; or

(e)   a review is being undertaken of part of the council's area and a petition is received relating to the whole or part of the council's area[6].

[1]   LGPIHA 2007, s 80.
[2]   LGPIHA 2007, s 80.
[3]   LGPIHA 2007, s 83.
[4]   LGPIHA 2007, s 84.
[5]   LGPIHA 2007, s 84(2).
[6]   LGPIHA 2007, s 85.

Recommendations of review

4.7 A review may make recommendations about what new parish or parishes (if any) should be created. A new parish may be created in any of the following ways:

(a)   by establishing a parish in an unparished area;
(b)   by aggregating one or more unparished areas with one or more parished areas;
(c)   by aggregating parts of parishes;
(d)   by amalgamating two or more parishes;
(e)   by separating part of a parish.

If a review recommends the creation of a new parish, the review must also recommend a name for the parish, whether or not the parish is to have a council and whether or not the parish should have one of the alternative styles (see section F below)[1].

In relation to each existing parish included within the area under review (if any), the review must make one of the following recommendations:

(a)   that the parish should not be abolished or its area altered;
(b)   that the area should be altered;
(c)   that the parish should be altered;
(d)   as to whether or not the name of the parish should be changed;
(e)   where the parish has no council: whether or not it should have one;

(f)   where the parish has a council: whether or not it should continue to have one[2].

Where a review recommends the creation of a new parish council, it must also make recommendations about electoral arrangements. If a review recommends the continuation of a parish council it must also make recommendations as to what changes (if any) should be made to that council's electoral arrangements[3].

[1]   LGPIHA 2007, s 87.
[2]   LGPIHA 2007, s 88.
[3]   LGPIHA 2007, ss 89, 90.

Recommendations to create parish councils

4.8 Where a review must recommend whether or not a parish should have a council, it must:

(a)   recommend that the parish should have a council where the number of local government electors exceeds 999;

(b)   recommend that the parish should not have a council if the number of those electors is fewer than 150, unless the parish already has a council or the parish is part of a parish with a council.

In any other case it is for the principal council to decide on these matters.

Elaborate provision is made for the electoral arrangements which should apply where a review recommends the creation of a new parish council or the alteration of an existing one.

Publicising and implementing a review

4.9 As soon as practicable after deciding to what extent it will implement the recommendations of a review the council must publish the decision and the reasons for making it. If the council makes a reorganisation order (see below), it must then deposit at its principal office a copy of the order and of a map showing the effects of the order in greater detail than on the map included in the order. These copies must be available for public inspection at all reasonable times and the council must publicise that fact. The council must also inform the following bodies as soon as practicable after making the order:

(a)   the Secretary of State;
(b)   the Electoral Commission;
(c)   the Office for National Statistics;
(d)   the Director General of the Ordnance Survey;
(e)   any other principal council whose area the order relates to[1].

Once a recommendation has been made, the principal council may give effect thereto by means of an order, but not so as to alter changes to the boundaries of the electoral areas of a principal council or to 'protected electoral arrangements' without, in both cases, the consent of the Electoral Commission. Protected electoral arrangements are those relating to a parish which have been established by an order under the Local Government Act 1992, s 17 or the Local Government and Rating Act 1997, s 14 within the five years preceding the start of a community governance review[2].

The Secretary of State has power to make general regulations of an incidental, consequential, transitional or supplementary nature[3].

Once an order has been made, the council must send two copies to the Secretary of State and the Electoral Commission and the Secretary of State must send two copies of any regulations he makes to the Commission[4].

A reorganisation order, or general regulations, may:

(a)   provide for the transfer and management of both real and personal property and with respect to the transfer of property rights and liabilities[5];

(b)   provide for the transfer of legal proceedings and staff and for legal succession between existing bodies and new or altered bodies[6];

(c)   make appropriate electoral arrangements[7].

Any public bodies (including parish councils) affected by an order may make agreements about property, income, rights, liabilities, expenses and financial arrangements. In default of agreement, any dispute is referred to a single arbitrator who, if not agreed by the parties, is appointed by the Secretary of State[8].

The Secretary of State may issue guidance about undertaking reviews and the Electoral Commission about electoral arrangements. The council must have regard to them[9]. The Commission's guidance may be viewed on the Commission's website[10].

A sum payable under an agreement or award may be paid out of such fund or rate as is therein provided, and in default of such provision it may be paid out of the fund from which the general expenses of the public body are defrayed, or out of such fund as it may itself direct[11].

Where capital payments have to be made under an agreement or award a local authority may borrow in order to raise the appropriate sums. The Secretary of State's consent is not required for such a loan, but the period within which it must be repaid has to be approved by him. Other public bodies may borrow for these purposes if they have statutory borrowing powers, and if not, the Secretary of State can by order empower them to borrow[12].

[1]   LGPIHA 2007, s 96.
[2]   See LGPIHA 2007, s 86.
[3]   LGPIHA 2007, s 97.
[4]   LGPIHA 2007, s 98(1), (2).
[5]   LGPIHA 2007, s 98(4).
[6]   LGPIHA 2007, s 98(5).
[7]   LGPIHA 2007, s 98(6).
[8]   LGPIHA 2007, s 99.
[9]   LGPIHA 2007, s 100.
[10]   www.electoralcommission.gov.uk.
[11]   As defined in the LGA 1972, s 270(1).
[12]   LGA 1972, s 68(1)–(2).

D   GROUPS

4.10 It is possible to alter the area administered by a local council without altering the status of a parish or the extent of a parish. This is done by grouping parishes together under a joint council or by dissolving such a group. The reorganisation of localities by means of grouping orders has certain advantages, for the units concerned retain their identity and their electors' meeting, and such orders can be made by the district council (T) without the formalities of review.

Formation[1]

[1]   LGA 1972, ss 11(1)–(3) and 29(1)–(3).

4.11 If an electors' meeting applies to the district council (T) for a grouping order, the latter may group that locality with a neighbouring locality or more than one in the same district (T) or the same London borough under a common local council. The inclusion of London borough councils is consequential upon the extension of the power to create parishes in Greater London[2]. This may be done by grouping units which previously had no council, or by adding one without a council to an existing group.

A group cannot be formed without the consent of the electors' meeting of each of the units concerned.

The order must name the group; it must provide for the separate representation on the local council of each unit or the wards of each unit, for the application of the Charities Act 2011, ss 298–303 (relating to the appointment of trustees and beneficiaries of parochial charities) to the units in the group, and for the application of the provisions of the Local Government Act 1972 relating to the custody of parish or community documents so as to preserve the separate rights of each unit; it must also dissolve the separate local council of any unit included, and it may provide for any necessary adaptations of the LGA 1972 to the group. Such an adaptation could, for example, enable an election to be held in a year when one would not otherwise have been expected.

The order can require that the consent of the parish meeting of a parish shall be necessary for any particular act of the parish council.

A group local council may adopt an alternative style (see section F below)[3].

[2]   LGPIHA 2007, Part 4, Chapter 3.
[3]   LGA 1972, ss 11A and 11B (added by the LGPIHA 2007).

Dissolution

4.12 If a common council of a group or an electors' meeting for a unit in it applies for the group to be dissolved or for the unit to be separated from it, the district council (T) or London borough council may order accordingly. Such an order must provide for the election of a local council for each unit in the group if it is dissolved, or for any unit separated from the group where it is not[1].

In the rare cases where parishes in a group happen to be in different districts (T), the group continues to exist until the two district councils (T) concerned jointly make orders dissolving the council or the group, or separating a parish from the group, or an order is made after a review, having such effects[2].

[1] LGA 1972, ss 11(4) and 29(4).
[2] LGA 1972, s 11(5).

E   PARISH WARDS

4.13 As a rule the local councillors are elected at large for the whole of their locality, but the parishes in a group must be separately represented on the common local councils[1], and it is possible for a locality to be divided into wards. Such division is effected either consequentially upon a community governance review (see section C above) or substantively, that is to say independently of such changes. Substantive changes in electoral arrangements are made by the Electoral Commission following a review by its statutory Boundary Committee[2].

For the position in Wales, see CHAPTER 35 C.

[1] LGA 1972, ss 11(3)(b) and 29(5)(a).
[2] LGA 1992, ss 13 and 14 (as amended by LGPIHA 2007). For the Commission's guidance notes see its website at **4.9** above.

F   CHANGES OF NAME AND STYLE

Changes of name

4.14 If a local council or, where there is no council, the electors' meeting so requests, the district or unitary council may change the name of the locality. It must send notice of the change to the Secretary of State, the Director-General of the Ordnance Survey and the Registrar-General, and publish it in the parish or community and elsewhere.

Changes of style

4.15 A parish council and a parish meeting in a parish without a council may resolve to adopt the alternative style of 'community', 'neighbourhood' or 'village'. Conversely, either body may resolve to drop an alternative style and revert to being called a parish[1]. The legislation makes elaborate provision for consequential changes, eg to the style of the chairman and vice-chairman.

As soon as practicable after adopting an alternative style, the council or meeting must give notice of the change to the Secretary of State, the Electoral Commission, the Office for National Statistics, the Director-General of the Ordnance Survey and the district council, the county council or London borough council in which the parish lies[2].

[1] LGA 1972, ss 12A, 12B and 17A (added by the LGPIHA 2007).
[2] LGA 1972, s 12A(5) (added by the LGPIHA 2007).

G   CITY AND TOWN STATUS

4.16 A local council which is not part of a group can resolve that its area shall have the status of a town. Such a resolution continues in effect until either the area ceases to exist, or it is resolved to the contrary by the local council, or by the electors' meeting, if the council has been dissolved[1].

A place which was a borough either immediately before 1 April 1974, or at some time in its history, especially if it keeps evidences of that status, such as a guildhall, may reasonably feel entitled to call itself a town, and so may parishes and communities which are towns in the ordinary sense of the word. In the latter case common observation and local speech habits may be a useful criterion. The fact, however, that a place was once an urban district is not necessarily relevant, for urban districts were originally only places where certain health functions were exercised, and many of them were really villages. In 1973 the National Association of Local Councils advised its members in doubtful cases to consult its electors' meeting, or to err on the side of modesty[2].

The statutory rules about town status do not affect the royal prerogative of conferring city status. Hence a parish, a community or a town can be made a city[3], and, indeed Ely, Ripon and Wells are cities.

The Electoral Commission's published guidance on changes of style can be viewed on the Commission's website (www.electoralcommission.gov.uk) on the pages devoted to community governance reviews.

[1]   LGA 1972, s 245(6)–(9). For its other effects see **8.1** (chairman); **9.22** (clerk); **10.16** (parish trustees) below.
[2]   NALC National Circular No 308.
[3]   LGA 1972, s 245(10). For the effect on honorary freedoms see **5.15** below.

H   MINOR BOUNDARY CHANGES

Accretion and diluvion

4.17 By force of law, land to low-water mark and accretions from the sea form part of coastal localities or non-parochial places in proportion to the extent of their common boundaries[1]. Areas may similarly be lost by encroachment (called diluvion) as at mediaeval Dunwich (Suffolk).

[1]   LGA 1972, s 72.

Watercourses

4.18 If a watercourse, used as a boundary, is altered by the responsible water undertaker or drainage board, it must inform the Secretary of State who, after consulting the appropriate commission, lays down a new boundary line by order. He is not bound to follow the realigned watercourse[1].

[1]   LGA 1972, s 73(2).

Chapter 5

THE PEOPLE

A   INHABITANTS AND PARISHIONERS

5.1 'Inhabitants', 'residents', 'parishioners' and 'the public' figure in many documents such as charitable trust instruments, tithe and inclosure awards, grants and in claims involving proof of customs. The exact meaning of these words has to be established in each case by reference to the facts and law at the time and place to which they relate. The following summary must therefore be read with caution because in any particular case the evidence may establish an interpretation which differs from the normal.

Custom

5.2 If a right is given to or an obligation imposed upon all the Queen's sub-jects, it must be established by authority of the general law. A local custom can therefore never be general and a customary claim in the name of the general public will fail. Similarly a custom must be capable of definition, and so the courts will not uphold a claim on behalf of a class whose membership cannot be ascertained.

The public

5.3 Except in relation to highways and admission to meetings of public bodies, the words 'the public' or 'the general public' are probably legally meaningless unless it is clear from the circumstances or wording of the document that the inhabitants of a definable locality are meant. In the context of the two exceptions mentioned above they probably mean 'everyone'.

Inhabitants

5.4 The right to create corporations is vested in the Sovereign (who may delegate it[1]) and such other persons as Parliament appoints[2]. A Crown grant to the inhabitants of a place might therefore be upheld on the ground that the Crown had intended the inhabitants to be incorporated for the purposes of the grant, but such a grant by a subject would fail for want of a grantee unless it were charitable. Practical difficulties of this kind are usually overcome by vesting property in trustees or the local council upon trust for the inhabitants, and such a trust will not fail for uncertainty, for the beneficiaries can, at any moment, be ascertained.

¹ Eg to the Bishops of Durham until 1834 within the ancient palatinate of Durham, which included not only the county but the shires of Bedlington, Norham and Islandshire in Northumberland and Craik in Yorkshire.

² Eg a district council (T) and a London borough council can create a local council in pursuance of a community governance review (see CHAPTER 4).

Residents

5.5 The words 'inhabitant' and 'resident' are generally held to mean the same thing. It is not necessary for a person to reside for any particular period in a parish to become an inhabitant[1] nor need the residence be exclusive[2]. The residence ought, however, to be of such a kind that the person in question may fairly be described as having some root or stake in the parish. The court would take into account not only whether he habitually or occasionally sleeps[3] in the parish, but whether his family come there[4], whether he occupies property[5] or is employed there and any other relevant matters. These rules would also apply to communities.

¹ Though residence for a certain period is in practice necessary in most cases to become an elector.

² *AG v Coote* (1817) 4 Price 183 and *Bond v The Overseers of St Georges, Hanover Square* (1870) LR 6 CP 312.

³ *R v The Mayor of Exeter, Dipstales Case* (1868) LR 4 QB 114.

⁴ *Whithorn v Thomas* (1844) 14 LJCP 38.

⁵ *Donne v Martyr* (1828) 8 B & C 62.

Occupation

5.6 Residence is not the same as occupation, for a man may occupy a house in which he does not reside[1].

¹ *Barlow v Smith* (1892) 9 TLR 57 (DC).

Parishioners

5.7 The word 'parishioners' in England is of wider import than the word 'inhabitants'[1], and includes people who merely own or occupy property in the parish. The statutory extinction of civil parishes in Wales leaves the word only with an ecclesiastical connotation in the principality.

Ecclesiastically, it seems that even the most temporary presence (for example, by walking across a parish) may for that space of time constitute a person a parishioner; hence the incumbent of the parish, if he happened to be killed by a passing car, would officiate at his funeral.

¹ *AG v Parker* (1747) 3 Atk 576 (the Report is corrupt).

B   THE ELECTORS

5.8 In a parish or community every elector may exercise direct authority by speaking and voting at electors' meetings[1]. In addition, where he has, or is represented upon, a local council, he may vote in elections of local councillors. No one is entitled to exercise either of these rights unless his name appears in the appropriate electoral register[2] currently in force, but a properly qualified person has an enforceable right to have his name placed upon the register if it has been wrongly omitted therefrom[3].

[1]   LGA 1972, ss 9(1) and 27(1).
[2]   Representation of the People Act 1983, s 2.
[3]   RPA 1983, s 4.

The register

5.9 The register of electors is maintained by the electoral registration officer (an official of the district council in England and the county or county borough council in Wales). He must undertake an annual canvass of persons in residence on 15 October and must publish the revised register by 1 December, or a later date prescribed by regulations[1]. Subsequent alterations may be made at any time to add or remove a name from the register[2]. This creates a 'rolling' register, the aim being to enable changes to be made quickly, rather than annually.

The registration process is due to switch from registration by household to individual registration when the Electoral Registration and Administration Act 2013 is brought into force. It is anticipated that this will be in 2014, in time for the general election due to be held in 2015.

Every resident in the parish or community is entitled to vote so long as: his name is on the register; he is a Commonwealth citizen (which includes a British subject) or a citizen of the Irish Republic or a citizen of a member state of the European Union; and he is of voting age (18 or over)[3].

[1]   Representation of the People Act 1983, s 10.
[2]   RPA 1983, s 13A (as amended by the Electoral Registration and Administration Act 2013).
[3]   RPA 1983, s 2.

Voting age

5.10 A person reaches voting age on[1] his 18th[2] birthday.

[1]   Representation of the People Act 1983, s 202(2).
[2]   RPA 1983, s 2(1).

Lunacy

5.11 At common law idiots are subject to a permanent legal incapacity to vote[1] but persons of unsound mind may vote during lucid intervals[2].

[1]   *Burgess' Case* (1785) 2 Lud EC.

² Robin's Case (1791) 1 Fras.

Crime and corruption

5.12 A convict detained in a penal institution in pursuance of his sentence is legally incapable of voting[1]. Incapacity may also arise from conviction or report for corrupt or illegal election practices or for corruption of public officials.

If a person is convicted on indictment or by an election court[2] or is reported by an election court[3] for a corrupt practice[4] he becomes incapable for five years of being registered as an elector or voting at any election in Great Britain to any public office. If he is similarly convicted or reported for any illegal practice[5] the period of incapacity is three years[6].

1 Representation of the People Act 1983, s 3.
2 RPA 1983, s 160.
3 RPA 1983, s 160.
4 For corrupt and illegal election practices see **6.6** below.
5 For corrupt and illegal election practices see **6.6** below.
6 RPA 1983, s 173.

Residence

5.13 There is no qualifying period to establish residence and an elector may have more than one residence[1].

1 See *R v Mayor of Exeter* (1868) 4 QB 110 per Blackburn J.

Proxies and postal votes

5.14 Absent voters may vote by post or by proxy provided that they apply well beforehand to the electoral registration officer to be included in the absent voters list. A proxy must be of voting age, not subject to any legal incapacity to vote at the election in question and either a Commonwealth citizen or a citizen of the Republic of Ireland or a citizen of a member state of the European Union[1].

1 Representation of the People Act 2000, Sch 4.

C   FREEMEN AND HONORARY FREEMEN

5.15 The LGA 1972 did not affect any person's status as, or his right to be admitted to the status of, a freeman of a previously existing borough. The freemen's roll is kept by the district council (T), whose chairman must examine and decide claims to be admitted. The Act also expressly preserved the special rights of freemen, their appropriate relatives or associates, the relatives by marriage of their widows or children and of existing or future inhabitants in any property or otherwise[1].

A local council and charter trustees may admit as honorary freemen or honorary freewomen persons of distinction and those who have rendered eminent service to the place or area[2]. This must be done at a meeting specially convened for the purpose and requires a two thirds majority of those voting. Such honorary freedom carries none of the special rights preserved by the Act[3].

[1] LGA 1972, s 248.
[2] LGA 1972, s 249(5) as amended by the Local Democracy, Economic Development and Construction Act 2009.
[3] LGA 1972, s 249(8).

Chapter 6

THE LOCAL COUNCIL AND ITS MEMBERS

A   THE NATURE OF A LOCAL COUNCIL

6.1 A local council is a body corporate with perpetual succession, and a name. It is composed of a chairman (or town mayor) and councillors[1]. The number of councillors is fixed by the district council (T). In England it must be not less than five[2]. In Wales no statutory minimum is specified[3] but the rules on quorum make five the minimum in practice. A council may elect one of its members to be vice-chairman.

If the local council resolves to call itself the town council the chairman is entitled to be called the town mayor and the vice-chairman the deputy town mayor. If the council resolves to adopt an alternative style (see Chapter **4**, section F) the title of the chairman and vice-chairman changes appropriately[4].

As a body corporate the council is a person[5] and is distinct from its members (either as individuals or collectively) for the time being[6]. Its lawful acts, assets and liabilities are its own and not those of its members[7]. A newly created council comes into existence on the day named in the order which establishes it; it is immaterial that its members are not elected until some later day[8], and therefore a gift of property to it made after its establishment will not be void for want of a grantee if made before the first election. Similarly it remains in uninterrupted existence from the moment of its creation until its lawful dissolution, even if all its members vacate office, or if its membership falls so low that it is unable to act for want of a quorum.

Where there are so many vacancies in the membership that a council cannot act, the district council (T) may, by order, appoint persons to fill vacancies pending the election of new councillors and their taking office[9]. If the council is the council of a group of parishes in different districts, the appointment must be made by the district councils (T) acting jointly[10]. As these appointees are not elected they are not required to make a declaration of acceptance of office, and apparently they cannot resign, but do vacate office for persistent absence[11].

---

[1]   LGA 1972, ss 14 (as amended by the Local Government and Public Involvement in Health Act 2007) and 33.
[2]   LGA 1972, s 16(1).
[3]   LGA 1972, s 35.
[4]   LGA 1972, ss 245(6), 15(11)–(14).
[5]   Interpretation Act 1978, Sch 1.
[6]   *Society for the Illustration of Practical Knowledge v Abbott* (1840) 2 Beav 559.

7   See also Public Health Act 1875, s 265 which was amended and applied to all local authorities
    by the Local Government (Miscellaneous Provisions) Act 1976, ss 27(2) and 39.
8   *The case of Sutton's Hospital* (1612) 10 Co Rep 1a at 31a.
9   LGA 1972, s 91(1).
10 LGA 1972, s 91(2).
11 Compare the words of LGA 1972, ss 83(1), 84 and 85.

B   ELIGIBILITY FOR OFFICE

6.2 Roughly speaking, electors over 18 years of age may become members of local councils, but certain additional qualifications and disqualifications have the effect of extending this class of eligible persons in one direction whilst restricting it in another.

Qualifications

6.3 Subject therefore to the rules on disqualification a person is qualified if he is a Commonwealth citizen (which includes a British subject) or a citizen of a member state of the European Union, is over 18, and is an elector. In addition he will be qualified if he has either during the whole of the twelve months before the day on which he is nominated as a candidate, or the day of the election, resided in the locality or within three miles of it or occupied as owner or tenant any land or premises therein or had his principal or only place of work there[1]. Such work need not be paid, but must be substantial; it may even include duties which the candidate was elected to perform before the election by the very same council as that to which he is now seeking election[2].

One effect of these rules is that it is possible to be a member of more than one local council.

1   LGA 1972, s 79.
2   *Parker v Yeo* (1992) 90 LGR 645 (Court of Appeal).

Disqualifications

6.4 A person may be disqualified from being elected or being a member in the following ways:

(1)   if he holds a paid office or other place of profit in the gift or disposal of the council or any committee or sub-committee thereof or under a company controlled by the council[1]; in the case of an office of profit it is immaterial that no profits were actually received[2]; where a paid officer is employed under the direction of a committee or board any of whose members are appointed by some other local authority, the disqualification extends to the other authority as well[1]; an appointment which can be vetoed by some other body or person does not seem to be caught by this rule, but an appointment made or confirmed by an officer holding any such office or employment, is[1];

(2)   being subject to a bankruptcy restrictions order or an interim order creates disqualification which dates from the judgment or execution and generally ends one year after the relevant order is made[3];

(3)   if he has within five years before the election or since his election been convicted in the United Kingdom, the Channel Islands or the Isle of Man of any offence and has been sentenced to not less than three months' imprisonment (whether suspended or not) without the option of a fine[4]. Imprisonment probably includes any type of custodial sentence[5]. This disqualification begins when the ordinary period for making an appeal has expired or when the appeal is finally dismissed or abandoned or fails for want of prosecution[6]. If the convict receives a free pardon, the disqualification ceases because the conviction upon which it depends is thereby expunged[7];

(4)   if he is convicted of offences involving corrupt or illegal practices[8];

(5)   if a person has been convicted for the failure to register or declare disclosable interests under the Localism Act 2011 (in England) or for breach of the council's code of conduct (in Wales).

See Chapter **7 G** for further details on councillors' conduct.

[1]   LGA 1972, s 80(1)(a) and (aa).
[2]   *Delane v Hillcoat* (1829) 9 B & C 310.
[3]   LGA 1972, s 80(1)(b).
[4]   LGA 1972, s 80(1)(d).
[5]   For imprisonment see Powers of Criminal Courts (Sentencing) Act 2000.
[6]   LGA 1972, s 80(5).
[7]   See *Hay v Justices of the Tower of London Division* (1890) 24 QBD 561 and the authorities quoted therein.
[8]   Representation of the People Act 1983, Part III.

C   HOW TO ATTAIN OFFICE

6.5 A suitably qualified person may become a member of a local council in six different ways. These are:

(1)   ordinary election;
(2)   bye-election;
(3)   appointment by the district council (T);
(4)   appointment by the council itself;
(5)   return after a successful election petition; and
(6)   co-option to a casual vacancy.

Ordinary election

6.6 *Date*

Ordinary elections coincide with the election year of the district (T) or Welsh principal councillor representing the locality[1] and must be held on the same day[2]. The interval between elections is four years[3].

The election day for district (T) or Welsh principal councillors is the first Thursday in May unless the Secretary of State otherwise orders. Such an order must be made before February in the year, or if an order affects more than one year, the first year in which it is to come into force[4].

There are special provisions for the rare cases where a poll has to be abandoned or countermanded[5] and where a parish is in a part of a district transferred to a unitary authority[6].

Election rules and officials

The election is conducted in accordance with the Representation of the People Acts, and elaborate rules[7] made by the Secretary of State under them.

A returning officer must be appointed by the district council (T)[8]. He may appoint persons to discharge all or any of his functions. Such appointments must be made by writing under his hand[9]. They will include, at each polling station, a presiding officer.

Notice of election and time

The returning officer must give notice of the election in a prescribed form and publish it in the same manner as notices of local council meetings are published.

Proceedings during the 32 days before the election must be conducted in accordance with a set timetable, and in computing the correct number of days Saturdays, Sundays, Christmas Eve, Christmas Day, Maundy Thursday, Good Friday, a bank holiday and any day of public thanksgiving or mourning must be disregarded.

The hours of poll commence at 7 am and end at 10 pm.

Nomination, adjudication and publication of names

Each candidate must be nominated on a separate nomination paper stating his full names, place of residence and description, but a misnomer or inaccurate description does not invalidate the paper if the description is such as to be commonly understood[10]. The description must not associate him with a party unless it is certified as authorised by the nominating officer of the party concerned. If it is so certified, the party emblem may be included[11]. The returning officer must supply nomination papers and prepare them for signature on request. Each nomination paper must be signed by a proposer and seconder ('subscribers') who must be electors for the locality or, if it is divided into wards, of the relevant ward for which the candidate is nominated. A nomination is void unless the candidate consents in writing, which must be attested by a witness and must contain a statement that the candidate is qualified and the particulars of the qualification.

Nomination papers must be delivered at the place fixed by the returning officer. It is desirable that this place should be easily accessible, but it need not be in the locality.

As soon as practicable after each nomination paper is delivered the returning officer must adjudicate upon it. He may hold it invalid only on the ground that the particulars of the candidate or subscribers are not as required by law or that the paper is not properly signed. His decision on these points is final. It is therefore desirable in any doubtful case for him to be required to prepare the papers for signature himself.

Having adjudicated, he must publish a list of candidates standing nominated and of persons who were nominated but who no longer stand nominated.

Withdrawal

A candidate may withdraw by notice in writing attested by one witness. If a candidate is validly nominated for more than one ward he must duly withdraw from all those wards except one; if he does not do so, he is deemed to have withdrawn altogether.

Method of election

If there are enough vacancies for the validly surviving candidates the returning officer must, not later than 11 o'clock on the day of the election, declare them elected.

If their number exceeds the number of vacancies, a poll must be held by the method of secret ballot. The rules contain lengthy provisions for the conduct of contested elections including provisions for the use of schools, notices of poll, issue of official poll cards, proxies, appointment by candidates of polling and counting agents, challenge of voters, and counting and recounting of votes.

If there is a tie, the returning officer may not use his brains but must decide by lot[12].

Agents

A candidate at a local council election may, but need not, appoint an election agent[13].

Expenses

A candidate's expenditure is limited to a lump sum in pounds, plus a fixed number of pence for each entry in the electoral register and for any less number of entries above a multiple of six[14]. Regulations made in 2005 fixed the lump sum at £600 and the pence figure at 5. In the case of a joint candidature the total figure is reduced by one-fourth each, and if more than two candidates stand jointly by one-third each[15]. Joint candidates are those who appoint the same election agent, or employ the same polling agents, clerks or messengers, or use the same committee rooms or publish a joint address or circular[16].

Claims for election expenses are barred and may not be paid if not made to the candidate (or his election agent) within 21 days of the election; claims lawfully made must be paid within 28 days of the election[17] but both these time limits may in particular cases be extended by the High or County Court, or an election court[18].

Within 35 days of the election the candidate must send a declaration of his expenses supported by all the bills and receipts to the proper officer[19], who must preserve them for two years. A candidate may be fined £100 for every day on which he sits or votes as a member of the council without having made this declaration[20].

Use of premises

A candidate may at all reasonable times and on reasonable notice use, free of charge, any suitable room in a community, or voluntary school in the locality, or any room which is maintained wholly or mainly out of public funds or out of any rate[21].

Election offences[22]

Election offences are classified into corrupt practices and illegal practices. The law regards corrupt practice as more serious than illegal practice[23], but there is, in addition, an important difference in their nature, for a person cannot be convicted of a corrupt practice unless he is proved to have had a corrupt intention when he committed the act for which he is prosecuted, whereas illegal practices are peremptorily forbidden and intention is consequently irrelevant.

The following are *corrupt* practices:

- treating;
- bribery;
- undue influence;
- personation;
- false declaration of election expenses;
- incurring or aiding and abetting the incurring of certain expenses without written authority from an election agent.

The following are *illegal* practices:

- illegal payments: that is payments for the conveyance of electors, or for prohibited premises such as licensed premises, or payments to an elector for exhibiting bills and notices. Corruptly inducing a candidate to withdraw in consideration of payment, or withdrawing in pursuance of such an inducement is also deemed an illegal payment;
- providing money or knowingly allowing money to be provided for making illegal payments;
- illegal employment: that is employing paid canvassers;
- illegal hiring (by candidates or agents) of conveyances for electors, or of prohibited premises such as licensed premises;
- improper conduct: that is the publication of false statements about the character or conduct of a candidate, or concerning the withdrawal of a candidate;
- illegal broadcasting.

[1] Representation of the People Act 1983, s 37; amended by the Representation of the People Act 1985.
[2] Representation of the People Act 1983, s 37; amended by the Representation of the People Act 1985.
[3] Local Government Act 1972, s 16.
[4] RPA 1983, s 37.
[5] RPA 1983, s 39.
[6] Local Government Act 1992, s 17(3)(ea).
[7] RPA 1983, s 36(1); Local Elections (Parishes and Communities) (England and Wales) Rules 2006, SI 2006/3305.
[8] RPA 1983, s 35(1).
[9] RPA 1983, s 35(4).
[10] RPA 1983, s 50.
[11] Local Elections (Parishes and Communities) (England and Wales) Rules 2006, SI 2006/3305, r 16 as amended by the Local Elections (Parishes and Communities) (England and Wales) (Amendment) Rules 2011, SI 2011/562.
[12] Local Elections (Parishes and Communities) (England and Wales) Rules 2006, r 48.
[13] RPA 1983, s 71.
[14] RPA 1983, ss 76, 76A and Representation of the People (Variation of Limits of Candidates' Election Expenses) Order 2005, SI 2005/269.
[15] RPA 1983, s 77(1).
[16] RPA 1983, s 76(2).
[17] RPA 1983, s 78(1)–(3).
[18] RPA 1983, s 78(4).
[19] RPA 1983, s 81.
[20] RPA 1983, s 85.

21 RPA 1983, s 95.
22 These will be found in RPA 1983, ss 60–66, 97–115.
23 See **5.12** above for the civil consequences. Offenders may in addition be fined or imprisoned or both.

Bye-elections

6.7 A bye-election of the *whole council* can occur when a local council comes into existence in some year other than the year in which the district (T) councillor for the locality is elected, and when an entire election is declared void on the trial of an election petition, and lastly when a new election is ordered by the district council (T) under its 'reserve power'[1].

A bye-election to a *particular vacancy* occurs either where the membership of a local council has been increased[2] during the term of office of the existing members or where a bye-election to fill a casual vacancy has been claimed. The vacancies in newly created offices are not 'casual' and must therefore be filled in any of the ways in which vacancies are filled at or immediately after the ordinary elections.

Bye-elections are conducted in the same way as ordinary elections.

1 Representation of the People Act 1983, s 39.
2 For the district council's (T) power to regulate the size of membership see **6.1** (above).

Insufficient candidates

6.8 If there are insufficient candidates, those who are and remain validly nominated (if any) are declared elected. If they constitute a quorum they may fill the remaining vacancies by co-option. If there is no quorum the district council (T) may fill the vacancies[1].

1 Representation of the People Act 1985, s 21. See also Chapter **22G** on Quality Councils.

Appointment

6.9 If there are so many vacancies in a local council that it cannot act, the district council (T) or (in the case of a common council whose area straddles a district (T) boundary) the district council (T) with the most parish or community electors for that council, may by order appoint persons to fill some or all the vacancies, but only until other councillors are elected and take up office. Two copies of the order must be sent to the Secretary of State[1].

A parish council may be able to appoint persons to be councillors, in accordance with regulations made by the Secretary of State[2].

The fact that these persons are appointed, not elected, appears to create special problems. If they are not qualified for election or are disqualified their acts can be challenged[3]; they do not have to make a declaration of acceptance of office[4]; they cannot resign[5] but can vacate office by failure to attend, because they are members of the council[6].

In Wales only, a community council may appoint no more than two persons over the age of 15 and under the age of 26 to be youth representatives on the council on such terms as the council may decide[7].

1   Local Government Act 1972, s 91.
2   LGA 1972, s 16A, added by Local Government and Public Involvement in Health Act 2007, s 76. At the time of going to press, no regulations had been made.
3   See the wording of LGA 1972, s 82.
4   See the wording of LGA 1972, s 83(4).
5   See the wording of LGA 1972, s 84.
6   LGA 1972, s 85.
7   Local Government (Wales) Measure 2011, ss 118 and 119.

Return after a successful election petition

6.10 An election court may either declare a particular place vacant (in which case a casual vacancy occurs)[1] or it may scrutinise the votes given and strike off any which ought not to be counted. A vote is struck off where the voter has been personated or treated or bribed or unduly influenced. Where votes have been given for a candidate who is disqualified, they will be struck off if the voters knew or can be or ought to be presumed to have known of the disqualification. When the scrutiny is complete the court may declare which of the candidates has been elected.

1   Local Government Act 1972, s 89.

Co-option to fill a casual vacancy

6.11 A casual vacancy is deemed to have occurred:

(a)   when a local councillor fails to make his declaration of acceptance of office within the proper time; or
(b)   when his notice of resignation is received; or
(c)   on the day of his death; or
(d)   in the case of a disqualification by conviction or an order under Part VIII of the Local Government Act 1972 on the day when either the time for appeal or application for relief expires, or such appeal or application is dismissed or abandoned; or
(e)   in the case of an election being declared void, upon the date of the report or certificate of the election court; or
(f)   where a person ceases to be qualified, or becomes disqualified for any reason other than conviction or order, or is persistently absent from meetings, upon the date when his office is declared vacant by the High Court or council as the case may be[1].

The date may be important; for example the quorum may be different before and after it.

1   Local Government Act 1972, s 87(1).

Procedure

6.12 Except where the vacancy arises from three cases, namely failure to accept office, resignation, or death, an interval of days must elapse. The office must be declared vacant by an authority competent to make such a declaration

48

or its equivalent; for instance the High Court may do so in appropriate cases (such as on conviction). Often, however, the local council must make the declaration itself; particularly where a member ceases to be qualified or becomes disqualified for any reason other than a conviction or breach of an enactment relating to corrupt or illegal election practices, or where he ceases to be a member through persistent absence[1].

The council must make the declaration within a reasonable time. This means that where the vacancy is created by the act of some body other than the council, it must take reasonable steps to ascertain the fact. It will, for example, not necessarily be informed by the court.

After the vacancy has been declared by the council, it must be publicly notified immediately[2]; in other cases it must be similarly notified as soon as possible[3]. Proper notification is important because the period within which a poll may be claimed begins with the date of notification.

[1]   Local Government Act 1972, s 86.
[2]   LGA 1972, s 87(2)(a), Local Government (Wales) Measure 2011, s 116.
[3]   LGA 1972, s 87(2)(b).

The claimed poll

6.13 If a poll is claimed by ten electors a bye-election of the usual kind by nomination and poll[1] takes place within 60 days of the notice of vacancy[2]. The poll must be claimed within 14 days of the public notification of the vacancy, not counting Saturdays, Sundays, Christmas Eve, Christmas Day, Maundy Thursday, Good Friday, a bank holiday and any day of public thanksgiving or mourning, and it cannot be claimed within six months of the day when the councillor whose office is declared vacant would ordinarily have retired.

[1]   See **6.6** above.
[2]   Local Elections (Parishes and Communities) (England and Wales) Rules 2006, SI 2006/3305, r 8(3).

No poll claimed

6.14 If no poll is claimed in time, the council fills the vacancy by co-option as soon as practicable. It must do this, if the period of vacancy has six months or more to run. It may, but is not bound to do so, if less[1].

[1]   Local Elections (Parishes and Communities) (England and Wales) Rules 2006, SI 2006/3305, r 5(5).

Voting in council on casual vacancies

6.15 A successful candidate must have received an absolute majority vote of those present and voting[1]. It follows that if there are more than two candidates for one vacancy and no one of them at the first count receives a majority over the aggregate votes given to the rest, steps must be taken to strike off the candidate with the least number of votes and the remainder must then be put to the vote again; this process must, if necessary, be repeated until an absolute majority is obtained.

This will mostly be a satisfactory procedure, but if several candidates have obtained the same number of least votes and the aggregate of the others is less than a normal quorum (eg 3:2:2:2:2) it may be thought wise not to strike off all those with the least votes together but, if negotiations for withdrawals fail, to strike them off one by one, in an order determined by vote.

If there is more than one vacancy and the number of candidates equals the number of vacancies, all the vacancies may be filled by a single composite resolution, but if the number of candidates exceeds the number of vacancies, each vacancy must be filled by a separate vote or series of votes.

The council is not obliged to consider the claims of candidates who were unsuccessful at a previous election.

[1] Local Government Act 1972, Sch 12, para 39.

D   DECLARATION AND UNDERTAKING

Acceptance of office

6.16 The chairman and councillors must make a declaration of acceptance of office in a prescribed form[1]. The vice-chairman (if any) is not required to make such a declaration.

The chairman must make his declaration at the meeting at which he is elected and each councillor must make his declaration at or before the first meeting after he is elected unless in either case the council at that meeting permits the declaration to be made at or before a later meeting. The declaration must be made in the presence of a member or the council's proper officer and delivered to the council[2].

If, therefore, a council meeting occurs between the ordinary elections and the fourth day thereafter, the declarations of the newly elected councillors must be made at that meeting in the presence of a member of the outgoing council.

Since the term of office of outgoing members is brought to an end by statute, re-elected councillors must execute new declarations as well as the others.

If the declaration is not executed at the proper time, a casual vacancy automatically arises, but this does not, by itself, affect the right of the person concerned to seek office again.

[1] Local Government Act 1972, s 83(4). The form of the English undertaking appears in Local Elections (Declaration of Acceptance of Office) Order 2012, SI 2012/1465, the Welsh in Local Elections (Declaration of Acceptance of Office) (Wales) Order 2004, SI 2004/1508.
[2] See note 1 above.

Code of conduct

6.17 In addition, each councillor must undertake in writing to abide by the council's code of conduct. If he fails to do so within two months from the date on which the council adopts its code he ceases to be a member of the council (and a casual vacancy thereby arises)[1]. In Wales only, the undertaking is incorporated in the declaration of acceptance of office, so that admission to office is not possible without signing it[2].

1   Local Government Act 2000, s 52(1) and (2).
2   Local Elections (Declaration of Acceptance of Office (Wales) Order 2004, SI 2004/1508.

6.18 All councillors are obliged to adhere to a code of conduct. This subject is dealt with in CHAPTER 7.

E   TERM OF OFFICE

Councillors

6.19 Apart from the chairman and vice-chairman, councillors retire together on the fourth day after the ordinary elections[1]; therefore, the ordinary term of office of an elected councillor will be four years (sometimes less three weeks if a poll has been postponed for a parliamentary or European Assembly election)[2], but occasionally there may be exceptions of two kinds. Where a local bye-election has to be held the term of office of the bye-elected local councillors will be shortened by the period which has elapsed since the ordinary election year, and where a district council's method of election is changed, the term of office of the local councillors in some of the localities in the district may be extended or reduced by order of the Secretary of State so as to bring their election timetable conveniently into step with that of their ward[3].

Bye-elected local councillors hold office until the end of the current term of office of the other local councillors[4].

Councillors appointed by the district council (T) (see **6.1**) hold office until their successors are elected.

Councillors appointed by the council (see **6.9** above) hold office in accordance with regulations made by the Secretary of State[5].

1   Local Government Act 1972, ss 16(3) and 35(2).
2   See **6.6**.
3   See **6.6**.
4   LGA 1972, ss 16(3) and 35(2).
5   LGA 1972, s 16A(3)(b) added by Local Government and Public Involvement in Health Act 2007, s 76. At the time of going to press no regulations had been made.

Area alterations

6.20 A parish councillor for an area altered by an order continues in office for the altered area until he would have retired if the order had not been made, and casual vacancies are treated as if they had arisen for the altered area. Members of an abolished parish council retire when the abolition takes effect[1].

1   Local Government (Parishes and Parish Councils) Regulations 1999, SI 1999/545, reg 11.

Chairman or town mayor

6.21 The chairman or town mayor is elected annually at the annual meeting, where his election must be the first business, and he holds office (unless he resigns or is persistently absent or ceases to be qualified or becomes disqualified) until his successor is elected[1]; his term of office is not affected by the time limit on the term of office of local councillors even where there has been a supervening election in which he, as a candidate, has failed to secure re-election; but if he is to retire immediately after the election of the new chairman he has only a casting vote[2].

[1] Local Government Act 1972, ss 15(4) and 34(4).
[2] LGA 1972, ss 15(2) and 34(2).

Vice-chairman or deputy town mayor

6.22 The vice-chairman or deputy town mayor may be appointed at any time and holds office until immediately after the appointment of the chairman at the next annual meeting[1].

[1] Local Government Act 1972, ss 15(7) and 34(7).

F   THE RESERVE POWERS OF THE DISTRICT COUNCIL (T)

6.23 A district council (T) has far-reaching powers designed to prevent such breakdowns as may result from a local council being improperly constituted in the first instance for reasons other than shortage of candidates or the abandonment of a poll, or from its becoming unable to act at a later stage.

First, if any difficulty arises with respect to any election or to the first meeting after an ordinary election or if for any reason a local council is not properly constituted, the district council (T) may make such appointment or do anything necessary or expedient for the proper holding of the election or meeting and properly constituting the council, and it may also direct and fix the dates for the holding of such an election or meeting[1]. An application under this power can be made, for instance, for the appointment of a councillor where the ordinary machinery for election has failed, or for leave to hold a first meeting out of time.

Second, if a local council (T) has so many vacancies that it cannot act, the district council (T) may by order appoint persons to fill the vacancies or some of them until other councillors are elected and take up office. In the case of a common local council whose localities are in different districts, this power is exercised by the district council (T) with the greater number of electors for the localities in the group. Two copies of any such order must be sent to the Secretary of State[2].

[1] Representation of the People Act 1983, s 39(4).
[2] Local Government Act 1972, s 91.

Chapter 7

MEETINGS AND PROCEDURE OF A LOCAL COUNCIL

A NUMBER, DATE AND TIME

7.1 A local council must meet annually. In an election year this annual meeting must take place on the day when the councillors take office, or within 14 days thereafter. In any other year it may be held on any day in May.

In addition a parish, but not a community[1], council must meet on at least three other occasions during the year[2] and may hold as many further meetings as it pleases. Such meetings may be held by virtue of a standing order, or they may be specially convened.

A meeting may be adjourned for any reasonable length of time but after the resumption it can consider only the remainder of the agenda being considered before the adjournment. A meeting cannot be adjourned to a date after the next regular meeting, because its minutes cannot then be completed in time, nor before an election to a date after the new councillors come into office, because the new councillors will not have received the old agenda.

A local council may meet at any time of day but the annual meeting is held at 6 pm if no other time has been fixed for it[3].

[1] Local Government Act 1972, Sch 12, para 8. There is no equivalent Welsh provision.
[2] LGA 1972, Sch 12, paras 10(1) and 26(1).
[3] LGA 1972, Sch 12, paras 7 and 23.

B PLACE OF MEETING

7.2 Meetings may not take place in licensed premises (see **24.5** below) unless no other suitable room is available free of charge or at reasonable cost[1].

If the council owns a suitable room in the locality which it can use free of charge, meetings must be held there; if not, then at all reasonable times and after reasonable notice, the council may use free of charge a room in any school maintained by the local education authority or any room maintainable out of any rate, but a room in a dwelling-house cannot be required for the purpose nor may a meeting be held so as to interfere with the hours in which a room is needed for education, justice or police[2].

It is generally inappropriate for a council to meet in a room in private house. The room may be of inadequate size and not compliant with rules or good practice relating to health and safety, public liability, disabled access and facilities for the press. It also may give the impression that the council is a private body.

Subject to the foregoing a council may meet outside its locality[3].

The local council or parish meeting must make good the cost of any expenses or damage incurred as a result of the meeting[4].

Before 1894 the vestry could meet in the church or vestry unless the Vestries Act 1850 had been applied to the parish by order. English parish councils (or, where there is no parish council, the parish meeting) inherited the rights of their respective vestries as they stood in 1894[5].

[1] Local Government Act 1972, Sch 12, paras 7 and 23.
[2] LGA 1972, s 134(1)–(3).
[3] LGA 1972, Sch 12, paras 10(1) and 26(1).
[4] LGA 1972, s 134(4).
[5] Local Government Act 1894, ss 6(1), 19 and 75(1).

C   RIGHT TO CONVENE

7.3 There is a distinction between ordinary and extraordinary meetings. An ordinary meeting is called by the clerk in pursuance of statutory rules or under standing orders, and includes a meeting convened by him to elect a chairman when a casual vacancy has arisen in the chair[1]. An extraordinary meeting is one specially called.

The chairman may convene an extraordinary meeting of the council at any time[2], and unless it by standing order otherwise directs, the vice-chairman may do so in the absence of the chairman[3]. In addition if two members sign a requisition that the council be convened and the chairman (or vice-chairman as the case may be) either refuses or neglects to do so for seven days, then any two members may convene[1]. The two convening members need not be the same as the requisitioning members.

[1] Local Government Act 1972, Sch 12, paras 8 and 24 and s 88(2).
[2] LGA 1972, Sch 12, paras 9 and 25. For special meetings to appoint honorary freemen see **5.15** above.
[3] LGA 1972, ss 15(9) and 34(9).

D   PUBLIC NOTICES AND AGENDA

Notice

7.4 At least three clear days before a meeting of the council (excluding the days of issue and meeting, Sundays, the days of the Christmas, Easter and bank holiday breaks and days appointed for public thanksgiving or mourning[1]) a notice of the time and place of the meeting must be affixed in some conspicuous place in the locality. If the meeting is called by councillors, they must sign it and it must specify the business to be transacted at the meeting[2]; if the business includes a statutory resolution under the Local Government

Superannuation Acts the terms of the resolution and the fact that it will be moved must be set out in the notice, which must be exhibited 28 clear days before the meeting[3]. For meetings to consider certain auditors' reports see **18.15–19** below.

[1] Local Government Act 1972,s 243.
[2] Local Government Act 1972, Sch 12, paras 10(2)(a) and 26(2)(a).
[3] Local Government Pension Scheme Regulations 1995, SI 1995/1019, reg B1(i) and Sch A1(i). (The latter defines "statutory resolution".)

Agenda

7.5 A similar period before the meeting a summons signed by the clerk must be left at or sent by post to the usual residence of every member of the council[1] (including the retiring chairman and vice-chairman after an ordinary election even if they have failed to secure re-election). This must specify the business which it is proposed to transact[1] in such a way that the member who receives it can identify the matters which he will be expected to discuss. A council cannot lawfully decide any matter which is not specified in the summons[2]. It is a common practice to send agendas (and accompanying documents) by email. NALC advises its members that the summons may be served electronically so long as the relevant email contains the electronic signature and title of the proper officer and the council has first passed a resolution authorising service of the summons by electronic means.

Some agendas conclude with the item 'Any Other Business'. Since this conceals rather than specifies the business, if any, to which it relates no decisions may lawfully be made on business brought up for discussion under it, unless the council has at a previous meeting passed a standing order which permits business left over from a previous meeting to be discussed under this head. There is, however, no objection to matters being discussed under the heading of 'Any Other Business' which involve no more than an exchange of information. The author's view is that an agenda should not include "Any Other Business" to avoid the possibility of decisions being taken unlawfully.

[1] Local Government Act 1972, Sch 12, paras 10(2)(b) and 26(2)(b).
[2] *Longfield Parish Council v Wright* (1918) 88 LJ Ch 119.

E   CONFIDENCE AND ADMISSION OF STRANGERS

7.6 A meeting of a council must be open to the public and the press. They can be excluded only by a resolution if publicity would prejudice the public interest by reason of the confidential nature of the business or for some other reason stated in the resolution and arising out of the business to be transacted. The power to exclude[1] is not exercisable generally but only for a particular occasion.

The press has no greater right to be present than the public, but it is entitled, on payment, to copies of the agenda. The council must also give the press facilities for taking their reports and (unless the meeting place is not owned by the council) for telephoning them.

These rules apply equally to committees of the council[2].

In few cases is there any good reason for excluding the press or the public from meetings, and in still fewer is it necessary to impose secrecy upon the members. As a rule, however, it is desirable to treat the discussion of the following types of business as confidential:

(a)   engagement, terms of service, conduct and dismissal of employees;
(b)   terms of tenders, and proposals and counter-proposals in negotiations for contracts;
(c)   preparation of cases in legal proceedings; and
(d)   the early stages of any dispute.

[1]   Public Bodies (Admission to Meetings) Act 1960.
[2]   Local Government Act 1972, ss 100 and 102.

Public participation

7.7 Many local councils set aside a period when the public can ask questions or even make statements. This is an excellent practice as long as the period is defined, and it is clearly understood that the public must not take part at any other time.

F   COUNCIL QUORUM

7.8 The quorum is three or one-third of the total membership, whichever is the greater, but where more than one-third of the members are disqualified at the same time the quorum is either three or one-third of the qualified members whichever is the greater, until such time as the membership has been increased to not less than two-thirds of the total[1].

[1]   Local Government Act 1972, Sch 12, paras 12, 28 and 45. For the temporary appointment of members pending the election of new councillors so as to expedite business see **6.22** above.

G   COUNCILLORS' CONDUCT

England

7.9 The power conferred by the Local Government Act 2000 on the Secretary of State to prescribe principles and codes of conduct for councillors was abolished by the Localism Act 2011. The 2011 Act requires every council to adopt a code of conduct. Parish councils may adopt the code of the principal authority within the area of which it lies[1]. NALC has prepared a model code which can be accessed by councils in membership on the Association's website. The code applies to elected and co-opted councillors but not to appointed councillors.

[1]   Localism Act 2011, s 27.

Wales

The Welsh Assembly may by order specify principles which are to govern the conduct of members and co-opted members of local councils. The Assembly may also issue model codes consistent with such principles or revise them[2]. The codes may contain optional as well as mandatory provisions. Most of the provisions are mandatory, the exceptions being where the relevant legislation underlying the code is not applicable to local councils. Within six months of their issue a local council must resolve to adopt or revise a code, make copies available for inspection, advertise them and send copies to the Public Services Ombudsman for Wales.

Principal authorities must appoint Standards Committees to promote high standards of conduct, assist members to observe their code, advise on the adoption or revision of it, monitor its operation and arrange for training on related matters[3]. At least one member of a standards committee must be a local councillor for the area.

The Public Services Ombudsman for Wales has issued guidance to community councillors. This can be viewed on the Ombudsman's website.

[2] LGA 2000, s 50; Local Authorities (Model Code of Conduct) (Wales) Order 2008, SI 2008/788.
[3] LGA 2000, ss 53–56.

Pursuit and adjudication (Wales only)

7.10 The Public Services Ombudsman for Wales appoints ethical standards officers who may investigate and report on complaints. The report may be referred to an adjudication panel and ultimately to a Case Tribunal to declare whether there has or has not been a breach of a code of conduct. If it declares a breach, it may decide to take no other action, or decide that a culprit be suspended for not more than a year or until the end of his term of office, or be disqualified from office in that or any other authority for not more than five years. It can also make recommendations to the council, which must consider them within three months.

H   INTERESTS

England

7.11 Councillors' conduct in relation to interests and the registration of them, are regulated by the Localism Act 2011 ss 26–34 and regulations made thereunder. The provisions of the 2011 Act require the monitoring officer of the relevant principal authority to establish and maintain a register of interests of elected and co-opted members. The register must be available for public inspection at a place within the principal authority's area at all reasonable hours and must be published on that authority's website. If a parish council has a website, the register must be published there as well[1].

Within 28 days after becoming an elected or co-opted member, a councillor must notify the monitoring officer of any disclosable pecuniary interests which he has at the time of notification[2]. Those interests are specified in the Relevant Authorities (Disclosable Interests) Regulations 2012, SI 2012/1464. A pecuniary interest is disclosable if it is either the interest of the member himself or that of his spouse, or civil partner, or person living with the member as husband or wife or as if they were civil partners. The member must be aware of the interest for it to be disclosable[3]. Where a member has a sensitive disclosable interest, the existence of the interest must be disclosed but not its nature. An interest is sensitive if member and the monitoring officer consider that disclosure could lead to the member being subject to violence or intimidation[4].

At a meeting of the council, a committee, a sub-committee or a joint committee or sub-committee at which he is present, a member must disclose any disclosable interest of which he is aware (including any such interest which is not registered). Having declared the interest, the member must not participate, or further participate, in discussion on the matter and must not take part in any vote or further vote thereon. If the declared interest is not on the register, it must be registered within 28 days of its declaration. Standing orders may provide for the exclusion of a member during discussion and voting on a matter in which he has declared a disclosable pecuniary interest. Furthermore, the member must not take any steps, or further steps, in relation to the matter, save for the purpose of enabling the matter to be dealt with otherwise than by the member[5].

The council may grant a member a dispensation from the ban on speaking or voting (one or both) if it considers: (a) that without a dispensation the number of persons prohibited from speaking and/or voting would be so great a proportion of the members that the council's business would be impeded; (b) that without the dispensation the party political balance on the council would be upset and alter the likely outcome of a vote; or (c) that it would otherwise be appropriate to grant a dispensation. The period of dispensation must be for a specified period not exceeding four years[6].

It is an offence without reasonable excuse: (a) to fail to register a disclosable pecuniary interest, or to fail to declare an unregistered interest at a meeting, or to fail to register an unregistered within 28 days after its declaration; (b) to speak or vote in relation to a declared pecuniary interest; (c) take any steps in relation to a matter in which he has declared an interest. The maximum penalty on summary conviction is a fine not exceeding level 5 on the standard scale. In addition, the court may disqualify a convicted person for a period not exceeding five years. A prosecution must be sanctioned by the Director of Public Prosecutions and must normally be brought within 12 months from the date on which the prosecutor obtained sufficient evidence to warrant proceedings with a long stop of three years[7].

1   Localism Act 2011, s 29.
2   Localism Act 2011, s 30(1).
3   Localism Act 2011, s 30(3).
4   Localism Act 2011, s 32.
5   Localism Act 2011, s 31.
6   Localism Act 2011, s 33.
7   Localism Act 2011, s 34.

Wales

The Localism Act 2011 does not apply in Wales, The law relating to interests in Wales is governed by Part III of the Local Government Act 2000. The registrable interests of members are specified in The Local Authorities (Model Code of Conduct) (Wales) Order 2008, SI 2008/788.

I   PERSISTENT ABSENCE

7.12 If a member fails throughout six consecutive months to attend any meetings of the council or of its committees or sub-committees of which he is a member, or of a joint committee, joint board or other body to which any of the council's powers have been transferred or delegated, he ceases automatically to be a member of the council[1] unless either he has a 'statutory excuse' (broadly speaking, military service during war or an emergency) or his failure is due to a reason approved by the council before the end of the period or he attended as a representative of the council at a meeting of any body of persons (such as a county association of local councils). The period begins with the last meeting attended[2].

[1]   Local Government Act 1972, s 85(1) and (2).
[2]   LGA 1972, s 85(1).

Employment

7.13 A councillor's employer must give his employee reasonable time off to attend to council affairs and perform approved duties, having regard to the employee's absence on the business and the amount of time required or already taken by the employee on trade union duties; and the councillor may complain to an employment tribunal if he fails to do so[1].

[1]   Employment Rights Act 1996, s 50.

Excuses

7.14 Membership of the armed forces in time of war is a statutory excuse and so is such service under the Crown in connection with a war or emergency as in the Secretary of State's opinion entitles the member to relief[1].

Apologies need not necessarily be conveyed in writing but reasons for absence known to the council should be minuted. Where a council is considering a reason for absence, some reason or explanation must be known to it and this must be approved by affirmative resolution at the earliest possible moment before the end of the six months. If at that moment the council fails to consider the question, the office falls vacant without further ado, and the vacancy must be declared and filled in the proper manner.

There is nothing to prevent a local council from approving a reason for absence in advance.

[1]   Local Government Act 1972, s 85(3).

J DISQUALIFICATION AND CESSATION OF QUALIFICATION

7.15 When a member ceases to be qualified or becomes disqualified he must at once cease to act and risks legal proceedings if he continues to do so[1]. The prohibition, which covers the signature of documents[2], is absolute, though for the purpose of filling the vacancy his office is not deemed vacant until so declared.

A member always ceases to be a member when he ceases to hold a qualifying nationality, but apart from this some may be more effectively entrenched than others; thus one who resided in the locality or within three miles of it during the whole twelve months before the election day, or who has, during the whole of that period, occupied land or had his principal place of work there, will remain a member for the whole of his term even though he leaves the qualifying area permanently on the day after he enters office, but another who is qualified only as an elector will cease to be eligible or to be a member when his name no longer appears on the electoral roll[3].

A disqualification is a consequence of a positive event[4] whereas a cessation of qualification is negative; disqualifications are therefore usually attended with greater publicity and are easier to ascertain.

[1]   Local Government Act 1972, s 92.
[2]   For the evidential effect of signed minutes in this context see **7.34** below.
[3]   For the right to be on the electoral roll and the date upon which it comes into force see **5.8** above.
[4]   See **6.2** above.

K ATTENDANCE REGISTER AND APOLOGIES

7.16 The names of members present at a meeting must be recorded[1] and this record should form part of the minutes of each meeting. It is unnecessary as a rule to record a late arrival, but it is important to record the grounds upon which apologies for absence are tendered in case they have to be approved to prevent a casual vacancy arising[2]. If a member withdraws on grounds of interest, his withdrawal should be recorded.

[1]   Local Government Act 1972, Sch 12, para 40.
[2]   See **7.12** above.

L ANNUAL AND FIRST MEETINGS

First meetings

7.17 Local councillors are, of course, entitled to be present at all meetings but in addition certain others may, for a short time, take part at certain first or annual meetings; these additional persons are, in the case of the first meeting after the creation of the council, the person appointed by the district council (T) to act in place of the chairman[1]; in the case of the first annual meeting after an ordinary election the chairman and vice-chairman who are about to retire; and in the case of any other annual meeting the retiring chairman[2].

[1]   Under Representation of the People Act 1983, s 39 and Local Government Act 1972, s 91.

² LGA 1972, ss 15(4), (7) and (8) and 34(4), (7) and (8).

Who may preside

7.18 The chairman, or in his absence the vice-chairman (if any), must preside. Only if these are both absent may the council appoint some other councillor to preside[1]. The once common practice whereby proceedings at first annual meetings after the elections were opened with the paid clerk in the chair is unlawful.

¹ Local Government Act 1972, Sch 12, paras 11 and 27.

First business

7.19 The first business of the meeting must be the election of the chairman[1], who must be an elected (ie not appointed—see Chapter 6) member of the council. The person presiding may vote and must, if necessary, give a casting vote in such an election and may vote for himself, unless, in either case, he is a retiring chairman who is about to cease to be a member of the council, in which case he has only a casting vote[2]. In his absence the retiring vice-chairman has the same voting rights as the chairman[3], but if the chairman is present, the vice-chairman may only vote if he is a councillor. The possibility of the vice-chairman not being a councillor can only occur immediately after an election.

At the moment when the new chairman accepts office the previous chairman and vice-chairman automatically retire[4] and if they are not councillors they at the same moment cease to be members.

¹ Local Government Act 1972, ss 15(2) and 34(2).
² LGA 1972, ss 15(2), (3) and 34(2), (3).
³ LGA 1972, ss 15(9) and 34(9). See also LGA 1972, Sch 12, paras 11 and 27.
⁴ LGA 1972, ss 15(4), (7) and 34(4), (7).

Removal of difficulties

7.20 The district council (T) has power to remove certain difficulties arising at first meetings. The appointment of a person to preside at the opening is a common example of the use of this power[1].

¹ Under Representation of the People Act 1983, s 39 and Local Government Act 1972, s 91.

Routine business at annual meetings

7.21 Apart from the appointment of the chairman the law does not require any particular business to be transacted at the annual meeting, but it is desirable to establish a routine list of matters which should always appear on its agenda. Such a list may conveniently be incorporated in a standing order and may include the checking of inventories of parish and community documents, the appointment of representatives to the local councils association and other bodies, the hearing of reports from such representatives, the payment of annual subscriptions and the election of committees.

M   TIMING OF MEETINGS AND PRECEPTS

7.22 In fixing the dates of its meetings the council should have regard both to the timing of its precepts in the financial year preceding the beginning of the financial year for which it is issued, and, in England, the date of the annual assembly of the parish meeting which takes place between 1 March and 1 June inclusive.

N   STANDING ORDERS ON BUSINESS[1]

[1]   For the compulsory standing orders on contracts see **19.9** below.

7.23 A council may make standing orders to regulate its business and proceedings, and may vary or revoke them[2]. Models are published by the National Association of Local Councils. It is usually not necessary for very small councils to have standing orders, but it is always desirable for every council to possess a copy of one of the recognised models, so that in a difficulty the chairman can give a decision based upon an established precedent.

Standing orders must obviously not conflict with the law, and the Secretary of State may by regulation require or forbid particular standing orders[3].

[2]   Local Government Act 1972, Sch 12, para 42.
[3]   Local Government and Housing Act 1989, s 20.

O   SUBJECTS FOR CONSIDERATION

7.24 A local council may obviously consider any matter in which it has statutory power to act, including the power to spend an amount of money for any purpose which in the council's opinion is for the benefit of its area or its inhabitants[1]. In addition it has the same power to discuss parish or community affairs as the parish or community meeting[2] because it may convene that body and therefore discuss the reason for doing so. In any event it is usually cheaper and better to discuss local affairs in the council than constantly to summon the electors to do so.

[1]   See **22.17** and also **22.35** below.
[2]   See **10.11** and **35.10** below.

Moving

7.25 A council may by standing order require that a resolution shall be seconded as well as moved (and many do) but a seconder is not required by any rule of law (or by either House of Parliament), and in the absence of such a standing order the chairman should permit resolutions and amendments to be discussed after they have been moved only.

Form

7.26 In all but the very simplest cases the mover of a resolution or amendment should be required to reduce it to writing.

A resolution should be specific and wherever possible vagueness should be avoided. If it is not possible to be specific, a person or committee should be instructed to fill in the details, or the matter should be adjourned pending inquiries.

Duplicity

7.27 A resolution should not deal with more than one subject and where a resolution combining more than one subject is moved, the chairman should require the mover to separate the component parts and move them one by one. Disregard of this rule usually leads to confused discussion and may lead to confused action, if different parts of a resolution affect different interests or require consents from other and different bodies. In considering whether a resolution is duplex or not regard must be had to its substantial effect and not only to its wording, which may be deceptively simple. A resolution 'that the parish field be sold' may turn out to be duplex if half the area happens to be held upon charitable trusts.

When the chairman has severed the resolution which he suspects of duplicity it may be convenient (if the subjects are in some way inter-dependent) to allow both resolutions to be moved together but to require that the discussion upon them shall proceed separately.

Discussion

7.28 In larger authorities it is common to limit the length of speeches and not to permit members other than the mover to speak more than once on any one resolution. In any but the largest local councils these rules seem unduly restrictive. On the other hand the chairman ought not to allow members to introduce into their speeches matters which do not relate to the issue before the council. A decision on relevance is often hard to make, and no doubt a chairman should allow some latitude rather than incur the suspicion that he is trying to gag debate, but the duty should not be shirked and when a matter is ruled out of order as irrelevant the ruling should be firmly enforced.

The direct negative

7.29 It is never necessary to move the rejection of a resolution because every decision must be reached by an affirmative vote of a majority present and voting, and if this is not secured the resolution is rejected in any case[1].

[1]   See 7.32 below.

Amendment

7.30 Amendments should be moved in the form of motions either to insert or to alter or to omit words in the resolution under discussion. A direct negative is not an amendment, and an amendment whose practical effect is to negative the resolution should not be permitted, because its sponsor can achieve his object by persuading the council to vote against the resolution.

In putting resolutions and amendments to the vote the chairman must put the amendment first. The fact that an amendment is rejected does not mean that the main resolution is accepted, nor does acceptance of the amendment mean that the resolution as amended is accepted. In every case voting on an amendment must be followed by a decision on the main resolution. For instance, on a motion, 'that a motor mower be purchased' an amendment might be moved to insert the words 'second-hand' before 'motor'. If the amendment is passed the motion under discussion will read 'that a second-hand motor mower be purchased' and it will still be open to move a further amendment (for instance to substitute 'hand' for 'motor'). After all amendments have been disposed of it will still be necessary to decide if a mower shall be purchased at all, and this is done by voting upon the resolution in its final form as amended or not amended.

Enforcing decisions

7.31 A decision on a topic ends discussion upon it. The council should proceed to the next business and the chairman must rule out of order (as irrelevant) any attempt at that meeting to reopen the previous topic.

P   VOTING

7.32 Every decision, save to appoint an honorary freeman, must be made by a majority of the members present and voting[1]. Provided that a quorum is present it is immaterial that a quorum of members take part in the voting. A motion may therefore be carried by a single voter if nobody votes against him[2].

The person presiding may vote even if by so doing he creates an equality of votes, and if there is an equality of votes he has a second or casting vote[3].

Members vote by show of hands unless they have provided otherwise by standing order. If any member so requires the manner in which each member voted on any particular question must be recorded in the minutes[4]; and a member who wishes the voting to be recorded may make his demand either before or after the vote.

[1]   Local Government Act 1972, Sch 12, para 39(1). For honorary freedoms see **5.15** above.
[2]   For voting on co-options see **6.7** and on elections to the chair see **6.21** and **7.17**.
[3]   LGA 1972, Sch 12, para 39(2) but see **8.1**. See the facts in *R v Jackson, ex p Pick* (1913) 3 KB 426. For casting vote at an electors' meeting see **10.7** and **35.11** below.
[4]   LGA 1972, Sch 12, paras 13 and 29.

Q   DEFAMATION

The subject matter of possible defamation is infinitely various and the law correspondingly complicated. The following paragraphs give only the barest outline of that part of the law which most commonly affects local council proceedings.

7.33

'A man disparages the good name of another when he publishes to some third person words or matter which are false and which injure his reputation . . . such disparagement, if embodied in some permanent form . . . is called libel: if expressed in some fugitive form . . . it is called slander'[1].

It is presumed that libel causes injury and a similar presumption arises in slanders which disparage a person in his office, profession, calling, trade, or business; in other cases of slander the person alleging injury must prove it[2].

[1]   *Gatley on Libel and Slander* (5th edn, 1960), p 3. The current edition of *Gatley* (the 11th, published in 2008) does not contain these words. In view of the Rehabilitation of Offenders Act 1974 this famous quotation may need some revision.
[2]   Defamation Act 1952, s 2.

Privilege

7.34 A person who has made a defamatory statement may claim privilege for it if he can show that he made it without malice and in pursuit of a public duty. For instance if a member has a good reason to believe that the local council's funds are being misappropriated he is under a public duty to inform the council. If, on investigation, the statement is found to be true, it is not defamatory at all, but if it is found to be untrue he may claim privilege if he acted without malice.

Fair comment

7.35 Fair comment on a matter of public interest is not actionable. The acts and proceedings of a local council are matters of public interest, and a local council or other local authority as such cannot maintain an action for defamation if it is criticised[1] even if such criticism is intemperately expressed. Criticism must, however, be fair and if it is so worded that it can reasonably be held to impute unworthy or corrupt motives to particular members they would, as individuals, be entitled to take action.

[1]   *Purcell v Sowler* (1876–77) LR 2 CPD 215; *Derbyshire County Council v Times Newspapers* [1993] AC 534.

R   MINUTES

7.36 Minutes of proceedings of a council and of its committees must be kept[1]. They are intended to be formal records of official acts and decisions, not reports, still less verbatim reports, of the speeches made by councillors. Minutes should, therefore, be as short as is consistent with clarity and accuracy, and the arguments used in the discussion need be recorded only if the decision cannot be clearly expressed in any other way. Short simple minutes are less likely to be defamatory than long reports.

1   Local Government Act 1972, Sch 12, para 41(1).

Minute book

7.37 The minutes must be entered in a book kept for the purpose[1]. Looseleaf minute books are lawful provided that the pages are consecutively numbered and initialled by the person signing the minutes at the time of signature[2].

Though minutes may be held in a computer database for convenience, the minute book remains the only lawful and authentic record.

1   Local Government Act 1972, Sch 12, para 41(1).
2   LGA 1972, Sch 12, para 41(2).

Signature

7.38 The minutes must be signed and looseleaf pages initialled at the meeting which they record or at the next meeting, by the person presiding thereat[1], but the Secretary of State has power to make regulations permitting some other day. In the world of local councils there does not seem to be any good reason for making them[2]. A council before allowing the chairman to sign should satisfy itself of their accuracy, but discussion of the words should not be allowed to stray into the merits of the decision which they express.

The practice of signing minutes at the next meeting should not be regarded as invariable. In a difficult or complicated matter, and especially when an interval of some months or a change of membership is expected, it is preferable to adjourn while the minutes are drawn up and to approve and sign them then and there. Minutes of an annual council meeting, if not signed on the same day, should be signed at the next ordinary council meeting and not held over for a year.

1   Local Government Act 1972, Sch 12, para 41(1).
2   LGA 1972, Sch 12, para 41(4).

Minutes of last meetings

7.39 The minutes of the last meeting of an abolished authority or one of its committees or of any joint committee which ceases to exist because of the abolition, should be drawn up and signed by the chairman at the end of the meeting, but if this is not practicable they must be circulated to every member present at the meeting and after seven days the chairman may sign them after considering representations from the recipients. If the chairman cannot sign, the proper officer of the district or unitary council may nominate someone else present to do so[1].

1   Local Government (Parishes and Parish Councils) Regulations 1999, SI 1999/545, reg 14.

Recording majorities

7.40 It is not necessary to record the majority by which a decision is made unless a member requires the voting to be recorded[1], and though a member cannot be prevented from insisting upon this requirement, there are cases where it is undesirable or invidious to insist. These arise mainly in relation to the appointment of employees and especially the clerk.

[1]   Local Government Act 1972, Sch 12, paras 13(2) and 29(2).

Minutes as evidence

7.41 Minutes purporting to be properly signed may be received in evidence without further proof. Until the contrary is proved, where the minutes relate to a meeting of the council, the meeting is deemed to have been duly convened and held and all members present are deemed to have been qualified; and where they relate to a meeting of a committee, the committee is deemed to have been properly constituted and to have had power to deal with the matter set out in the minutes[1].

A copy of a resolution, order, report or minute of a local council or of a precursor of that council (or, in either case, of their committees or sub-committees) is evidence as long as it bears a certificate signed by the clerk or other proper officer authorised by the council. This certificate must state that the original was made or passed on a date specified in the certificate and, in the case of a minute that it was signed in accordance with the Local Government Act 1972, Sch 12, para 41, or the corresponding enactment in force at the time[2]. The corresponding enactment between 1 June 1934 and 31 March 1974 was the Local Government Act 1933, Sch III, Part V, para 3; if before that date the precursor was a parish council or a committee of a rural district council, the enactment was the Local Government Act 1894, Sch I, Part 3, para 2; but where it was the council of an urban or rural district it was the Public Health Act 1875, Sch I, Part (1), para 10 and where, before 1895 the precursor was a sanitary authority it was the same enactment for the authority but Part (2), para 8 for its committees.

The following form of words may be thought suitable:

> 'I certify that I am the proper officer authorised by the Llanfair Community Council to make this certificate; that the Llanfair Parish Council was the precursor of the Llanfair Community Council; that the said Parish Council passed a minute on the 3rd January, 1943, which was signed on 7th February, 1943, in accordance with the Local Government Act, 1933, and that the within written matter is a true and faithful copy thereof.
>
> (Signed) . . . Dillwyn Miles . . .
>
> Clerk of the Llanfair Community Council'.

This certificate must be written or endorsed upon the same sheet, or one of the sheets of the copy which it certifies. It may sometimes be necessary to add identifying words after the word 'matter' such as marked DM1, DM2 and DM3.

Minutes which are not drawn up or signed in accordance with the law are not receivable in evidence.

For public rights of inspection see **11.9** below.

[1] Local Government Act 1972, Sch 12, para 41(3).
[2] Local Government (Miscellaneous Provisions) Act 1976, s 41.

S   SIGNING AND SEALING

7.42 A local council may have a common seal but if it has none it may execute documents requiring a seal under the hands and seals of two of its members[1]. Naturally such execution must not take place without the authority of a resolution, but the law neither requires that the resolution shall name the members concerned nor that the formalities shall be performed in the presence of the council, but the sealing of the documents must be witnessed and in practice the best witness is the clerk.

Where there is a common seal it is advisable and usual to lay down arrangements for its custody and use by standing order.

A private person acting on his own behalf no longer has to seal a deed[2], but a council still must; therefore in a deed between a local council and a private individual, the council must seal it or have it sealed by two of its members, but the individual need not.

[1] Local Government Act 1972, s 14(3).
[2] Law of Property (Miscellaneous Provisions) Act 1989, s 1(1). An example of a pointless change.

T   BRIBERY AND CORRUPTION

7.43 The statutory provisions relating to bribery and corruption are contained in the Bribery Act 2010, which replaces the Public Bodies Corrupt Practices Act 1889 and related legislation. It is an offence for a person ('P') to offer, promise or give a financial or other advantage to another person in either of the following cases. Case 1 is where P intends the advantage to induce the improper performance by another person of a relevant function or activity or to reward such improper performance. Case 2 is where P offers, promises or give a financial or other advantage to another person and knows or believes that the acceptance of the advantage would itself constitute an improper performance of a relevant function[1]. What constitutes improper performance is, in essence, a breach of an expectation that a person will act in good faith, impartially or in pursuance of a position of trust. A relevant function is any function of a public nature (and thus includes the functions of a local authority), any activity connected with a business, with employment or carried on by a body of persons (corporate or unincorporate). In order to decide whether a function or activity is performed improperly, the test is what a reasonable person in the United Kingdom would expect in relation to that functiom or activity[2].

Prosecution of an offender requires the consent of the Director of Public Prosecutions, or the Director of the Serious Fraud Office, or the Director of

Revenue and Customs Prosecutions[3]. The maximum penalty on summary conviction for an individual is a fine not exceeding the statutory maximum (currently £5,000) and for conviction on indictment a term of imprisonment not exceeding 10 years, or a fine, or both. The penalties on conviction for any other person (e.g. a body corporate such as a local authority) are same as for an individual without the option of a prison sentence[4].

It is an offence for an officer of a local authority to accept any fee or reward other than his proper remuneration. The maximum penalty on summary conviction is a level 4 fine[5].

[1] Bribery Act 2010, s 1.
[2] Bribery Act 2010, ss 3–5.
[3] Bribery Act 2010, s 10.
[4] Bribery Act 2101, s 11.
[5] Local Government Act 1972, s 117(2).

U   DISTURBANCES AT MEETINGS

7.44 Anyone (whether a member of the council or of the public) who disturbs the proceedings may be required by resolution to withdraw. It is not desirable for such a resolution to be moved until the chairman has at least once requested the offender to desist and the request has been ignored. Where the chairman's request has been disregarded, the resolution should be moved automatically and without comment by the senior councillor able to do so, though legally any councillor or the chairman may move it. Mere heat or anger in discussion is not of itself a ground for excluding a member, but almost any interruption by the public is technically a disturbance.

An offender who refuses to obey the resolution may be removed by force, but care should be taken to use no more force than is necessary. It is usually desirable (but not legally necessary) to secure the help of the police.

A resolution of exclusion ought not to extend to future meetings[1].

[1] *Barton v Taylor* (1886) 11 AC 197.

V   COMMITTEES—VOTING AND NON-VOTING MEMBERS

7.45 Committees and joint committees[1] may be appointed and they may appoint sub-committees. The council or councils concerned settle the area, if restricted, within which the committee is to operate and the number of its members. All the members of a finance committee must be members of the appointing council or councils. In other committees with executive functions non-members may be appointed but save in four cases the non-members have no vote. These four are the management of land, harbour functions if the council is a harbour authority, tourism functions and the management of a festival[2]. Advisory committees need have no council members at all. A committeeman who is a member of an appointing authority ceases to be a committeeman if he retires from the council, unless already re-elected[3]. The disqualifications for membership of a local council committee are the same as those for the local council[4].

A council can arrange to have any of its functions, except the issuing of precept, exercised by a committee which can, in turn, arrange to have them exercised by a sub-committee[5]. At least when exercising functions (as opposed merely to giving advice) a committee must consist of more than one member[6].

1   For uses of joint committees see **23.8** below.
2   Local Government and Housing Act 1989, s 13 and Parish and Community Councils (Committees) Regulations 1990, SI 1990/2476.
3   Local Government Act 1972, s 102.
4   LGA 1972, s 104.
5   LGA 1972, s 101.
6   *R v Secretary of State, ex p Hillingdon London Borough Council* [1986] 1 All ER 810. It is otherwise in the House of Lords.

W   CONTROLLED, INFLUENCED AND REGULATED COMPANIES

7.46 Some local authorities find it convenient to carry on activities through a company rather than directly. Companies and trusts which are controlled or influenced by local authorities (including local councils acting individually or jointly or through joint committees) are subject to a code whose purpose is to secure that the company's activities are treated financially as part of the council's activities. The legislation breaks down the legal screen between the council as one corporation and the company as another wherever the company is subject to the council's will. The rules apply to any limited or unlimited company together with any society registered under the Industrial and Provident Societies Act 1965. If such a body is for the time being a subsidiary or a subsidiary of a subsidiary of the council, or if the council controls a majority of the shares or appoints or removes a majority of the directors, the company is a controlled company; if the control touches in either case 20 per cent rather than a majority but more than half of the company's turn-over is derived from the council, it is an influenced company. Such orders also apply *pari passu* to non-charitable trusts which are similar in character. The main sanction is that expenditure or other financial transactions in defiance of orders may become illegal.

Such a regulated company must print on all its operative documents and stationery the fact that it is controlled by a local authority or authorities, naming it or them. Directors who are members of such an authority must not be paid more as total remuneration or as travelling or subsistence allowances for a given company duty than the most which they could receive from an authority alone.

The state of the company's finances must be reported by the company or its auditor to the authority's auditor or, as the case may be to the Audit Commission, and also sufficiently to any member of a relevant authority for the purpose of his duties, and it must obtain the Commission's consent to its first appointment of an auditor. A controlled company must make the minutes of its first four general meetings available to the public.

Special rules on capital transactions fill out the principle that the company's finances are to be treated as part of the controlling authority's finances. In general, company capital receipts including grants from the European Union, credit transactions or variations in liabilities which can be made by a council as such, are treated as having been made by the council unless the funds concerned come from the same local authority group or have been disposed for charitable purposes.

The council must have credit cover equivalent to the totals of these transactions, if the total exceeds £10,000. There are also rules on credit approvals, the calculation of liabilities and their relationship to the value of transferred shares, and on dealings between councils in a group and on the apportionment of the value of transactions between councils.

Companies (called arms-length companies) and trusts which are emancipated from the council's influence, for example by the appointment of irremovable directors, cease to be caught by the legislation[1].

Part V of the 1989 Act is repealed and replaced by Part 12 of the Local Government and Public Involvement in Health Act 2007 from a date to be appointed.

[1]   Local Government and Housing Act 1989 Part V and Local Authorities (Companies) Order 1995, SI 1995/849 (as amended).

X   COMPLAINTS AGAINST LOCAL COUNCILS

England

7.47 In England, a local council is not subject to investigation by the local government ombudsman. A complaint about the conduct of a clerk or other employee should be pursued through the council.

A complaint about the council itself can best be dealt with, if not through the ballot box, then through a complaints procedure which the council adopts and makes known to the public. The National Association of Local Councils has promulgated a model code of practice for handling complaints. If the complainant is not satisfied about the council's handling of a complaint, his ultimate remedy (if any) lies through the ballot box at the next election.

Wales

7.48 In Wales, community councils are subject to investigation by the Public Services Ombudsman for Wales (see **21.15** below). In addition, all employees of Welsh local authorities are subject to a code of conduct (the Code of Conduct (Qualifying Local Government Employees) (Wales) Order 2001, SI 2001/2280). However, as a matter of common sense and good practice, a community council would be well advised to consider the advice offered above.

Chapter 8

ELECTED OFFICERS

A   CHAIRMAN OR TOWN MAYOR

8.1 A local council is not properly constituted until it has appointed its chairman; therefore his appointment must be the first business at its annual meeting[1]. He must be a member of the council[2] and he remains in office until his successor is elected unless he resigns, ceases to be qualified or becomes disqualified.

If the locality is a town the chairman is entitled to be called the town mayor[3]. He cannot, apparently, be compelled to use or prevented from using this title.

[1]   Local Government Act 1972, ss 14(1), 15(2), 33(1) and 34(2); see **7.15** above.
[2]   LGA 1972, ss 15(1) and 34(1).
[3]   LGA 1972, s 245(6).

Precedence and representation

8.2 The chairman ought not, within his area, to yield precedence to the representative of any unofficial body. A mayor has precedence within his borough (that is to say the district (T) if it has a borough charter) before all others except the sovereign. A town mayor has precedence within his town immediately after the mayor[1]. The chairman or town mayor is the proper person to represent his parish, community or town on ceremonial occasions elsewhere.

[1]   This seems to follow from the general layout of Local Government Act 1972, ss 245 and 246.

Duties

8.3 If present at a council, the chairman must preside[1], and he has control of its procedure for the purpose of enforcing the law and good order. He must prevent decisions being taken on matters which are not on the agenda, but he cannot stop discussion of subjects properly brought up nor, if matters on the agenda remain to be settled, will his departure of itself bring proceedings to an end. He is the proper person to whom a notice of resignation must be given.

[1]   Local Government Act 1972, Sch 12, paras 11(1) and 27(1).

Casting vote

8.4 The person presiding at a council meeting (whether he is the chairman or not) has a second or casting vote[1], unless the chairman is presiding over the election of a new chairman as his last act before ceasing to be a member of the council. In this case he has only a casting vote[2]. Where there is a tie in the election of the chairman, the person presiding is required by law to give his casting vote one way or the other. In other cases there is no such requirement[2].

There is a convention, supported by good sense and the need to maintain, if possible, the impartiality of the chair, that the casting vote should be used in such a way as to leave the question in issue open for future reconsideration. There is, however, no rule of law to this effect[3].

[1] Local Government Act 1972, Sch 12, para 39(2).
[2] LGA 1972, ss 15(2) and 34(2).
[3] See *R v Bradford City Council, ex p Wilson* [1989] 3 All ER 14 where the subject is considered in detail.

Convening meetings

8.5 The chairman may, on three clear days' notice, convene the council at any time[1], and on seven[2] (or in certain cases relating to the establishment or dissolution of a parish council) 14 or (relating to the establishment or dissolution of a community council) 30[3]) days' notice he may convene the parish or community meeting at any time[4]. He presides at the latter meeting[5], but if he is not an elector for that parish or community he only has a casting vote[6].

In relation to the establishment and dissolution of a community council, see CHAPTER 35.

[1] Local Government Act 1972, Sch 12, paras 9(1), 10(2), 25(1) and 26(2).
[2] LGA 1972, Sch 12, paras 15(1) and 30(1).
[3] LGA 1972, Sch 12, paras 15(3) and 30(3).
[4] LGA 1972, Sch 12, paras 15(2) and 30(2).
[5] LGA 1972, Sch 12, paras 17(1) and 33(1).
[6] LGA 1972, Sch 12, paras 16 and 31.

Minutes

8.6 Minutes must be signed by the person presiding at a meeting[1].

[1] Local Government Act 1972, Sch 12, para 41.

Chairman's allowance

8.7 The chairman may be paid an allowance to meet the expenses of his office[1].

[1] Local Government Act 1972, ss 15(5) and 34(5). See CHAPTER 16 O for more details.

B   VICE-CHAIRMAN OR DEPUTY TOWN MAYOR

8.8 A local council may[1], but need not, appoint a vice-chairman. He may[2] but is not required to execute a declaration of acceptance of office and he holds office until immediately after the election of the chairman at the next annual meeting unless he resigns or ceases to be qualified or becomes disqualified[3].

Subject to any standing orders made by the council anything authorised or required to be done by, to or before the chairman, may be done by, to or before the vice-chairman[4]. A standing order whose effect was to create a distinction between the functions of a chairman and his deputy might thus be lawful, if inconvenient.

[1] Local Government Act 1972, ss 15(6) and 34(6).
[2] LGA 1972, s 83(4).
[3] LGA 1972, ss 15(7) and 34(7).
[4] LGA 1972, ss 15(9) and 34(9).

Inspection of property

8.9 Some local councils make their vice-chairman or deputy town mayor responsible for inspecting the council's property. This custom ensures that a reasonable number of members are personally familiar with the parish or community property[1].

[1] See Chapter **12**.

C   OFFICERS OF DIGNITY

8.10 Certain ancient boroughs elected officers of dignity such as a sheriff or high steward. Where such a borough became on 1 April 1974 a parish or a community with a separate council, the power to appoint these officers passed to the local council[1].

[1] Local Government Act 1972, s 246(3). For honorary freedoms see **5.15** above.

Chapter 9

EMPLOYEES

A   GENERAL

9.1 A local council is required to appoint only such proper officers as it thinks necessary[1], and it may appoint them on such reasonable terms, pay and conditions as it thinks fit[2]. It is not bound to appoint any specified officer[3], but must secure that one of its officers is responsible for its financial affairs[4]. Appointments to paid offices must be made on merit[5].

[1]   Local Government Act 1972, s 112(1).
[2]   LGA 1972, s 112(2).
[3]   LGA 1972, s 112(3).
[4]   LGA 1972, s 151.
[5]   This attempt to make people good by law is in Local Government and Housing Act 1989, s 7. There are some exceptions.

Trade union membership

9.2 A person must not be refused employment because he is or is not, or is unwilling to join, remain in or cease to be a member of a trade union, or to make payments or suffer deductions in the event of his not being such a member. Such a refusal gives him a right of complaint to an employment tribunal and posts must not be advertised on such conditions[1].

[1]   Trade Union and Labour Relations (Consolidation) Act 1992, s 137.

Councillors as officers

9.3 A local council may appoint one or more of its members to be officers of the council without remuneration[1]. An office of profit remains an office of profit even though no profits are actually received[2], and therefore an unpaid office must be specifically created before a councillor can be appointed to it. Moreover a councillor cannot be appointed to a paid office while he is a councillor and for twelve months after he ceases to be one[3], so he must not be appointed during the twelve months to a paid post on condition that he is not actually paid until after the period has elapsed. Such a bargain is contrary to law. If the holder of an unpaid post wishes to seek a paid one after the end of the year, the council must treat his candidacy in the same way as any other.

[1]   Local Government Act 1972, s 112(5).

2   *Delane v Hillcoat* (1829) 9 B & C 310.
3   LGA 1972, s 116.

Secondment

9.4 One local authority may lend personnel to another for the purposes of its functions. An officer involved must be consulted before any such agreement is made[1] and his superannuation rights are protected[2]. Accordingly local councils may lend their officers to each other; district or county councils may lend them to local councils or vice versa. The provisions for secondment might be used so that the officers at different levels of local government could get experience of work at a level not their own.

1   Local Government Act 1972, s 113(1).
2   LGA 1972, s 113(2).

Training

9.5 The success of local councils depends increasingly on administration by well educated as well as dedicated clerks. The National Association of Local Councils (NALC) and the Society of Local Council Clerks (SLCC) co-operate to this end with the Department for Communities and Local Government), the University of Gloucestershire, Local Government Improvement and Development and the Department for the Environment, Food and Rural Affairs. Together they have developed the National Training Strategy which includes the Certificate in Local Council Administration. This is gained by clerks who complete a portfolio of evidence showing their competence. Details are contained in the *Portfolio Guide* whichcan be viewed on NALC's and the SLCC's websites (see list of addresses in APPENDIX III for details).

In addition, the University of Gloucestershire provides certificate, diploma and honours degree courses in community governance[1].

The clerk of a council which seeks 'quality' status (see **22.9** below) or wishes to exercise the power of general competence (see **22.21** below) must have the Certificate in Local Council Administration.

Clerks who obtain the Certificate in Local Council Administration, and higher qualifications, can join the Institute of Local Council Management.

1   The NALC and SLCC's joint recommendations for the recognition of such success through the salary structure appear at **9.28** below.

Office machinery and the village computer

9.6 Local councils are increasingly using office machinery including voicemail, fax and computers and are securing access to electronic mail systems and the internet. Relatively speaking they need such things more than larger authorities, in order to keep their staffs small and personal. Voicemail is a boon to the clerk who cannot be in two places at once, and the cost of a computer can be partly met by selling spare time to local users. The proper and economical use of such equipment, however, requires a degree of training, for which a council will be wise to provide.

B   SECURITY AND ACCOUNTABILITY

9.7 The purpose of security is to ensure that if money or property is lost there will be a fund in existence from which it can be replaced. The purpose of accountability is to provide a simple method for settling accounts between a council and its officers and for recovering any outstanding debts owed by them to the council.

Security (fidelity bonds)

9.8 A local council must, at its own expense, take such security as it considers sufficient in the case of any of its officers likely to handle its money, and it may do so, also at its own expense, in the case of any other officer or any person who though not in its employ is likely to handle its money or property[1]. This is easily done by an insurance policy. The security must be produced to the auditor at audit[1].

The council may refuse to take out security if it considers that no security is 'sufficient', but there must be objective grounds for such a conclusion.

[1]   Local Government Act 1972, s 114.

Safekeeping

9.9 It is as a rule unwise to allow substantial sums to remain for any length of time in the hands of an officer. Money (for instance the rents of allotments) should if possible be banked the same day, and in particular all money should be safely lodged before a weekend. An unsecured officer may suffer great hardship if he loses (perhaps through burglary) money belonging to the council, and the method of safekeeping should be supervised as much in his interest as in that of the public.

Frankness

9.10 Where security involves entering into a contract of suretyship, there must be the utmost frankness and good faith between the parties. The sureties will be discharged if they have been misled by the council into a reasonable (but false) sense of security which put them off from making inquiries, or if the nature of the office or its duties changes materially so as to affect their risk. The same rules apply to insurance policies. The release of one surety automatically discharges the others, but death is not necessarily a release.

Satisfaction

9.11 Before cancelling a bond the council should be satisfied that no occasion to enforce it has actually arisen and that the public funds will be protected by other security from the time of cancellation.

Accountability

9.12 Every officer may be required whilst in office or within three months afterwards to account for money and property committed to his charge and for receipts and payments due to or from any person and must produce all the supporting vouchers and documents, and if he owes any money he must pay it in[1].

[1] Local Government Act 1972, s 115.

C   SUPERANNUATION

9.13 Employees of local councils and parish meetings are not automatically entitled to rights or subject to liabilities under the Local Government Pension Scheme[1], but (subject to certain exceptions and conditions) a local council may by 'statutory resolution' specify that any of its employees is a contributory employee[1] and thereupon he and the council must make proper periodical contributions to the appropriate superannuation fund (which is administered by the fund administrator, in most areas of England the county council (T) and in Wales the county or county borough council[2]) and the employee becomes entitled to such benefits as are specified by statutory instrument made under the Superannuation Acts.

[1] Local Government Pension Scheme (Benefits, Membership and Contributions) Regulations 2007, SI 2007/1166 (as amended); Local Government Pension Scheme (Transitional Provisions) Regulations 2008, SI 2008/238; Local Government Pension Scheme (Administration) Regulations 2008, SI 2008/239.
[2] SI 2008/239, reg 29.

Statutory resolution

9.14 As the statutory resolution has enduring effects, its terms, and the fact that it will be moved, must at least 28 days before the meeting be publicly notified in the usual manner for giving notices of meetings[1]. It is desirable to consult the administering authority before settling its terms.

The resolution cannot apply to any person under 16[2] nor generally to an employee who has attained the age of 75[3]. A person legally attains a specified age on the day of his appropriate birthday[4].

[1] Local Government Pension Scheme Regulations 1995, SI 1995/1019, reg B1(1) and sch A1.
[2] SI 1995/1019, reg B2(1).
[3] SI 2008/239, reg 12.
[4] Family Law Reform Act 1969, s 9.

Other types of pension

9.15 Under the Pensions Acts 2004, 2008 and 2011 employees generally who do not opt out will be automatically enrolled into a qualifying pension scheme from specified dates, as follows:

Employer size	Automatic enrolment duty date	
	From	To
250 or more members	1 October 2012	1 February 2014
50 to 249 members	1 April 2014	1 April 2015
Test tranche for less than 30 members	1 June 2015	30 June 2015
30 to 49 members	1 August 2015	1 October 2015
Less than 30 members	1 January 2016	1 April 2017
Employers without PAYE schemes	1 April 2017	

All employers with at least one employee (but a councillor who is an office holder, such as an unpaid clerk is not counted as an employee) must register with the Pensions Regulator[1].

For the purposes of the Pension Acts, employees (called 'jobholders') are placed in three categories: (a) eligible jobholders: those aged 22 or more and under the state pension age earning more than income tax personal allowance (£8,105 per annum in 2012-13); (b) non-eligible jobholders: those aged 22 or more and under the state pension age earning more than the lower income limit for National Insurance purposes (£5,564 in 2012–13) but less than the income tax personal allowance; those aged between 16 and 21 or state pension age and 74 who earn more than the income tax personal allowance; (c) entitled workers: those aged between 16 and 74 earning less than the lower income limit for National Insurance purposes.

An employer must enrol an eligible jobholder into a pension scheme during the appropriate period specified above or on the date on which the jobholder's employment begins, whichever is the later. A non-eligible jobholder has the right to opt into a pension scheme. An entitled jobholder has a right to join a pension scheme but not necessarily the same one as provided to a person with a right to automatic enrolment[2].

The government has established a pension scheme for employees called the National Employment Savings Trust (NEST), to which local councils will be able to subscribe.

[1] Pensions Act 2004, ss 59–65.
[2] Pensions Act 2008, Part 1, Chapter 1 (as amended by the Pensions Act 2011). The subject of pensions is complex. The text here is necessarily only a brief summary. More advice can be found on the websites of the Pensions Regulator and the Department of Work and Pensions.

D DISCRETIONARY PAYMENTS AND ADVANCES

Discretionary payments

9.16 The Local Government Superannuation (Discretionary Payments) Regulations 1996, SI 1996/1680 which enabled a local council to pay a gratuity to non-pensionable employees have been revoked. There is no longer any power for a council to pay a gratuity as such. However, the Local Government (Discretionary Payments) (Injury Allowances) Regulations 2011, SI 2011/2954 – in force from 16th January 2012 – enables a local council to make discretionary payments to an employee in the following circumstances:

(a) to an employee whose remuneration is reduced as a result of injury or disease;

(b) to an employee who through injury or disease is permanently incapacitated from work;

(c) to make up a shortfall in pension for an employee who has ceased to be employed by reason of (a) or (b) above;

(d) a death benefit to the spouse, civil partner, nominated cohabiting partner or dependant of an employee.

The amount of any discretionary payment is determined by the employer, but the Regulations provide for an initial decision to be reviewed if the claimant disagrees with that decision.

The revocation of the 1996 Regulations was a consequence of the enactment of the Pension Acts covered above.

Advances paid before death

9.17 A local council may forgo repayment of remuneration paid in advance of services if the employee dies after the payment, but not if the deceased is receiving a public pension at a rate equal to or more than the rate of the payment[1].

[1] Local Government (Miscellaneous Provisions) Act 1976, s 30.

E BRIBERY AND CORRUPTION

9.18 It is an offence to offer or give bribes to public officers and for such officers to accept or solicit them (see **7.43** above).

F PECUNIARY INTERESTS

9.19 An officer must, under pain of a level 4 fine, disclose his interest, direct or indirect, in any contract (including, for example, an insurance policy) into which the council or any of its committees intends to enter or has entered, and must give notice of his interest in writing[1].

[1] Local Government Act 1972, s 117.

G   CLERK OR TOWN CLERK

9.20 The title 'clerk' for a local council's chief executive officer is honourable, familiar and short; it seems more suitable to a small authority than the polysyllabic appellations gaining ground elsewhere. In a town, the clerk may be called the town clerk.

Duties

9.21 The extent to which the clerk's duties are defined by the general law is now obscure; for this reason his duties and remuneration should be specified in a written contract. Various model contracts exist, including one agreed between the National Association of Local Councils and the Society of Local Council Clerks. Such a contract should, amongst other matters, require him to attend at and keep the minutes of electors' meetings; the council may, however, pay special remuneration for such attendances if they are not included in the contract.

In the absence of specification in any contract the duties of the clerk in any given English parish will be those which his predecessors have hitherto been accustomed to perform. There is no general authority for the belief that he need not attend parish meetings; indeed where the parish meeting is exercising powers which were formerly exercisable by the vestry, the clerk, as successor to the vestry clerk, is probably bound to attend.

In Wales the abolition of the parishes probably ended such residual inheritances from the past, as a matter of law; but a clerk who continued after 1 April 1974, to perform for his community the same duties as he performed for his parish will be presumed to have adopted a contract (even if unwritten) in the same terms.

Subject to the direction of the council the clerk must keep the parish or community documents and records in his custody, and he is required to sign certain notices and summonses. (See **9.7** above for accountability; **6.11** for casual vacancy and **7.4** for summons.

Press advertisements

9.22 Though local councils are entitled to claim notification of planning applications (see **24.26** below) the increasing number of cases where matters, especially development and hazardous substance applications, have to be advertised in the local press, make it desirable for most local councils to acquire or have access to copies of local newspapers and the internet and to require (perhaps contractually) the clerk to read the advertisements in them, or make the necessary visits to websites.

Allotments

9.23 It is not the duty of the clerk as such to collect rents for allotments unless it has always been the custom of the parish for him to do so or it is part of his contract of employment, but as separate allotment accounts must in practice be kept that part of his pay which is referable to his activities in connection with allotments should be charged to the allotments account; it will usually be most convenient for the council to fix this amount by entering into a separate contract with him and dealing specifically with his allotments duties in that contract.

H   AUTHORITY OF PROPER OFFICER

9.24 The legislation has committed much work and many duties to an unspecified proper officer of a council. In other types of authority there will be several departmental heads who are the proper officers for the purposes of their respective departments. In a local council the proper officer will usually be the clerk. To ensure that outside bodies and other authorities are in no doubt, a local council may be wise to make a standing order in the following or equivalent form:

'The Clerk is the proper officer for any purpose in respect of which a proper officer is mentioned in any statute [except for any such purpose as is mentioned in Standing Order No .-.-.].'

I   CLERKS' PAY

This and the sections on part-time clerks' salaries, allowances, expenses and income tax are derived from the two organisations joint 'National agreement on salaries and conditions for local council clerks in England and Wales' 2008.

9.25 There are no rules for fixing the amount of a clerk's salary and councils vary widely in the amounts paid and in the methods by which they are calculated. Sometimes he is paid a salary or fee which may vary from the substantial to the nominal; in other cases he may be paid a fee for each meeting attended; or he is paid a sum which is the equivalent of a fixed percentage of the council's expenditure in each year. Combinations of these methods are not unknown, and some clerks are unpaid.

Where an employee is allowed time off to act as a member (other than chairman) of another local authority (including a local council), he may not be paid for more than 208 hours per year spent in the duties of such membership[1]. This rule affects a full-time job at a full-time salary, but under other employment regimes it is hard to envisage a situation in which it can apply.

A council may wish to take into account: (i) its population; (ii) its population density, for a scattered community is harder to administer than a compact one; (iii) the scope of the clerk's responsibility, which may range from mere routine, to work requiring leadership and versatility; and (iv) the range and balance of services which the council operates.

NALC has attempted to introduce some order into the payment of clerks. Since 1958 this has taken the shape of formulae agreed with the Society of Local Council Clerks.

In the view of the two organisations, clerks should be paid by reference to scales based upon four particular posts evaluated as of typical councils. In each, size, number of meetings, of delegated functions and of staff are taken into account. The salary range is that which is closest to a typical case. If it exactly matches it, the amount paid should be in the range indicated below. If the match is not exact, the amount should be set in accordance with a range above, below or overlapping it. The points are derived from the numbered positions on the spinal column chart of salaries in the 'Green Book', issued by the National Joint Council for Local Government Services (and obtainable from Provincial Councils of that Council).

The scales are as follows:

Scale	Points below substantive range (c)	Substantive benchmark range (b)	Points above substantive range (a)
LC1	(15–17)	(18–22)	(23–25)
LC2	(26–29)	(30–34)	(35–38)
LC3	(39–42)	(43–47)	(48–51)
LC4	(52–55)	(56–60)	(61–68)

[1] Local Government and Housing Act 1989, s 10.

Recommendations for part-time clerks

9.26 The two organisations recommend that the salary of a part-time clerk should be calculated by dividing that appropriate to a full-time clerk with the same population by 37 (the average hours in a local government working week) and multiplying by the number of hours specified or worked (as the case may be).

National minimum wage

9.27 A clerk is entitled to at least the national minimum wage (set in October 2012 at £3.68 for workers aged 16–17, £4.98 per hour for workers aged 18–21 and £6.19 per hour for those aged over 21). A salary which comes within the para **9.26** pay scale complies with this.

J   EXAMINATION SUCCESS

9.28 The two organisations recommend that a clerk's pay should be raised by the following (non-cumulative) number of annual increments for the successful passing of the following courses in local policy of the University of Gloucestershire.

Certificate in Local Council Administration or Certificate of Higher Education (first year)	1
Certificate of Higher Education, completion of Level 1	2
Diploma of Higher Education, completion of level 2	3
Award of BA (Honours), completion of level 3	4

These increments should not only accelerate progress through the scale, but increase the maximum, and should (obviously) not be applied to a clerk's disadvantage. Councils should give sympathetic consideration to equivalent qualifications from other institutions.

K   CLERKS' ALLOWANCES AND LOSS OF EARNINGS

9.29 Generally speaking, allowances (in the strict sense) are not payable to clerks (other than unpaid clerks who are councillors) because other arrangements can be made to produce the same result.

One consequence of the rule against allowances is that as most clerks are part-time and have another job, it can happen, especially in connection with conferences, that a clerk loses earnings as a result of his work as clerk, but cannot be paid a loss of earnings allowance in lieu. In calculating his salary this factor can be taken into account by averaging his annual losses over three years and increasing his 'formula salary' by the amount of the average. For a new clerk the amount can be estimated at the beginning and adjusted (up or down) later when more is known.

Expenses

9.30 A clerk who incurs inevitable expenditure in carrying out his duties is entitled at common law to be reimbursed, because the expenditure is really incurred on behalf of the council and is part of the cost of administration. An obvious example is the purchase of stamps, but the rule extends much further and a council can, for example, defray travelling costs, including out-of-pocket expenses of attending conferences on its behalf and as part of his duties. The council may also pay for the use of his communications equipment and, where the work is at all onerous, make a contribution towards rent, council tax (which is based on house valuation), lighting and heating of the clerk's house if it, or a room or even part of a room in it, is used as the council office[1]. In the case of premises the amount can be calculated by the proportion of a year during which one room in the house is used for council business. Similar principles apply to communications equipment.

Additionally a council may pay the clerk a contribution towards expenses incurred by him because he holds the post of clerk, for example a contribution towards expenditure on his residence because it is used as the council's office. Such payments of 'expenses' which are not reimbursements of expenditures directly incurred on behalf of the council, should nonetheless be related to actual additional costs borne by the clerk, because this should help to avoid difficulties in taxation assessments.

In Wales, the Welsh Assembly lays down for councillors maximum travelling allowances, mileage rates for different types of vehicle, permissible train and air fares and subsistence rates. A local council in Wales cannot go far wrong if it uses the same scales and principles for its clerk. It should, however, be noted that NALC and SLCC recommend that the clerk should be paid the mileage rates for different types of vehicles set out in the Green Book. In England, the Secretary of State no longer lays down maximum rates of allowance.

[1]   The inherent right of a local authority to pay the expenses of its officers is expressly preserved by the Local Government (Financial Provisions) Act 1963, s 5.

Income tax

9.31 In principle, a clerk's pay is liable to income tax as part of his income, and must be declared by him to HM Revenue and Customs (HMRC). On the other hand, expenses repaid to him by the council are not taxable because they are not part of his income but represent reimbursement of outlay on its behalf. It follows that repaid expenses should not be declared, and that payments of pay and repayments of expenses should always be kept separate.

If a paid clerk incurs expense in carrying out his duties he can either get the local council to reimburse him or he can set off the expenses against his pay and so declare a reduced amount to HMRC, but he cannot do both.

The general rule for all taxable employees is that the employing council must deduct income tax from their pay under the PAYE system and account for it to HMRC. PAYE documents are issued annually to councils by HMRC. In 2011 HMRC issued guidance stating that all local councils must operate a PAYE system for their employees. However, where a clerk or other employee's total income from all sources does not exceed the lower earnings limit for national insurance contributions, the council does not have to deduct tax under the PAYE system. From April 2013, an electronic method of sending PAYE returns to HMRC, called Real Time Information (RTI), has been introduced. A council operating a PAYE system will have to register online with HMRC. In any case of doubt the council should seek specific advice from HMRC.

Sums paid over by a local council as PAYE to HMRC, or an appropriate proportion of them, can be recovered by the clerk (or other employee) himself from HMRC if it turns out that too much tax has been paid on his total income.

L   NATIONAL INSURANCE CONTRIBUTIONS

9.32 Councils must, as employers, make National Insurance payments in respect of those employees whose pay exceeds the annually revised lower earnings limit. The amount is in two parts: the employer's contribution payable in respect of any employee, and the employee's contribution payable (if at all) only by employees over 16 and under pensionable age. They are paid together by the employer, who deducts the employee's contribution so as to include it in his payment.

M   RESPONSIBLE FINANCIAL OFFICER

9.33 Like any other local authority, a local council must arrange for the proper administration of its financial affairs, and secure that one of its officers has responsibility for the administration of those affairs[1]. This officer is called the 'responsible financial officer' and is almost invariably the clerk. It is his duty to determine the form and content of the accounts and supporting records, subject to any directions from the council and in compliance with the Accounts and Audit (England) Regulations 2011 SI 2011/817 or, in Wales, the Accounts and Audit (Wales) Regulations 2005, SI 2005/368. He must ensure that the records are maintained in accordance with 'proper practices' and kept up to date. The proper practices are prescribed by the Secretary of State in England and by the Welsh Assembly in Wales. These are contained in the NALC/SLCC publication *Governance and Accountability in Local Councils in England and Wales: A Practitioner's Guide*[2].

As a local council may appoint one or more of its members to be unpaid officers[3], it follows that one of them may be the unpaid treasurer.

[1] Local Government Act 1972, s 151. The opening words of the section are difficult if not impossible to interpret, and seem to indicate more suspicion than common sense in the legislature.
[2] LGA 1972, s 112(5); Audit Commission Act 1998, s 2; Accounts and Audit (England) Regulations 2011, SI 2011/817, reg 4(1); Accounts and Audit (Wales) Regulations 2005, SI 2005/368, reg. 5(1); Local Government Act 2003, s 21(2).
[3] Local Government Act 1972, s 112(5).

N HEALTH AND SAFETY AT WORK

9.34 Local councils, like other employers, are under a duty to ensure, so far as reasonably practicable, the health, safety and welfare at work of all their employees[1]. The obligation includes, amongst others, the maintenance of a place of work and a working environment in a condition which is safe and without risks to health. There is a correlative duty on employees to behave at work so as not to put at risk other employees or members of the public. These principles are supplemented or amplified in many regulations and codes of practice, notably:

- management of health and safety at work;
- workplace health, safety and welfare; and
- display screen equipment at work[2].

A local council which employs more than five people must produce a written health and safety statement of policy.

[1] Health and Safety at Work etc Act 1974, s 2. The details of this long Act are beyond the scope of this work.
[2] Obtainable from the Health and Safety Executive.

O EMPLOYMENT RIGHTS

9.35 The Employment Rights Act 1996 consolidated the statutory law on employment in general. Where someone was employed by an abolished or transferor authority and the termination of the employment was attributable to the winding-up and dissolution of the authority and where, additionally, another local council employs him within four weeks but the Act precludes him from receiving redundancy pay for his terminated employment, he is entitled to count the period of his previous employment as if it were continuous with his new employment for the purposes of the Act of 1996 or for any provisions in his contract which depends on length of service[1].

This Act has been supplemented by the Employment Relations Act 1999, the Employment Act 2002, the Employment Relations Act 2004 and the Employment Act 2008 which, amongst other things, provide respectively for leave for family reasons, for statutory dispute procedures, for the enforcement of the national minimum wage and for dispute resolution. The Work and Families Act 2006 has made further provision for paternity and maternity leave and flexible working.

In the comparatively unusual cases where difficulties arise, it will be wise to have a copy of the Acts available. The subject is, however, beyond the scope of this work.

1   Local Government (Parishes and Parish Councils) Regulations 1999, SI 1999/545, reg 13.

Chapter 10

THE ENGLISH PARISH OR TOWN'S MEETING AND PARISH OR CHARTER TRUSTEES

10.1 Every English parish must have a parish meeting[1].

Parish meetings are therefore of three types, namely:

- for the whole of a parish which has a separate parish council;
- for a parish which is grouped with other parishes under a common parish council; and finally
- for a parish which is not represented upon a parish council at all.

Where the council is called the town council, the meeting is often called the town's meeting. It is also sometimes called the village or town conference.

[1] Local Government Act 1972, s 9(1).

A   MEMBERSHIP AND RIGHT TO PRESIDE

10.2 A parish meeting consists of the local government electors registered for the area for which it is held[1] and, in addition, if there is a parish council its chairman may attend (whether he is an elector or not[2]) and if he is present he must preside[3]. The vice-chairman must preside in the chairman's absence. If both are absent, the meeting elects someone to preside[4].

In a parish without a separate council the chairman is elected at the annual parish meeting by the meeting itself, unless a grouping order otherwise provides[5].

The electoral registration officer must, at the request of the local council, provide a free copy of that part of the electoral register relating to the parish[6].

[1]   Local Government Act 1972, s 13(1).
[2]   LGA 1972, Sch 12, para 16.
[3]   LGA 1972, Sch 12, para 17(1).
[4]   LGA 1972, Sch 12, para 17(3).
[5]   LGA 1972, Sch 12, para 17(2).
[6]   Representation of the People (England and Wales) Regulations 2001, SI 2001/347, reg 107.

B   NUMBER, DATE AND TIME OF MEETINGS

10.3 The parish meeting must assemble annually between 1 March and 1 June (both inclusive); and where there is no separate parish council it must (subject to the provisions of any grouping order) meet on at least one other occasion in the year[1]. In addition it must meet when convened by the parish council or, if there is none, by the chairman of the parish meeting[2], and it may be convened as often as may be required.

There is no effective method of enforcing these rules.

Proceedings must not begin before 6pm.

1   Local Government Act 1972, Sch 12, para 14(1) and (3).
2   LGA 1972, Sch 12, para 14(2).

C   RIGHT TO CONVENE

10.4 A parish meeting may be convened by the chairman of the parish council or any two parish councillors, or in a parish without a parish council by the chairman of the parish meeting or by any representative of the parish upon the district council (T)[1], or in either case by six electors for the area for which it is to be held[2]. The parish council may also convene it but is under no obligation to do so unless its consent is required before the parish council does certain acts[3].

1   Local Government Act 1972, Sch 12, para 15(1)(a)–(c).
2   LGA 1972, Sch 12, para 15(1)(d).
3   See **10.11** below and LGA 1972, Sch 12, para 14(2).

D   NOTICES AND AGENDA

10.5 Notices specifying the time and place and business of an intended meeting and signed by the conveners[1] must be affixed in some conspicuous place or places in the parish and, in addition, the conveners may give such publicity to the meeting as seems desirable[2].

Ordinarily the minimum notice required is seven clear days[3] but if any of the business relates to the establishment or dissolution of a parish council, or to the grouping of the parish with another parish, it is 14 clear days[4] and if it is intended to move a statutory resolution relating to superannuation it is 28 clear days[5].

1   Local Government Act 1972, Sch 12, para 15(2).
2   LGA 1972, Sch 12, para 15(4).
3   LGA 1972, Sch 12, para 15(2).
4   LGA 1972, Sch 12, para 15(3).
5   See **9.14** above.

E   QUORUM

10.6 The quorum of a parish meeting is two[1] unless a document has to be executed, in which case it is three[2].

[1]   *Loughlin v Guinness* (1904) 23 NZLR 748, per Denniston J at 754.
[2]   Local Government Act 1972, s 13(2).

F   DECISIONS

10.7 Decisions are taken in the first instance by a majority of those present and voting. If the chairman is an elector he has an original as well as a casting vote; if he is not an elector he only has a casting vote. Unless a poll is demanded before the end of the meeting, the chairman's declaration of the result is final[1].

[1]   Local Government Act 1972, Sch 12, para 18(1)–(4).

Voting

10.8 Unlike a parish council, a parish meeting is not required to vote in any particular way, and so the chairman may ascertain the effect of the voting from any evidence which may in the circumstances lead to an accurate result: thus a voice vote may in the case of an overwhelming majority be sufficient, but when the opposing opinions are represented with approximate equality, a count, whether of persons or voting papers, must be taken.

Poll

10.9 A poll may be demanded not later than the end of the meeting on any question arising at it. Such a poll must be held only if ten or one-third of the electors present (whichever is the less) insist or if the person presiding at the meeting consents[1]. It is not clear what happens if the chairman alone calls for a poll, but the outcome probably depends on whether he is an elector or not. It is essential that the wording of any question to be answered in the poll be settled before the meeting ends. The chairman must immediately notify the district council (T) if a poll is required[2]. It is held in accordance with rules made by the Secretary of State and the procedure is generally similar to the procedure for electing a local councillor[3].

The returning officer must appoint an office for the purpose of the poll[4].

[1]   Local Government Act 1972, Sch 12, para 18(4).
[2]   Parish and Community Meetings (Polls) Rules 1987, SI 1987/1, r 4(1).
[3]   SI 1987/1, Schedule.
[4]   SI 1987/1, r 4(3).

G   PLACES OF MEETING

10.10 In a parish where there is no separate council, the parish meeting is entitled and not entitled to meet in the same places as a parish council. Where there is a separate parish council, the parish meeting has the same rights save that it is not entitled to meet in the church or vestry[1].

[1] See **7.2** above.

H RELATIONSHIP BETWEEN PARISH MEETING AND COUNCIL

10.11 Though a parish meeting may discuss parish affairs[1] its resolutions differ considerably in their legal consequences. In a few cases a resolution is legally binding. In all others a resolution is persuasive only; the parish council may legally disregard it and leave the electors to their remedy at the next election.

[1] Local Government Act 1972, s 9(1).

Binding resolutions and necessary consents

10.12 A resolution by a well-attended parish meeting that the parish council ought to provide allotments, legally obliges the council to provide them (see **29.4** below).

Sometimes a trust instrument will make certain resolutions binding upon a parish council acting as trustee, or require certain consents; the commonest case arises on a proposal to dissolve a village hall trust constituted under the model trust deed issued by the National Council for Voluntary Organisations or, now, by Action with Communities in Rural England (ACRE).

Other resolutions

10.13 The right of the parish meeting to discuss parish affairs extends to any public matter of a parochial nature and is not confined to the exercise of the statutory functions of the parish council. The parish meeting may accordingly pass resolutions on the public activities or policies in the parish of any other local authority, public or private[1] body, government department or public service provided that they affect the parish specially and are not such as are calculated to affect the whole country or all parishes equally[2].

[1] *R (on the application of Letchworth Garden Heritage Foundation) v (1) The returning officer for the District of North Hertfordshire and (2) The Chairman of the Parish Meeting of Letchworth Garden City* [2009] EWHC 841 (Admin)
[2] Cf the parliamentary distinction between public and local or private Bills.

Expenses

10.14 Where there is a parish council the expenses of parish meetings are met by it[1].

[1] Local Government Act 1972, s 150(2).

I PARISH MEETINGS WHERE THERE IS NO SEPARATE COUNCIL

10.15 A parish meeting is not a corporation and is therefore unable to own property or to sue or be sued[1]. Generally speaking it is not a local authority[2], though for certain limited purposes it may be regarded as one.

Its alleged lack of legal personality has not prevented Parliament from enabling it to exercise functions. These are as follows.

Allotments: a parish meeting may hold and administer allotments for cultivation. (See CHAPTER 29).

Burials: a parish meeting is a burial authority. It may therefore provide burial grounds and may contribute towards the cost of burial facilities provided by others. (See CHAPTER 33).

Charities: a parish meeting has the same powers as a parish council to appoint trustees to parochial charities. (See CHAPTER 13).

Churchyards: liability to maintain a closed Church of England churchyard may be transferred to a parish meeting by the same process by which such liability is transferred to a parish council. (See CHAPTER 33B).

Commons: a parish meeting may be registered as the owner of common land if it has inherited ownership from the appropriate pre-1894 authority (often the Churchwardens and Overseers of the poor). (See CHAPTER 26B).

Discretionary charges: a parish meeting may charge for the provision of discretionary services. (See CHAPTER 14.11).

Freedom of Information: a parish meeting is subject to the Freedom of Information Act 2000. It must adopt and maintain a publication scheme for the information it holds. (See CHAPTER 11E).

Land: a parish meeting has no general power to acquire land, but may acquire land to exercise its allotments or burial powers: it may appropriate land from one purpose to another with the approval of the Secretary of State. A parish meeting may dispose of land on the same conditions applicable to parish councils. (See CHAPTER 12).

Licensing: the chairman of a parish meeting is an interested party in relation to applications for licences for the sale of alcohol and for providing regulated entertainment and should be notified by the licensing authority of such applications. (See CHAPTER 16C).

Lighting: a parish meeting may provide footway lighting. (See CHAPTER 28).

Open Spaces: the county council may contribute to expenses incurred by a parish meeting in providing a public open space. (See CHAPTER 14.19).

Rights of Way: a parish meeting is entitled to be notified of a definitive map modification order, a public path creation order, an extinguishment order, a diversion order or a. A parish meeting is also entitled to be consulted by the county council before a definitive map modification order is made. A parish meeting is entitled to be notified of an application to the magistrates' court to stop up or divert a highway and may appear at the hearing. No application can be made if the chairman of the parish meeting refuses to consent to the application within two months of being notified. (See CHAPTER 31).

Village Greens: a parish meeting may prosecute a person who damages or encroaches upon a village green in the parish and commits an offence under section 12 of the Inclosure Act 1857 or section 29 of the Commons Act 1876. (See CHAPTER **26A**).

War memorials: a parish meeting may incur reasonable expenditure on the maintenance, repair and protection of war memorials. (See CHAPTER **33M**).

It may appoint committees to administer any of its functions[3].

1   Local Government Act 1972, s 222.
2   See the definition of 'local authority' in LGA 1972, s 270(1).
3   LGA 1972, s 108.

J   THE PARISH TRUSTEES

10.16 The parish trustees are a puppet corporation which in law exists (subject to the express terms of any grouping order) in every parish with no separate parish council, and nowhere else[1]. It consists of the chairman of the parish meeting and an officer appointed by the district council (T). It may have a common seal, but if it has not it may signify its acts under the hands or hands and seals of its members[2].

Its function is primarily to be the depository of the title to parish property. It must act as directed by the parish meeting, but it has power to act in any way necessary or desirable in the execution of its trust that does not conflict with a direction of the parish meeting[3].

1   Local Government Act 1972, s 13(3).
2   LGA 1972, s 13(5).
3   LGA 1972, s 13(4); *Taylor v Masefield and another* (1986) LGR 108.

K   CHARTER TRUSTEES

Nature

10.17 Charter trustees exist for the areas of dissolved pre-1974 boroughs now forming part of a new district (T) which is not a borough or for part of a principal area abolished by an order under the Local Government Act 1992, s 17 or the Local Government and Public Involvement in Health Act 2007, s 7 They are dissolved if their own area becomes a parish or a separate community or is wholly comprised within one or more parishes[1]. While they exist they administer the ceremonial and historical properties other than land and which belonged to the pre-1974 borough or part and which is appropriated to its area. They have precepting powers which are limited by statutory instruments of local application and they must pay any surplus income to the district council (T)[2].

1   Local Government (Parishes and Parish Councils) Regulations 1999, SI 1999/545, reg 16.
2   Local Government Act 1972, s 246 amended by the Charter Trustees Act 1985.

Devolution of property

10.18 Historic and ceremonial property may be extensive and valuable. In a disputed case 167 items were listed as possibly ceremonial, including a mace insured for £20,000, and 89 as possibly historic, besides much furniture and over 200 pictures. The accurate apportionment of such public chattels may be important now that new parish councils can be more easily created in urban areas, and might have to take them over.

The following are the principles for settling their destination. A chattel need not be both historic and ceremonial to pass to charter trustees.

Ceremony is an outward observance, the performance of a solemn act according to a prescribed form, or formal observances or usages collectively. The adjective ceremonial applied to an object implies necessary association with a ceremony or that it is an external accessory or symbolic attribute of worship, state or pomp[1]. It need not be old, elaborate, valuable or even in regular use. A pottery plate and a silver model of an aircraft were found to be ceremonial because they originated in a ceremony and would certainly be present at another of the same kind. A mayoral chair in a court room was ceremonial but the older and more valuable Chippendale chairs in the same room were not, because they formed the equipment for the everyday use of the room where ceremony was only a minor feature of events.

Historic means having an interest or importance due to connection with historical events or conveying or dealing with history or recording past events. It does not mean ancient or even old. Thus, some ancient and more modern charters were historic and so were other documents forming with them a coherent series, as being part of a single archive which should not be dispersed. A recent picture of the Sovereign performing a local ceremony is probably both ceremonial and historic. An old silver tea service was not historic as having no connection with historic events. The 200 pictures remained with the museums authority as pleasant artistic public exhibits[2].

[1]   *Oxford English Dictionary.*
[2]   These paragraphs are founded on the Joint Advice by Professor P Boylan and Professor C Arnold-Baker to the Charter Trustees of Beverley and the East Riding of Yorkshire Council, 15 January 1997.

L   MINUTES

10.19 The rules on the signature and admissibility of the minutes of a parish meeting and its committees are in effect the same as those in force for a parish council. Parish trustees have no minutes.

M   ADMISSION OF THE PUBLIC

10.20 The press and public have the same rights of admission to a parish meeting as they have to a meeting of a parish council[1]. It is therefore advisable to set aside a clearly marked place for strangers to avoid confusion when a vote is taken.

[1]   Public Bodies (Admission to Meetings) Act 1960. See **7.6** above.

Chapter 11

DOCUMENTATION

A   CUSTODY AND CUSTODIANS' MUTUAL RIGHTS OF INSPECTION

11.1 Before 1894 the public books, writings and papers of the parish and the three registers (of baptism, marriage and burial) were in the custody of the incumbent and churchwardens. These documents have since been divided into two groups: namely (1) the three registers together with documents containing entries wholly or partly relating to the affairs of the church other than documents specifically directed by law to be kept with the public books; and (2) all the other public books and the documents directed to be kept with them[1]. For group (1), inquiry should now be made with the incumbent[2], whilst the other remained in its existing custody as at 17 November 1933, until the parish council (or where there was no parish council the parish meeting) otherwise directed. Where a parish is co-extensive with a pre-existing rural parish on 1 April 1974, this position is preserved[3], and in the case of ex-borough and urban districts in England most of the documents of a parochial nature pass to the successor parish council or in some cases, where there is no such council to parish or charter trustees[4]. In Wales the devolution is from parish, urban district and borough councils to community councils for the same area, if any; but where there is no community council the documents pass to the district council (T).

Each side is entitled to have reasonable access to documents in the possession of the other, and disputes on custody and access are to be settled, where a parish is in a metropolitan district, by the Secretary of State, and elsewhere by the county council (T)[5]. It has been suggested that the parish and parochial church councils might advantageously inspect each other's documents annually, and that in the localities which hold a civic Sunday, such inspection might form part of the ceremonies.

1   Local Government Act 1933, s 281 (repealed).
2   Parochial Church Councils (Powers) Measure 1956, s 4; Parochial Register and Records Measure 1978 as amended by the Church of England (Miscellaneous Provisions) Measure 1992.
3   Local Government Act 1972, s 226(1)(a) and (2).
4   See **10.16–10.18** above.
5   LGA 1972, s 226(4).

B DEPOSIT AND SUPERVISION

11.2 The manner in which documents are kept and preserved is controlled by four different types of authority, some of whom may make conflicting orders.

Manorial documents

11.3 The Master of the Rolls may make enquiries regarding manorial documents and their proper preservation, and may transfer documents which are not being properly preserved to museums or other institutions for proper preservation. Such an order does not affect rights of inspection[1].

[1] Law of Property Act 1922, s 144A(5).

Tithe documents

11.4 Documents relating to tithes may have been placed in such custody as was ordered by Quarter Sessions[1] (now the Crown Court), but the county council is equally entitled to make orders for their custody[2]. Until an order is made, one copy of the confirmed instrument of apportionment or agreement should be kept by the local council[3]. Sealed copies (as opposed to originals) of instruments of apportionment are under the jurisdiction of the Master of the Rolls who may determine their places of deposit[4].

[1] Tithe Act 1846, s 17 (repealed).
[2] See **11.11** below and *Fox v Pett* [1918] 2 KB 196.
[3] Tithe Act 1836, s 64.
[4] Tithe Act 1836, s 36 (repealed).

Others

11.5 Of the remaining documents, those in the hands of the ecclesiastical and of the lay body are supervised respectively by the Bishop[1] and the county council (T)[1]. These supervisory powers are, in practice, only spasmodically effective.

The county council or metropolitan district council (T) must periodically inquire how the lay parish or community records are being preserved, and must make preservation orders as it thinks fit; these orders must be obeyed by the local council or parish meeting as the case may be[2], but Welsh district councils (T) in possession of community documents are under no such obligation. County (T) record offices are willing to preserve and maintain any parochial records entrusted to them. Deposit at such record offices makes no difference to ownership or rights of inspection and an undertaking to return at seven days' notice is usually given.

In relation to the three registers[3] the Bishop has powers of inquiry and control over his parochial organisations which are very similar to those possessed by a county council (T) over a local council[4], and where a diocesan record office has been established an incumbent may, with the consent of the Bishop and the parochial church council, deposit in it any such register which is not in actual use, such as deeds and documents of value as historical records or as evidence of legal rights. Where documents, which may be voluntarily deposited, are exposed to danger of loss or damage, the Bishop may order their deposit at the Diocesan Office[5].

1 Parochial Registers and Records Measure 1978, s 11.
2 Local Government Act 1972, s 226(5).
3 See **11.1** above.
4 Parochial Registers and Records Measure 1978, s 12.
5 Parochial Registers and Records Measure 1978, s 11.

C   PROMOTION OF USE

11.6 A local council may do anything necessary or expedient to enable adequate use to be made of records under its control and in particular it can permit persons, for example students and local history societies, with or without charge, to inspect and copy them; it can have them indexed and calendared, and can publish such indices and calendars, and it can hold exhibitions or entrust its records to others for exhibition[1].

It may also bear the expense incurred by anyone else in doing to its records what it may do itself, or in doing to records of local interest not under its control what it could do if they were[2]. In effect this means that if any records of parish or community interest are deposited in a museum or with a county archivist, the local council can pay to have them restored, indexed, calendared or otherwise made useful.

1 Local Government (Records) Act 1962, s 1.
2 Local Government (Records) Act 1962, s 4.

D   SAFES AND REPOSITORIES

11.7 Where there is a separate local council it must either provide proper 'repositories' for its records or request the district council (T) to do so, in which case the latter must comply with the request[1]. Where there is no local council the district council (T) must in England provide the repositories with the consent of the parish meeting[2], and in Wales without such consent.

1 Local Government Act 1972, s 227(1).
2 LGA 1972, s 227(2).

E   FREEDOM OF INFORMATION

11.8 A person who asks a public authority in writing for information on a given topic, is entitled to be told whether the authority has the information, and if it has, to be told what it is[1]. The rule applies to 50 categories of English and Welsh authorities and some 371 named ones outside those categories. The categories embrace local authorities including local councils, parish meetings and charter trustees, and governing bodies of maintained schools. The individually named bodies include those listed below. All are caught by the rule. They must reply promptly and in any case not later than the twentieth working day after receiving the request. There are, however, some common sense exceptions, including 23 kinds of sensitive types of information such as personal material or matters which, if published, might prejudice the conduct of the authority's functions. In certain arduous cases a fee may be charged. The authority is obliged to provide help and advice in relation to the information provided, but there is a code of practice, conformity with which satisfies the obligation.

Every local council and parish meeting where there is no council must prepare and regularly review a publication scheme for the information it holds which is available for public inspection. The scheme must be approved by the Information Commissioner, who has issued model schemes which no doubt most local councils and parish meetings follow[2].

The right may be enjoyed by any person, which includes all the bodies mentioned above. A local council may therefore ask, as well as answer, questions[3].

Some named bodies:

- Audit Commission;
- Commission for Local Administration in England;
- Natural England;
- Countryside Council for Wales;
- Electoral Commission;
- Environment Agency;
- Gambling Commission;
- National Heritage Memorial Fund;
- Public Services Ombudsman for Wales;
- Post Office;
- Sports Council for Wales;
- English Sports Council;
- UK Sports Council;
- Welsh Language Commissioner.

[1] Freedom of Information Act 2000, ss 1 and 12.
[2] Freedom of Information Act 2000, s 19.
[3] Interpretation Act 1978.

F   PUBLIC RIGHTS OF INSPECTION

11.9 The minutes of a local authority (including a parish meeting[1]) may be inspected by any elector for its area, and he may copy or make extracts from them[2]. This rule applies also to committee minutes which have been laid before the council for approval[3]. Such electors may also, free of charge[4], inspect and copy orders for payment[5] and the financial statement or abstract of accounts of the authority and of any proper officer, with any auditors' report upon them, and copies must be delivered to such electors upon payment of a reasonable sum[6]. The accounts themselves may be inspected and copied by any member of the council[7].

A document required by law or the standing orders of either House of Parliament to be deposited with the chairman of a local council or parish meeting or their respective proper officers[8] may be inspected at all reasonable hours by anyone interested in it, and he may make copies or extracts from it. He must, however, pay 10p for each inspection, plus 10p for each hour of an inspection after the first[9].

Documents which are legally open to inspection must be open at reasonable hours[10], and any custodian of them who obstructs lawful inspection or copying, or who refuses to give copies or extracts to persons entitled to them, is liable to a level 1 fine[11].

1   Local Government Act 1972, s 228(8).
2   LGA 1972, s 228(1).
3   *Williams v Manchester Corpn* (1897) 45 WR 412.
4   LGA 1972, s 228(6).
5   LGA 1972, s 228(2).
6   Audit Commission Act 1998, s 14.
7   LGA 1972, s 228(3).
8   See LGA 1972, s 225 and **11.11** below.
9   LGA 1972, s 228(5).
10 LGA 1972, s 228(6).
11 LGA 1972, s 228(7). See **21.40** below.

Agents

11.10 In general anyone (the principal) is entitled to appoint anyone else (the agent) to do for him anything which the principal can do himself unless the law otherwise requires (which, in the case of inspection or copying of public documents it does not). Consequently any person entitled to inspect or copy documents statutorily open to such treatment, is entitled to appoint an agent to do these things on his behalf, and that agent need not be an elector or himself be in any way entitled in his own right to inspect or, as the case may be, make copies. This happens most commonly where the principal wishes to employ an expert such as an accountant for the purpose[1].

No formalities of appointment are required. It may even be made by a telephone call, but as a matter of common sense, the custodian of the documents must be reasonably sure that the agent is really the principal's appointed agent.

1   *Norey v Keep* [1909] Ch 561 (accounts); *R v Bedwelty Urban District Council, ex p Price* [1934] 1 KB 333 (accounts); *R v Glamorgan County Council, ex p Collier* [1936] 2 All ER 166.

G   RETURNS

General information

11.11 Local councils, joint committees and joint boards must make to the Secretary of State such reports and returns and give such information on their functions as he may require or as may be required by either House of Parliament[1]. Parish meetings are not obliged to do this.

1   Local Government Act 1972, s 230.

Financial returns

11.12 Local councils and parish meetings are supposed annually to make a financial return to the Secretary of State showing their income and expenditure[1] and this obligation is enforceable by mandamus. He can dispense with this requirement[2], and seems to have done so for many years. However, local councils and parish meetings are required to prepare an annual return as part of their accounting obligations (see CHAPTER 17).

[1]   Local Government Act 1972, s 168.
[2]   LGA 1972, s 168(3).

H   SOME NOTES ON PARTICULAR DOCUMENTS

11.13 The following is a list of some of the more important documents together with suggestions for finding them.

(a)   *Inclosure awards*: If the local council has no copy, inquiry should be made to the parochial church council and incumbent, and failing them to the county council (T). If this fails to bring a copy to light, the National Archives should be consulted. If the award was made under a private Act, application to inspect the Act itself may be made to the House of Lords.

(b)   *Tithe apportionments, parochial agreements, etc (sometimes loosely called tithe awards)*: If the council has no copies, inquiry should be made to the parochial church council and the diocesan registry. Some of the original documents are in the possession of the Department for Environment, Food and Rural Affairs. If an order of the county council or of the justices has been made, inquiries should be addressed to the person named in the order or his successors in title or their respective solicitors. Where a firm of solicitors has ceased to function the documents may be in the possession of the Law Society.

(c)   *Manor rolls, terriers and court rolls*: These should be in the hands of the Lord of the Manor, or of his solicitor as, or in succession to, the steward of the manor. Sometimes they will have been deposited with a museum, library, record office or learned body, either voluntarily or as a result of an order made by the Master of the Rolls. In such cases the lord or his solicitor should know where they are. Occasionally, however, they will be found among papers formerly in the possession of the vestry with the result that they may have descended to the local council and the county council (T) on the one hand or to the parochial church council and (notwithstanding the law) to the diocesan registry.

(d)   *Private Acts of Parliament*: Private Acts which authorise the compulsory acquisition of land for a railway, canal or similar undertaking, should be in the hands of the county council (T) in whose area such land is situated[1].

(e)   *Plans and sections* of alterations from the original plan and section approved by Parliament for a railway must be deposited with the county council (T) and the relevant local councils[2]. Such plans should be in the custody of the local council but the older ones may be in the possession of the parochial church council or even of the diocesan registry. Both Houses of Parliament require the local deposit of plans in connection with certain private bills to authorise the construction of certain types of public works[3].

(f) *Local Acts and orders* conferring special powers upon a local council or its predecessors. The county council (T) will have copies.

(g) *Statutory instruments* relating to the parish or community, particularly boundary and transfer of property orders. Prints of maps made under the orders are deposited with the Secretary of State and the district or unitary council and in addition are supplied to the Ordnance Survey, the Registrar-General, the Land Registry and the Valuation Office.

There are also statutory instruments concerning limitations on charter trustee precepts, and orders about the use of coats of arms:

- *agreements and arbitration awards* arising out of boundary alterations;
- *orders of the county and district council* on the constitution and functions of the local council;
- *orders and schemes* made by the Charity Commission or the former Department of Education and Science or of Education and Employment for parochial charities;
- *trust instruments*;
- *deeds, leases and conveyances*;
- *property transfer orders* giving effect to agreements made in the course of a local government reorganisation;
- *mortgages and the mortgage register*;
- *written contracts*;
- *vehicle licences and inspection records*;
- *copies of statutory reports and returns*;
- *circulars* issued by government departments;
- *circulars* issued by the National Association of Local Councils;
- *minutes*; vestry minutes may be found with the parochial church council or in the diocesan registry;
- *transport schemes* (see **32.2** below).

NALC has issued guidance to member councils about the treatment of council documents and records.

[1] Lands Clauses Consolidation Act 1845, ss 150 and 151.
[2] Railway Clauses Consolidation Act 1845, ss 8–10.
[3] Local Government Act 1972, s 225 and House of Commons SO (Private Business) 27 and 36 and House of Lords SO 27 and 36.

I   PHOTOGRAPHIC COPIES

11.14 Any requirement imposed by statute upon a local authority to keep a document is satisfied by keeping a photographic copy, except that where colour is relevant to the interpretation of the document, for example in a plan, a photograph will suffice only if it distinguishes between the colours so as to enable the document to be interpreted[1].

[1] Local Government Act 1972, s 229.

J   CERTIFICATION OF COPIES

11.15 See **7.41** above.

Chapter 12
PROPERTY

A   GENERAL

12.1 Land is the most obvious form of property, but under the Law of Property Act 1925, s 205 it has a special definition. It

> 'includes land of any tenure and mines and minerals whether or not held apart from the surface, buildings or parts of buildings (whether the division is horizontal, vertical or made in any other way) and other corporeal hereditaments; also a manor, an advowson, and a rent or other incorporeal hereditaments, and an easement, right, privilege or benefit in, over or derived from land; but not an undivided share in land'

Of the 'other corporeal hereditaments', the most important are trees and fixtures. The latter are things which would be chattels were it not that they had become, like electric wiring or mantelpieces, part of the 'land' for its more convenient use, but things however large, not affixed to the land, like a Dutch barn, are not. Even strong attachment, if it is for the more convenient use of the thing not the land, like a heavy picture, may not result in annexation to the land.

The most important surviving incorporeal hereditaments are easements and rights of common. An easement is a private right, such as a private right of way or a wayleave for pipes, existing for the benefit of one piece of land across another. A right of common is a right (such as pasture) to enjoy a benefit from land in common with other owners of nearby land.

'Parish property' was a class of property whose rents and profits, before 1 April 1974, were applicable (or would have been applicable if let) to the general benefit of one or more parishes or of their ratepayers, parishioners or inhabitants, and also certain exhausted quarries, but it did not include charitable property not so applicable nor property acquired before 1 April 1930, by a board of guardians for the relief of the poor[1].

Corporate land was land belonging to or held in trust for a borough otherwise than for an express statutory purpose[2].

Not all parish property was necessarily owned by the parish council, and conversely not all property owned by a parish council was necessarily parish property; parish property owned by a parish council might have been 'inherited', 'transferred' or 'acquired'; acquired property either came to the parish council by gift or may have been acquired actively for the purpose of its functions; actively acquired property may have been obtained compulsorily or by agreement, and property acquired by agreement may have been obtainable by purchase, lease, exchange or gift.

In addition, in most parishes there were lands not vested in a public authority where the inhabitants had certain rights and over which the parish council had or may have had powers of repair, maintenance, control or contribution.

These and allied classifications are illustrated by the diagram below.

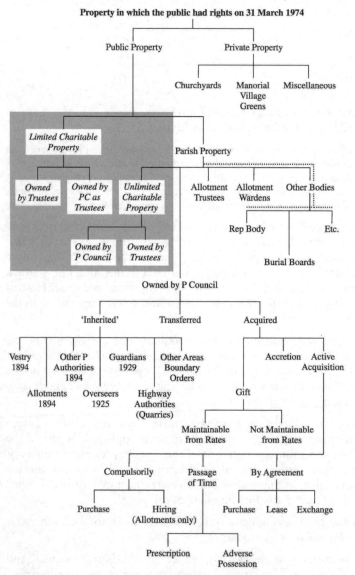

Property in which the public had rights on 31 March 1974

---

[1] See the repealed Local Government Act 1933, s 178 and the definition in s 305 which codified the definition in the Local Government Act 1929, s 115(6).
[2] LGA 1933, s 305 (repealed).

B   TYPES OF PROPERTY

12.2 The following is a list of the main kinds of property owned by a local council or parish trustees or in which they or the inhabitants have or may have rights or interests. The items in **bold type** are those which, unless otherwise agreed, will have passed to English successor councils:

- **allotment gardens, pasture grazing rights and stints;**
- almshouses;
- bathing places and beaches;
- **bus and public shelters;**
- car parks;
- chattels including safes, chests, furniture, typewriters, books, lawn mowers, pictures, rollers, nets, word processors, computers, printers, scanners, telephones;
- church and vestry;
- churchyards and burial grounds;
- **clocks;**
- **commons;**
- **cycle parks and racks;**
- fair charters;
- flag poles;
- fuel allotments;
- halls;
- historic and ceremonial things;
- investments;
- lavatories;
- lighting equipment;
- **litter bins;**
- markets;
- **mortuaries and hearses;**
- non-denominational chapels;
- parks, recreation grounds, playing fields and children's playgrounds;
- parochial offices provided under the Parochial Offices Act 1861;
- pounds, pumps, wells, hearse houses, etc, of ancient origin;
- public notice boards;
- quarries and gravel pits;
- regalia;
- rights of way (local only);
- schools;
- **seats;**
- surveillance equipment;
- swimming pools;
- **town greens;**
- undertakings such as water and harbour boards;
- vehicles;
- vestry rooms provided under the Vestries Act 1850;
- **village greens** and allotments for exercise and recreation;
- **war memorials;**
- workhouses, cottages and other property which were before 14 August 1834, vested in trustees or the churchwardens and overseers for the relief of the poor.

Miscellaneous or unusual possessions include a crematorium, two public houses, public wharves, a marina, a tower wagon and a holiday home.

C   THEORETICAL EXPOSITION (OLD SYSTEM)

12.3 Like parish meetings the vestries were not generally[1] corporations and had no legal personality. 'Their' property had therefore to be held on their behalf by other persons and so, immediately before the Local Government Act 1894 was passed, such property was vested in bodies of trustees of varying kinds and composition[2] who had, as a rule, to obey the directions of the vestry, though sometimes the property was subject to special trusts or to statutory appropriation for a particular purpose. The most important of these trustees were the churchwardens, the overseers and the guardians acting alone or in various combinations, but there also existed more specialised bodies of which the commonest were burial boards, inspectors of lighting, wardens, trustees, committees or managers of allotments, and commissioners for public baths.

The Act of 1894 secularised the civil administration of all parishes and therefore transferred property held for non-ecclesiastical purposes away from church officials to the new secular institutions. The authors of the original Bill in 1893 had intended that there should be a parish council in every parish, but their political opponents forced them to abandon this arrangement in small parishes, and it therefore became necessary to preserve alongside the new parish councils a slightly modernised version of the older system for use in the many parishes without separate councils; in these the Act did little to reduce the confusion which it had been intended to remedy, for it became necessary to preserve some of the specialised parish authorities and to introduce the unfortunately named 'representative body'.

[1]   Some select vestries were corporations.
[2]   No doubt these persons were in fact trustees but the word is not used here in a technical sense.

'Inheritance' through a representative body

12.4 In parishes without a separate parish council the Local Government Act 1894 created a corporation consisting of the chairman of a parish meeting and overseers[1] and transferred to it the legal interest in all property which would have been transferred to the parish council had one existed[2]. On 1 April 1927, overseers were abolished and their functions and interests transferred to other bodies[3]; the corporation was accordingly reconstituted, renamed the 'representative body'[4] and the property was transferred to it; this arrangement was re-enacted in statutory form in 1933[5].

Deeds, leases, conveyances and other instruments made between 1894 and 1 April 1927, in connection with property in these small parishes, were accordingly made in the name of the chairman and overseers acting as a corporate body and not as individuals, and they bound the representative body as successor in title.

On 17 July 1957, inspectors of lighting were abolished and their property transferred to the representative body[6].

In England its property, debts and liabilities passed to the parish trustees on

1 April 1974; in Wales they passed to the district council (T)[7].

1 Local Government Act 1894, s 19(6).
2 LGA 1894, s 19(7).
3 The Overseers Order 1927 No 55 made under authority of Rating and Valuation Act 1925, s 62.
4 Overseers Order 1927 No 55, art 7.
5 Local Government Act 1933, s 47 (repealed).
6 Parish Councils Act 1957, s 3(2)(b).
7 See **12.12** below.

'Inheritance' by or through a parish council

12.5 Where a burial authority's area did not coincide with the area administered by the parish council, the authority remained separately in existence and was the owner of the property which it had acquired for its functions. If a parish council was set up whose area coincided with the area of the authority, the latter ceased to exist and its property passed automatically to the parish council[1].

These specialist burial authorities ceased to exist on 1 April 1974 and their property passed to the authority or authorities exercising burial functions in the relevant area[2].

1 Local Government Act 1894, s 7(5).
2 See CHAPTER 33.

Vestries and Adoptive Act Authorities, 1894

12.6 Most parish councils inherited vestry property by the statutory transfer in 1894 of the parish property vested in the overseers or churchwardens and overseers; this included the village greens, and garden, recreational and all other types of allotments[1], and the property of those adoptive Act authorities whose area coincided with the area of the parish council[2].

1 Local Government Act 1894, s 6(1) and s 6(4) which was substantially re-enacted in the Small Holdings and Allotments Act 1908, s 33(3).
2 LGA 1894, s 7(5).

Overseers, 1927

12.7 Where no burial board had been appointed and a parish mortuary existed and had not been acquired by the parish council, the mortuary was transferred to it on 1 April 1927[1].

1 Rating and Valuation Act 1925 and Overseers Order 1927 No 55, arts 5, 6 and Schedule.

Guardians, 1930

12.8 Parish property which was vested in a board of guardians on 1 April 1930, including investments and money representing the proceeds of the sale of such property, were transferred to the parish council on that day. If the property was held on behalf of two or more parishes, it vested in their councils or representative bodies jointly, and where the parishes concerned were grouped, the property was vested in the common parish council unless the county council otherwise provided in the grouping order[1].

---

[1]   Local Government Act 1929, s 115.

Quarries and gravel pits, 1930 and their conversion

12.9 Inclosure Acts usually set aside land to provide materials for road making. Such quarries and gravel pits were sometimes allotted for the use of the inhabitants and vested in the Lord of the Manor as trustee, but more often they were vested in the surveyor of highways or other trustees. The surveyor could, with the consent of the vestry, sell them (giving the adjoining landowner first refusal) if they became exhausted, and with the like consent purchase others[1]. In due course the parish council succeeded to the functions of the vestry[2] and the surveyor's functions descended to the rural district council as highway authority. On 1 April 1930, the functions of the highway authority were transferred to the county council[3] which was obliged, if required by the rural district council, to purchase the quarries or materials belonging to it as highway authority.

The effect of this legislation was only to deal with the materials but not with the land itself, which was and remained parish property[4]; of the numerous exhausted quarries, therefore, those which were exhausted before 1894 were usually vested in the parish council or representative body whilst of the remainder some were vested in district councils (T) and others in county councils (T). None of them, however, can be sold without the consent of the local council (or parish meeting), and the income, if any, from such properties must be paid into the parochial or communal account. The proceeds of sale, which can be large, must be held in trust for the parish or community.

Some exhausted quarries have turned out to be valuable local assets and have been converted into playgrounds, recreational areas and similar amenities.

---

[1]   Highway Act 1835, s 48.
[2]   Local Government Act 1894, s 6(a).
[3]   Local Government Act 1929, s 30.
[4]   See Local Government Act 1933, s 305 (repealed) which was not affected by Highways Act 1959.

Creation of new parish councils

12.10 If a parish council was created for a single pre-existing parish, the property of the representative body passed to it automatically when the parish council came into office[1], but this was not necessarily the case where the new parish council came into existence as a result of a grouping order, for the parishes in the group retained their representative bodies[2] unless the county council decided to adapt the Local Government Act 1933, so as to abolish them in a particular instance[3].

---

[1]   Local Government Act 1894, s 7(6).
[2]   Local Government Act 1933, s 47(3).

Unclaimed village greens and commons

12.11 Where land was registered as a village green during the period for general registration (1967–1970) but no one laid claim to be the owner, the question of ownership was referred to a Commons Commissioner. If, after a public hearing, he was unable to discover an owner, he was required to direct the registration authority to register the parish council as owner, where there was one, and otherwise to register the district council. If a parish council, or in Wales after 1 April 1974 a community council, was or is subsequently established, ownership passed to that council[1].

If, however, a village green has been, or is, registered after 1970, ownership may remain undetermined until settled by legislation.

Where land was registered as common land in the period 1967 to 1970, the procedure for seeking an owner was the same as for village greens, but the Commons Commissioner had no power to direct the registration of a parish or other council as owner if no owner could be found. Instead, the land was subject to the Commons Registration Act 1965, s 9, which gave concurrent powers to county, district and parish or community councils to protect the land from unlawful interference and encroachment. Section 9 has been repealed and re-enacted as the Commons Act 2006, s 45 (see **26.12** below).

Where a village green has been vested in a local authority under s 8 of the 1965 Act, the authority holds it in accordance with the Open Spaces Act 1906, ss 10–15, unless a scheme of management has been made under the Commons Act 1899, in which case the scheme will apply[2].

[1]   Commons Registration Act 1965, s 8 (repealed).
[2]   Commons Registration Act 1965, s 8(4) (repealed).

D   THEORETICAL EXPOSITION (NEW SYSTEM)

12.12 The Local Government Act 1972, with its dependent statutory instruments, did not simplify things. The general distinction between England and Wales was compounded by the introduction into each country of successor councils (with differing characteristics); moreover, in England the old representative bodies were replaced by parish trustees, while in Wales they were simply abolished; and, finally, in both countries burial boards and joint burial committees disappeared.

England

12.13 In England the rural parishes and rural boroughs existing on 31 March 1974 continued to exist[1]. Hence on 1 April their councils (if any) remained in uninterrupted existence and possession of all the property which they owned the day before for statutory purposes or as trustees. The representative bodies of parishes not represented on a parish council were replaced at the same

113

moment by the more practically constituted parish trustees[2], to whom their property automatically passed[3].

In the case of ex-borough and urban district councils which acquired successor parish councils[4], and three rural district councils which became parish councils, there was a basic presumption that if property had been held before 1 April 1974, for the purposes of a function exercisable by a district council, then, even if that function was also exercisable concurrently by the successor parish council, the relevant property passed to the district council unless it and the successor council otherwise agreed[5]. To this presumption there were a number of specified exceptions[6], namely together with 'parish property'[7], charitable trust property[8], and historic and ceremonial property, especially charters, insignia and plate[9]; in all these cases the presumption was reversed.

Agreements between district and successor councils were embodied in property transfer orders made by the Secretary of State and these continued, occasionally, to be made. In addition, when a new parish council is created for, or in, an area which became non-parochial in 1974, such orders are made to vest property in them, or clauses similar to the provisions of such orders are included in the order creating them. These orders avoid the expense of conveyancing.

The property of burial boards and joint burial committees passed to whichever authority or authorities exercise burial functions in the relevant area[10].

[1] Local Government Act 1972, s 1(6) and (9).
[2] LGA 1972, ss 272 and 13(3).
[3] LGA 1972, Sch 29, para 5 and Local Authorities (England) (Property etc) Order 1973, SI 1973/1861, art 16.
[4] LGA 1972, Sch 1, Part V and Local Government (Successor Parishes) Orders 1973, SI 1973/1110, SI 1973/1939 and SI 1974/569.
[5] Local Authorities (England) (Property etc) Order 1973, SI 1973/1861, art 9.
[6] Local Government (Successor Parishes) Order 1974, SI 1974/406, art 4(18). The exceptions are printed in bold type in the list in **12.2** above.
[7] See **12.1** above.
[8] LGA 1972, s 210(2); see also CHAPTER **13** below.
[9] Local Authorities (England) (Property etc) Order 1973, SI 1973/1861, art 9.
[10] Local Authorities (England) (Property etc) Order 1973, SI 1973/1861, art 16 and see CHAPTER 33.

Wales

12.14 In Wales the rural parishes were abolished. The property of their councils passed to the community council which replaced them[1], but the property of the abolished representative bodies passed to the district council (T)[2].

Where, however, a community council succeeded to a borough or urban district council, it obtained, in default of agreement otherwise, only the 'parish property', such minor properties as were not held for functions exercisable by a county or district council, and historic and ceremonial property, with the charters, insignia and plate[3].

Property of burial boards and joint burial committees passed to whichever authority or authorities exercise burial functions in the relevant area[4].

[1] Local Authorities (Wales) (Property etc) Order 1973, SI 1973/1863, arts 9 and 16.
[2] SI 1973/1863, art 16.
[3] SI 1973/1863, art 9.
[4] SI 1973/1863, art 16.

User rights—both countries

12.15 Successor councils in both countries, and the parish councils of Alston with Garrigill, Disley and Tintwhistle became entitled for the proper discharge of their functions to the use of accommodation in property held by the predecessor council before 1 April 1974, and the district council (T) owning such property was forbidden to dispose of it without consulting the councils having the user rights and making agreed arrangements instead. Failing agreement, differences are settled by an agreed referee or, in default of agreement, by the Secretary of State[1].

[1] Local Authorities (England) (Property etc) Order 1973, SI 1973/1861, art 23(4A) and (8) inserted by Local Government (Successor Parishes) Order 1974, SI 1974/406 (England); Local Authorities (Wales) (Property etc) Order 1973, SI 1973/1863, art 23(4A) and (8) inserted by Local Authorities etc (Wales) (Property etc: Further Provision) Order 1974, SI 1974/404 (Wales).

E   NEW ACQUISITIONS BY AGREEMENT

12.16 A local council may by agreement acquire any land in or outside its area[1], for money or money's worth and as purchaser or lessee[2]. Land includes any interest or easement or right in or over land[3]. As an exchange involves a disposal certain consents may be needed[4].

The land may be acquired for any statutory function or simply for the benefit, improvement or development of the area[5].

Where boundary alterations occur, the authorities affected may adjust their property rights and liabilities by agreement or by arbitration in default of agreement. In such cases the right or duty to transfer or receive property will depend upon the terms of the agreement or award, and the title to the property itself will depend upon the deeds executed in pursuance of them[6].

If a parish council is to be abolished or its area partitioned, and if before the changes take effect, it and the contemplated transferee authority have not made agreements on the transfer of the relevant transferable property, the transfers are made in accordance with regulation 8[7]. Transferable property includes liabilities, contracts, deeds, bonds, agreements and other instruments and notices and also legal proceedings and their causes, provided in each case they relate exclusively to the area transferred. Consequential balancing payments (if needed) are made in such proportion as the population of a transferred area bears to that of the transferor council.

There may be more than one transferee authority and if, in the case of a partition, it is not a parish council, it will be the district council or, if none, the council of the county.

1   Local Government Act 1972, s 124(1).
2   LGA 1972, s 124(3).
3   LGA 1972, s 270(1).
4   See **12.30** and **12.31** below.
5   LGA 1972, s 124(1).
6   LGA 1972, s 68.
7   In the Local Government (Parishes and Parish Councils) Regulations 1999, SI 1999/545.

Transferred property

12.17 Trustees who hold property for the purposes of a public recreation ground or of allotments for the benefit of the inhabitants or any of them or for other charitable purposes other than an ecclesiastical charity may, with the consent of the Charity Commission, transfer the property to the local council or its appointees upon the same trusts[1].

1   Charities Act 2011, s 298(1).

Gifts

12.18 A council may, for the purposes of any of its functions, or for the benefit of the inhabitants of its area or part of it, accept, hold and administer any gift of property so long as the gift is not to be held in trust for an ecclesiastical or eleemosynary charity[1].

1   Local Government Act 1972, s 139(1) and (3). For the maintenance and improvement of these properties see **12.35** below.

F   COMMUNITY ASSETS AND RIGHT TO BID (ENGLAND ONLY)

Assets of community value

12.19 Chapter 3 of Part 5 of the Localism Act 2011 gives parish councils and community organisations the right to bid for land of community value (called "assets of community value" in the Act) when the owners wish to dispose of them. An asset is of community value if its current use furthers the social wellbeing or social interests of the local community. Principal authorities are required to maintain a list of land in their area which is of community value. There is an elaborate procedure for creating and maintaining lists of community assets.

A parish council, a neighbouring parish council, community organisation or neighbourhood forum may nominate an asset for listing as a community asset. Once on the list, the asset cannot be disposed of by the owner without giving the parish council or other local body a right to bid for the asset. In effect, any sale (or grant of a long lease) of an asset is delayed so as to give bidders time to make their own bid. The maximum delay period (or moratorium) is six months. The procedure does not provide for an enforced sale to a community bidder, which means that such a bidder must pay the proper market price for the asset.

The Department for Communities and Local Government has issued a non-statutory advice note to local authorities, published on the DCLG website.

G   FORESHORE, ACCRETION AND DILUVION

12.20 The imperceptible natural increase of land belonging to the council and situated on the seashore or beside running water is called accretion and will belong to it even though the increase is artificially caused by it, provided that the act is lawful[1], but this rule does not apply where the land is situated beside a lake, canal or pond[2], nor will it entitle a council to claim land artificially reclaimed by someone else[3]. Conversely land may be lost through natural encroachment (called diluvion).

Foreshore is the land between low and high water mark and the exact position of these marks varies. Foreshore usually belongs to the Crown or the Duchy of Cornwall but may belong to a council deriving ownership from a Crown or Duchy grant. Whether or not the council has such a movable freehold will depend on the wording of the grant[4].

[1]   *A G v Chambers* (1859) 4 de G & J 55 and *Mayor of Bradford v Pickles* [1895] AC 587.
[2]   *Trafford v Thrower* (1929) 45 TLR 502.
[3]   *A G of Southern Nigeria v John Holt and Co* [1915] AC 599.
[4]   *Baxendale v Instow Parish Council* [1982] Ch 14, [1981] 2 All ER 620; see CHAPTER **13**.

H   COMPULSORY ACQUISITION

Purchase

12.21 Unless in any particular case (such as the benefit, improvement or development of their area) a local council's power to acquire land is specifically limited to acquisition by agreement[1], it may make use of a special procedure for compulsory purchase where it is unable to purchase land by agreement and on reasonable terms. The following is an account of an important procedure in which, save at the outset, the local council takes little active part.

Compulsory purchase cannot be used to acquire for allotments land which is part of a park, garden, pleasure ground or home farm, or which is needed for the amenity or convenience of a dwelling, or which is woodland unless wholly surrounded by or adjacent to land already acquired by the local council for the purposes of the Allotments Acts 1908–1950[2], and the consent of the Secretary of State must, in the latter case, be obtained[3].

Where it is proposed compulsorily to acquire land owned inalienably by the National Trust, the compulsory purchase order is subject to special parliamentary procedure[4], and in the case of a common, open space, or fuel or field garden allotment special parliamentary procedure is required unless the appropriate minister certifies that equally advantageous land of equal extent has been given in exchange or that the land is needed for road widening and that the giving of land in exchange is unnecessary. He must give public notice of his intention to certify and must afford opportunity for representation at a public inquiry or otherwise[5].

1   Local Government Act 1972, s 125(1).
2   Small Holdings and Allotments Act 1908, s 41(1).
3   Small Holdings and Allotments Act 1908, s 39(1) amended by Compulsory Acquisition (Authorisation Procedure) Act 1946, s 1.
4   Acquisition of Land Act 1981, s 18.
5   Acquisition of Land Act 1981, Sch 3, Part II

Procedure

12.22 The local council represents the case to the district council (T), and the latter, if satisfied that the representation is true, may be authorised by the Secretary of State to purchase the whole or part of the land compulsorily.

Appeal

12.23 If the district council (T) refuses to make the order or does not make it within eight weeks of the representation or such longer period as may be agreed between the two councils, the local council may petition the Secretary of State who may hold the inquiry and 'step into the shoes' of the district council for the purpose of making the order[1].

The confirmed order is carried out by the district council (T), but the land is conveyed to the local council[2], which becomes liable to the vendor for the compensation and the cost of the conveyance and for interest on the compensation money if payment is delayed after the council has gone into possession. The rate of interest is 0.5 per cent below the standard rate. This is the base rate quoted by the seven largest banks on the reference day nearest before the date when the land was entered[3].

1   Local Government Act 1972, s 125(7).
2   Local Government Act 1972, s 125(4)(b).
3   Acquisition of Land (Rate of Interest after Entry) Regulations 1995, SI 1995/2262.

Hiring for allotments

12.24 A district council (T) may acquire land compulsorily for the purpose of letting it to a parish council for allotments[1]. This is seldom done.

1   Land Settlement (Facilities) Act 1919, s 17, amended by Local Government Act 1972, Sch 29; see **29.5** below.

Access to neighbouring land

12.25 Anyone may gain access to neighbouring land if it is necessary for preservation work on his own land. In default of agreement such access can be obtained by an application to the county court[1].

[1]   Access to Neighbouring Land Act 1992.

I   OPERATION OF TIME

Prescription and presumption of legality

12.26 Title to land may be acquired by prescription[1], and where rights of ownership have been publicly exercised over a long period without challenge the court will presume a lawful origin for the local council's rights[2].

[1]   *Blackstone v Martin* (1625) 81 ER 253.
[2]   *Haigh v West* [1893] 2 QB 19. This was a vestry case.

Limitation—unregistered land

12.27 The time within which an action for the recovery of unregistered land (ie land without a title registered at HM Land Registry) may be brought is limited to a fixed period from the time when the right of action accrued. Where the Crown wishes to recover foreshore, the period is 60 years, and in the case of other lands where the Crown or a spiritual or eleemosynary corporation sole intends to bring the action the period is 30 years. In all other cases such actions must be brought within twelve years[1].

There are rules for ensuring that the rights of action of persons under a disability are preserved until their disability ends and for dealing with cases of concealment, fraud and mistake[2].

The rules on limitation are purely negative. They merely extinguish at the end of a fixed period[3] the title of people who neglected to defend their property when they were able to do so. The rules do not create a new title in favour of the person in possession and against whom an action should have been brought. Thus it is not sufficient for the latter to show that he was in possession for the appropriate period of time: he must, in order to establish a complete title to the land, be able to prove what persons would be entitled but for limitation and then that all such persons have been barred.

The European Court of Human Rights has ruled that the statutory regime of adverse possession of unregistered land is not in breach of Article 1 of the First Protocol to the European Convention on Human Rights (right not to be deprived of possessions without paying proper compensation). The Convention is incorporated into English law by the Human Rights Act 1998[4]. However, the ruling only applies if the period of adverse possession ended before 2 October 2000 (the date on which the relevant parts of the Human Rights Act 1998 were brought into force). If that period ended or ends after that date, the 1998 Act applies and a claimant must be able to show that his use of the land in question was inconsistent with the use of the land by the owner, not merely without the owner's consent[5]. Since the European Court's decision in *Pye* continues to apply in the case of unregistered land, it is unlikely that a challenge to a claim for adverse possession on the ground of breach of the 1998 Act would succeed.

¹   Limitation Act 1980, s 15 and Sch 1, paras 10 and 11.
²   LA 1980, Pt II.
³   LA 1980, s 17.
⁴   *J A Pye (Oxford) Ltd v United Kingdom* (2008) 46 EHRR 45.
⁵   *Beaulane Properties Ltd v Palmer* [2006] Ch 79.

Limitation—registered land

12.28 Where the title to land is registered, as it mostly is, the Limitation Act 1980, ss 15 and 17 (see **12.27** above) do not apply¹. Instead, a person may apply to be the registered proprietor of registered land if he has been in adverse possession for ten years ending with the date of application. The land need not have been registered for the whole period of adverse possession. The land registrar must give notice of the application to the registered proprietor and to the registered proprietor of any charge over the land. If there is no opposition to the application, the applicant can be registered as proprietor. If the application is opposed, it will only succeed if three conditions are satisfied. Stated briefly, these are:

(a)   that it would be unconscionable because of an equity by estoppel for the registered proprietor to seek to displace the applicant. An equity by estoppel is a personal right which has come into existence by reason of some act or representation which the registered proprietor cannot reasonably be allowed to deny;

(b)   for some other reason (eg the applicant has entered into a valid contract to purchase the land) the applicant is entitled to be registered as proprietor; and

(c)   the land forms part of the boundary with the applicant's land and the applicant has been in possession for at least ten years and reasonably believes the land belongs to him².

In practice, save perhaps in the case of boundary land, it is likely that opposed applications will succeed.

¹   Land Registration Act 2002, s 96.
²   LRA 2002, s 97 and Sch 6.

J   PRIVATE PROPERTY SUBJECT TO PUBLIC RIGHTS¹

¹   See also Chapter 13 and Chapter 26.

12.29 In many localities there are private lands over which the inhabitants have rights of a more or less far-reaching nature. Such rights originate sometimes in custom, sometimes in a presumption that the right must have been granted by somebody able to make such a grant, and sometimes in statute—more especially in Inclosure Acts and the awards made under them.

The most usual lands in which such rights exist are village greens and churchyards, both of which may be controlled and to some extent maintained and managed by the local council even though they remain in private ownership. The most usual public rights are rights of exercise and recreation, and rights of way.

Village and town greens must be registered.

K   ORDINARY APPROPRIATIONS

12.30 Land acquired for a purpose is said to be 'appropriated' to that purpose, and can be used for no other, save as the law permits, but with certain exceptions[1] a local council, and (with the Secretary of State's consent) a parish meeting may reappropriate any land not required for the purpose for which it was acquired or appropriated, to some other purpose, subject, of course, to the rights of other persons over the land[2]. Appropriations and reappropriations must be made by resolution and are, in their nature, meant to be long lasting. There is no special restraint on the reappropriation of compulsorily purchased land as such.

[1]   For exceptional cases see **12.32** below.
[2]   Local Government Act 1972, s 126(1)–(3).

L   ORDINARY DISPOSALS OF LAND

12.31 A local council, and parish trustees with the consent of the parish meeting, may ordinarily dispose of land in any way they wish[1]. If, however, in the case of land not held on charitable trusts[2], the disposal is for less than the land is worth, the Secretary of State's consent is needed, unless either the disposal is by way of short tenancy, that is to say a term not exceeding seven years or the assignment of a term with no more than seven years still to run[3]. The Secretary of State has given a general consent for the disposal of land at less than full value where:

(a)   the local authority considers that the purpose for which the land is to be disposed is likely to contribute to the achievement of any one or more of the following objects in respect of the whole or any part of its area, or of all or any persons resident or present in its area:
      (i)   the promotion or improvement of economic well-being;
      (ii)   the promotion or improvement of social well-being;
      (iii) the promotion or improvement of environmental well-being; and
(b)   the difference between the unrestricted value of the land to be disposed of and the consideration for the disposal does not exceed £2,000,000[4].

The Welsh assembly has made similar provision[5].

[1]   Local Government Act 1972, ss 127(1) and 131(3).
[2]   See CHAPTER **13** below.
[3]   LGA 1972, s 127(2) and (5); Local Government (Miscellaneous Provisions) Act 1976.
[4]   LGA 1972, s 127(2) and (5); Department of Communities and Local Government Circular 06/03: Local Government Act 1972: General disposal consent (England) 2003; disposal of land for less than the best consideration that can reasonably be obtained.
[5]   National Assembly for Wales Circular 2003: Local Government Act 1972: General disposal consent (Wales) 2003.

M   EXCEPTIONAL REAPPROPRIATIONS AND DISPOSALS

12.32 In some cases (apart altogether from special covenants) a public authority owes a duty to the public that land in its possession shall be used for the purpose for which it was acquired. Reappropriation and disposal can threaten that purpose and therefore special formalities must be observed before they can take place.

Open spaces

12.33 A council or parish meeting cannot reappropriate or, save by way of short tenancy, dispose of an open space or part of one without first advertising its intention in two consecutive weeks in a local newspaper, and considering any objections[1].

Such a disposal or reappropriation frees the land from any trusts arising solely from its being held in trust for the enjoyment of the public under the Public Health Act 1875, s 164, or the Open Spaces Act 1906, s 10[2].

[1]   Local Government Act 1972, ss 123, 126 and 127.
[2]   See **12.30**, footnote 2 above.

Commons and allotments

12.34 A council wishing to reappropriate land forming part of a common[1] or fuel or field garden allotments[2] must first advertise its intention for two consecutive weeks in a local newspaper and consider objections. The council then makes the reappropriation by order which has to be confirmed by the Secretary of State unless the area to be appropriated does not exceed 250 square yards[3].

[1]   See **12.33** above.
[2]   See **29.1** below.
[3]   Local Government Act 1972, s 126(4). For metric equivalents see **20.5** below.

Cycle and car parks

12.35 A local council may, with the Secretary of State's consent, appropriate for the purposes of a cycle or car park any part of a recreation ground[1], open space[2] or land acquired under the repealed Physical Training and Recreation Act 1937, s 4, or its successor, the Local Government (Miscellaneous Provisions) Act 1976, s 19, provided that the land does not exceed the lesser of one-eighth of the total area or 800 square feet[3].

These parking places may be let for periods not exceeding seven days, but without prejudice to the local council's right to let the land, of which they form a part, for a longer period[4].

[1]   Acquired under Local Government Act 1894, s 8.
[2]   See Open Spaces Act 1906.
[3]   Road Traffic Regulation Act 1984, s 51. For metric equivalents see **20.5** below.
[4]   RTRA 1984, s 57(7).

N   MAINTENANCE AND IMPROVEMENT

12.36 A local council[1] and a parish meeting may execute any works including works of maintenance or improvement in relation to any parish property[2]. So far as gifts for non-statutory purposes are concerned the council must use its 'free resource'[3], for this purpose An eligible parish council which has adopted the power of general competence (see **22.22** below) must use that power. A Welsh community council may be able to use the power to promote well-being (see **35.21** below).

[1]   Local Government Act 1894, s 8(1)(i).
[2]   See **12.1** above.
[3]   See **22.17** below.

O   LAND REGISTRATION

12.37 Any local council which owns land can register its title in the Land Registry. This has advantages. Dealings in the land are simplified and there is thenceforth no doubt of the council's title even if the documents are subsequently lost or mislaid[1].

In addition, registration is compulsory within two months of the happening of certain events. These events are the conveyance of the fee simple (that is full ownership) by sale, gift, under a court order or by vesting assent, of the land, the grant of a lease for seven years or more, the assignment of a lease which has seven or more years to run and the vesting by way of an assent or vesting deed of the fee simple or of a lease with at least seven years to run. Where a local council acquires the land there will generally be little difficulty, save that it may be asked to pay part or the whole of the expense of registration, but where the council is disposing of it, it will be responsible for seeing that the registration is effected. Failure to register in time results in the grant becoming void, unless an extension of time is secured[2].

[1]   Land Registration Act 2002, ss 4 and 58.
[2]   LRA 2002, s 7.

P   INFORMATION ON INTERESTS IN LAND

12.38 If a local council thinks that with a view to performing one of its statutory functions it needs information connected with any land, it may serve a notice on the occupier, or manager or on anyone with any interest in the land. The notice must specify the land and the function and the enactment which confers the function and may require the person on whom it is served to give information about his own interest, and particulars of any other persons who may occupy or manage or have other interests. He must be given a date not earlier than a fortnight hence in which to reply, and failure to reply or false replies may lead to a level 3 fine[1].

[1]   Local Government (Miscellaneous Provisions) Act 1976, s 16; see **21.40** below for the maximum amount of each level of fine.

Q   INVESTMENTS AND PROCEEDS OF SALE

12.39 Where parish property had been sold the resulting proceeds and investments or other property into which they had been converted before 17 November 1933, remained vested and continued to be applied as they were on that date until the minister (now the Secretary of State) otherwise directed[1]. After that date capital received for the disposal of charitable land had to be applied in accordance with the directions of the scheme-making- authority[2], and capital received for other land had to be applied as the minister approved towards the reduction of debt or otherwise for any purpose for which capital might be applied[3].

Since the Local Government Act 1972 came into force the disposal of charitable capital is effected by conditions imposed upon consents to sell the land[4], and the disposal of other capital is subject to the control of the Secretary of State[5].

[1]   Local Government Act 1933, s 178.
[2]   LGA 1933, s 170(2)(i).
[3]   LGA 1933, s 170(2)(ii).
[4]   Charities Act 2011, Part 7
[5]   Local Government Act 2003, Part 1

LAMIT and CIF

12.40 Funds invested to bring income can be placed with the Local Authorities Mutual Investment Trust (LAMIT) or if charitable with the Common Investment Funds (CIF); these are approved methods of investment[1]; they are under the same management and have the same address and have been very successful. Alternatively funds needing to be invested for a short time only, can be lent to another local authority (see **15.36** below) which will often pay a higher rate of interest than a bank.

[1]   Trustee Act 2000, Part 2.

R   TRANSFER OF SECURITIES

12.41 Where local authorities have investments in the form of stocks, shares or other securities, the company concerned is required on production of the proper authority to transfer the investment into the name of another body or another name on the happening of certain events.

Where the event is a change of name, the local council requests the company to alter its records and the request is supported by a statutory declaration made by the clerk or other proper officer specifying the investments, verifying the change of name and the identity of the council.

Where a different event, such as a boundary alteration, results in some other council becoming entitled to the investment, the scheme, order or award affecting the change is sufficient authority, but if a statutory declaration is required, the proper officer of the district council (T) is the person who should make it.

In case of difficulty an application may be made to the High Court if the value exceeds £50,000; otherwise it must be made to the local county court[1].

1 Local Government Act 1972, s 146.

S   LOST PROPERTY

12.42 If property is found in buildings or premises owned or managed by the council or is deposited with the council but not collected in accordance with the terms under which it is deposited, the council may give the owner a clear month's written notice (or more) to collect it and must warn him that if he fails to do so, the property will vest in the council. If he fails to comply, the property passes to the council.

If it is impossible to serve a notice, then in the case of property found on the premises, the ownership passes to the council after one month. In the case of other property the period is six months, but perishables or property which cannot be looked after, save at unreasonable expense, may be sold at any time and the proceeds vest in the council at the time when the ownership would have passed if it had not been sold.

The property or its value or any part of it may be given to the finder.

A person who claims property before it has vested in the council may be charged the cost of the council's inquiries and custody[1].

A council which intends to operate these rules may think it wise to put up a permanent notice about it on the premises beforehand, to avoid bad blood.

1 Local Government (Miscellaneous Provisions) Act 1982, s 41.

T   OCCUPIERS' LIABILITY

Lawful visitors

12.43 If an occupier, such as a local council, of premises (including structures and appliances on the land) has a sufficient degree of control over them that he ought to realise that a failure on his part to use care may result in injury to a person coming lawfully there, he owes a so-called common duty of care to that person. This is 'a duty to take such care as in all the circumstances of the case is reasonable, to see that the visitor will be reasonably safe in using the premises for the purposes for which he is invited or permitted by the occupier to be there'[1]. Reasonable care involves consideration of the nature of any danger, the length of time that the danger was in existence, the steps necessary to remove it and the likelihood or otherwise of injury. The occupier does not owe the duty to someone who has willingly accepted the risk, and he can exclude his liability to some voluntary visitors (as opposed to persons with a statutory right of entry) contractually or by exhibiting a conspicuous, legible and suitably expressed notice[2]. Hence children may be expected to be more vulnerable and less able to understand a notice than adults, but an expert (such as an electrician) may be expected to guard against risks special to his field.

1 Occupiers' Liability Act 1957, s 2(2).
2 Occupiers' Liability Act 1957, s 2(1) and *Ashdown v Samuel Williams* [1957] 1 QB 409.

Trespassers

12.44 As against trespassers (who, in principle, must take other people's premises and their occupiers as they find them) there is a lesser duty, namely to take precautions against injury to the person, but not to property, if the council is aware of the danger or has reasonable grounds to believe that it exists, and knows or has reasonable grounds to believe that the trespasser is or may come near the danger, and that it may in all the circumstances be reasonably expected to offer protection[1].

[1] Occupiers' Liability Act 1984. See also Countryside and Rights of Way Act 2000 and *Tomlinson v Congleton Borough Council* [2003] UKHL 47.

Chapter 13

CHARITIES AND PUBLIC GIFTS

13.1 The law on charities and public gifts has had to be adapted to the special needs of localities, first and particularly to preserve the barrier between the secular and the ecclesiastical and to continue the century-old policy of relieving the locality of direct responsibility for the poor[1]. Second, provision has been made for the fact that many charities benefit more than one locality. Third, for reasons of convenience there is provision for the continuance in office or the future creation of independent bodies of trustees. Fourth, whilst all charities are public not all public gifts are charitable; under the general law only charities are perpetual, and the law has had, without making inroads upon the law of charity, to find a way of preserving non-charitable gifts from destruction under the rule against perpetuities. Fifth, Parliament has given to the parish or community, or its elected representatives, as much control over a public gift or charity affecting it as may reasonably be expected.

[1] See Local Government Act 1972, s 139(3).

A   THE NATURE OF LEGAL CHARITY

13.2 The law of legal charity comprises some of the most abstruse problems of English jurisprudence: it is essentially a matter for experts, and in practical questions of difficulty it will always be better to seek advice rather than to rely upon such general statements of principle as are contained in this work. The propositions in this section are, however, to some extent developed in later sections of this chapter.

Common characteristics

13.3 Valid gifts for charitable purposes must be couched in imperative language, the charitable intention of the donor must be beyond question, the property comprised in the gift must be certain, and in the case of a gift by a living person, the ownership of the property must have passed to the trust.

The question whether a trust is charitable or not depends upon its objects and not upon the character of the trustees, though that character may, of course, be evidence of the nature of the objects.

The objects must be public: that is to say a purpose must in order to be charitable be directed to the benefit of the community or a section of the community[1]. Thus an intention to benefit an individual or particular individuals (even though by so doing poverty will be relieved or education or religion

127

furthered) will not be charitable, but an intention to further a charitable object in the abstract without giving any individual person an enforceable claim on the funds will be charitable.

The purposes of the trust must not be contrary to the policy of the law. Infringements of this rule are now uncommon.

If the objects of a trust fall under one head or classification of charity, they will be valid even if they contravene another[2].

To escape certain fiscal burdens the trust must be charitable and nothing else, but this rigorous rule does not apparently apply in cases of discretionary relief from non-domestic rating[3].

Charitable trusts are perpetual and therefore if their objects become obsolete the Crown or its other representatives will intervene as guardians of the public to ensure, in accordance with the principles set out in **13.27** below, that the charitable intentions of the donor do not fail and that the funds are redirected for the public good.

[1]   The word 'community' in this quotation does not refer to a Welsh local government community.
[2]   See *A G v Lonsdale* (1827) 1 Sim 105 (education of sons of gentlemen).
[3]   Local Government Finance Act 1988, s 47.

B   CHARITABLE PURPOSES CLASSIFIED

Historical classification

13.4 Before Part 1 of the Charities Act 2006 came into force in April 2008, legal charity was mainly defined by reference to the preamble to the repealed statute 43 Eliz I cap 4 which did not so much define charity as give examples of it[1]. The courts always interpreted the spirit rather than the letter of the statute, and many attempts to classify the extensive case law were made. The most notable, and potentially misleading, of these attempts was made in 1891[2] in the following manner: (1) relief of poverty; (2) education; (3) advancement of religion; (4) other purposes beneficial to the community (in its general not specially Welsh sense) not falling under any of the preceding three heads. A fifth class—recreation—was recognised by statute in 1958.

The Charities Act 2006, and most other legislation relating to charities, has now been consolidated in the Charities Act 2011.

[1]   *Morice v Bishop of Durham* (1804) 9 Ves 399.
[2]   *Income Tax Special Purposes Commissioners v Pemsel* [1891] AC 583.

Charities Act 2011

13.5 Section 3(1) of the Charities Act 2011 provides that charitable purposes must be for the public benefit:

(a)   the prevention or relief of poverty;
(b)   the advancement of education;

(c)   the advancement of religion;

(d)   the advancement of health or the saving of lives;

(e)   the advancement of citizenship or community development;

(f)   the advancement of arts, culture, heritage or science;

(g)   the advancement of amateur sport;

(h)   the advancement of human rights, conflict resolution or reconciliation or the promotion of religious or racial harmony or equality or diversity;

(i)   the advancement of environmental protection or improvement;

(j)   the relief of those in need by reason of youth, age, ill health, disability, financial hardship or other disadvantage;

(k)   the advancement of animal welfare;

(l)   the promotion of the efficiency of the armed forces of the Crown, or of the efficiency of the police, fire and rescue services or ambulance services;

(m)   any other purposes which are not specifically comprised in the above categories but which are:

    (i)   recognised as charitable under the pre-2006 law or by virtue of the Recreational Charities Act 1958, s 1;

    (ii)   reasonably analogous to, or within the spirit of, any of those purposes;

    (iii)   reasonably analogous to, or within the spirit of, previous charity law.

The Charity Commission has a duty to issue guidance on the operation of the requirement for a charity to provide a public benefit[1].

[1]   Charities Act 2011, s 17(1). The Commission has issued 'Charities and Public Benefit', which can be viewed on the Commission's website: www.charity-commission.gov.uk

Relief of poverty (eleemosynary charities)

13.6 Gifts to benefit the poor either generally or of a particular parish[1], or for a particular class of poor persons or for institutions benefiting the poor are charitable, and a gift for the poor is charitable even if it happens incidentally to benefit the rich, but a trust benefiting the rich exclusively and without any other charitable object cannot be charitable.

[1]   *Whicker v Hume* (1858) 7 HLC 124, and see *Attorney-General v Charity Commission for England and Wales* [2012] WTLR 977 for a wide-ranging judgment on the meaning of the relief of poverty.

Education

13.7 Gifts for the advancement of education generally, or for the education of particular classes of persons, are charitable and the advancement of education has been held to include education in particular branches of study[1], the equipment of a school with a facility for playing a game[2], or with a sanatorium[3], the provision of a school treat[4], the endowment of scholarships[5] and prizes[3].

On the other hand, a gift for the promotion of a scientific or artistic pursuit is not charitable unless it promotes education[6].

1   *Re Allsop* (1884) I Th R 4.
2   *Re Mariette* [1915] 2 Ch 284.
3   *Re Harrow School* [1927] 1 Ch 556. *Thompson v Thompson* (1844) 1 Coll 398.
4   *Re Mellody* [1918] 1 Ch 228.
5   *R v Newman* (1670) 1 Lev 284.
6   *Re Ogden* (1909) 25 TLR 382.

Advancement of religion

13.8 Most, but not quite all, gifts which are technically for the advancement of religion are ecclesiastical charities (with which local councils are not concerned), but it is customary to include in this class gifts for the maintenance of a churchyard[1] or burial ground, even though restricted to members of one sect[2], gifts for the maintenance of a church[3] and for the provision of a church clock[4]. A gift for the maintenance of a particular tomb is not charitable[5] unless it is in a church.

1   *Re Vaughan* (1886) 33 Ch D 187; *Re Pardoe* [1906] 2 Ch 184.
2   *Re Manser* [1905] 1 Ch 68.
3   *A-G v Ruper* (1722) 2 P Wms 125.
4   *Re Church Estates Charity Wandsworth* (1871) 6 Ch App 296.
5   *Masters v Masters* (1718) 1 P Wms 422.

Recreation

13.9 It is charitable to provide or help to provide facilities for recreation or other leisure time occupation if (but only if) this is done to improve the condition of life of the intended beneficiaries, and either they need them because of age, youth, infirmity, poverty or social or economic circumstances or the facilities are to be open to all members of the public at large or to male, or to female, members of the public[1]. All these rules apply especially to village halls, women's institutes and recreation grounds.

1   Charities Act 2011, s 5.

Miscellaneous

13.10 Not all trusts which benefit the community are legally charitable. For local councils, however, the following types of trusts which have been held to be charitable, are the most important: gifts for the relief of the rates (or perhaps for the relief of council tax)[1], or to the local council in furtherance of its statutory duties[2]; for a burial ground[3]; for supplying public water[4]; for repairing public highways and bridges[5]; for the provision of a public car park[6].

1   *Doe d Preece v Howells* (1831) 2 B & Ad 744.
2   *Luckcraft v Pridham* (1877) 6 Ch D 205.
3   *Re St Pancras Burial Ground* (1866) LR 3 Eq 173.
4   *Jones v Williams* (1767) Amb 651.
5   *A-G v Corporation of Limerick* (1817) 6 Dowl 136.
6   Registered charity no. 278236. The income from the car park is spent on grants to local charities.

C   NON-CHARITABLE PUBLIC GIFTS

13.11 A local authority may for the benefit of the inhabitants of its area or part of it accept, hold and administer any non-charitable gift of property whether real or personal[1]. It may execute any works, including works of maintenance and improvement, incidental or consequential, on the acceptance, ownership and administration of the gift. If the purposes of the gift are purposes in relation to which the council has specific statutory powers (for example, a playing field), it may defray the cost under those powers. If the purposes are merely for the benefit of the area or its inhabitants or some or part of them and are not referable to some other specific power, the cost, in the absence of an endowment, must be defrayed from the 'free resource', or in exercise of the power of general competence[2].

[1]   Local Government Act 1972, s 139(1).
[2]   LGA 1972, s 139(2), Localism Act 2011, Part 1, Chapter 1. For the 'free resource' see **22.17** below and for the power of general competence see **22.21** below.

D   REGISTRATION AND INDEXES

13.12 Public registers of charities are maintained by the Charity Commission. County and district councils (T) may keep indexes of local charities which are in fact copies of their local portions of the main register[1].

It is the duty of charity trustees to register their charity unless it is: (a) exempted under the Charities Act 2011; or (b) is excepted by regulations and in receipt of a gross income not exceeding £100,000; or (c), in receipt of an income not exceeding £5,000[2]. A trust when registered is conclusively presumed for all purposes to be a charity[3]; this is a great practical advantage when recovering tax or negotiating rate settlements. A record of the registration number should always be kept. Nevertheless a charity which has not been registered (even if it should have been) will not, by that fact alone, be shut out from claiming tax relief for it is open to the trustees to prove charitable status by other means.

[1]   Charities Act 2011, s 295.
[2]   CA 2011, s 30.
[3]   CA 2011, s 37.

E   REVIEW AND CO-ORDINATION

13.13 With the consent of the charities concerned a county or district council (T) may review the working of charities in its area[1] and all councils may make arrangements with a charity for co-ordinating its activities with those of the council concerned[2].

[1]   Charities Act 2011, s 295.
[2]   CA 2011, s 297.

F PAROCHIAL CHARITIES

13.14 'Parochial charity' is a technical term meaning in relation to a locality, a charity, the benefits of which are confined either to its inhabitants, or those of an ancient ecclesiastical parish which included it or part of it or of an area consisting of that locality and not more than four neighbouring localities[1]. A reorganisation of boundaries sometimes results in a parochial charity ceasing to be technically parochial, with the result that the local councils and parish meetings formerly concerned in its management lose most of their rights.

[1]   Charities Act 2011, s 303.

G CHARITIES OUTSIDE LOCAL ADMINISTRATION

13.15 Ecclesiastical and eleemosynary charities cannot be administered by a local council.

Ecclesiastical

13.16 An ecclesiastical charity (as distinguished from the larger class of charities for the advancement of religion) includes a charity for any spiritual purpose which is lawful or for the benefit of any spiritual person or ecclesiastical officer as such, or (if a building) for a church, chapel, mission room or Sunday school or otherwise for any denomination, or for maintenance of Divine Service in such building, or otherwise for the benefit of any particular church or denomination or of any members thereof as such; and, in addition, it includes any building which, between 5 March 1854 and 5 March 1894, was provided mainly at the expense of the members of any particular denomination[1].

A partly ecclesiastical endowment other than a building is regarded as an ecclesiastical charity but must be apportioned by the Charity Commission on application, and provision must be made for the management of the non-ecclesiastical part[1].

[1]   Local Government Act 1894, s 75.

Eleemosynary

13.17 An eleemosynary charity is one which, in practical terms, exists to distribute its founder's bounty or alms and comprises "all charities directed to the relief of individual distress, whether due to poverty, age, sickness or other similar afflictions"[1].

It seems possible that this ancient type of charity may have been superseded by items (*a*), (*d*), (*j*) and (*m*) (see **13.5** above).

[1]   Goulding J in *Re Armitage, Dec'd, Ellam and Another v Norwich Corporation and Others* (1972) Ch 438.

H   CHARITY ADMINISTRATION AND APPOINTMENT OF TRUSTEES

Acceptance or transfer

13.18 A local council may accept, hold and administer or act as a holding trustee for[1] a charitable trust for the general benefit of the locality so long as it is not of an ecclesiastical or eleemosynary character[2], and it may also accept trusteeship of village greens, and recreational, agricultural and other allotments[3].

The trustees of such trusts and trustees who hold property for public purposes may, with the consent of the Charity Commission, transfer their property to the local council or its nominees upon the same trusts[4]. The trustees are not bound to transfer, nor the council to accept the property.

On a boundary change, charitable property with its rights and liabilities is transferred in accordance with common sense rules[5]. The trusts are not changed: the property is simply passed to the transferee authority in whose area the greater part of the area benefited by the trust lies. If there is more than one, the councils must agree which of them is to be the trustee. If they have not agreed three months before the boundary order takes effect, the Charity Commission decide for them. There is provision for the transfer of functions from an officer of the transferor authority to one of the transferee.

[1]   Public Trustee Rules 1912 (SR & O 1912/348) (as amended).
[2]   Local Government Act 1972, s 139(1).
[3]   Poor Relief Act (1819), s 17 (repealed) and Local Government Act 1894, s 6(1)(c).
[4]   Charities Act 2011, s 298.
[5]   Local Government (Parishes and Parish Councils) Regulations 1999, SI 1999/545, reg 9.

Parochial charities

13.19 Many local councils are entitled to appoint trustees under the terms of a trust deed. Apart from rights of this kind they also have powers of appointment accorded them by statute. Thus where there exists or it is intended to create a parochial charity not vested in the local council, it is subject to special rules and the local council has certain rights of appointment of trustees.

Formerly overseers and churchwardens

13.20 The local council is entitled to appoint one trustee of every parochial charity in the place of each overseer who was formerly entitled to be a trustee, and one trustee in place of each churchwarden who was formerly entitled to be a trustee of a non-ecclesiastical charity. Where there is no separate council these rights of appointment belong to the parish meeting[1], or in Wales, to the county or country borough council[2].

[1]   Charities Act 2011, s 299.
[2]   CA 2011, s 299(2).

No popular element

13.21 Where the body of trustees of a non-ecclesiastical parochial charity includes no representative appointed by the council, the parish meeting, or by rate or probably council tax payers, electors or inhabitants, the council may appoint additional trustees not exceeding the number permitted by the Charity Commission, and where the charity is managed by a single person, the trustees may be increased to three, one of whom may be appointed by the local council[1]. In Wales if there is no community council, these rights are exercised by the county or county borough council[2].

1   Charities Act 2011, s 299.
2   CA 2011, s 299(2).

Vestry

13.22 Any power to appoint trustees or beneficiaries of a non-ecclesiastical charity formerly exercisable by the vestry was transferred to the local council[1], or in Wales to the county or county borough council for a community without a council[2].

1   Charities Act 2011, s 299.
2   CA 2011, s 299(2).

Non-parochial places

13.23 In non-parochial places the rights of appointment are exercised by the district council (T) or, in Wales, the county or county borough council[1].

1   Charities Act 2011, s 299.

Forty-year moratorium

13.24 Save in the case of appointments in lieu of overseers, none of the powers of appointment may be exercised within 40 years of the foundation of the charity without the consent of the founder or surviving founders[1].

1   Charities Act 2011, s 299.

Term of office

13.25 Trustees appointed as described above hold office for four years, but half (as nearly as may be) of those first appointed hold office for only two years[1].

1   Charities Act 2011, s 302.

Audit

13.26 The accounts of a parochial charity administered by a local council form part of its ordinary accounts and are subject to statutory audit[1], but where a charity is administered by trustees its accounts do not form part of them and they are therefore not subject to statutory audit even though all the trustees are appointed by the local council. This does not, of course, exempt them from keeping accounts or having them audited[2].

[1]   Audit Commission Act 1998, s 2 and Sch 2.
[2]   The general provisions on trustee's audits are in the Charities (Accounts and Reports) Regulations 2008, SI 2008/629.

I   REDIRECTION OF OBSOLETE OR UNECONOMIC FUNDS

Summary

13.27 In principle obsolete charities are applied 'cy pres', that is to say, 'as nearly as possible to that which has failed'. There is a list of the circumstances in which the original purposes of a charitable gift may be altered in the Charities Act 2011, s 62. Though contained in five paragraphs, it will be seen that there are really ten such cases, one of which is residual and probably capable of indefinite extension. It is considered unpractical to allow trustees to be the sole judges of when original trusts have failed or what objects are cy pres the original trusts, and it would be equally difficult for an independent body to do so without powers of inquiry and control. Jurisdiction over charities is vested in the Crown acting through the Attorney-General or the Lord Chancellor or in a visitor (depending on circumstances), in the High or a county court, but mostly in the Charity Commission which exercises the Crown's power of reorganisation by means of so-called schemes for the future management of a given trust; but the Charities Act 2011 contains a simplified method for redirecting the funds of certain obsolete or small charities. The procedure by scheme (see below) will in most local cases be unnecessary because the assets will be low enough to bring it within the procedure by resolution.

Schemes

13.28 The draft of any scheme relating to a parochial charity (other than an ecclesiastical charity) must be communicated on or before the publication of the draft order making the scheme, to the local council or chairman of the parish meeting (as the case may be)[1]. In the case of a Welsh community without a council the draft must presumably be sent to the county or county borough council. A local council, with the consent of the electors' meeting, may appeal within three months to the High Court against the order creating the scheme. A certificate that the matter is a proper one for appeal must be obtained from the Commission or the leave of a High Court judge[2]. A parish meeting has no such right.

Where the charity property includes land other than buildings, the scheme must contain a clause permitting the trustees to let the land for allotments[3].

1   Charities Act 2011, s 88(2)
2   CA 2011, s 69.
3   Allotments Extensions Act 1882, s 14 (repealed).

Resolution with Commission's concurrence

13.29 In the case of a charity which in the last financial year:

(a)   had an income of £10,000 or less;
(b)   had no land required to be used for the purposes or a purpose of the trust (called 'designated land'); and
(c)   was not a company or other body,

the trustees may pass, by a two-thirds majority of those voting, a resolution to transfer the property to another charity (which must be registered or not required to be registered), or divide it between more than one[1].

The trustees may in like circumstances, instead replace the purposes of the charity by other charitable purposes, or to modify its procedural or administrative arrangements. They must beforehand have satisfied themselves that the purposes of the charity have ceased to be conducive to a suitable and effective application of the funds; that the purposes of the transferee charity or the new purposes, as the case may be, are similar to the existing ones, and that the transferee charity will accept the property[2].

Having in either case passed the resolution, the trustees must send a copy to the Commission with a statement of their reasons for passing it. The Commission may direct the trustees to give public notice and, if it does so, it must take into account representations made to it by interested persons within 28 days of the date on which the trustees give public notice of the resolution. The Commission may make its own objections to the resolution. If it gives no directions, or having advertised the resolution, there are no representations, the resolution takes effect after 60 days from the date on which it was submitted to the Commission. If directions are given and representations received, the 60-day period is in effect extended until the representations are dealt with to the satisfaction of the Commission but the length of the period cannot exceed 120 days. If that limit is breached, the resolution is treated as if never passed[3].

If the resolution takes effect, the Commission makes the necessary orders to transfer the property to the appropriate transferee charity or other person[4].

1   Charities Act 2011, ss 267, 271–278.
2   Charities Act 2011, s 275.
3   Charities Act 2011, s 273–274.
4   Charities Act 2011, s 272(4).

J   RELIEF FROM TAXES

Taxes

13.30 Where a trust is established for charitable purposes only[1] the trustees may for the most part claim exemption from income tax, and from corporation tax and both capital gains taxes upon most of their investments and in certain circumstances also upon trading profits[2]. HM Revenue and Customs cannot dispute the charitable status of a trust registered in the Register of Charities.

[1]   Income Tax Act 2007, Part 10 (ss 518–564).
[2]   Income Tax Act 2007, s 524. The details are beyond the scope of this work.

Payroll subscribers

13.31 An employee paying tax under PAYE can subscribe to a charity by asking his employer to divert some of his pay to the charity. Such payments must be made in accordance with a scheme made by the Treasury. The money so diverted counts as an expense in computing the employee's income[1].

[1]   Income Tax (Earnings and Pensions) Act 2003, ss 713–715.

K   INVESTMENT

13.32 The Trustee Act 2000 gives charity trustees (with a few exceptions, chiefly relating to charitable companies and the cases where the charity's governing instrument excludes or restricts the powers granted by the Act), a wide power to invest surplus funds in any form of investment authorised by trust law.

When managing a charity's investments, trustees must comply with the following requirements of the Act, whether they are using the investment powers in it or not:

There is the general duty to exercise such care and skill as is reasonable in the circumstances. This applies to the use of any power of investment and to the performance of the specific duties which the Act attaches to the use of investment powers. A trustee who has (or claims to have) any special knowledge or experience in investments, or who is paid, has a higher duty of care than one who is not so experienced or who is unpaid.

Trustees must consider the suitability for their charity of any investment. They must be satisfied that the type of any proposed investment (eg a common investment fund or a deposit account) is right for their charity (including whether it is consistent with an ethical investment policy if the charity has one). They must also consider whether a particular investment of that type is a suitable one for the charity to make.

Trustees must consider the need for diversification of their investments so as to reduce the risk of losses resulting from 'too many eggs in one basket' and must periodically review their investments. The Charity Commission recommends that for most charities a review should be carried out at least once a year.

Before exercising any power of investment, and when reviewing investments, trustees must obtain and consider proper advice from a suitably qualified adviser (who may be one of the trustees), unless the size of the funds available for investment is so small that seeking such advice would not be cost effective[1].

Capital money received on disposal of lands must be applied in accordance with any directions given by the Charity Commission. In practice a special direction is not needed if the above rules are observed.

[1] Trustee Act 2000, especially ss 1–7.

Need for vigilance

13.33 It was common to vest the property and investments of a charity in the Official Custodian of Charities. It was widely but wrongly thought that he managed investments in his name and in the 1960s and 1970s this led to a disastrous fall in the value of charity investments. As indicated immediately above, it is the duty of trustees, including local councils, actively to manage their investments themselves and since 1992 the Custodian has been obliged to divest himself of all property (including mortgages) except land.

L DECLARATION OF CHARITABLE TRUSTS

13.34 With four exceptions, of which only one is real, a council cannot declare trusts of its property because if the trusts agree with the purposes for which the property was acquired, the declaration is unnecessary, and if they are inconsistent with those purposes, they would be unlawful.

The three unreal exceptions are as follows:

- First, a donor may give property to a council upon charitable trusts which the latter is to declare. Here the property is already subject to charitable trusts when accepted by the council which only says what those trusts shall be.
- Second, a council may declare charitable trusts of property in a conveyance upon sale for full and valuable consideration. These trusts will come into operation only at the moment when the property ceases to belong to it. The trusts cannot govern the money or other consideration received for the property sold.
- Third, a council may let its land to 'clubs, societies or organisations having athletic, social or educational objects'[1], some of which may be charitable; but from the point of view of the council they are no different from other tenants. It is, however, sometimes financially advantageous, especially in connection with rating, to make a lease to a charitable organisation[2].

The real exception is that a charitable trust can be created for the benefit of the locality or its inhabitants, and sums paid from the 'free resource' to it for the trustees to disburse in accordance with the objects of the trust. This is lawful so long as the trusts' objects do not conflict with the purposes for which a council may apply its 'free resource'[3], but the trustees must each year tell the council in writing how the amount of any grant exceeding £500 has been applied[4]. It would seem, too, that an eligible parish council which has adopted the power of general competence under Part 1 of the Localism Act 2011 could set up a charitable trust without being limited by the restrictions of the 'free resource'[5].

1   Local Government (Miscellaneous Provisions) Act 1976, s 19(1)(d).
2   See **13.30** above.
3   This happened in *Manchester City Council v Greater Manchester Metropolitan County Council* (1980) Times, 11 July, where the House of Lords unanimously rejected a rating authority's attempt to upset such an arrangement. See **13.2** and **13.4** above and **22.17** below.
4   Local Government Act 1972, s 137A. See **22.21** below.
5   Localism Act 2011, Part 1. See **22.21** below.

M   RELIEF FROM RATES AND COUNCIL TAX

Council tax

13.35 A charity as such could not be liable for council tax, for this is payable only by individuals in domestic property. It may, however, occasionally be liable for the tax in circumstances and with the effects similar to those in which a local council may be liable.

Rates—mandatory relief

13.36 Where a charity occupies non-domestic property which is used wholly or mainly for charitable purposes (not necessarily its own), the amount payable for rates is one-fifth of the amount set for the non-domestic rate for the year[1]. In the case of unoccupied property falling within a prescribed description, the amount is zero[2].

1   Local Government Finance Act 1988, s 43(5).
2   LGFA 1988, s 45(A).

Rates—discretionary relief

13.37 The billing authority may reduce the amount payable to less than one-fifth or one-tenth or even to nothing. This power of discretionary relief applies to non-profit making bodies, not only with charitable objects, which are otherwise philanthropic, or religious, or concerned with education, social welfare, science, literature or the fine arts, and also to properties used wholly or mainly for recreation or occupied for the purposes of a club, society or other organisation not established or conducted for profit[1]. The discretion cannot be exercised in favour of a local authority in beneficial occupation, but it can be exercised where it is in occupation as a trustee[2].

1   Local Government Finance Act 1988, s 47(2).
2   LGFA 1988, s 47(9).

N   PROTECTION OF CHARITIES

13.38 The Charity Commission may, mostly after notice to each ascertainable trustee, inquire into the affairs of a charity. Once an inquiry is begun, it may, if satisfied either that there has been misconduct or mismanagement, or that it is necessary or desirable to protect the property or secure a proper application of it, by order suspend or remove trustees, appoint new ones, appoint trustees temporarily or permanently, transfer or forbid the transfer of property, suspend debts, restrict the nature or amount of the charity's transactions, appoint receivers or managers or establish a scheme of management. It must periodically review such orders and may discharge them. It is an offence (level 5 fine) to contravene some of these orders, mostly related to property and debts[1].

Receivers and managers must make to the Commission a report on appointment, annually, and on discharge. Those on appointment and annual reports must set out their 'strategy' for effecting the purposes of the charity; those after the report on appointment must set out the extent to which the 'strategy' has been followed. All must show the value of the charity[2].

[1]   The details are in Charities Act 2011, ss 76–87.
[2]   Charities (Receiver and Manager) Regulations 1992, SI 1992/2355, reg 5. It is uncertain what the military technical term 'strategy' means in this context.

Chapter 14

FINANCE—ASSETS

14.1 An average local council may obtain 'the money which it can call its own' from eight main types of sources. These are public funds, special trusts, rents and payment for services, subscriptions, grants, sales, lotteries and capital gifts. Of these the first three are always income and the last is capital, whilst the remainder may fall under one or other heading according to circumstances. Ex-boroughs may, in addition, have some former corporate property. Lastly, the council may itself have set up accumulation funds.

A   PUBLIC FUNDS AND LOCAL ACCOUNTS

14.2 A 'local' account is a parochial or communal account kept by the billing authority (the district council (T)) for each parish or community and to this are credited the proceeds of any trusts in aid of the rates or council tax, any contributions made (but see **16.8** below) by the Crown, and such sums as are raised by way of precepts, together with any surplus rents from allotments, parking fees and rents and surplus bathing receipts.

The expenses of a local council election and of a poll consequent on an electors' meeting are paid by the district council (T), which may reclaim the cost from the local council[1]. There is one exception: where a local council election is postponed so as not to coincide with a Parliamentary or European Parliamentary general election, the cost of the local council election is met from central government funds[2].

Where there is a local council the expenses of the electors' meeting (including any polls) are payable by the local council[3], but those of a community meeting[4] where there is no community council, are payable by the county or county borough council[2]. All these amounts, save the expenses met from central funds, are debited to the local account[5].

To levy the council tax, the billing authority may require a local council to supply information other than information in its possession as an employer, or, if personal, confined to a person's name and present and past address[6].

[1]   Representation of the People Act 1983, s 36(5).
[2]   Representation of the People Act 1985, s 16.
[3]   Local Government Act 1972, s 150(2).
[4]   LGA 1972, s 150(3).
[5]   RPA 1985, s 16(1)(c).
[6]   See generally Local Government Finance Act 1992, ss 39, 41, 42, 50, 51 and Council Tax (Administration and Enforcement) Regulations 1992, SI 1992/613, reg 4.

B   PRECEPTS

14.3 A precept is a peremptory order to a billing authority to pay to a local council or parish meeting a named sum, but this is payable in accordance with a schedule of instalments which the authority draws up by 31 January for the financial year beginning the following 1 April. The statutory timing of the instalments differs as between England and Wales, but if an instalment is paid late the billing authority must pay interest on a daily basis at 2 per cent above the highest base rate quoted by the seven reference banks authorised by the Bank of England. The interest is paid with the outstanding amount. In any event the billing authority must discharge its full liability under the precept by 31 March. If a substitute precept is larger than the original, the difference is not taken into account in paying the instalment due, as the case may be, for a one-month or three-month period during which it was issued.

English schedules of instalments

14.4 The English schedules depend upon whether the case is small (less than 5 per cent of the billing authority's budget) or larger as follows.

If the precept is issued before 31 March:

Small cases	*Larger cases*
Half by 1 May	Half by 1 July
Half by 1 October	Half by 1 January

If the precept is issued later the dates are one month and three months after the date of issue.

Welsh schedules of instalments

14.5 A Welsh schedule must specify not more than three instalments payable by the last working day of the months set out below.

Proportion of precept	*Where precept is issued*	
	Before 1 April	After 31 March
One third	in April	1st month following month of issue[1]
One third	in August	5th month following month of issue[1]
Remainder	in December	9th month following month of issue[1]

[1]   Local Authorities (Funds) (England) Regulations 1992, SI 1992/2428; Local Authorities (Precepts) (Wales) Regulations 1995, SI 1995/2562.

Precepts

14.6 A precept need not be a printed document but usually is. Its function, as will be seen, is similar to that of a cheque on a bank, and so long as it is regular upon its face the billing authority can be compelled to honour it.

A precept from a parish meeting is signed by the chairman. A precept from a local council may be signed by anyone so long as it is clear that it is issued by the direction of the council.

Supplementary precepts cannot be issued, but a new precept may be substituted for an old one. The local council, in calculating its precept, must as far as possible secure that it will suffice for four classes of items, namely:

(a)   next year's expenditure, including an allowance for contingencies;
(b)   outstanding expenditure incurred in previous years;
(c)   expenditure likely to be incurred before the precepted sum becomes available (for example interest on an overdraft);
(d)   payments to financial reserves[1].

In the case of a new or newly transferred parish, the billing authority has often to calculate the amount of a probable precept before it can be issued. In such cases the first real precept must not exceed the billing authority's calculation[2].

[1] Local Government Finance Act 1992, s 49A (added by the Localism Act 2011, s 78) (England), s 50 (Wales).
[2] Local Government Finance (Miscellaneous Provisions) Order 1993, SI 1993/22, and Local Government Finance (Miscellaneous Provisions) Order 1995, SI 1995/161.

Enforcement of precept

14.7 It will seldom be necessary to take action to enforce a precept because of the billing authority's mounting liability for interest on a late instalment, and in any event it may be enforced only after the end of the year to which it relates. This is done by application to the High Court for an order of mandamus[1] which can ultimately lead to imprisonment for contempt of court[2].

[1] *R v Poplar Borough Council (No 1)* [1922] 1 KB 72.
[2] *R v Poplar Borough Council (No 2)* [1922] 1 KB 95.

C   LIMITATIONS ON EXPENDITURE

14.8 The only statutory limitations on revenue expenditure arise in relation to the 'free resource' (see **22.17** below). For controls over capital expenditure see **14.27** below.

D   SPECIAL TRUSTS

14.9 Apart from charities a local council may have trust funds for special objects. These funds are commonly given, or acquired by lottery, as an endowment for the maintenance of gifts of a type which cannot be maintained from public funds (see **12.35** above) or they may exist to further a particular statutory function such as the provision of a playing field. The corporate lands of a rural borough were often of this character.

Where there is an endowment trust for a non-statutory purpose and the income is not sufficient for maintenance, it is a breach of trust to use the capital for maintenance unless the trust instrument specifically permits such use. It will accordingly be necessary to resort to public subscription (see **14.13** below) or lottery or to use the 'free resource'.

Where there is a trust for a statutory function the recurrent (as opposed to capital) costs of that function must be charged against the income of that fund unless the trust instrument otherwise provides.

In general the application of funds of this sort is governed by the terms of the trust deed, rather than by the law applicable to public funds.

E   PAYMENTS AND RENTS

14.10 Local councils may receive rents from tenants of their property or for herbage on their land, and charges and fees for the use of common pasture, for burials, for admission to playing fields and recreation grounds (but only on days when they may lawfully be closed), for admission to swimming pools, baths, boating pools and vehicle parks, and also for the use of the parish or communal hall and other offices. By analogy a local council which owns a computer, for which it may not itself have enough work, can charge others for the use of its surplus time.

It is normal for the income from these services to be applied towards the cost of maintaining them and to apply any surpluses in aid of rates or council tax, but there are exceptional cases connected with the management of allotments and recreation grounds (see **27.1** below) where such surpluses must be 'ploughed back' and not used for any other purpose without special leave.

Charges for discretionary services

14.11 It is a general rule of local government that a council cannot charge for a service which it may provide under statute, but local authorities (including parish councils, parish meetings and community councils) may charge for discretionary services which they already have power to provide[1]. The Secretary of State and the Welsh Assembly may disapply the power to charge for discretionary services, but has not done so in relation to local councils and parish meetings[2].

[1]   Local Government Act 2003, s 93.
[2]   Local Government Act 2003, s 94.

F   FEES

14.12 Certain fees are payable to a local council as follows:

For each copy of the confirmed bye-laws	Not more than 20p[1]
For each copy made by the clerk of the Financial Statement or Auditor's Report and given to an elector	A reasonable sum[2]
For each copy made by the clerk of the draft byelaws	Not more than 10p per 100 words[1]
For each compensation fund entry of the transfer of a mortgage	Not more than 5p for every £100 transferred with a minimum equal to the charge for £25[3]

[1]   Local Government Act 1972, s 236.

[2]   Audit Commission Act 1998, s 14.

[3]   Forged Transfers Acts 1891 and 1892.

G   SUBSCRIPTIONS

14.13 Local councils may[1] raise funds by public subscription for their statutory purposes, or in order to maintain property which they have no specific power to maintain from public funds. In most localities this practice, once common, has declined through the use of the 'free resource' or lotteries.

[1]   Local Government Act 1972, s 139.

Trusts

14.14 Money raised by subscription or lottery is impressed with a trust because those who gave the money are presumed to have given it for the purpose represented to them and no other. The first object of such a trust is naturally the purpose for which the fund was raised, but if the purpose fails, or if, after it has been achieved, there remains a surplus, then, if there is a general charitable intention, the ordinary law of charity applies, but if there was no such intention the money must be returned pro rata to those who gave it. To avoid these, often oppressive, difficulties, it is desirable to frame the objects of the appeal carefully and to insert a clause stating that if the objects fail or if there is a surplus, the fund will be applied in accordance with the directions of the local council or parish meeting.

Street and house-to-house collections

14.15 A district council (T) may make regulations about the streets and other public places where, and the conditions under which, money may be collected or articles sold for charitable or other purposes[1]. Disobedience may lead to a fine. Model regulations provide for the production of accounts in a specified form[2].

In the case of a house-to-house collection the promoter (for instance the local council) must obtain a licence from the district council (T)[3]. It is an offence to promote such a collection without a licence or to collect if no licence is in force.

A licence may be refused or revoked upon any of six specific grounds which between them are designed to prevent such collections degenerating into begging or becoming an encouragement to vagrancy[4].

The promoter must be prepared to furnish accounts.

The House to House Collections Act 1939 is repealed by the Charities Act 2006 and replaced by Chapter 1 of Part 3 of the Charities Act 2006 (ss 45–66) as from a date appointed by the Secretary of State. At the date of publication of this book these provisions had not been brought into force.

[1]   Police, Factories etc (Miscellaneous Provisions) Act 1916, s 5 amended by Local Government Act 1972, Sch 29, para 22.
[2]   Charitable Collections (Transitional Provisions) Order 1974, SI 1974/140, Schedule.
[3]   House to House Collections Act 1939, ss 1 and 2 amended by Local Government Act 1972, Sch 29, para 23.
[4]   House to House Collections Act 1939, s 2.

H   GRANTS

14.16 Local councils receive relatively much less in grants than any other type of authority.

Basic services in development and intermediate areas

14.17 A minister may, with Treasury consent, make grants to a local council in a development area or intermediate area to improve an inadequate basic service for which he is responsible[1]. Such areas are designated by order[2] of the Secretary of State for Trade and Industry.

A basic service means facilities for transport, power, lighting or heating, water or sewerage, and sewage disposal, or any other service or facility on which the development of the area or of industry therein depends[1]. Presumably the extension of burial grounds falls within this definition and also the improvement of public lighting and recreational facilities. The Secretary of State may make grants or loans, give guarantees or incur expenditure to regenerate or develop any area[3].

[1]   Industrial Development Act 1982, s 13.
[2]   IDA 1982, s 1.
[3]   Housing Grants, Construction and Regeneration Act 1996, s 126.

Halls and other recreational facilities

14.18 Grants may be available from district councils (T) and from National Lottery funds towards the building and equipment of village halls and other rural community buildings by voluntary bodies. There is also a scheme for providing advantageous loans, which is administered by the Rural Community Buildings Loan Fund of Action with Communities in Rural England (ACRE).

Any local authority may make grants towards expenditure for the provision of recreational facilities of all kinds including parish halls and playing fields (see **26.15** below).

Open spaces

14.19 A county council (T) may make grants towards the cost of providing land for use as a public open space[1]. Expenditure ranking for grant may include the cost of acquisition, such clearing and preliminary development as is approved by the county council (T), and any payment in connection with the imposition of planning restrictions.

A county council (T) may support or contribute to the support of public walks or pleasure grounds provided by anyone[2].

1   Local Government Act 1958, s 56 (2).
2   Open Spaces Act 1906, s 14.

Playing fields

14.20 The County Playing Fields Associations, affiliated to Fields in Trust (formerly called the National Playing Fields Association) can advise on sources of grants. Local councils wishing to provide or improve playing fields or to provide new types of equipment should always ask their county playing fields association for information before proceeding.

Countryside amenities

14.21 Natural England may give financial assistance to any person in order to further its general purpose (to ensure that the natural environment is conserved, enhanced and managed for the benefit of present and future generations)[1]. In accordance with arrangements approved by the Welsh Assembly, the Countryside Council for Wales can assist by grant or loan any person, including a local council, who incurs expenditure in doing anything conducive to the attainment of the purposes of the National Parks and Access to the Countryside Act 1949, the Countryside Act 1968 and of the Countryside and Rights of Way Act 2000[2]. These Acts confer upon the CCW certain functions for the conservation and enhancement of the natural beauty and amenity of the countryside or to encourage the provision and improvement of facilities for the enjoyment of the countryside, or of open-air recreation[3] or the study of nature[4] or the management of the right of access to open country[5]. For local councils the most interesting cases will arise in connection with specially important bridleways and footpaths (for which there is a system of grants), shelters, car parks and information.

1   Natural Environment and Rural Communities Act 2006, ss 2 and 6.
2   Local Government Act 1974, s 9 (as substituted by the Natural Environment and Rural Communities Act 2006, Sch 11, para 59.
3   Countryside Act 1968, s 1.
4   National Parks and Access to the Countryside Act 1949, s 1.
5   Countryside and Rights of Way Act 2000, Part I, Chapter I.

National Heritage and National Lottery

14.22 It seems that grants may sometimes be available from the National Heritage Memorial Fund (see **25.6** below), and from the National Lottery.

Countryside stewardship agreements

14.23 The Secretary of State for Environment, Food and Rural Affairs may make stewardship agreements with any person, including a local council, with an interest in land. An agreement must specify its own duration and the activity which is to be carried out on the land and the amount which he is required to pay towards such activity. The Schedule to the Countryside Stewardship Regulations 2000 contains a list of management and capital activities towards which grants may be paid. Many of these, such as public access facilities, restoration of walls and installation of fencing, may well be relevant to council property[1].

[1] Environment Act 1995, s 98 and Countryside Stewardship Regulations 2000, SI 2000/3048 (as amended).

Paths, ways, litter and forestry

14.24 A highway authority or district council (T) may make grants to a local council towards the maintenance of a footpath or bridleway[1].

A county council (T) may contribute to a local council's expenses in providing litter bins or disposing of the contents. The Secretary of State may make grants to any body to help it to encourage the public not to deface places by litter[2].

The Forestry Commission, with Treasury consent, may make grants or loans for the use or management of land for forestry purposes[3].

[1] Highways Act 1980, s 43(2).
[2] Litter Act 1983, s 36 (1).
[3] Forestry Act 1979, s 1.

I   SALES

Land

14.25 Capital received for the disposal of charitable land must be applied in accordance with the directions of the Secretary of State or the Charity Commission. Capital received for other land must be applied as the Secretary of State may consent, towards the discharge of any debt of the council or for any lawful capital purpose[1] or it may be paid into a capital fund (see **15.37** below). A receipt of less than £10,000 is not treated as a capital receipt (and may thus be treated as income)[2].

[1] Local Government Act 2003, s 11.
[2] Local Authorities (Capital Finance and Accounting) (England) Regulations 2003, SI 2003/3146, reg 10 and Local Authorities (Capital Finance and Accounting) (Wales) Regulations 2003, SI 2003/3239, reg 9.

Chattels

14.26 There are no statutory rules governing the sale of other kinds of property such as furniture, but the ordinary rules of good business management do not necessarily require that an article shall be worn out (and unsaleable) before it is replaced.

Difficulties may arise where a service is being discontinued. Cases of this kind have to be decided on individual merits, especially where equipment was acquired through the medium of grants, but where there is a substantial unappropriated surplus it should be invested and the income paid in aid of the rates and council tax, or used to reduce the council's debt, whilst a small surplus can be paid in aid of the rates and council tax in the current year.

J   CAPITAL GIFTS OF MONEY

14.27 A local council cannot hold a capital gift of money with no restrictions whatever on its use, for in the absence of special directions of an explicit kind it will be presumed that the gift is for local public purposes or for the benefit of the inhabitants of the area or of part of it. Such gifts must be invested until spent.

K   LOTTERIES

14.28 The statutory law relating to lotteries (and other forms of gambling) has been consolidated, with many changes, in the Gambling Act 2005.

Local councils may hold lotteries so long as they have a lottery operating licence issued by the Gambling Commission[1]. The Commission must attach the following conditions to the licence, and may attach others:

(1)   at least 20% of the proceeds of the lottery are spent on a purpose for which the council has power to spend money;

(2)   the amount of the proceeds of the lottery does not exceed £2,000,000 and the aggregate amount of the proceeds of all the lotteries promoted within a calendar year does not exceed £10,000,000;

(3)   it is not possible for the purchaser of a lottery ticket to win more than (a) £25,000 with that ticket, or (b) if more, 10 per cent of the proceeds of the lottery[2].

---

[1]   Gambling Act 2005, s 98.
[2]   GA 2005, s 99. Though local councils have been able to promote lotteries at least since 1976, the author knows of no case where this has been done.

Chapter 15

CAPITAL FINANCE

A   GENERAL

15.1 If a council wishes to do something which involves capital outlay, such as buying land, or constructing or reconstructing a building, or which involves expense noticeably exceeding that which it might wish to spend from income, such as re-equipping a hall, it will, in the absence or inadequacy of grant aid or lottery profits, have to choose between five ways of covering the cost. These are: sale of an asset or assets; payment by instalments; accumulation in advance; borrowing; or some combination of these.

Procedural distinctions

15.2 Some sales of assets and borrowing are subject to government controls; accumulation and the use of accumulated funds are statutorily regulated but payment by instalments is not.

Economic aspects

15.3 Under a stable currency, payment by instalments is cheaper than accumulation which, in its turn, is cheaper than borrowing, but during inflation the question which is really the cheapest method will depend upon the rate at which the fall in the value of money may be expected to offset the cost of borrowing.

Social considerations

15.4 The choice of method represents in part, at least, a decision on which generation of rate and council tax payers is to pay. In money terms, accumulation imposes a relatively light burden before the outlay creates the benefit; payment by instalments, being generally restricted to a fairly short time, imposes a slightly heavier burden at about the same time as the creation of the benefit; borrowing creates the benefit first and imposes a burden upon later generations which increases with the repayment period of the debt. The sale of assets may prevent the imposition of a burden altogether, but may have other, possibly serious, consequences. In arriving at a choice on social grounds, the incidence of the cost of maintenance and dilapidation will have to be taken into account, and this in its turn may influence the consideration of a repairs and renewals fund.

Relationship with a voluntary body

15.5 Especially where it is desired to provide a village hall, it is sometimes economical to finance the undertaking indirectly by making a capital grant or a loan to a non-profit-making voluntary organisation[1] (see **15.15–17** below) possibly with charitable status, and entrusting the building and subsequent management to it. The reason is that there are a number of foundations which will make grants or loans to such bodies, but which cannot make them to local authorities. Information on these foundations can be obtained from the county council or National Council for Voluntary Organisations or Action with Communities in Rural England (ACRE). The local council can raise the necessary capital for this type of arrangement in the same ways as it can raise it for its own direct purposes.

[1]   Under the Local Government (Miscellaneous Provisions) Act 1976, s 19.

Co-operation with another authority

15.6 The important provisions for co-operation with other authorities, which include not only other local councils but district (T) and county councils (T), may be relevant in financing substantial undertakings, especially those with multiple uses[1], but subject to the government control of capital expenditure experienced by the principal councils under legislation passed since 1980.

[1]   See Local Government Act 1972, ss 101–103 and **23.8** below.

B   WHAT IS AND IS NOT BORROWING?

15.7 With certain exceptions (see **15.14** below) the Secretary of State's approval is required for the purpose or class of purpose for which money is borrowed, and he may impose conditions in accordance with which the borrowing shall be carried out[1]. If the purposes can be attained without borrowing, the Secretary of State's approval is not needed, and it is not necessary to observe his conditions. Some transactions resemble borrowing in their practical effect but are not borrowing in law; and this fact can be important, especially in times of capital stringency.

[1]   Local Government Act 2003, Sch 1, para 2.

Loans defined

15.8 In a contract of loan the lender agrees to appropriate a fixed sum of money to the borrower's order[1], either by paying it to him, or to a third party at the borrower's direction, or by using the appropriated fund to pay off a debt already owed to the lender, or by any combination of these methods. In return, the borrower agrees to appropriate similarly the equivalent or a larger sum at an agreed time and on agreed conditions (usually involving payment of interest) to the lender's order. The only subject of a contract of loan is money, and only loans are governed by the code contained in the Local Government Act 2003, Part 1, Chapter 1, and regulations made under it.

1 *Lyle (B S) Ltd v Chappel* [1932] 1 KB 691.

Distinguished from bailments of chattels

15.9 The temporary custody and use of chattels (for example, lawn mowers, large musical instruments or furniture), is not in law a loan but a bailment, and is not restricted by any enactment even where the bailment is effected for money.

Distinguished from forbearance

15.10 A contract to purchase land or goods or to employ services may include a provision relieving the local council from the usual obligation to pay the whole of the consideration money at one time. From the council's point of view the effect may resemble that of a loan, but the transaction is not a loan because the other party is not appropriating money but transferring property or giving services whilst exercising forbearance in requiring full payment. Such contracts are merely varieties of ordinary contracts of sale, and the forbearance is not an appropriation of money because no money would be due at all if, for example, the goods were not delivered. Moreover, a council may even pay for such forbearance by agreeing in the contract that the total of the instalments shall be more than the lump sum and may well save its council tax and ratepayers by so doing, without risk of being charged with illegal borrowing. It is possible to spread a total payment over three accounting years, yet to ensure that the creditor receives all the money due to him within a period of a few days over twelve months.

Confusion with hire purchase

15.11 It sometimes happens that a provision for deferred payments may be, or may be converted into or replaced by, a contract of loan. Many hire purchase agreements are triangular, the third party being a finance house, and in agreements of this type there may be a loan requiring departmental approval. In other cases, the intentions of the parties will have to be discovered from the wording of the agreements between them. In the type of triangular hire purchase agreement common in the motor trade:

> 'the finance house has to discard the role of a lender of money on security and it has to become an owner of goods who let them out on hire. So it buys the goods from the dealer and lets them out on hire to the appellant. The appellant has discarded the role of a man who has agreed to buy the goods, and he has become a man who takes them on hire with only an option to purchase'[1].

An agreement providing for many instalments over a period of several years or for the payment of interest might raise a presumption of loan which would be hard to rebut; it could, however, be rebutted if each instalment was payable in return for an instalment of goods or services.

¹   *Bridge v Campbell Discount Co* [1962] AC 600 per Lord Denning at 627.

Credit arrangements

15.12 Detailed legislation[1] applying to other authorities regulates their relationship of credit arrangements such as hire purchase with their capital operations such as borrowing. This legislation may be extended to local councils by statutory instrument[2].

¹   Local Government Act 2003, Part 1, Ch 1.
²   LGA 2003, s 19(3)(b), but no such statutory instrument has yet been made.

C   PROCEDURE AND DEPARTMENTAL APPROVAL

15.13 Until April 2002, the Treasury and the relevant Secretary of State annually agreed on the global amount which English parish councils might borrow. Since then, the annual ceiling has been abolished, but the maximum amount an individual council may borrow in a single financial year is normally £500,000. The tiers of scrutiny have been reduced from three to two and a quick procedural timetable has been introduced.

Notwithstanding these relaxations, departmental consent must still be obtained for borrowing. In England, applications for approval are made through the County Associations of Local Councils to the National Association. There is a standard form of application and applications will be approved so long as the current criteria for approval are met.

In Wales, applications may be made either to the county associations of One Voice Wales or direct to the local government finance division of the National Assembly government. There is no specific limit on the amount a council can borrow, but the Assembly may set an annual cash limit on the total available for borrowing.

D   TEMPORARY BORROWING

15.14 A council may borrow temporarily (by way of overdraft or otherwise) without approval, in two cases where money is needed quickly and funds are expected, but have not yet reached the council. This can happen where expenses are to be defrayed pending either the receipt of revenue (for example by way of precept) or the raising of a loan already approved[1], but unapproved borrowing is not permissible pending receipt of a promised grant (unless the promise was made by deed) because a grant, not being enforceable, is not revenue; nor is it permissible pending receipt of capital money on a sale of land, because it is neither revenue nor the proceeds of a loan already approved. Where, therefore, it is desired to finance a project from the proceeds of a sale it is wise to seek approval for a temporary or 'bridging' loan at the same time as approval for the application of the proceeds is being sought.

¹   Local Government Act 2003, Sch 1, para 2.

E   SOURCES OF BORROWED CAPITAL

15.15 There are four types of sources of loan capital.

Private lenders and loans trusts

15.16 A council may borrow from any willing lender, including a private individual or bank; occasionally local benefactors have come forward to lend money at advantageous rates of interest. An extension of this principle is to form a non-profit-making local loans trust by receiving gifts, subscriptions and even loans; such a trust, if its trust deed were appropriately worded, could lend money to the local council or to local voluntary organisations, and its trustees could be nominated by the local council itself.

Public foundations

15.17 There are certain public trusts and foundations which can be important in parish or community finance, even when unable or unwilling to lend to the local council itself. Thus for open air recreation, a local council should inquire with Fields in Trust (formerly called the National Playing Fields Association) or County Playing Fields Associations, and where a village hall is to be provided or improved through a charitable trust, the Rural Community Buildings Loan Fund of ACRE may be approached.

Other councils

15.18 Another local council may lend money, and so may the county (T) and the district (T) council, both of which may borrow for the purpose[1]. Such loans may be made on any terms mutually agreed.

[1]   Local Government Act 2003, Sch 1, para 4.

Public Works Loans Board

15.19 The Public Works Loans Board may lend to councils for any purpose for which they may borrow money[1]. The board's willingness to lend and the conditions upon which its loans are made depend upon the financial policy of the government and the general state of the economy, and therefore no account of these topics can safely be given here. The board has, however, sometimes refused to allow its loans to be paid off before the date of the last instalment, and it charges a fee. Borrowing from private or local sources, though more complicated, is often cheaper in the long run.

[1]   National Loans Act 1968, s 3.

F   MODE OF BORROWING MONEY

Charges

15.20 Apart from temporary loans, a local council normally borrows by way of a charge on all the revenues of the council[1]. Councils mostly borrow from the Public Works Loans Board[2] by way of automatic charge.

1   Local Government Act 2003, s 13.
2   Public Works Loans Act 1965, s 2.

Stocks and bonds

15.21 A local council may borrow by issuing stocks or bonds or both.

In the case of stock the resolution to raise the money must either specify, or indicate the procedure for determining, the amount of stock to be issued, the issue price, the rate of interest, the dates when interest is payable, the date after which the council may redeem the stock at par, and the final date by which it must be redeemed[1]. Great care and the advice of a banker or stockbroker should be taken in drafting this resolution.

In the case of bonds the council must determine the rate of interest at the time of issue, and negotiable bonds cannot be issued for periods of less than a year[2].

Neither stocks nor bonds may be transferable by delivery, but every holder must be given a certificate containing prescribed particulars.

So far as the author is aware, no local council raises money by the issue of stocks or bonds.

1   Local Authority (Stocks and Bonds) Regulations 1974, SI 1974/519, reg 2.
2   SI 1974/519, reg 3.

G   SECURITY AND PRIORITY OF LOANS

15.22 All money borrowed by a local council is charged indifferently on all its revenues[1] not its property. It is, indeed, uncertain whether the council's land can ever be charged, for in case of default a property mortgage might lead to alienation of the land; the council's land cannot be disposed of for less than its value without the Secretary of State's consent, but he cannot consider the question in advance because it would be hypothetical, and if he refused his consent at the proper time the charge could not be enforced.

All securities rank equally without any priority[2].

1   Local Government Act 2003, s 13(3).
2   LGA 2003, s 13(4).

H   RECEIVERSHIP

15.23 If any sum of £10,000 or more due under a mortgage or in respect of stock or bonds remains unpaid for two months after it has been demanded in writing, the person or persons entitled may apply to the High Court for the appointment of a receiver, and the court may confer upon him all or any powers of collecting, receiving and recovering the council's revenues including the power of issuing and enforcing precepts[1].

[1]   Local Government Act 2003, s 13(5).

I   PERIOD OF LOAN

15.24 A local council must repay a loan within the maximum period determined by the Secretary of State. This is 50 years for fixed rate loans and 10 years for variable rate loans.

J   LENDING BY LOCAL COUNCILS

15.25 A local council may lend money to any other local authority[1] and this is often a convenient method of investing surplus funds. In addition, it may lend money, on any terms which may be mutually agreed, to any non-profit-making voluntary organisation providing or maintaining in its area or for the benefit of its inhabitants anything which the council could itself provide under the Local Government (Miscellaneous Provisions) Act 1976, s 19. Since the objects of the latter kind of loan are social rather than financial, such loans are often made interest-free.

It is essential to keep a separate account of such lendings and of repayments, distinguishing between capital repayments and interest.

[1]   Local Government Act 2003, Sch 1, para 4.

K   FUNDS AND ACCUMULATION

15.26 Local councils may establish a loans fund[1], and any other kind of fund such as a sinking fund, capital fund or renewal and repairs fund[2].

[1]   Local Government Act 1972, Sch 13, para 15.
[2]   LGA 1972, Sch 13, para 16(1).

Common features

15.27 Pending the application of a fund to the purposes for which it was set up, the sums in it must be invested[1] in securities in which superannuation funds may be invested[2]. Nevertheless, the council may, instead of borrowing, use money in a fund for a purpose for which it might legally have borrowed otherwise than temporarily, but if it does it must from revenue repay the money to the fund, either as and when the money is required for the purposes of the fund or within the period in which a loan would ordinarily be repayable, whichever is the sooner[3]. In effect the council must behave as if it had borrowed the money from somebody else.

[1]   Local Government Act 1972, Sch 13, para 16(1).
[2]   LGA 1972, Sch 13, para 16(2).
[3]   LGA 1972, Sch 13, para 19.

Loans fund

15.28 To establish a loans fund the council must make a scheme, which it may from time to time amend[1]. It is compelled to set up such a fund if it issues stocks or bonds[2]. The books of the fund must show the council's capital debt (including expenses of issuing bonds and stocks and the discount, if any, at which they were issued) and setting off premiums if any[3]; they must also show the actual amount of money raised, the expenditure which has been defrayed from it and the sums which have been credited to it for the repayment or redemption of the debt. These latter sums may, of course, derive from later borrowings, appreciation and interest on investments, or payments from the council's other income.

[1] Local Government Act 1972, Sch 13, para 15(1) and (2).
[2] Local Authority (Stocks and Bonds) Regulations 1974, SI 1974/519, reg 15(1).
[3] SI 1974/519, reg 15(2) and (3).

Other funds

15.29 Funds may be established to meet any expenditure of a local council in connection with its functions: for example a capital fund to accumulate money instead of borrowing or to repay money already borrowed, or a renewal and repairs fund to prevent violent oscillations in rates and charges arising from sudden calls for expensive repairs or replacements. Such funds must, until they are used for their purpose, be invested in such securities as are suitable for a superannuation fund, and the council may pay into the fund such sums as it thinks fit[1].

In calculating the amount which might regularly be paid into a renewal fund the basis of depreciation may be thought to be the same as the appropriate loan period if a loan had been raised.

A fund established for a purpose which is not an undertaking must not be used for any purpose of an undertaking. This can apply only to a local council harbour, ferry or market[2]. An insurance fund can be used to pay premiums[3].

[1] Local Government Act 1972, Sch 13, para 16.
[2] LGA 1972, Sch 13, para 17(1).
[3] LGA 1972, Sch 13, para 17(2).

L   SERVICE OF LOANS

15.30 Where a local council meets expenditure by borrowing, the repayments on the loan must be debited annually to the account from which the expenditure would otherwise be met[1].

[1] Local Government Act 2003, Sch 1.

M   REDUCING THE DEBT BURDEN

15.31 The table at the end of this chapter shows for various interest rates and repayment periods the half-yearly annuity payments which have to be made to a lender from whom a council has borrowed £100. The total cost of the operation can be calculated by multiplying the amount of each payment by the number of payments. In practice at any given moment the rate of interest for long periods may be slightly higher (say 0.5 per cent) than the rate for short ones.

Apart from those already mentioned in **15.7** above, there are several ways in which a debt can be kept down or its cost reduced.

Reborrowing

15.32 The rate of interest at which money can be borrowed fluctuates under the influence of factors related to the general prosperity of the country. If a council has had to borrow at a high rate of interest it is, unless prevented by the terms of the loan itself, entitled when market rates fall to borrow at the new lower rates and use the money to pay off the original loan. In this way the capital debt will remain the same in amount but the interest payable will be less. Reborrowing of this kind can be repeated whenever interest rates fall sufficiently to make it worth while. The Secretary of State's approval is not required[1], but contracts with the Public Works Loans Board have often been so drawn as to prevent repayment before the final date. This effectively prevents repayment by reborrowing.

It should, however, be observed that a lender will sometimes be in a position to require an increased rate of interest when interest rates rise.

[1]   Local Government Act 2003, Sch 1, para 2(3)(b).

Capital or sinking fund management

15.33 Since local councils, like other local authorities, have ceased to pay income tax on their investments and are liable neither for corporation tax nor for the capital gains taxes, the establishment of a fund to amortise debts has become attractive and important, particularly when interest rates are high, for it is then that the numerous low interest trustee 'dated' stocks can be purchased at less than the full amount at which they will eventually be repaid. For example on 29 January 1988, long-term loans could be obtained in the market only at about 9.5 per cent. On that day £100 worth of 3.5 per cent Funding Loan 1999–2004 could be bought on the market for £57, so for the present outlay of £57, £100 worth of debt would have been redeemed in not more than 16 years disregarding the yield of about £60 in simple interest.

Conclusion

15.34 By purchasing dated stocks below par when interest rates are high and by reborrowing when they fall, a vigilant local council can do a great deal to lighten the burden on its rate and council tax payers. Sound advice is obviously desirable and so when borrowing any substantial sum a local council ought to consult a stockbroker or accountant or investment consultant.

N INVESTMENTS

15.35 Trustees are allowed to invest the trust funds only in a manner permitted by law. Where a local council is a trustee of any special trust funds which it happens to administer (such as charitable trust funds), it may invest its funds in accordance with the Trustee Act 2000. In the case of a special trust fund the deed may (but will probably not) confer additional powers[1].

A local council has a general power to invest its funds for any purpose relevant to its functions and for the prudent management of its financial affairs. In exercising its powers, the council must have regard to any guidance issued by the Secretary of State and to any regulations he has made[2]. Guidance was issued in March 2004 by the Office of the Deputy Prime Minister. The guidance will in certain cases apply to parish councils (and charter trustees), depending upon the level of investments they expect to have in a particular financial year. If that level is expected to exceed £500,000 during the year, the guidance should be treated as applying in full in relation to the whole year. Where investments are expected to exceed £10,000 but not £500,000, the council should simply make a formal decision on the extent to which it would be reasonable to adopt this guidance, either wholly or in part. For councils not expecting their investments to exceed £10,000, no action is necessary. Such councils will, however, be free to adopt the guidance if they wish.

[1]   Trustee Act 2000, Part II.
[2]   Local Government Act 2003, ss 12 and 15.

Local authority investment schemes

15.36 Any local authority may invest its funds through the Local Authorities Mutual Investment Trust (LAMIT), which is described in **12.40**.

> **Example:** If it is desired to borrow £10,000 for 25 years at 8 per cent follow the 8 per cent line as far as the 25-year column where the figure 4.655020 appears. This is the periodical payment in pounds appropriate to £100. Therefore it will be necessary to multiply it by 100 giving a periodical payment of £465–5020. The total cost of the loan will be this figure multiplied by the number of payments (ie 50) = £23,275.1.

Half-yearly annuity payments required to repay a loan of £100

15.37

Rate of interest						Years					
	5	10	15	20	25	30	35	40	50	60	80
3%	10.843418	5.824574	4.163919	3.342710	2.857168	2.539343	2.317235	2.154832	1.937057	1.801852	1.652618
3.5%	10.987534	5.969122	4.312975	3.497209	3.017391	2.705336	2.488930	2.332093	2.124880	1.999317	1.866270
4%	11.132653	6.115672	4.454992	3.655575	3.182321	2.876797	2.666765	2.516071	2.320274	2.204810	2.087835
4.5%	11.278768	6.264207	4.619934	3.817738	3.351836	3.053533	2.850458	2.706376	2.522594	2.417398	2.315854
5%	11.425876	6.414713	4.777764	3.983623	3.525806	3.235340	3.039712	2.902605	2.731188	2.636179	2.549041
5.5%	11.573972	6.567173	4.938442	4.153151	3.704092	3.422002	3.234218	3.104342	2.945418	2.860304	2.786302
6%	11.723051	6.721571	5.101926	4.326238	3.886549	3.613296	3.433663	3.311175	3.164667	3.088992	3.026731
6.5%	11.873107	6.877888	5.268172	4.502794	4.073027	3.808993	3.637727	3.522690	3.388351	3.321537	3.269592
7%	12.024137	7.036108	5.437133	4.682728	4.263371	4.008862	3.846095	3.738489	3.615927	3.557317	3.514302
7.5%	12.176134	7.196210	5.608762	4.865946	4.457422	4.212670	4.058456	3.958184	3.846895	3.795786	3.760402
8%	12.329094	7.358175	5.783010	5.052349	4.655020	4.420185	4.274506	4.181408	4.080800	4.036476	4.007543
8.5%	12.483012	7.521983	5.959825	5.241839	4.856005	4.631178	4.493952	4.407811	4.317236		
9%	12.637882	7.687614	6.139154	5.434315	5.060215	4.845426	4.716511	4.637069	4.555839		
9.5%	12.793699	7.855047	6.320945	5.629675	5.267490	5.062710	4.941917	4.868879	4.796292		
10%	12.950457	8.024259	6.505144	5.827816	5.477674	5.282818	5.169915	5.102962	5.038314		
10.5%	13.108152	8.195228	6.691693	6.028637	5.690609	5.505549	5.400269	5.339063	5.281664		
11%	13.266777	8.367933	6.880539	6.232034	5.906145	5.730707	5.632754	5.576948	5.526132		
11.5%	13.426327	8.542350	7.071624	6.437907	6.124133	5.958107	5.867166	5.816409	5.771540		
12%	13.586796	8.817456	7.264891	6.646154	6.344429	6.187572	6.103313	6.057254	6.017736		
12.5%	13.748179	8.869227	7.460284	6.856675	6.566893	6.418938	6.341019	6.299315	6.264588		
13%	13.910469	9.075640	7.657744	7.069373	6.791393	6.652047	6.580124	6.542440	6.511988		
13.5%	14.073662	9.256670	7.857215	7.284150	7.017798	6.886754	6.820480	6.786493	6.759843		

Rate of interest	5	10	15	20	25	30	35	40	50	60	80
						Years					
14%	14.237750	9.439293	8.058640	7.500914	7.245985	7.122923	7.061953	7.031357	7.008076		
14.5%	14.402729	9.623484	8.261962	7.719571	7.475837	7.360424	7.304422	7.276926	7.256622		
15%	14.568593	9.809219	8.467124	7.940031	7.707241	7.599142	7.547778	7.523106	7.505427		

Chapter 16

MISCELLANEOUS LIABILITIES

A INCOME, CORPORATION AND CAPITAL GAINS TAXES, AND PAYE

16.1 If a council has employees who are paid a regular wage or salary it will be required to make the appropriate tax deductions from the amount payable to the employee and account for them to HM Revenue and Customs (HMRC).

Local councils and their district, county and national associations are exempt from income and corporation taxes, but in so far as the exemption from income tax calls for repayment of tax, they must claim it[1]. These same bodies are also exempt from capital gains taxes[2].

[1]   Income Tax Act 2007, s 838, Corporation Tax Act 2010, ss 984 and 1130.
[2]   Taxation of Chargeable Gains Act 1992, s 271(3).

B VALUE ADDED TAX

16.2 A local council must register with the appropriate Office of HMRC if it expects to make any taxable supply, however small[1]. A taxable supply by a local authority is said to arise from a 'business purpose', as opposed to a non-business purpose such as the provision of a public service charged wholly to the rates and council tax.

A supply is taxable within the meaning of the legislation if it is either 'standard rated' ('SR') or 'zero rated'.

VAT Notice No 749

Copies of any VAT notice may be obtained from HMRC.

The practical difference between standard rated and zero rated supplies is that the council must charge the standard rate on the service it provides (the output tax) but (strictly speaking) charges an output tax of zero on a zero rated service. As, however, in both cases, the service is taxable in law, it is entitled in both cases to recover from HMRC tax which it has itself paid (the input tax). Zero rating is, thus, more advantageous than exemption.

Any local council (registered or unregistered) may recover from HMRC any input tax invoiced to it in respect of a non-business activity. A registered council recovers it by way of a form (VAT 100) which it will receive monthly. Unregistered councils may apply periodically (more than monthly, not more than annually) to Banking/GABS, HMRC, 7th Floor, Alexander House, 21 Victoria Avenue, Southend-on-Sea, SS99 1AU.

The first such application is by letter. It should state the period for which the claim is made and the amount claimed, and should include a declaration that the tax was paid in respect of goods and services acquired for non-business activities.

The following wording for the declaration is suggested by HMRC in VAT notice 749:

'I am claiming a refund of £X for the period . . . . to . . . . to cover VAT charged on goods and services bought for [name of council] non-business activities. The tax claimed includes VAT incurred for exempt business activities that can be reclaimed under Notice 749 "Local Authorities and similar bodies".'

The first refund is made by money order which will be accompanied by a claim form for the next claim. Thereafter claims are made by form.

It is necessary to keep up to date accounts in such a complete form that input and output taxes can be correctly calculated and easily identified by auditors and HMRC officials. This involves identifying not only standard rated and zero rated transactions but exempt ones too, as well as such miscellaneous matters as amended tax invoices and credits for returned goods. Such accounts must be preserved for at least three years.

[1]   Value Added Tax Act 1994, s 42.

C   LICENSING

16.3 Parish and community halls are often used for entertainments; local councils have power to provide entertainments, and their property is often let to organisations and individuals which provide them.

This is not the place to explain licensing law. However, since even the most innocent infringement may have unfortunate consequences, anyone wishing to organise an entertainment should make certain that all proper steps have been taken. In cases involving public entertainment or the sale of alcohol the advice of the district council (T) should be sought. The district council (T) is the licensing authority both for the sale of alcohol and for the provision of public entertainment and applications for licences must be made to them[1].

[1]   Licensing Act 2003, Part 2. See CHAPTER **24B** for an outline of the licensing system under the Act.

D   VEHICLE OPERATORS' LICENCES

16.4 If a council operates a goods vehicle weighing more than 3.5 tonnes for hire or reward or in connection with any trade or business carried on by it, it must obtain an operator's licence from the Traffic Commissioner at one of the eleven traffic area offices[1]. The licence must show where the vehicle is kept (the so-called operating centre) and it contains conditions and undertakings which an operator must accept. Breach of these may lead to the forfeiture of the licence. The most important is that the vehicle must be maintained preventively, so as to anticipate things going wrong, and that repair and inspection records must be kept, and preserved for at least 15 months. The vehicle may be inspected at any time by an official vehicle examiner, besides undergoing its annual 'MOT' inspection.

Some councils may operate a community bus service. To operate such a service, the council requires a community bus permit[2].

[1]   Goods Vehicles (Licensing of Operators) Act 1995, s 2.
[2]   Transport Act 1985, s 22.

E   STAMP DUTY AND STAMP DUTY LAND TAX

Conveyance and transfers on sale

16.5 Transfers of stocks, shares or loan capital raised by a government or local authority, or of interests or dividends arising out of them, or of allotment or option rights, or of units in a unit trust scheme, are not liable to stamp duty.

In the case of land, stamp duty land tax is payable, depending upon the 'chargeable consideration' of the transaction as follows:

Value—Residential	*Stamp Duty Land Tax*
Not more than £125,000	nil
£125,000–£250,000	1%
£250,000–£500,000	3%
over £500,000	4%
over £1 million to £2 million	5%
over £2 million	7%
over £2 million purchased by certain persons including corporate bodies	15%
Not more than £150,000	nil
£150,000–£250,000	1%
£250,000–£500,000	3%
Over £500,000	4%

Stamp duty land tax, if payable, is assessed on the whole consideration, not merely on the excess above a limit. To claim concessionary rates, the transfer or conveyance must contain a statement certifying that the transaction thereby effected does not form part of a larger one or of a series of them in respect of which the amount or value or the aggregate amount or value of the consideration exceeds the appropriate threshold.

For solicitors' charges see **16.44** below.

16.6 *Miscellaneous liabilities*

Charities

16.6 A conveyance to a charity is free of stamp duty land tax[1].

[1] Finance Act 2003, s 68 and Sch 8.

F   AUDIT FEES

16.7 The Audit Commission (in Wales, the Auditor General for Wales) prescribes the standard audit fees and can fix a higher or lower fee in a particular case. The fees are in principle based upon hourly rates for the number of man-hours required to complete the audit.

G   LIABILITY TO RATES

16.8 With a modern exception to the disadvantage of the owners of unoccupied premises, rates are basically a personal charge levied in respect of the occupation of non-domestic property; and since 1 April 2000 Crown land has been rateable. With a few exceptions local authorities are subject to the same rules of liability to rates as every other non-domestic ratepayer. The purpose of the following paragraphs is to indicate the occasions when the rules enure to the advantage of a local council or parochial charity.

Property of public resort

16.9 A rateable occupier is one who can legally exclude other people from the relevant property. Accordingly, recreation grounds, parks, village greens, bus shelters and other property owned and maintained upon statutory trusts by a local council for the use of the public and to which the public resort by right, are occupied by the public at large and rates are not payable in respect of these properties any more than a private person is rateable for a public right of way across his property[1].

Parks, recreation and pleasure grounds, public walks, and open spaces if provided or managed by a local council are treated for rating purposes as if dedicated to perpetual public use so long as they are available for the free and unrestricted use of the public[2].

The same rule applies to playing fields provided under the Physical Training and Recreation Act 1937 but not, apparently, to those provided under the Local Government (Miscellaneous Provisions) Act 1976, s 19, which superseded the Act of 1937 on 14 February 1977[3].

[1] See the 'Brockwell Park Case' (*Lambeth Overseers v LCC* [1897] AC 625), the 'Putney Bridge Case' (*Hare v Overseers of Putney* (1881) 7 QBD 223), and *Trustees of Mitcham Golf Course v Ereaut* (1937) 3 All ER 450.
[2] Local Government Finance Act 1988, Sch 5, para 15.
[3] See the reference to the Physical Training and Recreation Act 1937 in LGFA 1988, Sch 5, para 15.

Allotments

16.10 Allotments, as agricultural land, are not rateable[1].

[1] Local Government Finance Act 1988, Sch 5, para 2.

Local Acts, orders, and Highway Act 1865

16.11 Within limits, rating privileges conferred by local Acts and orders (often of ancient date) may be preserved[1] and property exempted from statute duty or highway rate before 1835 may be exempted from that part of the rate attributable to the repair of the highways. If created before 22 December 1925 these local privileges subsisted only if continued by a scheme in force in 1967 or if enjoyed in practice then and until 29 July 1988. The power of preservation is exercised by departmental regulation.

[1] Local Government Finance Act 1988, Sch 5, para 20.

Not charitable

16.12 A local council cannot as such claim the rating privileges accorded to charitable and similar organisations and will therefore be liable to pay rates on its hall unless it is let to such an organisation (see CHAPTER 13).

Appeals

16.13 Appeals against assessment and other methods of resisting liability or payment of rates are discussed in CHAPTER 21.

H   COUNCIL TAX

Method of assessment

16.14 Council tax is based on the amount which a dwelling might reasonably have been expected to realise if it had been sold with vacant possession in the open market by a willing seller on 1 April 1991 (in Wales, 1 April 2003), upon eight assumptions, of which the most important are that the interest sold was a freehold, or in the case of a flat, a 99-year lease at a nominal rent; that it was in a reasonable state of repair and that the purchaser would have to contribute to the upkeep of common parts (if any)[1].

The values so calculated are grouped into eight successively widening bands, respectively for England and Wales, upon which the tax must be levied in steadily increasing proportions as shown by the figures in parentheses in the following table:

	England (£)	*Wales (£)*
A(6)	up to 40,000	Up to 44,000
B(7)	40,001–52,000	44,001–65,000
C(8)	52,001–68,000	65,001–91,000
D(9)	68,001–88,000	91,001–123,000
E(11)	88,001–120,000	123,001–162,000
F(13)	120,001–160,000	162,001–223,000
G(15)	160,001–320,000	223,001–324,000
H(18)	Over 320,000	324,001–424,000
I(21)		Over 424,000

The amount payable for dwellings in a given band is the same throughout the band, which might, for example, in English band G involve a value difference of £159,999 while a difference of as little as £1 (upwards or downwards) may make a very large difference at the extremities.

[1]   Council Tax (Situation and Valuation of Dwellings) Regulations 1992, SI 1992/550, reg 6 lists these and other less usual assumptions.

Liability

16.15 There is a hierarchical list of persons successively liable to pay the tax, each in default of the person before. For the purposes of this list a resident is a person who is over 18 and has his sole or main residence in the building. Those successively liable are:

(a)   an owner resident;
(b)   a resident with a leasehold not inferior to another leasehold held by another resident;
(c)   a resident who is a statutory or secure tenant;
(d)   a resident with a contractual licence;
(e)   a resident;
(f)   the owner.

A council which owns a dwelling such as a tied cottage, although it can never be a 'resident', may be liable if the dwelling becomes vacant and so remains for six months (save for repairs). In the interests of its council tax and rate-payers, and of its tenants, it should if possible exploit the anomalies of the system to secure the lowest possible tax band.

I   DRAINAGE CHARGES

16.16 Agricultural land and buildings not within an internal drainage district, but excluding rough grazing and woodlands may be assessed to the general drainage charge payable to a water undertaker which may in addition levy a special drainage charge for carrying out works in the interests of agriculture.

The special charge can only be levied under authority of a scheme approved by the Secretary of State. These charges will sometimes be leviable on allotments[1].

[1]   Water Resources Act 1991, ss 134–138.

J   CORN RENTS

16.17 Corn rents are payments charged on land in lieu of tithes when the old tithe system in a parish had become unworkable as a result of a private inclosure act. They are redeemable[1].

[1]   See Corn Rents Act 1963.

K   PERFORMANCE AND COPYING FEES

Copyright

16.18 Copyright in an original literary, dramatic or musical work subsists, generally speaking, for 70 years from the year of first publication or the author's death, whichever comes later[1]. In the first instance the copyright belongs to the author, who may assign it. In modern books the copyright owner is identified on a preliminary page by the symbol © with the year and name.

[1]   Copyright Designs and Patents Act 1988 amended to conform with EU Directive 93/98 by the Duration of Copyright and Rights in Performances Regulations 1995, SI 1995/3297.

Fees and inquiries

16.19 Generally a copyright owner charges a fee for the public performance of his work. The amount is negotiable. If it is intended to provide an entertainment in the form of a copyright play, the publisher should be approached; if in the form of recorded music, the local council should approach the Performing Rights Society which charges fees on the basis of standardised schemes, and pays them to the copyright owner.

Copying

16.20 The Copyright Licensing Agency operates standardised licensing schemes for fees for copies made by copying machines, and pays the fees to the copyright owners through the Authors' Licensing and Collecting Society.

L   SUBSCRIPTIONS

16.21 A local council may pay reasonable subscriptions annually or otherwise to any association of local authorities formed to consult upon matters of common interest or relating to local government, or to associations of officers or of members of local authorities[1].

[1] Local Government Act 1972, s 143.

M   INSURANCE

16.22 Any authority may insure its members against accident when on duty[1], and must take adequate security for the fidelity of its officers (see **9.7** above).

A council may, moreover, insure its property and funds against loss, destruction or outside claims because it is bound to preserve the property held by it as a trustee for the public and to conduct its affairs in a prudent and businesslike fashion: the right to effect such insurance is inherent in the duties of preservation and maintenance laid upon councils by law[2].

Similarly, where a risk exists, a council may (and ought to) protect its rate- and tax-payers against claims and litigation costs arising out of injury and damage to members of the public. Neglect of this precaution may lead to a heavy imposition on the public. An accident led, in 1951, to an action against the Stone Parish Council. In 1954 judgment was given against the council for the then large sum of £17,500 which was reduced to £9,000 in the Court of Appeal. The costs in such protracted cases are always high. The National Association of Local Councils launched a series of insurance schemes as a result.

The following are the main types of policy in which a council may be interested:

(1) public liability to protect the rate- and council tax-payers against claims for accidents caused to members of the public as a result of the council's activities;

(2) loss of property by fire, burglary and the like. There is a type of comprehensive policy in this class known as an 'all risks' policy, which is usually much less comprehensive than its name suggests;

(3) fidelity to protect the council against the loss of cash in the hands of its employees;

(4) members' accidents to cover members on duty. Such a policy is generally necessary only where meetings are numerous and distances long;

(5) employer's liability for injuries to the council's own employees;

(6) defamation: The council can insure itself against the rare event of its defaming other individuals in its documents or correspondence. It cannot insure its members.

[1] Local Government Act 1972, s 140(1) as amended.
[2] Local Government Act 1972, s 111.

Pitfalls

16.23 In scrutinising policies a council should pay particular attention to **exceptions** which set out types of risk which the policy does not cover, and **exclusions** which set out sums of money which the insurers will not pay even if the insured event comes to pass. Commercial insurers do not regard themselves as public benefactors, and are very ready to repudiate liability if they think that they can. Some have claims agents whose function is to negotiate repudiations. For dangers arising out of the proposal form see **19.8** below.

Regular review

16.24 Insurance policies insensibly but with surprising speed become out of date and a council would be wise to review its work at intervals and consider whether it is adequately insured and whether there are new risks against which insurance is advisable or old ones which no longer need it.

N   MEMBERS' ALLOWANCES IN ENGLAND

16.25 Before May 2003 allowances, other than the chairman's allowance, were, inside the United Kingdom, related to specific types of expenditure closely defined by detailed regulations. This is no longer so in England[1], but that control continues to apply in Wales (see **16.32** below). The annual parish basic allowance combined with the amended and now discretionary travel and subsistence allowances make the specific consideration of particulars in individual cases mostly unnecessary, for it seems that the amount of the parish basic allowance can be settled so as to include elements to cover expected expenditure on travel and subsistence, thereby obviating any need to claim for them separately.

In calculating the amount suitable for a parish basic allowance (which must be the same for all save the chairman) a local council should have regard not only to the district council's (T) recommendation and practices but also to the cost of genuinely probable expenses. The total will mostly be small.

The discretionary feature of these allowances is important. A council is not obliged to pay them and therefore may pay less than the amount incurred.

[1]   Local Authorities (Members' Allowances) (England) Regulations 2003, SI 2003/1021, Part 5.

Parish basic allowance

16.26 A parish council may pay a parish basic allowance to its members. This incitement to corruption is limited to a certain extent by special rules:

(a)   *recommendation*: the district council's (T) parish remuneration panel must have made a recommendation about the levels of this allowance. This must be made known to the parish council which must take it into account when taking decisions on these allowances, and at the end of the fiscal year it must publish details of the recommendation and of the amounts actually paid;

(b)   *equality*: save for the chairman, the allowance must be the same for every elected member. Appointed and co-opted members are not entitled to it[1];

(c)   *chairman*: the chairman may be paid a greater parish basic allowance than the elected members;

(d)   *annual*: the allowance is an annual allowance and is not, therefore, related to a specific expense;

(e)   *entitlement*: a member may elect to forego his entitlement to all or some of his allowances.

¹   Local Authorities (Members' Allowances) (England) Regulations 2003, SI 2003/1021, reg 25(10) (added by the Local Authorities (Members' Allowances) (England) (Amendment) Regulations 2004, SI 2004/2596, reg 4).

Taxation

16.27 The parish basic allowance is treated as income from an office (ie the office of councillor) under the Income Tax Acts. In principle, therefore, it is taxable under the PAYE system (see **9.31** above). It would be wise for the council to consult HMRC before resolving to pay parish basic allowances to establish their exact requirements.

Travel and subsistence allowances

16.28 Travel (including travel by bicycle, on horseback or other non-motorised form of transport) and subsistence allowances may be paid for 'approved duties' namely, a meeting:

(a)   of the council or any of its committees or subcommittees; or

(b)   of some other body to which the council make appointments or nominations; or

(c)   of a committee or subcommittee of such a body; or

(d)   of a local authority association of which the authority is a member; and

(e)   at which, in accordance with standing orders, a member or members are required to be present while tender documents are opened.

These allowances may also be paid for:

(f)   duties undertaken on behalf of the council in connection with the discharge of any statutory function empowering or requiring the council to inspect or authorise the inspection of premises; and

(g)   carrying out any other duty approved by the council or any duty of a class so approved, for the purpose of, or in connection with, the discharge of its functions or of any of its committees or subcommittees.

Allowances may be paid for travel and subsistence costs incurred both within and outside the parish.

The parish remuneration panel of the district (T) council may make recommendations about levels of travel and subsistence allowance. A parish council would be expected to follow these recommendations, even if there is no positive obligation to do so (as there is in relation to recommendations about the level of parish basic allowance).

Taxation

16.29 Allowances which simply reimburse expenditure and contain no element of remuneration are not taxable. Round sum allowances may contain an element of remuneration and that element is, or may be, taxable. As a general rule, therefore, a local council should try to avoid paying round sum allowances.

· O   CHAIRMAN'S ALLOWANCE

16.30 Instead of paying him a parish basic allowance, a local council may pay the chairman such allowance as it thinks reasonable to enable him to meet the expenses of his office[1]. This does not apply to the vice-chairman.

This allowance should be distinguished from the other allowances payable to councillors (including the chairman). These protect them against personal problems which might arise, and which might make activity in their office difficult. The chairman's allowance is designed to defray the expense of the chairmanship itself, in the same way as other sums are allocated to maintain buildings or provide a playing field.

In considering whether this allowance should be paid and, if so, the amount, the council may wish to consider what, besides taking the chair, the chairman as such should reasonably be expected to do in the future, not necessarily what, in the absence of an allowance, he has done in the past. His duties may generally be considered in two parts: first, the duties outside the council chamber but arising from the ordinary business of the council, and second, activities expected of him by the public.

The duties arising from ordinary business usually amount to regular communication with the clerk and committee chairmen by meeting, fax or telephone. The cost of this often mounts up, but it can be estimated.

The demands of the public arise because the chairman is a local figure. He may be expected to attend ceremonies (to which he must travel) and occasionally to entertain in the name of the council or of the locality. This is really a form of public relations and should be considered in that light. In a small village it may be that any special public relations exercise is seldom necessary; in a larger one it may well be important. One reason why local councils in the past have not received their proper recognition may be that they have not had the means to attract it.

The amount should be fixed by the council in advance on a rational basis. It may reasonably consider what the chairman may have to do, leaving the choice of what he actually does to him. It may also wish to take into account that the 'free resource' will enable a council to spend money lawfully in circumstances for which other authorities in the past could only have used the chairman's allowance. One such case is the provision of refreshments at the annual electors' meeting.

Some authorities pay the allowance quarterly or half-yearly. Others make advances on request, and, in some, the treasurer makes the disbursements on the chairman's behalf.

[1] Local Government Act 1972, ss 15(5) and 34(5).

Taxation

16.31 As long as the chairman's allowance is a reasonable reimbursement of the expenses of an unpaid office, and contains no element of remuneration for the holder, HMRC treat it as not chargeable for tax, but they ask councils how much is paid; and, where it is thought that there might be an element of remuneration, they might ask chairmen for details of the uses to which the allowances are put.

If the total of allowances and expenses paid to the chairman (or any councillor) exceeds £8,500 a year, they must be reported to HM Revenue and Customs unless a dispensation has been obtained[1].

[1] See generally the Income Tax (Earnings and Pensions) Act 2003.

P   MEMBERS' ALLOWANCES IN WALES

What allowances may be paid

16.32 Provided that the expenses have been necessarily incurred or losses suffered, payments may be made for approved duties, and official and courtesy visits in the following cases:

- travelling expenses outside the community[1];
- subsistence expenses but only outside the community[2];
- attendance allowance to councillors for either performing any approved duty, or attending any 'section 175 meeting' outside the community[3].

Members may elect to forgo entitlement to allowances.

[1] Local Government Act 1972, s 174.
[2] LGA 1972, s 174.
[3] LGA 1972, ss 173 and 175.

Financial loss allowance

16.33 Financial loss allowance is paid to councillors, and to any non-councillor who is a member of a committee or sub-committee, towards loss of earnings or additional expense incurred (apart from travelling and subsistence expenses) in performing approved duties or attending 'section 175 meetings' outside the community[1].

In the case of a councillor, however, it is only in lieu of attendance allowance, and only if he opts to receive it by a written financial loss allowance notice to the council. Such a notice, if made within a month of his election, entitles him to the allowance from the time of his election; if made at any other time, only from one month after it is given. It may be withdrawn[2].

[1] Local Government Act 1972, ss 173, 173A and 175.

[2]   LGA 1972, s 173A.

Outside the United Kingdom

16.34 Payments for travelling and subsistence may be made for visits outside the United Kingdom (which includes Northern Ireland) if the purposes of a visit would be permissible if made within the United Kingdom.

Amounts

Attendance and financial loss allowance

16.35 The initial maximum amounts of attendance and financial loss allowances were prescribed by regulations and applied to the year beginning on 1 April 2003[1]. Thereafter, until 31 March 2012, the council was entitled to make an annual adjustment in line with the percentage increase (if any) in the Average Male Non-manual Wage for Wales index in the New Earnings Survey published by the UK Statistics Authority. Since 1 April 2012 the Independent Remuneration Panel for Wales prescribes the maxima for payments to councillors and may set percentage rates and indices for adjustments in successive financial years[2].

[1]   Local Authorities (Allowances for Members of Community Councils) (Wales) Regulations 2003, SI 2003/895, regs 5 and 6 (repealed by the Local Government (Wales) Measure 2011 but continued in force until 31 March 2012 by virtue of reg 3 of the Local Government (Wales) Measure 2011 (Commencement No. 2 and Saving Provisions) Order 2012, SI 2012/1187.
[2]   Local Government (Wales) Measure 2011, s 142.

Travelling and subsistence allowances

16.36 Private motor vehicles: the rate of allowance must not exceed that payable to members of the Welsh Assembly[1].

Other travel and subsistence: as determined by the council[2].

[1]   Local Authorities (Allowances for Members of Community Councils) (Wales) Regulations 2003, SI 2003/895, reg 7.
[2]   SI 2003/895, reg 11.

General provisions

Entitlement to allowances and avoidance of duplication

16.37 The prescribed rates are maxima. Local councils may pay less. In no case may allowances be paid which exceed the amounts claimed and the expenses or losses actually incurred or suffered. No allowances may be paid except for activities authorised by the council.

Where a person performs duties for more than one body in the same period, he is not entitled to more in aggregate allowances than he would receive if he had performed all the duties for one body. Where he is entitled to payments under different enactments, his claims under one enactment must be reduced by the amount received under the other[1].

[1] Local Authorities (Allowances for Members of Community Councils) (Wales) Regulations 2003, SI 2003/895, reg 12.

Taxation

16.38 The attendance allowance is an emolument and therefore taxable: recipients must declare it to HMRC as part of their income, but may set off against it any expenses wholly and necessarily incurred by them (and not otherwise reimbursed) in the performance of the duties for which the allowance is paid. Travelling, subsistence and financial loss allowances are reimbursements of sums spent, or lost, and are therefore not taxable as income.

Claims

16.39 There are no prescribed forms of claim. Every claim must be accompanied by appropriate receipts proving actual expenses, subject to any limitation or requirement that the council may determine[1].

[1] Local Authorities (Allowances for Members of Community Councils) (Wales) Regulations 2003, SI 2003/895, reg 11.

Records

16.40 All payments must be recorded so as to show to whom and under what heads they were made. Where tickets are issued the amount must likewise be recorded, since the issue of a ticket is treated as constituting a payment of an equivalent amount. These records must be open to inspection by electors of the locality at all reasonable hours[1].

[1] Local Authorities (Allowances for Members of Community Councils) (Wales) Regulations 2003, SI 2003/895, reg 13.

Q   ALLOWANCES TO OFFICERS

16.41 Expenses properly incurred by an officer as such may and indeed must at common law be defrayed by the council because they have been incurred on the council's behalf. In paying these expenses the council is not obliged by law to have regard to the amounts prescribed for councillors, but if, in equivalent circumstances, these amounts are not exceeded it would be difficult to criticise the council for extravagance.

R   NATIONAL INSURANCE

16.42 See **9.32** above.

S   FREEMEN'S ADDRESSES

16.43 Where a local council has admitted somebody to the honorary freedom of the locality it may spend a reasonable sum for the purpose of presenting him with an address or a casket containing one[1].

[1]   Local Government Act 1972, s 249(6).

T   SOLICITORS' CHARGES

16.44 Solicitors commonly meter the time of interviews and telephone calls and, charged on a time basis, the expense of dealing with them can mount up. In 2013 it was generally around £200 an hour. For conveyancing some solicitors make a straight all-in charge; others charge a percentage of the value of the transactions. It is thus important to obtain an estimate in advance, because, as will be seen, the means for protecting the client are not strong.

Challenge

16.45 A solicitors' bill can be challenged by way of complaint to the Legal Ombudsman or by application to the High Court[1]

[1]   Solicitors (Non-Contentious Business) Remuneration Order 2009, SI 2009/1931. The Legal Ombudsman's website is www.legalombudsman.gov.uk.

Solicitors' lien

16.46 A solicitor is entitled to keep in his hands documents relating to a transaction until his bill has been paid. If it is desired to challenge the bill and the documents are urgently required, this lien can be discharged by paying the bill. The solicitor must then release the documents, but is liable to repay the difference (if any) between his bill and the final amount of the bill as determined by the Legal Ombudsman or the court (if not agreed).

Chapter 17

ACCOUNTS AND FINANCIAL ADMINISTRATION

17.1 Like every other local authority a local council may buy, own or sell property and goods, employ servants and contractors, and give or receive services. These transactions are connected with each other, with the council and with the rate- and tax-payers by the passing of money. An effective accounting system provides an accurate record of the origin, quantity, whereabouts and disposal of the council's property and money in a form which will make mistakes obvious.

A   RESPONSIBILITY FOR FINANCIAL MANAGEMENT

17.2 Every local council is responsible for ensuring that the financial management of the council is adequate and effective and that the council has a sound system of internal control[1]. The council must review the effectiveness of its system of internal control at least annually and must publish a statement on internal control, prepared in accordance with proper practices, with its annual statement of accounts or, as the case may be, its income and expenditure account and statement of balances (see CHAPTER 18).

'Proper practices' are practices which are regarded as proper practices in a generally recognised published code. For local councils such practices are to be found in the joint NALC/SLCC publications *Governance and accountability in local council: a practitioner's guide (England)* and *Governance and accountability in local council: a practitioner's guide (Wales)*[2].

[1]   Accounts and Audit (England) Regulations 2011, SI 2011/817, reg 4; Accounts and Audit (Wales) Regulations 2005, SI 2005/368, reg 4.
[2]   The most recent editions were published in 2010.

B   FORM OF ACCOUNTS

17.3 The council or parish meeting must see that its financial management is adequate and that there is a sound system of internal control in place[1]. The council may give instructions upon the form of the accounts and their supporting records and the systems of accounting control, but subject to this the responsible financial officer[2] (commonly the clerk) decides them himself[3]. He is responsible under the council for seeing that they are observed. His records must suffice to show the council's transactions so that he can ensure that all the accounts will conform with the Accounts and Audit Regulations. In particular they must show daily entries of receipts and expenditure and the matters to which they relate; the assets and liabilities; and the income and expenditure in relation to claims (past or contemplated) against European, government or principal council grants. Entries must be made as soon as possible and organised so that inaccuracies and fraud can be detected and lost records reconstituted; the duties of those concerned with financial transactions must be defined; and bad debts and uncollectable sums must not be written off without the clerk's approval. Though many local council accounts are adequately kept by hand or by mechanical accounting machine, computer-based systems with their limitations (see **17.5** below) are coming increasingly into vogue.

[1] Accounts and Audit (England) Regulations 2011, SI 2011/817, reg 4; Accounts and Audit (Wales) Regulations 2005, SI 2005/368, reg 4.
[2] Local Government Act 1972, s 151.
[3] Accounts and Audit (England) Regulations 2011, SI 2011/817, reg 5; Accounts and Audit (Wales) Regulations 2005, SI 2005/368, reg 5.

C   FINANCIAL ADMINISTRATION

Receiving small sums

17.4 Local councils often receive large numbers of small sums such as admission charges to tennis courts, bowling greens, bathing pools, recreation and camping grounds, vehicle parks, or as use charges for towels or boats, or as payments for refreshments. Hand-written receipts are a wasteful nuisance but ticket-printing machines often produce tickets which are difficult to read. A simple alternative is to use machine numbered tickets differently coloured for different amounts or uses, combined with a ticket register showing progressively the rolls in use (identified by number, colour and letter). At the beginning of each day the first unused number should be entered: this number should be the same as the number entered at the end of the previous day. At the end of the day the number of the first unused ticket should be entered. The difference between the numbers multiplied by the amount of each ticket should equal the money collected. The book should also show how much was banked, the amounts brought in and carried down and the totals of each day. A register of this kind ruled in columns is not difficult to enter up and is a useful safeguard. Electronic versions of such a system are available and provide automatic up-dating of records.

Where a turnstile is in use instead of tickets, it should be self-recording and a turnstile register should be kept in the same way as a ticket register.

Receiving larger sums

17.5 For larger sums (such as rent) it is desirable, though not essential, to use official receipt forms printed with or at least showing the council's name. The manifold carbon receipt book is better than the counterfoil type because it has to be written only once and exactly reproduces the original. The receipts should be machine numbered in duplicate, the original only being torn out. Similar principles apply in the use of machine or electronically produced accounts and receipts.

A register of receipt books should be kept showing the date when each was acquired and the dates when it was begun and finished. If a receipt book is issued out permanently, the person to whom it is issued should be required to sign for it and the person issuing it should also sign at the same time.

A computer can be programmed to replace receipt books and receipt-book registers, but storage in a computer memory can be dangerous because of the damage which can be done by an electrical failure. Regular print-outs are essential. All computer records should be regularly backed up on discs or external hard drives, which should be stored in a separate place from the computer.

Payments to the bank

17.6 Money ought to be paid into the bank at the earliest possible opportunity. The council is required to provide a paying-in book with counterfoils or duplicates for the use of anyone who pays money into its account or the account of any of its officers. Particulars of payments must be entered on a slip and its counterfoil (or duplicate) and in the case of cheques, the amount of each cheque and some reference, such as the number of the receipt given or the name of the debtor, which will connect the cheque with the debt. In addition, if a cheque was not received in discharge of a debt that fact should be noted.

Materials

Orders

17.7 Orders for goods should always be in writing. Orders, unless very small, should have the previous approval of the council, but in an emergency it may be necessary to order without specific authority; nevertheless all orders must ultimately be reported. There is, however, no objection to the council authorising the clerk permanently to order specified categories of materials as and when required, but it must then ensure that proper records are kept and produced.

Records

17.8 Stock books or lists should be kept showing particulars of each item, when and where purchased and showing also the date of issue and the date and place of use. Records of this kind are particularly desirable where the council owns numbers of small objects such as tennis balls or perishable equipment such as cricket nets.

It is also desirable to keep a register of plant and equipment such as old iron chests, mowers, rollers, tennis court markers or pleasure boats. This sort of equipment, especially if it is of an old-fashioned pattern, is easily forgotten and notwithstanding size and weight quite capable of being lost[1].

[1] It is said that the government of Ireland once lost a battery of heavy guns; the author is aware of a council which mislaid a half-ton roller.

Lighting

17.9 A council which maintains public lighting should have a large-scale map upon which each light is marked and numbered. Where it maintains its lights itself, labour and materials can be booked to each light by number; in this way the cost of each light can be quickly calculated and the council will be put on inquiry if one regularly costs more than the others. Contractors should, for the same reason, be required to keep a similar record and permit the council to inspect it.

Particular account books and financial statements

17.10 Forms are not prescribed generally for the accounts of local councils but forms and books which facilitate the keeping of the accounts appropriate to the accounting category of the body concerned (as described above) are obviously necessary. Apart from these the responsible financial officer should keep a treasurer's receipts and payments book, and if, as is usual, someone has authority to make small disbursements in cash he should keep a petty cash book in the form of a receipts and payments book.

Separate accounts

17.11 Separate accounts must be kept for the 'free resource'[1], for a forged transfer compensation fund[2], for members' allowances, and for publicity[3].

[1] Local Government Act 1972, s 137.
[2] This seems to follow from the terms of the Forged Transfer Acts 1891 and 1892.
[3] Local Government Act 1986, s 5.

Voluntary bodies' accountability

17.12 If the council has made a grant loan or guarantee exceeding £2,000 to a voluntary body, it must require from that body within a year a statement of the way in which the money has been applied[1].

[1] Local Government Act 1972, s 137A.

Bills, timesheets and wages records

17.13 Apart from disbursements of sums under a limit set by the council (eg £50) (petty cash) bills should be numbered consecutively, and when they are submitted to the council for approval they should be initialled by the chairman. When they have been paid they should, with the receipt (or paid cheque) attached, be filed in order of number in files (such as box or clutch files) from which they cannot be unintentionally detached.

Bills should be itemised and the council should refuse to consider a bill which does not set out with reasonable clarity the goods or services for which payment is demanded.

Where a council employs labour on a time basis, the timesheet is really the bill for work done. Like any other bill it should be specific, setting out the nature of each job and the time taken to do it. If the council employs a foreman he should certify the time-sheets.

The wages book (or sheet) is compiled primarily from the time-sheets. It shows the employee's name, the rates of pay, the hours worked, the total gross wages earned and the deductions for taxation, superannuation and so forth, together with the employer's contributions, and finally the net amounts payable by the council to the employee, and to HM Revenue & Customs.

Payment of bills

17.14 *By cheque:* when the payment of a bill has been authorised and generally speaking the amount exceeds £10 a cheque should be made out and signed by two members of the council[1] who should also initial the counterfoil. It is not essential that cheques should be signed at council meetings.

Any cheque which appears to have been paid by the banker upon whom it is drawn is evidence that the person to whom the cheque is made out (the creditor) has received the sum payable by the cheque. It is not, however, by itself evidence that any particular debt owed to the creditor has been paid, and therefore a covering letter should be sent stating that the cheque is sent in payment of a particular debt, or better still the cheque can be marked with the number of the bill to which it relates or some other cross reference to the bill; it is undesirable to insist upon a separate receipt, and auditors ought not to do so, for the multiplication of the formalities of receipt was the very thing which the Cheques Act 1957 was intended to abolish. If a cheque is crossed 'Account payee only' the banker becomes liable if the money finds its way into the hands of any other person.

Credit transfers, electronic transfers, internet banking, periodical payments and direct debits: an authority for a credit transfer must be signed by two members as if it were a cheque[2], and a counterfoil or duplicate kept. Periodical payments orders must be authorised in the same way.

It is doubtful whether a local authority can authorise regular direct debits against its bank in advance of even regular receipts of goods or services from contractors or tradespeople, who may go unexpectedly into liquidation; but it is probably lawful in the case of regularly renewable insurance policies, which might otherwise lapse. Direct debits are commonly used for the repayment instalments of a loan. Direct debit is practised more for the benefit of businesses than for their customers.

In July 2012, the Department for Communities and Local Government issued a consultation paper proposing that the requirement for cheques and other orders for the payment of money to be signed by two councillors be revoked; local councils and charter trustees would be allowed to develop their own controls on making payments in compliance with their general duty to have in place an effective system of internal controls. At the time of writing, the proposals had not been enacted.

In cash payments of small sums (eg under £20) are commonly made from a petty cash imprest of a few, say £100, in the hands of the clerk or treasurer. When small bills are paid, the transaction is entered in the petty cash book and a receipt or signature obtained. At each meeting the book should be presented and initialled in the same way as a bill, and a cheque should be issued to bring the imprest up to the original amount.

As banks usually charge for each item entered in the accounts, there are practical advantages in making small payments in cash rather than by cheque.

1   Local Government Act 1972, s 150(5).
2   LGA 1972, s 150(5).

D   FINANCIAL YEAR, BALANCING AND SIGNATURE

17.15 The financial year begins on 1 April and ends on 31 March[1].

In England, councils (and parish meetings in parishes without councils) with a gross income or expenditure (whichever is the higher) for the year, and for each of the two immediately preceding years, which is less than £200,000 must produce in accordance with, and in the form specified by, the annual return required by proper practices relating to accounts, a record of receipts and payments; or an income and expenditure account and statement of balances in relation to that year[2].

Councils and parish meetings with a gross income or expenditure (whichever is the higher) of £200,000 or more, but not exceeding £6.5 million, for the year and for each of the two immediately preceding years, must likewise produce an income and expenditure account and a statement of balances in relation to that year[2].

Councils with a gross expenditure exceeding £6.5 million must prepare a statement of accounts in accordance with proper practices[3].

In Wales, community councils with a gross income or expenditure (whichever is higher) for the year and for each of the two immediately preceding years which is less than £1,000,000 and is:

(a)   £200,000 or more for the year and each of the immediately preceding two years, the council may (but need not) produce a full statement of accounts in accordance in the same way as principal councils and to community councils with a gross expenditure exceeding £1,000,000);
(b)   £200,000 or more for those years, the council must prepare an income and expenditure account and a statement of balances;
(c)   less than £200,000 for those years, the council must prepare a record of receipts and payments or an income and expenditure account and statement of balances in relation to that year[4].

As soon as possible after 31 March the accounts must be made up. The record of receipts and payments, or the balance sheet, or (if more than one) the consolidated balance sheet or summary of them must be signed by the responsible financial officer. It must be approved by resolution as soon as practicable after the end of the financial year and in any event by the 30 June following the end of the year[5].

1   Audit Commission Act 1998, s 2.
2   Accounts and Audit (England) Regulations 2011, SI 2011/817, reg 12.
3   Accounts and Audit (England) Regulations 2011, SI 2011/817, reg 7.
4   Accounts and Audit (Wales) Regulations 2005, SI 2005/368, reg 8 (as amended by the Accounts and Audit (Wales) (Amendment) Regulations 2010 SI 2010/683).
5   Accounts and Audit (England) Regulations 2011, SI 2011/817, regs 13 and 8; Accounts and Audit (Wales) Regulations 2005, SI 2005/368, reg 9.

Chapter 18

AUDIT

A   INTRODUCTION

18.1 England and Wales now have largely separate statutory provisions relating to audit. The English provisions are contained in the Audit Commission Act 1998 and the Welsh provisions in the Public Audit (Wales) Act 2004. There are very few differences between the audit provisions in the two Acts; these are noted where appropriate below. In this chapter the Secretary of State through the Financial Reporting Council and the Auditor General for Wales are together called 'the supervising auditors'.

In July 2012, the Government published a draft Local Audit Bill which abolishes the Audit Commission and establishes a new local audit regime. The bill applies only to England. The bill provides an audit regime for smaller local audit bodies, defined as those with an annual turnover below £6.5 million. The regime is less rigorous than that for larger public bodies.

B   WHAT ACCOUNTS MAY BE AUDITED

18.2 The accounts of every local council, parish meeting or committee of either, of charter trustees, of any joint committee of which a local council is a constituent authority, and of any officer who handles money or property for which he should account to the council are liable to audit. Charities administered by the council are audited as part of the council's accounts but not charities to which the council appoints trustees, even if it appoints them all. Audit (which refers to the past) is quite separate from the auditor's powers of advice, which concerns the future. These powers are described in 22.9 below. Auditors are as much bound by the law as they are entitled to enforce it, but their legal opinions are not conclusive.

The accounts of an abolished council in England are audited with the accounts of the authority to which its property and accounts have been transferred, and which then has consequential powers of recovery[1]. There is no comparable provision in Wales. The whole of Wales is divided into communities and there is thus no need for a system for creating new communities.

[1]   Local Government (Parishes and Parish Councils) Regulations 1999, SI 1999/545, reg 15.

C   TIME FOR AUDIT

18.3 The audit is supposed to take place annually as soon as may be after the close of the financial year on 31 March. An extraordinary audit may take place at any time on three days' notice[1].

[1]   Audit Commission Act 1998, s 25; Public Audit (Wales) Act 2004, s 37.

D   WHO AUDITS THE ACCOUNTS?

18.4 Extraordinary audits are carried out by direction of the supervising auditors[1].

The auditors are either officers of the Commission or the Auditor General for Wales, or firms or private practitioners appointed by it. Fees are charged at the same rate in all cases[2].

[1]   Audit Commission Act 1998, s 25; Public Audit (Wales) Act 2004, s 37.
[2]   ACA 1998, s 3; PA(W)A 2004, s 20.

Internal control and statement of assurance

18.5 Every council must institute adequate and effective systems of internal control and must annually make (with the help, if necessary, of the supervising auditors or auditors) a statement of assurance confirming that it has such systems in operation. Without this statement the audit cannot go forward.

Basis of accounts

18.6 English parish councils and parish meetings with income or expenditure (whichever is higher) not exceeding £200,000 must prepare accounts as follows:

(a)   if one has a gross income or expenditure (whichever is the higher) for the year, and for each of the two immediately preceding years, of less than £200,000, it must produce in accordance with, and in the form specified by, the annual return required by proper practices relating to accounts:
      (i)   a record of receipts and payments in relation to that year; or
      (ii)   an income and expenditure account and statement of balances in relation to that year.
(b)   where gross income or expenditure (whichever is the higher) is £200,000 or more, but not exceeding £6.5 million, for the year and for each of the two immediately preceding years, it must likewise produce an income and expenditure account and a statement of balances in relation to that year[1].

In Wales, community councils of which the gross income or expenditure (whichever is higher) for the year and for each of the two immediately preceding years is less than £1,000,000 and is:

(a)　£200,000 or more for the year and each of the immediately preceding two years, may (but need not) produce a statement of accounts;

(b)　£200,000 or more for those years, must prepare an income and expenditure account and a statement of balances;

(c)　less than £200,000 for those years, must prepare:

　　(i)　a record of receipts and payments in relation to that year; or

　　(ii)　an income and expenditure account and statement of balances in relation to that year[2].

[1]　Accounts and Audit (England) Regulations 2011, SI 2011/817, reg 12.
[2]　Accounts and Audit (Wales) Regulations 2005, SI 2005/368, reg 8 (as amended by the Accounts and Audit (Wales) (Amendment) Regulations 2010, SI 2010/683).

E　PROCEDURE BEFORE ORDINARY AUDIT

Notice

18.7　The accounts having been made up to 31 March, balanced, certified by the clerk and signed[1], the clerk[2] (or chairman of the parish meeting) asks the auditor for an appointment. This request must be made more than five weeks in advance of the date of the proposed appointment because the accounts must be made available for at least 20 working days before that date, and public notice that the accounts will be available must be given at least 16 days before those working days begin. The notice must state the period, place and hours of availability, the name and address of the auditor and the public rights conferred by the Audit Commission Act 1998, s 15. In the case of a council with a gross income or expenditure of £6.5 million or more, this notice must be advertised and displayed on the council's website. For other councils and meetings the notice may be displayed in the usual manner. In Wales (but not England),when notice has been given the clerk must immediately send to the auditor a certificate that he has given it, or a copy of the advertisement with a statement of the date and name of the newspaper in which it appeared[3].

[1]　Accounts and Audit (England) Regulations 2011, SI 2011/817, reg 8; Accounts and Audit (Wales) Regulations 2005, SI 2005/368, reg 9.
[2]　Mostly called 'the responsible financial officer' in the legislation.
[3]　Accounts and Audit (Wales) Regulations 2005, SI 2005/368, reg 15.

Inspection

18.8　Every account, duly made up and balanced and all the relevant account books, deeds, contracts, bills, vouchers, and receipts must be open to inspection by all interested persons, who may make copies or extracts without payment[1].

The accounts should be deposited in the locality, but if the office is outside it their deposit there is not illegal if it is in the neighbourhood.

Accounts may not be altered after they have been made available for public inspection, without the auditor's consent[2]. It is an offence to obstruct inspection.

[1]　Audit Commission Act 1998, s 14; Public Audit (Wales) Act 2004, s 29.

2   Accounts and Audit England) Regulations 2011, SI 2011/817, reg 23; Accounts and Audit
     (Wales) Regulations 2005, SI 2005/368, reg 14.

F   PROCEEDINGS AT AUDIT

Code of audit practice

18.9 Auditors must carry out their functions in accordance with a code of
practice prepared by the supervising auditors with parliamentary approval.
The code is obtainable from the supervising auditors[1].

1   Audit Commission Act 1998, s 4, Public Audit (Wales) Act 2004, s 16.

Evidence

18.10 The auditor may require the production of any document which he
thinks necessary for the audit and may require anyone who has or should have
such a document to appear before him and give such information or
explanations as may be necessary. Anyone who fails to comply with the
auditor's requirements may be fined (level 3) plus £20 a day for a continuing
offence[1]. Anyone who knowingly makes or signs a false declaration may be
imprisoned for up to two years or fined or both[2].

1   Audit Commission Act 1998, s 6; Public Audit (Wales) Act 2004, s 18.
2   Perjury Act 1911, s 5.

Electors' rights

18.11 Though he cannot demand personal information about a member of the
staff[1] either by inspecting documents or by questions, any elector for the area
to which the accounts relate may question the auditor[2]. He may make
objections to the accounts as to any matter on which the auditor may make a
report or apply to the court, but he must give written notice of objection
beforehand to the auditor and to the body to whose accounts he is objecting[3].
This notice must state the facts upon which the objector proposes to rely and
give, as far as possible, particulars of any item of account which is alleged to
be contrary to law, particulars of the person from whom the money should be
recovered, the amount of the deficiency, and particulars of any matter upon
which it is proposed that the auditor should make a report[4].

1   Audit Commission Act 1998, s 15; Public Audit (Wales) Act 2004, s 30.
2   ACA 1998, s 15; PA(W)A 2004, s 30.
3   ACA 1998, s 16; PA(W)A 2004, s 31.
4   Accounts and Audit (England) Regulations 2011, SI 2011/817, reg 25; Accounts and Audit
     (Wales) Regulations 2005, SI 2005/368, reg 16.

Auditors' powers

18.12 The auditor may, first, report to the council at the conclusion of the audit, or second, he may report immediately without waiting[1]. Third, if it seems to him that an item of account is illegal, he may apply to a court for a declaration that the item is unlawful[2].

[1] Audit Commission Act 1998, s 8; Public Audit (Wales) Act 2004, s 22.
[2] ACA 1998, s 17; PA(W)A 2004, s 32.

Auditors' duties

18.13 Auditors must satisfy themselves that the accounts are prepared in accordance with statute and regulations, that proper accounting practices have been observed and that there are proper arrangements for securing economy, efficiency and effectiveness in the use of resources[1]. They must give electors or their representatives an opportunity to question them about the accounts and object to them, but an objector has no absolute right to have his objection heard in public[2].

If an auditor will not apply to the court on suspicion of illegality or certify a sum not brought into account or a loss or deficiency, an aggrieved objector may require his reasons; and where conversely, he has issued a certificate, a person aggrieved may equally require his reasons, in either event within six weeks (in Wales 14 days) after he has been notified of the decision[3].

[1] Audit Commission Act 1998, s 5; Public Audit (Wales) Act 2004, s 17. See **18.23** below.
[2] *R v Farmer, ex p Hargrave* (1982) 79 LGR 676.
[3] ACA 1998, s 17(4); PA(W)A 2004, s 32(6)

Conclusion

18.14 At the end of the proceedings the auditor must certify that he has completed the audit. This certificate may be included in any report which he makes to the council[1].

[1] Audit Commission Act 1998, s 9; Public Audit (Wales) Act 2004, s 23.

G   PROCEEDINGS AFTER AUDIT

Reports and recommendations

18.15 The auditor must send a report to the council or chairman of the parish meeting, and it or the parish meeting must consider it as soon as possible. A copy must accompany the agenda and it must be disclosed, on demand, to the press[1]. He may also make written recommendations and state which, if any, of them should be statutorily considered[2].

Immediate reports must be sent to the commission forthwith; other reports and certificates within 14 days[3].

[1] Audit Commission Act 1998, s 10; Public Audit (Wales) Act 2004, ss 24–25.
[2] ACA 1998, s 11; PA(W)A 2004, s 24.

3   ACA 1998, s 10; PA(W)A 2004, s 22.

Notice of right of inspection—ordinary reports

18.16 As soon as possible after the audit has been completed, the council must give public notice of the fact, and within 14 days after the meeting at which a report is considered public notice must be given that the report is available for inspection. The notice must set out the public rights of inspection and copying and give the address where and the hours when the report may be inspected or copied.

These notices must be given by advertisement in the same way as notice of audit[1].

1   Accounts and Audit (England) Regulations 2011, SI 2011/817, regs 11 and 16; Accounts and Audit (Wales) Regulations 2005, SI 2005/368, reg 17.

Immediate reports

18.17 Once an immediate report is received from the auditor, any member of the public may inspect and copy it at all reasonable times free of charge. The council or the chairman of the parish meeting must insert an advertisement in one or more local newspapers identifying the subject matter of the report and stating where and when it may be inspected and that it may be copied. A copy must be given to every member of the council, and the auditor may supply one to anyone he thinks fit. It is an offence (level 3 fine) to obstruct a person in the exercise of these rights or to refuse a copy to anyone entitled to it, or to fail to issue the advertisement as laid down, or to give copies of the report to the councillors[1].

1   Audit Commission Act 1998, s 13; Public Audit (Wales) Act 2004, s 27.

Ordinary reports and recommendations

18.18 Ordinary reports and the recommendations for statutory consideration must be considered within four months of receipt at a meeting for which at least seven clear days' notice has been published in a local newspaper, giving the time and place, stating that a report is to be considered and describing the subject matter of the report or recommendation; and after the end of that meeting the council's decisions must be communicated to the auditor and a summary of them published in a local newspaper (unless such decisions had to be taken at a closed meeting)[1].

1   Audit Commission Act 1998, s 11; Public Audit (Wales) Act 2004, s 29.

H   COURT PROCEEDINGS

Auditors' applications (illegality)

18.19 If an item of account appears to be illegal, the auditor may apply to the court for a declaration that it is contrary to law. If it makes the declaration it may order the accounts to be rectified[1].

[1]   Audit Commission Act 1998, s 17 as amended by the Local Government Act 2000; Public Audit (Wales) Act 2004, s 32.

Aggrieved persons' appeals

18.20 Objectors and others aggrieved by an auditor's decision may approach the court, as if the auditor had made the application or the certificate, and the court may give any certificate which the auditor could have given[1]. The High Court and the county courts have concurrent jurisdiction[2].

[1]   Audit Commission Act 1998, s 17(4); Public Audit (Wales) Act 2004, s 32(8).
[2]   ACA 1998, s 17(6); PA(W)A 2004, s 32(10).

Costs

18.21 On an application or an appeal, the court may make an order for the payment of the applicant's or the auditor's costs by the local council[1].

[1]   Audit Commission Act 1998, s 17(5); Public Audit (Wales) Act 2004, s 32(9).

I   OTHER OFFENCES

18.22 In Wales only, certain wilful acts are offences punishable on summary conviction with a level 3 fine. These acts include failure to balance the accounts as soon as practicable (and in any case within six months), failure to make documents available for public inspection at the proper time before audit, and to issue or to certify the proper notices at the proper time, and making unauthorised alterations in accounts once they have been made available for public inspection[1].

[1]   Accounts and Audit (Wales) Regulations 2005, SI 2005/368, reg 21.

J   THE THREE ES

18.23 To secure the economy, efficiency and effectiveness ('the three Es') mentioned in **18.13** above, auditors encourage authorities to make proper budgets, namely realistic (neither pessimistic, nor over-optimistic nor timid) forecasts of expected expenditure and of the means to meet it; this includes consideration and necessary updating of charges and the establishment of financial policies to deal with more distant likelihoods such as the replacement of obsolescent buildings. Second, a council will wish to ensure proper cash flow management to avoid embarrassments, and to put temporary balances to work in deposit accounts or other short term investments. Progress can then be monitored against the current budget and cash flow.

Some rare legislation concerns the supervising auditors. They may direct relevant bodies to acquire accurate and complete information about their activities so that comparisons of cost, and of the three Es, may be made as between one year and another, and as between authorities. The information on a financial year must be published in a local newspaper within nine months of the end of it, and a document embodying the information must be kept and made available for inspection by any elector. To obstruct such inspection is an offence (level 3 fine).

Relevant bodies do not include local councils, but the Secretary of State and the Welsh Assembly may include them by order, which may make different provision for different cases (perhaps distinguished by size of population) or areas[1].

[1]   Audit Commission Act 1998, s 44; Public Audit (Wales) Act 2004, s 47.

Chapter 19

CONTRACTS

A   THE POWER

19.1 A council may make all contracts necessary for the discharge of its functions. Accordingly a contract made in pursuance of action which is beyond the council's powers, is itself beyond those powers[1].

[1]   Local Government Act 1972, s 111. See **22.8** below.

B   NATURE OF CONTRACTS GENERALLY

Form

19.2 Save for contracts for the sale of land or an interest in land, contracts (called guarantees) to answer for the debt default or miscarriage of another, and contracts to deal in securities through a stockbroker, the general law does not require a contract to be in writing, either formally as a specially drafted contractual document, or informally by, for example, an exchange of letters[1]. In fact over 99 per cent of all contracts are made wholly or partly by word of mouth, but obviously it is often convenient both practically and legally to have the terms of a contract agreed in writing so as to ensure cheap and easy proof of them.

[1]   Statute of Frauds 1677, s 4.

Seven features of a real agreement

19.3 Whether or not an agreement is in writing, there must be a real agreement on the same issue and it must exhibit seven features for it to be enforceable as a contract in law. The following is a very short summary of a very big subject.

Qualified parties

19.4 First, the parties must be qualified. The commonest difficulty under this heading is where one of them is under 18. A contract of loan to such an infant is never enforceable against him, even if he ratifies it after coming of age. Other contracts are enforceable against him only if they are for his benefit, for example, employment at reasonable pay, or training for a profession, or for necessaries such as food, or clothing.

Offer and acceptance

19.5 Second, there must be an offer (which can be contained in an advertisement) which has not been changed or withdrawn, and third, that offer must be exactly accepted. A so-called counter-offer is a refusal followed by a further offer. Acceptances come into force when received or when made according to the terms of the offer, but in the absence of any other indication, a postal acceptance comes into effect when the letter is *posted*. It is, however, necessary to distinguish between a simple offer, which can be turned into a contract by acceptance, and an offer to treat, which is merely a readiness to negotiate. Priced goods in a shop window do not represent offers, but only readiness to negotiate. The shop is entitled to refuse to sell.

Consideration or quid pro quo

19.6 Fourth, there must be consideration or quid pro quo. Each party must do something for the other in return for the promise made by that other. The something (that is, the consideration) may take the form of a counter-promise ('I promise to pay you £100 if you promise to deliver ten tons of coal to me by Thursday'), or a promise for an act ('I will pay you £100 if you clear my drains') or a forbearance ('I will not sue you for the £1,000 which you owe me, if you will let your garage to me for ten years at £1 a year'). A request for a service or goods implies, in the absence of a named price, that if the service is performed or the goods delivered, the payment will be reasonable (and therefore fixed by the court in the event of a dispute). This is called *quantum meruit.*

The consideration must be real: for example, there will be no consideration if the benefit has already been conferred before the contract was made, or if it has to be conferred anyway under another legal obligation. On the other hand, contract law is not concerned with its adequacy: if a contract stipulates a gross imbalance of advantage ('£1,000 for a china orange') that fact by itself will not be enough to upset the contract (but it might be evidence of fraud or pressure which would have to be separately proved). Since 1999 it has been possible for persons to contract so as to confer upon a third person not a party to the contract rights which are enforceable by him.

Three other major features

19.7 Fifth, the agreement must be intended to create a legal relationship, not merely an obligation of honour. Where there is consideration this is very seldom a problem. Sixth, the agreement must not be void as being in undue restraint of trade or actually or inferentially a wager. Bets are unenforceable by the courts. The latter rule prevents a person from insuring against an event in which he has no interest. Seventh, the agreement must not be tainted by illegality or sexual immorality. The commonest illegalities involve evasion of rates, taxes and exchange controls, insider dealings and agreements to defame someone.

Special rules and practice in insurance

19.8 When someone wishes to insure against a particular risk in which he has an insurable interest, he invariably has special knowledge of the circumstances not possessed by the insurance company (or syndicate), and the latter must rely upon his frankness. An insurance policy is usually based upon a proposal form, which is a questionnaire issued by the company to him, in which he will be expected, in effect, to guarantee the truth of his answers to the questions. A single even innocent inaccuracy will make the policy void.

Second, insurance is a guarantee against loss, not a way of making a profit. If someone over-insures, for example, a building against fire, he will be entitled to its replacement value or less, but not more.

Third, where a collection of things is under-insured, and one of them is lost, the insured will be entitled only to the proportion of the real value represented by the amount for which the collection as a whole was in fact insured. For example, a small fire destroys the piano. The building and contents were insured for £100,000 but are now worth £200,000. The piano was worth £2,000. The company is not bound to pay more than £1,000. For this reason, it is wise to update one's policies.

C   LOCAL GOVERNMENT REQUIREMENTS AND STANDING ORDERS

19.9 Contracts made by a council or committee thereof must be made in accordance with standing orders which it must make. These must, in the case of contracts for the supply of goods or materials or for the execution of works, provide for securing competition and for regulating the way in which tenders are invited, but may exempt small contracts from such rules or permit the council to make an exemption in a particular case. It is sometimes desirable to relate these standing orders to any list of approved contractors kept by the district council (T). Persons contracting with a local council are not bound to inquire whether the standing orders have been complied with[1].

A contract need not be in the form of a deed if it is for work done or goods supplied in the ordinary course of business with the approval of the council or its authorised agent, but as a general rule contracts of a substantial nature should be signed by two members of the council under authority of a resolution.

[1]   Local Government Act 1972, s 135.

Ultra vires

19.10 For the effect of the *ultra vires* rule on contracts see **22.8** below.

Exclusion of non-commercial considerations

19.11 Non-commercial considerations must play no part in making supply or works contracts, or in including or excluding persons in or from lists or groups of persons, or their sub-contractors, from whom tenders are invited, selected or submitted. The rule is meant to prevent the rate- and council tax-payers being burdened with the cost of councillors' personal adherence to social or political ideals or philosophies which might obstruct the economical conduct of the council's proper business. There is an extensive definition of 'non-commercial' but the Secretary of State can alter the list of non-commercial considerations[1].

If a council decides to exclude someone from an approved contractors' list or not to invite a tender from someone who has asked to be invited, or not to accept the submission of a tender or to refuse a tender, or withhold approval of a sub-contractor, or to terminate an existing contract, it must on request give its reasons within 15 days[2].

[1]   Local Government Act 1988, ss 17 and 19.
[2]   LGA 1988, s 20.

Chapter 20

ANCILLARY MATTERS

20.1 The apparently miscellaneous matters raised in this chapter have a unifying feature, in that they do not arise by themselves but, if at all, as conditions precedent to something else or in understanding or pursuing a particular objective.

A   SAFEGUARDS FOR OTHER INTERESTS

20.2 There are some things which local councils cannot do or cannot do in particular ways without observing procedures which are intended to safeguard the interests of others. The safeguards which are peculiar to the provision of bus shelters are explained in **31.40** below, but there are also safeguards connected with the provision of vehicle parks and the placing upon land or premises of seats, shelters other than bus shelters, public clocks, and lighting equipment.

Where it is proposed to erect any of these installations it may be necessary to obtain certain consents (set out in the Parish Councils Act 1957) even (in some rare cases) if they are to be placed upon the council's own property.

The person from whom such consents must be obtained are the owner and occupier in the case of private property (including public paths across it and places obstructing access to it)[1], and certain public authorities in the case of highways (other than public paths) and land abutting onto them. The private owners and occupiers have an absolute right to withhold their consent; the public authorities, however, must not do so unreasonably but may impose reasonable conditions, including a condition requiring removal in due course[2]. Disputes on reasonableness are to be settled by an arbitrator who is appointed in default of agreement by the Secretary of State for Transport or the Welsh Assembly unless he or it is a party to the dispute, when the arbitrator is appointed by the President of the Institution of Civil Engineers[3].

The Secretary of State may contract out his functions[4].

[1]   Parish Councils Act 1957, s 5(1)(a) and (b).
[2]   PCA 1957, s 5(2).
[3]   PCA 1957, s 5(3).
[4]   Deregulation and Contracting Out Act 1994, s 69 and Contracting Out (Highway Functions) Order 2009, SI 2009/721.

B   DISCRIMINATION

20.3 In carrying out its functions a local or any other public authority must have due regard to the need to (a) eliminate discrimination, harassment, victimisation and any other conduct that is prohibited by the Equality Act 2010; (b) advance equality of opportunity between persons who share a relevant protected characteristic and persons who do not share it; (c) foster good relations between persons who share a relevant protected characteristic and persons who do not share it[1]. Relevant protected characteristics are: age, disability, gender reassignment, marriage and civil partnership, pregnancy and maternity, race, religion or belief, sex, sexual orientation[2].

It is unlawful for a local or public authority to discriminate against a person because of a protected characteristic[3].

A person who provides services to the public (whether for payment or not) must not discriminate against a person by not providing the service. A local council is a service provider. The duty includes a requirement to make reasonable adjustments to the means of providing services, including access to premises, so as to avoid or reduce discrimination. (For example, the duty may require the provision of a ramped access to premises to enable those in wheelchairs to enter and leave[3].)

In general it is unlawful to treat the remuneration of one person less favourably than another on account of a difference of sex[4].

The details of this large subject are beyond the scope of this work.

1   Equality Act 2010 s 149.
2   Equality Act 2010, s 4.
3   Equality Act 2010, ss 13, 20, 29, Sch 2.
4   Equality Act 2010, Part 5, Chapter 3.

C   POLITICAL PUBLICITY

20.4 No local authority may publish or assist anyone, financially or otherwise, to publish, by any means, any material which in whole or part appears to be designed to affect public support for a political party. In deciding whether material falls under the ban, regard must be had to whether it refers to a political party or promotes or opposes a point of view identifiable as the view of one political party, and, if part of a campaign, the apparent purpose of the campaign[1], and also to the provisions of the Secretary of State's Code of Recommended Practice on Publicity, the latest version of which was published in March 2011[2]. A separate account of publicity expenditure must be kept, but this need not include items where there is a legal obligation to publish, or of expenditure to inform the public about the council's services, or to encourage public order, road safety, waste collection, and so forth[3].

1   Local Government Act 1986, s 2.
2   LGA 1986, s 4.
3   LGA 1986, s 5.

E   NOTE ON DEFINITIONS

20.5 All Acts must be construed in the light of definitions contained in the Interpretation Act 1978 unless the contrary appears, or the words concerned are in an Act passed before a certain date (if any) mentioned in the Interpretation Act itself. The commonest words and dates are:

- land includes buildings and other structures, land covered with water, and any estate, interest, easement, servitude or right in or over land [1 January 1979];
- month means calendar month [1850];
- person includes a body of persons corporate or unincorporate [1889];
- representative body mentioned in pre-1972 legislation refers, in England only, to the parish trustees;
- Wales means the area consisting of the counties established by s 20 of the Local Government Act 1972 [1 April 1974]. Pre-1972 legislation (unless repealed) about parishes and their councils, now refers to communities in this area;
- writing includes any mode of representing or reproducing words in a visible form.

In addition, unless the context otherwise requires, the surviving words defined in s 100 of the Local Government Act 1888, are used in the same sense in the Act of 1894 which contains further definitions[1]; the 'vocabulary' thus created is used but not used consistently in the Acts of 1929 and 1948: the Act of 1972 contains many definitions[2] for its own peculiar purposes. Local authority tends to be specially defined for every Act and even parts of an Act:

- a pound weight is 0.453,592,37 kilogram;
- a yard is 0.9144 metre[3].

Where something is required to be done within a specified time, the day from which the time runs is not counted[4] and the period runs up to midnight of the last day[5].

---

1   Local Government Act 1894, s 75(2).
2   Local Government Act 1872, s 270.
3   Weights and Measures Act 1985, s 1(1).
4   *Goldsmiths Co v West Metropolitan Rly Co* [1904] 1 KB 1.
5   *Manorlike Ltd v Le Vitas Travel* [1986] 1 All ER 573.

Chapter 21

LEGAL AND SIMILAR BUSINESS AND INQUIRIES

A   GENERAL CONSIDERATIONS

Insurance

21.1 Litigation is expensive and the potential cost to the rate- and council tax-payers is increased by civil legal aid; for if a council is forced into contested proceedings by a legally-aided opponent it will generally be compelled to bear its own costs even if it succeeds. Hence councils which own any substantial property or which operate extensive services should insure and be certain that their insurance policy will cover them against the cost of any legal proceedings which may arise from the risks insured.

Timely preparation of cases

21.2 The importance of making an early start with the preparation of a case and the collection of evidence cannot be overstressed, whether in legal proceedings or in administrative inquiries. Witnesses' memories grow dim over long periods, and a good case hurriedly prepared may be lost because those who have to conduct it have not had time either to collect sufficient evidence or to reflect upon it; and where professional assistance is not, or cannot be, procured such reflection is doubly necessary.

Possible allies

21.3 It is always desirable, but especially in administrative inquiries, to consider who, or what organisations, may support or have similar or complementary interests to the local council and to co-ordinate the case with him or them. Sometimes it may be convenient for a local council to support another authority's case by providing a witness instead of itself appearing as a principal. This can save time and money and help to keep the inspector or court or parliamentary committee interested, without any loss of cogency.

Public petitions and letters of support

21.4 In public inquiries, petitions signed by many people seldom have much impact because it is notorious that people often sign them without being certain of their effect. If, however, a public petition is to be presented, each signatory should make his or her name clear and add his or her address; and the petition's effect will be enhanced if it is presented by a witness who canvassed for it. He should be prepared to stand up to cross-examination.

An individual letter of support is commonly held to be worth ten signatures on a petition, especially if couched in the writer's own language. The 600 local councils which petitioned the then Department of the Environment in 1971 about local government reorganisation in their own words created a powerful impression.

B   LEGAL PROCEEDINGS

General rules

21.5 If a council thinks that it is expedient for the promotion or protection of the interests of the inhabitants it may, subject to any specific exceptions (mostly concerned with charities and allotments) laid down in a few particular Acts, prosecute or defend legal proceedings[1]. There is also a special right to take proceedings to protect an ownerless common[2], and to prosecute for certain offences concerning the ploughing of footpaths[3]. In addition and independently of these statutory rights, it may as a local authority and trustee for the rate- and council tax-payers have recourse to the ordinary rights which trustees have to defend their position and the rights of their beneficiaries, and this enables it to take or defend proceedings with the object of defending its constitution, property, or rights[4].

[1]   Local Government Act 1972, s 222.
[2]   Commons Act 2006, s 45 and see **26.8** below.
[3]   See **31.15** below.
[4]   Per Jessel MR in *AG v Mayor of Brecon* (1878) 10 Ch D 204 at 214–219. For appeals against auditors' prohibitions see **22.9** below.

Representation

21.6 A local council may authorise a solicitor or any member or officer (but no one else[1]) to conduct proceedings on its behalf in a magistrates' court[2]. The authority must be given before proceedings are commenced[3]. A county court may allow a corporation to appear before it otherwise than by solicitor or by solicitor and counsel[4]. Otherwise the rule that a corporation must appear by counsel in legal proceedings applies to local councils.

[1]   *Kyle v Barbor* (1888) 58 LT 229.
[2]   Local Government Act 1972, s 223.
[3]   *Bowyer, Philpott and Payne Ltd v Mather* [1919] 1 KB 419.
[4]   *Kinnell (Charles P) & Co Ltd v Harding, Wace & Co* [1918] 1 KB 405.

Briefs and retainers

21.7 If a solicitor is retained for legal proceedings the retainer should be by deed[1].

A barrister may accept a brief from a clerk of a local authority who is not a solicitor.

A local council may in all proper cases take and pay for professional legal advice. This right is a necessary incident to its functions as a public authority[2], as well as a logical consequence of its power to take legal proceedings.

1 *Arnold v Poole Corporation* (1842) 4 Man & G 860.
2 Local Government Act 1972, s 111.

Evidence of byelaws

21.8 Byelaws are proved by producing a printed copy endorsed with a certificate signed by the clerk that the council made the byelaws, that the copy is a true copy, that it was confirmed on a specified date, and that it came into operation on a specified date[1].

1 Local Government Act 1972, s 238.

C   PROCEEDINGS IN PARLIAMENT

Private Bills

21.9 A local council cannot promote a private Bill in Parliament[1] but may, like other local authorities, oppose any private Bill.

Opposition in committee to private Bills is normally conducted through parliamentary agents and is somewhat expensive[2]. A local council will seldom wish to conduct such opposition alone, but may nevertheless sometimes wish to petition against Bills, in which case it is important to have regard to the timetable which is normally followed. As elections, particularly a general election, and other events may derange the parliamentary timetable, the council should consult the Private Bills' Office of each House.

1 Local Government Act 1972, s 239.
2 In 1960 the House of Lords, despite opposition from the promoters, heard a petition by the Brookthorpe-with-Waddon parish council against a British Transport Commission Bill under which it was proposed to take land in the parish not the property of the council. The council's case was conducted by its clerk.

Usual timetable

21.10 A petition for a Bill with a copy of the Bill annexed is deposited by the promoters at the House of Commons or the House of Lords on or before 27 November in each year and advertised, and copies of the Bill become available for sale, both in London and in the district to which it relates on 4 December. A petition against a Bill must be made to the Commons on or before 30 January and to the Lords on or before 6 February. If the Bill passes its first House a petition may be made to the second House.

These dates may be altered by the occurrence of a general election.

Procedure

21.11 Petitions on private Bills are heard by a committee of each House and the proceedings resemble those of a court.

Where a local council cannot afford the expense of a petition it should request a Member of Parliament or a Peer to oppose the Bill on second reading or at the report or third reading stage. The second reading takes place before the committee stage, the report and third reading afterwards.

Special parliamentary procedure

21.12 A few orders must undergo special parliamentary procedure. As in private Bill procedure, the timetable is very important. The following is a summary.

The body promoting the order must first comply with all the requirements of the enabling Act concerning the publication and service of notices, the consideration of objections and the holding of inquiries. If that Act contains no such requirements, the rules in the First Schedule to the Statutory Orders (Special Procedure) Act 1945, must be followed. The responsible minister (the minister who could confirm the order if it were not subject to special parliamentary procedure) then gives at least three days' notice in the London Gazette of his intention to lay the order before Parliament, and thereafter lays it before both Houses with a certificate of the requirements and that they have been complied with. Without this certificate the order cannot be confirmed.

An objector then has 21 days within which to petition Parliament against the order. There are two sorts of petitions: a petition for amendment which must specify the amendments desired, and a petition of general objection against the whole order. These two types of petitions must be submitted in different documents. At the expiry of this first period of 21 days, the order and any petitions against it are considered by the chairmen of committees, who must report on them to the Houses and especially whether the petitions disclose substantial grounds of objection and are fit to be received. There follows a second period of 21 days called the resolution period; if during this period a house resolves to annul the order, it becomes void—but can be resubmitted. If no such resolution is passed then petitions against it may be referred to a joint committee of the two Houses. Petitions of general objection must be specifically referred; petitions for amendment certified by the chairmen are referred automatically. If no petitions are referred, the order comes into force at the end of the resolution period or any later date mentioned in it.

After a third period of three weeks for counter-petitions against any petitions for amendment, the joint committee holds a hearing similar to the proceedings on a private bill[1].

[1] See generally Statutory Orders (Special Procedure) Acts 1945 and 1965.

Parliamentary Commissioner (Ombudsman)

21.13 Complaints to the Ombudsman against maladministration must be made by an individual. They cannot be made by local authorities.

D   LOCAL GOVERNMENT OMBUDSMAN

England: exhaustion of previous resorts

21.14 Complaints about maladministration in local government are made to the Commission for Local Administration in England. They must be in writing and must be submitted within 12 months after the person affected had notice of the subject matter of the complaint or, where that person has died without having had such notice, within 12 months after the person's personal representatives have first had such notice. If a complaint is made to a member of a local authority, the complaint may be referred to the Commissioner by the member it the complainant consents[1].

No local authority as such can make a complaint to the Commission, and therefore such complaints must be made, if at all, by councillors acting as individuals[2].

Local councils and parish meetings are not subject to the Commission's jurisdiction[3].

All principal authorities have complaints procedures. These should normally be exhausted before a complaint is made to the English Commission or the Welsh Ombudsman. (See **7.47** above for the handling of complaints about the conduct of local councils.)

[1]   Local Government Act 1974, ss 26, 26A, 26B, 26C,
[2]   LGA 1974, s 27.
[3]   LGA 1974, s 25(1).

Wales

21.15 The investigation of complaints in Wales is undertaken by the Public Services Ombudsman for Wales[1]. He can investigate alleged cases of:

(a)   maladministration;
(b)   failure in the provision of a 'relevant service';
(c)   failure to provide a 'relevant service' by a 'listed authority'[2].

Listed authorities include community councils. The Welsh Assembly has power to remove a person or body from the list[3]. So far as a community council is concerned, a relevant service is action taken by the council in discharge of any of its administrative functions[4].

The procedure for making a complaint is available only to individuals who claim to have suffered injustice or hardship as a result of maladministration etc by a listed authority. A complaint may be made either to the listed authority and, through it, to the Ombudsman or direct to him. A complaint direct to the

Ombudsman must be made within one year of the matter(s) which give raise to the complaint; if made through the listed authority, it must be referred by that authority to the Ombudsman within one year from the receipt of the complaint[5].

1 Public Services Ombudsman (Wales) Act 2005.
2 PSO(W)A 2005, s 7.
3 PSO(W)A 2005, Sch 3 and s 28.
4 PSO(W)A 2005, s 7(3)(e).
5 PSO(W)A 2005, ss 5 and 6.

E   PUBLIC LOCAL INQUIRIES

21.16 Ministers may hold local inquiries 'to determine any difference, to make or confirm any order, to frame any scheme or to give any consent, confirmation, sanction or approval to any matter or otherwise to act' under the Local Government Act 1972, or under any enactment relating to the functions of a local authority[1].

Such inquiries are held by an inspector appointed by the department concerned. He may (but seldom does) administer oaths, and may summon in writing any witness to attend and bring relevant documents, but if a witness must travel, his travelling expenses must be paid or tendered. Documents of title cannot be required unless they relate to the title of a local authority.

A local council may appear in the interests of the inhabitants and be represented at such an inquiry and may pay the expenses (including the expense of witnesses) of such representation[2].

1 Local Government Act 1972, s 250.
2 LGA 1972, s 222(1)(b).

Procedure

21.17 There is a statutory code for highway inquiries[1]. This sets out practices long observed at all inquiries.

When objections to a proposal have been made, the Secretary of State must within one month tell proposers and objectors whether a public inquiry will be held, and serve an outline statement on the objectors, who may be required to do the same in return. All the parties may then be called to a preliminary meeting over which the inspector presides. If this meeting fails to achieve a settlement, an inquiry timetable is fixed. Those with a statutory right to object (statutory objectors) are entitled to be heard and others may appear with the inspector's permission (which must not be unreasonably withheld) or may be called as witnesses by a statutory objector. Solicitors and counsel may appear for those taking part. Parties and witnesses exchange written copies (called proofs) of their evidence beforehand, and there may be site inspections. Sometimes the inspector may sit with a specialist assessor. His and his assessor's report to the Secretary of State are sent to the parties. The Secretary of State is not bound by the conclusions or recommendations in the report but if he disagrees he must say why, and as a Minister his decision may be attacked in Parliament. An inquiry may be (but seldom is) reopened.

¹   The Highways (Inquiries Procedure) Rules 1994, SI 1994/3263.

Examples

21.18 Inquiries are held into appeals against refusals of planning permission, but many such, mostly minor, appeals are now decided on documents and written submissions rather than at public hearings. Inquiries are also held in cases on the layout of motorways and trunk roads. Traffic Commissioners must hold public sittings to determine the fitness of vehicle operators, if challenged, and into the environmental suitability of an operating centre subject to objection or representation by owners or occupiers of neighbouring land. In such cases local councils cannot raise objections, but may as landowners make representations, or give evidence in support of a party if called to do so by that party[1].

¹   Transport Tribunal 1987 Y12 *Mid Suffolk DC v Dowell*. The legislation relating to the appointment and tenure of office of traffic commissioners is the Public Passenger Vehicles Act 1981. The statutory provisions covering vehicle operators are in the Goods Vehicles (Licensing of Operators) Act 1995.

Costs

21.19 The Secretary of State may (but seldom does) order any local authority or party to pay the department's costs (including a daily amount for the inspector) and these when certified are recoverable as a debt to the Crown or as a civil debt. He may also make orders as to the costs of the parties, and any party can make such an order a rule of court[1].

Traffic Commissioners cannot award costs but they can award certain expenses.

¹   Local Government Act 1972, s 250.

F   COURT PROCEEDINGS

Summary jurisdiction—compensation for damage ('damages')

21.20 Damages up to £20 may be recovered summarily in a magistrates' court for damage caused by negligence to any lamp, lamp-post, notice board, fence, rail, post, shelter or other equipment provided by a local council in a street or public place[1]. Where loss or damage results from an offence the magistrates may award compensation up to £5,000 on conviction[2], but for larger amounts or a civil claim the local council must proceed in the civil courts (see below).

Except as otherwise provided by a particular Act a magistrates' court cannot deal with a case unless the information or complaint has been laid or made within six months of the date of the offence or matter of complaint[3]. Unless the right to prosecute is limited by statute[4] any person may lay an information where the offence is not a matter merely of private grievance[5].

1   Public Health Act 1961, s 81 and Magistrates' Courts Act 1980, s 58.
2   Powers of Criminal Courts (Sentencing) Act 2000, s 131.
3   Magistrates' Courts Act 1980, s 127
4   Eg Public Health Act 1936, s 298.
5   *R v Hicks* (1855) 19 JP 515.

Costs—criminal and civil

21.21 An accused may, on conviction, be ordered to pay some or all of the prosecutor's costs, but if he is under 17 these must not exceed the fine imposed. If the information is dismissed the prosecutor may be ordered to pay his costs[1].

Courts, in addition, have power to order payment of costs out of central funds in certain cases.

A magistrates' court has a discretion to order the unsuccessful party to pay some or all of the successful party's costs[2], and in some particular cases it may order a successful party to pay the other party's costs. The amount may include witness expenses as well as solicitors' fees.

A party who claims such costs from the other side or from central funds should ask the court to incorporate the necessary clause in its order. It will not usually do so of its own motion.

1   See Prosecution of Offences Act 1985, s 18.
2   Magistrates' Courts Act 1980, s 64.

Civil court proceedings

21.22 To recover property or a larger debt or to secure damages for a civil wrong such as a grave trespass, a council may have to take action in the civil courts. Their jurisdiction is classified by the value of the claim, In a case of a debt worth less than £10,000 it should use the cheaper county court small claims procedure, and seek the advice of the court officials in operating it. A larger claim should be pursued through the formal county court proceedings or, if it exceeds £50,000, in the High Court.

G   PUBLIC NOTICES

21.23 Special statutory exceptions apart, any public notice required to be given by a local council, chairman of a parish meeting or joint committee of local councils must be given by affixing the notice in some conspicuous place or places in the locality and, in addition, in such other manner as appears to be desirable for giving publicity to the notice[1], such as by proclamation or advertisement in the press, or the employment of a town crier. Expenditure upon such publicity must be reasonable.

A notice of any meeting open to the public by statute must, in addition, be posted at the local council's offices (if any) and if none then in a central and conspicuous place[2].

1   Local Government Act 1972, s 232.

² Public Bodies (Admission to Meetings) Act 1960, s 1(4).

Destruction or damage

21.24 Destruction or damage to notices or notice boards is an offence punishable by fine or imprisonment[1].

¹ Criminal Damage Act 1971, ss 1 and 4.

Fixtures bulletins and newsletters

21.25 In many localities a monthly bulletin of future events and fixtures, or a newsletter, is published, usually by voluntary effort. A local council can assist this enterprise from the 'free resource', but apart from this it can pay to ensure that its own official notices are inserted.

H   SERVICE OF DOCUMENTS

21.26 Notices, orders and documents, other than those used in court proceedings, required to be sent, delivered or served upon a local council, its clerk or chairman must be left at or sent by post, addressed to the council at its office. For a parish meeting they go to the chairman[1].

A document contained in a letter which is properly addressed, stamped and posted is deemed, unless the contrary is proved, to have been served when the letter would have been delivered in the ordinary course of post[2], but this rule applies only to documents to be served under Acts passed since 1 January 1890.

Documents required by law to be sent by registered post may be sent by recorded delivery[3].

¹ Local Government Act 1972, s 231.
² Interpretation Act 1978.
³ Recorded Delivery Service Act 1962, s 1.

I   BYELAWS GENERALLY

Local council

21.27 Byelaws must be made under hand and seal and have no effect until confirmed[1]. The confirming authority is the Secretary of State for Communities and Local Government (in Wales, the Welsh Assembly) unless some other authority (for example, in the case of dog control and byelaws relating to the countryside, the Secretary of State for Environment, Food and Rural Affairs) is (rarely) specified in the enactment under which the byelaws are made[2]. Model byelaws have been issued by the Department for Communities and Local Government on pleasure grounds (model byelaw 2), amusement premises (model byelaw 3), pleasure fairs (model byelaw 4), promenades (model byelaw 5), seashore (model byelaw 6), good rule and government (model byelaw 8), markets (model byelaw 10). Where it is desired to pass a byelaw which departs from a standard model, it is wise to consult the relevant department beforehand.

[1] Local Government Act 1972, s 236(3).
[2] LGA 1972, s 236(11).

Good rule and government

21.28 Where a byelaw seems to be needed but the local council has no power to make one, the district council (T) should be asked to make it.

Procedure

21.29 At least one month before the council intends to apply for confirmation, notice of intention to apply must be advertised in a local newspaper and a copy of the proposed byelaws must be available for inspection at all reasonable hours at the council's offices. A copy, at a price not exceeding 10p per 100 words, must be furnished to every person applying for it[1].

The confirming authority may confirm or refuse to confirm and may fix the date when the byelaws are to come into operation, but if no date is so fixed they come into operation one month after confirmation[2]; they must be printed or reproduced by some mechanical process, and open to free inspection at all reasonable times, and copies must be furnished to any applicant at a price not exceeding 20p[3].

[1] Local Government Act 1972, s 236(4)–(6).
[2] LGA 1972, s 236(7).
[3] LGA 1972, s 236(8).

District council byelaws (special cases)

21.30 A district council (T) may make byelaws for the management of its cemeteries, and, if it does, a local council may adopt them for the management of its own[1].

In three cases a district council (T) must give notice to a local council if it intends to take power to exercise certain powers of regulation or byelaw making[2]. These cases relate to Hackney Carriage licences[3], and seashore and promenade byelaws[4].

[1] Local Government Act 1972, Sch 26, para 11.
[2] LGA 1972, Sch 14, para 25.
[3] Public Health Act 1875, s 171(4) and Public Health Act 1925, s 76.
[4] Public Health (Amendment) Act 1907, ss 82 and 83.

Enforcement

21.31 Constables may prosecute for the enforcement of byelaws[1].

[1] Local Government (Miscellaneous Provisions) Act 1982, s 12.

Penalties

21.32 Byelaws may fix reasonable fines, recoverable on summary conviction, not exceeding the amount fixed by the enabling Act or, if no amount is fixed, not exceeding level 1, and in the case of a continuing offence £5 for each day during which the offence continues after conviction[1].

[1] Local Government Act 1972, s 237.

Undesirability

21.33 Byelaws are seldom effective and therefore seldom desirable. Before seeking to make one, a council should consider whether the mischief can be cured in some other way; for example a shallow ditch is more likely to deter illicit parking in a village green than a byelaw on a notice board which nobody reads.

Obsolete byelaws

21.34 Byelaws in force before 1 April 1974 remain in force in their original area despite boundary changes or the repeal of the enactment under which they were made[1], but the Home Secretary can adapt them to new areas or circumstances, or revoke any such older byelaws if he thinks that they are spent, obsolete or unnecessary[2].

[1] Local Government Act 1972, ss 262(1)–(5), 272(2) and *DPP v Jackson* (1990) 88 LGR 876.
[2] LGA 1972, s 262(8).

New legislation

England

21.35 Part 6 of the Local Government and Public Involvement in Health Act 2007 (ss 129–135) simplifies procedures for making and enforcing local authority byelaws. Detailed proposals based on the legislation were published by the Secretary of State in August 2008 entitled *The making and enforcement of byelaws*[1]. They envisage that the powers in Part 6 will be used to introduce new procedures for local authorities to make byelaws and enforce them through fixed penalty notices, but only in relation to local authority byelaws which are confirmed by the Secretary of State for Communities and Local Government.

Part 6 of the Local Government and Public Involvement in Health Act 2007 enables the Secretary of State to make regulations establishing a new procedure for local authorities to follow in making byelaws. The intention is that this power will be used so that once local authorities have consulted on, prepared and advertised draft byelaws locally, they can be enacted without confirmation by the Secretary of State. He will have the power to make regulations dealing in particular with consultation on, and the advertisement of, byelaws locally and the power to issue guidance in relation to the new procedures. At the time of writing no regulations had been made.

Part 6 also provides for the enforcement of byelaws through fixed penalty notices, as an alternative to enforcement through magistrates' courts. This will bring the enforcement of byelaws on to the same footing as the enforcement of other low-level nuisance activities, and will facilitate a more coordinated approach to the enforcement of such matters.

Schedule 6 to the Act repeals some provisions relating byelaws. Section 82(4) of the Public Health Acts Amendment Act 1907 no longer provides that byelaws affecting the foreshore below high water require the consent of 'the Board of Trade' (which is now given by the Secretary of State for Transport). Section 231(1) of the Public Health Act 1936 is amended to repeal the provisions which relate to byelaws regulating the location of bathing-machines and the costumes to be worn by bathers. It also repeals the Public Health (Control of Disease) Act 1984, s 56(2) and (3), which provide for byelaws against the spread of infectious disease by the occupants or users of tents, vans, sheds and similar structures used for human habitation. This provision has never been used.

[1]   These can be viewed on the Communities and Local Government website at www.communities.gov.uk/publications/localgovernment/byelaws.

Wales

21.36 The Local Government Byelaws (Wales) Act 2012 makes new provision of the making of byelaws in Wales. The Act is not yet in force.

J   RATE AND COUNCIL TAX PROCEEDINGS

The following is a summary only, and mostly derived from various parts of the Local Government Finance Act 1988 (non-domestic rating) and the Local Government Finance Act 1992 (council tax), which is complicated and disorderly.

21.37 Any rate or council tax payer (including a council) may dispute the extent of his liability, or in some cases resist payment.

The first step is to write to the listing or valuation officer requesting a change in the relevant item in his register or valuation list. This is called a proposal. If this has no effect, more formal steps may be taken.

The local Valuation Tribunals hear council tax appeals, but first the aggrieved person must serve a written notice stating the matter by which and the grounds on which he is aggrieved. If the grievance concerns an estimate of the amount payable or the imposition of a penalty, the notice must be served on the billing authority: in other cases, on the officer. The aggrieved person must then wait two months or until (within that period) he has been notified that the grievance is rejected (with reasons for rejection) or that named steps are being taken to remedy it. Only if a grievance still remains may the appeal be taken to the tribunal. Where a proposal is rejected, the proposer may appeal to the tribunal or the dispute may be referred to arbitration. From the tribunal, valuation appeals go to the Lands Tribunal; appeals on points of law, to the High Court.

Judicial review

21.38 Certain large issues such as the setting of a council tax or precept can be challenged only by applying for judicial review to a High Court judge. If the judge gives leave to proceed, the review itself is conducted by a Divisional Court of two judges.

Liability orders and their enforcement

21.39 Where money is due to a billing authority, it may apply to a magistrates' court for a liability order which can be enforced by attachment of earnings or by a distress warrant for the seizure and sale of the debtor's goods. In either case the debtor may appeal to the magistrates.

K   FINES GENERALLY

21.40 The Criminal Justice Act 1991, s 17(1) substituted in Acts passed before 1977 a standard scale in five levels of fines instead of those laid down in those Acts. The highest amount in each level can be varied by statutory instrument. Thus the maximum fines are the amount in the standard scale next above the amount stated in the original Act, unless that stated amount is the same as a figure in the scale, in which case there is no change. The Act at present governs the upper limits in each level as follows:

Level 1	£200
Level 2	£500
Level 3	£1,000
Level 4	£2,500
Level 5	£5,000

Chapter 22

LOCAL COUNCILS IN LOCAL LIFE

22.1 The usefulness of a local council may be considered in terms of voluntary activities and legal powers. The voluntary activities arise from the versatility of village life. The members of the council may unite in their persons the majority of the leading positions in all the local clubs and societies. A council so constituted is locally influential even if it seldom exercises its legal powers, and it is in a position to focus the effort and opinion of those by whom it is elected.

A   SPECIFIC POWERS CLASSIFIED

Origin and juridical nature

22.2 The legal powers of local councils used to be classified according to their origin into powers descended respectively from the vestry, the churchwardens, the churchwardens and overseers, or overseers alone[1], 'additional' powers conferred in 1894[2], and miscellaneous powers conferred since 1894. These last have become numerous and are better considered by their juridical nature, namely into powers of provision, support and service, of supervision, consultation and complaint, of appointment and of bye-legislation and enforcement.

[1]   Local Government Act 1894, s 6.
[2]   LGA 1894, s 8(1).

Financial order

22.3 The legal powers may be considered from the point of view of the financial resources behind them and the, now few, limitations placed by law upon those resources. There are general powers whose expense is not restrained by law; powers whose expense is legally restricted; 'delegated' powers whose expense is borne wholly or partly by another authority; powers whose expense is borne by some fund other than rates and council tax; and powers involving no expenditure.

Degree of independence

22.4 Third, powers may be considered from the standpoint of the formalities which are needed before they can be exercised. Most, for example the purchase of land, can be exercised without any, but some such as the raising of a loan, require the previous intervention of another body.

Ancillary powers

22.5 Local authorities have ancillary powers to do anything calculated to facilitate or conducive or incidental to the discharge of any of their functions[1]; for instance, power to maintain a building is inherent in power to provide it, and includes authority to insure it against damage. The obligation to keep proper records, minutes and accounts and to issue notices implies power to make adequate office arrangements. The conduct of public affairs involves an obligation to be businesslike, and therefore to obtain necessary advice, and to give employees reasonable means of improving their skill.

[1] Local Government Act 1972, s 111.

Common law powers

22.6 Local councils had some common law powers conferred upon them by statute, because the powers, duties and liabilities of the vestry (including the inhabitants whether assembled in vestry or not and any select vestry by statute or common law[1]) were conferred upon parish councils in 1894[2] except in so far as they related to church affairs or ecclesiastical charities or were transferred from the vestry to some other authority. Hence, if it can be shown that a vestry exercised a power by a custom enforceable at common law, that power will have descended in the absence of legislative interference to the local council; it is, for instance, by virtue of this that some local councils are entitled to meet in the vestry or even in the church; and there are probably other examples.

[1] Local Government Act 1894, s 75(2).
[2] LGA 1894, s 6.

Local legislation

22.7 Local councils sometimes exercise functions conferred upon them by local Acts, or orders. They should make inquiries with county councils (T) concerning these, which were mostly promoted in Parliament by the latter but they ceased to have effect in metropolitan counties at the end of 1980 and elsewhere at the end of 1984 unless, in either case, replaced by new local enactments or orders[1].

[1] Local Government Act 1972, s 262.

B   ULTRA VIRES

22.8 Any body which acts beyond its legal powers is said to act *ultra vires*.

Local councils are statutory corporations and 'have therefore only such powers as are conferred upon them by statute and will be restrained by the courts if they act *ultra vires*'; after due allowance is made for ancillary powers this means in theory that a local authority can do nothing whatever without express statutory permission. The inconveniences, not to say absurdities, inherent in this rule if pushed to its logical conclusion, have led to limitations in its application and to some exceptions recognised by statute. Thus:

(a)   the Local Government Act 1972, s 111 empowers a local council to do anything (whether or not involving the expenditure, borrowing or lending of money or the acquisition or disposal of property or rights) which is calculated to facilitate, or is conducive or incidental to, the discharge of its functions. However, the raising of money by way of precept, rates or borrowing, and the lending of money, must be in accordance with the relevant statutory provisions governing these activities (eg the Local Government Finance Act 1992 governs the raising of precepts, and the Local Government Act 2003 governs borrowing);

(b)   the LGA 1972, s 137 empowers a local council to spend up to a prescribed amount in any one year (the 'free resource' described in **22.17** below) for the benefit of the inhabitants of the area or part of them;

(c)   the Localism Act 2011 empowers an 'eligible' parish council (but not a community council in Wales) to use the general power of competence conferred on principal authorities by section 1 of that Act (see **22.21** below);

(d)   the Local Government (Wales) Measure 2011 empowers community councils to use the power to promote well-being set out in the Local Government Act 2000 (see **35.21** below).

Advisory notices

22.9 Auditors, nowadays, are to some extent supervisors of future actions as well as investigators into the past. They may serve an advisory notice on a council or any of its committees or subcommittees or on an officer, if they have reason to believe that a decision is about to be or has been made involving unlawful expenditure, or a course of action is about to be taken or has been taken which, if pursued to its conclusion would be unlawful and likely to cause a deficiency, or an unlawful item of account is about to be entered.

The notice must be addressed to the body or officer concerned; it must specify the relevant paragraph of the Audit Commission Act 1998, s 19A(1) (in Wales, the Public Audit (Wales) Act 2004, s 33) under which it is issued, the matter to which it relates and the date when it is to take effect, and it requires the addressee to refer the matter to the auditor. It cannot, however, take effect unless the auditor has served a statement of his reasons on the addressee within seven days of service of the notice, and it may be revoked (but not varied). It remains in force until the addressee has considered the consequences of its intention and until the days (not exceeding 21) specified in the notice have expired.

Its effect, while in force, is to make the implementation of the decision, course of action or item of account unlawful[1] but where a contract relating to land was made before but not completed till after the notice was served, its existence does not prejudice any remedy in damages available to someone by reason of failure to complete the contract[2].

The body concerned, but not an officer, has a right of appeal to the High Court but this must be exercised within 28 days of the service of the statement of reasons. The auditor's expenses in connection with the notice can be recovered from the body or officer concerned.

It may be thought that supervision beforehand is undesirable as being incompatible with the auditor's duties exercisable after the event.

[1]   Audit Commission Act 1998, s 19A; Public Audit (Wales) Act 2004, s 33.
[2]   ACA 1998, s 19C; PA(W)A 2004, s 35.

Misuse of property

22.10 The foregoing exceptions to the rule of *ultra vires* relate only to unauthorised expenditure and cannot legalise something which would be illegal on other grounds. Action involving a crime or (more probably) a trespass or a breach of trust might still lead to proceedings in the courts based upon the nature of the acts complained of. Malice in the exercise of a council function, even where the council is exercising a private contractual right, is a cause of action for the tort of misfeasance in public office[1], giving rise to damages.

The general public has an interest in public property being used for the purposes for which it was acquired, and therefore proceedings are sometimes taken in the courts to restrain local authorities from putting property acquired for one purpose to a different use[2]. These vexations can now be mostly avoided by reappropriation (see **12.29** and **12.31** above).

[1]   *Jones v Swansea City Council* [1989] 3 All ER 162.
[2]   See *AG v Westminster City Council* (1924) 2 Ch 416, CA.

Judicial review

22.11 An auditor may apply to the High Court for judicial review of any decision by a council, its committees or sub-committees, or any failure of such a body to act, which it is reasonable to believe would affect the accounts, and may claim expenses for so doing from the body concerned.

It is not envisaged that councils should inform auditors of their intentions, nor that auditors should become their legal advisers.

Total absence of powers

22.12 A local authority can be restrained by injunction from doing something for which it has no statutory authority, even though it involves or has so far involved no expenditure. Such actions are rare and mostly brought by claimants whose property or commercial interests are affected.

Ultra vires contracts

22.13 An important effect of the rule of *ultra vires* is that a contract made by a local authority for a purpose not authorised by statute, or which in the case of a works contract is not made so as to comply with relevant legislation and regulations, is void and consequently a council cannot be sued upon it[1]; the liability falls personally upon, if anyone, the councillors or officials who authorised it; it also seems that the council cannot attempt to enforce such a contract.

[1] See *Ashbury Railway Carriage Co v Riche* (1875) LR 71 HL 653.

C   CONTROLS IN GENERAL

22.14 Besides the doctrine of *ultra vires*, British local government is still, despite recent pruning, riddled with controls. Many of these (such as the need to obtain agreement for a loan) are exercised by a central ministry. Others (such as planning) are administered by other local authorities. The details appear elsewhere; here it may be worth noticing certain general characteristics which they exhibit as a class.

The local man

22.15 For practical reasons, the more distant the controlling authority the more it has to depend upon local sources for information. An application for a speed limit will invariably result in the relevant department consulting the Chief Constable; negotiations for a loan may involve, besides the Association of Local Councils, specialist bodies such as the Regional Arts Association or Sports Council, depending on the purpose of the loan. It follows that a friendly acquaintanceship with the other authorities and the local representatives of central departments is increasingly important to sound administration.

Money and policy

22.16 There are subtle forms of control exercised through the manipulation of funds. It may, for instance, be difficult without great determination to carry out some operation (such as laying out a playing field) with local resources alone. A grant from another body may be a great relief to the local payers: but the body that offers grants may impose conditions; if the proportion of the grant to proposed expenditure is high, the conditions may not seem very onerous in comparison with the advantages achieved, and so the money is difficult to refuse. Thus grant-administering bodies (not all of which are statutory) can and do exercise a strong influence in local administration; in theory their ideas can be rejected: in fact acceptance of them can be less than voluntary. Again the funds are administered by central and by local bodies: amongst them are the Rural Community Buildings Loan Fund of ACRE and the Carnegie Trust, and these have to rely for guidance upon local organisations whom they trust. As a result, Voluntary Service Councils usually act as a channel for negotiations with the appropriate central body.

One way to rationalise these various forms of control is to use a Local Councils' Association, whose function (amongst others) is to obtain general principles to guide their administration. These organisations are often closely associated with Voluntary Service Councils and in some cases have played a leading part in forming them.

D   THE 'FREE RESOURCE'

22.17 Subject to certain formalities, a council, but not a parish meeting, may spend in a single financial year up to a prescribed limit for any purpose which in its opinion is in the interests of or will directly benefit the area or its inhabitants, or of part of it, or of some of them. The limit was set at £5 per head of the number of local government electors for the locality on 1 January before the commencement of the financial year for the financial year beginning on 1 April 2004[1]. Legislation also provides for the limit to rise in accordance with the movement of the Retail Prices Index in subsequent years. In England and Wales, the limit from 1 April 2013 is £6.98 per head.

To calculate whether the expenditure in a given year is within the limit, certain items are omitted as indicated in the following formula:

$E \times (D + G + L + S + R + C)$ must be less than $N \times £6.98$ (in England and Wales),

where:

- D = expenditure which would be part of the local council's gross expenditure if a principal (Donor) council had not made a donation of the money to the local council under section 137[2];
- E = expenditure from the Resource;
- G = the amount of any Grant towards E from the government, the European Regional Development Fund or Social Fund;
- L = the amount of the repayment of any Loan raised to finance E;
- S = the amount of any public Subscription spent by the council for the purpose of E;
- R = the amount of the Repayment of any loan made under section 137 by the council;
- C = the amount of any expenditure incurred by the council in Circumstances specified by the Secretary of State or defrayed by a grant or payment to the council of the specified description; and
- N = Number of local government electors[3].

The purpose cannot include political publicity or the promotion of homosexuality, and publicity expenditure in favour of a public body or voluntary organisation must be confined to the main purpose for which assistance is given to it. It follows that publicity expenditure by itself alone is not permitted[4]. The power includes power to contribute to the expenses of another local authority, and to contribute to charities for the furtherance of their work in the United Kingdom, to the funds of any body which provides a public service in the United Kingdom otherwise than for gain, and to any fund raised in connection with a particular event, directly affecting residents in the United Kingdom, by the Lord Mayor of London or the chairman of a principal council or by an appeal committee of which he or they are a member[5], but where assistance worth £2,000 or more is given to a voluntary body, the body must be required within twelve months to state in writing the use to which the money (or other help) has been put[6].

Where a local council accepts a gift of property for the benefit of the inhabitants of its area or part of it and not for the purpose of discharging one of its statutory functions, the cost of maintaining it is chargeable to this account[7].

1   Local Government Act 1972, Sch 12B, para 2 (inserted by Local Government Act 2003, s 118).
2   Local Authorities (Expenditure Powers) Order 1995, SI 1995/3304.
3   SI 2000/990.
4   Local Government Act 1986 as amended by Local Government Act 1988, ss 27 and 28, and Local Government (Discretionary Expenditure) (Relevant Population) Regulations 1993, SI 1993/40.
5   LGA 1972, s 137.
6   LGA 1972, s 137A.
7   LGA 1972, s 139.

Accounts and resolutions

22.18 A separate account must be kept and be open to public inspection and (which is a corollary) expenditure under the section must be specifically authorised by resolution[1]. It is not enough to plead at audit that if an item is unauthorised by a statute the section will cover it. The following form of resolution may be regarded as suitable:

> 'Resolved that the Council in accordance with its powers under sections 137 and 139 of the Local Government Act 1972, should incur the following expenditure which, in the opinion of the Council, is in the interests of the area or its inhabitants and will benefit them in a manner commensurate with the expenditure:—
>
> [here set it out]'

1   See para **22.17**, note 6 above.

Nature of the power

22.19 The council is the judge of what is or is not in the interests of the area or inhabitants provided that there is some ground for saying that the direct benefit is commensurate with the expenditure[1]. This probably lets in the auditor's judgment.

The powers of an existing statute must be used if there are any. The principle of this is simple enough, but the exact application may sometimes be complicated by a prohibition against '[Expenditure] for a purpose for which they are either unconditionally or subject to a limitation or to the satisfaction of any condition authorised or required by or by virtue of any enactment other than this section to make any payment.'

A limitation appears to mean a statutory clog on the exercise of a power within a place where it can otherwise be exercised without the limitation. The most obvious example was the limitation on the deficit on the allotments account.

It does not seem to refer to a geographical limitation: thus a council can under the War Memorials (Local Authorities' Powers) Act 1923 only maintain, repair and protect a war memorial in its area; therefore it can spend money under the section for a memorial outside; nor does it seem to apply to the definition of a power itself; a council could use the section to pay for doing something to a war memorial which was not maintenance, repair or protection, eg it could re-site it. An omission is not a limitation.

The satisfaction of any condition refers to something which is required to be done by a local council before it can exercise a power which it already has. For example, under s 5 of the Parish Councils Act 1957, it is required to obtain certain consents before exercising its powers to place seats and shelters in particular positions. The section cannot be used to evade such conditions but, on the other hand, it could be used to pay for seats, or shelters in situations (such as private property) which were not authorised by the Act of 1957 at all.

Though the section may not be used if there is already a power conferred upon the council by some other enactment, this does not prevent it being used to effect something which another type of authority has power to do.

1   Local Government Act 1972, s 137(1).

Actual uses

22.20 The following are examples of actual uses to which the power is known to have been put by local councils.

(a)   Class 1: *small public properties*
     (i)   seat outside the parish
     (ii)   memorial plaques
     (iii)   film projector
     (iv)   repair of a bier-house
     (v)   kerbing, resurfacing road or market
     (vi)   set of parish china
     (vii)   invalid wheelchair
     (viii)   public telephone
     (ix)   doctor's car radio
     (x)   culvert
     (xi)   bus turning-bay
     (xii)   village surgery
     (xiii)   duckhouse for village pond
     (xiv)   repair of sheepwash
     (xv)   repair of shipway
(b)   Class 2: *preservation or restoration of old objects or buildings*
     (i)   churches and chapels
     (ii)   stocks, firehooks, pinfolds
     (iii)   windmill
     (iv)   biers
     (v)   market and village cross
     (vi)   contribution to local preservation society
     (vii)   pounds
     (viii)   jubilee arch
(c)   Class 3: *improvement of appearance of villages*

       (i)   civic trust type 'face lift' scheme
       (ii)   removal of slaughterhouse
       (iii)   planning competition
       (iv)   landscaping
       (v)   garden competition prizes
       (vi)   local garden centre
       (vii) best-kept village competition
       (viii) litter competitions
       (ix)   village sweeper
       (x)   beach cleansing
       (xi)   junk disposal or bottle bank
       (xii) clearance of commons
       (xiii) tidying land of unknown ownership
       (xiv) planting trees, shrubs and flowers

(d)   Class 4: *influence*
       (i)   propaganda for civic centre
       (ii)   contribution to Anti-Third London Airport Campaign
       (iii)   support of organisations such as River Thames Society, Railway Protection Association

(e)   Class 5: *ceremonial and entertainment*
       (i)   Christmas trees
       (ii)   chains or badges of office
       (iii)   sports prizes
       (iv)   beating bounds
       (v)   civic entertainments and services
       (vi)   flower shows, festivals and fairs
       (vii) flags
       (viii) exhibitions

(f)   Class 6: *safety*
       (i)   fencing dangerous places
       (ii)   first-aid post
       (iii)   road warden
       (iv)   inshore rescue service
       (v)   old people's distress cards and lights
       (vi)   safety competitions
       (vii) road markings
       (viii) lectures on artificial respiration
       (ix)   safety posts and bollards
       (x)   ambulance competition entries
       (xi)   accident committees
       (xii) life-belts and lifeguards
       (xiii) flood prevention

(g)   Class 7: *public information*
       (i)   parish fixture lists and bulletins
       (ii)   local publicity association
       (iii)   letters of welcome to newcomers

(h)   Class 8: *contributions to voluntary bodies without premises*
       (i)   play groups and youth clubs

(i)   Class 9: *social welfare*
       (i)   flood relief
       (ii)   mobile physiotherapy unit

        (iii)   new ambulance
        (iv)   assistance for the handicapped
        (v)   meals on wheels
        (vi)   welfare organisations
        (vii)   marriage guidance and family planning
        (viii)   sickness fund
        (ix)   collection of medicines from distant dispensaries
        (x)   village librarian
        (xi)   day nursery
        (xii)   Samaritans

(j)   Class 10: *recognition of exceptional or outstanding public service*
        (i)   non-pecuniary testimonials on retirement
        (ii)   gratuity to youths making historical discoveries

(k)   Class 11: *communication*
        (i)   repair of ford
        (ii)   temporary roads, private streets
        (iii)   'no parking' signs

(l)   Class 12: *educational*
        (i)   history and local government lectures
        (ii)   further education grant
        (iii)   Duke of Edinburgh's scheme
        (iv)   compilation of village history
        (v)   Prince of Wales's Trust
        (vi)   essay competitions

(m)   Class 13: *miscellaneous*
        (i)   co-operative Christmas crib
        (ii)   restocking of river with trout
        (iii)   flower and vegetable show
        (iv)   village handyman
        (v)   purchase of South-East study

E   POWER OF GENERAL COMPETENCE

22.21 Part 1 of the Localism Act 2011 provides for local authorities in England to have a general power of competence. Section 1 of the Act gives principal authorities and "eligible" parish councils a power to do anything that generally individuals of full age (ie over 18) can do. The power (with some restrictions – see below, **22.25**) can be exercised in any way whatever, including:

(a)   anywhere in the United Kingdom or elsewhere;

(b)   for a commercial purpose or otherwise for a charge, or without charge; and

(c)   for, or otherwise than for, the benefit of the authority, its area or persons resident or present in its area.

The generality of the power is not limited by the existence of any other power of the authority which (to any extent) overlaps the general power.

Eligible parish councils

22.22 A parish council (but not a parish meeting of a parish where there is no parish council) is eligible if it comes within the compass of the Parish Councils (General Power of Competence) (Prescribed Conditions) Order 2012 (SI 2012/965). The Order lays down the following conditions for eligibility:

(1)   The council has resolved at a meeting of the council and each subsequent relevant annual meeting that it meets the conditions below.

(2)   At the time a resolution under paragraph 1 above is passed:

    (a)   the number of members of the council that have been declared to be elected, whether at ordinary elections or at a by-election, is equal to or greater than two-thirds of the total number of members of the council;

    (b)   the clerk to the parish council holds:

        (i)   the Certificate in Local Council Administration;

        (ii)   the Certificate of Higher Education in Local Policy;

        (iii)   the Certificate of Higher Education in Local Council Administration; or

        (iv)   the first level of the foundation degree in Community Engagement and Governance awarded by the University of Gloucestershire or its successor qualifications; and

    (c)   the clerk to the parish council has completed the relevant training, unless such training was required for the purpose of obtaining a qualification of a description mentioned in paragraph (b) above.

For the purposes of this paragraph "relevant training" means training:

    (a)   in the exercise of the general power;

    (b)   provided in accordance with the national training strategy for parish councils adopted by the National Association of Local Councils, as revised from time to time.

22.23 A parish council which has adopted the general power of competence cannot also incur expenditure under the Localism Act 2011, section 137, except under section 137(3) which empowers a council to donate to UK based charities, bodies providing a public service in the UK and public appeals for funds in relation to specific events affecting UK residents.

22.24 The power to promote well being enacted by the Local Government Act 2000 has been repealed in England but remains in force in Wales (see **35.21** below).

Limits on the general power

22.25 The Localism Act 2011, section 2 sets out the boundaries of the general power, requiring local authorities to act in accordance with statutory limitations or restrictions. Limitations that apply to existing powers that are overlapped by the general power are applied to the general power. So for instance if an existing power requires a particular procedure to be followed, the same procedure will apply to the use of the general power to do the same thing. It also applies any express prohibitions, restrictions and limitations within primary or secondary legislation, to the use of the general power. A distinction is drawn between restrictions in pre-commencement legislation, and those in post-commencement legislation. Restrictions in post-commencement legislation will only apply to the general power where they are expressed to do so. The general power does not enable a local authority to make arrangements for the discharge of its functions or for governance beyond what is permitted under the Local Government Acts 1972 and 2000.

22.26 The Localism Act 2011, section 3 restricts the ability of a local authority to charge for providing a service to a person using the general power, or where they are using an overlapped power. Local authorities can charge up to the full cost of recovery for discretionary services. Section 93 of the Local Government Act 2003 gives relevant authorities – including parish and community councils and parish meetings – power to charge for discretionary services related to specific statutory functions.

22.27 The Localism Act 2011, section 5 enables the Secretary of State:

- to remove or change statutory provisions that prevent or restrict use of the general power;
- to similarly amend or repeal etc legislation to remove overlaps between the general power and existing powers;
- to restrict what a local authority may do under the general power or to make its use subject to conditions.

F   PROMOTION OF WELL-BEING (WALES ONLY)

22.28 This subject is covered in **35.21** below.

G   'QUALITY' COUNCILS

22.29 The Quality Parish and Town Council Scheme is set out in *The Quality Parish and Town Council Scheme; the Quality Scheme Explained* published by the Department for Communities and Local Government. It is out of print but can be viewed on and downloaded from the Department's website.

The Scheme applies only in England. For the position in Wales, see **35.24** below.

H   CITIZENS' ADVICE BUREAUX AND SIMILAR BODIES

22.30 There is a separate power to assist bodies such as Citizens' Advice Bureaux in advising individuals and by making or receiving communications or by providing representation to or before 'any body or person in asserting' an individual's rights or obligations[1]. This remarkably wide enactment seems to amount to a form of legal aid, for it seems to enable a local council to assist an individual in asserting rights which it does not necessarily itself possess.

---

[1]   Local Government Act 1972, s 142(2A).

I   VOLUNTARY ACTIVITIES

22.31 In most localities (except the very large and the very small) there is a meeting point between the statutory or official organisation of the state and the voluntary bodies. This is often the local council. The most effective administration is one in which there is a marriage of minds between the statutory and the voluntary sides of social organisation. The older settled form of village and small town life is giving way to something more mobile. A village has to maintain its social life by a more self-conscious effort than was formerly needed, and this has led to the widespread rise of village societies of all kinds, and often to the creation of national organisations of such societies.

The table at the end of this chapter represents a conspectus of the kind of activity which nowadays leads to the formation of a voluntary organisation and will indicate the ways in which help from the statutory side may be needed: broadly these consist in preliminary encouragement, trusteeship, or the provision of premises (especially for meetings) or land, or a judicious combination of all these.

Most of the activities in the table will breed separate committees which need to meet somewhere, in addition to the gatherings which the activities themselves involve.

Weaknesses of voluntary bodies

22.32 In any fair-sized village many of the activities mentioned are either in progress or desired; some of them must in their nature be confined to daylight hours and are therefore restricted to the young, the unemployed or to weekends; others in practice have to be restricted to evenings. Tastes vary: it is not possible to be in more than one place at once, or to have two functions in the same place at the same time; in younger families someone has to stay at home to mind the baby, and there is always the pub. Bringing all these factors into account and making allowances for cross-membership, most voluntary organisations will obviously be small and poor. If a village has 1,000 inhabitants and its people indulge in only half the activities in the table, the average attendance per activity is unlikely to exceed 30, and the composition of each 30 will be changing continually.

The main weaknesses of such bodies are that they are hard to launch, liable to disintegrate, and mostly unable to provide their own premises or land. Local councils are equipped by law to provide most of the remedies for these defects.

Encouragement at the start

22.33 A local council can legitimately spend from the 'free resource' to encourage the formation or development of some potentially valuable organisation. Apart from this, however, it can help a new body by lending equipment or premises and by helping them to publicise their objects and meetings on noticeboards and in bulletins. A local council should ensure that its willingness to do these things is known.

Permanence

22.34 Most voluntary societies have funds and small bank accounts. If a society disintegrates and those entitled to operate the accounts die or leave the district or become otherwise disengaged, these balances may be wasted. This happens all too frequently.

A local council, being a corporation, never dies and this fact can be used to provide the required stiffening in two ways. Where funds or other property are provided with charitable or public objects it can itself act as trustee for the benefit of the organisations interested; this often happens in the case of village halls.

Its advantage is that no further appointment is necessary; the disadvantage that the funds have to be brought into account for the assessment of audit charges. Alternatively the council can be given power to nominate the trustees instead of acting as a trustee itself; this can be done whether or not the objects of the fund are charitable or public, and no question of audit or audit charges arises.

Lands and buildings

22.35 The legal powers of local councils to provide or help to provide lands and buildings for voluntary activities are very comprehensive. The practical problem is to provide an adequate and also economical substructure for a vigorous social life. Some villages have no meeting place; others have too many all in poor condition; lands have often been acquired haphazardly and without relation to each other or so that they are no longer adequate for their purpose, or simple or cheap to maintain; and bad siting and over-specialisation of types and poor insulation and heating may lead to underuse.

The ideal is a recreational and community centre[1] comprising all the necessary lands and buildings (with a caretaker's residence), the whole being situated so that it is not difficult for anyone in the village to walk to it. Such an ideal is worth stating even if it is rarely attainable.

A glance at the table will show that if the design is well thought out many different activities can be accommodated in one building, namely the village or parish hall with which a pavilion can sometimes be combined. A stage or platform is equally desirable for a play, a parish meeting, a dance band, or a lecture. Changing rooms can serve both actors and cricketers. The eventual (if not immediate) ownership and use of a projector and the likelihood of exhibitions should be foreseen. There should be a separate place for smaller meetings, a kitchen and lavatories. Some halls have a room with a separate door for occasional use as a village surgery; others have an outside booth with a public telephone. There must be a reasonable degree of bodily comfort; audiences become restive on ill designed chairs, and soon disperse in the cold. Insulation, double-glazed windows, and storage or infrared heating are good investments. The capital cost may at first seem high but the important factor in the long run is the cost (both on maintenance and on capital account) per hour of actual use. A village cannot afford a building which is not used.

Similar principles apply in satisfying other demands. Playing fields should be laid out so that they are capable of use both in winter and in summer, and if land of the right sort is scarce or prohibitively expensive, facilities for games playing in enclosures (such as tennis or bowls) or in small buildings (such as fives) should be considered.

Sports and Games

	Vigorous		Placid	
	I(L)	II(S)	I(L)	(II)S
In the open air	Football	Netball	Camping	Bowls
	Cricket	Tennis		Croquet
	Archery			Boule
In buildings	Gymnastics	Squash	Billiards	Chess
	Badminton	Fives	Bingo	Cards*
	Dancing	Rackets	Snooker	Darts
		Pelota	Pool	Other board games eg Backgammon, Monopoly, Wei-Chi
Water		Swimming		Fishing
		Boating		
		Sailing		

	Cultural	Welfare	Social and Official
In the open air			Fêtes
In buildings	Debating	Old people	Church functions
	Drama	Play groups*	Dances
	Music	Nursery schools	Occasional celebrations
	Literature*	Youth clubs	Local Council
	Local history*	Meals on wheels	Parochial church council
	Archaeology	Welfare cars	British Legion
	Civic societies		Electors' meetings
	Exhibitions		
	Best kept village		

I(L) — Large resources needed; II(S) — Small resources needed; *Often occur in private homes.

1   By a convention 'village hall' means a hall managed under a charitable trust deed usually
     modelled on that provided by ACRE; 'parish hall' or 'community hall' means a hall provided
     and managed by a local council under its statutory powers. 'Community centre' means much
     the same but is in a town. It is not here used in this restricted sense.

J   CRIME AND DISORDER

22.36 Local councils must exercise their functions with due regard to their likely effect, if any, on crime and disorder and the need to prevent them[1]. They may find it convenient to require the subject to be mentioned in each relevant agenda item.

1   Crime and Disorder Act 1998, s 17.

K   MARKETS

22.37 A local council has power to establish a market within its area or acquire (by agreement only) an existing market there. The council may provide a market place and necessary buildings, such as a market house. A market established by a council must not interfere with the rights of an already existing market without the consent of that market's proprietor[1].

The council may make byelaws for the regulation of its markets[2]. Model byelaws for markets are published by the Department for Communities and Local Government[3]. (For the making etc of byelaws generally see **21.27–21.29** above.)

1   Food Act 1984, ss 50–61.
2   Food Act 1984, s 61.
3   They can be viewed on their website at www.communities.gov.uk/publications/localgovernm
     ent/modelbyelaw7.

Chapter 23

CONCURRENCY, INDEPENDENCE AND CO-OPERATION

A   CONCURRENT FUNCTIONS

23.1 Before 1974 there had, broadly speaking, been a relationship of differing specialisation between the old parish and rural district councils, and even where powers, such as those under the former Physical Training and Recreation Acts, had been concurrent in law, rural district and parish councils generally agreed (tacitly or otherwise) to share out the responsibilities so as not to interfere with each other.

With certain important exceptions (mentioned in **23.5** below) the Local Government Act 1972 conferred upon district councils (T) the powers possessed by local councils, probably because the former were an amalgam of rural with urban areas, and the councils of the latter (where no parish councils had existed) had always had parish functions anyway. In many new districts the majority of district council members and many of the new staffs were unfamiliar with the uses of the local council and found it natural to attempt to provide, from a district centre, facilities which were more normally provided by local councils or local effort. In the long run the procedure for creating parish councils in English unparished areas is likely to change this.

Overlapping finance

23.2 Connected with this development was the existence in many English districts of the non-parochial place, and, in some Welsh ones, of the community without a council. In these 'blank' areas (which in England were numerous and often substantial) the district council (T) has to provide the 'local council' facilities itself if they are not to depend wholly on voluntary effort. The blank areas were strongly represented upon many district councils where their members were sometimes in a majority. Some yielded to the temptation to subsidise the local council facilities in the blank areas at the expense of the localities with councils, by charging the cost to the general district rate. This, though unfair, was seldom as serious as some of the local taxpayers tried to claim.

Uniform district (T) charges

23.3 A different type of development, loosely related to the subsidisation of blank areas, was represented by efforts to establish a uniform rate level for the whole of a given district. Such uniformity was, of course, reasonable in a town where it was easy for all the inhabitants to have access to all the services, but in large districts (T), the necessarily uneven nature of services provided for disparate, dissimilar and scattered villages made the fairness of such uniformity illusory; it resulted in some people paying for services they were not receiving, while others received services for which they underpaid.

These considerations justified the changes which came into effect on 1 April 1993. The district council (T) must, unless it specifically resolves otherwise, now set different amounts for its council tax on dwellings in areas for which a precept has been issued to it, to the extent that an item is not provided for by other means[1].

[1]   Local Government Finance Act 1992, ss 33–35.

Principles of good (or better) practice

23.4 In June 2003 the government issued guidance on best practice for England to avoid or minimise overlapping finance (called 'double taxation'). The guidance, issued in agreement with the National Association of Local Councils and the Local Government Association, provides some principles of good practice such as the imposition of a charge only upon taxpayers living in an area where a service is being provided, or the institution by a principal council of a system of grants to parish councils which provide a service on its behalf, or the transfer to a parish council of a package of services, some of which (for example parking) generate income. The guidance forms Appendix 3 to *The Quality Parish and Town Council Scheme* (see CHAPTER **22G**).

B   NON-CONCURRENT ACTIVITIES

Functions

23.5 The definition of a function is important, because with some exceptions authorities can arrange to discharge the 'functions' of other authorities[1] or pay for their discharge by other authorities[2]. It is not generally defined by statute. It appears to mean an activity specifically defined by law, decided by the authority as such, leading to action by its servants or agents, which directly affects the inhabitants of its area.

The most important non-concurrent function is that of providing allotments in England, where most of them are. A district council (T) may not provide allotments in a parish[3], and cannot provide them in exercise of the general power of competence (see CHAPTER **22E**)[4]. It is otherwise in Wales.

[1]   Local Government Act 1972, s 101.
[2]   LGA 1972, s 136.
[3]   LGA 1972, Sch 29, para 9(1).
[4]   Localism Act 2011, s 2(2).

Non-functions

23.6 The holding of meetings of an authority is not a function, nor is the holding of electors' meetings nor the payment of allowances.

The use of the 'free resource' is probably not a function; it is rather a legal right whose application is defined (within very wide limits) by the authority making use of it.

Other cases

23.7 Where one authority is obliged to notify another about something and to take into account its views on the matter notified, there is no concurrency, for the two authorities' activities with respect to the matter are complementary. Hence there is insufficient ground upon which one authority can contribute to the expenses, which might include the cost of expert advice, of the other save from the 'free resource'. This class of case includes the notification of intention to make use of certain powers of regulation and of intention to establish a cemetery[1].

[1]   See 33.8–33.19 below.

C   CO-OPERATION

Central provision and mutual assistance

23.8 There is a distinction between activity on a large scale (such as is required both by law and common sense in planning, water or the provision of roads) and the multiplication of small-scale activities (such as the management of many widely scattered properties). The former, being unavoidable, has to be accepted. The latter, particularly in large, mainly rural areas can be wasteful[1]. On the other hand a locality may need a facility (such as playing fields, swimming pool or a community centre) which, owing to local conditions such as the high cost of land, is financially over-burdensome. Between these two considerations there is much room for co-operation between the local and the district council (T). In particular the latter can help by looking favourably upon applications by local councils for compulsory purchase orders, and by being ready, especially in expanding villages, to help with capital finance in the form of grants or loans on favourable terms. The number of occasions when any particular local council will need assistance of these kinds is small—save in exceptional cases, probably not more than once in a generation.

Conversely the local councils can often help the district (T) authority by providing or managing properties which are of interest primarily to their own people. The cost per unit will be less, the district council's (T) overheads will be reduced, and local interest and satisfaction increased[2].

[1]   Eg in three large Berkshire parishes a proposal in 1965 to amalgamate their three lighting systems was rejected when costings revealed that the unified system would cost a 1d rate more than the three systems run separately, without the addition of a single light.

[2]   It is widely known (but so far unexplained) that usually village halls are better managed by representatives of the users than by public authorities, but that playing fields are better managed by local councils than by the users.

Arrangements between authorities generally

23.9 A local authority may arrange for any of its functions (except those mentioned in **7.43** above) to be discharged by a committee, subcommittee, or joint committee, or by one of its officers, or by any other local authority, which may in turn arrange for the business to be discharged by a committee or officer[1]. Delegation in the sense implied in the system existing before 1974 appears to have been abolished and arrangements between authorities can be extremely varied. The authorities concerned need not be adjacent nor in the same district or county; they need not be in adjacent tiers of local government; and there is legally no limit to the number of participating authorities.

[1]   Local Government Act 1972, s 101(1), (5) and (6).

Five main types of arrangement

23.10 The following approximate classification of co-operative arrangements may perhaps be found useful:

(a)   in *joint arrangements* managed by a joint committee, the co-operating authorities are exercising a function jointly over the whole of their areas or over such parts of them as they may agree;

(b)   in *consortia*, also usually managed by joint committees, the co-operating authorities create joint organisations (for example a works' department) of which each makes use for its own purposes, subject to the terms of the agreement between them;

(c)   in *agency arrangements* a (dominant) council empowers another (agent) council to carry out a function on its behalf. This kind of agency can be committed 'downwards' by a greater council to a lesser, or 'upwards' by a lesser to a greater or 'sideways' by one council to another of equal status. The agent necessarily has powers of decision;

(d)   *loan of staff.* some activities may need the help of another authority in a manner falling short of agency. Here the dominant authority keeps power to make or revise all the decisions, the loan of staff may be a suitable means of co-operation;

(e)   *joint teams* are numbers of officers pooled by different authorities to work upon a particular project of mutual concern.

The Quality Parish and Town Council Scheme gives information about model 'charters' whereby principal and local councils in England can work in partnership (see **22.29**).

NALC and the Local Government Association have jointly published advice entitled *Modellling Devolution*.

In Wales, a joint publication by the Welsh Assembly Government, the Welsh Local Government Association and One Voice Wales—*A shared community:*

relationship building and charters for unitary authorities and community and town councils—covers similar ground. For model charter agreements in Wales, see **35.23**.

D   POWERS OF APPOINTMENT

23.11 The power to appoint representatives to another body can be a vehicle for useful co-operation.

Primary schools

England

23.12 An English local council has no specific right to appoint a governor to a primary school. The legislation regarding school governors was re-cast by the Education Act 2002 and the right of English local councils to appoint a governor in certain cases was abolished, although existing governors continued to hold office until, at the latest, 31 August 2006.

Under the Education Act 2002 (as amended by the Education Act 2011) and regulations made thereunder, the governing body of a maintained school consists of a number of different categories of governor, two of which are foundation governor and co-opted governor. A foundation governor is defined, *inter alia*, as a person who is appointed for the purpose of securing that the character of the school is preserved and developed. A co-opted governor defined as a person whom the governing body thinks has the skills to contribute to the effective governance and success of the school[1]. Such persons could be local councillors.

[1]   School Governance (Constitution) (England) Regulations 2012, 2012/1034.

Wales

23.13 The Education Act 2002 applies in Wales and the general provisions relating to the appointment of governors are the same as for England. However, the instrument of government of a community, voluntary or foundation school which is a primary school and a maintained nursery school which serves the area of one or more community councils must provide for one community governor to be nominated by the community council. If the school serves the area of one of more community councils, the governors may seek nominations from one or more of those councils[1].

[1]   Government of Maintained Schools (Wales) Regulations 2005, SI 2005/2914, reg 20.

Trusts

23.14 Many trust deeds not caught by the law on charities, provide for local council representation on the trust (see **13.10** and **13.11** above).

E   PARISH MEMBERS OF ENGLISH NATIONAL PARK AUTHORITIES

23.15 Of the members of an English National Park authority, a number are appointed by the district (T) councils and the same number less two by the Secretary of State. Of this latter number half less one must be parish councillors for a parish or part of a parish within the park, or if there is no such parish council, the chairman of such a parish meeting. They hold their appointments till they cease to hold their respective offices but are eligible for reappointment on re-election. The terms of appointment are laid down by the Secretary of State[1].

[1]   Environment Act 1995, s 63 and Sch 7.

Chapter 24

CONSULTATION, REPRESENTATION AND NOTIFICATION

24.1 As observed in the Preface, the oversight and representational duties of local councils have, in a practical sense, become vastly widened as a result of the Local Government Acts of 1972 and 1992 (England) and 1994 (Wales). The Local Government Act 1972 contains complementary provisions for voluntary consultation and co-operation including the formation of joint executive and advisory committees (see CHAPTER 23). There are, however, cases where opportunities for consultation are imposed by law.

A   LESSER CASES

24.2 Though bodies such as British Telecom are not, generally speaking, required to notify their intentions about works to local councils, it is obviously important that they should do so particularly if the works involve digging up roads or footpaths. Life in a neighbourhood can be materially eased if people know what to expect. This is perhaps an issue upon which associations of local councils might negotiate.

The Secretary of State or a local highway authority intending to construct a road hump must consult organisations representing road users or others likely to be affected[1].

[1]   Highways (Road Humps) Regulations 1999, SI 1999/1025, reg 3.

District council (T) byelaws, etc

24.3 For the three types of case where a district council (T) wishing to take byelaw-making or regulating powers must notify the local council beforehand see **21.30** above.

Litter

24.4 For the special arrangements on litter see **30.5** below.

B   LICENSING ACT 2003

24.5 The Licensing Act 2003 reorganised the system of licensing in England and Wales. A licence is required for:

(a)   the retail sale of alcohol;
(b)   the supply of alcohol by a club to a member of the club or to the order of a club member;
(c)   the provision of regulated entertainment; and
(d)   the provision of night refreshment.

Supply to a club

24.6 Part 4 of the Licensing Act 2003 (ss 60–97) applies to clubs. Various conditions are laid down with which a club must comply in order to become a 'qualifying club' and able to be granted a licence. These conditions relate to membership, whether or not the club is a *bona fide* non-profit making body and whether or not the club intends to provide alcohol for members or members and their guests. The conditions are more stringent if the club wishes to provide alcohol.

As well as the factors in **24.5** above, the following are licensable activities in relation to a club:

(a)   the sale by retail of alcohol to a guest of a club member for consumption on the premises where the sale takes place; and
(b)   the provision of regulated entertainment by or on behalf of club members or club members and their guests.

Provision of regulated entertainment

24.7 'The provision of regulated entertainment' is defined in great detail in the Licensing Act 2003, Part 1, and Sch 1 (as amended by the Live Music Act 2012). It includes the performance of a play, the exhibition of a film, an indoor sporting event, a performance of live or recorded music and the performance of dance, so long as the activity takes place in the presence of an audience or of spectators and is provided for the purpose, wholly or partly, of entertaining the audience or the spectators.

To be a licensable activity, the entertainment must comply with two conditions. The first is that the entertainment is:

(a)   provided for members of the public or a section of the public;
(b)   provided for members of a qualifying club or for members and their guests;
(c)   if neither (a) or (b) applies, charged for with a view to making a profit.

The second condition is that the premises where the entertainment takes place are made available for the purpose of enabling the entertainment to take place (this obscure wording seems to mean that entertainment in premises which have not been specifically provided for the purpose—eg without the consent of the owner—does not qualify as regulated entertainment and is unlawful unless a licence has been obtained).

Late night refreshment

24.8 'The provision of late night refreshment' is defined in the Licensing Act 2003, Sch 2. A person provides late night refreshment if he supplies hot food or drink to members of the public between 11 pm and 5 am from any premises (defined in the LA 2003, s 193 as any place, including a vehicle, vessel or moveable structure). There are a number of exemptions. These include supplying hot food or drink to members of a recognised club, to persons staying in a hotel or comparable premises for the night in question, to a particular employee by his employer and where the premises are licensed under other legislation.

Licensing authorities

24.9 The licensing authorities are:

(a)   the council of a district in England;
(b)   the council of a county in England in which there are no district councils;
(c)   the council of a county or county borough in Wales;
(d)   the council of a London borough;
(e)   the Sub-Treasurer of the Inner Temple;
(f)   the Under-Treasurer of the Middle Temple; and
(g)   the Council of the Isles of Scilly.

The Licensing Act 2003 provides for the establishment of licensing committees by licensing authorities, the keeping of a register of licensed premises and the procedures for granting licences. Every licensing authority must prepare and publish a statement of licensing policy, following the general guidance given by the Secretary of State, currently for Culture, Media and Sport. The statement must be updated every three years.

Licences

24.10 In order to apply for a premises licence (ie a licence for any place including a vehicle, vessel or moveable structure) or a club premises certificate (in effect a premises licence for a club) an application must be completed and sent or delivered to the appropriate licensing authority accompanied by an operating schedule, a plan of the premises and, if the application is for a premises licence which includes authorisation for the supply of alcohol, a form of consent given by the individual whom the applicant wishes to have designated in the premises licence as the premises supervisor.

An operating schedule is a document which is in a prescribed form and includes a statement of the following matters:

(a)   the relevant licensable activities;
(b)   the times during which it is proposed that these activities are to take place;
(c)   any other times during which it is proposed that the premises are to be open to the public;

(d)   where the applicant wishes the licence to have effect for a limited period, that period;
(e)   where the activities include the supply of alcohol prescribed information in respect of the individual whom the applicant wishes to have specified in the premises licence as the premises supervisor. He may be the licensee;
(f)   where the activities include the supply of alcohol, whether the supplies are proposed to be for consumption on the premises or off the premises, or both;
(g)   the steps which it is proposed to take to promote the licensing objectives; and
(h)   such other matters as may be prescribed.

If alcohol is to be supplied on the premises the premises supervisor must hold a personal licence (see below).

The applicant is required to advertise his application and notify it to specified bodies. A fee is payable.

Under the wholly repealed Licensing Act 1964, notice of application for new justices' licences and for the transfer of existing licences had to be given to local councils and to the chairmen of parish meetings of parishes where there was no council. This requirement has not been reproduced in the Licensing Act 2003. However, the Secretary of State may by regulation require an applicant for a licence to ensure that the application is brought to the attention of interested parties. An 'interested party' is defined to include 'a body representing persons who live in that vicinity' (ie the vicinity of the premises to which the application relates). That definition is wide enough to include a local council and the chairman of a parish meeting. Regulations have been made[1] which require an applicant to give public notice of an application and allow 28 days from the date of deposit of the application with the licensing authority for interested parties to make representations.

A personal licence can be issued to an individual to authorise him or her to supply alcohol in accordance with a premises licence. It is valid initially for ten years and may be renewed for further periods of five years. It can be surrendered and may be revoked or forfeited if the licence holder is convicted of certain 'relevant offences' listed in LA 2003, Sch 4.

A premises licence remains valid until it is revoked by the licensing authority (which can only happen following a review under LA 2003, s 52) or, if granted for a limited period, it expires at the end of the period. The licence lapses if the licence holder dies, becomes mentally incapable, insolvent, is dissolved (if a company) or, if a club, ceases to be a recognised club.

A club premises certificate ceases to be valid if is surrendered or it is revoked following a review or if the club ceases to be a qualifying club.

[1]   Licensing Act 2003 (Premises Licences and Club Premises Certificates) Regulations 2005, SI 2005/42, as amended by the Licensing Act 2003 (Premises Licences and Club Premises Certificates) Regulations 2012, SI 2012/955.

Permitted temporary activities

24.11 Part 5 of the Licensing Act 2003 makes special provision for licensable activities which are temporary in nature. Instead of having to obtain a licence, a person organising a temporary activity may give a temporary event notice to the licensing authority which provides full (and prescribed) details of the activity in question. At least 10 working days' notice must be given both to the licensing authority and to the police. The authority must send an acknowledgement in the prescribed form within one working day after receipt of the notice. If there is no objection by the police, the notice is valid unless the authority serves a counter notice, which will normally occur where the permitted limits on the number of temporary events in a calendar year would be exceeded.

A temporary activity is one which comprises one or more licensable activities and lasts for no more than 96 hours. There must be at least 24 hours between successive permitted temporary activities. There is also a limit on the number of temporary event notices which can be given in a year. That limit is 12 in each year subject to an overall limit of 15 days in a calendar year. Furthermore, the numbers of persons attending a permitted temporary activity must be fewer than 500.

Exemptions from licensing

24.12 Part 2 of Schedule 1 to the Licensing Act 2003 provides mostly unnecessarily for exemptions from licensing of various types of entertainment (as broadly interpreted). These include religious meetings or services, the provision of a film as part of an exhibit in a museum or art gallery, garden fetes and similar events, morris dancing and dancing of a similar nature where only unamplified live music is used and entertainment provided in a vehicle in motion. A vehicle is defined in s 193 as a vehicle intended or adapted for use on the roads.

Parish and community halls, village halls, church halls, chapel halls and similar buildings will not be exempt from the licensing requirements but may be exempt from having to pay a fee for a licence simply for the provision of regulated entertainment. If, however, the licence also authorises the use of the premises for the supply of alcohol or the provision of late night refreshment, a fee will be required for those activities.

C PLANNING

24.13 It is not possible, in a work of this scope, to do more than describe the main signposts to an understanding of the planning system. For detail the reader is invited to consult the Town and Country Planning Act 1990, combined with the Planning and Compensation Act 1991, the Planning (Listed Buildings and Conservation Areas) Act 1991, the Planning (Hazardous Substances) Act 1990, the Planning and Compulsory Purchase Act 2004, the Planning Act 2008, the Localism Act 2011 and a large number of statutory instruments made under them.

The authorities

England

24.14 Local planning authorities (district councils, London borough councils, metropolitan district councils, county councils in areas in England where there are no district councils, the Broads Authority and National Park Authorities) are responsible for the preparation of local development plans, in consultation with local councils and local communities. In addition, county councils in counties where there are district councils are responsible for keeping under review any county matters (which, broadly speaking, relate to mineral working and the use of land for the processing of minerals).

Local planning authorities are also responsible for development control. This includes statutory requirements on publicising, consulting on and determining most applications for planning permission, taking into account the opinions of local councils and others. They also operate discretionary services, including pre-application advice to prospective developers, and enforcement against breaches of planning legislation.

The Secretary of State has promulgated a national planning policy framework which sets out government planning policies in broad terms. Local planning authorities are expected to follow those policies.

The Localism Act 2011 has introduced a system of neighbourhood planning in England under which local communities can produce their own neighbourhood development plans. Any such plans must conform to local development plans. Local councils are expected to play a prominent part in the preparation of neighborhood plans. The Secretary of State has issued guidance on neighborhood planning which can be viewed on the Department for Communities and Local Government website.

Wales

24.15 In Wales, there is a single spatial plan, prepared, kept under review and, when necessary, revised by the Welsh Assembly. The local planning authorities (the county and county borough councils) must prepare local development plans, which are broadly similar to the local development plans in England.

D   DEVELOPMENT CONTROL

24.16 Local development schemes and plans are given effect by a variety of means, of which development control is the most pervasive.

What is development? The principle

24.17 In principle, development is the 'carrying out of any building, engineering, mining or other operations in, on, over or under land or the making of any material change in the use of any buildings or other land'[1], and it is necessary for an intending developer to seek permission for his proposed development. Since, however, the full rigour of the rule would rapidly bring everything to a halt, there are a number of far-reaching exceptions and general permissions.

[1] Town and Country Planning Act 1990, s 55(1).

Exceptions defined by the Act

24.18 Certain acts and activities are treated as not involving development. These are, first, maintenance, improvement or alteration of a building affecting only its interior or not materially affecting its external appearance; second, road works by highway authorities; third, works on sewers, mains, pipes, cables and other apparatus by local authorities or statutory undertakers; fourth, uses incidental to the enjoyment of a dwelling-house and within its curtilage; and fifth, agriculture which, amongst other things, includes horticulture, fruit and seed growing, and the keeping of livestock including any creature kept for the production of food; forestry, and the use of buildings for agriculture and forestry[1].

[1] Town and Country Planning Act 1990, ss 55(2) and 336. The use of land for allotments is classed as an agricultural use: *Crowborough Parish Council v Secretary of State for the Environment and Wealden District Council* [1980] JPL 590.

Exceptions defined by Use Class

24.19 A further important relaxation arises from classifications of uses, which are made by the Secretary of State in so-called Use Classes orders.

The Town and Country Planning (Use Classes) Order 1987 (as amended) divides the Use Classes into four categories (A, B, C and D). Generally speaking, land used for a purpose in any one of the categories may be used for any other purpose in the same category without the new use being considered to be a development requiring planning permission. In outline (only) the relevant Use Classes are as follows:

A1   (eleven types) shops, post offices, hairdressers, funeral parlours, travel agents, internet cafés etc but not places selling hot food (the list for Wales is slightly different, comprising eight types);

A2   (three types) financial and professional services such as banks, solicitors and estate agents;

A3   places selling food and drink for consumption on the premises and, in Wales only, off the premises;

A4   pubs, wine bars and other drinking establishments;

A5   places selling hot food for consumption off the premises;

B1   (three types) business offices other than those within class A2, research and development premises and general industrial premises;

B2   industrial premises other than within class B1;

B8   storage premises and distribution centres;

C1   use as a hotel, or as a boarding or guest house where, in each case, no significant element of care is provided;

C2   residential institutions such as old people's and nursing homes, hospitals and colleges;

C2A secure residential institutions, including prisons and young offenders institutions;

C3 dwellings for single persons, families or for not more than six residents living together;

C4 houses in multiple occupation occupied by not more than six residents;

D1 (nine types) non-residential buildings such as medical and day centres, schools, museums, art galleries, libraries, public halls, churches and chapels and law courts;

D2 (five types) assembly or leisure including cinemas (but not theatres), concert, bingo and dance halls and facilities for sport and recreation not involving motor vehicles or firearms.

[1] Town and Country Planning (Use Classes) Order 1987, SI 1987/764 (as amended).

Permitted development and enterprise zones

24.20 Many developments are permitted by the Secretary of State by General Development Order[1]. These are set out in the Town and Country Planning (Permitted General Development) Order 1995, Sch 2. Many are subject to detailed conditions. There are minor variations between the provisions applying to England and to Wales.

The Schedule is divided into 43 Parts each containing a varying number of classes, viz:

1 development within the curtilage of a dwellinghouse;

2 minor operations such as gates, fences, walls, access roads and painting of buildings;

3 various changes of use from one Use Class to another;

4 certain temporary buildings and uses;

5 caravan sites;

6 agricultural buildings and operations including fish farming;

7 forestry buildings and operations;

8 industry and warehousing;

9 repairs to unadopted streets and private ways;

10 repairs to services (sewers, mains, pipes, cables and other apparatus);

11 development under local or private Acts or Orders;

12 small developments by local authorities including local councils. (These are small buildings on their own land needed for the exercise of their functions on that land, and street furniture such as lamps, information kiosks, shelters, seats, telephone boxes, fire alarms, public drinking fountains, horse troughs, bus stop barriers, and the dumping of rubbish on a rubbish dump in use on 1 April 1948.)

Development consisting mostly of or incidental to maintenance or improvement of works by:

13–15 highway authorities, drainage bodies and the Environment Agency;

16   sewerage undertakers;

17   works by statutory undertakers[2];

18   aviation development;

19–23 various limited developments relating to mining, ancillary tipping and mineral exploration;

24   development by electronic telecommunications code operators;

25   other telecommunications development;

26   developments by the Historic Buildings and Monuments Commission for England;

27   uses by rescreational organisations with exemption certificates under the Public Health Act 1936, s 269;

28   amusement parks and piers;

29   driver information systems;

30   toll road facilities;

31   demolition of buildings;

32   schools, colleges, universities and hospitals;

33   closed circuit television cameras;

34   development by the Crown;

35   aviation development by the Crown;

36   Crown railways, dockyards etc and lighthouses;

37   emergency development by the Crown;

38   development for national security purposes;

39   temporary protection of poultry and other captive birds;

40   installation of domestic microgeneration equipment;

41   office buildings;

42   shops or catering, financial or professional service establishments;

43   installation of non-domestic microgeneration equipment.

In addition an Enterprise Zone Order with its important financial and planning effect may in advance permit any development or class of development within the zone[3]. Such zones may be created anywhere, but only after the district council (T), at the Secretary of State's invitation, has proposed a scheme and he has accepted it.

[1]   See the Town and Country Planning (Permitted General Development) Order 1995, SI 1995/418 (as frequently amended).

[2]   A statutory undertaker is a body which manages a public undertaking under statutory authority. It has nothing to do with burials.

[3]   Local Government Planning and Land Act 1980, Part XVIII and Sch 32, para 17.

Application for planning permission

24.21 If a proposed operation falls within none of the exceptions or permissions sketched above, it is a development for which permission is required, and for which the intending developer must apply to the district planning authority or, as the case may be, to the national park planning board. The authority to which he applies may pass it to a different authority. In any case his application will not fail because it was made to the wrong authority, and the district planning authority must tell him the name of the authority to which the application has been passed.

The application is made on a form supplied by the authority or board or downloaded from the authority or board's website), and must be accompanied by appropriate plans and specifications and a fee. Unless the authority indicates a lesser number, it must be accompanied by three copies of the form, plans and specification[1]. It has long been a practice to pass one of these to the local council (see section E below).

Applications may initially be for outline planning permission for the erection of a building, followed by a further application for detailed planning permission for such matters as have been reserved by the authority for further approval under the outline planning permission.

In some cases, notice of an application has to be publicised by the local planning authority. These cases are where:

(a)   an environmental impact assessment is required (see below);
(b)   the development is not in accordance with the development plan;
(c)   the application would affect a right of way;
(d)   the application is for a major development (mineral working or extraction, waste development, building 10 or more houses or building houses on a site of 0.5 hectares or more, provision of a building of 1,000 square metres or more, development on a site of 1 hectare or more).

For the type of publicity required, see section E below.

In addition, there are extensive requirements for local planning authorities to consult specified bodies before granting planning permission for specified types of development. For example, if a development is likely to prejudice or lead to the loss of use of, a playing field or is on land which has been used as a playing field in the five years before the application but remains undeveloped, the planning authority must consult the English, or as the case may be, the Welsh Sports Council[2].

[1]   Town and Country Planning (Applications) Regulations 1988, SI 1988/1812, and Town and Country Planning (Development Management Procedure) (England) Order 2010, SI 2010/2184, and Town and Country Planning (Development Management Procedure) (Wales) Order 2012, SI 2012/801.
[2]   Town and Country Planning (Development Management Procedure) (England) Order 2010, SI 2010/2184, and Town and Country Planning (Development Management Procedure) (Wales) Order 2012, SI 2012/801.

Time factor

24.22 If an application is not granted within two months, or such longer time as may be agreed between the applicant and the authority dealing with it, it is deemed to have been refused, and the applicant may therefore appeal against the refusal.

Environmental effects in important cases

24.23 There is a special procedure for developments which are either very large or potentially very deleterious to the environment. These are described in the Town and Country Planning (Environmental Impact Assessment) (England and Wales) Regulations 1999, SI 1999/293, Schs 1 and 2 (as amended).

Schedule 1 cases include:

- refineries, gas plants and large thermal power stations;
- storage of radioactive waste, incinerators for treating special waste, and deposits of special waste;
- smelting;
- asbestos extraction and processing;
- integral chemical installations manufacturing olefins from petrol, or sulphuric, nitric or hydrofluoric acids, or chlorine or fluorine;
- motorways, long distance railway lines, aerodromes with a basic runway of 2,100m, trading ports and large inland waterways.

Schedule 2 contains 13 classes, viz:

- agriculture (five cases);
- extractive industries (five); energy industries (nine); metal processing (eleven); mineral industry (six); chemical industry (three);
- food (nine);
- textiles, leather, wood and paper (four);
- rubber (one);
- infrastructure projects such as railways, airfields, pipelines and motorway service areas (sixteen);
- other projects such as motor racing circuits, storage of scrap and knackers' yards (nine);
- tourism and leisure (five); ski-runs and lifts, holiday villages, marinas, permanent camp and caravan sites and golf courses;
- modifications of Sch 1 developments;
- temporary Sch 1 developments.

The basic rule is that the planning authority or the Secretary of State or an inspector must not in these cases grant planning permission without first taking environmental information into account. The applicant must supply this in an environmental statement, which must contain specified information about his proposals; the data needed to identify their environmental effect; a description of the likely significant effects direct and indirect by reference to the impact on the following matters:

(1)   human beings;
(2)   flora;
(3)   fauna;
(4)   soil;
(5)   water;
(6)   air;
(7)   climate;
(8)   material assets, including the architectural and archaeological heritage;
(9)   the landscape; and
(10)   the interaction between any of these.

Where significant adverse effects are identified, there must be a description of measures envisaged to avoid, reduce or remedy them, and there must be a summary of all the above information in non-technical language.

As the preparation of such a statement will often be a major undertaking involving research, sometimes in fields unfamiliar to prospective applicants, the latter may seek a preliminary written opinion from the local planning authority as to whether an application falls within one of the Schedules, or apply for directions from the Secretary of State if it fails to give an opinion or holds that it does fall within them. Conversely, if the prospective applicant thinks that his case does not fall within the Schedules and makes his application without the environmental statement, the authority may nevertheless tell him to submit one. He may then apply for directions from the Secretary of State if he thinks that the authority is wrong, and in either event the application may be refused.

There are provisions for publicising the environmental statement (copies of which must be available) and for publicising requests for preliminary opinions and directions, and the documents supporting such requests together with the opinions and directions themselves.

European Wildlife Sites

24.24 In principle, where there is one of the rare European Wildlife Sites in or adjacent to the locality, its council, as a competent authority, must, in forming an opinion about a planning application, make an appropriate assessment of the implications for the site and its conservation objectives, but it is not bound to do this if another competent authority can do it more appropriately. As the latter will usually be a principal council, action by a local council will seldom be required[1].

[1]   See Conservation (Natural Habitats, &c) Regulations 1994, SI 1994/2716, which implements EU Directive 92/43/EEC (OJ No L 206).

E   DEVELOPMENT PUBLICITY AND REPRESENTATIONS

24.25 A local council has a right to claim notification of planning applications. These must relate to land in the locality and include an application for planning permission and an application for planning approval of a matter reserved under an outline planning permission. The claim must be made in writing. The local council has 14 days in which to respond to any application of which it is informed (unless it can negotiate a longer period with the local planning authority). The authority must within 21 days take into account any representations made by a local council within the statutory or negotiated time limit and it may consider later representations. The authority must notify the local council of the terms of its decision on an application on which the local council has made representations and also of the decision of the Secretary of State in relation to any application referred to him[1].

Legislation has also extended a right of representation to a wide segment of the public.

¹ Town and Country Planning Act 1990, Sch 1, para 8, Town and Country Planning (Development Management Procedure) (England) Order 2010, SI 2010/2184, art 23 and Town and Country Planning (Development Management Procedure) (Wales) Order 2012, SI 2010/8014, art 16.

Types of required publicity

24.26 Depending on the nature of the application, a local planning authority must advertise it at least 21 days before it considers it and advertise it by:

(a)   a statutory form on or near the site (site display);
(b)   service of a similar form on adjacent landowners; or
(c)   an advertisement in a newspaper circulating in the area, as follows:

Type of Application	*Type of Advertisement*
(1) Those which are accompanied by an environmental statement and do not accord with the development plan, or would affect a public right of way	(a) and (c)
(2) Major developments, namely those concerned with mineral workings treating, storing, processing and disposal of refuse or waste; the provision of ten or more houses, or an unknown number of houses, on a site of 0.5 hectares; buildings with 100m sq of floor space or more; development of site of 1 hectare or more	(a) or (b) and (c)
(3) Other minor developments	(a) or (b)

Notification of upshot

24.27 A district planning authority must inform a local council of the terms of its decision on an application in relation to which the council has made representations to the local planning authority¹.

¹ Town and Country Planning (Development Management Procedure) (England) Order 2010, SI 2010/2184, art 23 and Town and Country Planning (Development Management Procedure) (Wales) Order 2012, SI 2010/8014, art 16

F   HAZARDOUS SUBSTANCES

24.28 Subject to some exceptions, the district council (T) has control over the presence of hazardous substances, but the appropriate minister has the control in the case of a statutory undertaker, and the county council (T) in the case of a national park, land used for winning minerals or for dumping waste or refuse, and a housing trust which has planning powers.

Sixty-seven hazardous substances are listed in regulations made in 1992[1], together with the quantities beyond which those who wish to deposit them must apply for a hazardous substance consent. Twenty-one days' notice must be given by site notice and in a local newspaper. Before determining the application the authority must consult the local council unless it has notified the authority that it does not wish to be consulted.

[1]   Planning (Hazardous Substances) Regulations 1992, SI 1992/656, Sch 1.

G   NEW TOWNS

24.29 The site of a new town is designated by the Secretary of State[1] after consulting any local authorities, including local councils[2] who appear to him to be concerned. Notice of intention to make the order must be published in local newspapers and served on county (T) and district councils (T) involved, and may be served on the local councils. A public inquiry must be held into objections validly made within the time limit specified in the order, and when the order has eventually been made, notice must again be given to those bodies who received the original notice and to the objectors to give them an opportunity, within six weeks, to challenge the legality (as opposed to the expediency) of the order in the courts.

Where land or rights over land are needed for the purposes of the new town and new town corporation, the highway authority and the Secretary of State respectively can acquire them by agreement or compulsorily. Once acquired in this way the purposes for which the land was previously used can be overridden: public[3] and private[4] rights of way can be extinguished; subject to planning permission being obtained, burial grounds can be cleared and used for other purposes[5] and commons, open spaces and fuel and field garden allotments can be put to other uses[6].

[1]   New Towns Act 1981, s 1(1).
[2]   NTA 1981, Sch 1, para 2(3) and s 80.
[3]   NTA 1981, s 23.
[4]   NTA 1981, s 19.
[5]   NTA 1981, s 20.
[6]   NTA 1981, s 21.

H   RENEWAL AREAS

24.30 Housing authorities may declare renewal areas, where living conditions are unsatisfactory, but only after receiving a report from a qualified person (who may be one of their own staff) on, amongst other things, the living conditions and the way in which they may be improved including the cost. When the declaration has been made, it must be advertised and local residents and landowners informed. The general effect of the declaration is to empower the authority to acquire housing accommodation compulsorily or by agreement and to improve or replace it and to extinguish vehicular rights of way; and from time to time it must publicise the action which it proposes to take[1].

There is no required procedure for consulting local councils, but the person drawing up the original report may find it convenient to do so and this is probably the best time for it.

Associations of local councils may perhaps approach the housing authorities to gain their co-operation by, as a matter of policy, persuading their consultant to approach the local councils for information and views.

1 Local Government Housing Act 1989, Part VII.

I COMPULSORY PLANNING LOSSES

24.31 It occasionally (if rarely) happens that a local council is the victim of a compulsory acquisition made in connection with a comprehensive development by a minister for his own purposes or by principal councils or statutory undertakers for theirs with planning permission. These may result in the taking and reuse of consecrated land and consecrated or unconsecrated burial grounds (but in either case the new use cannot proceed until proper measures have been taken, if necessary in accordance with ecclesiastical law, to dispose of human remains and the monuments and tombstones)[1]. Common land, open spaces and field garden allotments[2] may also be taken and public rights of way extinguished[3].

1 Town and Country Planning Act 1990, ss 238–241.
2 TCPA 1990, s 229.
3 TCPA 1990, s 251.

Procedure

24.32 In the case of an order extinguishing rights of way, the Secretary of State must serve on the local council a copy of a notice stating its general effect, when and where the draft of the order may be inspected and the 28-day period within which objections may be made. This notice must also be published in a local newspaper and in the London Gazette, and posted at each end of the way to be extinguished. The Secretary of State may hold an inquiry if he thinks it necessary[1].

In other cases there will be opportunities for representation because the order will have to be confirmed by a minister, and in any case the planning application will have to proceed in the usual way (see section D above).

1 Town and Country Planning Act 1990, s 252.

J CONSULTATION WITH PRINCIPAL AND NATIONAL PARK AUTHORITIES

24.33 The Welsh Assembly may, by order, designate subjects upon which a principal council must either, always consult its community councils, or must do so if a local council notifies its wish to be consulted[1]. It must without delay notify its decision to a council concerned, but contravention of these duties does not invalidate a decision[1]. For model charter agreements in Wales, see **35.23**.

A National Park authority must arrange with the local councils of its park so as to inform and consult them about its work. The arrangements are likely to be more effective in England, where the authorities have parish members, than in Wales where there is no equivalent[2].

[1]   Local Government Act 1972, s 33A.
[1]   Local Government Act 1972, s 33A.
[2]   Environment Act 1995, Sch 7, para 16 and see **23.15** above.

K   REPRESENTATIONS—SHOPS, POST OFFICES, CRIME

24.34 Local councils are increasingly concerned to make representations to other bodies. It is not possible to mention here all the cases, but provisions were enacted in 1997 to reduce the economic pressure on village shops and post offices which may represent a novel, if indirect, interest for local councils[1], and the police and principal authorities in co-operating against crime and disorder must also co-operate with local councils[2].

[1]   Local Government and Rating Act 1997, Sch 1. For these rural settlements see **2.1** above.
[2]   Crime and Disorder Act 1998, s 6.

Chapter 25

APPEARANCE OF VILLAGES

25.1 Local councils can statutorily take a certain part in maintaining or improving the general appearance of villages, and can also exert a persuasive influence to the same effect on other people. The sum total of these powers is greater than is sometimes supposed.

A   KEY BUILDINGS AND SITES

25.2 Many places have a visual focus, of which the church and its churchyard are usually the most conspicuous; other striking features may include greens, memorials or market crosses, tithe barns, avenues or clumps of trees, ponds, and verges. These things individually or in combination set the local character: they may be good or bad, well designed or ugly, well or badly sited. Under modern conditions it will be rare for a local council to be wholly powerless in dealing with them, for where a specific power is lacking, the 'free resource'[1] is generally available. The following paragraphs are examples of the uses to which specific powers have been put.

Where a churchyard is open a local council may contribute to its maintenance (see 33.43 below). This can be used, in the case of an impecunious parochial church council, either to improve the appearance of an unkempt churchyard or, by taking the financial burden of churchyard maintenance off the parochial church council, to help that body to improve the appearance of the church.

In some places the greens are being degraded by parking and litter, and some seem to be disappearing through encroachment, erosion and clutter. This process can be reversed by a judicious combination of measures: prosecutions for litter can be publicised, and litterbins can be provided[2]. Large stones, ditches, or posts and chains can be placed to hinder vehicles[3], and drivers can be prosecuted for damaging the surface[4]. Car parks can be provided elsewhere[5]. If the green is big enough, local clubs can be encouraged to play games on it and take an interest in it, and sometimes trees or shrubs can be planted.

[1]   Local Government Act 1972, s 137.
[2]   Litter Act 1983, s 5.
[3]   Local Government Act 1894, s 8.
[4]   Inclosure Act 1857, s 12.
[5]   Road Traffic Regulation Act 1984, s 57.

Trees

25.3 Often a village can be improved by tree planting or tree preservation. Apart from the power to plant highway verges (see **25.8** below), the power to provide public walks can be invoked. Where trees are privately owned, the county council (T) can be asked to make a preservation order or in an appropriate case an open space agreement can be negotiated[1].

Dust and carbon dioxide pollution, especially from motor vehicles with catalytic converters, is absorbed in huge amounts by trees. Tree planting is thus an adjunct to public health as well as amenity.

[1] Open Spaces Act 1906, s 10.

Ponds

25.4 There are instances where neglected village ponds have been rescued and made agreeable to the eye, and subsequently stocked with goldfish to keep down the mosquitoes.

B CIVIC SOCIETIES

25.5 No place will ever look better than its people want. If a local council can set in motion the process of improvement by paying attention to the key sites, the general level can often be maintained by voluntary action through a civic society organised with the help of, for example, Civic Voice. The formation of such a society can by itself be a valuable service, and a local council can encourage or even initiate the process by providing a meeting place, offering help with publicity and subscribing to its funds[1]. The society can embark on undertakings of wide scope once its membership is adequate. It can organise street and house improvement schemes similar to the Magdalen Street Scheme in Norwich; it can act as the organising body in best-kept village competitions and in garden and window box competitions—for which the local council can provide prizes, and it can by persuasion or pressure help to eliminate eyesores and derelict buildings.

[1] From the free resource (Local Government Act 1972, s 137 or in exercise of the power of general competence (see CHAPTER 22) or (in Wales) the power to promote well-being (see CHAPTER 35)).

C NATIONAL HERITAGE GRANTS

25.6 The trustees of the National Heritage Memorial Fund may lend or grant money to help acquire, maintain or preserve things of any kind which are of scenic, historic, archaeological, aesthetic, architectural, engineering, artistic or scientific interest and which are important to the national heritage. Eligible projects include any which have as a purpose the provision, improvement or preservation of amenities enjoyed by the public or the acquisition of land to be used by the public[1]. The enabling Acts do not exclude local authorities.

[1] National Heritage Act 1980, s 3.

D   GOOD DESIGN

25.7 Apart from buildings, local councils provide a surprisingly large amount of street furniture such as lamp-posts, bus shelters, litterbins, public seats and notice boards. These are not always as apt for their purpose or as durable or as suitable for their surroundings as they might be, because the existence of better designs is not invariably known. Well-designed articles of the kind are usually worth their higher price, because they look better, and because they attract vandalism less and so last better. Moreover, the habitual planting of cheap or ill-designed objects in public places diminishes the moral authority of a council interested in amenity. A council which intends to provide street furniture can usually obtain independent information on designs through its association or Civic Voice, and should invariably do so before placing large contracts.

E   ROADSIDE VERGES

25.8 With the consent of the Highway Authority a local council may, in any publicly repairable highway, plant trees and shrubs and plants and lay out grass verges; it may fence or otherwise protect them or similar plantings effected by private persons. These powers must not be exercised so as to obstruct public rights of passage or so as to be a nuisance to a frontager[1].

[1]   Highways Act 1980, s 96(5).

F   MILITARY MANOEUVRES

25.9 Manoeuvres can only be held under authority of a manoeuvres order, which defines the area in which they may be held. At least two months before the order is to be made, a draft of it must be sent to every local council in the area. Manoeuvres under an order may not last more than three months and no further order for the same area may be made within five years without the consent of the county council (T) and (in the case of the New Forest) of the verderers.

During the currency of the order a manoeuvres commission has power to pay compensation for damage, and to impose requirements on owners of property; disregard of such requirements destroys the right to compensation. Magistrates' courts also have power on application from the military authorities, and after seven days' notice, to close highways and footpaths during certain hours of the day[1].

[1]   Manoeuvres Act 1958, s 3.

G   PUBLIC CLOCKS

25.10 A local council may provide and light public clocks in its area, and, subject to the safeguards mentioned in **20.2** above, it may install them on or against any premises or in any convenient situation. It may, moreover, maintain any public clock whether provided by it or some other person such as a parochial church council[1]. For these purposes it may combine with any other local council or parish meeting with like powers or may contribute to their expenses or to those of any other person in providing lighting or maintaining a public clock; it is therefore possible, for instance, for a local council to maintain or help to maintain a church clock[2].

There are restrictions on the placing of public clocks in walkways similar to the restrictions on lighting[3].

[1] Parish Councils Act 1957, s 2.
[2] PCA 1957, ss 2 and 6.
[3] Walkways Regulations 1973, SI 1973/686, reg 3. In relation to lighting see **28.6** below.

Chapter 26

OPEN AIR AND EXERCISE

26.1 Local councils have many powers relating to open-air and other recreational facilities; they are derived from many general enactments passed in the course of more than a century and may also be derived from local (especially inclosure) Acts. It is difficult to reconcile all these powers.

A   VILLAGE GREENS AND RECREATIONAL ALLOTMENTS

Definitions

26.2 Historically, a village green was either a piece of land (usually but not necessarily common or waste of the manor) where the inhabitants had by enforceable custom a right to indulge in lawful sports and pastimes[1], or a piece of land set aside under an Inclosure Award for the recreation of the inhabitants. Such allotments were sometimes made in substitution for old village greens and sometimes the village green was converted into a recreational allotment, with or without its older characteristics. From 1845 onwards recreation allotments were (save in exceptional cases) required to be made as a condition of inclosure[2], and were awarded under general legislation[3]. Nowadays, the best definition of a green is land which is registered as such[4] but there is an entitlement to registration if a significant number of the inhabitants of a locality have indulged regularly in lawful sports and pastimes on the land openly and without protest or permission for at least 20 years and either continue to do so, or have ceased to do so for a prescribed period. The relevant periods are:

(a)   where application is made to register land as a green after 6 April 2007 in England, one year after the use ceased or after 6 September 2007 in Wales, two years after the use ceased[5];

(b)   where application was made to register the land as a green before these dates five years after the use ceased[6].

Restrictions on applying to register a new green where the land in question is subject to certain development proposals have been introduced in England by the Growth and Infrastructure Act 2013[7].

The list of registered greens is therefore never completely closed.

---

[1]   *Fitch v Rawling* (1795) 2 Hy Bl 393 (games, sports and pastimes in a particular close). *Hall v Nottingham* (1875) 1 Ex D 1 (maypole in old glebe). *Warwick v Queen's College, Oxford* (1870) LR 10 Eq 105 (sports on a common and unfenced green). See also Commons Act 2006, s 15.

[2]   Inclosure Act 1845, s 30 (repealed).
[3]   Inclosure Act 1845, s 73; Commons Act 1876, s 27; Commons Act 1879, s 2; Commons Act 1899, s 16.
[4]   Commons Registration Act 1965, s 1(2)(a) and Commons Act 2006, s 15.
[5]   Commons Act 2006, s 15(3).
[6]   Commons Act 2006, s 15(4).
[7]   Commons Act 2006, s 15C and Sch 1A (added by the Growth and Infrastructure Act 2013).

How acquired

26.3 Most greens came to be controlled or owned by the local council or parish meeting by statutory transfer in 1894[1], by subsequent acquisitions, or as a result of procedures under the Commons Registration Act 1965, for where ownership was unclaimed and a commons commissioner's investigation fails to reveal an owner, the green was eventually vested in the local council if there was one, and in the district council (T) if not[2].

[1]   Local Government Act 1894, s 6.
[2]   Commons Registration Act 1965, s 8 (repealed). There is no provision in the legislation for the vesting of 'new' greens (ie those registered after the initial registrations made under the CRA 1965 in 1967–1970) in local authorities.

Herbage

26.4 On recreational allotments the local council or parish meeting may let the herbage and must apply the rents towards maintenance and the payment of taxes, rates and charges. Any surplus may be used to acquire further recreational allotments or to acquire or improve field gardens, and for no other purpose; if these opportunities are not available the income must be accumulated.

Modification of Inclosure Acts

26.5 Save in Epping and the New Forests and in the Forest of Dean, a local council or parish meeting may apply to the Charity Commission to modify the recreational and other allotments provisions in an Inclosure Act[1].

[1]   Commons Act 1899, s 18.

B   COMMONS REGULATION SCHEMES

For New Towns see **24.30** above.

26.6 A district council (T) (after three months' notice by advertisement[1]) may make a scheme for the management of any common in the district (T) with a view to the expenditure of money on drainage, levelling, improvement and the making of byelaws and regulations for the prevention of nuisances and the preservation of order on the common[2]. As from a date to be appointed by the Secretary of State, the words from 'within their district . . . order on the common' will be replaced by the words 'in the public interest'[3],such interest being defined to include:

(a)   nature conservation;
(b)   the conservation of the landscape;
(c)   the protection of public rights of access to any area of land; or
(d)   the protection of archaeological remains and features of historic interest[4].

A local council may contribute to the expense of preparing and executing the scheme (including any compensation to be paid)[5]. These schemes are made in a standard statutory form[6]. Many commons were managed by parish councils under a form of permanent delegation[7] and these are now managed by arrangement[8].

Schemes of this sort are intended only to simplify bringing into use commons for purposes of recreation, and as they may interfere with the agricultural uses they may be vetoed by either the lord of the manor or one-third (by value) of the commoners. The district council (T) may hold a local inquiry before approving a scheme[9].

Byelaws made under a regulation scheme require the confirmation of the Secretary of State (W)[10].

Regulation schemes cannot be made for a common regulated by a provisional order made under the Inclosure Acts 1845–1882, or which is subject to byelaws made by a parish council under the (repealed) Local Government Act 1894, s 8[11] or for a common any part of which is in the Metropolitan Police District, for such a metropolitan common as defined in 1866 may not be inclosed[12] and, subject to the making of any schemes, the public is entitled to rights of access for air and exercise over it unless the county council (T) resolves to exclude the public, and the Secretary of State (W) approves the resolution[13].

[1]   Commons Act 1899, s 2, as amended by the Commons Act 2006, s 50(5).
[2]   CA 1899, s 1(1).
[3]   CA 1899, s 1(1), as amended by the Commons Act 2006, s 50(2)(a).
[4]   CA 1899, s 1(1A), inserted by the Commons Act 2006, s 50(2)(b).
[5]   CA 1899, s 5.
[6]   Set out in the Commons (Schemes) Regulations 1982, SI 1982/209.
[7]   Under the repealed CA 1899, s 4.
[8]   Under Local Government Act 1972, s 101.
[9]   CA 1899, s 2.
[10] CA 1899, s 10, amended by LGA 1972.
[11] CA 1899, s 14, amended as from a day to be appointed by the Secretary of State by the Commons Act 2006, s 50(5).
[12] Metropolitan Commons Act 1866, ss 4 and 5.
[13] Law of Property Act 1925, s 193(1).

C   PUBLIC ACCESS TO COMMONS

26.7 The public has rights of access for air and exercise (only) to manorial waste and common land:

(a)   wholly or partly in the Metropolitan Police District as defined in 1866;
(b)   in a borough or in the area of a former borough or urban district as it existed on 31 March 1974; or
(c)   under the Countryside and Rights of Way Act 2000 (see E below).

In other cases the lord of a manor or other person such as a local council entitled to the soil may by deed revocable or irrevocable give the public a right of access to a rural common, and this right begins when the deed is deposited with the Secretary of State[1], who may on application by the lord impose limitations or conditions upon such right[2]; these must be published[3].

The power to make a deed of declaration was repealed by the Countryside and Wildlife Act 2000, s 46(1). In Wales, the power was repealed as from 21 June 2004[4]. However, s 46 itself was repealed by the Commons Act 2006, s 50, on 1 October 2006. As a result, in England, the power to make a deed of declaration remains in force.

Any person who brings a vehicle on to such a common without lawful authority or who camps or lights fires or fails to observe any of the limitations or conditions commits an offence (level 3 fine)[5].

1   Law of Property Act 1925, s 193(2).
2   LPA 1925, s 193(1)(b).
3   LPA 1925, s 193(3).
4   Countryside and Rights of Way Act 2000 (Commencement No 5) (Wales) Order 2004, SI 2004/1489.
5   LPA 1925, s 193(4). For the maximum amount of each level of fine, see **21.40** above.

D   OLD AGREED ACCESS LAND

26.8 Where land is subject to an access agreement[1] between a local planning authority and a landowner, or to an access order[2], a person who enters such land for open-air recreation cannot be treated as a trespasser unless he does damage or goes upon 'excepted land'.

The main types of excepted land are agricultural land (other than rough grazing), nature reserves, the curtilage of a house, private parks, gardens and pleasure grounds so used at the date of the agreement or order, surface workings for minerals and quarries, land used for a rail or tramway, golf course, racecourse or aerodrome or for a statutory undertaking, and land upon which certain works are being erected[3].

The authority may suspend the effect of the agreement or order during periods of exceptional fire risk[4]. An access agreement or order cannot confer these rights in respect of rural commons to which the public has a right of access conferred by deed deposited with the Secretary of State[5].

1   Under the National Parks and Access to the Countryside Act 1949, s 64.
2   NPACA 1949, s 65.
3   NPACA 1949, s 60.
4   NPACA 1949, s 69, substituted by Local Government Planning and Land Act 1980, Sch 3.
5   NPACA 1949, s 60(5)(h) and see **26.7** above.

E   MODERN ACCESS LAND

26.9 In February 2001[1] a new type of access land came into existence by statute. This is of two kinds: open country and registered common land outside Inner London.

Open country is access land if it is shown on a special map prepared in conclusive form by (as the case may be) the access authority, namely the local National Park Authority, or the Highway Authority, or if there is no map, if the land is above the 600 metre contour or has been dedicated by the owner or by a long lessee for the remainder of his term.

Registered common land is access land whether it is shown on such a map, or (outside London) not. There are 13 types of exceptions to the general rule including: cultivated or wooded land, built-up land or land within 20 metres of a dwelling, parks and gardens, surface mineral workings, rail and tramways, golf and racecourses, airfields, statutory undertakings, land whose development will place it in any of the above groups, livestock byres and pens, racehorse training grounds and military lands[2].

Since 31 October 2005, the whole of England and Wales has been subject to Part 1 of the Act.

[1]   Countryside and Rights of Way Act 2000, s 103.
[2]   CRWA 2000, s 1 and Sch 1.

Public rights

26.10 Any person may enter access land for personal recreation as long as he does no damage, but he may not indulge in some 20 (rather obvious) activities, viz:

- public offences (driving vehicles, using boats, committing crimes, bringing any animal other than a dog, lighting fires);
- interfering with fauna (failing to shut gates);
- bathing;
- using a metal detector;
- interfering with nature (destroying plants or blocking drains or ditches);
- interfering with walls and fences;
- interfering with lawful users of the land (intimidation, games, camping, gliding, graffiti); or
- carrying on a commercial activity.

Someone who breaks the rules on any land may not return to it or land in the same ownership for 72 hours.

It is an offence (level 3 fine) to display on access land any notice likely to deter the exercise of public rights[1]. Access authorities can make byelaws (level 2 fine)[2] to preserve order, prevent damage and enforce good behaviour. Local councils as well as other authorities can enforce them by prosecution.

[1]   Countryside and Rights of Way Act 2000, s 14.
[2]   CRWA 2000, s 17.

Exclusion of rights

26.11 Owners can suspend access for 28 days, which must not include Christmas, Good Friday or any Bank Holiday or more than four Sundays in the year or on a Saturday between 1 June and 11 August or on a Sunday between 1 June and 30 September, and they may exclude dogs from grouse moors and sheep enclosures[1].

Access authorities can protect land against fire risks[2]; and the Secretary of State can exclude persons in the interests of national security[3].

[1] Countryside and Rights of Way Act 2000, s 23.
[2] CRWA 2000, s 25.
[3] CRWA 2000, s 28.

F   PROTECTION OF COMMONS

General

26.12 The governing legislation is Part 3 (ss 38–44) of the Commons Act 2006, replacing, with modifications, the Law of Property Act 1925, s 194.

The carrying out of 'restricted works' (ie works which prevent or impede access to the land in respect of which consent is sought or which are resurfacing works) is prohibited on:

(a)   registered common land; and
(b)   land which is regulated by a provisional order confirmation act made under the Commons Act 1876 or a scheme under the Commons Act 1899; and
(c)   land within the New Forest which is subject to rights of common but not within (a) or (b), unless the consent of the appropriate national authority (in England, the Secretary of State; in Wales, the Welsh assembly) is obtained[1].

Works include, in particular, fencing, the erection of buildings and other structures, the digging of trenches and the building of embankments. Resurfacing consists of the laying of concrete, tarmacadam, coated roadstone or the like, but not the repair of an existing surface made of such material (s 38(4)). There are various exceptions relating to works authorised under other enactments or relating to the installation of electronic communications apparatus[2].

When considering an application for consent, the authority must have regard to:

(a)   the interests of the occupiers and those having rights on or over the land and in particular the rights of commoners;
(b)   the interests of the neighbourhood;
(c)   the public interest, including nature conservation, landscape conservation, protection of public rights of access to any area of land (not just the application area) and protection of archaeological remains and features of historic interest[3];
(d)   any other matter considered to be relevant.

The authority may:

(1)   give consent to all or part of the proposed works, with or without modifications;

(2)   take into consideration any previous consent given under s 38(1) or under the Law of Property Act 1925, s 194;

(3)   on the application of the person to whom the consent was given, vary or revoke any modification or condition attached to a consent;

(4)   give consent to works which have been started or completed, with the consent running from the date on which the works began[4].

Detailed procedural regulations have been made covering England only[5].

[1]   Commons Act 2006, s 38(1).
[2]   Commons Act 2006, s 38(3)–(6).
[3]   Commons Act 2006, s 39(1)–(2).
[4]   Commons Act 2006, s 39(3).
[5]   Works on Common Land etc (Procedure) (England) Regulations 2007, SI 2007/2588.

26.13 Where works are carried out in contravention of s 38(1), any person may apply to the county court which may:

(1)   in any case, order the removal of the works and restoration of the land to its previous condition;

(2)   where works have not been carried out in accordance with a consent granted under s 38(1), order that the works be carried out in such manner and subject to such conditions as the order may specify[1].

The authority may exempt some kinds of work from the necessity to obtain consent under s 38(1), but only where the works are necessary or expedient for one or more of the following purposes:

(a)   use of the land by members of the public for open-air recreation in exercise of a right of access;

(b)   exercise of common rights;

(c)   nature conservation;

(d)   protection of archaeological remains and features of historic interest;

(e)   use of the land for sporting or recreational purposes[2].

[1]   Commons Act 2006, s 41.
[2]   Commons Act 2006, s 43.

Collective trespass

26.14 The police may direct two or more trespassers apparently intending to reside on land to leave it, provided that the occupier has asked them to leave and if they have damaged the land or abused or insulted him, his family or an employee or agent of his and have six or more vehicles on the land. Disobedience is an offence, and the police may remove vehicles.

This general rule applies to common land, in such a way that occupiers include commoners and, if the public has access, a local authority with powers in relation to the land. This may include a local council[1].

[1]   Criminal Justice and Public Order Act 1994, ss 61–62E. For the details see the sections themselves printed in Appendix I.

Ownerless commons

26.15 If land is registered as a common but no one is registered as the owner, a local council or any other local authority in whose area it lies may take such steps to protect it against illegal interference as would be open to an owner in possession, and may also launch criminal proceedings for any offence committed in respect of the land[1]. Primarily these powers enable the council to warn off trespassers, prevent encroachments and institute proceedings, whether criminal or civil, as may be appropriate to the situation, but it also enables the council sometimes to execute works.

[1]   Commons Act 2006, s 45.

G   OPEN SPACES ACT POWERS

General power

26.16 A local council may (with the appropriate consent) convey, with or without conditions, land to another local authority for the purpose of its being preserved as an open space for the enjoyment of the public, and may similarly accept or appropriate land for that purpose[1].

The remaining provisions of the Open Spaces Act 1906 fall into two classes and certain safeguards.

[1]   Open Spaces Act 1906, s 7.

Freedom to transfer

26.17 The first class makes possible the transfer to local councils (amongst others) of certain kinds of lands which are open spaces in fact but to whose transfer legal obstacles would otherwise exist. Accordingly trustees of open spaces under local and private acts or held otherwise than under such acts[1], charitable trustees of open spaces[2], owners of land subject to rights of exercise and recreation vested in neighbouring owners or occupiers[3], and owners of disused burial grounds[4] may after obtaining the consents proper to each case[5] convey or let the land or transfer its management or entire or partial control to the local council. Usually, but not invariably, the land must be held upon the same trusts as bound the previous owner, and in each class of case the type of agreement is defined in the Act[6].

[1]   Open Spaces Act 1906, ss 2 and 3.
[2]   OSA 1906, s 4.
[3]   OSA 1906, s 5.
[4]   OSA 1906, s 6; 'disused burial ground' is defined in s 20.
[5]   See note 4 above.
[6]   The details will be found in OSA 1906, ss 2–6 and 8.

Acquisition

26.18 The second class confers upon a local council numerous powers of acquisition and administration. It may acquire by agreement and for any valuable, nominal or no consideration the freehold or lease of or any limited interest in or any right or easement in on or over any open space[1] or burial ground[2] in its area or outside; and it may undertake the entire or partial care, management or control whether any interest in the soil is transferred to it or not; and for these purposes it may make any agreement with any person authorised to convey or agree with reference to such land or with any person interested therein[3].

[1] Specially defined in Open Spaces Act 1906, s 20.
[2] Specially defined in OSA 1906, s 20.
[3] OSA 1906, s 9.

Trusts

26.19 Subject to any conditions under which the estate, interest or control was acquired, the council must hold the land in trust to allow and with a view to enjoyment by the public as an open space and under proper control and regulation, and for no other purpose, and must maintain it in a good and decent state[1]. The land can, however, be freed from these statutory trusts (but not the contractual conditions) by disposal or reappropriation after a special procedure (see **12.31** above).

[1] Open Spaces Act 1906, s 11(1). For the special circumstances which can arise in a New Town see **24.30** above.

Administrative powers

26.20 To carry out the trusts a local council may enclose the land with proper railings and gates and may drain, level, lay out, turf, plant, ornament, light, provide with seats and otherwise improve it, and do all such works and employ such officers and servants as may be requisite[1].

[1] Open Spaces Act 1906, s 10.

Consecrated land, and games

26.21 The powers of management may not be exercised in consecrated land until a faculty or licence has been obtained from the bishop[1]. Games may not be played in a burial ground without the consent, in the case of consecrated land, of the bishop (given by licence or faculty), and in the case of other land, of the person from whom the estate, interest or control was obtained. Such consent may be given subject to conditions[2].

[1] Open Spaces Act 1906, s 11(1).
[2] OSA 1906, s 11(2).

Tombstones

26.22 Headstones, tombstones or monuments in a disused burial ground may be moved by a local council, but if it wishes to do so it must at least three months beforehand prepare a statement sufficiently describing by name, date and other necessary particulars the tombstones and monuments in the ground, and this statement must be open to public inspection; it must on three occasions advertise in a newspaper circulating in the area its intention, the existence and place of deposit of the statement and the hours when it is open to inspection, and, in addition, it must place a copy of the advertisement on the door of the church (if any) and send a copy by post to any known near relatives[1]. Further, if the ground is consecrated the council must wait for at least one month after the appearance of the last of the advertisements, and must then apply for a faculty or licence to the bishop. No monuments or tombstones in consecrated ground may be moved until such licence or faculty has been obtained[2].

For buildings on disused burial grounds see **33.6** below.

[1] Open Spaces Act 1906, s 16. Photographs are sometimes taken of the tombstones.
[2] OSA 1906, s 11(3) and (4).

Byelaws

26.23 For open spaces managed under the Act a local council may, with the approval of the Secretary of State (W), make byelaws to regulate their use (for instance for games), preserve order, prevent nuisances and for the removal of persons infringing the byelaws. Fines may be imposed and are recoverable summarily[1].

[1] Open Spaces Act 1906, s 15.

Extension to other property

26.24 A local council is entitled to exercise the powers of the Act respecting open spaces and burial grounds transferred to it under the Act in relation to open spaces and burial grounds of a similar nature which may be vested in it by any other title[1].

[1] Open Spaces Act 1906, s 12.

Co-operation

26.25 In carrying out the Act a local council may act jointly with any other local authority, and there is a right of mutual contribution[1].

[1] Open Spaces Act 1906, s 15.

Exceptions

26.26 The Open Spaces Act 1906 cannot apply to Royal Parks, land vested in the Crown or the Duchy of Lancaster, land belonging to the Honourable Societies of the Inner and Middle Temples, or any metropolitan common.

H   NATIONAL TRUST

26.27 With the Secretary of State's consent any local authority may contribute to the expenses of the National Trust in acquiring, maintaining or preserving any land (or building) in or in the neighbourhood of its area[1].

[1]   National Trust Act 1937, s 7(2).

I   RECREATIONAL FACILITIES INCLUDING BATHING

26.28 A local council or any other local authority may provide inside or outside[1] its area such recreational facilities as it thinks fit. The enabling legislation is very widely drawn and includes power to provide premises for the use of clubs or societies having athletic, social or recreational objects, to provide staff and instructors, to provide ancillary facilities such as car parks and places for the sale of food, drink and tobacco, and generally to provide buildings, equipment, supplies and assistance of any kind.

It can make the facilities available with or without charge.

The authorities may also make grants to other local authorities for these purposes and grants or loans to non-profit making voluntary bodies, in providing the facilities which the authorities cannot provide themselves[2]. Grants and loans cannot, however, be made to a voluntary body (such as a society which always meets in the private house of one of its members) which neither provides nor intends to provide the facilities, save from the 'free resource'[3].

A property held before 14 February 1977 for the purposes of the Public Health Act 1936, s 221(b) (bathing) or the Physical Training and Recreation Act 1937, s 4 (recreation and meetings) or the Local Government Act 1972, s 144(1)(b) (conferences, trade fairs and exhibitions) is now held under the Local Government (Miscellaneous Provisions) Act 1976.

[1]   The Swanley Town Council has a seaside holiday home. Swanley is far inland.
[2]   Local Government (Miscellaneous Provisions) Act 1976, s 19.
[3]   Local Government Act 1972, s 137.

J   PLEASURE GROUNDS AND PUBLIC WALKS

26.29 A local council may provide public walks and pleasure grounds, and may lay out, plant, improve and maintain them and may support or contribute to the support or purchase of such places provided by any person and whether they are in its area or not so long as they are situated conveniently for the inhabitants[1]; it may provide and let or license someone to provide and let pleasure boats together with the necessary buildings and equipment[2]; it may close the land for not more than 12 days in the year and grant its use (free or for payment) to any public charity or institution or for any agricultural, horticultural or other show or public purpose, or may use it for any such show or purpose itself, and on 'closed' days admission to the land may be free or for such payment as is directed by the local council; closure may not be imposed on a Sunday nor for more than six days consecutively nor upon more than a quarter of the total 'recreational land' available on a Bank Holiday or at

269

Christmas, Good Friday, or a day of public mourning or thanksgiving[3].

1   Public Health Act 1875, s 164.
2   Public Health (Amendment) Act 1890, s 44(2) and Public Health Act 1961, s 54.
3   Public Health (Amendment) Act 1890, s 44(1) and Public Health Act 1936, s 53.

Byelaws for land and boating

26.30 A council may make byelaws for the regulation of the land for the removal of any person infringing them[1]; and also on the naming and numbering of boats, the numbers of persons to be carried in them, boathouses and mooring places, rates of hire, qualifications of boatmen and for securing their good and orderly conduct while in charge of a boat[2].

1   Public Health Act 1875, s 164.
2   Public Health (Amendment) Act 1890, s 44(2).

K   SWIMMING POOLS AND BATHING PLACES

Management

26.31 Local councils now provide swimming pools and bathing places under their general power to provide recreational facilities (see **26.16** above). They may also close them temporarily so as to grant their exclusive use (either free or for payment) to a school or club or to persons organising swimming practices or contests, aquatic sports or other entertainments or may organise such events themselves[1]; and between 1 October and 30 April they may close the pool and use or allow it to be used or let it for such purpose and subject to such conditions as they think fit. There is also power to provide bathing huts and other conveniences for bathing and to charge for them[2].

1   Public Health Act 1936, s 225.
2   PHA 1936, ss 226 and 232.

Byelaws

26.32 A local council may make byelaws regulating its bathing places and persons resorting thereto; for excluding undesirables and for regulating such matters as bathing times, management of huts, and safety. The byelaws may provide for penalties and for the removal of persons infringing them. A printed copy or abstract must be exhibited at the bathing place[1]. There is also a certain power to make byelaws for places not under the council's management[2].

1   Public Health Act 1936, ss 223 and 231.
2   PHA 1936, s 233.

L   FACILITIES FOR COUNTRYSIDE VISITORS

For other sorts of visitors see **27.2** below.

26.33 Natural England has a general power to undertake experimental schemes to facilitate enjoyment of the countryside. The Countryside Council for Wales has a specific power to prepare schemes for experimental projects facilitating the enjoyment of the countryside. In both cases, the body must consult such persons (including local councils) as appear to it to have an interest. Schemes made by the Countryside Council for Wales must be confirmed by the Secretary of State[2].

Country parks, with or without facilities for sailing, boating, bathing and fishing may be provided by the councils of counties, districts and by a London borough council and the Common Council of the City of London. They can also provide camping and picnic sites with the necessary road access, car parks and conveniences, and in the case of commons in which a public right of access exists they can provide, on or near them, means for facilitating their enjoyment by persons going there for open-air recreation[3].

---

[2]   Countryside Act 1968, s 4.
[3]   Natural Environment and Rural Communities Act 2006, s 8; Countryside Act 1968, ss 6–10.

Chapter 27

GATHERINGS

A GENERAL

27.1 Local people gather at recurrent moments in pursuit of permanent introvert interests or social purposes, or intermittently to consider a local issue, and they form more or less permanent voluntary organisations to satisfy some local need.

There are also activities, loosely called 'entertainment', which increase the pleasure of life and which are carried on, generally speaking, in the context of large assemblies. Finally, there are gatherings of visitors whose motive may be curiosity, the holiday instinct or a rumoured or advertised attraction. The Cotswold parishes are famous for their beauty; hundreds of coastal communities and parishes have magnificent sands or scenery; Llangollen is not the only community which regularly shelters a large eisteddfod; the annual Aldeburgh Festival is held at the Maltings at Snape; and there have been jazz festivals in parishes in Hampshire and Northumberland. The popular mobility is at the bottom of new developments, to which a more extrovert attitude by the parishes and communities is required. This has brought about a recasting of the relevant law.

B TOURISM

Publicity, etc

27.2 Local councils, alone or jointly with others, may encourage visitors for recreation or health, or to hold conferences, trade fairs or exhibitions, and such encouragement may be given by advertisement or otherwise in Great Britain or abroad[1]. Arrangements could, for example, be made with a publisher of travel information to draw attention to the area and its beauties, or to advertise it suitably at travel agencies, or with a tour operator to make it a coach stopping place, or to assemble and publish information, for example on accommodation, which visitors might need.

[1] Local Government Act 1972, s 144.

Facilities

27.3 Similarly there is power to provide or join in facilities for recreation, conferences, trade fairs and exhibitions, or to encourage others to improve them. This is far-reaching. It would, for example, enable a local council to operate a conference, information and accommodation centre, or lend[1] money to a golf club for improvements provided that it was open to visitors, or design its hall or adapt an existing hall, with an eye to conferences, or let a building, not otherwise required at the time, to the organisers of a trade fair, or make a grant to harbour trustees or commissioners to improve facilities for the increasing number of yachtsmen.

[1] Under Local Government Act 1972, s 111.

C ENTERTAINMENT AND ARTS

Provision

27.4 A local council may do anything necessary or expedient to provide an entertainment of any kind, or facilities for dancing, or to maintain a band or orchestra, and there is a very general power to develop and improve the knowledge and practice of the arts, and of the crafts which serve them[1]. It may do these things itself, or arrange for them to be done or contribute to the expenses of so doing. It is under these powers that communities sponsor and organise eisteddfods; and by way of further example, local councils can back village choir festivals, and help local colonies of artists, potters, or sculptors by lending them premises in which to exhibit their works; it is possible even to engage instructors or teachers of music or painting.

Encouragement and advice can often be obtained from, or through, the Arts Council.

[1] Local Government Act 1972, s 145.

Suitable premises, properties and incidentals

27.5 Naturally the authorities may provide suitable premises, so that local councils may provide (but are much more likely to join in or encourage providing) theatres, concert and dance halls, and other such places and without infringing any contrary covenants or the licensing laws, any part of a park or pleasure ground may be set aside for these purposes, or may be used by or let to others for them, and the local council may incidentally provide refreshments and programmes, and may charge for them or for admission, and may advertise the proceedings.

D HALLS AND CENTRES

27.6 The powers possessed by local authorities (and originally enacted in 1925)[1] for providing or encouraging the provision of playing fields, gymnasiums or camping and holiday sites (see **26.16** above) for their own people are equally available for providing halls and (so-called) community centres for the use of clubs, societies or organisations with athletic, social or educational objects. It is hard to imagine an organisation (other than a criminal conspiracy) which is not covered by this definition; the type of facility originally envisaged was, however, intended for the use of local people, and experience showed that such halls and centres were well managed by representatives of the users; hence the practice of committing them to charitable trusts managed by committees representing local voluntary organisations and the local council. The standard vehicle for this method was a model trust deed drawn up by ACRE. The later versions of this model deed were agreed with NALC.

The legislation on tourism, entertainment and the arts has, certainly in some places, disturbed the position. It is desirable that relatively large and expensive buildings should be capable of varied and frequent use. Where many strangers are expected, some of these uses may, without forethought, conflict with those to which residents are accustomed. Moreover there seems to be no way in which the permanent representation of casual outsiders can be incorporated into the terms of a trust deed. A local council of a locality with hotel and similar interests, faced with a problem of community centre or public hall management, may have to approach the charitable trust method with caution.

[1] In a repealed part of the Public Health Act 1925.

Grants and loans

27.7 Grants and loans towards the construction, improvement and alteration of village halls are available from several sources. The National Lottery fund distribution bodies make grants for a wide range of purposes to charitable and similar bodies as well as to local authorities for the provision of recreational, social and cultural projects and buildings. Many district councils (T) make grants available for new halls and improvements to existing halls. ACRE operates the rural community buildings loan fund on behalf of the Commission for Rural Communities.

Parish or community halls

27.8 Independently of the community centre or village hall powers which local councils possess, they can also provide and furnish buildings for public meetings and assemblies, or contribute towards the expenses of any other local council or person who does so[1].

[1] Local Government Act 1972, s 133. For the right to use other places see **7.2** and **12.12** above.

E   WARDENS AND LEADERS

27.9 Wardens, teachers and leaders may be provided and trained so that effective use can be made of the facilities[1]. This power, which is being increasingly used, has been found especially valuable in areas with a large youth population.

[1] Local Government (Miscellaneous Provisions) Act 1976, s 19(1)(e).

F LANDS FOR LITERARY AND SCIENTIFIC INSTITUTES AND SCHOOLS

27.10 A local council or parish meeting may, with the consent of the Secretary of State[1] (or in the case of charity land, of the Charity Commission), convey land not exceeding one acre for each institute, to any number of literary or scientific institutes[2]. Similarly an acre may be conveyed for a school or schoolmaster's house[3], but there may not be more than one such site in the same ecclesiastical parish[4].

In all these cases the land reverts to the council or meeting if it ceases to be used for the purpose for which it was granted[5]. Some vigilance is required. Many transactions under this legislation are old and the documents have sometimes been forgotten. Lands have in the past been sold (for example by the local education authority) regardless of the reverter rule and the rights lost by operation of time. To cure this defect the land has since 1987 become subject to a trust for sale for the benefit of the person who would have been entitled to the ownership by virtue of the reverter[6]. Hence, the seller (whoever he may be) is a trustee of the property as long as he is in possession and becomes a trustee of the proceeds if he sells it, and in either case can be forced to hand it over.

[1] Literary and Scientific Institutions Act 1854, ss 6 and 8.
[2] Literary and Scientific Institutions Act 1854, ss 1 and 10.
[3] Schools Sites Act 1841, s 2.
[4] Schools Sites Act 1841, s 9 and Schools Sites Act 1857.
[5] Schools Sites Act 1841, s 2; Literary and Scientific Institutions Act 1854, s 4.
[6] Reverter of Sites Act 1987.

G TWINNING

27.11 Local councils take part in the growing practice of forming alliances and exchanging visits with foreign places. This ability stems from the powers described in sections A to D of this chapter combined with the 'free resource' and the power to pay allowances abroad. Councils wishing to make contact with a foreign authority should obtain advice and assistance from the European and International Unit of the Local Government Association.

H FLAGPOLES IN HIGHWAYS

27.12 Local councils may erect flagpoles in highways with the consent of the highway authority or, in the case of a bridge or its approaches, with the consent of the body responsible for them; these authorities or bodies must be indemnified for possible payments which they may have to make and the council must see that the poles are safe and properly maintained[1]. Outside highways no such conditions apply.

[1] Highways Act 1980, s 144.

Chapter 28

PUBLIC LIGHTING AND CRIME PREVENTION

A SUMMARY

28.1 Lighting is of three major kinds, namely open space, road and footway lighting. 'Road lighting' and 'footway lighting' are technical terms describing not the function but the layout and dimensions of a lighting system.

Open space lighting

28.2 Any local council may light an open space acquired or controlled under the Open Spaces Act 1906[1].

[1]   Parish Councils Act 1957, s 8(1) and Open Spaces Act 1906, s 10.

Road lighting

28.3 A highway authority may provide road lighting in any highway for which it is responsible[1]. Road lighting is any such lighting other than footway lighting[2]. On 1 April 1967, all road lighting (including lamps, apparatus and property) was transferred from the lighting authority to the highway authority, and agreements were made respecting the transfer, and defining the property and rights to be transferred[3].

Where the highway authority is the Secretary of State no liability for outstanding loans or loan charges can be transferred to him[4], but where it is a county council (T), the agreement might transfer such liabilities.

A highway authority can delegate its road lighting powers to a lighting authority, which exercises them as agent. Works and expenditure must be approved by the highway authority; the lighting authority must comply with any requirements on the manner in which works are to be carried out, and with any directions about the terms of agreements made with contractors. Works must be carried out to the satisfaction of the highway authority[5], and if the system is not in proper repair or condition the highway authority can by notice require it to be put in order, and if the notice is not complied with it may do the work itself[6].

Delegation agreements may be terminated by notice. Such a notice must not be given in the last three months of a calendar year and must not take effect until 1 April in the year after which it is given[7].

This is a rare case where delegation has not been abolished. A delegate cannot delegate further, whereas an authority exercising another's functions by arrangement, can arrange for their discharge by a committee, sub-committee or officer. If there is a practical problem in such a distinction, it seems that lighting authorities can make mutual arrangements instead of delegation agreements[8].

[1] Highways Act 1980, s 97.
[2] Highways Act 1980, s 270.
[3] Highways Act 1980, s 270 and see below.
[4] Highways Act 1980, s 272(4).
[5] Highways Act 1980, s 98(1) and (2).
[6] Highways Act 1980, s 98(3).
[7] Highways Act 1980, s 98(5).
[8] See Local Government Act 1972, s 101(1).

Footway lighting

28.4 Footway lighting has no necessary connection with a footway at all. It is simply lighting where either no lamp is more than 13 feet above the ground, or no lamp is more than 20 feet above ground and there is in addition at least one interval exceeding 50 yards between adjacent lamps in the system[1], but the Secretary of State may by order vary these definitions.

Lighting authorities may provide or, as the case may be, continue to provide footway lighting, but even these systems are liable to transfer to the highway authority in any one of three obvious contingencies. The first is where the lighting authority itself alters the system so that it ceases to comply with the definition of footway lighting; the second is where the old definition is altered and the system does not comply with the new definition; the third is where the highway authority proposes to provide road lighting along the same road and gives notice to that effect to the lighting authority[2]. In each of these cases the method of transfer is the same as if it had happened on 1 April 1967.

New lighting requires the consent of the highway authority[3].

[1] Highways Act 1980, s 270(1).
[2] Highways Act 1980, s 272(2) and (7).
[3] Highways Act 1980, s 301.

Footway lighting authorities

28.5 A district council (T) may light streets (up to footway standard), markets and public buildings[1]. A local council (or parish meeting where no parish council exists) may provide footway lighting[2].

Where a road hitherto lit by a local council or parish meeting becomes a special road[3] an order may authorise or even require the special road authority to light the road concurrently with or to the exclusion of the local council[4]. The

Secretary of State makes the order if he is providing the special road, otherwise the highway authority makes it and he confirms it[5]. Motorways are the commonest type of special road.

Wherever an area is represented upon a local council the latter (either alone or in combination with other lighting authorities)[6] is the administering authority under the section, and where there is no local council the section is administered in England by the parish meeting which may appoint a committee for the purpose.

1   Public Health Act 1875, s 161.
2   Parish Councils Act 1957, ss 3 and 1A.
3   Highways Act 1980, s 16.
4   Highways Act 1980, s 18(1)(e) and (8).
5   Highways Act 1980, s 18(3).
6   Parish Councils Act 1957, s 6.

B   POWERS

28.6 The lighting powers may be used to light any highway, except a special road, including any footpath or bridleway and any other road, lane, footway, square, court, alley or passage, whether a thoroughfare or not, and also any other place to which the public has access[1]. It is not necessary that the lighting equipment shall be actually situated in those places so long as they are designed to light them, for a lighting authority is expressly empowered (subject, however, to safeguards mentioned in **20.2** above) to cause the apparatus to be installed on or against any premises or in such other places as may be convenient[2].

Lighting authorities may provide and maintain such lamps, lampposts and other materials and apparatus as they think fit, contract for the supply of gas, electricity or other means of lighting and employ with or without remuneration the necessary maintenance and superintendent staff[3]. They also have a power of contribution towards the expense incurred by any other council or person in the provision of lighting, and there is also power to combine[4].

In the unusual case of a walkway, the lighting powers cannot be exercised unless the walkway agreement specifies that they may be exercised, or the building's owner has given his consent[5].

1   Parish Councils Act 1957, s 3(1) and s 7.
2   Parish Councils Act 1957, s 3(1)(b).
3   Parish Councils Act 1957, s 3(1)(a), (c) and (d).
4   Parish Councils Act 1957, s 6.
5   Walkways Regulations 1973, SI 1973/686.

C   FINANCE

28.7 The expenses of footway lighting and lighting under the Open Spaces Act 1906 are chargeable upon the whole parish or community in the ordinary way.

D   LIGHTING AUTHORITY'S LIABILITY

28.8 In some rare cases a lighting authority may be liable to a householder for the depreciation of his interest in the house by physical factors, which include artificial lighting[1].

[1]   Land Compensation Act 1973, s 1.

E   FRONTAGERS' LIABILITY IN PRIVATE STREETS

Need for vigilance

28.9 In ordinary cases the expense of lighting installation must be defrayed by the lighting authority, but in private streets it is occasionally possible to impose the cost on private persons, with the result that the frontager will pay in the end. This can be important in the case of new housing estates whether built by a local authority or by a private developer, but the occasions for taking advantage of the law are fugitive, and vigilance is necessary to ensure that the opportunity does not slip away.

The two codes

28.10 The Private Street Works Code (PSWC) is in force in all districts; the Advance Payments Code only in certain parishes and communities, to which the county council (T) may add, by resolution. Notice that the resolution has been passed must be exhibited in the locality[1].

Of these two codes the universal PSWC[2] empowers a county council to resolve to execute certain works (including lighting) in a private street and the cost of this operation is eventually apportioned between the frontagers. There is provision for publishing specifications, hearing objections to them by the magistrates, apportioning the cost and hearing appeals to the magistrates against the apportionments, and finally for recovering the sums due. There is also an independent right of appeal in some cases to the Secretary of State, who may on such appeal order a local authority to contribute to the cost. Once the procedure has been completed the street becomes a highway maintainable at the public expense and nothing more can be done. It follows that when a housing estate is being built, efforts should be made to ensure that the county council includes lighting to the satisfaction of the local council in the specification.

The Advance Payments Code[3] (where in force) lays down that anyone who erects a building on a road may be required to deposit or secure a sum which will suffice to pay for the cost of such works (including lighting) as may have to be carried out in future under the PSWC. The deposit exonerates the frontager from future liability, and efforts should therefore be made to ensure that the cost of lighting is included in the estimate.

[1]   Highways Act 1980, Sch 15.
[2]   Highways Act 1980, ss 205–218.
[3]   Highways Act 1980, ss 219–225.

F   SURVEILLANCE ETC

28.11 The (repealed) Lighting and Watching Act 1834 was passed as much to prevent night crime as to light streets. Parish authorities could adopt it and many did. As the police forces and the traffic grew, watching was slowly taken over by the police, while lighting came to be seen mainly as part of traffic management. By 1997 the need to watch against crime had reappeared and the local councils were empowered, for the detection or prevention of crime to install equipment, establish any scheme or assist others to do these things, or make grants for these purposes[1]. In 1998 they were required to exercise all their functions with due regard to crime and disorder and to co-operate with other bodies in so doing[2]. In practice where a need seems to have arisen a local council will wish to consult the police. The term 'equipment' is not necessarily confined to detection apparatus such as cameras, but may include alarms and special lights. 'Schemes' might include neighbourhood watch arrangements or police security advice and lectures.

[1]   Local Government and Rating Act 1997, s 31.
[2]   Crime and Disorder Act 1998, ss 5 and 17; and see **22.28** above.

Chapter 29

ALLOTMENTS FOR CULTIVATION AND COMMON PASTURE

A   DEFINITIONS

29.1 Strictly speaking an allotment is a piece of land *allotted* to a person or for a particular purpose under an Inclosure Award, but the word soon came to mean land allotted for a public purpose, such as recreation or poor relief[1], and finally land which is let in small plots for cultivation. These, however, are lay, not legal usages, and though definitions exist for the purposes of particular Acts, there is no general technical definition.

About one quarter of all allotment land in England and Wales is privately owned. This chapter is not concerned with such land.

Poor allotments were cultivation allotments provided as part of the general poor law[2]. Fuel allotments were provided under Inclosure Acts and awards as compensation for turbary, estovers and other fuel rights. Field gardens are cultivation allotments provided under the general Inclosure Acts from 1845 onwards[3]. Parochial charity allotments were carved out of lands held for the purposes of parochial charities[4].

An allotment garden is a plot not exceeding 1,210 square yards (for metric equivalent see **20.5** above) which is wholly or mainly cultivated by the occupier to produce vegetables or fruit for consumption by himself and his family[5]. It cannot be agricultural land for the purposes of the Agriculture Act 1947[6], and it is not an agricultural holding within the Agricultural Holdings Act 1986[7], because an agricultural holding is the aggregate of agricultural land comprised in a contract (other than 'tied land') for an agricultural tenancy and which is used for a trade or business, or land which is designated as agricultural land by the Secretary of State. Tenancies of agricultural land entered into after 31 August 1995 are farm business tenancies subject to the Agricultural Tenancies Act 1995. An allotment garden cannot be the subject of such a farm business tenancy because it is not cultivated as part of a trade or business.

[1] It is often used in this sense in statutes.
[2] See Poor Relief Acts 1819 and 1831; Crown Allotments Act 1831. All the relevant provisions of these Acts have now been repealed.
[3] Inclosure Act 1845, s 31. See also ss 34, 73 and 87.
[4] Allotments Extension Act 1882, now repealed.
[5] Allotments Act 1922, s 22(1).
[6] Agriculture Act 1947, s 109(1).

29.1 *Allotments for cultivation and common pasture*

[7] Agricultural Holdings Act 1948, s 1 amended by Agricultural Holdings Act 1986.

B OWNERSHIP, TRUSTS AND AUTHORITIES

29.2 Usually allotments (whatever their origin) will nowadays be vested for the benefit of the locality in the local council, parish trustees or Welsh county or county borough[1], but exceptional cases still occur where they have not been transferred, usually by charitable trustees.

Whatever their origin, an allotments authority manages its allotments as one unit; the great majority are provided under the Allotments Acts 1908–1950, but these Acts apply whether the allotments are provided under them or not[2]; nevertheless, the trusts upon which a given allotment was originally held will remain in force.

[1] Local Government Act 1894, s 6(1)(c) and s 19, and Small Holdings and Allotments Act 1908, ss 33 and 61.
[2] Small Holdings and Allotments Act 1908, s 23(2).

Other authorities (T)

29.3 In England district councils (T) have allotments functions only in non-parochial places; consequently where a parish is constituted by an order and land in it is held by a district council as or for allotments, the land automatically passes to the parish council or, as the case may be, to the parish meeting[1]. In Wales counties or county boroughs have allotments powers concurrently with the communities[2].

[1] Local Government (Parishes and Parish Councils) Regulations 1999, SI 1999/545, reg 10.
[2] Local Government Act 1972, s 179 as excluded in England by Sch 29, para 9.

C OBLIGATION TO PROVIDE ALLOTMENT GARDENS

29.4 A local council must formally consider any written request by six or more electors to operate the Allotments Acts[1] and, in addition, if it is of the opinion that there is a demand it is bound to provide allotments[2] but the duty is restricted to the provision of allotment gardens[3]. It would be difficult to be of any other opinion in the face of a resolution from a well-attended electors' meeting.

As long as the allotments, provided to satisfy the obligation, are reasonably accessible to users, it is not essential that they should be within the locality[4].

[1] Small Holdings and Allotments Act 1908, s 23(2).
[2] Small Holdings and Allotments Act 1908, s 23(1).
[3] Allotments Act 1950, s 9.
[4] Small Holdings and Allotments Act 1908, s 25(1).

D   PROVISION

Usual modes

29.5 Land for allotments can be provided in the manners usual for other purposes, namely by appropriation[1], purchase[2] or compulsory purchase[3].

[1]   Local Government Act 1972, s 126.
[2]   LGA 1972, s 124.
[3]   Small Holdings and Allotments Act 1908, ss 39–41.

Hiring by district council (T)

29.6 District councils (T) (which in England are not allotments authorities) may hire land compulsorily for leasing to a local council for the purpose of allotments[1]. The compulsory hiring order must be confirmed by the Secretary of State and the procedure resembles the procedure for compulsory purchase. The order must incorporate regulations made by him, and these place the local council in much the same position as to covenants, compensation at the end of the tenancy and rent as it would hold under an ordinary lease[2]; in particular it must not confer a power to cut timber or take, sell or carry away minerals without the landlord's consent save in so far as such operations may be necessary to adapt the land for allotments or erect the associated buildings, and even then only upon payment of compensation for minerals, sand, gravel or clay removed[3].

The Secretary of State must not confirm an order to hire and break up pasture, unless no arable land is available, and consequently the order if made must specifically permit such breaking up in the case of allotment gardens[4]; in other cases he must satisfy himself that breaking up will not depreciate the land or that the allotments cannot otherwise be successfully cultivated[5].

The land must be acquired for not less than 14 nor more than 35 years, but the tenancy is renewable if the council gives notice to the landlord not more than two years nor less than one year before the expiration of the lease. The renewed tenancy will then be upon the same terms as before save that in default of agreement on rent, the rent will be fixed by a valuer appointed by the Secretary of State[6]. The tenancy is perpetually renewable in this way at the option of the council[7] but the landlord may at any stage resume the land on twelve months' notice if he needs it for building, mining or industrial purposes[8].

[1]   The regulations appear in the Small Holdings and Allotments (Compulsory Hiring) Regulations 1936, SI 1936/196.
[2]   See note 1 above.
[3]   Small Holdings and Allotments Act 1908, s 39(2) and Sch 1, Part II, para 2.
[4]   Allotments Act 1922, s 8.
[5]   Small Holdings and Allotments Act 1908, s 29(2) and Sch 1, Part II, para 2; Land Settlement Facilities Act 1919, s 25; see also *Knowles v Salford Corporation* [1922] 1 Ch 328.
[6]   Small Holdings and Allotments Act 1908, s 44(1).
[7]   Law of Property Act 1922, s 145 and Sch 15, para 9.
[8]   Small Holdings and Allotments Act 1908, s 46(6).

New Forest

29.7 In the New Forest the Crown Estate Commissioners may lease a limited amount of land to a local council for allotments. Such a lease becomes void if the land is used for any other purpose, but while it lasts it suspends any common rights exercisable over the land[1].

[1] Allotments Act 1922, s 21.

E BUILDINGS AND ADAPTATION OF LAND

29.8 The allotments authority may improve and adapt land for letting for allotments, by draining, fencing, dividing, acquiring approaches, making roads and otherwise as it thinks fit, and this power of adaptation includes power to erect buildings and adapt existing buildings, but so that no more than one house is erected for occupation with any one allotment nor with an allotment of less than one acre[1].

In the case of field gardens buildings are prohibited and the local council or trustees must pull them down if put up[2].

[1] Small Holdings and Allotments Act 1908, s 26.
[2] Inclosure Act 1845, s 109.

F TOWN AND COUNTRY PLANNING

29.9 The use of land for agriculture and the use of buildings occupied together with agricultural land is not to be taken to involve development, for which, therefore, development permission is unnecessary. This makes development permission for allotments equally unnecessary. Sheds and similar structures not covered by this rule are permitted development so long as they are provided by the relevant local authority[1] (see **24.21** above).

[1] Town and Country Planning Act 1990, ss 55(2)(e) and 336; Town and Country Planning (General Permitted Development) Order 1995, SI 1995/418, Sch 2, Part 12, Class A.

G LETTING AND RENT

Field gardens

29.10 Field gardens must be offered to the poor of the locality in plots not exceeding a quarter of an acre on tenancies for a year or from year to year, upon such terms as the allotments authority thinks fit, but free of all rates and taxes[1] and at a fair agricultural rent if sufficient to cover the rates and taxes[2]. If they cannot be let in these amounts and at these rents, they may be let in plots not exceeding one acre at the best annual rent (without premium or fine) and on such terms that they may be resumed at twelve months' notice[3].

If the rent is 40 days in arrears or if at any time after the third month of the tenancy, the tenant is not carrying out the terms of the tenancy or has gone to live more than a mile from the locality, a month's notice to quit must be given.

If he lives there this must be served on him: if he lives outside, it must be fixed in some conspicuous manner on the allotment[4].

Arrears of rent are recoverable by distress or other ordinary means[5], but possession may be recovered by application to a county court[6].

1   Inclosure Act 1845, s 109.
2   Commons Act 1876, s 26.
3   Commons Act 1876, s 26.
4   Small Holdings and Allotments Act 1908, s 30(2).
5   Inclosure Act 1845, s 112.
6   Inclosure Act 1845, s 111.

Modern allotments

29.11 'Modern' allotments under the Allotments Acts 1908–1950 may not without the consent of the allotments authority be sub-let[1]. The duration of a lease is governed by the ordinary law[2]. The rent must be such as a tenant can reasonably be expected to pay for the land on the terms on which it is in fact let to him, but may be less if there exist special circumstances affecting him personally which render it proper to reduce it[3]. If the rent is £1.25p a year or less, the whole of it may be demanded in advance; in other cases not more than one quarter's rent may be required in advance[4].

In relation to modern allotments which are not allotment gardens[5], the rules on arrears, breaches of covenant, departure from the locality and (with one exception) the consequent notice to quit together with their relevant legal remedies are the same as the rules relating to field gardens.

Holders of modern allotments may have certain compensation rights, and accordingly the court may stay delivery of possession until any compensation due has been made or secured[6].

1   Small Holdings and Allotments Act 1908, s 27.
2   Local Government Act 1972, s 127.
3   Allotments Act 1950, s 10(1).
4   Allotments Act 1950, s 10(2).
5   Allotments Act 1922, s 1.
6   Small Holdings and Allotments Act 1908, s 30.

Allotment gardens

29.12 The rules on the letting and rent of allotment gardens are the same as those for other modern allotments, but the rules on the ending of tenancies are far more rigid. Such a tenancy may (notwithstanding any agreement to the contrary) only be ended in six ways.

Notice to quit First, notice to quit must be of at least one year's duration expiring on or after 29 September or on or before 6 April, in any year[1].

Re-entry for breach Second, there is a right of re-entry if the tenant fails to pay the rent or breaks any term or condition of the tenancy or becomes bankrupt or compounds with his creditors, or, where the tenant is an association, if it goes into liquidation.

Re-entry in the contract In the remaining four cases the right of re-entry can be exercised only if it is contained in or affects the contract of tenancy; they are (third) re-entry on land let by a corporation and needed for a railway, dock, canal water or other public undertaking (other than agricultural land); in this case three months' written notice is required save in an emergency; (fourth) re-entry upon land acquired for housing under the Housing Acts and now required by a local authority for housing; (fifth) re-entry upon land acquired by a local authority for one of its statutory purposes and now required for that purpose; (sixth) re-entry after three months' written notice upon land required for building, mining or other industrial purposes or for roads or sewers connected therewith[2].

Most of these cases will affect the allotments authority's relationship with its tenants only where the land has been taken on lease and sub-let, but care must be taken in allotments agreements to make provision for them, and it is generally simplest to word such agreements so that the authority's rights of entry on allotment gardens shall be similar to those provided by law for field gardens.

[1]   Allotments Act 1922, s 1(a) amended by Allotments Act 1950, s 1.
[2]   Allotments Act 1922, s 1(b)–(e).

Agricultural holdings and farm business tenancies

29.13 If an allotment exceeds 1,210 square yards (for the metric equivalent, see **20.5** above), let for commercial cultivation because nobody can be found to cultivate it for personal consumption and it was granted before 1 September 1995, it may become an agricultural holding and the special rules on notice to quit agricultural holdings will apply. Broadly speaking such notices are invalid if they purport to terminate a tenancy before the end of 12 months from the end of the current year of the tenancy[1] and, in addition, a valid notice cannot operate if the tenant has within one month of service served a counter notice and if thereafter the Agricultural Land Tribunal does not consent to the notice to quit[2].

If such an allotment is let after 1 September 1995 the tenancy may become a farm business tenancy subject to the Agricultural Tenancies Act 1995.

Covenant against commercial use It is, therefore, desirable that where allotment land is to be let in plots exceeding 40 poles, the tenant should be required to covenant that the land is to be cultivated exclusively for his own consumption.

[1]   Agricultural Holdings Act 1986, s 25.
[2]   AHA 1986, s 24.

H   OFFENCES

29.14 It is an offence under the general law to destroy or damage anyone else's property intentionally or recklessly[1] or to steal anything[2].

[1]   Criminal Damage Act 1971, s 1(1).

² Theft Act 1968, s 1.

I   RULES

Modern allotments

29.15 An allotments authority may make allotments rules which are binding upon all persons¹. They may contain provisions to prevent undue preferences, to define the qualifications of tenants, the length of notice to quit and the conditions of cultivation and rent. They may be published as the authority thinks fit, but free copies must be given on demand.

¹   Small Holdings and Allotments Act 1908, s 28, amended by Local Government Planning and Land Act 1980, Sch 5.

J   ALLOTMENT MANAGERS

29.16 Allotment managers may be appointed; they may consist partly of members of the council and partly of locally resident individuals who, as such, are liable to pay the rate or council tax. They may do anything in relation to the management of allotments which the council could do, and may incur expenses up to a limit authorised by it, and any such expenses are deemed to be expenses of the council¹.

¹   Small Holdings and Allotments Act 1908, s 29.

K   COMPENSATION AT THE END OF TENANCIES (OTHER THAN ALLOTMENT GARDENS)

29.17 Parties cannot contract out of their rights to and liabilities for compensation, but may by agreement increase the rights of the tenant.

Prohibited improvements

29.18 An allotments authority may in writing prohibit improvements, and if a tenant is aggrieved by such prohibition he may appeal to the Minister of Agriculture who may confirm, vary or annul the prohibition. His decision is final¹. The tenant is not entitled to compensation for an improvement which has been effectively prohibited².

¹   Small Holdings and Allotments Act 1908, s 47.
²   Small Holdings and Allotments Act 1908, s 47(2).

'Compensation crops'

29.19 A tenant (provided that he has carried out the improvement himself¹) may claim compensation for the 'compensation crops' which include permanent fruit trees and bushes, strawberry plants, asparagus, rhubarb and other vegetable crops likely to be productive for two or more years[2].

1 Small Holdings and Allotments Act 1908, Sch 2, Part I.
2 Small Holdings and Allotments Act 1908, s 47(4).

'Removables'

29.20 The tenant may before, but not after, the expiration of the tenancy remove any trees, bushes, toolhouse, shed, greenhouse, fowl-house or pigsty for which he has no claim to compensation. In the alternative he may, even though the allotment exceeds two acres[1], claim compensation for crops (including fruit), for labour expended and manure applied, for fruit trees and bushes planted with the previous written consent of the authority and for drains, outbuildings, pigsties, fowl-houses and other structural improvements made at the tenant's expense and with such consent. From the amount of such claim is deducted amounts due for rent, breach of contract, and wilful or negligent damage[2]. In case of dispute the amount is settled by a valuer appointed by the local county court judge upon written application by either party, and is recoverable, if not paid, within 14 days as a debt within the ordinary jurisdiction of the county court[3].

1 Small Holdings and Allotments Act 1908, s 47(3) and Allotments Act 1922, s 3(5).
2 Allotments Act 1922, s 3(2) and (3).
3 Allotments Act 1922, ss 3(4) and 6(1).

Compensation by landlord

29.21 Subject to any provisions to the contrary in the tenancy agreement, the allotments authority is entitled on quitting land which it has hired for allotments, to compensation for the 'compensation crops' and, in addition (if such improvement was necessary to adapt the land for allotments), for the erection, alteration or enlargement of buildings, formation of silos, laying down of permanent pasture, making and planting osier beds, making of water meadows, irrigation works, gardens, roads, bridges, water courses, ponds, wells, reservoirs or works for agricultural water supply and fences; for planting hops, orchards or fruit bushes; for protecting young trees; for reclaiming waste; for warping and weiring; for embankments and sluices against floods; for wire work in hop gardens; for drainage; for removal of bracken, gorse, tree roots, boulders and other obstructions and for permanent sheep dips[1].

Moreover where the tenancy is determined by notice to quit or re-entry for industrial, housing, or statutory purposes or for purposes of a public undertaking (see **29.10** above), the allotments authority may claim compensation for growing crops and manure[2], and also for disturbance up to the amount of one year's rent[3].

1 Small Holdings and Allotments Act 1908, Sch 2, Part II.
2 Allotments Act 1922, s 2.
3 Allotments Act 1950, s 3.

L COMPENSATION AT THE END OF ALLOTMENT GARDEN'S TENANCY

29.22 A tenant of an allotment garden has the same rights of compensation for growing crops, manure and disturbance against the allotments authority as it has against a superior landlord, and may exercise them in like circumstances, and in cases where the parish or community authority's tenancy has come to an end[1].

He may also before but not after the end of the tenancy, remove fruit trees and bushes and any erection, fencing or other improvement provided by him, making good any damage done in the process[2].

Compensation may also be recovered from a foreclosing mortgagee as if he were the landlord, and a tenant who compensates an outgoing tenant is entitled to claim for improvements as if he had made them himself[3].

[1] Allotments Act 1922, s 2 and Allotments Act 1950, s 3.
[2] Allotments Act 1922, s 4.
[3] Allotments Act 1922, s 5.

M ARBITRATION AND VALUATION

Act of 1908

29.23 Compensation disputes under the Act of 1908 are settled by an arbitrator appointed by the parties or in default of agreement by the Secretary of State (currently for Environment, Food and Rural Affairs), and the arbitration is held under the Agricultural Holdings Act 1986, and not under the Arbitration Acts. The arbitrator may state a case for the opinion of the county court, whence an appeal may be made to the Court of Appeal.

Act of 1922

29.24 Compensation disputes under the Act of 1922 are settled by a valuer.

The essential difference between the two procedures is that an arbitrator decides upon evidence placed before him by the parties, whereas a valuer uses his own knowledge and skill.

N SALES AND EXCHANGES OF ALLOTMENT LAND

29.25 Poor and recreational allotments may be exchanged for better land under orders made, on application by the local council or trustees, by the Secretary of State[1].

Field gardens may be sold with the approval of the Secretary of State for the purchase within a reasonable time of other land to be held upon the same trusts[2].

Modern allotments must not be sold without the consent of the Secretary of State[3]. Before giving his consent, the Secretary of State must be satisfied that:

(a) the allotment is not necessary or is surplus to requirements;

(b)   adequate provision will be made for displaced plotholders or that such provision is impracticable;

(c)   the number of people on the waiting list has been taken into account; and

(d)   the authority has actively promoted and publicised the availability of allotment sites and has consulted the National Society of Allotment and Leisure Gardeners.

Fuel and field garden allotments can be acquired compulsorily for the purposes of a New Town, and the land used for other purposes (see **24.32** above).

1   See Inclosure Acts 1845, s 149; 1852, s 21. For appropriations see **12.29** and **12.31** above.
2   Commons Act 1876, s 27.
3   Allotments Act 1925, s 8, amended by Agricultural Land (Utilisation) Act 1931, Sch 2.

O   ASSOCIATIONS

29.26 An allotments authority may sell allotments to persons working on a co-operative system provided that the system is approved by the county council (T)[1].

Lettings to allotments associations are now made under the authority's ordinary letting powers.

1   Small Holdings and Allotments Act 1908, ss 27(6) and 61(4) and Small Holdings and Allotments Act 1926, s 3.

P   COMMON PASTURE

29.27 An allotments authority may acquire land, stints and other alienable common rights and let them to tenants of allotments[1]. If it wishes to provide common pasture for other people it must apply to the county council (T) for a scheme[2].

1   Small Holdings and Allotments Act 1908, s 42.
2   Small Holdings and Allotments Act 1908, s 34.

Q   ACCOUNTS

29.28 There is no legal obligation to keep separate allotments accounts but in practice the rules and laws on the subject cannot be administered without them.

Chapter 30

HEALTH

A   WASHHOUSES, LAUNDERETTES AND BATHS

30.1 A local council may provide open or covered public baths and it may provide washhouses equipped with washing machines, with or without drying grounds and may lay the necessary pipes and make charges and byelaws of a nature similar to those which apply to swimming facilities[1]. The provision of these facilities is classed as a business activity for VAT purposes and is standard rated. Councils should therefore levy VAT on charges for their use.

[1] Public Health Act 1936, ss 221(a), 222, 223 and 227. There is at least one local council launderette.

B   PUBLIC CONVENIENCES

30.2 A local council may provide public conveniences but must not do so in, or under, a highway or proposed highway without the consent of the highway authority nor in relation to a walkway without the consent of the owner of the building[1]. It may make byelaws on conduct, and it may let the conveniences or charge for them, except for urinals. Access must not be impeded by turnstiles[2].

[1] Walkways Regulations 1973, SI 1973/686.
[2] Public Health Act 1936, s 87, as amended by Local Government Act 1974, Sch 14, para 9.

C   WATER

30.3 A local council may utilise any well, spring or stream in its area and provide facilities for obtaining water therefrom and may execute the necessary consequential works, and this can, as at Blockley in Gloucestershire, be lucrative but the powers must not be exercised so as to interfere with any private right or the powers of the district council (T). It may also contribute to the expenses of any other local council or person in doing these things[1].

[1] Public Health Act 1936, s 125.

D   DRAINAGE AND PONDS

30.4 A local council may drain, clean or cover or otherwise deal with any pond, pool, ditch, gutter or place containing or used for the collection of any drainage, filth, stagnant water or matter likely to be prejudicial to health, but not so as to interfere with any private right or any public drainage, sewerage or sewage disposal works, and may carry out any incidental or consequential works or contribute to the expense incurred by any other person in so doing[1]. These powers can be used to improve the many village ponds for example by introducing goldfish to keep down mosquitoes.

[1]   Public Health Act 1936, s 260(1).

E   LITTER AND GRAFFITI

Bins

30.5 A local council may provide, and must regularly empty and cleanse litter bins which it provides, in public places and may erect anti-litter notices. Such bins and notices cannot be placed in open spaces without the consent of the controlling authority nor on land not forming part of a street without the consent of the owner and occupier. In addition, certain other consents may be needed. These are much the same as for a bus shelter (see **31.40** below). It may empty and cleanse such bins provided by other authorities. Refuse and litter collected may be sold[1].

A county council (T) and a metropolitan district council may contribute to the expenses of a local council in providing litter bins. A local council may contribute to the reasonable expenses of any person providing etc them and to the expenses of another local council exercising its functions under the Litter Act 1983[2].

[1]   Litter Act 1983, s 5.
[2]   LA 1983, s 6.

Proceedings

30.6 A local council may complain to a magistrates' court if it is aggrieved by the defacement of certain lands by litter, including dog faeces, or refuse. In the case of a highway or motorway the defendant must be the responsible authority or the Secretary of State; in the case of land in the open air open to public access, it must be the county (T) or district (T) council, the Crown or a statutory undertaker in charge of the land, or the occupier of such land if situated in a litter control area.

Five days' notice must be given before laying the complaint before the court, which may make a litter abatement order requiring the land to be cleared by a certain date. Disobedience is an offence (level 4 fine).

A similar procedure applies to dirty roads.

The council may be awarded costs if the court is satisfied that the complaint is true and that it was reasonable to make it[1].

[1]   Environmental Protection Act 1990, ss 89–91.

Dropping litter—powers of local councils

30.7 It is an offence to throw down, drop or otherwise deposit any litter in any place (whether on land or in water) in the area of a principal litter authority which is open to the air, so long as the public have access to it, with or without payment[1].

If an authorised officer of a principal litter authority finds a person whom he believes has just committed the offence of dropping litter he may give notice to him offering an opportunity of discharging any liability to conviction for that offence by payment of a fixed penalty. The amount of the fixed penalty is specified by a principal litter authority in relation to its area or, if no such amount is specified, £75. If this is paid within 14 days after receiving the notice, the offender cannot be convicted of the offence of dropping litter. The officer may require a person to whom he intends to give a fixed penalty notice to give his name and address. Failure to do so, or the giving of false particulars, is an offence (level 3 fine). Local councils are litter authorities for the purpose of issuing fixed penalty notices for dropping litter. The Secretary of State has power to prescribe conditions to be applied to a local council in relation to the authorisation of persons to give fixed penalty notices[2].

[1] Environmental Protection Act 1990, s 87, as amended by the Clean Neighbourhoods and Environment Act 2005.
[2] EPA 1990, s 88, as amended by Clean Neighbourhoods and Environment Act 2005.

Graffiti and fly-posting

30.8 In the case of analogous offences involving graffiti or fly-posting, fixed penalty notices of the same kind may be issued by the same persons and subject to the same sanctions[1].

A local authority may arrange for a local council to carry out its function of issuing penalty notices. The Secretary of State may by regulations prescribe conditions which must be satisfied by a person before he is authorised by a local council to issue penalty notices[2].

[1] Anti-social Behaviour Act 2003, ss 43 and 43B.
[2] ABA 2003, s 47.

Co-operation between authorities

30.9 County councils (T) must consult their local authorities, including the local councils and parish meetings, from time to time and also such voluntary bodies as they shall agree upon, about the steps which it and the authorities and bodies shall take for abating litter. It must prepare, publicise and revise a statement of the steps agreed to be taken and must keep a copy of it available for public inspection[1]. Not many of these documents seemed to be available in 2009.

[1] Litter Act 1983, s 4.

F   STATUTORY NUISANCES

30.10 A few matters are specially declared to be statutory nuisances, but most 'prejudicial to health or a nuisance' are in the form of badly maintained premises; smoke, fumes, gases or noise emitted from premises; dust, steam, smell or other effluvia arising on industrial, trade or business premises; accumulations or deposits; noise emitted from or caused by a vehicle, machinery or equipment in a street; or animals kept in a place or in a manner likely to prejudice health or be a nuisance.

District councils (T) must try to discover and take action against these, mainly by serving abatement notices, but a local council may complain independently to a magistrates' court that it is aggrieved by such a nuisance, but it must give written notice of intention to complain to the person responsible. In the case of noise, at least three days is required, in other cases 21 days. The court may issue the abatement notices, or, after hearing the district council (T) order the latter to abate the nuisance; and it must order the defendant to pay to the council sufficient compensation to cover the cost of its proceedings[1].

Obviously the local council will not go to court without informing the district council (T) of the nuisance beforehand and finding that there has been no effective response.

[1]   Environmental Protection Act 1990, s 82.

G   DOGS AND STRAYS

30.11 Apart from hunting-pack hounds and sporting or sheep dogs and dogs used against vermin or in emergency rescues, and registered guide-dogs for the blind, a dog must wear a collar showing its owner's name and address. Failure to comply with this rule is an offence (level 5 fine) and the dog may be seized and treated as a stray. A seized stray must be returned to its owner or taken to the district council's dog-catcher who must be told where it was found[1]. The police are not concerned.

[1]   Environmental Protection (Stray Dogs) Regulations 1992, SI 1992/288, and Environmental Protection Act 1990, s 149. He is called the officer in the legislation.

Dog control

30.12 A primary authority and a local council has power to make an order providing for an offence or offences in relation to the control of dogs in its area. A primary authority is a district council in England, a county council in England for an area for which there are no district councils, a London borough council, the Common Council of the City of London, a Welsh county or county borough council. A local council is a secondary council.

Such orders may only apply to land in the open air to which the public are entitled or permitted to have access with or without payment. Covered land is in the open air if it is open to the air on at least one side. The Secretary of State may designate land which is not to be subject to dog control orders. Where land is regulated under a private Act otherwise than by a primary or a secondary authority, the person who has the powers of regulation may by notice in writing to those authorities in whose area the land is situated exclude the land from the ambit of the legislation.

Such an order may relate to one or more of the following:

(a)   fouling of land by dogs and the removal of dog faeces;
(b)   keeping of dogs on leads;
(c)   exclusion of dogs from land;
(d)   the number of dogs which a person may take on to any land.

The Secretary of State has power to make regulations prescribing the penalties for breach of a dog control order (which cannot exceed level 3 on the standard scale) and prescribing its form and content.

An authorised officer of a primary authority or local council may issue a fixed penalty notice where he has reason to believe that an offence has been committed under a dog control order made by the authority. The amount of the fixed penalty is the amount specified by the authority (which may differ for different offences) or, if none, £75. The Secretary of State has power to prescribe maximum and minimum penalty amounts.

Where a primary authority or local council has byelaws which make similar provision to a dog control order, the byelaws cease to have effect in relation to any land once it becomes subject to a dog control order[1].

[1]   Clean Neighbourhoods and Environment Act 2005, Part 6. The practical need for this legislation is not obvious.

H   DISEASED ANIMALS

30.13 Ministers and the county council (T) may regulate the care and pasturing of diseased animals particularly cattle and sheep, by, amongst other things, declaring infected areas involving restrictions on animal movements, and by notices requiring animals to be removed from commons or gathered together in a specified place. These powers are aimed at those who own or control the animals, but may affect local councils if such animals are on their land. The commonest occasions for the use of these powers are outbreaks of sheep scab, foot and mouth and 'mad cow disease'[1].

[1]   Animal Health Act 1981 and the many orders made under it.

Chapter 31

POWERS RELATING
TO COMMUNICATIONS

A RIGHTS OF WAY—SUMMARY

31.1 Sometimes there are elongated strips of land owned by a public authority and dedicated or held in trust for public use as roads or footpaths. This, however, is a surprisingly rare situation. Much more commonly the land is private, but various kinds of rights of way subsist across it. These are of two basic types: (i) private rights of way; and (ii) highways or public rights of way.

Private rights of way

31.2 A private right of way exists for the benefit of, and is attached to, a particular piece of land (called the dominant tenement) and runs across another piece of land (called the servient tenement). It is simply a right of passage, and it is private property, conferring rights only on the owner of the dominant tenement. Like any other kind of private property it can be bought and sold. Usually it will be sold with the dominant tenement, whose owner could, on the other hand, extinguish it by selling it to the owner of the servient tenement. If both tenements come into the same ownership in the same right, the right of way is said to merge, and would have to be created anew if the previously dominant tenement were sold away later. So-called 'accommodation roads' are nearly always private rights of way.

Special private rights of way

31.3 There is a class of extensive and well known rights of way which seem to be public but are not. These are usually created by a local or private Act of Parliament for a special purpose, or if not directly created by the words of an Act, are deducible from a special legal situation. The commonest examples are canal and river towpaths, used by members of the public for their casual convenience, but where usually only those actually towing boats have a right of way. The power of a local council to acquire a right of way and hold it in trust for its inhabitants is in this class.

31.4 *Powers relating to communications*

Highways or rights of way and their scope

31.4 A highway (or public right of way) is a place where all the Queen's lieges have a right to pass and repass without hindrance. They have, in principle, no right to stop, save incidentally for the exercise of their right of passage. A walker may retie his shoelaces.

The scope of rights of way is classified in an ascending order of magnitude in which each greater class includes the rights in the classes below. The lowest is a right of passage on foot; a footway is a place alongside a public road where such a right is exercisable; a footpath is such a place not alongside a public road. A walkway is a footway which goes through or over or across a private building. This is almost exclusively an urban phenomenon. Next come bridleways which are rights of passage on horse or leading a horse. A bridleway may or may not also be a droveway or driftway over which there is a right to drive cattle. A cycle track is a public right of way only for pedal cycles, beside a carriageway, which is a right of way for vehicles[1]. A byway is an ordinary carriageway used mainly by pedestrians and riders. This is relevant mainly in connection with signs (see **31.28** below).

[1] Highways Act 1980, s 329(1). 'Drove' and 'driftway' are not terms of art.

Dedication

31.5 A public right of way comes into existence when a landowner dedicates it or when he is presumed to have done so, or when the public has exercised a right of passage without protest or permission across the land continuously for 20 years before a dispute arises in which the right is called in question. Dedication may be a formal act such as an agreement with a highway authority or local council, or it may be informal, amounting to no more than spoken words, or it may be positively inferred from behaviour. Such an inference cannot, however, be drawn if the landowner is a statutory corporation without power of dedication such as some of the older railway and canal companies, nor where a landowner has denied the public right of way by a publicly visible notice maintained since 1 January 1934[1].

No right of way for mechanically propelled vehicles can be created after 2 May 2006 in England and 16 November 2006 in Wales save by statute or by instrument (eg a deed of dedication)[2].

[1] Highways Act 1980, s 31(3).
[2] Natural Environment and Rural Communities Act 2006, s 66.

The rights of the public

31.6 Since dedication confers only a right of passage against the landowner, it confers in general no rights against other members of the public, and the public must take the way as they find it at the moment of dedication. A walker on a footpath cannot complain if the landowner allows horsemen to ride along the footpath, nor that he has to climb over walls or stiles if they were there originally. Conversely the landowner must not derogate from or attempt to minimise his grant. He may thus make passage easier by substituting (for

300

example) a gate for a stile, but he may not make it harder by substituting a stile for a gate. It sometimes happens, too, that a public right of way of one kind (for example on foot) may exist along a private right of way of another kind (such as an accommodation road).

Extinction

31.7 Since February 2001 the rule that a highway cannot be extinguished by mere disuse has been slightly modified. In summary, where a footpath or bridleway existed as such on 1 January 1949, and is still one on 1 January 2026 and has been neither a highway of any other sort between those dates nor is shown on 1 January 2026 on a definitive map as any sort of highway[1], all public rights of way will be extinguished on the latter date unless it is an excepted highway[2]. An excepted highway cannot be a footway beside a road but must have become a footpath or bridleway on or after 1 January 1949 by widening or extension or stopping up, passing over a bridge or through a tunnel and which connects a footpath or bridleway with a retained highway[3]. There is much statutory verbiage on this topic, which will doubtless be expounded in greater detail when this work reaches an edition closer to 2026.

Special provisions apply to the extinction of certain unrecorded rights of way for mechanically propelled vehicles[4].

[1] Countryside and Rights of Way Act 2000, s 53.
[2] CRWA 2000, ss 53–54.
[3] CRWA 2000, s 56.
[4] Natural Environment and Rural Communities Act 2006, s 67.

B   RIGHTS OF WAY MAPS

31.8 Before 1981 the county council was required to survey the footpaths and bridleways and mark them on a map. There was an elaborate procedure for establishing the legal validity of these maps, and the definitive map which emerged was conclusive of certain matters, at least until revised. Where a footpath was shown on a definitive map, this was conclusive that a right of way existed on foot only and that no other right of way existed along it. Where a bridleway or road used as a public path was shown, there is no such presumption against other rights. It will be obvious from the nature of the law on dedication that the absence of markings raises no presumptions at all. Many footpaths, though not marked, are nevertheless public footpaths. This is one of the reasons why the map was supposed to be revised regularly. Originally (in 1949) the interval was five years but in most counties it was and is many years longer[1]. The maps are still useful as evidence of rights of way.

[1] National Parks and Access to the Countryside Act 1949, s 33.

Certain reclassifications

31.9 In 1981 the county councils were required to reclassify those roads used as public paths which appeared as such in the definitive maps as byways open to all traffic, bridleways or footpaths[1]. The procedure involved notices to the same bodies as those which must be notified when a public path is to be extinguished or diverted (see below).

In 2002 the duty to reclassify roads used as public paths was abolished[2]. All such paths are redesignated as restricted byways, over which as a general rule there are no public rights of way for mechanically propelled vehicles.

[1]   Wildlife and Countryside Act 1981, s 54.
[2]   Countryside and Rights of Way Act 2000, s 47.

C   CREATION OF RIGHTS OF WAY BY LOCAL COUNCILS

Rights held in trust

31.10 A local council may by agreement acquire any right of way in or in an adjoining parish or community, the acquisition of which is beneficial to the inhabitants of the area or part of it, and may execute any necessary works (including maintenance and improvement) or may contribute to the expense of, or combine with any other local council in so doing[1]. This power does not create a highway: it is not limited to footpaths but may include bridle, drift and carriageways, and the effect of using it is to create a private right of way held in trust for the inhabitants. The main value of this power is to create approaches to playing fields and other public properties, but it can be used for a wider purpose such as a convenient short cut to a housing estate[2].

The acquisition of a right of way does not necessarily involve ownership of the strip of soil along which it passes, but in an appropriate case this soil could be acquired if it were needed.

[1]   Local Government Act 1894, s 8(1)(g), (i) and (k) and Highways Act 1959, Sch 25.
[2]   For roads and approaches in connection with allotments see **29.8** above.

Street management

31.11 The effect of such arrangements is to convert the council into a street authority for the right of way and entitle it to license works in it. It becomes an offence to place unlicensed works in it (level 3 fine)[1].

[1]   New Roads and Street Works Act 1991, ss 48–49.

Dedication agreements

31.12 In addition a local council may make an agreement with a landowner for the dedication of a highway in its area or an adjoining locality, and has in relation to such a highway the same powers as if it had acquired it on trust[1].

[1]   Highways Act 1980, s 30.

D   PROTECTION OF RIGHTS OF WAY AND ROADSIDE WASTES

31.13 If a highway is unlawfully obstructed or if a roadside waste is unlawfully encroached upon, the local council may assert and protect the rights of the public to their use, or impose upon the highway authority a duty to take proper proceedings to remove the obstruction or encroachment, by making an official representation which the authority must obey unless satisfied that it is incorrect[1].

The power of representation does not derogate from the general right of a local council to take legal proceedings for the promotion or protection of the interests of its inhabitants (as, for instance, where the opposing party is the district council (T) itself) but enables it in most such cases to impose the cost of litigation on the highway authority.

It is an offence, without lawful authority, to drive a motor vehicle on a common or moor or other land not forming part of a road[2] or a footpath or bridleway except a vehicle for cleaning or repairing it[3] but subject to local byelaws, a person may ride a bicycle upon a bridleway provided that he gives way to pedestrians and riders[4].

[1]   Highways Act 1980, s 130.
[2]   Road Traffic Act 1988, s 34.
[3]   HA 1980, s 300.
[4]   Countryside Act 1968, s 30, which, however, seems to conflict with the definition of a 'bridleway' in the HA 1980, s 329(1).

Misleading notices

31.14 It is an offence (level 1 fine) to exhibit a false or misleading notice likely to deter the public from using a public path shown on the definitive or revised footpath survey map. The offender may be ordered to remove the notice within not less than four days, and fined a further £2 for every day on which he fails to comply with the order[1]. Only the highway authority may prosecute for this offence.

[1]   National Parks and Access to the Countryside Act 1949, s 57.

Ploughing up and disturbing surfaces

31.15 A farmer may plough up a public path but must make it good within two weeks of the ploughing (under liability for a level 3 fine plus £1 for each day that the offence continues) or, if prevented by exceptional weather, as soon as practicable. The highway authority may extend the time, for up to 28 days. The rule on making good is almost unworkable unless the local council is prepared to report failures or itself prosecute them[1].

Apart from this it is an offence (level 3 fine) to disturb the surface of a footway, bridleway or unmade carriageway without lawful authority or excuse, but the highway authority may for a period of not more than three months authorise works necessary to agriculture or concomitant diversions or both, and may in either case impose conditions, breach of which is also an offence. A local council, non-metropolitan district council (T) and the highway authority may prosecute for disturbance and the last is supposed to see that necessary prosecutions are brought[2]. A local council may prosecute for breach of condition with the highway authority's consent[3].

[1]   Highways Act 1980, ss 134 and 135.
[2]   HA 1980, s 131A.
[3]   HA 1980, s 135.

Wardens

31.16 Any local authority including a local council may appoint wardens for footpaths, bridleways and byways. Their function is to advise and assist the public in their use[1]. They are not common.

[1]   Wildlife and Countryside Act 1981, s 62.

E   DIVERSIONS AND CLOSURES

New Towns

31.17 Public and private rights of way can be extinguished over land acquired compulsorily for the purposes of a New Town.

Manoeuvres

31.18 Public rights of way can be suspended for short daily periods during military manoeuvres[1].

[1]   See 25.9 above.

Magistrates' court procedures

31.19 In the case of any highway other than a trunk or special road, a highway authority may apply to the magistrates' court for authority to stop it up or divert it on the ground that it is unnecessary or that a diversion will be more commodious to the public. If the highway is a classified road the local council or the chairman of the parish meeting must, amongst others, be given at least 28 days' notice and is entitled to appear before the magistrates' court and be heard[1]. Any other person likely to be aggrieved may also be heard and this presumably includes a council of a neighbouring parish or community.

If, however, the highway is an unclassified road the highway authority must give notice that it proposes to make the application, to both the district council (T) and the local council or chairman of the parish meeting, and if within two months any of these give notice to the highway authority that they have refused their consent, the latter may not make the application at all[2].

Any two magistrates of the court may view the highway in question; and an order can reserve a footway or bridleway[3].

[1]   Highways Act 1980, s 116(6) and (7) and Sch 12.
[2]   HA 1980, s 116(3).

3   HA 1980, s 116(4).

Order procedures

31.20 Whilst the magistrates' court procedure is available only to highway authorities, but applies, apart from trunk and special roads, to all highways, principal councils (T) and joint planning boards have a special procedure available to them for extinguishing by order a public right of way over any footpath or bridleway in their area. The order (called a public path extinguishment order) can be made only on the ground that the path or way is not needed for public use[1]. If the order is opposed it must be confirmed by the Secretary of State, and before it is submitted to him for confirmation the order-making body must give at least 28 days' notice in the London Gazette, a local newspaper and to the local council or parish meeting, and must post a notice near the land concerned. Certain societies must also be notified. These are:

The Auto-Cycle Union, the British Horse Society, the Byways and Bridleways Trust, the Open Spaces Society, the Ramblers Association and the Cyclists' Touring Club. In Cheshire, Derbyshire, Greater Manchester, Lancashire, Merseyside, South and West Yorkshire and Staffordshire notice must be given to the Peak and Northern Footpaths Society; in 27 parishes in Bedfordshire, Buckinghamshire and Hertfordshire, to the Chiltern Society and in Wales, to the Welsh Trail Riders Association[2].

The Secretary of State may hold a public inquiry, and must do so if the objector is a local authority including a local council, or parish meeting. If the order is not opposed the authority may confirm the order itself[3].

A similar procedure exists for the diversion of public footpaths and bridleways in the interests of landowners, but the order cannot be made unless the new line is substantially as convenient to the public as the old. The landowner may be required to contribute to the expenses or compensation resulting from the diversion order[4].

Rail crossing and diversion orders can also be made on the application of the rail operator, but only for the safety of the public[5].

To combat crime highway authorities may make 'gating orders' to close or limit the use of highways (except motorways, trunk roads and other classified roads). In practice, the power is likely to be used to close or restrict use of paths and alleyways adjacent or close to dwellings. The authority must be satisfied that:

(a)   premises adjoining or adjacent to the highway are affected by crime or anti-social behaviour;

(b)   the existence of the highway is facilitating the persistent commission of such activities; and

(c)   it is in all the circumstances expedient to make the order to reduce crime or anti-social behaviour (such circumstances to include: the likely effect of making the order on the occupiers of premises adjoining or adjacent to the highway and on other persons in the locality; and in a case where the highway constitutes a through route, the availability of a reasonably convenient alternative route).

A gating order may restrict the public right of way at all times, or at specified times, days or periods and may authorise the installation, operation and maintenance of a barrier or barriers for the purpose of enforcing the restrictions provided for in the order[6].

1 Highways Act 1980, s 118.
2 Town and Country Planning (Public Path Orders) Regulations 1993, SI 1993/11.
3 HA 1980, s 118(4) and Sch 6.
4 HA 1980, s 119.
5 HA 1980, ss 118A and 119A. Rail Crossing Extinguishment and Diversion Orders Regulations 1993, SI 1993/9.
6 HA 1980, Part 8A (ss 129A–129G), inserted by Clean Neighbourhoods and Environment Act 2005, s 2.

Charges

31.21 The authority making a public path order may charge the applicant for the cost of making the order and for placing an advertisement in a local newspaper. The amount of the charge is at the authority's discretion. It must repay the charge if ultimately the order is not confirmed[1].

1 Local Authorities (Recovery of Costs for Public Path Orders) Regulations 1993, SI 1993/407 (as amended).

New special and trunk roads

31.22 The Secretary of State can close or divert side roads, including paths, in connection with the building of new motorways or classified roads. Diversion can include over bridges or in tunnels[1]. The draft order has to be published in the London Gazette, in a local newspaper and on the path itself. It will say where the relevant map can be inspected, and six weeks must be allowed for objections. Since a single draft order may deal with many side roads they need to be closely scrutinised. The Secretary of State must not confirm the order unless he is satisfied that equally convenient routes are available or will be provided[2].

1 Highways Act 1980, s 18 and Sch 1.
2 HA 1980, s 18(6).

Town and country planning

31.23 Highways may be closed or diverted to facilitate a redevelopment, which may itself involve the building of new roads or the alteration of alignments. In the case of carriageways the order is made by the Secretary of State, in others, by him or by a planning authority. The procedure resembles that for Public Path Extinguishment Orders[1], but such draft orders can sometimes be made before a relevant planning permission has been granted, primarily when the developer is a local authority or statutory undertaker[2], or where the Secretary of State has called the application in or is considering an appeal[3]. Notice must be given to the same societies as those mentioned above in relation to Public Path Orders[4]. There is also provision for temporary closures to facilitate, for example, mineral workings[5].

1 Town and Country Planning Act 1990, ss 257–259.
2 TCPA 1990, s 253.
3 TCPA 1990, s 261.
4 Public Path Orders Regulations 1993, SI 1993/11.
5 TCPA 1990, s 253.

Sporting and social events and entertainments

31.24 A traffic authority may temporarily restrict or prohibit traffic including even pedestrians on a road (but probably not a footpath or bridleway) to facilitate a sporting or social event or an entertainment to be held on a road and so as to enable people to watch it, or to reduce traffic disruption[1].

1 Road Traffic Regulation (Special Events) Act 1994.

F   RALLIES AND CYCLING OFFENCES

31.25 It is an offence to organise a motor vehicle trial on a footpath or bridleway without the county council's (T) authorisation which must not be given unless the owner and occupier of the land have given their consent in writing[1]. Apart from rallies, it is also an offence to cycle recklessly, inconsiderately, carelessly or under the influence of drink or drugs on a road or bridleway[2].

1 Road Traffic Act 1988, s 33.
2 RTA 1988, ss 30–32.

G   WORKS ON FOOTPATHS AND BRIDLEWAYS

Repair and maintenance

31.26 A local council may repair and maintain bridleways and footpaths in its area (but not footways), and the highway authority or district council may contribute to the cost, but this does not relieve any other authority or person whose duty it may be to repair them[1]. Unless there is an agreement or condition to the contrary, the landowner is bound to keep gates and stiles safe and to the standard of repair necessary to prevent unreasonable interference with users, but may claim a quarter of his expenses from the highway authority. If he fails in his duty, the latter may do the work at his expense after 14 days' notice[2].

The council must not carry out works on a walkway or do or place anything in it without the consent of the owner of the building unless such consent has already been given in the walkway agreement[3].

1 Highways Act 1980, s 43.
2 Highways Act 1980, s 146.
3 Walkways Regulations 1973, SI 1973/686, reg 3.

Improvement

31.27 Except where rights of way have been acquired on trust or created under a dedication agreement (see **31.1** above) a power to repair and maintain does not include a power to improve, but reasonable expenditure designed to reduce maintenance costs in the future is not, in this sense, improvement, nor is expenditure upon an improvement (such as drainage) if the public right would become inoperative without it.

H   SIGNS

Footpath signposts

31.28 A highway authority may in consultation with a landowner signpost a footpath, bridleway or byway along its length; it must do so at every point where they leave a metalled road unless the local council or chairman of the parish meeting agree that it is unnecessary. In addition, any other person, including a local council may signpost a footpath, bridleway or byway with the consent of the highway authority[1].

[1]   Countryside Act 1968, s 27, as amended.

Dangers

31.29 A local council may warn the public of any danger in its area[1]. In an emergency such a warning could take any form ready to hand. If it is a permanent sign on a footpath or bridleway, the consent of the landowner is needed; if on a highway the permission of the highway authority is required as well[2].

[1]   Road Traffic Regulation Act 1984, s 72.
[2]   Road Traffic Regulation Act 1984, s 72.

Bus stops and place-names

31.30 With the permission of the highway authority, and, if necessary, the landowner, a local council may erect bus stop signs and place-name signs on roadsides[1].

[1]   Road Traffic Regulation Act 1984, s 72.

I   LIABILITY FOR THE STATE OF HIGHWAYS

31.31 A local council has a power but no duty to repair public foot- and bridleways and cannot therefore be made liable for their condition if they fall into disrepair. It is only if someone is injured by a positive act of the council (for instance, by leaving an unlit obstruction at night) that the local council may be liable in damages to that person.

Highway authority

31.32 The duty of a highway authority to maintain publicly repairable highways (including bridges forming part of them) in a proper state of repair is more positive and can be enforced by court proceedings. The complainant begins by serving a notice requiring the highway authority (or other person who may be liable) to state whether it admits that the way is a highway and that it is liable to maintain it. If the necessary notice of admission is not forthcoming within a month, the Crown Court may order it to put the highway in proper repair within a specified time. If the notice of admission is given the complainant can within six months obtain a similar order from the local magistrates' court. If the time allowed expires without the work having been done, the complainant may apply to the magistrates, who may authorise him to do it himself and recover the cost[1].

In a few cases a footpath or bridleway repairable by the public, is in fact repairable by a private person by reason of tenure of the land, prescription or under the terms of an inclosure award. In such a case, if the highway authority thinks that it is out of repair it may do the work itself and recover the cost under a magistrates order of similar character[2].

[1]   Highways Act 1980, s 56.
[2]   Highways Act 1980, s 57.

Standards for new footpaths and bridleways

31.33 Where a new footpath or bridleway has been created by agreement with a local authority other than a local council or by order, the highway authority certifies what work needs to be done; the Secretary of State may quash or vary such a certificate on appeal by the local authority, and where this has happened the liability to repair is limited to the standard which obtained before the certificate was quashed, or as established by the variation[1].

[1]   Highways Act 1980, s 27.

J   TRAFFIC CALMING

31.34 If a local council thinks that traffic calming works (for example, humps, curves, lights or signs) will benefit the locality, it may contribute to the highway authority's expenses in providing them[1] but it cannot provide them itself save by arrangement with the authority.

[1]   Local Government and Rating Act 1997, s 30.

K   VEHICLE PARKS AND CYCLE RACKS

Purchase and appropriation

31.35 A local council may by purchase, order, or appropriation provide and maintain within its area structures or places suitable for parking. In a showpiece village a car park can be profitable. The ordinary rules on compulsory purchase and purchase by agreement apply; the council may also appropriate part of any recreation ground or playing field which it provides or maintains or part of any open space controlled or maintained by it; but appropriation of this sort is limited to an area not exceeding 800 square feet or one-eighth of the land concerned and to land held for purposes of the Local Government Act 1894, s 8, the Open Spaces Act 1906, and the Local Government (Miscellaneous Provisions) Act 1976, s 19[1].

If the council wishes to provide a car park, the car park must be off the street, and it must secure the permission of the highway authority. It must apply for such permission in writing and must send a copy to the district council (T).

[1]   Road Traffic Regulation Act 1984, s 57. For metric equivalents see **20.5** above.

Orders for cycle parks

31.36 The local council may, subject to the safeguards mentioned in **20.2** above, adapt and by order authorise the use as a cycle park of any part of a 'road', that is to say any of the places (not being open spaces) where a parish or community lighting authority may put lamps. Such an order cannot authorise the creation of a cycle park so as to be a nuisance, or so as unreasonably to prevent access to adjoining premises or the use of the 'road' by anyone entitled to use it.

Attendants, byelaws and orders

31.37 A local council which has provided a parking place may employ paid or unpaid parking attendants. In the case of cycle parks it may make byelaws (subject to the confirmation of the Home Secretary) as to their use, the conditions upon which they may be used and, provided that the parking place is not in a 'road', the parking charges. Copies of byelaws must be posted at every place to which they relate.

In the case of car parks, the local council cannot make byelaws, but may make orders regulating the uses of a park, the classes of vehicles which may use it, the conditions and charges for use, and the removal and custody of a vehicle placed in defiance of the order. The order can also specify the use of meters as long as they are of a type approved by the Secretary of State. A draft of a proposed order must be sent to the county council (T), and it cannot come into force without the latter's approval.

Liability for losses

31.38 In the case of a cycle park in a 'road' a local council cannot be made liable for loss of or damage to any vehicle parked there or its fittings or contents.

Letting

31.39 A local council may let its parking places other than those in a 'road' but no single letting must exceed seven days; this restriction is not, however, to prejudice the right of the council under other enactments to let the land of which the park forms a part[1].

[1]   Road Traffic Regulation Act 1984, ss 57–60.

L   SHELTERS AND SEATS

At bus stops

31.40 A local council (or other local authority) may provide and maintain bus shelters 'or other accommodation' at bus stops or land abutting a bus route for the use of intending passengers and may make agreements with the bus operators or any other local authority for such provision and maintenance including agreements on the manner in which the cost is to be defrayed[1]. 'Other accommodation' includes queue barriers and probably seats.

[1]   Local Government (Miscellaneous Provisions) Act 1953, s 4.

Consultation and consents

31.41 The Commissioner of the Metropolitan Police must be consulted on the position if they are to be erected in his district[1], and the power may not be exercised in the following cases without obtaining the consent of:

- in or on land abutting any highway for which there is a highway authority other than the local authority, the highway authority;
- if the shelter is to be placed in any highway belonging to or repairable by any railway, dock, harbour, canal, inland navigation or passenger road transport undertakers and forming the approach to any station, dock, wharf, or depot belonging to them, the consent of the undertakers;
- in the case of a bridge or approaches to a bridge the consent of the person in whom the bridge is vested and where the bridge carries a highway over a railway canal or inland navigation or where a bridge carries a railway, canal, or inland navigation over a highway, the consent of the relevant undertakers must also be obtained;
- if the shelter is to be placed in a position obstructing or interfering with any existing access to any land or premises abutting on a highway, the consent of the owner must be obtained[2].

[1]   Local Government (Miscellaneous Provisions) Act 1953, s 4(3).
[2]   Local Government (Miscellaneous Provisions) Act 1953, s 5. The 'owner' is defined in Public Health Act 1936, s 343.

Disputes

31.42 Consent must not be unreasonably withheld, but may be given subject to reasonable conditions including a condition that it shall be removed after a period if reasonably required by the person giving the consent. Disputes on reasonableness with the Secretaries of State for Environment, Food and Rural Affairs or Transport are to be settled by an arbitrator to be appointed in default of agreement by the President of the Institution of Civil Engineers[1]. There is no provision for statutory arbitration between other parties.

If the shelter or accommodation obstructs access to telegraphic lines the local council must at request either remove it or pay to the Post Office or British Telecom the additional cost of gaining access[2]. Similar provisions apply to sewers, pipe subways or wires belonging to or maintained by a local authority or any gas, electricity, water, hydraulic power, tramcar or trolley undertakers. Disputes on the amount payable are settled by arbitration or (if the amount does not exceed £50 and either party so requests) by a magistrates' court[3].

A local council may maintain bus shelters and other accommodation and queue-barriers which were erected without statutory authority before 14 July 1953[4].

[1] Local Government (Miscellaneous Provisions) Act 1953, s 5, amended by Local Government Planning and Land Act 1980, Sch 7.
[2] Local Government (Miscellaneous Provisions) Act 1953, s 6(1).
[3] Local Government (Miscellaneous Provisions) Act 1953, s 6 and Public Health Act 1936, s 278.
[4] Local Government (Miscellaneous Provisions) Act 1953, s 7.

Elsewhere than at bus stops

31.43 Subject to safeguards (see **20.2** above) a local council may provide and maintain seats and shelters in, or on, any land abutting on any 'road' within the parish; for this purpose a 'road' excludes a 'special road' (such as a motorway) but includes any highway, road, lane, footway, square, court, alley or passage to which the public has access[1]. There are restrictions on the placing of shelters in walkways similar to the restrictions on lighting[2].

[1] Parish Councils Act 1957, ss 1(1) and 7.
[2] Walkways Regulations 1973, SI 1973/686; in relation to lighting, see **28.1** above.

Chapter 32

TRANSPORT

A   INVESTIGATIONS AND TRANSPORT SCHEMES

32.1 Local councils may investigate public transport and the use of roads or the need for either of them, and the management and control of traffic in their locality[1].

In practice such investigations are likely to precede consideration of transport schemes which they were empowered in 1997 to establish for the benefit of their people. These are schemes for car sharing[2], the increasingly important taxi-fare concessions[3], and for bus service grants[4].

[1]   Local Government and Rating Act 1997, s 29.
[2]   LGRA 1997, s 26.
[3]   LGRA 1997, s 28.
[4]   Transport Act 1985, ss 22–23 and s 106A inserted by LGRA 1997.

Car sharing

32.2 There is power to establish and maintain any car-sharing scheme or to help others to do so and to impose any conditions which the council thinks fit in the process[1]. This may be of great value in isolated areas or to parents with children at schools a car journey away from home.

[1]   Local Government and Rating Act 1997, s 26.

Taxi-fare concessions

32.3 The council may arrange with any licensed taxi or hire car operator to grant fare concessions to eligible residents, namely anyone over 60 or under 16, between 16 and 18 in full-time education, the blind, the partially sighted, the deaf, those without speech, people with serious walking difficulties, without arms or with long-term loss of use of arms, people with learning disabilities, persons refused a driving licence because of lack of appropriate physical fitness (other than that caused by persistent misuse of alcohol or drugs), a person travelling as a companion of someone in the foregoing categories and anyone else specified by the Secretary of State[1], and to reimburse the difference. It may impose any conditions it thinks fit[2], but plainly the arrangements, which are sometimes likely to be related to reorganisations of the National Health Service, must be carefully drafted and not so as to drive out one operator by favouring another.

1 Transport Act 1985, s 93(7).
2 Local Government and Rating Act 1997, s 28.

Bus service grants

32.4 A local council may subsidise a community bus service, namely one provided on a non-profit making basis by a body concerned with local social welfare needs, using a 9- to 16-seater vehicle under a community bus permit granted by the Traffic Commissioner. It may also make grants towards the cost of a permitted bus service wholly or mainly for the elderly or disabled. As usual, it may impose conditions[1].

1 Transport Act 1985, ss 22–23 and s 106A, inserted by Local Government and Rating Act 1997.

B   PUBLICITY FOR PUBLIC PASSENGER SERVICES

32.5 A local council may publicise public passenger services or help others to do so[1]. These are not confined to services which it supports or helps to organise, but may include services of any use to residents including railways and ferries. Notice boards, some of which may already exist, may be provided for the purpose. The cost should be small.

1 Local Government and Rating Act 1997, s 29.

Chapter 33

POWERS RELATING TO THE DEAD

A ANGLICAN AREAS DEFINED

33.1 For the purposes of this chapter, an 'Anglican area' is an area of England plus some parishes close to the Welsh border subject to the Welsh Church Act 1914.

B CLOSED AND DISUSED CHURCHYARDS

Order in Council

33.2 Parishioners have a right of burial in their churchyard even when it is full. A regular procedure is therefore needed for extinguishing this right when a churchyard is full. This is done by an order made by the Sovereign in Council on the representation of the Secretary of State[1]. Anybody may inform him of the need for such a representation. At least one month's public notice must be given and also at least ten days' notice to the parochial church council[2]. The order can apply to Jewish, or Quaker or private non-parochial burial grounds but only if it specifically mentions them, and its operation may be postponed or varied by a later order[2]. Its sole effect is under penalty (level 1 fine) to forbid further burials. Ashes may be buried in a closed churchyard, subject to the obtaining of a faculty (if required) but only where the burial does not involve the disturbance of human remains[3].

[1] For special circumstances arising in New Towns see **24.30** above.
[2] Burial Act 1853, s 1.
[3] This opinion is supported by observed practice.

Responsibility for maintenance

33.3 The parochial church council remains responsible for maintenance[1], but if a final certificate was issued[2] by it before 1 April 1974, in respect of a previously closed churchyard, the responsibility for maintenance lies with the local council, or in a Welsh community not represented on a community council with the district council (T)[3]. Final certificates were abolished from 1 April 1974, and since then a parochial church council which is still liable for maintenance may serve a written request to take the responsibility over. Outside the Anglican area, the written request is served upon the local council, but if the churchyard is in a parish without a separate parish council it is served on the chairman of the parish meeting, and if not in a parish, on the district council (T). In the Anglican area the procedure does not apply (but, as in England, a community council may contribute towards the cost of maintenance of a closed churchyard)[4]. The primary effect of the request is that the body on which it is served becomes responsible for maintenance three months after the date of service, but if the local council or parish meeting resolve to pass the responsibility to the district council (T) and give notice before that date to the parochial church council, the responsibility passes to the district council (T)[5].

[1]   Local Government Act 1972, s 215(1). For contributions towards the cost see 33.43 below.
[2]   Under Burial Act 1855, s 18 now repealed.
[3]   LGA 1972, s 215 (4).
[4]   LGA 1972, s 215(2).
[5]   LGA 1972, s 215(2) and (3).

Miscellaneous characteristics of written requests

33.4 A written request cannot be made until an Order in Council applies to the churchyard in question, nor can a liability which has already been imposed under a final certificate be altered by a resolution. In England a parish meeting which is grouped under a common parish council can, instead of passing the liability to the district council (T), request the parish council to maintain the churchyard and the latter may do so. The financial effects appear at **33.43** below. The transfer of liability to maintain, in no way affects the ownership or any other legal interest in the churchyard; the fruit of the trees, for instance, continues to belong to the person entitled to it before the request became effective. There are practical advantages in the responsibility remaining with the local rather than the district council (T), particularly if it is desired later on to improve the churchyard under the Open Spaces Act 1906.

Standard of maintenance and Open Spaces Act improvements

33.5 The responsible body must maintain the churchyard in decent order[1], that is, it must not offend the susceptibilities of a reasonable Christian bearing in mind that ground levels always rise. It must also keep the walls (which are often retaining walls) and the fences in good repair, and effective for their purpose. All this amounts, if circumstances warrant, to an obligation to bring an 'indecent' closed churchyard up to a standard of decency and to put walls and fences in good repair, even at great expense[2].

If the local council wishes to make improvements beyond the standard of decency, it may use its open space powers. The effective use of these powers will be greatly complicated if the responsibility for maintenance is in the hands of another authority, which will have to be consulted at every turn.

[1]   Local Government Act 1972, s 215(1).
[2]   A few grazing sheep will often mow a churchyard cluttered with monuments more cheaply and efficiently than anything else!

New buildings

33.6 Building in disused burial grounds is prohibited[1] save where the land or part of it belongs or belonged to a religious body and is unconsecrated (according to the laws of the Church of England) and either no burial has ever taken place in it or if any have taken place within 50 years, no relatives or personal representatives duly object, or if they do, the objections are withdrawn.

There are three distinct procedural cases:

(1)   if no burials are known to have taken place the proposer simply applies for planning permission for the building which he proposes;

(2)   if burials have taken place an additional procedure for dealing with them, with monuments and those concerned (as above) may have to be followed; but

(3)   if the building is to be erected without disturbing remains, the proposer may apply to the Secretary of State for an order dispensing with procedural requirements[2].

The effect in each case is to discharge the land from all rights and interests of relatives or personal representatives and also all other trusts, uses, obligations, disabilities and restrictions related to use as a burial ground except charitable trusts. These continue to apply until the land is sold and are then transferred to the proceeds. It also makes a Secretary of State's licence to remove the relevant remains unnecessary.

The discharge takes effect in the first case when planning permission has been granted; otherwise when the procedure for dealing with human remains and monuments has been completed or dispensed with[3].

[1]   Disused Burial Grounds Act 1884, s 3.
[2]   Disused Burial Grounds (Amendment) Act 1981, Schedule.
[3]   Disused Burial Grounds (Amendment) Act 1981 *passim.*

C   BURIAL AND CREMATION AUTHORITIES

33.7 The councils of districts (T), parishes and communities are burial and cremation authorities. The parish meetings of English parishes without a parish council (whether separate or common) are burial authorities only. When burial boards, joint boards, and the joint committees with burial board powers, were abolished[1], their property and functions were transferred to the relevant burial authority or authorities jointly[2]; but in the case of a joint transfer the authorities concerned had to set up a joint committee[3], unless the Secretary of State had created a joint board for a united district[4]. Such joint committees may be dissolved by agreement; but if the constituent authorities disagree, then if they are all parish or communal authorities the district council (T) may effect the dissolution, but if one or more of them is a district council (T), the Secretary of State may do so[5].

[1]   Local Government Act 1972, s 214(1).
[2]   For details see LGA 1972, Sch 26, para 1.
[3]   LGA 1972, Sch 26, para 2.
[4]   LGA 1972, Sch 26, para 3.

5   LGA 1972, Sch 26, para 4.

D   BURIAL FACILITIES GENERALLY

33.8 When it becomes apparent that a churchyard's further usefulness for burials is limited, the local and parochial church councils should consider in good time what should be done.

Churchyard extension

33.9 One possibility is that the parochial church council should acquire land, preferably but not necessarily adjacent to the churchyard, as an extension to it. If this is done before the churchyard is full, it becomes unnecessary to obtain an Order in Council, and the local burial customs and responsibilities remain unchanged. A burial authority may contribute to the expense[1] and often saves its taxpayers considerable sums in the long run by so doing. Even if an Order in Council has had to be made, it is possible to make an agreement (which must be in writing) between the two councils, that in return for financial assistance, the parochial church council will not issue a written request to transfer the liability for maintenance.

1   Local Government Act 1972, s 214(6).

Joint operations

33.10 Burial authorities may provide cemeteries outside their own area[1]; they have powers of mutual contribution[2] and they can arrange to have their functions discharged by a committee or other authority[3]. Hence it may be convenient, when churchyard extension is not feasible, to make joint arrangements between neighbouring councils.

1   Local Government Act 1972, s 214(2).
2   LGA 1972, s 214(6).
3   LGA 1972, s 101.

Notice of termination

33.11 Any agreement between authorities for one of them to provide burial facilities for another (second) authority, may be held to be perpetual[1] unless it specifically includes a provision for termination by notice. This is important, especially where the second authority is to be obliged under the agreement to contribute a proportion of the annual cost.

1   This happened in *Watford Borough Council v Watford Rural Parish Council* (1988) 86 LGR 524.

E PROVIDING A CEMETERY

33.12 A burial authority may provide cemeteries in or outside its area[1]. It can no longer purchase burial rights in a private cemetery, or appropriate charity land for the purpose[2], but it can often appropriate land which it owns for some other purpose[3]. Otherwise land will have to be purchased by agreement or compulsorily.

[1] Local Government Act 1972, s 214(2).
[2] This follows from the repeal of the Burial Act 1952 especially ss 25 and 29.
[3] See **12.29** and **12.31** above.

Amount of land

33.13 At two burials per grave, one acre may be expected to last 70 years for each 2,000 inhabitants; the amount of land to be bought should suffice to provide graves for at least the duration of the loan period.

Type of land and tests

33.14 The land should preferably have a medium soil; it should not be on a slope, but should be well drained, but with no risk of contaminating underground water. The water undertaker should be consulted.

Having chosen the proposed site, outline planning permission should be obtained; trial boreholes should be sunk and a medical officer of health should be asked to certify the suitability of the soil. If the owner will not permit entry, the burial authority should serve a notice of entry for between three and 14 days under the Lands Clauses Consolidation Act 1845, s 84, and then enter the land. It remains liable for any damage and for fencing the holes.

Finance, purchase and layout

33.15 The district valuer should be asked to negotiate a price and, when his figure is known, the burial authority should start proceedings for raising the money[1] and, if the owner will not sell, for compulsory purchase[2], and it should apply for planning approval for the layout of the site. The land should then actually be purchased and conveyed to the burial authority, and laid out in accordance with the terms of the planning approval.

[1] Eg by sale, precept or borrowing.
[2] See **12.20** above.

Consecration and setting apart

33.16 A burial authority in any area to which the Welsh Church Act 1914 does not apply may apply to the bishop of the diocese, where the cemetery is situated, for the consecration of part of it, and any burial authority anywhere may set apart part of it for the use of a particular denomination, provided, in either case, that it is satisfied that enough land remains over. In areas subject to the Welsh Church Act 1914, land consecrated or the subject of a ceremony of consecration is treated as having been set apart, not consecrated[1].

Consecrated land must be marked off from other land[2]; land set apart should, as a matter of good management, be marked off as well[3].

1 Local Authorities' Cemeteries Order 1977, SI 1977/204, art 5(1), (2) and (3).
2 SI 1977/204, art 5(4).
3 SI 1977/204, art 3(1).

Layout and repair

33.17 A burial authority may enclose, lay out and embellish a cemetery as it thinks fit and improve it, and it is obliged to keep it and its associated buildings, walls and fences in good repair[1].

It is, generally speaking, wise to provide the foundations for a solid retaining wall (even if the wall is not initially built to its full height) because the level of the ground in cemeteries invariably rises unless soil excavated from graves is carted away. The power of embellishment enables the authority to do anything (such as tree planting) which makes the cemetery appear more attractive[2].

1 Local Authorities' Cemeteries Order 1977, SI 1977/204, art 4(1).
2 Best Kept Churchyard competitions notably improved the appearance of many midland cemeteries after 1964.

Access

33.18 Roads to a cemetery may be built, improved or widened, but if an existing road is to be improved or widened, the consent of the highway authority or other owner must first be obtained. If a burial authority or its predecessor has built a road, the authority is responsible for maintaining it, unless it has become a publicly maintainable highway[1].

1 Local Authorities' Cemeteries Order 1977, SI 1977/204, art 4 and Sch 1.

Chapels

33.19 Chapels may be provided, equipped and maintained for funeral services, but if they are on land which is not consecrated or set apart, they must be built only at the request of the appropriate denomination, and the expense must not be borne by the burial authority. If (but only if) a denominational chapel becomes dangerous, may the authority take proper action (including removal) to obviate the danger[1]. The authority may make a chapel for one denomination available for the ceremonies of another at the request of the denomination for which it was originally provided.

1 Local Authorities' Cemeteries Order 1977, SI 1977/204, art 6.

F   MANAGEMENT

33.20 Except in relation to chapels, existing tombstones and other memorials (where special rules apply) a burial authority may do all that is necessary or desirable for the proper management, regulation and control of the cemetery[1]. It can, therefore, determine such matters as the future design and treatment of monuments, and whether or not kerbs shall be used or mounds levelled. These powers cannot be used capriciously so as, for instance, to infringe rights acquired by someone else under a contract or agreement with a religious denomination[2].

[1]   Local Authorities' Cemeteries Order 1977, SI 1977/204, art 3.
[2]   For removal of tombstones in disused burial grounds in new towns, see **24.30** above.

Regulation of graves

33.21 The Secretary of State can make orders on the management, regulation and control of cemeteries[1], and his predecessors made such regulations[2]. The older ones (in so far as they are not superseded) required grave spaces to measure at least 9 ft x 4 ft for adults; and either 6 ft x 3 ft or 4½ ft x 4 ft for children under twelve; only one body might be buried at one time in a common grave except in the case of members of the same family; no unwalled grave might be opened in the case of adults for at least 14 years, and in the case of children for at least eight, save to bury another member of the same family, and the bricks of vaults and walled graves containing coffins are never to be disturbed.

More recent regulations make additional provision[3], of which the most important is that no burial, scattering of ashes, erection of a tombstone or memorial or the making of any additional inscription on such, is to be carried out without the permission of the proper officer of the authority.

[1]   Local Government Act 1972, s 214(3).
[2]   Under Burial Act 1852, s 44. These regulations were not printed in the series of Statutory Rules and Orders.
[3]   Local Authorities' Cemeteries Order 1977, SI 1977/204, Sch 2, Part I.

Mortuaries and biers

33.22 A burial authority may provide a mortuary and furnish it for use in connection with a cemetery, and biers and other things necessary or desirable for use at funerals[1].

[1]   Local Authorities' Cemeteries Order 1977, SI 1977/204, art 7.

Joint arrangements

33.23 Arrangements can be made to use non-denominational chapels, mortuaries, biers and other things provided by other persons or to use such things owned by the authority in connection with burials elsewhere. Arrangements of these types can include arrangements to employ staff[1].

[1] Local Authorities' Cemeteries Order 1977, SI 1977/204, art 8.

Inspection

33.24 The Secretary of State may appoint inspectors to inspect burial grounds, cemeteries and mortuaries to ascertain their condition and whether the applicable regulations have been complied with. It is an offence (level 1 fine) for anyone having care of them to violate, neglect or fail to observe such regulations or to obstruct such inspection[1].

[1] Burial Act 1855, s 8.

G   CEREMONIES

33.25 A burial in consecrated land or land set apart may take place without any religious service, or with such Christian and orderly service as those in charge of the burial think fit[1], but the burial authority may at the request of a denomination prohibit the burial or scattering of cremated remains in a part set apart for that denomination[2].

In a cemetery in an Anglican area, the incumbent of an ecclesiastical parish wholly or partly chargeable with the expense of maintaining the cemetery is under the same obligation to perform on request funeral services in the consecrated part for Anglicans who are his parishioners or who die in his parish, as he is in one of his own churchyards[3]. His obligations at a cremation are described at **33.42** below.

[1] Local Authorities' Cemeteries Order 1977, SI 1977/204, art 5(5).
[2] SI 1977/204, art 5(6).
[3] SI 1977/204, art 17.

H   GRANTS AND AGREEMENTS

33.26 A burial authority may grant a simple right of burial (in a common grave) or an exclusive right in an ordinary grave or with the right to construct a walled grave or vault. Where the right is exclusive, the written consent of the owner is required before a body or ashes can be buried there or ashes scattered there[1].

[1] Local Authorities' Cemeteries Order 1977, SI 1977/204, art 10(1) and (6).

Duration and resumption

33.27 Where an old grant in perpetuity or for more than 75 years has been made, but the rights have not been exercised for 75 years, the burial authority may serve a notice on the owner of the right, or, if he cannot be found, exhibit a notice in the cemetery and also publish it in two successive weeks in a local newspaper. If within six months of service or of the first newspaper publication, the owner does not in writing notify his intention to retain the right, it then comes to an end[1].

New rights may be granted for not more than 100 years, but may be renewed from time to time for periods not exceeding 100 years, not necessarily upon the same terms[2].

1 Local Authorities' Cemeteries Order 1977, SI 1977/204, art 10(3).
2 SI 1977/204, art 10(4).

Tombstones at graves

33.28 A right to place a tombstone or other memorial over a grave may be granted to the owner of the right of burial in that grave, or to any person who satisfies the authority that he is a relative, and that the owner of the right cannot be traced[1].

1 Local Authorities' Cemeteries Order 1977, SI 1977/204, art 10(1). For the special case of grants to the Commonwealth War Graves Commission, see art 20.

Memorials elsewhere

33.29 A burial authority may grant to anyone a right to place and maintain a memorial in a cemetery elsewhere than over a grave, but if it is to be in a denominational chapel the consent of the denomination is required, and if it is to be an inscription additional to an existing memorial, the consent of the person entitled to place and maintain the memorial is required[1].

1 See footnote 1 to **33.28** above.

Inscriptions in consecrated parts

33.30 A bishop may object to an inscription on a memorial in a consecrated part[1]. Such an objection can, if necessary, be tried in the appropriate ecclesiastical court which in Anglican areas[2] can order the inscriptions to be removed.

1 Local Authorities' Cemeteries Order 1977, SI 1977/204, art 13.
2 SI 1977/204, art 5(3).

Removal of unauthorised memorials

33.31 A burial authority can remove a memorial or tombstone placed otherwise than in accordance with a grant or approval given by it or its predecessor, and may recover the cost as a simple contract debt from the person who ordered it to be placed, or (if he is dead) within two years of its being placed, from his personal representatives[1].

1 Local Authorities' Cemeteries Order 1977, SI 1977/204, art 14.

Maintenance agreements

33.32 A burial authority may agree to maintain a grave or memorial in a cemetery for a period not exceeding 100 years. Such an agreement may contain such terms and conditions as may be proper[1] and is generally based upon the payment by the person concerned to the authority of an endowment in the form of a lump sum which the authority invests.

[1] Local Authorities' Cemeteries Order 1977, SI 1977/204, art 10(7) which keeps alive agreements made under Parish Councils and Burial Authorities (Miscellaneous Provisions) Act 1970, s 3 (now repealed).

I   FEES

Authority's fees and charges

33.33 A burial authority may charge such fees as it thinks proper, for cremations, or in connection with burials, or for the grant of any rights except the right to place a memorial in a denominational chapel, and also for searches in its records and for certified copies of entries in them[1]. The provision of these facilities is treated for VAT purposes as a business and is standard rated. Councils should therefore charge VAT on burial etc fees.

[1] Local Authorities' Cemeteries Order 1977, SI 1977/204, art 15(1) and Sch 2, Part II, para 6.

Minister's and sexton's fees

33.34 The authority may and normally does collect fees due (for actual services only) to ministers of religion and sextons to whom it pays them over[1]. The fees payable to ministers etc of the Church of England are fixed under Parochial Fees Orders made periodically by the Church Commissioners and approved by the General Synod.

[1] Local Authorities' Cemeteries Order 1977, SI 1977/204, art 15(2) and (4).

Table of fees

33.35 The authority must keep and make available a table of the nature and amount of every fee or charge payable to it[1]. The table should contain a note about maintenance agreements if it is the policy of the council to enter into them.

[1] Local Authorities' Cemeteries Order 1977, SI 1977/204, art 15(3).

J   RECORDS

33.36 All grants must be in writing signed by the officer appointed by the authority for the purpose[1]. It must also maintain a register of all grants showing the date, name and address of the grantee, the consideration, the place where it is exercisable and the duration, and it must keep a plan showing the grave spaces with a distinguishing number allotted to each one in which a right has been granted, and a book setting out the numbers and the relevant names and addresses of the grantees[2].

1 Local Authorities' Cemeteries Order 1977, SI 1977/204, Sch 2, Pt II, para 1.
2 SI 1977/204, Sch 2, Pt II.

Preservation

33.37 The burial authority must preserve registers of rights granted under earlier general or local burial legislation and transferred to it, but may do so by photographing them[1].

1 Local Authorities' Cemeteries Order 1977, SI 1977/204, art 12 and Local Government Act 1972, s 229.

K   TRANSMISSION OF RIGHTS

33.38 The owner of a registered right may assign it to someone else by deed or will, but the assignee cannot exercise it until he has in writing notified the burial authority, which is bound to alter its records accordingly[1] when satisfied that the notification is true. When in doubt, he should be asked to produce a copy of the deed or will.

1 Local Authorities' Cemeteries Order 1977, SI 1977/204, Sch 2, Pt II, paras (3) and (4).

L   OTHER OFFENCES AND PENALTIES

33.39 Certain acts, described in the Local Authorities' Cemeteries Order, arts 18 and 19 (qv), are offences (level 3 fine) and, for a continuing offence, £10 a day may be imposed during which it continues after conviction[1].

1 Local Authorities' Cemeteries Order 1977, SI 1977/204, art 19; for the punishable acts see art 18.

M   OTHER MEMORIALS

33.40 A local council or parish meeting may maintain, repair and protect any war memorial whether vested in it or not, and may adapt it to serve for any war subsequent to that for which it was erected[1]. A burial authority could also formerly agree with someone in consideration of a sum of money paid by him, to maintain a memorial or monument in any place to which it has a right of access. Such an agreement could not last for more than 99 years[2]. Agreements of this type made before 10 March 1977 remain valid, but the power to make new agreements can now be exercised only in cemeteries.

1 War Memorials Act 1923, ss 1 and 3.
2 Parish Councils and Burial Authorities (Miscellaneous Provisions) Act 1970, s 1(1) repealed by Local Authorities' Cemeteries Order 1977, SI 1977/204, art 10(7).

N   WALES

33.41 For Welsh burial facilities and churchyards see Chapter **36**.

O   CREMATION

33.42 A cremation authority[1] must not place a crematorium within 50 yards of a highway, nor on consecrated land, nor within 200 yards of a house without the written consent of the owner, tenant and occupier[2], and burnings must not take place until the authority has certified to the Secretary of State for Justice that it is complete in accordance with the plans and properly equipped[3].

He also regulates by order the maintenance and inspection of crematoria and the circumstances in which burnings may take place. There are heavy penalties for breach of these regulations[4].

An incumbent may, but is not bound to, officiate at a cremation, but if he (in Anglican areas) refuses, any other priest may do so at the request of the executor or of the burial authority, and with the permission of the Bishop[5].

[1]   See **33.7** above.
[2]   Cremation Act 1902, s 5.
[3]   Cremation Act 1952, s 1.
[4]   Cremation Act 1902, ss 7–8 and Cremation Act 1952, s 2; see also the Cremation (England and Wales) Regulations 2008, SI 2008/2841.
[5]   Canon B38 of the Revised Canons Ecclesiastical.

P   SPECIAL FINANCIAL MATTERS

Special charging and application of fees

33.43 The cost of cemeteries and crematoria can be charged, if provided by a district council, upon the whole district or only part of it[1], but a local council or parish meeting cannot charge only part of its own area.

[1]   Local Government Finance Act 1992, s 35.

Transfers of assets

33.44 If a burial ground, crematorium or responsibility for maintenance is to be transferred to a burial authority, such a transfer can take place only by agreement and the authority can in practice require that the person previously responsible shall transfer any assets held for the purposes of maintenance to the authority. If any such assets are impressed with a trust, the trust will bind the authority.

Powers of contribution

33.45 Any burial authority may contribute to the expenses of any other person in providing or maintaining a cemetery in which inhabitants of its area may be buried[1]. Such a cemetery need not be situated in its area.

1   Local Government Act 1972, s 214(6).

Part II

MATTERS PECULIAR TO WALES

Chapter 34

WELSH CENTRAL INSTITUTIONS

34.1 Recent legislation, notably the Government of Wales Act 1998, the Public Audit (Wales) Act 2004, the Public Services Ombudsman (Wales) Act 2005 and the Government of Wales Act 2006, while not directly affecting the constitution of the community councils, has already changed the circumstances in which they work, so that one may detect a process likely to create conditions in which adaptations of their functions are made as a consequence, mainly but perhaps not wholly of changed practices. Hence, some understanding of the agencies external to the community councils able to initiate or make, accelerate or slow down changes may be useful.

A   THE NATIONAL ASSEMBLY

Constitution

34.2 The National Assembly, which sits at Cardiff, consists of 40 members elected for the ordinary parliamentary constituencies of Wales by the same system as Members of Parliament are elected, and 20 members for the five electoral regions related to European institutions, elected by a kind of proportional representation.

The Assembly appoints committees. These are: Children and Young People, Committee for scrutiny of the First Minister, Communities Equality and Local Government, Constitutional and Legislative Affairs, Enterprise and Business, Environment and Sustainability, Finance, Health and Social Care, Petitions, Public Accounts and Standards of Conduct.

Powers

34.3 The Secretary of State for Wales ceded almost all his administrative powers exercisable within Wales to the Assembly, leaving him with his parliamentary and supervisory functions. These and other powers created for Wales by particular Acts of Parliament are all subordinate to United Kingdom primary legislation.

The Assembly cannot make, alter or repeal an Act of Parliament unless specifically permitted to do so by the terms of such an Act. The Government of Wales Act 2006 empowers the Assembly to make Acts in relation to matters specified in Schedule 7 to the Act. The Assembly can also pass secondary laws arising out of powers created by an Act. These are known as Assembly Measures. The fields within which the Assembly can make Measures are specified in Schedule 5 to the 2006 Act. The list of matters relating to both Acts and Measures is identical and covers: agriculture, fisheries, forestry and rural development; ancient monuments and historic buildings; culture; economic development; education and training; environment; fire and rescue services and promotion of road safety; food, health and health services; highways and transport; housing; local government; National Assembly for Wales; public administration; social welfare; sport and recreation; tourism; town and country planning; water and flood defence; Welsh language. By means of legislative competence orders, Her Majesty in Council may specify particular matters within a field on which the Assembly may exercise its legislative powers. She may also amend the list of fields by addition, variation or removal[1].

[1] Government of Wales Act 2006, ss 109, 95

Subordinate legislation

34.4 The Assembly handles five types of subordinate legislation, namely:

(a)   that which is subject to specific approval by the Assembly before it takes effect;

(b)   that which is subject to annulment by the Assembly and thus takes effect unless annulled by the Assembly;

(c)   that which is subject to no formal procedure other than that it is laid before the Assembly;

(d)   that which is subject to specific procedures set out in the Act or Measure which contains the power to make it;

(e)   those which are special procedure orders. These are similar to orders that are subject to special parliamentary procedure as especially affecting a private interest. Petitions on this type are made to the Assembly rather than to Parliament.

Procedure

34.5 The procedures for dealing with Measures and subordinate legislation are set out in the Standing Orders of the Assembly.

B   THE PARTNERSHIP COUNCIL

Constitution

34.6 The Partnership Council, which is unique to Wales, has arisen out of the Assembly's obligation[1] to 'make a scheme to sustain and promote local government in Wales'. Local government comprises principal and community councils and the authorities for police, fire and National Parks. The Partnership Council is composed of ministers of the Welsh Assembly Government; representatives from principal Welsh local authorities, the Welsh Local Government Association, One Voice Wales (representing community councils),

Police, Fire and National Parks Authorities; and observers from Welsh service reform partners. It meets approximately three times a year, one such meeting being outside Cardiff.

¹   Government of Wales Act 2006, s 72.

Functions

34.7 The statutory functions of the Partnership Council are:

(a)   to give advice to the Welsh Ministers about matters affecting the exercise of any of their functions;

(b)   to make representations to the Welsh Ministers about any matters affecting, or of concern to, those involved in local government in Wales; and

(c)   to give advice to those involved in local government in Wales¹.

The Partnership Council is designed to advise the Assembly and to assist in the preparation of advice to councils. This implies no authority but a two-way traffic of information. There is consultation on financial issues (including grants); the preparation of new Assembly legislation; on Westminster and European legislation and policy where this is likely to affect local government; and appointment of representatives of local government at local, national and international level.

¹   Government of Wales Act 2006, s 72.

Scheme and periodic review

34.8 The arrangements of the Partnership Council are set out in the *Local Government Partnership Scheme 2008*. The Welsh Ministers publish an annual report of how the proposals set out in the scheme have been implemented in that financial year and lay it before the National Assembly.

Welsh Ministers in conjunction with the local government associations keep the scheme under periodic review and consider whether it should be revised or remade.

In December 2011, the Partnership Council, the Welsh Government and Local Government signed a joint commitment to reform aimed at delivering improved and cost effective services to communities across Wales.

Chapter 35

WELSH COMMUNITIES

A   DEFINITION OF A COMMUNITY

35.1 Up to 1 April 1974, the progression described in the section on parishes applied equally in England and Wales except that no rural boroughs had been set up in Wales. The Local Government Act 1972, however, abolished all previously existing local government areas including the rural parishes, as from that date[1], but provided that the area of every previously existing borough, urban district and rural parish and six specially constituted communities should thenceforth constitute a community[2]. As, however, the term 'community' now embraced great cities with six-figure populations, and hamlets with only two or three people, this was, geographically speaking, clearly a provisional arrangement which the Local Government Boundary Commission for Wales (Welsh Commission), by means of an initial review, rationalised[3]. The definition of a community thus depends upon the Local Government Act 1972 and orders made as a result of, or after the initial review.

[1]   Local Government Act 1972, s 20(6) as originally enacted.
[2]   LGA 1972, s 20(4) and Sch 4, Part III.
[3]   LGA 1972, s 64 and Sch 10 as originally enacted (now repealed).

B   ALTERATIONS OF STATUS—GENERAL

Communities

35.2 The procedure for altering the Anglo-Welsh border under the Local Government Act 1972 was never used and has been repealed. Hence a Welsh community cannot cease to be a community by becoming an English parish. Every part of Wales is in a community[1]; therefore, a community can be abolished only by amalgamation with another community, or by the dismemberment of its area among adjacent communities[2].

[1]   Local Government Act 1972, s 20(3) and (4).
[2]   LGA 1972, s 54(1)(c).

C   REVIEWS OF COMMUNITY ARRANGEMENTS

35.3 The boundaries of the principal areas have been set by statute[1] and a special community review by the Commission settled those of the communities in the 1970–80s. It is the duty both of the Welsh Commission to keep under review principal areas and of principal councils to keep under review community areas. A review of community areas must be carried out by a principal council at least every fifteen years and the council must publish a report showing what it has done in the previous fifteen years. The report must be sent to the Commission, which may make proposals, based on the report, for changes in community arrangements[2]. The Welsh Assembly may direct the Commission to conduct a review of the whole of Wales or one or more local government[3]. It is open to the a principal council and the Welsh Commission to arrange for the Commission to undertake the council's functions in reviewing community arrangements[4].Where a review of community arrangements has been carried out by a principal council and a report submitted to the Welsh commission, the Commission may submit proposals to the Welsh Assembly. If adopted by the Assembly (wholly or in part) they are put into effect by an order made by statutory instrument[5]. The Assembly may give directions to the Welsh Commission and to principal councils for guidance on the conduct of reviews[6].

Each principal council is responsible for keeping under review the electoral arrangements for the communities in its area. It must consider any request made by a community council relating to electoral arrangements and any request made by at least 30 electors in that community relating to any proposed changes. The Local Government Boundary Commission for Wales may on a request by a local council or 30 electors review the electoral arrangements of a locality and make proposals to the district council (T), which may make an order giving effect to them or, if the commission agrees, giving effect to them with modifications. If a district council (T) refuses to make an order, or for six months neglects to make one, the Commission can make its proposals to the Secretary of State instead, and he may put them into effect[7]. It is doubtful whether these rules are much operated.

[1]   Under Local Government (Wales) Act 1994.
[2]   Local Government Act 1972, s 55.
[3]   LGA 1972, s 56.
[4]   LGA 1972, s 57A.
[5]   LGA 1972, s 58.
[6]   LGA 1972, s 59.
[7]   LGA 1972, s 57.

Application by a community meeting to establish a community council

35.4 If a community has no separate community council and is not co-extensive with a county or county borough area, its community meeting may, subject to the following conditions, apply to the county or county borough council (T) for an order establishing a community council.[1]

The conditions are:

(i)   the meeting has taken an effective decision to hold a poll on the proposal to establish a separate council for the community. A decision is only effective if 10% of the local government electors for the community, or 150 electors (if 10% of the electorate exceeds 150), are present and voting at the meeting;

(ii)   the poll is not held before the end of 42 days beginning with the day on which the decision to hold the poll was taken;

(iii) the poll is not held within two years from the day on which an earlier poll was held which resulted in the rejection of a proposal to establish a separate community council;

(iv)   a majority of those voting in the poll support the proposal to establish a separate community council.

[1]   Local Government Act 1972, s 27A.

35.5 If the foregoing conditions are met, the county or county borough council must make an order establishing the community council.[1]

[1]   Local Government Act 1972, s 27B.

Application by a community meeting to dissolve a community council

35.6 A community meeting may apply for an order dissolving its separate community council, subject to complying with the following conditions:

(i)   the meeting has taken an effective decision to hold a poll on the proposal to establish a separate council for the community. A decision is only effective if not less than 30% of the local government electors for the community, or 300 electors (if 30% of the electorate exceeds 300), are present and voting at the meeting;

(ii)   the poll is not held before the end of 42 days beginning with the day on which the decision to hold the poll was taken;

(iii) the poll is not held within two years from the day on which an earlier poll was held which resulted in the rejection of a proposal to dissolve the separate community council;

(iv)   two thirds of those voting in the poll support the proposal to dissolve the separate community council[1].

[1]   Local Government Act 1972, s 30.

35.7 If the foregoing conditions are met, the county or county borough council must make an order dissolving the community council.

35.8 No community application to establish or dissolve a separate or a group council can be made within two years after the coming into force of an order altering community arrangements[1].

[1]   Local Government Act 1972, s 30.

D   GROUPS

35.9 The grouping of communities under a common council can occur following a procedure identical to that for the establishment of a separate community council (see **35.4** above), with the added condition that all the communities must concur before a grouping order can be made by the county or county borough council.

E   THE COMMUNITY OR TOWN'S MEETING

35.10 In a community, a meeting of the electors may, but need not, be convened to discuss community affairs; but the nature and structure of such a meeting, and its powers, differ in many ways from those of the English parish or town's meeting. Nevertheless the three main types resemble their English equivalents. These three are:

- a meeting for the whole of a community which has a separate community council;
- a meeting for a community grouped with other communities under a common council; and
- a meeting for a community which is not represented on a community council at all.

Membership and right to preside

35.11 The meeting consists of all the local government electors for the community[1] and, in addition, if there is a community council, its chairman may attend whether he is an elector or not[2], and if he attends he must preside[3]. The vice-chairman, however, has no right to take his place in his absence[4]; consequently, if the chairman of the council is absent or if there is no community council the meeting must appoint a person to be chairman at that meeting[5]. The authority of this person is not permanent even in a community without a council; it lasts, at the most, until the commencement of the next community meeting.

The electoral registration officer must, at the request of the community council, provide a free copy of the electoral register relating to the community[6].

[1]   Local Government Act 1972, s 32.
[2]   LGA 1972, Sch 12, para 31.
[3]   LGA 1972, Sch 12, para 33(1).
[4]   This follows from a comparison of LGA 1972, Sch 12, paras 17 and 33.
[5]   LGA 1972, Sch 12, para 33(2).
[6]   Representation of the People (England and Wales) Regulations 2001, SI 2001/341, reg 107 (as amended).

Right to convene

35.12 Where there is a community council, a community meeting may be convened by the chairman of, or any two councillors representing the community on, the community council.[1]. In addition, a community meeting may be convened, whether or not the community has a community council, by not less than 10% of the local government electors for the community, or 50 electors if 10% of the electorate exceeds 50 electors).

[1] Local Government Act 1972, Sch 12, para 30.

Time and notice

35.13 A meeting must not commence before 6 pm[1]. Where the meeting is convened by the chairman or by two or more community councillors, notices specifying the time and place and business of an intended meeting and signed by the conveners[2] must be affixed in some conspicuous place or places in the community, and in addition the conveners may publicise the meeting in such other ways as they think desirable[3]. Normally seven clear days' notice is required, but if the business is to concern the establishment or dissolution of a community council or the grouping of the community under a common community council, the notice required is 30 clear days. In most cases of dissolution of groups, a 30-day notice will be necessary because dissolution of the group may bring about the dissolution of the common council.

[1] Local Government Act 1972, Sch 12, para 30A.
[2] LGA 1972, Sch 12, para 30(2) and (3).
[3] LGA 1972, Sch 12, para 30.

35.14 Where the meeting is convened by electors, notice must be given to the community council, if there is one, or to the county or county borough council, if there is not. The notice must contain the names, addresses and signatures of the individuals convening the meeting. The notice must be in writing if given to the community council; if given to the county or county borough council the notice may be in electronic form[1]. On receipt of the notice, the community or county/county borough council, as the case may be, must check the validity of the notice and be sure that a sufficient number of identifiable electors has signed the notice. If so satisfied, the council must give public notice of the meeting in the same way as for a meeting convened by the chairman or councillors (see **35.12** above) and the notice must be signed by the proper officer of the council.[2]

[1] Local Government Act 1972, Sch 12, para 30B and 30C.
[2] LGA 1972, Sch 12, para 30E.

Quorum

35.15 The quorum of a community meeting is two[1], unless the meeting concerns the establishment of a community council, the establishment or dissolution of a group council or the dissolution of a community council and there is a demand for a poll (see **35.4-35.9** above).

[1] *Loughlin v Guinness* (1904) 23 NZLR 748, per Denniston J at 754.

Decisions

35.16 Decisions and the consequent polls are taken in the same way as decisions by parish meetings and polls consequent upon them[1].

[1]   See **10.7** above and Local Government Act 1972, Sch 12, paras 18 and 34.

Places of meeting

35.17 Community meetings may be held and are forbidden to meet in the same places as community councils[1].

[1]   Local Government Act 1972, s 134(2).

Community meetings where there is no council

35.18 A community meeting, not being a corporation, cannot own property or sue or be sued[1]; it is not a local authority[2], and where there is no community council it has not even a permanent chairman. As a result there is no institution similar to the English parish trustees. The community property is vested in the county or country borough council (T)[3], there is no power to appoint committees but if something needs to be done or an instrument signed, a community meeting may authorise the person presiding and two other electors present at the meeting to do it[4]. It seems that the authority of these three cannot extend beyond the commencement of the next meeting.

A resolution demanding the establishment of a community council, if passed in the same manner as a resolution to dissolve a community council, binds the district council (T).

[1]   See Local Government Act 1972, s 222.
[2]   LGA 1972, s 270(1).
[3]   Local Authorities (Wales) (Property etc) Order 1973, SI 1973/1863, Sch 4.
[4]   LGA 1972, s 32(2) and (3).

Minutes and procedure

35.19 Minutes of community meetings must be kept. They must be drawn up and entered in a book by the proper officer of the community council if there is one, and by the proper officer of the county or county borough council (T) if there is not. They must be signed at the conclusion of the meeting to which they relate by the person presiding[1]. Time must therefore be allowed for the drafting and signature of the minutes before the meeting breaks up.

It will be observed that these rules indirectly require the attendance of a district council (T) officer at any community meeting where there is no community council.

A community meeting, whether there is a community council or not, regulates its own procedure[2].

[1]   Local Government Act 1972, Sch 12, para 35(1).

² LGA 1972, Sch 12, para 36.

Admission of the public

35.20 The press and public have the same rights at a community meeting as at a community council. A clearly marked area for strangers should be set aside to avoid confusion when a vote is taken.

F   PROMOTION OF WELL-BEING

35.21 Principal authorities and community councils in Wales have the power to do anything which they consider likely to achieve one or more of the following objects:

(a)   the promotion or improvement of the economic well-being of their area;

(b)   the promotion or improvement of the social well-being of their area; and

(c)   the promotion or improvement of the environmental well-being of their area.

The power may be used:

- to incur expenditure;
- to give financial assistance to any person;
- to enter into arrangements or agreements with any person;
- to co-ordinate or facilitate or co-ordinate the activities of any person;
- to exercise on behalf of any person the functions of that person; and
- to provide staff, goods, services or accommodation to any person[1].

The power may not be used in contravention of any prohibition, restriction or limitation on the powers of local authorities contained in enactments whenever passed. The Welsh Ministers (ie the First Minister and other ministers in the Welsh Assembly government appointed by him) have power to impose further limitations[1].

In exercising the power, a local authority (ie a principal council and a community council) must have regard to the community strategy for its area (see **35.22** below)[2].

¹   Local Government Act 2000, ss 1.
²   LGA 2000, s 2(3B).

G   COMMUNITY STRATEGIES

35.22 Every principal authority must have a community planning strategy for its area. The strategy must indentify long-term objectives for improving the social, economic and environmental well-being for the area. The strategy must be implemented jointly with the principal council's community planning partners[1]. Those partners are community councils, the fire and rescue authority, local health board, NHS trust, national park authority, police authority and chief constable[2]. Local residents, voluntary organisations, local businesses and others interested in the well-being of the area must be able to express their views on community planning[3]. Once produced, the strategy must be kept under review and monitored[4]. Welsh Ministers have power to issue guidance about community planning[5]. Guidance was issued in June 2010 and can be viewed on the Welsh Assembly Government website[6].

[1] Local Government (Wales) Measure 2009, s37.
[2] LG(W)A 2009, s 38.
[3] LG(W)A 2009, s 44.
[4] LG(W)A 2009, ss 39–43.
[5] LG(W)A 2009, s 45.
[6] See www.wales.gov.uk.

H   MODEL CHARTER AGREEMENTS

35.23 Welsh Ministers may make by order provision for a model charter agreement between a principal council and a community council, or community councils, in its area. The order may include provisions about the way in which functions are exercised and may direct that the principal council and the community council or councils adopt a charter agreement[1].

Welsh Ministers may, after consultation with principal authorities, community councils and others ministers consider it appropriate to consult, issue guidance about model charter agreements[2]. No model agreement has yet been published by the Welsh Ministers.

[1] Local Government (Wales) Measure 2011, s 130 and 131.
[2] LG(W)M 2011, s 132 and 133.

I   ACCREDITATION SCHEMES

35.24 Chapter 9 (ss 130–140) of the Local Government (Wales) Measure 2011 empowers Welsh Ministers to make schemes for the accreditation of quality in community government. Ministers have expressed the view that such a scheme should be developed and operated on a non-statutory basis, with the statutory provisions being a reserve power for possible use in the future (presumably, if a non-statutory scheme cannot be agreed).

It is likely that any accreditation scheme will be similar to the quality parish council scheme in England (see CHAPTER **22G**).

Chapter 36

WELSH BURIAL FACILITIES

36.1 On 31 March 1920[1], the churchyards and burial grounds of the Welsh Church were vested in the Welsh Church Commissioners[2]; those given as private benefactions were transferred to the Representative Body of the Church in Wales[3]; most of the rest (comprising, amongst others, most of the old churchyards), passed to that body on 1 December 1946[4].

In some cases (the 'transferred churchyards') the churchyard or burial ground was transferred to the existing incumbent, and at the end of his incumbency to the burial authority, if any, and if none to the parish (now community) council, or if no parish council to the representative body of the parish, through which it has now passed to the county or county borough council[5]. If it adjoins a church vested in the Welsh Representative Body it is held subject to a right of way for clergy and worshippers; funerals are forbidden during hours of Divine Service; the authority must maintain any road or path through it, and where any land is needed to enlarge the church it may be so used[6]. Subject to these four rules it is to be held at the incumbent's death as if it were a cemetery[7], but the burial authority can by agreement transfer it to the Welsh Representative Body, and thereupon the four rules and the law on cemeteries cease to apply[8].

The Welsh Representative Body must maintain its own burial grounds, and when a burial ground vests in it, any other liability to maintain it ceases[9], including any liability previously imposed upon a burial authority.

For closed churchyards, see **33.2** above.

[1] Welsh Church (Temporalities) Act 1919, s 2.
[2] Welsh Church Act 1914, s 4.
[3] WCA 1914, s 8(a).
[4] Welsh Church (Burial Grounds) Act 1945.
[5] See **13.11** above.
[6] WCA 1914, s 24(1)–(3).
[7] WCA 1914, s 24(1) and Local Government Act 1972, Sch 26, para 1.
[8] WC(BG)A 1945, s 2.
[9] WC(BG)A 1945, s 3.

Chapter 37

THE WELSH LANGUAGE

37.1 Though there are hardly any monoglot Welshmen left, proceedings at meetings may be (and often are) in Welsh and where this is the common language of communication it is advisable for the minutes to be available in the language best understood by the members. It is, all the same, desirable for the accounts to be kept in English in case they become the subject of an appeal, because the making of an official translation will increase the cost of the proceedings.

The Welsh Language (Wales) Measure 2011 makes comprehensive provision for promoting and supporting use of Welsh and enables community councils, among others, to adhere to service delivery standards specified by Welsh ministers.

A   SERVICE DELIVERY STANDARDS

37.2 There is a duty on community councils to comply with the service delivery standards in relation to the Welsh language specified by Welsh Ministers[1]. At the time of writing no standards have been specified.

[1]   Welsh Language (Wales) Measure 2011, s 28 and Sch 6.

B   WELSH COMMUNITY NAMES

37.3 Every community council must have an English and a Welsh name consisting of the name of the community with the addition, in English, of 'Community Council' (eg 'Dale Community Council') and, in Welsh, of 'Cyngor Cymuned' (eg 'Cyngor Cymuned Dale')[1].

[1]   Local Government Act 1972, s 33(2).

Appendix I

STATUTES

Contents

Acts of Parliament

Localism Act 2011

Local Authorities (Goods and Services) Act 1970

Local Government (Financial Provisions) Act 1963

Local Government (Miscellaneous Provisions) Act 1953

Local Government (Miscellaneous Provisions) Act 1976

Local Government (Miscellaneous Provisions) Act 1982

Local Government (Records) Act 1962

Local Government (Wales) Act 1994

Local Government Act 1894

Local Government Act 1929

Local Government Act 1948

Local Government Act 1958

Local Government Act 1972

Local Government Act 1986

Local Government Act 1988

Local Government Act 2000

Local Government Act 2003

Local Government and Housing Act 1989

Local Government and Public Involvement in Health Act 2007

Local Government and Rating Act 1997

Local Government Finance Act 1988

Local Government Finance Act 1992

Natural Environment and Rural Communities Act 2006

Open Spaces Act 1906

Parish Councils Act 1957

Parish Councils and Burial Authorities (Miscellaneous Provisions) Act 1970

Public Audit (Wales) Act 2004

Public Bodies (Admission to Meetings) Act 1960

Introduction

The condition of parish and community law is not as good as it should be and there remain acts and instruments which have been amended, partially repealed, extended, restricted or reinterpreted.

In the texts which follow, irrelevant and repealed legislation has, so far as possible, been omitted altogether and amended legislation is printed as amended, the amending enactment being likewise, if possible, omitted. The author's comments appear within square brackets and are printed in italics.

Local councils may need to know of the existence of some provisions (mostly concerning parliament, ministers and principal councils) but are unlikely to find the exact and often lengthy wording useful to their needs; in these special cases the provisions have been summarised.

The expressions parish and parish council in pre-1972 statutes are nearly always taken to include the Welsh community and its council. On the other hand the expression 'parish meeting' is now only seldom to be taken to include the community meeting, and the expression 'representative body' now means the parish trustees in England but until 1 April 1996 the district council in Wales. (See also note on the symbol T below.)

The expression poor rate meant, until 31 March 1990, the rate. Thereafter it must be taken (as the context requires) either to include the council tax, or to mean the money obtained by precept.

349

The symbol T

For the meaning of the symbol T used in the first part of this book, see the note on p xii. The symbol is not used in this appendix, but the user should bear in mind that references in the statutes to counties, districts and their councils may have to be read in England as references either to counties or to districts and their council, and in Wales to counties, county boroughs and their councils.

The marks E and P

The Environment Act 1995, s 70 and Sch 9 adapts the enactments marked below so as to include National Parks authorities in the definition of local authorities, but in the case of the Commons Act 1899, ss 1, 7, 12 and 18 and the Commons Act 2006, s 45 (marked P), those authorities are included only where they are the local planning authority, and the registered common involved is not vested in some other local authority.

NOTE: The texts of the Inclosure Acts 1845, 1852, 1857 and the Commons Acts 1876, 1878, 1879 and 1882 though still, with amendments, in force, have been omitted because the author has not been asked to advise on them for over 30 years. Their effects are summarised in the main text, notably in CHAPTER 26 and CHAPTER 29.

DISUSED BURIAL GROUNDS ACT 1884

2 Interpretation
In this Act—

'building' includes any temporary or movable building;

'burial ground' includes any churchyard, cemetery or other ground, whether consecrated or not, which has been at any time set apart for the purpose of interment;

'disused burial ground' means any burial ground which is no longer used for interments, whether or not the ground has been partially or wholly closed for burials under the provisions of a statute of Order in Council.

3 No buildings to be erected upon disused burial grounds except for enlargement, etc
It shall not be lawful to erect any buildings upon any disused burial ground, except for the purpose of enlarging a church, chapel, meeting house, or other places of worship[1].

---

[1] But see Disused Burial Grounds (Amendment) Act 1981.

PUBLIC HEALTH ACTS AMENDMENT ACT 1890

44[1] Parks and pleasure grounds
(1) An urban authority may on such days as they think fit (not exceeding twelve days in any one year nor four consecutive days on any one occasion) close to the public any park or pleasure ground provided by them or any part thereof, and may grant the use of the same, either gratuitously or for payment, to any public charity or institution, or for any agricultural, horticultural, or other show, or any other public purpose, or may use the same for any such show or purpose; and the admission to the said park or pleasure ground, or such part thereof, on the days when the same shall be so closed to the public may be either with or without payment, as directed by the urban authority, or, with the consent of the urban authority, by the society or persons to whom the use of the park or pleasure ground, or such part thereof, may be granted: Provided that no such park or pleasure ground shall be closed on any Sunday ...

(2) An urban authority may either themselves provide and let for hire, or may license any person to let for hire, any pleasure boats on any lake or piece of water in any such park or pleasure ground, and may make byelaws for regulating the numbering and naming of such boats, the number of persons to be carried therein, the boathouses and mooring places for the same, and for fixing rates of hire and the qualifications of boatmen, and for securing their good and orderly conduct while in charge of any boat.

¹ See PHA 1961, s 53; and LGA 1972, Sch 14, para 27.

45 Extension of 38 & 39 Vict c 55, s 164

The powers of an urban authority under section one hundred and sixty-four of the Public Health Act 1875, to contribute to the support of public walks or pleasure grounds, shall include a power to contribute towards the cost of the laying out, planting, or improvement of any lands provided by any person which have been permanently set apart as public walks or pleasure grounds, and which, whether in the district of the urban authority or not, are so situated as to be conveniently used by the inhabitants of the district, and shall also include a power to contribute towards the purchase by any person of lands so situate and to be so set apart as aforesaid.

LOCAL GOVERNMENT ACT 1894

5 Parish council to appoint overseers

(2)

- (b) References in any Act to the churchwardens and overseers shall, as respects any rural parish, except so far as those references relate to the affairs of the church, be construed as references to the overseers and

6 Transfer of certain powers of vestry and other authorities to parish council

(1) Upon the parish council of a rural parish coming into office, there shall be transferred to that council—

- (a) The powers, duties, and liabilities of the vestry of the parish except—
  - (i) so far as relates to the affairs of the church or to ecclesiastical charities; and
  - (ii) any power, duty, or liability transferred by this Act from the vestry to any other authority:
- (b) The powers, duties, and liabilities of the churchwardens of the parish, except so far as they relate to the affairs of the church or to charities, or are powers and duties of overseers
- (c) The powers, duties, and liabilities of the overseers or of the churchwardens and overseers of the parish with respect to—
  - (ii) the provision of parish books or matters relating thereto; and
  - (iii) the holding or management of parish property, not being property relating to affairs of the church or held for an ecclesiastical charity, and the holding or management of village greens, or of allotments, whether for recreation grounds or for gardens or otherwise for the benefit of the inhabitants or any of them;

8 Additional powers of parish council

(1) A parish council shall have the following additional powers, namely, power—

- (d) sections one hundred and eighty-three to one hundred and eighty-six of the Public Health Act 1875, shall apply as if the parish council were a local authority within the meaning of those sections; and

(i) to execute any works (including works of maintenance or improvement) incidental to or consequential on the exercise of any of the foregoing powers, or in relation to any parish property, not being property relating to affairs of the church or held for an ecclesiastical charity; and

(k) to contribute towards the expense of doing any of the things above mentioned, or to agree or combine with any other parish council to do or contribute towards the expense of doing any of the things above mentioned.

19 Provisions as to small parishes

In a rural parish not having a separate parish council, the following provisions shall, subject to provisions made by a grouping order, if the parish is grouped with some other parish or parishes, have effect—

(4) All powers, duties, and liabilities of the vestry shall, except so far as they relate to the affairs of the Church or to ecclesiastical charities, or are transferred by this Act to any other authority, be transferred to the parish meeting;

26 Duties and powers of district council as to . . . rights of common . . .

(2) A district council may with the consent of the county council for the county within which any common land is situate aid persons in maintaining rights of common where, in the opinion of the council, the extinction of such rights would be prejudicial to the inhabitants of the district.

(3) A district council may, for the purpose of carrying into effect this section, institute or defend any legal proceedings, and generally take such steps as they deem expedient.

52 Supplemental provisions as to transfer of powers

(5) All enactments in any Act, whether general or local and personal, relating to any powers, duties, or liabilities transferred by this Act to a parish council or parish meeting from justices or the vestry or overseers or churchwardens and overseers shall, subject to the provisions of this Act and so far as circumstances admit, be construed as if any reference therein to justices or to the vestry, or to the overseers, or to the churchwardens and overseers, referred to the parish council or parish meeting as the case requires, and the said enactments shall be construed with such modifications as may be necessary for carrying this Act into effect.

75 Construction of Act

(1) The definition of 'parish' in section one hundred of the Local Government Act, 1888, shall not apply to this Act, but, save as aforesaid, expressions used in this Act shall, unless the context otherwise requires, have the same meaning as in the said Act.

(2) In this Act, unless the context otherwise requires—

The expression 'ecclesiastical charity' includes a charity, the endowment whereof is held for some one or more of the following purposes—

(a) for any spiritual purpose which is a legal purpose; or

(b) for the benefit of any spiritual person or ecclesiastical officer as such; or

(c) for use, if a building, as a church, chapel, mission room, or Sunday school, or otherwise by any particular church or denomination; or

(d) for the maintenance, repair, or improvement of any such building as aforesaid, or for the maintenance of divine service therein; or

(e) otherwise for the benefit of any particular church or denomination, or of any members thereof as such.

Provided that where any endowment of a charity, other than a building held for any of the purposes aforesaid, is held in part only for some of the purposes aforesaid, the charity, so far as that endowment is concerned, shall be an ecclesiastical charity within the meaning of this Act; and the Charity Commission shall, on application by any person interested, make such provision for the apportionment and management of that endowment as seems to it necessary or expedient for giving effect to this Act.

The expression shall also include any building which in the opinion of the Charity Commission has been erected or provided within forty years before the passing of this Act mainly by or at the cost of members of any particular church or denomination.

The expression 'affairs of the church' shall include the distribution of offertories or other collections made in any church.

The expression 'vestry' in relation to a parish means the inhabitants of the parish whether in vestry assembled or not, and includes any select vestry either by statute or at common law.

The expression 'local and personal Act' includes a Provisional Order confirmed by an Act and the Act confirming the Order.

COMMONS ACT 1899

PART I

REGULATION OF COMMONS

1 Power for district council to make scheme for regulation of common[1]
(1) The council of a district may make a scheme for the regulation and management of any common within their district with a view to the expenditure of money on the drainage, levelling, and improvement of the common, and to the making of byelaws and regulations for the prevention of nuisances and the preservation of order on the common.
(2) The scheme may contain any of the statutory provisions for the benefit of the neighbourhood mentioned in section seven of the Commons Act 1876.
(3) The scheme shall be in the prescribed form, and shall identify by reference to a plan the common to be thereby regulated, and for this purpose an ordnance survey map shall, if possible, be used.

---

[1] This section has been amended, in relation to Wales only, by the addition of a sub-s (4), as follows (see the Commons Act 2006):

(4) Regulations under subsection (3) may—

(a) prescribe alternative forms;
(b) permit exceptions or modifications to be made to any prescribed form.

2 Procedure for making scheme[1]
(1) Not less than three months before the making of a scheme under this Part of this Act the council shall give the prescribed notice of their intention to make it, and shall state thereby where copies of the draft of the scheme may be obtained, and where the plan therein referred to may be inspected.
(2) During the three months aforesaid any person may obtain copies of the draft on payment of a sum not exceeding 2p per copy, and may inspect the plan at the prescribed place, and may make in writing to the council any objection or suggestion with respect to the scheme or plan.
(3) After the expiration of the said three months the council shall take into consideration any objections or suggestions so made, and for that purpose may, if they think fit, direct that an inquiry be held by an officer of the council.

(4)   The Council may by order approve of the scheme, subject to such modifications, if any, as they may think desirable, and thereupon the scheme shall have full effect.

Provided that if, at any time before the Council have approved of the scheme, they receive a written notice of dissent either—

(a)   from the person entitled as lord of the manor or otherwise to the soil of the common; or

(b)   from persons representing at least one-third in value of such interests in the common as are affected by the scheme,

and such notice is not subsequently withdrawn, the Council shall not proceed further in the matter.

[1]   This section has been amended in relation to Wales only. The section applicable to Wales reads as follows:

(1)   A council is to make and approve a scheme under this Part of this Act in the prescribed manner.

(2)   Provided that if, at any time before the Council have approved of the scheme, they receive a written notice of dissent either—

(a)   from the person entitled as lord of the manor or otherwise to the soil of the common; or

(b)   from persons representing at least one-third in value of such interests in the common as are affected by the scheme,

and such notice is not subsequently withdrawn, the Council shall not proceed further in the matter.

3 Management of regulated commons

The management of any common regulated by a scheme made by a district council under this Part of this Act shall be vested in the district council.

5 Power for parish council to contribute to expenses

A parish council may agree to contribute the whole or any portion of the expenses of and incidental to the preparation and execution of a scheme for the regulation and management of any common within their parish (including any compensation paid under this Act).

6 Provision for compensation

No estate, interest, or right of a profitable or beneficial nature in, over, or affecting any common shall, except with the consent of the person entitled thereto, be taken away or injuriously affected by any scheme under this Part of this Act without compensation being made or provided for the same by the council making the scheme, and such compensation shall, in case of difference, be ascertained and provided in the same manner as if it were for the compulsory purchase and taking, or the injurious affecting, of lands under the Lands Clauses Acts.

7 Power for district council to acquire property in regulated common

A district council may acquire the fee simple or any estate in or any rights in or over any common regulated by a scheme under this Part of this Act by gift or by purchase by agreement, and hold the same for the purposes of the scheme.

8 Digging of gravel

Section twenty of the Commons Act 1876 (which relates to the digging of gravel), shall apply to any common regulated by a scheme under this Part of this Act.

9 Power to amend scheme[1]

The power to make a scheme under this Part of this Act shall include power to amend or supplement any such scheme.

¹   This section has been substituted, in relation to Wales only, as follows (see the Commons Act 2006):

9 Power to amend or revoke scheme

(1)   A scheme under this Part of this Act for any common may, in prescribed circumstances, be amended in the prescribed manner.

(2)   A scheme under this Part of this Act for any common may, where a new scheme is made under this Part of this Act for the whole of that common, be revoked in the prescribed manner.

10 Provisions as to byelaws

The provisions with respect to byelaws contained in sections one hundred and eighty-two to one hundred and eighty-six, both inclusive, of the Public Health Act 1875, and any enactment amending or extending those sections, shall apply to all byelaws made in pursuance of a scheme under this Part of this Act, and any fine imposed by any such byelaw shall be recoverable summarily and be payable to the council in whom the management of the common is vested.

11 Expenses

All expenses of and incidental to the preparation and execution of a scheme under this Part of this Act shall be paid by the district council.

12 Power for district council to contribute towards expenses

The council of any district may, with a view to the benefit of the inhabitants of their district, enter into an undertaking with any other council making or having made a scheme under this Part of this Act to contribute any portion of the expenses incurred by that council in executing the scheme.

14 Saving for commons regulated under other Acts

A scheme under this Part of this Act, shall not apply to any common which is or might be the subject of a scheme made under the Metropolitan Commons Acts 1866 to 1878, or is regulated by a Provisional Order under the Inclosure Acts 1845 to 1882, or . . . is the subject of any private or local and personal Act of Parliament having for its object the preservation of the common as an open space, or is subject to byelaws made by a parish council under section eight of the Local Government Act 1894.

15 Definitions

In this Part of this Act, unless the context otherwise requires,—

The expression 'common' shall include any land subject to be inclosed under the Inclosure Acts 1845 to 1882, and any town or village green;

The expression 'prescribed' shall mean prescribed by regulations made by the Board of Agriculture.

PART II

MISCELLANEOUS

16 Surplus rents from field gardens and recreation grounds

(1)   Surplus rents arising from field gardens may, in addition to the purposes for which they are now applicable, be applied for any of the purposes for which surplus rents arising from recreation grounds may be applied.

(2)   Surplus rents arising from any field garden or recreation ground may be applied towards the redemption of any land tax, tithe rentcharge, or other charge on the garden or ground.

18 Power to modify provisions as to recreation grounds, etc

Any provisions with respect to allotments for recreation grounds, field gardens or other public or parochial purposes contained in any Act relating to inclosure or in any award or order made in pursuance thereof, and any provisions with respect to the management of any such allotments contained in any such Act, order, or award, may, on the application of any district or parish council interested in any such allotment, be dealt with by a scheme of the Charity Commission in the exercise of its ordinary jurisdiction, as if those provisions had been established by the founder in the case of a charity having a founder.

For the purposes of this section the Broads Authority shall be treated as a district council.

22[1] Restrictions on inclosures under scheduled Acts

(1) A grant or inclosure of common purporting to be made under the general authority of any of the Acts mentioned in the First Schedule hereto or any Act incorporating the same, or any provisions thereof, shall not be valid unless it is either—

    (a)   specially authorised by Act of Parliament; or

    (b)   made to or by any Government Department; or

    (c)   made with the consent of the Board of Agriculture.

(2) The Board of Agriculture, in giving or withholding their consent under this section, shall have regard to the same considerations, and shall, if necessary, hold the same inquiries as are directed by the Commons Act 1876, to be taken into consideration and held by the Board before forming an opinion whether an application under the Inclosure Acts shall be acceded to or not.

[1]   See Compulsory Purchase Act 1965, s 21(2) and Countryside Act 1969, s 9.

23 Repeal

This repeal shall not affect the construction or effect of any local and personal Act of Parliament passed before the commencement of this Act, whereby any provisions of the said enactments are intended to be incorporated.

24 Short title

This Act may be cited as the Commons Act 1899, and shall be read with the Inclosure Acts 1845 to 1882.

SCHEDULE 1

ENACTMENTS RELATING TO INCLOSURES SUBJECT TO RESTRICTION
UNDER THIS ACT

Session and Chapter[1]	Title or Short Title
51 Geo 3 c 115	*The Gifts for Churches Act 1811.*
4 & 5 Vict c 38	*The Schools Sites Act 1841.*
8 & 9 Vict c 18	The Lands Clauses Consolidation Act 1845.
17 & 18 Vict c 112	*The Literary and Scientific Institutions Act 1854.*

[1]   Entries in italics were repealed by the Commons Act 2006.

OPEN SPACES ACT 1906

Local authorities

1 Local authorities
Each of the following bodies shall be a local authority for the purposes of this Act, namely—

The council of any county, of any municipal borough, or of any district:

. . .

Any parish council.

Power to transfer open spaces and burial grounds to local authorities

2 Power of trustees under local Act to transfer open space to local authority or admit other persons to enjoyment thereof
(1)   Where an open space is, in pursuance of a local or private Act of Parliament, placed under the care and management of trustees or other persons (in this section referred to as trustees), with a view to the preservation and regulation thereof as a garden or open space, the trustees may, in pursuance of a special resolution, and with the consent, signified by a special resolution, of the owners and occupiers of any houses which front upon the open space, or of which the owners and occupiers are liable to be specially rated for the maintenance of the open space—

(a)   convey, for or without any consideration, to any local authority, their estate or interest in the open space or, if they have no such estate or interest, transfer to any local authority the entire care and management of the open space, to the end that the space may be preserved for the enjoyment of the public; or

(b)   grant, for or without any consideration, to any local authority any term of years or other limited interest in or any right or easement over the open space; or

(c)   make any agreement with any local authority for the opening to the public of the open space and the care and management thereof by the local authority, either at all times or at any specified time or

(d)   notwithstanding anything in the Act or any instrument under which the trustees are constituted or act, admit persons not owning, occupying, or residing in any house fronting on the open space to the enjoyment of the open space, either at all times or at any specified time or times, and regulate the admission of such persons thereto on such terms and conditions as the trustees think proper.

(2)   Where the freehold of the open space and the freehold of all or the greater part of the houses round the open space are vested in the same person the powers conferred by this section shall not be exercised without the consent of that person.

(3)   Any such conveyance, transfer, grant, or agreement shall be made, if the trustees are a corporation, by an instrument under the common seal of the trustees, and if the trustees are not a corporation, by an instrument under the hands and seals of any five of the trustees, or of all the trustees if for the time being they are less than five in number.

(4)   Any conveyance, transfer, grant, or agreement under this section shall be deemed a good execution of the trusts, powers, and duties imposed or conferred upon the trustees by the Act or instrument under which they are constituted or act, and where the trustees convey their entire interest in, or transfer the entire care and management of, the open space they shall, on the execution of the conveyance or transfer, be

relieved and discharged from all trusts, powers, and duties under the Act or instrument or otherwise with reference to the open space.

(5)   The trustees shall hold any purchase money or rent paid for or in respect of the open space in trust for the benefit of the persons or class of persons for whose benefit the open space was previously preserved and managed by the trustees, or, as the case may be, for the benefit of the objects to which any rates previously imposed in respect of the open space had been applied, and such persons or class of persons shall be discharged either absolutely, or, if the grant was for a term of years or other limited interest, during the continuance of that interest, from any special rate or other obligation previously imposed on them in respect of the open space.

3 Transfer to local authority of spaces held by trustees for purposes of public recreation

(1)   Where any land is held by trustees (not being trustees elected or appointed under any local or private Act of Parliament) upon trust for the purposes of public recreation, the trustees may, in pursuance of a special resolution, transfer the land to any local authority by a free gift absolutely or for a limited term, and, if the local authority accept the gift, they shall hold the land on the trusts and subject to the conditions on and subject to which the trustees held the same, or on such other trusts and subject to such other conditions (so that the land be appropriated to the purposes of public recreation) as may be agreed on between the trustees and the local authority with the approval of the Charity Commission.

(2)   Subject to the obligation of the land so transferred being used for the purposes of public recreation, the local authority may hold the land as and for the purposes of an open space under this Act.

4 Transfer by charity trustees of open space to local authority

(1)   Where an open space is vested in trustees, other than such as are mentioned in the foregoing provisions of this Act, for any charitable purpose and as part of their trust estate, and it appears to the majority of the trustees that the open space is no longer required for the purposes of their trust, or may with advantage to the trust be dealt with under this section, the trustees may, in pursuance of a special resolution, and in accordance with subsection (1A), convey or demise the open space to any local authority on such terms as they may agree, and the local authority shall thenceforth be entitled to hold the same as an open space on the terms and under the conditions specified in the conveyance or demise, or on such terms or under such conditions as may be so authorised or approved, or as the court may from time to time order, as the case may be.

(1A)   The trustees act in accordance with this subsection if they convey or demise the open space as mentioned in subsection (1)—

  (a)   with the sanction of an order of the Charity Commission or with that of an order of the court to be obtained as provided in the following provisions of this section, or

  (b)   in accordance with such provisions of sections 117(2) and 119 to 121 of the Charities Act 2011 as are applicable.

(2)   The court for the purposes of this section shall be either the High Court or the county court of the district in which the whole or any part of the open space is situate.

(3)   An order of the court for the purposes of this section may be made upon application by the trustees, in manner directed by rules of court, and the court, before making any order, may direct such inquiries to be made, such consents to be obtained, and notice to be given to such persons, as to the court seem expedient, and may make such order thereon as in the discretion of the court appears proper.

(4)   Section 337 of the Charities Act 2011 (provisions as to orders under that Act) applies to any order of the Charity Commission under this section as it applies to orders made by it under that Act.

5 Transfer to local authority by owners of open spaces subject to rights of user

(1)   Where any open space is subject to rights of user for exercise and recreation in the owners or occupiers, or both, of any houses round or near the same, whether the rights are secured by covenant or not, the owner of the open space may, with the consent, signified by a special resolution, of such owners or occupiers, or both, as the case may require,—

   (a)   convey to any local authority his estate or interest in the open space in trust for the enjoyment of the public; or

   (b)   grant to any local authority in trust as aforesaid any term of years or other limited interest in or any right or easement over the open space; or

   (c)   make an agreement with any local authority for the opening to the public of the open space and the care and management thereof by the local authority either at all times or at any specified times:

and thereupon the owner shall be discharged from any liability to any person entitled to any right of user in respect of any act done in accordance with the consent so given.

(2)   Where any person has any term of years or other limited interest in any such open space this section shall apply to him with reference to that interest in like manner as it applies to the owner of the open space.

(3)   Where any open space is used as a place of exercise and recreation for the inhabitants of certain houses, and the property and right of user is vested in one or more persons as owners or occupiers of the houses, those owners and occupiers (if any) may convey to a local authority in trust for the public a right to enter upon, use, and enjoy the open space subject to such terms and conditions as may be agreed upon.

6 Transfer of disused burial grounds to local authority

The owner of any disused burial ground may convey the burial ground to, or grant any term of years or other limited interest therein to, or make any agreement with, any local authority for the purpose of giving the public access to the burial ground, and preserving the same as an open space accessible to the public and under the control of the local authority, and for the purpose of improving and laying out the same.

7 Power of corporation, etc, to convey land for open space

(1)   Any corporation (other than a municipal corporation) or persons having power, either with or without the consent of any other corporation or persons, to sell any land may, but with the like consent (if any), convey, for or without any consideration, to any local authority that land, or any part thereof, for the purpose of the same being preserved as an open space for the enjoyment of the public under this Act, and may so convey the same with or without conditions, and the local authority may accept the land for that purpose, and, if conditions are imposed, subject to such conditions.

(2)   Where a corporation having power under this section to convey land are themselves a local authority, this section shall enable the authority to appropriate their land as an open space for the enjoyment of the public, and shall, with the necessary modifications, apply to the appropriation in like manner as it applies to the conveyance.

8 Special resolutions and consents

(1)   A resolution shall for the purposes of this Act be a special resolution when it has been—

   (a)   passed by a majority of at least two-thirds of the persons present at a meeting summoned as herein-after provided; and

   (b)   confirmed by another resolution passed by a majority of at least two-thirds of the persons present at a meeting summoned as hereinafter provided and held after an interval of not less than one month from the first meeting.

(2)   A meeting of trustees for the purposes of this Act shall be summoned by a notice stating generally the object of the meeting, which notice shall be left at or sent by post, at least one month before the date of the meeting, to the last known or usual place of abode of each trustee.

(3)   A meeting of owners and occupiers of houses under this Act shall be summoned by a notice stating generally the object of the meeting, which notice shall be left at, or sent through the post to, each of such houses, at least one month before the date of the meeting, and shall be inserted as an advertisement at least three times in any two or more papers circulating in the neighbourhood.

(4)   If at any meeting of trustees or of owners and occupiers under this Act a resolution with respect to an open space is rejected, no meeting of the trustees, or, as the case may be, the owners or occupiers, shall be called or held with the same object and with respect to the same open space until the expiration of three years from the date of the rejection.

(5)   A meeting of owners or occupiers of houses for the purposes of this Act shall not be held between the first day of August in one year and the thirty-first day of January in the following year.

Powers of local authorities with respect to open spaces and burial grounds

9 Powers of local authority to acquire open space or burial ground
A local authority may, subject to the provisions of this Act,—
- (a) acquire by agreement and for valuable or nominal consideration by way of payment in gross, or of rent, or otherwise, or without any consideration, the freehold of, or any term of years or other limited estate or interest in, or any right or easement in or over, any open space or burial ground, whether situate within the district of the local authority or not; and
- (b) undertake the entire or partial care, management, and control of any such open space or burial ground, whether any interest in the soil is transferred to the local authority or not; and
- (c) for the purposes aforesaid, make any agreement with any person authorised by this Act or otherwise to convey or to agree with reference to any open space or burial ground, or with any other persons interested therein.

10 Maintenance of open spaces and burial grounds by local authority
A local authority who have acquired any estate or interest in or control over any open space or burial ground under this Act shall, subject to any conditions under which the estate, interest, or control was so acquired—
- (a) hold and administer the open space or burial ground in trust to allow, and with a view to, the enjoyment thereof by the public as an open space within the meaning of this Act and under proper control and regulation and for no other purpose; and
- (b) maintain and keep the open space or burial ground in a good and decent state,

and many inclose it or keep it inclosed with proper railings and gates, and may drain, level, lay out, turf, plant, ornament, light, provide with seats, and otherwise improve it, and do all such works and things and employ such officers and servants as may be requisite for the purposes aforesaid or any of them.

11 Special provisions as to management of burial grounds and removal of tombstones
(1)   A local authority shall not exercise any of the powers of management under this Act with reference to any consecrated burial ground unless and until they are authorised so to do by the licence or faculty of the bishop.

(2)   The playing of any games or sports shall not be allowed in any burial ground in or over which a local authority have acquired any estate, interest, or control under this Act, except that—

(a)   in the case of a consecrated burial ground, the bishop by licence or faculty; and

(b)   in the case of any burial ground which is not consecrated, the persons from whom the local authority have acquired the estate, interest, or control in or over the same

may expressly sanction any such use of the burial ground, and may specify any conditions as to the extent or nature of such use.

(3)   In the case of any disused burial ground, at least three months before removing or changing the position of any tombstone or monument, a local authority shall—

(a)   prepare a statement sufficiently describing by the name and date appearing thereon the tombstones and monuments standing or being in the ground, and such other particulars as may be necessary, and shall cause this statement to be deposited with the clerk of the local authority, and to be open to inspection by all persons; and

(b)   insert an advertisement of the intention to remove or change the position of such tombstones and monuments three times at least in some newspaper circulating in the neighbourhood, and by that advertisement give notice of the deposit of the statement herein-before described, and of the place at which and the hours within which the same may be inspected; and

(c)   place a notice in terms similar to the advertisement on the door of the church (if any) to which the burial ground is attached, and deliver or send by post a notice to any person known or believed by the local authority to be a near relative of any person whose death is recorded on any such tombstone or monument.

(4)   In the case of a consecrated ground, no tombstone or monument shall be removed or its position changed without a licence or faculty from the bishop, and no application for such licence or faculty shall be made until the expiration of one month at least after the appearance of the last of such advertisements as aforesaid:

Provided that on an application for a licence or faculty nothing shall prevent the bishop from directing or sanctioning the removal or change of position of any tombstone or monument, if he is of opinion that reasonable steps have been taken to bring the intention to effect such removal or change of position to the notice of some person having a family interest in the tombstone or monument.

(5)   A licence or faculty for the purposes of this section may be granted by the bishop of the diocese within which the consecrated burial ground is situate on the application of the local authority who have acquired any estate, interest, or control in or over the burial ground, and may be granted subject to such conditions and restrictions as to the bishop may seen fit.

12 Powers over open spaces and burial grounds already vested in local authority

A local authority may exercise all the powers given to them by this Act respecting open spaces and burial grounds transferred to them in pursuance of this Act in respect of any other spaces and burial grounds of a similar nature which may be vested in them in pursuance of any other statute, or of which they are otherwise the owners.

13 Provision for compensation

No estate, interest, or right of a profitable or beneficial nature in, over, or affecting an open space or burial ground shall, except with the consent of the person entitled thereto, be taken away or injuriously affected by anything done under this Act without compensation being made for the same; and such compensation shall be paid by the local authority by whom the estate, interest, or right is taken away or injuriously affected, and shall, in case of difference, be ascertained and provided in the same manner as if the same were compensation for lands purchased and taken otherwise than by agreement or injuriously affected under the Lands Clauses Acts.

14 Power of county councils as to public walks or pleasure grounds
A county council may purchase or take on lease, lay out, plant, improve, and maintain lands for the purpose of being used as public walks or pleasure grounds, and may support or contribute to the support of public walks or pleasure grounds provided by any person whomsoever.

15 Byelaws
(1)   A local authority may, with reference to any open space or burial ground in or over which they have acquired any estate, interest, or control under this Act, make byelaws for the regulation thereof, and of the days and times of admission thereto, and for the preservation of order and prevention of nuisances therein, and may by such byelaws impose penalties recoverable summarily for the infringement thereof, and provide for the removal of any person infringing any byelaws by any officer of the local authority or police constable.

(2)   All byelaws made under this Act by any local authority shall be made—

- (a)   in the case of a county council, subject and according to the provisions of section sixteen of the Local Government Act 1888; and
- (c)   in the case of the Common Council of the City of London, subject and according to the Corporation of London (Open Spaces) Act 1878; and
- (e)   in the case of a municipal borough or district or parish council, subject and according to the provisions with respect to byelaws contained in sections one hundred and eighty-two to one hundred and eighty-six of the Public Health Act 1875 and those sections shall apply to a parish council in like manner as if they were a local authority within the meaning of that Act, except that byelaws made by a parish council need not be under common seal.

(3)   The trustees or other persons having the care and management of any open space, who in pursuance of this Act admit to the enjoyment of the open space any persons not owning, occupying, or residing in any house fronting thereon, shall have the same powers of making byelaws as are conferred on a committee of the inhabitants of a square by section four of the Town Gardens Protection Act 1863, and that section shall apply accordingly.

16 Power of local authorities to act jointly
Any two or more local authorities may jointly carry out the provisions of this Act and may make any agreement on such terms as may be arranged between them for so doing and for defraying the expenses of the execution of this Act, and any local authority may defray the whole or any part of the expenses incurred by any other local authority in the execution of this Act.

18 Borrowing
A local authority may borrow for the purposes of this Act . . .

Supplemental

19 Savings
(1)   This Act shall not apply to—

- (a)   the royal parks; nor
- (b)   any land belonging to His Majesty in right of His Crown or of His Duchy of Lancaster; nor
- (e)   any land belonging to either of the honourable Societies of the Inner Temple and Middle Temple.

(2) Nothing in this Act other than section 15 shall apply to any metropolitan common within the meaning of the Metropolitan Commons Acts 1866 to 1898, which does not fall within the provision made by article 32 of the London Authorities (Property etc) Order 1964.

20 Definitions

In this Act, unless the context otherwise requires,—

The expression 'open space' means any land, whether inclosed or not, on which there are no buildings or of which not more than one-twentieth part is covered with buildings, and the whole or the remainder of which is laid out as a garden or is used for purposes of recreation, or lies waste and unoccupied;

The expression 'common council of the City of London' means the mayor, alderman, and commons of the City of London in common council assembled:

The expression 'owner'—

(a) used in relation to an open space (not being a burial ground), means any person in whom the open space is vested for an estate in possession during his life or for any larger estate;

(b) used in relation to a house, includes any person entitled to any term of years in the house;

(c) used in relation to a burial ground, means the person in whom the freehold of the burial ground is vested whether as appurtenant or incident to any benefice or cure of souls or otherwise:

The expression 'occupier', used in relation to a house, means the person rated to the relief of the poor in respect of the house:

The expression 'burial ground' includes any churchyard, cemetery, or other ground, whether consecrated or not, which has been at any time set apart for the purpose of interment:

The expression 'disused burial ground' means any burial ground which is no longer used for interments, whether or not the ground has been partially or wholly closed for burials under the provisions of a statute or Order in Council:

The expression 'building' includes any temporary or movable building.

23 Repeal

(a) Nothing in this repeal shall affect the validity or operation of any byelaw made under any enactment so repealed, but all such byelaws shall continue in force as if made under that Act, and may be revoked and altered accordingly.

PUBLIC HEALTH ACTS AMENDMENT ACT 1907

76[1] Powers as to parks and pleasure gardens

(1) The local authority shall, in addition to any powers under any general Act, have the following powers with respect to any public park or pleasure ground provided by them or under their management and control, namely, powers—

(a) To enclose during time of frost any part of the park or ground for the purpose of protecting ice for skating, and charge admission to the part inclosed, but only on condition that at least three-quarters of the ice available for the purpose of skating is open to the use of the public free of charge;

(b) To set apart any such part of the park or ground as may be fixed by the local authority, and may be described in a notice board affixed or set up in some conspicuous position in the park or ground for the purpose of cricket, football, or any other game or recreation, and to exclude the public from the part set apart while it is in actual use for that purpose;

    (c)   To provide any apparatus for games and recreations, and charge for the use thereof, or let the right of providing any such apparatus for any term not exceeding three years to any person;

    (f)   To place, or authorise any person to place, chairs or seats in any such park or ground, and charge for, or authorise any person to charge for, the use of the chairs so provided;

    (g)   To provide and maintain any reading rooms, pavilions, or other buildings and conveniences, and to charge for admission thereto, subject in the case of reading rooms to the limitation that such a charge shall not be made on more than twelve days in any one year, nor on more than four consecutive days;

    (i)   To provide and maintain refreshment rooms in any such park, and either manage them themselves, or, if they think fit, let them to any person for any term not exceeding three years.

(2)   Any expenses of the local authority incurred in the exercise of the powers given to them by this section shall be defrayed out of the fund or rate out of which the expenses of the park or ground, as to which the powers are exercised, are payable, and any receipts arising from the exercise of any such powers shall be carried to the credit of the same fund or rate.

(4)   No power given by this section shall be exercised in such a manner as to contravene any covenant or condition subject to which a gift or lease of a public park or pleasure ground has been accepted or made, without the consent of the donor, grantor, lessor, or other person or persons entitled in law to the benefit of such covenant or condition.

---

[1]   See PHA 1961, s 52.

77 Power to appoint officers
The local authority may appoint officers for securing the observance of this Part of this Act, and of the regulations and byelaws made thereunder, and may procure such officers to be sworn in as constables for that purpose, but any such officer shall not act as a constable unless in uniform or provided with a warrant.

SMALL HOLDINGS AND ALLOTMENTS ACT 1908

PART II

ALLOTMENTS

Provision of allotments

23 Duty of certain councils to provide allotments
(1)   If the council of any borough, urban district, or parish are of opinion that there is a demand for allotments in the parish, the council shall provide a sufficient number of allotments, and shall let such allotments to persons resident in the parish, and desiring to take the same.

(2)   On a representation in writing to the council of any parish, by any six registered parliamentary electors or persons who are liable to pay an amount in respect of council tax[1] resident in the parish, that the circumstances of the parish are such that it is the duty of the council to take proceedings under this Part of this Act therein, the council shall take such representation into consideration.

[1] See CHAPTER **16**.

Powers of councils in relation to the provision of allotments

25 Acquisition of land for purpose of Act
(1) The Council of a borough, urban district, or parish may, for the purpose of providing allotments, by agreement purchase or take on lease land, whether situate within or without their borough, district, or parish or may purchase such land compulsorily in accordance with the provisions of this Act and of the Acquisition of Land Act 1981 in that behalf.

26 Improvement and adaptation of land for allotments
(1) The council of a borough, urban district, or parish may improve any land acquired by them for allotments and adapt the same for letting in allotments, by draining, fencing, and dividing the same, acquiring approaches, making roads and otherwise, as they think fit, and may from time to time do such things as may be necessary for maintaining such drains, fences, approaches, and roads, or otherwise for maintaining the allotments in a proper condition.
(2) The council may also adapt the land for allotments by erecting buildings and making adaptations of existing buildings, but so that not more than one dwelling-house shall be erected for occupation with any one allotment; and no dwelling-house shall be erected for occupation with any allotment of less than one acre.

27[1] Provisions as to letting of allotments
(4) An allotment shall not be sublet except with the consent of the council.
(5) If at any time an allotment cannot be let in accordance with the provisions of this Act and the rules made thereunder, the same may be let to any person whatever at the best annual rent which can be obtained for the same, without any premium, and on such terms as may enable possession thereof to be resumed within a period not exceeding twelve months if it should at any time be required to be let under the provisions aforesaid.
(6) A council shall have the same power of letting one or more allotments to persons working on a co-operative system or of letting or selling to an association formed for the purposes of creating or promoting the creation of allotments as may be exercised as respects small holdings by a county council.

[1] See Agriculture Act 1970, s 44.

28[1] Rules as to letting allotments
(1) Subject to the provisions of this Act, a borough, urban district, or parish council may make such rules as appear to be necessary or proper for regulating the letting of allotments under this Act, and for preventing any undue preference in the letting thereof, and generally for carrying the provisions of this Part of this Act into effect.
(2) Rules under this section may define the persons eligible to be tenants of allotments, the notices to be given for the letting thereof, the size of the allotments, the conditions under which they are to be cultivated, and the rent to be paid for them.
(3) All such rules shall make provision for reasonable notice to be given to a tenant of any allotment of the determination of his tenancy.
(4) Rules for the time being in force under this section shall be binding on all persons whatsoever; and the council shall cause them to be from time to time made known, in such manner as the council think fit, to all persons interested, and shall cause a copy thereof to be given gratis to any inhabitant of the district or parish demanding the same.

¹ Model rules are issued by the Secretary of State

29 Management of allotments

(1) The council of a borough, urban district, or parish may from time to time appoint, and, when appointed, remove allotment managers of land acquired by the council for allotments, and the allotment managers shall consist either partly of members of the council and partly of other persons, or wholly of other persons, so that in either case such other persons be persons residing in the locality and liable to pay to the district or London borough council in whose area the land is situated an amount in respect of council tax.

(2) The proceedings and powers of allotment managers shall be such as, subject to the provisions of this Act, may be directed by the council; the allotment managers may be empowered by the council to do anything in relation to the management of the allotments which the council are authorised to do and to incur expenses to such amount as the council authorise, and any expenses properly so incurred shall be deemed to be expenses of the council under this Act.

30 Recovery of rent and possession of allotments

(1) The rent for an allotment let by a council in pursuance of this Act, and the possession of such an allotment in the case of any notice to quit, or failure to deliver up possession thereof as required by law, may be recovered by the council as landlords, in the like manner as in any other case of landlord and tenant.

(2) If the rent for any allotment is in arrear for not less than forty days, or if it appears to the council that the tenant of an allotment not less than three months after the commencement of the tenancy thereof has not duly observed the rules affecting the allotment made by or in pursuance of this Act, or is resident more than one mile out of the borough, district, or parish for which the allotments are provided, the council may serve upon the tenant, or, if he is residing out of the borough, district, or parish, leave at his last known place of abode in the borough, district, or parish, or fix in some conspicuous manner on the allotment, a written notice determining the tenancy at the expiration of one month after the notice has been so served or affixed, and thereupon the tenancy shall be determined accordingly.

(3) Upon the recovery of an allotment from any tenant, the court directing the recovery may stay delivery of possession until payment of the compensation (if any) due to the outgoing tenant has been made or secured to the satisfaction of the court.

32 Sale of superfluous or unsuitable land

(1) Where the council of any borough, urban district, or parish are of opinion that any land acquired by them for allotments or any part thereof is not needed for the purpose of allotments, or that some more suitable land is available, they may sell or let such land otherwise than under the provisions of this Act, or exchange the land for other land more suitable for allotments, and may pay or receive money for equality of exchange.

(2) The proceeds of a sale under this Act of land acquired for allotments, and any money received by the council on any such exchange as aforesaid by way of equality of exchange, shall be applied in discharging, either by way of a sinking fund or otherwise, the debts and liabilities of the council in respect of the land acquired by the council for allotments, or in acquiring, adapting, and improving other land for allotments, and any surplus remaining may be applied for any purpose for which capital money may be applied; and the interest thereon (if any) and any money received from the letting of the land may be applied in acquiring other land for allotments, or shall be applied in like manner as receipts from allotments under this Act are applicable.

33 Transfer of allotments to borough, district, and parish councils

(1) The allotment wardens under the Inclosure Acts 1845 to 1882 having the management of any land appropriated under those Acts either before or after the

passing of this Act for allotments or field gardens for the labouring poor of any place, may, by agreement with the council of the borough, urban district, or parish, within whose borough, district or parish that place is wholly or partly situate, transfer the management of that land to the council, upon such terms and conditions as may be agreed upon with the sanction, as regards the allotment wardens, of the Board, and thereupon the land shall vest in the council.

(3)   Where, as respects any rural parish, any Act constitutes any persons wardens of allotments, or authorises or requires the appointment or election of any wardens, committee, or managers for the purpose of allotments, the powers and duties of the wardens, committee, or managers shall, subject to the provisions of this Act, be exercised and performed by the parish council, or, in the case of a parish not having a parish council, by persons appointed by the parish meeting, and it shall not be necessary to make the said appointment or to hold the said election.

(4)   The provisions of this Act relating to allotments shall apply to land vested in, or the management whereof has been transferred to, a council under this section or the corresponding provision of any enactment repealed by this Act in like manner as if the land had been acquired by the council under the general powers of this Part of this Act.

Supplemental

34 Power to make scheme for provision of common pasture
(1)   Where it appears to the council of any borough, urban district, or parish that, as regards their borough, district, or parish, land can be acquired for affording common pasture at such price or rent that all expenses incurred by the council in acquiring the land and otherwise in relation to the land when acquired may reasonably be expected to be recouped out of charges paid in respect thereof, and that the acquisition of such land is desirable in view of the wants and circumstances of the population, the council may prepare and carry into effect a scheme for providing such common pasture.

(2)   Upon such a scheme being carried into effect the provisions of this Act relating to allotments shall, with the necessary modifications, apply in like manner as if 'allotments' in those provisions included common pasture, and 'rent' included a charge for turning out an animal:

Provided that the rules made under those provisions may extend to regulating the turning out of animals on the common pasture, to defining the persons entitled to turn them out, the number to be turned out, and the conditions under which animals may be turned out, and fixing the charges to be made for each animal, and otherwise to regulating the common pasture.

PART III

GENERAL

Acquisition of land

38[1] Purchase of land by agreement
For the purpose of the purchase of land by agreement under this Act by a council, the provisions of Part I of the Compulsory Purchase Act 1965 (so far as applicable) other than sections 4 to 8, section 10, subsections (1) to (5) of section 23, and section 31, shall apply.

---

[1]   See LGA 1972, s 130.

39 Procedure for compulsory acquisition of land
(1)   Where a council propose to purchase land compulsorily under this Act, the council may be authorised so to do by the[1] Minister of Agriculture, Fisheries and Food.

[*Sub-ss (2)–(3) provide a procedure whereby a district council may compulsorily hire land in order to let it to a local council for allotments.*]

(4)   An order for the compulsory purchase or hiring of land under this Act may provide for the continuance of any existing easement or the creation of any new easement over the land authorised to be acquired, and every such order shall, if so required by the owner of the land to be acquired, provide for the creation of such new easements as are reasonably necessary to secure the continued use and enjoyment by such owner and his tenants of all means of access, drainage, water supply, and other similar conveniences theretofore used or enjoyed by them over the land to be acquired:

Provided that, notwithstanding anything contained in this subsection, no new easement created by or in pursuance of the order over land hired by a council shall continue beyond the determination of such hiring.

(5)   In determining the amount of any disputed compensation under any such order, no additional allowance shall be made on account of the purchase or hiring being compulsory.

(6)   Where land authorised to be compulsorily hired by an order under this section is subject to a mortgage, any lease made in pursuance of the order by the mortgagor or mortgagee in possession shall have the like effect as if it were a lease authorised by section eighteen of the Conveyancing and Law of Property Act 1881.

(7)   Where the council proposing to acquire land compulsorily is a parish council, the council shall, instead of themselves making and submitting to the Board the order, represent the case to the district council, and thereupon the district council may, on behalf of the parish council, exercise the powers in relation to compulsory purchase or hiring conferred on councils by this Act, and the order shall be carried into effect by the district council, but the land shall be assured or demised to the parish council, and all expenses incurred by the district council shall be paid by the parish council:

Provided that, if the parish council are aggrieved by the refusal of the district council to proceed under this section, the parish council may petition the Board, and thereupon the Board, after such inquiry as they think fit, may make such an order as the district council might have made, and this subsection shall apply as if the order had been made by the district council.

(8)   If, after the determination of the amount of the compensation (including in the case of land hired compulsorily the rent) to be paid to any person in respect of his interest in the land proposed to be compulsorily acquired, it appears to the council that the land cannot be let for small holdings or allotments, as the case may be, at such rent as will secure the council from loss, the council may at any time within six weeks after the determination of the amount by notice in writing withdraw any notice to treat served on that person or on any other person interested in the land, and in such case any person on whom such notice of withdrawal has been served shall be entitled to obtain from the council compensation for any loss or expenses which he may have sustained or incurred by reason or in consequence of the notice to treat and of the notice of withdrawal, and the amount of such compensation shall, in default of agreement, be determined by arbitration.

---

[1]   MAFF has been abolished and its functions transferred to the Department for Environment, Food and Rural Affairs.

40 Powers of certain limited owners to sell and lease land for small holdings or allotments

(1)   Any person having power to lease land for agricultural purposes for a limited term, whether subject to any consent or conditions or not, may, subject to the like consent and conditions (if any), lease land to a council for the purposes of allotments for a term not exceeding thirty-five years, either with or without such right of renewal as is conferred by this Act in the case of land hired compulsorily for those purposes.

(2)   The like powers of leasing may be exercised, in the case of land forming part of the possessions of the Duchy of Cornwall, by the Duke of Cornwall or other the persons for the time being having power to dispose of land belonging to that Duchy.

41 Restrictions on the acquisition of land[1]
(1)   No land shall be authorised by an order under this Act to be acquired compulsorily which at the date of the order forms part of any park, garden, or pleasure ground, or forms part of the home farm attached to and usually occupied with a mansion house, or is otherwise required for the amenity or convenience of any dwelling-house, or which is woodland not wholly surrounded by or adjacent to land acquired by a council under this Act.
(2)   A council in making, and the Board in confirming, an order for the compulsory acquisition of land shall have regard to the extent of land held or occupied in the locality by any owner or tenant and to the convenience of other property belonging to or occupied by the same owner or tenant, and shall, so far as practicable, avoid taking an undue or inconvenient quantity of land from any one owner or tenant, and for that purpose, where part only of a holding is taken, shall take into consideration the size and character of the existing agricultural buildings not proposed to be taken which were used in connection with the holding, and the quantity and nature of the land available for occupation therewith, and shall also, so far as practicable, avoid displacing any considerable number of agricultural labourers or others employed on or about the land.

[1]   See also Land Settlement Facilities Act 1919, s 16 (below).

42 Grazing rights, etc, to be attached to small holdings or allotments
(1)   The powers of a council to acquire land for small holdings or allotments shall, subject to the restrictions by this Act imposed, include power to acquire land for the purpose of letting to tenants of small holdings and allotments rights of grazing and other similar rights over the land so acquired, and to acquire for that purpose stints and other alienable common rights of grazing.
(2)   Any rights created or acquired by the council under this section shall be let to tenants of small holdings or allotments in such manner and subject to such regulations as the council think expedient.

Provisions affecting land acquired

45 Interchange of land for small holdings and allotments
A county council may sell or let to a borough, urban district, or parish council for the purpose of allotments any land acquired by them for small holdings, and a borough, urban district, or parish council may sell or let to the county council for the purpose of small holdings any land acquired by them for allotments.

47[1] Compensation for improvements
(1)   Where a council has let a small holding or allotment to any tenant otherwise than under a farm business tenancy, the tenant shall as against the council have the same rights with respect to compensation for the improvements mentioned in Part I of the Second Schedule to this Act as he would have had if the holding had been a holding to which subsections (2) to (5) of section 79 of the Agricultural Holdings Act 1986 applied:
  Provided that the tenant shall not be entitled to compensation in respect of any such improvement if executed contrary to an express prohibition in writing by the council affecting either the whole or any part of the holding or allotment.
(2)   Where land has been hired by a council for small holdings or allotments otherwise than under a farm business tenancy, the council shall (subject to any provision to the contrary in the agreement or order for hiring) be entitled at the

determination of the tenancy on quitting the land to compensation under the Agricultural Holdings Act 1986 for any improvement mentioned in Part I of the Second Schedule to this Act, and for any improvement mentioned in Part II of that Schedule which was necessary or proper to adapt the land for small holdings or allotments, as if the land were a holding to which subsections (2) to (5) of section 79 of the Agricultural Holdings Act 1986 applied, and the improvements mentioned in Part II of the said Schedule were improvements mentioned in Schedule 8 to the Agricultural Holdings Act 1986:

Provided that, in the case of land hired compulsorily, the amount of the compensation payable to the council for those improvements shall be such sum as fairly represents the increase (if any) in the value to the landlord and his successors in title of the holding due to those improvements.

(3) The tenant of an allotment to which Part II of this Act applies may, if he is not a tenant under a farm business tenancy and he so elects, claim compensation for improvements under section 3 of the Allotments Act 1922 instead of under the Agricultural Holdings Act 1986 as amended by this section, notwithstanding that the allotment exceeds two acres in extent.

(4) A tenant of any small holding or allotment who is not a tenant under a farm business tenancy may, before the expiration of his tenancy, remove any fruit and other trees and bushes planted or acquired by him for which he has no claim for compensation, and may remove any toolhouse, shed, greenhouse, fowl-house, or pigsty built or acquired by him for which he has no claim for compensation.

. . .

---

[1]   See also Opencast Coal Act 1958, s 41 and Sch 8 (not printed).

Expenses and borrowing

53 Expenses and borrowing

(4) The council of a borough, urban district, or parish may borrow for the purposes of acquiring, improving, and adapting land for allotments and the council of a borough or urban district may borrow for the purpose of grants or advances to a co-operative society.

Supplemental

57 Local inquiries

(1) The Board and officers of the Board shall have for the purpose of an inquiry in pursuance of this Act the same powers as the Local Government Board and their inspectors respectively have for the purpose of an inquiry under the Public Health Acts.

(2) Notices of the inquiries shall be given and published in accordance with such general or special directions as the Board may give.

58 Arbitrations and valuations

(1) All questions which under this Act are referred to arbitration shall, unless otherwise expressly provided by this Act, be determined by a single arbitrator in accordance with the Agricultural Holdings Act 1986.

(3) The remuneration of an arbitrator or valuer appointed under this Act shall be fixed by the Board.

61 Interpretation

(1) For the purposes of this Act—

The expression 'small holding' means an agricultural holding which exceeds one acre and either does not exceed fifty acres, or, if exceeding fifty acres, is at the date of sale or letting of an annual value for the purposes of income tax not exceeding one hundred pounds:

The expression 'allotment' includes a field garden:

The expressions 'agriculture' and 'cultivation' shall include horticulture and the use of land for any purpose of husbandry, inclusive of the keeping or breeding of live stock, poultry, or bees, and the growth of fruit, vegetables, and the like:

The expression 'prescribed' means prescribed by regulations made by the Board:

The expression 'landlord', in relation to any land compulsorily hired by a council, means the person for the time being entitled to receive the rent of the land from the council.

(2)   In this Act and in the enactments incorporated with this Act the expression 'land' shall include any right or easement in or over land.

(3)   For the purposes of this Act, any expenses incurred by a council in the purchase or redemption of any quit rent, chief rent, tithe, or other rentcharge, or other perpetual annual sum issuing out of land so acquired, shall be deemed to have been incurred in the purchase of the land.

(4)   In this Act references to a parish council shall, in the case of a rural parish not having a parish council, include references to the parish meeting.

(5)   Any notice required by this Act to be served or given may be sent by registered post.

SCHEDULE 2
IMPROVEMENTS REFERRED TO IN SECTION FORTY-SEVEN

PART I

(1)   Planting of standard or other fruit trees permanently set out;
(2)   Planting of fruit bushes permanently set out;
(3)   Planting of strawberry plants;
(4)   Planting of asparagus, rhubarb, and other vegetable crops which continue productive for two or more years.

PART II

(1)   Erection, alteration, or enlargement of buildings;
(2)   Formation of silos;
(3)   Laying down of permanent pasture;
(4)   Making and planting of osier beds;
(5)   Making of water meadows or works of irrigation;
(6)   Making of gardens;
(7)   Making or improving of roads or bridges;
(8)   Making or improving of watercourses, ponds, wells, or reservoirs, or of works for the application of water power or for supply of water for agricultural or domestic purposes;
(9)   Making or removal of permanent fences;
(10)   Planting of hops;
(11)   Planting of orchards or fruit bushes;
(12)   Protecting young fruit trees;
(13)   Reclaiming of waste land;
(14)   Warping or weiring of land;
(15)   Embankments and sluices against floods;
(16)   The erection of wirework in hop gardens;
(17)   Drainage;

(18)   Provision of permanent sheep-dipping accommodation;

(19)   In the case of arable land, the removal of bracken, gorse, tree roots, boulders, and other like obstructions to cultivation.

LAND SETTLEMENT (FACILITIES) ACT 1919

PART I

PROVISIONS AS TO THE ACQUISITION OF LAND

2 Power of entry on land

(1)   Where the council authorised to purchase any land compulsorily under the principal Act have, by virtue of section 11(1) of the Compulsory Purchase Act 1965 entered on the land, the council shall not be entitled to exercise the powers conferred by subsection (8) of section thirty-nine of the principal Act.

(2)   Where a council have agreed for the purposes of the principal Act, to purchase land subject to the interest of the person in possession thereof, and that interest is not greater than that of a tenant for a year, or from year to year, then at any time after such agreement has been made the council may, after giving not less than fourteen days' notice to the person so in possession, enter on and take possession of the land or of such part thereof as is specified in the notice without previous consent, but subject to the payment to the person so in possession of the like compensation for the land of which possession is taken, with such interest thereon as aforesaid, as if the council has been authorised to purchase the land compulsorily and such person had, in pursuance of such power, been required to quit possession before the expiration of his term or interest in the land, but without the necessity of compliance with sections eighty-four to ninety of the Lands Clauses Consolidation Act 1845.

(3)   Where a notice of entry given in the circumstances mentioned in subsection (1) of this section, or given under the last foregoing subsection relates to land on which there is a dwelling-house and the length of notice is less than three calendar months, the occupier of the dwelling-house may, by notice served on the council within ten days after the service on him of the notice of entry, appeal against such notice, and in any such case the appeal shall be determined by an arbitrator under and in accordance with the provisions of the Agricultural Holdings Act 1986 (except that the arbitrator shall, in default of agreement, be appointed by the President of the Surveyors' Institution), and the council shall not be entitled to enter on the land except on such date and on such conditions as the arbitrator may award.

(4)   This section shall with such necessary adaptations as may be prescribed apply in the case of an order authorising the compulsory hiring of land, or of an agreement to hire land.

PART II

AMENDMENT OF THE SMALL HOLDINGS AND ALLOTMENTS ACT 1908

16 Amendment of section 41 of principal Act

(1)   An order under the principal Act may, notwithstanding anything in section forty-one thereof, authorise the compulsory acquisition—

(a)   of any land which at the date of the order forms part of any park or of any home farm attached to and usually occupied with a mansion house, if the land is not required for the amenity or convenience of the mansion house; or

(b)   of a holding of fifty acres or less in extent or any part of such a holding.

(2) Where it is proposed to acquire any land forming part of a park or any such home farm, or, except where required for purposes of allotments, a holding of fifty acres or less in extent or of an annual value not exceeding one hundred pounds for the purposes of income tax, or any part of such a holding, the order authorising the acquisition of the land shall not be valid unless confirmed or made by the Board of Agriculture and Fisheries.

(3) A holding to which the preceding subsection applies shall not in whole or in part be compulsorily acquired under the principal Act by a council where it is shown to the satisfaction of the council, that the holding is the principal means of livelihood of the occupier thereof, except where the occupier is a tenant and consents to the acquisition.

17 Power of district council to acquire land for letting to parish council for allotments

A district council may acquire land for the purpose of leasing it to the council of a parish within the district for the provision of allotments, and the provisions of the principal Act relating to the acquisition, and to proceedings in relation to the acquisition, of land for the purpose of providing small holdings shall apply to such acquisition as if the land were to be acquired for the provision of small holdings.

19 Power of entry to inspect land

A council, with a view to ascertaining whether any land is suitable for any purpose for which the council has power to acquire land under the principal Act, may by writing in that behalf authorise any person (upon production, if so required, of his authority), to enter and inspect the land specified in the authority, and any one who obstructs or impedes any person acting under and in accordance with any such authority shall be liable on summary conviction to a fine not exceeding level 2 on the standard scale.

21 Provisions as to allotments

(1) The council of any borough, urban district or parish may purchase any fruit trees, seeds, plants, fertilizers or implements required for the purposes of allotments cultivated as gardens, whether provided by the council or otherwise, and sell any article so purchased to the cultivators, or, in the case of implements, allow their use, at a price or charge sufficient to cover the cost of purchase.

(2) The powers conferred by the preceding subsection shall be exerciseable by a council only where in the opinion of the council the facilities for the purchase or hire of the articles therein referred to from a society on a co-operative basis are inadequate.

(3) Rules made by a council under section twenty-eight of the principal Act, shall, unless otherwise expressly provided, apply to an allotment, though held under a tenancy made before the rules come into operation.

22 Power of appropriation of land

(1) A council of a borough, urban district, or parish may, in a case where no power of appropriation is otherwise provided,

    (a)   appropriate for the purpose of allotments any land held by the council for other purposes of the council; or

    (b)   appropriate for other purposes of the council land acquired by the council for allotments.

23[1] Agreement as to compensation where land is let for provision of allotments

Where land is let for the provision of allotments either to a council under the principal Act or to an association formed for the purpose of creating or promoting the creation of allotments, the right of the council or association to claim compensation from the landlord on the determination of the tenancy shall be subject to the terms of the contract of tenancy, notwithstanding the provision of any Act to the contrary:

Provided that this section shall not prejudice or affect any right on the part of a person holding under a tenancy granted by the council or association to claim compensation from the council or association on the determination of his tenancy.

[1] This section may be spent. See AA 1922, s 2(6).

PART IV

GENERAL

28 Provisions as to commons and open spaces

(1) Any land which is, or forms part of, a metropolitan common within the meaning of the Metropolitan Commons Act 1866[1], or which is subject to regulation under an order or scheme made in pursuance of the Inclosure Acts 1845 to 1899, or under any local Act or otherwise, or which is or forms part of any town or village green, or of any area dedicated or appropriated as a public park, garden, or pleasure ground, or for use for the purposes of public recreation, shall not be appropriated under this Act by a council for small holdings or allotments, and shall not be acquired by a council or by the Board of Agriculture and Fisheries under the principal Act except under the authority of an order for compulsory purchase made under the principal Act, which so far as it relates to such land shall be provisional only, and shall not have effect unless it is confirmed by Parliament.

(2) The Board of Agriculture and Fisheries, in giving or withholding their consent under this Act to the appropriation and in confirming an order for compulsory acquisition by a council for the purpose of small holdings or allotments of any land which forms part of any common, and in the exercise by the Board of their powers of acquiring land under this Act, shall have regard to the same considerations and shall hold the same inquiries as are directed by the Commons Act 1876 to be taken into consideration and held by the Board before forming an opinion whether an application under the Inclosure Acts shall be acceded to or not. Any consent by the Board of Agriculture and Fisheries for the appropriation of land forming part of any common for the purpose of small holdings or allotments shall be laid before Parliament while Parliament is sitting, and, if within twenty-one days in either House of Parliament a motion is carried dissenting from such appropriation, the order of the Board shall be cancelled.

(3) Where an order for compulsory purchase to which this section applies or a consent by the Board to the appropriation of land provides for giving other land in exchange for the common or open space to be purchased or appropriated, the order for compulsory purchase or an order made by the Board in relation to the consent for appropriation may vest the land given in exchange in the persons in whom the common or open space purchased or appropriated was vested subject to the same rights, trusts, and incidents as attached to the common or open space and discharges the land purchased or appropriated from all rights, trusts, and incidents to which it was previously subject.

(4) Nothing in the principal Act shall be deemed to authorise the acquisition of any land which forms part of the trust property to which the National Trust Act 1907 applies.

[1] That is, a common wholly or partly within the Metropolitan Police District.

32 Construction

(1) This Act, so far as it amends the principal Act, shall be construed as one with that Act, and references in this Act to the principal Act, or to any provision of the principal Act, shall, where the context permits, be construed as references to the principal Act, or the provisions of the principal Act as amended by this Act.

(2) References to small holdings provided, and to land acquired, under the principal Act shall be construed as including references to small holdings provided and land acquired under any enactment repealed by the principal Act.

34 Short title
. . . the Small Holdings and Allotments Acts 1908 and 1910 and so much of this Act as amends those Acts may be cited together as the Small Holdings and Allotments Acts 1908 to 1919.

ALLOTMENTS ACT 1922

1 Determination of tenancies of allotment gardens
(1) Where land is let on a tenancy for use by the tenant as an allotment garden or is let to any local authority or association for the purpose of being sub-let for such use the tenancy of the land or any part shall not (except as hereinafter provided) be terminable by the landlord by notice to quit or re-entry, notwithstanding any agreement to the contrary, except by—

(a) twelve months' or longer notice to quit expiring on or before the sixth day of April or on or after the twenty-ninth day of September in any year; or

(b) re-entry, after three months' previous notice in writing to the tenant, under a power of re-entry contained in or affecting the contract of tenancy on account of the land being required for building, mining, or any other industrial purpose or for roads or sewers necessary in connection with any of those purposes; or

(c) re-entry under a power in that behalf contained in or affecting the contract of tenancy in the case of land let by a corporation or company being the owners or lessees of a railway, dock, canal, water, or other public undertaking on account of the land being required by the corporation, or company, for any purpose (not being the use of the land for agriculture) for which it was acquired or held by the corporation, or company, or has been appropriated under any statutory provision, but so that, except in a case of emergency, three months' notice in writing of the intended re-entry shall be given to the tenant; or

(d) re-entry under a power in that behalf contained in or affecting the contract of tenancy, in the case of land let by a local authority after three months' previous notice in writing to the tenant on account of the land being required by the local authority for a purpose (not being the use of land for agriculture) for which it was acquired by the local authority, or has been appropriated under any statutory provision; or

(e) re-entry for non-payment of rent or breach of any term or condition of the tenancy or on account of the tenant becoming bankrupt or compounding with his creditors, or where the tenant is an association, on account of its liquidation.

(4) This section shall not apply to land held by or on behalf of the Secretary of State for Defence or Minister of Supply, and so let as aforesaid when possession of the land is required for naval, military, or air force purposes or for purposes of the Ministry of Supply as the case may be.

2 Compensation on quitting allotment gardens
(1) Where under any contract of tenancy land is, before or after the passing of this Act, let for use by the tenant as an allotment garden, the tenant shall, subject to the provisions of this section and notwithstanding any agreement to the contrary, be entitled at the termination of the tenancy, on quitting the land, to obtain from the landlord compensation as provided by this section.

(2) Subject to the provisions of this section, compensation shall be recoverable under this section only if the tenancy is terminated by the landlord by notice to quit or by re-entry under paragraph (b), (c) or (d) of subsection (1) of the last preceding section.

(3) The compensation recoverable from the landlord under this section shall be for crops growing upon the land in the ordinary course of the cultivation of the land as an allotment garden or allotment gardens, and for manure applied to the land.

(4) A tenant whose tenancy is terminated by the termination of the tenancy of his landlord shall be entitled to recover from his landlord such compensation (if any) as would have been recoverable if his tenancy had been terminated by notice to quit given by his landlord.

(6) This section shall also apply to any contract of tenancy made after the passing of this Act by which land is let to any local authority or association for the purpose of being sub-let for use by the tenants as allotment gardens and, notwithstanding that the crops have been grown and the manure applied by the tenants of the local authority or association. Section twenty-three of the Land Settlement (Facilities) Act 1919 shall not apply to land let after the passing of this Act to any local authority or association for the purpose of being sub-let for use by the tenants as allotment gardens.

(7) This section shall apply to the termination of the tenancy of the whole or any part of the land the subject of a contract of tenancy.

(8) Except as provided by this section or by the contract of tenancy, the tenant of land under a contract of tenancy to which this section applies shall not be entitled to recover compensation from the landlord at the termination of the tenancy.

(9) If the tenancy of the tenant is terminated on the twenty-ninth day of September or the eleventh day of October, or at any date between those days, either by notice to quit given by the landlord or by the termination of the tenancy of the landlord, the tenant whose tenancy is so terminated shall be entitled at any time within twenty-one days after the termination of the tenancy to remove any crops growing on the land.

3 Provision as to cottage holdings and certain allotments

(1) The foregoing provisions of this Act as to determination of tenancies of allotment gardens and compensation to a tenant on quitting the same shall not apply to any parcel of land attached to a cottage.

(2) In the case of any allotment within the meaning of this section (not being an allotment garden), the tenant shall, on the termination of his tenancy by effluxion of time, or from any other cause, be entitled, notwithstanding any agreement to the contrary, to obtain from the landlord compensation for the following matters:—

    (a)   For crops, including fruit, growing upon the land in the ordinary course of cultivation and for labour expended upon and manure applied to the land; and

    (b)   For fruit trees or bushes provided and planted by the tenant with the previous consent in writing of the landlord, and for drains, outbuildings, pigsties, fowl-houses, or other structural improvements made or erected by and at the expense of the tenant on the land with such consent.

(3) Any sum due to the landlord from the tenant in respect of rent or of any breach of the contract of tenancy under which the land is held, or wilful or negligent damage committed or permitted by the tenant, shall be taken into account in reduction of the compensation.

(4) The amount of the compensation shall, in default of agreement, be determined and recovered in the same manner as compensation is, under this Act, to be determined and recovered in the case of an allotment garden.

(5) The Agricultural Holdings Act 1986 shall, in the case of an allotment within the meaning of this section which is an agricultural holding within the meaning of that Act, have effect as if the provisions of this section as to the determination and recovery of compensation were substituted for the provisions of that Act as to the determination and recovery of compensation, and a claim for compensation for any matter or thing

for which a claim for compensation can be made under this section, may be made either under that Act or under this section, but not under both.

(7)   In this section the expression 'allotment' means any parcel of land, whether attached to a cottage or not, of not more than two acres in extent, held by a tenant under a landlord otherwise than under a farm business tenancy (within the meaning of the Agricultural Tenancies Act 1995) and cultivated as a farm or a garden, or partly as a garden and partly as a farm.

4 Further provision as to allotment gardens and allotments

(1)   A tenant of land held under a contract of tenancy to which any of the foregoing provisions of this Act apply may, before the termination of the tenancy, remove any fruit trees or bushes provided and planted by the tenant and any erection, fencing or other improvement erected or made by and at the expense of the tenant, making good any injury caused by such removal.

(2)   A tenant of land held under a contract of tenancy to which any of the foregoing provisions of this Act apply and which is made with a mortgagor but is not binding on the mortgagee, shall, on being deprived of possession by the mortgagee, be entitled to recover compensation from him as if he were the landlord and had then terminated the tenancy, but subject to the deduction from such compensation of any rent or other sum due from the tenant in respect of the land.

5 Rights of tenant who has paid compensation to outgoing tenant

Where a tenant of an allotment has paid compensation to an outgoing tenant for any fruit trees or bushes or other improvement, he shall have the same rights as to compensation or removal as he would have had under this Act if the fruit trees or bushes had been provided and planted or the improvement had been made by him and at his expense.

6 Assessment and recovery of compensation

(1)   The compensation under the foregoing provisions of this Act, and such further compensation (if any) as is recoverable under the contract of tenancy (not being a farm business tenancy within the meaning of the Agricultural Tenancies Act 1995) shall, in default of agreement, be determined by a valuation made by a person appointed in default of agreement by the judge of the county court having jurisdiction in the place where the land is situated, on an application in writing being made for the purpose by the landlord or tenant, and, if not paid within fourteen days after the amount is agreed or determined, shall be recoverable upon order made by the county court as money ordered to be paid by a county court under its ordinary jurisdiction, is recoverable.

(2)   The proper charges of the valuer for the valuation shall be borne by the landlord and tenant in such proportion as the valuer shall direct, but be recoverable by the valuer from either of the parties and any amount paid by either of the parties in excess of the amount (if any) directed by the valuer to be borne by him shall be recoverable from the other party and may be deducted from any compensation payable to such party.

7 Application to Crown lands

The foregoing provisions of this Act shall not apply to any land forming part of a royal park; but, save as aforesaid, the foregoing provisions of this Act shall apply to land vested in His Majesty in right of the Crown or the Duchy of Lancaster, and to land forming part of the possessions of the Duchy of Cornwall, and, except as otherwise hereinbefore expressly provided, to land vested in any Government department for public purposes.

8 Amendment of statutory provisions as to compulsory acquisition of land for allotments

(3)   Notwithstanding anything contained in any other enactment, counsel shall not be heard in any arbitration under this Act or as to compensation payable for land

acquired for allotments under the Allotments Acts unless the Minister otherwise directs.

11 Determination of questions arising on resumption of land

(1)   Where land has been let to a local authority or to an association for the purpose of being sub-let for use as allotment gardens, or is occupied by a council under the powers of entry conferred by this Act, and the landlord, or the person who but for such occupation would be entitled to the possession of the land, proposes to resume possession of the land in accordance with the provisions of this Act for any particular purpose, notice in writing of the purpose for which resumption is required shall be given to the local authority or association.

(2)   The local authority or association may, by a counter notice served within twenty-one days after receipt of such notice on the person requiring possession, demand that the question as to whether resumption of possession is required in good faith for the purpose specified in the notice shall be determined by arbitration under and in accordance with the provisions of the Agricultural Holdings Act 1986.

(3)   Possession of the land shall not be resumed until after the expiration of the said period of twenty-one days or the determination of such question as aforesaid where such determination is demanded under this section.

(4)   This section shall not apply to any case where resumption of possession is required by a corporation or company being the owners or lessees of a railway, dock, canal, water, or other public undertaking.

12 Time limit for serving notice to treat for compulsory acquisition of land

(1)   Where an order has been made for the compulsory acquisition of any land and notice to treat thereunder is not served by the acquiring authority within three calendar months after the date of the said order, or where confirmation of the said order is necessary, then after the date of the confirmation thereof the order so far as it relates to land in respect of which notice to treat has not been so served shall become null and void.

(2)   Where an order has so become null and void as respects any land, no order authorising the compulsory acquisition of that land or any part of such land shall, if made within three years after the expiration of the said three calendar months, be valid, unless confirmed by the Minister, or be so confirmed, unless it is proved to the satisfaction of the Minister that there are special reasons justifying the failure to exercise the powers under the original order and the making of the order submitted for confirmation.

21 Provision as to parts of New Forest now used for allotment gardens

(1)   Notwithstanding anything in any other Act, the Commissioners of Woods[1] may let for any term to a local authority under the Allotments Acts, and the local authority may take for the purpose of providing allotment gardens any land in the Forest (as defined in the New Forest Act 1877) which is vested in His Majesty and was on the fifth day of April, nineteen hundred and twenty-two, being used for the provision of allotment gardens, and, with the consent of the Minister, such further land in the Forest not exceeding sixty acres, as may be agreed between the Commissioners of Woods and the Verderers of the Forest:

Provided that, if at any time any land so let is used for any purpose other than the provision of allotment gardens, the lease shall become void and the land shall revert to His Majesty and be held in the same manner as it was held before its use for the provision of allotment gardens and subject to the same rights and liabilities so far as practicable.

(2)   While a lease under this section has effect any land let thereunder shall be free from all rights of common and all other similar rights and privileges except the right of the public to use any highway on the land.

---

[1]   Now the Forestry Commission.

22 Interpretation

(1) For the purposes of this Act, where the context permits—

The expression 'allotment garden' means an allotment not exceeding forty poles[1] in extent which is wholly or mainly cultivated by the occupier for the production of vegetable or fruit crops for consumption by himself or his family;

The expression 'landlord' means in relation to any land the person for the time being entitled to receive the rents and profits of the land;

The designations of landlord and tenant shall continue to apply to the parties until the conclusion of any proceedings taken under this Act in respect of compensation and shall include the legal personal representative of either party;

The expression 'council' shall, in the case of a rural parish not having a parish council, mean the parish meeting;

The expression 'industrial purpose' shall not include use for agriculture or sport, and the expression 'agriculture' includes forestry, horticulture, or the keeping and breeding of livestock;

The expression 'the Allotments Acts' means the provisions of the Small Holdings and Allotments Acts 1908 to 1919, which relate to allotments and this Act;

(3) Compensation recoverable by a tenant under this Act for crops or other things shall be based on the value thereof to an incoming tenant.

(4) Where land is used by the tenant thereof as an allotment garden, then, for the purposes of this Act, unless the contrary is proved—

 (a) the land shall be deemed to have been let to him to be used by him as an allotment garden; and

 (b) where the land has been sublet to him by a local authority or association which holds the land under a contract of tenancy, the land shall be deemed to have been let to that authority or association for the purpose of being sub-let for such use as aforesaid.

---

[1] A quarter of an acre.

WAR MEMORIALS (LOCAL AUTHORITIES' POWERS) ACT 1923

1 Expenditure in maintenance, etc, of war memorials

A local authority may incur reasonable expenditure in the maintenance, repair and protection of any war memorial within their district whether vested in them or not.

3 Application

The provisions of this Act shall not apply to a war memorial provided or maintained by a local authority in the exercise of any other statutory power.

4 Definition

In this Act the expression 'local authority' means the council of a county, borough district or parish, and the parish meeting of a rural parish with no parish council.

LAW OF PROPERTY ACT 1925

Commons and Waste Lands

193¹ Rights of the public over commons and waste lands

(1)   Members of the public shall, subject as hereinafter provided, have rights of access for air and exercise to any land which is a metropolitan common within the meaning of the Metropolitan Commons Acts, 1866 to 1898, or manorial waste, or a common, which is wholly or partly situated within an area which immediately before 1st April 1974 was a borough or urban district, and to any land which at the commencement of this Act is subject to rights of common and to which this section may from time to time be applied in manner hereinafter provided:

Provided that—

(a)   such rights of access shall be subject to any Act, scheme, or provisional order for the regulation of the land, and to any byelaw, regulation or order made thereunder or under any other statutory authority; and

(b)   the Minister shall, on the application of any person entitled as lord of the manor or otherwise to the soil of the land, or entitled to any commonable rights affecting the land, impose such limitations on and conditions as to the exercise of the rights of access or as to the extent of the land to be affected as, in the opinion of the Minister, are necessary or desirable for preventing any estate, right or interest of a profitable or beneficial nature in, over, or affecting the land from being injuriously affected, for conserving flora, fauna or geological or physiographical features of the land, or for protecting any object of historical interest and, where any such limitations or conditions are so imposed, the rights of access shall be subject thereto; and

(c)   such rights of access shall not include any right to draw or drive upon the land a carriage, cart, caravan, truck, or other vehicle, or to camp or light any fire thereon; and

(d)   the rights of access shall cease to apply—

(i)   to any land over which the commonable rights are extinguished under any statutory provision;

(ii)   to any land over which the commonable rights are otherwise extinguished if the council of the county, county borough or metropolitan district in which the land is situated by resolution assent to its exclusion from the operation of this section, and the resolution is approved by the Minister.

(2)   *The lord of the manor or other person entitled to the soil of any land subject to rights of common may by deed, revocable or irrevocable, declare that this section shall apply to the land, and upon such deed being deposited with the Minister the land shall, so long as the deed remains operative, be land to which this section applies.*

(3)   Where limitations or conditions are imposed by the Minister under this section, they shall be published by such person and in such manner as the Minister may direct.

(4)   Any person who, without lawful authority, draws or drives upon any land to which this section applies any carriage, cart, caravan, truck, or other vehicle, or camps or lights any fire thereon, or who fails to observe any limitation or condition imposed by the Minister under this section in respect of any such land, shall be liable on summary conviction to a fine not exceeding level 1 on the standard scale for each offence.

(5)   Nothing in this section shall prejudice or affect the right of any person to get and remove mines or minerals or to let down the surface of the manorial waste or common.

(6) This section does not apply to any common or manorial waste which is for the time being held for Naval, Military or Air Force purposes and in respect of which rights of common have been extinguished or cannot be exercised.

---

[1] See also RTA 1988, s 34.

[2] Sub-s (2) repealed, in relation to Wales only, by the Countryside and Rights of Way Act 2000.

ALLOTMENTS ACT 1925

1 Interpretation
In this Act, unless the context otherwise requires,—
'Allotment' means an allotment garden as defined by the Allotments Act 1922, or any parcel of land not more than five acres in extent cultivated or intended to be cultivated as a garden or farm, or partly as a garden and partly as a farm;

8 Sale, etc, of land used as allotments
Where a local authority has purchased or appropriated land for use as allotments the local authority shall not sell, appropriate, use, or dispose of the land for any purpose other than use for allotments without the consent of the Minister of Agriculture, Fisheries and Food, and such consent may be given unconditionally or subject to such conditions as the Minister thinks fit, but shall not be given unless the Minister is satisfied that adequate provision will be made for allotment holders displaced by the action of the local authority or that such provision is unnecessary or not reasonably practicable.

SMALL HOLDINGS AND ALLOTMENTS ACT 1926

17 Amendment of law as to the acquisition of land
(3) For removing doubts as to the effect of the Acquisition of Land (Assessment of Compensation) Act 1919[1] it is hereby declared:—
    (a)   that the said Act does not apply to the determination of a dispute as to the amount of compensation payable on the withdrawal of a notice to treat under subsection (8) of section thirty-nine of the principal Act;
    . . .

---

[1] The Act of 1919 was superseded by the Land Compensation Act 1961. See especially s 40 and Sch 8 (not printed).

LOCAL GOVERNMENT ACT 1929

115 Parish property
(3) The council of any county borough or urban district and the parish meeting of any rural parish not having a parish council may exercise the powers of executing works in relation to parish property which are by paragraph (*i*) of subsection (1) of section eight of the Local Government Act 1894, conferred on parish councils.
    . . .

(6) For the purposes of this section 'parish property' means any property the rents and profits of which are applicable or, if the property were let, would be applicable to the general benefit of one or more parishes, or the ratepayers, parishioners or inhabitants thereof, but does not include—

(a)   property given or bequeathed by way of charitable donation or allotted in right of some charitable donation or otherwise for the poor persons of any parish or parishes if the income of the property is not applicable to the general benefit of the ratepayers or other persons as aforesaid;

(b)   property acquired by a board of guardians for the purposes of their functions in the relief of the poor.

PUBLIC HEALTH ACT 1936

1 Local authorities for purposes of Act

(1)   Subject to the provisions of this Act with respect to certain special authorities, districts and areas, it shall be the duty of the following authorities to carry this Act, excluding Part VI except section 198, into execution, that is to say—

(a)   except in Wales, in a county, the county council as respects certain matters and the district councils as respects all other matters, without prejudice, however, to the exercise by a parish council of any powers conferred upon such councils;

(aa)   in Wales, the county council or county borough council as respects all matters, without prejudice, however, to the exercise by a community council of any powers conferred upon such a council;

(b)   in a London borough, the borough council;

. . .

(2)   In this Act—

'community', in relation to a common community council acting for two or more grouped communities, means those communities;

'district', in relation to a local authority in Greater London, means a London borough, the City of London, the Inner Temple or the Middle Temple, as the case may be [and, in relation to a local authority in Wales, means a county or (as the case may be) county borough;

'local authority' means the council of a district or London borough, the Common Council of the City of London, the Sub-Treasurer of the Inner Temple and the Under Treasurer of the Middle Temple but, in relation to Wales, means the council of a county or county borough;

'parish', in relation to a common parish council acting for two or more grouped parishes, means those parishes.

87 Provision of public conveniences

(1)   A county council, a local authority or a parish or community council may, subject to subsection (2) of this section, provide sanitary conveniences in proper and convenient situations.

(2)   Any such council or authority shall not provide any such convenience in or under a highway or proposed highway for which they are not the highway authority without the consent of the highway authority.

(3)   Any such council or authority who provide any public sanitary conveniences, may—

(a)   make byelaws as to the conduct of persons using or entering them;

(b)   let them for such term, at such rent, and subject to such conditions as they think fit;

(c) charge such fees for the use of any such conveniences as they think fit.

(4) In this section the expression 'sanitary conveniences' includes lavatories.

124 Certain public pumps, wells, cisterns, etc, vested in local authority

(1) All public pumps, wells, cisterns, reservoirs, conduits, and other works used for the gratuitous supply of water to the inhabitants of any part of the district of a local authority shall vest in and be under the control of the authority, and the authority may cause the works to be maintained and supplied with wholesome water, or may substitute, maintain and supply with wholesome water other such works equally convenient.

(2) If the local authority are satisfied that any such works are no longer required, or that the water obtained from any such works is polluted and that it is not reasonably practicable to remedy the cause of the pollution, they may close those works or restrict the use of the water obtained therefrom.

125 Power of parish council to utilise wells, springs or streams for obtaining water

(1) A parish council may utilise any well, spring or stream within their parish and provide facilities for obtaining water therefrom, and may execute any works, including works of maintenance or improvement, incidental to, or consequential on, any exercise of that power:

Provided that nothing in this subsection shall be construed as authorising them to interfere with the rights of any person, or as restricting, in the case of a public well or other works, any powers of the local authority under the last preceding section.

(2) A parish council may contribute towards the expenses incurred by any other parish council, or by any other person, in doing anything authorised by the preceding subsection.

198 Provision of mortuaries and post-mortem rooms

(1) A local authority or a parish council may, and if required by the Minister shall, provide—

    (a) a mortuary for the reception of dead bodies before interment;

    (b) a post-mortem room for the reception of dead bodies during the time required to conduct any post-mortem examination ordered by a coroner or other duly authorised authority;

and may make byelaws with respect to the management, and charges for the use, of any such place provided by them.

(2) A local authority or parish council may provide for the interment of any dead body which may be received into their mortuary.

PART VIII[1]

BATHS, WASHHOUSES, BATHING PLACES, ETC

---

[1] See LGA 1972, Sch 14, para 18 which confers the powers of this part on all local authorities including local councils.

Provision of baths, etc

221 Power of local authority to provide baths, bathing places and washhouses

A local authority may provide—

    (a) public baths and washhouses, either open or covered, and with or without drying grounds

or any of those conveniences.

222 Charges for use of baths, etc

(1)   Subject to the provisions of this section, a local authority may make such charges for the use of, or for admission to, any baths, or wash-house under their management as they think fit.

(2)   One month at least before fixing any charges to be made under this section, the local authority shall publish by advertisement in a local newspaper circulating in their district a notice stating their intention to consider a proposed table of charges and naming a place where a copy of the proposed table may be inspected at all reasonable hours by any person free of charge.

223 Byelaws for regulation of baths, etc

(1)   A local authority may make byelaws for the regulation of any baths, washhouses, swimming baths and bathing places under their management, and for the regulation of persons resorting thereto, including the exclusion therefrom of undesirable persons.

Any such byelaws may, in addition to providing for the imposition of penalties, empower any officer of the local authority to exclude or remove from any baths, washhouse, swimming bath or bathing place under the management of the authority any person contravening any of the byelaws applicable to the premises in question.

(2)   A printed copy, or abstract, of the byelaws relating to any baths, washhouse, swimming bath or bathing place shall be exhibited in a conspicuous place therein.

224 Baths, etc, to be public places for certain purposes

Any baths, washhouse, swimming bath or bathing place under the management of a local authority shall be deemed to be a public and open place for the purposes of any enactment relating to offences against decency.

225 Use of baths and bathing places for swimming contests, etc, or by schools or clubs

(1)   A local authority may close temporarily to the public any swimming bath or bathing place under their management and may—

    (a)   grant, either gratuitously or for payment, the exclusive use thereof to a school or club, or to persons organising swimming practices or contests, aquatic sports or similar entertainments; or,

    (b)   themselves use it for such practices, contests, sports or entertainments.

(2)   The authority may make, or authorise the making of, charges for admission to, or for the use of, any swimming bath or bathing place while it is closed to the public under this section.

226 Closing of baths and bathing places during winter months, and use for other purposes

(1)   A local authority may, during any period between the first day of October and the last day of the following April, close any swimming bath or bathing place under their management, and may, at any time when it is closed, use it, or allow it to be used, or let it, for such purposes, and upon such conditions as they think fit, and may adapt it for the purpose of being so used or let.

(2)   The power of the local authority to make byelaws under the foregoing provisions of this Part of this Act shall extend to the making of byelaws with respect to a swimming bath or bathing place when used for any purpose authorised by this section.

(3)   Nothing in this section shall authorise the use of a swimming bath or bathing place for the provision of regulated entertainment (within the meaning of the Licensing Act 2003), unless that activity is carried on under and in accordance with an authorisation (within the meaning given in section 136 of that Act).

227[1] Power of local authority to lay pipes for purposes connected with baths, etc

A local authority may provide, lay down and maintain such pipes and apparatus as may be necessary for conducting water to or from any baths, washhouse, swimming bath or bathing place which is under their management, or which they propose to provide and for the purposes of the provision, laying down or maintenance in any street of any such pipes or apparatus—

(a)   the authority shall be entitled in relation to any such pipes or apparatus to exercise the same powers as, for the purpose of carrying out its functions, are conferred on a water undertaker in relation to relevant pipes by section 158 of the Water Industry Act 1991 (street works); and

(b)   the provisions of that Act shall apply, with the necessary modifications, in relation to the power conferred by virtue of paragraph (a) above as they apply in relation to the power conferred by the said section 158;

and in this section 'street' has the same meaning as in that Act.

---

[1]   The Water Act 1989 gives the authority, for the purposes of the provision, laying down or maintenance in any street of any such pipes or apparatus, the street works powers conferred on a water undertaker.

228 Power of trustees to sell existing baths, etc, to local authority

The trustees of any public baths, washhouse, swimming bath or bathing place may, with the consent of the committee of management, if any, sell or lease the baths, washhouse, swimming bath or bathing place to a local authority.

229 Power of statutory undertakers to supply water, gas or electricity to baths, etc, on favourable terms

Any statutory undertakers supplying water or electricity may supply water or electricity to any public baths, washhouse, swimming bath or bathing place, either without charge or on such other favourable terms as they think fit.

Public bathing

231[1] Byelaws with respect to public bathing

(1)   A local authority may make byelaws with respect to public bathing, and may by such byelaws—

(a)   regulate the areas in which, and the hours during which, public bathing shall be permitted;

(aa)   prohibit or restrict public bathing at times when and places as respects which warning is given, by the display of flags or by other means specified in the byelaws, that bathing is dangerous;

(b)   fix the places at which bathing-machines may be stationed, or bathing huts or tents may be erected;

(c)   regulate the manner in which bathing-machines, huts or tents may be used, and the charges which may be made for the use thereof;

(d)   regulate, so far as decency requires, the costumes to be worn by bathers;

(e)   require persons providing accommodation for bathing to provide and maintain life-saving appliances, or other means of protecting bathers from danger; and

(f)   regulate, for preventing danger to bathers, the navigation of vessels used for pleasure purposes within any area allotted for public bathing during the hours allowed for bathing.

(2)   If and so far as a byelaw made under the preceding subsection is inconsistent with a byelaw made by dock undertakers, the latter shall prevail.

---

[1]   Under LG(MP)A 1976, s 17 (not printed). Byelaws under this section may extend seawards.

232 Provision of bathing huts, etc
A local authority may provide huts or other conveniences for bathing on any land belonging to them or under their control, and may make charges for the use thereof.

233 Byelaws with respect to swimming baths and bathing pools not under the management of a local authority
(1) A local authority may make byelaws with respect to swimming baths and bathing pools, whether open or covered, which are not under their management for—

    (a)   securing the purity of the water therein;

    (b)   ensuring the adequacy and cleanliness of the accommodation thereat;

    (c)   regulating the conduct of persons resorting thereto; and

    (d)   the prevention of accidents:

Provided that this section shall not apply to any swimming bath or bathing pool which is not open to the public and for, or in connection with, the use of which no charge is made.

(2) Byelaws made under this section may require the person responsible for any swimming bath or bathing pool to which the byelaws apply to keep a printed copy of the byelaws exhibited in a conspicuous place on the premises.

234 Provision of life-saving appliances
A local authority may provide life-saving appliances at such places, whether places used for bathing or not, as they think fit.

Watercourses, ditches, ponds, etc

259 Nuisances in connection with watercourses, ditches, ponds, etc
(1) The following matters shall be statutory nuisances for the purposes of Part III of the Environmental Protection Act 1990, that is to say—

    (a)   any pond, pool, ditch, gutter or watercourse which is so foul or in such a state as to be prejudicial to health or a nuisance;

    (b)   any part of a watercourse, not being a part ordinarily navigated by vessels employed in the carriage of goods by water, which is so choked or silted up as to obstruct or impede the proper flow of water and thereby to cause a nuisance, or give rise to conditions prejudicial to health:

Provided that in the case of an alleged nuisance under paragraph (b) nothing in this subsection shall be deemed to impose any liability on any person other than the person by whose act or default the nuisance arises or continues.

260 Power of parish council, or local authority, to deal with ponds, ditches, etc
(1) A parish council may—

    (a)   deal with any pond, pool, ditch, gutter or place containing, or used for the collection of, any drainage, filth, stagnant water, or matter likely to be prejudicial to health, by draining, cleansing or covering it, or otherwise preventing it from being prejudicial to health, but so as not to interfere with any private right, or with any public drainage, sewerage or sewage disposal works;

    (b)   execute any works, including works of maintenance or improvement, incidental to or consequential on any exercise of the foregoing power;

    (c)   contribute towards the expenses incurred by any other person in doing anything mentioned in this subsection.

(2) Without prejudice to their right to take action in respect of any statutory nuisance, a local authority may exercise any powers which a parish council may exercise under this section.

266 Saving for land drainage authorities, the London County Council, railway companies and dock undertakers
(1)   The powers conferred by the foregoing provisions of this Part of this Act shall not be exercised—

> (i)   with respect to any stream, watercourse, ditch or culvert within the jurisdiction of a land drainage authority, except after consultation with that authority;

Provided that nothing in this subsection shall apply in relation to the taking of proceedings in respect of a statutory nuisance.
(2)   Nothing in the foregoing provisions of this Part of this Act shall prejudice or affect the powers of any railway company or dock undertakers to culvert or cover in any stream or watercourse, or, without the consent of the railway company or dock undertakers concerned, extend to any culvert or covering of a stream or watercourse constructed by a railway company and used by them for the purposes of their railway, or constructed by dock undertakers and used by them for the purposes of their undertaking.

322 Power of Minister to enforce exercise of powers by local authorities, etc, in default
(2)   If the Minister is satisfied that any council or joint board have failed to discharge their functions under this Act in any case where they ought to have done so, he may make an order declaring them to be in default and directing them for the purpose of removing the default to discharge such of their functions, and in such manner and within such time or times, as may be specified in the order.
(3)   [*Provides for enforcement of default order by mandamus or transfer of the function.*]

324 Provisions as to exercise by Minister of functions of body in default
(1)   Where under the last but one preceding section the Minister has by order transferred to himself any functions of a council or joint board, any expenses incurred by him in discharging the said functions shall be paid in the first instance out of moneys provided by Parliament, but the amount of those expenses as certified by the Minister shall on demand be paid to him by the body in default, and shall be recoverable by him from them as a debt due to the Crown, and that body shall have the like power of raising the money required as they have of raising money for defraying expenses incurred directly by them.
(2)   The payment of any such expenses as aforesaid shall, to such extent as may be sanctioned by the Minister, be a purpose for which a local authority or joint board may borrow money in accordance with the statutory provisions relating to borrowing by such an authority or board.

325 Power to vary and revoke orders relating to defaults
In any case where under this Part of this Act an order has been made by the Minister transferring to a county council or to himself any functions of a council or joint board, the Minister may at any time by a subsequent order vary or revoke that order, but without prejudice to the validity of anything previously done thereunder; and when any order is so revoked the Minister may, either by the revoking order or by a subsequent order, make such provision as appears to him to be desirable with respect to the transfer, vesting and discharge of any property or liabilities acquired or incurred by the county council or by him in discharging any of the functions to which the order so revoked related.

Savings

328 Powers of Act to be cumulative

All powers and duties conferred or imposed by this Act shall be deemed to be in addition to, and not in derogation of, any other powers and duties conferred or imposed by Act of Parliament, law or custom, and, subject to any repeal effected by, or other express provision of, this Act, all such other powers and duties may be exercised and shall be performed in the same manner as if this Act had not been passed.

Interpretation, transitory provisions, repeals, etc

343 Interpretation

(1)   In this Act, unless the context otherwise requires, the following expressions have the meanings hereby assigned to them—

. . .

'owner' means the person for the time being receiving the rackrent of the premises in connection with which the word is used, whether on his own account or as agent or trustee for any other person, or who would so receive the same if those premises were let at a rackrent;

. . .

LOCAL GOVERNMENT ACT 1948

133 War memorials

(1)   [*Amends section 1 of the* War Memorials (Local Authorities' Powers) Act 1923.]

(2)   The matters on which expenditure may be incurred under the said section one shall include the alteration of any memorial to which that section applies so as to make it serve as a memorial in connection with any war subsequent to that in connection with which it was erected and the correction of any error or omission in the inscription on any such memorial.

ALLOTMENTS ACT 1950

3 Compensation to tenant of an allotment garden for disturbance

(1)   Where a tenancy under which land let, whether before or after the passing of this Act, for use by the tenant as an allotment garden or to a local authority or association for the purpose of being sub-let for such use is terminated, as to the whole or any part of the land comprised in the tenancy—

- (a)   by re-entry under paragraph (b), (c) or (d) of subsection (1) of section one of the Allotments Act 1922; or
- (b)   where the landlord is himself a tenant, by the termination of his tenancy; or
- (c)   where the landlord is a local authority who have let the land under section ten of the Allotments Act 1922 by the termination of the right of occupation of the authority;

the tenant shall, notwithstanding any agreement to the contrary, be entitled, on quitting the land or that part thereof, as the case may be, to recover from the landlord compensation for the disturbance of an amount determined in accordance with subsection (2) of this section.

(2)   The amount of any compensation recoverable under this section shall be—

(a)   where the tenancy terminates as to the whole of the land, an amount equal to one year's rent of the land at the rate at which rent was payable immediately before the termination of the tenancy;

(b)   where the tenancy terminates as to part of the land, an amount bearing to the amount mentioned in the foregoing paragraph the same proportion that the area of that part bears to the area of the whole of the land.

(3)   Compensation under this section shall be in addition to any compensation to which the tenant may be entitled under the Allotments Act 1922.

(4)   Subsection (2) of section four of the Allotments Act 1922 (which enables the tenant of an allotment garden to recover compensation from a mortgagee who deprives him of possession) shall apply to compensation under this section as it applies to compensation under that Act.

4 Right of landlord of an allotment garden to compensation for deterioration

(1)   Where the tenant of land let, whether before or after the passing of this Act, on a tenancy for use by the tenant as an allotment garden quits the land on the termination of the tenancy, the landlord shall, notwithstanding any agreement to the contrary, be entitled to recover from the tenant compensation in respect of any deterioration of the land caused by failure of the tenant to maintain it clean and in a good state of cultivation and fertility.

(2)   The amount of any compensation recoverable under this section shall be the cost, as at the date of the tenant's quitting the land, of making good the deterioration.

(3)   Where the tenant of land let on a tenancy for use by him as an allotment garden has remained therein during two or more tenancies, his landlord shall not be deprived of his right to compensation under this section in respect of deterioration of the land by reason only that the tenancy during which an act or omission occurred which in whole or in part caused the deterioration was a tenancy other than the tenancy at the termination of which the tenant quits the land.

5 Set-off of compensation against rent, etc

(1)   Out of any money payable to a tenant by way of compensation under section two of the Allotments Act 1922 or section three of this Act, the landlord shall be entitled to deduct any sum due to him from the tenant under or in respect of the tenancy (including any sum due by way of compensation under section four of this Act).

(2)   Out of any money due to the landlord from the tenant under or in respect of the tenancy (including any money due by way of compensation under section four of this Act), the tenant shall be entitled to deduct any sum payable to him by the landlord by way of compensation under section two of the Allotments Act 1922 or section three of this Act.

6[1] Exclusion of cottage holdings, and provisions as to war-time allotments

The foregoing provisions of this Act shall not apply to any parcel of land attached to a cottage, and the said provisions, other than those of section two, shall not apply to land let by a local authority under Regulation sixty-two A of the Defence (General) Regulations 1939.

---

[1]   See Emergency Laws (Misc Prov) Act 1953, s 5(1) (not printed). The regulations were revoked in 1952 with a saving for existing allotments.

7 Application of provisions of the Allotments Act 1922 for purposes of preceding sections

Section six of the Allotments Act 1922 (which relates to the determination and recovery of compensation under the foregoing provisions of that Act) and section seven of that Act (which provides for the application of those provisions to Crown lands) shall have effect as if the references to those provisions included references to the foregoing provisions of this Act, and subsection (4) of section twenty-two of that Act (which provides, amongst other things, that, for the purposes of that Act, where land is used by the tenant thereof as an allotment garden, it shall, unless the contrary is proved, be deemed to have been let to him to be used as an allotment garden) shall have effect as if the reference to that Act included a reference to this Act.

9 Restriction of obligations of local authorities to provide allotments

The obligation under the Allotments Acts 1908 to 1931 of the council of a borough, urban district or parish and of the parish meeting of a rural parish not having a parish council to provide allotments shall—

(a) except in the case of the council of a borough or urban district the population whereof is, according to the last published census for the time being, ten thousand or upwards, be limited to the provision of allotment gardens; and

(b) in the said excepted case, be limited to the provision of allotment gardens not exceeding twenty poles in extent.

10 Rents to be charged for allotments let by local authorities

(1) Land let by a council under the Allotments Acts 1908 to 1931 for use as an allotment shall be let at such rent as a tenant may reasonably be expected to pay for the land if let for such use on the terms (other than terms as to rent) on which it is in fact let:

Provided that land may be let by a council as aforesaid to a person at a less rent if the council are satisfied that there exist special circumstances affecting that person which render it proper for them to let the land to him at a less rent.

(2) Not more than a quarter's rent for land let by a council as mentioned in subsection (1) of this section shall be required to be paid in advance:

Provided that this subsection shall not apply where the yearly rent is £1.25 or less.

(3) In this section the references to a council shall be construed as including references to the parish meeting of a rural parish not having a parish council.

12 Abolition of contractual restrictions on keeping hens and rabbits

(1) Notwithstanding any provision to the contrary in any lease or tenancy or in any covenant, contract or undertaking relating to the use to be made of any land, it shall be lawful for the occupier of any land to keep, otherwise than by way of trade or business, hens or rabbits in any place on the land and to erect or place and maintain such buildings or structures on the land as are reasonably necessary for that purpose:

Provided that nothing in this subsection shall authorise any hens or rabbits to be kept in such a place or in such a manner as to be prejudicial to health or a nuisance or affect the operation of any enactment.

Supplementary

14 Interpretation

(1) In this Act the expressions 'allotment garden' and 'landlord' have the same meanings as they have for the purposes of the Allotments Act 1922 and the provisions of subsection (1) of section twenty-two of that Act relating to the continued application to parties of the designations of landlord and tenant shall apply for the purposes of this Act as they apply for the purposes of that Act.

(2) References in this Act to any other enactment shall, except so far as the context otherwise requires, be construed as references to that enactment as amended by any subsequent enactment, including this Act.

15 Short title, citation, extent and repeal

(1) This Act may be cited as the Allotments Act 1950 and the Allotments Acts 1908 to 1931 and this Act may be cited together as the Allotments Acts 1908 to 1950.

. . .

LOCAL GOVERNMENT (MISCELLANEOUS PROVISIONS) ACT 1953

Powers of local authorities in respect of omnibus shelters, etc

4 Provision of omnibus shelters, etc

(1) Subject to the following provisions of this Act, a local authority may provide and maintain in any highway within their district which is comprised in the route of public service vehicles, or on any land abutting on such a highway, shelters or other accommodation at stopping places on the route for the use of persons intending to travel on such vehicles.

(2) Any local authority, or any persons authorised to run public service vehicles, may enter into and carry into effect any agreement with a local authority with respect to the provision and maintenance of shelters or other accommodation under this section by the last-mentioned authority; and any such agreement may in particular provide for the payment by the first-mentioned authority or persons of the whole or any part of the cost of the provision and maintenance of the shelter or accommodation.

(3) A local authority shall consult the Commissioner of Police of the Metropolis with regard to the position of any shelter or other accommodation which they propose to provide under this section in a highway in the metropolitan police district.

(4) In this and the next three following sections, 'local authority' includes the council of a rural parish; and 'public service vehicle' has the meaning which it would have in the Public Passenger Vehicles Act 1981 if in section 1(1) of that Act the words '(other than a tramcar)' were omitted.

5 Consents to exercise of powers under s 4

(1) A local authority shall not have power by virtue of the last foregoing section to provide a shelter or other accommodation in any such situation or position as is described in the first column of the following Table, except with the consent of the person described in relation thereto in the second column of that Table:—

TABLE

In any highway for which there is a highway authority other than the local authority, or on land abutting on any such highway.	The highway authority.
In any highway belonging to and repairable by any railway, dock, harbour, canal, inland navigation or passenger road transport undertakers and forming the approach to any station, dock, wharf or depot of those undertakers.	The undertakers.
On any bridge not vested in the local authority or on the approaches to any such bridge.	The authority or other person in whom the bridge is vested.
On any bridge carrying a highway over any railway, canal or inland navigation, or on the approaches to any such bridge, or under any bridge carrying a railway, canal or inland navigation over a highway.	The railway, canal or inland navigation undertakers concerned.

In a position obstructing or interfering with any existing access to any land or premises abutting on a highway.	The owner (as defined by the Public Health Act 1936) of the land or premises.

(2) Any consent required by this section in respect of a shelter or other accommodation shall not unreasonably be withheld but may be given subject to any reasonable conditions, including a condition that the local authority shall remove the shelter or other accommodation either at any time or at or after the expiration of a period if reasonably required so to do by the person giving the consent.

(3) Where the consent of the Secretary of State or the Minister of Transport is required under this section, disputes between the Minister whose consent is required and the local authority as to whether the consent of that Minister is unreasonably withheld or is given subject to reasonable conditions, or whether the removal of any shelter or other accommodation in accordance with any condition of the consent is reasonably required shall be referred to and determined by an arbitrator to be appointed in default of agreement by the President of the Institution of Civil Engineers.

6 Supplementary provisions as to omnibus shelters, etc

(1) Where a shelter or other accommodation is provided by a local authority under section four of this Act in a position obstructing access to any electronic communications apparatus kept installed for the purposes of an electronic communications code network and the operator of that network notifies the local authority that he requires to obtain access to the apparatus, the authority shall, unless they temporarily remove the shelter or accommodation for the purpose of affording such access or so much thereof as is necessary for that purpose, be liable to repay to the operator so much of the expenses reasonably incurred by him in obtaining such access as is attributable to the situation of the shelter or accommodation.

(2) The provisions of the foregoing subsection shall apply in relation to any sewers, pipe-subways, pipes, wires or other apparatus belonging to or maintained by any local authority or any gas, electricity, water, hydraulic power, tramcar or trolley vehicle undertakers, as they apply in relation to any such electronic communications apparatus as is therein mentioned, and as if for any reference therein to the operator of the network in question there were substituted a reference to the local authority or the undertakers, as the case may be.

(3) Any dispute as to the amount (if any) payable by a local authority under the foregoing provisions of this section shall be determined in accordance with subsection (2) of section two hundred and seventy-eight of the Public Health Act 1936.

7 Maintenance of existing bus shelters and queue barriers

(1) Where, at any time before the commencement of this Act, a local authority, acting in the exercise of powers conferred under Regulation 54B of the Defence (General) Regulations 1939, or without statutory powers, have provided any such accommodation as follows, that is to say—

(a) any such shelter or accommodation as is described in section four of this Act;

(b) any barriers or posts for the regulation of persons waiting to enter public service vehicles,

the local authority shall have power by virtue of this section to maintain that accommodation.

(2) The provisions of sections five and six of this Act shall apply to the maintenance of any accommodation under this section, and to accommodation maintained thereunder, as they apply to the provision of accommodation under section four of this Act, and to accommodation provided under that section: . . . .

PARISH COUNCILS ACT 1957

PART I[1]

POWERS TO PROVIDE PUBLIC AMENITIES

[1]   See Walkway Regulations 1973 No 686, reg 3.

1 Power to provide seats and shelters in roads

(1)   Subject to the provisions of section five of this Act, a parish council may provide and maintain seats and shelters for the use of the public and cause them to be installed or erected in proper and convenient situations in, or on any land abutting on, any road within the parish.

(2)   In parishes in which the Public Improvements Act 1860 (in this section referred to as 'the Act of 1860') has effect, the powers conferred by this section shall be in substitution for any powers under that Act to place seats and shelters.

2 Power to provide public clocks

A parish council may provide, maintain and light such public clocks within the parish as they consider necessary, and (subject to the provisions of section five of this Act) may cause them to be installed on or against any premises or in any other place the situation of which may be convenient.

3 Power to light roads and public places

(1)   The council of a parish or community or, in the case of a parish for which there is no parish council the parish meeting may (subject to the provisions of section five of this Act) for the purpose of lighting the roads and other public places in the parish, or community, or in any part thereof

   (a)   provide and maintain such lamps, lamp posts and other materials and apparatus as they think necessary;

   (b)   cause such lamps, lamp posts and other materials and apparatus to be erected or installed on or against any premises or in such other places as may be convenient;

   (c)   contract with any person for the supply of gas, electricity or other means of lighting; and

   (d)   employ, with or without remuneration, such persons as may be necessary for the maintenance and superintendence of anything provided under this subsection.

(10)   In this section 'road' includes a highway comprised in the route of a special road (as defined by the Highways Act 1980), being a highway in relation to which a parish council or parish meeting, as the case may be, are exercising the powers conferred by subsection (1) of this section on the date on which a scheme made under section 16 of the said Act of 1980 authorising the provision of the special road comes into force.

5 Provisions as to consents and access[1]

(1)   A parish council or parish meeting shall not have power by virtue of the foregoing provisions of this Part of this Act to provide any seat, shelter, clock, lamp or lamp post, any other material or apparatus,   . . .

   (a)   on any land or premises not forming part of a road, or in a position obstructing or interfering with any existing access to any such land or premises, except with the consent of the owner and the occupier of the land or premises; or

   (b)   in any road which is not a highway or in any public path, except with the consent of the owner and the occupier of the land over which the road or path runs; or

(c)   in any such situation or position as is described in the first column of the following Table, except with the consent of the persons described in relation thereto in the second column of that Table.

TABLE

In any trunk road or any other road maintained by the Minister of Transport, or on land abutting on any such road.	The Minister.
In any road which is a highway (other than a trunk road or a road maintained as aforesaid or a public path) or on land abutting on any such road.	The county council or metropolitan district council.
In any road which is a highway belonging to and repairable by any railway, dock, harbour, canal, inland navigation or passenger road transport undertakers and forming the approach to any station, dock, wharf or depot of those undertakers.	The undertakers concerned.
On any bridge carrying a highway over any railway, dock, harbour, canal or inland navigation, or on the approaches to any such bridge or under any bridge carrying a railway, canal or inland navigation over a highway.	The railway, dock, harbour, canal or inland navigation undertakers concerned.

(2)   Any consent required by paragraph (c) of subsection (1) of this section shall not unreasonably be withheld, but may be given subject to any reasonable conditions, including a condition that the parish council or parish meeting, as the case may be, shall remove any thing to the provision of which the consent relates either at any time or at or after the expiration of a period if reasonably required so to do by the person giving the consent.

(3)   Any dispute between a parish council or parish meeting and a person whose consent is required under paragraph (c) of subsection (1) of this section whether that consent is unreasonably withheld or is given subject to reasonable conditions, or whether the removal of any thing to the provision of which the consent relates in accordance with any condition of the consent is reasonably required, shall—

(a)   in the case of a dispute between the parish council or parish meeting and the Minister of Transport, be referred to and determined by an arbitrator to be appointed in default of agreement by the President of the Institution of Civil Engineers; and

(b)   in any other case be referred to and determined by the Minister of Transport, who may cause a local inquiry to be held for the purpose;

and section two hundred and ninety of the Local Government Act 1933, shall apply in relation to a local inquiry held under this subsection as it applies in relation to such an inquiry held under that Act.

(4)   Section six of the Local Government (Miscellaneous Provisions) Act 1953 (which makes provision as to access to telegraphic lines, sewers, pipe-subways, pipes, wires and other apparatus) shall apply in relation to a thing provided by a parish council or parish meeting under this Part of this Act, and to the council or meeting by which the thing is so provided, as it applies in relation to a shelter or other accommodation provided, and to the local authority by which it is provided, under section four of that Act.

[1]   See also PHA 1961, s 45(10).

6 Supplementary powers

(1)   A parish council or parish meeting may contribute towards—

(a) the reasonable expenses incurred by any person in doing anything which by virtue of the foregoing provisions of this Act that council or meeting has power to do; and

(b) the expenses incurred by any other parish council or parish meeting in exercising their powers under any such provision as aforesaid.

(2) Where before the commencement of this Act any parish council or parish meeting have provided anything which, after the said commencement, could be provided by them under any of the foregoing provisions of this Act, or where either before or after the said commencement any other person has provided any such thing, the parish council or parish meeting shall have the like power to maintain that thing as if it had been provided by them under those provisions.

7 Interpretation of Part I

In this Part of this Act except so far as the context otherwise requires—

'in' in a context referring to things in a road includes a reference to things under, over, across, along or upon the road;

'owner' has the meaning assigned to it by section three hundred and forty-three of the Public Health Act 1936;

'public path' has the meaning assigned to it by the Wildlife and Countryside Act 1981, s 66;[1]

'road' means any highway (including a public path) and any other road, lane, footway, square, court, alley or passage (whether a thoroughfare or not) to which the public has access, but does not include a special road (as defined by the Special Roads Act 1949).

[1] Ie 'a highway being either a footpath or a bridleway'.

PART II

EXTENSION AND ADAPTATION OF OTHER POWERS

8 Powers to be exercisable without reference to county council

(1) Every parish council shall be a local authority for the purposes of the Open Spaces Act 1906, whether or not invested with the powers of that Act by the council of the county within which the parish is situate.

(2) The approval or consent of the county council shall no longer be required for any of the following matters—

(b) by reason that it will involve a loan, for the incurring by a parish council of any other expense or liability; or

(c) for the borrowing by a parish council of such sums as may be required for any of the purposes mentioned in section one hundred and ninety-five of the Local Government Act 1933.

PART III

MISCELLANEOUS

14 Interpretation

(1) Any reference in this Act to any other enactment shall, except so far as the context otherwise requires, be construed as a reference to that enactment as amended or applied by or under any other enactment, including this Act.

(2) In this Act 'parish', in relation to a common parish council acting for two or more grouped parishes, means those parishes.

LAND POWERS (DEFENCE) ACT 1958

8 Stopping up and diversion of highways

(1)   The powers conferred on the Minister of Transport by section forty-nine of the Town and Country Planning Act 1947 (which empowers that Minister to authorise by order the stopping up or diversion of a highway where he is satisfied that it is necessary to do so to enable land to be developed) shall also be exercisable where—

  (a)   land is, or is to be, used by a Secretary of State for the purposes of an installation provided or to be provided for defence purposes, or is used by a manufacturer of aircraft as an airfield wholly or mainly in connection with the manufacture of aircraft for defence purposes; and

  (b)   the Minister of Transport is satisfied that, for the land to be so used efficiently without danger to the public, it is necessary that a highway should be stopped up or diverted.

(2)   Where, in the circumstances specified in paragraphs (a) and (b) of the foregoing subsection, it appears to the Minister of Transport that it is not necessary that the highway should be stopped up or diverted for more than a limited period, an order under the said section forty-nine, including an order made by virtue of subsection (7) of that section (which authorises the stopping up or diversion of a highway temporarily stopped up or diverted under any other enactment) instead of providing for the permanent stopping up or diversion of the highway may provide for its stopping up or diversion during such period as may be prescribed by or under the order and for its restoration at the expiration of that period:

Provided that, for the purposes of any subsequent order by virtue of the said subsection (7), any order made by virtue of the foregoing provisions of this subsection shall be regarded as having been made otherwise than under the said section forty-nine.

(3)   Any order made by virtue of the last foregoing subsection which provides for the provision of another highway in substitution for a highway stopped up by the order may also contain such provisions as appear to the Minister of Transport to be expedient for the stopping up, at the expiration of the period prescribed by or under the order, of that other highway and for the original highway to be reconstructed at the expense of such of the Ministers referred to in paragraph (a) of subsection (1) of this section as may be specified in the order and thereafter maintained by any person who would for the time being have been liable for its maintenance if it had never been stopped up.

9 Supplementary provisions with respect to stopping up and diversion of highways

(1)   The powers to make orders conferred on the Minister of Transport—

  (a)   by section fifteen of the Requisitioned Land and War Works Act 1945, with respect to the permanent stopping up or diversion of a highway which has been stopped up or diverted in the exercise of emergency powers or as respects which a Minister has certified as mentioned in subsection (1) of section three of the Requisitioned Land and War Works Act 1948; and

  (b)   by section sixteen of the said Act of 1945 with respect to the use and maintenance until other provision is made by or under any Act of certain works placed along, across, over or under a highway in the exercise of emergency powers or for war purposes,

shall include power to vary or revoke any previous order made under the section in question; and subsection (1) of section twenty of the said Act of 1945 (which restricts the period during which orders may be made under the said section fifteen or sixteen) shall not apply to any order so far as it is made by virtue of this subsection.

. . .

(3)   Any person authorised in that behalf by the Minister of Transport or a local authority may enter on any land for the purpose of surveying it in connection with, or with proposals for, the diversion, provision or improvement of any highway by virtue of an order under the said section fifteen, and the provisions of the Fourth Schedule to this Act shall have effect in relation to the powers conferred by this subsection.

In this subsection and in the said Fourth Schedule the expression 'local authority' means the council of a county, borough or urban district or, in relation to Scotland, a county or town council.

LOCAL GOVERNMENT ACT 1958

PART IV

GENERAL AND SUPPLEMENTARY

General amendments relating to local government finance

56 Contributions by county councils to expenses of county district councils
. . .
(2)   A county council may make any contribution the council think fit towards expenditure by a parish council or parish meeting in connection with the exercise of the functions of the council or meeting relating to public open spaces.

PUBLIC BODIES (ADMISSION TO MEETINGS) ACT 1960[1]

[1]   See LGA 1972, ss 100A–100K; and ACA 1998, s 10.

1 Admission of public to meetings of local authorities and other bodies
(1)   Subject to subsection (2) below, any meeting of a body exercising public functions, being a body to which this Act applies, shall be open to the public.
(2)   A body may, by resolution, exclude the public from a meeting (whether during the whole or part of the proceedings) whenever publicity would be prejudicial to the public interest by reason of the confidential nature of the business to be transacted or for other special reasons stated in the resolution and arising from the nature of that business or of the proceedings; and where such a resolution is passed, this Act shall not require the meeting to be open to the public during proceedings to which the resolution applies.
(3)   A body may under subsection (2) above treat the need to receive or consider recommendations or advice from sources other than members, committees or sub-committees of the body as a special reason why publicity would be prejudicial to the public interest, without regard to the subject or purport of the recommendations or advice; but the making by this subsection of express provision for that case shall not be taken to restrict the generality of subsection (2) above in relation to other cases (including in particular cases where the report of a committee or sub-committee of the body is of a confidential nature).
(4)   Where a meeting of a body is required by this Act to be open to the public during the proceedings or any part of them, the following provisions shall apply, that is to say,—

(a)   public notice of the time and place of the meeting shall be given by posting it at the offices of the body (or, if the body has no offices, then in some central and conspicuous place in the area with which it is concerned) three clear days at least before the meeting or, if the meeting is convened at shorter notice, then at the time it is convened;

(b)   there shall, on request and on payment of postage or other necessary charge for transmission, be supplied for the benefit of any newspaper a copy of the agenda for the meeting as supplied to members of the body (but excluding, if thought fit, any item during which the meeting is likely not to be open to the public), together with such further statements or particulars, if any, as are necessary to indicate the nature of the items included or, if thought fit in the case of any item, with copies of any reports or other documents supplied to members of the body in connection with the item;

(c)   while the meeting is open to the public, the body shall not have power to exclude members of the public from the meeting and duly accredited representatives of newspapers attending for the purpose of reporting the proceedings for those newspapers shall, so far as practicable, be afforded reasonable facilities for taking their report and, unless the meeting is held in premises not belonging to the body or not on the telephone, for telephoning the report at their own expense.

(5)   Where a meeting of a body is required by this Act to be open to the public during the proceedings or any part of them, and there is supplied to a member of the public attending the meeting, or in pursuance of paragraph (b) of subsection (4) above there is supplied for the benefit of a newspaper, any such copy of the agenda as is mentioned in that paragraph, with or without further statements or particulars for the purpose of indicating the nature of any item included in the agenda, the publication thereby of any defamatory matter contained in the agenda or in the further statements or particulars shall be privileged, unless the publication is proved to be made with malice.

(6)   When a body to which this Act applies resolves itself into committee, the proceedings in committee shall for the purposes of this Act be treated as forming part of the proceedings of the body at the meeting.

(7)   Any reference in this section to a newspaper shall apply also to a news agency which systematically carries on the business of selling and supplying reports or information to newspapers, and to any organisation which is systematically engaged in collecting news for sound or television broadcasts or for programme services (within the meaning of the Broadcasting Act 1990) other than sound or television broadcasting services; but nothing in this section shall require a body to permit the taking of photographs of any proceedings, or the use of any means to enable persons not present to see or hear any proceedings (whether at the time or later), or the making of any oral report on any proceedings as they take place.

(8)   The provisions of this section shall be without prejudice to any power of exclusion to suppress or prevent disorderly conduct or other misbehaviour at a meeting.

2 Application of Act, and consequential provisions

(1)   This Act shall apply to the bodies specified in the Schedule to this Act, and to such bodies as may for the time being be added to that Schedule by order made under subsection (3) below; and where this Act applies to a body, the foregoing section shall apply in relation to any committee of the body whose members consist of or include all members of the body, as that section applies in relation to the body itself, but so that for the purposes of paragraph (c) of subsection (4) of that section premises belonging to the body shall be treated as belonging to the committee.

(3)   Any body established by or under any Act may be added to the Schedule to this Act, and any body so added may be removed from the Schedule, by order of the appropriate Minister made by statutory instrument, but a statutory instrument made

by a Minister under this section shall be of no effect unless it is approved by resolution of each House of Parliament; and for this purpose the appropriate Minister is, in the case of any body, the Minister of the Crown in charge of the Government department concerned or primarily concerned with the matters dealt with by that body, but an order made under this subsection by any Minister of the Crown shall be effective, whether or not he is the appropriate Minister.

SCHEDULE
BODIES TO WHICH THIS ACT APPLIES

1

The bodies to which in England and Wales this Act applies are—

(a)   parish or community councils, the Council of the Isles of Scilly and joint boards or joint committees which discharge functions of any of those bodies (or of any of those bodies and of a principal council, within the meaning of the Local Government Act 1972, or a body falling within paragraph (a), (b) or (c) of section 100J(1) of that Act);

(b)   the parish meetings of rural parishes;

(bca)   the Professional Standards Authority for Health and Social Care;

(bd)   the Care Council for Wales;

(bj)   the Care Quality Commission;

(bk)   Monitor;

(ea)   Strategic Health Authorities;

(fa)   the National Health Service Commissioning Board, except in exercise of functions under the National Health Service (Service Committees and Tribunals) Regulations 1992, or any regulations amending or replacing those Regulations;

(g)   if the order establishing a Special Health Authority so provides, the Special Health Authority;

(gg)   Primary Care Trusts, except as regards the exercise of functions under the National Health Service (Service Committees and Tribunal) Regulations 1992 or any regulations amending or replacing those Regulations;

(gh)   Local Health Boards;

(i)   regional and local flood defence committees;

(j)   advisory committees established and maintained under section 12 or 13 of the Environment Act 1995;

(k)   regional committees of the Consumer Council for Water established under section 27A of the Water Industry Act 1991;

(l)   National Health Service trusts established under section 25 of the National Health Service Act 2006 or section 18 of the National Health Service (Wales) Act 2006;

(m)   the Wales Centre for Health.

PUBLIC HEALTH ACT 1961

45 Attachment of street lamps to buildings

(1) Subject to the provisions of this section, a county council, local authority or parish council or parish meeting (hereafter in this section referred to as a 'street lighting authority') may affix to any building such lamps, brackets, pipes, electric lines and apparatus (hereafter in this section referred to as 'attachments') as may be required for the purposes of street lighting.

(2) A street lighting authority shall not under this section affix attachments to a building without the consent of the owner of the building:

Provided that, where in the opinion of the street lighting authority any consent required under this subsection is unreasonably withheld, they may apply to the appropriate authority, who may either allow the attachments subject to such conditions, if any, as to rent or otherwise as the appropriate authority thinks fit, or disallow the attachments.

(3) Where any attachments have been affixed to a building under this section and the person who gave his consent under subsection (2) of this section, or who was the owner of the building when the attachments were allowed by the appropriate authority, ceases to be the owner of the building, the subsequent owner may give to the street lighting authority notice requiring them to remove the attachments; and, subject to the provisions of this subsection, the street lighting authority shall comply with the requirements within three months after the service of the notice:

Provided that, where in the opinion of the street lighting authority any such requirement is unreasonable, they may apply to the appropriate authority, who may either annul the notice subject to such conditions, if any, as to rent or otherwise as the appropriate authority thinks fit or confirm the notice subject to such extension, if any, of the said period of three months as the appropriate authority thinks fit.

(4) Where any attachments have been affixed to a building under this section, the owner of the building may give the street lighting authority by whom they were affixed not less than fourteen days notice requiring them at their own expense temporarily to remove the attachments where necessary during any reconstruction or repair of the building.

(5) Where attachments are affixed to a building under this section, the street lighting authority shall have the right as against any person having an interest in the building to alter or remove them, or to repair or maintain them.

(6) If the owner of a building suffers damage by, or in consequence of, the affixing to the building of any attachments under this section, or by or in consequence of the exercise of the rights conferred by subsection (5) of this section, he shall be entitled to be paid by the street lighting authority compensation to be determined in case of dispute by the Lands Tribunal, and, so far as the compensation is properly to be calculated by reference to the depreciation of the value of his interest in the building, Rules 2 to 4 of the Rules[1] set out in section five of the Land Compensation Act 1961, shall apply.

(7) A street lighting authority shall not do anything under this section which would, to their knowledge, be in contravention of a building preservation order under section twenty-nine of the Town and Country Planning Act 1947[2].

(8) In this section 'appropriate authority' means a magistrates' court . . .

(9) In this section—

    'building' includes a structure and a bridge or aqueduct over a street;

    'owner'—

        (a)   in relation to a building occupied under a tenancy for a term of years whereof five years or more remain unexpired, means the occupier of the building, and

        (b)   in relation to any other building, has the same meaning as in the Public Health Act 1936, and

    'owned' shall be construed accordingly;

    'street lighting' includes the lighting of markets and public buildings under section one hundred and sixty-one of the Public Health Act 1875 (which relates to the powers conferred on urban authorities within the meaning of that Act), and the lighting of public places under section three of the Parish Councils Act 1957,

and the definitions in this section shall apply for the purposes of the Fourth Schedule to this Act.

(10)   Section five of the Parish Councils Act 1957 (which contains provisions as to the consents required for the exercise of the powers of street lighting conferred by that Act) shall not apply in relation to the affixing after the commencement of this Act of any attachments to a building within the meaning of this section but those powers shall not be taken to authorise anything to be done without consent for which consent is required by this section.

¹   That is ordinary market value disregarding uses by virtue of statutory provisions and unlawful uses.

²   The Act of 1947 was repealed but these words remain here. It is uncertain (but likely) that this subscription now applies to listed buildings and to unlisted buildings subject to a buildings preservation notice.

Parks and open spaces

52 Management of parks and pleasure-grounds

(1)   Sections seventy-six and seventy-seven of the Public Health Acts Amendment Act 1907 (which give a local authority certain powers as regards their parks and pleasure-grounds), together with Part VI of the Public Health Act 1925 (which extends the said section seventy-six), shall be in force throughout the district of every local authority.

(2)   When any part of a park or pleasure-ground is set apart by a local authority under paragraph (b) of subsection (1) of the said section seventy-six for the purpose of cricket, football or any other game or recreation, the local authority may, subject to the restrictions or conditions, if any, prescribed by rules made under that section, permit the exclusive use by any club or other body of persons of—

(a)   any portion of the part set apart as aforesaid, and

(b)   the whole or any part of any pavilion, convenience, refreshment room or other building provided under that section,

subject to such charges and conditions as the local authority think fit.

(3)   Subsection (2) of this section shall not empower a local authority to permit at one and the same time the exclusive use of—

(a)   more than one-third of the area of any park or pleasure-ground, or

(b)   more than one-quarter of the total area of all the parks and pleasure-grounds provided by them or under their management and control,

and in exercising their powers under paragraph (a) of that subsection, the local authority must satisfy themselves that they have not unfairly restricted the space available to the public for games and recreations.

(4)   Subsections (2) and (3) of this section shall be read as one with the said section seventy-six.

53 Closing of parks and pleasure-grounds

(1)   Subsection (1) of section forty-four of the Public Health Acts Amendment Act 1890 (which empowers a local authority to close their parks and pleasure-grounds or to allow their use for a show or other special purposes), shall be amended as follows.

. . .

(4)   The proviso to the said subsection (which prohibits the closing of a park or pleasure-ground on a Sunday or public holiday) shall cease to apply to a public holiday, but on any bank holiday, or on Christmas Day or Good Friday, or on a day appointed for public thanksgiving or mourning, a local authority shall not have power under the subsection to close any park or pleasure-ground, or any part thereof, if the area so closed, together with any other area so closed, exceeds one-quarter of the total area of all the parks or pleasure-grounds provided by the local authority.

54¹ Boating pools and lakes

(1) Subject to the provisions of this section, a local authority or parish council may in any park or pleasure-ground provided by them, or under their management and control, provide a boating pool.

(2) The local authority or parish council may provide such buildings and execute such work as may be necessary or expedient in connection with the provision of a boating pool under this section, and may also provide boats for the boating pool and such other equipment as may be reasonably required in connection with the use of the boating pool and buildings.

References in this section to a boating pool so provided shall include references to anything else provided under this subsection.

(3) The local authority or parish council may either—

  (a) themselves manage a boating pool provided under this section, making such reasonable charges for its use, or for admission, as they think fit, or

  (b) let it, or any part of it, for such consideration, and on such terms and conditions, as they think fit.

(4) Where the existence of a boating pool is likely to interfere with any water flowing directly or indirectly out of or into any watercourse which is vested in or controlled by the Environment Agency or any internal drainage board, the local authority or parish council shall before providing a boating pool under this section consult with that Agency or, as the case may be, that board.

(5) No power given by this section shall be exercised in such a manner as to contravene any covenant or condition subject to which a gift or lease of a park or pleasure-ground has been accepted or made without the consent of the donor, grantor, lessor or other person or persons entitled in law to the benefit of the covenant or condition.

(6) Subsection (2) of section forty-four of the Public Health Acts Amendment Act 1890 (which gives a local authority certain powers as regards lakes and water in parks and pleasure-grounds)—

  (a) shall apply in relation to a park or pleasure-ground under the management and control of a local authority as it applies in relation to a park or pleasure-ground provided by them, and

  (b) shall be in force throughout the district of every local authority;

(7) Section two hundred and seventy-eight of the Public Health Act 1936 (under which compensation may be paid for damage incurred in consequence of the exercise by the local authority of their powers under that Act), shall apply as if this section were contained in that Act.

(9) Sections three hundred and thirty-one and three hundred and thirty-four of the Public Health Act 1936 (which contain savings for water rights and for the works of land drainage authorities), shall apply as if this section were contained in that Act and as if references in those sections to a local authority included references to a parish council.

(10) It is hereby declared that this section does not authorise a local authority or parish council to do anything in contravention of byelaws made by virtue of paragraph 5 of Schedule 25 to the Water Resources Act 1991 or section 66 of the Land Drainage Act 1991.

¹ See LGA 1972, Sch 14, para 42.

PART VI

MISCELLANEOUS

81 Summary recovery of damages for negligence

Damages recoverable by a county council, local authority or parish council or parish meeting for damage caused by negligence to any lamp, lamp-post, notice board, fence, rail, post, shelter or other apparatus or equipment provided by them in a street or public place shall, if the amount thereof does not exceed twenty pounds, be recoverable summarily as a civil debt.

SCHEDULE 4

ATTACHMENT OF STREET LIGHTING EQUIPMENT TO
CERTAIN BUILDINGS

As regards buildings of the descriptions in the first column of the following Table the appropriate authority for the purposes of section forty-five of this Act shall be the person specified in the second column of that Table (and not a magistrates' court).

TABLE

A building which is for the time being included in a list published under section 12 of the Ancient Monuments Consolidation and Amendment Act 1913.	The Secretary of State.
A building which is included in a list compiled or approved under section 1 of the Planning (Listed Buildings and Conservation Areas) Act 1990.	The Secretary of State.
A building owned by railway, canal, dock, harbour or inland navigation undertakers.	The Secretary of State.
A building owned by electricity or gas undertakers.	The Secretary of State.
A building owned by statutory water undertakers.	The Secretary of State.
A building forming part of an aerodrome licensed under the Civil Aviation Act 1949, or any enactment repealed by that Act.	The Secretary of State.
A building owned by a county council, local authority or parish council or parish meeting who are not the street lighting authority concerned.	The Secretary of State.
A building owned by a development corporation established under the New Towns Act 1946, or the Homes and Communities Agency so far as exercising functions in relation to anything transferred (or to be transferred) to it as mentioned in section 52(1)(a) to (d) of the Housing and Regeneration Act 2008.	The Secretary of State.
A building owned by British Telecommunications.	The Secretary of State.

LOCAL GOVERNMENT (RECORDS) ACT 1962

1 Powers to promote adequate use of records

(1)   A local authority may do all such things as appear to it necessary or expedient for enabling adequate use to be made of records under its control, and in relation to such records may in particular—

(a)   make provision for enabling persons, with or without charge and subject to such conditions as the authority may determine, to inspect records and to make or obtain copies thereof;

(b)   prepare, or procure or assist in the preparation of, indexes and guides to and calendars and summaries of the records;

(c)   publish, or procure or assist in the publication of, the records or any index or guide to or calendar or summary of the records;

(d)   hold exhibitions of the records and arrange for the delivery of explanatory lectures, with or without charging for admission to such exhibitions or lectures;

(e)   direct that the records be temporarily entrusted to other persons for exhibition or study.

(2)   Nothing in subsection (1) above shall be taken to authorise the doing of any act which infringes copyright or contravenes conditions subject to which records are under the control of a local authority.

2 Acquisition and deposit of records

(1)   A local authority to which this subsection applies may—

(a)   by agreement acquire by way of purchase records which, or (in the case of a collection) the majority of which, appear to the authority to be of local interest;

(b)   accept the gift of records which, or (in the case of a collection) the majority of which, appear to the authority to be of general or local interest.

(2)   A local authority to which this subsection applies may accept the deposit of records—

(a)   which appear to the authority to be of general or local interest; or

(b)   which are the subject of an arrangement made under subsection (4) below.

(3)   A local authority may accept the deposit of records authorised to be deposited with it by any enactment other than this section.

(4)   A local authority other than a parish council or parish meeting may arrange to deposit any records under its control with an authority to which subsections (1) and (2) above apply or, if the Minister of Housing and Local Government consents, with any other person.

(5)   Where by virtue of this section records are under the control of a local authority in relation to which a provision of the following sections applies, namely, section two hundred and seventy-nine of the Local Government Act 1933[1], applies that provision shall apply as respects those records notwithstanding that apart from this subsection it would not so apply.

(6)   Subsections (1) and (2) above apply to the council of every country, county borough, metropolitan district or London borough to the Common Council of the City of London, to the London Fire and Emergency Planning Authority, to a joint authority established by Part IV of the Local Government Act 1985, to an authority established under section 10 of that Act (waste regulation and disposal authorities), to an economic prosperity board established under section 88 of the Local Democracy, Economic Development and Construction Act 2009, to a combined authority established under section 103 of that Act and to the council of any non-metropolitan district specified in an order made in that behalf by the Secretary of State.

(7)   In the application of this section to the Common Council of the City of London 'local interest' shall be construed as if the area of the Council included the whole of Greater London.

---

[1]   See now LGA 1972, s 224.

4 Financial

(1)   A local authority may contribute a sum equal to the whole or a part of any such expenses as the following, that is to say—

(a)   as respects records under the authority's control, expenses which have been incurred by any person in doing, by arrangement with the authority, anything relating to the records which the authority itself was empowered to do;

(b)   as respects records not under the authority's control, being records which in the opinion of the authority are nevertheless of local interest,—

(i)   expenses which have been incurred by any person in doing any such thing relating to the records as the authority is empowered by subsection (1) of section one above to do in relation to records under its control;

(ii)   expenses which have been incurred by any person in looking after the records in a case where the authority are of opinion that reasonable provision is made for enabling persons to inspect and make copies of them.

5   Modification of local Acts

Where at the commencement of this Act there is in force—

(a)   in a county borough a local Act the Bill for which was promoted by the council of the borough, or

(b)   in a county or county district a local Act the Bill for which was promoted either by the council of the county or by the council of the county district,

and the said local Act contains provisions appearing to the Minister of Housing and Local Government either to be inconsistent with any of the provisions of this Act, or to be redundant having regard to any of the provisions of this Act, the said Minister on the application of the council by which the said Bill was promoted may by order make such alterations, whether by amendment or repeal, in the local Act as appear to him to be necessary for the purpose of bringing its provisions into conformity with the provisions of this Act, or for the purpose of removing redundant provisions, as the case may be.

6   Orders by Minister

(1)   Any power to make orders conferred by this Act shall be exercisable by statutory instrument; and any instrument containing an order made under section five thereof shall be subject to annulment in pursuance of a resolution of either House of Parliament.

(2)   Any order made under subsection (6) of section two of this Act may be varied or revoked by a subsequent order made thereunder.

7   Minor amendments

[*Confers powers upon the Master of the Rolls to direct the transfer of manorial documents and copies of instruments of apportionment to a local authority.*]

8   Interpretation

(1)   In this Act—

'local authority' means the council of a county, county borough, London borough or county district the Broads Authority the Common Council of the City of London, the London Fire and Emergency Planning Authority, or a joint authority established by Part IV of the Local Government Act 1985 or an authority established under section 10 of that Act (waste regulation and disposal authorities), or an economic prosperity board established under section 88 of the Local Democracy, Economic Development and Construction Act 2009 or a combined authority established under section 103 of that Act, or a parish council or parish meeting, or the Council of the Isles of Scilly;

'records' means materials in written or other form setting out facts or events or otherwise recording information.

(2) For the purposes of this Act records shall be treated as being under the control of a local authority if they are in the possession of the authority by virtue of section two of this Act or otherwise, or if the authority has power to give directions as to their custody.

LOCAL GOVERNMENT (FINANCIAL PROVISIONS) ACT 1963

5 Payment of expenses of local authority officers

Nothing in any enactment providing for the payment by a local authority of expenses of their members shall be taken to limit the power of the local authority to defray expenses properly incurred by an officer of the authority as such.

PUBLIC WORKS LOANS ACT 1964

6 Re-borrowing powers of public authorities

(1) The provisions of this section shall have effect notwithstanding anything in any of the following enactments (which relate to the re-borrowing powers of local authorities), that is to say, Schedule 3 to the Local Government (Scotland) Act 1975 (including any of those enactments as applied by or under any other enactment), or any other enactment with respect to the re-borrowing powers of any other public authority.

(2) Where a local authority or other public authority have borrowed moneys in pursuance of powers conferred by or under any Act and the loan is repayable by instalments or annual payments, any power of the authority to borrow under any of the enactments referred to in subsection (1) of this section shall be exercisable in connection with the repayment of that loan, but, subject to subsection (4) of this section, shall be so exercisable only—

(a) for the purpose of repaying forthwith, and before they would otherwise become due for repayment, all sums for the time being outstanding by way of principal on the loan; or

(b) where the authority borrowed the moneys for a period less than the maximum period for which they were authorised so to do, for the purpose of the payment of any amount by which any instalment or annual payment exceeds what it would have been if it had been calculated by reference to that maximum period.

(3) Where a local authority or other public authority have borrowed moneys in pursuance of powers conferred by or under any Act, not being a loan repayable by instalments or annual payments, and payments towards the repayment of the loan have been made by the authority into any sinking or other fund maintained by the authority wholly or partly for the purpose of that repayment, any power of the authority to borrow under any of the enactments referred to in subsection (1) of this section shall be exercisable with respect to that loan, but, subject to subsection (4) of this section, shall be so exercisable only for the purpose of the repayment of the

amount, if any, by which the principal of the loan exceeds the aggregate amount of those payments.

(4) Any power of a local authority or other public authority to borrow under any of the enactments referred to in subsection (1) of this section shall be exercisable for the purpose of replacing moneys which, during the preceding twelve months, have been temporarily applied from other moneys of the authority in making such a repayment or payment as is authorised by subsection (2) or (3) of this section, and which at the time of that repayment or payment it was intended to replace by borrowed moneys.

COUNTRYSIDE ACT 1968

6 Country parks and commons: preliminary

(1) The powers conferred by this and the three next following sections shall be exercisable for the purpose of providing, or improving, opportunities for the enjoyment of the countryside by the public, and a local authority in exercising those powers in any area in the countryside shall have regard—

    (a)   to the location of that area in the countryside in relation to an urban or built-up area, and

    (b)   to the availability and adequacy of existing facilities for the enjoyment of the countryside by the public.

(2) In this and the three next following sections 'local authority' means—

    (a)   the council of a county, or county district, or

    (b)   the Common Council of the City of London or any London borough council,

(3) A local authority may exercise the powers conferred by the three next following sections inside or outside their area.

7 Power to provide country parks

(1) Subject to section 6 above, a local authority shall have power, on any site in the countryside appearing to them suitable or adaptable for the purpose set out in section 6(1) above, to provide a country park, that is to say a park or pleasure ground to be used for that purpose.

(2)–(6) [*Powers ancillary to subsection (1).*]

(7) A country park provided under this section shall not be subject to any of the following enactments (which relate to parks and pleasure grounds):

    Section 164 of the Public Health Act 1875.

    Section 44 of the Public Health Acts Amendment Act 1890.

    Sections 76 and 77 of the Public Health Acts Amendment Act 1907.

    Section 56(5) of the Public Health Act 1925.

    Section 132 of the Local Government Act 1948.

8 Country parks: sailing, boating, bathing and fishing

(1) Without prejudice to the generality of section 7(2) of this Act, where a country park comprises any waterway the kinds of open-air recreation for which the local authority may provide facilities and services under that subsection shall include sailing, boating, bathing and fishing.

(2) If a country park is bounded by the sea, or by any waterway which is not part of the sea, the local authority providing the country park shall have power to carry out such work and do such things as may appear to them necessary or expedient for facilitating the use of the waters so adjoining the country park by the public for sailing, boating, bathing and fishing and other forms of recreation.

(3) The powers conferred by subsections (1) and (2) above include power to erect buildings or carry out works on land adjoining the sea or other waters but outside the country park, and to construct jetties or other works wholly or partly in the sea or other waters.

(4) The local authority, before acting under the foregoing provisions of this section, shall consult with, and seek the consent of, the Environment Agency and such authorities, being authorities which under any enactment have functions relating to the sea or other waters in question, as the Minister may either generally or in particular case direct, and Schedule 1 to this Act shall have effect where any authority so consulted withhold their consent.

(5) A local authority may make byelaws regulating the use of works carried out by them pursuant to this section and of any facilities or services provided in connection with the works, but before making any such byelaws the local authority shall consult Natural England (if the works are in England) or the Council (if the works are in Wales):

Provided that byelaws made under this subsection shall not interfere with the exercise of any functions relating to the waters or land to which the byelaws apply which are exercisable by any authority under any enactment.

Section 106 of the Act of 1949 (supplementary provisions as to byelaws) shall have effect as if byelaws under this subsection were byelaws under that Act.

(6) Nothing in this section shall authorise the carrying out of any operation in contravention of section 34 of the Coast Protection Act 1949 (works detrimental to navigation) or section 9 of the Harbours Act 1964 (control of harbour development).

9 Powers exercisable over or near common land

(1) This section has effect as respects any common land to which the public have rights of access, and the powers conferred by this section are to be exercised in the interests of persons resorting to the common land for open-air recreation.

(2) Subject to the provisions of section 6 above, a local authority may exercise the powers conferred by this section on land taken out of the common land in accordance with this section and Schedule 2 to this Act, or on other land in the neighbourhood of the common land.

(3) A local authority shall have power to do anything appearing to the local authority to be desirable for the purpose set out in section 6(1) above, and in the interests of persons resorting to the common land, and in particular—

    (a)   to provide facilities and services for the enjoyment or convenience of the public, including meals and refreshments, parking places for vehicles, shelters and lavatory accommodation,

    (b)   to erect buildings and carry out works:

Provided that a local authority shall not under this section provide accommodation, meals or refreshments except in so far it appears to them that the facilities therefor in the neighbourhood of the common land are inadequate or unsatisfactory, either generally or as respects any description of accommodation, meals or refreshments, as the case may be.

(4) Schedule 2 to this Act shall have effect for the purposes of this section, and in that Schedule 'the principal section' means this section.

(5) A local authority shall have power to acquire compulsorily any land in the neighbourhood of the common land which is required by them for the purposes of their functions under this section and which is not common land.

(6) In this section—

    'common land' has the meaning given by section 22(1) of the Commons Registration Act 1965;

    'common land to which the public have rights of access' means—

(a)   land to which section 193 of the Law of Property Act 1925 for the time being applies, other than land to which that section applies by virtue of a revocable instrument, or

(b)   common land comprised in an access agreement or access order under Part V of the Act of 1949, other than a revocable access agreement or an access agreement expressed to have effect only for a period specified in the agreement, or

(c)   any other common land to which the public have rights of access permanently or for an indefinite period.

Public rights of way

27 Signposting of footpaths and bridleways

(1)   A highway authority, after consultation with the owner or occupier of the land concerned, shall have power to erect and maintain signposts along any footpath, bridleway, restricted byway or byway for which they are the highway authority.

(2)   Subject to subsection (3) below, at every point where a footpath, bridleway, restricted byway or byway leaves a metalled road the highway authority shall in exercise of their power under subsection (1) above erect and maintain a signpost.

(a)   indicating that the footpath, bridleway, restricted byway or byway is a public footpath, bridleway, restricted byway or byway, and

(b)   showing, so far as the highway authority consider convenient and appropriate, where the footway, bridleway, restricted byway or byway leads, and the distance to any place or places named on the signpost.

(3)   A highway authority need not erect a signpost in accordance with subsection (2) above at a particular site if the highway authority, after consulting the council of the parish in which the site is situated, or as the case may be the chairman of the parish meeting for the parish, not having a parish council, in which the site is situated, are satisfied that it is not necessary, and if the parish council, or as the case may be the chairman of the parish meeting, agree.

(4)   It shall also be the duty of a highway authority in exercise of their powers under subsection (1) above to erect such signposts as may in the opinion of the highway authority be required to assist persons unfamiliar with the locality to follow the course of a footpath, bridleway, restricted byway or byway.

(5)   With the consent of the highway authority, any other person may erect and maintain signposts along a footpath, bridleway, restricted byway or byway.

. . .

(7)   In this section (and in the amendments made by this section in other enactments) references to other signs or notices serving the same purpose and references to the erection of a signpost shall include references to positioning any such other sign or notice.

(8)   In this section 'byway' means a byway open to all traffic, that is to say, a highway over which the public have a right of way for vehicular and all other kinds of traffic, but which is used by the public mainly for the purposes for which footpaths and bridleways are so used, and 'restricted byway' has the same meaning as in Part 2 of the Countryside and Rights of Way Act 2000.

30 Riding of pedal bicycles on bridleways

(1)   Any member of the public shall have, as a right of way, the right to ride a bicycle, not being a mechanically propelled vehicle, on any bridleway, but in exercising that right cyclists shall give way to pedestrians and persons on horseback.

(2)   Subsection (1) above has effect to any orders made by a local authority, and to any byelaws.

(3)   The rights conferred by this section shall not affect the obligations of the highway authority, or of any other person, as respects the maintenance of the bridleway, and this section shall not create any obligation to do anything to facilitate the use of the bridleway by cyclists.

(4)   Subsection (1) above shall not affect definition of 'bridleway' in this or any other Act.

(5)   In this section 'mechanically propelled vehicle' does not include a vehicle falling within paragraph (c) of section 189(1) of the Road Traffic Act 1988.

49 Interpretation

(1)   Section 114 of the Act of 1949 shall apply for the construction of this Act.

(2)   In this Act, unless the context otherwise requires—

> 'the Act of 1949' means the National Parks and Access to the Countryside Act 1949;
>
> 'boat' includes any hover vehicle or craft being a vehicle or craft designed to be supported on a cushion of air and which is used on or over water;
>
> 'bridleway' and 'footpath' have the meanings given by section 329 (1) of the Highways Act 1980;
>
> 'the Council' means the Countryside Council for Wales;
>
> 'land' includes any interest in or right over land;
>
> 'the Minister', as respects Wales and Monmouthshire, means the Secretary of State, and otherwise means the Minister of Housing and Local Government[1];
>
> 'public body' includes any local authority or statutory undertaker, and any trustees, commissioners, board or other persons, who, as a public body and not for their own profit, act under any enactment for the improvement of any place or the production or supply of any commodity or service;

(3)   In this Act 'parish' means a rural parish.

(4)   References in this Act to the conservation of the natural beauty of an area shall be construed as including references to the conservation of its flora, fauna and geological and physiographical features.

---

[1]   Now the Secretary of State for the Environment, Food and Rural Affairs.

SCHEDULE 1
PROPOSALS SUBMITTED TO STATUTORY UNDERTAKERS AND OTHER AUTHORITIES

1

This Schedule has effect where any authority are consulted in accordance with section 8, section 12(4) or section 16(7) of this Act.

2

(1)   If the authority withhold their consent to the proposals about which they are consulted, the proposals shall not be proceeded with unless, on an application in that behalf specifying the proposals and the grounds for withholding consent, the Minister so directs, and subject to any conditions or modifications specified in the direction.

(2)   Before giving a direction under this paragraph the Minister shall afford to the objecting authority, and the authority by whom the proposals are made, an opportunity of being heard by a person appointed by him for the purpose, and shall consider that person's report.

SCHEDULE 2
PROCEDURE FOR TAKING COMMON LAND

1

(1)   For the purpose of enabling a local authority to exercise their powers under the principal section on land taken out of the common land the Minister may in accordance with this Schedule authorise a local authority to acquire any part of the common land, including all commonable and other rights in or over the land, and, where the local authority already hold the land, to appropriate that land for the purposes of the principal section.

(2)   Where the local authority already hold the land, but subject to any commonable or other rights in or over the land, they shall not appropriate the land until they have, under sub-paragraph (1) above, acquired all those rights.

(3)   Land acquired or appropriated as authorised under this paragraph shall be held by the local authority free from the public right of access, but shall be used for the benefit of the public resorting to the common land.

(4)   The Minister shall not give his authority under this paragraph unless he is satisfied—

(a)   that there has been or will be given in exchange for the land, other land, not being less in area and being equally advantageous to the persons, if any, entitled to commonable and other rights, and to the public, and that the land given in exchange has been or will be vested in the persons in whom the land taken was vested, and subject to the like rights, trusts and incidents as attached to the land taken, or

(b)   that the giving in exchange of such other land is unnecessary, whether in the interests of the persons, if any, entitled to commonable or other rights or in the interests of the public.

Preliminary notices

2

(1)   Before a local authority apply to the Minister for authority under paragraph 1 above as respects any part of the common land, they shall in two successive weeks publish in one or more newspapers circulating in the locality of the land a notice—

(a)   stating that the local authority propose to make the application;

(b)   giving particulars of the land which it is proposed to take out of the common land;

(c)   stating whether land has been or is to be given in exchange, and, if so, giving particulars of that land, and stating the respective areas of the land to be taken and of the land given or to be given in exchange.

(2)   If all or any part of the land to be taken is in a parish, the local authority shall, not later than the time of first publication of the notice, serve a copy of the notice on the parish council or, in the case of a parish not having a parish council, on the chairman of the parish meeting.

(3)   The notice shall name a place within the locality where a map showing the said land, and any land given or to be given in exchange, may be inspected, and shall specify the time (not being less than twenty-eight days from first publication of the notice) within which and the manner in which representations with respect to the proposals in the notice may be made to the Minister.

(4)   The Minister shall before giving his decision on the application take into consideration every representation which has been duly made and which has not been withdrawn, and may if he thinks fit either afford to each person making such a representation an opportunity of appearing before and being heard by a person appointed by the Minister for the purpose, or cause a public inquiry to be held.

Compulsory purchase

3

(1) A local authority shall have power to acquire compulsorily any land which is required by them for the purposes of their functions under the principal section, and which is part of the common land (or any commonable or other rights in or over that land), but the Minister shall not confirm a compulsory purchase order made in pursuance of this section except after giving his authority under paragraph 1 above as respects the land.

(2) Any notice which relates to a compulsory purchase order made in pursuance of this paragraph and which is published, affixed or served under section 11 or 12 of the Acquisition of Land Act 1981 shall refer to the provisions of this Schedule and shall state whether land has been, or is to be, given in exchange.

(3) The notice to be published under paragraph 2 of this Schedule may be combined with a notice to be published under the said section 11 of the said Act of 1981 in the same newspaper and relating to the same land.

(4) If land has been, or is to be, given in exchange—

    (a)   the notice to be published, affixed and served under section 11 or 12 of the said Act of 1981 shall give particulars of that land and state the respective areas of the land to be taken and of the land given or to be given in exchange,

    (b)   the map in the compulsory purchase order shall show that land,

    (c)   the compulsory purchase order may provide for vesting any land to be given in exchange in the persons, and subject to the rights, trusts and incidents, mentioned in paragraph 1(4) above.

(5) A compulsory purchase order made in pursuance of this paragraph may provide for discharging the land purchased from all rights, trusts and incidents to which it was previously subject.

(6) Section 19 of the Acquisition of Land Act 1981 (special provisions for acquisition of common land) shall not apply to a compulsory purchase order made in pursuance of this paragraph, and section 22 of the Commons Act 1899 (consent of Minister required for purchase of common land) shall not apply to the acquisition of land in pursuance of such a compulsory purchase order.

Acquisition by agreement and appropriation

4

(1) A local authority shall not acquire by agreement, or appropriate, any common land for the purposes of the principal section except as authorised under paragraph 1 of this Schedule.

(2) Subject to sub-paragraph (1) above, a local authority may appropriate any common land for the purposes of the principal section except as authorised under paragraph 1 of this Schedule.

(2) Subject to sub-paragraph (1) above, a local authority may appropriate any common land for the purposes of the principal section without compliance with the provisions of section 163 of the Local Government Act 1933 or section 104 of the Act of 1949 as amended by section 23 of the Town and Country Planning Act 1959 (under which the approval of the Minister is required).

(3) On an appropriation of land under this paragraph such adjustment shall be made in the accounts of the local authority as the Minister may direct.

Power to override restrictions affecting common land

5

No restrictions applying to commons generally, or to any particular common, contained in or having effect under any enactment, and no trust subject to which the common land is held, shall prevent a local authority from taking part of common land in accordance with the Schedule.

Protection for statutory undertakers

6

References in this Schedule to commonable and other rights in or over common land shall not be taken as including references to any right vested in statutory undertakers for the purpose of the carrying on of their undertaking or to any right conferred by or in accordance with the electronic communications code on the operator of an electronic communications code network.

Interpretation

7

In this Schedule 'common land' has the meaning given by section 22(1) of the Commons Registration Act 1965.

PARISH COUNCILS AND BURIAL AUTHORITIES[1] (MISCELLANEOUS PROVISIONS) ACT 1970

[1]   See LGA 1972, s 214 and Sch 26, para 25.

1 Maintenance of private graves

(1) A burial authority or a local authority may agree with any person in consideration of the payment of a sum by him, to maintain—

      (b)   a monument or other memorial to any person situated in any place within the area of the authority to which the authority have a right of access;

so, however, that no agreement or, as the case may be, none of the agreements made under this subsection by any authority with respect to a particular monument or other memorial may impose on the authority an obligation with respect to maintenance for a period exceeding 99 years from the date of that agreement.

(2) On the transfer of a burial ground or crematorium or of responsibility for the maintenance of a burial ground to a burial authority or local authority, any person who was responsible before the transfer for the maintenance of the burial ground or crematorium may transfer to the authority any assets held by him for the general purpose of the maintenance of the burial ground or crematorium, other than any such assets the devolution of which is affected by any condition of a trust, being a condition relating to the maintenance of a particular grave, vault, tombstone or other memorial.

(3) If assets are transferred to an authority by any person under subsection (2) of this section, any agreement binding on that person and made with a third party for the maintenance of any grave, vault, tombstone or other memorial in the burial ground or crematorium to which those assets relate shall also be binding on the authority.

(4) In this section, the expression 'local authority' shall be construed as if contained in the Local Government Act 1933, but it shall also be deemed, for the purposes of this section, to include the Council of the Isles of Scilly.

2 Form of grants

Where a burial authority has power under any enactment (whether local or general) to grant, with respect to a burial ground, any right relating to burial, the construction and use of a vault or other place of burial, or the placing of any tombstone or other memorial therein, that right may be granted under the hand of the town clerk, clerk, or other authorised officer of the burial authority.

4 Power to amend local Acts

Subsections (1), (2), (4) and (5) of section 82 of the Public Health Act 1961 shall apply for the purpose of conferring power on the Minister of Housing and Local Government to repeal or amend any such provision as is mentioned in subsection (1) of that section, being a provision appearing to him to be inconsistent with, or unnecessary in consequence of, any provision of this Act, as if references in those subsections to that Act were references to this Act.

5 Interpretation

(2)   In this Act 'burial ground' has the same meaning as in the Open Spaces Act 1906.

LOCAL AUTHORITIES (GOODS AND SERVICES) ACT 1970

1 Supply of goods and services by local authorities

(1)   Subject to the provisions of this section, a local authority and any public body within the meaning of this section may enter into an agreement for all or any of the following purposes, that is to say—

- (a)   the supply by the authority to the body of any goods or materials;
- (b)   the provision by the authority for the body of any administrative, professional or technical services;
- (c)   the use by the body of any vehicle, plant or apparatus belonging to the authority and, without prejudice to paragraph (b) above, the placing at the disposal of the body of the services of any person employed in connection with the vehicle or other property in question;
- (d)   the carrying out by the authority of works of maintenance in connection with land or buildings for the maintenance of which the body is responsible;

and a local authority may purchase and store any goods or materials which in their opinion they may require for the purposes of paragraph (a) of this subsection.

. . .

(2)   Nothing in paragraphs (a) to (c) of the preceding subsection authorises a local authority—

- (a)   to construct any buildings or works; or
- (b)   to be supplied with any property or provided with any service except for the purposes of functions conferred on the authority otherwise than by this Act.

(3)   Any agreement made in pursuance of subsection (1) of this section may contain such terms as to payment or otherwise as the parties consider appropriate.

(4)   In this Act—

'local authority', in relation to England and Wales, means the council of any county, county borough, county district or London borough, the Greater London Authority, the Broads Authority, the Common Council of the City of London, the Council of the Isles of Scilly and any joint board, joint committee and combined authority and any joint authority established by

Part IV of the Local Government Act 1985, [any economic prosperity board established under section 88 of the Local Democracy, Economic Development and Construction Act 2009, any combined authority established under section 103 of that Act, any authority established for an area in England by an order under section 207 of the Local Government and Public Involvement in Health Act 2007 (joint waste authorities), a Mayoral development corporation and the London Fire and Emergency Planning Authority, Transport for London and the London Development Agency and Transport for London and, in relation to Scotland, means a council constituted under section 2 of the Local Government etc (Scotland) Act 1994 or any joint board or combination of two or more such councils councils;

'public body' means any local authority, any police and crime commissioner, any housing action trust established under Part III of the Housing Act 1988, any probation trust, any person who is a public body by virtue of subsection (5) of this section and, in relation to England and Wales, any parish council, and representative[1] body of a rural parish; and

'works of maintenance' include minor renewals, minor improvements and minor extensions

. . .

(5)–(6)   [*The Secretaries of State for the Environment and for Wales may by statutory instrument provide that persons performing public functions are public bodies for the purposes of this Act, and may impose restrictions upon the agreements which those persons may make.*]

---

[1]   Now parish trustees.

2 Supplemental

(1)   Nothing in section 1 of this Act shall be construed as derogating from any powers exercisable by any public body apart from that section.

(2)   The accounts of a local authority by whom agreements in pursuance of the said section 1 are entered into under which the authority are to provide any such property or service or do such work as is mentioned in subsection (1) of that section shall include a separate account in respect of the agreements; and subsections (4), (6) and (7) of section 283 of the Local Government Act 1933 and sections 101 and 105 of the Local Government (Scotland) Act 1973 (which relate to the inspection and taking of copies of the abstract of accounts of authorities) shall have effect as if any reference to an abstract of the accounts of an authority included a reference to such a separate account as aforesaid.

(3)   [*Secretary of State empowered to adapt other legislation so as to make it consistent with this Act.*]

(5)   An order under section 1(5) of this Act may be revoked or varied by a subsequent order thereunder, and the subsequent order may contain such transitional provisions as the person making it considers appropriate.

LOCAL GOVERNMENT ACT 1972

Author's note: extensively amended by the Local Government (Wales) Measure 2011

PART I

LOCAL GOVERNMENT AREAS AND AUTHORITIES IN ENGLAND

Parishes

9 Parish meetings and councils

(1) For every parish there shall be a parish meeting for the purpose of discussing parish affairs and exercising any functions conferred on such meetings by any enactment and, subject to the provisions of this Act or any instrument made thereunder, for every parish or group of parishes having a parish council before 1st April 1974 there shall continue to be a parish council.

(4) Subject to any order under section 10 or 11 below Part II of the Local Government Act 1992 or section 86 of the Local Government and Public Involvement in Health Act 2007, there shall be a separate parish council for—

    (a)   every parish which immediately before the passing of this Act was a borough included in a rural district;

    (b)   every parish which immediately before the passing of this Act was co-extensive with a rural district;

    (c)   every parish established by paragraph 1 of Part IV of Schedule 1 to this Act;

    (d)   every parish to which part of another parish is added by paragraph 2 of the said Part IV and which immediately before the passing of this Act had no parish council; and

    (e)   every parish constituted under Part V of Schedule 1 to this Act.

(6) An order shall not be made under section 86 of the Local Government and Public Involvement in Health Act 2007 establishing a separate parish council for a parish grouped under a common parish council unless by that order or an order under section 11(4) below the parish is separated from the group or the group is dissolved, and where the group is not dissolved, the order under section 86 of the 2007 Act shall make such provision as appears to the district council to be necessary for the alteration of the parish council of the group.

10 Power to dissolve parish councils in small parishes

(1) Where the population of a parish having a separate parish council includes not more than 150 local government electors, the parish meeting may apply to the district council or London borough council for the dissolution of the parish council, and thereupon the district council or London borough council may by order dissolve the parish council.

(2) Where an application under this section by a parish meeting is rejected, another such application may not be presented by that meeting within two years from the making of the previous application.

11 Orders for grouping parishes, dissolving groups and separating parishes from groups

(1) The parish meeting of a parish may apply to the district council or London borough council for an order grouping the parish with some neighbouring parish or parishes in the same district or London borough under a common parish council or by adding the parish to an existing group of such parishes under such a council, and the district council or London borough council may thereupon make an order accordingly, but subject to subsection (2) below.

(2)   Parishes shall not be grouped without the consent of the parish meeting of each of the parishes.

(3)   A grouping order shall make the necessary provision—

    (a)   for the name of the group;

    (b)   the electoral arrangements that are to apply to the council;

    (c)   for the application to the parishes included in the group of all or any of the provisions of sections 298 to 303 of the Charities Act 2011 (parochial charities) and of any of the provisions of this Act with respect to the custody of parish documents, so as to preserve the separate rights of each parish;

    (d)   for the dissolution of the separate parish council of any parish included in the group,

and the order may provide for the consent of the parish meeting of a parish being required to any particular act of the parish council and for any necessary adaptations of this Act to the group of parishes or to the parish meetings of the parishes in the group.

(3A)   In this section 'electoral arrangements', in relation to a council, means all of the following—

    (a)   the year in which ordinary elections of councillors are to be held;

    (b)   the number of councillors to be elected to the council by each parish;

    (c)   the division (or not) of any of the parishes, into wards for the purpose of electing councillors;

    (d)   the number and boundaries of any such wards;

    (e)   the number of councillors to be elected for any such ward;

    (f)   the name of any such ward.

(4)   The district council or London borough council may on the application of the council of a group of parishes or of the parish meeting of any parish included in a group of parishes make an order dissolving the group or separating one or more of those parishes from the group, and an order so made shall make such provision as appears to the district council or London borough council to be necessary for the election of a parish council for any of the parishes in the group, where it is dissolved, and for any of the parishes separated from the group, where it is not.

(5)   Parishes grouped under a common parish council before 1st April 1974 and situated in different districts on and after that date shall, notwithstanding that they are so situated, continue to be grouped under that council—

    (a)   unless an order is made under subsection (4) above or Part II of the Local Government Act 1992 or section 86 of the Local Government and Public Involvement in Health Act 2007 dissolving the group; or

    (b)   except so far as such an order separates one or more of the parishes from the group;

and any order under subsection (4) above or section 86 of the Local Government and Public Involvement in Health Act 2007 in relation to any parishes so situated shall be made by the district councils concerned acting jointly.

11A   Grouping: alternative styles

(1)   An order under section 11(1) which forms a new group may make the provision set out in subsection (3).

(2)   But the order must make that provision in either of these cases—

    (a)   if at least one of the parishes which is to be grouped does not have an alternative style, and at least one of them does have an alternative style;

    (b)   if at least one of the parishes which is to be grouped has an alternative style, and at least one of them has a different alternative style.

(3)   The provision referred to in subsections (1) and (2) is—

     (a)   provision that each of the parishes in the group shall have an alternative style, or

     (b)   provision that each of the parishes in the group which has an alternative style shall cease to have an alternative style.

(4) Provision made by virtue of subsection (3)(a)—

     (a)   must provide for each of the parishes to have the same alternative style;

     (b)   may provide for each of the parishes to have an alternative style which any of them already has;

     (c)   has the effect that each parish in the new group shall cease to have any different alternative style which it had before the provision was made.

(5) An order under section 11(1) which adds one or more parishes to an existing group must make the provision set out in subsection (6) if—

     (a)   the parishes in the group do not have an alternative style, and

     (b)   at least one of the parishes which is to be added has an alternative style.

(6) The provision referred to in subsection (5) is provision that each added parish which has an alternative style shall cease to have an alternative style.

(7) An order under section 11(1) which adds one or more parishes to an existing group must make the provision set out in subsection (8) if—

     (a)   the parishes in the group have an alternative style, and

     (b)   at least one of the parishes which is to be added—

         (i)   has a different alternative style, or

         (ii)   does not have any of the alternative styles.

(8) The provision referred to in subsection (7) is provision that each added parish shall (if it does not already have the style) have the same alternative style as the parishes already in the group.

(9) If an order makes provision under subsection (1) or (2) for parishes to have an alternative style, the group shall have the appropriate one of the following styles—

     (a)   'group of communities';

     (b)   'group of neighbourhoods';

     (c)   'group of villages'.

(10) As soon as practicable after making an order which includes any provision under this section, the council which makes the order must give notice of the change of style to all of the following—

     (a)   the Secretary of State;

     (b)   the Local Government Boundary Commission for England;

     (c)   the Office of National Statistics;

     (d)   the Director General of the Ordnance Survey;

     (e)   any district council or county council within whose area the parish lies.

11B De-grouping: alternative styles

(1) This section applies if—

     (a)   the parishes in a group of parishes have an alternative style, and

     (b)   an order under section 11(4) dissolves the group or separates one or more parishes from the group.

(2) The order under section 11(4) must provide for each de-grouped parish to continue to have the alternative style.

(3) In subsection (2) 'de-grouped parish' means—

     (a)   in the case of dissolution of the group, each parish in the group;

     (b)   in the case of separation of one or more parishes from the group, each parish that is separated.

12 Provision supplementary to sections 9 to 11

(1)   An order made by a district council or district councils or by a London borough council under section 10 or 11 above may contain such incidental, consequential, transitional or supplementary provision as may appear to the district council or district councils or the London borough council to be necessary or proper for the purposes or in consequence of the order or for giving full effect thereto, and may include provision with respect to the transfer and management or custody of property (whether real or personal) and the transfer of rights and liabilities.

(2)   When any such order is made, section 16 of the Local Government and Public Involvement in Health Act 2007 (agreements about incidental matters) shall apply as if—

    (i)   the reference in subsection (1) to an order under section 7 or 10 of that Act were to an order under section 10 or 11 of this Act; and

    (ii)   the reference in subsection (5)(b) to any order or regulations under Chapter 1 of Part 1 of that Act were to an order under section 10 or 11 of this Act.

(3)   Two copies of every order under section 10 or 11 above shall be sent to the Secretary of State.

12A Parishes: alternative styles

(1)   This section applies to a parish which is not grouped with any other parish.

(2)   The appropriate parish authority may resolve that the parish shall have one of the alternative styles.

(3)   If the parish has an alternative style, the appropriate parish authority may resolve that the parish shall cease to have that style.

(4)   A single resolution may provide for a parish—

    (a)   to cease to have an alternative style, and

    (b)   to have another of the alternative styles instead.

(5)   As soon as practicable after passing a resolution under this section, the appropriate parish authority must give notice of the change of style to all of the following—

    (a)   the Secretary of State;

    (b)   the Local Government Boundary Commission for England;

    (c)   the Office of National Statistics;

    (d)   the Director General of the Ordnance Survey;

    (e)   any district council, county council or London borough council within whose area the parish lies.

(6)   In this section 'appropriate parish authority' means—

    (a)   the parish council, or

    (b)   if the parish does not have a parish council, the parish meeting.

12B Groups of parishes: alternative styles

(1)   This section applies to a group of parishes.

(2)   The common parish council of the group may resolve that each of the grouped parishes shall have the same alternative style.

(3)   If each of the grouped parishes has an alternative style, the common parish council of the group may resolve that each of the grouped parishes shall cease to have that style.

(4)   A single resolution may provide for each of the grouped parishes—

    (a)   to cease to have an alternative style, and

    (b)   to have the same one of the other alternative styles instead.

(5)   If the common parish council passes a resolution under this section for each of the grouped parishes to have an alternative style, the group of parishes shall have the appropriate one of the following styles—

  (a) 'group of communities';

  (b) 'group of neighbourhoods';

  (c) 'group of villages'.

(6) As soon as practicable after passing a resolution under this section, the common parish council of a group must give notice of the change of style to all of the following—

  (a) the Secretary of State;

  (b) the Local Government Boundary Commission for England;

  (c) the Office of National Statistics;

  (d) the Director General of the Ordnance Survey;

  (e) any district council, county council or London borough council within whose area the group lies.

13 Constitution of parish meeting, etc

(1) The parish meeting of a parish shall consist of the local government electors for the parish.

(2) Any act of a parish meeting may be signified by an instrument signed by the person presiding and two other local government electors present at the meeting, or, if an instrument under seal is required, by an instrument signed by those persons and sealed with the seal of the parish council in the case of a parish having a separate parish council or the parish trustees in any other case, if that council or those trustees have a seal, or, if they do not, with the seals of those persons.

(3) In a parish not having a separate parish council the chairman of the parish meeting and the proper officer of the district council shall be a body corporate by the name of 'the Parish Trustees' with the addition of the name of the parish.

(4) The parish trustees of a parish shall act in accordance with any directions given by the parish meeting.

(5) Notwithstanding anything in any rule of law the parish trustees need not have a common seal, but where they have no seal any act of theirs which requires to be signified by an instrument under seal may be signified by an instrument signed and sealed by the persons who are the parish trustees.

(5A) If the parish has the style of community—

  (a) the parish meeting shall have the style of 'community meeting';

  (b) the parish trustees shall be known by the name of 'The Community Trustees' with the addition of the name of the community.

(5B) If the parish has the style of neighbourhood—

  (a) the parish meeting shall have the style of 'neighbourhood meeting';

  (b) the parish trustees shall be known by the name of 'The Neighbourhood Trustees' with the addition of the name of the neighbourhood.

(5C) If the parish has the style of village—

  (a) the parish meeting shall have the style of 'village meeting';

  (b) the parish trustees shall be known by the name of 'The Village Trustees' with the addition of the name of the village.

14 Constitution and powers of parish council

(1) A parish council shall consist of the chairman and parish councillors and shall have all such functions as are vested in the council by this Act or otherwise.

(2) The parish council shall be a body corporate by the name 'The Parish Council' with the addition of the name of the particular parish.

(2A) If the parish has the style of community, the council shall be known by the name 'The Community Council' with the addition of the name of the community.

(2B) If the parish has the style of neighbourhood, the council shall be known by the name 'The Neighbourhood Council' with the addition of the name of the neighbourhood.

(2C)   If the parish has the style of village, the council shall be known by the name 'The Village Council' with the addition of the name of the village.

(2D)   If parishes are grouped under a common parish council—

- (a)   subsection (2), (2A), (2B) or (2C) (as appropriate) applies to that council as the subsection would apply in the case of the council of an individual parish; but
- (b)   the names of all of the parishes, communities, neighbourhoods or villages in the group are to be included in the name of the common council.

(3)   Notwithstanding anything in any rule of law, a parish council need not have a common seal, but where a parish council have no seal any act of theirs which is required to be signified by an instrument under seal may be signified by an instrument signed and sealed by two members of the council.

15 Chairman and vice-chairman of parish council or meeting

(1)   The chairman of a parish council shall be elected annually by the council from among the [elected]¹ councillors.

(2)   The election of a chairman shall be the first business transacted at the annual meeting of the parish council and if, apart from subsection (8) below, the person presiding at the meeting would have ceased to be a member of the parish council, he shall not be entitled to vote in the election except in accordance with subsection (3) below.

(3)   In the case of an equality of votes in the election of a chairman the person presiding at the meeting shall give a casting vote in addition to any other vote he may have.

(4)   The chairman shall, unless he resigns or becomes disqualified, continue in office until his successor becomes entitled to act as chairman.

(5)   A parish council may pay the chairman for the purpose of enabling him to meet the expenses of his office such allowance as the council think reasonable.

(6)   The parish council may appoint *a member* [one of the elected members] of the council to be vice-chairman of the council.

(7)   The vice-chairman shall, unless he resigns or becomes disqualified, hold office until immediately after the election of a chairman at the next annual meeting of the council.

(8)   During their term of office the chairman and vice-chairman shall continue to be members of the council notwithstanding the provisions of this Act relating to the retirement of parish councillors.

(9)   Subject to any standing orders made by the parish council, anything authorised or required to be done by, to or before the chairman may be done by, to or before the vice-chairman.

(10)   In a parish not having a separate parish council, the parish meeting shall, subject to any provisions of a grouping order, at their annual assembly elect a chairman for the year who shall continue in office until his successor is elected.

(11)   If the parish has the style of community, the chairman and vice-chairman shall (respectively) have the style—

- (a)   'chairman of the community council';
- (b)   'vice-chairman of the community council'.

(12)   If the parish has the style of neighbourhood, the chairman and vice-chairman shall (respectively) have the style—

- (a)   'chairman of the neighbourhood council';
- (b)   'vice-chairman of the neighbourhood council'.

(13)   If the parish has the style of village, the chairman and vice-chairman shall (respectively) have the style—

- (a)   'chairman of the village council';
- (b)   'vice-chairman of the village council'.

(14)   If parishes which have an alternative style are grouped under a common parish council, subsection (11), (12) or (13) (as appropriate) applies to the chairman and vice-chairman of that council as the subsection would apply in the case of the council of an individual parish.

---

1   The word 'elected' in sub-s (1) is in force only in so far as it confers powers to make regulations under s 16A below. In sub-s (6) the words in italics should be treated as substituted by the subsequent words in square brackets, but only in so far as it confers powers to make regulations under s 16A below.

16 Parish councillors

(1)   The number of [elected][1] parish councillors for each parish shall not be less than five.
(2)   Parish councillors shall be elected by the local government electors for the parish in accordance with this Act and Part I of the Representation of the People Act 1983.
(2A)   In their application to the election of parish councillors, this Act and Part 1 of the Representation of the People Act 1983 (c 2) are subject to the relevant electoral arrangements that apply to the election.
(2B)   For the purposes of this section 'relevant electoral arrangements' means—

> (a)   any arrangements about the election of councillors that are made in, or applicable by virtue of, provision made by virtue of section 245(6)(b) of the Local Government and Public Involvement in Health Act 2007 (transitional, saving or transitory provision), and
>
> (b)   any electoral arrangements applicable to the council by virtue of an order under section 7 or 10 or an order under section 86 of the Local Government and Public Involvement in Health Act 2007.

(3)   Subject to any provision included in an order by virtue of section 67 below and to the provisions of paragraphs 12 and 13 of Schedule 3 to this Act, the ordinary elections of parish councillors shall take place in 1976, 1979 and every fourth year thereafter, their term of office shall be . . . four years in the case of those elected at ordinary elections held thereafter, and the whole number of parish councillors shall retire together in every ordinary year of election of such councillors on the fourth day after the ordinary day of election of such councillors, and the newly elected councillors shall come into office on the day on which their predecessors retire.
(4)   Where a parish is not divided into parish wards there shall be one election of parish councillors for the whole parish.
(5)   Where a parish is divided into parish wards there shall be a separate election of parish councillors for each ward.
(6)   If the parish has the style of community, the councillors shall have the style of 'councillors of the community council'.
(7)   If the parish has the style of neighbourhood, the councillors shall have the style of 'councillors of the neighbourhood council'.
(8)   If the parish has the style of village, the councillors shall have the style of 'councillors of the village council'.
(9)   If parishes which have an alternative style are grouped under a common parish council, subsection (6), (7) or (8) (as appropriate) applies to the councillors of that council as the subsection would apply in the case of the council of an individual parish.

---

1   The word 'elected' in sub-s (1) is in force only in so far as it confers powers to make regulations under s 16A below.

16A Appointed councillors

(1)   A parish council may appoint persons to be councillors of the council.
(2)   The Secretary of State may by regulations make provision about—

> (a)   the appointment of persons under this section;

    (b)   the holding of office after appointment under this section.

(3)   The regulations may, in particular, make provision about any of the following matters—

    (a)   persons who may be appointed;

    (b)   the number of persons who may be appointed;

    (c)   the term of office of persons appointed;

    (d)   the right of persons appointed to participate in decision-making by the council (including voting);

    (e)   purposes for which a person appointed is to be treated as an elected councillor;

    (f)   the filling of vacancies.

(4)   In exercising a function under or by virtue of this section a parish council must have regard to any guidance issued by the Secretary of State about the exercise of that function.

(5)   A statutory instrument containing regulations under this section is subject to annulment in pursuance of a resolution of either House of Parliament.

[1]   This section was inserted by the Local Government and Public Involvement in Health Act 2007. As at 29 May 2013 it was in force only in so far as it confers powers to make regulations.

17A Alternative styles: supplementary

(1)   This section applies for the purposes of sections 9 to 16A.

(2)   'Alternative style' means one of the following styles—

    (a)   'community';

    (b)   'neighbourhood';

    (c)   'village'.

(3)   References to a parish having an alternative style, or a particular alternative style, are references to the parish having that style by virtue of—

    (a)   a relevant order, or

    (b)   a resolution under section 12A or 12B.

(4)   The provisions of a relevant order which provide for a parish to have, or to cease to have, an alternative style are subject to any resolution under section 12A or 12B relating to that parish.

(5)   A resolution under section 12A or 12B relating to a parish is subject to any provisions of a relevant order which provide for a parish to have, or to cease to have, an alternative style.

(6)   A parish shall cease to have an alternative style if the parish begins to have the status of a town by virtue of section 245(6).

(7)   In this section 'relevant order' means an order under—

    (a)   section 11 of this Act, or

    (b)   section 86 of the Local Government and Public Involvement in Health Act 2007.

Miscellaneous

18 Establishment of new authorities in England

Schedule 3 to this Act shall have effect with respect to . . . the establishment of the new local authorities in England . . . and related matters.

19 Extent of Part I

This Part of this Act shall extend to England only.

PART II

LOCAL GOVERNMENT AREAS AND AUTHORITIES IN WALES

New local government areas

20 New principal local government areas in Wales

(1)   For the administration of local government on and after 1st April 1996, the local government areas in Wales shall be—

(a)   the new principal areas; and

(b)   the communities.

(2)   The new principal areas (determined by reference to areas which, immediately before the passing of the Local Government (Wales) Act 1994, are local government areas) are set out in Parts I and II of Schedule 4 to this Act.

(3)   Each of the new principal areas shall have the name given to it in Schedule 4.

(4)   The new principal areas set out in Part I of Schedule 4 shall be counties and those set out in Part II of that Schedule shall be county boroughs.

(5)   In this Act 'principal area', in relation to Wales, means a county or county borough.

(6)   The counties which were created by this Act, as originally enacted, as counties in Wales, and the districts within them, shall cease to exist on 1st April 1996 except that the preserved counties shall continue in existence (with, in some cases, modified boundaries) for certain purposes.

(7)   The councils of the counties and districts mentioned in subsection (6) above shall cease to exist on 1st April 1996.

(8)   The areas of the preserved counties are set out in Part III of Schedule 4 and are determined by reference to local government areas in existence immediately before the passing of the Local Government (Wales) Act 1994.

(9)   The Secretary of State may by order change the name by which any of the preserved counties is for the time being known.

(10)   Any such order shall be subject to annulment in pursuance of a resolution of either House of Parliament.

(11)   The Welsh name of each of the new principal areas is shown in Schedule 4 immediately after its English name.

Communities

27 Community meetings and continuation of community councils

(1)   A meeting of the local government electors for a community ('a community meeting') may be convened for the purpose of discussing community affairs and exercising any functions conferred by any enactment on such meetings.

(2)   The community councils in existence on 1st April 1996 shall, subject to any provision made under this Act, continue in existence after that date.

(3)   Subsection (4) below applies where—

(a)   the name of a community was given only in its English form or only in its Welsh form; but

(b)   there is a generally accepted alternative form of that name, or alternative name, in Welsh or (as the case may be) in English.

(4)   The principal council within whose area the community lies shall, before 1st October 1997, take such steps as may be prescribed with a view to securing that there is both an English and a Welsh name for the community.

27A Power of community meeting to apply for an order establishing a community council

(1)   This section sets out the conditions that must be met before an application may be made by a community meeting of a community which does not have a separate council for an order under section 27B establishing a separate council for the community.

(2)   The first condition is that the community meeting has taken an effective decision to hold a poll on a proposal to establish a separate council for the community.

(3)   For the purposes of the first condition a decision is only effective if not less than—

      (a)   10% of the local government electors for the community, or

      (b)   150 of the electors (if 10% of the electors exceeds 150 electors),

are present and voting at the community meeting.

(4)   The second condition is that the poll is not held before the end of the period of 42 days beginning with the day on which the decision to hold the poll was taken.

(5)   The third condition is that the poll is not held within two years of an earlier poll which resulted in a rejection of a proposal to establish a separate council for the community (that period of two years beginning with the day on which the earlier poll was held).

(6)   The fourth condition is that a majority of those voting in the poll support the proposal to establish a separate council for the community.

(7)   Paragraph 34 of Schedule 12 to this Act (voting at community meetings) shall have effect subject to the provisions of this section.

27B Orders establishing separate community councils for communities

(1)   This section applies where a community meeting of a community which does not have a separate council applies to the principal council within whose area it lies for an order establishing a separate council for the community.

(2)   The principal council must consider whether it is satisfied that—

      (a)   the conditions in section 27A are met; and

      (b)   any relevant requirements of Schedule 12 have been met.

(3)   If the council is so satisfied, the council must make the order applied for (but this is subject to subsections (4) to (6) below).

(4)   The order shall make such provision as appears to the principal council to be necessary for the election of a community council in accordance with this Act and Part I of the Representation of the People Act 1983.

(5)   No order shall be made so as to establish a separate community council for a community grouped under a common community council unless—

      (a)   the community is separated from the group, or

      (b)   the group is dissolved,

by the order, or by an order under section 27J or section 27L below.

(6)   Where, in a case to which subsection (5) above applies, the group is not dissolved, the order under this section shall make such provision as appears to the principal council to be necessary for the alteration of the group's community council.

27C Power of community meeting to apply for an order dissolving its separate community council

(1)   This section sets out the conditions that must be met before an application may be made by a community meeting of a community which has a separate council for an order under section 27D dissolving the council.

(2)   The first condition is that the community meeting has taken an effective decision to hold a poll on a proposal to dissolve the council for the community.

(3)   For the purposes of the first condition a decision is only effective if not less than—

      (a)   30% of the local government electors for the community, or

      (b)   300 of the electors (if 30% of the electors exceeds 300 electors), are present and voting at the community meeting.

(4) The second condition is that the poll is not held before the end of the period of 42 days beginning with the day on which the decision to hold the poll was taken.

(5) The third condition is that the poll is not held within two years of an earlier poll which resulted in a rejection of a proposal to dissolve the separate council for the community (that period of two years beginning with the day on which the earlier poll was held).

(6) The fourth condition is that at least two-thirds of those voting in the poll support the proposal to dissolve the separate council for the community.

(7) Paragraph 34 of Schedule 12 to this Act (voting at community meetings) shall have effect subject to the provisions of this section.

27D Orders dissolving separate community councils for communities

(1) This section applies where a community meeting of a community which has a separate council applies to the principal council within whose area it lies for an order dissolving the council for the community.

(2) The principal council must consider whether it is satisfied that—

    (a)   the conditions in section 27C are met; and

    (b)   any relevant requirements of Schedule 12 have been met.

(3) If the council is so satisfied, the council must make the order applied for.

27E Power of community meeting to apply for an order grouping its community with other communities under a common community council

(1) This section sets out the conditions that must be met before an application may be made by a community meeting for an order under section 27F grouping the community with some neighbouring community or communities which lie in the same principal area as the community, under a common community council.

(2) The first condition is that the community meeting has taken an effective decision to hold a poll on a proposal to group the community with a neighbouring community or communities which lie in the same principal area as the community, under a common community council.

(3) For the purposes of the first condition a decision is only effective if not less than—

    (a)   10% of the local government electors for the community, or

    (b)   150 of the electors (if 10% of the electors exceeds 150 electors),

are present and voting at the community meeting.

(4) The second condition is that the poll is not held before the end of the period of 42 days beginning with the day on which the decision to hold the poll was taken.

(5) The third condition is that the poll is not held within two years of an earlier poll which resulted in a rejection of an identical proposal to group the community with a neighbouring community or communities (that period of two years beginning with the day on which the earlier poll was held).

(6) The fourth condition is that a majority of those voting in the poll support the proposal to group the community with a neighbouring community or communities which lie in the same principal area as the community, under a common community council.

(7) The fifth condition is that the application is made jointly with the community meeting, or meetings, for the community, or communities to be grouped under the common community council.

(8) Paragraph 34 of Schedule 12 to this Act (voting at community meetings) shall have effect subject to the provisions of this section.

27F Orders grouping a community with other communities under a common community council

(1) This section applies where a community meeting of a community applies to the principal council within whose area it lies for an order grouping the community with

some neighbouring community or communities which lie in the same principal area as the community, under a common community council.

(2) The principal council must consider whether it is satisfied that—

    (a) the conditions in section 27E are met; and

    (b) any relevant requirements of Schedule 12 have been met.

(3) If the council is so satisfied, the council must make the order applied for (but this is subject to subsections (4) to (7) below).

(4) The order shall provide for the name of the group in both an English and a Welsh form.

(5) The order shall—

    (a) make such provision as appears to the principal council to be necessary for the election, in accordance with this Act and Part I of the Representation of the People Act 1983, of separate representatives on the community council for each community or for the wards of any community, and

    (b) provide for the dissolution of the separate community council of any community included in the group.

(6) The order shall make such provision as appears to the principal council to be necessary for the application to the communities included in the group of all or any of the provisions of sections 298 to 303 of the Charities Act 2011 (parochial charities) and of any of the provisions of this Act with respect to the custody of community documents, so as to preserve the separate rights of each community.

(7) The order may provide for any necessary adaptations of this Act in relation to the group of communities.

27G Power of community meeting to apply for an order adding its community to a group of communities with a common council

(1) This section sets out the conditions that must be met before an application may be made by a community meeting for an order under section 27H adding the community to a group of communities all of which lie in the same principal area as the community and for which there is a common community council.

(2) The first condition is that the community meeting has taken an effective decision to hold a poll on a proposal to add the community to a group of communities all of which lie in the same principal area as the community and for which there is a common community council.

(3) For the purposes of the first condition a decision is only effective if not less than—

    (a) 10% of the local government electors for the community, or

    (b) 150 of the electors (if 10% of the electors exceeds 150 electors),

are present and voting at the community meeting.

(4) The second condition is that a majority of those voting in the poll support the proposal to add the community to a group of communities all of which lie in the same principal area as the community and for which there is a common community council.

(5) The third condition is that a community meeting of each of the communities in the group has made an effective decision to hold a poll on a proposal to consent to the community in question becoming a member of the group.

(6) For the purposes of the third condition a decision is only effective if not less than—

    (a) 10% of the local government electors for the community, or

    (b) 150 of the electors (if 10% of the electors exceeds 150 electors),

are present and voting at the community meeting.

(7) The fourth condition is that a majority of those voting in a poll following an effective decision for the purposes of the third condition support the proposal to consent to the community in question becoming a member of the group.

(8)   The fifth condition is that none of the above polls are held within two years of an earlier poll which resulted in a rejection of an identical proposal to add the community in question to the group of communities (that period of two years beginning with the day on which the earlier poll was held).

(9)   The sixth condition is that none of the above polls are held before the end of the period of 42 days beginning with the day on which the decision to hold that poll was taken.

(10)   Paragraph 34 of Schedule 12 to this Act (voting at community meetings) shall have effect subject to the provisions of this section.

27H Orders adding a community to a group of communities with a common council

(1)   This section applies where a community meeting of a community applies to the principal council within whose area it lies for an order adding the community to a group of communities all of which lie in the same principal area as the community and for which there is a common community council.

(2)   The principal council must consider whether is it satisfied that—

>   (a)   the conditions in section 27G are met; and
>   (b)   any relevant requirements of Schedule 12 have been met.

(3)   If the council is so satisfied, the council must make the order applied for (but this is subject to subsections (4) to (7) below).

(4)   order shall provide for the name of the group in both an English and a Welsh form.

(5)   The order shall—

>   (a)   make such provision as appears to the principal council to be necessary for the election, in accordance with this Act and Part I of the Representation of the People Act 1983, of separate representatives on the community council for the community that is added to the group or for the wards of that community, and
>   (b)   provide for the dissolution of any separate community council for the community that is added to the group.

(6)   The order shall make such provision as appears to the principal council to be necessary for the application to the communities included in the group of all or any of the provisions of sections 298 to 303 of the Charities Act 2011 (parochial charities) and of any of the provisions of this Act with respect to the custody of community documents, so as to preserve the separate rights of each community.

(7)   The order may provide for any necessary adaptations of this Act in relation to the group of communities.

27I Power of council for a group of communities to apply for an order dissolving the group

(1)   This section sets out the conditions that must be met before an application may be made by a council for a group of communities to the principal council in whose area the communities lie for an order under section 27J below dissolving the group.

(2)   The first condition is that a community meeting of each of the communities in the group has taken an effective decision to hold a poll on a proposal to dissolve the group.

(3)   For the purposes of the first condition a decision is only effective if not less than—

>   (a)   30% of the local government electors for the community, or
>   (b)   300 of the electors (if 30% of the electors exceeds 300 electors),

are present and voting at the community meeting.

(4)   The second condition is that no poll is held before the end of the period of 42 days beginning with the day on which the decision to hold the poll was taken.

(5)   The third condition is that no poll is held within two years of an earlier poll which resulted in a rejection of a proposal to dissolve the group (that period of two years beginning with the day on which the earlier poll was held).

(6)   The fourth condition is that at least two thirds of those voting in each poll support the proposal to dissolve the group.

(7)   Paragraph 34 of Schedule 12 to this Act (voting at community meetings) shall have effect subject to the provisions of this section.

27J Orders dissolving a group of communities

(1)   This section applies where the council for a group of communities applies to the principal council within whose area the communities lie for an order dissolving the group.

(2)   The principal council must consider whether is it satisfied that—

    (a)   the conditions in section 27I are met; and

    (b)   any relevant requirements of Schedule 12 have been met.

(3)   If the council is so satisfied, the council must make the order applied for (but this is subject to subsection (4)).

(4)   The order shall make such provision as appears to the principal council to be necessary for the election of a community council for any of the communities in the group in accordance with this Act and Part I of the Representation of the People Act 1983.

27K Power of community meeting to apply for an order separating community from a group of communities

(1)   This section sets out the conditions that must be met before an application may be made by a community meeting of a community included in a group of communities for an order under section 27L separating the community from the group.

(2)   The first condition is that a community meeting of the community has taken an effective decision to hold a poll on a proposal to separate the community from its group.

(3)   For the purposes of the first condition a decision is only effective if not less than—

    (a)   30% of the local government electors for the community, or

    (b)   300 of the electors (if 30% of the electors exceeds 300 electors),

are present and voting at the community meeting.

(4)   The second condition is that the poll is not held before the end of the period of 42 days beginning with the day on which the decision to hold the poll was taken.

(5)   The third condition is that the poll is not held within two years of an earlier poll which resulted in a rejection of a proposal to separate the community from its group (that period of two years beginning with the day on which the earlier poll was held).

(6)   The fourth condition is that at least two-thirds of those voting in the poll support the proposal to separate the community from its group.

(7)   Paragraph 34 of Schedule 12 to this Act (voting at community meetings) shall have effect subject to the provisions of this section.

27L Orders separating a community from a group of communities

(1)   This section applies where a community meeting of a community included in a group of communities applies to the principal council within whose area the community lies for an order separating the community from the group.

(2)   The principal council must consider whether is it satisfied that—

    (a)   the conditions in section 27K are met; and

    (b)   any relevant requirements of Schedule 12 have been met.

(3)   If the council is so satisfied, the council must make the order applied for (but this is subject to subsection (4)).

(4)   The order shall make such provision as appears to the principal council to be necessary for the election of a community council for the community in accordance with this Act and Part I of the Representation of the People Act 1983.

27M Power of Welsh Ministers to alter voting thresholds in connection with organisation of community councils

(1)   The Welsh Ministers may by order amend the following provisions of this Act—

    (a)   section 27A(3) and (6);

    (b)   section 27C(3) and (6);

    (c)   section 27E(3) and (6);

    (d)   section 27G(3), (4), (6) and (7);

    (e)   section 27I(3) and (6);

    (f)   section 27K(3) and (6).

(2)   That power includes power to amend provision previously made by an order under subsection (1).

(3)   No order may be made under subsection (1) unless the Welsh Ministers have carried out such consultation as they consider appropriate with the following—

    (a)   principal councils in Wales or a body representative of such councils; and

    (b)   community councils in Wales or a body representative of such councils.

(4)   The power of the Welsh Ministers to make an order under subsection (1) is exercisable by statutory instrument.

(5)   A statutory instrument which contains an order under subsection (1) may not be made unless a draft of the instrument has been laid before, and approved by a resolution of, the National Assembly for Wales.

28 Establishment or dissolution of community councils

(1)   A community meeting of a community which does not have a separate council may apply to the principal council within whose area it lies for an order establishing a council for the community.

(2)   A community meeting of a community which has a separate community council may apply to the principal council within whose area it lies for an order dissolving the community council.

(3)   If, on any application under this section, the principal council are satisfied that the relevant requirements of section 29B below and Schedule 12 to this Act have been complied with, they shall make the order applied for.

(4)   An order under this section establishing a separate community council for a community shall make such provision as appears to the council making it to be necessary for the election of a community council in accordance with this Act and Part I of the Representation of the People Act 1983.

(5)   An order under this section establishing a separate community council for a community grouped under a common community council shall not be made unless—

    (a)   the community is separated from the group, or

    (b)   the group is dissolved,

by the order, or by an order under section 29A below.

(6)   Where, in a case to which subsection (5) above applies, the group is not dissolved, the order under this section shall make such provision as appears to the principal council making it to be necessary for the alteration of the group's community council.

(7)   Subject to section 30 below, an application under subsection (1) or (2) above may be made at any time.

(8)   This section is subject to section 29B below.

29 Community councils for groups of communities

(1)   A community meeting of a community may apply to the principal council within whose area the community is situated—

    (a)   for an order grouping the community with some neighbouring community or communities which lie in the same principal area as the applicant, under a common community council, or

    (b)   for an order adding the community to a group of communities—

> (i)   which are all in the area of the same principal council as the community; and
>
> (ii)   for which there is a common community council.

(2) If, on any application under this section, the principal council are satisfied that—

> (a)   the relevant requirements of section 29B below and Schedule 12 to this Act have been complied with, and
>
> (b)   in the case of an application under subsection (1)(b) above, that a community meeting of each of the communities in the group has consented to the applicant becoming a member of the group,

they shall make the order applied for.

(3) Subject to section 30 below, an application under subsection (1) above may be made at any time.

(4) An order under this section shall provide for the name of the group in both an English and a Welsh form.

(5) An order under this section shall—

> (a)   make such provision as appears to the council making it to be necessary for the election, in accordance with this Act and Part I of the Representation of the People Act 1983, of separate representatives on the community council for each community or for the wards of any community or, in the case of an order which adds a community to a group, for that community or for the wards of that community; and
>
> (b)   provide for the dissolution of the separate community council of any community included in the group.

(6) An order under this section shall make such provision as appears to the council making it to be necessary for the application to the communities included in the group of all or any of the provisions of section 79 of the Charities Act 1993 (parochial charities) and of any of the provisions of this Act with respect to the custody of community documents, so as to preserve the separate rights of each community.

(7) An order under this section may provide for any necessary adaptations of this Act in relation to the group of communities.

(8) This section is subject to section 29B below.

29A Community councils for groups of communities: dissolution

(1) The council of a group of communities may apply to the principal council within whose area the communities lie for an order dissolving the group.

(2) A community meeting of a community included in a group of communities may apply to the principal council within whose area the community lies for an order separating the community from the group.

(3) If, on any application under this section, the principal council are satisfied that—

> (a)   the relevant requirements of section 29B below and Schedule 12 to this Act have been complied with, and
>
> (b)   in the case of an application under subsection (1) above, that a community meeting of each of the communities in the group has consented to the dissolution of the community council,

they shall make the order applied for.

(4) Where a community council are dissolved by an order under this section, the order shall make such provision as appears to the principal council to be necessary for the election of a community council for any of the communities in the group in accordance with this Act and Part I of the Representation of the People Act 1983.

(5) Where a community is separated from a group by an order under this section, the order shall make such provision as appears to the principal council to be necessary for the election of a community council for the community in accordance with this Act and Part I of the Representation of the People Act 1983.

(6)   Subject to section 30 below, an application under subsection (1) above may be made at any time.

(7)   This section is subject to section 29B below.

29B   Community councils: applications under section 28, 29 or 29A

(1)   An application under section 28, 29 or 29A above may be made only if—

(a)   a poll of the local government electors in the community has been held;

(b)   a majority of those voting in the poll supports the proposal; and

(c)   in the case of an application under section 29(1)(a), the application is made jointly with the communities to be grouped under the common community council.

(2)   In the case of an application under section 29A(1), paragraphs (a) and (b) of subsection (1) above apply in relation to each of the communities concerned.

(3)   The consent required by section 29(2)(b) or 29A(3)(b) above may be given by a community meeting only if—

(a)   a poll of the local government electors in the community has been held; and

(b)   a majority of those voting in the poll supports the proposal.

(4)   At any community meeting at which there is discussed a proposal—

(a)   for the establishment, or for the dissolution, of a community council,

(b)   for the grouping of the community with another community or communities (on an application under section 29(1)(a) or (b) above), under a common community council;

(c)   for the separation of the community from the communities with which it is grouped under a common community council;

(d)   for the dissolution of the common community council for the communities with which it is grouped;

(e)   for the giving of the consent required by section 29(2)(b) or 29A(3)(b) above,

a decision to hold a poll on the question shall be effective only if not less than the required number of local government electors is present and voting.

(5)   The required number of local government electors is such number as is equal to 30% of the local government electorate or, if that number exceeds 300, is 300.

(6)   No poll shall be held for the purposes of this section before the end of the period of 42 days beginning with the day on which the decision to hold the poll was taken.

(7)   Paragraph 34 of Schedule 12 to this Act (voting at community meetings) shall have effect subject to the provisions of this section.

(8)   Where the result of any poll ('the previous poll') held for the purposes of this section is the rejection of the proposal with respect to which the poll was held, no further poll on that question shall be held before the end of the period of two years beginning with the date on which the previous poll was held.

30   Restriction on community applications during and after reviews

(1)   Subject to subsection (3) below, no community application shall be made in relation to any community—

(b)   during the two years beginning with the coming into force of an order relating to the community under Part IV of this Act consequent on the report or proposals of the Welsh Commission on a review under that Part of this Act of any area of which the community forms part or, as the case may be, of the community; or

(c)   during the two years beginning with the coming into force of an order made under this Part of this Act on a community application in relation to the community.

(3)   The Secretary of State may, on an application made by the Welsh Commission at any time when conducting a review under Part IV of this Act or on an application by a principal council at any time when conducting such a review, direct that no community application shall be made in relation to any community affected by the review until the Secretary of State further directs.

(4)   Notwithstanding anything in subsection (1) above but without prejudice to subsection (3) above, the Secretary of State may permit the making of a community application in relation to a community if requested to do so by the council of the area in which the community is situated or by the community council (if any) or a community meeting of the community.

(5)   In this section 'community application' means any application under section 28, 29 or 29A referred to in section 27B, 27D, 27F, 27H, 27J or 27L above.

31 Provision supplementary to sections 27A to 27L

(1)   An order made by a principal council under section 27B, 27D, 27F, 27H, 27J or 27L above may contain such incidental, consequential, transitional or supplementary provision as may appear to the principal council to be necessary or proper for the purposes or in consequence of the order or for giving full effect thereto, and may include provision with respect to the transfer and management or custody of property (whether real or personal) and the transfer of rights and liabilities.

(2)   Where any such order is made, section 68 below shall apply as if the order were made under Part IV of this Act.

(3)   Two copies of every such order shall be sent to the Secretary of State.

32 Constitution of community meeting

(1)   A community meeting of a community shall consist of local government electors for the community.

(2)   A community meeting may authorise the person presiding and two other local government electors present at the meeting to do anything or any class of things authorised by the meeting.

(3)   Any act of a community meeting may be signified by an instrument signed by the person presiding and two other local government electors present at the meeting.

33 Constitution and powers of community councils

(1)   A community council shall be a body corporate consisting of the chairman and community councillors and shall have the functions given to them by this Act or otherwise.

(2)   Each community council shall have the name of the community, with the addition—

  (a)   in   English,   of   the   words   'Community   Council'   (as   in 'Dale Community Council' or 'Llandrillo Community Council'); and

  (b)   in Welsh, of the words 'Cyngor Cymuned' (as in 'Cyngor Cymuned Dale' or 'Cyngor Cymuned Llandrillo').

(3)   A community council need not have a common seal.

(4)   Where a community council do not have a seal, any act of theirs which is required to be signified by an instrument under seal may be signified by an instrument signed and sealed by two members of the council.

33A Consultation with community councils

(1)   The Secretary of State may by order designate any matter—

  (a)   for the purposes of subsection (2) below; or

  (b)   for the purposes of subsection (3) below.

(2)   Where a new principal council are to consider any proposal which relates to a matter which is designated for the purposes of this subsection, the council shall—

(a)   afford the relevant community councils an opportunity to make representations to them about the proposal;

(b)   before making any decision in relation to the proposal, take into account any representations made to them by any relevant community council with respect to the proposal; and

(c)   when they take a decision with respect to the proposal, notify without delay any relevant community council by whom any such representations have been made.

(3) If a community council have given written notice to the relevant principal council—

(a)   that they wish to be consulted about a specified proposal which is to be considered by the principal council, and which relates to a matter designated for the purposes of this subsection, or

(b)   that they wish to be consulted about any proposal which is to be considered by the principal council and which relates to such a matter,

the principal council shall take the steps mentioned in subsection (2) above in relation to that community council.

(4) An order under this section may—

(a)   prescribe circumstances (including, in particular, the need to act with urgency) in which subsections (2) and (3) above do not apply;

(b)   give the Secretary of State power, in such circumstances as may be prescribed by the order, to provide that in relation to any principal council specified by him, those subsections shall not apply or shall apply only to the extent specified by him.

(5) A contravention of the duty imposed by subsection (2) or (3) above shall not affect the validity of any decision of a principal council or of anything done in pursuance of any such decision.

(6) In this section—

'relevant community council', in relation to a principal council, means the council of any community which is, or group of communities which are, within the area of the principal council; and

'relevant principal council', in relation to any community council, means the principal council within whose area the community is, or group of communities are, situated.

(7) The power to make an order under this section shall include power—

(a)   to make such incidental, consequential, transitional or supplemental provision as the Secretary of State thinks necessary or expedient; and

(b)   to make different provision for different areas, including different provision for different localities and for different authorities.

33B Principal council's response to a community poll

(1) This section applies where a principal council has been given a notice under paragraph 38B(3) or (5)(a) of Schedule 12 to this Act which contains a determination that a question in relation to which a poll consequent on a community meeting was taken relates to the council's functions.

(2) The council must, during the relevant period, perform one of the actions described in subsection (4).

(3) If the council chooses to perform more than one action, the council may do so during or after the relevant period.

(4) The actions referred to in subsection (2) are as follows—

(a)   to exercise the council's functions in accordance with the question in relation to which the poll was taken;

(b)   to include the question of what action (if any) the council should take in response to the community poll within the business to be transacted at a meeting of the principal council held within the relevant period (and for this purpose a meeting of a committee or sub-committee of the council does not count);

(c)   to initiate a consultation exercise which seeks the views of such members of the public as the council considers appropriate about what action (if any) the council should take in response to the community poll;

(d)   to hold a meeting open to members of the public, at such venue as the council considers appropriate, for the purpose of seeking the views of members of the public about what action (if any) the council should take in response to the community poll;

(e)   to initiate research for the purpose of assisting the council to decide what action (if any) it should take in response to the community poll;

(f)   to refer the question of what action (if any) the council should take in response to the community poll to an overview and scrutiny committee with a request that the committee reports its conclusions to the council.

(5)   In this section the "relevant period" means the period of two months beginning on the day following that on which the notice referred to in subsection (1) was given.

33C Principal council's explanation of its response to a community poll

(1)   As soon as is reasonably practicable following the end of the relevant period for the purposes of section 33B of this Act, a principal council must take all reasonable steps to give the chairman of, or person who presided at, the community meeting referred to in subsection (1) of that section a notice in writing which—

(a)   describes what action the council has taken in response to the community poll to which the notice relates, and

(b)   describes what further action (if any) the council intends to take.

(2)   If notice cannot be given to the chairman of, or person who presided at, the community meeting—

(a)   in the case of a community meeting convened under paragraph 30 of Schedule 12 to this Act, the notice must instead be given to the chairman of the community council for the community;

(b)   in the case of a community meeting convened under paragraph 30A of Schedule 12 to this Act, the principal council must instead take all reasonable steps to give notice to each of the individuals who convened the community meeting.

(3)   Subject to subsection (5), notice under subsection (2)(b) is to be given by sending the notice to the address given in respect of an individual in the relevant convening notice.

(4)   In subsection (3), "relevant convening notice" means the notice given to the council under paragraph 30B of Schedule 12 to this Act which preceded the holding of the community meeting at which the poll in question was demanded.

(5)   Where an individual is an anonymous registrant in the register of local government electors (within the meaning of paragraph 29A of Schedule 12 to this Act), the duty under subsection (3) does not apply and notice shall instead be given, and related functions performed, in accordance with sub-paragraphs (4) to (8) of paragraph 29A of Schedule 12 to this Act.

(6)   The council must publish the notice on its website for a period of at least six months, beginning with the day on which the notice was given.

34 Chairman and vice-chairman of community council

[*With the substitution of references to a 'community' for references to a 'parish', the nine subsections of this section are identical with the first nine subsections of s 15 above.*]

35 Community councillors

(1)   Community councillors shall be elected by the local government electors for the community in accordance with this Act and Part I of the Representation of the People Act 1983.

(2)   There shall be ordinary elections of community councillors in 2004 and in every fourth year thereafter.

(2A)   The term of office of the community councillors shall be four years.

(2B)   On the fourth day after any such ordinary election—

    (a)   the persons who were councillors immediately before the election shall retire; and

    (b)   the newly elected councillors shall assume office.

(3)   Where a community is not divided into community wards there shall be one election of community councillors for the whole community.

(4)   Where a community is divided into community wards there shall be a separate election of community councillors for each ward.

Miscellaneous

38 Extent of Part II

This Part of this Act shall extend to Wales only.

PART IV

CHANGES IN LOCAL GOVERNMENT AREAS

Proposals by Local Government Boundary Commission for Wales

53 Local Government Boundary Commission for Wales

(1)   There shall be a Local Government Boundary Commission for Wales (in this Act referred to as 'the Welsh Commission') who shall carry out the functions conferred on them by or under this Act.

   . . .

54 Proposals for changes in local government areas in Wales

(1)   Subject to subsection (2) below, the Welsh Commission may in consequence of a review conducted by them or a principal council under this Part of this Act make proposals to the Secretary of State for effecting changes appearing to the Commission desirable in the interests of effective and convenient local government by any of the following means or any combination of those means (including the application of any of the following paragraphs to an area constituted or altered under any of those paragraphs):—

    (a)   the alteration of a local government area;

    (b)   the constitution of a new local government area by—

        (i)   amalgamating two or more principal areas or two or more communities;

        (ii)   aggregating parts of principal areas or parts of communities; or

        (iii)   separating part of a principal area or part of a community;

    (c)   the abolition of a principal area and its distribution among other principal areas;

    (cc)   the abolition of a community and its distribution among other areas of the like description;

    (d)   the constitution of a new community by—

        (i)   the establishment of any area which is not a community or part of one as a community;

        (ii)   the aggregation of the whole or any part of any such area with one or more communities or parts of communities;

    (e)   a change of electoral arrangements for any local government area which is either consequential on any change in local government areas proposed under the foregoing paragraphs or is a change (hereafter in this Part referred to as a substantive change) which is independent of any change in local government areas so proposed;

    (f)   a change in police areas (including a change resulting in a reduction or increase in the number of police areas) in connection with a change in local government areas.

(1A)   The Welsh Commission may, in consequence of a review conducted by them under this Part of this Act make proposals to the Secretary of State for effecting changes in the area of a preserved county which appear to the Commission to be desirable having regard, in particular, to the purposes for which the preserved counties are retained.

(1B)   Where the Welsh Commission make proposals for the constitution of a new principal area, those proposals shall specify whether the new area should be a county or a county borough.

(2)   The Welsh Commission shall not make any proposals to the Secretary of State under this section for a substantive change of electoral arrangements for a community except in accordance with section 57(7) below.

55 Review of local government areas in Wales

(1)   It shall be the duty of the Welsh Commission to keep under review all principal areas in Wales for the purpose of considering whether or not to make such proposals in relation to them as are authorised by section 54 above and what proposals, if any, to make, and the Commission shall, unless to do so would in their opinion impede the proper discharge of their functions, consider any request made to them by any local authority appearing to the Commission to be interested in any such principal area that the Commission should make such proposals, and in either case the Commission shall, if they think fit, formulate such proposals accordingly.

(2)   It shall be the duty of each Welsh principal council to keep the whole of their area under review for the purpose of considering whether or not to make recommendations to the Welsh Commission for such proposals with respect to the constitution of new communities, the abolition of communities or the alteration of communities in their area as are authorised by section 54 above and what recommendations, if any, to make and the council shall, unless to do so would in their opinion impede the proper discharge of their functions under this Part of this Act, consider any request made with respect to any of those matters by any community council or community meeting appearing to the principal council to be interested, and the principal council shall from time to time report to the Commission accordingly.

(2A)   Each Welsh principal council must, every fifteen years, publish a report which describes what the council has done in the previous fifteen years in order to discharge its duty to keep the whole of their area under review for the purpose described in subsection (2).

(2B)   The council must send a copy of any report published under subsection (2A) to the Welsh Commission.

(2C)   The first report under subsection (2A) must be published within four years of the day on which that subsection comes into force.

(2D)   Further reports must be published within fifteen years of the date on which the last report under subsection (2A) was published.

(3)   The Welsh Commission shall consider any report made under subsection (2) above with respect to any principal area in Wales and, if they think fit, make the proposals recommended, either as submitted to them or with modifications, but if the Commission are of the opinion that the proposals recommended are not, as

submitted or with modifications, apt for securing effective and convenient local government in that principal area or the principal council have reported that they will not recommend the Commission to make proposals, the Commission may themselves review the whole or part of that principal area for the purpose of considering whether or not to make such proposals in relation to it as are authorised by section 54 above and what proposals, if any, to make and may, if they think fit, formulate such proposals accordingly.

(4)   In any case where the Secretary of State has made an order under section 1 of the New Towns Act 1965 designating any land as, or as an extension of, a new town and the area of the new town as so designated or so extended is not wholly comprised within one principal area, he shall, as soon as practicable after the order has become operative, send to the Welsh Commission a notice stating that the order is in operation and specifying the principal areas within which that area is situated, and on receipt of such a notice it shall be the duty of the Commission to review the areas of those principal areas for the purpose of considering whether or not to make such proposals in relation to them as are authorised by section 54 above and what proposals, if any, to make, and the Commission shall, if they think fit, formulate such proposals accordingly.

(5)   If in conducting a review under this section the Commission or a principal council intend to make, or recommend the making of, proposals for a change in local government areas they shall also consider whether or not in consequence of that change to make or recommend the making of proposals for any of the following:—

(a)   the constitution of a council for a community or a group of such communities;

(b)   the dissolution of a community council, whether separate or common;

(c)   the separation of a community from a group of communities having a common community council;

(d)   the addition of a community to a group of communities having a common community council;

(e)   the making of provision for electoral arrangements for any community or group of communities which is consequential on any change proposed under the foregoing paragraphs;

(f)   the alteration of the boundaries of any preserved county;

and subsections (1) to (3) above shall apply in relation to proposals for any of those matters and recommendations for such proposals as they apply in relation to proposals authorised by section 54 above and recommendations for such proposals.

56 Power of Secretary of State to direct holding of reviews

(1)   The Secretary of State may direct the Welsh Commission to conduct a review of—

(a)   Wales as a whole,

(b)   any one or more local government areas or parts of such areas in Wales, or

(c)   any one or more preserved counties or parts of such counties,

for the purpose of considering whether or not to make such proposals in relation to the area reviewed as are authorised by section 54 above and what proposals, if any, to make; and the Commission shall, if they think fit, formulate such proposals accordingly.

(2)   The Secretary of State may, at the request of the Welsh Commission or otherwise, direct a principal council in Wales to conduct a review of the whole or any part of their area for the purpose of considering whether or not to make recommendations to the Commission for such proposals with respect to the constitution of new communities, the abolition of communities or the alteration of communities in their area as are authorised by section 54 above and what recommendations, if any, to make, and to report to the Commission accordingly within a period specified in the direction.

(3)   The Welsh Commission shall consider any report made under subsection (2) above with reference to any principal area in Wales and, if they think fit, make the proposals recommended, either as submitted to them or with modifications, but if the Commission are of the opinion that the proposals recommended are not, as submitted or with modifications, apt for securing effective and convenient local government in that principal area or the principal council have reported that they will not recommend the Commission to make proposals, the Commission may themselves review the whole or part of that principal area for the purpose of considering whether or not to make such proposals in relation to it as are authorised by section 54 above and what proposals, if any, to make and may, if they think fit, formulate such proposals accordingly.

(4)   If a principal council fail within the period specified in a direction under subsection (2) above to submit a report to the Welsh Commission, the Secretary of State may direct the Welsh Commission to conduct the review which the principal council were directed to conduct for the purpose of considering whether or not to make any such proposals as aforesaid and what, if any, proposals to make, and the Commission shall, if they think fit, formulate such proposals accordingly.

(4A)   A direction given to the Welsh Commission under subsection (4) may require the principal council to pay to the Commission such sum as is specified, or calculated according to a formula contained, in the direction.

(4B)   Any dispute as to the sum payable under the direction is to be determined by the Welsh Ministers.

(4C)   Any sum payable under a direction under subsection (4) is to be recoverable as a debt due to the Welsh Commission.

(5)   If in conducting a review under this section the Commission or a principal council intend to make, or recommend the making of, proposals for a change in any areas, they shall also consider whether or not in consequence of that change to make or recommend the making of proposals for any such matters as are mentioned in section 55(5) above, and subsections (1) to (3) of that section shall apply in relation to such proposals and recommendations as they apply in relation to proposals authorised by section 54 above and recommendations for such proposals.

57 Substantive changes in electoral arrangements

(1)   No review shall be conducted under section 55 or 56 above for the purpose of making proposals for a substantive change of electoral arrangements, but the following provisions of this section shall have effect with respect to the making of such proposals.

(2)   It shall be the duty of the Welsh Commission not less than ten or more than fifteen years after the completion of the initial review of the electoral arrangements for principal areas under section 64 of this Act (as substituted by the Local Government (Wales) Act 1994) and thereafter, so far as is reasonably practicable, at intervals of not less than ten or more than fifteen years from the submission of the last report of the Commission on the previous review under this subsection in relation to the area in question, to review the electoral arrangements for every principal area in Wales for the purpose of considering whether or not to make proposals to the Secretary of State for a substantive change in those electoral arrangements and what proposals, if any, to make, and the Commission shall, if they think fit, formulate such proposals accordingly.

(3)   Without prejudice to subsection (2) above, the Welsh Commission may at any time, whether at the request of a local authority or otherwise, review the electoral arrangements for a principal area in Wales for the purpose of considering whether or not to make proposals to the Secretary of State for a substantive change in those electoral arrangements and what proposals, if any, to make, and the Commission shall, if they think fit, formulate such proposals accordingly.

(4) It shall be the duty of each principal council in Wales to keep under review the electoral arrangements for the communities in their area for the purpose of considering whether or not to make substantive changes in those arrangements and what changes, if any, to make and the council shall consider any requests made with respect to those arrangements by the council for, or not less than thirty local government electors of, any community appearing to the principal council to be likely to be affected by those changes, and the principal council may, if they think fit, make an order giving effect to those changes.

(4A) Each Welsh principal council must, every fifteen years, publish a report which describes what the council has done in the previous fifteen years in order to discharge its duty to keep the whole of the area under review for the purpose described in subsection (4).

(4B) The council must send a copy of any report published under subsection (4A) to the Welsh Commission.

(4C) The first report under subsection (4A) must be published within four years of the day on which that subsection comes into force.

(4D) Further reports must be published within fifteen years of the date on which the last report under subsection (4A) was published.

(5) The Welsh Commission may, on a request made by the council for, or not less than thirty local government electors of, any community, review the electoral arrangements for the community for the purpose of considering whether or not to make proposals to the principal council for an order under subsection (6) below changing those arrangements and what proposals, if any, to make, and may, if they think fit, formulate such proposals and send them to the principal council accordingly.

(6) Where a principal council have received proposals from the Welsh Commission under subsection (5) above for an order under this subsection they may, if they think fit, make the order proposed or may suggest modifications to the proposals and, where the Commission agree to the modifications suggested, may make the order with those modifications.

(7) If after receiving any such proposals a principal council inform the Welsh Commission that in their opinion the order proposed should not be made (whether with or without modifications) or if, within six months of receiving any such proposals, the principal council have not made the order proposed (whether with or without modifications), the Commission may report that fact to the Secretary of State and make to him the proposals which they made to the principal council.

57A Exercise of functions by the Welsh Commission on behalf of principal councils

(1) Arrangements may be made between the Welsh Commission and a principal council in Wales under which the Commission exercises, to whatever extent and subject to whatever terms the parties may agree, all or any of the functions of the principal council referred to in subsection (2).

(2) The functions are—

    (a)   the principal council's function of keeping under review the whole of their area for the purpose specified in section 55(2) or the purpose specified in section 57(4);

    (b)   the principal council's function of considering requests specified in section 55(2) or section 57(4).

58 Commission's reports and their implementation

(1) Where the Welsh Commission have—

    (a)   in accordance with section 55 or 56 above been conducting a review of any area or considering any recommendations made by a principal council; or

    (b)   in accordance with section 57 above or in accordance with a direction under section 167 of the Local Government (Wales) Measure 2011 been conducting a review of electoral arrangements on which they have a power or duty to formulate proposals to, or submit a report to, the Secretary of State;

and in either case are of the opinion that they are in a position to submit to the Secretary of State a report on the review or any part of it or any of the recommendations, they shall submit a report to him on the review or that part or those recommendations, together with the proposals they have formulated thereon, or, as the case may be, a notification that they have no proposals to put forward thereon.

(2) The Secretary of State may if he thinks fit by order give effect to any proposals made to him by the Welsh Commission, either as submitted to him or with modifications:

Provided that an order giving effect to any such proposals shall not be made until after the expiry of six weeks from the day on which those proposals were submitted to him.

(3) If in relation to any area the Secretary of State decides to make an order under this section giving effect with modifications to proposals made to him by the Commission, he may, if he thinks fit, direct the Commission to conduct a further review of that area or, as the case may be, of its electoral arrangements and to make revised proposals with respect to that area or those arrangements within a time specified in the direction.

(3A) The Secretary of State shall exercise his power to make orders under this section in relation to police areas in such a way as to ensure that no county or county borough is divided between two or more police areas.

(4) Any statutory instrument containing an order under this section which—

  (a)   alters the area of a principal council,

  (b)   alters the area of a preserved county, or

  (c)   abolishes a principal area,

shall be subject to annulment in pursuance of a resolution of either House of Parliament.

59 Directions about reviews

[This section provides that, subject to consultation with appropriate local authority associations, the Secretary of State may issue guidance on the conduct and order of reviews.]

Conduct of reviews

60 Procedure for reviews

(1) The Welsh Commission or a Welsh principal council proposing to conduct a review under the foregoing provisions of this Part of this Act or in accordance with a direction under section 167 of the Local Government (Wales) Measure 2011 shall take such steps as they think fit to secure that persons who may be interested in the review are informed of the proposal to conduct it and of any directions of the Secretary of State which are relevant to it.

(2) In conducting any such review the Welsh Commission or Welsh principal council shall—

  (a)   consult—

    (i)   the council of any local government area and the police and crime commissioner for any police area affected by the review, and such other local authorities and public bodies as appear to them to be concerned;

    (ii)   any bodies representative of staff employed by local authorities who have asked the Commission or the council, as the case may be, to be consulted; and

(iii)   such other persons as they think fit;

(b)   take such steps as they think fit for securing that persons who may be interested in the review are informed of any draft proposals or recommendations, any draft of an order under section 57(4) above or any interim decision not to make proposals or recommendations or any such order and of the place or places where those proposals or recommendations or that order or decision can be inspected;

(c)   in particular, deposit copies of those proposals or recommendations or that order or decision at the offices of any principal council or police and crime commissioner whose area may be affected thereby and require any such principal council to keep the copies available for inspection at their offices for a period specified in the requirement; and

(d)   take into consideration any representations made to them within that period.

(3) In considering any recommendations made by a Welsh principal council in consequence of a review conducted by them under this Part of this Act the Welsh Commission may consult the council of any local government area affected by the review, such other local authorities and public bodies as appear to them to be concerned and such other persons as they think fit.

(4) Where the Welsh Commission propose to modify any proposals recommended by a Welsh principal council as aforesaid or not to submit any such proposals, the Commission shall—

(a)   take such steps as they think fit for securing that persons who may be interested in any modification or decision are informed of it and of the place or places where it can be inspected;

(b)   deposit copies of any draft modification or the decision at the offices of the principal council and of any other principal council in Wales whose area may be affected thereby and require any such council to keep the copies available for inspection at their offices for a period specified in the requirement; and

(c)   take into consideration any representations which may be made to them with respect to any such modification or decision within that period.

(5) Where the Welsh Commission make a report, proposals or recommendations under this Part of this Act they shall—

(a)   take such steps as they think fit for securing that persons who may be interested in the report, proposals or recommendations are informed of the report, proposals or recommendations and of the place or places where they can be inspected;

(b)   in particular, deposit copies of the report, proposals or recommendations at the offices of any principal council or police and crime commissioner whose area may be affected thereby and require any such principal council to keep the copies available for inspection at their offices until the expiration of six months after the making of an order giving effect, with or without modifications, to the proposals or recommendations or after a notification by the Commission that they have no proposals to put forward or, as the case may be, by the Secretary of State that he does not propose to give effect to the proposals of the Commission.

(5A) Where a Welsh principal council make a report, proposals or recommendations under this Part of this Act they shall—

(a)   make copies of the report, proposals or recommendations available for inspection at their offices for the period mentioned in subsection (5)(b) above;

(b)   take the steps mentioned in subsection (5)(a); and

(c)   comply with the requirements of subsection (5)(b) above in relation to any other principal council in Wales whose area may be affected by the report, proposals or recommendations.

(6) Subject to subsections (1) to (5A) above, the Secretary of State may make regulations prescribing the procedure by which the Welsh Commission or, as the case may be, a Welsh principal council are to conduct a review under this Part of this Act or by which the Welsh Commission are to consider recommendations of a Welsh principal council thereunder.

(7) Subject to those subsections and to any regulations made under subsection (6) above, the procedure of the Welsh Commission or a Welsh principal council in conducting any such review and the procedure of the Commission in considering any such recommendations shall be such as they may determine.

61 Local inquiries

(1) The Welsh Commission or a Welsh principal council may cause a local inquiry to be held with respect to any review carried out by them under this Part of this Act.

(2) Section 250(2), (3) and (5) below shall apply in relation to an inquiry held under this section with the substitution for references to a Minister of references to the Commission or Welsh principal council causing the inquiry to be held.

Supplementary provisions

65 Delegation of functions of Commission

[*This section empowers the Welsh Commission to delegate investigations and consultations to certain individuals.*]

67 Consequential and transitional arrangements relating to Part IV

(1) The Secretary of State may by regulations of general application make such incidental, consequential, transitional or supplementary provision as may appear to him to be necessary or proper for the purposes or in consequence of orders under this Part of this Act or for giving full effect thereto; and nothing in any other provision of this Act shall be construed as prejudicing the generality of this subsection.

(2) Regulations under this section may in particular include, in addition to any provision made by virtue of section 255 below, provision of general application with respect to—

    (a)   the transfer and management or custody of property (whether real or personal) and the transfer of rights and liabilities;

    (b)   the functions or areas of jurisdiction of any public body, justice of the peace other than a District Judge (Magistrates' Courts), coroner, custos rotulorum, lord-lieutenant, lieutenant, high sheriff and other officers (including police officers), and the functions of any District Judge (Magistrates' Courts), within any area affected by any such order, and the costs and expenses of such public bodies and persons as aforesaid;

    (c)   the transfer of legal proceedings;

and may apply, with or without modifications, or extend, exclude or amend, or repeal or revoke, with or without savings, any provision of an Act, an instrument made under an Act or a charter.

(3) A statutory instrument containing regulations under this section shall be subject to annulment in pursuance of a resolution of either House of Parliament.

(4) An order under this Part of this Act may include the like provision in relation to the order as may be made by regulations of general application under this section by virtue of subsections (1) and (2) above; and nothing in any other provision of this Act shall be construed as prejudicing the generality of this subsection.

(5) Any such order may also include provision with respect to—

    (a)   the name of any altered area;

    (b)   the constitution, election and membership of public bodies in any area affected by the order;

    (c)   the total number of councillors, the apportionment of councillors among electoral areas, the assignment of existing councillors to new or altered electoral areas and the first election of councillors for any new or altered electoral area;

    (d)   without prejudice to paragraph (c) above, the holding of a fresh election of councillors for all electoral areas in the local government area in question in a case where substantial changes have been made to some of those areas;

    (e)   without prejudice to paragraph (c) above, the order of retirement of councillors for any such electoral area;

    (g)   the abolition or establishment, or the restriction or extension, of the jurisdiction of any public body in or over any part of the area affected by the order.

(5A) Without prejudice to subsection (5), an order under section 58 which makes provision altering any police areas may make provision as to who is to be a police and crime commissioner, including—

    (a)   provision for the police and crime commissioner for a police area affected by the order to become the police and crime commissioner for a police area resulting from the order;

    (B)   provision for the holding of an election for the police and crime commissioner for any police area resulting from the order.

(5B) Such an order which includes provision within subsection (5A)(b) may, in particular, require the election in question to be held before the alteration of police areas takes effect.

68 Transitional agreements as to property and finance

(1) Any public bodies affected by the alteration, abolition or constitution of any area by an order under this Part of this Act or by an order under section 162 of the Local Government (Wales) Measure 2011 may from time to time make agreements with respect to any property, income, rights, liabilities and expenses (so far as affected by the alteration, abolition or constitution) of, and any financial relations between, the parties to the agreement.

(2) The agreement may provide—

    (a)   for the transfer or retention of any property, rights and liabilities, with or without conditions, and for the joint use of any property;

    (b)   for the making of payments by either party to the agreement in respect of property, rights and liabilities so transferred or retained, or of such joint use, and in respect of the remuneration or compensation payable to any person; and

    (c)   for the making of any such payment either by way of a capital sum or of a terminable annuity.

(3) In default of agreement as to any matter, the matter shall be referred to the arbitration of a single arbitrator agreed on by the parties, or in default of agreement appointed by the Secretary of State, and the award of the arbitrator may provide for any matter for which an agreement under this section might have provided.

(4) Any sum required to be paid by a public body in pursuance of an agreement or award under this section may be paid out of such fund or rate as may be specified in the agreement or award, or if no fund or rate was specified, either out of the fund or rate from which the general expenses of the public body are defrayed, or out of such fund or rate as the public body may direct.

(5) For the purposes of paying any capital sum required to be paid by a public body in pursuance of any such agreement or award—

(a)   a local authority may borrow without the approval of the Secretary of State, but so that the sum borrowed shall be repaid within such period as the authority with the consent of the Secretary of State may determine;

(b)   any other public body having power under any enactment or any instrument made under any Act to borrow may borrow under that enactment or instrument; and

(c)   a public body having no power under any enactment or any such instrument to borrow may be empowered by an order made by the Secretary of State to borrow in such manner and in accordance with such conditions as may be provided by the order.

(8)   Any agreement or award under this section which relates to the profits of local taxation licences shall, so far as it so relates, be carried out in accordance with regulations made by the Secretary of State.

(9)   Subsection (8) above shall apply to—

(a)   an adjustment made under section 151 of the 1933 Act, whether as originally enacted or as applied by any other enactment or any instrument made under any Act; and

(b)   an adjustment made under section 32 or 62 of the Local Government Act 1888, whether as originally enacted or as so applied, and consequent on an alteration of areas effected after 31st March 1930;

as it applies in relation to an agreement or award under this section.

69 Variation and revocation of orders under Part IV, etc

(1)   The power conferred by section 266 below to vary and revoke orders under this Act shall, in the case of orders under this Part of this Act, apply only in relation to any supplementary provision contained in any such order, and an order varying or revoking any such provision shall only be made after compliance with subsections (2) and (3) below.

(2)   The Secretary of State or Welsh principal council proposing to make any such varying or revoking order shall prepare a draft of the order, shall send copies of the draft to such local or public authorities as appear to him or them to be concerned, and shall give public notice, in such manner as appears to him or them sufficient for informing persons likely to be concerned, that the draft has been prepared, that a copy of the draft is available for inspection at a place specified in the notice and that representations with respect to the draft may be made to him or them within two months of the publication of the notice.

(3)   The Secretary of State or Welsh principal council shall consider any representations duly made with respect to the draft and may, if he or they think fit, make an order either in the form of the draft or subject to modifications.

(4)   The Secretary of State or a Welsh principal council may cause a local inquiry to be held with respect to the draft and section 250(2), (3) and (5) below shall apply in relation to an inquiry held under this subsection by a council with the substitution for references to a Minister of references to the council.

(5)   Any supplementary provision contained in an order made by a Minister of the Crown under any of the following enactments (being enactments making provision corresponding to some or all of the foregoing provisions of this Part of this Act), that is to say—

(a)   section 46 of the Local Government Act 1929;

(b)   Part VI of the 1933 Act;

(c)   Part II of the Local Government Act 1958;

(d)   section 6 of the 1963 Act;

(e)   any enactment repealed by the 1933 Act and corresponding to any enactment in the said Part VI;

may be varied or revoked by an order made by the Secretary of State, and subsections (2) to (4) above shall apply in relation to any such order as they apply in relation to orders varying or revoking orders under this Part of this Act.

(6) Any supplementary provision contained in an order made under any of the enactments mentioned in subsection (5) above by any predecessor of a Welsh principal council may be varied or revoked in relation to any Welsh principal area to which or part of which that provision relates by an order made by the council of that area, and subsections (2) to (4) above shall apply with all necessary modifications in relation to any such order as they apply in relation to orders varying or revoking orders under this Part of this Act.

(7) In this section 'supplementary provision' means any such provision as could be made by an order under this Part of this Act by virtue of section 67 above or section 255 below.

Miscellaneous

70 Restriction on promotion of Bills for changing local government areas, etc
[*Local authorities deprived of power to promote Bills affecting the area, status or electoral arrangements of local authorities or executive arrangements, alternative arrangements or the election of an elected mayor.*]

71 Modification of seaward boundaries of local government areas
(1) The Welsh Commission may at any time review so much of the boundary of any area as lies below the high-water mark of medium tides and does not form a common boundary with another area and may make proposals to the Secretary of State for making alterations to any part of the boundary so as to include in the area any area of the sea which at the date of the proposals is not, in whole or in part, comprised in any other area or to exclude from the area any area of the sea which at that date is comprised in the area.

(2)–(5) [*These consequential subsections align the procedure and the Secretary of State's powers with those in other types of review, but subject the Secretary of State's order to annulment by resolution of either Houses of Parliament.*]

(6) In subsection (1) above, 'area' (except in 'area of the sea') means any local government area in Wales and any preserved county.

(7) No order may be made under this section extending any area into England.

72 Accretions from the sea, etc
(1) Subject to subsection (3) below, every accretion from the sea, whether natural or artificial, and any part of the sea-shore to the low water-mark, which does not immediately before the passing of this Act form part of a parish shall be annexed to and incorporated with—

  (a)   in England, the parish or parishes which the accretion or part of the sea-shore adjoins, and

  (b)   in Wales, the community or communities which the accretion or part of the sea-shore adjoins,

in proportion to the extent of the common boundary.

(2) Every accretion from the sea or part of the sea-shore which is annexed to and incorporated with a parish under this section shall be annexed to and incorporated with the district and county in which that parish is situated.

(2A) Every accretion from the sea or part of the sea-shore which is annexed to and incorporated with a community under this section shall be annexed to and incorporated with the principal area and the preserved county in which that community is situated.

(3) In England, in so far as the whole or part of any such accretion from the sea or part of the sea-shore as is mentioned in subsection (1) above does not adjoin a parish, it shall be annexed to and incorporated with the district which it adjoins or, if it adjoins more than one district, with those districts in proportion to the extent of the

common boundary; and every such accretion or part of the sea-shore which is annexed to and incorporated with a district under this section shall be annexed to and incorporated with the county in which that district is situated.

73 Alteration of local boundaries consequent on alteration of water-course

(1) Where, in the exercise of any power conferred by the Water Resources Act 1991, the Land Drainage Act 1991 or any other enactment, a water-course forming a boundary line between two or more areas of local government is straightened, widened or otherwise altered so as to affect its character as a boundary line, the drainage board or other persons under whose authority the alteration is made shall forthwith send notice of the alteration to the Secretary of State.

(2) If after consultation with the Local Government Boundary Commission for England or the Welsh Commission, as the case may require, the Secretary of State is satisfied that, having regard to the alteration specified in the notice, a new boundary line may conveniently be adopted, he may by order declare that such line as may be specified in the order (whether or not consisting wholly or in part of the line of the water-course as altered) shall be substituted for so much of the boundary line as, before the alteration, lay along the line of the water-course; and where such an order is made the limits of the areas of which the water-course, before the alteration, was the boundary shall be deemed to be varied accordingly.

(3) The Secretary of State shall, in such manner as he thinks appropriate, publish notice of any order made by him under this section.

(4) For the purposes of this section a preserved county is an area of local government.

75 Change of name of parish

(1) At the request of the parish council or, where there is no parish council, at the request of the parish meeting, the council of the district in which the parish is situated may change the name of the parish.

(2) Notice of any change of name made under this section—

    (a)   shall be sent by the district council concerned to the Secretary of State, to the Director General of the Ordnance Survey and to the Registrar General; and

    (b)   shall be published by the district council in the parish and elsewhere in such manner as they consider appropriate.

(3) A change of name made in pursuance of this section shall not affect any rights or obligations of any parish or of any council, authority or person, or render defective any legal proceedings; and any legal proceedings may be commenced or continued as if there had been no change of name.

76 Change of name of community

[*Apart from the substitution of the word 'community' for the word 'parish' and references to a principal area instead of a district, this section is identical with s 75 above.*]

78 Supplementary

(1) In this Part of this Act—

    'electoral arrangements' means—

    (a)   in relation to a principal area, the number of councillors of the council for that area, the number and boundaries of the electoral areas into which that area is for the time being divided for the purpose of the election of councillors, the number of councillors to be elected for any electoral area in that principal area and the name of any electoral area;

    (b)   in relation to a parish or community council or a common parish or community council, the number of councillors, the question whether the parish or community or any parish or community, as the case may be, should or should not be or continue to be divided into wards for the purpose of the election of councillors, the number and boundaries of any such wards, the number of councillors to be elected for any such ward or in the case of a common parish or community council for each parish or community and the name of any such ward;

. . .

'substantive change' has the meaning assigned to it by section 54(1)(e) above.

(2) In considering the electoral arrangements for local government areas for the purposes of this Part of this Act, the Secretary of State, the Welsh Commission and every Welsh principal council and district council shall so far as is reasonably practicable comply with the rules set out in Schedule 11 to this Act.

PART V

GENERAL PROVISIONS AS TO MEMBERS AND PROCEEDINGS OF LOCAL AUTHORITIES

Qualifications and disqualifications

79 Qualifications for election and holding office as member of local authority

(1) A person shall, unless disqualified by virtue of this Act or any other enactment, be qualified to be elected and to be a member of a local authority if he is qualifying Commonwealth citizen or a citizen of the Republic of Ireland or a relevant citizen of the Union and on the relevant day he has attained the age of eighteen years and—

(a) on that day he is and thereafter he continues to be a local government elector for the area of the authority; or

(b) he has during the whole of the twelve months preceding that day occupied as owner or tenant any land or other premises in that area; or

(c) his principal or only place of work during that twelve months has been in that area; or

(d) he has during the whole of those twelve months resided in that area; or

(e) in the case of a member of a parish or community council he has during the whole of those twelve months resided either in the parish or community or within three miles of it.

(2) In this section 'relevant day', in relation to any candidate, means—

(a) except in the case of an election not preceded by the nomination of candidates, the day on which he is nominated as a candidate and also, if there is a poll, the day of election; and

(b) in the said excepted case, the day of election.

(2A) In this section the expression 'citizen of the Union' shall be construed in accordance with Article 20(1) of the Treaty on the Functioning of the European Union, and 'relevant citizen of the Union' means such a citizen who is not a qualifying Commonwealth citizen or a citizen of the Republic of Ireland.

(2B) For the purposes of this section, a person is a qualifying Commonwealth citizen if he is a Commonwealth citizen who either—

(a) is not a person who requires leave under the Immigration Act 1971 to enter or remain in the United Kingdom, or

(b) is such a person but for the time being has (or is, by virtue of any enactment, to be treated as having) indefinite leave to remain within the meaning of that Act.

(2C)   But a person is not a qualifying Commonwealth citizen by virtue of subsection (2B)(a) if he does not require leave to enter or remain in the United Kingdom by virtue only of section 8 of the Immigration Act 1971 (exceptions to requirement for leave in special cases).

. . .

80 Disqualifications for election and holding office as member of local authority
(1)   Subject to the provisions of section 81 below, a person shall be disqualified for being elected or being a member of a local authority if he—

- (a)   holds any paid office or employment (other than the office of chairman, vice-chairman or deputy chairman or, in the case of a local authority which are operating executive arrangements which involve a leader and cabinet executive, the office of executive leader or member of the executive) appointments or elections to which are or may be made or confirmed by the local authority or any committee or sub-committee of the authority or by a joint committee or National Park authority on which the authority are represented or by any person holding any such office or employment; or
- (aa)   holds any employment in an entity which is under the control of the local authority; or
- (b)   is the subject of a bankruptcy restrictions order or an interim bankruptcy restrictions order, or a debt relief restrictions order or interim debt relief restrictions order under Schedule 4ZB of the Insolvency Act 1986; or
- (d)   has within five years before the day of election or since his election been convicted in the United Kingdom, the Channel Islands or the Isle of Man of any offence and has had passed on him a sentence of imprisonment (whether suspended or not) for a period of not less than three months without the option of a fine; or
- (e)   is disqualified for being elected or for being a member of that authority under Part III of the Representation of the People Act 1983 *or under the Audit Commission Act 1998.*

(2)   Subject to the provisions of section 81 below, a paid officer of a local authority who is employed under the direction of—

- (a)   a committee or sub-committee of the authority any member of which is appointed on the nomination of some other local authority; or
- (b)   a joint board, joint authority, economic prosperity board, combined authority,] joint waste authority or joint committee on which the authority are represented and any member of which is so appointed;

shall be disqualified for being elected or being a member of that other local authority.
(2AA)   A paid member of staff of the Greater London Authority who is employed under the direction of a joint committee the membership of which includes—

- (a)   one or more persons appointed on the nomination of the Authority acting by the Mayor, and
- (b)   one or more members of one or more London borough councils appointed to the committee on the nomination of those councils,

shall be disqualified for being elected or being a member of any of those London borough councils.
(2A)   Subsection (2) above shall have effect as if the reference to a joint board included a reference to a National Park authority.
(2B)   For the purposes of this section a local authority shall be treated as represented on a National Park authority if it is entitled to make any appointment of a local authority member of the National Park authority.
(3)   Subsection (1)(a) shall have effect in relation to a teacher in a school maintained by the local authority who does not hold an employment falling within that provision as it has effect in relation to a teacher in such a school who holds such an employment.

(3A) In subsection (1)(aa) as it applies in relation to a local authority in England, the reference to an entity under the control of the local authority has the meaning given by order under section 217 of the Local Government and Public Involvement in Health Act 2007.

(3B) In subsection (1)(aa) as it applies in relation to a local authority in Wales, that reference has the meaning given by order under section 218 of that Act.

(5) For the purposes of subsection (1)(d) above, the ordinary date on which the period allowed for making an appeal or application with respect to the conviction expires or, if such an appeal or application is made, the date on which the appeal or application is finally disposed of or abandoned or fails by reason of the non-prosecution thereof shall be deemed to be the date of the conviction.

82 Validity of acts done by unqualified persons

(1) The acts and proceedings of any person elected to an office under this Act or elected or appointed to an office under Part IV of the Local Government Act 1985 or elected as elected mayor or executive leader and acting in that office shall, notwithstanding his disqualification or want of qualification, be as valid and effectual as if he had been qualified.

(2) Subsection (1) above shall have effect, in relation to the Broads Authority, as if the references to this Act included a reference to the Norfolk and Suffolk Broads Act 1988.

Acceptance, resignation and vacation of office, and casual vacancies

83 Declaration of acceptance of office

. . .

(4) A person elected to the office of chairman of a parish or community council or parish or community councillor shall—

>(a)   in the case of the chairman, at the meeting at which he is elected;
>
>(b)   in the case of a councillor, before or at the first meeting of the parish or community council after his election; or
>
>(c)   in either case if the council at that meeting so permit, before or at a later meeting fixed by the council;

make in the presence of a member of the council or of the proper officer of the council and deliver to the council a declaration of acceptance of office in a form prescribed by an order made by the Secretary of State, and if he fails to do so his office shall thereupon become vacant.

(5) Any person before whom a declaration is authorised to be made under this section may take the declaration.

84 Resignation

(1) A person elected to any office under this Act or elected as an elected mayor may at any time resign his office by written notice delivered—

. . .

>(c)   in the case of a parish or community councillor, to the chairman of the parish or community council;
>
>(d)   in the case of a chairman of a parish or community council or of a parish meeting, to the council or the meeting, as the case may be;

and his resignation shall take effect upon the receipt of the notice by the person or body to whom it is required to be delivered.

(2) A person elected or appointed to an office under Part IV of the Local Government Act 1985 may at any time resign his office by written notice delivered to the proper officer of the authority of which he is a member and his resignation shall take effect upon the receipt of the notice by that officer.

85 Vacation of office by failure to attend meetings

(1)   Subject to subsections (2) and (3) below, if a member of a local authority fails throughout a period of six consecutive months from the date of his last attendance to attend any meeting of the authority, he shall, unless the failure was due to some reason approved by the authority before the expiry of that period, cease to be a member of the authority.

(2)   Attendance as a member at a meeting of any committee or sub-committee of the authority, or at a meeting of any joint committee, joint board or other body by whom for the time being any of the functions of the authority are being discharged, or who were appointed to advise the authority on any matter relating to the discharge of their functions, and attendance as representative of the authority at a meeting of any body of persons, shall be deemed for the purposes of subsection (1) above to be attendance at a meeting of the authority.

(2A)   Subject to subsections (2B) and (3), if a member of a local authority which are operating executive arrangements, who is also a member of the executive of that local authority, fails throughout a period of six consecutive months from the date of his last attendance to attend any meeting of the executive, he shall, unless the failure was due to some reason approved by the local authority before the expiry of that period, cease to be a member of the local authority.

(2B)   For the purposes of this section—

(a)   the discharge by a member, acting alone, of any function which is the responsibility of the executive; and

(b)   in respect of a mayor and cabinet executive or leader and cabinet executive, attendance as a member at a meeting of a committee of the executive,

shall each be deemed to be attendance at a meeting of the executive.

(3)   A member of any branch of Her Majesty's naval, military or air forces when employed during war or any emergency on any naval, military or air force service, and a person whose employment in the service of Her Majesty in connection with war or any emergency is such as, in the opinion of the Secretary of State, to entitle him to relief from disqualification on account of absence, shall not cease to be a member of a local authority by reason only of a failure to attend meetings of the local authority or of a failure to attend meetings of the executive if the failure is due to that employment.

(3A)   Any period during which a member of a local authority is suspended or partially suspended under section 66, 73, 78, or 79 of the Local Government Act 2000 shall be disregarded for the purpose of calculating the period of six consecutive months under subsection (1) or (2A) above (and, accordingly, a period during which a member fails to attend meetings of the authority or, as the case may be, meetings of the executive that falls immediately before, and another such period that falls immediately after, a period of suspension or partial suspension shall be treated as consecutive).

(3B)   Subsections (3C) and (3D) apply for the purpose of calculating the period of six consecutive months under subsection (1) or (2A).

(3C)   Any period during which a member of a local authority in Wales is exercising a right to absence under Part 2 of the Local Government (Wales) Measure 2011 is to be disregarded.

(3D)   The following two periods are to be treated as consecutive—

(a)   the period during which a member of a local authority in Wales fails to attend meetings of the authority or, as the case may be, meetings of the executive that falls immediately before the period described in subsection (3C), and

(b)   the period that falls immediately after the period described in subsection (3C).

(4)   In this section 'local authority' includes a joint authority, an economic prosperity board, a combined authority and a joint waste authority

86 Declaration by local authority of vacancy in office in certain cases

(1)   Where a member of a local authority—

  (a)   ceases to be qualified to be a member of the authority; or

  (b)   becomes disqualified for being a member of the authority otherwise than under the Audit Commission Act 1998 or section 79 of the Local Government Act 2000 or section 34 of the Localism Act 2011 or by virtue of a conviction or a breach of any provision of Part II of the Representation of the People Act 1983; or

  (c)   ceases to be a member of the authority by reason of failure to attend meetings of the authority;

the authority shall, except in any case in which a declaration has been made by the High Court under this Part of this Act, forthwith declare his office to be vacant.

(2)   In this section 'local authority' includes a joint authority, an economic prosperity board, a combined authority and a joint waste authority.

87 Date of casual vacancies

(1)   For the purpose of filling a casual vacancy in any office for which an election is held under this Act, the date on which the vacancy is to be deemed to have occurred shall be—

  (a)   in the case of non-acceptance of office by any person who is required to make and deliver a declaration of acceptance of office, on the expiration of the period appointed under this Part of this Act for the delivery of the declaration;

  (b)   in the case of resignation, upon the receipt of the notice of resignation by the person or body to whom the notice is required to be delivered;

  (c)   in the case of death, on the date of death;

  (d)   in the case of a disqualification under the Audit Commission Act 1998 or by virtue of a conviction, on the expiration of the ordinary period allowed for making an appeal or application with respect to the relevant order or decision under that Act or (as the case may be) that conviction or, if an appeal or application is made, on the date on which that appeal or application is finally disposed of or abandoned or fails by reason of non-prosecution thereof;

  (e)   in the case of an election being declared void on an election petition, on the date of the report or certificate of the election court;

  (ee) in the case of a disqualification under section 79 of the Local Government Act 2000 or section 34 of the Localism Act 2011 or, on the expiration of the ordinary period allowed for making an appeal or application with respect to the relevant decision or order under that section or, if an appeal or application is made, on the date on which that appeal or application is finally disposed of or abandoned or fails by reason of non-prosecution thereof;

  (f)   in the case of a person ceasing to be qualified to be a member of a local authority, or becoming disqualified, for any reason other than one mentioned in paragraphs (a) to (ee) above, or ceasing to be a member of a local authority by reason of failure to attend meetings, on the date on which his office is declared to have been vacated either by the High Court or by the local authority, as the case may be.

(2)   Public notice of a casual vacancy in any such office as is referred to in subsection (1) above shall be given by the local authority in which the office exists; and the steps required to be taken to give public notice in accordance with section 232 below shall be taken—

  (a)   in a case where the local authority declare the office to be vacant, immediately after the declaration; and

(b)   in any other case, as soon as practicable after the date on which, by virtue of subsection (1) above, the vacancy is deemed to have occurred.

88 Filling of casual vacancy in case of chairman, etc

(1)   On a casual vacancy occurring in the office of chairman of any council, an election to fill the vacancy shall be held not later than the next ordinary meeting of the council held after the date on which the vacancy occurs, or if that meeting is held within fourteen days after that date, then not later than the next following ordinary meeting of the council, and shall be conducted in the same manner as an ordinary election.

(2)   A meeting of the council for the election may be convened by the proper officer of the authority.

(3)   In a parish not having a separate parish council, a casual vacancy in the office of chairman of the parish meeting shall be filled by the parish meeting, and a parish meeting shall be convened for the purpose of filling the vacancy forthwith.

89 Filling of casual vacancies in case of councillors

. . .

(6)   A casual vacancy among parish or community councillors shall be filled by election or by the parish or community council in accordance with rules made under section 36 of the Representation of the People Act 1983.

(7)   Where under this section any question is required to be determined by lot—

(a)   in the case of a contested election, the lot shall be drawn by the returning officer immediately after the question has arisen; and

(b)   in any other case, the lot shall be drawn at the next meeting of the council after the question has arisen, and the drawing shall be conducted under the direction of the person presiding at the meeting.

90 Term of office of persons filling casual vacancies

A person elected or appointed under the foregoing provisions of this Act in England or Wales or under Part IV of the Local Government Act 1985 to fill any casual vacancy shall hold office until the date upon which the person in whose place he is elected or appointed would regularly have retired, and he shall then retire.

91 Temporary appointment of members of parish and community councils

(1)   Where there are so many vacancies in the office of parish or community councillor that the parish or community council are unable to act, the district council or Welsh principal council may by order appoint persons to fill all or any of the vacancies until other councillors are elected and take up office.

(2)   In the case of a common parish council under which are grouped, by virtue of section 11(5) above, parishes situated in different districts, the reference in subsection (1) above to the district council shall be construed as a reference to the council of the district in which there is the greater number of local government electors for the parishes in the group.

(3)   Two copies of every order made under this section shall be sent to the Secretary of State.

Proceedings for disqualification

92 Proceedings for disqualification

(1)   Proceedings against any person on the ground that he acted or claims to be entitled to act as a member of a local authority while disqualified for so acting within the meaning of this section may be instituted by, and only by, any local government elector for the area concerned—

(a)   in the High Court or a magistrates' court if that person so acted;

(b)   in the High Court if that person claims to be entitled so to act;

but proceedings under paragraph (a) above shall not be instituted against any person after the expiration of more than six months from the date on which he so acted.

(2)   Where in proceedings instituted under this section it is proved that the defendant has acted as a member of a local authority while disqualified for so acting, then—

    (a)   if the proceedings are in the High Court, the High Court may—

        (i)   make a declaration to that effect and declare that the office in which the defendant has acted is vacant;

        (ii)   grant an injunction restraining the defendant from so acting;

        (iii)   order that the defendant shall forfeit to Her Majesty such sum as the court think fit, not exceeding £50 for each occasion on which he so acted while disqualified;

    (b)   if the proceedings are in a magistrates' court, the magistrates' court may, subject to the provisions of this section, convict the defendant and impose on him a fine not exceeding level 3 on the standard scale for each occasion on which he so acted while disqualified.

(3)   Where proceedings under this section are instituted in a magistrates' court, then—

    (a)   if the court is satisfied that the matter would be more properly dealt with in the High Court, it shall by order discontinue the proceedings;

    (b)   if the High Court, on application made to it by the defendant within fourteen days after service of the summons, is satisfied that the matter would be more properly dealt with in the High Court, it may make an order, which shall not be subject to any appeal, requiring the magistrates' court by order to discontinue the proceedings.

(4)   Where in proceedings instituted under this section in the High Court it is proved that the defendant claims to act as a member of a local authority and is disqualified for so acting, the court may make a declaration to that effect and declare that the office in which the defendant claims to be entitled to act is vacant and grant an injunction restraining him from so acting.

(5)   No proceedings shall be instituted against a person otherwise than under this section on the ground that he has, while disqualified for acting as a member of a local authority, so acted or claimed to be entitled so to act.

(6)   For the purposes of this section a person shall be deemed to be disqualified for acting as a member of a local authority—

    (a)   if he is not qualified to be, or is disqualified for being, a member of the authority; or

    (b)   if by reason of failure to make and deliver the declaration of acceptance of office within the period required, or by reason of resignation or failure to attend meetings of the local authority, he has ceased to be a member of the authority.

(7)   In this section 'local authority' includes a joint authority, an economic prosperity board and a combined authority, and in relation to a joint authority, an economic prosperity board or a combined authority the reference in subsection (1) above to a local government elector for the area concerned shall be construed as a reference to a local government elector for any local government area in the area for which the authority is established.

(7A)   In this section 'local authority' also includes a joint waste authority.

(7B)   The reference in subsection (1) above to a local government elector for the area concerned shall—

    (a)   in relation to a joint waste authority established for an area that includes a local government area, be construed as including a reference to a local government elector for that local government area;

    (b)   in relation to a joint waste authority established for an area that includes the City of London, be construed as including a reference to a person whose name appears in a ward list published under section 7 of the City of London (Various Powers) Act 1957;

    (c)   in relation to a joint waste authority established for an area that includes the Inner Temple or the Middle Temple, be construed as including a reference to a person whose name appears in the ward list published with respect to the ward of Farrington Without in the City under section 7 of the City of London (Various Powers) Act 1957.

(8)   In relation to the Broads Authority, the reference in subsection (1) above to a local government elector for the area concerned shall be construed as a reference to a local government elector for the area of any of the local authorities mentioned in section 1(3)(a) of the Norfolk and Suffolk Broads Act 1988.

Meetings and proceedings

99 Meetings and proceedings of local authorities

The provisions of Schedule 12 to this Act shall have effect with respect to the meetings and proceedings of local authorities, joint authorities, economic prosperity boards, combined authorities, and their committees, parish meetings and their committees and community meetings.

100 Admission of public and press to local authority committee meetings

(1)   For the purpose of securing the admission, so far as practicable, of the public (including the press) to all meetings of committees of local authorities as well as to meetings of local authorities themselves, the Public Bodies (Admission to Meetings) Act 1960 (in this section referred to as 'the 1960 Act') shall have effect subject to the following provisions of this section.

(2)   Without prejudice to section 2(1) of the 1960 Act (application of section 1 of that Act to any committee of a body whose membership consists of or includes all members of that body) section 1 of the 1960 Act shall apply to any committee appointed by one or more local authorities under section 102 below, not being a committee falling within section 2(1) of the 1960 Act or section 100E(3)(a) or (b) below (whether or not by virtue of section 100J below).

(3)   Where section 1 of the 1960 Act applies to a committee by virtue of subsection (2) above, then, for the purposes of subsection (4)(c) of that section, premises belonging to the local authority or one or more of the local authorities which appointed the committee shall be treated as belonging to the committee.

PART VA

ACCESS TO MEETINGS AND DOCUMENTS OF CERTAIN AUTHORITIES, COMMITTEES AND SUB-COMMITTEES

100A Admission to meetings of principal councils

(1)   A meeting of a principal council shall be open to the public except to the extent that they are excluded (whether during the whole or part of the proceedings) under subsection (2) below or by resolution under subsection (4) below.

(2)   The public shall be excluded from a meeting of a principal council during an item of business whenever it is likely, in view of the nature of the business to be transacted or the nature of the proceedings, that, if members of the public were present during that item, confidential information would be disclosed to them in breach of the obligation of confidence; and nothing in this Part shall be taken to authorise or require the disclosure of confidential information in breach of the obligation of confidence.

(3)   For the purposes of subsection (2) above, 'confidential information' means—

(a) information furnished to the council by a Government department upon terms (however expressed) which forbid the disclosure of the information to the public; and

(b) information the disclosure of which to the public is prohibited by or under any enactment or by the order of a court;

and, in either case, the reference to the obligation of confidence is to be construed accordingly.

(4) A principal council may by resolution exclude the public from a meeting during an item of business whenever it is likely, in view of the nature of the business to be transacted or the nature of the proceedings, that if members of the public were present during that item there would be disclosure to them of exempt information, as defined in section 100I below.

(5) A resolution under subsection (4) above shall—

(a) identify the proceedings, or the part of the proceedings, to which it applies, and

(b) state the description, in terms of Schedule 12A to this Act, of the exempt information giving rise to the exclusion of the public,

and where such a resolution is passed this section does not require the meeting to be open to the public during proceedings to which the resolution applies.

(6) The following provisions shall apply in relation to a meeting of a principal council, that is to say—

(a) public notice of the time and place of the meeting shall be given by posting it at the offices of the council *three clear days* [five clear days][1] at least before the meeting or, if the meeting is convened at shorter notice, then at the time it is convened;

(b) while the meeting is open to the public, the council shall not have power to exclude members of the public from the meeting; and

(c) while the meeting is open to the public, duly accredited representatives of newspapers attending the meeting for the purpose of reporting the proceedings for those newspapers shall, so far as practicable, be afforded reasonable facilities for taking their report and, unless the meeting is held in premises not belonging to the council or not on the telephone, for telephoning the report at their own expense.

(7) Nothing in this section shall require a principal council to permit the taking of photographs of any proceedings, or the use of any means to enable persons not present to see or hear any proceedings (whether at the time or later), or the making of any oral report on any proceedings as they take place.

(8) This section is without prejudice to any power of exclusion to suppress or prevent disorderly conduct or other misbehaviour at a meeting.

---

[1] Words 'three clear days' in italics repealed and subsequent words in square brackets substituted, in relation to England only.

100B–100K

[Ss 100B–100K *represent a code ancillary to s 100A above. In principle, and subject to exceptions mainly detailed in Sch 12A:*

s 100B deals with rights of access to agendas and their connected reports;

ss 100C and100D deal with the public right of inspection of minutes and related documents and background papers;

s 100E applies s 100A with adaptations to committees and sub-committees;

s 100F confers on members of principal councils the right to inspect any documents in the possession of their council;

s 100G requires principal councils to maintain public registers of their members and committee members, public lists of their powers exercisable by their officers and public written summaries of rights of attendance at committees and sub-committees and of rights to inspect and copy their documents;

s 100H supplements ss 100A to 100G, protects the relevant copyrights and makes obstructions of lawful inspection an offence;

s 100I and Sch 12A (below) describe the (so-called) exempt information which may be withheld from public rights of access under ss 100A to 100H;

s 100K defines certain terms used in ss 100A to 100I and Sch 12A.]

PART VI

DISCHARGE OF FUNCTIONS

101¹ Arrangements for discharge of functions by local authorities

(1) Subject to any express provision contained in this Act or any Act passed after this Act, a local authority may arrange for the discharge of any of their functions—

    (a)   by a committee, a sub-committee or an officer of the authority; or

    (b)   by any other local authority.

(1A) A local authority may not under subsection (1)(b) above arrange for the discharge of any of their functions by another local authority if, or to the extent that, that function is also a function of the other local authority and is the responsibility of the other authority's executive.

(1B) Arrangements made under subsection (1)(b) above by a local authority ('the first authority') with respect to the discharge of any of their functions shall cease to have effect with respect to that function if, or to the extent that,—

    (a)   the first authority are operating or begin to operate executive arrangements, and that function becomes the responsibility of the executive of that authority; or

    (b)   the authority with whom the arrangements are made ('the second authority') are operating or begin to operate executive arrangements, that function is also a function of the second authority and that function becomes the responsibility of the second authority's executive.

(1C) Subsections (1A) and (1B) above do not affect arrangements made by virtue of section 9EA or 19 of the Local Government Act 2000 (discharge of functions of and by another authority).

(2) Where by virtue of this section any functions of a local authority may be discharged by a committee of theirs, then, unless the local authority otherwise direct, the committee may arrange for the discharge of any of those functions by a sub-committee or an officer of the authority and where by virtue of this section any functions of a local authority may be discharged by a sub-committee of the authority, then, unless the local authority or the committee otherwise direct, the sub-committee may arrange for the discharge of any of those functions by an officer of the authority.

(3) Where arrangements are in force under this section for the discharge of any functions of a local authority by another local authority, then, subject to the terms of the arrangements, that other authority may arrange for the discharge of those functions by a committee, sub-committee or officer of theirs and subsection (2) above shall apply in relation to those functions as it applies in relation to the functions of that other authority.

(4) Any arrangements made by a local authority or committee under this section for the discharge of any functions by a committee, sub-committee, officer or local authority shall not prevent the authority or committee by whom the arrangements are made from exercising those functions.

(5) Two or more local authorities may discharge any of their functions jointly and, where arrangements are in force for them to do so,—

   (a)   they may also arrange for the discharge of those functions by a joint committee of theirs or by an officer of one of them and subsection (2) above shall apply in relation to those functions as it applies in relation to the functions of the individual authorities; and

   (b)   any enactment relating to those functions or the authorities by whom or the areas in respect of which they are to be discharged shall have effect subject to all necessary modifications in its application in relation to those functions and the authorities by whom and the areas in respect of which (whether in pursuance of the arrangements or otherwise) they are to be discharged.

(5A)   Arrangements made under subsection (5) above by two or more local authorities with respect to the discharge of any of their functions shall cease to have effect with respect to that function if, or to the extent that, the function becomes the responsibility of an executive of any of the authorities.

(5B)   Subsection (5A) above does not affect arrangements made by virtue of section 9EB or 20 of the Local Government Act 2000 (joint exercise of functions).

(6)   A local authority's functions with respect to levying, or issuing a precept for, a rate shall be discharged only by the authority.

. . .

(12)   References in this section and section 102 below to the discharge of any of the functions of a local authority include references to the doing of anything which is calculated to facilitate, or is conducive or incidental to, the discharge of any of those functions.

(13)   In this Part of this Act 'local authority' includes the Common Council, the Sub-Treasurer of the Inner Temple, the Under Treasurer of the Middle Temple, the London Fire and Emergency Planning Authority, any joint authority, an economic prosperity board, a combined authority, a joint waste authority, a joint board on which a local authority within the meaning of this Act or any of the foregoing authorities are represented and, without prejudice to the foregoing, any port health authority.

(14)   Nothing in this section affects the operation of section 5 of the 1963 Act or the Local Authorities (Goods and Services) Act 1970.

(15)   Nothing in this section applies in relation to any function under the Licensing Act 2003 of a licensing authority (within the meaning of that Act).

[1]   This section does not apply to the approval of schemes for local lotteries or the consideration of audit reports.

102 Appointment of committees

(1)   For the purpose of discharging any functions in pursuance of arrangements made under section 101 above or section 53 of the Children Act 1989—

   (a)   a local authority may appoint a committee of the authority; or

   (b)   two or more local authorities may appoint a joint committee of those authorities; or

   (c)   any such committee may appoint one or more sub-committees.

(1A)   For the purpose of discharging any function in pursuance of arrangements made under section 9E(2)(b)(iv), (3)(b), (4)(a) or (5)(a) of the Local Government Act 2000 or under regulations made under section 18 of that Act (discharge of functions by area committees)—

   (a)   a local authority may appoint a committee of the authority; or

   (b)   any such committee may appoint one or more sub-committees.

(2)   Subject to the provisions of this section, the number of members of a committee appointed under subsection (1) or (1A) above, their term of office, and the area (if restricted) within which the committee are to exercise their authority shall be fixed by

the appointing authority or authorities or, in the case of a sub-committee, by the appointing committee.

(3) A committee appointed under subsection (1) or (1A) above, other than a committee for regulating and controlling the finance of the local authority or of their area, may, subject to section 104 below, include persons who are not members of the appointing authority or authorities or, in the case of a sub-committee, the authority or authorities of whom they are a sub-committee.

(4) A local authority may appoint a committee, and two or more local authorities may join in appointing a committee, to advise the appointing authority or authorities, or, where the appointing authority or each of the authorities operate executive arrangements, any executive of that or those authorities, or a committee or member of that executive, on any matter relating to the discharge of their functions, and any such committee—

  (a)   may consist of such persons (whether members of the appointing authority or authorities or not) appointed for such term as may be determined by the appointing authority or authorities; and

  (b)   may appoint one or more sub-committees to advise the committee with respect to any such matter.

(5) Every member of a committee appointed under this section who at the time of his appointment was a member of the appointing authority or one of the appointing authorities shall upon ceasing to be a member of that authority also cease to be a member of the committee; but for the purposes of this section a member of a local authority shall not be deemed to have ceased to be a member of the authority by reason of retirement if he has been re-elected a member thereof not later than the day of his retirement.

103 Expenses of joint committees

The expenses incurred by a joint committee of two or more local authorities whether appointed or established under this Part of this Act or any other enactment shall be defrayed by those authorities in such proportions as they may agree or in case of disagreement as may be determined—

  (a)   in any case in which those authorities are the councils of parishes or groups of parishes situated in the same district, by the district council;

  (aa) in any case in which those authorities are the councils of communities or groups of communities situated in the same principal area, by the council of that area; and

  (b)   in any other case, by a single arbitrator agreed on by the appointing authorities or, in default of agreement, appointed by the Secretary of State.

104 Disqualification for membership of committees and joint committees

(1) Subject to subsection (2) below, a person who is disqualified under Part V of this Act for being elected or being a member of a local authority shall be disqualified for being a member of a committee (including a sub-committee) of that authority, or being a representative of that authority on a joint committee (including a sub-committee) of the authority and another local authority, whether the committee or joint committee are appointed under this Part of this Act or under any other enactment.

  . . .

(3) Section 92 above shall, so far as applicable, apply with respect to membership of or a claim to be entitled to act as a member of a committee of a local authority or a joint committee of two or more local authorities as it applies to membership of or claims to be entitled to act as a member of a local authority.

  . . .

106 Standing orders

Standing orders may be made as respects any committee of a local authority by that authority or as respects a joint committee of two or more local authorities, whether appointed or established under this Part of this Act or any other enactment, by those authorities with respect to the quorum, proceedings and place of meeting of the committee or joint committee (including any sub-committee) but, subject to any such standing orders, the quorum, proceedings and place of meeting shall be such as the committee, joint committee or sub-committee may determine.

108 Committees of parish meetings

In a parish not having a separate parish council the parish meeting may, subject to any provisions made by a grouping order and subject to such conditions as the meeting may impose, arrange for the discharge of any of their functions by a committee of local government electors for the parish, but any such arrangement shall not prevent the meeting from exercising those functions.

109 Conferring functions of parish council on parish meeting

(1) On the application of the parish meeting of a parish not having a separate parish council, the district council may, subject to the provisions of the grouping order if the parish is grouped with any other parish, by order confer on the parish meeting any functions of a parish council.

(2) Two copies of every order made under this section shall be sent by the district council to the Secretary of State.

PART VII

MISCELLANEOUS POWERS OF LOCAL AUTHORITIES

Subsidiary powers

111 Subsidiary powers of local authorities

(1) Without prejudice to any powers exercisable apart from this section but subject to the provisions of this Act and any other enactment passed before or after this Act, a local authority shall have power to do any thing (whether or not involving the expenditure, borrowing or lending of money or the acquisition or disposal of any property or rights) which is calculated to facilitate, or is conducive or incidental to, the discharge of any of their functions.

(2) For the purposes of this section, transacting the business of a parish or community meeting or any other parish or community business shall be treated as a function of the parish or community council.

(3) A local authority shall not by virtue of this section raise money, whether by means of rates, precepts or borrowing, or lend money except in accordance with the enactments relating to those matters respectively.

(4) In this section 'local authority' includes the Common Council.

Staff

112 Appointment of staff

(1) Without prejudice to section 111 above but subject to the provisions of this Act, a local authority shall appoint such officers as they think necessary for the proper discharge by the authority of such of their or another authority's functions as fall to be discharged by them and the carrying out of any obligations incurred by them in connection with an agreement made by them in pursuance of section 113 below.

(2)   An officer appointed under subsection (1) above shall hold office on such reasonable terms and conditions, including conditions as to remuneration, as the authority appointing him think fit.

(2A)   A local authority's power to appoint officers on such reasonable terms and conditions as the authority thinks fit is subject to section 41 of the Localism Act 2011 (requirement for determinations relating to terms and conditions of chief officers to comply with pay policy statement).]

....

(5)   Without prejudice to the provisions of subsection (1) above, a parish or community council may appoint one or more persons from among their number to be officers of the council, without remuneration.

(6)   Nothing in this section affects the operation of section 5 of the 1963 Act or the Local Authorities (Goods and Services) Act 1970.

113   Placing of staff of local authorities at disposal of other local authorities

(1)   Without prejudice to any powers exercisable apart from this section, a local authority may enter into an agreement with another local authority for the placing at the disposal of the latter for the purposes of their functions, on such terms as may be provided by the agreement, of the services of officers employed by the former, but shall not enter into any such agreement with respect to any officer without consulting him.

(1A)   [*Provides for the interchange of staff between local authorities and health authorities.*]

(2)   For superannuation purposes service rendered by an officer of a local authority whose services are placed at the disposal of another local authority in pursuance of this section is service rendered to the authority by whom he is employed, but any such officer shall be treated for the purposes of any enactment relating to the discharge of local authorities' functions as an officer of that other local authority.

114   Security to be taken in relation to officers

(1)   A local authority shall, in the case of an officer employed by them, whether under this or any other enactment, who by reason of his office or employment is likely to be entrusted with the custody or control of money, and may in the case of any other officer employed by them, take such security, for the faithful execution of his office and for his duly accounting for all money or property which may be entrusted to him, as the local authority consider sufficient.

(2)   A local authority may, in the case of a person not employed by them but who is likely to be entrusted with the custody or control of money or property belonging to the local authority, take such security as they think sufficient for the person duly accounting for all such money or property.

(3)   A local authority shall defray the cost of any security taken under this section, and every such security shall be produced to the auditor at the audit of the accounts of the local authority.

. . .

115   Accountability of officers

(1)   Every officer employed by a local authority, whether under this Act or any other enactment, shall at such times during the continuance of his office or within three months after ceasing to hold it, and in such manner as the local authority direct, make out and deliver to the authority, or in accordance with their directions, a true account in writing of all money and property committed to his charge, and of his receipts and payments, with vouchers and other documents and records supporting the entries therein, and a list of persons from whom or to whom money is due in connection with his office, showing the amount due from or to each.

(2)   Every such officer shall pay all money due from him to the proper officer of the local authority or in accordance with their directions.

116 Members of local authorities not to be appointed as officers

A person shall, so long as he is, and for twelve months after he ceases to be, a member of a local authority, be disqualified for being appointed or elected by that authority to any paid office, other than to the office of chairman or vice-chairman or, in the case of a local authority which are operating executive arrangements which involve a leader and cabinet executive, the office of executive leader or member of the executive.

117 Disclosure by officers of interest in contracts

(1) If it comes to the knowledge of an officer employed, whether under this Act or any other enactment, by a local authority that a contract in which he has any pecuniary interest, whether direct or indirect (not being a contract to which he is himself a party), has been, or is proposed to be, entered into by the authority or any committee thereof, he shall as soon as practicable give notice in writing to the authority of the fact that he is interested therein.

For the purposes of this section an officer shall be treated as having indirectly a pecuniary interest in a contract or proposed contract if he would have been so treated by virtue of section 95 above had he been a member of the authority.

(2) An officer of a local authority shall not, under colour of his office or employment, accept any fee or reward whatsoever other than his proper remuneration.

(3) Any person who contravenes the provisions of subsection (1) or (2) above shall be liable on summary conviction to a fine not exceeding level 4 on the standard scale.

(4) References in this section to a local authority shall include references to a joint committee appointed under Part VI of this Act or any other enactment.

119 Payments due to deceased officers

(1) If, on the death of any person who is or has been an officer of a local authority, there is due to him or his legal personal representatives from a local authority a sum not exceeding £5,000 and not being a pension, allowance or gratuity payable by virtue of section 7 of the Superannuation Act 1972, the authority may, without requiring the production of probate or letters of administration of the estate of the officer, pay the whole or any part of that sum to the officer's personal representatives or to the person, or to or among any one or more of any persons, appearing to the authority to be beneficially entitled to the estate of the officer, and any person to whom such a payment is made, and not the authority, shall be liable to account for the sum paid to him under this subsection.

(2) The authority may, if they think fit, pay out of the said sum the funeral expenses of the officer or so much thereof as they consider reasonable.

(3) Subsection (1) above shall be included among the provisions with respect to which the Treasury may make an order under section 6(1) of the Administration of Estates (Small Payments) Act 1965, substituting for references to £500 references to such higher amount as may be specified in the order.

(4) Where provision has been made by regulations under section 7(1)(b) of the said Act of 1972 with respect to the pensions, allowances or gratuities which in certain circumstances are to be, or may be, paid to or in respect of any persons or classes of persons, the Secretary of State may by regulations provide for the application of the foregoing provisions of this section to such of those persons or classes of persons as may be specified in the regulations.

Land transactions—principal councils

120 Acquisition of land by agreement by principal councils

(1) For the purposes of—

    (a)   any of their functions under this or any other enactment, or

    (b)   the benefit, improvement or development of their area, a principal council may acquire by agreement any land, whether situated inside or outside their area.

(2) A principal council may acquire by agreement any land for any purpose for which they are authorised by this or any other enactment to acquire land, notwithstanding that the land is not immediately required for that purpose; and, until it is required for the purpose for which it was acquired, any land acquired under this subsection may be used for the purpose of any of the council's functions.

(3) Where under this section a council are authorised to acquire land by agreement, the provisions of Part I of the Compulsory Purchase Act 1965 (so far as applicable) other than section 31 shall apply, and in the said Part I as so applied the word 'land' shall have the meaning assigned to it by this Act.

(3A) Police and crime commissioners and the Mayor's Office for Policing and Crime are to be treated as principal councils for the purposes of—

(a)   this section (apart from subsection (1)(b)), and

(b)   section 121.

(4) Where two or more councils acting together would have power to acquire any land by agreement by virtue of this section, nothing in any enactment shall prevent one of those councils from so acquiring the land on behalf of both or all of them in accordance with arrangements made between them, including arrangements as to the subsequent occupation and use of the land.

(5) References in the foregoing provisions of this section to acquisition by agreement are references to acquisition for money or money's worth, as purchaser or lessee.

121 Acquisition of land compulsorily by principal councils

(1) Subject to subsection (2) below, for any purpose for which they are authorised by this or any other public general Act to acquire land, a principal council may be authorised by the Minister concerned with that purpose to purchase compulsorily any land, whether situated inside or outside their area.

(2) A council may not be authorised under subsection (1) above to purchase land compulsorily—

(a)   for the purpose specified in section 120(1)(b) above, or

(b)   for the purpose of any of their functions under the Local Authorities (Land) Act 1963, or

(c)   for any purpose in relation to which their power of acquisition is by any enactment expressly limited to acquisition by agreement.

(3) Where one or more councils propose, in exercise of the power conferred by subsection (1) above, to acquire any land for more than one purpose, the Minister or Ministers whose authorisation is required for the exercise of that power shall not be concerned to make any apportionment between those purposes nor, where there is more than one council, between those councils, and—

(a)   the purposes shall be treated as a single purpose and the compulsory acquisition shall be treated as requiring the authorisation of the Minister, or the joint authorisation of the Ministers, concerned with those purposes; and

(b)   where there is more than one council concerned, the councils may nominate one of them to acquire the land on behalf of them all and the council so nominated shall accordingly be treated as the acquiring authority for the purposes of any enactment relating to the acquisition.

(4) The Acquisition of Land Act 1981 shall apply in relation to the compulsory purchase of land in pursuance of subsection (1) above.

122 Appropriation of land by principal councils

(1) Subject to the following provisions of this section, a principal council may appropriate for any purpose for which the council are authorised by this or any other enactment to acquire land by agreement any land which belongs to the council and is

no longer required for the purpose for which it is held immediately before the appropriation; but the appropriation of land by a council by virtue of this subsection shall be subject to the rights of other persons in, over or in respect of the land concerned.

(2)   A principal council may not appropriate under subsection (1) above any land which they may be authorised to appropriate under section 229 of the Town and Country Planning Act 1990 (land forming part of a common, etc) unless—

    (a)   the total of the land appropriated in any particular common, or fuel or field garden allotment (giving those expressions the same meanings as in the said section 229) does not in the aggregate exceed 250 square yards, and

    (b)   before appropriating the land they cause notice of their intention to do so, specifying the land in question, to be advertised in two consecutive weeks in a newspaper circulating in the area in which the land is situated, and consider any objections to the proposed appropriation which may be made to them.

(2A)   A principal council may not appropriate under subsection (1) above any land consisting or forming part of an open space unless before appropriating the land they cause notice of their intention to do so, specifying the land in question, to be advertised in two consecutive weeks in a newspaper circulating in the area in which the land is situated, and consider any objections to the proposed appropriation which may be made to them.

(2B)   Where land appropriated by virtue of subsection (2A) above is held—

    (a)   for the purposes of section 164 of the Public Health Act 1875 (pleasure grounds); or

    (b)   in accordance with section 10 of the Open Spaces Act 1906 (duty of local authority to maintain open spaces and burial grounds),

the land shall by virtue of the appropriation be freed from any trust arising solely by virtue of its being land held in trust for enjoyment by the public in accordance with the said section 164 or, as the case may be, the said section 10.

(4)   Where land has been acquired under this Act or any other enactment or any statutory order incorporating the Lands Clauses Acts and is subsequently appropriated under this section, any work executed on the land after the appropriation has been effected shall be treated for the purposes of section 68 of the Lands Clauses Consolidation Act 1845 and section 10 of the Compulsory Purchase Act 1965 as having been authorised by the enactment or statutory order under which the land was acquired.

123   Disposal of land by principal councils

(1)   Subject to the following provisions of this section, and to those of the Playing Fields (Community Involvement in Disposal Decisions) (Wales) Measure 2010, a principal council may dispose of land held by them in any manner they wish.

(2)   Except with the consent of the Secretary of State, a council shall not dispose of land under this section, otherwise than by way of a short tenancy, for a consideration less than the best that can reasonably be obtained.

(2A)   A principal council may not dispose under subsection (1) above of any land consisting or forming part of an open space unless before disposing of the land they cause notice of their intention to do so, specifying the land in question, to be advertised in two consecutive weeks in a newspaper circulating in the area in which the land is situated, and consider any objections to the proposed disposal which may be made to them.

(2AA)   Subsection (2A) does not apply to a disposal to which the provisions of regulations made under section 1 of the Playing Fields (Community Involvement in Disposal Decisions) (Wales) Measure 2010 apply.

(2B)   Where by virtue of subsection (2A) above or in accordance with the provisions of regulations made under section 1 of the Playing Fields (Community Involvement in Disposal Decisions) (Wales) Measure 2010 a council dispose of land which is held—

(a)   for the purposes of section 164 of the Public Health Act 1875 (pleasure grounds); or

(b)   in accordance with section 10 of the Open Spaces Act 1906 (duty of local authority to maintain open spaces and burial grounds),

the land shall by virtue of the disposal be freed from any trust arising solely by virtue of its being land held in trust for enjoyment by the public in accordance with the said section 164 or, as the case may be, the said section 10.

. . .

Land transactions—parish and community councils

124 Acquisition of land by agreement by parish and community councils

(1)   For the purposes of—

(a)   any of their functions under this or any other public general Act, or

(b)   the benefit, improvement or development of their area,

a parish or community council may acquire by agreement any land, whether situated inside or outside their area.

(2)   Where under this section a parish or community council are authorised to acquire land by agreement, the provisions of Part I of the Compulsory Purchase Act 1965 (so far as applicable) other than section 31 shall apply, and in the said Part I as so applied the word 'land' shall have the meaning assigned to it by this Act.

(3)   References in the foregoing provisions of this section to acquisition by agreement are references to acquisition for money or money's worth, as purchaser or lessee.

125 Compulsory acquisition of land on behalf of parish or community councils

(1)   If a parish or community council are unable to acquire by agreement under section 124 above and on reasonable terms suitable land for a purpose for which they are authorised to acquire land other than—

(a)   the purpose specified in section 124(1)(b) above, or

(b)   a purpose in relation to which the power of acquisition is by an enactment expressly limited to acquisition by agreement,

they may represent the case to the council of the district in which the parish or community is situated.

(2)   If the district council are satisfied that suitable land for the purpose cannot be acquired on reasonable terms by agreement, they may be authorised by the Secretary of State to purchase compulsorily the land or part of it; and the Acquisition of Land Act 1981 shall apply in relation to the purchase.

(3)   The district council in making and the Secretary of State in confirming an order for the purposes of this section shall have regard to the extent of land held in the neighbourhood by an owner and to the convenience of other property belonging to the same owner and shall, as far as practicable, avoid taking an undue or inconvenient quantity of land from any one owner.

(4)   The order shall be carried into effect by the district council but the land when acquired shall be conveyed to the parish or community council; and accordingly in construing for the purposes of this section and of the order any enactment applying in relation to the compulsory acquisition, the parish or community council or the district council, or the two councils jointly, shall, as the case may require, be treated as the acquiring authority.

(5)   The district council may recover from the parish or community council the expenses incurred by them in connection with the acquisition of land under this section.

(6)   If a parish or community council make representations to a district council with a view to the making of an order under this section and the district council—
 (a) refuse to make an order, or
 (b) do not make an order within 8 weeks from the making of the representations or such longer period as may be agreed between the two councils,
the parish or community council may petition the Secretary of State who may make the order, and this section and the provisions of the Acquisition of Land Act 1981 shall apply as if the order had been made by the district council and confirmed by the Secretary of State.

(7)   In the application of this section to a parish or community council for a group of parishes or communities—
 (a) references to the parish or community shall be construed as references to the area of the group, and
 (b) if different parts of the area of the group lie in different districts, references to the council of the district in which the parish or community is situated shall be construed as references to the councils of each of the districts acting jointly.

(8)   In relation to Wales—
 (a) references in this section to a district council are to be read as references to a principal council; and
 (b) references to a district are to be read as references to a principal area.

126   Appropriation of land by parish and community councils and by parish meetings

(1)   Any land belonging to a parish or community council which is not required for the purposes for which it was acquired or has since been appropriated may, subject to the following provisions of this section, be appropriated by the council for any other purpose for which the council are authorised by this or any other public general Act to acquire land by agreement.

(2)   In the case of a parish which does not have a separate parish council, any land belonging to the parish meeting which is not required for the purposes for which it was acquired or has since been appropriated may, subject to the following provisions of this section, be appropriated by the parish meeting for any other purpose approved by the Secretary of State.

(3)   The appropriation of land by virtue of this section by a parish or community council or by a parish meeting shall be subject to the rights of other persons in, over or in respect of the land concerned.

(4)   Neither a parish or community council nor a parish meeting may appropriate by virtue of this section any land which they may be authorised to appropriate under section 229 of the Town and Country Planning Act 1990 (land forming part of a common, etc) unless—
 (a) the total of the land appropriated in any particular common or fuel or field garden allotment (giving those expressions the same meanings as in the said section 229) does not in the aggregate exceed 250 square yards, and
 (b) before appropriating the land they cause notice of their intention to do so, specifying the land in question, to be advertised in two consecutive weeks in a newspaper circulating in the area in which the land is situated, and consider any objections to the proposed appropriation which may be made to them,

(4A)   Neither a parish or community council nor a parish meeting may appropriate by virtue of this section any land consisting or forming part of an open space unless before appropriating the land they cause notice of their intention to do so, specifying the land in question, to be advertised in two consecutive weeks in a newspaper circulating in the area in which the land is situated, and consider any objections to the proposed appropriation which may be made to them.

(4B)   Where land appropriated by virtue of subsection (4A) above is held—

(a)   for the purposes of section 164 of the Public Health Act 1875 (pleasure grounds); or

(b)   in accordance with section 10 of the Open Spaces Act 1906 (duty of local authority to maintain open spaces and burial grounds),

the land shall by virtue of the appropriation be freed from any trust arising solely by virtue of its being land held in trust for enjoyment by the public in accordance with the said section 164 or, as the case may be, the said section 10.

(6)   Where land has been acquired under this Act or any other enactment or any statutory order incorporating the Lands Clauses Acts and is subsequently appropriated under this section any work executed on the land after the appropriation has been effected shall be treated for the purposes of section 68 of the Lands Clauses Consolidation Act 1845 and section 10 of the Compulsory Purchase Act 1965 as having been authorised by the enactment or statutory order under which the land was acquired.

127 Disposal of land held by parishes and communities

(1)   Subject to the following provisions of this section, and to those of the Playing Fields (Community Involvement in Disposal Decisions) (Wales) Measure 2010, a parish or community council, or the parish trustees of a parish acting with the consent of the parish meeting, may dispose of land held by them in any manner they wish.

(2)   Except with the consent of the Secretary of State, land shall not be disposed of under this section, otherwise than by way of a short tenancy, for a consideration less than the best that can reasonably be obtained.

(3)   Subsections (2A) and (2B) of section 123 above shall apply in relation to the disposal of land under this section as they apply in relation to the disposal of land under that section, with the substitution of a reference to a parish or community council or the parish trustees of a parish for the reference to a principal council in the said subsection (2A).

(4)   Capital money received in respect of a disposal under this section of land held for charitable purposes shall be applied in accordance with any directions given under the Charities Act 2011.

(5)   For the purposes of this section a disposal of land is a disposal by way of a short tenancy if it consists—

(a)   of the grant of a term not exceeding seven years, or

(b)   of the assignment of a term which at the date of the assignment has not more than seven years to run.

Land transactions—general provisions

128 Consents to land transactions by local authorities and protection of purchasers

(1)   In any case where under the foregoing provisions of this Part of this Act the consent of any Minister is required to a dealing in land by a local authority, that consent may be given—

(a)   in relation to any particular transaction or transactions or in relation to a particular class of transactions; and

(b)   in relation to local authorities generally, or local authorities of a particular class, or any particular local authority or authorities; and

(c)   either unconditionally or subject to such conditions as the Minister concerned may specify (either generally, or in relation to any particular transaction or transactions or class of transactions).

(2)   Where under the foregoing provisions of this Part of this Act or under any other enactment, whether passed before, at the same time as, or after, this Act, a local authority purport to acquire, appropriate or dispose of land, then—

(a)   in favour of any person claiming under the authority, the acquisition, appropriation or disposal so purporting to be made shall not be invalid by reason that any consent of a Minister which is required thereto has not been given or that any requirement as to advertisement or consideration of objections has not been complied with, and

(b)   a person dealing with the authority or a person claiming under the authority shall not be concerned to see or enquire whether any such consent has been given or whether any such requirement has been complied with.

. . .

(4)   In this section 'local authority' includes a parish meeting and the parish trustees of a parish.

129   Payment of purchase or compensation money by one local authority to another
(1)   With the consent of the Secretary of State, any purchase money or compensation payable in pursuance of the foregoing provisions of this Part of this Act by a local authority in respect of any land acquired from another local authority, being money or compensation which would, apart from this section, be required to be paid into court in accordance with the Compulsory Purchase Act 1965, may, instead of being so paid, be paid and applied as the Secretary of State may determine.
(2)   A decision of the Secretary of State under this section shall be final.

130   Acquisition by local authorities of lands belonging to the Duchy of Lancaster
The Chancellor and Council of the Duchy of Lancaster may sell to a local authority any land belonging to Her Majesty in right of that Duchy which the local authority think fit to purchase, and the land may be granted to the local authority and the proceeds of sale shall be paid and dealt with as if the land had been sold under the authority of the Duchy of Lancaster Lands Act 1855.

131   Savings
(1)   Nothing in the foregoing provisions of this Part of this Act or in Part VIII below—

(a)   shall authorise the disposal of any land by a local authority in breach of any trust, covenant or agreement which is binding upon them, excluding any trust arising solely by reason of the land being held as public walks or pleasure grounds or in accordance with section 10 of the Open Spaces Act 1906; or

(b)   shall affect, or empower a local authority to act otherwise than in accordance with, any provision contained in, or in any instrument made under, any of the enactments specified in subsection (2) below and relating to any dealing in land by a local authority or the application of capital money arising from any such dealing.

(2)   The enactments referred to in subsection (1)(b) above are—

(a)   the Technical and Industrial Institutions Act 1892;
(b)   the Military Lands Acts 1892 to 1903;
(d)   the Allotments Acts 1908 to 1950;
(e)   the Small Holdings and Allotments Acts 1908 to 1931;
(f)   the Ancient Monuments and Archaeological Areas Act 1979;
(g)   section 28 of the Land Settlement (Facilities) Act 1919;
(j)   Part III of the Agriculture Act 1970; and
(k)   any local Act (including an Act confirming a provisional order);
(m)   the Housing Act 1985.

(3) Nothing in the foregoing provisions of this Part of this Act shall affect the operation of sections 117 to 121 of the Charities Act 2011 (restrictions on dispositions of charity land) and, in particular none of those provisions shall be treated as giving any such authority for a transaction as is referred to in section 117(3)(a) (certain statutorily authorised dispositions not to require the sanction of the Charity Commission).

(4) In this section 'local authority' includes a parish meeting and the parish trustees of a parish.

Premises and contracts

132 Provision of offices, etc, by principal councils

A principal council may acquire or provide and furnish halls, offices and other buildings, whether within or without the area of the authority, for use for public meetings and assemblies.

133 Provision of parish and community buildings

A parish or community council may acquire or provide and furnish buildings to be used for public meetings and assemblies or contribute towards the expenses incurred by any other parish or community council or any other person in acquiring or providing and furnishing such a building.

134 Use of schoolroom, etc in parish or community

(1) If in a parish there is no suitable public room vested in the parish council or the parish trustees, as the case may be, which can be used free of charge, a suitable room in premises of a school maintained by the local authority or a suitable room the expenditure of maintaining which is payable out of any rate may, subject to subsection (3) below, be used free of charge at all reasonable times and after reasonable notice for any of the following purposes, that is to say, for the purpose of—

- (a) a parish meeting or any meeting of the parish council, where there is one; or
- (b) meetings convened by the chairman of the parish meeting or by the parish council, where there is one; or
- (c) the administration of public funds within or for the purposes of the parish where those funds are administered by any committee or officer appointed by the parish council or parish meeting or by the county council or district council.

(2) If in a community there is no suitable public room vested in the community council which can be used free of charge or there is no community council, a suitable room in premises of a school maintained by the local authority or a suitable room the expenditure of maintaining which is payable out of any rate may, subject to subsection (3) below, be used free of charge at all reasonable times and after reasonable notice for any of the following purposes, that is to say, for the purpose of—

- (a) a community meeting or any meeting of the community council, where there is one; or
- (b) meetings convened by the community council, where there is one; or
- (c) the administration of public funds within or for the purposes of the community where those funds are administered by any committee or officer appointed by the community council, where there is one, or by the principal council.

(3) Nothing in this section shall authorise—

- (a) the use of a room used as part of a private dwelling; or
- (b) any interference with the hours during which a room in the premises of a school is used for educational purposes; or

(c)   any interference with the hours during which a room used for the purposes of the administration of justice, or for the purposes of the police, is used for those purposes.

(4) If, by reason of the use of a room for any of the purposes mentioned in subsection (1) or (2) above, any expense is incurred by persons having control of the room, or any damage is done to the room or the building of which it is part or to its appurtenances, or to the furniture of the room or any teaching aids, the expense or the cost of making good the damage shall be defrayed as an expense of the parish or community council or parish or community meeting.

(5) If any question arises under this section as to what is reasonable or suitable it may be determined by the Secretary of State.

(6) In subsections (1) and (2) "local authority" has the meaning given by section 579(1) of the Education Act 1996.

135 Contracts of local authorities

(1) A local authority may make standing orders with respect to the making of contracts by them or on their behalf.

(2) A local authority shall make standing orders with respect to the making by them or on their behalf of contracts for the supply of goods or materials or for the execution of works.

(3) Standing orders made by a local authority with respect to contracts for the supply of goods or materials or for the execution of works shall include provision for securing competition for such contracts and for regulating the manner in which tenders are invited, but may exempt from any such provision contracts for a price below that specified in standing orders and may authorise the authority to exempt any contract from any such provision when the authority are satisfied that the exemption is justified by special circumstances[1].

(4) A person entering into a contract with a local authority shall not be bound to inquire whether the standing orders of the authority which apply to the contract have been complied with, and non-compliance with such orders shall not invalidate any contract entered into by or on behalf of the authority.

[1]   See also LGA 1988.

Miscellaneous

136 Contributions towards expenditure on concurrent functions

Two or more local authorities may make arrangements for defraying any expenditure incurred by one of them in exercising any functions exercisable by both or all of them.

137 Power of local authorities to incur expenditure for certain purposes not otherwise authorised

(1) A local authority may, subject to the provisions of this section, incur expenditure which in their opinion is in the interests of, and will bring direct benefit to, their area or any part of it or all or some of its inhabitants, but a local authority shall not, by virtue of this subsection, incur any expenditure:

(a)   for a purpose for which they are, either unconditionally or subject to any limitation or to the satisfaction of any condition, authorised or required to make any payment by or by virtue of any other enactment; nor

(b)   unless the direct benefit accruing to their area or any part of it or to all or some of the inhabitants of their area will be commensurate with the expenditure to be incurred.

(1A) In any case where—

(a)   by virtue of paragraph (a) of subsection (1) above, a local authority are prohibited from incurring expenditure for a particular purpose, and

(b)   the power or duty of the authority to incur expenditure for that purpose is in any respect limited or conditional (whether by being restricted to a particular group of persons or in any other way),

the prohibition in that paragraph shall extend to all expenditure to which that power or duty would apply if it were not subject to any limitation or condition.

(2) It is hereby declared that the power of a local authority to incur expenditure under subsection (1) above includes power to do so by contributing towards the defraying of expenditure by another local authority in or in connection with the exercise of that other authority's functions.

(2C) A local authority may incur expenditure under subsection (1) above on publicity only—

(b)   by way of assistance to a public body or voluntary organisation where the publicity is incidental to the main purpose for which the assistance is given;

but the following provisions of this section apply to expenditure incurred by a local authority under section 142 below on information as to the services provided by them under this section, or otherwise relating to their functions under this section, as they apply to expenditure incurred under this section.

(2D) In subsection (2C) above—

'publicity' means any communication, in whatever form, addressed to the public at large or to a section of the public; and

'voluntary organisation' means a body which is not a public body but whose activities are carried on otherwise than for profit.

(3) A local authority may, subject, in the case of a parish or community council, to the following provisions of this section, incur expenditure on contributions to any of the following funds, that is to say—

(a)   the funds of any charitable body in furtherance of its work in the United Kingdom; or

(b)   the funds of any body which provides any public service (whether to the public at large or to any section of it) in the United Kingdom otherwise than for the purposes of gain; or

(c)   any fund which is raised in connection with a particular event directly affecting persons resident in the United Kingdom on behalf of whom a public appeal for contributions has been made by the Lord Mayor of London or the chairman of a principal council or by a committee of which the Lord Mayor of London or the chairman of a principal council is a member or by such a person or body as is referred to in section 83(3)(c) of the Local Government (Scotland) Act 1973.

(4) The expenditure of a local authority under this section in any financial year shall not exceed the amount produced by multiplying—

(a)   such sum as is for the time being appropriate to the authority under Schedule 12B to this Act, by

(b)   the relevant population of the authority's area.

(4AB) For the purposes of subsection (4)(b) above the relevant population of a local authority's area shall be determined in accordance with regulations made by the Secretary of State; and a statutory instrument containing such regulations shall be subject to annulment in pursuance of a resolution of the House of Commons.

(4A) For the purpose of determining whether a local authority have exceeded the limit set out in subsection (4) above, their expenditure in any financial year under this section shall be taken to be the difference between their gross expenditure under this section for that year and the aggregate of the amounts specified in subsection (4B) below.

(4B) The amounts mentioned in subsection (4A) above are—

(a)   the amount of any expenditure which forms part of the authority's gross expenditure for that year under this section and in respect of which any grant has been or is to be paid under any enactment by a Minister of the Crown, within the meaning of the Ministers of the Crown Act 1975 (whether or not the grant covers the whole of the expenditure);

(b)   the amount of any repayment in that year of the principal of a loan for the purpose of financing expenditure under this section in any year;

(c)   so much of any amount raised by public subscription as is spent in that year for a purpose for which the authority are authorised by this section to incur expenditure;

(d)   any grant received by the authority for that year out of the European Regional Development Fund or the Social Fund of the European Economic Community, in so far as the grant is in respect of an activity in relation to which the authority incurred expenditure in that year under this section;

(e)   the amount of any repayment in that year of a loan under this section made by the authority in any year; and

(f)   the amount of any expenditure—

　　(i)   which is incurred by the authority in that year in circumstances specified in an order made by the Secretary of State; or

　　(ii)   which is incurred by the authority in that year and is of a description so specified; or

　　(iii)   which is defrayed by any grant or other payment to the authority which is made in or in respect of that year and is of a description so specified.

(5)   A statutory instrument containing an order under this section may apply to all local authorities or may make different provision in relation to local authorities of different descriptions.

(6)   Any such instrument shall be subject to annulment in pursuance of a resolution of either House of Parliament.

(7)   The accounts of a local authority by whom expenditure is incurred under this section shall include a separate account of that expenditure.

(7A)   In relation to England, section 14 of the Audit Commission Act 1998 (rights of inspection) applies in relation to a separate account included in a local authority's accounts by virtue of subsection (7) above as it applies in relation to a statement of accounts prepared by the authority pursuant to regulations under section 27 of that Act.

(7B)   In relation to Wales, section 29 of the Public Audit (Wales) Act 2004 (rights of inspection) applies in relation to a separate account included in a local authority's accounts by virtue of subsection (7) above as it applies in relation to a statement of accounts prepared by the authority pursuant to regulations under section 39 of that Act.

(9)   Subject to subsection (10) below, in this section 'local authority' means—

(a)   a parish council which is not an eligible parish council for the purposes of Chapter 1 of Part 1 of the Localism Act 2011 (general power of competence), or

(b)   a community council.

(10)   In subsection (3) above 'local authority' means—

(a)   in relation to England, a county council, a district council, a London borough council, the Common Council or a parish council,

(b)   in relation to Wales, a county council, a county borough council or a community council.

137A Financial assistance to be conditional on provision of information

(1) If in any financial year a local authority provides financial assistance—

    (a)   to a voluntary organisation, as defined in subsection (2D) of section 137 above, or

    (b)   to a body or fund falling within subsection (3) of that section,

and the total amount so provided to that organisation, body or fund in that year equals or exceeds the relevant minimum, then, as a condition of the assistance, the authority shall require the organisation, body or fund, within the period of twelve months beginning on the date when the assistance is provided, to furnish to the authority a statement in writing of the use to which that amount has been put.

(2) In this section 'financial assistance' means assistance by way of grant or loan or by entering into a guarantee to secure any money borrowed and, in relation to any financial assistance,—

    (a)   any reference to the amount of the assistance is a reference to the amount of money granted or lent by the local authority or borrowed in reliance on the local authority's guarantee; and

    (b)   any reference to the date when the assistance is provided is a reference to the date on which the grant or loan is made or, as the case may be, on which the guarantee is entered into.

(3) The relevant minimum referred to in subsection (1) above is £2,000 or such higher sum as the Secretary of State may by order specify.

(4) It shall be a sufficient compliance with a requirement imposed by virtue of subsection (1) above that there is furnished to the local authority concerned an annual report or accounts which contain the information required to be in the statement.

(5) A statement (or any report or accounts) provided to a local authority in pursuance of such a requirement shall be deposited with the proper officer of the authority.

138 Powers of principal councils with respect to emergencies or disasters

[*Principal councils are empowered to deal with emergencies and to undertake contigency planning to avert them.*]

139 Acceptance of gifts of property

(1) Subject to the provisions of this section a local authority may accept, hold and administer—

    (a)   for the purpose of discharging any of their functions, gifts of property, whether real or personal, made for that purpose; or

    (b)   for the benefit of the inhabitants of their area or of some part of it, gifts made for that purpose;

and may execute any work (including works of maintenance or improvement) incidental to or consequential on the exercise of the powers conferred by this section.

(2) Where any such work is executed in connection with a gift made for the benefit of the inhabitants of the area of a local authority or of some part of that area, the cost of executing the work shall be added to any expenditure under section 137 above in computing the limit imposed on that expenditure by subsection (4) of that section.

(3) This section shall not authorise the acceptance by a local authority of property which, when accepted, would be held in trust for an ecclesiastical charity or for a charity for the relief of poverty.

(4) Nothing in this section shall affect any powers exercisable by a local authority under or by virtue of the Education Act 1996.

140 Insurance by local authorities against accidents to members

(1) A local authority may enter into a contract of accident insurance against risks of any member of the authority meeting with a personal accident, whether fatal or not, while engaged on the business of the authority.

(2)   Any sum received by the authority under any such contract shall, after deduction of any expenses incurred in the recovery thereof, be paid by them to, or to the personal representatives of, the member of the authority in respect of an accident to whom that sum is received.

(3)   The provisions of the Life Assurance Act 1774 shall not apply to any such contract.

(3A)   References to accident insurance must be read with—

    (a)   section 22 of the Financial Services and Markets Act 2000;

    (b)   any relevant order under that section; and

    (c)   Schedule 2 to that Act.

(4)   In this section, the expression 'member of the authority' includes a member of a committee or sub-committee of the authority who is not a member of that authority.

140A   Insurance of voluntary assistants of local authorities

(1)   A local authority may enter into a contract of insurance of a relevant class against risks of any voluntary assistant of the authority meeting with a personal accident, whether fatal or not, while engaged as such, or suffering from any disease or sickness, whether fatal or not, as the result of being so engaged.

(2)   In this section—

        'local authority' includes—

            (a)   a board constituted in pursuance of section 2 of the Town and Country Planning Act 1990 . . . ;

        'voluntary assistant' means a person who, at the request of the local authority or an authorised officer of the local authority, performs any service or does anything otherwise than for payment by the local authority (except by way of reimbursement of expenses), for the purposes of, or in connection with, the carrying out of any of the functions of the local authority.

140C   Provisions supplementary to sections 140A and 140B

(1)   The relevant classes of contracts of insurance for the purposes of sections 140A and 140B above are—

    (a)   contracts of permanent health insurance; and

    (b)   contracts of accident insurance.

(1A)   Subsection (1) must be read with—

    (a)   section 22 of the Financial Services and Markets Act 2000;

    (b)   any relevant order under that section; and

    (c)   Schedule 2 to that Act.

(2)   Any sum received under a contract of insurance made by virtue of section 140A or 140B above shall, after deduction of any expenses incurred in the recovery thereof, be paid by the authority receiving it to, or to the personal representatives of, the voluntary assistant who suffered the accident, disease or sickness in respect of which the sum is received or to such other person as the authority consider appropriate having regard to the circumstances of the case; and a sum paid to any person other than the assistant or his personal representatives shall be applied by that person in accordance with any directions given by the authority for the benefit of any dependant of the voluntary assistant.

(3)   The provisions of the Life Assurance Act 1774 shall not apply to any such contract.

(4)   Section 119 above shall apply to any sum which is due by virtue of subsection (2) above and does not exceed the amount for the time being specified in section 119(1) above.

141 Research and the collection of information

[*Principal councils may conduct or assist research into matters concerning their area and its publication; and ministers may require local authorities, and such councils may require other authorities in their county area, to make available to them information in their possession.*]

142 Provision of information, etc, relating to matters affecting local government

(1) A local authority may make, or assist in the making of, arrangements whereby the public may on application readily obtain, either at premises specially maintained for the purpose or otherwise, information concerning the services available within the area of the authority provided either by the authority or by other authorities mentioned in subsection (1B) below or by government departments or by charities and other voluntary organisations, and other information relating to the functions of the authority.

(1A) A local authority may arrange for the publication within their area of information as to the services available in the area provided by them or by other authorities mentioned in subsection (1B) below.

(1AA) A local authority may—

    (a) for the purpose of broadcasting or distributing information falling within subsection (1AB), provide an electronic communications network or electronic communications service, or

    (b) arrange with the provider of such a network or service for the broadcasting or distribution of such information by means of the network or service.

(1AB) Information falls within this subsection, in relation to a local authority, if it is one or both of the following—

    (a) information concerning the services within the area of the authority that are provided either by the authority themselves or by other authorities mentioned in subsection (1B) below;

    (b) information relating to the functions of the authority.

(1AC) Nothing in subsection (1AA) entitles a local authority to do anything in contravention of a requirement or restriction imposed by or under—

    (a) Part 2 of the Wireless Telegraphy Act 2006,

    (b) the Broadcasting Act 1990,

    (c) the Broadcasting Act 1996, or

    (d) the Communications Act 2003,

and in that subsection 'electronic communications network' and 'electronic communications service' each has the same meaning as in the Communications Act 2003.

(1B) The other authorities referred to above are any other local authority, a joint authority established by Part IV of the Local Government Act 1985, an economic prosperity board, a combined authority and any authority, board or committee which discharges functions which would otherwise fall to be discharged by two or more local or other such authorities.

(2) A local authority may—

    (a) arrange for the publication within their area of information relating to the functions of the authority; and

    (b) arrange for the delivery of lectures and addresses and the holding of discussions on such matters; and

    (c) arrange for the display of pictures, cinematograph films or models or the holding of exhibitions relating to such matters; and

    (d) prepare, or join in or contribute to the cost of the preparation of, pictures, films, models or exhibitions to be displayed or held as aforesaid.

(2A) A local authority may assist voluntary organisations to provide for individuals—

    (a)   information and advice concerning those individuals' rights and obligations; and

    (b)   assistance, either by the making or receiving of communications or by providing representation to or before any person or body, in asserting those rights or fulfilling those obligations.

(3) In this section 'local authority' includes the Common Council and 'voluntary organisation' means a body which is not a public body but whose activities are carried on otherwise than for profit.

 . . .

143 Subscriptions to local government associations

(1) A local authority may pay reasonable subscriptions, whether annually or otherwise, to the funds—

    (a)   of any association of local authorities formed (whether inside or outside the United Kingdom) for the purpose of consultation as to the common interests of those authorities and the discussion of matters relating to local government, or

    (b)   of any association of officers or members of local authorities which was so formed.

(2) In this section 'local authority' includes the Common Council.

144 Power to encourage visitors and provide conference and other facilities

(1) A local authority may (either alone or jointly with any other person or body)—

    (a)   encourage persons, by advertisement or otherwise, to visit their area for recreation, for health purposes, or to hold conferences, trade fairs and exhibitions in their area; and

    (b)   provide, or encourage any other person or body to provide, facilities for conferences, trade fairs and exhibitions or improve, or encourage any other person or body to improve, any existing facilities for those purposes.

(2) Without prejudice to subsection (1) above, a local authority may contribute to any organisation approved by the Secretary of State for the purposes of this subsection and established for the purpose of encouraging persons to visit the United Kingdom or any part thereof.

 . . .

145 Provision of entertainments

(1) A local authority may do, or arrange for the doing of, or contribute towards the expenses of the doing of, anything (whether inside or outside their area) necessary or expedient for any of the following purposes, that is to say—

    (a)   the provision of an entertainment of any nature or of facilities for dancing;

    (b)   the provision of a theatre, concert hall, dance hall or other premises suitable for the giving of entertainments or the holding of dances;

    (c)   the maintenance of a band or orchestra;

    (d)   the development and improvement of the knowledge, understanding and practice of the arts and the crafts which serve the arts;

    (e)   any purpose incidental to the matters aforesaid, including the provision of refreshments or programmes and the advertising of any entertainment given or dance or exhibition of arts or crafts held by them.

(2) Without prejudice to the generality of the provisions of subsection (1) above, a local authority—

   (a)   may for the purposes therein specified enclose or set apart any part of a park or pleasure ground belonging to the authority or under their control;

   (b)   may permit any theatre, concert hall, dance hall or other premises provided by them for the purposes of subsection (1) above and any part of a park or pleasure ground enclosed or set apart as aforesaid to be used by any other person, on such terms as to payment or otherwise as the authority think fit, and may authorise that other person to make charges for admission thereto;

   (c)   may themselves make charges for admission to any entertainment given or dance or exhibition of arts or crafts held by them and for any refreshment or programmes supplied thereat.

(3) Subsection (2) above shall not authorise any authority to contravene any covenant or condition subject to which a gift or lease of a public park or pleasure ground has been accepted or made without the consent of the donor, grantor, lessor or other person entitled in law to the benefit of the covenant or condition.

(4) Nothing in this section shall affect the provisions of any enactment by virtue of which a licence is required for the public performance of a stage play or the public exhibition of cinematograph films, or for boxing or wrestling entertainments or for public music or dancing, or for the sale of alcohol.

   . . .

146 Transfer of securities on alteration of area, etc

(1) Where any securities are standing in the books of a company in the name of a local authority, the following provisions shall have effect—

   (a)   if the name of the authority is changed, then at the request of the authority and on production of a statutory declaration by the proper officer of the authority specifying the securities and verifying the change of name and identity of the authority, the company shall enter the securities in the new name of the local authority in like manner as if the securities had been transferred to the authority under that name;

   (b)   if by virtue of anything done under any provision of this Act or the 1963 Act or any enactment similar to any such provision (whenever passed), any other local authority have become entitled to the securities or any dividends or interest thereon, as the case may be, a certificate of the proper officer of the council of the county in which the area of that other authority is situated, or the scheme, order or award under which that other authority have become so entitled, shall be a sufficient authority to the company to transfer the securities into the name of the local authority specified in that behalf in the certificate, or in the scheme, order or award, as the case may be, and to pay the dividends or interest to that authority;

   (c)   if in any other case any other local authority have become entitled to the securities or any dividends or interest thereon, as the case may be, the court may on application make an order vesting in that other authority the right to transfer the securities or to receive the dividends or interest, as the case may be, and the Trustee Act 1925 shall apply in like manner as if the vesting order were made under section 51 of that Act.

(1A) In relation to Wales, subsection (1)(b) above shall have effect as if the reference to a county council were a reference to a principal council.

(2) In this section, the expression—

       'company' includes the Bank of England and any company or person keeping books in which any securities are registered or inscribed;

'local authority' means a local authority within the meaning of the 1933 Act, the London Government Act 1939 or this Act or a joint board on which, or a joint committee on which, a local authority or parish meeting are represented, a burial board, a joint burial board or the parish trustees of a parish;

'securities' has the meaning given in section 98(1) above.

(3) The jurisdiction of the court under this section may be exercised by the High Court or, in cases in which a county court would have jurisdiction if the application were an application made under the Trustee Act 1925, by that court.

146A Joint Authorities and Inner London Education Authority

(1) Subject to subsections (1ZA), (1ZB), (1ZC), (1ZD) or (1ZE) below, a joint authority, an economic prosperity board, a combined authority, a joint waste authority, and the London Fire and Emergency Planning Authority shall each be treated—

(a)   as a local authority for the purposes of sections 111 to 119, 128 to 131, 135, 136, 139 (except subsections (1)(b) and (2)), 140, 140A, 140C, 143 and 146 above; and

(b)   as a principal council for the purposes of section 120 (except subsection (1)(b)) and sections 121 to 123 above.

(1ZA) In its application by virtue of subsection (1) to an economic prosperity board, section 111 has effect as if it did not permit the borrowing of money.

(1ZB) In its application by virtue of subsection (1) to a combined authority, section 111 has effect as if it permitted the borrowing of money for the purposes of the exercise by the authority of its transport functions only.

(1ZC) Neither a metropolitan county fire and rescue authority, nor the London Fire and Emergency Planning Authority, is to be treated as a local authority for the purposes of section 111 above (but see section 5A of the Fire and Rescue Services Act 2004).

(1ZD) An Integrated Transport Authority is not to be treated as a local authority for the purposes of section 111 above (but see section 102B of the Local Transport Act 2008).

(1ZE) Neither an economic prosperity board, nor a combined authority, is to be treated as a local authority for the purposes of section 111 above (but see section 113A of the Local Democracy, Economic Development and Construction Act 2009).

PART VIII

FINANCE

Expenses and receipts

150 Expenses of parish and community councils

(2) In a parish having a separate parish council or in a community having a council, whether separate or common, the expenses of the parish meeting or any community meeting shall be paid by the parish or community council.

(3) In a community not having a community council, whether separate or common, the expenses of any community meeting shall be paid by the council of the principal area in which the community is situated.

(5) Every cheque or other order for the payment of money by a parish or community council shall be signed by two members of the council.

(6) Every parish or community council and the chairman of the parish meeting for a parish not having a separate parish council shall keep such accounts as may be prescribed of the receipts and payments of the council or parish meeting, as the case may be.

(7) References in this section to the expenses of a parish or community meeting include references to the expenses of any poll consequent on a parish or community meeting.

151 Financial administration

Without prejudice to section 111 above, every local authority shall make arrangements for the proper administration of their financial affairs and shall secure that one of their officers has responsibility for the administration of those affairs.

152 Revenues from undertakings

Nothing in sections 147 to 150 above shall be construed as requiring or authorising a local authority to apply or dispose of the surplus revenue arising from any undertaking carried on by them otherwise than in accordance with any enactment or instrument applicable to the undertaking.

Miscellaneous provisions as to finance and rating

168 Local financial returns

(1) Subject to subsection (3) below, every local authority and the chairman of the parish meeting of every parish not having a separate parish council shall make a return to the Secretary of State for each year ending on 31st March, or such other day as the Secretary of State may direct,—

    (a)   of their income and expenditure or, in the case of the chairman of a parish meeting, the income and expenditure of the parish meeting;

   . . .

(2) Returns under this section shall be in such form, shall contain such particulars, shall be submitted to the Secretary of State by such date in each year and shall be certified in such manner as the Secretary of State may direct, and a direction under this subsection may impose different requirements in relation to returns of different classes.

(3) If it appears to the Secretary of State that sufficient information about any of the matters mentioned in subsection (1) above has been supplied to him by a local authority or by or on behalf of a parish meeting under any other enactment, he may exempt the authority or the chairman of the meeting from all or any of the requirements of this section so far as they relate to that matter.

  . . .

Allowances to members of local authorities and other bodies

173 Attendance allowance and financial loss allowance

(1) Subject to subsection (6) below, any member of a parish or community council who is a councillor shall be entitled to receive a payment by way of attendance allowance, that is to say, a payment for the performance of any approved duty, being a payment of such reasonable amount, not exceeding the prescribed amount, as the parish or community council may determine unless a notice under section 173A below is effective in relation to him.

(2) The amount prescribed under subsection (1) above may be prescribed by reference to any period of twenty-four hours.

(3) The amount of any allowance determined by a parish or community council under subsection (1) above may vary according to the time of day and the duration of the duty, but shall be the same for all members of the council entitled to the allowance in respect of a duty of any description at the same time of day and of the same duration.

(4) Subject to subsection (6) below, any member of a parish or community council who is not entitled under subsection (1) above to receive attendance allowance for the performance of an approved duty shall be entitled to receive a payment by way of

financial loss allowance, that is to say, a payment not exceeding the prescribed amount in respect of any loss of earnings necessarily suffered, or any additional expenses (other than expenses on account of travelling or subsistence) necessarily suffered or incurred by him for the purpose of enabling him to perform that duty.

(6)   A member of a parish or community council shall not be entitled to any payment under this section in respect of the performance as such a member of an approved duty within the parish or community or, in the case of a parish or community grouped under a common parish or community council, the area of the group.

173A Right to opt for financial loss allowance

(1)   If a councillor gives notice in writing to the parish or community council of which he is a member that he wishes to receive financial loss allowance, he shall be entitled, subject to and in accordance with the following provisions of this section, to receive that allowance instead of any payment by way of attendance allowance to which he would otherwise be entitled.

(2)   A notice under this section is referred to in this section as a 'financial loss allowance notice'.

(3)   If a councillor gives a financial loss allowance notice to the parish or community council not later than the end of the period of one month beginning with the day of his election as a member of the council then, subject to subsection (4A) below, he shall be entitled to receive financial loss allowance for the performance of any approved duty since his election, whether performed before or after the giving of the notice.

(4)   If a councillor gives a financial loss allowance notice to the parish or community council otherwise than in accordance with subsection (3) above, then, subject to subsection (4A) below, he shall be entitled to receive financial loss allowance for the performance of any approved duty after the end of the period of one month beginning with the day on which the notice is given.

(4A)   If a councillor who has given a parish or community council a financial loss allowance notice gives them notice in writing that he withdraws that notice, it shall not have effect in relation to any duty performed after the day on which the notice of withdrawal is given.

174 Travelling allowance and subsistence allowance

(1)   Subject to subsections (2) and (3) below, a member of a body to which this section applies shall be entitled to receive payments by way of travelling allowance or subsistence allowance where expenditure on travelling (whether inside or outside the United Kingdom) or, as the case may be, on subsistence is necessarily incurred by him for the purpose of enabling him to perform any approved duty as a member of that body, being payments at rates determined by that body, but not exceeding, in the case of travel or subsistence for the purpose of an approved duty within the United Kingdom, such rates as may be specified by the Secretary of State.

(2)   A member of a parish or community council shall not be entitled to any payment under this section in respect of the performance as such a member of an approved duty within the parish or community or, in the case of a parish or community grouped under a common parish or community council, the area of the group.

175 Allowances for attending conferences and meetings

(1)   The following bodies, that is to say—

> (a)   *any local authority;*
> (b)   *any other body to which this section applies and which has power by virtue of any enactment to send representatives to any conference or meeting to which this section applies;*

may pay any member of the authority or other body attending any such conference or meeting such allowances in the nature of an attendance allowance and an allowance for travelling and subsistence, as they think fit.

(1A)   Payments made under subsection (1) above shall be of such reasonable amounts as the body in question may determine in a particular case or class of case but shall not exceed—

 (a) in the case of payments of an allowance in the nature of an attendance allowance, such amounts as may be specified in or determined under regulations made by the Secretary of State; and

 (b) in the case of payments of an allowance in the nature of an allowance for travel and subsistence in respect of a conference or meeting held in the United Kingdom, such amounts as may be specified under section 174 above for the corresponding allowance under that section;

and regulations made by the Secretary of State may make it a condition of any payment mentioned in paragraph (a) above that, in the financial year to which the payment would relate, the aggregate amount which the body in question has paid or is already liable to pay in respect of any prescribed allowance or allowances does not exceed such maximum amount as may be specified in or determined under the regulations.

(2)   Where a body mentioned in subsection (1)(b) above has power under any enactment other than this Act or any instrument under such an enactment to pay expenses incurred in attending a conference or meeting to which this section applies, the amount payable under that enactment or instrument shall not exceed the amount which would be payable in respect of the attendance under that subsection.

(3)   In relation to a local authority this section applies to a conference or meeting held inside or outside the United Kingdom and convened by any person or body (other than a person or body convening it in the course of a trade or business or a body the objects of which are wholly or partly political) for the purpose of discussing matters which in their opinion relate to the interests of their area or any part of it or the interests of the inhabitants of their area or any part of it.

(3B)   In relation to the London Fire and Emergency Planning Authority, a joint waste authority, an economic prosperity board, a combined authority or any [body which is a joint board, joint authority or other combined body all the members of which are representatives of local authorities] this section applies to a conference or meeting held and convened as mentioned in subsection (3) above for the purpose of discussing matters which in the body's opinion relate—

 (a) to the functions of the body; or

 (b) to any functions of local authorities in which the body has an interest.

(4)   In relation to any other body to which this section applies this section applies to a conference or meeting convened by one or more such bodies or by an association of such bodies.

176 Payment of expenses of official and courtesy visits, etc

(1)   Subject to subsection (2) below, a local authority may—

 (a) defray any travelling or other expenses reasonably incurred by or on behalf of any members in making official and courtesy visits, whether inside or outside the United Kingdom, on behalf of the authority;

 (b) defray any expenses incurred in the reception and entertainment by way of official courtesy of distinguished persons visiting the area of the authority and persons representative of or connected with local government or other public services whether inside or outside the United Kingdom and in the supply of information to any such persons.

(2)   In the case of a visit within the United Kingdom, the amount defrayed under this section by a local authority in respect of the expenses of any member of the authority in making a visit within the United Kingdom shall not exceed the payments which he would have been entitled to receive by way of travelling allowance or subsistence allowance under section 174 above if the making of the visit had been an approved duty of that member.

(3) In this section "local authority" includes a joint authority, an economic prosperity board, a combined authority, a joint waste authority and the London Fire and Emergency Planning Authority

177 Provisions supplementary to sections 173 to 176
(1) Sections 174 and 175 above apply—
   . . .
     (c)   to any parish or community council.
. . .
(2) In sections 173 to 176 above 'approved duty', in relation to a member of a body, means such duties as may be specified in or determined under regulations made by the Secretary of State.
(3) For the purposes of sections 173 to 176 above a member of a committee or sub-committee of a local authority or other body mentioned in subsection (1) above shall be deemed to be a member of that body.
(4) Section 94(5) above shall apply in relation to a member of any body mentioned in subsection (1) above to whom it would not otherwise apply as it applies in relation to a member of a local authority; and no other enactment or instrument shall prevent a member of any such body from taking part in the consideration or determination of any allowance or other payment under any of the provisions of sections 173 to 176 above or under any scheme made by virtue of section 18 of the Local Government and Housing Act 1989.

178 Regulations as to allowances
(1) The Secretary of State may make regulations as to the manner in which sections 173 to 176 above are to be administered, and in particular, and without prejudice to the generality of the foregoing provision, may make regulations—
     (a)   providing for the avoidance of duplication in payments under those sections, or between payments under any of those sections and any other Act, and for the determination of the body or bodies by whom any payments under those sections are to be made, and, where such payments are to be made by more than one body, for the apportionment between those bodies of the sums payable;
     (b)   specifying the forms to be used and the particulars to be provided for the purpose of claiming payments under those sections;
     (c)   providing for the publication by a body to which sections 173 to 175 above apply, in the minutes of that body or otherwise, of details of such payments.
(2) A statutory instrument containing regulations under section 173 or 177 above or this section shall be subject to annulment in pursuance of a resolution of either House of Parliament.

PART IX

FUNCTIONS

General

179 General provision for transfer of functions
(1)–(3) [Substitution of references to new counties and districts for pre-1973 legislative references to administrative counties and urban districts.]
(4) In any such provision any reference to a rural parish (whether as such or as a parish) or the council or meeting of such a parish, or any reference which is to be construed as such a reference, shall, except where it is a reference to a specified parish or its council or meeting, be construed—

- (a) as respects England, as a reference to a parish or, as the case may be, its council or meeting; and
- (b) as respects Wales, as a reference to a community or, as the case may be, its council, if any.

The environment

187 Local highway authorities and maintenance powers of district councils

(3) With respect to footpaths, bridleways and restricted byways within their area a district council or, where they are not the highway authority, a Welsh principal council shall have—

- (a) the like powers as a highway authority under section 57(3) of the National Parks and Access to the Countryside Act 1949 (prosecution of offences of displaying on footpaths notices deterring public use), and

(3A) 'Restricted byway' has the same meaning as in Part 2 of the Countryside and Rights of Way Act 2000.

189 Commons

(3) The references in section 12 of the Inclosure Act 1857 (prevention of nuisances in town and village greens, etc) to a churchwarden or overseer of the parish in which the town or village green or land is situated shall be construed—

- (a) with respect to a green or land in a parish, as references to the parish council, or, where there is no parish council, the parish meeting;
- (b) with respect to a green or land in a community where there is a community council, as references to the community council;
- (c) with respect to any other green or land, as references to the council of the district or Welsh principal area in which the green or land is situated;

and where those references fall to be construed in accordance with paragraph (c) above, the reference in the said section 12 to highways in the parish shall be construed as a reference to highways in the district or (as the case may be) area.

Miscellaneous functions

210 Charities

(1) Where, immediately before 1st April 1974, any property is held, as sole trustee, exclusively for charitable purposes by an existing local authority for an area outside Greater London, other than the parish council, parish meeting or representative body of an existing rural parish in England (but including the corporation of a borough included in a rural district), that property shall vest (on the same trusts) in a new local authority in accordance with subsections (2) to (5) below.

(2) Subject to subsection (3) below, where the property is held by one of the existing authorities specified below, and is so held for the benefit of, or of the inhabitants of, or of any particular class or body of persons in, a specified area, the property shall vest in the new authority specified below, the area of which comprises the whole or the greater part of that specified area, and where the property is so held but is not held for such a benefit, it shall vest in the new authority specified below, the area of which comprises the whole or the greater part of the area of the existing authority, that is to say—

- (a) where the existing authority is a county council, the new authority is the council of the new county;
- (b) where the existing authority is the council of a borough or urban district in England, the new authority is the council of the parish constituted under Part V of Schedule 1 to this Act or, where there is no such parish, the council of the district;

    (c)   where the existing authority is the council of a borough or urban district in Wales, the new authority is the council of the community or, where there is no such council, the council of the district; and

    (d)   where the existing authority is a rural district council, then, if the rural district is co-extensive with a parish, the new authority is the parish council, and in any other case the new authority is the council of the district.

(4) Where the property is held by the corporation of a borough included in a rural district, it shall vest in the parish council for the parish consisting of the area of the existing borough.

(5) Where the property is held by the parish council, parish meeting or representative body of an existing rural parish in Wales, then—

    (a)   in the case of property held by an existing parish council, the property shall vest in the community council for the community or group of communities, the area or areas of which are co-extensive with the area of the parish or parishes for which the existing parish council act;

    (b)   in the case of property held by the parish meeting or representative body of an existing parish the area of which is comprised in a community for which there is a community council, the property shall vest in that community council; and

    (c)   in any other case, the property shall vest in the council of the district which comprises the area of the existing rural parish.

(6) Where, immediately before 1st April 1974, any power with respect to a charity, not being a charity incorporated under the Companies Acts or by charter, is under the trusts of the charity or by virtue of any enactment vested in, or in the holder of an office connected with, any existing local authority to which subsection (1) above applies, that power shall vest in, or in the holder of the corresponding office connected with, or (if there is no such office) the proper officer of, the corresponding new authority, that is to say, the new authority in which, had the property of the charity been vested in the existing local authority, that property would have been vested under subsections (1) to (5) above.

(7) References in subsection (6) above to a power with respect to a charity do not include references to a power of any person by virtue of being a charity trustee thereof; but where under the trusts of any charity, not being a charity incorporated under the Companies Acts or by charter, the charity trustees immediately before 1st April 1974 include either an existing local authority to which subsection (1) above applies or the holder of an office connected with such an existing local authority, those trustees shall instead include the corresponding new authority as defined in subsection (6) above or, as the case may require, the holder of the corresponding office connected with, or (if there is no such office) the proper officer of, that authority.

. . .

(11) In this section the expression 'local authority', in relation to a parish, includes a parish meeting and the representative body of a parish, and the expressions 'charitable purposes', 'charity', 'charity trustees', 'court' and 'trusts' have the same meanings as in the Charities Act 1960.

214 Cemeteries and crematoria

(1) The following authorities, that is to say, the councils of Welsh counties, county boroughs districts, London boroughs, parishes and communities, the Common Council and the parish meetings of parishes having no parish council, whether separate or common, shall be burial authorities for the purposes of, and have the functions given to them by, the following provisions of this section and Schedule 26 to this Act; and—

    (a)   the powers conferred by the Burial Acts 1852 to 1906 to provide burial grounds shall cease to be exercisable; and

(b)   any existing burial board, joint burial board or joint committee with the powers of such a board established under the Burial Act 1852 or section 53(2) of the Local Government Act 1894 or by any local statutory provision shall cease to exist.

(2)   Burial authorities may provide and maintain cemeteries whether in or outside their area.

(3)   The Secretary of State may by order make provision with respect to the management, regulation and control of the cemeteries of burial authorities and any such order may—

(a)   impose a fine for any contravention of the order; and

(b)   contain such provision amending or repealing any enactment (including any enactment in Schedule 26 to this Act) or revoking any instrument made under any enactment as appears to the Secretary of State to be necessary or proper in consequence of the order.

(4)   An order under this section may only be made after consultation with associations appearing to the Secretary of State to be representative of local authorities and with other bodies appearing to him to be concerned, and any such order shall be of no effect unless approved by a resolution of each House of Parliament.

(5)   A burial authority within the meaning of this section, other than a parish meeting, shall also be a burial authority for the purposes of the Cremation Acts 1902 and 1952.

(6)   A burial authority may contribute towards any expenses incurred by any other person in providing or maintaining a cemetery in which the inhabitants of the authority's area may be buried.

(7)   Schedule 26 to this Act shall have effect with respect to the exercise of functions of burial authorities and the management of cemeteries and crematoria and for making amendments and modifications of the enactments relating to cemeteries and crematoria.

(8)   In this section and that Schedule 'cemetery' includes a burial ground or any other place for the interment of the dead (including any part of any such place set aside for the interment of a dead person's ashes).

215   Maintenance of a closed churchyard

(1)   Subject to subsection (2) below, where outside the area subject to the Welsh Church Act 1914 a churchyard has been closed by an Order in Council, the parochial church council shall maintain it by keeping it in decent order and its walls and fences in good repair.

(2)   A parochial church council which is liable under subsection (1) above to maintain a closed churchyard may—

(a)   if the churchyard is in a parish or community having a separate parish or community council, serve a written request on that council to take over the maintenance of the churchyard;

(b)   if the churchyard is in a parish not having a separate parish council, serve such a request on the chairman of the parish meeting;

(c)   if the churchyard is in a community not having a separate community council, serve such a request on the council of the county or county borough in which the community is situated; or

(d)   if the churchyard is in England elsewhere than the City and the Temples and is not in any parish, serve such a request on the council of the district or London borough in which the churchyard is situated;

and, subject to subsection (3) below, the maintenance of the churchyard shall be taken over by the authority on whom the request is served or the parish meeting, as the case may be, three months after service of the request.

(3)   If, pursuant to subsection (2) above, a request is served on a parish or community council or the chairman of a parish meeting and, if that council or meeting so resolve

and, before the expiration of the said three months, give written notice of the resolution to the council of the district, Welsh county or (as the case may be) county borough and to the parochial church council maintaining the churchyard, the local authority to whom the notice is given, and not the parish or community council or parish meeting, shall take over the maintenance of the churchyard at the expiration of the said three months.

(4) Where before the passing of this Act a church council established under the constitution of the Church in Wales, in purported exercise of the powers conferred by section 18 of the Burial Act 1855 (maintenance of closed churchyard payable out of rates), issued a certificate with respect to a closed churchyard to a local authority, and that authority thereupon took over the maintenance of the churchyard, the authority's action shall be deemed to have been lawful for all purposes, and the authority for the time being responsible for the maintenance of the churchyard shall have the like duty with respect to its maintenance as a parochial church council elsewhere than the area subject to the Welsh Church Act 1914.

(5) In subsection (1) above, 'the area subject to the Welsh Church Act 1914' means the area in which the Church of England was disestablished by that Act.

PART XI

GENERAL PROVISIONS AS TO LOCAL AUTHORITIES

Legal proceedings

[Note: In this Part, all the sections as far as s 234 (except ss 222 and 237) have been extended so as to apply to joint authorities, and, where appropriate, to the electors of their joint area.]

222 Power of local authorities to prosecute or defend legal proceedings

(1) Where a local authority consider it expedient for the promotion or protection of the interests of the inhabitants of their area—

    (a)   they may prosecute or defend or appear in any legal proceedings and, in the case of civil proceedings, may institute them in their own name, and

    (b)   they may, in their own name, make representations in the interests of the inhabitants at any public inquiry held by or on behalf of any Minister or public body under any enactment.

. . .

223 Appearance of local authorities in legal proceedings

(1) Any member or officer of a local authority who is authorised by that authority to prosecute or defend on their behalf, or to appear on their behalf in, proceedings before a magistrates' court shall be entitled to prosecute or defend or to appear in any such proceedings, and, notwithstanding anything contained in the Solicitors Act 1974, to conduct any such proceedings although he is not a solicitor holding a current practising certificate.

(2) In this section "local authority" includes the Common Council, a joint authority, an economic prosperity board, a combined authority, a joint waste authority, the Greater London Authority, police and crime commissioner and the Mayor's Office for Policing and Crime.

Documents and notices, etc

225 Deposit of documents with proper officer of authority, etc

(1) In any case in which a document of any description is deposited with the proper officer of a local authority, or with the chairman of a parish or community council or with the chairman of a parish meeting, pursuant to the standing orders of either House

of Parliament or to any enactment or instrument, the proper officer or chairman, as the case may be, shall receive and retain the document in the manner and for the purposes directed by the standing orders or enactment or instrument, and shall make such notes or endorsements on, and give such acknowledgments and receipts in respect of, the document as may be so directed.

(2) All documents required by any enactment or instrument to be deposited with the proper officer of a parish or community shall, in the case of a parish or community not having a separate parish or community council, be deposited in England with the chairman of the parish meeting or in Wales with the proper officer of the principal council.

. . .

226 Custody of parish and community documents

(1) All specified papers of a parish or community shall—

    (a)   in the case of a parish which is co-extensive with an existing rural parish, remain in the same custody as before 1st April 1974; and

    (b)   in the case of any other parish or any community, be in the custody of the body to which the documents of that area, other than documents of a specified class, are transferred on that date;

but the parish or community council or, in the case of a parish or community not having a separate parish or community council, the parish meeting in England or the principal council in Wales may direct that any such papers shall be deposited in such custody as may be specified in the direction.

(2) Nothing in this Act shall affect the custody of registers of baptisms, marriages and burials and of all other documents containing entries wholly or partly relating to the affairs of the church, as defined by the Local Government Act 1894, or to ecclesiastical charities, as so defined, except documents directed by law to be kept with the papers of a parish or community.

(3) Any person having the custody of any documents mentioned in subsection (2) above shall have reasonable access to the papers mentioned in subsection (1) above and—

    (a)   in a parish or community having a separate parish or community council, that council;

    (b)   in any other parish, the parish meeting;

    (c)   in any other community, the principal council; and

    (d)   in any area in England not falling within paragraph (a) or (b) above, the district council, London borough council or Common Council, as the case may be;

shall have reasonable access to the documents mentioned in subsection (2) above.

(4) Any difference about the custody of or access to any documents mentioned in subsection (1) or (2) above shall, if the area is in Wales or in a metropolitan district, London borough or the City, be determined by the Secretary of State and in any other case by the county council.

(5) The council of every county or metropolitan district shall from time to time enquire into the manner in which specified papers under the control of a parish or parish meeting in their area are kept with a view to their proper preservation, and shall make such orders as they think necessary for their preservation, and those orders shall be complied with by the parish or parish meeting.

(6) Subsection (5) above shall also apply in relation to community councils but as if the functions conferred by it were functions of the principal council.

227 Provision of depositories for parish and community documents

(1) In the case of a parish or community having a separate parish or community council that council or, if they so request, the council of the district in which the parish is situated or the council of the principal area in which the community is situated, shall

provide proper depositories for all the specified papers belonging to the parish or community for which no provision is otherwise made.

(2)   In the case of a parish or community not having a separate parish or community council, the council of the district in which the parish is situated or the council of the principal area in which the community is situated shall provide proper depositories for all the specified papers under the control of the parish meeting or belonging to the community but in England only with the consent of the parish meeting of the parish.

228[1]   Inspection of documents

(1)   The minutes of proceedings of a parish or community council shall be open to the inspection of any local government elector for the area of the council and any such local government elector may make a copy of or extract from the minutes.

(2)   A local government elector for the area of a local authority may inspect and make a copy of or extract from an order for the payment of money made by the local authority.

(3)   The accounts of a local authority and of any proper officer of a local authority shall be open to the inspection of any member of the authority, and any such member may make a copy of or extract from the accounts.

(5)   Subject to any provisions to the contrary in any other enactment or instrument, a person interested in any document deposited as mentioned in section 225 above may, at all reasonable hours, inspect and make copies thereof or extracts therefrom on payment to the person having custody thereof of the sum of 10p for every such inspection, and of the further sum of 10p for every hour during which such inspection continues after the first hour.

(6)   A document directed by this section to be open to inspection shall be so open at all reasonable hours and, except where otherwise expressly provided, without payment.

(7)   If a person having the custody of any such document—

    (a)   obstructs any person entitled to inspect the document or to make a copy thereof or extract therefrom in inspecting the document or making a copy or extract,

    (b)   refuses to give copies or extracts to any person entitled to obtain copies or extracts,

he shall be liable on summary conviction to a fine not exceeding level 1 on the standard scale.

(7A)   This section shall apply to the minutes of proceedings and the accounts of a joint authority, an economic prosperity board, or a combined authority as if that authority were a local authority and as if, references to a local government elector for the area of the authority were a reference to a local government elector for any local government area in the area for which the authority is established.

(7B)   This section shall apply to the minutes of proceedings and the accounts of a joint waste authority as if that authority were a local authority; and in relation to a joint waste authority the reference to a local government elector for the area of the authority is to be construed in accordance with section 92(7B).

(8)   This section shall apply to the minutes of proceedings and to the accounts of a parish meeting as if that meeting were a parish council.

(9)   In relation to the Broads Authority, the references in this section to a local government elector for the area of the authority shall be construed as references to a local government elector for the area of any of the local authorities mentioned in section 1(3)(a) of the Norfolk and Suffolk Broads Act 1988.

---

[1]   See also LGFA 1982, ss 17 and 24.

229 Photographic copies of documents

(1) Subject to subsections (3) and (7) below, any requirement imposed by any enactment that a local authority or parish meeting shall keep a document of any description shall be satisfied by their keeping a photographic copy of the document.

(2) Subject to subsection (7) below, any requirement imposed by any enactment that a document of any description in the custody or under the control of a local authority or parish meeting shall be made available for inspection shall be satisfied by their making available for inspection a photographic copy of the document.

(3) Subsection (1) above shall not apply to any document deposited with a local authority under the Public Records Act 1958.

(4) In legal proceedings a photographic copy of a document in the custody of a local authority or parish meeting, or of a document which has been destroyed while in the custody of a local authority or parish meeting, or of any part of any such document, shall, subject to subsection (6) below, be admissible in evidence to the like extent as the original.

(5) A certificate purporting to be signed by the proper officer of the local authority, or the chairman of the parish meeting, concerned that a document is such a photographic copy as is mentioned in subsection (4) above, shall, subject to subsection (7) below, be evidence to that effect.

(6) The court before which a photographic copy is tendered in evidence in pursuance of subsection (4) above may, if the original is in existence, require its production and thereupon that subsection shall not apply to the copy.

(7) A photographic copy of a document in colour where the colours are relevant to the interpretation of the document shall not suffice for the purposes of this section unless it so distinguishes between the colours as to enable the document to be interpreted.

(8) In this section "court" and "legal proceedings" have the same meanings as in the Civil Evidence Act 1968 and "local authority" includes a joint authority, an economic prosperity board, a combined authority, a joint waste authority, a police and crime commissioner and the Mayor's Office for Policing and Crime

230 Reports and returns

(1) Every local authority, every joint board and every joint committee of local authorities shall send the Secretary of State such reports and returns, and give him such information with respect to their functions, as he may require or as may be required by either House of Parliament.

(2) In this section 'local authority' includes a joint authority and a joint waste authority.

231 Service of notices on local authorities, etc

(1) Subject to subsection (3) below, any notice, order or other document required or authorised by any enactment or any instrument made under an enactment to be given to or served on a local authority or the chairman or an officer of a local authority shall be given or served by addressing it to the local authority and leaving it at, or sending it by post to, the principal office of the authority or any other office of the authority specified by them as one at which they will accept documents of the same description as that document.

(2) Any notice, order or other document so required or authorised to be given to or served on a parish meeting, or the chairman of the parish meeting, shall be given or served by addressing it to the chairman of the parish meeting and by delivering it to him, or by leaving it at his last known address, or by sending it by post to him at that address.

(3) The foregoing provisions of this section do not apply to a document which is to be given or served in any proceedings in court, but except as aforesaid the methods of giving or serving documents provided for by those provisions are in substitution for

the methods provided for by any other enactment or any instrument made under an enactment so far as it relates to the giving or service of documents to or on a local authority, the chairman or an officer of a local authority or a parish meeting or the chairman of a parish meeting.

(4) In this section "local authority" includes a joint authority, an economic prosperity board, a combined authority, a joint waste authority, a police and crime commissioner and the Mayor's Office for Policing and Crime

232 Public notices

(1) Save as otherwise expressly provided, a public notice required to be given by a local authority shall be given—

(a) by posting the notice in some conspicuous place or places within the area of the local authority; and

(b) in such other manner, if any, as appears to the local authority to be desirable for giving publicity to the notice.

(1A) In subsection (1) above "local authority" includes a joint authority, an economic prosperity board, a combined authority, a joint waste authority, a police and crime commissioner and the Mayor's Office for Policing and Crime.

(2) This section shall apply to a public notice required to be given by the chairman of a parish meeting as it applies to public notices required to be given by a parish council.

233 Service of notices by local authorities

(1) Subject to subsection (8) below, subsections (2) to (5) below shall have effect in relation to any notice, order or other document required or authorised by or under any enactment to be given to or served on any person by or on behalf of a local authority or by an officer of a local authority.

(2) Any such document may be given to or served on the person in question either by delivering it to him, or by leaving it at his proper address, or by sending it by post to him at that address.

(3) Any such document may—

(a) in the case of a body corporate, be given to or served on the secretary or clerk of that body;

(b) in the case of a partnership, be given to or served on a partner or a person having the control or management of the partnership business.

(4) For the purposes of this section and of section 26 of the Interpretation Act 1889 (service of documents by post) in its application to this section, the proper address of any person to or on whom a document is to be given or served shall be his last known address, except that—

(a) in the case of a body corporate or their secretary or clerk, it shall be the address of the registered or principal office of that body;

(b) in the case of a partnership or a person having the control or management of the partnership business, it shall be that of the principal office of the partnership;

and for the purposes of this subsection the principal office of a company registered outside the United Kingdom or of a partnership carrying on business outside the United Kingdom shall be their principal office within the United Kingdom.

(5) If the person to be given or served with any document mentioned in subsection (1) above has specified an address within the United Kingdom other than his proper address within the meaning of subsection (4) above as the one at which he or someone on his behalf will accept documents of the same description as that document, that address shall also be treated for the purposes of this section and section 26 of the Interpretation Act 1889 as his proper address.

(7) If the name or address of any owner, lessee or occupier of land to or on whom any document mentioned in subsection (1) above is to be given or served cannot after reasonable inquiry be ascertained, the document may be given or served either by

leaving it in the hands of a person who is or appears to be resident or employed on the land or by leaving it conspicuously affixed to some building or object on the land.

(8)   This section shall apply to a document required or authorised by or under any enactment to be given to or served on any person by or on behalf of the chairman of a parish meeting as it applies to a document so required or authorised to be given to or served on any person by or on behalf of a local authority.

(9)   The foregoing provisions of this section do not apply to a document which is to be given or served in any proceedings in court.

(10)   Except as aforesaid and subject to any provision of any enactment or instrument excluding the foregoing provisions of this section, the methods of giving or serving documents which are available under those provisions are in addition to the methods which are available under any other enactment or any instrument made under any enactment.

(11)   In this section "local authority" includes a joint authority, an economic prosperity board, a combined authority, a joint waste authority, a police and crime commissioner and the Mayor's Office for Policing and Crime.

234   Authentication of documents

(1)   Any notice, order or other document which a local authority are authorised or required by or under any enactment (including any enactment in this Act) to give, make or issue may be signed on behalf of the authority by the proper officer of the authority.

(2)   Any document purporting to bear the signature of the proper officer of the authority shall be deemed, until the contrary is proved, to have been duly given, made or issued by the authority of the local authority.

   In this subsection the word 'signature' includes a facsimile of a signature by whatever process reproduced.

(3)   Where any enactment or instrument made under an enactment makes, in relation to any document or class of documents, provision with respect to the matters dealt with by one of the two foregoing subsections, that subsection shall not apply in relation to that document or class of documents.

(4)   In this section "local authority" includes a joint authority, an economic prosperity board, a combined authority, a joint waste authority, a police and crime commissioner and the Mayor's Office for Policing and Crime.

Byelaws

235   Power of councils to make byelaws for good rule and government and suppression of nuisances

(1)   The council of a district the council of a principal area in Wales and the council of a London borough may make byelaws for the good rule and government of the whole or any part of the district principal area or borough, as the case may be, and for the prevention and suppression of nuisances therein.

(2)   The confirming authority in relation to byelaws made under this section shall be the Secretary of State.

(3)   Byelaws shall not be made under this section for any purpose as respects any area if provision for that purpose as respects that area is made by, or is or may be made under, any other enactment.

236   Procedure, etc, for byelaws

(1)   Subject to subsection (2) below, the following provisions of this section shall apply to byelaws to be made by a local authority under this Act and to byelaws made by a local authority, the Greater London Authority, Transport for London, an Integrated Transport Authority for an integrated transport area in England or a

combined authority under any other enactment and conferring on the authority a power to make byelaws and for which specific provision is not otherwise made.
. . .

(3) Subject to subsection (3A) below, the byelaws shall be made under the common seal of the authority, or, in the case of byelaws made by a parish or community council not having a seal, under the hands and seals of two members of the council, and shall not have effect until they are confirmed by the confirming authority.

(3A) Byelaws made by the Greater London Authority shall be made under the hand of the Mayor and shall not have effect until they are confirmed by the confirming authority.

(4) At least one month before application for confirmation of the byelaws is made, notice of the intention to apply for confirmation shall be given in one or more local newspapers circulating in the area to which the byelaws are to apply.

(5) For at least one month before application for confirmation is made, a copy of the byelaws shall be deposited at the offices of the authority by whom the byelaws are made, and shall at all reasonable hours be open to public inspection without payment.

(6) The authority by whom the byelaws are made shall, on application, furnish to any person a copy of the byelaws, or of any part thereof on payment of such sum, not exceeding 10p for every hundred words contained in the copy, as the authority may determine.

(7) The confirming authority may confirm, or refuse to confirm, any byelaw submitted under this section for confirmation, and may fix the date on which the byelaw is to come into operation and if no date is so fixed the byelaw shall come into operation at the expiration of one month from the date of its confirmation.

(8) A copy of the byelaws, when confirmed, shall be printed and deposited at the offices of the authority by whom the byelaws are made, and shall at all reasonable hours be open to public inspection without payment, and a copy thereof shall, on application, be furnished to any person on payment of such sum, not exceeding 20p for every copy, as the authority may determine.

(9) The proper officer of a district council or in Wales of a principal council shall send a copy of every byelaw made by the council, and confirmed, to the proper officer of the council, whether separate or common, of every parish or community to which they apply or, in the case of a parish not having a council, to the chairman of the parish meeting, and the proper officer of the parish or community council or chairman of the parish meeting, as the case may be, shall cause a copy to be deposited with the public documents of the parish or community.

A copy so deposited shall at all reasonable hours be open to public inspection without payment.

(10) The proper officer of a county council shall send a copy of every byelaw made by the council, and confirmed, to the council of every district in the county, and the proper officer of the council of a district shall send a copy of every byelaw made by the council, and confirmed, to the council of the county.

(10A) Subsection (10) above does not apply to a principal council in Wales.
. . .

(11) In this section the expression 'the confirming authority' means the authority or person, if any, specified in the enactment (including any enactment in this Act) under which the byelaws are made, or in any enactment incorporated therein or applied thereby, as the authority or person by whom the byelaws are to be confirmed, or if no authority or person is so specified, means the Secretary of State.

237 Offences against byelaws
Byelaws to which section 236 above applies may provide that persons contravening the byelaws shall be liable on summary conviction to a fine not exceeding such sum as may be fixed by the enactment conferring the power to make the byelaws, or, if no sum is so fixed, the sum of £20, and in the case of a continuing offence a further fine not

exceeding such sum as may be fixed as aforesaid, or, if no sum is so fixed, the sum of £5 for each day during which the offence continues after conviction thereof.

23ZA Offences against byelaws
A byelaw made under section 235 may include provision for or in connection with—

(a)   the seizure and retention of any property in connection with any contravention of the byelaw, and

(b)   the forfeiture of any such property on a person's conviction of an offence of contravention of the byelaw.

238 Evidence of byelaws
The production of a printed copy of a byelaw purporting to be made by a local authority, the Greater London Authority, an Integrated Transport Authority for an integrated transport area in England or a combined authority upon which is endorsed a certificate purporting to be signed by the proper officer of the authority stating—

(a)   that the byelaw was made by the authority;

(b)   that the copy is a true copy of the byelaw;

(c)   that on a specified date the byelaw was confirmed by the authority named in the certificate or, as the case may require, was sent to the Secretary of State and has not been disallowed;

(d)   the date, if any, fixed by the confirming authority for the coming into operation of the byelaw;

shall be prima facie evidence of the facts stated in the certificate, and without proof of the handwriting or official position of any person purporting to sign the certificate.

Miscellaneous provisions

239 Power to promote or oppose local or personal Bills
(1)   Subject to the provisions of this Act, where a local authority, other than a parish or community council, are satisfied that it is expedient to promote, or any local authority are satisfied that it is expedient to oppose, any local or personal Bill in Parliament, the local authority may, but only in accordance with the procedure hereinafter provided by this section, promote or oppose the Bill accordingly, and may defray the expenses incurred in relation thereto.

(2)   A resolution of a local authority to promote or oppose a Bill under subsection (1) above shall be—

(a)   passed by a majority of the whole number of the members of the authority at a meeting of the authority held after the requisite notice of the meeting and of its purpose has been given by advertisement in one or more local newspapers circulating in the area of the authority, such notice being given in addition to the ordinary notice required to be given for the convening of a meeting of the authority;

. . .

(3)   For the purposes of subsection (2) above the requisite notice is thirty clear days' notice in the case of promotion of a Bill and ten clear days' notice in the case of opposition to a Bill.

(4)   The power conferred on a local authority by subsection (1) above shall be in substitution for any power conferred on that authority by a local Act.

(4A)   The powers conferred on a local authority by subsection (1) above shall also be exercisable by a joint authority, an economic prosperity board, a combined authority and a joint waste authority

(5)   No payment shall be made by an authority to a member of the authority for acting as counsel or agent in promoting or opposing a Bill under this section.

240 Provisional orders and orders subject to special parliamentary procedure

(1)   Where the Secretary of State is authorised to make a provisional order under this Act or any enactment passed on or after 1st June 1934 (being the date of commencement of the 1933 Act), the following provisions shall have effect—

(a)   before a provisional order is made, notice of the purport of the application for the order shall be given by the applicants by advertisement in the London Gazette and in one or more local newspapers circulating in the area to which the order will relate;

(b)   the Secretary of State shall consider any objections to the application which may be made by any persons affected thereby and shall, unless he considers that for special reasons an inquiry is unnecessary, cause a local inquiry to be held, of which notice shall be given in such manner as the Secretary of State may direct and at which all persons interested shall be permitted to attend and make objections;

(c)   the Secretary of State may submit the provisional order to Parliament for confirmation, and the order shall have no effect until it is confirmed by Parliament;

(d)   if while the Bill for the confirmation of the order is pending in either House of Parliament a petition is presented against the order, the petitioner shall be allowed to appear before the Select Committee to which the Bill is referred, and oppose the order, as in the case of a private Bill.

(2)   The reasonable costs incurred by a local authority in promoting or opposing a provisional order, and of the preliminary inquiry, or in supporting or opposing a Bill to confirm a provisional order, as sanctioned by the Secretary of State, shall be deemed to be expenses properly incurred by the local authority interested or affected by the order and shall be paid accordingly, and a local authority may borrow for the purpose of defraying any such costs.

(3)   Where the Secretary of State is authorised to make an order under this Act which is subject to special parliamentary procedure or an order under any enactment passed on or after 1st June 1934 which is so subject by virtue of section 8(3) of the Statutory Orders (Special Procedure) Act 1945, the following provisions shall have effect—

(a)   before the order is made, notice of the purport of the application for the order shall be given by the applicants by advertisement in the London Gazette and in one or more local newspapers circulating in the area to which the order will relate;

(b)   the Secretary of State shall consider any objections to the application which may be made by any persons affected thereby and shall, unless he considers that for special reasons an inquiry is unnecessary, cause a local inquiry to be held, of which notice shall be given in such manner as he may direct and at which all persons interested shall be permitted to attend and make objections.

(4)   Any order mentioned in subsection (1) or (3) above may repeal, revoke, modify or amend any Act confirming a provisional order or any order which has been subject to parliamentary procedure.

(5)   At any time before submitting any order mentioned in subsection (1) or (3) above to Parliament, the Secretary of State may revoke the order, either wholly or in part.

(6)   The making of any order mentioned in subsection (1) or (3) above shall be prima facie evidence that all the requirements of this section and any other enactment with respect to the steps to be taken before the making of the order have been complied with.

(7)   Subsections (3) to (6) above shall be included among the enactments which may be adapted or modified by an Order in Council under section 8(3) of the Statutory Orders (Special Procedure) Act 1945.

242 Effect of inaccurate description

No misnomer or inaccurate description of any person or place named in any voting paper or notice relating to an election under Part I or II of this Act shall affect its full operation with respect to that person or place, in any case where the description of the person or place is such as to be commonly understood.

243 Computation of time and timing of elections, etc

(1) Where the day or the last day on which anything is required or permitted to be done by or by virtue of any provision to which this subsection applies is a Sunday, day of the Christmas break, of the Easter break or of a bank holiday break or a day appointed for public thanksgiving or mourning, the requirement or permission shall be deemed to relate to the first day thereafter which is not one of the days specified above.

(2) Subsection (1) above applies to any provision of this Act or of an instrument under this Act, except a provision in Part IX or X or a provision of rules under paragraph 18 or 34 of Schedule 12 to this Act and applies also to sections 31 and 32 of the Local Government Act 1985.

(3) Where under subsection (4) below the day of a poll consequent on a parish or community meeting is postponed, the day to which it is postponed shall be treated for the purposes of this Act as the day of the poll.

(4) In computing any period of time for the purpose of any rules mentioned in subsection (2) above or for the purposes of 89(1) above any day specified in subsection (1) above shall be disregarded, but where between the giving of a notice of the poll and the completion of the poll a day is declared to be a bank holiday or day of public thanksgiving or mourning, the foregoing provision, so far as it relates to any such rules, shall not operate to invalidate any act which would have been valid apart from that provision.

(5) Subsection (4) above, so far as it relates to any such rules, shall have effect subject to the provisions of those rules.

PART XII

MISCELLANEOUS AND GENERAL

Status, etc

245 Status of certain districts, parishes and communities

. . .

(6) The council of a parish which is not grouped with any other parish may resolve that the parish shall have the status of a town and thereupon—

    (a)   the council of the parish shall bear the name of the council of the town;

    (b)   the chairman and vice-chairman of the council shall be respectively entitled to the style of town mayor and deputy town mayor;

    (c)   the parish meeting shall have the style of town meeting.

(7) A resolution under subsection (6) above shall cease to have effect if the parish to which it relates ceases to exist.

(7A) A resolution under subsection (6) shall cease to have effect if the parish has an alternative style (within the meaning of section 17A) by virtue of any of the following—

    (a)   an order under section 11;

    (b)   a resolution under section 12A;

    (c)   an order under section 86 of the Local Government and Public Involvement in Health Act 2007.

(8) If a parish council which has passed a resolution under subsection (6) above is dissolved without the parish ceasing to exist, the dissolution shall not affect the status

of the parish or the application to it of paragraph (c) of that subsection and in England the parish trustees shall have the style of town trustees.

(9) A parish council by whom a resolution under subsection (6) above has been passed or, if the council has been dissolved, the parish meeting in England may resolve that the parish shall cease to have the status of a town and thereupon subsection (6)(a) to (c) above and subsection (8) above shall cease to apply to the parish.

(10) The foregoing provisions of this section shall have effect subject to any provision made by a grant under Her Majesty's prerogative and, in particular, to any such provision granting the status of a city or royal borough or conferring the style of lord mayor, deputy lord mayor or right honourable.

245A Change of status of Welsh county to county borough

(1) Where a petition is presented to Her Majesty by the council of a county in Wales praying for the grant of a charter under this section, Her Majesty, on the advice of Her Privy Council, may by charter confer on that county the status of a county borough.

(2) No such petition shall be presented unless a resolution of the council has been passed by not less than two-thirds of the members voting at a meeting of the council specially convened for the purpose.

(3) No charter under this section shall take effect before 1st April 1996.

(4) A county borough which has acquired that status by a charter under this section—

    (a)   shall be a county borough; but

    (b)   shall not be treated as a borough for the purposes of any Act passed before 1st April 1974.

(5) This section shall have effect subject to any provision made by a grant under Her Majesty's prerogative and, in particular, to any provision granting the status of a royal borough or conferring any style on any person.

245B Community having the status of a town

(1) The council of a community which is not grouped with any other community may, subject to subsection (3) below, resolve that the community shall have the status of a town.

(2) Where a community has the status of a town—

    (a)   the town council shall have the name of the community with the addition—

        (i)   in English, of the words 'Town Council'; and

        (ii)   in Welsh, of the words 'Cyngor Tref';

    (b)   the chairman of the town council shall be entitled to the style of 'town mayor' or 'maer y dref'; and

    (c)   the vice-chairman of the town council shall be entitled to the style of 'deputy town mayor' or 'dirprwy faer y dref'.

(3) Where the provisions of section 27(4) above apply in relation to a community, the council of that community shall not pass a resolution under subsection (1) above unless it is satisfied that those provisions have been complied with in relation to the community.

(4) Any such resolution shall cease to have effect if the community to which it relates ceases to exist.

(5) If a community council which has passed such a resolution is dissolved without the community ceasing to exist, the dissolution shall not affect the status of the community.

(6) A community council by whom a resolution has been passed under subsection (1) above or, if the council has been dissolved, a community meeting of the community may resolve that the resolution shall cease to have effect.

(7) On the passing of a resolution under subsection (6) above, the community shall cease to have the status of a town.

(8)   This section shall have effect subject to any provision made by a grant under Her Majesty's prerogative and, in particular, to any provision conferring any style on any person.

246 Preservation of powers, privileges and rights of existing cities or boroughs

(1)   Any privileges or rights belonging immediately before 1st April 1974 to the citizens or burgesses of an existing city or borough shall belong on and after that date to the inhabitants of the area of the existing city or borough.

(2)   A charter granted by Her Majesty under section 245 above with respect to a district may—

(a)   provide that any powers to appoint local officers of dignity exercisable immediately before 1st April 1974 by the corporation of an existing city or borough, the area of which becomes wholly or partly comprised by virtue of Part I or II of this Act in the district being powers which are not exercised pursuant to subsection (4) or (5) below by charter trustees, shall be exercisable on the coming into force of the charter by the council of the district in relation to the whole or any part of the district;

(b)   provide that any privileges or rights belonging immediately before 1st April 1974 to the citizens or burgesses of any such city or borough for which charter trustees are not constituted pursuant to subsection (4) or (5) below shall belong on the coming into force of the charter to the inhabitants of the whole or any part of the district;

(c)   contain such incidental, consequential or supplementary provision as may appear to Her Majesty to be necessary or proper in connection with the aforesaid matters.

(2A)   Any powers to appoint local officers of dignity exercisable immediately before 1st April 1996 in relation to any area by the council of a district in Wales by virtue of a charter granted under section 245 above shall, on and after that date, be exercisable in relation to that area by the council of the principal area in which, on that date, that area becomes comprised.

(2B)   Where on 1st April 1996 that area becomes comprised partly in each of two or more principal areas, those powers shall be exercised on and after that date by such of the councils of those principal areas as may be agreed between them, or, in default of agreement, as the Secretary of State may designate.

(3)   Where by virtue of Part I or II of this Act, the area of an existing city or borough on 1st April 1974 becomes a parish in England or becomes a community in Wales having a separate community council, any powers to appoint local officers of dignity exercisable immediately before that date by the corporation of the city or borough shall be exercisable on and after that date by the parish or community council.

(4)   Where by virtue of Part I or II of this Act the area of an existing city or borough on 1st April 1974 becomes wholly comprised in a district not having the status, or entitled to the style, of a borough by virtue of subsection (1) or (4) of section 245 above and that city or borough does not on that date become a parish in England or a community in Wales having a separate community council—

(a)   there shall as from that date be a body corporate by the name of 'the Charter Trustees of the City' or 'the Charter Trustees of the Town', as the case may be, with the addition of the name of the existing city or borough, consisting of the district councillors for the wards wholly or partly comprising the area of the city or borough or, if the number of those councillors is less than three, consisting of those councillors and such number of local government electors for that area appointed by the district council as will make the number of charter trustees up to three;

(b)   the charter trustees may in every year elect one of their number to be city or town mayor and another to be deputy city or town mayor; and

(c)   any powers to appoint local officers of dignity exercisable immediately before that date by the corporation of the city or borough shall be exercisable on and after that date by the charter trustees.

(5) Where by virtue of Part I of this Act part of the area of an existing city or borough in England on 1st April 1974—

(a)   becomes a parish; or

(b)   becomes comprised in a district not having the status, or entitled to the style, of a borough by virtue of subsection (1) or (4) of section 245 above and does not become a parish;

the Secretary of State may by order provide that subsection (3) or (4) above, as the case may be, shall apply to that part of that area, but if the order so provides with the substitution for the name of the existing city or borough in question of a name specified in the order.

(6) Subsections (1) and (3) above and any order applying subsection (3) made pursuant to subsection (5) above shall have effect subject to subsection (2A) above, any provision made by a grant under Her Majesty's prerogative or any provision of a charter granted by Her Majesty under section 245 above and any other provision of this Act or an instrument thereunder, and a charter under subsection (2) above shall have effect subject to any provision made by any such grant or any other provision of this Act or an instrument thereunder.

(8) If an area or part of an area for which charter trustees have been constituted under subsection (4) above becomes, or becomes comprised in, a parish or a separate community council is established for a community consisting of such an area, that subsection shall cease to apply to the area or part and accordingly the charter trustees shall cease to act therefor.

(9) Where charter trustees have been constituted for an area which is altered by an order under Part IV of this Act and subsection (8) does not apply in relation to the alteration, the order may make such provision with respect to the charter trustees as may appear to the Secretary of State to be appropriate.

(10) The sums required to meet the expenses of charter trustees shall be chargeable on, but only on, the area for which the charter trustees act, and for the purpose of obtaining those sums the charter trustees shall issue precepts to the council of the district in which that area is situated.

(11) Where the amount of the income received by charter trustees in any year from their property exceeds any expenditure incurred in connection with that property, they shall pay the excess to the rating authority for the rating area in which the area for which the charter trustees act is situated to be credited to the last-mentioned area.

(12) Every cheque or other order for the payment of money by charter trustees shall be signed by two of them.

(13) Charter trustees shall keep such accounts as may be prescribed of their receipts and payments.

(14) Sections 15(5) and 34(5) above shall apply in relation to a city or town mayor holding office by virtue of this section as they apply to the chairman of a parish or community council.

(15) Section 168 above and section 228 above, except subsection (5), shall apply in relation to charter trustees as if the charter trustees were the council of a parish or community consisting of the area for which they act.

(16) Sections 173 to 178 above and (in relation to Wales) Part 8 of the Local Government (Wales) Measure 2011 shall apply in relation to charter trustees as if the charter trustees were the members of the council of a parish or community consisting of the area for which they act.

247 Transfer of armorial bearings from old to new authorities

(1) Subject to subsection (2) below, Her Majesty may by Order in Council authorise any new local authority specified in the Order to bear and use any armorial bearings

which may be so specified and which, immediately before 1st April 1974, were lawfully borne and used by an existing local authority which ceases to exist by virtue of section 1 or section 20 above.

(2)   An Order in Council under this section shall provide that before any armorial bearings of an existing local authority may be borne and used by a new local authority in accordance with the Order, they shall be exemplified according to the laws of arms and recorded in the College of Arms.

(3)   Subsections (1) and (2) above also apply in relation to new principal councils in Wales and authorities which ceased to exist as a result of the Local Government (Wales) Act 1994 but as if the reference to April 1, 1974 were a reference to 1st April 1996.

248   Freemen and inhabitants of existing boroughs

(1)   Subject to the following provisions of this section and Schedule 28A, nothing in this Act shall affect any person's status, or the right of any person to be admitted, as a freeman of a place which is an existing borough; and in this section and Schedule 28A any such place is referred to as a city or town.

(1A)   Where the son of a freeman of a city or town may claim to be admitted as a freeman of that place, the daughter of a freeman may likewise claim to be so admitted.

(1B)   The son or daughter of a freeman of a city or town shall be admitted as a freeman whether born before or after the admission, as a freeman, of his or her freeman parent and wherever he or she was born.

(1C)   In subsections (1A) and (1B) "freeman" excludes a freeman of the City of London.

(1D)   Schedule 28A (amendment of laws relating to freedom of city or town) shall have effect.

(2)   On and after 1st April 1974 the roll of persons admitted to the freedom of a city or town shall be kept by the proper officer of the relevant district council, that is to say, the council of the district which comprises the whole or the greater part of the city or town.

(3)   If at any time on or after 1st April 1974 any person claims to be admitted to the freedom of a city or town, the person's claim for admission shall be examined by the chairman of the relevant district council, as defined in subsection (2) above, and, if the person's claim is established, the person's name shall be entered on the roll of persons admitted to the freedom of that city or town.

(4)   After 31st March 1974—

    (a)   a person admitted to the freedom of a city or town,

    (b)   any person who by marriage, descent, employment or otherwise is or has been related to or associated with a person admitted to the freedom of a city or town, and

    (c)   any person who is or has been related by marriage to the widow or a child of a person admitted to the freedom of a city or town,

shall have and enjoy the same rights, whether in respect of property or otherwise, as were held and enjoyed on that date by a freeman of that city or town, by a person correspondingly related to or associated with such a freeman or, as the case may be, by a person correspondingly related by marriage to the widow or a child of such a freeman.

(5)   A person who is on 1st April 1974, or becomes thereafter, an inhabitant of a city or town shall, as such, have and enjoy the same rights, whether in respect of property or otherwise, as were held and enjoyed immediately before that date by an inhabitant of that city or town.

(6)   This section shall have effect in relation to Wales as if—

    (a)   in subsections (2) and (3) the references to the relevant district council were references to the relevant principal council; and

(b)   in subsection (2) the reference to the council of the district were a reference to the council of the principal area.

249 Honorary titles

(1)   A principal council may, by a resolution passed by not less than two-thirds of the members voting thereon at a meeting of the council specially convened for the purpose with notice of the object, confer the title of honorary aldermen or honorary alderwomen on persons who have, in the opinion of the council, rendered eminent services to the council as past members of that council, but who are not then members of the council.

(2)   No honorary alderman or honorary alderwoman shall, while serving as a [member] of the council, be entitled to be addressed as alderman or alderwoman or to attend or take part in any civic ceremonies of the council as an alderman or alderwoman.

(3)   Services rendered to the council of an existing county, county borough, borough or urban or rural district the area of which becomes wholly or partly included in a new county or district shall be treated for the purposes of subsection (1) above as services rendered to the council of the new county or district, as the case may be.

(4)   An honorary alderman [or honorary alderwoman] of a principal council may attend and take part in such civic ceremonies as the council may from time to time decide, but shall not, as such, have the right—

(a)   to attend meetings of the council or a committee of the council (including a joint committee upon which they are represented); or

(b)   to receive any such allowances or other payments as are payable under sections 173 to 176 above or Part 8 of the Local Government (Wales) Measure 2011.

(4A)   A principal council may spend such reasonable sum as they think fit for the purpose of presenting an address, or a casket containing an address, to a person on whom they have conferred the title of honorary alderman or honorary alderwoman.

(5)   Subject as follows, a relevant authority may admit to be honorary freemen or honorary freewomen of the place or area for which it is the authority—

(a)   persons of distinction, and

(b)   persons who have, in the opinion of the authority, rendered eminent services to that place or area.

(6)   In this section "relevant authority" means—

(a)   a principal council;

(b)   a parish or community council;

(c)   charter trustees in England constituted—

(i)   under section 246 of the Local Government Act 1972,

(ii)   by the Charter Trustees Regulations 1996 (SI 1996/263), or

(iii)   under Part 1 of the Local Government and Public Involvement in Health Act 2007.

(7)   The power in subsection (5) above is exercisable by resolution of the relevant authority.

(8)   A resolution under subsection (7) above must be passed—

(a)   at a meeting of the relevant authority which is specially convened for the purpose and where notice of the object of the meeting has been given; and

(b)   by not less than two-thirds of the members of the relevant authority (or, in the case of charter trustees, of the trustees) who vote on it.

(9)   A relevant authority may spend such reasonable sum as it thinks fit for the purpose of presenting an address or a casket containing an address to a person on whom the authority has conferred the title of honorary freeman or honorary freewoman under subsection (5) above.

(10) The admission of a person as honorary freeman or honorary freewoman does not confer on that person any of the rights referred to in section 248(4) above.

Inquiries

250 Power to direct inquiries

(1) Where any Minister is authorised by this Act to determine any difference, to make or confirm any order, to frame any scheme, or to give any consent, confirmation, sanction or approval to any matter, or otherwise to act under this Act, and where the Secretary of State is authorised to hold an inquiry, either under this Act or under any other enactment relating to the functions of a local authority, he may cause a local inquiry to be held.

(2) For the purpose of any such local inquiry, the person appointed to hold the inquiry may by summons require any person to attend, at a time and place stated in the summons, to give evidence or to produce any documents in his custody or under his control which relate to any matter in question at the inquiry, and may take evidence on oath, and for that purpose administer oaths.

Provided that—

    (a)   no person shall be required, in obedience to such summons, to attend to give evidence or to produce any such documents, unless the necessary expenses of his attendance are paid or tendered to him; and

    (b)   nothing in this section shall empower the person holding the inquiry to require the production of the title, or of any instrument relating to the title, of any land not being the property of a local authority.

(3) Every person who refuses or deliberately fails to attend in obedience to a summons issued under this section, or to give evidence, or who deliberately alters, suppresses, conceals, destroys, or refuses to produce any book or other document which he is required or is liable to be required to produce for the purposes of this section, shall be liable on summary conviction to a fine not exceeding level 3 on the standard scale or to imprisonment for a term not exceeding six months, or to both.

(4) Where a Minister causes an inquiry to be held under this section, the costs incurred by him in relation to the inquiry shall be paid by such local authority or party to the inquiry as he may direct, and the Minister may cause the amount of the costs so incurred to be certified, and any amount so certified and directed to be paid by any authority or person shall be recoverable from that authority or person by the Minister summarily as a civil debt.

(5) The Minister causing an inquiry to be held under this section may make orders as to the costs of the parties at the inquiry and as to the parties by whom the costs are to be paid, and every such order may be made a rule of the High Court on the application of any party named in the order.

(6) This section shall extend to local inquiries held by the Secretary of State under the provisions of the Local Government Act 1929 or the Ferries (Acquisition by Local Authorities) Act 1919.

General

253 Transfer of powers of certain public bodies

(1) Any functions of any such public body as is specified in subsection (2) below may with their approval be transferred by an order made by the Secretary of State to any local authority whose area comprises the district of that body, or jointly to two or more local authorities whose areas together comprise that district.

(2) This section applies to the following public bodies, that is to say, any trustees, commissioners or other persons who, for public purposes and not for their own profit,

act under any enactment or instrument for the improvement of any place, or for providing or maintaining a cemetery or market in any place.

(3) Any order under this section may contain such incidental, consequential, transitional and supplementary provision as may appear to the Secretary of State to be necessary or proper; and a statutory instrument containing an order under this section shall be subject to annulment in pursuance of a resolution of either House of Parliament.

. . .

254 Consequential and supplementary provision

(1) The Secretary of State or any appropriate Minister may at any time by order make such incidental, consequential, transitional or supplementary provision as may appear to him—

(a) to be necessary or proper for the general or any particular purposes of this Act or in consequence of any of the provisions thereof or for giving full effect thereto; or

(b) to be necessary or proper in consequence of such of the provisions of any other Act passed in the same session as this Act as apply to any area or authority affected by this Act;

and nothing in any other provision of this Act shall be construed as prejudicing the generality of this subsection.

(2) An order under this section may in particular include provision—

(a) with respect to the transfer and management or custody of property (whether real or personal) and the transfer of rights and liabilities;

(b) with respect to the membership of any body so far as that membership consists of persons elected by, or appointed by or on the nomination of, any authority affected by this Act or any two or more bodies who include such an authority;

(c) for applying with or without modifications, or amending, repealing, or revoking, with or without savings, any provision of an Act passed or an instrument under an Act made before 1st April 1974 and for making savings or additional savings from the effect of any repeal made by this Act;

(d) for any of the matters specified in section 67 above;

(e) without prejudice to paragraph (d) above, for dissolving any body corporate established by any Act passed or by any instrument under an Act made before 1st April 1974;

(h) for treating anything duly done before 1st April 1974 by any authority in the exercise of functions which on and after that date become functions of some other authority as having, from that date, been duly done by that other authority and for treating any instrument made before that date, if or so far as it was made in the exercise of those functions, as continuing in force on and after that date until varied or revoked in the exercise of those functions by that other authority;

(i) for securing the continued discharge of functions in relation to the Confederation of the Cinque Ports and its courts (including so far as is necessary for that purpose, provision for the constitution of a body to replace any existing corporation), for appropriating property or providing funds for the discharge of functions as aforesaid, and otherwise for securing that anything required or authorised to be done by, to or in relation to the Confederation or any of its courts may continue to be done.

(3) Subject to subsection (5) below any of the following things done or treated by virtue of any enactment as having been done by or to or in relation to an existing local

authority outside Greater London in connection with the discharge of any of their functions, that is to say—

    any written agreement or other instrument in writing or any determination or declaration made or treated as made by such an authority,

    any notice or direction given or treated as given by or to such an authority,

    any licence, permission, consent, approval, exemption, dispensation or relaxation granted or treated as granted by or to such an authority,

    any application, proposal or objection made or treated as made by or to such an authority,

    any condition or requirement imposed or treated as imposed by or on such an authority, or

    any appeal allowed by or in favour of or against such an authority,

shall, as from 1st April 1974, be treated as having been done by, to or in relation to the new local authority by whom those functions become exercisable on and after that date by or by virtue of this Act, and any such thing shall as from that date have effect as if any reference therein to a specified existing local authority outside Greater London by whom those functions were exercisable before that date were a reference to the new local authority by whom those functions become exercisable.

(4)   If there is any doubt as to the identity of a local authority to whom any particular functions are so transferred, that authority shall be taken to be such authority as may be specified in a direction given by a Minister of the Crown concerned with the discharge of those functions.

(5)   Subsection (3) above is without prejudice to any express provision made by, or by any instrument made under, this Act, but has effect subject to any provision to the contrary so made and in particular may be excluded from applying, either wholly or to any specified extent, in any particular case by an order made by the Secretary of State by statutory instrument.

(6)   Section 68 above shall apply for the purposes of Parts I and II, section 214(1)(b) and this Part of this Act as if any reference to an order under Part IV of this Act included a reference to any provision of Part I or II of this Act or to section 214(1)(b) of this Act or to any provision of any instrument made under Part I or II or this Part of this Act.

(7)   A local authority to whom any charters or insignia of a borough abolished by Part I or II of this Act have been transferred by virtue of subsection (2)(a) above shall if practicable preserve them in the area of the borough as it existed immediately before 1st April 1974.

(8)   An order under this section which extends the area for which any local statutory provision is in force shall be provisional only.

(9)   Any statutory instrument containing any other order under this section shall be subject to annulment in pursuance of a resolution of either House of Parliament.

262 Local Acts and instruments

(1)   Subject to subsection (2) below, any local statutory provision to which this section applies and which is not continued in force by any other provision of this Act shall—

    (a)   notwithstanding the changes of administrative areas and local authorities effected by or under this Act and, in the case of an instrument made under any enactment, notwithstanding the repeal of that enactment, continue to apply on and after 1st April 1974 to, but only to, the area, things or persons to which or to whom it applies before that date;

    (b)   have effect subject to any necessary modifications and to the modifications made by subsections (3) to (5) below;

but the continuation by this subsection of an instrument made under any enactment shall not be construed as prejudicing any power to vary or revoke the instrument which is exercisable apart from this subsection.

(2)   Subsection (1) above shall have effect subject to the provisions of—
  (a)   this Act, other than Part I of Schedule 29;
  (b)   any Act passed after this Act and before 1st April 1974; and
  (c)   any order made under section 254 above or the following provisions of this section.

(3)   Any local statutory provision to which this section applies and which relates to functions exercisable by a local authority of any description by virtue of any public general enactment shall have effect as if for any reference to the authority by whom the functions are exercised immediately before 1st April 1974 or to their area there were substituted a reference to the authority by whom those functions are exercisable on and after that date or, as the case may be, to so much of the area of the latter authority as comprises the area of the former authority or any part thereof.

(4)   In any local statutory provision to which this section applies and which does not fall within subsection (3) above—
  (a)   for any reference to an existing county or its council there shall be substituted a reference to so much of the new county or counties as comprises the area of the existing county or any part thereof or, as the case may be, the council of that new county or the councils of those new counties;
  (b)   for any reference to an existing county borough or county district or the council of either there shall be substituted a reference to so much of the new district or districts as comprises the area of the existing borough or district or any part thereof or, as the case may be, the council of that new district or the councils of those new districts.

(5)   In any local statutory provision to which this section applies which has effect in an area in Wales and which does not fall within subsection (3) above—
  (a)   for any reference to a rural parish there shall be substituted a reference to the corresponding community;
  (b)   for any reference to the council of any such parish which has a council, whether separate or common, there shall be substituted a reference to the council of the corresponding community; and
  (c)   for any reference to the parish meeting of any such parish which has no council there shall be substituted a reference to the council of the new district which comprises the corresponding community.

(6)   Subsections (3) to (5) above shall have effect subject to any provision to the contrary made by, or by any instrument made under, this Act and, without prejudice to the foregoing, the Secretary of State may by order provide for the exercise of functions conferred by any local statutory provision to which this section applies and exclude the operation of any of those subsections where it would otherwise conflict with any provision of the order.

(7)   So much of any local statutory provision—
  (a)   as confers functions on the Secretary of State with respect to the determination of tolls or other charges with respect to any fair, or
  (b)   as requires the submission to the Secretary of State of, or of proposals relating to, any scale of tolls or other charges with respect to any fair,
shall cease to have effect.

(8)   Where any local statutory provision is continued in force in any area by subsection (1) above or is amended or modified in its application to any area by an order under section 254 above, the Secretary of State or any appropriate Minister may by that order, or in the case of a provision continued as aforesaid, by an order under this subsection—
  (a)   extend the provision throughout the new local government area in which it is continued in force;

(b)   provide that that provision as so continued, amended, modified or extended shall have effect in that area to the exclusion of any enactment for corresponding purposes, including any enactment contained in or applied by this Act;

(c)   make such modifications of any such enactment in its application to that area as will secure that the enactment will operate harmoniously with the said provision in that area;

(d)   repeal or revoke any local statutory provision to which this section applies and which appears to the Secretary of State or that Minister to have become spent, obsolete or unnecessary or to have been substantially superseded by any enactment or instrument which applies or may be applied to the area, persons or things to which or to whom that provision applies;

(e)   transfer to any authority appearing to the Secretary of State or that Minister to be appropriate any functions of an existing local authority under a local statutory provision to which this section applies which are not to become functions of some other authority under any provision of this Act except section 254 above and this section, or under any other instrument made under this Act, being functions exercisable by any existing local authority abolished by this Act;

(f)   without prejudice to paragraph (e) above, make such modifications of any local statutory provision to which this section applies in its application to any new local government area as appear to the Secretary of State or that Minister to be expedient.

(9)–(13)   [*Spent.*]

270 General provisions as to interpretation

(1) In this Act, except where the context otherwise requires, the following expressions have the following meanings respectively, that is to say—

'appropriate Minister', in relation to the making of an order or regulation or the giving of a direction with respect to any matter, means the Minister in charge of any Government department concerned with that matter; but the validity of any order, regulation or direction purporting to be made or given by any Minister by virtue of a power conferred on the appropriate Minister by this Act shall not be affected by any question as to whether or not that Minister was the appropriate Minister for the purpose;

'bank holiday break' means any bank holiday not included in the Christmas break or the Easter break and the period beginning with the last week day before that bank holiday and ending with the next week day which is not a bank holiday;

. . .

'Christmas break' means the period beginning with the last week day before Christmas Day and ending with the first week day after Christmas Day which is not a bank holiday;

. . .

'combined authority' means a combined authority established under section 103 of the Local Democracy, Economic Development and Construction Act 2009;

'county' without more, means, in relation to England, a metropolitan county or a non-metropolitan county, but in the expressions 'county council', 'council of a county', 'county councillor' and 'councillor of a county' means, in relation to England, a non-metropolitan county only;

'district', without more, means, in relation to England, a metropolitan district or a non-metropolitan district;

505

'Easter break' means the period beginning with the Thursday before and ending with the Tuesday after Easter Day;

'economic prosperity board' means an economic prosperity board established under section 88 of the Local Democracy, Economic Development and Construction Act 2009;

'elected mayor' has—

(a)   in relation to England, the same meaning as in Part 1A of the Local Government Act 2000, and

(a)   in relation to Wales, the same meaning as in Part II of the Local Government Act 2000;

'electoral area' means any area for which councillors are elected to any local authority;

'executive', 'executive arrangements' and 'executive leader' have—

(a)   in relation to England, the same meaning as in Part 1A of the Local Government Act 2000, and

(a)   in relation to Wales, the same meaning as in Part II of the Local Government Act 2000;

'existing', in relation to a local government or other area or a local authority or other body, except in sections 1 and 20 above, means that area or body as it existed immediately before the passing of this Act;

'financial year' means the period of twelve months ending with 31st March in any year;

'grouped', in relation to a parish or community, means grouped by or by virtue of any provision of this Act or any previous corresponding enactment under a common parish or community council, and 'grouping order' shall be construed accordingly;

'joint authority' means an authority established by Part IV of the Local Government Act 1985;

'joint waste authority' means an authority established for an area in England by an order under section 207 of the Local Government and Public Involvement in Health Act 2007;

'land' includes any interest in land and any easement or right in, to or over land;

'leader and cabinet executive' means—

(a)   in relation to England: a leader and cabinet executive (England);

(b)   in relation to Wales: a leader and cabinet executive (Wales);

'leader and cabinet executive (England)' has the same meaning as in Part 2 of the Local Government Act 2000;

'leader and cabinet executive (Wales)' has the same meaning as in Part 2 of the Local Government Act 2000;

'local authority' means a county council, a district council, a London borough council or a parish council but, in relation to Wales, means a county council, county borough council or community council;

'local government area' means—

(a)   in relation to England, a county, Greater London, a district, a London borough or a parish;

(b)   in relation to Wales, a county, county borough or community;

'local government elector' means a person registered as a local government elector in the register of electors in accordance with the provisions of the Representation of the People Acts;

'local statutory provision' means a provision of a local Act (including an Act confirming a provisional order) or a provision of a public general Act passed with respect only to the whole or part of an existing local government area or a provision of an instrument made under any such local or public general Act or of an instrument in the nature of a local enactment made under any other Act;

'mayor and cabinet executive' has—

    (a)   in relation to England, the same meaning as in Part 1A of the Local Government Act 2000, and

    (b)   in relation to Wales, the same meaning as in Part II of the Local Government Act 2000;

'new', in relation to any area or authority, means an area or authority established by or under this Act including one established by virtue of any provision of the Local Government (Wales) Act 1994;

'1933 Act' means the Local Government Act 1933;

'1963 Act' means the London Government Act 1963;

'open space' has the meaning assigned to it by section 336(1) of the Town and Country Planning Act 1990;

'prescribed' means prescribed by regulations made by the Secretary of State;

'preserved county' means any county created by this Act as a county in Wales, as it stood immediately before the passing of the Local Government (Wales) Act 1994 but subject to any provision of the Act of 1994, or any provision made under this Act, redrawing its boundaries;

'principal area' means a non-metropolitan county, a district or a London borough but, in relation to Wales, means a county or county borough;

'principal council' means a council elected for a principal area;

'public body' includes—

    (a)   a local authority and a joint board on which, and a joint committee on which, a local authority or parish meeting are represented;

    (b)   any trustees, commissioners or other persons who, for public purposes and not for their own profit, act under any enactment or instrument for the improvement of any place, for the supply of water to any place, or for providing or maintaining a cemetery or market in any place; and

    (c)   any other authority having powers of levying or issuing a precept for any rate for public purposes;

and 'district' means, in relation to a public body other than a local authority, the area for which the public body acts;

'specified papers', in relation to a parish or community, means the public books, writings and papers of the parish or community (including any photographic copies thereof) and all documents directed by law to be kept therewith;

'the Temples' means the Inner Temple and the Middle Temple;

'Welsh Commission' has the meaning assigned to it by section 53 above.

(2) In this Act and in any other enactment, whether passed before, at the same time as, or after this Act, the expression 'non-metropolitan county' means any county other than a metropolitan county, and the expression 'non-metropolitan district' means any district other than a metropolitan district.

(3) Any reference in this Act to a proper officer and any reference which by virtue of this Act is to be construed as such a reference shall, in relation to any purpose and any local authority or other body or any area, be construed as a reference to an officer appointed for that purpose by that body or for that area, as the case may be.

. . .

(5) In this Act, except where the context otherwise requires, references to any enactment shall be construed as references to that enactment as amended, extended or

applied by or under any other enactment, including any enactment contained in this Act.

271 Savings

(2)   Nothing contained in, or done by virtue of, any provision of this Act other than section 253 or section 254(2)(b) shall affect the functions of the conservators of any common.

(3)   The provisions of Part I of this Act shall not affect the continuance of the Confederation of the Cinque Ports.

(4)   Any enabling provision contained in this Act shall be in addition to, and not in derogation of, any powers exercisable by Her Majesty by virtue of Her Royal Prerogative.

(5)   Except as provided by Part X of this Act, nothing in this Act shall prejudice any right, duty or privilege of Her Majesty in right of the Duchy of Lancaster.

273 Commencement

[*The whole Act was in force by 1 April 1974.*]

SCHEDULE 1

COUNTIES AND METROPOLITAN DISTRICTS IN ENGLAND

. . .

PART III

RULES AS TO BOUNDARIES

1

The boundaries of the new local government areas shall be mered by Ordnance Survey.

2

Any such boundary defined on the map annexed to any order under Part VI of the 1933 Act or Part II of the Local Government Act 1958 or section 6 of the 1963 Act by reference to proposed works shall, if the works have not been executed at the time of the completion of the first survey made after the passing of this Act for a new edition of Ordnance Survey large-scale plans including that boundary, be mered as if the boundary had not been so defined.

[*Paras 3–12 of Part III, and Parts IV and V of Sch 1 are of local effect and are not printed.*]

SCHEDULE 11

RULES TO BE OBSERVED IN CONSIDERING ELECTORAL ARRANGEMENTS

Counties

1

(1)   This paragraph applies to the consideration by *the Secretary of State or* either of the Commissions of the electoral arrangements for elections of county councillors but does not apply in relation to any county in Wales.

(2)   Having regard to any change in the number or distribution of the local government electors of the county likely to take place within the period of five years immediately following the consideration—

  (a)   the number of local government electors shall be, as nearly as may be, the same in every electoral division of the county;

  (b)   every electoral division shall lie wholly within a single district;

   (c)   every ward of a parish having a parish council (whether separate or common) shall lie wholly within a single electoral division; and

   (d)   every parish which is not divided into parish wards shall lie wholly within a single electoral division.

(3) Subject to sub-paragraph (2) above, in considering the electoral arrangements referred to in sub-paragraph (1) above regard shall be had to—

   (a)   the desirability of fixing boundaries which are and will remain easily identifiable;

   (b)   any local ties which would be broken by the fixing of any particular boundary; and

   (c)   the boundaries of the wards of the districts in the county.

Welsh counties and county boroughs

1A

(1) This paragraph applies to the consideration by the Secretary of State or the Welsh Commission of the electoral arrangements for elections of councillors for principal areas in Wales.

(2) Subject to any direction under sub-paragraph (3) below, the Welsh Commission shall, when considering the arrangements for elections of councillors for any principal area in Wales, provide for there to be a single member for each electoral division.

(3) The Secretary of State may give a direction to the Welsh Commission requiring it to consider the desirability of providing for multi-member electoral divisions for the area to which the direction relates (which may be the whole or a specified part of a principal area in Wales).

(4) For the purposes of this paragraph, an electoral division is a multi-member division if the arrangements made for the elections of councillors provide for a specified number of councillors (greater than one) to be elected for that division.

(5) Having regard to any change in the number or distribution of the local government electors of the principal area likely to take place within the period of five years immediately following the consideration—

   (a)   subject to paragraph (b), the number of local government electors shall be, as nearly as may be, the same in every electoral division in the principal area;

   (b)   where there are one or more multi-member divisions, the ratio of the number of local government electors to the number of councillors to be elected shall be, as nearly as may be, the same in every electoral division in the principal area (including any that are not multi-member divisions);

   (c)   every ward of a community having a community council (whether separate or common) shall lie wholly within a single electoral division; and

   (d)   every community which is not divided into community wards shall lie wholly within a single electoral division.

(6) Subject to sub-paragraph (5) above, in considering the electoral arrangements referred to in sub-paragraph (1) above, regard shall be had to—

   (a)   the desirability of fixing boundaries which are and will remain easily identifiable; and

   (b)   any local ties which would be broken by the fixing of any particular boundary.

Districts and London boroughs

3

(1) This paragraph applies to the consideration by *the Secretary of State or* either of the Commissions of the electoral arrangements for elections of councillors of a district or London borough.

(2) Having regard to any change in the number or distribution of the local government electors of the district or borough likely to take place within the period of five years immediately following the consideration—

(a) the ratio of the number of local government electors to the number of councillors to be elected shall be, as nearly as may be, the same in every ward of the district or borough;

(b) in a district every ward of a parish having a parish council (whether separate or common) shall lie wholly within a single ward of the district;

(c) in a district every parish which is not divided into parish wards shall lie wholly within a single ward of the district.

(3) Subject to sub-paragraph (2) above, in considering the electoral arrangements referred to in sub-paragraph (1) above, regard shall be had to—

(a) the desirability of fixing boundaries which are and will remain easily identifiable; and

(b) any local ties which would be broken by the fixing of any particular boundary.

Parishes and communities

4

(1) This paragraph applies to the consideration *the Secretary of State*, by either of the Commissions by a Welsh principal council or by a district council of the electoral arrangements for a parish or community having a parish or community council (whether separate or common).

(2) In considering whether any such parish or community is to be divided into parish or community wards, regard shall be had to the questions whether—

(a) the number or distribution of the local government electors for the parish or community is such as to make a single election of parish or community councillors impracticable or inconvenient; and

(b) it is desirable that any area or areas of the parish or community should be separately represented on the parish or community council.

(3) Where it is decided to divide any such parish or community into parish or community wards, in considering the size and boundaries of the wards and in fixing the number of parish or community councillors to be elected for each ward, regard shall be had to—

(a) any change in the number or distribution of the local government electors of the parish or community which is likely to take place within the period of five years immediately following the consideration;

(b) the desirability of fixing boundaries which are and will remain easily identifiable; and

(c) any local ties which will be broken by the fixing of any particular boundaries.

(4) Where it is decided not to divide the parish or community into parish or community wards, in fixing the number of councillors to be elected for each parish or community regard shall be had to the number and distribution of the local government electors of the parish or community and any change in either which is likely to take place within the period of five years immediately following the fixing of the number of parish or community councillors.

¹   Words in italics have been repealed, in relation to England but not to Wales.

SCHEDULE 12

MEETINGS AND PROCEEDINGS OF LOCAL AUTHORITIES

. . .

PART II

PARISH COUNCILS

7

(1)   A parish council shall in every year hold an annual meeting.

(2)   In a year which is a year of ordinary elections of parish councillors, the annual meeting of a parish council shall be held on, or within fourteen days after, the day on which the councillors elected at that election take office, and in any other year the annual meeting shall be held on such day in May as the parish council may determine.

(3)   The annual meeting of a parish council shall be held at such hour as the council may fix or, if no hour is so fixed, 6 o'clock in the evening.

8

(1)   A parish council shall in every year hold, in addition to the annual meeting, such other meetings (not less than three) as they may determine.

(2)   Those other meetings shall be held at such hour and on such days as the council may determine.

9

(1)   An extraordinary meeting of a parish council may be called at any time by the chairman of the council.

(2)   If the chairman refuses to call an extraordinary meeting of the council after a requisition for that purpose, signed by two members of the council, has been presented to him, or if, without so refusing, the chairman does not call an extraordinary meeting within seven days after such a requisition has been presented to him, any two members of the council, on that refusal or on the expiration of those seven days, as the case may be, may forthwith convene an extraordinary meeting of the council.

10

(1)   Meetings of a parish council shall be held at such place, either within or without their area, as they may direct, but shall not be held in premises which at the time of such a meeting may, by virtue of a premises licence or temporary event notice under the Licensing Act 2003, be used for the supply of alcohol (within the meaning of section 14 of that Act) unless no other suitable room is available either free of charge or at a reasonable cost.

(2)   Three clear days at least before a meeting of a parish council—

    (a)   notice of the time and place of the intended meeting shall be fixed in some conspicuous place in the parish and, where the meeting is called by members of the council, the notice shall be signed by those members and shall specify the business proposed to be transacted at the meeting; and

    (b)   a summons to attend the meeting, specifying the business proposed to be transacted at the meeting and signed by the proper officer of the council, shall be left at or sent by post to the usual place of residence of every member of the council.

(3)   Want of service of any such summons as is referred to in sub-paragraph (2)(*b*) above on any member of the parish council concerned shall not affect the validity of the meeting.

11

(1) At a meeting of a parish council the chairman of the council, if present, shall preside.

(2) If the chairman of the council is absent from a meeting of the council, the vice-chairman of the council, if present, shall preside.

(3) If both the chairman and the vice-chairman of the council are absent from a meeting of the council, such councillor as the members of the council present shall choose shall preside.

12

Subject to paragraph 45 below, no business shall be transacted at a meeting of a parish council unless at least one-third of the whole number of members of the council are present at the meeting; but, notwithstanding anything in that paragraph, in no case shall the quorum be less than three.

13

(1) Unless otherwise provided by the council's standing orders the manner of voting at meetings of a parish council shall be by a show of hands.

(2) On the requisition of any member of the council the voting on any question shall be recorded so as to show whether each member present and voting gave his vote for or against that question.

PART III

PARISH MEETINGS

14

(1) The parish meeting of a parish shall assemble annually on some day between 1st March and 1st June, both inclusive, in every year.

(2) Subject to sub-paragraph (1) above and to sub-paragraph (3) below, parish meetings shall be held on such days and at such times as may be fixed by the parish council or, if there is no parish council, by the chairman of the parish meeting.

(3) In a parish which does not have a separate parish council the parish meeting shall, subject to any provision made by a grouping order, assemble at least twice in every year.

(4) The proceedings at a parish meeting shall not commence earlier than 6 o'clock in the evening.

(5) A parish meeting shall not be held in premises which at the time of the meeting may, by virtue of a premises licence or temporary event notice under the Licensing Act 2003, be used for the supply of alcohol (within the meaning of section 14 of that Act), except in cases where no other suitable room is available for such a meeting either free of charge or at a reasonable cost.

15

(1) A parish meeting may be convened by—

    (a)   the chairman of the parish council, or

    (b)   any two parish councillors for the parish, or

    (c)   where there is no parish council, the chairman of the parish meeting or any person representing the parish on the district council, or

    (d)   any six local government electors for the parish.

(2) Not less than seven clear days, or, in a case falling within sub-paragraph (3) below, not less than fourteen clear days, before a parish meeting, public notice of the meeting shall be given, specifying the time and place of the intended meeting and the business to be transacted at the meeting, and signed by the person or persons convening the meeting.

(3)   The fourteen-day period of notice specified in sub-paragraph (2) above is applicable if any business proposed to be transacted at a parish meeting relates to—

(a)   the establishment or dissolution of a parish council, or

(b)   the grouping of the parish with another parish or parishes under a common parish council.

(4)   Public notice of a parish meeting shall be given—

(a)   by posting a notice of the meeting in some conspicuous place or places in the parish, and

(b)   in such other manner, if any, as appears to the person or persons convening the meeting to be desirable for giving publicity to the meeting.

16

The chairman of a parish council shall be entitled to attend a parish meeting for the parish (or, where a grouping order is in force, for any of the parishes comprised in the group) whether or not he is a local government elector for the parish, but if he is not such an elector he shall not be entitled to give any vote at the meeting other than any casting vote which he may have by virtue of paragraph 18(3) below.

17

(1)   In a parish having a separate parish council the chairman of the parish council, if present, shall preside at a parish meeting and if he is absent the vice-chairman (if any) shall, if present, preside.

(2)   In a parish which does not have a separate parish council the chairman chosen for the year in question under section 15(10) or 88(3) above, if present, shall preside.

(3)   If the chairman and the vice-chairman of the parish council or the chairman of the parish meeting, as the case may be, is absent from an assembly of the parish meeting, the parish meeting may appoint a person to take the chair, and that person shall have, for the purposes of that meeting, the powers and authority of the chairman.

18

(1)   Subject to the provisions of this Act, each local government elector may, at a parish meeting or at a poll consequent thereon, give one vote and no more on any question.

(2)   A question to be decided by a parish meeting shall, in the first instance, be decided by the majority of those present at the meeting and voting thereon, and the decision of the person presiding at the meeting as to the result of the voting shall be final unless a poll is demanded.

(3)   In the case of an equality of votes, the person presiding at the meeting shall have a casting vote, in addition to any other vote he may have.

(4)   A poll may be demanded before the conclusion of a parish meeting on any question arising at the meeting; but no poll shall be taken unless either the person presiding at the meeting consents or the poll is demanded by not less than ten, or one-third, of the local government electors present at the meeting, whichever is the less.

(5)   A poll consequent on a parish meeting shall be a poll of those entitled to attend the meeting as local government electors, and shall be taken by ballot in accordance with rules made by the Secretary of State, and the provisions of the rules with respect to the elections of parish councillors under section 36 of the Representation of the People Act 1983 and of the enactments mentioned in section 187(1) of that Act shall, subject to any adaptations, alterations or exceptions made by the first-mentioned rules, apply in the case of a poll so taken as if it were a poll for the election of parish councillors.

(6)   Rules made under sub-paragraph (5) above shall be laid before each House of Parliament as soon as may be after they are made.

19

(1) Minutes of the proceedings of a parish meeting, or a committee thereof, shall be drawn up and entered in a book provided for the purpose and shall be signed at the same or the next following assembly of the parish meeting, or, as the case may be, meeting of the committee, by the person presiding at the meeting, and any minute purporting to be so signed shall be received in evidence without further proof.

(2) Until the contrary is proved, a parish meeting, or a meeting of a committee thereof, in respect of the proceedings of which a minute has been made and signed as mentioned in sub-paragraph (1) above shall be deemed to have been duly convened and held, and all the persons present at the meeting shall be deemed to have been duly qualified, and where the proceedings are those of a committee, the committee shall be deemed to have been duly constituted and to have had power to deal with the matters referred to in the minutes.

20

(1) Subject to the provisions of this Act, in a parish having a separate parish council the parish council may make, vary and revoke standing orders for the regulation of proceedings and business at parish meetings for the parish.

(2) In a parish which does not have a separate parish council, the parish meeting may, subject to the provisions of this Act, regulate their own proceedings and business.

21

(1) Any ballot boxes, fittings and compartments provided for parliamentary elections out of moneys provided by Parliament may on request be lent to the returning officer at a poll consequent on a parish meeting on such terms and conditions as the Treasury may determine.

(2) Any ballot boxes, fittings and compartments provided by or belonging to a local authority shall, on request and if not required for immediate use by that authority, be lent as aforesaid on such terms and conditions as may be agreed.

22

If any person, in a poll consequent on a parish meeting—

    (a)   fraudulently defaces or fraudulently destroys any ballot paper or the official mark; or

    (b)   without due authority supplies a ballot paper to any person; or

    (c)   fraudulently puts into a ballot box any paper other than the ballot paper which he is authorised by law to put in; or

    (d)   fraudulently takes out of the polling station any ballot paper; or

    (e)   without due authority destroys, takes, opens or otherwise interferes with any ballot box or packet of ballot papers then in use for the purposes of the poll;

he shall—

    (i)   if he is a returning officer, or an authorised person appointed to assist in taking the poll or counting the votes, be liable on conviction on indictment to imprisonment for a term not exceeding two years; and

    (ii)   in any other case, be liable, on conviction on indictment or summary conviction, to imprisonment for a term not exceeding six months or to a fine not exceeding £50, or both.

PART IV

COMMUNITY COUNCILS

[*Except for para 24 and the substitution of the word 'community' for the word 'parish' wherever it occurs, the paras in Part IV are identical with the paras of Part III (above) as indicated below.*]

23

[*See para 7 above.*]

24

(1)   A community council may in every year hold, in addition to the annual meeting, such other meetings as the council may determine to hold for the transaction of their business.

(2)   Any of those other meetings shall be held at such hour and on such day as the council may determine.

25

[*See para 9 above.*]

26

[*See para 10 above.*]

27

[*See para 11 above.*]

28

[*See para 12 above.*]

29

[*See para 13 above.*]

PART V

COMMUNITY MEETINGS

30

(1)   Where there is a community council for a community, a community meeting may be convened at any time by the chairman of the council or by any two councillors representing the community on the council.

(2)   Except in a case falling within sub-paragraph (3) below, public notice of a community meeting convened under sub-paragraph (1) above shall be given not less than 7 clear days before the meeting.

(3)   Where any business proposed to be transacted at a community meeting convened under sub-paragraph (1) above relates to the existence of the community council or the grouping of the community with other communities, public notice of the meeting shall be given not less than 30 clear days before the meeting.

(3A)   The notice required by sub-paragraph (2) or (3) above shall—

    (a)   specify the time and place of the intended meeting;

    (b)   specify the business to be transacted at the meeting; and

    (c)   be signed by the person or persons convening the meeting.

(4)   Public notice of a community meeting a community meeting convened under sub-paragraph (1) above shall be given—

    (a)   by posting a notice of the meeting in some conspicuous place or places in the community, and

    (b)   in such other manner, if any, as appears to the person or persons convening the meeting to be desirable for giving publicity to the meeting.

(5)   For the purposes of sub-paragraph (3) above, business relates to the existence of the community council or the grouping of the community with other communities if it relates to any function of a community meeting under sections 27A to 27L of this Act.

30A

A community meeting may also be convened at any time by not less than—

    (a)   10% of the local government electors for the community, or

(b)   50 of the electors (if 10% of the electors exceeds 50 electors).

30B

(1)   Where a group of individuals assert that they have convened a community meeting under paragraph 30A above, those individuals must ensure that a notice which complies with the following requirements of this paragraph is given—

(a)   in a case where there is a community council for the community, to the community council, or

(b)   in a case where there is no community council for the community, to the principal council within whose area the community lies.

(2)   The notice must contain—

(a)   unless sub-paragraph (5) below applies to an individual, the name and address of each of the individuals who assert that they have convened a community meeting under paragraph 30A;

(b)   unless sub-paragraph (5) below applies to an individual, the signature of each of those individuals;

(c)   the business which is proposed to be transacted at the meeting;

(d)   the proposed time and place at which the meeting is to be held.

(3)   The notice must—

(a)   where it is given under sub-paragraph (1)(a) above, be in writing (but not in an electronic form);

(b)   where it is given under sub-paragraph (1)(b) above, be—

(i)   in writing (but not in an electronic form), or

(ii)   in an electronic form which meets the technical requirements set by the principal council under paragraph 30C below.

(4)   In sub-paragraph (2) above—

(a)   "address" means the individual's qualifying address for the purposes of the register of local government electors maintained under section 9(1)(b) of the Representation of the People Act 1983 for the local government area (within the meaning of that Act) in which the community lies;

(b)   "signature" means—

(i)   where a notice is in writing, an individual's signature or, if the individual cannot give a signature, a signature given on the individual's behalf by a duly authorised individual who, in giving that signature, declares that he or she is so authorised;

(ii)   where a notice is in an electronic form, an electronic signature in respect of an individual which meets the authentication requirements for such signatures set by the principal council under paragraph 30C below.

(5)   This sub-paragraph applies to an individual in respect of whom an anonymous entry under section 9B of the Representation of the People Act 1983 has been made in a register of local government electors.

(6)   Where sub-paragraph (5) above applies to an individual, the notice referred to in sub-paragraph (2) above—

(a)   need not include the individual's name and address and, if it does not do so, must instead include the contents of the anonymous entry made in respect of the individual in the register of local government electors, and

(b)   need not include a signature in respect of the individual.

(7)   Where a notice is in electronic form, it is to be treated as given to a principal council when the notice is given in accordance with whatever requirements the council has set as to the giving of such notices under paragraph 30C(2) below.

30C

(1) A principal council must provide a facility so that notices under paragraph 30B(1)(b) above may be given to the council in electronic form ("electronic notices").

(2) The council must set and, to such extent as the council considers appropriate, publicise the following requirements for electronic notices—

    (a)   the authentication requirements to be met by an electronic signature included within an electronic notice, and

    (b)   the other technical requirements to be met by and in relation to an electronic notice.

30D

(1) Where a principal council or a community council has been given a notice under paragraph 30B above, the council must consider—

    (a)   whether the group of individuals to whom the notice relates is comprised of—

        (i)   at least 50 local government electors for the community in question, or

        (ii)   at least 10% of the local government electors for the community in question, and

    (b)   whether the notice meets the requirements of paragraph 30B above.

(2) If the council is of the opinion that—

    (a)   the group of individuals to whom the notice relates is comprised of electors as described in paragraph (1)(a)(i) or (ii) above, and

    (b)   the notice meets the requirements of paragraph 30B above,

the council must give a public notice in accordance with paragraph 30E below.

(3) If the council is not of the opinion described in paragraph (2) above, the council must take all reasonable steps to give notice to the individuals to whom the notice relates as to why the council is not of that opinion.

(4) The relevant registration officer must supply the council with any information in relation to an individual in respect of whom the notice under paragraph 30B includes an anonymous entry, by virtue of sub-paragraph (6)(a) of that paragraph, that it is necessary for the council to have in order to perform the council's functions under this paragraph.

(5) In sub-paragraph (4) above, "relevant registration officer" means the registration officer under section 8 of the Representation of the People Act 1983 in relation to the register of local government electors maintained under section 9(1)(b) of that Act for the local government area (within the meaning of that Act) in which the community in question lies.

30E

(1) The public notice required by paragraph 30D(2) above must be given within a period of 30 days beginning with the day on which the council became of the opinion described in that paragraph.

(2) Except in a case falling within sub-paragraph (3) below, the public notice must be given not less than seven clear days before the community meeting.

(3) Where any business proposed to be transacted at the meeting relates to the existence of the community council or the grouping of the community with other communities, the public notice must be given not less than 30 clear days before the meeting.

(4) The public notice must—

    (a)   specify the time and place of the intended meeting;

    (b)   specify the business to be transacted at the meeting;

    (c)   be signed by the proper officer.

(5)   In specifying a time and place for the purposes of sub-paragraph (4)(a) above, the council must take into account the proposed time and place contained in the notice given to the council under paragraph 30B(2)(d) above.

(6)   The business specified for the purposes of sub-paragraph (4)(b) above must be the same as that contained in the notice given to the council under paragraph 30B(2)(c) above.

(7)   Public notice of a community meeting shall be given—

(a)   by posting a notice of the meeting in some conspicuous place or places in the community,

(b)   in such other manner, if any, as appears to the council to be desirable for giving publicity to the meeting.

(8)   For the purposes of sub-paragraph (3) above, business relates to the existence of the community council or the grouping of the community with other communities if it relates to any function of a community meeting under sections 27A to 27L of this Act.

31

The chairman of a community council shall be entitled to attend a community meeting for the community (or, where a grouping order is in force, for any of the communities comprised in the group)whether or not he is a local government elector for the community, but if he is not such an elector he shall not be entitled to give any vote at the meeting other than any casting vote which he may have by virtue of paragraph 34(3) below.

32

(1)   The proceedings at a community meeting shall not commence earlier than 6 o'clock in the evening.

(2)   A community meeting shall not be held in premises which at the time of the meeting may, by virtue of a premises licence or temporary event notice under the Licensing Act 2003, be used for the supply of alcohol (within the meaning of section 14 of that Act), except in cases where no other suitable room is available for such a meeting either free of charge or at a reasonable cost.

33

(1)   In a community for which there is a community council, the chairman of the council, if present, shall preside at a community meeting.

(2)   In any other case, a community meeting shall appoint a person to be chairman at that meeting.

34

(1)   Subject to the provisions of this Act, each local government elector may, at a community meeting or at a poll consequent thereon, give one vote and no more on any question.

(2)   A question to be decided by a community meeting shall, in the first instance, be decided by the majority of those present at the meeting and voting thereon, and the decision of the person presiding at the meeting as to the result of the voting shall be final unless a poll is demanded.

(3)   In the case of an equality of votes, the person presiding at the meeting shall have a casting vote, in addition to any other vote he may have.

(4)   A poll may be demanded before the conclusion of a community meeting on any question arising at the meeting; but no poll shall be taken unless—

(a)   the poll is demanded by a majority of the local government electors present at the meeting, and

(b)   the electors demanding a poll constitute not less than—

(i)   10% of the local government electors for the community, or

(ii)   150 of the electors (if 10% of the electors exceeds 150 electors).

(5) A poll consequent on a community meeting shall be a poll of those entitled to attend the meeting as local government electors, and shall be taken by ballot in accordance with rules made by the Secretary of State, and the provisions of the rules with respect to elections of community councillors under section 36 of the Representation of the People Act 1983 and of the enactments mentioned in section 187(1) of that Act shall, subject to any adaptations, alterations or exceptions made by the first-mentioned rules, apply in the case of a poll so taken as if it were a poll for the election of community councillors.

(6) Rules made under sub-paragraph (5) above shall be laid before each House of Parliament as soon as may be after they are made.

35

(1) Minutes of the proceedings of a community meeting shall be drawn up and entered in a book provided for the purpose by the proper officer of the community council where there is one or, where there is not, the proper officer of the council of the principal area in which the community is situated and shall be signed at the conclusion of the community meeting by the person presiding at the meeting, and any minute purporting to be so signed shall be received in evidence without further proof.

(2) Until the contrary is proved, a community meeting in respect of the proceedings of which a minute has been made and signed as mentioned in sub-paragraph (1) above shall be deemed to have been duly convened and held, and all the persons present at the meeting shall be deemed to have been duly qualified.

36

Subject to the provisions of this Act a community meeting may regulate their own proceedings and business.

37

[*Save for a reference to 'community' instead of 'parish', this para is identical to para 21 above.*]

38

[*Save for a reference to 'community' instead of 'parish', this para is identical to para 22 above.*]

38A

(1) This paragraph applies to a poll (other than a poll to which sub-paragraph (2) below refers) consequent on a community meeting where a majority of those voting were in favour of the question in relation to which the poll was taken.

(2) This paragraph does not apply to a poll taken on a question of a type specified in regulations made by the Welsh Ministers.

(3) The returning officer in relation to the poll must give notice in writing to the monitoring officer (within the meaning of section 5 of the Local Government and Housing Act 1989) of the relevant principal council of—

    (a)   the question posed by the poll, and

    (b)   the fact that that a majority of those voting were in favour of that question.

(4) In sub-paragraph (3) above, "relevant principal council" means the principal council in whose area lies the community of the community meeting at which the poll was demanded.

(5) The power of the Welsh Ministers to make regulations under sub-paragraph (2) above is exercisable by statutory instrument.

(6) A statutory instrument which contains regulations under sub-paragraph (2) above is subject to annulment in pursuance of a resolution of the National Assembly for Wales.

38B

(1) Within a period of 14 days beginning with the day on which notice was given under paragraph 38A(3) above, the monitoring officer must determine whether, in the officer's opinion, the question in relation to which the poll was taken corresponds to any of the descriptions in sub-paragraph (2) below.

(2) Those descriptions are—

    (a)   a question which relates only to the functions of the principal council,

    (b)   a question which relates only to the functions of a community council for the relevant community,

    (c)   a question which relates to the functions of the principal council and the functions of a community council for the relevant community.

(3) If the monitoring officer determines that the question in relation to which the poll was taken corresponds to the description in sub-paragraph (2)(a) above, the officer must give notice of that determination to the principal council (see section 33B of this Act for the duties of the council upon being given such notice).

(4) If the monitoring officer determines that the question in relation to which the poll was taken corresponds to the description in sub-paragraph (2)(b) above, the officer must give notice of that determination to the community council (see paragraphs 26A and 29A above for the duties arising following the giving of such a notice).

(5) If the monitoring officer determines that the question in relation to which the poll was taken corresponds to the description in sub-paragraph (2)(c) above, the officer must—

    (a)   to the extent that the determination concludes that the question relates to the functions of the principal council, give notice of the determination to the principal council (see section 33B of this Act for the duties of the council upon being given such notice), and

    (b)   to the extent that the determination concludes that the question relates to the functions of the community council, give notice of the determination to the community council (see paragraphs 26A and 29A above for the duties arising following the giving of such a notice).

(6) A notice required to be given by this paragraph must—

    (a)   be given in writing,

    (b)   be given as soon as is reasonably practicable after the date of determination, and

    (c)   include the monitoring officer's reasons for the determination to which the notice relates.

PART VI

PROVISIONS RELATING TO LOCAL AUTHORITIES GENERALLY

39

(1) Subject to the provisions of any enactment (including any enactment in this Act) all questions coming or arising before a local authority shall be decided by a majority of the members of the authority present and voting thereon at a meeting of the authority.

(2) Subject to those provisions in the case of an equality of votes, the person presiding at the meeting shall have a second or casting vote.

40

The names of the members present at a meeting of a local authority shall be recorded.

41

(1) Minutes of the proceedings of a meeting of a local authority shall, subject to sub-paragraph (2) below, be drawn up and entered in a book kept for that purpose and

shall be signed at the same or next suitable meeting of the authority by the person presiding thereat, and any minute purporting to be so signed shall be received in evidence without further proof.

(2)   Notwithstanding anything in any enactment or rule of law to the contrary, the minutes of the proceedings of meetings of a local authority may be recorded on loose leaves consecutively numbered, the minutes of the proceedings of any meeting being signed, and each leaf comprising those minutes being initialled, at the same or next suitable meeting of the authority, by the person presiding thereat, and any minute purporting to be so signed shall be received in evidence without further proof.

(3)   Until the contrary is proved, a meeting of a local authority a minute of whose proceedings has been made and signed in accordance with this paragraph shall be deemed to have been duly convened and held, and all the members present at the meeting shall be deemed to have been duly qualified.

(4)   For the purposes of sub-paragraphs (1) and (2) above the next suitable meeting of a local authority is their next following meeting or, where standing orders made by the authority in accordance with regulations under section 20 of the Local Government and Housing Act 1989 provide for another meeting of the authority to be regarded as suitable, either the next following meeting or that other meeting.

42

Subject to the provisions of this Act, a local authority may make standing orders for the regulation of their proceedings and business and may vary or revoke any such orders.

43

The proceedings of a local authority shall not be invalidated by any vacancy among their number or by any defect in the election or qualifications of any member thereof.

44

(1)   Paragraphs 39 to 43 above (except paragraph 41(3)) shall apply in relation to a committee of a local authority (including a joint committee) or a sub-committee of any such committee as they apply in relation to a local authority.

(2)   Until the contrary is proved, where a minute of any meeting of any such committee or sub-committee has been made and signed in accordance with paragraph 41 above as applied by this paragraph, the committee or sub-committee shall be deemed to have been duly constituted and to have had power to deal with the matters referred to in the minute, the meeting shall be deemed to have been duly convened and held and the members present at the meeting shall be deemed to have been duly qualified.

45

Where more than one-third of the members of a local authority become disqualified at the same time, then, until the number of members in office is increased to not less than two-thirds of the whole number of members of the authority, the quorum of the authority shall be determined by reference to the number of members of the authority remaining qualified instead of by reference to the whole number of members of the authority.

46

In this Part of this Schedule 'local authority' includes a joint authority and in relation to any such authority the reference in paragraph 43 above to election shall include a reference to appointment.

SCHEDULE 12A
ACCESS TO INFORMATION: EXEMPT INFORMATION

[*See s 100A and the summary note on ss 100B–100K above.*]

PART 1

DESCRIPTIONS OF EXEMPT INFORMATION: ENGLAND

1

Information relating to any individual.

2

Information which is likely to reveal the identity of an individual.

3

Information relating to the financial or business affairs of any particular person (including the authority holding that information).

4

Information relating to any consultations or negotiations, or contemplated consultations or negotiations, in connection with any labour relations matter arising between the authority or a Minister of the Crown and employees of, or office holders under, the authority.

5

Information in respect of which a claim to legal professional privilege could be maintained in legal proceedings.

6

Information which reveals that the authority proposes—

    (a)   to give under any enactment a notice under or by virtue of which requirements are imposed on a person; or

    (b)   to make an order or direction under any enactment.

7

Information relating to any action taken or to be taken in connection with the prevention, investigation or prosecution of crime.

PART 2

QUALIFICATIONS: ENGLAND

8

Information falling within paragraph 3 above is not exempt information by virtue of that paragraph if it is required to be registered under—

    (a)   the Companies Act 1985;

    (b)   the Friendly Societies Act 1974;

    (c)   the Friendly Societies Act 1992;

    (d)   the Industrial and Provident Societies Acts 1965 Co-operative and Community Benefit Societies and Credit Unions Acts 1965 to 1978;

    (e)   the Building Societies Act 1986; or

    (f)   the Charities Act 2011.

9

Information is not exempt information if it relates to proposed development for which the local planning authority may grant itself planning permission pursuant to regulation 3 of the Town and Country Planning General Regulations 1992.

10

Information which—

    (a)   falls within any of paragraphs 1 to 7 above; and

    (b)   is not prevented from being exempt by virtue of paragraph 8 or 9 above, is exempt information if and so long, as in all the circumstances of the case, the public interest in maintaining the exemption outweighs the public interest in disclosing the information.

PART 3

INTERPRETATION: ENGLAND

11

(1)   In Parts 1 and 2 and this Part of this Schedule—

'employee' means a person employed under a contract of service;

'financial or business affairs' includes contemplated, as well as past or current, activities;

'labour relations matter' means—

(a)   any of the matters specified in paragraphs (a) to (g) of section 218(1) of the Trade Union and Labour Relations (Consolidation) Act 1992 (matters which may be the subject of a trade dispute, within the meaning of that Act); or

(b)   any dispute about a matter falling within paragraph (a) above;

and for the purposes of this definition the enactments mentioned in paragraph (a) above, with the necessary modifications, shall apply in relation to office-holders under the authority as they apply in relation to employees of the authority;

'office-holder', in relation to the authority, means the holder of any paid office appointments to which are or may be made or confirmed by the authority or by any joint board on which the authority is represented or by any person who holds any such office or is an employee of the authority;

'registered' in relation to information required to be registered under the Building Societies Act 1986, means recorded in the public file of any building society (within the meaning of that Act).

(2)   Any reference in Parts 1 and 2 and this Part of this Schedule to 'the authority' is a reference to the principal council or, as the case may be, the committee or sub-committee in relation to whose proceedings or documents the question whether information is exempt or not falls to be determined and includes a reference—

(a)   in the case of a principal council, to any committee or sub-committee of the council; and

(b)   in the case of a committee, to—

(i)   any constituent principal council;

(ii)   any other principal council by which appointments are made to the committee or whose functions the committee discharges; and

(iii)   any other committee or sub-committee of a principal council falling within sub-paragraph (i) or (ii) above; and

(c)   in the case of a sub-committee, to—

(i)   the committee, or any of the committees, of which it is a sub-committee; and

(ii)   any principal council which falls within paragraph (b) above in relation to that committee.

PART 4

DESCRIPTIONS OF EXEMPT INFORMATION: WALES

12

Information relating to a particular individual.

13

Information which is likely to reveal the identity of an individual.

14

Information relating to the financial or business affairs of any particular person (including the authority holding that information).

15

Information relating to any consultations or negotiations, or contemplated consultations or negotiations, in connection with any labour relations matter arising between the authority or a Minister of the Crown and employees of, or office holders under, the authority.

16

Information in respect of which a claim to legal professional privilege could be maintained in legal proceedings.

17

Information which reveals that the authority proposes—

(a)   to give under any enactment a notice under or by virtue of which requirements are imposed on a person; or

(b)   to make an order or direction under any enactment.

18

Information relating to any action taken or to be taken in connection with the prevention, investigation or prosecution of crime.

PART 5

QUALIFICATIONS: WALES

19

Information falling within paragraph 14 above is not exempt information by virtue of that paragraph if it is required to be registered under—

(a)   the Companies Acts (as defined in section 2 of the Companies Act 2006);

(b)   the Friendly Societies Act 1974;

(c)   the Friendly Societies Act 1992;

(d)   the Industrial and Provident Societies Acts 1965 Co-operative and Community Benefit Societies and Credit Unions Acts 1965 to 1978;

(e)   the Building Societies Act 1986; or

(f)   the Charities Act 2011.

20

Information is not exempt information if it relates to proposed development for which the local planning authority may grant itself planning permission pursuant to regulation 3 of the Town and Country Planning General Regulations 1992.

21

Information which—

(a)   falls within any of paragraphs 12 to 15, 17 and 18 above; and

(b)   is not prevented from being exempt by virtue of paragraph 19 or 20 above,

is exempt information if and so long, as in all the circumstances of the case, the public interest in maintaining the exemption outweighs the public interest in disclosing the information.

PART 6

INTERPRETATION: WALES

22

(1) In Parts 4 and 5 and this Part of this Schedule—

'employee' means a person employed under a contract of service;

'financial or business affairs' includes contemplated, as well as past or current, activities;

'labour relations matter' means—

(a)   any of the matters specified in paragraphs (a) to (g) of section 218(1) of the Trade Union and Labour Relations (Consolidation) Act 1992 (matters which may be the subject of a trade dispute, within the meaning of that Act); or

(b)   any dispute about a matter falling within paragraph (a) above;

and for the purposes of this definition the enactments mentioned in paragraph (a) above, with the necessary modifications, shall apply in relation to office-holders under the authority as they apply in relation to employees of the authority;

'office-holder', in relation to the authority, means the holder of any paid office appointments to which are or may be made or confirmed by the authority or by any joint board on which the authority is represented or by any person who holds any such office or is an employee of the authority;

'registered' in relation to information required to be registered under the Building Societies Act 1986, means recorded in the public file of any building society (within the meaning of that Act).

(2) Any reference in Parts 4 and 5 and this Part of this Schedule to 'the authority' is a reference to the principal council or, as the case may be, the committee or sub-committee in relation to whose proceedings or documents the question whether information is exempt or not falls to be determined and includes a reference—

(a)   in the case of a principal council, to any committee or sub-committee of the council; and

(b)   in the case of a committee, to—

(i)   any constituent principal council;

(ii)   any other principal council by which appointments are made to the committee or whose functions the committee discharges; and

(iii) any other committee or sub-committee of a principal council falling within sub-paragraph (i) or (ii) above; and

(c)   in the case of a sub-committee, to—

(i)   the committee, or any of the committees, of which it is a sub-committee; and

(ii)   any principal council which falls within paragraph (b) above in relation to that committee.

SCHEDULE 12B

APPROPRIATE SUM UNDER SECTION 137(4)

1

This Schedule has effect to determine for the purposes of section 137(4)(a) above the sum that is for the time being appropriate to a local authority.

2

The sum appropriate to the local authority for the financial year in which section 118 of the Local Government Act 2003 comes into force is £5.00.

3

(1)   For each subsequent financial year, the sum appropriate to the local authority is the greater of the sum appropriate to the authority for the financial year preceding the year concerned and the sum produced by the following formula—

$$(A \times B) / C$$

(2)   A is the sum appropriate to the local authority for the financial year preceding the year concerned.

(3)   B is the retail prices index for September of the financial year preceding the year concerned.

(4)   C is the retail prices index for September of the financial year which precedes that preceding the year concerned except where sub-paragraph (5) below applies.

(5)   Where the base month for the retail prices index for September of the financial year mentioned in sub-paragraph (4) above (the first year) differs from that for the index for September of the financial year mentioned in sub-paragraph (3) above (the second year), C is the figure which the Secretary of State calculates would have been the retail prices index for September of the first year if the base month for that index had been the same as the base month for the index for September of the second year.

(6)   References in sub-paragraphs (3) to (5) above to the retail prices index are to the general index of retail prices (for all items) published by the Statistics Board.

(7)   If that index is not published for a month for which it is relevant for the purposes of any of those sub-paragraphs, the sub-paragraph shall be taken to refer to any substituted index or index figures published by the Board.

(8)   For the purposes of sub-paragraph (5) above, the base month for the retail prices index for September of a particular year is the month—

    (a)   for which the retail prices index is taken to be 100, and

    (b)   by reference to which the index for the September in question is calculated.

(9)   In calculating the sum produced by the formula in sub-paragraph (1) above a part of a whole (if any) shall be calculated to two decimal places only—

    (a)   adding one hundredth where (apart from this sub-paragraph) there would be five, or more than five, one-thousandths, and

    (b)   ignoring the one-thousandths where (apart from this sub-paragraph) there would be less than five one-thousandths.

4

Before the beginning of a financial year, the appropriate person may by order provide for a different sum to have effect as the sum appropriate to a local authority for the year in place of the sum calculated for the year in accordance with paragraph 3 above.

5

In paragraph 4 above 'the appropriate person' means—

    (a)   as respects England, the Secretary of State;

    (b)   as respects Wales, the National Assembly for Wales.

6

An order under paragraph 4 above may make different provision in relation to local authorities of different descriptions.

7

An order under paragraph 4 above made by the Secretary of State shall be subject to annulment in pursuance of a resolution of either House of Parliament.

SCHEDULE 14

AMENDMENT AND MODIFICATION OF PUBLIC HEALTH ACTS, ETC

PART I

THE PUBLIC HEALTH ACT 1936

. . .

18

The powers conferred by Part VIII on local authorities within the meaning of the Public Health Act 1936 shall be exercisable not only by such authorities but also by all local authorities within the meaning of this Act, whether or not they are local authorities within the meaning of that Act, and references in that Part to a local authority shall be construed accordingly.

. . .

PART II

OTHER ENACTMENTS

Public Health Acts 1875 to 1925

23

Subject to the following provisions of this Schedule and the provisions of Schedule 26 to this Act, all the provisions of the Public Health Acts 1875 to 1925 shall extend throughout England and Wales, whether or not they so extended immediately before 1st April 1974.

24

Paragraph 23 above shall not apply to the following enactments, that is to say—

    (a)   so much of section 160 of the Public Health Act 1875 as incorporates the provisions of the Towns Improvement Clauses Act 1847 with respect to the naming of streets (hereafter in this Schedule referred to as 'the original street-naming enactment');

    (b)   section 171(4) of the said Act of 1875;

    (d)   sections 21, 82, 83 . . . of the Public Health Acts Amendment Act 1907; and

    (e)   sections 17 to 19 and 76 of the Public Health Act 1925;

and those enactments shall, subject to paragraph 25 below, apply to those areas, and only those, to which they applied immediately before 1st April 1974.

27

(1) [*This sub-paragraph extends the powers of the enactments mentioned in sub-paragraph (2) to all local authorities.*]

(2) This paragraph applies to the following enactments, that is to say—

    (a)   section 164 of the Public Health Act 1875;

    (b)   section 44 of the Public Health Acts Amendment Act 1890;

    (c)   Part VI of the Public Health Acts Amendment Act 1907, as amended by Part VI of the Public Health Act 1925.

. . .

42

The powers conferred by sections 52 to 54 of that Act on local authorities shall be exercisable not only by such authorities, but also by all local authorities within the meaning of this Act, whether or not they are local authorities within the meaning of that Act, and references in those sections to a local authority shall be construed accordingly.

SCHEDULE 26[1]
CEMETERIES AND CREMATORIA

[1]   See Local Authorities Cemeteries Order 1977, SI 1977/204.

Discharge of functions of burial authorities

1

In relation to a cemetery or crematorium maintained immediately before 1st April 1974 by a burial board, joint burial board or committee which ceases to exist by virtue of section 214 above the functions conferred by the said section 214 and this Schedule shall, subject to the provisions of any order made under section 254 above, be exercised on and after that date by whichever of the following burial authorities is relevant:—

(a)   where the area of the board or committee becomes wholly comprised on that date in a parish or community having a parish or community council, whether separate or common, that council;

(b)   where that area becomes comprised in two or more such parishes or communities, the councils of those parishes or communities, acting jointly;

(c)   where that area becomes wholly comprised in a parish not having a parish council, the parish meeting of the parish;

(d)   where that area becomes wholly comprised in two or more parishes not having parish councils, the parish meetings for those parishes acting jointly;

(e)   where that area becomes wholly comprised in two or more parishes of which one or more have, and one or more have not, parish councils, the parish council or councils and the parish meeting or meetings of the parish or parishes not having parish councils, acting jointly;

(f)   where that area becomes wholly comprised in a community not having a community council or in two or more such communities, the council of the district in which that community or those communities become comprised or, where they become comprised in different districts, the councils of those districts acting jointly;

(g)   where that area becomes wholly comprised in two or more communities of which one or more have, and one or more have not, community councils, the community council or councils and the council or councils of the district or districts in which the community or communities not having community councils become comprised, acting jointly;

(h)   in the case of an area in England none of which becomes comprised in a parish, the council of the district in which it becomes comprised or, where it becomes comprised in two or more districts, the councils of those districts acting jointly;

(i)   where that area becomes comprised partly in a parish or parishes and partly in an area which is not a parish, the parish council or councils or parish meeting or meetings, as the case may be, of that parish or those parishes and the council or councils of the district or districts in which it becomes comprised, acting jointly.

2

Where by virtue of paragraph 1 above the functions conferred by section 214 above and this Schedule become exercisable by two or more burial authorities, then, unless a joint board is established under section 6 of the Public Health Act 1936 to exercise those functions, it shall be their duty to make arrangements under Part VI of this Act for the discharge of those functions by a joint committee of those authorities.

3

Section 6 of the Public Health Act 1936 (establishment of joint boards to perform the functions of local authorities under the Public Health Acts) shall have effect as if the provisions of the Cremation Acts 1902 and 1952, section 214 above and this Schedule were part of that Act and as if the reference to local authorities and their districts—

(a) so far as those sections relate to functions with respect to cemeteries, included references to burial authorities and their areas; and

(b) so far as those sections relate to functions with respect to crematoria, included references to burial authorities, other than parish meetings, and the areas of such authorities.

4

Where in pursuance of paragraph 2 above two or more burial authorities make arrangements under Part VI of this Act for the discharge of their functions by a joint committee, and if any of those authorities wish, and one or more of the others do not wish, to alter the arrangements, the arrangements may be changed or ended—

(a) where those authorities are the councils of parishes or groups of parishes situated in the same district, by the council of that district;

(aa) where those authorities are the councils of communities or groups of communities situated in the same principal area, by the council of that principal area;

(b) in any other case, by the Secretary of State.

5

In the following provisions of this Act, that is to say, sections 101 to 106, 111, 112, 124, 125, 139 and Part I of Schedule 13 so far as they relate to functions conferred by section 214 above and this Schedule, any reference to a local authority or a parish council shall include a reference to a parish meeting or, as may be appropriate, the parish trustees of a parish, and section 109 above shall not apply to those functions.

6

Notwithstanding anything in section 150 above, a parish or community council or parish meeting may by resolution declare any expenses incurred by them in the discharge of functions under section 214 above and this Schedule to be chargeable only on such part of their area as may be specified in the resolution, and any such resolution may be varied or revoked by a subsequent resolution of the council or meeting, as the case may be.

7

If the constituent local authorities of a joint committee of burial authorities are unable to purchase by agreement and on reasonable terms suitable land for the purpose of enabling the committee to exercise their powers under section 214 above and none of those authorities is a district council or Welsh principal council, the committee may represent the case to the council of the district or Welsh principal area in which their area or any part of it is situated, and thereupon section 125 above shall apply as if the committee were a parish or community council and their area were a parish or community.

8

The district council or Welsh principal council in making and the Secretary of State in confirming an order under that section as applied by paragraph 7 above shall take account of the needs of the whole area of the committee even if it is partly outside the district or (as the case may be) principal area.

9

Land acquired in pursuance of paragraph 7 above shall be conveyed to one or more of, or of the bodies qualified to hold land on behalf of[1], the constituent local authorities.

[1] The curious grammar is probably meant to refer to Parish Trustees in England and district councils in Wales.

Provision and management of cemeteries

11

(1) Subject to the provisions of any order made under section 214(3) above; the council of a district . . . may make byelaws with respect to the management of any cemeteries provided by them and a parish council or parish meeting may adopt for any cemetery provided by them any byelaws made under this paragraph by the district council and duly confirmed.

(1A) Subject to the provisions of any order made under section 214(3) above, a Welsh principal council may make byelaws with respect to the management of any cemetery provided by them and a community council may adopt for any cemetery provided by them any byelaws made under this paragraph by the principal council and duly confirmed.

(2) The confirming authority in relation to byelaws made under this paragraph shall be the Secretary of State.

Saving, amendments and modifications of enactments

15

Section 214(1) above shall not affect the power to make an Order in Council under section 1 of the Burial Act of 1853 or section 1 of the Burial Act 1855 with respect to the discontinuance of burials; and—

> (a) the power to make such an Order shall, notwithstanding anything in section 5 of the said Act of 1853 (which precludes the exercise of that power in the case of cemeteries provided under any Act of Parliament or with the approval of the Secretary of State) be exercisable in relation to all cemeteries provided under section 214 above or in Greater London provided otherwise; and
>
> (b) section 51 of the Burial Act 1852 shall apply to cemeteries in which burials are discontinued by virtue of this paragraph as it applies to burial grounds in which interments are discontinued under that Act;

but nothing in any such Order shall prevent the interment of the body of any person in the Cathedral Church of St. Paul, London, or in the Collegiate Church of St. Peter, Westminster, if Her Majesty signifies Her approval that the body be so interred.

17

In Part III of Schedule 5 to the Public Health Act 1875, the paragraph relating to section 83 of the Act 11 and 12 Vict c 63 shall . . . apply only within the outer London boroughs and shall outside Greater London apply to, and only to, a church or other place of public worship—

> (a) to which it applies immediately before 1st April 1974 or would have so applied if the building had then been completed; or
>
> (b) the building of which begins on or after that date.

24

It shall not be necessary for the Secretary of State to approve any table of fees as required by section 9 of the Cremation Act 1902, but any burial authority for the purposes of that Act shall keep such a table and it shall be available for inspection by the public at all reasonable times.

25

A burial authority within the meaning of section 214 above shall also be a burial authority for the purposes of the Parish Councils and Burial Authorities (Miscellaneous Provisions) Act 1970.

SCHEDULE 29

ADAPTATION, MODIFICATION AND AMENDMENT OF ENACTMENTS

PART I

GENERAL ADAPTATION OF ENACTMENTS

1

(1)   This paragraph applies to any enactment passed before, or during the same session as, this Act, and any instrument made before this Act under any enactment.

(2)   Any reference in any such enactment or instrument to a local authority within the meaning of the 1933 Act shall be construed as a reference to a local authority within the meaning of this Act.

2

In any enactment or instrument to which paragraph 1 above applies any reference to a district which is such a reference by virtue only of a provision of this Act shall be construed as a reference to a district within the meaning of this Act.

4

(1)   Subject to sub-paragraph (2) below, in any enactment or instrument to which paragraph 1 above applies—

  (a)   any reference to a specified officer of a local authority shall be construed as a reference to the proper officer of a local authority;

  (b)   any reference to a specified officer of a county council shall be construed as a reference to the proper officer of a county council;

  (c)   any reference to a specified officer of a borough or of the council of a county district (whether referred to as such or as the council of a borough or urban or rural district) shall be construed as a reference to the proper officer of a district council;

  (d)   any reference to a specified officer of a rural parish (whether referred to as such or as a parish) shall be construed as a reference to the proper officer of a parish or community council, as the case may be.

(2)   Sub-paragraph (1) above shall not apply in any case where the reference is to any officer of a specified local authority which ceases to exist by virtue of section 1 or 20 of this Act, and shall not apply to any reference in any enactment to an officer specified in section 112(4) above.

5

In any enactment or instrument to which paragraph 1 above applies any reference to a representative body of a parish—

  (a)   as respects England, shall be construed as a reference to the parish trustees of the parish; and

  (b)   as respects Wales, shall be disregarded.

6

(1)   This paragraph applies for the construction of any enactment passed before 22nd March 1967, and shall have effect subject to any contrary intention which may appear in any such enactment.

(2) In any such enactment any reference to a parish shall—

    (a) as respects those areas in England outside Greater London which immediately before 1st April 1974 constituted urban parishes, other than urban parishes in a rural district, be construed as a reference to each such area or, where the area is divided between more than one district, as a reference to each part of the area so divided; and

(3) In any such enactment any reference to an urban parish shall, as respects those areas of England outside Greater London which immediately before 1st April 1974 constituted urban parishes, be construed as a reference to each such area or, where the area is divided between more than one district, as a reference to each part of the area so divided.

(4) In any such enactment any reference to a rural parish shall as respects the areas mentioned in paragraph 3 of Part IV of Schedule 1 to this Act be construed as a reference to each such area.

(5) In any such enactment any reference to an urban parish shall as respects Wales be construed as a reference to a community.

8

The foregoing provisions of this Schedule shall have effect subject to any provision to the contrary made by, or by any instrument made under, this Act.

PART II

PARTICULAR MODIFICATIONS AND AMENDMENTS

Allotments

9

(1) As respects a parish in England those functions under the Allotments Acts 1908 to 1950 which, apart from this paragraph, would be exercisable both by the district council and the parish council or parish meeting shall not be exercisable by the district council.

LOCAL GOVERNMENT (MISCELLANEOUS PROVISIONS) ACT 1976

16[1] Power of local authorities to obtain particulars of persons interested in land

(1) Where, with a view to performing a function conferred on a local authority by any enactment, the authority considers that it ought to have information connected with any land, the authority may serve on one or more of the following persons, namely—

    (a) the occupier of the land; and

    (b) any person who has an interest in the land either as freeholder, mortgagee or lessee or who directly or indirectly receives rent for the land; and

    (c) any person who, in pursuance of an agreement between himself and a person interested in the land, is authorised to manage the land or to arrange for the letting of it,

a notice specifying the land and the function and the enactment which confers the function and requiring the recipient of the notice to furnish to the authority, within a period specified in the notice (which shall not be less than fourteen days beginning with the day on which the notice is served), the nature of his interest in the land and the name and address of each person whom the recipient of the notice believes is the occupier of the land and of each person whom he believes is, as respects the land, such

a person as is mentioned in the provisions of paragraphs (b) and (c) of this subsection.
(2) A person who—

(a)   fails to comply with the requirements of a notice served on him in pursuance of the preceding subsection; or

(b)   in furnishing any information in compliance with such a notice makes a statement which he knows to be false in a material particular or recklessly makes a statement which is false in a material particular,

shall be guilty of an offence and liable on summary conviction to a fine not exceeding level 5 on the standard scale.

---

[1]   The Land Registration Act 2002 makes it possible in the case of registered land to obtain most of the information direct from the Land Registry.

Places of entertainment

19 Recreational facilities

(1) A local authority may provide, inside or outside its area, such recreational facilities as it thinks fit and, without prejudice to the generality of the powers conferred by the preceding provisions of this subsection, those powers include in particular powers to provide—

(a)   indoor facilities consisting of sports centres, swimming pools, skating rinks, tennis, squash and badminton courts, bowling centres, dance studios and riding schools;

(b)   outdoor facilities consisting of pitches for team games, athletics grounds, swimming pools, tennis courts, cycle tracks, golf courses, bowling greens, riding schools, camp sites and facilities for gliding;

(c)   facilities for boating and water ski-ing on inland and coastal waters and for fishing in such waters;

(d)   premises for the use of clubs or societies having athletic, social or recreational objects;

(e)   staff, including instructors, in connection with any such facilities or premises as are mentioned in the preceding paragraphs and in connection with any other recreational facilities provided by the authority;

(f)   such facilities in connection with any other recreational facilities as the authority considers it appropriate to provide including, without prejudice to the generality of the preceding provisions of this paragraph, facilities by way of parking spaces and places at which food, drink and tobacco may be bought from the authority or another person;

and it is hereby declared that the powers conferred by this subsection to provide facilities include powers to provide buildings, equipment, supplies and assistance of any kind.
(2) A local authority may make any facilities provided by it in pursuance of the preceding subsection available for use by such persons as the authority thinks fit either without charge or on payment of such charges as the authority thinks fit.
(3) A local authority may contribute—

(a)   by way of grant or loan towards the expenses incurred or to be incurred by any voluntary organisation in providing any recreational facilities which the authority has power to provide by virtue of subsection (1) of this section; and

(b)   by way of grant towards the expenses incurred or to be incurred by any other local authority in providing such facilities;

and in this subsection 'voluntary organisation' means any person carrying on or proposing to carry on an undertaking otherwise than for profit.

(5) Any property which, immediately before the date when this subsection comes into force, is held by a local authority for the purposes of section 221(b) of the Public Health Act 1936 or section 4 of the Physical Training and Recreation Act 1937 or, in pursuance of section 144(1)(b) of the Local Government Act 1972, for the purposes of recreation shall on and after that date be held by the local authority for the purposes of this section.

Financial provisions

30 Power to forgo repayment of advances of remuneration paid to deceased employees

(1) If a person in the employment of a local authority—

(a) receives from the authority remuneration in respect of a future period on the assumption that he will be employed in that employment throughout that period; and

(b) dies before the expiration of that period,

the authority may, subject to the following subsection, forgo the repayment of so much of the remuneration as relates to the period after his death.

(2) An authority shall not be entitled to forgo such a repayment in respect of a period after the relevant death if—

(a) a pension is payable for that period in respect of the deceased out of money provided by Parliament or out of a fund which is maintained by the authority or into which contributions have been paid by the authority in respect of service of the deceased; and

(b) the rate of the pension is not less than the rate of relevant remuneration which was received by the deceased for his last year of service in the employment in question or, if relevant remuneration at different rates was received by him for that year, is not less than the highest of those rates;

and in paragraph (b) of this subsection 'relevant remuneration', in relation to a deceased person and a year, means remuneration which would have fallen to be taken into account in respect of that year in calculating a retirement pension payable to him in respect of the employment in question on his attaining pensionable age and being granted such a retirement pension.

. . .

Miscellaneous

36 Power of local authorities to appoint times and charges for markets

(1) Any provision of a local Act which confers power on a local authority to make byelaws appointing days on which or the hours during which markets or fairs are to be or may be held shall be construed as conferring on the authority a power to appoint such days or hours by resolution.

(2) A local authority which maintains a market in pursuance of a local Act may, notwithstanding anything in any enactment relating to the market, make in connection with the market such charges as the authority determines from time to time.

39 Protection of members and officers etc of local authorities from personal liability

. . .

(2) A person who is appointed as a member of a committee of a local authority or a joint committee of two or more local authorities by virtue of subsection (3) or (4) of section 102 of the Local Government Act 1972 (which authorises among other things the appointment to such a committee of a person who is not a member of a relevant authority) shall, if he is not a member of the authority which appointed him, be treated

as such a member for the purposes of the said section 265 as modified by the preceding subsection.

41 Evidence of resolutions and minutes of proceedings etc

(1)   A document which—

    (a)   purports to be a copy of—

        (i)   a resolution, order or report of a local authority or a precursor of a local authority, or

        (ii)   the minutes of the proceedings at a meeting of a local authority or a precursor of a local authority; and

    (b)   bears a certificate purporting to be signed by the proper officer of the authority or a person authorised in that behalf by him or the authority and stating that the resolution was passed or the order or report was made by the authority or precursor on a date specified in the certificate or, as the case may be, that the minutes were signed in accordance with paragraph 41 of Schedule 12 to the Local Government Act 1972 or the corresponding provision specified in the certificate of the enactments relating to local government which were in force when the minutes were signed,

shall be evidence in any proceedings of the matters stated in the certificate and of the terms of the resolution, order, report or minutes in question.

(2)   In the preceding subsection references to a local authority, except the first and second references in paragraph (b), include references to a committee of a local authority and a sub-committee of such a committee and references to a precursor of a local authority include references to a committee of such a precursor and a sub-committee of such a committee.

(2A)   In the case of a local authority which are operating executive arrangements, a document which—

    (a)   purports to be a copy of a record of any decision made by the executive of that authority, or a member of that executive or any person acting on behalf of that executive, where that record is required to be kept or produced by section 22 of the Local Government Act 2000 or any regulations made under that section; and

    (b)   bears a certificate purporting to be signed by the proper officer of the authority or by a person authorised in that behalf by him or any other person who, by virtue of regulations made under section 22 of the Local Government Act 2000, is authorised or required to produce such a record, stating that the decision was made on the date specified in the certificate by that executive, or as the case may be, by the member of that executive or by the person acting on behalf of that executive,

shall be evidence in any proceedings of the matters stated in the certificate and of the terms of the decision in question.

(2B)   Subsection (2C) applies to a record if—

    (a)   it records a decision made or action taken by a member of a local authority or of a precursor of a local authority in exercise of a function of the authority or precursor by virtue of arrangements made under section 236 of the Local Government and Public Involvement in Health Act 2007, and

    (b)   it is required to be made by regulations under section 100EA of the Local Government Act 1972.

(2C)   If a document which purports to be a copy of a record to which this subsection applies bears a certificate—

    (a)   purporting to be signed by—

        (i)   the proper officer of the local authority, or

    (ii) a person authorised in that behalf by that officer or by the local authority, and

  (b) stating that the decision was made or the action was taken by the member of the local authority on the date specified in the certificate,

the document shall be evidence in any proceedings of the matters stated in the certificate and of the terms of the decision, or nature of the action, in question.

(3) A document which—

  (a) purports to be a copy of an instrument by which the proper officer of a local authority appointed a person to be an officer of the authority or authorised a person to perform functions specified in the instrument; and

  (b) bears a certificate purporting to be signed as mentioned in subsection (1)(b) of this section and stating that the document is a copy of the instrument in question,

shall be evidence in any proceedings of the fact that the instrument was made by the said proper officer and of the terms of the instrument.

(4) In the preceding provisions of this section 'precursor', in relation to a local authority, means any authority which has ceased to exist but which when it existed was constituted, in pursuance of the enactments relating to local government which were then in force, for an area any part of which is included in the area of the local authority.

Supplemental

44 Interpretation etc of Part I

(1) In this Part of this Act, except where the contrary intention appears—

  . . .

  'local authority' means a county council, a county borough council, a district council, a London borough council, the Common Council, the Council of the Isles of Scilly and—

   (a) in sections 13 to 16, 29, 30, 38, 39 and 41 of this Act, a police authority established under section 3 of the Police Act 1996, the Metropolitan Police Authority, a joint authority established by Part IV of the Local Government Act 1985, an authority established for an area in England by an order under section 207 of the Local Government and Public Involvement in Health Act 2007 (joint waste authorities) and the London Fire and Emergency Planning Authority;

   (b) in sections 1, 16, 19, 30, 36, 39 and 41 of this Act, a parish council and a community council;

   (c) in section 40 of this Act, a joint authority established by Part IV of the Local Government Act 1985, an authority established under section 10 of that Act (waste regulation and disposal authorities), an authority established for an area in England by an order under section 207 of the Local Government and Public Involvement in Health Act 2007 (joint waste authorities), the London Fire and Emergency Planning Authority and the South Yorkshire Pensions Authority;

  . . .

REFUSE DISPOSAL (AMENITY) ACT 1978

3 Removal of abandoned vehicles

(1) Where it appears to a local authority that a motor vehicle in their area is abandoned without lawful authority on any land in the open air or on any other land forming part of a highway, it shall be the duty of the authority, subject to the following provisions of this section, to remove the vehicle.

(2) Where it appears to a local authority that the land on which a motor vehicle is abandoned as aforesaid is occupied by any person, the authority shall give him notice that they propose to remove the vehicle in pursuance of subsection (1) above but shall not be entitled to remove it if he objects to the proposal within the prescribed period.

(2A) Subsection (2) does not apply where the vehicle is abandoned on a road (within the meaning of the Road Traffic Regulation Act 1984).

(3) A local authority shall not be required by virtue of subsection (1) above to remove a vehicle situated otherwise than on a carriageway within the meaning of the Highways Act 1980 if it appears to them that the cost of its removal to the nearest convenient carriageway within the meaning of that Act would be unreasonably high.

. . .

(8) While a vehicle is in the custody of a local authority . . . in pursuance of this section, it shall be the duty of that body to take such steps as are reasonably necessary for the safe custody of the vehicle.

6 Removal and disposal etc of other refuse

(1) Where it appears to a local authority that any thing in their area, other than a motor vehicle, is abandoned without lawful authority on any land in the open air or on any other land forming part of a highway, the authority may if they think fit, subject to subsection (2) below, remove the thing.

(2) A local authority shall not be entitled to exercise their powers under subsection (1) above as respects a thing situated on land appearing to the authority to be occupied by any person unless the authority have given him notice that they propose to remove the thing and he has failed to object to the proposal within the prescribed period.

(3) Section 76 of the Public Health Act 1936 (which relates to the deposit and disposal of refuse) shall, with the exception of subsection (3)(a) of that section, apply to any thing removed in pursuance of subsection (1) above as it applies to other refuse.

(4) . . . A local authority by whom any thing is removed in pursuance of subsection (1) above shall be entitled to recover the cost of removing and disposing of it from—

    (a) any person by whom it was put in the place from which it was so removed, or

    (b) any person convicted of an offence under section 2(1) above in consequence of the putting of the thing in that place.

. . .

11 Interpretation

(1) In this Act, unless the contrary intention appears, the following expressions have the following meanings, that is to say—

    . . .

    'local authority' means—

        (a) in relation to England, a district council, London borough council or the Common Council;

    . . .

    'prescribed' means prescribed by regulations made by the Secretary of State;

. . .

HIGHWAYS ACT 1980

PART III

CREATION OF HIGHWAYS

30 Dedication of highway by agreement with parish or community council

(1)   The council of a parish or community may enter into an agreement with any person having the necessary power in that behalf for the dedication by that person of a highway over land in the parish or community or an adjoining parish or community in any case where such a dedication would in the opinion of the council be beneficial to the inhabitants of the parish or community or any part thereof.

(2)   Where the council of a parish or community have entered into an agreement under subsection (1) above for the dedication of a highway they may carry out any works (including works of maintenance or improvement) incidental to or consequential on the making of the agreement or contribute towards the expense of carrying out such works, and may agree or combine with the council of any other parish or community to carry out such works or to make such a contribution.

PART IV

MAINTENANCE OF HIGHWAYS

Maintenance of highways maintainable at public expense

42 Power of district councils to maintain certain highways

(1)   . . . the council of a non-metropolitan district may undertake the maintenance of any eligible highway in the district which is a highway maintainable at the public expense.

(2)   For the purposes of subsection (1) above the following are eligible highways:—
   (a)   footpaths,
   (b)   bridleways,
   (ba) restricted byways, . . .

43 Power of parish and community councils to maintain footpaths, bridleways and restricted byways

(1)   The council of a parish or community may undertake the maintenance of any footpath, bridleway or restricted byway within the parish or community which is, in either case, a highway maintainable at the public expense; but nothing in this subsection affects the duty of any highway authority or other person to maintain any such footpath, bridleway or restricted byway.

(2)   The highway authority for any footpath, bridleway or restricted byway which a parish or community council have power to maintain under subsection (1) above, and a non-metropolitan district council for the time being maintaining any such footpath, bridleway or restricted byway by virtue of section 42 above, may undertake to defray the whole or part of any expenditure incurred by the parish or community council in maintaining the footpath, bridleway or restricted byway.

(3)   The power of a parish or community council under subsection (1) above is subject to the restrictions for the time being imposed by any enactment on their expenditure, but for the purposes of any enactment imposing such a restriction their expenditure is to be deemed not to include any expenditure falling to be defrayed by a highway authority or district council by virtue of subsection (2) above.

47 Power of magistrates' court to declare unnecessary highway to be not maintainable at public expense

(1) Where a highway authority are of opinion that a highway maintainable at the public expense by them is unnecessary for public use and therefore ought not to be maintained at the public expense, they may, subject to subsections (2) to (4) below, apply to a magistrates' court for an order declaring that the highway shall cease to be so maintained.

(2) No application shall be made under this section for an order relating to a trunk road, special road, metropolitan road, footpath, bridleway or restricted byway.

(3) Where a county council, as highway authority, propose to make an application under this section for an order relating to any highway in England, they shall give notice of the proposal to the council of the district in which the highway is situated, and the application shall not be made if, within 2 months from the date of service of the notice by the county council, notice is given to the county council by the district council that the district council have refused to consent to the making of the application.

(4) If a highway authority propose to make an application under this section for an order relating to a highway situated in a parish or a community they shall give notice of the proposal—

    (a)   to the council of the parish or community, or

    (b)   in the case of a parish not having a separate parish council, to the chairman of the parish meeting,

and the application shall not be made if, within 2 months from the date of service of the notice by the highway authority, notice is given to the highway authority by the council of the parish or community or the chairman of the parish meeting, as the case may be, that the council or meeting have refused to consent to the making of the application.

(5)–(11)   [*These subsections relate to procedure if an application is properly made.*]

48 Power of magistrates' court to order a highway to be again maintainable at public expense

(1) Subject to subsection (2) below, if it appears to a magistrates' court that, in consequence of any change of circumstances since the time at which an order was made under section 47 above, the highway to which the order relates has again become of public use and ought to be maintained at the public expense, the court may by order direct that the highway shall again become for the purposes of this Act a highway maintainable at the public expense.

(2) An order under this section shall not be made except on the application of a person interested in the maintenance of the highway to which the application relates, and on proof that not less than 1 month before making the application he gave notice to the highway authority for the highway of his intention to make an application under this section.

Maintenance of privately maintainable highways

50 Maintenance of privately maintainable footpaths and bridleways

. . .

(2)   The council of a non-metropolitan district, parish or community may undertake by virtue of this subsection the maintenance of any footpath or bridleway within the district, parish or community (other than a footpath or bridleway the maintenance of which they have power to undertake under section 42 or, as the case may be, section 43 above) whether or not any other person is under a duty to maintain the footpath or bridleway; but nothing in this subsection affects the duty of any other person to maintain any such footpath or bridleway.

. . .

Enforcement of liability for maintenance

56 Proceedings for an order to repair highway

(1) A person ('the complainant') who alleges that a way or bridge—

  (a) is a highway maintainable at the public expense or a highway which a person is liable to maintain under a special enactment or by reason of tenure, enclosure or prescription, and

  (b) is out of repair,

may serve a notice on the highway authority or other person alleged to be liable to maintain the way or bridge ('the respondent') requiring the respondent to state whether he admits that the way or bridge is a highway and that he is liable to maintain it.

(2) If, within 1 month from the date of service on him of a notice under subsection (1) above, the respondent does not serve on the complainant a notice admitting both that the way or bridge in question is a highway and that the respondent is liable to maintain it, the complainant may apply to the Crown Court for an order requiring the respondent, if the court finds that the way or bridge is a highway which the respondent is liable to maintain and is out of repair, to put it in proper repair within such reasonable period as may be specified in the order.

(3) The complainant for an order under subsection (2) above shall give notice in writing of the application to the appropriate officer of the Crown Court and the notice shall specify—

  (a) the situation of the way or bridge to which the application relates,

  (b) the name of the respondent,

  (c) the part of the way or bridge which is alleged to be out of repair, and

  (d) the nature of the alleged disrepair;

and the complainant shall serve a copy of the notice on the respondent.

(4) If, within 1 month from the date of service on him of a notice under subsection (1) above, the respondent serves on the complainant a notice admitting both that the way or bridge in question is a highway and that he is liable to maintain it, the complainant may, within 6 months from the date of service on him of that notice, apply to a magistrates' court for an order requiring the respondent, if the court finds that the highway is out of repair, to put it in proper repair within such reasonable period as may be specified in the order.

(5) A court in determining under this section whether a highway is out of repair shall not be required to view the highway unless it thinks fit, and any such view may be made by any 2 or more of the members of the court.

(6) If at the expiration of the period specified in an order made under subsection (2) or (4) above a magistrates' court is satisfied that the highway to which the order relates has not been put in proper repair, then, unless the court thinks fit to extend the period, it shall by order authorise the complainant (if he has not the necessary power in that behalf) to carry out such works as may be necessary to put the highway in proper repair.

(7) Any expenses which a complainant reasonably incurs in carrying out works authorised by an order under subsection (6) above are recoverable from the respondent summarily as a civil debt.

(8) Where any expenses recoverable under subsection (7) above are recovered from the respondent, then, if the respondent would have been entitled to recover from some other person the whole or part of the expenses of repairing the highway in question if he had repaired it himself, he is entitled to recover from that other person the whole or the like part, as the case may be, of the expenses recovered from him.

(9) Where an application is made under this section for an order requiring the respondent to put in proper repair a footpath or bridleway which, in either case, is a highway maintainable at the public expense and some other person is liable to

Highways Act 1980

maintain the footpath or bridleway under a special enactment or by reason of tenure, enclosure or prescription, that other person has a right to be heard by the court which hears the application, but only on the question whether the footpath or bridleway is in proper repair.

PART V

IMPROVEMENT OF HIGHWAYS

Miscellaneous improvements

95A Power to install equipment for detection of traffic offences etc
A highway authority may install and maintain on or near a highway structures and equipment for the detection of traffic offences or offences under section 11 of the HGV Road User Levy Act 2013 (using or keeping heavy goods vehicle if HGV road user levy not paid).

96 Powers of highway and local authorities to plant trees, lay out grass verges etc
(1)   Subject to the provisions of this section, a highway authority may, in a highway maintainable at the public expense by them, plant trees and shrubs and lay out grass verges, and may erect and maintain guards or fences and otherwise do anything expedient for the maintenance or protection of trees, shrubs and grass verges planted or laid out, whether or not by them, in such a highway.
(2)   A highway authority may alter or remove any grass verge laid out, whether or not by them, in a highway maintainable at the public expense by them and any guard, fence or other thing provided, whether or not by them, for the maintenance or protection of any tree, shrub or verge in such a highway.
   . . .
(5)   . . . the council of a parish or community may, with the consent of the highway authority for a highway maintainable at the public expense in the parish or community, exercise with respect to that highway any of the powers conferred by subsections (1) and (2) above on the highway authority.
(6)   No tree, shrub, grass verge, guard or fence shall be planted, laid out or erected under this section, or, if planted, laid out or erected under this section, allowed to remain, in such a situation as to hinder the reasonable use of the highway by any person entitled to use it, or so as to be a nuisance or injurious to the owner or occupier of premises adjacent to the highway.
(7)   If damage is caused to the property of any person by anything done in exercise of the powers conferred by this section, that person is entitled, subject to subsection (8) below, to recover compensation for it from the authority or parish or community council by whom the powers were exercised.
(8)   A person is not entitled to compensation under subsection (7) above if his negligence caused the damage; and if his negligence contributed to the damage the compensation under that subsection shall be reduced accordingly.
   . . .
(10)   References in this section to trees or shrubs are to be construed as including references to plants of any description.

98 Delegation of lighting functions of highway authority
(1)   A highway authority may agree with a lighting authority for the delegation to the lighting authority of any of the functions of the highway authority with respect to the lighting of any highway or part of a highway within the area of the lighting authority.
(2)   A lighting authority shall, in the discharge of any functions delegated to them under subsection (1) above, act as agents for the highway authority; and it shall be a condition of the delegation—

    (a)   that the works to be executed or expenditure to be incurred by the lighting authority in the discharge of the delegated functions are to be subject to the approval of the highway authority;

    (b)   that the lighting authority are to comply with any requirement of the highway authority as to the manner in which any such works are to be carried out, and with any directions of the highway authority as to the terms of contracts to be entered into for the purposes of the discharge of the delegated functions; and

    (c)   that any such works are to be completed to the satisfaction of the highway authority.

(3) If at any time the highway authority are satisfied that a lighting system in respect of which the functions of that authority are delegated under this section is not in proper repair or condition, they may give notice to the lighting authority requiring them to place it in proper repair or condition, and if the notice is not complied with within a reasonable time may themselves do anything which seems to them necessary to place the system in proper repair or condition.

(4) A highway authority may agree with a lighting authority for the carrying out by the lighting authority of any works in connection with a lighting system provided or to be provided by the highway authority within the area of the lighting authority; and subsections (2) and (3) above apply to the conditions to be included in and to the discharge of functions pursuant to any such agreement, as they apply to the conditions to be attached to a delegation of functions under subsection (1) above and the discharge of functions so delegated.

(5) A delegation to a lighting authority under this section may be determined by notice given to that authority by the highway authority during the first 9 months of any calendar year, and functions delegated to a lighting authority under this section may be relinquished by notice given by that authority to the highway authority during any such period; and any such notice shall take effect as from 1st April in the calendar year following that in which it is given.

PART VIII

STOPPING UP AND DIVERSION OF HIGHWAYS AND STOPPING UP OF
MEANS OF ACCESS TO HIGHWAYS

Stopping up and diversion of highways

116 Power of magistrates' court to authorise stopping up or diversion of highway
(1) Subject to the provisions of this section, if it appears to a magistrates' court, after a view, if the court thinks fit, by any two or more of the justices composing the court, that a highway (other than a trunk road or a special road) as respects which the highway authority have made an application under this section—

    (a)   is unnecessary, or

    (b)   can be diverted so as to make it nearer or more commodious to the public,

the court may by order authorise it to be stopped up or, as the case may be, to be so diverted.

(3) If an authority propose to make an application under this section for an order relating to any highway (other than a classified road) they shall give notice of the proposal to—

    (a)   if the highway is in a non-metropolitan district, the council of that district; and

    (aa)   if the highway is in Wales, the Welsh council for the area in which it is situated if they are not the highway authority for it; and

(b)   if the highway is in England, the council of the parish (if any) in which the highway is situated or, if the parish does not have a separate parish council, to the chairman of the parish meeting; and

(c)   if the highway is in Wales, the council (if any) of the community in which the highway is situated;

and the application shall not be made if within 2 months from the date of service of the notice by the authority notice is given to the authority by the district council or Welsh council or by the parish or community council or, as the case may be, by the chairman of the parish meeting that the council or meeting have refused to consent to the making of the application.

(4)   An application under this section may be made, and an order under it may provide, for the stopping up or diversion of a highway for the purposes of all traffic, or subject to the reservation of a footpath, bridleway or restricted byway.

. . .

(8)   An order under this section authorising the diversion of a highway—

(a)   shall not be made unless the written consent of every person having a legal interest in the land over which the highway is to be diverted is produced to and deposited with the court; and

(b)   except in so far as the carrying out of the diversion may necessitate temporary interference with the highway, shall not authorise the stopping up of any part of the highway until the new part to be substituted for the part to be stopped up (including, where a diversion falls to be carried out under orders of 2 different courts, any necessary continuation of the new part in the area of the other court) has been completed to the satisfaction of 2 justices of the peace acting in the same local justice area as the court by which the order was made and a certificate to that effect signed by them has been transmitted to the clerk of the applicant authority.

. . .

(10)   Part II of Schedule 12 to this Act applies where, in pursuance of an order under this section, a highway is stopped up or diverted and, immediately before the order is made, there is under, in, upon, over, along or across the highway any apparatus belonging to or used by any statutory undertakers for the purpose of their undertaking.

(11)   In this section 'statutory undertakers'[1] includes operators of driver information systems.

[1]   Not printed. It concerns apparatus belonging to statutory undertakers.

117 Application for order under section 116 on behalf of another person

A person who desires a highway to be stopped up or diverted but is not authorised to make an application for that purpose under section 116 above may request the highway authority to make such an application; and if the authority grant the request they may, as a condition of making the application, require him to make such provision for any costs to be incurred by them in connection with the matter as they deem reasonable.

118 Stopping up of footpaths, bridleways and restricted byways

(1)   Where it appears to a council as respects a footpath, bridleway or restricted byway in their area (other than one which is a trunk road or a special road) that it is expedient that the path or way should be stopped up on the ground that it is not needed for public use, the council may by order made by them and submitted to and confirmed by the Secretary of State, or confirmed as an unopposed order, extinguish the public right of way over the path or way.

An order under this section is referred to in this Act as a 'public path extinguishment order'.

(2)   The Secretary of State shall not confirm a public path extinguishment order, and a council shall not confirm such an order as an unopposed order, unless he or, as the case may be, they are satisfied that it is expedient so to do having regard to the extent (if any) to which it appears to him or, as the case may be, them that the path or way would, apart from the order, be likely to be used by the public, and having regard to the effect which the extinguishment of the right of way would have as respects land served by the path or way, account being taken of the provisions as to compensation contained in section 28 above as applied by section 121(2) below.

. . .

(4)   Schedule 6 to this Act has effect as to the making, confirmation, validity and date of operation of public path extinguishment orders.

(5)   Where, in accordance with regulations made under paragraph 3 of the said Schedule 6, proceedings preliminary to the confirmation of the public path extinguishment order are taken concurrently with proceedings preliminary to the confirmation of a public path creation order, public path diversion order or rail crossing diversion order then, in considering—

(a)   under subsection (1) above whether the path or way to which the public path extinguishment order relates is needed for public use, or

(b)   under subsection (2) above to what extent (if any) that path or way would apart from the order be likely to be used by the public,

the council or the Secretary of State, as the case may be, may have regard to the extent to which the public path creation order, public path diversion order or rail crossing diversion order would provide an alternative path or way.

(6)   For the purposes of subsections (1) and (2) above, any temporary circumstances preventing or diminishing the use of a path or way by the public shall be disregarded.

(6A)   The considerations to which—

(a)   the Secretary of State is to have regard in determining whether or not to confirm a public path extinguishment order, and

(b)   a council are to have regard in determining whether or not to confirm such an order as an unopposed order,

include any material provision of a rights of way improvement plan prepared by any local highway authority whose area includes land over which the order would extinguish a public right of way.

118A Stopping up of footpaths and bridleways crossing railways
[*This section empowers a council to stop up a level crossing footpath or bridleway where, in general, public safety cannot be otherwise achieved.*] [E]

118B Stopping up of certain highways for purposes of crime prevention, etc
[*This section provides a stopping up procedure in cases where crime would otherwise disrupt the community or to protect school staff and pupils from violence, harassment or distress.*]

119 Diversion of footpaths and bridleways
(1)   Where it appears to a council as respects a footpath or bridleway in their area (other than one that is a trunk road or special road) that, in the interests of the owner, lessee or occupier of land crossed by the path or way or of the public, it is expedient that the line of the path or way, or part of that line, should be diverted (whether on to land of the same or of another owner, lessee or occupier), the council may, subject to subsection (2) below, by order made by them and submitted to and confirmed by the Secretary of State, or confirmed as an unopposed order,—

(a)   create, as from such date as may be specified in the order, any such new footpath, bridleway or restricted byway as appears to the council requisite for effecting the diversion, and

(b)   extinguish, as from such date as may be specified in the order or determined in accordance with the provisions of subsection (3) below, the public right of way over so much of the path or way as appears to the council requisite as aforesaid.

An order under this section is referred to in this Act as a 'public path diversion order'.

(2) A public path diversion order shall not alter a point of termination of the path or way—

(a)   if that point is not on a highway, or

(b)   (where it is on a highway) otherwise than to another point which is on the same highway, or a highway connected with it, and which is substantially as convenient to the public.

(3) Where it appears to the council that work requires to be done to bring the new site of the footpath, bridleway or restricted byway into a fit condition for use by the public, the council shall—

(a)   specify a date under subsection (1)(a) above, and

(b)   provide that so much of the order as extinguishes (in accordance with subsection (1)(b) above) a public right of way is not to come into force until the local highway authority for the new path or way certify that the work has been carried out.

(4) A right of way created by a public path diversion order may be either unconditional or (whether or not the right of way extinguished by the order was subject to limitations or conditions of any description) subject to such limitations or conditions as may be specified in the order.

(5) Before determining to make a public path diversion order on the representations of an owner, lessee or occupier of land crossed by the path or way, the council may require him the person who made the application or representations to enter into an agreement with them to defray, or to make such contribution as may be specified in the agreement towards,—

(a)–(c) [*these paragraphs cover compensation and expenses*].

(6) The Secretary of State shall not confirm a public path diversion order, and a council shall not confirm such an order as an unopposed order, unless he or, as the case may be, they are satisfied that the diversion to be effected by it is expedient as mentioned in subsection (1) above, and further that the path or way will not be substantially less convenient to the public in consequence of the diversion and that it is expedient to confirm the order having regard to the effect which—

(a)   the diversion would have on public enjoyment of the path or way as a whole,

(b)   the coming into operation of the order would have as respects other land served by the existing public right of way, and

(c)   any new public right of way created by the order would have as respects the land over which the right is so created and any land held with it,

so, however, that for the purposes of paragraphs (b) and (c) above the Secretary of State or, as the case may be, the council shall take into account the provisions as to compensation referred to in subsection (5)(a) above.

(6A) [*This sub-s covers the consideration of rights of way of improvement plan.*]

. . .

(8) Schedule 6 to this Act has effect as to the making, confirmation, validity and date of operation of public path diversion orders.

. . .

119A Diversion of footpaths, bridleways and restricted byways crossing railways
[*This section completes the powers conferred on a council by s 118A by enabling it to divert rather than stop up a level crossing footpath, bridleway or restricted byway. S 119D similarly in places of scientific interest.* [E]]

119B Diversion of certain highways for purposes of crime prevention, etc

(1) This section applies where it appears to a council—

   (a) that, as respects any relevant highway for which they are the highway authority and which is in an area designated by the Secretary of State by order under section 118B(1)(a) above, the conditions in subsection (3) below are satisfied and it is expedient, for the purpose of preventing or reducing crime which would otherwise disrupt the life of the community, that the line of the highway, or part of that line should be diverted (whether on to land of the same or another owner, lessee or occupier), or

   (b) that, as respects any relevant highway for which they are the highway authority and which crosses land occupied for the purposes of a school, it is expedient, for the purpose of protecting the pupils or staff from—

   (i)   violence or the threat of violence,

   (ii)   harassment,

   (iii) alarm or distress arising from unlawful activity, or

   (iv) any other risk to their health or safety arising from such activity,

that the line of the highway, or part of that line, should be diverted (whether on to land of the same or another owner, lessee or occupier).

(2) In subsection (1) above "relevant highway" means—

   (a) any footpath, bridleway or restricted byway,

   (b) any highway which is shown in a definitive map and statement as a footpath, a bridleway, or a restricted byway, but over which the public have a right of way for vehicular and all other kinds of traffic, or

   (c) any highway which is shown in a definitive map and statement as a byway open to all traffic,

but does not include a highway that is a trunk road or a special road.

(3) The conditions referred to in subsection (1)(a) above are—

   (a) that premises adjoining or adjacent to the highway are affected by high levels of crime, and

   (b) that the existence of the highway is facilitating the persistent commission of criminal offences.

(4) Where this section applies, the council may by order made by them and submitted to and confirmed by the Secretary of State, or confirmed as an unopposed order—

   (a) create, as from such date as may be specified in the order, any such—

   (i)   new footpath, bridleway or restricted byway, or

   (ii)   in a case falling within subsection (2)(b) or (c) above, new highway over which the public have a right of way for vehicular and all other kinds of traffic,

as appears to the council requisite for effecting the diversion, and

   (b) extinguish, as from such date as may be specified in the order or determined in accordance with the provisions of subsection (8) below, the public right of way over so much of the highway as appears to the council to be requisite for the purpose mentioned in paragraph (a) or (b) of subsection (1) above.

(5) An order under subsection (4) above is in this Act referred to as a "special diversion order".

(6) Before making a special diversion order, the council shall consult the police authority for the area in which the highway is situated.

(7) A special diversion order shall not alter a point of termination of the highway—

    (a)   if that point is not on a highway, or

    (b)   (where it is on a highway) otherwise than to another point which is on the same highway, or a highway connected with it.

(8) Where it appears to the council that work requires to be done to bring the new site of the highway into a fit condition for use by the public, the council shall—

    (a)   specify a date under subsection (4)(a) above, and

    (b)   provide that so much of the order as extinguishes (in accordance with subsection (4)(b) above) a public right of way is not to come into force until the local highway authority for the new highway certify that the work has been carried out.

(9) A right of way created by a special diversion order may be either unconditional or (whether or not the right of way extinguished by the order was subject to limitations or conditions of any description) subject to such limitations or conditions as may be specified in the order.

(10) The Secretary of State shall not confirm a special diversion order made by virtue of subsection (1)(a) above, and a council shall not confirm such an order as an unopposed order unless he or, as the case may be, they are satisfied that the conditions in subsection (3) above are satisfied, that the diversion of the highway is expedient as mentioned in subsection (1)(a) above and that it is expedient to confirm the order having regard to all the circumstances, and in particular to—

    (a)   whether and, if so, to what extent the order is consistent with any strategy for the reduction of crime and disorder prepared under section 6 of the Crime and Disorder Act 1998,

    (b)   the effect which the coming into operation of the order would have as respects land served by the existing public right of way, and

    (c)   the effect which any new public right of way created by the order would have as respects the land over which the right is so created and any land held with it,

so, however, that for the purposes of paragraphs (b) and (c) above the Secretary of State or, as the case may be, the council shall take into account the provisions as to compensation contained in section 28 above as applied by section 121(2) below.

(11) The Secretary of State shall not confirm a special diversion order made by virtue of subsection (1)(b) above, and a council shall not confirm such an order as an unopposed order unless he or, as the case may be, they are satisfied that the diversion of the highway is expedient as mentioned in subsection (1)(b) above and that it is expedient to confirm the order having regard to all the circumstances, and in particular to—

    (a)   any other measures that have been or could be taken for improving or maintaining the security of the school,

    (b)   whether it is likely that the coming into operation of the order will result in a substantial improvement in that security,

    (c)   the effect which the coming into operation of the order would have as respects land served by the existing public right of way, and

    (d)   the effect which any new public right of way created by the order would have as respects the land over which the right is so created and any land held with it,

so, however, that for the purposes of paragraphs (c) and (d) above the Secretary of State or, as the case may be, the council shall take into account the provisions as to compensation contained in section 28 above as applied by section 121(2) below.

(12) A special diversion order shall be in such form as may be prescribed by regulations made by the Secretary of State and shall contain a map, on such scale as may be so prescribed—

(a)   showing the existing site of so much of the line of the highway as is to be diverted by the order and the new site to which it is to be diverted,

(b)   indicating whether a new right of way is created by the order over the whole of the new site or whether some part of it is already comprised in a highway, and

(c)   where some part of the new site is already so comprised, defining that part.

(13)   Schedule 6 to this Act has effect as to the making, confirmation, validity and date of operation of special diversion orders.

(14)   Section 27 above (making up of new footpaths, bridleways and restricted byways) applies to a highway created by a special diversion order with the substitution—

(a)   for references to a footpath, bridleway or restricted byway of references to a footpath, a bridleway, a restricted byway or a highway over which the public have a right of way for vehicular and all other kinds of traffic,

(b)   for references to a public path creation order of references to a special diversion order, and

(c)   for references to section 26(2) above of references to section 120(3) below.

(15)   Neither section 27 nor section 36 above is to be regarded as obliging a highway authority to provide on any highway created by a special diversion order a metalled carriage-way.

119D Diversion of certain highways for protection of sites of special scientific interest

(1)   Subsection (3) below applies where, on an application made in accordance with this section by the appropriate conservation body, it appears to a council, as respects any relevant highway for which they are the highway authority and which is in, forms part of, or is adjacent to or contiguous with, a site of special scientific interest—

(a)   that public use of the highway is causing, or that continued public use of the highway is likely to cause, significant damage to the flora, fauna or geological or physiographical features by reason of which the site of special scientific interest is of special interest, and

(b)   that it is expedient that the line of the highway, or part of that line should be diverted (whether on to land of the same or another owner, lessee or occupier) for the purpose of preventing such damage.

(2)   In subsection (1) 'relevant highway' means—

(a)   a footpath, bridleway or restricted byway,

(b)   a highway which is shown in a definitive map and statement as a footpath, a bridleway or a restricted byway but over which the public have a right of way for vehicular and all other kinds of traffic, or

(c)   any highway which is shown in a definitive map and statement as a byway open to all traffic,

but does not include any highway that is a trunk road or special road.

(3)   Where this subsection applies, the council may, by order made by them and submitted to and confirmed by the Secretary of State, or confirmed as an unopposed order,—

(a)   create, as from such date as may be specified in the order, any such—

(i)   new footpath, bridleway or restricted byway, or

(ii)   in a case falling within subsection (2)(b) or (c) above, new highway over which the public have a right of way for vehicular and all other kinds of traffic,

as appears to the council requisite for effecting the diversion, and

(b)   extinguish, as from such date as may be specified in the order or determined in accordance with the provisions of subsection (6) below, the public right of way over so much of the way as appears to the council to be requisite for the purpose mentioned in subsection (1)(b) above.

(4) An order under this section is referred to in this Act as an 'SSSI diversion order'.

(5) An SSSI diversion order shall not alter a point of termination of the highway—

    (a)   if that point is not on a highway, or

    (b)   (where it is on a highway) otherwise than to another point which is on the same highway, or a highway connected with it.

(6) Where it appears to the council that work requires to be done to bring the new site of the highway into a fit condition for use by the public, the council shall—

    (a)   specify a date under subsection (3)(a) above, and

    (b)   provide that so much of the order as extinguishes (in accordance with subsection (3)(b) above) a public right of way is not to come into force until the local highway authority for the new highway certify that the work has been carried out.

(7) A right of way created by an SSSI diversion order may be either unconditional or (whether or not the right of way extinguished by the order was subject to limitations or conditions of any description) subject to such limitations or conditions as may be specified in the order.

(8) Before determining to make an SSSI diversion order, the council may require the appropriate conservation body to enter into an agreement with them to defray, or to make such contribution as may be specified in the agreement towards,—

    (a)   any compensation which may become payable under section 28 above as applied by section 121(2) below,

    (b)   to the extent that the council are the highway authority for the highway, any expenses which they may incur in bringing the new site of the highway into fit condition for use for the public, or

    (c)   to the extent that the council are not the highway authority, any expenses which may become recoverable from them by the highway authority under the provisions of section 27(2) above as applied by section 119E(6) below.

(9) The Secretary of State shall not confirm an SSSI diversion order, and a council shall not confirm such an order as an unopposed order, unless he, or as the case may be, they are satisfied that the conditions in subsection (1)(a) and (b) are satisfied, and that it is expedient to confirm the order having regard to the effect which—

    (a)   the diversion would have on public enjoyment of the right of way as a whole;

    (b)   the coming into operation of the order would have as respects other land served by the existing public right of way; and

    (c)   any new public right of way created by the order would have as respects the land over which the right is so created and any land held with it,

so, however, that for the purposes of paragraphs (b) and (c) above the Secretary of State or, as the case may be, the council shall take into account the provisions as to compensation referred to in subsection (8)(a) above.

(10) Schedule 6 to this Act has effect as to the making, confirmation, validity and date of operation of SSSI diversion orders.

(11) This section has effect subject to section 119E below.

(12) In this section—

    'the appropriate conservation body' means—

        (a)   as respects England, Natural England, and

        (b)   as respects Wales, the Countryside Council for Wales;

    'site of special scientific interest' has the same meaning as in the Wildlife and Countryside Act 1981.

¹ This section is in force in relation to England, but as at 24 March 2013, not in relation to Wales.

119E Provisions supplementary to section 119D

(1) An application under section 119D above shall be in such form as may be prescribed and shall be accompanied by—

    (a)   a map, on such scale as may be prescribed,—

        (i)   showing the existing site of so much of the line of the highway as would be diverted if the order were made and the new site to which it would be diverted,

        (ii)   indicating whether a new right of way would be created by the order over the whole of the new site or whether some of it is already comprised in a highway, and

        (iii)   where some part of the new site is already so comprised, defining that part,

    (b)   by an assessment in the prescribed form of the effects of public use of the right of way on the site of special scientific interest, and

    (c)   by such other information as may be prescribed.

(2) At least fourteen days before making an application under section 119D above, the appropriate conservation body shall give a notice in the prescribed form of their intention to do so—

    (a)   to any owner, lessee or occupier of land over which the proposed order would create or extinguish a public right of way; and

    (b)   to such other persons as may be prescribed;

(3) A council, in determining whether it is expedient to make or confirm an SSSI diversion order, and the Secretary of State, in determining whether to confirm such an order, shall, in particular, have regard to the following questions—

    (a)   whether the council would be able to prevent damage of the kind referred to in section 119D(1) above by making a traffic regulation order, and

    (b)   if so, whether the making of a traffic regulation order would cause less inconvenience to the public than that which would be caused by the diversion of the highway.

(4) The Secretary of State, in determining whether it is expedient to make an SSSI diversion order under section 120(3) below in a case where by virtue of section 22(4) of the Road Traffic Regulation Act 1984 he has power to make a traffic regulation order shall, in particular, have regard to the following questions—

    (a)   whether he would be able to prevent damage of the kind referred to in section 119D(1) above by making a traffic regulation order, and

    (b)   if so, whether the making of a traffic regulation order would cause less inconvenience to the public than that which would be caused by the diversion of the highway.

(5) An SSSI diversion order shall be in such form as may be prescribed and shall contain a map, on such scale as may be prescribed,—

    (a)   showing the existing site of so much of the line of the highway as is to be diverted by the order and the new site to which it is to be diverted,

    (b)   indicating whether a new right of way is created by the order over the whole of the new site or whether some part of it is already comprised in a highway, and

    (c)   where some part of the new site is already so comprised, defining that part.

(6) Section 27 above (making up of new footpaths, bridleways and restricted byways) applies to a highway created by an SSSI diversion order with the substitution—

(a)   for references to a footpath, bridleway or restricted byway of references to a footpath, a bridleway, a restricted byway or a highway over which the public have a right of way for vehicular and all other kinds of traffic,

(b)   for references to a public path creation order, of references to an SSSI diversion order, and

(c)   for references to section 26(2) above, of references to section 120(3) below.

(7)   Neither section 27 nor section 36 above is to be regarded as obliging a highway authority to provide on any highway created by an SSSI diversion order a metalled carriage-way.

(8)   In this section—

'the appropriate conservation body' has the same meaning as in section 119D above;

'prescribed' means prescribed by regulations made by the Secretary of State;

'site of special scientific interest' has the same meaning as in the Wildlife and Countryside Act 1981;

'traffic regulation order' means an order under section 1 or 6 of the Road Traffic Regulation Act 1984.

---

¹   This section is in force in relation to England, but as at 24 March 2013, not in relation to Wales.

120 Exercise of powers of making public path extinguishment and diversion orders

(1)   Where a footpath or bridleway lies partly within and partly outside the area of a council the powers conferred by sections 118, 118A, 119 and 119A above on the council extend, subject to subsection (2) below, to the whole of the path or way as if it lay wholly within their area.

(1A)   Where a council are the highway authority for only part of a highway, the powers conferred on the council by sections 118B, 119B and 119D above are exercisable with respect to the whole of the highway, but subject to subsection (2) and only with the consent of every other council which is a highway authority for any other part with respect to which the powers are exercised¹.

(2)   The powers of making orders under sections 118 to 119D above are not exercisable by a council—

(a)   with respect to any part of a highway which is within their area, without prior consultation with any other council in whose area that part of the highway is situated;

(b)   with respect to any part of a highway which is outside their area, without the consent of every council in whose area it is; and

(c)   with respect to any part of a highway in a National Park, without prior consultation with the Countryside Agency (if the National Park is in England) or the Countryside Council for Wales (if the National Park is in Wales).

(3)   Where it appears to the Secretary of State as respects a footpath, bridleway or restricted byway that it is expedient as mentioned in section 118(1) or 118A(1) or 119A(1) above that the path or way should be stopped up or diverted, or where it appears to the Secretary of State as respects a relevant highway as defined by section 118B(2), 119B(2) or 119D(2) that it is expedient as mentioned in section 118B(1)(a) or (b), 119B(1)(a) or (b) or 119D(1)(b) that the highway should be stopped up or diverted, or where an owner, lessee or occupier of land crossed by a footpath, bridleway or restricted byway satisfies the Secretary of State that a diversion of it is expedient as mentioned in section 119(1) above, then if—

(a)   no council having power to do so have made and submitted to him a public path extinguishment order, a rail crossing extinguishment order, a special extinguishment order, a public path diversion order, a rail crossing diversion order, a special diversion order or an SSSI diversion order, as the case may be, and

(b)   the Secretary of State is satisfied that, if such an order were made and submitted to him, he would have power to confirm the order in accordance with the provisions in that behalf of sections 118 to 119D above,

he may himself make the order after consultation (subject to the following provisions of this section) with the appropriate authority and, in the case of an SSSI diversion order, with the appropriate conservation body.

(3A) Where—

(a)   the operator of a railway makes a request to a council to make an order under section 118A or 119A above in respect of a crossing over the railway,

(b)   the request is in such form and gives such particulars as are prescribed by regulations made by the Secretary of State, and

(c)   the council have neither confirmed the order nor submitted it to the Secretary of State within 6 months of receiving the request,

the power conferred on the Secretary of State by subsection (3) above may be exercised without consultation with the council.

(3B) Unless an appeal to the Secretary of State is brought under section 121D(1) below, the power conferred on the Secretary of State by subsection (3) above to make a special extinguishment order or a special diversion order is exercisable only after consultation with the local policing body in whose area the highway lies.

(3C) The power conferred on the Secretary of State by subsection (3) above to make an SSSI diversion order may be exercised even though the appropriate conservation body has not made an application under section 119D above to the council who are the highway authority for the highway.

(3D) Where—

(a)   the appropriate conservation body has made an application under section 119D above to a council in respect of a highway for which the council are the highway authority, and

(b)   the council have neither confirmed the order nor submitted it to the Secretary of State for confirmation within 6 months of receiving the application,

the power conferred on the Secretary of State by subsection (3) above to make an SSSI diversion order may be exercised without consultation with the council.

. . .

(5) Where under subsection (3) above the Secretary of State decides to make a public path diversion order, or, on the representations of the operator of the railway concerned, a rail crossing diversion order, he may require the person on whose representations he is acting to enter into an agreement with such council as he may specify for that person to defray, or to make such contribution as may be specified in the agreement towards any such compensation or expenses as are specified in paragraphs (a), (b) and (c) of section 119(5), or as the case may be 119A(8), above[2].

[*Note: the remaining wordings of this section (subsection (3A) onwards), as a result of the Countryside and Rights of Way Act 2000, set out procedures which bind the Secretary of State.*]

---

[1]   Sub-s (1A) is in force in relation to England, and in force in Wales for certain purposes: see SI 2005/1314.

[2]   Sub-s (5) has been substituted by the following. The amendment is in force in relation to England and Wales for certain purposes only (see SIs 2003/272, 2005/1314, 2007/1493 for full details).

(5) The Secretary of State may, before determining—

(a) under subsection (3) above, to make a public path diversion order,

(b) under subsection (3) above, to make a public path extinguishment order, special extinguishment order, public path diversion order or special diversion order on an appeal under section 121D(1)(a) below,

(c) to confirm a public path extinguishment order, special extinguishment order, public path diversion order or special diversion order in respect of which an appeal under section 121D(1)(b) or (c) below has been brought, or

(d) under subsection (3) above, to make a rail crossing diversion order on the representations of the operator of the railway concerned,

require the appropriate person to enter into such agreement as he may specify with such council has he may specify for that person to defray, or to make such contribution as may be specified in the agreement towards, any such compensation or expenses as are specified in paragraphs (a), (b) and (c) of section 119(5), or as the case may be, section 118ZA(6), 119A(8) or 119C(3) above.

123 Saving and interpretation

(1) The provisions of any enactment contained in the foregoing provisions of this Part of this Act do not prejudice any power conferred by any other enactment (whether contained in this Part of this Act or not) to stop up or divert a highway, and do not otherwise affect the operation of any enactment not contained in this Part of this Act relating to the extinguishment, suspension, diversion or variation of public rights of way.

(2) Unless the context otherwise requires, expressions in the foregoing provisions of this Part of this Act, other than expressions to which meanings are assigned by sections 328 and 329 below, have the same meanings respectively as in the Town and Country Planning Act 1990.

PART IX

LAWFUL AND UNLAWFUL INTERFERENCE WITH HIGHWAYS AND STREETS

Protection of public rights

130 Protection of public rights

(1) It is the duty of the highway authority to assert and protect the rights of the public to the use and enjoyment of any highway for which they are the highway authority, including any roadside waste which forms part of it.

(2) Any council may assert and protect the rights of the public to the use and enjoyment of any highway in their area for which they are not the highway authority, including any roadside waste which forms part of it.

(3) Without prejudice to subsections (1) and (2) above, it is the duty of a council who are a highway authority to prevent, as far as possible, the stopping up or obstruction of—

(a) the highways for which they are the highway authority, and

(b) any highway for which they are not the highway authority, if, in their opinion, the stopping up or obstruction of that highway would be prejudicial to the interests of their area.

(4) Without prejudice to the foregoing provisions of this section, it is the duty of a local highway authority to prevent any unlawful encroachment on any roadside waste comprised in a highway for which they are the highway authority.

(5) Without prejudice to their powers under section 222 of the Local Government Act 1972, a council may, in the performance of their functions under the foregoing

provisions of this section, institute legal proceedings in their own name, defend any legal proceedings and generally take such steps as they deem expedient.

(6) If the council of a parish or community or, in the case of a parish or community which does not have a separate parish or community council, the parish meeting or a community meeting, represent to a local highway authority—

(a)   that a highway as to which the local highway authority have the duty imposed by subsection (3) above has been unlawfully stopped up or obstructed, or

(b)   that an unlawful encroachment has taken place on a roadside waste comprised in a highway for which they are the highway authority,

it is the duty of the local highway authority, unless satisfied that the representations are incorrect, to take proper proceedings accordingly and they may do so in their own name.

(7) Proceedings or steps taken by a council in relation to an alleged right of way are not to be treated as unauthorised by reason only that the alleged right is found not to exist.

Damage to highways, streets etc

131 Penalty for damaging highway etc

(1) If a person, without lawful authority or excuse—

(a)   makes a ditch or excavation in a highway which consists of or comprises a carriageway, or

(b)   removes any soil or turf from any part of a highway, except for the purpose of improving the highway and with the consent of the highway authority for the highway, or

(c)   deposits anything whatsoever on a highway so as to damage the highway, or

(d)   lights any fire, or discharges any firearm or firework, within 50 feet from the centre of a highway which consists of or comprises a carriageway, and in consequence thereof the highway is damaged,

he is guilty of an offence.

(2) If a person without lawful authority or excuse pulls down or obliterates a traffic sign placed on or over a highway, or a milestone or direction post (not being a traffic sign) so placed, he is guilty of an offence; but it is a defence in any proceedings under this subsection to show that the traffic sign, milestone or post was not lawfully so placed.

(3) A person guilty of an offence under this section is liable to a fine not exceeding level 3 on the standard scale.

131A Disturbance of surface of certain highways

(1) A person who, without lawful authority or excuse, so disturbs the surface of—

(a)   a footpath,

(b)   a bridleway, or

(c)   any other highway which consists of or comprises a carriageway other than a made-up carriageway,

as to render it inconvenient for the exercise of the public right of way is guilty of an offence and liable to a fine not exceeding level 3 on the standard scale.

(2) Proceedings for an offence under this section shall be brought only by the highway authority or the council of the non-metropolitan district, parish or community in which the offence is committed; and, without prejudice to section 130 (protection of public rights) above, it is the duty of the highway authority to ensure that where desirable in the public interest such proceedings are brought.

134 Ploughing etc of footpath or bridleway

(1)   Where in the case of any footpath or bridleway (other than a field-edge path) which passes over a field or enclosure consisting of agricultural land, or land which is being brought into use for agriculture—

    (a)   the occupier of the field or enclosure desires in accordance with the rules of good husbandry to plough, or otherwise disturb the surface of, all or part of the land comprised in the field or enclosure, and

    (b)   it is not reasonably convenient in ploughing, or otherwise disturbing the surface of, the land to avoid disturbing the surface of the path or way so as to render it inconvenient for the exercise of the public right of way,

the public right of way shall be subject to the condition that the occupier has the right so to plough or otherwise disturb the surface of the path or way.

(2)   Subsection (1) above does not apply in relation to any excavation or any engineering operation.

(3)   Where the occupier has disturbed the surface of a footpath or bridleway under the right conferred by subsection (1) above he shall within the relevant period, or within an extension of that period granted under subsection (8) below,—

    (a)   so make good the surface of the path or way to not less than its minimum width as to make it reasonably convenient for the exercise of the right of way; and

    (b)   so indicate the line of the path or way on the ground to not less than its minimum width that it is apparent to members of the public wishing to use it.

(4)   If the occupier fails to comply with the duty imposed by subsection (3) above he is guilty of an offence and liable to a fine not exceeding level 3 on the standard scale.

(6)   Without prejudice to section 130 (protection of public rights) above, it is the duty of the highway authority to enforce the provisions of this section.

(7)   For the purposes of this section 'the relevant period',—

    (a)   where the disturbance of the surface of the path or way is the first disturbance for the purposes of the sowing of a particular agricultural crop, means fourteen days beginning with the day on which the surface of the path or way was first disturbed for those purposes; or

    (b)   in any other case, means twenty-four hours beginning with the time when it was disturbed.

(8)   On an application made to the highway authority before the disturbance or during the relevant period, the authority may grant an extension of that period for an additional period not exceeding twenty-eight days.

(9)   In this section 'minimum width', in relation to a highway, has the same meaning as in Schedule 12A to this Act.

135 Authorisation of other works disturbing footpath or bridleway

(1)   Where the occupier of any agricultural land, or land which is being brought into use for agriculture, desires to carry out in relation to that land an excavation or engineering operation, and the excavation or operation—

    (a)   is reasonably necessary for the purposes of agriculture, but

    (b)   will so disturb the surface of a footpath or bridleway which passes over that land as to render it inconvenient for the exercise of the public right of way,

he may apply to the highway authority for an order that the public right of way shall be subject to the condition that he has the right to disturb the surface by that excavation or operation during such period, not exceeding three months, as is specified in the order ('the authorisation period').

(2)   The highway authority shall make an order under subsection (1) above if they are satisfied either—

(a)   that it is practicable temporarily to divert the path or way in a manner reasonably convenient to users; or

(b)   that it is practicable to take adequate steps to ensure that the path or way remains sufficiently convenient, having regard to the need for the excavation or operation, for temporary use while it is being carried out.

(3)   An order made by a highway authority under subsection (1) above—

(a)   may provide for the temporary diversion of the path or way during the authorisation period, but shall not divert it on to land not occupied by the applicant unless written consent to the making of the order has been given by the occupier of that land, and by any other person whose consent is needed to obtain access to it;

(b)   may include such conditions as the authority reasonably think fit for the provision, either by the applicant or by the authority at the expense of the applicant, of facilities for the convenient use of any such diversion, including signposts and other notices, stiles, bridges, and gates;

(c)   shall not affect the line of a footpath or bridleway on land not occupied by the applicant;

and the authority shall cause notices of any such diversion, together with a plan showing the effect of the diversion and the line of the alternative route provided, to be prominently displayed throughout the authorisation period at each end of the diversion.

(4)   An order made by a highway authority under subsection (1) above may include such conditions as the authority reasonably think fit—

(a)   for the protection and convenience during the authorisation period of users of the path or way;

(b)   for making good the surface of the path or way to not more than its minimum width before the expiration of the authorisation period;

(c)   for the recovery from the applicant of expenses incurred by the authority in connection with the order.

(5)   An order under this section shall not authorise any interference with the apparatus or works of any statutory undertakers.

(6)   If the applicant fails to comply with a condition imposed under subsection (3)(b) or (4)(a) or (b) above he is guilty of an offence and liable to a fine not exceeding level 3 on the standard scale.

(7)   Proceedings for an offence under this section in relation to a footpath, bridleway or restricted byway shall be brought only by the highway authority or (with the consent of the highway authority) the council of the non-metropolitan district, parish or community in which the offence is committed.

(8)   Without prejudice to section 130 (protection of public rights) above, it is the duty of the highway authority to enforce the provisions of this section.

(9)   In this section 'minimum width', in relation to a highway, has the same meaning as in Schedule 12A to this Act.

Obstruction of highways and streets

137 Penalty for wilful obstruction

(1)   If a person, without lawful authority or excuse, in any way wilfully obstructs the free passage along a highway he is guilty of an offence and liable to a fine not exceeding level 3 on the standard scale.

137ZA Power to order offender to remove obstruction

(1)   Where a person is convicted of an offence under section 137 above in respect of the obstruction of a highway and it appears to the court that—

(a)   the obstruction is continuing, and

(b) it is in that person's power to remove the cause of the obstruction,

the court may, in addition to or instead of imposing any punishment, order him to take, within such reasonable period as may be fixed by the order, such steps as may be specified in the order for removing the cause of the obstruction.

(2) The time fixed by an order under subsection (1) above may be extended or further extended by order of the court on an application made before the end of the time as originally fixed or as extended under this subsection, as the case may be.

(3) If a person fails without reasonable excuse to comply with an order under subsection (1) above, he is guilty of an offence and liable to a fine not exceeding level 5 on the standard scale; and if the offence is continued after conviction he is guilty of a further offence and liable to a fine not exceeding one-twentieth of that level for each day on which the offence is so continued.

(4) Where, after a person is convicted of an offence under subsection (3) above, the highway authority for the highway concerned exercise any power to remove the cause of the obstruction, they may recover from that person the amount of any expenses reasonably incurred by them in, or in connection with, doing so.

(5) A person against whom an order is made under subsection (1) above is not liable under section 137 above in respect of the obstruction concerned—

(a) during the period fixed under that subsection or any extension under subsection (2) above, or

(b) during any period fixed under section 311(1) below by a court before whom he is convicted of an offence under subsection (3) above in respect of the order.

137A Interference by crops

(1) Where a crop other than grass has been sown or planted on any agricultural land the occupier of the land shall from time to time take such steps as may be necessary—

(a) to ensure that the line on the ground of any relevant highway on the land is so indicated to not less than its minimum width as to be apparent to members of the public wishing to use the highway; and

(b) to prevent the crop from so encroaching on any relevant highway, whether passing over that or adjoining land, as to render it inconvenient for the exercise of the public right of way.

(2) For the purposes of subsection (1) above, a crop shall be treated as encroaching on a highway if, and only if, any part of the crop grows on, or otherwise extends onto or over, the highway in such a way as to reduce the apparent width of the highway to less than its minimum width.

(3) For the purposes of the application of subsection (1) above in the case of a particular crop, the crop shall be treated as grass if, and only if—

(a) it is of a variety or mixture commonly used for pasture, silage or haymaking, whether or not it is intended for such a use in that case; and

(b) it is not a cereal crop.

(4) If the occupier fails to comply with the duty imposed by subsection (1) above he is guilty of an offence and liable to a fine not exceeding level 3 on the standard scale.

(5) Without prejudice to section 130 (protection of public rights) above, it is the duty of the highway authority to enforce the provisions of this section.

(6) In this section—

'minimum width', in relation to a highway, has the same meaning as in Schedule 12A to this Act; and

'relevant highway' means—

(a) a footpath,

(b) a bridleway, or

(c) any other highway which consists of or comprises a carriageway other than a made-up carriageway.

144 Power to erect flagpoles etc on highways

(1) Subject to subsection (2) below, a local authority may—

(a)   erect flagpoles, pylons and other structures on any highway in their area for the purpose of displaying decorations;

(b)   make slots in such a highway for the purpose of erecting the structures; and

(c)   remove any structure erected or slot made by the authority in pursuance of paragraph (a) or (b) above;

and any structures or slots which may be erected or made by virtue of this subsection are hereafter in this section referred to as 'relevant works'.

(2) A local authority are not entitled to exercise the powers conferred on them by subsection (1) above in respect of a highway for which they are not the highway authority except with the consent in writing of the highway authority for the highway, and are not entitled to exercise those powers in respect of so much of a highway as—

(a)   is carried by a bridge which a body other than the local authority and the highway authority has a duty to maintain; or

(b)   forms part of the approaches to such a bridge and is supported or protected by works or materials which a body other than the local authority and the highway authority has a duty to maintain,

except with the consent in writing of that body.

   In this subsection 'bridge' includes a structure which carries a highway superimposed over a cutting.

(3) A highway authority or other body may give their consent in pursuance of subsection (2) above on such terms as they think fit (including in particular, without prejudice to the generality of the preceding provisions of this subsection, terms providing for the highway authority or body to remove any of the relevant works and reinstate the highway and to recover the reasonable cost of doing so from the local authority to whom the consent was given).

(4) It is the duty of an authority by whom relevant works are erected or made by virtue of the preceding provisions of this section—

(a)   to ensure that the works are erected or made so as to obstruct the highway in question as little as is reasonably possible, so as not to obscure or conflict with traffic signs connected with the highway and so as to interfere as little as is reasonably possible with the enjoyment of premises adjacent to the highway and with, and with access to, any apparatus in or on the highway which belongs to or is used or maintained by statutory undertakers; and

(b)   to ensure that while the works are retained they are properly maintained and, so far as it is necessary to light them to avoid danger to users of the highway, are properly lit; and

(c)   if the authority are not the highway authority for the highway, to indemnify the highway authority against any payments falling to be made by the highway authority in consequence of the works.

(5) A person who without lawful authority interferes with or removes any relevant works is guilty of an offence and liable to a fine not exceeding level 3 on the standard scale.

(6) In this section—

'local authority' means any of the following, namely, the council of a county, district or London borough . . . and a parish or community council; and 'statutory undertakers' means any of the following, namely, any body which is a statutory undertaker within the meaning provided by section 329(1) below, any universal service provider in connection with the provision of a universal postal service, any licensee under a street works licence and the operator of an electronic communications code network or a driver information system.

146 Duty to maintain stiles etc on footpaths, bridleways and restricted byways

(1) Any stile, gate or other similar structure across a footpath, bridleway or restricted byway shall be maintained by the owner of the land in a safe condition, and to the standard of repair required to prevent unreasonable interference with the rights of the persons using the footpath, bridleway or restricted byway.

(2) If it appears to the appropriate authority that the duty imposed by subsection (1) above is not being complied with, they may, after giving to the owner and occupier not less than 14 days' notice of their intention, take all necessary steps for repairing and making good the stile, gate or other works.

For the purposes of this section the appropriate authority is—

(a) in the case of a footpath, bridleway or restricted byway which is for the time being maintained by a non-metropolitan district council by virtue of section 42 or 50 above, that council, and

(b) in the case of any other footpath, bridleway or restricted byway, the highway authority.

(3) The appropriate authority may recover from the owner of the land the amount of any expenses reasonably incurred by the authority in and in connection with the exercise of their powers under subsection (2) above, or such part of those expenses as the authority think fit.

(4) [*The appropriate authority must contribute 25% of the owner's expenses in carrying out subsection (1) and may contribute more.*]

. . .

PART XII

ACQUISITION, VESTING AND TRANSFER OF LAND ETC

Transfer of property and liabilities on change of status of highway etc

270 Transfer of lighting systems

(1) In this section—

'footway lighting system' means a system of lighting, provided for a highway, which satisfies the following conditions, namely, that either:—

(a) no lamp is mounted more than 13 feet above ground level, or

(b) no lamp is mounted more than 20 feet above ground level and there is at least one interval of more than 50 yards between adjacent lamps in the system,

or such other conditions as may be prescribed by order of the Minister in substitution for the above mentioned conditions;

'road lighting system' means a lighting system that is not a footway lighting system;

and references in this section, as respects a transfer from a lighting authority to a highway authority, to 'the agreed date' are references to such date as may be determined by agreement between the two authorities or, in default of such agreement, as the Minister may direct.

(2) Subsections (3) to (6) below have effect where a road lighting system is at any time provided by a lighting authority for the purposes of a highway for which they are not the highway authority, and this includes cases where a footway lighting system maintained by a lighting authority other than the highway authority becomes a road lighting system—

    (a)   in consequence of any order made by the Minister under subsection (1) above (as respects the conditions referred to in the definition of 'footway lighting system'), or

    (b)   in consequence of any alterations effected by the lighting authority.

(3)   On the agreed date there are transferred to the highway authority—

    (a)   all lamps, lamp-posts and other apparatus which, immediately before the agreed date, were vested in the lighting authority as part of the road lighting system; and

    (b)   except as provided by subsection (4) below, all other property or rights which, immediately before the agreed date, were vested in the lighting authority for the purposes of that system, and all liabilities incurred by that authority for those purposes and not discharged before that date.

and any property or rights so transferred vest, by virtue of this section, in the highway authority.

(4)   There is not transferred to a highway authority by virtue of this section any right or liability of a lighting authority in respect of work done, services rendered, goods (including gas and electricity) supplied or money due for payment before the agreed date, and there is not transferred to the Minister by virtue of this section any liability of a lighting authority in respect of loans or loan charges.

(5)   A highway authority and a lighting authority, or any two or more highway authorities, may make agreements with respect to the transfer of property, rights and liabilities under this section, including agreements—

    (a)   for defining the property, rights and liabilities thereby transferred to the highway authority or any of those authorities, and

    (b)   for the transfer or retention of property, rights or liabilities held or incurred for the purposes of two or more road lighting systems, or partly for the purposes of such a lighting system and partly for other purposes.

(6)   Any dispute between the authorities concerned as to the property, rights or liabilities transferred by this section shall be determined—

    (a)   where the Minister is one of those authorities, by arbitration;

    (b)   in any other case, by the Minister.

(7)   If in the case of a road or part of a road in which a footway lighting system is maintained by a lighting authority other than a highway authority the highway authority propose to provide a road lighting system (either as a separate system or by means of alterations of the footway lighting system), they may give notice to that effect to the lighting authority; and where such notice is given subsections (2) to (6) above apply in relation to the footway lighting system as if for the references in subsections (3) and (4) to the agreed date there were substituted references to such date as may be specified for the purpose in the notice.

PART XIII

FINANCIAL PROVISIONS

274A Contributions by parish or community councils

A parish council or community council may contribute towards any expenses incurred or to be incurred by a highway authority in constructing, removing or maintaining—

    (a)   traffic calming works, or

    (b)   other works (including signs or lighting) required in connection with traffic calming works,

if, in the opinion of the council, the expenditure is or will be of benefit to their area.

PART XIV

MISCELLANEOUS AND SUPPLEMENTARY PROVISIONS

Interpretation

328 Meaning of 'highway'

(1)   In this Act, except where the context otherwise requires, 'highway' means the whole or a part of a highway other than a ferry or waterway.

(2)   Where a highway passes over a bridge or through a tunnel, that bridge or tunnel is to be taken for the purposes of this Act to be a part of the highway.

(3)   In this Act, 'highway maintainable at the public expense' and any other expression defined by reference to a highway is to be construed in accordance with the foregoing provisions of this section.

329 Further provision as to interpretation

(1)   In this Act, except where the context otherwise requires—

> . . .
>
> 'adjoining' includes abutting on, and 'adjoins' is to be construed accordingly;
>
> 'apparatus' includes any structure constructed for the lodging therein of apparatus;
>
> 'bridge' does not include a culvert, but, save as aforesaid, means a bridge or viaduct which is part of a highway, and includes the abutments and any other part of a bridge but not the highway carried thereby;
>
> 'bridleway' means a highway over which the public have the following, but no other, rights of way, that is to say, a right of way on foot and a right of way on horseback or leading a horse, with or without a right to drive animals of any description along the highway;
>
> . . .
>
> 'carriageway' means a way constituting or comprised in a highway, being a way (other than a cycle track) over which the public have a right of way for the passage of vehicles;
>
> . . .
>
> 'contravention' in relation to a condition, restriction or requirement, includes failure to comply with that condition, restriction or requirement, and 'contravene' is to be construed accordingly;
>
> 'council' means a county council or a local authority;
>
> 'cycle track' means a way constituting or comprised in a highway, being a way over which the public have the following, but no other, rights of way, that is to say, a right of way on pedal cycles (other than pedal cycles which are motor vehicles within the meaning of the Road Traffic Act 1988) with or without a right of way on foot;
>
> . . .
>
> 'enactment' includes an enactment in a local or private Act of Parliament and a provision of an order, scheme, regulations or other instrument made under or confirmed by a public general, local or private Act of Parliament;
>
> 'field-edge path' means a footpath or bridleway that follows the sides or headlands of a field or enclosure;
>
> . . .
>
> 'footpath' means a highway over which the public have a right of way on foot only, not being a footway;

'footway' means a way comprised in a highway which also comprises a carriageway, being a way over which the public have a right of way on foot only;

'functions' includes powers and duties;

. . .

'highway maintainable at the public expense' means a highway which by virtue of section 36 above or of any other enactment (whether contained in this Act or not) is a highway which for the purposes of this Act is a highway maintainable at the public expense;

'horse' includes pony, ass and mule, and 'horseback' is to be construed accordingly;

. . .

'improvement' means the doing of any act under powers conferred by Part V of this Act and includes the erection, maintenance, alteration and removal of traffic signs, and the freeing of a highway or road-ferry from tolls;

. . .

'land' includes land covered by water and any interest or right in, over or under land;

'lease' includes an underlease and an agreement for a lease or underlease, but does not include an option to take a lease or mortgage, and 'lessee' is to be construed accordingly;

'lighting authority' means a council or other body authorised to provide lighting under section 161 of the Public Health Act 1875 or under section 3 of the Parish Councils Act 1957 or any corresponding local enactment;

'local authority' means the council of a district or London borough or the Common Council but, in relation to Wales, means a Welsh council;

'local highway authority' means a highway authority other than the Minister;

'local planning authority' has the same meaning as in the Town and Country Planning Act 1990;

. . .

'made-up carriageway' means a carriageway, or a part thereof, which has been metalled or in any other way provided with a surface suitable for the passage of vehicles;

'maintenance' includes repair, and 'maintain' and 'maintainable' are to be construed accordingly;

. . .

'the Minister', subject to subsection (5) below, means as respects England, the Minister of Transport[1] and as respects Wales, the Secretary of State; and in section 258 of, and paragraphs 7, 8(1) and (3), 14, 15(1) and (3), 18(2), 19 and 21 of Schedule 1 to, this Act, references to the Minister and the Secretary of State acting jointly are to be construed, as respects Wales, as references to the Secretary of State acting alone;

. . .

'owner', in relation to any premises, means a person, other than a mortgagee not in possession, who, whether in his own right or as trustee or agent for any other person, is entitled to receive the rack rent of the premises or, where the premises are not let at a rack rent, would be so entitled if the premises were so let;

. . .

'premises' includes land and buildings;

'proposed highway' means land on which, in accordance with plans made by a highway authority, that authority are for the time being constructing or intending to construct a highway shown in the plans;

. . .

'public general enactment' means an enactment in an Act treated as a public general Act under the system of division of Acts adopted in the regnal year 38 George 3, other than an Act for confirming a provisional order;

'public path creation agreement' means an agreement under section 25 above;

'public path creation order' means an order under section 26 above;

'public path diversion order' means an order under section 119 above;

'public path extinguishment order' means an order under section 118 above;

. . .

'rail crossing diversion order' means an order under section 119A above;

'rail crossing extinguishment order' means an order under section 118A above;

'railway' includes a light railway;

'railway undertakers' means persons authorised by any enactment to carry on a railway undertaking;

. . .

'restricted byway' has the same meaning as in Part II of the Countryside and Rights of Way Act 2000;

. . .

'special enactment' means any enactment other than a public general enactment;

. . .

'special road' means a highway, or a proposed highway, which is a special road in accordance with section 16 above;

. . .

'statutory undertakers' means persons authorised by any enactment to carry on any of the following undertakings:—

    (a)   a railway, tramway, road transport, water transport, canal, inland navigation, dock, harbour, pier or lighthouse undertaking, or

    (b)   an undertaking for the supply of hydraulic power,

and 'statutory undertaking' is to be construed accordingly;

'street' has the same meaning as in Part III of the New Roads and Street Works Act 1991;

. . .

'traffic' includes pedestrians and animals;

. . .

'traffic sign' has the same meaning as in section 64 of the Road Traffic Regulation Act 1984;

. . .

'Welsh council' means the council of a Welsh county or county borough.

(2)   A highway at the side of a river, canal or other inland navigation is not excluded from the definition in subsection (1) above of 'bridleway', 'footpath' or 'restricted byway', by reason only that the public have a right to use the highway for purposes of navigation, if the highway would fall within that definition if the public had no such right thereover.

(2A)   In this Act—

    (a)   any reference to a county shall be construed in relation to Wales as including a reference to a county borough;

    (b)   any reference to a county council shall be construed in relation to Wales as including a reference to a county borough council; and

(c)   section 17(4) and (5) of the Local Government (Wales) Act 1994 (references to counties and districts to be construed generally in relation to Wales as references to counties and county boroughs) shall not apply.

(3)   In a case where two or more parishes are grouped under a common parish council, references in this Act to a parish are to be construed as references to those parishes.

(3A)   In a case where two or more communities are grouped under a common community council, references in this Act to a community are to be construed as references to those communities.

. . .

[1]   Now a Secretary of State.

SCHEDULE 6

PROVISIONS AS TO MAKING, CONFIRMATION, VALIDITY AND DATE OF OPERATION OF CERTAIN ORDERS RELATING TO FOOTPATHS, BRIDLEWAYS AND RESTRICTED BYWAYS

PART I

PROCEDURE FOR MAKING AND CONFIRMING CERTAIN ORDERS RELATING TO FOOTPATHS, BRIDLEWAYS AND RESTRICTED BYWAYS

1

(1)   Before a public path creation order, a public path extinguishment order, a rail crossing extinguishment order, a special extinguishment order, a public path diversion order, a rail crossing diversion order, a special diversion order or an SSSI diversion order is submitted to the Secretary of State for confirmation or confirmed as an unopposed order, the authority by whom the order was made shall give notice in the prescribed form—

(a)   stating the general effect of the order and that it has been made and is about to be submitted for confirmation or to be confirmed as an unopposed order,

(b)   naming a place in the area in which the land to which the order relates is situated where a copy of the order and of the map referred to therein may be inspected free of charge and copies thereof may be obtained at a reasonable charge at all reasonable hours, and

(c)   specifying the time (which shall not be less than 28 days from the date of the first publication of the notice) within which, and the manner in which, representations or objections with respect to the order may be made.

(2)   Before the Secretary of State makes a public path creation order, a public path extinguishment order, a rail crossing extinguishment order, a special extinguishment order, a public path diversion order, a rail crossing diversion order, a special diversion order or an SSSI diversion order, he shall prepare a draft of the order and shall give notice—

(a)   stating that he proposes to make the order and the general effect of it,

(b)   naming a place in the area in which the land to which the order relates is situated where a copy of the order and of the map referred to therein may be inspected free of charge and copies thereof may be obtained at a reasonable charge at all reasonable hours, and

(c)   specifying the time (which shall not be less than 28 days from the date of the first publication of the notice) within which, and the manner in which, representations or objections with respect to the order may be made.

(3)   The notices to be given under sub-paragraph (1) or (2) above shall be given—

    (a)   by publication in at least one local newspaper circulating in the area in which the land to which the order relates is situated;

    (b)   by serving a like notice on—

        (i)   every owner, occupier and lessee (except tenants for a month or any period less than a month and statutory tenants within the meaning of the Rent (Agriculture) Act 1976 or the Rent Act 1977 and licensees under an assured agricultural occupancy within the meaning of Part I of the Housing Act 1988) of any of that land;

        (ii)   every council, the council of every parish or community and the parish meeting of every parish not having a separate parish council being a council, parish or community whose area includes any of that land;

        (iii)   every person on whom notice is required to be served in pursuance of sub-paragraph (3A) or (3B) below; and

        (iv)   such other persons as may be prescribed in relation to the area in which that land is situated or as the authority or, as the case may be, the Secretary of State may consider appropriate[1]; and

    (c)   by causing a copy of the notice to be displayed in a prominent position—

        (i)   at the ends of so much of any footpath, bridleway or restricted byway as is created, stopped up or diverted by the order;

        (ii)   at council offices in the locality of the land to which the order relates; and

        (iii)   at such other places as the authority or, as the case may be, the Secretary of State may consider appropriate.

(3A)   Any person may, on payment of such reasonable charge as the authority may consider appropriate, require an authority to give him notice of all such public path creation orders, public path extinguishment orders, rail crossing extinguishment orders, special extinguishment orders, public path diversion orders, rail crossing diversion orders, special diversion orders and SSSI diversion orders as are made by the authority during a specified period, are of a specified description and relate to land comprised in a specified area; and in this sub-paragraph 'specified' means specified in the requirement.

(3B)   Any person may, on payment of such reasonable charge as the Secretary of State may consider appropriate, require the Secretary of State to give him notice of all such draft public path creation orders, draft public path extinguishment orders, draft rail crossing extinguishment orders, draft special extinguishment orders, draft public path diversion orders, draft rail crossing diversion orders, draft special diversion orders and draft SSSI diversion orders as are prepared by the Secretary of State during a specified period, are of a specified description and relate to land comprised in a specified area; and in this sub-paragraph 'specified' means specified in the requirement.

(3C)   The Secretary of State may, in any particular case, direct that it shall not be necessary to comply with sub-paragraph (3)(b)(i) above; but if he so directs in the case of any land then in addition to publication the notice shall be addressed to 'The owner and any occupiers' of the land (describing it) and a copy or copies of the notice shall be affixed to some conspicuous object or objects on the land.

(4)   Where under this paragraph a notice is required to be served on an owner of land and the land belongs to an ecclesiastical benefice of the Church of England, a like notice shall be served on the Diocesan Board of Finance for the diocese in which the land is situated.

(4A)   Sub-paragraph (3)(b) and (c) and, where applicable, sub-paragraphs (3C) and (4) above shall be complied with not less than 28 days before the expiration of the time specified in the notice.

(4B)   A notice required to be served by sub-paragraph (3)(b) (i), (ii) or (iv) above shall be accompanied by a copy of the order.

(4C)   A notice required to be displayed by sub-paragraph (3)(c) (i) above at the ends of so much of any way as is affected by the order shall be accompanied by a plan showing the general effect of the order so far as it relates to that way.

(4D)   In sub-paragraph (3)(c)(ii) above 'council offices' means offices or buildings acquired or provided by a council or by the council of a parish or community or the parish meeting of a parish not having a separate parish council.

---

[1]   The Town and Country Planning (Public Path Orders) Regulations 1993, SI 1993/10, and the Public Path Orders Regulations 1993, SI 1993/11 (not printed) both for their respective purposes require notices to be served on the organisations mentioned in Chapter 31.

2

(1)   If no representations or objections are duly made, or if any so made are withdrawn, then—

    (a)   the Secretary of State may, if he thinks fit, confirm or make the order, as the case may be, with or without modifications;

    (b)   the authority by whom the order was made (where not the Secretary of State) may, instead of submitting the order to the Secretary of State, themselves confirm the order (but without any modification).

(2)   If any representation or objection duly made is not withdrawn, the Secretary of State shall, before confirming or making the order, as the case may be, if the objection is made by a local authority cause a local inquiry to be held, and in any other case either—

    (a)   cause a local inquiry to be held, or

    (b)   afford to any person by whom any representation or objection has been duly made and not withdrawn an opportunity of being heard by a person appointed by him for the purpose,

and, after considering the report of the person appointed to hold the inquiry or to hear representations or objections, may, subject as provided below, confirm or make the order, as the case may be, with or without modifications.

    In the case of a public path creation order, a public path diversion order, a special diversion order or an SSSI diversion order, if objection is made by statutory undertakers on the ground that the order provides for the creation of a public right of way over land covered by works used for the purposes of their undertaking or the curtilage of such land, and the objection is not withdrawn, the order is subject to special parliamentary procedure.

(3)   Notwithstanding anything in the foregoing provisions of this paragraph, the Secretary of State shall not confirm or make an order so as to affect land not affected by the order as submitted to him or the draft order prepared by him, as the case may be, except after—

    (a)   giving such notice as appears to him requisite of his proposal so to modify the order, specifying the time (which shall not be less than 28 days from the date of the first publication of the notice) within which, and the manner in which, representations or objections with respect to the proposal may be made,

    (b)   holding a local inquiry or affording to any person by whom any representation or objection has been duly made and not withdrawn an opportunity of being heard by a person appointed by him for the purpose, and

    (c)   considering the report of the person appointed to hold the inquiry or to hear representations or objections, as the case may be,

and, in the case of a public path creation order, a public path diversion order, a special diversion order or an SSSI diversion order, if objection is made by statutory undertakers on the ground that the order as modified would provide for the creation of a public right of way over land covered by works used for the purposes of their undertaking or the curtilage of such land, and the objection is not withdrawn, the order is subject to special parliamentary procedure.

2A

[*Secretary of State to be entitled (save in prescribed classes of case or cases specified in directions) to delegate his powers of decision and to withdraw or transfer such powers provided that he states his reasons and notifies the delegate and the representers and objectors concerned.*]

2B

(1) Subject to sub-paragraph (2), subsections (2) to (5) of section 250 of the Local Government Act 1972 (giving of evidence at, and defraying of costs of, inquiries) apply to a hearing which the Secretary of State causes to be held under paragraph 2 above as they apply (by virtue of section 302(1) of this Act) to a local inquiry which he causes to be held under this Act.

(2) In its application to a hearing or local inquiry held under paragraph 2 above by a person appointed under paragraph 2A(1) above, subsection (5) of section 250 of that Act shall have effect as if the reference to the Minister causing the inquiry to be held were a reference to the person so appointed or the Secretary of State.

(3) Section 322A of the Town and Country Planning Act 1990 (orders as to costs where no hearing or inquiry takes place) applies in relation to a hearing or inquiry under paragraph 2 above as it applies in relation to a hearing or local inquiry for the purposes referred to in that section.

3

[*Secretary of State may make procedural regulations.*]

SCHEDULE 12

PROVISIONS AS TO ORDERS UNDER SECTION 116 AND CONVEYANCES UNDER SECTION 256

PART I

NOTICES TO BE GIVEN BY APPLICANT FOR ORDER UNDER SECTION 116

1

At least 28 days before the day on which an application for an order under section 116 of this Act is made in relation to a highway the applicant authority shall give notice of their intention to apply for the order, specifying the time and place at which the application is to be made and the terms of the order applied for (embodying a plan showing what will be the effect thereof)—

    (a)   to the owners and occupiers of all lands adjoining the highway;

    (b)   to any statutory undertakers having apparatus under, in, upon, over, along or across the highway;

    (c)   if the highway is a classified road, to the Minister;

    (d)   if the highway is a classified road in a non-metropolitan district, to the district council, if the highway is a classified road in a Welsh county or county borough and the council of that county or county borough is not the highway authority, to the council of that county or county borough, and if the highway is a classified road in, or partly in, a parish or community which has a separate parish council or community council, to the parish or community council, as the case may require or, in the case of a parish which does not have a separate parish council, to the chairman of the parish meeting.

2

Not later than 28 days before the day on which the application is made the applicant authority shall cause a copy of the said notice to be displayed in a prominent position at the ends of the highway.

3

At least 28 days before the day on which the application is made the applicant authority shall publish in the London Gazette and in at least one local newspaper circulating in the area in which the highway is situated a notice containing the particulars specified in paragraph 1 above, except that there may be substituted for the plan a statement of a place in the said area where the plan may be inspected free of charge at all reasonable hours.

DISUSED BURIAL GROUNDS (AMENDMENT) ACT 1981

1 Exclusion of Disused Burial Grounds Act 1884 in certain cases

(1) Notwithstanding section 3 of the principal Act (which prohibits the erection of buildings on disused burial grounds except in certain cases) but subject to section 2 of this Act a building may be erected on a disused burial ground or part thereof which is or has been owned by or on behalf of a church or other religious body provided that either—

(a) no interments have ever taken place in such land, or

(b) no personal representative or relative of any deceased person whose remains have been interred in such land during the period of fifty years immediately before the proposal to erect a building thereon has in accordance with subsection (2) of this section duly objected to the proposal or all such objections have been withdrawn.

(2) Notice of any proposal to erect a building on land in which human remains are interred shall be given by or on behalf of the church or other religious body by whom or on whose behalf the land is held by—

(a) advertisement in two successive weeks in one or more newspapers circulating in the area where such land is situated, and

(b) notice displayed on or near such land

specifying the time (not being less than six weeks from the date of the first publication of the newspaper advertisement) within which and the manner in which objections thereto can be made.

2 Disposal of human remains

(1) Where any human remains are interred in such land no building shall be erected upon it otherwise than in accordance with section 3 of the principal Act unless:—

(a) the human remains have been removed and reinterred or cremated in accordance with the provisions of the Schedule to this Act; and

(b) any tombstones, monuments or memorials commemorating the deceased persons have been dealt with in accordance with those provisions

and the other requirements of the said Schedule have been complied with in respect thereof.

(2) Where it appears to the Secretary of State that the erection of a building on such land or any part of it will not involve the disturbance of human remains, he may on the application by or on behalf of the church or other religious body owning the land or on whose behalf it is held, and (where appropriate) after consultation with the Commission, by order provide for dispensing with the requirements (so far as they

concern human remains) of subsection (1) of this section and of the said Schedule, subject to such conditions, restrictions and requirements as he may prescribe.

(3)   Any order made under the last foregoing subsection may be amended or revoked by a subsequent order made in like manner and subject to the like conditions on the application by or on behalf of such church or other religious body and if at any time the requirements of subsection (1) of this section and of the said Schedule are complied with in respect of the land, the order shall cease to have effect.

(4)   Where an order is made under this section in respect of any land, a copy thereof, certified by or on behalf of the Secretary of State to be a true copy, shall be deposited with the registering authority (within the meaning of the Local Land Charges Act 1975) and the order shall be a local land charge.

(5)   Where by virtue of any such order human remains are not removed and reinterred or cremated;

    (a)   notice shall be given in accordance with the provisions of the said Schedule if a grave will be rendered inaccessible by the erection of a building; and

    (b)   the requirements of subsection (1) of this section and of the said Schedule so far as they relate to tombstones, monuments and memorials shall nonetheless apply.

(6)   Where there is situated on such land any monument or memorial commemorating a deceased person whose remains are not interred in the land, no building shall be erected upon it unless the monument or memorial has been dealt with in such manner as the church or other religious body owning the land or on whose behalf it is held, or (where appropriate) the Commission, has determined.

(7)   The provisions of section 25 of the Burial Act 1857 (prohibition of removal of human remains without the licence of the Secretary of State except in certain cases) shall not apply to a removal carried out in accordance with the provisions of the said Schedule.

3 Rights, powers and duties of subsequent owners

Where a church or other religious body disposes of an interest in a disused burial ground, then the owner for the time being of that interest shall have the same rights and powers and be subject to the same obligations, restrictions, duties and liabilities conferred or imposed by this Act on that church or other religious body, as if that interest had not been so disposed of.

4 Discharge of trusts and restrictions

(1)   As from the date specified in the next subsection and subject to subsection (3) of this section the said land shall be freed and discharged from all rights and interests of any person who is a personal representative or relative of any deceased person whose remains are interred in the land and from all other trusts, uses, obligations, disabilities and restrictions whatsoever, insofar as the same relate to use as a burial ground which attached thereto immediately before that date:

Provided that notwithstanding the provisions of this subsection such land shall remain subject to charitable trusts unless or until, and subject to such consents as may from time to time be required by law, it is sold; and in the event of the sale of the whole or any part of the said land any charitable trusts which formerly attached to the land the subject of the sale shall attach to the net proceeds of that sale.

(2)   Subsection (1) of this section shall apply as from

    (a)   the date when the provisions of section 2 of this Act have been complied with; or

    (b)   where no interments have ever taken place in such land the date of the granting of planning permission for the erection of a building thereon on the application by or on behalf of the church or other religious body owning the land or on whose behalf it is held and on the sale of the land it shall be sufficient for the purposes of subsection (1) of this section if a certificate is given by or on behalf of the church or other religious body owning the land or on whose behalf it is held as to the fact and date of compliance with the provisions of section 2 of this Act or the fact and date of the granting of planning permission as the case may be.

(3)   Any person entitled to burial rights in the said land may claim compensation in respect thereof from the church or other religious body owning the land or on whose behalf it is held.

5 Saving for consecrated land

This Act shall not apply to any consecrated land and shall not affect the jurisdiction of the Consistory Court.

7 Saving for town and country planning

The provisions of the planning Acts (within the meaning of the Town and Country Planning Act 1990) and any restrictions or powers thereby imposed or conferred in relation to land shall apply and may be exercised in relation to any land notwithstanding that the erection of a building thereon is or may be authorised by this Act.

8 Determination of questions

If any person claiming compensation under subsection (3) of section 4 of this Act, or giving such notice as is mentioned in paragraph 3 of the said Schedule, fails to satisfy the church or other religious body owning the land or on whose behalf it is held that he is the person entitled to burial rights in the said land or that he is such personal representative or relative as he claims to be, or if any question arises about the amount of compensation for loss of such rights, or as to the reasonableness of the expenses or proposed expenses of the removal and reinterment or cremation of human remains or the removal and disposal of any tombstone, monument or memorial under the said paragraph, the question shall be determined on the application of either party by the County Court in whose district the land is situated who shall have power to make an order determining such question and as to the payment of the costs of the application, and any jurisdiction conferred on the county court by this section may be exercised by the registrar of the court.

9 Interpretation

In this Act unless the context otherwise requires:—

> 'the Commission' means the Commonwealth War Graves Commission;
> 'Commonwealth war burial' means a burial of any member of the forces of His Majesty fallen in the war of 1914–21 or in the war of 1939–1947;
> 'consecrated land' means land which has been consecrated according to the rites and ceremonies of the Church of England and is outside the area subject to the Welsh Church Acts 1914 to 1945;
> 'the principal Act' means the Disused Burial Grounds Act 1884;
> 'relative' means in relation to any person whose remains are interred, a spouse or civil partner, parent or grand-parent, or child or grandchild, including a legitimated child, and any person who is, or is the child of, a brother, sister, uncle or aunt.

10 Short title and extent

(1)   This Act may be cited as the Disused Burial Grounds (Amendment) Act 1981 and shall be construed as one with the Disused Burial Grounds Act 1884, and that Act and this Act may be cited together as the Disused Burial Grounds Act 1884 and 1981.

SCHEDULE
DISPOSAL OF HUMAN REMAINS AND TOMBSTONES, MONUMENTS OR OTHER MEMORIALS

1

The church or other religious body in whom the land in question is vested or on whose behalf it is held (hereinafter referred to as 'the church') shall before removing any human remains, or before any work is undertaken which does not involve the disturbance of the remains of any deceased person buried in a grave but which will render the grave inaccessible, or before removing any tombstones, monuments or other memorials commemorating the deceased persons—

    (a)   publish in a newspaper circulating in the locality a notice of intention to do so at least once during each of two successive weeks; and

    (b)   display a like notice in a conspicuous place where the remains are interred; and

    (c)   serve a like notice on the Commission; and

    (d)   if the remains were interred within twenty-five years before the date of the first publication of the notice serve a like notice on the personal representatives or a relative of the deceased person in so far as the names and addresses of such personal representatives or relative can be ascertained on reasonable enquiry.

2

[*Particulars to be included in the above notice.*]

3

(1)   The personal representatives or relatives of any deceased person whose remains are interred in the land or whose grave will be rendered inaccessible or, in the case of any Commonwealth war burial the Commission, may on giving the required notice, themselves remove and reinter any such remains or cremate them in any crematorium and may remove and dispose of any tombstone, monument or other memorial commemorating the deceased and the church shall defray the reasonable expenses of such removal and reinterment or cremation and of such removal and disposal.

Provided also that where the Commission themselves remove from the land and dispose of any memorial erected or owned by the Commission commemorating deceased persons whose remains are not interred in the land, the church shall defray the reasonable expenses of such removal and disposal.

(2)   If the removal and reinterment or cremation or disposal, as the case may be, has not been carried out by the personal representatives or relatives or the Commission in accordance with the provisions of this Schedule within two months from the date of the required notice the church may carry out the removal and reinterment or cremation or disposal, or work may be undertaken which will render the grave inaccessible as the case may be, as if the required notice had not been given.

4

Any human remains interred in the land which have not been removed and reinterred or cremated by the personal representatives or relatives of the deceased or the Commission within the said two months shall after removal by the church be reinterred in such cemetery or burial ground or cremated in such crematorium as the church thinks fit.

5

Any tombstone, monument or other memorial commemorating any deceased person whose remains are reinterred or cremated in accordance with the provisions of the last preceding paragraph may, where reasonably practicable, be removed and re-erected by the church over the grave in the cemetery or burial ground where the remains are reinterred or on some other appropriate site.

6

Any tombstone, monument or other memorial not dealt with in accordance with paragraph 3 or 5 above may be allowed to remain where it is or be removed and re-erected in such place on the land as the church may determine.

7

The removal of all human remains shall be effected, and the remains reinterred or cremated, in accordance with the directions of the Secretary of State.

8

Upon any removal of remains a certificate of removal and reinterment or cremation shall within two months be sent to the Registrar General by the church giving the dates of removal and reinterment or cremation respectively and identifying the place from which the remains are removed and the place in which they were reinterred or cremated showing the particulars of each removal separately, and every such certificate shall be deposited at the General Register Office with the miscellaneous records in the custody of the Registrar General.

9

Any tombstone, monument or other memorial not dealt with in accordance with the foregoing provisions of this Schedule shall be broken and defaced before being otherwise disposed of.

10

(1) Where any tombstone, monument or other memorial is removed from the land, the church shall within two months from the date of removal—

    (a)   deposit with the council of the district, or Welsh county or county borough, a record of the removal with sufficient particulars to identify the memorial (including a copy of any inscription thereon) and showing the date and manner of its removal and disposal and the place (if any) to which it is transferred; and

    (b)   send to the Registrar General a copy of such record for deposit with the miscellaneous records in the custody of the Registrar General.

(2) Where any tombstone, monument or other memorial is not removed from a grave which will be rendered inaccessible by work done on the land the church shall cause a record to be made of every such grave containing a copy of any legible inscription on any monument or inscription on the grave, and copies of such record shall be deposited with the same council as in the case of the record of tombstones, monuments and memorials removed from the land referred to in the foregoing sub-paragraph.

LOCAL GOVERNMENT (MISCELLANEOUS PROVISIONS) ACT 1982

PART VII

BYELAWS

12 General provisions relating to byelaws

(1) Notwithstanding anything in section 298 of the Public Health Act 1936 or section 253 of the Public Health Act 1875 or any other enactment, a constable may take proceedings in respect of an offence against a byelaw made by a relevant local authority under any enactment without the consent of the Attorney General.

(2) In subsection (1) above 'relevant local authority' means—

   (a)   a local authority, as defined in section 270 of the Local Government Act 1972; and

   (b)   any body that was the predecessor of a local authority as so defined.

(3) It is immaterial for the purposes of this section that a byelaw was made after the passing of this Act.

PART XII

MISCELLANEOUS

41 Lost and uncollected property

(1) This section has effect where—

   (a)   property comes into the possession of a local authority after being found on buildings or premises owned or managed by them; or

   (b)   property which has been deposited with a local authority is not collected from them in accordance with the terms under which it was deposited.

(2) Where—

   (a)   property is found on any building or premises owned or managed by a local authority; and

   (b)   it is subsequently handed over to the authority,

any right of possession of the property which was vested in a person by virtue of its having been found is extinguished.

(3) If—

   (a)   the local authority gives the owner or, as the case may be, the depositor of the property notice in writing—

       (i)   that they require him to collect the property by a date specified in the notice; and

      (ii)   that if he does not do so the property will vest in the local authority on that date; and

   (b)   he fails to comply with the notice,

the property shall vest in the local authority on the specified date.

(4) The date to be specified in a notice under subsection (3) above shall be not less than one month from the date of the notice.

(5) Where it appears to the local authority, on the date when property comes into their possession as mentioned in paragraph (a) of subsection (1) above, that it is impossible to serve a notice under subsection (3) above, the property shall vest in the authority one month from that date.

(6) Where the local authority are satisfied after reasonable inquiry that it is impossible to serve a notice under subsection (3) above in relation to any property, it shall vest in them six months from the relevant date.

(7) Where—

   (a)   any property is of a perishable nature; or

   (b)   to look after it adequately would involve the local authority in unreasonable expense or inconvenience,

the authority may sell or otherwise dispose of it at such time and in such manner as they think fit.

(8) Where property is sold or otherwise disposed of under subsection (7) above—

   (a)   any person to whom the property is transferred shall have a good title to it; and

   (b)   any proceeds of sale shall vest in the local authority on the day when the property would have vested in them under this section if it had not been sold.

(9) Where any property which came into the possession of a local authority as mentioned in paragraph (a) of subsection (1) above vests in the authority under this

section, the authority may give the whole or any part of the property to the person through whom it came into their possession.

(10)   Where the proceeds of sale of property which came into the possession of a local authority as mentioned in the said paragraph (a) vest in the authority under this section, the authority may make a payment not exceeding the value of the property to the person through whom it came into their possession.

(11)   Where property is claimed by its owner or depositor before it vests in a local authority under this section, he may collect it on payment to the local authority of any sum which they require him to pay in respect of costs incurred by them—

    (a)   in making inquiries for the purposes of this section or serving any notice under subsection (3) above; and

    (b)   in looking after the property adequately.

. . .

(13)   In this section—

   . . .

'local authority' means—

    (a)   a local authority as defined in section 270(1) of the Local Government Act 1972; and

    . . .

'the relevant date' means—

    (a)   in relation to property which came into the possession of a local authority as mentioned in paragraph (a) of subsection (1) above, the date when it came into their possession; and

    (b)   in relation to uncollected property,—

        (i)   the date when the local authority accepted custody of it; or

        (ii)   the date when the period for which it was deposited with them expired,

whichever is the later.

45   Arrangements under Employment and Training Act 1973

(1)   A local authority to whom this section applies shall have power and shall be deemed always to have had power to enter into arrangements with the Secretary of State under any provision of the Employment and Training Act 1973.

(2)   The local authorities to whom this section applies are—

    (a)   a local authority as defined in section 270(1) of the Local Government Act 1972;

   . . .

REPRESENTATION OF THE PEOPLE ACT 1983

Conduct of local government elections in England and Wales

36   Local elections in England and Wales

(1)   Elections of councillors for local government areas in England and Wales shall be conducted in accordance with rules made by the Secretary of State.

. . .

(3)   Where the polls at—

    (a)   the ordinary election of district councillors for any district ward or an election to fill a casual vacancy occurring in the office of such a councillor, and

(b)   the ordinary election of parish councillors for any parish or an election to fill a casual vacancy occurring in the office of such a councillor,

are to be taken on the same day and the elections are for related electoral areas, the polls at those elections shall be taken together.

(3AB) Where the polls at—

(a)   the ordinary election of councillors for any electoral division of a Welsh county or county borough or an election to fill a casual vacancy occurring in the office of such a councillor, and

(b)   the ordinary election of community councillors for any community or an election to fill a casual vacancy occurring in the office of such a councillor,

are to be taken on the same day and the elections are for related electoral areas, the polls at those elections shall be taken together.

(3AC) Where the polls at—

(a)   the ordinary election of councillors for any electoral division of a county in England in which there are no district councils or an election to fill a casual vacancy occurring in the office of such a councillor, and

(b)   the ordinary election of parish councillors for any parish or an election to fill a casual vacancy occurring in the office of such a councillor,

are to be taken on the same day and the elections are for related electoral areas, the polls at those elections shall be taken together.

(3A) For the purposes of this section electoral areas are related if they are coterminous or if one is situated within the other.

(3B) Where the polls at any elections are combined under this section the cost of taking the combined polls (excluding any cost solely attributable to one election) and any cost attributable to their combination shall be apportioned equally among the elections.

. . .

(5) All expenditure properly incurred by a returning officer in relation to the holding of an election of a parish councillor shall, in so far as it does not, in cases where there is a scale fixed for the purposes of this section by the council of the district in which the parish is situated, exceed that scale, be paid by the district council, but any expenditure so incurred shall, if the district council so require, be repaid to that council by the council of the parish for which the election is held.

(5A) All the expenditure properly incurred by a returning officer in relation to the holding of an election of a community councillor shall, in so far as it does not, in cases where there is a scale fixed for the purposes of this section by the council of the county or county borough in which the community is situated ('the principal council'), exceed that scale, be paid by the principal council; and if the principal council so require, any expenditure so incurred shall be repaid to them by the community council.

. . .

LITTER ACT 1983

3 Grants for publicity discouraging litter

The Secretary of State may with the consent of the Treasury make grants to any body for the purpose of assisting the body to encourage the public not to deface places by litter.

4 Consultations and proposals for abatement of litter

(1) In England and Wales, it shall be the duty of[1]—

(a)   the council of each non-metropolitan county and the other litter authorities whose areas are included in the county,

to consult from time to time together, and with such voluntary bodies as they consider appropriate and as agree to participate in the consultations, about the steps which the county council, each of the other litter authorities, and each of the bodies are to take for the purpose of abating litter in the county; and it shall be the duty of the county council—

(i)   to prepare and from time to time revise a statement of the steps which the council, each of the other litter authorities, and each of the bodies agree to take for that purpose, and

(ii)   to take such steps as in their opinion will give adequate publicity in the county to the statement, and

(iii)   to keep a copy of the statement available at their principal office for inspection by the public free of charge at all reasonable hours.

. . .

(3)   In subsection (1) above, 'litter authority' includes a parish meeting but not a joint body.

. . .

---

[1]   This duty does not appear to be much honoured in practice.

5 Litter bins in England and Wales

(1)   A litter authority in England and Wales may provide and maintain in any street or public place receptacles for refuse or litter (in this section referred to as 'litter bins').

(2)   It shall be the duty of a litter authority in England and Wales to make arrangements for the regular emptying and cleansing of any litter bins provided or maintained by them under this section or under section 185 of the Highways Act 1980; and such an authority shall have power to cleanse and empty litter bins provided in any street or public place by them or any other person.

(3)   The regular emptying mentioned in subsection (2) above shall be sufficiently frequent to ensure that no such litter bin or its contents shall become a nuisance or give reasonable ground for complaint.

(4)   In any place where a litter bin may be provided or maintained under this section or under section 185 of the Highways Act 1980, a litter authority may put up notices about the leaving of refuse and litter, and for that purpose may, subject to the provisions of this section, erect and maintain notice boards.

(5)   . . . a litter authority shall not have power under this section to place any litter bin or any notice board—

(a)   on any land forming part of an open space as defined in the Open Spaces Act 1906 which is provided by or under the management and control of some other litter authority or a parish meeting, without the consent of that authority or meeting, or

(b)   on any other land not forming part of a street, without the consent of the owner and of the occupier of that land.

(6)   The powers conferred by this section shall only be exercisable with the consent of the persons mentioned in the Table in paragraph 1 of Schedule 1 to this Act, and paragraphs 2 and 3 of that Schedule shall have effect in relation to those consents.

(7)   A litter authority may sell refuse or litter removed by them from any litter bins.

(8)   A litter authority may not, under this section, do anything that is unlawful under the law relating to ancient monuments or to town and country planning.

(9)   Any person who wilfully removes or otherwise interferes with any litter bin or notice board provided or erected under this section or section 185 of the Highways Act 1980 shall be liable on summary conviction to a fine not exceeding level 1 on the standard scale.

(10) The court by which a person is convicted under subsection (9) above may order him to pay a sum not exceeding £20 as compensation to the litter authority concerned, and any such order shall be enforceable in the same way as an order for costs to be paid by the offender.

. . .

6 Provisions supplementary to s 5

(1) A county council and a metropolitan district council may if they think fit make a contribution to any expenditure incurred by a parish council or a community council under section 5 above.

(2) A parish council or community council may contribute towards—

    (a)   the reasonable expenses incurred by any person in doing anything which the council have power to do under section 5 above, and

    (b)   the expenses incurred by any other parish council or community council in exercising their powers under that section.

(3) Two or more parish councils or community councils may by agreement combine for the purpose of exercising their powers under section 5 above.

(4)–(5) [*These subsections set out powers of the Secretary of State to amend or repeal inconsistent or unnecessary legislation.*]

(6) Where—

    (a)   a resolution under subsection (3) of section 147 of the Local Government Act 1972 (resolution declaring expenses to be special expenses chargeable only on part of a district council's area), or

    (b)   an order under section 190(3) of the Local Government Act 1933 that, by virtue of subsection (6) of the said section 147, continues to have effect as if it were such resolution,

contains, or has effect as if it included, a reference to section 51 of the Public Health Act 1961 (litter bins), that reference shall have effect as if it were a reference to the said section 51 or section 5 above.

(7) Sections . . . and 343 of the Public Health Act 1936 apply in relation to section 5 above, this section and Schedule 1 to this Act as if section 5, this section and that Schedule were contained in the said Act of 1936.

. . .

10 Interpretation

(1) In this Act—

    'joint body' means a joint body constituted solely of two or more such councils as are mentioned in paragraphs (a) to (f) of the definition of 'litter authority' below;

    'litter authority', in relation to England and Wales, means, except so far as is otherwise provided—

        (a)   a county council,

        (b)   a district council,

        (c)   a London borough council,

        (d)   the Common council of the City of London,

        (e)   a parish council,

        (f)   a community council,

        (g)   a joint body,

. . .

(2) In the application of this Act in relation to Wales, any reference to a county shall be read as including a reference to a county borough and any reference to a county council shall be read as including a reference to a county borough council.

SCHEDULE 1
CONSENTS REQUIRED UNDER SECTION 5

1

A litter authority shall not carry out works under section 5 above in any such situation or position as is described in an entry in column 1 of the following Table except with the consent of the person described in the corresponding entry in column 2.

Table

1.	2.
1. In a street which is a highway for which the litter authority are not the highway authority.	1. The highway authority for the street.
2. In a street belonging to and repairable by any railway, dock, harbour, canal, inland navigation or passenger road transport undertakers and forming the approach to a station, dock, wharf or depot of those undertakers.	2. The undertakers.
3. On a bridge not vested in the litter authority or on the approaches to such a bridge.	3. The authority or other person in whom the bridge is vested.
4. On a bridge carrying a street over a railway, canal or inland navigation, or on the approaches to such a bridge, or under a bridge carrying a railway, canal or inland navigation over a street.	4. The railway, canal or inland navigation undertakers concerned.
5. In a position obstructing or interfering with any existing access to land or premises abutting upon a street.	5. The owner and the occupier of the land or premises.

2

A consent required by this Schedule shall not unreasonably be withheld but may be given subject to any reasonable conditions, including a condition that the authority shall remove a litter bin or notice board either at any time or after the expiration of a period if reasonably required so to do by the person giving the consent.

3

Where the consent of the Secretary of State is required under this Schedule, any dispute between him and the authority as to—

    (a)   whether the consent is unreasonably withheld or is given subject to reasonable conditions, or

    (b)   whether the removal of anything to the provision of which the consent relates in accordance with any condition of the consent is reasonably required,

shall be referred to and determined by an arbitrator to be appointed in default of agreement by the President of the Institution of Civil Engineers.

ROAD TRAFFIC REGULATION ACT 1984

Provision of parking places by parish or community councils

[*Sections 32 and 35 incorporate Parts I to III of Schedule 9. They enable orders to be made on the management and use of parking places and meters in them, enforceable by prosecution. They also lay down procedures in the case of orders applying to roads, for consultation with Chief Constables, and consents by the Secretary of State.*]

57 General powers of parish or community councils for provision of parking places

(1) Where for the purposes of relieving or preventing congestion of traffic or preserving local amenities it appears to the council of a parish in England or a community in Wales to be necessary to do so, the council, subject to sections 58 and 59 of this Act, may—

    (a)   provide within their area and maintain suitable parking places for bicycles and motor cycles, or

    (b)   provide within their area and maintain suitable parking places, otherwise than on roads, for vehicles of other descriptions or for vehicles generally.

(2) For the purpose of providing and maintaining any such parking place, or for the purpose of providing means of entrance to and egress from any parking place provided under this section, a parish or community council may—

    (a)   utilise and adapt any land purchased by the council for the purpose or appropriated for the purpose under subsection (3) below, or

    (b)   in the case of a parking place provided under subsection (1)(a) above, but subject to the provisions of section 58 of this Act, adapt, and by order authorise the use of, any part of a road in the parish or community;

and any power under subsection (1) above to provide and maintain parking places shall include power to provide and maintain structures for use as parking places.

(3) Notwithstanding anything in any other enactment, but subject to subsection (4) below, a parish or community council may appropriate for the purpose of providing a parking place under this section—

    (a)   any part of a recreation ground provided by the council under section 8 of the Local Government Act 1894;

    (b)   any part of an open space controlled or maintained by the council under the Open Spaces Act 1906, other than a part which has been consecrated as a burial ground or in which burials have taken place;

    (c)   any part of any land provided by the council as a playing field or for any other purpose and held by that council for the purposes of section 19 of the Local Government (Miscellaneous Provisions) Act 1976 (recreational facilities).

(4) Any part of a recreation ground, open space or other land appropriated under subsection (3) above shall not exceed one-eighth of its total area or 800 square feet, whichever is the less.

(5) No order under subsection (1) above shall authorise the use of any part of a road as a parking place so as unreasonably to prevent access to any premises adjoining the road, or the use of the road by any person entitled to use it, or so as to be a nuisance.

(6) A parish or community council may employ, with or without remuneration, such persons as may be necessary for the superintendence of parking places provided by the council under this section.

(7) A parish or community council may make byelaws (subject to confirmation by the Secretary of State) as to the use of parking places provided under subsection (1)(a) above, and in particular as to the conditions upon which any such parking place may be used and as to the charges to be paid to the council in connection with the use of

any such parking place, not being part of a road; and a copy of any byelaws made under this subsection shall be exhibited on or near every parking place to which they relate.

(8)   A parish or community council may let for use as a parking place any parking place provided by them (not being a part of a road) under this section; but, without prejudice to any power of a parish or community council under any other enactment to let a playing field or other land of which a parking place forms part, no single letting under this subsection shall be for a longer period than 7 days.

(9)   The exercise by a parish or community council of their powers under this section with respect to the use as a parking place of any part of a road shall not render them subject to any liability in respect of loss of or damage to any vehicle or the fittings or contents of any vehicle parked in such a parking place.

58   Consents for purposes of s 57(1)

(1)   A parish or community council shall not have power by virtue of section 57(1) of this Act to provide a parking place—

   (a)   in a position obstructing or interfering with any existing access to any land or premises not forming part of a road, except with the consent of the owner and the occupier of the land or premises, or

   (b)   in a road which is not a highway, in a public path or in a restricted byway, except with the consent of the owner and the occupier of the land over which the road, path or way runs, or

   (c)   in any such situation or position as is described in the first column of the following Table, except with the consent of the persons described in relation to it in the second column of that Table.

Table

(i) In a trunk road or any other road maintained by the Secretary of State or on land abutting on any such road.	The Secretary of State.
(ii) In a road which is a highway (other than a trunk road or a road maintained as mentioned in sub-paragraph (i) above or a public path) or on land abutting on any such road.	The county council or metropolitan district council.
(iii) In a road which is a highway belonging to and repairable by the persons carrying on any railway, dock, harbour, canal, inland navigation or passenger road transport undertaking and forming the approach to any station, dock, wharf or depot of theirs.	The persons carrying on the undertaking concerned.
(iv) On a bridge carrying a highway over a railway, dock, harbour, canal or inland navigation, or on the approaches to any such bridge, or under a bridge carrying a railway, canal or inland navigation over a highway.	The persons carrying on the railway, dock, harbour, canal or inland navigation undertaking concerned.

(2)   Any consent required by subsection (1)(c) above shall not be unreasonably withheld, but may be given subject to any reasonable conditions, including a condition that the parish or community council shall remove any thing to the provision of which the consent relates, either at any time or at or after the expiry of a period, if reasonably required to do so by the person giving the consent.

(3)   Any dispute between a parish or community council and a person whose consent is required under subsection (1)(c) above, on the question whether that consent is unreasonably withheld or is given subject to reasonable conditions, or whether the removal of any thing to the provision of which the consent relates in accordance with any condition of the consent is reasonably required, it shall—

(a)   in the case of a dispute between the parish or community council and the Secretary of State, be referred to and determined by an arbitrator to be appointed, in default of agreement, by the President of the Institution of Civil Engineers; and

(b)   in any other case, be referred to and determined by the Secretary of State, who may cause a public inquiry to be held for the purpose.

(4)   Section 6 of the Local Government (Miscellaneous Provisions) Act 1953 (which makes provision as to access to telegraphic lines, sewers, pipe-subways, pipes, wires, and other apparatus) shall apply in relation to a parking place (including a structure for use as a parking place) provided by a parish or community council under section 57(1) of this Act, and to the council by whom the parking place is so provided, as it applies in relation to a shelter or other accommodation provided, and to the local authority by whom it is provided, under section 4 of that Act.

(5)   In this section, and in section 6 of that Act, as they apply in relation to a parking place provided under section 57(1)(a) of this Act which forms part of a road, references to removal shall be construed as including references to the suspension or revocation of the order authorising the use of that part of the road as a parking place.

59 Consents for, and provisions as to use of, parking places under s 57(1)(b)

(1)   A parish or community council shall not exercise their powers under section 57(1)(b) of this Act without the consent of the council of the county or metropolitan district in which the parish or community is situated; and any consent given by the county council or metropolitan district council may be subject to such conditions or restrictions as they think fit.

(2)   A parish or community council proposing to exercise their powers under section 57(1)(b) of this Act shall—

(a)   for the purpose of obtaining the consent of the county council or metropolitan district council under subsection (1) above, make an application in writing to that council giving details of the parking place which they propose to provide, and

(b)   in the case of an application to a county council, send a copy of it to the council of the district in which the parish is situated;

and, in that case, the county council, in considering whether or not to give their consent, or to make their consent subject to any conditions or restrictions, shall have regard to any representations made to them by that district council.

(2A)   In subsection (2) above, paragraph (b) and the words which follow it do not apply in relation to Wales.

(3)   Subject to subsections (4) to (6) below, section 35 of this Act shall apply in relation to a parking place provided under section 57(1)(b) of this Act as if—

(a)   the parish or community council were a local authority for the purposes of sections 32 and 35 of this Act, and

(b)   the parking place were provided by the parish or community council under section 32 of this Act.

(4)   A parish or community council shall not, by virtue of subsection (3) above, make an order under section 35(1) of this Act without the consent of the county council or metropolitan district council; and any consent given by the county council or metropolitan district council may be subject to such conditions or restrictions as they think fit.

(5)   Where, by virtue of subsection (3) above, a parish or community council proposes to make an order under section 35(1) of this Act, the council shall submit a draft of the order to the county council or metropolitan district council, who (without prejudice to their power to give or withhold consent to the making of the order) may require such modifications of the terms of the proposed order as they think appropriate.

(6) The powers of a county council or metropolitan district council under section 35 of this Act shall apply in relation to a parking place provided by a parish or community council under section 57(1)(b) of this Act as they apply in relation to a parking place provided by a county council or metropolitan district council; and the power to vary or revoke an order made by a parish or community council under section 35(1) of this Act shall be exercisable by the county council or metropolitan district council as well as by the parish or community council.

(7) If, by virtue of subsection (6) above, a county council or metropolitan district council proposes to make an order under section 35(1) of this Act in relation to a parking place provided by a parish or community council, they shall send a copy of the proposed order to the parish or community council.

60 Supplementary provisions relating to ss 57–59

(1) A parish or community council may contribute towards—

    (a)   the reasonable expenses incurred by any person in doing anything which by virtue of section 57 of this Act that council has power to do, and

    (b)   the expenses incurred by any other parish or community council in exercising their powers under that section.

(2) Without prejudice to any other power of combination, a parish or community council may by agreement combine with any other parish or community council for the purpose of exercising their powers under section 57 of this Act.

(3) Where before 17th July 1957 a parish council has provided anything which could be provided by a parish council under section 57 of this Act, or where any other person has at any time provided anything which could be provided by a parish council under that section, the parish or community council shall have the like power to maintain that thing as if it had been provided by them under that section.

(4) In sections 57 to 59 of this Act and in subsections (1) and (2) above, except in so far as the context otherwise requires,—

    'in', in a context referring to things in a road, includes a reference to things under, over, across, along or upon the road;

    'owner' has the meaning assigned to it by section 343 of the Public Health Act 1936;

    'parish' or 'community', in relation to a common parish council or common community council acting for two or more grouped parishes or communities, means those parishes or communities;

    'public path' has the meaning assigned to it by section 27 of the National Parks and Access to the Countryside Act 1949; and

    'road' means a highway (including a public path) and any other road, lane, footway, square, court, alley or passage (whether a thoroughfare or not) to which the public has access, but does not include a road provided or to be provided in pursuance of a scheme made, or having effect as if made, under section 16 of the Highways Act 1980 (which relates to special roads).

PART V

TRAFFIC SIGNS

General provisions

69 General provisions as to removal of signs

[*This section empowers highway authorities and the Secretary of State to secure the removal of unauthorised signs on highways, if necessary at the owner's expense.*]

72 Powers exercisable by parish or community councils

(1)   A parish or community council may, with the permission of the highway authority and subject to any conditions imposed by that authority, provide on or near any road, other than a footpath or bridleway, or may contribute, either wholly or in part, towards the cost of providing on or near any such road, traffic signs indicating—

    (a)   a stopping place for public service vehicles;

    (b)   a warning of the existence of any danger; or

    (c)   the name of the parish or community or of any place in it.

(2)   A parish or community council may provide, or may contribute, either wholly or in part, towards the cost of providing, on or near any footpath or bridleway, any object or device (not being a traffic sign) for conveying to users of that footpath or bridleway a warning of the existence of danger.

(3)   No traffic sign, object or device provided by a parish or community council in pursuance of this section shall be placed on any land (not being a road or part of a road) without the consent of the owner and occupier of the land.

(4)   Nothing in this section shall prejudice the exercise by the highway authority or the Secretary of State of their powers under section 69 of this Act; but where any such object or device as is mentioned in subsection (1) of that section is an object or device—

    (a)   provided by a parish or community council in pursuance of this section, and

    (b)   so provided on land which the council neither own nor occupy,

the powers conferred on the highway authority by that subsection shall be exercisable in relation to the council and not in relation to the owner or occupier of the land.

(5)   For the purpose of complying with a notice under section 69(1) of this Act which, by virtue of subsection (4) above, requires a parish or community council to remove an object or device, the council may enter any land and exercise such other powers as may be necessary for that purpose.

(6)   A parish or community council may warn the public of any danger in or apprehended in their area, subject, however, in the case of a warning given by providing any traffic sign, object or device, to the provisions of subsections (1) and (3) above.

. . .

FOOD ACT 1984

PART III

MARKETS

50 Establishment or acquisition

(1)   A local authority may—

    (a)   establish a market within their area;

    (b)   acquire by agreement (but not otherwise), either by purchase or on lease, the whole or any part of an existing market undertaking within their area, and any rights enjoyed by any person within their area in respect of a market and of tolls,

and, in either case, may provide—

    (i)   a market place with convenient approaches to it;

    (ii)   a market house and other buildings convenient for the holding of a market.

(2)   A market shall not be established in pursuance of this section so as to interfere with any rights, powers or privileges enjoyed within the authority's area in respect of a market by any person, without that person's consent.

(3)   For the purposes of subsection (2), a local authority shall not be regarded as enjoying any rights, powers or privileges within another local authority's area by reason only of the fact that they maintain within their own area a market which has been established under paragraph (a) of subsection (1) or under the corresponding provision of any earlier enactment.

51 Power to sell to local authority

(1)   The owner of a market undertaking, or of any rights in respect of a market and of tolls, whether established under, or enjoyed by virtue of, statutory powers or not, may sell or lease to a local authority the whole or any part of his market undertaking or rights, but subject to all attached liabilities.

(2)   A sale by a company under this section must be authorised—

    (a)   if the company is a company within the meaning of the Companies Act 1985, by special resolution;

    (b)   if the company is not such a company, by a resolution passed by three-fourths in number and value of the members present, either personally or by proxy, at a meeting specially convened for the purpose with notice of the business to be transacted.

52 Market days and hours

A market authority may appoint the days on which, and the hours during which, markets are to be held.

53 Charges

(1)   A market authority may demand in respect of the market, such charges as they may from time to time determine.

(2)   A market authority who provide—

    (a)   a weighing machine for weighing cattle, sheep or swine; or

    (b)   a cold air store or refrigerator for the storage and preservation of meat and other articles of food,

may demand in respect of the weighing of such animals or, as the case may be, the use of the store or refrigerator such charges as they may from time to time determine.

(3)   The authority—

    (a)   shall keep exhibited in conspicuous places in the market place, and in any market house, tables stating in large and legibly printed characters the several charges payable under this Part; and

    (b)   shall keep so much of the tables as relates to charges payable in respect of the weighing of animals, conspicuously exhibited at every weighing machine provided by them in connection with the market for the purpose.

(4)   A person who demands or accepts a charge greater than that for the time being authorised shall be liable to a fine not exceeding level 2 on the standard scale.

(5)   Nothing in this section applies in relation to rents charged by a market authority in respect of the letting of accommodation within their market for any period longer than one week.

54 Time for payment of charges

(1)   Charges payable in respect of the market shall be paid from time to time on demand to an authorised market officer.

(2)   Charges payable in respect of the weighing of cattle, sheep or swine shall be paid in advance to an authorised market officer by the person bringing the animals to be weighed.

584

(3)   Charges payable in respect of animals brought to the market for sale shall be payable, and may be demanded by an authorised market officer—

(a)   as soon as the animals in respect of which they are payable are brought into the market place, and

(b)   before they are put into any pen, or tied up in the market place,

but further charges shall be payable and may be demanded in respect of any of the animals which are not removed within one hour after the close of the market.

55   Recovery of charges

If a person liable to pay any charge authorised under this Part does not pay it when lawfully demanded, the market authority may, by any authorised market officer, levy it by distress—

(a)   of all or any of the animals, poultry or other articles in respect of which the charge is payable, or

(b)   of any other animals, poultry or articles in the market belonging to, or in the charge of, the person liable,

and any such charge may also be recovered either summarily as a civil debt or in any court of competent jurisdiction.

56   Prohibited sales in market hours

(1)   A person (other than a pedlar holding a certificate under the Pedlars Act 1871) who on a market day and during market hours sells or exposes for sale any articles—

(a)   which are specified in a byelaw made by the market authority, and

(b)   which are commonly sold in the market,

and such sale or exposure for sale—

(i)   is in any place within the authority's area, and

(ii)   is within such distance from the market as the authority may by byelaw declare,

is liable to a fine not exceeding level 2 on the standard scale.

This subsection does not apply to a sale or exposure for sale in a person's own dwelling place or shop, or in, or at the door of, any premises to a person resident in those premises.

(2)   The market authority shall keep exhibited in conspicuous positions in the vicinity of the market notices stating the effect of any byelaw made under this section.

57   Weighing machines and scales

(2)   A market authority in whose market cattle, sheep or swine are sold shall, unless there is in force an order of the Minister declaring that the circumstances are such as to render compliance with this subsection unnecessary—

(a)   provide to that Minister's satisfaction one or more weighing machines adapted for weighing such animals; and

(b)   appoint officers to attend to the weighing of such animals.

A weighing machine provided under this subsection shall for the purposes of section 1 of the Markets and Fairs (Weighing of Cattle) Act 1926, be deemed to have been provided for the purpose of complying with the provisions of the principal Act referred to in that Act of 1926.

57A   Provision of cold stores

(1)   A market authority may provide a cold air store or refrigerator for the storage and preservation of meat and other articles of food.

(2)   Any proposal by a market authority to provide under this section a cold air store or refrigerator within the area of another local authority requires the consent of that other authority, which shall not be unreasonably withheld.

(3)   Any question whether or not such a consent is unreasonably withheld shall be referred to and determined by the Ministers.

(4) Subsections (1) to (5) of section 250 of the Local Government Act 1972 (which relate to local inquiries) shall apply for the purposes of this section as if any reference in those subsections to that Act included a reference to this section.

59 Information for market officer

The person in charge of any vehicle in which, and any other person by whom, animals, poultry or other articles are brought for sale in the market shall give to any authorised market officer such information—

    (a)   as to their number and kind, or

    (b)   in the case of articles on which charges are made by reference to weight, as to their weight,

as that officer may require.

60 Market byelaws

A local authority who maintain a market, whether or not they are a market authority within the meaning of this Act, may make byelaws—

    (a)   for regulating the use of the market place, and the buildings, stalls, pens and standings in that market place;

    (b)   for preventing nuisances or obstructions in the market place, or in the immediate approaches to it;

    (c)   for regulating porters and carriers resorting to the market, and fixing the charges to be made for carrying articles from the market within the district;

    (d)   after consulting the fire and rescue authority, for preventing the spread of fires in the market.

61 Interpretation of Part III, and exclusion of City of London

In this Part, unless the context otherwise requires—

    'authorised market officer' means an officer of a market authority specially authorised by them to collect charges in their market;

    'charges' includes stallage or tolls;

    'fire and rescue authority' in relation to a market, means—

        (a)   where the Regulatory Reform (Fire Safety) Order 2005 applies to the market, the enforcing authority within the meaning given by article 25 of that Order; or

        (b)   in any other case, the fire and rescue authority under the Fire and Rescue Services Act 2004 for the area in which the market is situated;

    'food' has the same meaning as in the Food Safety Act 1990;

    'local authority' means a district council, a London borough council or a parish council but, in relation to Wales, means a county council, county borough council or community council;

    'market authority' means a local authority who maintain a market which has been established or acquired under section 50(1) or under the corresponding provisions of any earlier enactment.

CYCLE TRACKS ACT 1984

3 Conversion of footpaths into cycle tracks

(1) A local highway authority may in the case of any footpath for which they are the highway authority by order made by them or either—

    (a)   submitted to and confirmed by the Secretary of State, or

    (b)   confirmed by them as an unopposed order,

designate the footpath or any part of it as a cycle track, with the effect that, on such date as the order takes effect in accordance with the following provisions of this section, the footpath or part of the footpath to which the order relates shall become a highway which for the purposes of the 1980 Act is a highway maintainable at the public expense and over which the public have a right of way on pedal cycles (other than pedal cycles which are motor vehicles) and a right of way on foot.

(2) A local highway authority shall not make an order under this section designating as a cycle track any footpath or part of a footpath which crosses any agricultural land unless every person having a legal interest in that land has consented in writing to the making of the order.

In this subsection 'agricultural land' has the meaning given by section 1(4) of the Agricultural Holdings Act 1986; and 'legal interest' does not include an interest under a letting of land having effect as a letting for an interest less than a tenancy from year to year.

(3) An order made under this section by a local highway authority—

    (a)   may be confirmed by the Secretary of State either in the form in which it was made or subject to such modifications as he thinks fit;

    (b)   may be confirmed by the authority as an unopposed order only in the form in which it was made.

(4)–(5) [*These subsections empower the Secretary of State to make regulations on procedure for making, submission and confirming orders.*]

(6) If a person aggrieved by an order under this section desires to question its validity on the ground that it is not within the powers of this section or on the ground that any requirement of regulations made under subsection (4) above has not been complied with in relation to the order, he may, within six weeks from the date on which any such notice as is mentioned in subsection (4)(c) above is first published, make an application for the purpose of the High Court.

(7) On any such application, the High Court—

    (a)   may by interim order suspend the operation of the order, either wholly or to such extent as it thinks fit, until the final determination of the proceedings; and

    (b)   if satisfied that the order is not within the powers of this section or that the interests of the applicant have been substantially prejudiced by a failure to comply with any such requirement as aforesaid, may quash the order, either wholly or to such extent as it thinks fit.

(8) Subject to subsection (7) above, an order under this section shall not, either before or after it has been confirmed, be questioned in any legal proceedings whatever, and shall take effect on the date on which any such notice as is mentioned in subsection (4)(c) above is first published, or on such later date, if any, as may be specified in the order.

(9) A local highway authority may (subject to and in accordance with the provisions of subsections (3) to (8) above) by order made by them and either—

    (a)   submitted to and confirmed by the Secretary of State, or

    (b)   confirmed by them as an unopposed order,

revoke an order made by them under this section with the effect that, on such date as the order takes effect in accordance with those provisions, the way designated by the original order as a cycle track shall revert to being a footpath or a part of a footpath (as the case may be) and, as such, it shall only be maintainable at the public expense for the purposes of the 1980 Act if, prior to the original order taking effect, it constituted a highway so maintainable or, on the order under this subsection taking effect, it forms part of a highway so maintainable.

(10) A local highway authority shall have power to carry out any works necessary for giving effect to an order under this section; and in so far as the carrying out of any such works, or any change in the use of land resulting from any such order, constitutes

development within the meaning of the Town and Country Planning Act 1990, permission for that development shall be deemed to be granted under Part III of that Act.

(11)   The power to make regulations under subsection (4) above shall be exercisable by statutory instrument, which shall be subject to annulment in pursuance of a resolution of either House of Parliament.

4 Provision of barriers in cycle tracks, etc

(1)   A highway authority may provide and maintain in any cycle track such barriers as they think necessary for the purpose of safeguarding persons using the cycle track.

(2)   A highway authority may, in the case of any cycle track which is adjacent to a footpath or footway, provide and maintain such works as they think necessary for the purpose of separating, in the interests of safety, persons using the cycle track from those using the footpath or footway.

(3)   A highway authority may alter or remove any works provided by them under subsection (1) or (2) above.

(4)   Any reference in this section to a cycle track is a reference to a cycle track constituting or comprised in a highway maintainable at the public expense, and any reference to a footpath or a footway is a reference to a footpath constituting or a footway comprised in such a highway.

5 Compensation

(1)   Where any person suffers damage by reason of the execution by a highway authority of any works under section 3(10) or 4 above, he shall be entitled to recover compensation in respect of that damage from that authority.

(2)   Where in consequence of the coming into operation of an order under section 3 above any person suffers damage by the depreciation in value of any interest in land to which he is entitled, he shall be entitled to recover compensation in respect of that damage from the local highway authority which made the order; but a person shall not be entitled to recover any compensation under this subsection in respect of any depreciation—

>   (a)   in respect of which compensation is recoverable by him under subsection (1) above; or

>   (b)   which is attributable to the prospect of the execution of any such works as are referred to in that subsection.

(3)   [*This subsection provides for disputes on compensation to be referred to the Lands Tribunal.*]

8 Interpretation

(1)   In this Act—

>   'the 1980 Act' means the Highways Act 1980; and

>   'motor vehicle' means a motor vehicle within the meaning of the Road Traffic Act 1988.

(2)   Except where the context otherwise requires, any expression used in this Act which is also used in the 1980 Act has the same meaning as in that Act.

REPRESENTATION OF THE PEOPLE ACT 1985

Miscellaneous and supplemental

21 Ordinary elections of parish and community councillors: insufficient nominations
(1)   This section applies where, at an ordinary election of parish or community councillors in England and Wales, an insufficient number of persons are or remain validly nominated to fill the vacancies in respect of which the election is held.
(2)   Unless the number of newly elected members of the council in question is less than the number that constitutes a quorum for meetings of the council—

    (a)   those members may co-opt any person or persons to fill the vacancy or vacancies remaining unfilled,

    (b)   the district council or, in the case of a community council, the county council or county borough council may exercise the powers conferred by section 39(4) of the principal Act (power by order to do anything necessary for the proper holding of an election etc) in relation to any such vacancy or vacancies as are not so filled, and

    (c)   section 39(1) of that Act (duty of returning officer to order an election) shall not apply;

but the powers mentioned in paragraph (b) above shall not be exercised before the expiry of the period of 35 days (computed according to section 40 of that Act) beginning with the day on which the election was held.
(3)   Subsection (7) of section 39 of that Act (parishes in different districts grouped) shall apply for the purposes of subsection (2) above as it applies for the purposes of subsections (4) and (6) of that section and section 40(3) of that Act (computation of time) shall apply for the purposes of subsection (2) above as it applies for the purposes of section 39.

TRANSPORT ACT 1985

106A Grants for bus services
(1)   A parish council or community council may make grants to any body towards expenditure incurred or to be incurred by that body in connection with the operation of—

    (a)   a bus service appearing to the council to be wholly or mainly for the benefit of members of the public who are elderly or disabled; or

    (b)   a community bus service (as defined in section 22 of this Act).

(2)   The power in subsection (1) above may only be exercised if—

    (a)   the bus service benefits, or appears to the council likely to benefit, persons living in the council's area, and

    (b)   a permit in relation to the use of the vehicle by means of which the service is, or is to be, provided has been granted to the body concerned under section 19 or 22 of this Act.

(3)   Grants under this section may be made in such cases and subject to such terms and conditions as the council think fit.

LOCAL GOVERNMENT ACT 1986

PART II

LOCAL AUTHORITY PUBLICITY

2 Prohibition of political publicity

(1) A local authority shall not publish, or arrange for the publication of, any material which, in whole or in part, appears to be designed to affect public support for a political party.

(2) In determining whether material falls within the prohibition regard shall be had to the content and style of the material, the time and other circumstances of publication and the likely effect on those to whom it is directed and, in particular, to the following matters—

    (a)   whether the material refers to a political party or to persons identified with a political party or promotes or opposes a point of view on a question of political controversy which is identifiable as the view of one political party and not of another;

    (b)   where the material is part of a campaign, the effect which the campaign appears to be designed to achieve.

(3) A local authority shall not give financial or other assistance to a person for the publication of material which the authority are prohibited by this section from publishing themselves.

4 Codes of recommended practice as regards publicity

(1) The Secretary of State may issue one or more codes of recommended practice as regards the content, style, distribution and cost of local authority publicity, and such other related matters as he thinks appropriate; and local authorities shall have regard to the provisions of any such code in coming to any decision on publicity.

(2)–(4) [*These subsections provide that Codes may deal with different kinds of publicity or local authority or circumstances. Their issue, revision or withdrawal must take place only after consultation with local authority associations.*]

(5) A code shall not be issued unless a draft of it has been laid before and approved by a resolution of each House of Parliament.

(6) [*This subsection sets out Parliamentary procedure on revision of code.*]

. . .

5 Separate account of expenditure on publicity

(1) A local authority shall keep a separate account of their expenditure on publicity.

(2) Any person interested may at any reasonable time and without payment inspect the account and make copies of it or any part of it.

(3) A person having custody of the account who intentionally obstructs a person in the exercise of the rights conferred by subsection (2) commits an offence and is liable on summary conviction to a fine not exceeding level 3 on the standard scale.

(4) The regulation making power conferred by section 27(1)(e) of the Audit Commission Act 1998, section 39(1)(e) of the Public Audit (Wales) Act 2004 . . . (power to make provision as to exercise of right of inspection and as to informing persons of those rights) applies to the right of inspection conferred by subsection (2).

(5) The Secretary of State may by order provide that subsection (1) does not apply to publicity or expenditure of a prescribed description.

(6) Before making an order the Secretary of State shall consult such associations of local authorities as appear to him to be concerned and any local authority with whom consultation appears to him to be desirable.

(7) An order shall be made by statutory instrument which shall be subject to annulment in pursuance of a resolution of either House of Parliament.

6 Interpretation and application of Part II

(1) References in this Part to local authorities and to publicity, and related expressions, shall be construed in accordance with the following provisions.

(2) 'Local authority' means—

(a) in England and Wales—

a county, district or London borough council,

. . .

a joint authority established by Part IV of the Local Government Act 1985,

. . .

a parish or community council;

. . .

and includes any authority, board or committee which discharges functions which would otherwise fall to be discharged by two or more such authorities.

. . .

(4) 'Publicity', 'publish' and 'publication' refer to any communication, in whatever form, addressed to the public at large or to a section of the public.

(5) This Part applies to any such publicity expressly or implied authorised by any statutory provision, including—

[*sections 111, 141 and 145(1)(a) of the Local Government Act 1972*]

. . .

(6) Nothing in this Part shall be construed as applying to anything done by a local authority in the discharge of their duties under Part VA of the Local Government Act 1972 . . . (duty to afford public access to meetings and certain documents).

(7) Nothing in this Part shall be construed as applying to anything done by a person in the discharge of any duties under regulations made under section 22 of the Local Government Act 2000 (access to information etc).

LOCAL GOVERNMENT ACT 1988

PART II

PUBLIC SUPPLY OR WORKS CONTRACTS

17 Local and other public authority contracts: exclusion of non-commercial considerations

(1) It is the duty of every public authority to which this section applies, in exercising, in relation to its public supply or works contracts, any proposed or any subsisting such contract, as the case may be, any function regulated by this section to exercise that function without reference to matters which are non-commercial matters for the purposes of this section.

(2) The public authorities to which this section applies are those specified in Schedule 2 to this Act.

(3) The contracts which are public supply or works contracts for the purposes of this section are contracts for the supply of goods or materials, for the supply of services or for the execution of works; but this section does not apply in relation to contracts entered into before the commencement of this section.

(4) The functions regulated by this section are—

(a) the inclusion of persons in or the exclusion of persons from—

(i)   any list of persons approved for the purposes of public supply or works contracts with the authority, or

(ii)   any list of persons from whom tenders for such contracts may be invited;

(b)   in relation to a proposed public supply or works contract with the authority—

(i)   the inclusion of persons in or the exclusion of persons from the group of persons from whom tenders are invited,

(ii)   the accepting or not accepting the submission of tenders for the contract,

(iii)   the selecting the person with whom to enter into the contract, or

(iv)   the giving or withholding approval for, or the selecting or nominating, persons to be sub-contractors for the purposes of the contract; and

(c)   in relation to a subsisting public supply or works contract with the authority—

(i)   the giving or withholding approval for, or the selecting or nominating, persons to be sub-contractors for the purposes of the contract, or

(ii)   the termination of the contract.

(5) The following matters are non-commercial matters as regards the public supply or works contracts of a public authority, any proposed or any subsisting such contract, as the case may be, that is to say—

(a)   the terms and conditions of employment by contractors of their workers or the composition of, the arrangements for the promotion, transfer or training of or the other opportunities afforded to, their workforces;

(b)   whether the terms on which contractors contract with their sub-contractors constitute, in the case of contracts with individuals, contracts for the provision by them as self-employed persons of their services only;

(c)   any involvement of the business activities or interests of contractors with irrelevant fields of Government policy;

(d)   the conduct of contractors or workers in industrial disputes between them or any involvement of the business activities of contractors in industrial disputes between other persons;

(e)   the country or territory of origin of supplies to, or the location in any country or territory of the business activities or interests of, contractors;

(f)   any political, industrial or sectarian affiliations or interests of contractors or their directors, partners or employees;

(g)   financial support or lack of financial support by contractors for any institution to or from which the authority gives or withholds support;

(h)   use or non-use by contractors of technical or professional services provided by the authority under the Building Act 1984.

(6) The matters specified in subsection (5) above include matters which have occurred in the past as well as matters which subsist when the function in question falls to be exercised.

(7) Where any matter referable to a contractor would, as a matter specified in subsection (5) above, be a non-commercial matter in relation to him, the corresponding matter referable to—

(a)   a supplier or customer of the contractor;

(b)   a sub-contractor of the contractor or his supplier or customer;

(c)   an associated body of the contractor or his supplier or customer; or

(d)   a sub-contractor of an associated body of the contractor or his supplier or customer;

is also, in relation to the contractor, a non-commercial matter for the purposes of this section.

(8) In this section—

'approved list' means such a list as is mentioned in subsection (4)(a) above;

'associated body', in relation to a contractor, means any company which (within the meaning of the Companies Acts (see section 1159 of the Companies Act 2006)) is the contractor's holding company or subsidiary or is a subsidiary of the contractor's holding company;

'business' includes any trade or profession;

'business activities' and 'business interests', in relation to a contractor or other person, mean respectively any activities comprised in, or any investments employed in or attributable to, the carrying on of his business and 'activity' includes receiving the benefit of the performance of any contract;

'contractor', except in relation to a subsisting contract, means a 'potential contractor', that is to say—

    (a) in relation to functions as respects an approved list, any person who is or seeks to be included in the list; and

    (b) in relation to functions as respects a proposed public supply or works contract, any person who is or seeks to be included in the group of persons from whom tenders are invited or who seeks to submit a tender for or enter into the proposed contract, as the case may be;

'exclusion' includes removal;

'Government policy' falls within 'irrelevant fields' for the purposes of this section if it concerns matters of defence or foreign or Commonwealth policy and 'involve', as regards business activities and any such field of policy, includes the supply of goods or materials or services to, or the execution of works for, any authority or person having functions or carrying on business in that field and, as regards business interests and any such field of policy, includes investment in any authority or person whose business activities are so involved;

'industrial dispute' has, as regards a dispute in Great Britain, the same meaning as trade dispute in Part V of the Trade Union and Labour Relations (Consolidation) Act 1992 and 'involve', as regards business activities and an industrial dispute, includes the supply of goods, materials or services to or by, or the execution of works for or by, any party to the dispute, any other person affected by the dispute, or any authority concerned with the enforcement of law and order in relation to the dispute;

'political, industrial or sectarian affiliations or interests' means actual or potential membership of, or actual or potential support for, respectively, any political party, any employers' association or trade union or any society, fraternity or other association;

'suppliers or customers' and 'sub-contractors' includes prospective suppliers or customers and sub-contractors; and 'supplier', in relation to a contractor, includes any person who, in the course of business, supplies him with services or facilities of any description for the purposes of his business;

and 'employers' association' and 'trade union' have, as regards bodies constituted under the law of England and Wales or Scotland, the same meaning as in the Trade Union and Labour Relations (Consolidation) Act 1992.

(9) This section is subject to section 18 below.

(10) This section does not prevent a public authority to which it applies from exercising any function regulated by this section with reference to a non-commercial

matter to the extent that the authority considers it necessary or expedient to do so to enable or facilitate compliance with—

(a) the duty imposed on it by section 149 of the Equality Act 2010 (public sector equality duty), or

(a) any duty imposed on it by regulations under section 153 or 154 of that Act (powers to impose specific duties).

(11) This section does not prevent a public authority to which it applies from exercising any function regulated by this section with reference to a non-commercial matter to the extent that the authority considers it necessary or expedient to do so to enable or facilitate compliance with a duty imposed on it by section 1 of the Public Services (Social Value) Act 2012.

19 Provisions supplementary to or consequential on section 17

(1)–(5) [*These subsections provide for The Secretary of State to have power by statutory instrument subject to parliamentary approval to add to the list of non-commercial matters in section 17 above.*]

(6) Where a public authority makes arrangements under section 101 of the Local Government Act 1972, regulations under section 19 of the Local Government Act 2000 (discharge of functions of and by another local authority) or in relation to Scotland section 56 of the Local Government (Scotland) Act 1973 for the exercise by another public authority of any function regulated by section 17 above, section 17 shall apply to that other public authority in exercising that function as if it were exercising the function in relation to its own public supply or works contracts, any proposed or any subsisting such contract, as the case may be.

(7) The duty imposed by section 17(1) above does not create a criminal offence but—

(a) in proceedings for judicial review, the persons who have a sufficient interest or, in Scotland, title and interest in the matter shall include any potential contractor or, in the case of a contract which has been made, former potential contractor (or, in any case, any body representing contractors), as such; and

(b) a failure to comply with it is actionable by any person who, in consequence, suffers loss or damage.

(8) In any action under section 17(1) above by a person who has submitted a tender for a proposed public supply or works contract arising out of the exercise of functions in relation to the proposed contract the damages shall be limited to damages in respect of expenditure reasonably incurred by him for the purpose of submitting the tender.

(9) Nothing in section 17 above or subsection (1) above implies that the exercise of any function regulated by that section may not be impugned; in proceedings for judicial review, on the ground that it was exercised by reference to other matters than those which are non-commercial matters for the purposes of that section.

(10) If a public authority, in relation to public supply or works contracts or any proposed such contract, as the case may be—

(a) asks a question of any potential contractor relating to any non-commercial matter other than a question consideration of the answer to which is permitted by section 18 above, or

(b) submits to any potential contractor a draft contract or draft tender for a contract which includes terms or provisions relating to any non-commercial matter other than a term or provision the inclusion of which in the contract is permitted by section 18 above,

the authority shall be treated, for the purposes of section 17 above, as exercising functions regulated by that section by reference to non-commercial matters.

(11) In consequence of section 17 above, the following provisions (which require local authorities to secure the insertion of fair wages clauses in all housing contracts), namely—

(a) section 52(a) of the Housing Act 1985, and

. . .

shall cease to have effect.

(12) Expressions used in this section and section 17 above have the same meaning in this section as in that section.

20 Duty of public authorities to give reasons for certain decisions within section 17

(1) Where a public authority exercises a function regulated by section 17 above by making, in relation to any person, a decision to which this section applies, it shall be the duty of the authority forthwith to notify that person of the decision and, if that person so requests in writing within the period of 15 days beginning with the date of the notice, to furnish him with a written statement of the reasons for the decision.

(2) This section applies to the following decisions in relation to any person, namely—

    (a)   in relation to an approved list, a decision to exclude him from the list,

    (b)   in relation to a proposed public supply or works contract—

        (i)   where he has asked to be invited to tender for the contract, a decision not to invite him to tender,

        (ii)   a decision not to accept the submission by him of a tender for the contract,

        (iii)   where he has submitted a tender for the contract, a decision not to enter into the contract with him, or

        (iv)   a decision to withhold approval for, or to select or nominate, persons to be sub-contractors for the purposes of the contract, or

    (c)   in relation to a subsisting public supply or works contract with him—

        (i)   a decision to withhold approval for, or to select or nominate, persons to be sub-contractors for the purposes of the contract, or

        (ii)   a decision to terminate the contract.

(3) A statement of reasons under subsection (1) above shall be sent to the person requesting it within the period of 15 days beginning with the date of the request.

(4) The Secretary of State may by order amend subsection (1) or (3) above so as to substitute for the period specified in that subsection such other period as he thinks fit and such an order may make different amendments of subsections (1) and (3).

(5) The power to make an order under subsection (4) above is exercisable by statutory instrument which shall be subject to annulment in pursuance of a resolution of either House of Parliament.

(6) Expressions used in this section and section 17 above have the same meaning in this section as in that section.

22 Exclusion of charges for inclusion in approved list

(1) A public authority which maintains an approved list shall not require a person to pay any sum as a condition of his inclusion or continued inclusion in the list or of his being considered for such inclusion.

(2) Subsection (1) above does not create an offence but a contravention of it is actionable by the person seeking to be included or retained in the list.

(3) Expressions used in this section and section 17 above have the same meaning in this section as in that section.

LOCAL GOVERNMENT FINANCE ACT 1988

PART III

NON-DOMESTIC RATING

Local rating

42A Rural settlement list

(1)   Each billing authority in England shall compile and maintain, in accordance with section 42B below, a list (to be called its rural settlement list).

(2)   A rural settlement list shall have effect for each chargeable financial year and shall identify for each such year any settlements mentioned in subsection (3) below.

(3)   The settlements referred to in subsection (2) above are those which—

    (a)   are wholly or partly within the authority's area,

    (b)   appear to the authority to have had a population of not more than 3,000 on the last 31st December before the beginning of the chargeable financial year in question, and

    (c)   in that financial year are wholly or partly within an area designated by the Secretary of State by order as a rural area for the purposes of this section.

(4)   A rural settlement list must identify the boundaries of each settlement (whether by defining the boundaries or referring to boundaries defined in a map or other document), but if a settlement is not wholly within the area of a billing authority the list need not identify the boundaries outside the authority's area.

(5)   An order under subsection (3)(c) above may provide for designating as a rural area any area for the time being identified by any person, in any manner, specified in the order.

(6)   Subsection (1) above does not apply to a billing authority in respect of any chargeable financial year for which there are no such settlements as are mentioned in subsection (3) above (and, accordingly, if the authority has compiled a rural settlement list, it shall cease to maintain that list).

42B Preparation and maintenance of lists

(1)   The billing authority shall, throughout the period of three months preceding the beginning of the first chargeable financial year for which a rural settlement list is to have effect, make available for inspection a draft of the list in the form in which the authority proposes that it should have effect for that year.

(2)   In each chargeable financial year for which a rural settlement list has effect the billing authority shall (if it appears to the authority that section 42A(1) above will apply to the authority in respect of the next chargeable financial year) review the list and consider whether or not, for the next chargeable financial year, any alterations are required to the list in order to give effect to section 42A(2) above.

(3)   If following the review the authority considers that any such alterations are required for that year, it shall, throughout the three months preceding the beginning of that year, make available for inspection a draft of the list in the form in which the authority proposes that it should have effect for that year.

(4)   A billing authority which has compiled a rural settlement list shall make it available for inspection in the form in which the list has effect for each chargeable financial year to which it relates.

(5)   Where a billing authority is required to make any list or draft available for inspection under this section, it shall make the list or draft available at any reasonable hour (and free of charge) at its principal office.

43 Occupied hereditaments: liability

(1) A person (the ratepayer) shall as regards a hereditament be subject to a non-domestic rate in respect of a chargeable financial year if the following conditions are fulfilled in respect of any day in the year—

    (a)   on the day the ratepayer is in occupation of all or part of the hereditament, and

    (b)   the hereditament is shown for the day in a local non-domestic rating list in force for the year.

(2) In such a case the ratepayer shall be liable to pay an amount calculated by—

    (a)   finding the chargeable amount for each chargeable day, and

    (b)   aggregating the amounts found under paragraph (a) above.

(3) A chargeable day is one which falls within the financial year and in respect of which the conditions mentioned in subsection (1) above are fulfilled.

(4) Subject to subsections (4A), (5) and (6A) below, the chargeable amount for a chargeable day shall be calculated in accordance with the formula—

    (A x B) divided by C

(4A) Where subsection (4B) below applies, the chargeable amount for a chargeable day shall be calculated—

    (a)   in relation to England, in accordance with the formula—

        $(A \times D) / (C \times E)$

    (b)   in relation to Wales, in accordance with the formula—

        $(A \times B) / (C \times E)$

(4B) This subsection applies—

    (a)   in relation to England, where—

        (i)   the rateable value of the hereditament shown in the local non-domestic rating list for the first day of the chargeable financial year is not more than any amount prescribed by the Secretary of State by order,

        (ii)   on the day concerned any conditions prescribed by the Secretary of State by order are satisfied, and

        (iii)   the ratepayer has made an application for the purposes of this subsection to the billing authority concerned by such date as may be prescribed by the Secretary of State by order,

    (b)   in relation to Wales, where—

        (i)   the rateable value of the hereditament shown in the local non-domestic rating list for the first day of the chargeable financial year is not more than any amount prescribed by the National Assembly for Wales by order, and

        (ii)   on the day concerned any conditions prescribed by the National Assembly for Wales by order are satisfied.

(4C) An application under subsection (4B)(a)(iii) above shall be made in such form, and contain such information, as may be prescribed by the Secretary of State by order.

(4D) If the ratepayer—

    (a)   makes a statement in an application under subsection (4B)(a)(iii) above which he knows to be false in a material particular, or

    (b)   recklessly makes a statement in such an application which is false in a material particular,

he shall be liable on summary conviction to imprisonment for a term not exceeding 3 months or to a fine not exceeding level 3 on the standard scale or to both.

(5) Where subsection (6) below applies the chargeable amount for a chargeable day shall be calculated in accordance with the formula—

    (A x B) divided by (C x 5)

(6) This subsection applies where on the day concerned—

> (a)   the ratepayer is a charity or trustees for a charity and the hereditament is wholly or mainly used for charitable purposes (whether of that charity or of that and other charities), or
>
> (b)   the ratepayer is a registered club for the purposes of Schedule 18 to the Finance Act 2002 (community amateur sports clubs) and the hereditament is wholly or mainly used—
>
>> (i)   for the purposes of that club, or
>>
>> (ii)   for the purposes of that club and of other such registered clubs.

(6A)   Where subsection (6B) below applies, [or, subject to subsection (6I) below, subsection (6F) below applies,][1] the chargeable amount for a chargeable day shall be calculated in accordance with the formula—

(A x B) divided by (C x 2)

(6B)   This subsection applies where—

> (aa)   the hereditament is situated in England,
>
> (a)   on the day concerned the hereditament is within a settlement identified in the billing authority's rural settlement list for the chargeable financial year,
>
> (b)   the rateable value of the hereditament shown in the local non-domestic rating list at the beginning of that year is not more than any amount prescribed by the Secretary of State by order, and
>
> (c)   on the day concerned—
>
>> (i)   the whole or part of the hereditament is used as a qualifying general store[, a qualifying food store][1] or qualifying post office, or
>>
>> (ii)   any conditions prescribed by the Secretary of State by order are satisfied;

and subsections (6C) to (6E) below apply for the purposes of this subsection.

(6C)   A hereditament, or part of a hereditament, is used as a qualifying general store on any day in a chargeable financial year if—

> (a)   a trade or business consisting wholly or mainly of the sale by retail of both food for human consumption (excluding confectionery) and general household goods is carried on there, and
>
> (b)   such a trade or business is not carried on in any other hereditament, or part of a hereditament, in the settlement concerned.

[(6CA)   A hereditament, or part of a hereditament, is used as a qualifying food store on any day in a chargeable financial year if a trade or business consisting wholly or mainly of the sale by retail of food for human consumption (excluding confectionery and excluding the supply of food in the course of catering) is carried on there.

(6CB)   In subsection (6CA) above the supply of food in the course of catering includes—

> (a)   any supply of food for consumption on the premises on which it is supplied; and
>
> (b)   any supply of hot food for consumption off those premises;

and for the purposes of paragraph (b) above 'hot food' means food which, or any part of which—

>> (i)   has been heated for the purposes of enabling it to be consumed at a temperature above the ambient air temperature; and
>>
>> (ii)   is at the time of supply above that temperature.][1]

(6D)   A hereditament, or part of a hereditament, is used as a qualifying post office on any day in a chargeable financial year if—

> (a)   it is used for the purposes of a universal service provider (within the meaning of the Postal Services Act 2000) and in connection with the provision of a universal postal service (within the meaning of that Act), and

(b)   no other hereditament, or part of a hereditament, in the settlement concerned is so used.

(6E)   Where a hereditament or part is used as a qualifying general store or qualifying post office on any day in a chargeable financial year, it is not to be treated as ceasing to be so used on any subsequent day in that year merely because the condition in subsection (6C)(b) or (6D)(b) above ceases to be satisfied.

[(6F)   This subsection applies where—

(a)   on the day concerned the condition mentioned in subsection (6G) below is fulfilled in respect of the hereditament; and

(b)   the rateable value of the hereditament shown in the local non-domestic rating list at the beginning of the chargeable financial year is not more than any amount prescribed by the Secretary of State by order.

(6G)   The condition is that the hereditament—

(a)   consists wholly or mainly of land or buildings which were, on at least 183 days during the period of one year ending immediately before this subsection comes into effect, agricultural land or agricultural buildings for the purposes of the exemption under paragraph 1 of Schedule 5 to this Act; and

(b)   includes land or a building which is not agricultural for the purposes of that exemption but was agricultural for those purposes on at least 183 days during the period mentioned in paragraph (a) above.

(6H)   For the purposes of subsection (6G) above—

(a)   in relation to any hereditament which includes property which is domestic within the meaning of section 66 below, paragraph (a) has effect as if that part of the hereditament which does not consist of such property were the entire hereditament; and

(b)   a building which has replaced a building which was an agricultural building for the purposes of the exemption mentioned in that subsection ('the original building') is to be treated as if it were the original building.

(6I)   Subsection (6A) above shall not have effect, in relation to a hereditament to which subsection (6F) above applies, on a chargeable day on which paragraph 2A of Schedule 6 to this Act applies in relation to the hereditament.

(6J)   Subject to subsection (6K) below, subsections (6F) to (6I) above shall cease to have effect at the end of the period of five years beginning with the day on which those subsections come into effect.

(6K)   The Secretary of State may by order extend or further extend the period mentioned in subsection (6J).

(6L)   If the period is so extended or further extended—

(a)   subsection (6F) above cannot apply to a hereditament after the end of the period of five years beginning with the day on which it first applies; and

(b)   where a hereditament to which subsection (6F) above applies ('the original hereditament') includes land or a building which is subsequently included in a different hereditament, that subsection cannot apply to the different hereditament after the end of the period of five years beginning with the day on which it first applies to the original hereditament.]¹

. . .

(8)   The liability to pay any such amount shall be discharged by making a payment or payments in accordance with regulations under Schedule 9 below.

(8A)   In relation to any hereditament in respect of which both subsections (4A) and (6A) above (but not subsection (5) above) have effect on the day concerned, the chargeable amount—

(a)   in relation to England, shall be calculated in accordance with subsection (6A) above,

(b)   in relation to Wales, shall be calculated in accordance with whichever of subsections (4A) and (6A) above produces the smaller amount.

(8B) In relation to any hereditament in respect of which—

(a)   subsections (4A), (5) and (6A) above each have effect on the day concerned,

(b)   subsections (4A) and (5) above both have effect on that day, or

(c)   subsections (5) and (6A) above both have effect on that day,

the chargeable amount shall be calculated in accordance with subsection (5) above.

---

[1]   Words in square brackets are in force in relation to England but not, as at 29 May 2013, in relation to Wales: see the Rating (Former Agricultural Premises and Rural Shops) Act 2001.

44 Occupied hereditaments: supplementary

[*This section defines 'A' (above) as the rateable value or, in exceptional cases, a lesser amount defined by regulations made by the Secretary of State; 'B' as the non-domestic rating multiplier; and 'C' as the number of days in the financial year.*]

44A Partly occupied hereditaments

(1) Where a hereditament is shown in a billing authority's local non-domestic rating list and it appears to the authority that part of the hereditament is unoccupied but will remain so for a short time only the authority may require the valuation officer for the authority to apportion the rateable value of the hereditament between the occupied and unoccupied parts of the hereditament and to certify the apportionment to the authority.

(2) The reference in subsection (1) above to the rateable value of the hereditament is a reference to the rateable value shown under section 42(4) above as regards the hereditament for the day on which the authority makes its requirement.

(3) For the purposes of this section an apportionment under subsection (1) above shall be treated as applicable for any day which—

(a)   falls within the operative period in relation to the apportionment, and

(b)   is a day for which the rateable value shown under section 42(4) above as regards the hereditament to which the apportionment relates is the same as that so shown for the day on which the authority requires the apportionment.

(4) References in this section to the operative period in relation to an apportionment are references to the period beginning—

(a)   where requiring the apportionment does not have the effect of bringing to an end the operative period in relation to a previous apportionment under subsection (1) above, with the day on which the hereditament to which the apportionment relates became partly unoccupied, and

(b)   where requiring the apportionment does have the effect of bringing to an end the operative period in relation to a previous apportionment under subsection (1) above, with the day immediately following the end of that period,

and ending with the first day on which one or more of the events listed below occurs.

(5) The events are—

(a)   the occupation of any of the unoccupied part of the hereditament to which the apportionment relates;

(b)   the ending of the rate period in which the authority requires the apportionment;

(c)   the requiring of a further apportionment under subsection (1) above in relation to the hereditament to which the apportionment relates;

(d)   the hereditament to which the apportionment relates becoming completely unoccupied.

(6)   Subsection (7) below applies where—
    (a)   a billing authority requires an apportionment under subsection (1) above, and
    (b)   the hereditament to which the apportionment relates—
        (i)   does not fall within a class prescribed under section 45(1)(d), or
        (ii)   would (if unoccupied) be zero-rated under section 45A.

(7)   In relation to any day for which the apportionment is applicable, section 43 above shall have effect as regards the hereditament as if the following subsections were substituted for section 44(2)—

    '(2)   A is such part of the rateable value shown for the day under section 42(4) above as regards the hereditament as is assigned by the relevant apportionments to the occupied part of the hereditament.

    (2A)   In subsection (2) above 'the relevant apportionment' means the apportionment under section 44A(1) below which relates to the hereditament and is treated for the purposes of section 44A below as applicable for the day.'

(8)   Subsection (9) below applies where—
    (a)   a billing authority requires an apportionment under subsection (1) above, and
    (b)   the hereditament to which the apportionment relates—
        (i)   falls within a class prescribed under section 45(1)(d), and
        (ii)   would (if unoccupied) not be zero-rated under section 45A, and
    (c)   an order under section 45(4A) is in force and has effect in relation to the hereditament.

(9)   In relation to any day for which the apportionment is applicable, section 43 above shall have effect as regards the hereditament as if the following subsections were substituted for section 44(2)—

'(2)   A is the sum of—
    (a)   such part of the rateable value shown for the day under section 42(4) above as regards the hereditament as is assigned by the relevant apportionment to the occupied part of the hereditament, and
    (b)   one half of such part of that rateable value as is assigned by the relevant apportionment to the unoccupied part of the hereditament.

(2A)   In subsection (2) above 'the relevant apportionment' means the apportionment under section 44A(1) below which relates to the hereditament and is treated for the purposes of section 44A below as applicable for the day.'.

(10)   References in subsections (1) to (5) above to the hereditament, in relation to a hereditament which is partly domestic property or partly exempt from local non-domestic rating, shall, except where the reference is to the rateable value of the hereditament, be construed as references to such part of the hereditament as is neither domestic property nor exempt from local non-domestic rating.

45 Unoccupied hereditaments: liability

(1)   A person (the ratepayer) shall as regards a hereditament be subject to a non-domestic rate in respect of a chargeable financial year if the following conditions are fulfilled in respect of any day in the year—
    (a)   on the day none of the hereditament is occupied,
    (b)   on the day the ratepayer is the owner of the whole of the hereditament,
    (c)   the hereditament is shown for the day in a local non-domestic rating list in force for the year, and
    (d)   on the day the hereditament falls within a class prescribed by the Secretary of State by regulations.

(2)   In such a case the ratepayer shall be liable to pay an amount calculated by—
    (a)   finding the chargeable amount for each chargeable day, and

(b)   aggregating the amounts found under paragraph (a) above.

(3) A chargeable day is one which falls within the financial year and in respect of which the conditions mentioned in subsection (1) above are fulfilled.

(4) Subject to subsection (4A) and to section 45A below, the chargeable amount for a chargeable day shall be calculated in accordance with the formula—

$$(A \times B) / C$$

where A, B and C have the meanings given by section 46.

(4A) An order may provide that subsection (4) shall have effect as if the following formula were substituted—

$$(A \times B) / (C \times N)$$

where N is such number (greater than one but not greater than two) as may be prescribed.

(4B) An order under subsection (4A) may be made—

(a)   in relation to England, by the Secretary of State;

(b)   in relation to Wales, by the Welsh Ministers.

$$(A \times B) \text{ divided by } (C \times 10)$$

(7) The amount the ratepayer is liable to pay under this section shall be paid to the billing authority in whose local non-domestic rating list the hereditament is shown.

(8) The liability to pay any such amount shall be discharged by making a payment or payments in accordance with regulations under Schedule 9 below.

(9) For the purposes of subsection (1)(d) above a class may be prescribed by reference to such factors as the Secretary of State sees fit.

(10) Without prejudice to the generality of subsection (9) above, a class may be prescribed by reference to one or more of the following factors—

(a)   the physical characteristics of the hereditaments;

(b)   the fact that hereditaments have been unoccupied at any time preceding the day mentioned in subsection (1) above;

(c)   the fact that the owners of hereditaments fall within prescribed descriptions.

45A Unoccupied hereditaments: zero-rating

(1) Where section 45 applies in relation to a hereditament, the chargeable amount for a chargeable day is zero in the following cases.

(2) The first case is where—

(a)   the ratepayer is a charity or trustees for a charity, and

(b)   it appears that when next in use the hereditament will be wholly or mainly used for charitable purposes (whether of that charity or of that and other charities).

(3) The second case is where—

(a)   the ratepayer is a registered club for the purposes of Schedule 18 to the Finance Act 2002 (community amateur sports clubs), and

(b)   it appears that when the hereditament is next in use—

(i)   it will be wholly or mainly used for the purposes of that club and that club will be such a registered club, or

(ii)   it will be wholly or mainly used for the purposes of two or more clubs including that club, and each of those clubs will be such a registered club.

46 Unoccupied hereditaments: supplementary

[*This section defines A, B and C in the same way as s 44 save that there is no power to make exceptions by regulation.*]

46A Unoccupied hereditaments: new buildings

(1)   Schedule 4A below (which makes provision with respect to the determination of a day as the completion day in relation to a new building) shall have effect.

(2)   Where—

    (a)   a completion notice is served under Schedule 4A below, and

    (b)   the building to which the notice relates is not completed on or before the relevant day,

then for the purposes of section 42 above and Schedule 6 below the building shall be deemed to be completed on that day.

(3)   For the purposes of subsection (2) above the relevant day in relation to a completion notice is—

    (a)   where an appeal against the notice is brought under paragraph 4 of Schedule 4A below, the day stated in the notice, and

    (b)   where no appeal against the notice is brought under that paragraph, the day determined under that Schedule as the completion day in relation to the building to which the notice relates.

(4)   Where—

    (a)   a day is determined under Schedule 4A below as the completion day in relation to a new building, and

    (b)   the building is not occupied on that day,

it shall be deemed for the purposes of section 45 above to become unoccupied on that day.

(5)   Where—

    (a)   a day is determined under Schedule 4A below as the completion day in relation to a new building, and

    (b)   the building is one produced by the structural alteration of an existing building,

the hereditament which comprised the existing building shall be deemed for the purposes of section 45 above to have ceased to exist, and to have been omitted from the list, on that day.

(6)   In this section—

    (a)   'building' includes part of a building, and

    (b)   references to a new building include references to a building produced by the structural alteration of an existing building where the existing building is comprised in a hereditament which, by virtue of the alteration, becomes, or becomes part of, a different hereditament or different hereditaments.

47 Discretionary relief

(1)   Where the first and second conditions mentioned in subsections (2) and (3) below or the rural settlement condition and the second condition mentioned in subsection (3) below[, or the condition relating to relief for former agricultural premises mentioned in subsection (3C) below and the second condition mentioned in subsection (3) below,] ₁ or the small business condition and the second condition mentioned in subsection (3) below, are fulfilled for a day which is a chargeable day within the meaning of section 43 or 45 above (as the case may be)—

    (a)   the chargeable amount for the day shall be such as is determined by, or found in accordance with rules determined by, the billing authority concerned, and

    (b)   sections 43(4) to (6B) and 44 above, sections 45(4) to (4B) and 46 above, regulations under section 57A or 58 below or any provision of or made under Schedule 7A below (as the case may be) shall not apply as regards the day.

.....

(3) The .... condition is that, during a period which consists of or includes the chargeable day, a decision of the billing authority concerned operates to the effect that this section applies as regards the hereditament concerned.

.....

(4) A determination under subsection (1)(a) above—

    (a)   must be such that the chargeable amount for the day is less than the amount it would be apart from this section;

    (b)   may be such that the chargeable amount for the day is 0;

    (c)   may be varied by a further determination of the authority under subsection (1)(a) above.

(5) In deciding what the chargeable amount for the day would be apart from this section the effect of any regulations under section 57A or 58 below and of any provision of or made under Schedule 7A below shall be taken into account but anything which has been done or could be done under section 49 below shall be ignored.

(5A) So far as a decision under subsection (3) above would have effect where none of section 43(6) above, section 43(6B) above and subsection (5B) below applies, the billing authority may make the decision only if it is satisfied that it would be reasonable for it to do so, having regard to the interests of persons liable to pay council tax set by it.

(5B) This subsection applies on the chargeable day if—

    (a)   all or part of the hereditament is occupied for the purposes of one or more institutions or other organisations—

        (i)   none of which is established or conducted for profit, and

        (ii)   each of whose main objects are charitable or are otherwise philanthropic or religious or concerned with education, social welfare, science, literature or the fine arts, or

    (b)   the hereditament—

        (i)   is wholly or mainly used for purposes of recreation, and

        (ii)   all or part of it is occupied for the purposes of a club, society or other organisation not established or conducted for profit.

(5C) A billing authority in England, when making a decision under subsection (3) above, must have regard to any relevant guidance issued by the Secretary of State.

(5D) A billing authority in Wales, when making a decision under subsection (3) above, must have regard to any relevant guidance issued by the Welsh Ministers.

(6) A decision under subsection (3) above may be revoked by a further decision of the authority.

(7) A decision under subsection (3) above is invalid as regards a day if made more than six months after the end of the financial year in which the day falls.

(8) The Secretary of State may make regulations containing provision—

    (a)   requiring notice to be given of any determination or decision;

    (b)   limiting the power to revoke a decision or vary a determination;

    (c)   as to other matters incidental to this section.

(8A) This section does not apply where the hereditament is an excepted hereditament.

(9) A hereditament is an excepted hereditament if all or part of it is occupied (otherwise than as trustee) by

    (a)   a billing authority; or

    (b)   a precepting authority . . . *or* charter trustees; or

    (c)   a functional body, within the meaning of the Greater London Authority Act 1999.

(10) This section does not apply where the hereditament is zero-rated under section 45A.

48 Discretionary relief: supplementary

(1)   This section applies for the purposes of section 47 above.

(3)   A hereditament not in use shall be treated as wholly or mainly used for purposes of recreation if it appears that when next in use it will be wholly or mainly used for purposes of recreation.

(4)   A hereditament which is wholly unoccupied shall be treated as an excepted hereditament if it appears that when any of it is next occupied the hereditament will be an excepted hereditament.

(5)   If a hereditament is wholly unoccupied but it appears that it or any part of it when next occupied will be occupied for particular purposes, the hereditament or part concerned (as the case may be) shall be treated as occupied for those purposes.

SCHEDULE 5

NON-DOMESTIC RATING: EXEMPTION

Agricultural premises

1

A hereditament is exempt to the extent that it consists of any of the following—

  (a)   agricultural land;

  (b)   agricultural buildings;

2

(1)   Agricultural land is—

  . . .

  (d)   anything which consists of a market garden, nursery ground, orchard or allotment (which here includes an allotment garden within the meaning of the Allotments Act 1922),

  . . .

(2)   But agricultural land does not include—

  (a)   land occupied together with a house as a park,

  (b)   gardens (other than market gardens),

  (c)   pleasure grounds,

  (d)   land used mainly or exclusively for purposes of sport or recreation, or

  (e)   land used as a racecourse.

3

A building is an agricultural building if it is not a dwelling and—

  (a)   it is occupied together with agricultural land and is used solely in connection with agricultural operations on that or other agricultural land, or

  (b)   it is or forms part of a market garden and is used solely in connection with agricultural operations at the market garden.

  . . .

Places of religious worship etc

11

(1)   A hereditament is exempt to the extent that it consists of any of the following—

  (a)   a place of public religious worship which belongs to the Church of England or the Church in Wales (within the meaning of the Welsh Church Act 1914) or is for the time being certified as required by law as a place of religious worship;

(b) a church hall, chapel hall or similar building used in connection with a place falling within paragraph (a) above for the purposes of the organisation responsible for the conduct of public religious worship in that place.

(2) A hereditament is exempt to the extent that it is occupied by an organisation responsible for the conduct of public religious worship in a place falling within sub-paragraph (1)(a) above and—

(a) is used for carrying out administrative or other activities relating to the organisation of the conduct of public religious worship in such a place; or

(b) is used as an office or for office purposes, or for purposes ancillary to its use as an office or for office purposes.

(3) In this paragraph 'office purposes' include administration, clerical work and handling money; and 'clerical work' includes writing, book-keeping, sorting papers or information, filing, typing, duplicating, calculating (by whatever means), drawing and the editorial preparation of matter for publication.

Parks

15

(1) A hereditament is exempt to the extent that it consists of a park which—

(a) has been provided by, or is under the management of, a relevant authority or two or more relevant authorities in combination, and

(b) is available for free and unrestricted use by members of the public.

(2) The reference to a park includes a reference to a recreation or pleasure ground, a public walk, an open space within the meaning of the Open Spaces Act 1906, and a playing field provided under the Physical Training and Recreation Act 1937.

(3) Each of the following is a relevant authority—

(aa) a Minister of the Crown or Government department or any officer or body exercising functions on behalf of the Crown,

(a) a county council,

(aa) a county borough council,

(b) a district council,

(c) a London borough council,

(d) the Common Council,

(e) the Council of the Isles of Scilly,

(f) a parish or community council, and

(g) the chairman of a parish meeting.

(4) In construing sub-paragraph (1)(b) above any temporary closure (at night or otherwise) shall be ignored.

. . .

ROAD TRAFFIC ACT 1988

Cycling offences and cycle racing

28 Dangerous cycling

(1) A person who rides a cycle on a road dangerously is guilty of an offence.

(2) For the purposes of subsection (1) above a person is to be regarded as riding dangerously if (and only if)—

(a) the way he rides falls far below what would be expected of a competent and careful cyclist, and

(b)   it would be obvious to a competent and careful cyclist that riding in that way would be dangerous.

(3)   In subsection (2) above 'dangerous' refers to danger either of injury to any person or of serious damage to property; and in determining for the purposes of that subsection what would be obvious to a competent and careful cyclist in a particular case, regard shall be had not only to the circumstances of which he could be expected to be aware but also to any circumstances shown to have been within the knowledge of the accused.

29 Careless, and inconsiderate, cycling

If a person rides a cycle on a road without due care and attention, or without reasonable consideration for other persons using the road, he is guilty of an offence.

30 Cycling when under influence of drink or drugs

(1)   A person who, when riding a cycle on a road or other public place, is unfit to ride through drink or drugs (that is to say, is under the influence of drink or a drug to such an extent as to be incapable of having proper control of the cycle) is guilty of an offence.

. . .

31 Regulation of cycle racing on public ways

(1)   A person who promotes or takes part in a race or trial of speed on a public way between cycles is guilty of an offence, unless the race or trial—

(a)   is authorised, and

(b)   is conducted in accordance with any conditions imposed,

by or under regulations under this section.

(2)   The Secretary of State may by regulations authorise, or provide for authorising, for the purposes of subsection (1) above, the holding on a public way other than a bridleway—

(a)   of races or trials of speed of any class or description, or

(b)   of a particular race or trial of speed,

in such cases as may be prescribed and subject to such conditions as may be imposed by or under the regulations.

(3)   Regulations under this section may—

(a)   prescribe the procedure to be followed, and the particulars to be given, in connection with applications for authorisation under the regulations, and

(b)   make different provision for different classes or descriptions of race or trial.

(4)   Without prejudice to any other powers exercisable in that behalf, the chief officer of police may give directions with respect to the movement of, or the route to be followed by, vehicular traffic during any period, being directions which it is necessary or expedient to give in relation to that period to prevent or mitigate—

(a)   congesting or obstruction of traffic, or

(b)   danger to or from traffic,

in consequence of the holding of a race or trial of speed authorised by or under regulations under this section.

(5)   Directions under subsection (4) above may include a direction that any road or part of a road specified in the direction shall be closed during the period to vehicles or to vehicles of a class so specified.

(6)   In this section 'public way' means, in England and Wales, a highway, and in Scotland, a public road but does not include a footpath.

Use of motor vehicles away from roads

33 Control of use of footpaths, bridleways and restricted byways for motor vehicle trials

(1) A person must not promote or take part in a trial of any description between motor vehicles on a footpath, bridleway or restricted byway unless the holding of the trial has been authorised under this section by the local authority.

(2) A local authority shall not give an authorisation under this section unless satisfied that consent in writing to the use of any length of footpath, bridleway or restricted byway for the purposes of the trial has been given by the owner and by the occupier of the land over which that length of footpath, bridleway or restricted byway runs, and any such authorisation may be given subject to compliance with such conditions as the authority think fit.

(3) A person who—

    (a)   contravenes subsection (1) above, or

    (b)   fails to comply with any conditions subject to which an authorisation under this section has been granted,

is guilty of an offence.

(4) The holding of a trial authorised under this section is not affected by any statutory provision prohibiting or restricting the use of footpaths, bridleways or restricted byways or a specified footpath, bridleway or restricted byway; but this section does not prejudice any right or remedy of a person as having any interest in land.

(5) In this section 'local authority'—

    (a)   in relation to England and Wales, means the council of a county, metropolitan district or London borough, and

    . . .

(6) In this section 'restricted byway' means a way over which the public have restricted byway rights within the meaning of Part 2 of the Countryside and Rights of Way Act 2000, with or without a right to drive animals of any description along the way, but no other rights of way.

34 Prohibition of driving mechanically propelled vehicles elsewhere than on roads

(1) Subject to the provisions of this section, if without lawful authority a person drives a mechanically propelled vehicle—

    (a)   on to or upon any common land, moorland or land of any other description, not being land forming part of a road, or

    (b)   on any road being a footpath, bridleway or restricted byway,

he is guilty of an offence.

(2) For the purposes of subsection (1)(b) above, a way shown in a definitive map and statement as a footpath, bridleway or restricted byway is, without prejudice to section 56(1) of the Wildlife and Countryside Act 1981, to be taken to be a way of the kind shown, unless the contrary is proved.

(2A) It is not an offence under this section for a person with an interest in land, or a visitor to any land, to drive a mechanically propelled vehicle on a road if, immediately before the commencement of section 47(2) of the Countryside and Rights of Way Act 2000, the road was—

    (a)   shown in a definitive map and statement as a road used as a public path, and

    (b)   in use for obtaining access to the land by the driving of mechanically propelled vehicles by a person with an interest in the land or by visitors to the land.

(3)   It is not an offence under this section to drive a mechanically propelled vehicle on any land within fifteen yards of a road, being a road on which a motor vehicle may lawfully be driven, for the purpose only of parking the vehicle on that land.

(4)   A person shall not be convicted of an offence under this section with respect to a vehicle if he proves to the satisfaction of the court that it was driven in contravention of this section for the purpose of saving life or extinguishing fire or meeting any other like emergency.

(5)   It is hereby declared that nothing in this section prejudices the operation of—

    (a)   section 193 of the Law of Property Act 1925 (rights of the public over commons and waste lands), or

    (b)   any byelaws applying to any land,

or affects the law of trespass to land or any right or remedy to which a person may by law be entitled in respect of any such trespass or in particular confers a right to park a vehicle on any land.

(6)   Subsection (2) above and section 34A of this Act do not extend to Scotland.

(7)   In this section—

    'definitive map and statement' has the same meaning as in Part III of the Wildlife and Countryside Act 1981;

    'interest', in relation to land, includes any estate in land and any right over land (whether exercisable by virtue of the ownership of an estate or interest in the land or by virtue of a licence or agreement) and, in particular, includes rights of common and sporting rights;

    'mechanically propelled vehicle' does not include a vehicle falling within paragraph (a), (b) or (c) of section 189(1) of this Act; and

    'restricted byway' means a way over which the public have restricted byway rights within the meaning of Part II of the Countryside and Rights of Way Act 2000, with or without a right to drive animals of any description along the way, but no other rights of way.

(8)   A person—

    (a)   entering any land in exercise of rights conferred by virtue of section 2(1) of the Countryside and Rights of Way Act 2000, or

    (b)   entering any land which is treated by section 15(1) of that Act as being accessible to the public apart from that Act,

is not for the purposes of subsection (2A) a visitor to the land.

LOCAL GOVERNMENT AND HOUSING ACT 1989

Appointment and management etc of staff

7 All staff to be appointed on merit

(1)   Every appointment of a person to a paid office or employment under—

    (a)   a local authority or parish or community council in England and Wales,

    . . .

shall be made on merit.

(2)   Subsection (1) above applies to all appointments made by, or by any committee of, a local authority or parish or community council . . . under section 112 of the Local Government Act 1972 or . . . otherwise, but has effect subject to—

    (c)   section 7 of the Sex Discrimination Act 1975 (discrimination permitted in relation to employment where sex of employee is a genuine occupational qualification);

(d)   section 5 of the Race Relations Act 1976 (discrimination permitted in relation to employment where being of a particular racial group is a genuine occupational qualification);

(e)   section 113 of the Local Government Finance Act 1988 and section 6 above (qualifications of officers responsible for administration of financial affairs of certain authorities); and

(f)   sections 4, 4A, 4D and 4E of the Disability Discrimination Act 1995 (discrimination and duties to make adjustments in relation to employees and office-holders).

. . .

10 Limit on paid leave for local authority duties

(1)   Notwithstanding anything in section 50(4) of the Employment Rights Act 1996 (conditions of time off for public duties), where—

(a)   a local authority permit an employee of theirs to take time off for the purpose of performing the duties of a member of a relevant council; and

(b)   those duties do not include the duties of chairman of the council,

it shall be unlawful for the authority to make any payment of remuneration or other payment to that employee in respect of so much (if any) of any time off for that purpose as is in excess of two hundred and eight hours in any one financial year and is time off to which the employee would not be entitled apart from his membership of that council.

(2)   [*This subsection defines 'chairman', 'employee' and 'financial year' as might be expected and includes Scottish councils in the term 'relevant council'.*]

11 Confidentiality of staff records

(1)   Nothing in the Local Government Act 1985 . . . shall entitle any person—

(a)   to inspect so much of any document as contains personal information about a member of the relevant body's staff; or

(b)   to require any such information to be disclosed in answer to any question.

(2)   Information shall be regarded as personal information about a member of the relevant body's staff if it relates specifically to a particular individual and is available to that body for reasons connected with the fact—

(a)   that that individual holds or has held any office or employment under that body; or

(b)   that payments or other benefits in respect of any office or employment under any other person are or have been made or provided to that individual by that body.

(3)   [*This subsection sets out the obvious definitions.*]

Duty to adopt certain procedural standing orders

20 Duty to adopt certain procedural standing orders

(1)   The Secretary of State may by regulations require relevant authorities, subject to such variations as may be authorised by the regulations—

(a)   to incorporate such provision as may be prescribed by the regulations in standing orders for regulating their proceedings and business; and

(b)   to make or refrain from making such other modifications of any such standing orders as may be so prescribed.

(2)   Without prejudice to the generality of subsection (1) above, regulations under this section may require such standing orders as are mentioned in that subsection to contain provision which, notwithstanding any enactment or the decision of any

relevant authority or committee or sub-committee of a relevant authority, authorises persons who are members of such an authority, committee or sub-committee—

(a) to requisition meetings of the authority or of any of their committees or sub-committees;

(b) to require a decision of a committee or sub-committee of the authority to be referred to and reviewed by the authority themselves or by a committee of the authority;

(c) to require that a vote with respect to a matter falling to be decided by the authority or by any of their committees or sub-committees is to be taken in a particular manner.

(3) Regulations under this section may contain such incidental provision and such supplemental, consequential and transitional provision in connection with their other provisions as the Secretary of State considers appropriate.

(4) In this section 'relevant authority'—

(a) in relation to England and Wales, means a local authority of any of the descriptions specified in paragraphs (a) to (j) of section 21(1) below or any parish or community council; . . .

PART VII

RENEWAL AREAS

89

[*This section provides that a local housing authority may, after taking appropriate qualified advice, declare that an area where living conditions are unsatisfactory shall be a renewal area.*]

91 Renewal area: steps to be taken after declaration or extension

(1) As soon as may be after—

(a) declaring an area to be a renewal area; or

(b) extending (or further extending) the period for which an area is to be a renewal area,

a local housing authority shall take the steps required by subsection (2) below.

(2) Those steps are such as appear to the authority best designed to secure—

(a) that the resolution to which the declaration, or extension (or further extension) of the period, relates is brought to the attention of persons residing or owning property in the area; and

(b) that those persons are informed of the name and address of the person to whom should be addressed inquiries and representations concerning action to be taken with respect to the renewal area.

92 Duty to publish information

(1) Where a local housing authority have declared an area to be a renewal area, they shall from time to time publish, in such manner as appears to them best designed to secure that the information is brought to the attention of persons residing or owning property in the area, information with respect to—

(a) the action they propose to take in relation to the area,

(b) the action they have taken in relation to the area, and

(c) the assistance available for the carrying out of works in the area,

being such information as appears to them best designed to further the purpose for which the area was declared a renewal area.

93 General powers of local housing authority

(1) Where a local housing authority have declared an area to be a renewal area, the authority may exercise the powers conferred by this section.

(2) For the purpose of securing or assisting in securing all or any of the objectives mentioned in subsection (3) below, the authority may acquire by agreement, or be authorised by the Secretary of State to acquire compulsorily, any land in the area on which there are premises consisting of or including housing accommodation or which forms part of the curtilage of any such premises; and the authority may provide housing accommodation on land acquired under this subsection.

(3) The objectives referred to in subsection (2) above are—

  (a) the improvement or repair of the premises, either by the authority or by a person to whom they propose to dispose of the premises;

  (b) the proper and effective management and use of the housing accommodation, either by the authority or by a person to whom they propose to dispose of the premises comprising the accommodation; and

  (c) the well-being of the persons for the time being residing in the area.

(4) For the purpose of effecting or assisting the improvement of the amenities in the area, the authority may acquire by agreement, or be authorised by the Secretary of State to acquire compulsorily, any land in the area (including land which the authority propose to dispose of to another person who intends to effect or assist the improvement of those amenities).

(5) The authority may—

  (a) carry out works (including works of demolition) on land owned by the authority in the area (whether or not that land was acquired under subsection (2) or subsection (4) above).

(6) The authority may enter into an agreement with a housing association or other person under which, in accordance with the terms of the agreement, the authority's functions under subsection (5) above are to be exercisable by that association or other person.

(7) If after—

  (a) the authority have entered into a contract for the acquisition of land under subsection (2) or subsection (4) above, or

  (b) a compulsory purchase order authorising the acquisition of land under either of those subsections has been confirmed,

the renewal area concerned ceases to be such an area or the land is excluded from the area, the provisions of the subsection in question shall continue to apply as if the land continued to be in a renewal area.

(8) The powers conferred by this section are without prejudice to any power which a local housing authority may have under or by virtue of any other enactment.

94 Power to apply for orders extinguishing right to use vehicles on highway

(1) A local housing authority who have declared a renewal area may exercise the powers of a local planning authority under sections 249 and 250 of the Town and Country Planning Act 1990 (extinguishment of right to use vehicles on certain highways) with respect to a highway in that area notwithstanding that they are not the local planning authority, but subject to the following provisions.

(2) The local housing authority shall not make an application under subsection (2) or subsection (6) of section 249 (application to Secretary of State to make or revoke order extinguishing right to use vehicles) except with the consent of the local planning authority.

(3) If the local housing authority are not also the highway authority, any such application made by them shall in the first place be sent to the highway authority who shall transmit it to the Secretary of State.

(4) Where an order under subsection (2) of section 249 (order extinguishing right to use vehicles) has been made on an application made by a local housing authority by virtue of this section, any compensation under subsection (1) of section 250 (compensation for loss of access to highway) is payable by them instead of by the local planning authority.

95 Exclusion of land from, or termination of, renewal area

(1)   Subject to subsection (2) below, a local housing authority may by resolution—

(a)   exclude land from a renewal area; or

(b)   declare that an area shall cease to be a renewal area;

and as soon as may be after passing such a resolution the authority shall take the steps required by subsection (5) below.

(2)   Before exercising any power under subsection (1) above, an authority shall take such steps as appear to the authority best designed to secure—

(a)   that the proposed exclusion or cessation, as the case may be, is brought to the attention of persons residing or owning property in the area; and

(b)   that those persons are informed of the name and address of the person to whom should be addressed representations concerning the proposed exclusion or cessation.

(5)   The authority shall take such steps as appear to them best designed to secure that the resolution is brought to the attention of persons residing or owning property in the renewal area.

(6)   A resolution under subsection (1) above has effect from the day on which it is passed.

(7)   A resolution under subsection (1) above does not affect the continued operation of the provisions of this Part, or any other enactment relating to renewal areas, in relation to works begun before the date on which the exclusion or cessation takes effect; but the resolution does have effect with respect to works which have not been begun before that date, notwithstanding that expenditure in respect of the works has been approved before that date.

TOWN AND COUNTRY PLANNING ACT 1990

PART IX

ACQUISITION AND APPROPRIATION OF LAND FOR PLANNING PURPOSES, ETC

Acquisition for planning and public purposes

229 Appropriation of land forming part of common, etc

(1)   Any local authority may be authorised, by an order made by that authority and confirmed by the Secretary of State, to appropriate for any purpose for which that authority can be authorised to acquire land under any enactment any land to which this subsection applies which is for the time being held by them for other purposes.

(2)   Subsection (1) applies to land which is or forms part of a common or fuel or field garden allotment (including any such land which is specially regulated by any enactment, whether public general or local or private), other than land which is Green Belt land within the meaning of the Green Belt (London and Home Counties) Act 1938.

(3)   Section 19 of the Acquisition of Land Act 1981 (special provision with respect to compulsory purchase orders under that Act relating to land forming part of a common, open space or fuel or field garden allotment) shall apply to an order under this section authorising the appropriation of land as it applies to a compulsory purchase order under that Act.

(4)   Where land appropriated under this section was acquired under an enactment incorporating the Lands Clauses Acts, any works executed on the land after the appropriation has been effected shall, for the purposes of section 68 of the Lands

Clauses Consolidation Act 1845 and section 10 of the Compulsory Purchase Act 1965, be deemed to have been authorised by the enactment under which the land was acquired.

(5)   On an appropriation of land by a local authority under this section, where—

(a)   the authority is not an authority to whom Part II of the 1959 Act applies;

(b)   the land was immediately before the appropriation held by the authority for the purposes of a grant-aided function (within the meaning of that Act); or

(c)   the land is appropriated by the authority for the purposes of such a function,

such adjustments shall be made in the accounts of the local authority as the Secretary of State may direct.

(6)   On an appropriation under this section which does not fall within subsection (5), such adjustment of accounts shall be made as is required by section 24(1) of the 1959 Act.

230 Acquisition of land for purposes of exchange

(1)   Without prejudice to the generality of the powers conferred by sections 226 and 227, any power of a local authority to acquire land under those sections, whether compulsorily or by agreement, shall include power to acquire land required for giving in exchange—

(a)   for land appropriated under section 229; or

(b)   for Green Belt land appropriated in accordance with the Green Belt (London and Home Counties) Act 1938 for any purpose specified in a development plan.

(2)   In subsection (1) 'Green Belt land' has the same meaning as in that Act.

Extinguishment of certain rights affecting acquired or appropriated land

238 Use and development of consecrated land

(1)   Notwithstanding any obligation or restriction imposed under ecclesiastical law or otherwise in respect of consecrated land, any such land, which has been the subject of a relevant acquisition or appropriation, may subject to the following provisions of this section—

(a)   if it has been acquired by a Minister, be used in any manner by him or on his behalf for any purpose for which he acquired the land; and

(b)   in any other case, be used by any person in any manner in accordance with planning permission.

(2)   Subsection (1) applies whether or not the land includes a building but it does not apply to land which consists of or forms part of a burial ground.

(3)   Any use of consecrated land authorised by subsection (1) shall be subject—

(a)   to compliance with the prescribed requirements with respect—

(i)   to the removal and reinterment of any human remains, and

(ii)   to the disposal of monuments and fixtures and furnishings; and

(b)   to such provisions as may be prescribed for prohibiting or restricting the use of the land, either absolutely or until the prescribed consent has been obtained, so long as any church or other building used or formerly used for religious worship, or any part of it, remains on the land.

(4)   Any use of land other than consecrated land which—

(a)   has been the subject of a relevant acquisition or appropriation, and

(b)   at the time of acquisition or appropriation included a church or other building used or formerly used for religious worship or the site of such a church or building, shall be subject to compliance with such requirements as are mentioned in subsection (3)(a).

(5) Any regulations made for the purposes of subsection (3) or (4)—

    (a)   shall contain such provisions as appear to the Secretary of State to be requisite for securing that any use of land which is subject to compliance with the regulations shall, as nearly as may be, be subject to the same control as is imposed by law in the case of a similar use authorised by an enactment not contained in this Act or by a Measure, or as it would be proper to impose on a disposal of the land in question otherwise than in pursuance of an enactment or Measure;

    (b)   shall contain such requirements relating to the disposal of any such land as is mentioned in subsection (3) or (4) as appear to the Secretary of State requisite for securing that the provisions of those subsections are complied with in relation to the use of the land; and

    (c)   may contain such incidental and consequential provisions (including provision as to the closing of registers) as appear to the Secretary of State to be expedient for the purposes of the regulations.

(6) Nothing in this section shall be construed as authorising any act or omission on the part of any person which is actionable at the suit of any person on any grounds other than contravention of any such obligation, restriction or enactment as is mentioned in subsection (1).

239 Use and development of burial grounds

(1) Notwithstanding anything in any enactment relating to burial grounds or any obligation or restriction imposed under ecclesiastical law or otherwise in respect of them, any land consisting of a burial ground or part of a burial ground, which has been the subject of a relevant acquisition or appropriation, may—

    (a)   if it has been acquired by a Minister, be used in any manner by him or on his behalf for any purpose for which he acquired the land; and

    (b)   in any other case, be used by any person in any manner in accordance with planning permission.

(2) This section does not apply to land which has been used for the burial of the dead until the prescribed requirements with respect to the removal and reinterment of human remains, and the disposal of monuments, in or upon the land have been complied with.

(3) Nothing in this section shall be construed as authorising any act or omission on the part of any person which is actionable at the suit of any person on any grounds other than contravention of any such enactment, obligation or restriction as is mentioned in subsection (1).

240 Provisions supplemental to ss 238 and 239

(1) Provision shall be made by any regulations made for the purposes of sections 238(3) and (4) and 239(2)—

    (a)   for requiring the persons in whom the land is vested to publish notice of their intention to carry out the removal and reinterment of any human remains or the disposal of any monuments;

    (b)   for enabling the personal representatives or relatives of any deceased person themselves to undertake—

        (i)   the removal and reinterment of the remains of the deceased, and

        (ii)   the disposal of any monument commemorating the deceased,

and for requiring the persons in whom the land is vested to defray the expenses of such removal, reinterment and disposal (not exceeding such amount as may be prescribed);

    (c)   for requiring compliance—

(i)   with such reasonable conditions (if any) as may be imposed in the case of consecrated land, by the bishop of the diocese, with respect to the manner of removal and the place and manner of reinterment of any human remains and the disposal of any monuments, and

(ii)   with any directions given in any case by the Secretary of State with respect to the removal and reinterment of any human remains.

(2)   Subject to the provisions of any such regulations, no faculty is required—

(a)   for the removal and reinterment in accordance with the regulations of any human remains, or

(b)   for the removal or disposal of any monuments,

and section 25 of the Burial Act 1857 (prohibition of removal of human remains without the licence of the Secretary of State except in certain cases) does not apply to a removal carried out in accordance with the regulations.

(3)   In sections 238 and 239 and this section—

'burial ground' includes any churchyard, cemetery or other ground, whether consecrated or not, which has at any time been set apart for the purposes of interment,

'monument' includes a tombstone or other memorial, and

'relevant acquisition or appropriation' means an acquisition made by a Minister, a local authority or statutory undertakers under this Part or Chapter V of Part I of the Planning (Listed Buildings and Conservation Areas) Act 1990 or compulsorily under any other enactment, or an appropriation by a local authority for planning purposes.

241 Use and development of open spaces

(1)   Notwithstanding anything in any enactment relating to land which is or forms part of a common, open space or fuel or field garden allotment or in any enactment by which the land is specially regulated, such land which has been acquired by a Minister, a local authority or statutory undertakers under this Part or under Chapter V of Part I of the Planning (Listed Buildings and Conservation Areas) Act 1990 or compulsorily under any other enactment, or which has been appropriated by a local authority for planning purposes—

(a)   if it has been acquired by a Minister, may be used in any manner by him or on his behalf for any purpose for which he acquired the land; and

(b)   in any other case, may be used by any person in any manner in accordance with planning permission.

(2)   Nothing in this section shall be construed as authorising any act or omission on the part of any person which is actionable at the suit of any person on any grounds other than contravention of any such enactment as is mentioned in subsection (1).

PART X

HIGHWAYS

Orders made by Secretary of State

251 Extinguishment of public rights of way over land held for planning purposes

(1)   Where any land has been acquired or appropriated for planning purposes and is for the time being held by a local authority for the purposes for which it was acquired or appropriated, the Secretary of State may by order extinguish any public right of way over the land if he is satisfied—

(a)   that an alternative right of way has been or will be provided; or

(b)   that the provision of an alternative right of way is not required.

(2) In this section any reference to the acquisition or appropriation of land for planning purposes shall be construed in accordance with section 246(1) as if this section were in Part IX.

(3) Subsection (1) shall also apply (with the substitution of a reference to the Broads Authority for the reference to the local authority) in relation to any land within the Broads which is held by the Broads Authority and which was acquired by, or vested in, the Authority for any purpose connected with the discharge of any of its functions.

252 Procedure for making of orders

(1) Before making an order under section 247, 248, 249 or 251 the Secretary of State or, as the case may be, the council of a London borough shall publish in at least one local newspaper circulating in the relevant area, and in the London Gazette, a notice—

    (a)   stating the general effect of the order;

    (b)   specifying a place in the relevant area where a copy of the draft order and of any relevant map or plan may be inspected by any person free of charge at all reasonable hours during a period of 28 days from the date of the publication of the notice ('the publication date'); and

    (c)   stating that any person may within that period by notice to the Secretary of State or, as the case may be, the council of the London borough object to the making of the order.

(2) Not later than the publication date, the Secretary of State or, as the case may be, the council of the London borough shall serve a copy of the notice, together with a copy of the draft order and of any relevant map or plan—

    (a)   on every local authority in whose area any highway or, as the case may be, any land to which the order relates is situated, and

    (aa)   on any National Park authority which is the local planning authority for the area in which any highway or, as the case may be, any land to which the order relates is situated, and

    (b)   on any water, sewerage, hydraulic power or electricity undertakers or gas transporter having any cables, mains, sewers, pipes or wires laid along, across, under or over any highway to be stopped up or diverted, or, as the case may be, any land over which a right of way is proposed to be extinguished, under the order.

(3) Not later than the publication date, the Secretary of State or, as the case may be, the council of the London borough shall also cause a copy of the notice to be displayed in a prominent position at the ends of so much of any highway as is proposed to be stopped up or diverted or, as the case may be, of the right of way proposed to be extinguished under the order.

(4) If before the end of the period of 28 days mentioned in subsection (1)(b) an objection is received by the Secretary of State or, as the case may be, the council of the London borough from any local authority National Park authority or undertakers or gas transporter on whom a notice is required to be served under subsection (2), or from any other person appearing to the Secretary of State or, as the case may be, the council to be affected by the order, and the objection is not withdrawn, then

    (a)   in a case where the Secretary of State is proposing to make an order, he shall cause a local inquiry to be held unless subsection (5) applies, or

    (b)   in a case where the council of a London borough is proposing to make an order, it shall notify the Mayor of London of the objections and shall cause a local inquiry to be held unless subsection (5A) applies.

(5) If, in a case where the Secretary of State is proposing to make an order and the objection is made by a person other than such a local authority or undertakers or transporter, the Secretary of State is satisfied that in the special circumstances of the case the holding of such an inquiry is unnecessary he may dispense with the inquiry.

(5A) In a case where—

    (a)   the council of a London borough is proposing to make the order,

(b)   the council has under subsection (4)(b) notified the Mayor of London of the objections, and

(c)   none of the objections notified is made by such a local authority or undertakers or transporter as are mentioned in that subsection,

the Mayor of London shall decide whether, in the special circumstances of the case, the holding of such an inquiry is unnecessary, and if he decides that it is unnecessary he shall so notify the council which may dispense with the inquiry.

(6)   Subsections (2) to (5) of section 250 of the Local Government Act 1972 (local inquiries: evidence and costs) shall apply in relation to an inquiry caused to be held by the Secretary of State or the council of a London borough under subsection (4).

(6A)   In their application to an inquiry caused to be held by the council of a London borough—

(a)   subsection (4) of section 250 of the Local Government Act 1972 shall be treated as if—

    (i)   for the reference to a Minister there were substituted a reference to the council of a London borough,

    (ii)   for the reference to him there were substituted a reference to the council,

    (iii)   for the reference to he there were substituted a reference to the council acting with the consent of the Mayor of London, and

    (iv)   for the references to the Minister there were substituted references to the council of the London borough, and

(b)   subsection (5) of that section shall be treated as if—

    (i)   for the reference to the Minister there were substituted a reference to the council of a London borough, and

    (ii)   the power to make an order as to the costs of parties were subject to a requirement to act with the consent of the Mayor of London.

(7)   Where publication of the notice mentioned in subsection (1) takes place on more than one day, the references in this section to the publication date are references to the latest date on which it is published.

(8)   Where the Secretary of State is proposing to make an order, after considering any objections to the order which are not withdrawn and, where a local inquiry is held, the report of the person who held the inquiry, the Secretary of State may, subject to subsection (9), make the order either without modification or subject to such modifications as he thinks fit.

(8A)   Where the council of a London borough is proposing to make an order, after—

(a)   considering any objections to the order which are not withdrawn, and

(b)   where a local inquiry is held—

    (i)   considering the report of the person who held the inquiry, and

    (ii)   obtaining the consent of the Mayor of London to the making of the order,

the council may, subject to subsection (9), make the order either without modification or subject to such modification as it thinks fit.

(9)   Where—

(a)   the order contains a provision requiring any such payment, repayment or contribution as is mentioned in section 247(4)(a); and

(b)   objection to that provision is duly made by an authority or person who would be required by it to make such a payment, repayment or contribution; and

(c)   the objection is not withdrawn,

the order shall be subject to special parliamentary procedure.

(10)   Immediately after the order has been made, the Secretary of State or, as the case may be, the council of the London borough shall publish, in the manner specified in

subsection (1), a notice stating that the order has been made and naming a place where a copy of the order may be seen at all reasonable hours.

(10A) Nothing in subsection (2) shall require the council of a London borough to serve anything on itself.

(11) Subsections (2), (3) and (7) shall have effect in relation to a notice under subsection (10) as they have effect in relation to a notice under subsection (1).

(12) In this section—

'the relevant area', in relation to an order, means the area in which any highway or land to which the order relates is situated;

'local authority' means the council of a county, county borough, district, parish, community or London borough, a police authority established under section 3 of the Police Act 1996, the Metropolitan Police Authority, a joint authority established by Part IV of the Local Government Act 1985, the London Fire and Emergency Planning Authority, a housing action trust established under Part III of the Housing Act 1988, the Residuary Body for Wales (Corff Gweddilliol Cymru) and the parish meeting of a parish not having a separate parish council;

and in subsection (2)—

(i) the reference to water undertakers shall be construed as including a reference to the Environment Agency, and

(ii) the reference to electricity undertakers shall be construed as a reference to holders of licences under section 6 of the Electricity Act 1989 who are entitled to exercise any power conferred by paragraph 1 of Schedule 4 to that Act.

253 Procedure in anticipation of planning permission

(1) Where—

(a) the Secretary of State or the council of a London borough would, if planning permission for any development had been granted under Part III, have power to make an order under section 247 or 248 authorising the stopping up or diversion of a highway in order to enable that development to be carried out, and

(b) subsection (2), (3) or (4) applies,

then, notwithstanding that such permission has not been granted, the Secretary of State or, as the case may be, the council of the London borough may publish notice of the draft of such an order in accordance with section 252.

(2) This subsection applies where the relevant development is the subject of an application for planning permission and either—

(a) that application is made by a local authority National Park authority or statutory undertakers; or

(b) that application stands referred to the Secretary of State in pursuance of a direction under section 77; or

(c) the applicant has appealed to the Secretary of State under section 78 against a refusal of planning permission or of approval required under a development order [or a local development order][1], a local development order or a neighbourhood development order or against a condition of any such permission or approval.

(3) This subsection applies where—

(a) the relevant development is to be carried out by a local authority National Park authority or statutory undertakers and requires, by virtue of an enactment, the authorisation of a government department; and

(b) the developers have made an application to the department for that authorisation and also requested a direction under section 90(1) that planning permission be deemed to be granted for that development.

(4) This subsection applies where the council of a county, county borough, metropolitan district or London borough. a National Park authority or a joint planning board certify that they have begun to take such steps, in accordance with regulations made by virtue of section 316, as are required to enable them to obtain planning permission for the relevant development.

(5) Section 252(8) shall not be construed as authorising the Secretary of State or the council of a London borough to make an order under section 247 or 248 of which notice has been published by virtue of subsection (1) until planning permission is granted for the development which occasions the making of the order.

¹ Words in square brackets are in force in relation to England but not, as at 29 May 2013, in relation to Wales: see the Planning and Compulsory Purchase Act 2004.

254 Compulsory acquisition of land in connection with highways

(1) The Secretary of State, or a local highway authority on being authorised by the Secretary of State to do so, may acquire land compulsorily—

(a) for the purpose of providing or improving any highway which is to be provided or improved in pursuance of an order under section 247, 248 or 249 or for any other purpose for which land is required in connection with the order; or

(b) for the purpose of providing any public right of way which is to be provided as an alternative to a right of way extinguished under an order under section 251.

(2) The Acquisition of Land Act 1981 shall apply to the acquisition of land under this section.

255 Concurrent proceedings in connection with highways

(1) In relation to orders under sections 247, 248 and 249, regulations made under this Act may make provision for securing that any proceedings required to be taken for the purposes of the acquisition of land under section 254 (as mentioned in subsection (1)(a) of that section) may be taken concurrently with any proceedings required to be taken for the purposes of the order.

(2) In relation to orders under section 251, regulations made under this Act may make provision for securing—

(a) that any proceedings required to be taken for the purposes of such an order may be taken concurrently with any proceedings required to be taken for the purposes of the acquisition of the land over which the right of way is to be extinguished; or

(b) that any proceedings required to be taken for the purposes of the acquisition of any other land under section 254 (as mentioned in subsection (1)(b) of that section) may be taken concurrently with either or both of the proceedings referred to in paragraph (a).

Orders by other authorities

257 Footpaths, bridleways and restricted byways affected by development: orders by other authorities

(1) Subject to section 259, a competent authority may by order authorise the stopping up or diversion of any footpath, bridleway or restricted byway if they are satisfied that it is necessary to do so in order to enable development to be carried out—

(a) in accordance with planning permission granted under Part III or section 293A, or

(b) by a government department.

(2) An order under this section may, if the competent authority are satisfied that it should do so, provide—

(a) for the creation of an alternative highway for use as a replacement for the one authorised by the order to be stopped up or diverted, or for the improvement of an existing highway for such use;

(b) for authorising or requiring works to be carried out in relation to any footpath, bridleway or restricted byway for whose stopping up or diversion, creation or improvement provision is made by the order;

(c) for the preservation of any rights of statutory undertakers in respect of any apparatus of theirs which immediately before the date of the order is under, in, on, over, along or across any such footpath, bridleway or restricted byway;

(d) for requiring any person named in the order to pay, or make contributions in respect of, the cost of carrying out any such works.

(3) An order may be made under this section authorising the stopping up or diversion of a footpath, bridleway or restricted byway which is temporarily stopped up or diverted under any other enactment.

(4) In this section 'competent authority' means—

(a) in the case of development authorised by a planning permission, the local planning authority who granted the permission or, in the case of a permission granted by the Secretary of State, who would have had power to grant it; and

(b) in the case of development carried out by a government department, the local planning authority who would have had power to grant planning permission on an application in respect of the development in question if such an application had fallen to be made.

258 Extinguishment of public rights of way over land held for planning purposes

(1) Where any land has been acquired or appropriated for planning purposes and is for the time being held by a local authority for the purposes for which it was acquired or appropriated, then, subject to section 259, the local authority may by order extinguish any public right of way over the land, being a footpath, bridleway or restricted byway, if they are satisfied—

(a) that an alternative right of way has been or will be provided; or

(b) that the provision of an alternative right of way is not required.

(2) In this section any reference to the acquisition or appropriation of land for planning purposes shall be construed in accordance with section 246(1) as if this section were in Part IX.

(3) Subsection (1) shall also apply (with the substitution of a reference to the Broads Authority for the reference to the local authority) in relation to any land within the Broads which is held by the Broads Authority and which was acquired by, or vested in, the Authority for any purpose connected with the discharge of any of its functions.

259 Confirmation of orders made by other authorities

(1) An order made under section 257 or 258 shall not take effect unless confirmed by the Secretary of State or unless confirmed, as an unopposed order, by the authority who made it.

(2) The Secretary of State shall not confirm any such order unless satisfied as to every matter as to which the authority making the order are required under section 257 or, as the case may be, section 258 to be satisfied.

(3) The time specified—

(a) in an order under section 257 as the time from which a footpath, bridleway or restricted byway is to be stopped up or diverted; or

(b) in an order under section 258 as the time from which a right of way is to be extinguished,

shall not be earlier than confirmation of the order.

(4)   Schedule 14 shall have effect with respect to the confirmation of orders under section 257 or 258 and the publicity for such orders after they are confirmed.

Temporary highway orders: mineral workings

261 Temporary stopping up of highways for mineral workings
(1)   Where the Secretary of State or the council of a London borough is satisfied—
- (a)   that an order made by him or, as the case may be, the council under section 247 for the stopping up or diversion of a highway is required for the purpose of enabling minerals to be worked by surface working; and
- (b)   that the highway can be restored, after the minerals have been worked, to a condition not substantially less convenient to the public,

the order may provide for the stopping up or diversion of the highway during such period as may be prescribed by or under the order and for its restoration at the expiration of that period.

(2)   Where a competent authority within the meaning of section 257 are satisfied—
- (a)   that an order made by them under that section for the stopping up or diversion of a footpath, bridleway or restricted byway is required for the purpose of enabling minerals to be worked by surface working; and
- (b)   that the footpath, bridleway or restricted byway can be restored, after the minerals have been worked, to a condition not substantially less convenient to the public,

the order may provide for the stopping up or diversion of the footpath, bridleway or restricted byway during such period as may be prescribed by or under the order and for its restoration at the expiration of that period.

(3)   Without prejudice to the provisions of section 247 or 257, any such order as is authorised by subsection (1) or (2) may contain such provisions as appear to the Secretary of State, the council of the London borough or the competent authority (as the case may be) to be expedient—
- (a)   for imposing upon persons who, apart from the order, would be subject to any liability with respect to the repair of the original highway during the period prescribed by or under the order a corresponding liability in respect of any highway provided in pursuance of the order;
- (b)   for the stopping up at the expiry of that period of any highway so provided and for the reconstruction and maintenance of the original highway;

and any provision included in the order in accordance with subsection (4) of section 247 or subsection (2) of section 257 requiring payment to be made in respect of any cost or expenditure under the order may provide for the payment of a capital sum in respect of the estimated amount of that cost or expenditure.

(4)   In relation to any highway which is stopped up or diverted by virtue of an order under section 247 or 248, sections 271 and 272 shall have effect—
- (a)   as if for references to land which has been acquired as there mentioned and to the acquiring or appropriating authority there were substituted respectively references to land over which the highway subsisted and to the person entitled to possession of that land; and
- (b)   as if references in subsection (5) of each of those sections to a local authority or statutory undertakers included references to any person (other than a Minister) who is entitled to possession of that land,

and sections 275 to 278 shall have effect accordingly.

(5)   Subsection (4) shall not apply to land constituting the site of a highway in respect of which opencast planning permission (within the meaning of section 51 of the Opencast Coal Act 1958) has been granted.

SCHEDULE 1

LOCAL PLANNING AUTHORITIES: DISTRIBUTION OF FUNCTIONS

Planning and special control

8

(1) A local planning authority who have the function of determining applications for planning permission shall, if requested to do so by the council of any parish situated in their area, notify the council of—

    (a)   any relevant planning application; and

    (b)   any alteration to that application accepted by the authority.

(2) In sub-paragraph (1) 'a relevant planning application' means an application which—

    (a)   relates to land in the parish; and

    (b)   is an application for—

        (i)   planning permission; or

        (ii)   approval of a matter reserved under an outline planning permission within the meaning of section 92.

(3) Any request made for the purposes of sub-paragraph (1) shall be in writing and state that the council wishes to be notified of all relevant applications or all applications of a description specified in the request.

(4) An authority shall comply with the duty to notify a council of an application by—

    (a)   sending the council a copy of the application; or

    (b)   indicating to the council the nature of the development which is the subject of the application and identifying the land to which it relates,

and any notification falling within paragraph (b) shall be in writing.

(5) An authority shall comply with their duty to notify a council of an alteration by—

    (a)   sending a copy of the alteration to the council; or

    (b)   informing the council in writing of its general effect,

but they need not notify a council of an alteration which in their opinion is trivial.

(6) A development order may require a local planning authority which is dealing with an application of which a council is entitled to be notified—

    (a)   to give the council an opportunity to make representations to them as to the manner in which the application should be determined;

    (b)   to take into account any such representations;

    (c)   to notify the council of the terms of their decision or, where the application is referred to the Secretary of State, the date when it was so referred and, when notified to them, the terms of his decision.

SCHEDULE 14

PROCEDURE FOR FOOTPATHS AND BRIDLEWAYS ORDERS

PART I

CONFIRMATION OF ORDERS

1

(1) Before an order under section 257 or 258 is submitted to the Secretary of State for confirmation or confirmed as an unopposed order, the authority by whom the order was made shall give notice in the prescribed form—

(a)   stating the general effect of the order and that it has been made and is about to be submitted for confirmation or to be confirmed as an unopposed order;

(b)   naming a place in the area in which the land to which the order relates is situated where a copy of the order may be inspected free of charge and copies of it may be obtained at a reasonable charge at all reasonable hours; and

(c)   specifying the time (which must not be less than 28 days from the date of the first publication of the notice) within which, and the manner in which, representations or objections with respect to the order may be made.

(2) Subject to sub-paragraphs (6) and (7), the notice to be given under sub-paragraph (1) shall be given—

(a)   by publication in at least one local newspaper circulating in the area in which the land to which the order relates is situated; and

(b)   by serving a similar notice on—

    (i)   every owner, occupier and lessee (except tenants for a month or a period less than a month and statutory tenants within the meaning of the Rent Act 1977) of any of that land;

    (ii)   every council, the council of every parish or community and the parish meeting of every parish not having a separate council, being a council or parish whose area includes any of that land; and

    (iia)   any National Park authority for a National Park which includes any of that land; and

    (iii)   any statutory undertakers to whom there belongs, or by whom there is used, for the purposes of their undertaking, any apparatus under, in, on, over, along or across that land; and

    (iv)   every person on whom notice is required to be served in pursuance of sub-paragraph (4); and

    (v)   such other persons as may be prescribed in relation to the area in which that land is situated or as the authority may consider appropriate; and

(c)   by causing a copy of the notice to be displayed in a prominent position—

    (i)   at the ends of so much of any footpath, bridleway or restricted byway as is to be stopped up, diverted or extinguished by the order;

    (ii)   at council offices in the locality of the land to which the order relates; and

    (iii)   at such other places as the authority may consider appropriate.

(3) In sub-paragraph (2)—

'council' means a county council, a county borough council, a district council, a London borough council, the London Fire and Emergency Planning Authority, or a joint authority established by Part IV of the Local Government Act 1985;

'council offices' means offices or buildings acquired or provided by a council or by the council of a parish or community or the parish meeting of a parish not having a separate parish council.

(4) Any person may, on payment of such reasonable charge as the authority may consider appropriate, require an authority to give him notice of all such orders under section 257 or 258 as are made by the authority during a specified period, are of a specified description and relate to land comprised in a specified area.

(5) In sub-paragraph (4) 'specified' means specified in the requirement.

(6)   Except where an owner, occupier or lessee is a local authority National Park authority or statutory undertaker, the Secretary of State may in any particular case direct that it shall not be necessary to comply with sub-paragraph (2)(b)(i).

(7)   If the Secretary of State gives a direction under sub-paragraph (6) in the case of any land, then—

    (a)   in addition to publication the notice shall be addressed to 'the owners and any occupiers' of the land (describing it); and

    (b)   a copy or copies of the notice shall be affixed to some conspicuous object or objects on the land.

(8)   Sub-paragraph (2)(b) and (c) and, where applicable, sub-paragraph (7) shall be complied with not less than 28 days before the expiry of the time specified in the notice.

(9)   A notice required to be served by sub-paragraph (2)(b)(i), (ii), (iii) or (v) shall be accompanied by a copy of the order.

(10)   A notice required to be displayed by sub-paragraph (2)(c)(i) at the ends of so much of any way as is affected by the order shall be accompanied by a plan showing the general effect of the order so far as it relates to that way.

2

If no representations or objections are duly made, or if any so made are withdrawn, the authority by whom the order was made may, instead of submitting the order to the Secretary of State, themselves confirm the order (but without any modification).

3

(1)   This paragraph applies where any representation or objection which has been duly made is not withdrawn.

(2)   If the objection is made by a local authority or a National Park authority the Secretary of State shall, before confirming the order, cause a local inquiry to be held.

(3)   If the representation or objection is made by a person other than a local authority the Secretary of State shall, before confirming the order, either—

    (a)   cause a local inquiry to be held; or

    (b)   give any person by whom any representation or objection has been duly made and not withdrawn an opportunity of being heard by a person appointed by the Secretary of State for the purpose.

(4)   After considering the report of the person appointed under sub-paragraph (2) or (3) to hold the inquiry or hear representations or objections, the Secretary of State may confirm the order, with or without modifications.

(5)   In the case of an order under section 257, if objection is made by statutory undertakers on the ground that the order provides for the creation of a public right of way over land covered by works used for the purpose of their undertaking, or over the curtilage of such land, and the objection is not withdrawn, the order shall be subject to special parliamentary procedure.

(6)   Notwithstanding anything in the previous provisions of this paragraph, the Secretary of State shall not confirm an order so as to affect land not affected by the order as submitted to him, except after—

    (a)   giving such notice as appears to him requisite of his proposal so to modify the order, specifying the time (which must not be less than 28 days from the date of the first publication of the notice) within which, and the manner in which, representations or objections with respect to the proposal may be made;

    (b)   holding a local inquiry or giving any person by whom any representation or objection has been duly made and not withdrawn an opportunity of being heard by a person appointed by the Secretary of State for the purpose; and

(c)   considering the report of the person appointed to hold the inquiry or, as the case may be, to hear representations or objections.

(7) In the case of an order under section 257, if objection is made by statutory undertakers on the ground that the order as modified would provide for the creation of a public right of way over land covered by works used for the purposes of their undertaking or over the curtilage of such land, and the objection is not withdrawn, the order shall be subject to special parliamentary procedure.

4

(1) A decision of the Secretary of State under paragraph 3 shall, except in such classes of case as may for the time being be prescribed or as may be specified in directions given by the Secretary of State, be made by a person appointed by the Secretary of State for the purpose instead of by the Secretary of State.

(2) A decision made by a person so appointed shall be treated as a decision of the Secretary of State.

(3) The Secretary of State may, if he thinks fit, direct that a decision which, by virtue of sub-paragraph (1) and apart from this sub-paragraph, falls to be made by a person appointed by the Secretary of State shall instead be made by the Secretary of State.

(4) A direction under sub-paragraph (3) shall—

(a)   state the reasons for which it is given; and

(b)   be served on the person, if any, so appointed, the authority and any person by whom a representation or objection has been duly made and not withdrawn.

(5) Where the Secretary of State has appointed a person to make a decision under paragraph 3 the Secretary of State may, at any time before the making of the decision, appoint another person to make it instead of the person first appointed to make it.

(6) Where by virtue of sub-paragraph (3) or (5) a particular decision falls to be made by the Secretary of State or any other person instead of the person first appointed to make it, anything done by or in relation to the latter shall be treated as having been done by or in relation to the former.

(7) Regulations under this Act may provide for the giving of publicity to any directions given by the Secretary of State under this paragraph.

5

(1) The Secretary of State shall not confirm an order under section 257 which extinguishes a right of way over land under, in, on, over, along or across which there is any apparatus belonging to or used by statutory undertakers for the purposes of their undertaking, unless the undertakers have consented to the confirmation of the order.

(2) Any such consent may be given subject to the condition that there are included in the order such provisions for the protection of the undertakers as they may reasonably require.

(3) The consent of statutory undertakers to any such order shall not be unreasonably withheld.

(4) Any question arising under this paragraph whether the withholding of consent is unreasonable, or whether any requirement is reasonable, shall be determined by whichever Minister is the appropriate Minister in relation to the statutory undertakers concerned.

6

Regulations under this Act may, subject to this Part of this Schedule, make such provision as the Secretary of State thinks expedient as to the procedure on the making, submission and confirmation of orders under sections 257 and 258.

PART II

PUBLICITY FOR ORDERS AFTER CONFIRMATION

7

(1)   As soon as possible after an order under section 257 or 258 has been confirmed by the Secretary of State or confirmed as an unopposed order, the authority to whom the order was made—

> (a)   shall publish, in the manner required by paragraph 1(2)(a), a notice in the prescribed form—
>
> > (i)   describing the general effect of the order,
> >
> > (ii)   stating that it has been confirmed, and
> >
> > (iii)   naming a place in the area in which the land to which the order relates is situated where a copy of the order as confirmed may be inspected free of charge and copies of it may be obtained at a reasonable charge at all reasonable hours;
>
> (b)   shall serve a similar notice on any persons on whom notices were required to be served under paragraph 1(2)(b) or (7); and
>
> (c)   shall cause similar notices to be displayed in a similar manner as the notices required to be displayed under paragraph 1(2)(c).

(2)   No such notice or copy need be served on a person unless he has sent to the authority a request in that behalf, specifying an address for service.

(3)   A notice required to be served by sub-paragraph (1)(b) on—

> (a)   a person on whom notice was required to be served by paragraph 1(2)(b)(i), (ii) or (iii); or
>
> (b)   in the case of an order which has been confirmed with modifications, a person on whom notice was required to be served by paragraph 1(2)(b)(v),

shall be accompanied by a copy of the order as confirmed.

(4)   As soon as possible after a decision not to confirm an order under section 257 or 258, the authority by whom the order was made shall give notice of the decision by serving a copy of it on any persons on whom notices were required to be served under paragraph 1(2)(b) or (7).

8

Where an order under section 257 or 258 has come into force otherwise than—

> (a)   on the date on which it was confirmed by the Secretary of State or confirmed as an unopposed order; or
>
> (b)   at the expiration of a specified period beginning with that date,

then as soon as possible after it has come into force the authority by whom it was made shall give notice of its coming into force by publication in at least one local newspaper circulating in the area in which the land to which the order relates is situated.

ENVIRONMENTAL PROTECTION ACT 1990

PART III

STATUTORY NUISANCES AND CLEAN AIR

Statutory nuisances

79 Statutory nuisances and inspections therefor

(1) Subject to subsections (1A) to (6A) below, the following matters constitute 'statutory nuisances' for the purposes of this Part, that is to say—

   (a)   any premises in such a state as to be prejudicial to health or a nuisance;

   (b)   smoke emitted from premises so as to be prejudicial to health or a nuisance;

   (c)   fumes or gases emitted from premises so as to be prejudicial to health or a nuisance;

   (d)   any dust, steam, smell or other effluvia arising on industrial, trade or business premises and being prejudicial to health or a nuisance;

   (e)   any accumulation or deposit which is prejudicial to health or a nuisance;

   (f)   any animal kept in such a place or manner as to be prejudicial to health or a nuisance;

   (fa)   any insects emanating from relevant industrial, trade or business premises and being prejudicial to health or a nuisance;

   (fb)   artificial light emitted from premises so as to be prejudicial to health or a nuisance;

   (g)   noise emitted from premises so as to be prejudicial to health or a nuisance;

   (ga)   noise that is prejudicial to health or a nuisance and is emitted from or caused by a vehicle, machinery or equipment in a street . . . ;

   (h)   any other matter declared by any enactment to be a statutory nuisance;

and it shall be the duty of every local authority to cause its area to be inspected from time to time to detect any statutory nuisances which ought to be dealt with under section 80 below or sections 80 and 80A below and, where a complaint of a statutory nuisance is made to it by a person living within its area, to take such steps as are reasonably practicable to investigate the complaint.

. . .

(1A) No matter shall constitute a statutory nuisance to the extent that it consists of, or is caused by, any land being in a contaminated state.

(1B) Land is in a 'contaminated state' for the purposes of subsection (1A) above if, and only if, it is in such a condition, by reason of substances in, on or under the land, that—

   (a)   harm is being caused or there is a possibility of harm being caused; or

   (b)   pollution of controlled waters is being, or is likely to be, caused;

and in this subsection 'harm', 'pollution of controlled waters' and 'substance' have the same meaning as in Part IIA of this Act.

(2) Subsection (1)(b), (fb), (fba) and (g) above do not apply in relation to premises (or, in respect of paragraph (fba)(ii) above, a stationary object located on premises)—

   (a)   occupied on behalf of the Crown for naval, military or air force purposes or for the purposes of the department of the Secretary of State having responsibility for defence, or

   (b)   occupied by or for the purposes of a visiting force;

and 'visiting force' means any such body, contingent or detachment of the forces of any country as is a visiting force for the purposes of any of the provisions of the Visiting Forces Act 1952.

(3) Subsection (1)(b) above does not apply to—

    (i)   smoke emitted from a chimney of a private dwelling within a smoke control area,

    (ii)   dark smoke emitted from a chimney of a building or a chimney serving the furnace of a boiler or industrial plant attached to a building or for the time being fixed to or installed on any land,

    (iii)   smoke emitted from a railway locomotive steam engine, or

    (iv)   dark smoke emitted otherwise than as mentioned above from industrial or trade premises.

(4) Subsection (1)(c) above does not apply in relation to premises other than private dwellings.

(5) Subsection (1)(d) above does not apply to steam emitted from a railway locomotive engine.

    . . .

(5A) Subsection (1)(fa) does not apply to insects that are wild animals included in Schedule 5 to the Wildlife and Countryside Act 1981 (animals which are protected), unless they are included in respect of section 9(5) of that Act only.

(5B) Subsection (1)(fb) does not apply to artificial light emitted from—

    (a)   an airport;

    (b)   harbour premises;

    (c)   railway premises, not being relevant separate railway premises;

    (d)   tramway premises;

    (e)   a bus station and any associated facilities;

    (f)   a public service vehicle operating centre;

    (g)   a goods vehicle operating centre;

    (h)   a lighthouse;

    (i)   a prison.

(6) Subsection (1)(g) above does not apply to noise caused by aircraft other than model aircraft.

(6A) Subsection (1)(ga) above does not apply to noise made—

    (a)   by traffic,

    (b)   by any naval, military or air force of the Crown or by a visiting force (as defined in subsection (2) above), or

    (c)   by a political demonstration or a demonstration supporting or opposing a cause or campaign.

(7) In this Part—

    . . .

    'appropriate person' means—

        (a)   in relation to England, the Secretary of State;

        (b)   in relation to Wales, the National Assembly for Wales;

    'associated facilities', in relation to a bus station, has the meaning given by section 83 of the Transport Act 1985;

    'bus station' has the meaning given by section 83 of the Transport Act 1985;

    'chimney' includes structures and openings of any kind from or through which smoke may be emitted;

    'dust' does not include dust emitted from a chimney as an ingredient of smoke;

    'equipment' includes a musical instrument;

    'fumes' means any airborne solid matter smaller than dust;

'gas' includes vapour and moisture precipitated from vapour;

'goods vehicle operating centre', in relation to vehicles used under an operator's licence, means a place which is specified in the licence as an operating centre for those vehicles, and for the purposes of this definition 'operating centre' and 'operator's licence' have the same meaning as in the Goods Vehicles (Licensing of Operators) Act 1995;

'harbour premises' means premises which form part of a harbour area and which are occupied wholly or mainly for the purposes of harbour operations, and for the purposes of this definition 'harbour area' and 'harbour operations' have the same meaning as in Part 3 of the Aviation and Maritime Security Act 1990;

'industrial, trade or business premises' means premises used for any industrial, trade or business purposes or premises not so used on which matter is burnt in connection with any industrial, trade or business process, and premises are used for industrial purposes where they are used for the purposes of any treatment or process as well as where they are used for the purposes of manufacturing;

'lighthouse' has the same meaning as in Part 8 of the Merchant Shipping Act 1995;

'local authority' means, subject to subsection (8) below,—

    (a)   in Greater London, a London borough council, the Common Council of the City of London and, as respects the Temples, the Sub-Treasurer of the Inner Temple and the Under-Treasurer of the Middle Temple respectively;

    (b)   in England outside Greater London, a district council;

    (bb)   in Wales, a county council or county borough council; . . . .

'noise' includes vibration;

'person responsible'—

    (a)   in relation to a statutory nuisance, means the person to whose act, default or sufferance the nuisance is attributable;

    (b)   in relation to a vehicle, includes the person in whose name the vehicle is for the time being registered under the Vehicle Excise and Registration Act 1994 and any other person who is for the time being the driver of the vehicle;

    (c)   in relation to machinery or equipment, includes any person who is for the time being the operator of the machinery or equipment;

'prejudicial to health' means injurious, or likely to cause injury, to health;

'premises' includes land . . . and, subject to subsection (12) and, in relation to England and Wales section 81A(9) below, any vessel;

'prison' includes a young offender institution;

'private dwelling' means any building, or part of a building, used or intended to be used, as a dwelling;

'public service vehicle operating centre', in relation to public service vehicles used under a PSV operator's licence, means a place which is an operating centre of those vehicles, and for the purposes of this definition 'operating centre', 'PSV operator's licence' and 'public service vehicle' have the same meaning as in the Public Passenger Vehicles Act 1981;

'railway premises' means any premises which fall within the definition of 'light maintenance depot', 'network', 'station' or 'track' in section 83 of the Railways Act 1993;

'relevant separate railway premises' has the meaning given by subsection (7A);

'road' has the same meaning as in Part IV of the New Roads and Street Works Act 1991;

'smoke' includes soot, ash, grit and gritty particles emitted in smoke;

'street' means a highway and any other road, footway, square or court that is for the time being open to the public;

'tramway premises' means any premises which, in relation to a tramway, are the equivalent of the premises which, in relation to a railway, fall within the definition of 'light maintenance depot', 'network', 'station' or 'track' in section 83 of the Railways Act 1993;

and any expressions used in this section and in the Clean Air Act 1993 have the same meaning in this section as in that Act and section 3 of the Clean Air Act 1993 shall apply for the interpretation of the expression 'dark smoke' and the operation of this Part in relation to it.

(7A)   Railway premises are relevant separate railway premises if—

(a)   they are situated within—

(i)   premises used as a museum or other place of cultural, scientific or historical interest, or

(ii)   premises used for the purposes of a funfair or other entertainment, recreation or amusement, and

(b)   they are not associated with any other railway premises.

(7B)   For the purposes of subsection (7A)—

(a)   a network situated as described in subsection (7A)(a) is associated with other railway premises if it is connected to another network (not being a network situated as described in subsection (7A)(a));

(b)   track that is situated as described in subsection (7A)(a) but is not part of a network is associated with other railway premises if it is connected to track that forms part of a network (not being a network situated as described in subsection (7A)(a));

(c)   a station or light maintenance depot situated as described in subsection (7A)(a) is associated with other railway premises if it is used in connection with the provision of railway services other than services provided wholly within the premises where it is situated.

In this subsection 'light maintenance depot', 'network', 'railway services', 'station' and 'track' have the same meaning as in Part 1 of the Railways Act 1993.

(7C)   In this Part 'relevant industrial, trade or business premises' means premises that are industrial, trade or business premises as defined in subsection (7), but excluding—

(a)   land used as arable, grazing, meadow or pasture land,

(b)   land used as osier land, reed beds or woodland,

(c)   land used for market gardens, nursery grounds or orchards,

(d)   land forming part of an agricultural unit, not being land falling within any of paragraphs (a) to (c), where the land is of a description prescribed by regulations made by the appropriate person, and

(e)   land included in a site of special scientific interest (as defined in section 52(1) of the Wildlife and Countryside Act 1981),

and excluding land covered by, and the waters of, any river or watercourse, that is neither a sewer nor a drain, or any lake or pond.

(7D)   For the purposes of subsection (7C)—

'agricultural' has the same meaning as in section 109 of the Agriculture Act 1947;

'agricultural unit' means land which is occupied as a unit for agricultural purposes;

'drain' has the same meaning as in the Water Resources Act 1991;

'lake or pond' has the same meaning as in section 104 of that Act;

'sewer' has the same meaning as in that Act.

. . .

(9)   In this Part 'best practicable means' is to be interpreted by reference to the following provisions—

- (a)   'practicable' means reasonably practicable having regard among other things to local conditions and circumstances, to the current state of technical knowledge and to the financial implications;
- (b)   the means to be employed include the design, installation, maintenance and manner and periods of operation of plant and machinery, and the design, construction and maintenance of buildings and structures;
- (c)   the test is to apply only so far as compatible with any duty imposed by law;
- (d)   the test is to apply only so far as compatible with safety and safe working conditions, and with the exigencies of any emergency or unforeseeable circumstances;

and, in circumstances where a code of practice under section 71 of the Control of Pollution Act 1974 (noise minimisation) is applicable, regard shall also be had to guidance given in it.

(10)   A local authority shall not without the consent of the Secretary of State institute summary proceedings under this Part in respect of a nuisance falling within paragraph (b), (d), (e), (fb) or (g) and, in relation to Scotland, paragraph (ga), of subsection (1) above if proceedings in respect thereof might be instituted under Part I or under regulations under section 2 of the Pollution Prevention and Control Act 1999.

(11)   The area of a local authority which includes part of the seashore shall also include for the purposes of this Part the territorial sea lying seawards from that part of the shore; and subject to subsection (12) and, in relation to England and Wales, section 81A below, this Part shall have effect, in relation to any area included in the area of a local authority by virtue of this subsection—

- (a)   as if references to premises and the occupier of premises included respectively a vessel and the master of a vessel; and
- (b)   with such other modifications, if any, as are prescribed in regulations made by the Secretary of State.

(12)   A vessel powered by steam reciprocating machinery is not a vessel to which this Part of this Act applies.

80 Summary proceedings for statutory nuisances

(1)   Subject to subsection (2A) where a local authority is satisfied that a statutory nuisance exists, or is likely to occur or recur, in the area of the authority, the local authority shall serve a notice ('an abatement notice') imposing all or any of the following requirements—

- (a)   requiring the abatement of the nuisance or prohibiting or restricting its occurrence or recurrence;
- (b)   requiring the execution of such works, and the taking of such other steps, as may be necessary for any of those purposes,

and the notice shall specify the time or times within which the requirements of the notice are to be complied with.

(2)   Subject to section 80A(1) below, the abatement notice shall be served—

- (a)   except in a case falling within paragraph (b) or (c) below, on the person responsible for the nuisance;
- (b)   where the nuisance arises from any defect of a structural character, on the owner of the premises;
- (c)   where the person responsible for the nuisance cannot be found or the nuisance has not yet occurred, on the owner or occupier of the premises.

(2A)   Where a local authority is satisfied that a statutory nuisance falling within paragraph (g) of section 79(1) above exists, or is likely to occur or recur, in the area of the authority, the authority shall—

    (a)   serve an abatement notice in respect of the nuisance in accordance with subsections (1) and (2) above; or

    (b)   take such other steps as it thinks appropriate for the purpose of persuading the appropriate person to abate the nuisance or prohibit or restrict its occurrence or recurrence.

(2B)   If a local authority has taken steps under subsection (2A)(b) above and either of the conditions in subsection (2C) below is satisfied, the authority shall serve an abatement notice in respect of the nuisance.

(2C)   The conditions are—

    (a)   that the authority is satisfied at any time before the end of the relevant period that the steps taken will not be successful in persuading the appropriate person to abate the nuisance or prohibit or restrict its occurrence or recurrence;

    (b)   that the authority is satisfied at the end of the relevant period that the nuisance continues to exist, or continues to be likely to occur or recur, in the area of the authority.

(2D)   The relevant period is the period of seven days starting with the day on which the authority was first satisfied that the nuisance existed, or was likely to occur or recur.

(2E)   The appropriate person is the person on whom the authority would otherwise be required under subsection (2A)(a) above to serve an abatement notice in respect of the nuisance.

(3)   A person served with an abatement notice may appeal against the notice to a magistrates' court . . . within the period of twenty-one days beginning with the date on which he was served with the notice.

(4)   If a person on whom an abatement notice is served, without reasonable excuse, contravenes or fails to comply with any requirement or prohibition imposed by the notice, he shall be guilty of an offence.

(4A)   Where a local authority have reason to believe that a person has committed an offence under subsection (4) above, the local authority may give that person a notice (a 'fixed penalty notice') in accordance with section 80ZA offering the person the opportunity of discharging any liability to conviction for that offence by payment of a fixed penalty.

(5)   Except in a case falling within subsection (6) below, a person who commits an offence under subsection (4) above shall be liable on summary conviction to a fine not exceeding level 5 on the standard scale together with a further fine of an amount equal to one-tenth of that level for each day on which the offence continues after the conviction.

(6)   A person who commits an offence under subsection (4) above on industrial, trade or business premises shall be liable on summary conviction to a fine not exceeding £20,000.

(7)   Subject to subsection (8) below, in any proceedings for an offence under subsection (4) above in respect of a statutory nuisance it shall be a defence to prove that the best practicable means were used to prevent, or to counteract the effects of, the nuisance.

(8)   The defence under subsection (7) above is not available—

    (a)   in the case of a nuisance falling within paragraph (a), (d), (e), (f), (fa) or (g) of section 79(1) above except where the nuisance arises on industrial, trade or business premises;

    (aza)   in the case of a nuisance falling within paragraph (fb) of section 79(1) above except where—

       (i)   the artificial light is emitted from industrial, trade or business premises, or

      (ii)   the artificial light (not being light to which sub-paragraph (i) applies) is emitted by lights used for the purpose only of illuminating an outdoor relevant sports facility;

(aa)   in the case of a nuisance falling within paragraph (ga) of section 79(1) above except where the noise is emitted from or caused by a vehicle, machinery or equipment being used for industrial, trade or business purposes;

(b)   in the case of a nuisance falling within paragraph (b) of section 79(1) above except where the smoke is emitted from a chimney; and

(c)   in the case of a nuisance falling within paragraph (c) or (h) of section 79(1) above.

(8A) For the purposes of subsection (8)(aza) a relevant sports facility is an area, with or without structures, that is used when participating in a relevant sport, but does not include such an area comprised in domestic premises.

(8B) For the purposes of subsection (8A) 'relevant sport' means a sport that is designated for those purposes by order made by the Secretary of State, in relation to England, or the National Assembly for Wales, in relation to Wales.

A sport may be so designated by reference to its appearing in a list maintained by a body specified in the order.

(8C) In subsection (8A) 'domestic premises' means—

(a)   premises used wholly or mainly as a private dwelling, or

(b)   land or other premises belonging to, or enjoyed with, premises so used.

(9) In proceedings for an offence under subsection (4) above in respect of a statutory nuisance falling within paragraph (g) or (ga) of section 79(1) above where the offence consists in contravening requirements imposed by virtue of subsection (1)(a) above it shall be a defence to prove—

(a)   that the alleged offence was covered by a notice served under section 60 or a consent given under section 61 or 65 of the Control of Pollution Act 1974 (construction sites, etc); or

(b)   where the alleged offence was committed at a time when the premises were subject to a notice under section 66 of that Act (noise reduction notice), that the level of noise emitted from the premises at that time was not such as to a constitute a contravention of the notice under that section; or

(c)   where the alleged offence was committed at a time when the premises were not subject to a notice under section 66 of that Act, and when a level fixed under section 67 of that Act (new buildings liable to abatement order) applied to the premises, that the level of noise emitted from the premises at that time did not exceed that level.

(10) Paragraphs (b) and (c) of subsection (9) above apply whether or not the relevant notice was subject to appeal at the time when the offence was alleged to have been committed.

80A Abatement notice in respect of noise in the street

(1) In the case of a statutory nuisance within section 79(1)(ga) above that—

(a)   has not yet occurred, or

(b)   arises from noise emitted from or caused by an unattended vehicle or unattended machinery or equipment,

the abatement notice shall be served in accordance with subsection (2) below.

(2) The notice shall be served—

(a)   where the person responsible for the vehicle, machinery or equipment can be found, on that person;

(b) where that person cannot be found or where the local authority determines that this paragraph should apply, by fixing the notice to the vehicle, machinery or equipment.

(3) Where—

(a) an abatement notice is served in accordance with subsection (2)(b) above by virtue of a determination of the local authority, and

(b) the person responsible for the vehicle, machinery or equipment can be found and served with a copy of the notice within an hour of the notice being fixed to the vehicle, machinery or equipment,

a copy of the notice shall be served on that person accordingly.

(4) Where an abatement notice is served in accordance with subsection (2)(b) above by virtue of a determination of the local authority, the notice shall state that, if a copy of the notice is subsequently served under subsection (3) above, the time specified in the notice as the time within which its requirements are to be complied with is extended by such further period as is specified in the notice.

(5) Where an abatement notice is served in accordance with subsection (2)(b) above, the person responsible for the vehicle, machinery or equipment may appeal against the notice under section 80(3) above as if he had been served with the notice on the date on which it was fixed to the vehicle, machinery or equipment.

(6) Section 80(4) above shall apply in relation to a person on whom a copy of an abatement notice is served under subsection (3) above as if the copy were the notice itself.

(7) A person who removes or interferes with a notice fixed to a vehicle, machinery or equipment in accordance with subsection (2)(b) above shall be guilty of an offence, unless he is the person responsible for the vehicle, machinery or equipment or he does so with the authority of that person.

(8) A person who commits an offence under subsection (7) above shall be liable on summary conviction to a fine not exceeding level 3 on the standard scale.

81 Supplementary provisions

(1) Subject to subsection (1A) below, where more than one person is responsible for a statutory nuisance section 80 above shall apply to each of those persons whether or not what any one of them is responsible for would by itself amount to a nuisance.

(1A) In relation to a statutory nuisance within section 79(1)(ga) above for which more than one person is responsible (whether or not what any one of those persons is responsible for would by itself amount to such a nuisance), section 80(2)(a) above shall apply with the substitution of 'any one of the persons' for 'the person'.

(1B) In relation to a statutory nuisance within section 79(1)(ga) above caused by noise emitted from or caused by an unattended vehicle or unattended machinery or equipment for which more than one person is responsible, section 80A above shall apply with the substitution—

(a) in subsection (2)(a), of 'any of the persons' for 'the person' and of 'one such person' for 'that person',

(b) in subsection (2)(b), of 'such a person' for 'that person',

(c) in subsection (3), of 'any of the persons' for 'the person' and of 'one such person' for 'that person',

(d) in subsection (5), of 'any person' for 'the person', and

(e) in subsection (7), of 'a person' for 'the person' and of 'such a person' for 'that person'.

(2) Where a statutory nuisance which exists or has occurred within the area of a local authority, or which has affected any part of that area, appears to the local authority to be wholly or partly caused by some act or default committed or taking place outside the area, the local authority may act under section 80 above as if the act or default were wholly within that area, except that any appeal shall be heard by a magistrates' court . . . having jurisdiction where the act or default is alleged to have taken place.

(3) Where an abatement notice has not been complied with the local authority may, whether or not they take proceedings for an offence . . . under section 80(4) above, abate the nuisance and do whatever may be necessary in execution of the notice.

. . .

(4) Any expenses reasonably incurred by a local authority in abating, or preventing the recurrence of, a statutory nuisance under subsection (3) above may be recovered by them from the person by whose act or default the nuisance was caused and, if that person is the owner of the premises, from any person who is for the time being the owner thereof; and the court . . . may apportion the expenses between persons by whose acts or defaults the nuisance is caused in such manner as the court consider . . . fair and reasonable.

(5) If a local authority is of opinion that proceedings for an offence under section 80(4) above would afford an inadequate remedy in the case of any statutory nuisance, they may, subject to subsection (6) below, take proceedings in the High Court . . . for the purpose of securing the abatement, prohibition or restriction of the nuisance, and the proceedings shall be maintainable notwithstanding the local authority have suffered no damage from the nuisance.

(6) In any proceedings under subsection (5) above in respect of a nuisance falling within paragraph (g) or (ga) of section 79(1) above, it shall be a defence to prove that the noise was authorised by a notice under section 60 or a consent under section 61 (construction sites) of the Control of Pollution Act 1974.

(7) The further supplementary provisions in Schedule 3 to this Act shall have effect.

81A Expenses recoverable from owner to be a charge on premises

(1)–(5) [*These sections cover expenses recoverable under s 81(4) above to be a change in the premises carrying interest.*]

(6) A person served with a notice or copy of a notice under this section may appeal against the notice to the county court within the period of twenty-one days beginning with the date of service.

(7) On such an appeal the court may—
    (a)   confirm the notice without modification,
    (b)   order that the notice is to have effect with the substitution of a different amount for the amount originally specified in it, or
    (c)   order that the notice is to be of no effect.

(8) A local authority shall, for the purpose of enforcing a charge under this section, have all the same powers and remedies under the Law of Property Act 1925, and otherwise, as if it were a mortgagee by deed having powers of sale and lease, of accepting surrenders of leases and of appointing a receiver.

(9) In this section—
        'owner', in relation to any premises, means a person (other than a mortgagee not in possession) who, whether in his own right or as trustee for any other person, is entitled to receive the rack rent of the premises or, where the premises are not let at a rack rent, would be so entitled if they were so let, and
        'premises' does not include a vessel.

. . .

81B Payment of expenses by instalments

(1) Where any expenses are a charge on premises under section 81A above, the local authority may by order declare the expenses to be payable with interest by instalments within the specified period, until the whole amount is paid.

(2) In subsection (1) above—
        'interest' means interest at the rate determined by the authority under section 81A (1) above, and

'the specified period' means such period of thirty years or less from the date of service of the notice under section 81A above as is specified in the order.

(3) Subject to subsection (5) below, the instalments and interest, or any part of them, may be recovered from the owner or occupier for the time being of the premises.

(4) Any sums recovered from an occupier may be deducted by him from the rent of the premises.

(5) An occupier shall not be required to pay at any one time any sum greater than the aggregate of—

(a) the amount that was due from him on account of rent at the date on which he was served with a demand from the local authority together with a notice requiring him not to pay rent to his landlord without deducting the sum demanded, and

(b) the amount that has become due from him on account of rent since that date.

. . .

82 Summary proceedings by persons aggrieved by statutory nuisances

(1) A magistrates' court may act under this section on a complaint . . . made by any person on the ground that he is aggrieved by the existence of a statutory nuisance.

(2) If the magistrates' court . . . is satisfied that the alleged nuisance exists, or that although abated it is likely to recur on the same premises or, in the case of a nuisance within section 79(1)(ga) above, in the same street . . . , the court . . . shall make an order for either or both of the following purposes—

(a) requiring the defendant . . . to abate the nuisance, within a time specified in the order, and to execute any works necessary for that purpose;

(b) prohibiting a recurrence of the nuisance, and requiring the defendant . . . , within a time specified in the order, to execute any works necessary to prevent the recurrence;

and, in England and Wales, may also impose on the defendant a fine not exceeding level 5 on the standard scale.

(3) If the magistrates' court . . . is satisfied that the alleged nuisance exists and is such as, in the opinion of the court . . . , to render premises unfit for human habitation, an order under subsection (2) above may prohibit the use of the premises for human habitation until the premises are, to the satisfaction of the court . . . , rendered fit for that purpose.

(4) Proceedings for an order under subsection (2) above shall be brought—

(a) except in a case falling within paragraph (b), (c) or (d) below, against the person responsible for the nuisance;

(b) where the nuisance arises from any defect of a structural character, against the owner of the premises;

(c) where the person responsible for the nuisance cannot be found, against the owner or occupier of the premises.

(d) in the case of a statutory nuisance within section 79(1)(ga) above caused by noise emitted from or caused by an unattended vehicle or unattended machinery or equipment, against the person responsible for the vehicle, machinery or equipment.

(5) Subject to subsection (5A) below, where more than one person is responsible for a statutory nuisance, subsections (1) to (4) above shall apply to each of those persons whether or not what any one of them is responsible for would by itself amount to a nuisance.

(5A) In relation to a statutory nuisance within section 79(1)(ga) above for which more than one person is responsible (whether or not what any one of those persons is responsible for would by itself amount to such a nuisance), subsection (4)(a) above shall apply with the substitution of 'each person responsible for the nuisance who can be found' for 'the person responsible for the nuisance'.

(5B)   In relation to a statutory nuisance within section 79(1)(ga) above caused by noise emitted from or caused by an unattended vehicle or unattended machinery or equipment for which more than one person is responsible, subsection (4)(d) above shall apply with the substitution of 'any person' for 'the person'.

(6)   Before instituting proceedings for an order under subsection (2) above against any person, the person aggrieved by the nuisance shall give to that person such notice in writing of his intention to bring the proceedings as is applicable to proceedings in respect of a nuisance of that description and the notice shall specify the matter complained of.

(7)   The notice of the bringing of proceedings in respect of a statutory nuisance required by subsection (6) above which is applicable is—

    (a)   in the case of a nuisance falling within paragraph (g) or (ga) of section 79(1) above, not less than three days' notice; and

    (b)   in the case of a nuisance of any other description, not less than twenty-one days' notice;

but the Secretary of State may, by order, provide that this subsection shall have effect as if such period as is specified in the order were the minimum period of notice applicable to any description of statutory nuisance specified in the order.

(8)   A person who, without reasonable excuse, contravenes any requirement or prohibition imposed by an order under subsection (2) above shall be guilty of an offence and liable on summary conviction to a fine not exceeding level 5 on the standard scale together with a further fine of an amount equal to one-tenth of that level for each day on which the offence continues after the conviction.

(9)   Subject to subsection (10) below, in any proceedings for an offence under subsection (8) above in respect of a statutory nuisance it shall be a defence to prove that the best practicable means were used to prevent, or to counteract the effects of, the nuisance.

(10)   The defence under subsection (9) above is not available—

    (a)   in the case of a nuisance falling within paragraph (a), (d), (e), (f), (fa) or (g) of section 79(1) above except where the nuisance arises on industrial, trade or business premises;

    (aza)   in the case of a nuisance falling within paragraph (fb) of section 79(1) above except where—

        (i)   the artificial light is emitted from industrial, trade or business premises, or

        (ii)   the artificial light (not being light to which sub-paragraph (i) applies) is emitted by lights used for the purpose only of illuminating an outdoor relevant sports facility;

    (aa)   in the case of a nuisance falling within paragraph (ga) of section 79(1) above except where the noise is emitted from or caused by a vehicle, machinery or equipment being used for industrial, trade or business purposes;

    (b)   in the case of a nuisance falling within paragraph (b) of section 79(1) above except where the smoke is emitted from a chimney;

    (c)   in the case of a nuisance falling within paragraph (c) or (h) of section 79(1) above; and

    (d)   in the case of a nuisance which is such as to render the premises unfit for human habitation.

(10A)   For the purposes of subsection (10)(aza) 'relevant sports facility' has the same meaning as it has for the purposes of section 80(8)(aza).

(11)   If a person is convicted of an offence under subsection (8) above, a magistrates' court . . . may, after giving the local authority in whose area the nuisance has

occurred an opportunity of being heard, direct the authority to do anything which the person convicted was required to do by the order to which the conviction relates.

(12) Where on the hearing of proceedings for an order under subsection (2) above it is proved that the alleged nuisance existed at the date of the making of the complaint or summary application, then, whether or not at the date of the hearing it still exists or is likely to recur, the court . . . shall order the defendant or defender (or defendants or defenders) in such proportions as appears fair and reasonable to pay to the person bringing the proceedings such amount as the court . . . considers reasonably sufficient to compensate him for any expenses properly incurred by him in the proceedings.

(13) If it appears to the magistrates' court . . . that neither the person responsible for the nuisance nor the owner or occupier of the premises or (as the case may be) the person responsible for the vehicle, machinery or equipment can be found the court . . . may, after giving the local authority in whose area the nuisance has occurred an opportunity of being heard, direct the authority to do anything which the court . . . would have ordered that person to do.

PART IV

LITTER ETC

Provisions relating to litter

87 Offence of leaving litter

(1) A person is guilty of an offence if he throws down, drops or otherwise deposits any litter in any place to which this section applies and leaves it.

(2) This section applies to any place in the area of a principal litter authority which is open to the air, subject to subsection (3) below.

(3) This section does not apply to a place which is 'open to the air' for the purposes of this Part by virtue of section 86(13) above if the public does not have access to it, with or without payment.

(4) It is immaterial for the purposes of this section whether the litter is deposited on land or in water.

(4A) No offence is committed under subsection (1) above where the depositing of the litter is—

    (a)   authorised by law; or

    (b)   done by or with the consent of the owner, occupier or other person having control of the place where it is deposited.

(4B) A person may only give consent under subsection (4A)(b) above in relation to the depositing of litter in a lake or pond or watercourse if he is the owner, occupier or other person having control of—

    (a)   all the land adjoining that lake or pond or watercourse; and

    (b)   all the land through or into which water in that lake or pond or watercourse directly or indirectly discharges, otherwise than by means of a public sewer.

(4C) In subsection (4B) above, 'lake or pond', 'watercourse' and 'public sewer' have the same meanings as in section 104 of the Water Resources Act 1991.

(5) A person who is guilty of an offence under this section shall be liable on summary conviction to a fine not exceeding level 4 on the standard scale.

(6) A local authority, with a view to promoting the abatement of litter, may take such steps as the authority think appropriate for making the effect of subsection (5) above known to the public in their area.

PART VIII

MISCELLANEOUS

Control of dogs

149 Seizure of stray dogs

(1) Every local authority shall appoint an officer (under whatever title the authority may determine) for the purpose of discharging the functions imposed or conferred by this section for dealing with stray dogs found in the area of the authority.

(2) The officer may delegate the discharge of his functions to another person but he shall remain responsible for securing that the functions are properly discharged.

(3) Where the officer has reason to believe that any dog found in a public place or on any other land or premises is a stray dog, he shall (if practicable) seize the dog and detain it, but, where he finds it on land or premises which is not a public place, only with the consent of the owner or occupier of the land or premises.

(4) Where any dog seized under this section wears a collar having inscribed thereon or attached thereto the address of any person, or the owner of the dog is known, the officer shall serve on the person whose address is given on the collar, or on the owner, a notice in writing stating that the dog has been seized and where it is being kept and stating that the dog will be liable to be disposed of if it is not claimed within seven clear days after the service of the notice and the amounts for which he would be liable under subsection (5) below are not paid.

(5) A person claiming to be the owner of a dog seized under this section shall not be entitled to have the dog returned to him unless he pays all the expenses incurred by reason of its detention and such further amount as is for the time being prescribed.

(6) Where any dog seized under this section has been detained for seven clear days after the seizure or, where a notice has been served under subsection (4) above, the service of the notice and the owner has not claimed the dog and paid the amounts due under subsection (5) above the officer may dispose of the dog—

(a) by selling it or giving it to a person who will, in his opinion, care properly for the dog;

(b) by selling it or giving it to an establishment for the reception of stray dogs; or

(c) by destroying it in a manner to cause as little pain as possible;

but no dog seized under this section shall be sold or given for the purposes of vivisection.

(7) Where a dog is disposed of under subsection (6)(a) or (b) above to a person acting in good faith, the ownership of the dog shall be vested in the recipient.

(8) The officer shall keep a register containing the prescribed particulars of or relating to dogs seized under this section and the register shall be available, at all reasonable times, for inspection by the public free of charge.

(9) The officer shall cause any dog detained under this section to be properly fed and maintained.

(10) Notwithstanding anything in this section, the officer may cause a dog detained under this section to be destroyed before the expiration of the period mentioned in subsection (6) above where he is of the opinion that this should be done to avoid suffering.

(11) In this section—

'local authority', in relation to England, means a district council, a London borough council, the Common Council of the City of London or the Council of the Isles of Scilly, in relation to Wales, means a county council or a county borough council . . . ;

'officer' means an officer appointed under subsection (1) above;

'prescribed' means prescribed in regulations made by the Secretary of State; and

'public place' means—

    (i)   as respects England and Wales, any highway and any other place to which the public are entitled or permitted to have access;

    . . .

and, for the purposes of section 160 below in its application to this section, the proper address of the owner of a dog which wears a collar includes the address given on the collar.

150 Delivery of stray dogs to local authority officer

(1)   Any person (in this section referred to as 'the finder') who takes possession of a stray dog shall forthwith either—

    (a)   return the dog to its owner; or

    (b)   take the dog—

        (i)   to the officer of the local authority for the area in which the dog was found;

and shall inform the officer of the local authority where the dog was found.

(2)   Where a dog has been taken under subsection (1) above to the officer of a local authority, then—

    (a)   if the finder desires to keep the dog, he shall inform the officer of this fact and shall furnish his name and address and the officer shall, having complied with the procedure (if any) prescribed under subsection (6) below, allow the finder to remove the dog;

    (b)   if the finder does not desire to keep the dog, the officer shall, unless he has reason to believe it is not a stray, treat it as if it had been seized by him under section 149 above.

(3)   Where the finder of a dog keeps the dog by virtue of this section he must keep it for not less than one month.

    . . .

(5)   If the finder of a dog fails to comply with the requirements of subsection (1) or (3) above he shall be liable on summary conviction to a fine not exceeding level 2 on the standard scale.

(6)   The Secretary of State may, by regulations, prescribe the procedure to be followed under subsection (2)(a) above.

(7)   In this section 'local authority' and 'officer' have the same meaning as in section 149 above.

LOCAL GOVERNMENT FINANCE ACT 1992

PART I

COUNCIL TAX: ENGLAND AND WALES

CHAPTER IV

PRECEPTS
Preliminary

39 Precepting and precepted authorities

. . .

(2) Each of the following is a local precepting authority for the purposes of this Part, namely—

. . .

    (c)   a parish or community council;

    (d)   the chairman of a parish meeting; and

    (e)   charter trustees.

(3) A precept may only be issued to an appropriate billing authority.

(4) If the whole or part of a billing authority's area falls within a precepting authority's area, it is an appropriate billing authority in relation to the precepting authority to the extent of the area which so falls.

Issue of precepts

41 Issue of precepts by local precepting authorities

(1) For each financial year a local precepting authority may issue a precept in accordance with this section.

(2) A precept issued to a billing authority under this section must state, as the amount payable by that authority for the year, the amount which has been calculated (or last calculated)—

    (a)   in the case of a precepting authority in England, by that authority under section 49A below as its council tax requirement for the year, and

    (b)   in the case of a precepting authority in Wales, by that authority under section 50 below as its budget requirement for the year.

(2A) The Secretary of State may by regulations make provision that a billing authority in England making calculations in accordance with section 31A above (originally or by way of substitute) may anticipate a precept under this section; and the regulations may include provision as to—

    (a)   the amounts which may be anticipated by billing authorities in pursuance of the regulations;

    (b)   the sums (if any) to be paid by such authoritiesin respect of amounts anticipated by them; and

    (c)   the sums (if any) to be paid by such authorities in respect of amounts not anticipated by them.

(3) The Welsh Ministers may by regulations make provision that a billing authority in Wales making calculations in accordance with section 32 above (originally or by way of substitute) may anticipate a precept under this section; and the regulations may include provision as to—

    (a)   the amounts which may be anticipated by billing authorities in pursuance of the regulations;

(b)   the sums (if any) to be paid by such authorities in respect of amounts anticipated by them; and

(c)   the sums (if any) to be paid by such authorities in respect of amounts not anticipated by them.

(4)   A precept under this section must be issued before 1st March in the financial year preceding that for which it is issued, but is not invalid merely because it is issued on or after that date.

42 Substituted precepts

(1)   Where—

(a)   a precepting authority has issued a precept or precepts for a financial year (originally or by way of substitute); and

(b)   at any later time it makes substitute calculations under section 49, 49A, 52ZU, 52J or 52U or (as the case may be) section 51 below or section 95 of the Greater London Authority Act 1999,

it shall as soon as reasonably practicable after that time issue a precept or precepts in substitution so as to give effect to those calculations.

(2)   Any precept issued in substitution under subsection (1) above must be issued in accordance with section 40 or (as the case may be) section 41 above, but subsection (5) of section 40 and subsection (4) of section 41 shall be ignored for this purpose.

(3)   Where a precepting authority issues a precept in substitution (a new precept) anything paid to it by reference to the precept for which it is substituted (the old precept) shall be treated as paid by reference to the new precept.

(4)   If the amount stated in the old precept exceeds that of the new precept, the following shall apply as regards anything paid if it would not have been paid had the amount of the old precept been the same as that of the new precept—

(a)   it shall be repaid if the billing authority by whom it was paid so requires;

(b)   in any other case it shall (as the precepting authority determines) either be repaid or be credited against any subsequent liability of the billing authority in respect of any precept of the precepting authority.

(5)   Any reference in subsection (4) above to the amount stated in a precept shall be construed, in relation to a precept issued by a major precepting authority, as a reference to the amount stated in the precept in accordance with section 40(2)(b) above.

Calculations by local precepting authorities

50 Calculation of budget requirement by authorities in Wales

(1)   In relation to each financial year a local precepting authority in Wales shall make the calculations required by this section.

(2)   The authority must calculate the aggregate of—

(a)   the expenditure the authority estimates it will incur in the year in performing its functions and will charge to a revenue account for the year;

(b)   such allowance as the authority estimates will be appropriate for contingencies in relation to expenditure to be charged to a revenue account for the year;

(c)   the financial reserves which the authority estimates it will be appropriate to raise in the year for meeting its estimated future expenditure; and

(d)   such financial reserves as are sufficient to meet so much of the amount estimated by the authority to be a revenue account deficit for any earlier financial year as has not already been provided for.

(3)   The authority must calculate the aggregate of—

    (a)   the sums which it estimates will be payable to it for the year and in respect of which amounts will be credited to a revenue account for the year, other than sums which it estimates will be so payable in respect of any precept issued by it; and

    (b)   the amount of the financial reserves which the authority estimates that it will use in order to provide for the items mentioned in paragraphs (a) and (b) of subsection (2) above.

(4) If the aggregate calculated under subsection (2) above exceeds that calculated under subsection (3) above, the authority must calculate the amount equal to the difference; and the amount so calculated shall be its budget requirement for the year.

(5) For the purposes of subsection (2)(c) above an authority's estimated future expenditure is—

    (a)   that which the authority estimates it will incur in the financial year following the year in question, will charge to a revenue account for the year and will have to defray in the year before the following sums are sufficiently available, namely, sums—

        (i)   which will be payable to it for the year; and

        (ii)   in respect of which amounts will be credited to a revenue account for the year; and

    (b)   that which the authority estimates it will incur in the financial year referred to in paragraph (a) above or any subsequent financial year in performing its functions and which will be charged to a revenue account for that or any other year.

51 Substitute calculations

(1) A local precepting authority which has made calculations in accordance with section 50 above in relation to a financial year (originally or by way of substitute) may make calculations in substitution in relation to the year in accordance with that section.

(2) None of the substitute calculations shall have any effect if the amount calculated under section 50(4) above would exceed that so calculated in the previous calculations.

(3) Subsection (2) above shall not apply if the previous calculation under subsection (4) of section 50 above has been quashed because of a failure to comply with that section in making the calculation.

Supplemental

52 Information for purposes of Chapter IV

If the Secretary of State so requires by regulations, a billing authority shall supply prescribed information within a prescribed period to any precepting authority which has power to issue a precept to the billing authority.

PART IV

MISCELLANEOUS

English and Welsh provisions

106 Council tax and community charges: restrictions on voting

(1) This section applies at any time to a member of a local authority, or a member of a committee of a local authority or of a joint committee of two or more local authorities (including in either case a sub-committee), or a council manager within the meaning of section 11(4)(b) of the Local Government Act 2000, if at that time—

    (a)   a sum falling within paragraph 1(1)(a) of Schedule 4 to this Act; or

(b)   a sum falling within paragraph 1(1)(a), (b), (d) or (ee) of Schedule 4 to the 1988 Act (corresponding provisions with respect to community charges),

has become payable by him and has remained unpaid for at least two months.

(2)   Subject to subsection (5) below, if a member or a council manager to whom this section applies is present at a meeting of the authority or committee or in the case of an authority which are operating executive arrangements the executive of that authority or any committee of that executive at which any of the following matters is the subject of consideration, namely—

(a)   any calculation required by Chapter III, IV, 4ZA or IVA of Part I of this Act;

(b)   any recommendation, resolution or other decision which might affect the making of any such calculation; or

(c)   the exercise of any functions under Schedules 2 to 4 to this Act or Schedules 2 to 4 to the 1988 Act (corresponding provisions with respect to community charges),

he shall at the meeting and as soon as practicable after its commencement disclose the fact that this section applies to him and shall not vote on any question with respect to the matter.

(2A)In the case of an authority which are operating executive arrangements, if or to the extent that any matter listed in paragraphs (a), (b) or (c) of subsection (2) is the responsibility of the executive of that authority, no member of the executive to whom this section applies shall take any action or discharge any function with respect to that matter.

(3)   If a person fails to comply with subsection (2) above, he shall for each offence be liable on summary conviction to a fine not exceeding level 3 on the standard scale, unless he proves that he did not know—

(a)   that this section applied to him at the time of the meeting; or

(b)   that the matter in question was the subject of consideration at the meeting.

(4)   A prosecution for an offence under this section shall not be instituted except by or on behalf of the Director of Public Prosecutions.

(5)   Subsections (1) to (3) of section 97 of the Local Government Act 1972 (removal or exclusion of liability etc) shall apply in relation to this section and any disability imposed by it as they apply in relation to section 94 of that Act and any disability imposed by that section.

(6)   In this section 'local authority' has the same meaning as in sections 94 and 97 of the Local Government Act 1972.

LOCAL GOVERNMENT (WALES) ACT 1994

PART II

FUNCTIONS

General

17 General provision for transfer of functions

(1)   This section has effect for the purpose of adapting relevant legislative provisions and in particular for the purpose of providing for the exercise of functions conferred by such provisions.

(2)   A provision is a 'relevant legislative provision' for the purposes of this section if it is a provision of—

    (a)   any public general Act passed before, or during the same Session as, this Act; or

    (b)   an instrument which—

        (i)   was made before the passing of this Act, under a public general Act; and

        (ii)   is of a legislative character but is not in the nature of a local enactment.

(3)   This section has effect subject to any provision made by, or by any instrument under, this Act and is not to be taken as affecting any provision so made.

(4)   In any relevant legislative provision—

    (a)   any reference to an area which is the area of a county council or the area of a district council, and

    (b)   any reference which is to be construed as a reference to such an area,

shall be construed, in relation to Wales, as a reference to a new principal area.

(5)   In any relevant legislative provision—

    (a)   any reference to the council of a county or district, and

    (b)   any reference which is to be construed as such,

shall be construed, in relation to Wales, as a reference to the council of a new principal area.

(6)   Where, in relation to any relevant legislative provision, any question arises as to which new principal area is the appropriate new principal area for the purposes of that provision, that question shall be determined by order made by the Secretary of State.

(7)   Where any relevant legislative provision is by virtue of this section to be construed in accordance with subsection (4) or (5)—

    (a)   it shall be so construed subject to any modifications necessary to give full effect to the provision; and

    (b)   the Secretary of State may by order make such amendments or other modifications of the provision as he considers necessary or expedient in consequence of any provision made by or under this Act.

PART III

DECENTRALISATION AND JOINT WORKING

Decentralisation schemes

27 and 28 Decentralisation schemes: preparation

[These sections provide that decentralisation schemes by the establishment of area committees may be made on application made before 1 January 1996.]

29 Area committees: safeguards

(1)   Where an area committee has been established by a council in accordance with an approved decentralisation scheme—

    (a)   the council shall not, except with the agreement of the committee, abolish the committee or alter any arrangements in force with respect to the committee which were made in accordance with the scheme as originally approved or which have subsequently been agreed with the committee; and

    (b)   nothing in section 101(4) of the 1972 Act (power of local authority to exercise functions otherwise discharged by committee) shall be taken to authorise the council to exercise any functions which are to be discharged by the committee, except as provided for by the scheme.

(2)   Every decentralisation scheme shall include provision, to be given effect to by the standing orders of the council concerned, for the majority required in order for any suspending resolution to be passed to be such majority greater than a simple majority as may be specified by the scheme.

(3)   In subsection (2) 'suspending resolution', in relation to a decentralisation scheme, means a resolution to suspend any of the arrangements in force with respect to an area committee established in accordance with the scheme.

30 Area committees: membership etc

(1)   This section applies where an area committee has been established by a council in accordance with an approved decentralisation scheme.

(2)   The provisions of the 1972 Act with respect to arrangements for the discharge of functions by committees of local authorities and sub-committees, and the appointment of such committees and sub-committees, shall be subject to this section and section 31.

(3)   Every person who is a member of the council for an electoral division which falls within the area for which the committee is established shall be entitled to be appointed to the committee at his request.

(4)   The committee may appoint additional persons, including members of the council who are not entitled to membership of the committee under subsection (3), as members of the committee.

(5)   No other persons shall be eligible for appointment to the committee.

(6)   In this section, in relation to an area committee, 'co-opted member' means any member appointed by the committee under subsection (4).

. . .

(8)   A co-opted member of an area committee shall not be entitled to vote at any meeting of the committee on any question which falls to be decided at that meeting.

(9)   Nothing in subsection (8) shall prevent the appointment of a person, in compliance with a direction under section 499 of the Act of 1996, as a voting member of an area committee.

(10)   In the application of section 101 of the 1972 Act (arrangement for discharge of functions by local authorities) in relation to the committee—

(a)   subsection (1) shall have effect as if it gave power to the committee, if authorised to do so by the decentralisation scheme, to arrange for the discharge of any of its functions by a local authority other than the authority who made the scheme;

(b)   subsection (2) shall have effect with the omission of the words 'unless the local authority otherwise direct' and (in the second place where they occur) the words 'the local authority or'.

(11)   Sections 102(3) of the 1972 Act (power to include persons who are not members of the local authority concerned) and 15 of the Local Government and Housing Act 1989 (political balance on committees) shall not apply in relation to membership of the committee.

(12)   The term of office of each of the co-opted members of an area committee shall be fixed by the committee.

(13)   Section 102(2) of the 1972 Act (number of members of committee and terms of office) shall not apply in relation to the committee.

(14)   In the case of an appointment made in order to comply with a direction under section 499 of the Act of 1996, the committee shall exercise its powers under subsection (12) subject to any provision of the direction relating to terms of office.

31 Sub-committees of area committees

(1)   In this section 'sub-committee' means a sub-committee of an area committee.

(2)   The members of a sub-committee shall be appointed by the area committee from among persons who are—

(a)   members of the area committee appointed under subsection (3) of section 30; or

(b)   entitled to be members of the area committee by virtue of that subsection.

(3)   Subject to subsection (10), a sub-committee may appoint additional persons, including persons who are not members of the area committee concerned, as members of the sub-committee.

(4)   No other persons shall be eligible for appointment to a sub-committee.

(5)   In this section, in relation to a sub-committee, 'co-opted member' means any member of the sub-committee appointed under subsection (3).

(6)   Where the Secretary of State has given a direction under section 499 of the Education Act 1996 (power to direct appointment of members of certain committees) which applies to a sub-committee, it shall be the duty of the area committee concerned and the sub-committee to secure compliance with the direction.

(7)   A co-opted member of a sub-committee shall not be entitled to vote at any meeting of the sub-committee on any question which falls to be decided at that meeting.

(8)   Nothing in subsection (7) shall prevent the appointment of a person in compliance with a direction under section 499 of the Act of 1996 as a voting member of a sub-committee.

(9)   Sections 102(3) of the 1972 Act (power to include persons who are not members of the local authority concerned) and 15 of the Local Government and Housing Act 1989 (political balance on committees) shall not apply in relation to membership of a sub-committee.

(10)   The number of members of a sub-committee and their terms of office shall be fixed by the area committee concerned.

(11)   Section 102(2) of the 1972 Act (number of members of committee and terms of office) shall not apply in relation to the sub-committee.

(12)   In the case of an appointment made in order to comply with a direction under section 499 of the Act of 1996, the area committee shall exercise its powers under subsection (10) subject to any provision of the direction relating to terms of office.

CRIMINAL JUSTICE AND PUBLIC ORDER ACT 1994

PART V

PUBLIC ORDER: COLLECTIVE TRESPASS OR NUISANCE ON LAND

Powers to remove trespassers on land

61 Power to remove trespassers on land

(1)   If the senior police officer present at the scene reasonably believes that two or more persons are trespassing on land and are present there with the common purpose of residing there for any period, that reasonable steps have been taken by or on behalf of the occupier to ask them to leave and—

(a)   that any of those persons has caused damage to the land or to property on the land or used threatening, abusive or insulting words or behaviour towards the occupier, a member of his family or an employee or agent of his, or

(b)   that those persons have between them six or more vehicles on the land, he may direct those persons, or any of them, to leave the land and to remove any vehicles or other property they have with them on the land.

(2)   Where the persons in question are reasonably believed by the senior police officer to be persons who were not originally trespassers but have become trespassers on the land, the officer must reasonably believe that the other conditions specified in subsection (1) are satisfied after those persons became trespassers before he can exercise the power conferred by that subsection.

(3)   A direction under subsection (1) above, if not communicated to the persons referred to in subsection (1) by the police officer giving the direction, may be communicated to them by any constable at the scene.

(4)   If a person knowing that a direction under subsection (1) above has been given which applies to him—

(a)   fails to leave the land as soon as reasonably practicable, or

(b)   having left again enters the land as a trespasser within the period of three months beginning with the day on which the direction was given,

he commits an offence and is liable on summary conviction to imprisonment for a term not exceeding three months or a fine not exceeding level 4 on the standard scale, or both.

. . .

(6)   In proceedings for an offence under this section it is a defence for the accused to show—

(a)   that he was not trespassing on the land, or

(b)   that he had a reasonable excuse for failing to leave the land as soon as reasonably practicable or, as the case may be, for again entering the land as a trespasser.

(7)   In its application in England and Wales to common land this section has effect as if in the preceding subsections of it—

(a)   references to trespassing or trespassers were references to acts and persons doing acts which constitute either a trespass as against the occupier or an infringement of the commoners' rights; and

(b)   references to 'the occupier' included the commoners or any of them or, in the case of common land to which the public has access, the local authority as well as any commoner.

(8)   Subsection (7) above does not—

(a)   require action by more than one occupier; or

(b)   constitute persons trespassers as against any commoner or the local authority if they are permitted to be there by the other occupier.

(9)   In this section—

'common land' means

(a)   land registered as common land in a register of common land kept under Part 1 of the Commons Act 2006; and

(b)   land to which Part 1 of that Act does not apply and which is subject to rights of common as defined in that Act;

'commoner' means a person with rights of common as so defined;

'land' does not include—

(a)   buildings other than—

(i)   agricultural buildings within the meaning of, in England and Wales, paragraphs 3 to 8 of Schedule 5 to the Local Government Finance Act 1988 or, in Scotland, section 7(2) of the Valuation and Rating (Scotland) Act 1956, or

(ii)   scheduled monuments within the meaning of the Ancient Monuments and Archaeological Areas Act 1979;

(b)   land forming part of—

(i)   a highway unless it is a footpath, bridleway or byway open to all traffic within the meaning of Part III of the Wildlife and Countryside Act 1981, is a restricted byway within the meaning of Part II of the Countryside and Rights of Way Act 2000 or is a cycle track under the Highways Act 1980 or the Cycle Tracks Act 1984; or

. . .

'the local authority', in relation to common land, means any local authority which has powers in relation to the land under section 45 of the Commons Act 2006;

'occupier' (and in subsection (8) 'the other occupier') means—

(a)   in England and Wales, the person entitled to possession of the land by virtue of an estate or interest held by him; and

. . .

'property', in relation to damage to property on land, means—

(a)   in England and Wales, property within the meaning of section 10(1) of the Criminal Damage Act 1971; and

. . .

and 'damage' includes the deposit of any substance capable of polluting the land;

'trespass' means, in the application of this section—

(a)   in England and Wales, subject to the extensions effected by subsection (7) above, trespass as against the occupier of the land;

. . .

'trespassing' and 'trespasser' shall be construed accordingly;

'vehicle' includes—

(a)   any vehicle, whether or not it is in a fit state for use on roads, and includes any chassis or body, with or without wheels, appearing to have formed part of such a vehicle, and any load carried by, and anything attached to, such a vehicle; . . .

and a person may be regarded for the purposes of this section as having a purpose of residing in a place notwithstanding that he has a home elsewhere.

62 Supplementary powers of seizure

(1) If a direction has been given under section 61 and a constable reasonably suspects that any person to whom the direction applies has, without reasonable excuse—

(a)   failed to remove any vehicle on the land which appears to the constable to belong to him or to be in his possession or under his control; or

(b)   entered the land as a trespasser with a vehicle within the period of three months beginning with the day on which the direction was given,

the constable may seize and remove that vehicle.

(2) In this section, 'trespasser' and 'vehicle' have the same meaning as in section 61.

LOCAL GOVERNMENT AND RATING ACT 1997

PART I

NON-DOMESTIC RATING

England and Wales

1 General stores etc in rural settlements
The Local Government Finance Act 1988 (referred to in this Part as 'the 1988 Act') is amended as set out in Schedule 1 (which provides for mandatory or discretionary relief from non-domestic rates for certain hereditaments in rural settlements).

PART III

POWERS OF PARISH COUNCILS AND COMMUNITY COUNCILS

Transport etc

26 Car-sharing schemes
(1)   A parish council or community council may—
    (a)   establish and maintain any car-sharing scheme, or
    (b)   assist others to establish and maintain any car-sharing scheme,
for the benefit of persons in the council's area.
(2)   A parish or community council may impose any conditions they think fit—
    (a)   on the participation of persons in any scheme established and maintained by the council under subsection (1)(a) (including conditions requiring persons who receive fares under the scheme to contribute to the costs of establishing and maintaining it), or
    (b)   on the giving of any assistance under subsection (1)(b).
(3)   For the purposes of this section—
    (a)   a car-sharing scheme is a scheme for the provision of private cars for use on journeys in the course of which one or more passengers may be carried at separate fares, and
    (b)   the participants in a car-sharing scheme are those who make private cars available for use under the scheme or who are eligible for carriage as passengers under the scheme.
(4)   In this section—
    (a)   'private car' means a motor vehicle other than a public service vehicle, a licensed taxi, a licensed hire car or a motor cycle,
    (b)   'motor vehicle', 'public service vehicle' and 'fares' have the same meaning as in section 1 of the Public Passenger Vehicles Act 1981, and
    (c)   'licensed taxi' and 'licensed hire car' have the meaning given by section 13(3) of the Transport Act 1985.

28 Taxi fare concessions
(1)   A parish council or a community council may enter into arrangements with any licensed taxi operator or licensed hire car operator under which—
    (a)   the operator grants fare concessions on local journeys specified in the arrangements to some or all of the persons falling within subsection (2), and
    (b)   the council reimburse the cost incurred in granting the concessions.
(2)   The persons falling within this subsection are persons who are—

    (a)   resident in the council's area, and

    (b)   specified for the time being in or under subsection (7) of section 93 of the Transport Act 1985 as eligible to receive travel concessions under a scheme established under that section.

(3) Arrangements made under subsection (1) may specify such other terms and conditions as the council think fit.

(4) In subsection (1) 'licensed taxi operator' and 'licensed hire car operator' mean a person who provides a service for the carriage of passengers by licensed taxi (as defined by section 13(3) of the Transport Act 1985) or by licensed hire car (as so defined).

29 Information about transport

(1) A parish council or community council may investigate—

    (a)   the provision and use of, and the need for, public passenger transport services in their area,

    (b)   the use of and need for roads in their area, and

    (c)   the management and control of traffic in their area.

(2) A parish council or community council may publicise information on public passenger transport services in their area or, on any conditions they think fit, assist others to do so.

(3) In this section 'public passenger transport services' has the same meaning as in the Transport Act 1985 (see section 63(10)).

Crime prevention

31 Crime prevention

(1) A parish council or community council may, for the detection or prevention of crime in their area—

    (a)   install and maintain any equipment,

    (b)   establish and maintain any scheme, or

    (c)   assist others to install and maintain any equipment or to establish and maintain any scheme.

(2) In section 92 of the Police Act 1996 (grants by local authorities)—

    (a)   in subsection (1)—

        (i)   for 'or London borough' there is substituted 'London borough, parish or community', and

        (ii)   for 'county, district, county borough or borough' there is substituted 'council's area', and

    (b)   in subsection (2), for 'or district' there is substituted 'district or parish'.

PART IV

GENERAL

35 Short title and extent

(2) Sections 1 to 4, 9 to 31 and Schedule 1 extend to England and Wales only.

AUDIT COMMISSION ACT 1998

PART II

ACCOUNTS AND AUDIT OF PUBLIC BODIES

Audit of accounts

2 Required audit of accounts

(1) The accounts to which this section applies—

    (a)   shall be made up each year to 31st March or such other date as the Secretary of State may generally or in any special case direct, and

    (b)   shall be audited in accordance with this Act by an auditor or auditors appointed by the Commission.

(2) This section applies to the accounts mentioned in Schedule 2.

3 Appointment of auditors

(1) An auditor appointed by the Commission to audit the accounts of a body whose accounts are required to be audited in accordance with this Act ('a body subject to audit') may be—

    (a)   an officer of the Commission,

    (b)   an individual who is not an officer of the Commission, or

    (c)   a firm.

(2) Where two or more auditors are appointed in relation to the accounts of a body, some but not others may be officers of the Commission and they may be appointed—

    (a)   to act jointly;

    (b)   to act separately in relation to different parts of the accounts; or

    (c)   to discharge different functions in relation to the audit.

(3) Before appointing an auditor or auditors to audit the accounts of a body other than a health service body the Commission shall consult that body.

(4) For the purpose of assisting the Commission in deciding on the appointment of an auditor or auditors in relation to the accounts of a body other than a health service body, the Commission may require the body to make available for inspection by or on behalf of the Commission such documents relating to any accounts of the body as the Commission may reasonably require for that purpose.

(5) A person appointed by the Commission as an auditor must—

    (a)   be eligible for appointment as a statutory auditor (see Part 42 of the Companies Act 2006),

    (b)   be a member of one or more of the bodies listed in subsection (7) below, or

    (c)   have such other qualifications as may be approved for the purposes of this section by the Secretary of State.]

(6) ....

(7) The bodies referred to in subsection (5)(b) are—

    (a)   the Institute of Chartered Accountants in England and Wales;

    (b)   the Institute of Chartered Accountants of Scotland;

    (c)   the Association of Chartered Certified Accountants;

    (d)   the Chartered Institute of Public Finance and Accountancy;

    (e)   the Institute of Chartered Accountants in Ireland; and

    (f)   any other body of accountants for the time being approved by the Secretary of State for the purposes of this section.

. . .

4 Code of audit practice

(1)   The Commission shall prepare, and keep under review, a code of audit practice prescribing the way in which auditors are to carry out their functions under this Act.

. . .

(3)   A code prepared under this section shall embody what appears to the Commission to be the best professional practice with respect to the standards, procedures and techniques to be adopted by auditors.

(4)   A code does not come into force until approved by a resolution of each House of Parliament, and its continuation in force is subject to its being so approved at intervals of not more than five years.

(5)   Subsection (4) does not preclude alterations to a code being made by the Commission in the intervals between its being approved in accordance with that subsection.

(7)   Before preparing or altering a code applicable to any accounts, the Commission shall consult—

. . .

    (b)   if the accounts are or include those of other bodies, such associations of local authorities as appear to the Commission to be concerned; and

    (c)   in any case, the National Assembly for Wales, the Care Quality Commission and such bodies of accountants as appear to the Commission to be appropriate.

. . .

5 General duties of auditors

(1)   In auditing accounts required to be audited in accordance with this Act, an auditor shall by examination of the accounts and otherwise satisfy himself—

. . .

    (b)   . . . that they are prepared in accordance with regulations under section 27;

    (c)   that they comply with the requirements of all other statutory provisions applicable to the accounts;

    (d)   that proper practices have been observed in the compilation of the accounts;

    (e)   that the body whose accounts are being audited has made proper arrangements for securing economy, efficiency and effectiveness in its use of resources.

(2)   The auditor shall comply with the code of audit practice applicable to the accounts being audited as that code is for the time being in force.

6 Auditors' right to documents and information

(1)   An auditor has a right of access at all reasonable times to every document relating to a body subject to audit which appears to him necessary for the purposes of his functions under this Act.

(1A)   The right conferred by subsection (1) includes power to inspect, copy or take away the document.

(2)   An auditor may—

    (a)   require a person holding or accountable for any such document to give him such information and explanation as he thinks necessary for the purposes of his functions under this Act; and

    (b)   if he thinks it necessary, require the person to attend before him in person to give the information or explanation or to produce the document.

(4)   Without prejudice to subsection (2), the auditor may—

(a)   require any officer or member of a body subject to audit to give him such information or explanation as he thinks necessary for the purposes of his functions under this Act; and

(b)   if he thinks it necessary, require the officer or member to attend before him in person to give the information or explanation.

(4A)   In relation to a document kept in electronic form, the power in subsection (2)(b) to require a person to produce a document includes power to require it to be produced in a form in which it is legible and can be taken away.

(4B)   In connection with inspecting such a document, an auditor—

(a)   may obtain access to, and inspect and check the operation of, any computer and associated apparatus or material which he considers is or has been used in connection with the document;

(b)   may require a person within subsection (4C) to afford him such reasonable assistance as he may require for that purpose.

(4C)   A person is within this subsection if he is—

(a)   the person by whom or on whose behalf the computer is or has been used; or

(b)   a person having charge of, or otherwise concerned with the operation of, the computer, apparatus or material.

(5)   Without prejudice to subsections (1) to (4C), every body subject to audit shall provide the auditor with every facility and all information which he may reasonably require for the purposes of his functions under this Act.

(6)   A person who without reasonable excuse obstructs the exercise of any power conferred by this section or fails to comply with any requirement of an auditor under this section is guilty of an offence and liable on summary conviction—

(a)   to a fine not exceeding level 3 on the standard scale, and

(b)   to an additional fine not exceeding £20 for each day on which the offence continues after conviction for that offence.

(7)   Any expenses incurred by an auditor in connection with proceedings for an offence under subsection (6) alleged to have been committed in relation to the audit of the accounts of any body, so far as not recovered from any other source, are recoverable from that body.

7 Fees for audit

(1)   The Commission shall prescribe a scale or scales of fees in respect of the audit of accounts which are required to be audited in accordance with this Act.

(2)   Before prescribing any scale of fees under subsection (1) the Commission shall consult—

. . .

(b)   . . . such associations of local authorities as appear to the Commission to be concerned; and

(c)   in any case, the Care Quality Commission and such bodies of accountants as appear to the Commission to be appropriate.

(3)   A body subject to audit shall, subject to subsection (4), pay to the Commission the fee applicable to the audit in accordance with the appropriate scale.

(4)   If it appears to the Commission that the work involved in a particular audit was substantially more or less than that envisaged by the appropriate scale, the Commission may charge a fee which is larger or smaller than that referred to in subsection (3).

(5)   For the purpose of determining the fee payable for an audit, a body whose accounts are being audited or (if it is a parish meeting) its chairman shall—

(a)   complete a statement containing such information as the Commission may require and submit it to the auditor, and

    (b)   provide the Commission with such further information as it may at any time require.

(6) The auditor shall send the statement mentioned in subsection (5)(a) to the Commission on the conclusion of the audit with a certificate that the statement is correct to the best of his knowledge and belief.

(7) The fee payable for an audit shall be the same whether the auditor who carries it out is an officer of the Commission or not.

. . .

Auditors' reports and recommendations

8 Immediate and other reports in public interest

In auditing accounts required to be audited in accordance with this Act, the auditor shall consider—

    (a)   whether, in the public interest, he should make a report on any matter coming to his notice in the course of the audit, in order for it to be considered by the body concerned or brought to the attention of the public, and

    (b)   whether the public interest requires any such matter to be made the subject of an immediate report rather than of a report to be made at the conclusion of the audit.

9 General report

(1) When an auditor has concluded his audit of the accounts of any body under this Act he shall, subject to subsection (2), enter on the relevant statement of accounts prepared pursuant to regulations under section 27 (or, where no such statement is required to be prepared, on the accounts)—

    (a)   a certificate that he has completed the audit in accordance with this Act, and

    (b)   his opinion on the statement (or, as the case may be, on the accounts).

(2) Where an auditor makes a report to the body concerned under section 8 at the conclusion of the audit, he may include the certificate and opinion referred to in subsection (1) in that report instead of making an entry on the statement or accounts.

10 Transmission and consideration of section 8 reports

(1) Any report under section 8 shall be sent by the auditor to the body concerned or (if it is a parish meeting) to its chairman—

    (a)   forthwith if it is an immediate report;

    (b)   otherwise not later than 14 days after conclusion of the audit.

(2) A copy of the report shall be sent by the auditor to the Commission and (in the case of a health service body) to the Secretary of State and (in the case of a functional body or the London Pensions Fund Authority) to the Mayor of London—

    (a)   forthwith if it is an immediate report;

    (b)   otherwise not later than 14 days after conclusion of the audit.

(3) The body concerned (and, in the case of the Greater London Authority, the London Assembly) shall take the report into consideration—

    (a)   in accordance with sections 11, 11A and 12, or

    (b)   if section 11 does not apply to the body, as soon as practicable after receiving it.

(4) The agenda supplied to the members for the meeting of the body at which the report is considered shall be accompanied by the report.

. . .

(5) The report shall not be excluded—

(a) from the matter supplied under section 1(4)(b) of the Public Bodies (Admission to Meetings) Act 1960 or section 100B(7) of the 1972 Act (supply of agenda etc to newspapers); or

(b) from the documents open to inspection under section 100B(1) of the 1972 Act (public access to agenda and reports before meetings).

(6) Part VA of the 1972 Act has effect in relation to the report as if section 100C(1)(d) of that Act (public access to copies of reports for six years after meeting) were not limited to so much of the report as relates to an item during which the meeting was open to the public.

11 Consideration of reports or recommendations

(1) A body to which this section applies shall consider in accordance with this section and section 12 (and, in the case of a report or recommendations sent to the Greater London Authority, section 11A)—

(a) any report under section 8, and

(b) any written recommendation within subsection (3),

sent to the body or (if a parish meeting) its chairman in connection with the audit of its accounts.

(2) This section applies to every body subject to audit except—

(a) charter trustees constituted under section 246 of the 1972 Act;

. . .

(3) A written recommendation is within this subsection if it is made to the body concerned by an auditor and is stated in the document containing it to be one which in the auditor's opinion should be considered under this section.

. . .

(4) The body concerned shall consider the report or recommendation at a meeting held before the end of one month beginning with the day on which the report or recommendation was sent to the body or its chairman (as the case may be).

(5) At that meeting the body shall decide—

(a) whether the report requires the body to take any action or whether the recommendation is to be accepted; and

(b) what, if any, action to take in response to the report or recommendation.

(6) If an auditor is satisfied that it is reasonable to allow more time for the body to comply with its duties under subsections (4) and (5) in relation to a report or recommendation, the auditor may, in relation to that report or recommendation, extend the period of one month mentioned in subsection (4).

(7) A period may be extended under subsection (6) whether or not it has already been extended under that subsection once or more than once.

. . .

(8) Nothing in section 101 of the 1972 Act (delegation of functions) applies to a duty imposed on a body by this section.

. . .

(9) This section is without prejudice to any duties (so far as they relate to the subject-matter of a report or recommendation sent to a body to which this section applies) which are imposed by or under this Act, sections 114 to 116 of the Local Government Finance Act 1988 (functions and reports of finance officers), section 5 of the Local Government and Housing Act 1989 (functions of monitoring officers) or any other enactment.

12 Publicity for meetings under section 11

(1) A meeting shall not be held for the purposes of section 11 or 11A unless, at least seven clear days before the meeting, there has been published, in a newspaper circulating in the area of the body concerned, a notice which—

    (a)   states the time and place of the meeting,

    (b)   indicates that the meeting is to be held to consider an auditor's report or recommendation (as the case may be), and

    (c)   describes the subject-matter of the report or recommendation.

(2)   The body concerned shall ensure that, as soon as practicable after the meeting (or, in the case of the Greater London Authority, the making of the decisions under section 11A(6))—

    (a)   the auditor of its accounts is notified of the decisions made in pursuance of section 11(5) or 11A(6); and

    (b)   a notice containing a summary of those decisions which has been approved by the auditor is published in a newspaper circulating in that body's area.

(3)   The notice required by subsection (2)(b) in relation to a meeting—

    (a)   need not summarise any decision made while the public were excluded from the meeting—

        (i)   under section 100A(2) of the 1972 Act (confidential matters);

        (ii)   in pursuance of a resolution under section 100A(4) of that Act (exempt information); or

        (iii)   in pursuance of a resolution under section 1(2) of the Public Bodies (Admission to Meetings) Act 1960 (protection of public interest);

    but

    (b)   if sections 100C and 100D of the 1972 Act (availability for inspection after meetings of minutes, background papers and other documents) apply in relation to the meeting, shall indicate the documents in relation to the meeting which are open for inspection in accordance with those sections.

(4)   This section is without prejudice to, and in addition to, any provision made in relation to meetings of the body in question by section 10(4) to (6) or by or under the 1972 Act, the Public Bodies (Admission to Meetings) Act 1960 or any other enactment.

13 Additional publicity for immediate reports

(1)   This section applies where under section 10(1) an auditor has sent an immediate report to a body or its chairman, except where the body is a health service body.

(2)   From the time when the report is received by virtue of section 10(1), any member of the public may—

    (a)   inspect the report at all reasonable times without payment,

    (b)   make a copy of it, or of any part of it, and

    (c)   require the body or chairman to supply him with a copy of it, or of any part of it, on payment of a reasonable sum.

(3)   On receiving the report by virtue of section 10(1), the body or (if a parish meeting) its chairman shall forthwith publish in one or more local newspapers circulating in the area of the body a notice which—

    (a)   identifies the subject-matter of the report, and

    (b)   states that any member of the public may inspect the report and make a copy of it or any part of it between such times and at such place or places as are specified in the notice;

and the body, if not a parish meeting, shall in addition forthwith supply a copy of the report to every member of the body.

(4)   The auditor may—

    (a)   notify any person he thinks fit of the fact that he has made the report, and

    (b)   supply a copy of it or of any part of it to any person he thinks fit.

(5)   A person who has the custody of an immediate report and—

- (a) obstructs a person in the exercise of a right conferred by subsection (2)(a) or (b), or
- (b) refuses to supply a copy of the report or of part of it (as the case may be) to a person entitled to the copy by virtue of subsection (2)(c),

is guilty of an offence and liable on summary conviction to a fine not exceeding level 3 on the standard scale.

(6) A person who fails to comply with a requirement of subsection (3) is guilty of an offence and liable on summary conviction to a fine not exceeding level 3 on the standard scale.

(7) Nothing in this section affects the operation of section 10(4) to (6).

Public inspection etc and action by the auditor

14 Inspection of statements of accounts and auditors' reports

(1) A local government elector for the area of a body subject to audit, other than a health service body, may—

- (a) inspect and make copies of any statement of accounts prepared by the body pursuant to regulations under section 27;
- (b) inspect and make copies of any report, other than an immediate report, made to the body by an auditor; and
- (c) require copies of any such statement or report to be delivered to him on payment of a reasonable sum for each copy.

(2) A document which a person is entitled to inspect under this section may be inspected by him at all reasonable times and without payment.

(3) A person who has the custody of any such document and—

- (a) obstructs a person in the exercise of a right under this section to inspect or make copies of the document, or
- (b) refuses to give copies of the document to a person entitled under this section to obtain them,

is guilty of an offence and liable on summary conviction to a fine not exceeding level 3 on the standard scale.

(4) References in this section to copies of a document include references to copies of any part of it.

15 Inspection of documents and questions at audit

(1) At each audit under this Act, other than an audit of accounts of a health service body, any persons interested may—

- (a) inspect the accounts to be audited and all books, deeds, contracts, bills, vouchers and receipts relating to them, and
- (b) make copies of all or any part of the accounts and those other documents.

(2) At the request of a local government elector for any area to which the accounts relate, the auditor shall give the elector, or any representative of his, an opportunity to question the auditor about the accounts.

(3) Nothing in this section entitles a person—

- (a) to inspect so much of any accounts or other document as contains personal information about a member of the staff of the body whose accounts are being audited; or
- (b) to require any such information to be disclosed in answer to any question.

(3A) Information is personal information if—

- (a) it identifies a particular individual or enables a particular individual to be identified; and
- (b) the auditor considers that it should not be inspected or disclosed.

(4) Information is personal information if it is information about a member of the staff of the body whose accounts are being audited which relates specifically to a particular individual and is available to the body for reasons connected with the fact—

(a) that that individual holds or has held an office or employment under that body; or

(b) that payments or other benefits in respect of an office or employment under any other person are or have been made or provided to that individual by that body.

(5) For the purposes of subsection (4)(b), payments made or benefits provided to an individual in respect of an office or employment include any payment made or benefit provided to him in respect of his ceasing to hold the office or employment.

16 Right to make objections at audit

(1) At each audit of accounts under this Act . . . a local government elector for an area to which the accounts relate may make objections to the auditor—

(a) as to any matter in respect of which the auditor could take action under section 17; or

(b) as to any other matter in respect of which the auditor could make a report under section 8.

(2) An objection under subsection (1) must be sent to the auditor in writing.

(3) At the same time as the objection is sent to the auditor, a copy of the objection must be sent to the body whose accounts are being audited.

17 Declaration that item of account is unlawful

(1) Where—

(a) it appears to the auditor carrying out an audit under this Act, other than an audit of accounts of a health service body, that an item of account is contrary to law; . . .

the auditor may apply to the court for a declaration that the item is contrary to law.

(2) On an application under this section the court may make or refuse to make the declaration asked for, and if it makes the declaration then it may also—

(c) order rectification of the accounts.

(4) A person who has made an objection under section 16(1)(a) and is aggrieved by a decision of an auditor not to apply for a declaration under this section may—

(a) not later than six weeks after being notified of the decision, require the auditor to state in writing the reasons for his decision, and

(b) appeal against the decision to the court;

and on such an appeal the court has the same powers in relation to the item of account to which the objection relates as if the auditor had applied for the declaration.

(5) On an application or appeal under this section relating to the accounts of a body, the court may make such order as it thinks fit for the payment by the body of expenses incurred, in connection with the application or appeal, by—

(a) the auditor,

(c) the person by whom the appeal is brought.

(6) The High Court and the county courts have jurisdiction for the purposes of this section.

Prevention of unlawful expenditure etc

24 Power of auditor to apply for judicial review

(1) Subject to section 31(3) of the Supreme Court Act 1981 (no application for judicial review without leave) the auditor appointed in relation to the accounts of a body other than a health service body may make an application for judicial review with respect to—

(a)   any decision of that body, or

(b)   any failure by that body to act,

which it is reasonable to believe would have an effect on the accounts of that body.

(2)   The existence of the powers conferred on an auditor under this Act is not a ground for refusing an application falling within subsection (1) (or an application for leave to make such an application).

(3)   On an application for judicial review made as mentioned in subsection (1), the court may make such order as it thinks fit for the payment, by the body to whose decision the application relates, of expenses incurred by the auditor in connection with the application.

Miscellaneous

25 Extraordinary audit

(1)   The Commission may direct an auditor or auditors appointed by it to hold an extraordinary audit of the accounts of a body subject to audit—

(a)   if it appears to the Commission to be desirable to do so in consequence of a report made under this Act by an auditor or for any other reason; or

(b)   where the accounts are not those of a health service body, if an application for such an audit is made by a local government elector for the area of the body in question.

(2)   If it appears to the Secretary of State that it is desirable in the public interest that there should be an extraordinary audit of the accounts of a body subject to audit he may require the Commission to direct such an audit by an auditor or auditors appointed by it.

(3)   The following provisions apply to an extraordinary audit under this section as they apply to an ordinary audit under this Act—

(a)   in relation to the accounts of a body other than a health service body, sections 3, 5, 6, 8 to 13 and 16 to 18; and

(b)   in relation to the accounts of a health service body, sections 3, 5, 6 and 8 to 10.

(4)   An extraordinary audit under this section may be held after three clear days' notice in writing to be given to the body whose accounts are to be audited or (if it is a parish meeting) to be given to its chairman.

(5)   The expenditure incurred in holding an extraordinary audit of the accounts of any body—

(a)   shall be defrayed in the first instance by the Commission, but

(b)   may be recovered by the Commission, if it thinks fit, in whole or part from the body concerned.

26 Audit of accounts of officers

(1)   Where an officer of a body subject to audit receives money or other property—

(a)   on behalf of that body, or

(b)   for which he ought to account to that body,

the accounts of the officer shall be audited by the auditor of the accounts of that body, and the provisions mentioned in subsection (2) apply with the necessary modifications to the accounts and audit.

(2)   Those provisions are—

. . .

(b)   . . . sections 2(1), 5 to 10, 13 to 18, 25 and 27.

27 Accounts and audit regulations

(1)   The Secretary of State may by regulations applying to bodies subject to audit other than health service bodies make provision with respect to—

(a) the keeping of accounts;

(b) the form, preparation and certification of accounts and of statements of accounts;

(c) the deposit of the accounts of any body at the offices of the body or at any other place;

(d) the publication of information relating to accounts and the publication of statements of accounts;

(e) the exercise of any rights of objection or inspection conferred by section 14, 15 or 16 and the steps to be taken by any body for informing local government electors for the area of that body of those rights.

(3) Before making any regulations under this section the Secretary of State shall consult—

(a) the Commission,

(b) such associations of local authorities as appear to him to be concerned, and

(c) such bodies of accountants as appear to him to be appropriate.

. . .

PART IV

GENERAL

Information etc

48 Provision of information and documents to Commission

(1) Without prejudice to any other provision of this Act, the Commission may require—

(a) any body subject to audit, and

(b) any officer or member of such a body,

to provide the Commission or a person authorised by it with all such information as the Commission or that person may reasonably require for the discharge of the functions under this Act of the Commission or of that person, including the carrying out of any study under section 33 or 34.

(2) Subsection (1) does not apply to functions under section 36 or 47A.

(3) For the purpose of assisting the Commission to maintain proper standards in the auditing of the accounts of a body subject to audit the Commission may require that body to make available for inspection by or on behalf of the Commission—

(a) the accounts concerned; and

(b) such other documents relating to the body as might reasonably be required by an auditor for the purposes of the audit.

(4) A person who without reasonable excuse fails to comply with a requirement of the Commission under subsection (1)(b) is guilty of an offence and liable on summary conviction—

(a) to a fine not exceeding level 3 on the standard scale, and

(b) to an additional fine not exceeding £20 for each day on which the offence continues after conviction for that offence.

. . .

49 Restriction on disclosure of information

(1) No information relating to a particular body or other person and obtained by the Commission or an auditor, or by a person acting on behalf of the Commission or an auditor, pursuant to any provision of this Act or of Part I of the Local Government Act 1999 or in the course of any audit or study under any such provision shall be disclosed except—

    (a)   with the consent of the body or person to whom the information relates;

    (b)   for the purposes of any functions of the Commission or an auditor under this Act or under Part I of the 1999 Act;

. . .

    (f)   for the purposes of any criminal proceedings.

(2)   References in subsection (1) to studies and to functions of the Commission do not include studies or functions under section 36.

. . .

(3)   A person who discloses information in contravention of this section is guilty of an offence and liable—

    (a)   on summary conviction to a fine not exceeding the statutory maximum;

51 Publication of information by the Commission

(1)   The Commission may publish such information as it thinks fit except where the publication would, or would be likely to, prejudice the effective performance of a function imposed or conferred on the Commission or an auditor by or under an enactment.

(4)   Information published under this section shall be published in such manner as the Commission considers appropriate for bringing the information to the attention of those members of the public who may be interested.

51A Co-operation with the Auditor General for Wales

The Commission must co-operate with the Auditor General for Wales where it seems to it appropriate to do so for the efficient and effective discharge of—

    (a)   its functions under sections 33 and 34, or

    (b)   its functions in relation to bodies mentioned in paragraph 1(g) of Schedule 2.

51B Provision of information to Auditor General for Wales

The Commission must, on request, provide the Auditor General for Wales with any information he may reasonably require for the purpose of making comparisons, in the discharge of his functions under sections 41 and 42 of the Public Audit (Wales) Act 2004, between local government bodies in Wales and other local government bodies.

Supplementary

52 Orders and regulations

(1)   Any power conferred on the Secretary of State by this Act to make orders or regulations is exercisable by statutory instrument.

(1A)   No order shall be made under section 32H unless a draft of the order has been laid before and approved by a resolution of each House of Parliament.

(2)   No order shall be made under paragraph 9(2) of Schedule 1 unless a draft of the order has been approved by a resolution of the House of Commons.

(3)   In any other case, an order or regulations contained in a statutory instrument made by the Secretary of State under this Act shall be subject to annulment in pursuance of a resolution of either House of Parliament.

53 Interpretation

(1)   In this Act—

. . .

    'the 1972 Act' means the Local Government Act 1972;

. . .

LOCAL GOVERNMENT ACT 2000

[The sections reproduced below apply only in Wales]

PART I

PROMOTION OF ECONOMIC, SOCIAL OR ENVIRONMENTAL
WELL-BEING ETC

Interpretation

1 Meaning of "local authority" in Part I

(1)   In this Part "local authority" means—

...

(b)   in relation to Wales, a county council or a county borough council or a community council.

...

Promotion of well-being

2 Promotion of well-being

(1)   Every local authority [in Wales] are to have power to do anything which they consider is likely to achieve any one or more of the following objects—

(a)   the promotion or improvement of the economic well-being of their area;

(b)   the promotion or improvement of the social well-being of their area, and

(c)   the promotion or improvement of the environmental well-being of their area.

(2)   The power under subsection (1) may be exercised in relation to or for the benefit of—

(a)   the whole or any part of a local authority's area, or

(b)   all or any persons resident or present in a local authority's area.

(3)   ...

(3A)   ...

(3B)   In determining whether or how to exercise the power under subsection (1), a local authority in Wales must have regard to the community strategy for its area published under section 39(4) of the Local Government (Wales) Measure 2009 or, where the strategy has been amended following a review under section 41 of that Measure, the strategy most recently published under section 41(6).

(3C)   The community strategy for the area of a community council is the strategy referred to in subsection (3B) that is published by the county council or county borough council in whose area lies the community or communities for which the community council is established.

(4)   The power under subsection (1) includes power for a local authority to—

(a)   incur expenditure,

(b)   give financial assistance to any person,

(c)   enter into arrangements or agreements with any person,

(d)   co-operate with, or facilitate or co-ordinate the activities of, any person,

(e)   exercise on behalf of any person any functions of that person, and

(f)   provide staff, goods, services or accommodation to any person.

(5)   The power under subsection (1) includes power for a local authority to do anything in relation to, or for the benefit of, any person or area situated outside their area if they consider that it is likely to achieve any one or more of the objects in that subsection.

(6)   Nothing in subsection (4) or (5) affects the generality of the power under subsection (1).

3 Limits on power to promote well-being

(1)   The power under section 2(1) does not enable a local authority to do anything which they are unable to do by virtue of any prohibition, restriction or limitation on their powers which is contained in any enactment (whenever passed or made).

(2)   The power under section 2(1) does not enable a local authority to raise money (whether by precepts, borrowing or otherwise).

(3)   The [Welsh Ministers] may by order make provision preventing local authorities from doing, by virtue of section 2(1), anything which is specified, or is of a description specified, in the order.

(3A)   The power under subsection (3) may be exercised in relation to—

    (a)   all local authorities,

    (b)   particular local authorities, or

    (c)   particular descriptions of local authority.

(4)   Subject to subsection (4A),] before making an order under subsection (3), the [Welsh Ministers] must consult such representatives of local government and such other persons (if any) as he considers appropriate.

(4A)   Subsection (4) does not apply to an order under this section which is made only for the purpose of amending an earlier order under this section—

    (a)   so as to extend the earlier order, or any provision of the earlier order, to a particular authority or to authorities of a particular description, or

    (b)   so that the earlier order, or any provision of the earlier order, ceases to apply to a particular authority or to authorities of a particular description.

(5)   Before exercising the power under section 2(1), a local authority must have regard to any guidance for the time being issued by the [Welsh Ministers] about the exercise of that power.

(6)   Before issuing any guidance under subsection (5), the [Welsh Ministers] must consult such representatives of local government and such other persons (if any) as he considers appropriate

(7)   ...

(8)   In this section "enactment" includes an enactment comprised in subordinate legislation (within the meaning of the Interpretation Act 1978).

4 Strategies for promoting well-being

(1)   Every local authority [in England] must prepare a strategy (referred to in this section as a [sustainable community strategy]) for promoting or improving the economic, social and environmental well-being of their area and contributing to the achievement of sustainable development in the United Kingdom.

(2)   A local authority may from time to time modify their [sustainable community strategy.

(3)   In preparing or modifying their [sustainable community strategy], a local authority—

    (a)   must consult and seek the participation of—

        (i)   in the case of a responsible local authority, each partner authority and such other persons as the responsible local authority consider appropriate, or

        (ii)   in any other case, such persons as the authority consider appropriate, . . .

    (aa)   must, if it is a local authority in England, have regard to the following, so far as they relate to the authority's area—

> > (i) any arrangements made under section 21 of the Child Poverty Act 2010 (co-operation to reduce child poverty in local area);
> >
> > (ii) any local child poverty needs assessment prepared under section 22 of that Act (local child poverty needs assessment);
> >
> > (iii) any joint child poverty strategy prepared under section 23 of that Act (joint child poverty strategy for local area), and
>
> (b) must have regard to any guidance for the time being issued by the Secretary of State.

(4) Before issuing any guidance under this section, the Secretary of State must consult such representatives of local government and such other persons (if any) as he considers appropriate.

(5) ...

(6) In subsection (3)(a), "responsible local authority" and "partner authority", in relation to a responsible local authority, have the same meanings as in Chapter 1 (local area agreements) of Part 5 of the Local Government and Public Involvement in Health Act 2007 (see sections 103 and 104 of that Act).

5 Power to amend or repeal enactments

(1) If the Secretary of State thinks that an enactment (whenever passed or made) prevents or obstructs local authorities from exercising their power under section 2(1) he may by order amend, repeal, revoke or disapply that enactment.

(2) The power under subsection (1) may be exercised in relation to—

> (a) all local authorities,
>
> (b) particular local authorities, or
>
> (c) particular descriptions of local authority.

(3) The power under subsection (1) to amend or disapply an enactment includes a power to amend or disapply an enactment for a particular period.

(4) In exercising the power under subsection (1), the Secretary of State must not make any provision which has effect in relation to Wales unless he has consulted the Welsh Ministers.

(4A) In exercising the power under subsection (1), the Secretary of State—

> (a) must not make any provision amending, repealing or disapplying any Measure or Act of the National Assembly for Wales without the consent of the National Assembly for Wales, and
>
> (b) must not make any provision amending, revoking or disapplying subordinate legislation made by the Welsh Ministers (or the National Assembly for Wales established under the Government of Wales Act 1998) without the consent of the Welsh Ministers.

(4B) Subsection (4A) does not apply to the extent that the Secretary of State is making incidental or consequential provision.]

(5) The Welsh Ministers may submit proposals to the Secretary of State that the power under subsection (1) should be exercised in relation to Wales in accordance with those proposals.

(6) In this section "enactment" includes an enactment comprised in subordinate legislation (within the meaning of the Interpretation Act 1978).

(7) The reference to local authorities in subsection (1) does not include community councils.

Modification of certain enactments

7 Power to modify enactments concerning plans etc: Wales

(1) Subject to subsections (4) and (6), [the Welsh Ministers] may by order amend, repeal, revoke or disapply any enactment [(whenever passed or made) which requires

a local authority to prepare, produce or publish any plan or strategy relating to any particular matter] so far as that enactment has effect in relation to a local authority in Wales.

(2) ...

(3) The power under subsection (1) may be exercised in relation to—

(a) all local authorities in Wales,

(b) particular local authorities in Wales, or

(c) particular descriptions of local authority in Wales.

(4) The power under subsection (1) may be exercised in relation to a local authority only if [the Welsh Ministers consider]—

(a) that it is not appropriate for any such enactment as is mentioned in that subsection to apply to the authority, or

(b) that any such enactment should be amended so that it operates more effectively in relation to the authority.

(5) The power under subsection (1) to amend or disapply an enactment includes a power to amend or disapply an enactment for a particular period.

(6) ...

(7) In this section "enactment" includes an enactment comprised in subordinate legislation (within the meaning of the Interpretation Act 1978).

(8) An order under this section may not make a provision which, if it were a provision of [an Act] of the National Assembly for Wales, would be outside the Assembly's legislative competence.

(9) For the purposes of subsection (8), [section 108(4) of the Government of Wales Act 2006 (Legislative competence) has effect as if paragraph (a) were omitted].

(10) Subject to subsection (11), a statutory instrument which contains an order under this section is not to be made unless a draft of the instrument has been laid before and approved by a resolution of the National Assembly for Wales.

(11) A statutory instrument containing an order under this section which is made only for the purpose of amending an earlier such order—

(a) so as to extend the earlier order, or any provision of the earlier order, to a particular authority or to authorities of a particular description, or

(b) so that the earlier order, or any provision of the earlier order, ceases to apply to a particular authority or to authorities of a particular description,

is to be subject to annulment in pursuance of a resolution of the National Assembly for Wales.]

9A Procedure for orders under section 7

(1) Before the Welsh Ministers make an order under section 7 they must consult—

(a) such local authorities in Wales,

(b) such representatives of local government in Wales, and

(c) such other persons (if any),

as appear to them to be likely to be affected by their proposals.

(2) If, following consultation under subsection (1), the Welsh Ministers propose to make an order under section 7 they must lay before the National Assembly for Wales a document which—

(a) explains their proposals,

(b) sets them out in the form of a draft order, and

(c) gives details of consultation under subsection (1).

(3) Where a document relating to proposals is laid before the National Assembly for Wales under subsection (2), no draft of an order under section 7 to give effect to the proposals (with or without modifications) is to be laid before the National Assembly for Wales until after the expiry of the period of sixty days beginning with the day on which the document was laid.

(4) In calculating the period mentioned in subsection (3) no account is to be taken of any time during which the National Assembly is dissolved or is in recess for more than four days.

(5) In preparing a draft order under section 7 the Welsh Ministers must consider any representations made during the period mentioned in subsection (3).

(6) A draft order under section 7 which is laid before the National Assembly for Wales must be accompanied by a statement of the Welsh Ministers giving details of—

    (a) any representations considered in accordance with subsection (5), and

    (b) any changes made to the proposals contained in the document laid before the National Assembly for Wales under subsection (2).

(7) Nothing in this section applies to an order under section 7 which is made only for the purpose of amending an earlier order under that section—

    (a) so as to extend the earlier order, or any provision of the earlier order, to a particular authority or to authorities of a particular description, or

    (b) so that the earlier order, or any provision of the earlier order, ceases to apply to a particular authority or to authorities of a particular description.

PART III

CONDUCT OF LOCAL GOVERNMENT MEMBERS AND EMPLOYEES

CHAPTER I

CONDUCT OF MEMBERS
Standards of conduct

49 Principles governing conduct of members of relevant authorities

(1) ....

(2) The National Assembly for Wales may by order specify the principles which are to govern the conduct of members and co-opted members of relevant authorities

(2A) An order under subsection (1) must provide as respects each specified principle—

    (a) that it applies to a person only when acting in an official capacity; or

    (b) that it applies to a person only when not acting in an official capacity;

but the order may provide as mentioned in paragraph (b) only as respects a principle within subsection (2B).[1]

(2B) A principle is within this subsection if it prohibits particular conduct (or conduct of a particular description) where that conduct would constitute a criminal offence.

(2C) ....

(2D) An order under subsection (2)—

    (a) may specify principles which are to apply to a person at all times;

    (b) may specify principles which are to apply to a person otherwise than at all times.

(3) ....

(4) ....

(5) Before making an order under this section, the National Assembly for Wales must consult—

    (a) such representatives of relevant authorities in Wales as it considers appropriate,

    (b) the Auditor General for Wales,

    (c) the Public Services Ombudsman for Wales, and

    (d) such other persons (if any) as it considers appropriate.

(6) In this Part 'relevant authority' means—

    (a)   a county council,

    (b)   a county borough council,

    (c)   ....

    (e)   ....

    (f)   a community council,

    . . .

(7) In this Part 'co-opted member', in relation to a relevant authority, means a person who is not a member of the authority but who—

    (a)   is a member of any committee or sub-committee of the authority, or

    (b)   is a member of, and represents the authority on, any joint committee or joint sub-committee of the authority,

and who is entitled to vote on any question which falls to be decided at any meeting of that committee or sub-committee.

---

[1]   Subsections (2A)–(2D) were inserted by the Local Government and Public Involvement in Health Act 2007. As at 29 May 2013, they were in force in so far as they relate to sub-ss (2C), (2D), and not for other purposes.

50 Model code of conduct

(1)   ....

(2) The National Assembly for Wales may by order issue a model code as regards the conduct which is expected of members and co-opted members of relevant authorities in Wales (also referred to in this Part as a model code of conduct).

(3) The power under subsection (2) to issue a model code of conduct includes power to revise any such model code which has been issued.

(4) A model code of conduct—

    (a)   must be consistent with the principles for the time being specified in an order under section 49(2),

    (b)   may include provisions which are mandatory, and

    (c)   may include provisions which are optional.

(4A) A model code of conduct issued under subsection (1) must provide, as respects each provision of the code which relates to the conduct expected of the persons mentioned in that subsection—

    (a)   that the provision applies to a person only when acting in an official capacity; or

    (b)   that it applies to a person only when not acting in an official capacity;

but the code may provide as mentioned in paragraph (b) only as respects a provision within subsection (4B).

(4B) A provision is within this subsection if it prohibits particular conduct (or conduct of a particular description) where that conduct would constitute a criminal offence.

(4C)   ....

(4D)   ....

(4E) A model code of conduct issued under subsection (2) may include—

    (a)   provisions which are to apply to a person at all times;

    (b)   provisions which are to apply to a person otherwise than at all times.

(5) Before making an order under this section, the Secretary of State or the National Assembly for Wales must carry out such consultation as is required, by virtue of section 49, before an order is made under that section.

(6)   ....

(7)   ....

¹   Subsections (4A)–(4E) were inserted by the Local Government and Public Involvement in Health Act 2007. As at 29 May 2013, they were in force in so far as they relate to sub-ss (4C)–(4E), and not for other purposes.

51 Duty of relevant authorities to adopt codes of conduct

(1)   It is the duty of a relevant authority, before the end of the period of six months beginning with the day on which the first order under section 50 which applies to them is made, to pass a resolution adopting a code as regards the conduct which is expected of members and co-opted members of the authority (referred to in this Part as a code of conduct).

(2)   It is the duty of a relevant authority, before the end of the period of six months beginning with the day on which any subsequent order under section 50 which applies to them is made, to pass a resolution—

> (a)   adopting a code of conduct in place of their existing code of conduct under this section, or
>
> (b)   revising their existing code of conduct under this section.

(3)   A relevant authority may by resolution—

> (a)   adopt a code of conduct in place of their existing code of conduct under this section, or
>
> (b)   revise their existing code of conduct under this section.

(4)   A code of conduct or revised code of conduct—

> (a)   must incorporate any mandatory provisions of the model code of conduct which for the time being applies to that authority,
>
> (b)   may incorporate any optional provisions of that model code, and
>
> (c)   may include other provisions which are consistent with that model code.

(4A)   Where under subsection (4)(c) a provision relating to the conduct expected of persons is included in the code of a relevant authority in England, the code must provide—

> (a)   that the provision applies to a person only when acting in an official capacity (within the meaning given by the code); or
>
> (b)   that it applies to a person only when not acting in an official capacity (within that meaning);

but the code may provide as mentioned in paragraph (b) only as respects a provision within subsection (4B).

(4B)   A provision of a code is within this subsection if it prohibits particular conduct (or conduct of a particular description) where that conduct would constitute a criminal offence within the meaning of the code.

(4C)   The provisions which may be included under subsection (4)(c) include—

> (a)   provisions which are to apply to a person at all times;
>
> (b)   provisions which are to apply to a person otherwise than at all times.

(5)   Where a relevant authority fail to comply with the duty under subsection (1) or (2) before the end of the period mentioned in that subsection—

> (a)   they must comply with that duty as soon as reasonably practicable after the end of that period, and
>
> (b)   any mandatory provisions of the model code of conduct which for the time being applies to the authority are to apply in relation to the members and co-opted members of the authority for so long as the authority fail to comply with that duty.

(6)   As soon as reasonably practicable after adopting or revising a code of conduct under this section, a relevant authority must—

> (a)   ensure that copies of the code or revised code are available at an office of the authority for inspection by members of the public at all reasonable hours,

(b)   publish in one or more newspapers circulating in their area a notice which—

    (i)   states that they have adopted or revised a code of conduct,

    (ii)   states that copies of the code or revised code are available at an office of the authority for inspection by members of the public at such times as may be specified in the notice, and

    (iii) specifies the address of that office, and

(c)   send a copy of the code or revised code—

    (i)   ....

    (ii)   to the Public Services Ombudsman for Wales.

(7)   Where a relevant authority themselves publish a newspaper, the duty to publish a notice under subsection (6)(b) is to be construed as a duty to publish that notice in their newspaper and at least one other newspaper circulating in their area.

(8)   A relevant authority may publicise their adoption or revision of a code of conduct under this section in any other manner that they consider appropriate.

(9)   A relevant authority's function with respect to the passing of a resolution under this section may be discharged only by the authority (and accordingly, in the case of a relevant authority to which section 101 of the Local Government Act 1972 applies, is not to be a function to which that section applies).

---

[1]   Subsections (4A)–(4C) were inserted by the Local Government and Public Involvement in Health Act 2007. As at 29 May 2013, they were in force in so far as they relate to sub-s (4C), and not for other purposes.

52 Duty to comply with code of conduct

(1)   A person who is a member or co-opted member of a relevant authority at a time when the authority adopt a code of conduct under section 51 for the first time—

(a)   must, before the end of the period of two months beginning with the date on which the code of conduct is adopted, give to the authority a written undertaking that *in performing his functions*[1] he will observe the authority's code of conduct for the time being under section 51, and

(b)   if he fails to do so, is to cease to be a member or co-opted member at the end of that period.

(2)   The form of declaration of acceptance of office which may be prescribed by an order under section 83 of the Local Government Act 1972 in relation to a relevant authority may include an undertaking by the declarant that *in performing his functions* ₁ he will observe the authority's code of conduct for the time being under section 51.

(3)   A person who becomes a member of a relevant authority to which section 83 of that Act does not apply at any time after the authority have adopted a code of conduct under section 51 for the first time may not act in that office unless he has given the authority a written undertaking that *in performing his functions*[1] he will observe the authority's code of conduct for the time being under section 51.

(4)   A person who becomes a co-opted member of a relevant authority at any time after the authority have adopted a code of conduct under section 51 for the first time may not act as such unless he has given the authority a written undertaking that *in performing his functions*[1] he will observe the authority's code of conduct for the time being under section 51.

(5)   In relation to a relevant authority whose members and co-opted members are subject to mandatory provisions by virtue of section 51(5)(b)—

(a)   the references in subsections (2) to (4) to the authority's code of conduct for the time being under section 51 include the mandatory provisions which for the time being apply to the members and co-opted members of the authority, and

(b)   the references in subsections (3) and (4) to any time after the authority have adopted a code of conduct under section 51 for the first time are to be read as references to any time after the coming into force of section 184 of the Local Government and Public Involvement in Health Act 2007.

¹ Words in italics were repealed by the Local Government and Public Involvement in Health Act 2007. These amendments are in force in relation to Wales but not, as at 29 May 2013, in relation to England.

Standards committees

54 Functions of standards committees

(1) The general functions of a standards committee of a relevant authority are—

    (a)   promoting and maintaining high standards of conduct by the members and co-opted members of the authority, and

    (b)   assisting members and co-opted members of the authority to observe the authority's code of conduct.

(2) Without prejudice to its general functions, a standards committee of a relevant authority has the following specific functions—

    (a)   advising the authority on the adoption or revision of a code of conduct,

    (b)   monitoring the operation of the authority's code of conduct, and

    (c)   advising, training or arranging to train members and co-opted members of the authority on matters relating to the authority's code of conduct.

(3) A relevant authority may arrange for their standards committee to exercise such other functions as the authority consider appropriate.

(3A) In relation to a relevant authority whose members and co-opted members are subject to mandatory provisions by virtue of section 51(5)(b), references in subsection (1)(b) and (2)(b) and (c) to the authority's code of conduct are to those mandatory provisions.

(4) ....

(5) The National Assembly for Wales may by regulations make provision with respect to the exercise of functions by standards committees of relevant authorities in Wales . . . .

(6) ....

(7) The National Assembly for Wales may issue guidance with respect to the exercise of functions by standards committees of relevant authorities in Wales . . . .

54A Sub-committees of standards committees

(1) A standards committee of a relevant authority may appoint one or more sub-committees for the purpose of discharging any of the committee's functions, whether or not to the exclusion of the committee.

(2) Subsection (1) does not apply to functions under section 56.

(3) A sub-committee under subsection (1) shall be appointed from among the members of the standards committee by which it is appointed.

(4) ....

(5) As regards sub-committees appointed under subsection (1) by a standards committee of a relevant authority—

    (a)   regulations under section 53(11) may make provision in relation to such sub-committees, and

    (b)   section 54(5) and (7) apply in relation to such sub-committees as they apply in relation to standards committees.

(6) Subject to any provision made by regulations under section 53(11)(a) (as applied by this section)—

    (a)   the number of members of a sub-committee under subsection (1), and

    (b)   the term of office of those members,

are to be fixed by the standards committee by which the sub-committee is appointed.

56 Standards committees or sub-committees for community councils

(1)   A standards committee of a county council in Wales is to have the same functions in relation to—

(a)   the community councils which are situated in the area of the county council, and

(b)   the members of those community councils,

as the standards committee has under section 54(1) and (2) in relation to the county council and the members of the county council.

(2)   A standards committee of a county borough council is to have the same functions in relation to—

(a)   the community councils which are situated in the area of the county borough council, and

(b)   the members of those community councils,

as the standards committee has under section 54(1) and (2) in relation to the county borough council and the members of the county borough council.

(3)   A standards committee of a county council or county borough council may appoint a sub-committee for the purpose of discharging all of the functions conferred on the standards committee by this section.

(4)   In deciding whether it will be their standards committee, or a sub-committee of their standards committee, which is to discharge the functions conferred by this section, a county council or county borough council must consult the community councils which are situated in their area.

(5)   Regulations under section 53(11) may make provision in relation to sub-committees appointed under this section.

(6)   Subsections (5) and (7) of section 54 apply in relation to sub-committees of standards committees appointed under this section as they apply in relation to standards committees.

(7)   Any function which by virtue of the following provisions of this Part is exercisable by or in relation to the standards committee of a relevant authority which is a community council is to be exercisable by or in relation to—

(a)   the standards committee of the county council or county borough council in whose area the community council is situated, or

(b)   where that standards committee has appointed a sub-committee under this section, that sub-committee;

and any reference in the following provision of this Part to the standards committee of a relevant authority which is a community council is to be construed accordingly.

CHAPTER III

INVESTIGATIONS ETC: WALES
Public Services Ombudsman for Wales

68 Public Services Ombudsman for Wales

(1)   The Public Services Ombudsman for Wales is to have the functions conferred on him by this Part and such other functions as may be conferred on him by order made by the National Assembly for Wales under this subsection.

(2)   The Public Services Ombudsman for Wales—

(a)   may issue guidance to relevant authorities on matters relating to the conduct of members and co-opted members of those authorities,

(b)   may issue guidance to relevant authority in relation to the qualifications or experience which monitoring officers should possess, and

(c)   may arrange for any such guidance to be made public.

(3)   The National Assembly for Wales may by regulations make provision which, for the purpose of any provisions of the Public Services Ombudsman (Wales) Act 2005 specified in the regulations, treats—

    (a)   functions of the Public Services Ombudsman for Wales under that Act as including his functions under this Part, or

    (b)   expenses of the Public Services Ombudsman for Wales under that Act as including his expenses under this Part.

(4)   The provision which may be made by virtue of subsection (3) includes provision which modifies, or applies or reproduces (with or without modifications), any provisions of that Act.

Investigations

69 Investigations by the Public Services Ombudsman for Wales

(1)   The Public Services Ombudsman for Wales may investigate—

    (a)   cases in which a written allegation is made to him by any person that a member or co-opted member (or former member or co-opted member) of a relevant authority has failed, or may have failed, to comply with the authority's code of conduct, and

    (b)   other cases in which he considers that a member or co-opted member (or former member or co-opted member) of a relevant authority has failed, or may have failed, to comply with the authority's code of conduct and which have come to his attention as a result of an investigation under paragraph (a).

(2)–(5)   [*With the substitution of references to the Public Services Ombudsman for Wales to the Standards Board for England or, as the case may be, to an ethical standards officer, the subsections are the same as s 58(2) and s 59(3)–(5) above.*]

70 Investigations: further provisions

(1)   The National Assembly for Wales may by order make provision with respect to investigations under section 69 (including provision with respect to the obtaining or disclosure of documents or information).

(2)   The provision which may be made by virtue of subsection (1) includes provision which applies or reproduces (with or without modifications)—

    (a)   any provisions of sections 60 to 63, or

    (b)   any provisions of sections 13 to 15, 25 to 27 and 32 of the Public Services Ombudsman (Wales) Act 2005.

(3)   The Public Services Ombudsman for Wales may cease an investigation under section 69 at any stage before its completion.

(4)   Where the Public Services Ombudsman for Wales ceases an investigation under section 69 before its completion, he may refer the matters which are the subject of the investigation to the monitoring officer of the relevant authority concerned.

(5)   Where a person is no longer a member or co-opted member of the relevant authority concerned but is a member or co-opted member of another relevant authority, the Public Services Ombudsman for Wales may, if he thinks it more appropriate than making such a reference as is mentioned in subsection (4), refer the matters which are the subject of the investigation to the monitoring officer of that other relevant authority.

Reports etc

71 Reports etc

(1)   Where the Public Services Ombudsman for Wales determines in relation to any case that a finding under section 69(4)(a) or (b) is appropriate—

(a) he may produce a report on the outcome of his investigation,

(b) he may provide a summary of any such report to any newspapers circulating in the area of the relevant authority concerned,

(c) he must send to the monitoring officer of the relevant authority concerned a copy of any such report, and

(d) where he does not produce any such report, he must inform the monitoring officer of the relevant authority concerned of the outcome of the investigation.

(2) Where the Public Services Ombudsman for Wales determines in relation to any case that a finding under section 69(4)(c) is appropriate he must—

(a) produce a report on the outcome of his investigation,

(b) subject to subsection (4)(b), refer the matters which are the subject of the investigation to the monitoring officer of the relevant authority concerned, and

(c) send a copy of the report to the monitoring officer, and the standards committee, of the relevant authority concerned.

(3) Where the Public Services Ombudsman for Wales determines in relation to any case that a finding under section 69(4)(d) is appropriate he must—

(a) produce a report on the outcome of his investigation,

(b) refer the matters which are the subject of the investigation to the president of the Adjudication Panel for Wales for adjudication by a tribunal falling within section 76(1), and

(c) send a copy of the report to the monitoring officer of the relevant authority concerned and to the president of the Adjudication Panel for Wales.

(4) Where a person is no longer a member or co-opted member of the relevant authority concerned but is a member or co-opted member of another relevant authority—

(a) the references in subsections (1)(b), (c) and (d), (2)(c) and (3)(c) to the relevant authority concerned are to be treated as including references to that other relevant authority, and

(b) if the Public Services Ombudsman for Wales reaches a finding under section 69(4)(c) he must refer the matters concerned either to the monitoring officer of the relevant authority concerned or to the monitoring officer of that other relevant authority.

(5) A report under this section may cover more than one investigation under section 69 in relation to any members or co-opted members (or former members or co-opted members) of the same relevant authority.

(6) The Public Services Ombudsman for Wales must—

(a) inform any person who is the subject of an investigation under section 69, and

(b) take reasonable steps to inform any person who made any allegation which gave rise to the investigation,

of the outcome of the investigation.

72 Interim reports

(1) Where he considers it necessary in the public interest, the Public Services Ombudsman for Wales may, before the completion of an investigation under section 69, produce an interim report on that investigation.

(2) An interim report under this section may cover more than one investigation under section 69 in relation to any members or co-opted members (or former members or co-opted members) of the same relevant authority.

(3) Where the prima facie evidence is such that it appears to the Public Services Ombudsman for Wales—

(a)   that the person who is the subject of the interim report has failed to comply with the code of conduct of the relevant authority concerned,

(b)   that the nature of that failure is such as to be likely to lead to disqualification under section 79(4)(b), and

(c)   that it is in the public interest to suspend or partially suspend that person immediately,

the interim report may include a recommendation that that person should be suspended or partially suspended from being a member or co-opted member of the relevant authority concerned for a period which does not exceed six months or (if shorter) the remainder of the person's term of office.

(4) Where the Public Services Ombudsman for Wales produces an interim report under this section which contains such a recommendation as is mentioned in subsection (3), he must refer the matters which are the subject of the report to the president of the Adjudication Panel for Wales for adjudication by a tribunal falling within section 76(2).

(5) A copy of any report under this section must be given—

(a)   to any person who is the subject of the report,

(b)   to the monitoring officer of the relevant authority concerned, and

(c)   to the president of the Adjudication Panel for Wales.

(6) Where a person is no longer a member or co-opted member of the relevant authority concerned but is a member or co-opted member of another relevant authority—

(a)   the second reference in subsection (3) to the relevant authority concerned is to be treated as a reference to that other relevant authority, and

(b)   the reference in subsection (5)(b) to the relevant authority concerned is to be treated as including a reference to that other relevant authority.

References to monitoring officers

73 Matters referred to monitoring officers

[*Substituting references to 'the Secretary of State' with references to 'the National Assembly for Wales', and references to sections 60(2) and 64(2) with sections 70(4) and 71(2), respectively, and a reference to 'an ethical standards officer' with 'the Public Services Ombudsman for Wales', this section is the same as s 66 above.*]

CHAPTER IV

ADJUDICATIONS
Adjudication Panels

75 Adjudication Panels

[*This section creates Adjudication Panels for Wales.*]

Case tribunals and interim case tribunals

76–80

[*These sections cover procedure, decisions and recommendations.*]

CHAPTER V

SUPPLEMENTARY
Disclosure and registration of members' interests etc

81 Disclosure and registration of members' interests etc

(1) The monitoring officer of each relevant authority must establish and maintain a register of interests of the members and co-opted members of the authority.

(2) The mandatory provisions of the model code applicable to each relevant authority ('the mandatory provisions') must require the members and co-opted members of each authority to register in that authority's register maintained under subsection (1) such financial and other interests as are specified in the mandatory provisions.

(3) The mandatory provisions must also—

    (a) require any member or co-opted member of a relevant authority who has an interest specified in the mandatory provisions under subsection (2) to disclose that interest before taking part in any business of the authority relating to that interest,

    (b) make provision for preventing or restricting the participation of a member or co-opted member of a relevant authority in any business of the authority to which an interest disclosed under paragraph (a) relates.

(4) Any participation by a member or co-opted member of a relevant authority in any business which is prohibited by the mandatory provisions is not a failure to comply with the authority's code of conduct if the member or co-opted member has acted in accordance with a dispensation from the prohibition granted by the authority's standards committee in accordance with regulations made under subsection (5).

(5) The Welsh Ministers may prescribe in regulations the circumstances in which standards committees may grant dispensations under subsection (4).

(6) A relevant authority must ensure that copies of the register for the time being maintained by their monitoring officer under this section are available at an office of the authority for inspection by members of the public at all reasonable hours.

(7) As soon as practicable after the establishment by their monitoring officer of a register under this section, a relevant authority must—

    (a) publish in one or more newspapers circulating in their area a notice which—

        (i) states that copies of the register are available at an office of the authority for inspection by members of the public at all reasonable hours, and

        (ii) specifies the address of that office, and

    (b) ....

    (c) inform the Public Services Ombudsman for Wales that copies of the register are so available,

(8) ....

Code of conduct for local government employees

82 Code of conduct for local government employees

. . .

(2) The National Assembly for Wales may by order issue a code as regards the conduct which is expected of qualifying employees of relevant authorities.

(3) The power under subsection (2) to issue a code includes power—

    (a) to issue a separate code for council managers (within the meaning of Part II of this Act), and

  (b)   to revise any code which has been issued.

. . .

(6) Before making an order under this section, the National Assembly for Wales must consult—

  (a)   such representatives of relevant authorities and of employees of those authorities, as it considers appropriate,
  (b)   the Auditor General for Wales, and
  (c)   the Public Services Ombudsman for Wales.

(7) The terms of appointment or conditions of employment of every qualifying employee of a relevant authority (whether appointed or employed before or after the commencement of this section) are to be deemed to incorporate any code for the time being under this section which is applicable.

(8) In this section 'qualifying employee', in relation to a relevant authority, means an employee of the authority other than an employee falling within any description of employee specified in regulations under this subsection.

(9) The power to make regulations under subsection (8) is to be exercised—

  . . .

  (b)   by the National Assembly for Wales.

Interpretation

83 Interpretation of Part III

. . .

(5) Any reference in this Part to a joint committee or joint sub-committee of a relevant authority is a reference to a joint committee on which the authority is represented or a sub-committee of such a committee.

(6) Any reference in this Part to a failure to comply with a relevant authority's code of conduct includes a reference to a failure to comply with the mandatory provisions which apply to the members or co-opted members of the authority by virtue of section 51(5)(b).

(7) Any reference in this Part to a person being partially suspended from being a member or co-opted member of a relevant authority includes a reference to a person being prevented from exercising particular functions or having particular responsibilities as such a member or co-opted member.

(8) The reference in subsection (7) to particular functions or particular responsibilities as a member of a relevant authority, in the case of a relevant authority to which Part II of this Act applies, includes a reference to particular functions or particular responsibilities as a member of an executive of the authority.

(9) A person who is suspended under this Part from being a member of a relevant authority shall also be suspended from being a member of any committee, sub-committee, joint committee or joint sub-committee of the authority, but this subsection does not apply to a person who is partially suspended under this Part.

. . .

(11) A person who is disqualified under this Part for being or becoming a member of a relevant authority shall also be disqualified—

  (a)   for being or becoming a member of any committee, sub-committee, joint committee or joint sub-committee of the authority, . . .

. . .

(13) Any function which by virtue of this Part is exercisable by or in relation to the monitoring officer of a relevant authority which is a community council is to be exercisable by or in relation to the monitoring officer of the county council or county

borough council in whose area the community council is situated; and any reference in this Part to the moni toring officer of a relevant authority which is a community council is to be construed accordingly.

(14)   Any functions which are conferred by virtue of this Part on a relevant authority to which Part II of this Act applies are not to be the responsibility of an executive of the authority under executive arrangements.

. . .

PART IV

ELECTIONS

84 Meaning of 'local authority' and 'principal council' in Part IV

(1)   In relation to England—

    'local authority' means a principal council or a parish council,

    'principal council' means a county council, a district council or a London borough council.

(2)   In relation to Wales—

    'local authority' means a principal council or a community council,

    'principal council' means a county council or a county borough council.

(3)   This section applies for the purposes of this Part.

85 Options for elections

(1)   For the purposes of this Part the three options for the scheme for the ordinary elections of councillors of a principal council are those set out in this section.

(2)   The first option is for a scheme under which—

    (a)   the term of office of councillors is four years,

    (b)   the elections are held in a given year and every fourth year after it,

    (c)   all the councillors are elected in each year in which the elections are held, and

    (d)   the councillors retire together.

(3)   The second option is for a scheme under which—

    (a)   the term of office of councillors is four years,

    (b)   the elections are held in a given year and every second year after it,

    (c)   one half (or as nearly as may be) of the councillors are elected in each year in which the elections are held, and

    (d)   one half (or as nearly as may be) of the councillors retire in each year in which the elections are held.

(4)   The third option is for a scheme under which—

    (a)   the term of office of councillors is four years,

    (b)   the elections are held in a given year and every year after it other than every third year after it,

    (c)   one third (or as nearly as may be) of the councillors are elected in each year in which the elections are held, and

    (d)   one third (or as nearly as may be) of the councillors retire in each year in which the elections are held.

86 Power to specify a scheme for elections

(A1)   The Secretary of State may by order make provision to secure that the scheme for the ordinary elections of councillors of any specified council in England is the scheme under the first option set out in section 85.

(1)   The Secretary of State may by order make provision to secure that the scheme for the ordinary elections of councillors of any specified council in Wales is the scheme under such of the options set out in section 85 as is specified in the order.

(2)   A council is specified if it is—

    (a)   a principal council (or one of the principal councils) specified by name in the order, or

    (b)   a principal council falling within any description of principal council specified in the order.

(3)   An order may make provision in relation to a council if the scheme specified in the order is different from the scheme which prevails (whether by virtue of an earlier order under this section or otherwise) for the ordinary elections of its councillors.

(4)   An order may include provision specifying the years in which the ordinary elections are to be held.

(5)   In a case where the specified scheme is that under the second or third option, an order may include provision for identifying which councillors are to retire in a particular year, and such provision may include—

    (a)   provision for identifying the electoral divisions or wards affected,

    (b)   provision for identifying the councillors affected within particular electoral divisions or wards.

(6)   Provision under subsection (5) may include—

    (a)   provision allowing the Secretary of State to direct councils to propose methods (complying with any guidance he may issue) for identifying electoral divisions, wards or councillors,

    (b)   provision allowing him to give directions as to the methods to be adopted (whether those proposed or otherwise).

(7)   An order may include provision designed to secure the transition from a prevailing scheme to the one specified in the order, and such provision may include—

    (a)   provision to secure the retirement of existing councillors at times different from those applying under a prevailing scheme,

    (b)   in a case where the specified scheme is that under the second or third option, provision for the initial election of all the councillors, for the retirement of some of them before the end of the normal term of four years, and for identifying which of them are so to retire.

87 Power to change years in which elections held

(1)   The Secretary of State may by order make provision which changes the years in which the ordinary elections of councillors of any specified local authority are to be held but which does not change the scheme which prevails (whether by virtue of an order under section 86 or otherwise) for the ordinary elections of those councillors.

(2)   A local authority is specified if it is—

    (a)   a local authority (or one of the local authorities) specified by name in the order, or

    (b)   a local authority falling within any class or description of local authority specified in the order.

(3)   An order may include provision to secure the retirement of existing councillors at times different from those at which they would otherwise retire.

88 Separate power to make incidental provisions etc

(1)   If the Secretary of State makes an order under section 86 or 87 he may make a separate order containing such incidental, consequential, transitional or supplemental provision as could have been included in the order made under that section.

(2)   This applies whether or not the order under section 86 or 87 itself includes incidental, consequential, transitional or supplemental provision.

LOCAL GOVERNMENT ACT 2003

CHAPTER 1

CAPITAL FINANCE ETC
Borrowing

2 Control of borrowing

. . .

(3)   A local authority may not, without the consent of the Treasury, borrow otherwise than in sterling.

(4)   This section applies to borrowing under any power for the time being available to a local authority under any enactment, whenever passed.

6 Protection of lenders

A person lending money to a local authority shall not be bound to enquire whether the authority has power to borrow the money and shall not be prejudiced by the absence of any such power.

Capital receipts

9 'Capital receipt'

(1)   Subject to subsection (3), references in this Chapter to a capital receipt, in relation to a local authority, are to a sum received by the authority in respect of the disposal by it of an interest in a capital asset.

(2)   An asset is a capital asset for the purposes of subsection (1) if, at the time of the disposal, expenditure on the acquisition of the asset would be capital expenditure.

(3)   The Secretary of State may by regulations—

    (a)   make provision for the whole of a sum received by a local authority in respect of the disposal by it of an interest in a capital asset, or such part of such a sum as may be determined under the regulations, to be treated as not being a capital receipt for the purposes of this Chapter;

    (b)   make provision for the whole of a sum received by a local authority otherwise than in respect of the disposal by it of an interest in a capital asset, or such part of such a sum as may be determined under the regulations, to be treated as being a capital receipt for the purposes of this Chapter.

(4)   Where a sum becomes payable to a local authority before it is actually received by the authority, it shall be treated for the purposes of this section as received by the authority when it becomes payable to it.

10 Non-money receipts

(1)   The Secretary of State may by regulations apply section 9 to cases where—

    (a)   a local authority makes a disposal of the kind mentioned in subsection (1) of that section and the consideration for the disposal does not consist wholly of money payable to the authority, or

    (b)   a local authority receives otherwise than in the form of money anything which, if received in that form, would be a capital receipt under that section.

(2)   Regulations under subsection (1) may, in particular—

    (a)   make provision for a local authority to be treated as receiving a sum of such an amount as may be determined under the regulations;

(b)   make provision about when the deemed receipt is to be treated as taking place.

11 Use of capital receipts

(1) The Secretary of State may by regulations make provision about the use of capital receipts by a local authority.

(2) Regulations under subsection (1) may, in particular—

(a)   make provision requiring an amount equal to the whole or any part of a capital receipt to be used only to meet—

(i)   capital expenditure, or

(ii)   debts or other liabilities;

(b)   make provision requiring an amount equal to the whole or any part of a capital receipt to be paid to the Secretary of State.

(3) The power under subsection (1), so far as relating to provision of the kind mentioned in subsection (2)(b), shall only apply to receipts which a local authority derives from the disposal of an interest in housing land.

(4) The reference in subsection (3) to housing land is to any land, house or other building in relation to which the local authority is, or has been, subject to the duty under section 74 of the Local Government and Housing Act 1989 (c 42) (duty to keep Housing Revenue Account).

(5) Regulations under subsection (1) may include provision authorising the Secretary of State to set off any amount which an authority is liable to pay to him under this section against any amount which he is liable to pay to it.

Investment

12 Power to invest

A local authority may invest—

(a)   for any purpose relevant to its functions under any enactment, or

(b)   for the purposes of the prudent management of its financial affairs.

Miscellaneous

13 Security for money borrowed etc

(1) Except as provided by subsection (3), a local authority may not mortgage or charge any of its property as security for money which it has borrowed or which it otherwise owes.

(2) Security given in breach of subsection (1) shall be unenforceable.

(3) All money borrowed by a local authority (whether before or after the coming into force of this section), together with any interest on the money borrowed, shall be charged indifferently on all the revenues of the authority.

(4) All securities created by a local authority shall rank equally without any priority.

(5) The High Court may appoint a receiver on application by a person entitled to principal or interest due in respect of any borrowing by a local authority if the amount due remains unpaid for a period of two months after demand in writing.

(6) The High Court may appoint a receiver under subsection (5) on such terms, and confer on him such powers, as it thinks fit.

(7) The High Court may confer on a receiver appointed under subsection (5) any powers which the local authority has in relation to—

(a)   collecting, receiving or recovering the revenues of the local authority,

(b)   issuing levies or precepts, or

(c)   setting, collecting or recovering council tax.

(8)   No application under subsection (5) may be made unless the sum due in respect of the borrowing concerned amounts to not less than £10,000.

(9)   The Secretary of State may by order substitute a different sum for the one for the time being specified in subsection (8).

Supplementary

15 Guidance

(1)   In carrying out its functions under this Chapter, a local authority shall have regard—

> (a)   to such guidance as the Secretary of State may issue, and
>
> (b)   to such other guidance as the Secretary of State may by regulations specify for the purposes of this provision.

(2)   The power under subsection (1)(b) is not to be read as limited to the specification of existing guidance.

16 'Capital expenditure'

(1)   Subject to subsection (2), references in this Chapter to capital expenditure, in relation to a local authority, are to expenditure of the authority which falls to be capitalised in accordance with proper practices.

(2)   The Secretary of State may—

> (a)   by regulations provide that expenditure of local authorities shall be treated for the purposes of this Chapter as being, or as not being, capital expenditure;
>
> (b)   by direction provide that expenditure of a particular local authority shall be treated for the purposes of this Chapter as being, or as not being, capital expenditure.

17 External funds

(1)   For the purposes of this Chapter—

> (a)   borrowing of money by a local authority for the purposes of an external fund shall be treated as not being borrowing by the authority;
>
> (b)   the temporary use by a local authority of money forming part of an external fund, if not for a purpose of the fund, shall be treated as borrowing by the authority;
>
> (d)   a disposal by a local authority of—
>
> > (i)   an interest in an asset which, at the time of the disposal, is an asset of an external fund, or
> >
> > (ii)   an investment held for the purposes of such a fund,
>
> shall be treated as not being a disposal by the authority;
>
> (e)   the making of an investment by a local authority for the purposes of an external fund shall be treated as not being the making of an investment by the authority;
>
> (f)   expenditure incurred by a local authority in respect of payments out of an external fund shall be treated as not being expenditure of the authority.

(2)   In this section, references to an external fund, in relation to a local authority, are to—

> (a)   a superannuation fund which the authority is required to keep by virtue of the Superannuation Act 1972 (c 11), or
>
> (b)   a trust fund of which the authority is a trustee.

18 Local authority companies etc

(1)   The Secretary of State may, for the purposes of this Chapter, by regulations make provision for things done by or to a body mentioned in subsection (2) to be treated, in

such cases and to such extent as the regulations may provide, as done by or to a local authority specified in, or determined in accordance with, the regulations.

(2) Those bodies are—

    (a)   a Passenger Transport Executive,

    (b)   a company which, in accordance with Part 5 of the Local Government and Housing Act 1989 (c 42) (companies in which local authorities have interests), is under the control, or for the time being subject to the influence, of a local authority or a Passenger Transport Executive, and

    (c)   a trust to which the provisions of section 69 of that Act (companies subject to local authority influence) are applicable because of an order under section 72 of that Act (trusts influenced by local authorities).

(3) A local authority to which regulations under this section apply and any body or bodies falling within subsection (2)(a) or (b) with which the regulations link the authority are referred to in this section as the members of a local authority group.

(4) Regulations under this section may include—

    (a)   provision for the application of any of the provisions of this Chapter to members of a local authority group subject to such modifications as the regulations may specify;

    (b)   provision as to the way in which—

        (i)   dealings between members of a local authority group, or

        (ii)   changes in the capitalisation or capital structure of a company in a local authority group,

are to be brought into account for the purposes of this Chapter.

19 Application to parish and community councils

(1) In sections 2(3) and (4), 6, 9 to 13, 15, 16, 17(1)(a), (b) and (d) to (f) and (2) and 18, references to a local authority include a parish council, a community council and charter trustees.

(2) Schedule 1 (which makes provision about capital finance in relation to parish and community councils and charter trustees) has effect.

(3) The appropriate person may by regulations—

    (a)   apply any of the other provisions of this Chapter to parish or community councils or charter trustees, or parish or community councils or charter trustees of any description, with or without modifications, and

    (b)   make any corresponding disapplication of any of the provisions of Schedule 1.

SCHEDULE 1
CAPITAL FINANCE: PARISH AND COMMUNITY COUNCILS AND CHARTER TRUSTEES

Introductory

1

The following are local authorities for the purposes of this Schedule—

    (a)   a parish council;

    (b)   a community council;

    (c)   charter trustees.

Borrowing

2

(1) Subject to sub-paragraph (2), a local authority may borrow money—

    (a)   for any purpose relevant to its functions under any enactment, or

    (b)   for the purposes of the prudent management of its financial affairs.

(2)   A local authority may only borrow money (whether under sub-paragraph (1) or otherwise)—

    (a)   for a purpose or class of purpose approved for the purposes of this provision by the appropriate person, and

    (b)   in accordance with any conditions subject to which the approval is given.

(3)   Sub-paragraph (2) does not apply—

    (a)   to borrowing by way of temporary loan or overdraft from a bank or otherwise of sums which a local authority may temporarily require—

        (i)   for the purpose of meeting expenses pending the receipt of revenues receivable by it in respect of the period of account in which the expenses are chargeable, or

        (ii)   for the purpose of meeting expenses intended to be met by means of borrowing in accordance with approval under sub-paragraph (2), or

    (b)   to borrowing for the purpose of repaying money borrowed in accordance with approval under sub-paragraph (2), where the new borrowing takes place during the fixed period relating to the existing borrowing.

(4)   A local authority's functions under this paragraph shall be discharged only by the authority.

3

(1)   Where a local authority meets any expenditure by borrowing, it shall in each financial year debit the appropriate amount to the account from which that expenditure would otherwise fall to be met; but that duty shall not prevent the authority debiting a larger amount to that account.

(2)   The appropriate amount for the purposes of sub-paragraph (1) is a sum equivalent to an instalment of principal and interest combined such that if paid annually it would secure the payment of interest at the due rate on the outstanding principal together with the repayment of the principal not later than the end of the fixed period.

(3)   Sub-paragraph (1) has effect subject to sub-paragraph (4) if—

    (a)   a local authority makes an advance to any other person and the expenditure incurred in making the advance is met by borrowing, and

    (b)   the terms of that advance are such that repayment is to be made otherwise than by equal instalments of principal and interest combined.

(4)   The local authority may debit to the account from which the expenditure met by the borrowing would otherwise fall to be met sums of different amounts (whether or not including instalments of principal) in respect of different financial years in order to take account of the terms on which its advance falls to be repaid.

Loans

4

(1)   A local authority may lend to a qualifying local government body, on such terms as they may agree, such sums as the body may require for any purpose for which it is authorised by or under any enactment to borrow money.

(2)   In sub-paragraph (1), 'qualifying local government body' means a body with local government functions which is specified for the purposes of this paragraph by regulations made by the appropriate person.

'Fixed period'

5
In this Schedule, references to the fixed period, in relation to borrowing by a local authority, are to the period within which the money borrowed is to be repaid as determined by the local authority with the consent of the appropriate person.

PUBLIC AUDIT (WALES) ACT 2004

[*This Act makes effectively identical provision for the audit of accounts of local authorities in Wales as the Audit Commission Act 1998 does for local authorities in England.*]

PUBLIC SERVICES OMBUDSMAN (WALES) ACT 2005

PART 1

THE PUBLIC SERVICES OMBUDSMAN FOR WALES

1 The Public Services Ombudsman for Wales
(1) There is to be a Public Services Ombudsman for Wales or Ombwdsmon Gwasanaethau Cyhoeddus Cymru (in this Act referred to as 'the Ombudsman').
(2) Schedule 1 makes further provision about the Ombudsman.

PART 2

INVESTIGATION OF COMPLAINTS

Power of investigation

2 Power of investigation
(1) The Ombudsman may investigate a complaint in respect of a matter if—
    (a) the complaint has been duly made or referred to him, and
    (b) the matter is one which he is entitled to investigate under sections 7 to 11.
(2) A complaint is 'duly made' to the Ombudsman if (but only if)—
    (a) it is made by a person who is entitled under section 4 to make the complaint to the Ombudsman, and
    (b) the requirements of section 5 are met in respect of it.
(3) A complaint is 'duly referred' to the Ombudsman if (but only if)—
    (a) it is referred to him by a listed authority, and
    (b) the requirements of section 6 are met in respect of it.
(4) The Ombudsman may investigate a complaint in respect of a matter even if the requirements of section 5(1) or (as the case may be) section 6(1)(b) or (d) are not met in respect of the complaint, if—
    (a) the matter is one which he is entitled to investigate under sections 7 to 11, and
    (b) he thinks it reasonable to do so.
(5) It is for the Ombudsman to decide whether to begin, continue or discontinue an investigation.

(6) The Ombudsman may take any action which he thinks may assist in making a decision under subsection (5).

(7) The Ombudsman may begin or continue an investigation into a complaint even if the complaint, or the referral of the complaint, has been withdrawn.

3 Alternative resolution of complaints

(1) The Ombudsman may take any action he thinks appropriate with a view to resolving a complaint which he has power to investigate under section 2.

(2) The Ombudsman may take action under this section in addition to or instead of conducting an investigation into the complaint.

(3) Any action under this section must be taken in private.

Complaints

4 Who can complain

(1) The persons entitled to make a complaint to the Ombudsman are—
- (a) a member of the public (in this Act referred to as 'the person aggrieved') who claims or claimed to have sustained injustice or hardship in consequence of a matter which the Ombudsman is entitled to investigate under sections 7 to 11;
- (b) a person authorised by the person aggrieved to act on his behalf;
- (c) if the person aggrieved is not capable of authorising a person to act on his behalf (for example because he has died), a person who appears to the Ombudsman to be appropriate to act on behalf of the person aggrieved.

(2) 'Member of the public' means any person other than a listed authority acting in its capacity as such.

(3) It is for the Ombudsman to determine any question of whether a person is entitled under this section to make a complaint to him.

5 Requirements: complaints made to the Ombudsman

(1) The requirements mentioned in section 2(2)(b) are that—
- (a) the complaint must be made in writing;
- (b) the complaint must be made to the Ombudsman before the end of the period of one year starting on the day on which the person aggrieved first has notice of the matters alleged in the complaint.

(2) It is for the Ombudsman to determine any question of whether the requirements of subsection (1) are met in respect of a complaint.

6 Requirements: complaints referred to the Ombudsman

(1) The requirements mentioned in section 2(3)(b) are that—
- (a) the complaint must have been made to the listed authority by a person who would have been entitled under section 4 to make the complaint to the Ombudsman;
- (b) the complaint must have been made to the listed authority before the end of the period of one year starting on the day on which the person aggrieved first had notice of the matters alleged in the complaint;
- (c) the complaint must be referred to the Ombudsman in writing;
- (d) the complaint must be referred to the Ombudsman before the end of the period of one year starting on the day on which the complaint was made to the listed authority.

(2) It is for the Ombudsman to determine any question of whether the requirements of subsection (1) are met in respect of a complaint.

Matters which may be investigated

7 Matters which may be investigated

(1) The matters which the Ombudsman is entitled to investigate are—
- (a) alleged maladministration by a listed authority in connection with relevant action;
- (b) an alleged failure in a relevant service provided by a listed authority;
- (c) an alleged failure by a listed authority to provide a relevant service.

(2) Subsection (1) is subject to sections 8 to 11.

(3) Relevant action is—
- (a) in the case of a listed authority which is a family health service provider in Wales or an independent provider in Wales, action taken by the authority in connection with the provision of a relevant service;
- (b) in the case of a listed authority which is a social landlord in Wales or a Welsh health service body other than the Assembly, action taken by the authority in the discharge of any of its functions;
- (c) in the case of a listed authority which is a person with functions conferred by regulations made under section 113(2) of the Health and Social Care (Community Health and Standards) Act 2003 (c 43), action taken by the authority in the discharge of any of those functions;
- (d) in the case of a listed authority which is a listed authority by virtue of an order under section 28(2) adding it to Schedule 3, action taken by the authority in the discharge of any of its specified functions;
- (e) in any other case, action taken by the authority in the discharge of any of its administrative functions.

(4) A relevant service is—
- (a) in the case of a listed authority which is a family health service provider in Wales, any of the family health services which the authority had, at the time of the action which is the subject of the complaint, entered into a contract, undertaken, or made arrangements, to provide;
- (b) in the case of a listed authority which is an independent provider in Wales, any service which the authority had, at that time, made arrangements with a Welsh health service body or a family health service provider in Wales to provide;
- (c) in the case of a listed authority falling within subsection (3)(c), any service which it was, at that time, the authority's function to provide in the discharge of any of the functions mentioned in that paragraph;
- (d) in the case of a listed authority falling within subsection (3)(d), any service which it was, at that time, the authority's function to provide in the discharge of any of its specified functions;
- (e) in any other case, any service which it was, at that time, the authority's function to provide.

(5) For the purposes of subsections (3)(d) and (4)(d), a listed authority's specified functions are the functions specified in relation to the authority in an order under section 28(2) as falling within the Ombudsman's remit.

(6) An administrative function which may be discharged by a person who is a member of the administrative staff of a relevant tribunal is to be treated as an administrative function of a listed authority for the purposes of subsection (3) if—
- (a) the person was appointed by the authority, or
- (b) the person was appointed with the consent of the authority (whether as to remuneration and other terms and conditions of service or otherwise).

8 Exclusion: matters not relating to Wales

(1) The Ombudsman may not investigate a matter arising in connection with the discharge by a listed authority of any of the authority's functions otherwise than in relation to Wales.

(2) Subsection (1) does not apply in relation to the Welsh Assembly Government.

(3) To the extent that a function of a listed authority is discharged in relation to the Welsh language or any other aspect of Welsh culture, it is to be regarded for the purposes of subsection (1) as discharged in relation to Wales.

9 Exclusion: other remedies

(1) The Ombudsman may not investigate a matter if the person aggrieved has or had—

>   (a)   a right of appeal, reference or review to or before a tribunal constituted under an enactment or by virtue of Her Majesty's prerogative,

>   (b)   a right of appeal to a Minister of the Crown, the Welsh Ministers, the First Minister for Wales or the Counsel General to the Welsh Assembly Government, or

>   (c)   a remedy by way of proceedings in a court of law.

(2) But subsection (1) does not apply if the Ombudsman is satisfied that, in the particular circumstances, it is not reasonable to expect the person to resort, or to have resorted, to the right or remedy.

(3) The Ombudsman may investigate a matter only if he is satisfied that—

>   (a)   the matter has been brought to the attention of the listed authority to which it relates by or on behalf of the person aggrieved, and

>   (b)   the authority has been given a reasonable opportunity to investigate and respond to it.

(4) But subsection (3) does not prevent the Ombudsman from investigating a matter if he is satisfied that it is reasonable in the particular circumstances for him to investigate the matter despite the fact that the requirements of that subsection have not been met.

10 Other excluded matters

(1) The Ombudsman may not investigate a matter specified in Schedule 2.

(2) The Welsh Ministers may by order amend Schedule 2 by—

>   (a)   adding an entry;

>   (b)   removing an entry;

>   (c)   changing an entry.

(3) Before making an order under subsection (2), the Assembly must consult the Ombudsman.

(3A) No order is to be made under subsection (2) unless a draft of the statutory instrument containing it has been laid before, and approved by a resolution of, the Assembly.

(4) Subsection (1) does not prevent the Ombudsman from investigating action of a listed authority in operating a procedure established to examine complaints or review decisions.

11 Decisions taken without maladministration

(1) The Ombudsman may not question the merits of a decision taken without maladministration by a listed authority in the exercise of a discretion.

(2) Subsection (1) does not apply to the merits of a decision to the extent that the decision was taken in consequence of the exercise of professional judgement which appears to the Ombudsman to be exercisable in connection with the provision of health or social care.

28 Listed authorities

(1)   The persons specified in Schedule 3 are listed authorities for the purposes of this Act.

(2)   The Welsh Ministers may by order amend Schedule 3 by—

(a)   adding a person;

(b)   omitting a person;

(c)   changing the description of a person.

(3)   An order under subsection (2) adding a person to Schedule 3 may provide for this Act to apply to the person with the modifications specified in the order.

(4)   Before making an order under subsection (2), the Welsh Ministers must consult the Ombudsman and any other persons it thinks appropriate.

(4A)   No order is to be made under subsection (2) unless a draft of the statutory instrument containing it has been laid before, and approved by a resolution of, the Assembly.

(5)   Sections 29 and 30 contain further restrictions on the power in subsection (2).

29 Restrictions on power to amend Schedule 3

(1)   An order under section 28(2) may not omit the Welsh Assembly Government or the National Assembly for Wales Commission from Schedule 3.

(2)   An order under section 28(2) may add a person to Schedule 3 only if—

(a)   the person has functions dischargeable in relation to Wales or a part of Wales (whether or not the functions are also dischargeable otherwise than in relation to Wales),

(b)   all or some of the person's functions are in a field in which the Welsh Ministers have, or the First Minister for Wales or the Counsel General to the Welsh Assembly Government has, functions, and

(c)   the person falls within subsection (3), (4) or (5).

(3)   A person falls within this subsection if—

(a)   it is a body established by or under an enactment or by virtue of Her Majesty's prerogative or in any other way by a Minister of the Crown, a government department, the Welsh Ministers, the First Minister for Wales, the Counsel General to the Welsh Assembly Government or another listed authority,

(b)   it is a body wholly or partly constituted by appointment made by Her Majesty, a Minister of the Crown, a government department, the Welsh Ministers, the First Minister for Wales, the Counsel General to the Welsh Assembly Government or another listed authority, and

(c)   at least half of its expenditure on the discharge of its functions in relation to Wales is met out of the Welsh Consolidated Fund or is met directly from payments made by other listed authorities.

(4)   A person falls within this subsection if—

(a)   it is a body established by or under an enactment, and

(b)   it has power to issue a precept or a levy.

(5)   A person falls within this subsection if—

(a)   it appears to the Welsh Ministers that the person discharges functions of a public nature, and

(b)   at least half of the person's expenditure on the discharge of those functions in relation to Wales is met out of the Welsh Consolidated Fund or directly or indirectly from payments made by other listed authorities.

(6)   An order under section 28(2) may not add to Schedule 3—

(a)   a Special Health Authority discharging functions only or mainly in England;

(b)   a person who carries on under national ownership an industry or undertaking or part of an industry or undertaking.

30 Provisions in orders adding persons to Schedule 3

(1)   If the Welsh Ministers propose to make an order under section 28(2) adding a person to Schedule 3, they must also specify in the order—

(a)   whether all or only some of the person's functions are to fall within the remit of the Ombudsman under this Part;

(b)   if only some of the person's functions are to fall within the remit of the Ombudsman under this Part, which those functions are.

(2)   If the person is to be added to Schedule 3 on the basis that the person falls within section 29(3) or (4), the order may specify a function under subsection (1) only if the function is in a field in which the Welsh Ministers have, or the First Minister for Wales or the Counsel General to the Welsh Assembly Government has, functions.

(3)   If the person is to be added to Schedule 3 on the basis that the person falls within section 29(5), the order may specify a function under subsection (1) only if—

(a)   the function is in a field in which the Welsh Ministers have, or the First Minister for Wales or the Counsel General to the Welsh Assembly Government has, functions, and

(b)   the function appears to the Welsh Ministers to be a function of a public nature.

(4)   The order may specify all a person's functions under subsection (1) only if all the person's functions satisfy the requirements of subsection (2) or (as the case may be) subsection (3).

Miscellaneous

31 Power to issue guidance

(1)   The Ombudsman may issue to one or more listed authorities such guidance about good administrative practice as he thinks appropriate.

(2)   Before issuing guidance under this section the Ombudsman must consult such listed authorities, or persons appearing to him to represent them, as he thinks appropriate.

(3)   If guidance issued under this section is applicable to a listed authority, the authority must have regard to the guidance in discharging its functions.

(4)   In conducting an investigation in respect of a listed authority, the Ombudsman may have regard to the extent to which the authority has complied with any guidance issued under this section which is applicable to the authority.

(5)   The Ombudsman may publish any guidance issued under this section in any manner that he thinks appropriate, including in particular by putting the guidance in an annual or extraordinary report.

(6)   Guidance issued under this section may contain different provision for different purposes.

(7)   Subject to subsection (8), guidance issued under this section must not—

(a)   mention the name of any person other than the listed authorities to which it is applicable or a listed authority in respect of which a complaint has been made or referred to the Ombudsman under this Act, or

(b)   include any particulars which, in the opinion of the Ombudsman, are likely to identify any such person and which, in his opinion, can be omitted without impairing the effectiveness of the guidance.

(8)   Subsection (7) does not apply if, after taking account of the interests of any persons he thinks appropriate, the Ombudsman considers it to be in the public interest to include that information in the guidance.

PART 3

MISCELLANEOUS AND GENERAL

Conduct of local government members and employees

35 Conduct of local government members and employees
Schedule 4 (which confers functions on the Ombudsman in relation to the conduct of local government members and employees) has effect.

Abolition of existing bodies and offices

36 Abolition of existing bodies and offices
(1)   The Commission for Local Administration in Wales is abolished.
(2)   The office of Welsh Administration Ombudsman is abolished.
(3)   The office of Health Service Commissioner for Wales is abolished.
(4)   The office of Social Housing Ombudsman for Wales is abolished.

General

41 Interpretation
(1)   In this Act—
      . . .
      'local authority in Wales' means a county council, county borough council or community council in Wales;
      . . .

SCHEDULE 3
LISTED AUTHORITIES

Local government, fire and police

. . .

A local authority in Wales.
. . .

CLEAN NEIGHBOURHOODS AND ENVIRON-MENT ACT 2005

PART 6

DOGS

CHAPTER 1

CONTROLS ON DOGS
Dog control orders

55 Power to make dog control orders

(1)   A primary or secondary authority may in accordance with this Chapter make an order providing for an offence or offences relating to the control of dogs in respect of any land in its area to which this Chapter applies.

(2)   An order under subsection (1) is to be known as a 'dog control order'.

(3)   For the purposes of this Chapter an offence relates to the control of dogs if it relates to one of the following matters—

   (a)   fouling of land by dogs and the removal of dog faeces;
   (b)   the keeping of dogs on leads;
   (c)   the exclusion of dogs from land;
   (d)   the number of dogs which a person may take on to any land.

(4)   An offence provided for in a dog control order must be an offence which is prescribed for the purposes of this section by regulations made by the appropriate person.

(5)   Regulations under subsection (4) may in particular—

   (a)   specify all or part of the wording to be used in a dog control order for the purpose of providing for any offence;
   (b)   permit a dog control order to specify the times at which, or periods during which, an offence is to apply;
   (c)   provide for an offence to be defined by reference to failure to comply with the directions of a person of a description specified in the regulations.

(6)   A dog control order may specify the land in respect of which it applies specifically or by description.

(7)   A dog control order may be revoked or amended by the authority which made it; but this Chapter applies in relation to any amendment of a dog control order as if it were the making of a new order.

56 Dog control orders: supplementary

(1)   The appropriate person must by regulations prescribe the penalties, or maximum penalties, which may be provided for in a dog control order in relation to any offence.

(2)   Regulations under subsection (1) may not in any case permit a dog control order to provide for a penalty other than a fine not exceeding level 3 on the standard scale in relation to any offence.

(3)   The appropriate person must by regulations prescribe such other requirements relating to the content and form of a dog control order as the appropriate person thinks fit.

(4)   The appropriate person must by regulations prescribe the procedure to be followed by a primary or secondary authority before and after making a dog control order.

(5)   Regulations under subsection (4) must in particular include provision as to—

   (a)   consultation to be undertaken before a dog control order is made;

(b)   the publicising of a dog control order after it has been made.

57 Land to which Chapter 1 applies

(1)   Subject to this section, this Chapter applies to any land which is open to the air and to which the public are entitled or permitted to have access (with or without payment).

(2)   For the purposes of this section, any land which is covered is to be treated as land which is 'open to the air' if it is open to the air on at least one side.

(3)   The appropriate person may by order designate land as land to which this Chapter does not apply (generally or for such purposes as may be specified in the order).

(4)   Land may be designated under subsection (3) specifically or by description.

(5)   Where a private Act confers powers on a person other than a primary or secondary authority for the regulation of any land, that person may, by notice in writing given to the primary and secondary authorities in whose area the land is situated, exclude the application of this Chapter to that land.

58 Primary and secondary authorities

(1)   Each of the following is a 'primary authority' for the purposes of this Chapter—
    (a)   a district council in England;
    (b)   a county council in England for an area for which there is no district council;
    (c)   a London borough council;
    (d)   the Common Council of the City of London;
    (e)   the Council of the Isles of Scilly;
    (f)   a county or county borough council in Wales.

(2)   Each of the following is a 'secondary authority' for the purposes of this Chapter—
    (a)   a parish council in England;
    (b)   a community council in Wales.

(3)   The appropriate person may by order designate any person or body exercising functions under an enactment as a secondary authority for the purposes of this Chapter in respect of an area specified in the order.

Fixed penalty notices

59 Fixed penalty notices

(1)   This section applies where on any occasion—
    (a)   an authorised officer of a primary or secondary authority has reason to believe that a person has committed an offence under a dog control order made by that authority; or
    (b)   an authorised officer of a secondary authority has reason to believe that a person has in its area committed an offence under a dog control order made by a primary authority.

(2)   The authorised officer may give that person a notice offering him the opportunity of discharging any liability to conviction for the offence by payment of a fixed penalty.

(3)   A fixed penalty payable under this section is payable to the primary or secondary authority whose officer gave the notice.

(4)   Where a person is given a notice under this section in respect of an offence—
    (a)   no proceedings may be instituted for that offence before the expiration of the period of fourteen days following the date of the notice; and
    (b)   he may not be convicted of that offence if he pays the fixed penalty before the expiration of that period.

(5) A notice under this section must give such particulars of the circumstances alleged to constitute the offence as are necessary for giving reasonable information of the offence.

(6) A notice under this section must also state—

    (a)   the period during which, by virtue of subsection (4), proceedings will not be taken for the offence;

    (b)   the amount of the fixed penalty; and

    (c)   the person to whom and the address at which the fixed penalty may be paid.

(7) Without prejudice to payment by any other method, payment of the fixed penalty may be made by pre-paying and posting a letter containing the amount of the penalty (in cash or otherwise) to the person mentioned in subsection (6)(c) at the address so mentioned.

(8) Where a letter is sent in accordance with subsection (7) payment is to be regarded as having been made at the time at which that letter would be delivered in the ordinary course of post.

(9) The form of a notice under this section is to be such as the appropriate person may by order prescribe.

(10) In any proceedings a certificate which—

    (a)   purports to be signed on behalf of the chief finance officer of a primary or secondary authority, and

    (b)   states that payment of a fixed penalty was or was not received by a date specified in the certificate,

is evidence of the facts stated.

(11) In this section—

    'authorised officer', in relation to a primary or secondary authority, means—

        (a)   an employee of the authority who is authorised in writing by the authority for the purpose of giving notices under this section;

        (b)   any person who, in pursuance of arrangements made with the authority, has the function of giving such notices and is authorised in writing by the authority to perform that function; and

        (c)   any employee of such a person who is authorised in writing by the authority for the purpose of giving such notices;

    'chief finance officer', in relation to a primary or secondary authority, means the person having responsibility for the financial affairs of the authority.

(12) The appropriate person may by regulations prescribe conditions to be satisfied by a person before a secondary authority may authorise him in writing for the purpose of giving notices under this section.

60 Amount of fixed penalties

(1) The amount of a fixed penalty payable to a primary or secondary authority in pursuance of a notice under section 59 in respect of an offence under a dog control order—

    (a)   is the amount specified by the authority which made the order;

    (b)   if no amount is so specified, is £75.

(2) A primary or secondary authority may under subsection (1)(a) specify different amounts in relation to different offences.

(3) A primary or secondary authority may make provision for treating a fixed penalty payable to that authority in pursuance of a notice under section 59 as having been paid if a lesser amount is paid before the end of a period specified by the authority.

(4) The appropriate person may by regulations make provision in connection with the powers conferred on primary and secondary authorities under subsections (1)(a) and (3).

(5) Regulations under subsection (4) may (in particular)—

(a) require an amount specified under subsection (1)(a) to fall within a range prescribed in the regulations;

(b) restrict the extent to which, and the circumstances in which, a primary or secondary authority can make provision under subsection (3).

(6) The appropriate person may by order substitute a different amount for the amount for the time being specified in subsection (1)(b).

61 Power to require name and address

(1) If an authorised officer of a primary or secondary authority proposes to give a person a notice under section 59, the officer may require the person to give him his name and address.

(2) A person commits an offence if—

(a) he fails to give his name and address when required to do so under subsection (1), or

(b) he gives a false or inaccurate name or address in response to a requirement under that subsection.

(3) A person guilty of an offence under subsection (2) is liable on summary conviction to a fine not exceeding level 3 on the standard scale.

(4) In this section 'authorised officer' has the same meaning as in section 59.

Supplementary

63 Overlapping powers

(1) Where a primary authority makes a dog control order providing for an offence relating to a matter specified in any of paragraphs (a) to (d) of section 55(3) as respects any land—

(a) a secondary authority may not make a dog control order providing for any offence which relates to the matter specified in that paragraph as respects that land;

(b) any dog control order previously made by a secondary authority providing for any offence which relates to the matter specified in that paragraph shall, to the extent that it so provides, cease to have effect.

(2) Where the area of an authority designated as a secondary authority under section 58(3) is to any extent the same as that of a parish or community council, subsection (1) applies in relation to orders made by the designated authority and that council as if the council were a primary authority.

64 Byelaws

(1) Where, apart from this subsection, a primary or secondary authority has at any time power to make a byelaw in relation to any matter specified in any of paragraphs (a) to (d) of section 55(3) as respects any land, it may not make such a byelaw if at that time it has power under this Chapter to make a dog control order as respects that land in relation to the matter specified in that paragraph.

(2) Subsection (1) does not affect any byelaw which the authority had power to make at the time it was made.

(3) Where a dog control order is made in relation to any matter specified in any of paragraphs (a) to (d) of section 55(3) as respects any land, any byelaw previously made by a primary or secondary authority which has the effect of making a person guilty of any offence in relation to the matter specified in that paragraph as respects that land shall cease to have that effect.

(4) Where any act or omission would, apart from this subsection, constitute an offence under a dog control order and any byelaw, the act or omission shall not constitute an offence under the byelaw.

65 Dogs (Fouling of Land) Act 1996
The Dogs (Fouling of Land) Act 1996 (c 20) shall cease to have effect.

NATURAL ENVIRONMENT AND RURAL COMMUNITIES ACT 2006

PART 6

RIGHTS OF WAY

Rights of way and mechanically propelled vehicles

66 Restriction on creation of new public rights of way
(1) No public right of way for mechanically propelled vehicles is created after commencement unless it is—

(a) created (by an enactment or instrument or otherwise) on terms that expressly provide for it to be a right of way for such vehicles, or

(b) created by the construction, in exercise of powers conferred by virtue of any enactment, of a road intended to be used by such vehicles.

(2) For the purposes of the creation after commencement of any other public right of way, use (whenever occurring) of a way by mechanically propelled vehicles is to be disregarded.

67 Ending of certain existing unrecorded public rights of way
(1) An existing public right of way for mechanically propelled vehicles is extinguished if it is over a way which, immediately before commencement—

(a) was not shown in a definitive map and statement, or

(b) was shown in a definitive map and statement only as a footpath, bridleway or restricted byway.

But this is subject to subsections (2) to (8).

(2) Subsection (1) does not apply to an existing public right of way if—

(a) it is over a way whose main lawful use by the public during the period of 5 years ending with commencement was use for mechanically propelled vehicles,

(b) immediately before commencement it was not shown in a definitive map and statement but was shown in a list required to be kept under section 36(6) of the Highways Act 1980 (c 66) (list of highways maintainable at public expense),

(c) it was created (by an enactment or instrument or otherwise) on terms that expressly provide for it to be a right of way for mechanically propelled vehicles,

(d) it was created by the construction, in exercise of powers conferred by virtue of any enactment, of a road intended to be used by such vehicles, or

(e) it was created by virtue of use by such vehicles during a period ending before 1st December 1930.

(3) Subsection (1) does not apply to an existing public right of way over a way if—

(a) before the relevant date, an application was made under section 53(5) of the Wildlife and Countryside Act 1981 (c 69) for an order making modifications to the definitive map and statement so as to show the way as a byway open to all traffic,

697

    (b)   before commencement, the surveying authority has made a determination under paragraph 3 of Schedule 14 to the 1981 Act in respect of such an application, or

    (c)   before commencement, a person with an interest in land has made such an application and, immediately before commencement, use of the way for mechanically propelled vehicles—

        (i)   was reasonably necessary to enable that person to obtain access to the land, or

        (ii)   would have been reasonably necessary to enable that person to obtain access to a part of that land if he had had an interest in that part only.

(4) 'The relevant date' means—

    (a)   in relation to England, 20th January 2005;

    (b)   in relation to Wales, 19th May 2005.

(5) Where, immediately before commencement, the exercise of an existing public right of way to which subsection (1) applies—

    (a)   was reasonably necessary to enable a person with an interest in land to obtain access to the land, or

    (b)   would have been reasonably necessary to enable that person to obtain access to a part of that land if he had had an interest in that part only,

the right becomes a private right of way for mechanically propelled vehicles for the benefit of the land or (as the case may be) the part of the land.

(6) For the purposes of subsection (3), an application under section 53(5) of the 1981 Act is made when it is made in accordance with paragraph 1 of Schedule 14 to that Act.

(7) For the purposes of subsections (3)(c)(i) and (5)(a), it is irrelevant whether the person was, immediately before commencement, in fact—

    (a)   exercising the existing public right of way, or

    (b)   able to exercise it.

(8) Nothing in this section applies in relation to an area in London to which Part 3 of the Wildlife and Countryside Act 1981 (c 69) does not apply.

(9) Any provision made by virtue of section 48(9) of the Countryside and Rights of Way Act 2000 (c 37) has effect subject to this section.

COMMONS ACT 2006

PART 1

REGISTRATION

Introductory

1 Registers of common land and greens

Each commons registration authority shall continue to keep—

    (a)   a register known as a register of common land; and

    (b)   a register known as a register of town or village greens.

2 Purpose of registers

(1) The purpose of a register of common land is—

    (a)   to register land as common land; and

    (b)   to register rights of common exercisable over land registered as common land.

(2)   The purpose of a register of town or village greens is—

    (a)   to register land as a town or village green; and

    (b)   to register rights of common exercisable over land registered as a town or village green.

3 Content of registers

(1)   The land registered as common land in a register of common land is, subject to this Part, to be—

    (a)   the land so registered in it at the commencement of this section; and

    (b)   such other land as may be so registered in it under this Part.

(2)   The land registered as a town or village green in a register of town or village greens is, subject to this Part, to be—

    (a)   the land so registered in it at the commencement of this section; and

    (b)   such other land as may be so registered in it under this Part.

(3)   The rights of common registered in a register of common land or town or village greens are, subject to this Part, to be—

    (a)   the rights registered in it at the commencement of this section; and

    (b)   such other rights as may be so registered in it under this Part.

(4)   The following information is to be registered in a register of common land or town or village greens in respect of a right of common registered in it—

    (a)   the nature of the right;

    (b)   if the right is attached to any land, the land to which it is attached;

    (c)   if the right is not so attached, the owner of the right.

(5)   Regulations may—

    (a)   require or permit other information to be included in a register of common land or town or village greens;

    (b)   make provision as to the form in which any information is to be presented in such a register.

(6)   Except as provided under this Part or any other enactment—

    (a)   no land registered as common land or as a town or village green is to be removed from the register in which it is so registered;

    (b)   no right of common registered in a register of common land or town or village greens is to be removed from that register.

(7)   No right of common over land to which this Part applies is to be registered in the register of title.

4 Commons registration authorities

(1)   The following are commons registration authorities—

    (a)   a county council in England;

    (b)   a district council in England for an area without a county council;

    (c)   a London borough council; and

    (d)   a county or county borough council in Wales.

(2)   For the purposes of this Part, the commons registration authority in relation to any land is the authority in whose area the land is situated.

(3)   Where any land falls within the area of two or more commons registration authorities, the authorities may by agreement provide for one of them to be the commons registration authority in relation to the whole of the land.

5 Land to which Part 1 applies

(1)   This Part applies to all land in England and Wales, subject as follows.

(2)   This Part does not apply to—

    (a)   the New Forest; or

    (b)   Epping Forest.

(3)   This Part shall not be taken to apply to the Forest of Dean.

(4) If any question arises under this Part whether any land is part of the forests mentioned in this section it is to be referred to and decided by the appropriate national authority.

Registration of rights of common

6 Creation

(1) A right of common cannot at any time after the commencement of this section be created over land to which this Part applies by virtue of prescription.

(2) A right of common cannot at any time after the commencement of this section be created in any other way over land to which this Part applies except—

    (a)   as specified in subsection (3); or

    (b)   pursuant to any other enactment.

(3) A right of common may be created over land to which this Part applies by way of express grant if—

    (a)   the land is not registered as a town or village green; and

    (b)   the right is attached to land.

(4) The creation of a right of common in accordance with subsection (3) only has effect if it complies with such requirements as to form and content as regulations may provide.

(5) The creation of a right of common in accordance with subsection (3) does not operate at law until on an application under this section—

    (a)   the right is registered in a register of common land; and

    (b)   if the right is created over land not registered as common land, the land is registered in a register of common land.

(6) An application under this section to register the creation of a right of common consisting of a right to graze any animal is to be refused if in the opinion of the commons registration authority the land over which it is created would be unable to sustain the exercise of—

    (a)   that right; and

    (b)   if the land is already registered as common land, any other rights of common registered as exercisable over the land.

7 Variation

(1) For the purposes of this section a right of common is varied if by virtue of any disposition—

    (a)   the right becomes exercisable over new land to which this Part applies instead of all or part of the land over which it was exercisable;

    (b)   the right becomes exercisable over new land to which this Part applies in addition to the land over which it is already exercisable;

    (c)   there is any other alteration in what can be done by virtue of the right.

(2) A right of common which is registered in a register of common land or town or village greens cannot at any time after the commencement of this section be varied so as to become exercisable over new land if that land is at the time registered as a town or village green.

(3) A right of common which is registered in a register of town or village greens cannot at any time after the commencement of this section be varied so as to extend what can be done by virtue of the right.

(4) The variation of a right of common which is registered in a register of common land or town or village greens—

    (a)   only has effect if it complies with such requirements as to form and content as regulations may provide; and

    (b)   does not operate at law until, on an application under this section, the register is amended so as to record the variation.

(5)   An application under this section to record a variation of a right of common consisting of a right to graze any animal is to be refused if in the opinion of the commons registration authority the land over which the right is or is to be exercisable would, in consequence of the variation, be unable to sustain the exercise of—

   (a)   that right; and

   (b)   if the land is already registered as common land, any other rights of common registered as exercisable over the land.

8 Apportionment

(1)   Regulations may make provision as to the amendments to be made to a register of common land or town or village greens where a right of common which is registered in a register of common land or town or village greens as attached to any land is apportioned by virtue of any disposition affecting the land.

(2)   Regulations under subsection (1) may provide that a register is only to be amended when—

   (a)   a disposition relating to an apportioned right itself falls to be registered under this Part; or

   (b)   the register falls to be amended under section 11.

(3)   Where at any time—

   (a)   a right of common which is registered in a register of common land or town or village greens as attached to any land has been apportioned by virtue of any disposition affecting the land, and

   (b)   no amendments have been made under subsection (1) in respect of the apportionment of that right,

the rights of common subsisting as a result of the apportionment shall be regarded as rights which are registered in that register as attached to the land to which they attach as a result of the apportionment.

9 Severance

(1)   This section applies to a right of common which—

   (a)   is registered in a register of common land or town or village greens as attached to any land; and

   (b)   would, apart from this section, be capable of being severed from that land.

(2)   A right of common to which this section applies is not at any time on or after the day on which this section comes into force capable of being severed from the land to which it is attached, except—

   (a)   where the severance is authorised by or under Schedule 1; or

   (b)   where the severance is authorised by or under any other Act.

(3)   Where any instrument made on or after the day on which this section comes into force would effect a disposition in relation to a right of common to which this section applies in contravention of subsection (2), the instrument is void to the extent that it would effect such a disposition.

(4)   Where by virtue of any instrument made on or after the day on which this section comes into force—

   (a)   a disposition takes effect in relation to land to which a right of common to which this section applies is attached, and

   (b)   the disposition would have the effect of contravening subsection (2),

the disposition also has effect in relation to the right notwithstanding anything in the instrument to the contrary.

(5)   Where by virtue of any instrument made on or after the day on which this section comes into force a right of common to which this section applies falls to be apportioned between different parts of the land to which it is attached, the instrument is void to the extent that it purports to apportion the right otherwise than rateably.

(6)   Nothing in this section affects any instrument made before, or made pursuant to a contract made in writing before, the day on which this section comes into force.

(7)   This section and Schedule 1 shall be deemed to have come into force on 28 June 2005 (and an order under paragraph 2 of that Schedule may have effect as from that date).

10 Attachment

(1)   This section applies to any right of common which is registered in a register of common land or town or village greens but is not registered as attached to any land.

(2)   The owner of the right may apply to the commons registration authority for the right to be registered in that register as attached to any land, provided that—

(a)   he is entitled to occupy the land; or

(b)   the person entitled to occupy the land has consented to the application.

11 Re-allocation of attached rights

(1)   Where—

(a)   a right of common is registered in a register of common land or town or village greens as attached to any land, and

(b)   subsection (2), (3) or (4) applies in relation to part of the land ('the relevant part'),

the owner of the land may apply to the commons registration authority for the register to be amended so as to secure that the right does not attach to the relevant part.

(2)   This subsection applies where the relevant part is not used for agricultural purposes.

(3)   This subsection applies where planning permission has been granted for use of the relevant part for purposes which are not agricultural purposes.

(4)   This subsection applies where—

(a)   an order authorising the compulsory purchase of the relevant part by any authority has been made in accordance with the Acquisition of Land Act 1981 (c 67) (and, if the order requires to be confirmed under Part 2 of that Act, has been so confirmed);

(b)   the relevant part has not vested in the authority; and

(c)   the relevant part is required for use other than use for agricultural purposes.

(5)   Regulations may for the purposes of subsections (2) to (4) make provision as to what is or is not to be regarded as use of land for agricultural purposes.

(6)   Regulations may provide that an application under this section is not to be granted without the consent of any person specified in the regulations.

12 Transfer of rights in gross

The transfer of a right of common which is registered in a register of common land or town or village greens but is not registered as attached to any land—

(a)   only has effect if it complies with such requirements as to form and content as regulations may provide; and

(b)   does not operate at law until, on an application under this section, the transferee is registered in the register as the owner of the right.

13 Surrender and extinguishment

(1)   The surrender to any extent of a right of common which is registered in a register of common land or town or village greens—

(a)   only has effect if it complies with such requirements as to form and content as regulations may provide; and

(b)   does not operate at law until, on an application under this section, the right is removed from the register.

(2)   The reference in subsection (1) to a surrender of a right of common does not include a disposition having the effect referred to in section 7(1)(a).

(3)   A right of common which is registered in a register of common land or town or village greens cannot be extinguished by operation of common law.

Registration, deregistration and exchange of land

14 Statutory dispositions

(1)   Regulations may make provision as to the amendment of a register of common land or town or village greens where by virtue of any relevant instrument—

    (a)   a disposition is made in relation to land registered in it as common land or as a town or village green; or

    (b)   a disposition is made in relation to a right of common registered in it.

(2)   Regulations may provide that, where—

    (a)   by virtue of any relevant instrument a disposition is made in relation to land registered as common land or as a town or village green,

    (b)   by virtue of regulations under subsection (1) the land ceases to be so registered, and

    (c)   in connection with the disposition other land is given in exchange,

the land given in exchange is to be registered as common land or as a town or village green.

(3)   In this section, 'relevant instrument' means—

    (a)   any order, deed or other instrument made under or pursuant to the Acquisition of Land Act 1981 (c 67);

    (b)   a conveyance made for the purposes of section 13 of the New Parishes Measure 1943 (No 1);

    (c)   any other instrument made under or pursuant to any enactment.

(4)   Regulations under this section may require the making of an application to a commons registration authority for amendment of a register of common land or town or village greens.

(5)   Regulations under this section may provide that a relevant instrument, so far as relating to land registered as common land or as a town or village green or to any right of common, is not to operate at law until any requirement for which they provide is complied with.

15 Registration of greens

(1)   Any person may apply to the commons registration authority to register land to which this Part applies as a town or village green in a case where subsection (2), (3) or (4) applies.

(2)   This subsection applies where—

    (a)   a significant number of the inhabitants of any locality, or of any neighbourhood within a locality, have indulged as of right in lawful sports and pastimes on the land for a period of at least 20 years; and

    (b)   they continue to do so at the time of the application.

(3)   This subsection applies where—

    (a)   a significant number of the inhabitants of any locality, or of any neighbourhood within a locality, indulged as of right in lawful sports and pastimes on the land for a period of at least 20 years;

    (b)   they ceased to do so before the time of the application but after the commencement of this section; and

    (c)   the application is made within the relevant period.

(3A)   In subsection (3), "the relevant period" means——

    (a)   in the case of an application relating to land in England, the period of one year beginning with the cessation mentioned in subsection (3)(b);

(b)   in the case of an application relating to land in Wales, the period of two years beginning with that cessation..

(4)   This subsection applies (subject to subsection (5)) where—

    (a)   a significant number of the inhabitants of any locality, or of any neighbourhood within a locality, indulged as of right in lawful sports and pastimes on the land for a period of at least 20 years;

    (b)   they ceased to do so before the commencement of this section; and

    (c)   the application is made within the period of five years beginning with the cessation referred to in paragraph (b).

(5)   Subsection (4) does not apply in relation to any land where—

    (a)   planning permission was granted before 23 June 2006 in respect of the land;

    (b)   construction works were commenced before that date in accordance with that planning permission on the land or any other land in respect of which the permission was granted; and

    (c)   the land—

        (i)   has by reason of any works carried out in accordance with that planning permission become permanently unusable by members of the public for the purposes of lawful sports and pastimes; or

        (ii)   will by reason of any works proposed to be carried out in accordance with that planning permission become permanently unusable by members of the public for those purposes.

(6)   In determining the period of 20 years referred to in subsections (2)(a), (3)(a) and (4)(a), there is to be disregarded any period during which access to the land was prohibited to members of the public by reason of any enactment.

(7)   For the purposes of subsection (2)(b) in a case where the condition in subsection (2)(a) is satisfied—

    (a)   where persons indulge as of right in lawful sports and pastimes immediately before access to the land is prohibited as specified in subsection (6), those persons are to be regarded as continuing so to indulge; and

    (b)   where permission is granted in respect of use of the land for the purposes of lawful sports and pastimes, the permission is to be disregarded in determining whether persons continue to indulge in lawful sports and pastimes on the land 'as of right'.

(8)   The owner of any land may apply to the commons registration authority to register the land as a town or village green.

(9)   An application under subsection (8) may only be made with the consent of any relevant leaseholder of, and the proprietor of any relevant charge over, the land.

(10)   In subsection (9)—

        'relevant charge' means—

    (a)   in relation to land which is registered in the register of title, a registered charge within the meaning of the Land Registration Act 2002 (c 9);

    (b)   in relation to land which is not so registered—

        (i)   a charge registered under the Land Charges Act 1972 (c 61); or

        (ii)   a legal mortgage, within the meaning of the Law of Property Act 1925 (c 20), which is not registered under the Land Charges Act 1972;

        'relevant leaseholder' means a leaseholder under a lease for a term of more than seven years from the date on which the lease was granted.

15A Registration of greens: statement by owner

(1) Where the owner of any land in England to which this Part applies deposits with the commons registration authority a statement in the prescribed form, the statement is to be regarded, for the purposes of section 15, as bringing to an end any period during which persons have indulged as of right in lawful sports and pastimes on the land to which the statement relates.

(2) Subsection (1) does not prevent a new period commencing

(3) A statement under subsection (1) must be accompanied by a map in the prescribed form identifying the land to which the statement relates.

(4) An owner of land may deposit more than one statement under subsection (1) in respect of the same land.

(5) If more than one statement is deposited in respect of the same land, a later statement (whether or not made by the same person) may refer to the map which accompanied an earlier statement and that map is to be treated, for the purposes of this section, as also accompanying the later statement.

(6) Where a statement is deposited under subsection (1), the commons registration authority must take the prescribed steps in relation to the statement and accompanying map and do so in the prescribed manner and within the prescribed period (if any).

(7) Regulations may make provision—

(a) for a statement required for the purposes of this section to be combined with a statement or declaration required for the purposes of section 31(6) of the Highways Act 1980;

(b) for the requirement in subsection (3) to be satisfied by the statement referring to a map previously deposited under section 31(6) of the Highways Act 1980;

(c) as to the fees payable in relation to the depositing of a statement under subsection (1) (including provision for a fee payable under the regulations to be determined by the commons registration authority);

(d) as to when a statement under subsection (1) is to be regarded as having been deposited with the commons registration authority.

(8) An agreement under section 4(3) of this Act or section 2(2) of the Commons Registration Act 1965 which would have the effect of requiring an owner of land to deposit a statement under subsection (1) with a registration authority in Wales is to be disregarded for the purposes of this section.

(9) In this section "prescribed" means prescribed in regulations.

15B Register of section 15A statements

(1) Each commons registration authority must keep, in such manner as may be prescribed, a register containing prescribed information about statements deposited under section 15A(1) and the maps accompanying those statements.

(2) The register kept under this section must be available for inspection free of charge at all reasonable hours.

(3) A commons registration authority may discharge its duty under subsection (1) by including the prescribed information in the register kept by it under section 31A of the Highways Act 1980 (register of maps and statements deposited and declarations lodged under section 31(6) of that Act).

(4) Regulations may make provision—

(a) where a commons registration authority discharges its duty under subsection (1) in the way described in subsection (3), for the creation of a new part of the register kept under section 31A of the Highways Act 1980 for that purpose;

(b) as to the circumstances in which an entry relating to a statement deposited under section 15A(1) or a map accompanying such a statement, or anything relating to the entry, is to be removed from the register kept under this section or (as the case may be) the register kept under section 31A of the Highways Act 1980.

(5)　In this section "prescribed" means prescribed in regulations.

15C Registration of greens: exclusions

(1)　The right under section 15(1) to apply to register land in England as a town or village green ceases to apply if an event specified in the first column of the Table set out in Schedule 1A has occurred in relation to the land ("a trigger event").

(2)　Where the right under section 15(1) has ceased to apply because of the occurrence of a trigger event, it becomes exercisable again only if an event specified in the corresponding entry in the second column of the Table occurs in relation to the land ("a terminating event").

(3)　The Secretary of State may by order make provision as to when a trigger or a terminating event is to be treated as having occurred for the purposes of this section.

(4)　The Secretary of State may by order provide that subsection (1) does not apply in circumstances specified in the order.

(5)　The Secretary of State may by order amend Schedule 1A so as to—

    (a)　specify additional trigger or terminating events;

    (b)　amend or omit any of the trigger or terminating events for the time being specified in the Schedule.

(6)　A trigger or terminating event specified by order under subsection (5)(a) must be an event related to the development (whether past, present or future) of the land.

(7)　The transitional provision that may be included in an order under subsection (5)(a) specifying an additional trigger or terminating event includes provision for this section to apply where such an event has occurred before the order is made or before it comes into force and as to its application in such a case.

(8)　For the purposes of determining whether an application under section 15 is made within the period mentioned in section 15(3)(c), any period during which an application to register land as a town or village green may not be made by virtue of this section is to be disregarded.

16 Deregistration and exchange: applications

(1)　The owner of any land registered as common land or as a town or village green may apply to the appropriate national authority for the land ('the release land') to cease to be so registered.

(2)　If the release land is more than 200 square metres in area, the application must include a proposal under subsection (3).

(3)　A proposal under this subsection is a proposal that land specified in the application ('replacement land') be registered as common land or as a town or village green in place of the release land.

(4)　If the release land is not more than 200 square metres in area, the application may include a proposal under subsection (3).

(5)　Where the application includes a proposal under subsection (3)—

    (a)　the replacement land must be land to which this Part applies;

    (b)　the replacement land must not already be registered as common land or as a town or village green; and

    (c)　if the owner of the release land does not own the replacement land, the owner of the replacement land must join in the application.

(6)　In determining the application, the appropriate national authority shall have regard to—

    (a)　the interests of persons having rights in relation to, or occupying, the release land (and in particular persons exercising rights of common over it);

    (b)　the interests of the neighbourhood;

(c) the public interest;

(d) any other matter considered to be relevant.

(7) The appropriate national authority shall in a case where—

(a) the release land is not more than 200 square metres in area, and

(b) the application does not include a proposal under subsection (3),

have particular regard under subsection (6) to the extent to which the absence of such a proposal is prejudicial to the interests specified in paragraphs (a) to (c) of that subsection.

(8) The reference in subsection (6)(c) to the public interest includes the public interest in—

(a) nature conservation;

(b) the conservation of the landscape;

(c) the protection of public rights of access to any area of land; and

(d) the protection of archaeological remains and features of historic interest.

(9) An application under this section may only be made with the consent of any relevant leaseholder of, and the proprietor of any relevant charge over—

(a) the release land;

(b) any replacement land.

(10) In subsection (9) 'relevant charge' and 'relevant leaseholder' have the meanings given by section 15(10).

17 Deregistration and exchange: orders

(1) Where the appropriate national authority grants an application under section 16 it must make an order requiring the commons registration authority to remove the release land from its register of common land or town or village greens.

(2) Where the application included a proposal to register replacement land, the order shall also require the commons registration authority—

(a) to register the replacement land as common land or as a town or village green in place of the release land; and

(b) to register as exercisable over the replacement land any rights of common which, immediately before the relevant date, are registered as exercisable over the release land.

(3) A commons registration authority must take such other steps on receiving an order under this section as regulations may require.

(4) Where immediately before the relevant date any rights of common are registered as exercisable over the release land, those rights are on that date extinguished in relation to that land.

(5) Where immediately before the relevant date any rights are exercisable over the release land by virtue of its being, or being part of, a town or village green—

(a) those rights are extinguished on that date in respect of the release land; and

(b) where any replacement land is registered in its place, those rights shall become exercisable as from that date over the replacement land instead.

(6) Where immediately before the relevant date the release land was registered as common land and any relevant provision applied in relation to it—

(a) the provision shall on that date cease to apply to the release land; and

(b) where any replacement land is registered in its place, the provision shall on that date apply to the replacement land instead.

(7) An order under this section may contain—

(a) provision disapplying the effect of subsection (5)(b) or (6)(b) in relation to any replacement land;

(b) supplementary provision as to the effect in relation to any replacement land of—

(i)   any rights exercisable over the release land by virtue of its being, or being part of, a town or village green;

(ii)   any relevant provision;

(c)   supplementary provision as to the effect in relation to the release land or any replacement land of any local or personal Act.

(8)   In subsections (6) and (7) 'relevant provision' means a provision contained in, or made under—

(a)   section 193 of the Law of Property Act 1925 (c 20);

(b)   a scheme under the Metropolitan Commons Act 1866 (c 122);

(c)   an Act under the Commons Act 1876 (c 56) confirming a provisional order of the Inclosure Commissioners;

(d)   a scheme under the Commons Act 1899 (c 30);

(e)   section 1 of the Commons Act 1908 (c 44).

(9)   In this section, 'relevant date' means the date on which the commons registration authority amends its register as required under subsections (1) and (2).

(10)   Regulations may make provision for the publication of an order under this section.

Conclusiveness and correction of the registers

18 Conclusiveness

(1)   This section applies to land registered as common land, or as a town or village green, which is registered as being subject to a right of common.

(2)   If the land would not otherwise have been subject to that right, it shall be deemed to have become subject to that right, as specified in the register, upon its registration.

(3)   If the right is registered as attached to any land, the right shall, if it would not otherwise have attached to that land, be deemed to have become so attached upon registration of its attachment.

(4)   If the right is not registered as attached to any land, the person registered as the owner of the right shall, if he would not otherwise have been its owner, be deemed to have become its owner upon his registration.

(5)   Nothing in subsection (2) affects any constraint on the exercise of a right of common where the constraint does not appear in the register.

(6)   It is immaterial whether the registration referred to in subsection (2), (3) or (4) occurred before or after the commencement of this section.

19 Correction

(1)   A commons registration authority may amend its register of common land or town or village greens for any purpose referred to in subsection (2).

(2)   Those purposes are—

(a)   correcting a mistake made by the commons registration authority in making or amending an entry in the register;

(b)   correcting any other mistake, where the amendment would not affect—

(i)   the extent of any land registered as common land or as a town or village green; or

(ii)   what can be done by virtue of a right of common;

(c)   removing a duplicate entry from the register;

(d)   updating the details of any name or address referred to in an entry;

(e)   updating any entry in the register relating to land registered as common land or as a town or village green to take account of accretion or diluvion.

(3)   References in this section to a mistake include—

(a)   a mistaken omission, and

    (b)   an unclear or ambiguous description,

and it is immaterial for the purposes of this section whether a mistake was made before or after the commencement of this section.

(4)   An amendment may be made by a commons registration authority—

    (a)   on its own initiative; or

    (b)   on the application of any person.

(5)   A mistake in a register may not be corrected under this section if the authority considers that, by reason of reliance reasonably placed on the register by any person or for any other reason, it would in all the circumstances be unfair to do so.

(6)   Regulations may make further provision as to the criteria to be applied in determining an application or proposal under this section.

(7)   The High Court may order a commons registration authority to amend its register of common land or town or village greens if the High Court is satisfied that—

    (a)   any entry in the register, or any information in an entry, was at any time included in the register as a result of fraud; and

    (b)   it would be just to amend the register.

Information etc

20 Inspection

(1)   Any person may inspect and make copies of, or of any part of—

    (a)   a register of common land or town or village greens;

    (b)   any document kept by a commons registration authority which is referred to in such a register;

    (c)   any other document kept by a commons registration authority which relates to an application made at any time in relation to such a register.

(2)   The right in subsection (1) is subject to regulations which may, in particular—

    (a)   provide for exceptions to the right;

    (b)   impose conditions on its exercise.

(3)   Conditions under subsection (2)(b) may include conditions requiring the payment of a fee (which may be a fee determined by a commons registration authority).

21 Official copies

(1)   An official copy of, or of any part of—

    (a)   a register of common land or town or village greens,

    (b)   any document kept by a commons registration authority which is referred to in such a register, or

    (c)   any other document kept by a commons registration authority which relates to an application made at any time in relation to such a register,

is admissible in evidence to the same extent as the original.

(2)   Regulations may make provision for the issue of official copies and may in particular make provision about—

    (a)   the form of official copies;

    (b)   who may issue official copies;

    (c)   applications for official copies;

    (d)   the conditions to be met by applicants for official copies.

(3)   Conditions under subsection (2)(d) may include conditions requiring the payment of a fee (which may be a fee determined by a commons registration authority).

Transitory and transitional provision

22 Non-registration or mistaken registration under the 1965 Act

Schedule 2 (non-registration or mistaken registration under the Commons Registration Act 1965 (c 64)) has effect.

23 Transitional

(1)   Schedule 3 (transitional provision) has effect.

(2)   Nothing in Schedule 3 affects the power to make transitional provision and savings in an order under section 56; and an order under that section may modify any provision made by that Schedule.

Supplementary

24 Applications etc

(1)   Regulations may make provision as to the making and determination of any application for the amendment of a register of common land or town or village greens under or for the purposes of this Part.

(2)   Regulations under subsection (1) may in particular make provision as to—

    (a)   the steps to be taken by a person before making an application;

    (b)   the form of an application;

    (c)   the information or evidence to be supplied with an application;

    (d)   the fee payable on an application (which may be a fee determined by the person to whom the application is made);

    (e)   the persons to be notified of an application;

    (f)   the publication of an application;

    (g)   the making of objections to an application;

    (h)   the persons who must be consulted, or whose advice must be sought, in relation to an application;

    (i)   the holding of an inquiry before determination of an application;

    (j)   the evidence to be taken into account in making a determination and the weight to be given to any evidence;

    (k)   the persons to be notified of any determination;

    (l)   the publication of a determination;

    (m)   the amendments to be made by a commons registration authority to a register of common land or town or village greens pursuant to a determination;

    (n)   the time at which any such amendments are to be regarded as having been made.

(2A)   Regulations under subsection (1) made by the Secretary of State may make provision as to the fees payable in relation to an application (including provision for a fee payable under the regulations to be determined by the person to whom the application is made or (if different) the person by whom the application is to be determined).

(2B)   Regulations under subsection (1) made by the Welsh Ministers may make provision as to the fee payable on an application (which may be a fee determined by the person to whom the application is made).

(3)   In the case of an application made for the purposes of any of—

    (a)   sections 6 to 8, 12 and 13,

    (b)   paragraph 1 or 3 of Schedule 1,

    (c)   paragraph 2 or 3 of Schedule 2, and

    (d)   paragraph 2(5)(a) of Schedule 3,

regulations under subsection (1) may make provision as to the persons entitled to make the application.

(4)   An application made for the purposes of any of—

(a)   sections 6, 7, 10, 11, 12, 13 and 15, and

(b)   paragraph 1 or 3 of Schedule 1,

shall, subject to any provision made by or under this Part, be granted.

(5)   Regulations under subsection (1) may include provision for the appropriate national authority to appoint a person to discharge any or all of its functions in relation to an application made to it under section 16.

(6)   Regulations may make provision as to the making and determination of any proposal by a commons registration authority to amend a register on its own initiative pursuant to section 19, Schedule 2 or paragraph 2(5)(b) of Schedule 3.

(7)   Regulations under subsection (6) may in particular make provision as to—

(a)   the persons to be notified of a proposal;

(b)   the publication of a proposal (and the information or evidence to be published with a proposal);

(c)   the making of objections to a proposal;

(d)   the persons who must be consulted, or whose advice must be sought, in relation to a proposal;

(e)   the holding of an inquiry before determination of a proposal;

(f)   the evidence to be taken into account in making a determination and the weight to be given to any evidence;

(g)   the persons to be notified of any determination;

(h)   the publication of a determination;

(i)   the amendments to be made by a commons registration authority to a register of common land or town or village greens pursuant to a determination.

(8)   Regulations under this section may include provision for—

(a)   the appropriate national authority to appoint persons as eligible to discharge functions of a commons registration authority in relation to applications made to, or proposals made by, the commons registration authority; and

(b)   the appointment of one or more of those persons to discharge functions of the commons registration authority in the case of any description of application or proposal.

(9)   Regulations under this section may provide for the Diocesan Board of Finance for the diocese in which the land is situated to act with respect to any land or rights belonging to an ecclesiastical benefice of the Church of England which is vacant.

25   Electronic registers

(1)   Regulations may require or permit the whole or any part of a register kept under this Part to be kept in electronic form.

(2)   Regulations under subsection (1) may include provision as to—

(a)   requirements to be complied with in relation to the recording of information in electronic form;

(b)   the certification of information recorded in electronic form (including the status of print-outs of such information).

(3)   Regulations under subsection (1) may also include provision as to the process of converting a register, or part of a register, into electronic form.

(4)   The provision referred to in subsection (3) includes in particular provision—

(a)   as to the publicity to be given to such a conversion;

(b)   requiring a provisional electronic version to be made available for inspection and comment;

(c)   as to the holding of an inquiry in relation to any question arising as a result of the conversion.

PART 2

MANAGEMENT

Commons councils

26 Establishment

(1)   The appropriate national authority may, for any area or areas of land to which this section applies, establish a body corporate to carry out functions conferred under this Part.

(2)   This section applies to any land that—

(a)   is registered as common land; or

(b)   is registered as a town or village green and is subject to rights of common.

(3)   A body corporate established under this section is to be known as a 'commons council'.

(4)   A commons council is to be established by order.

(5)   An order establishing a commons council must specify—

(a)   the name of the council;

(b)   the area or areas of land for which the council is established.

27 Procedure for establishment

(1)   This section applies where the appropriate national authority proposes to make an order under section 26 establishing a commons council.

(2)   The appropriate national authority must—

(a)   publish a draft of the proposed order in such manner as it thinks fit; and

(b)   invite representations about it.

(3)   The appropriate national authority may cause a local inquiry to be held.

(4)   The appropriate national authority may not make the proposed order unless, having regard to—

(a)   any representations received pursuant to subsection (2)(b), and

(b)   the result of any local inquiry held under subsection (3),

it is satisfied that there is substantial support for the making of the order.

(5)   For the purposes of subsection (4) the appropriate national authority must have particular regard to representations received pursuant to subsection (2)(b) from—

(a)   persons having rights (other than rights of common) in relation to, or occupying, land specified in the draft order;

(b)   persons who are entitled to exercise rights of common (and in particular persons exercising rights of common) over any such land; and

(c)   persons with functions under an enactment which relate to the maintenance or management of any such land.

Status and constitution of commons councils

28 Status

(1)   A commons council is not to be regarded as the servant or agent of the Crown or as enjoying any status, immunity or privilege of the Crown.

(2)   The property of a commons council is not to be regarded as the property of, or as property held on behalf of, the Crown.

(3)   A commons council is not to be regarded as an authority to which section 28G of the Wildlife and Countryside Act 1981 (c 69) applies.

29 Constitution

(1)   The appropriate national authority must by regulations prescribe standard terms as to the constitution and administration of commons councils (in this Part, the 'standard constitution').

(2)   The terms of the standard constitution apply to every commons council, subject as follows.

(3)   An order under section 26 may also make provision as to the constitution and administration of a commons council.

(4)   Provision which may be made under subsection (3) includes in particular—

   (a)   provision supplementary to any term of the standard constitution;

   (b)   provision disapplying any such term;

   (c)   provision replacing any such term.

(5)   Where in relation to a commons council—

   (a)   provision is made under subsection (3) that is inconsistent with any term of the standard constitution, and

   (b)   any such term has not been expressly disapplied under that subsection,

the provision made under subsection (3) prevails, to the extent of the inconsistency, over the term of the standard constitution.

(6)   Terms of the standard constitution prescribed by regulations under subsection (1) may be amended by further regulations under that subsection; and this section applies in relation to such terms as amended as it applies in relation to the terms as first prescribed.

30 Constitution: supplementary

(1)   This section applies in relation to terms as to the constitution and administration of a commons council contained in—

   (a)   the standard constitution; or

   (b)   an order under section 26.

(2)   The terms may in particular include terms as to—

   (a)   the membership of the council;

   (b)   participation in the council by persons other than members;

   (c)   the proceedings of the council;

   (d)   the keeping and publication of accounts, annual reports and other information relating to the council.

(3)   The terms referred to in subsection (2)(a) include in particular terms as to—

   (a)   the appointment of members (by election or otherwise);

   (b)   the term for which members are appointed;

   (c)   co-option of members;

   (d)   the conduct of members;

   (e)   resignation and disqualification of members;

   (f)   termination and renewal of membership;

   (g)   payment of allowances to members.

(4)   The terms referred to in subsection (2)(b) include in particular terms as to—

   (a)   entitlement to elect members;

   (b)   entitlement to attend meetings.

(5)   The terms referred to in subsection (2)(c) include in particular terms as to—

   (a)   the frequency of meetings;

   (b)   voting procedures at meetings;

   (c)   committees and sub-committees.

(6)   The terms referred to in subsection (2)(d) include in particular terms as to—

   (a)   the appointment of auditors;

   (b)   the preparation and publication of accounts;

(c) the preparation and publication of annual reports.

(7) Subject to any terms made of the kind referred to in subsection (2)(c), a commons council may regulate its own proceedings.

Functions of commons councils

31 Functions

(1) An order under section 26 is to confer on a commons council functions relating to any one or more of the following—

(a) the management of agricultural activities on the land for which the council is established;

(b) the management of vegetation on the land;

(c) the management of rights of common on the land.

(2) The functions conferred on a commons council under subsection (1) must be those the appropriate national authority considers appropriate in the case of that council.

(3) The functions which may be conferred on a commons council under subsection (1) include in particular functions of—

(a) making rules relating to agricultural activities, the management of vegetation and the exercise of rights of common on the land for which the council is established;

(b) making rules relating to the leasing or licensing of rights of common;

(c) preparing and maintaining a register of grazing;

(d) establishing and maintaining boundaries;

(e) removing unlawful boundaries and other encroachments;

(f) removing animals unlawfully permitted to graze.

(4) Rules made by virtue of subsection (3)(a) may have the effect of—

(a) limiting or imposing conditions on the exercise of rights of common over, or the exercise of rights to use the surplus of, the land for which the council is established;

(b) requiring the provision of information to the commons council in relation to the exercise of those rights.

(5) In exercising a function conferred under subsection (3)(f), a commons council may—

(a) dispose of any animal it removes; and

(b) recover from the owner of the animal the costs that it may reasonably incur in removing and disposing of it.

(6) A commons council must discharge its functions having regard to—

(a) any guidance given by the appropriate national authority; and

(b) the public interest in relation to the land for which it is established.

(7) The reference in subsection (6)(b) to the public interest includes the public interest in—

(a) nature conservation;

(b) the conservation of the landscape;

(c) the protection of public rights of access to any area of land; and

(d) the protection of archaeological remains and features of historic interest.

32 Ancillary powers

(1) A commons council has the power to do anything which it considers will facilitate, or is conducive or incidental to, the carrying out of its functions.

(2) The power conferred by subsection (1) includes power to—

(a) enter into agreements;

(b) prepare and adopt management plans;

(c)   raise money (including by applying for funds from any source);

(d)   acquire or dispose of land;

(e)   employ staff.

(3)   The power of a commons council to raise money as specified in subsection (2)(c) includes power to require the payment of fees in connection with—

(a)   the exercise of rights of common over, or the exercise of rights to use the surplus of, the land for which the council is established, and

(b)   participation in the council,

and any such fees owed to the council may be recovered as a debt due to it.

33 Consent

(1)   Subject to subsections (2) and (3), nothing in this Part authorises a commons council to do anything on the land for which it is established without the consent of a person with an interest in the land, where that person's consent would otherwise be required.

(2)   A commons council does not need the consent of a person who has a right of common over the land for which it is established in order to do anything on the land.

(3)   A commons council does not need the consent of any other person with an interest in the land for which it is established in order to do anything on the land where what is proposed to be done could be done without that person's consent by any person who has a right of common over the land.

(4)   Where a commons council wishes to obtain the consent of any person with an interest in the land for which the council is established in respect of anything it proposes to do on the land, it may serve a notice on him.

(5)   A notice under subsection (4) must specify—

(a)   what the commons council proposes to do;

(b)   the time within which the person on whom it is served may object (which may not be less than 28 days after service of the notice); and

(c)   the manner in which he may object.

(6)   If the person on whom a notice under subsection (4) is served does not object within the time and in the manner specified in the notice, he is to be regarded as having given his consent in relation to the proposal specified in the notice.

(7)   Where a commons council proposes to serve a notice on a person under subsection (4) but is unable after reasonable enquiry to ascertain his name or proper address—

(a)   the council may post the notice on the land; and

(b)   the notice is to be treated as having been served on the person at the time the notice is posted.

(8)   An order under section 26 may make further provision as to the form and service of notices under subsection (4).

(9)   For the purposes of this section, a person with an interest in any land is a person who—

(a)   owns the land; or

(b)   is entitled to exercise any right over the land.

34 Enforcement of rules

(1)   A person who breaches a rule to which subsection (2) applies is guilty of an offence.

(2)   This subsection applies to a rule which—

(a)   is made with the consent of the appropriate national authority pursuant to a function of making rules conferred on a commons council under section 31; and

(b)   specifies that a person who contravenes it is guilty of an offence under this section.

(3) A person guilty of an offence under subsection (1) is liable on summary conviction to—

    (a)   a fine not exceeding level 4 on the standard scale; and

    (b)   in the case of a continuing offence, to a further fine not exceeding one half of level 1 on the standard scale for each day during which the offence continues after conviction.

(4) A commons council may bring proceedings in relation to an offence under subsection (1) in respect of breach of any rule made by it to which subsection (2) applies.

(5) A commons council may apply to a county court for an order to secure compliance with any rule that it has made pursuant to a function of making rules conferred on it under section 31.

(6) But a commons council may only make an application under subsection (5) for the purpose of securing compliance with a rule to which subsection (2) applies if it is of the opinion that proceedings for an offence under subsection (1) would provide an ineffectual remedy against the person who has failed to comply with the rule.

(7) On an application under subsection (5) the court may make such an order as it thinks fit.

35 Rules: supplementary

(1) Any power to make rules conferred on a commons council under section 31 includes power to vary or revoke the rules made by the council.

(2) An order under section 26 conferring a power to make rules may provide for the procedure to be followed in the exercise of the power (and may in particular require the consent of the appropriate national authority to be obtained before rules are made).

(3) The appropriate national authority may by direction revoke any rule made by a commons council.

(4) A direction under subsection (3) must set out the reason why the rule is being revoked.

(5) Before revoking any rule under subsection (3) the appropriate national authority must consult—

    (a)   the commons council; and

    (b)   any other person it thinks appropriate.

Commons councils: supplementary

36 Consequential provision

(1) The appropriate national authority may by order under section 26 make any provision specified in subsection (2) if it appears to the authority desirable to do so in consequence of functions conferred on a commons council in relation to any land.

(2) The provision referred to in subsection (1) is provision to—

    (a)   vary or abolish the jurisdiction so far as relating to the land of any court of a description referred to in Part 1 of Schedule 4 to the Administration of Justice Act 1977 (c 38) (certain ancient courts);

    (b)   vary or revoke any regulations or arrangement made under the Commons Act 1908 (c 44);

    (c)   vary or revoke any scheme made under the Commons Act 1899 (c 30), or any arrangement arising under such a scheme;

    (d)   vary or revoke any Act made under the Commons Act 1876 (c 56) confirming a provisional order of the Inclosure Commissioners or any arrangement arising under such an Act;

(e)   vary or revoke any local or personal Act, or any scheme or arrangement under such an Act, which relates to the management or maintenance of, or the exercise of rights of common over, the land.

(3)   The appropriate national authority may not under subsection (1) make provision specified in subsection (2)(c) to (e) to the extent that to do so would have the effect of abolishing or restricting a right of access of whatever nature exercisable by members of the public generally or by any section of the public.

37 Variation and revocation of establishment orders

(1)   The appropriate national authority may by order under section 26 revoke a previous order under that section establishing a commons council only if it is satisfied that—

(a)   the council has ceased to operate;

(b)   the council is failing to discharge its functions in an effective manner; or

(c)   the council is, in discharging its functions, failing to have sufficient regard to the public interest as required by section 31.

(2)   An order under section 26 revoking a previous order under that section may include—

(a)   provision for the transfer of rights, property and liabilities of the commons council;

(b)   provision amending any enactment previously amended under section 36 in relation to the council.

(3)   Section 27 applies to an order under section 26 varying or revoking a previous order under that section as it applies to an order under that section establishing a commons council (but as if the references in section 27 to land specified in the order were to land affected by the variation or revocation).

PART 3

WORKS

38 Prohibition on works without consent

(1)   A person may not, except with the consent of the appropriate national authority, carry out any restricted works on land to which this section applies.

(2)   In subsection (1) 'restricted works' are—

(a)   works which have the effect of preventing or impeding access to or over any land to which this section applies;

(b)   works for the resurfacing of land.

(3)   The reference to works in subsection (2)(a) includes in particular—

(a)   the erection of fencing;

(b)   the construction of buildings and other structures;

(c)   the digging of ditches and trenches and the building of embankments.

(4)   For the purposes of subsection (2)(b) works are for the resurfacing of land if they consist of the laying of concrete, tarmacadam, coated roadstone or similar material on the land (but not if they consist only of the repair of an existing surface of the land made of such material).

(5)   This section applies to—

(a)   any land registered as common land;

(b)   land not so registered which is—

(i)   regulated by an Act made under the Commons Act 1876 (c 56) confirming a provisional order of the Inclosure Commissioners; or

(ii)   subject to a scheme under the Metropolitan Commons Act 1866 (c 122) or the Commons Act 1899 (c 30);

(c)   land not falling within paragraph (a) or (b) which is in the New Forest and is subject to rights of common.

(6)   The prohibition in subsection (1) does not apply to—

  (a)   works on any land where those works, or works of a description which includes those works, are carried out under a power conferred in relation to that particular land by or under any enactment;

  (b)   works on any land where the works are carried out under a power conferred by or under any enactment applying to common land;

  (c)   works authorised under a scheme under the Metropolitan Commons Act 1866 or the Commons Act 1899 without any requirement for any person to consent to the works;

  (d)   works for the installation of electronic communications apparatus for the purposes of an electronic communications code network.

(7)   In subsection (6)(a) the reference to an enactment does not include Part 2 of this Act.

(8)   For the purposes of subsection (6)(b), an enactment applies to common land if it is expressed to apply (generally) to—

  (a)   registered common land;

  (b)   common land; or

  (c)   any common or commons, commonable land, land subject to inclosure under any enactment or other land of a similar description.

(9)   Subject to the following provisions of this Part, consent given to works under subsection (1) of this section constitutes consent for the purposes of that subsection only.

39 Consent: general

(1)   In determining an application for consent under subsection (1) of section 38 in relation to works on land to which that section applies, the appropriate national authority shall have regard to—

  (a)   the interests of persons having rights in relation to, or occupying, the land (and in particular persons exercising rights of common over it);

  (b)   the interests of the neighbourhood;

  (c)   the public interest;

  (d)   any other matter considered to be relevant.

(2)   The reference in subsection (1)(c) to the public interest includes the public interest in—

  (a)   nature conservation;

  (b)   the conservation of the landscape;

  (c)   the protection of public rights of access to any area of land; and

  (d)   the protection of archaeological remains and features of historic interest.

(3)   Consent may be given under section 38(1)—

  (a)   in relation to all or part of the proposed works;

  (b)   subject to such modifications and conditions relating to the proposed works as the appropriate national authority thinks fit.

(4)   In considering the effect in relation to any land of proposed works under this section, the appropriate national authority may consider that effect in conjunction with the effect in relation to that land of any other works for which consent has previously been given under section 38(1) above or section 194 of the Law of Property Act 1925 (c 20).

(5)   Where the appropriate national authority imposes any modification or condition in relation to any consent given under section 38(1), it may on the application of any person carrying out or proposing to carry out works in accordance with the consent vary or revoke that modification or condition.

(6)   Regulations may specify a time limit for the making of applications under subsection (5).

(7) Consent may be given under section 38(1) in relation to works which have been commenced or completed; and any consent so given has effect from the time of commencement of the works.

40 Consent: procedure

(1) Regulations may make provision as to the procedure to be followed in the making and determination of applications under sections 38(1) and 39(5).

(2) Regulations under this section may in particular include provision—

(a) as to the steps to be taken by an applicant before submitting an application;

(b) as to the form and content of an application;

(c) as to the procedure to be followed in making an application;

(d) as to the evidence to be supplied in support of an application;

(e) as to the fees payable in relation to an application;

(f) as to the steps to be taken by the appropriate national authority upon receipt of an application;

(g) for the appointment by the appropriate national authority of a person to discharge any (or all) of its functions in relation to the determination of an application;

(h) for the making of representations or objections in relation to an application;

(i) for the holding of a hearing or local inquiry in relation to an application;

(j) for the publication of a determination of an application and the notification of interested persons.

41 Enforcement

(1) Where any works are carried out on land to which section 38 applies in contravention of subsection (1) of that section, any person may apply to the county court in whose area the land is situated.

(2) On an application under this section the court may make an order—

(a) in any case, for removal of the works and restoration of the land to the condition it was in before the works were carried out;

(b) in a case where consent has been given under section 38(1) but the works have not been carried out in accordance with any term of that consent, for the works to be carried out in such manner and subject to such conditions as the order may specify.

42 Schemes

(1) This section applies in relation to works on relevant land where, by virtue of section 38(1), the works may not be carried out without the consent of the appropriate national authority.

(2) In subsection (1) 'relevant land' means land which is subject to—

(a) a scheme under the Metropolitan Commons Act 1866 (c 122) which is in force at the commencement of this section; or

(b) a scheme under the Commons Act 1899 (c 30) which is in force at the commencement of this section.

(3) Where—

(a) any provision of the scheme referred to in subsection (2) would also prohibit the carrying out of the works, and

(b) the scheme does not allow for any person to consent to the works to be carried out,

the works do not contravene that provision if they are carried out with (and in accordance with the terms of) the consent of the appropriate national authority under section 38(1) and of any owner of the land (if not the person carrying out the works).

(4) Regulations may make provision as to the procedure to be followed in obtaining the consent of an owner under subsection (3) (and may include provision for the consent of an owner to be regarded as having been given where he has not objected within a period of time specified in the regulations).

(5) Where any provision of the scheme referred to in subsection (2) would also prohibit the carrying out of the works without the consent of the appropriate national authority—

    (a)   consent given under section 38(1) is to be regarded as consent given under the scheme; and

    (b)   consent may not be sought separately under the scheme.

43 Power to exempt

(1) The appropriate national authority may by order provide that section 38 is not to apply to—

    (a)   the carrying out by a specified person of specified works on specified land; or

    (b)   the carrying out by a specified person, or a person of a specified description, of works of a specified description on—

        (i)   any land; or

        (ii)   land of a specified description.

(2) The appropriate national authority may only make an order under subsection (1)(a) if it is satisfied that the works specified in the order are necessary or expedient for any of the purposes in subsection (4).

(3) The appropriate national authority may only make an order under subsection (1)(b) if it is satisfied that works of the description specified in the order are likely to be necessary or expedient on any land, or on land of the description specified in the order, for any of the purposes in subsection (4).

(4) The purposes referred to in subsections (2) and (3) are—

    (a)   use of land by members of the public for the purposes of open-air recreation pursuant to any right of access;

    (b)   the exercise of rights of common;

    (c)   nature conservation;

    (d)   the protection of archaeological remains or features of historic interest;

    (e)   the use of the land for sporting or recreational purposes.

(5) Where—

    (a)   any land was at any time before the commencement of this section land to which section 194 of the Law of Property Act 1925 (c 20) applied, but

    (b)   at any such time that section ceased to apply to the land by virtue of subsection (3)(a) of that section,

the appropriate national authority may by order provide that section 38 is not to apply to the carrying out of works, or works of a description specified in the order, on that land.

(6) Where any land is the subject of a resolution under section 194(3)(b) of the Law of Property Act 1925 (c 20) immediately before the commencement of this section, the appropriate national authority may by order provide that section 38 is not to apply to the carrying out of works, or works of a description specified in the order, on that land.

(7) An order under this section may provide that section 38 is not to apply only if the works to which the order relates are carried out in accordance with the terms of the order.

(8) In subsection (1) 'specified' means specified in an order under that subsection.

44 Supplementary

(1)   Schedule 4 (which makes supplementary provision relating to works on common land) has effect.

(2)   A national authority may for any purpose specified in subsection (3) by order amend—

(a)   any local or personal Act passed before this Act which contains provision for that authority to consent to works on land which is common land; and

(b)   any Act made under the Commons Act 1876 (c 56) confirming a provisional order of the Inclosure Commissioners which contains provision for that authority to consent to works on land to which the Act applies.

(3)   The purposes referred to in subsection (2) are—

(a)   that of securing that sections 39 and 40 apply to an application for the consent referred to in paragraph (a) or (b) of subsection (2) as they apply to an application for consent under section 38(1);

(b)   that of securing that section 41 applies in relation to the carrying out of works in contravention of the provision referred to in paragraph (a) or (b) of subsection (2) as it applies to works carried out in contravention of section 38(1).

(4)   In subsection (2)—

'national authority' means—

(a)   the Secretary of State; and

(b)   the National Assembly for Wales;

'common land' means—

(a)   any land registered as common land; and

(b)   any land not so registered which is subject to a scheme under the Metropolitan Commons Act 1866 (c 122) or the Commons Act 1899 (c 30).

PART 4

MISCELLANEOUS

Intervention powers

45 Powers of local authorities over unclaimed land

(1)   This section applies where—

(a)   land is registered as common land or a town or village green;

(b)   no person is registered in the register of title as the owner of the land; and

(c)   it appears to a local authority in whose area the land or any part of it is situated that the owner cannot be identified.

(2)   The local authority may—

(a)   take any steps to protect the land against unlawful interference that could be taken by an owner in possession of the land; and

(b)   institute proceedings against any person for any offence committed in respect of the land (but without prejudice to any power exercisable apart from this section).

(3)   In this section 'local authority' means—

(a)   a county, district or parish council in England;

(b)   a London borough council; and

(c)   a county, county borough or community council in Wales.

46 Powers relating to unauthorised agricultural activities

(1) This section applies where it appears to the appropriate national authority that—

    (a)   a person is carrying out, or causing to be carried out by virtue of any arrangements, an agricultural activity on land which—

        (i)   is registered as common land; or

        (ii)   is registered as a town or village green and is subject to rights of common;

    (b)   the activity is unauthorised; and

    (c)   the activity is detrimental to—

        (i)   the interests of persons having rights in relation to, or occupying, the land; or

        (ii)   the public interest.

(2) The appropriate national authority may, subject to the following provisions of this section, serve a notice on the person requiring him to do any one or more of the following—

    (a)   within such reasonable period as may be specified in the notice to stop carrying out the activity, or stop causing it to be carried out, to the extent that it is unauthorised;

    (b)   not to carry out, or cause to be carried out, any other unauthorised agricultural activity on the land which would be detrimental to the matters specified in subsection (1)(c)(i) and (ii);

    (c)   to supply the authority with such information relating to agricultural activities on the land carried out, or caused to be carried out, by him as it may reasonably require.

(3) Before serving a notice under this section the appropriate national authority must, to the extent that it is appropriate and practicable in all the circumstances to do so—

    (a)   notify the persons specified in subsection (4) of its intention to serve the notice; and

    (b)   publicise its intention to do so (in such manner as it thinks fit).

(4) The persons referred to in subsection (3)(a) are—

    (a)   any commons council for the land;

    (b)   any other person with functions under any enactment which relate to the maintenance or management of the land; and

    (c)   any person appearing to the authority to own or occupy the land.

(5) Any notification or publication under subsection (3) may specify a period within which representations about the proposed notice may be made.

(6) In deciding whether to serve a notice under this section the appropriate national authority must have regard to—

    (a)   any criminal or civil proceedings that have been or may be commenced in relation to the activity; and

    (b)   any steps taken by a commons council in relation to the activity.

(7) If a person on whom a notice is served under this section fails to comply with it—

    (a)   the appropriate national authority may apply to a county court for an order requiring him to do so; and

    (b)   the court may make such an order for the purpose of securing compliance with the notice as it thinks fit.

(8) For the purposes of this section, activity is unauthorised if the person carrying it out or causing it to be carried out—

    (a)   has no right or entitlement by virtue of his ownership or occupation of the land, or pursuant to any right of common, to do so; or

    (b)   is not doing so with the authority of the person or persons entitled to give such authority.

(9)   The reference in subsection (1)(c)(ii) to the public interest includes the public interest in—

   (a)   nature conservation;

   (b)   the conservation of the landscape;

   (c)   the protection of public rights of access to any area of land; and

   (d)   the protection of archaeological remains and features of historic interest.

(10)   Section 123(1) to (5) of the Environment Act 1995 (c 25) applies in relation to the service of a notice under this section as it applies in relation to the service of a notice under that Act.

Abolition of powers of approvement and inclosure etc

47 Approvement

(1)   The Commons Act 1285 (13 Edw 1 c. 46) (power of approvement) shall cease to have effect.

(2)   Any power of approvement of a common which subsists at common law is abolished.

48 Inclosure

(1)   Section 147 of the Inclosure Act 1845 (c 118) (power to exchange common land for other land) shall cease to have effect.

(2)   The following shall cease to have effect—

   (a)   section 2 of the Gifts for Churches Act 1811 (c 115);

   (b)   in section 2 of the School Sites Act 1841 (c 38), the words from 'Provided also, that where any portion' to 'such conveyance;';

   (c)   in section 1 of the Literary and Scientific Institutions Act 1854 (c 112), the words from 'Provided also' to the end.

49 Notice of inclosure

(1)   Section 31 of the Commons Act 1876 (c 56) (three months' notice of claim to inclose to be given in local papers) shall cease to have effect.

(2)   In section 3 of the Metropolitan Commons Act 1878 (c 71), for 'Sections thirty and thirty-one' substitute 'Section 30'.

Vehicular access

51 Vehicular access

Section 68 of the Countryside and Rights of Way Act 2000 (c 37) shall cease to have effect.

PART 5

SUPPLEMENTARY AND GENERAL

Amendments and repeals

52 Minor and consequential amendments

Schedule 5 (minor and consequential amendments) has effect.

53 Repeals

Schedule 6 (repeals, including consequential repeals and repeals of spent and obsolete enactments) has effect.

54 Power to amend enactments relating to common land or greens

(1)   The appropriate national authority may by order amend any relevant Act so as to secure that—

  (a)   a provision of that Act applying to common land does not apply to land to which Part 1 applies and which is not registered as common land;

  (b)   such a provision applies to either or both of the following—

    (i)   land registered as common land, or particular descriptions or areas of such land;

    (ii)   land to which Part 1 does not apply, or particular descriptions or areas of such land.

(2)   The appropriate national authority may by order amend any relevant Act so as to secure that—

  (a)   a provision of that Act which is expressed to apply to a town or village green does not apply to land to which Part 1 applies and which is not registered as a town or village green;

  (b)   such a provision applies to either or both of the following—

    (i)   land registered as a town or village green, or particular descriptions or areas of such land;

    (ii)   land to which Part 1 does not apply, or particular descriptions or areas of such land.

(3)   In this section, 'relevant Act' means any public general Act passed before this Act.

(4)   For the purposes of subsection (1) a provision applies to common land if it is expressed to apply (generally) to common land, any common or commons, commonable land, land subject to inclosure under any enactment or other land of a similar description.

55 Power to amend enactments conferring functions on national authorities

(1)   A national authority may by order amend or repeal any provision of a local or personal Act passed before this Act which applies to common land for any of the following purposes—

  (a)   to remove any function of the national authority which relates to the common land;

  (b)   to transfer such a function from the national authority to another person;

  (c)   to remove a requirement that the national authority be consulted, or that its consent be obtained, in respect of—

    (i)   any act or omission relating to the common land; or

    (ii)   any act or omission of a person concerned with the management of the common land;

  (d)   to substitute for a requirement referred to in paragraph (c) a requirement that a person other than the national authority be consulted, or his consent obtained, in relation to the act or omission.

(2)   In subsection (1), 'common land' means—

  (a)   any land registered as common land or as a town or village green;

  (b)   any land referred to in section 5(2); and

  (c)   any land not falling within paragraph (a) or (b) which is subject to a scheme under the Metropolitan Commons Act 1866 (c 122) or the Commons Act 1899 (c 30).

(3)   A national authority may by order amend or repeal any provision of an Act made under the Commons Act 1876 (c 56) confirming a provisional order of the Inclosure Commissioners for any of the following purposes—

  (a)   to remove any function of the national authority which relates to land to which the Act applies;

  (b)   to transfer such a function from the national authority to another person;

(c)   to remove a requirement that the national authority be consulted, or that its consent be obtained, in respect of—

      (i)   any act or omission relating to land to which the Act applies; or

      (ii)   any act or omission of a person concerned with the management of such land;

(d)   to substitute for a requirement referred to in paragraph (c) a requirement that a person other than the national authority be consulted, or his consent obtained, in relation to the act or omission.

(4)   In this section 'national authority' means—

    (a)   the Secretary of State; and

    (b)   the National Assembly for Wales.

Commencement and transitional provision

56 Commencement

(1)   The preceding provisions of this Act, except section 9 and Schedule 1 and sections 54 and 55, come into force in accordance with provision made by order by the appropriate national authority.

(2)   Sections 54 and 55 come into force at the end of the period of two months beginning with the day on which this Act is passed.

57 Severance: transitional

(1)   In relation to any area of England and Wales, the reference in subsection (1) of section 9 to a register of common land or town or village greens shall, during the relevant period in relation to that area, be read as a reference to such a register kept under the Commons Registration Act 1965 (c 64).

(2)   Sub-paragraph (6) of paragraph 1 of Schedule 1 shall not have effect in relation to a right of common severed (in accordance with that paragraph) from land in any area of England and Wales during the relevant period in relation to that area.

(3)   In this section, the 'relevant period', in relation to an area of England and Wales, is the period which—

    (a)   begins with the coming into force of this section; and

    (b)   ends with the coming into force of section 1 in relation to that area.

(4)   This section is deemed to have come into force on 28 June 2005.

58 Natural England

Any reference in a provision of this Act to Natural England shall, in relation to any time after the coming into force of that provision but before the coming into force of section 1(4) of the Natural Environment and Rural Communities Act 2006, be read as a reference to English Nature.

General

59 Orders and regulations

(1)   An order or regulations under this Act may make—

    (a)   transitional, consequential, incidental and supplemental provision or savings;

    (b)   different provision for different purposes or areas.

(2)   An order or regulations under this Act, other than an order under section 17, must be made by statutory instrument.

(3)   A statutory instrument containing regulations under section 29(1) or an order under section 54 or 55 may not be made by the Secretary of State (alone or jointly with the National Assembly for Wales) unless a draft has been laid before and approved by a resolution of each House of Parliament.

(3A) A statutory instrument containing an order under section 15C(5) may not be made unless a draft has been laid before and approved by a resolution of each House of Parliament.

(4) Subject to subsection (3) or (3A), a statutory instrument containing any order or regulations made under this Act by the Secretary of State (alone or jointly with the National Assembly for Wales) other than an order under section 56 shall be subject to annulment in pursuance of a resolution of either House of Parliament.

60 Crown application

(1) This Act (and any provision made under it) binds the Crown.

(2) This section does not impose criminal liability on the Crown in relation to an offence under section 34(1).

(3) Subsection (2) does not affect the criminal liability of persons in the service of the Crown.

61 Interpretation

(1) In this Act—

'appropriate national authority' means—

    (a)   the Secretary of State, in relation to England; and

    (b)   the National Assembly for Wales, in relation to Wales;

'commons council' means a commons council established under Part 2;

'land' includes land covered by water;

'nature conservation' means the conservation of flora and fauna and geological and physiographical features;

'regulations' means regulations made by the appropriate national authority;

'register of title' means the register kept under section 1 of the Land Registration Act 2002 (c 9);

'right of common' includes a cattlegate or beastgate (by whatever name known) and a right of sole or several vesture or herbage or of sole or several pasture, but does not include a right held for a term of years or from year to year.

(2) In this Act—

    (a)   any reference to land registered as common land or a town or village green is to land so registered in a register of common land or town or village greens;

    (b)   any reference to a register of common land or town or village greens is to such a register kept under Part 1 of this Act.

(3) In this Act—

    (a)   references to the ownership or the owner of any land are references to the ownership of a legal estate in fee simple in the land or to the person holding that estate;

    (b)   references to land registered in the register of title are references to land the fee simple of which is so registered.

62 Short title

This Act may be cited as the Commons Act 2006.

63 Extent

This Act extends to England and Wales only.

SCHEDULE 1
AUTHORISED SEVERANCE

Section 9

Severance by transfer to public bodies

1

(1) A right of common to which section 9 applies may on or after the day on which this Schedule comes into force be severed permanently from the land to which it is attached by being transferred on its own to—

(a) any commons council established for the land over which the right is exercisable;

(b) Natural England (where the land or any part of it is in England); or

(c) the Countryside Council for Wales (where the land or any part of it is in Wales).

(2) Where a person proposes to sever a right of common to which section 9 applies by a transfer under sub-paragraph (1)(b) or (c), Natural England or the Countryside Council for Wales as the case may be must—

(a) give notice of the proposal to the owner of the land over which the right is exercisable unless his name and address cannot reasonably be ascertained;

(b) in a case where there is no commons council established for the land, give notice of the proposal to such persons (if any) as they consider represent the interests of persons exercising rights of common over the land.

(3) A notice under sub-paragraph (2) must be given at least two months before the transfer and must—

(a) specify the name and address of the owner of the land to which the right is attached;

(b) describe the right proposed to be transferred, giving such details as regulations may specify;

(c) state the proposed consideration for the transfer; and

(d) give such other information as regulations may specify.

(4) Where a right of common to which section 9 applies is exercisable over land for which a commons council is established, the right may only be severed by a transfer under sub-paragraph (1)(b) or (c) if that council consents to the transfer.

(5) In a case where there is no commons council established for the land over which a right of common to which section 9 applies is exercisable, the appropriate national authority may by order provide that a person with functions of management conferred by any enactment in relation to that land is to be regarded, for any or all purposes of this paragraph, as a commons council established for the land.

(6) The severance of a right of common by its transfer under sub-paragraph (1)—

(a) only has effect if the transfer complies with such requirements as to form and content as regulations may provide; and

(b) does not operate at law until, on an application under this Schedule, the transferee is registered as the owner of the right in the register of common land or of town or village greens in which the right is registered.

Temporary severance by letting or leasing

2

(1) A right of common to which section 9 applies may, on or after the day on which this Schedule comes into force, to any extent be severed temporarily from the land to

which it is attached by virtue of the right, or all or part of the land, being leased or licensed on its own in accordance with—

    (a)   provision made by order by the appropriate national authority; or

    (b)   rules made in relation to the land by a commons council under section 31.

(2) Provision under sub-paragraph (1)(a) and rules referred to in sub-paragraph (1)(b) may be framed by reference to—

    (a)   particular land or descriptions of land;

    (b)   descriptions of persons to whom rights of common may be leased or licensed.

(3)   Where—

    (a)   provision under sub-paragraph (1)(a) applies in relation to any land, and

    (b)   rules referred to in sub-paragraph (1)(b) also apply in relation to that land and are inconsistent with that provision,

the rules prevail over that provision, to the extent of the inconsistency, in relation to that land.

(4)   The appropriate national authority may by order provide that the leasing or licensing of a right of common (whether authorised by provision under sub-paragraph (1)(a) or by rules referred to in sub-paragraph (1)(b)) must comply with such requirements as to form and content as the order may provide.

Severance authorised by order

3

(1)   The appropriate national authority may by order make provision authorising rights of common to which section 9 applies to be severed permanently from the land to which they are attached by transfer in accordance with that provision.

(2)   Provision under sub-paragraph (1) is to be framed by reference to—

    (a)   particular land over which the rights of common are exercisable, or

    (b)   particular descriptions of such land,

and may authorise transfers to particular persons, particular descriptions of persons or any person.

(3)   The appropriate national authority must, before making any provision under sub-paragraph (1) in relation to any land, consult such persons (if any) as it considers represent the interests of—

    (a)   persons who own the land;

    (b)   persons who exercise rights of common over the land.

(4)   Provision under sub-paragraph (1) may include provision securing that the owner of any land over which a right of common is exercisable is to be notified, and his consent obtained, before the right may be transferred.

(5)   Provision referred to in sub-paragraph (4) may include—

    (a)   provision as to the circumstances in which notification may be regarded as having been given; or

    (b)   provision as to the circumstances in which consent may be regarded as having been obtained.

(6)   Provision referred to in sub-paragraph (5)(b) may include—

    (a)   provision for consent to be regarded as having been obtained if it is withheld unreasonably;

    (b)   provision for the circumstances in which consent is to be regarded as withheld unreasonably;

    (c)   provision for the resolution of disputes.

(7)   The severance of a right of common by its transfer under provision under sub-paragraph (1)—

(a) only has effect if the transfer complies with such requirements as to form and content as regulations may provide; and

(b) does not operate at law until, on an application under this Schedule, the transferee is registered as the owner of the right in the register of common land or of town or village greens in which the right is registered.

(8) Provision under sub-paragraph (1) may include provision to secure the result that where—

(a) the person to whom the right of common is transferred is the owner of land to which rights of common are attached, and

(b) those rights are exercisable over the same land, or substantially the same land, as the right of common being transferred,

the transferee must, when making an application as specified in sub-paragraph (7)(b), apply to the commons registration authority for the right to be registered as attached to the land referred to in paragraph (a).

SCHEDULE 1A
EXCLUSION OF RIGHT UNDER SECTION 15

Section 15C

Trigger events	*Terminating events*
1. An application for planning permission in relation to the land which would be determined under section 70 of the 1990 Act is first publicised in accordance with requirements imposed by a development order by virtue of section 65(1) of that Act.	(a) The application is withdrawn.
	(b) A decision to decline to determine the application is made under section 70A of the 1990 Act.
	(c) In circumstances where planning permission is refused, all means of challenging the refusal in legal proceedings in the United Kingdom are exhausted and the decision is upheld.
2. An application for planning permission made in relation to the land under section 293A of the 1990 Act is first publicised in accordance with subsection (8) of that section.	(d) In circumstances where planning permission is granted, the period within which the development to which the permission relates must be begun expires without the development having been begun.
	(a) The application is withdrawn.
	(b) In circumstances where planning permission is refused, all means of challenging the refusal in legal proceedings in the United Kingdom are exhausted and the decision is upheld.
3. A draft of a development plan document which identifies the land for potential development is published for consultation in accordance with regulations under section 17(7) of the 2004 Act.	(c) In circumstances where planning permission is granted, the period within which the development to which the permission relates must be begun expires without the development having been begun.
	(a) The document is withdrawn under section 22(1) of the 2004 Act.

Trigger events	Terminating events
4. A development plan document which identifies the land for potential development is adopted under section 23(2) or (3) of the 2004 Act.	(b) The document is adopted under section 23(2) or (3) of that Act (but see paragraph 4 of this Table). (a) The document is revoked under section 25 of the 2004 Act.
5. A proposal for a neighbourhood development plan which identifies the land for potential development is published by a local planning authority for consultation in accordance with regulations under paragraph 4(1) of Schedule 4B to the 1990 Act as it applies by virtue of section 38A(3) of the 2004 Act.	(b) A policy contained in the document which relates to the development of the land in question is superseded by another policy by virtue of section 38(5) of that Act. (a) The proposal is withdrawn under paragraph 2(1) of Schedule 4B to the 1990 Act (as it applies by virtue of section 38A(3) of the 2004 Act). (b) The plan is made under section 38A of the 2004 Act (but see paragraph 6 of this Table).
6. A neighbourhood development plan which identifies the land for potential development is made under section 38A of the 2004 Act.	(a) The plan ceases to have effect. (b) The plan is revoked under section 61M of the 1990 Act (as it applies by virtue of section 38C(2) of the 2004 Act). (c) A policy contained in the plan which relates to the development of the land in question is superseded by another policy by virtue of section 38(5) of the 2004 Act.
7. A development plan for the purposes of section 27 or 54 of the 1990 Act, or anything treated as contained in such a plan by virtue of Schedule 8 to the 2004 Act, continues to have effect (by virtue of that Schedule) on the commencement of section 16 of the Growth and Infrastructure Act 2013 and identifies the land for potential development.	The plan ceases to have effect by virtue of paragraph 1 of Schedule 8 to the 2004 Act.
8. A proposed application for an order granting development consent under section 114 of the 2008 Act in relation to the land is first publicised in accordance with section 48 of that Act.	(a) The period of two years beginning with the day of publication expires. (b) The application is publicised under section 56(7) of the 2008 Act (but see paragraph 9 of this Table).
9. An application for such an order in relation to the land is first publicised in accordance with section 56(7) of the 2008 Act.	(a) The application is withdrawn. (b) In circumstances where the application is refused, all means of challenging the refusal in legal proceedings in the United Kingdom are exhausted and the decision is upheld. (c) In circumstances where an order granting development consent in relation to the land is made, the period within which the development to which the consent relates must be begun expires without the development having been begun.

(5)   For the purposes of this Schedule, all means of challenging a decision in legal proceedings in the United Kingdom are to be treated as exhausted and the decision is to be treated as upheld if, at any stage in the proceedings, the time normally allowed for the making of an appeal or further appeal or the taking of any other step to challenge the decision expires without the appeal having been made or (as the case may be) the other step having been taken.

(6)   Paragraph 7 of the first column of the Table does not apply in relation to a part of a development plan for the purposes of section 27 or 54 of the 1990 Act which consists of—

(a)   Part 1 of a unitary development plan or alterations to such a Part, or

(b)   a structure plan or alterations to such a plan.

SCHEDULE 2
NON-REGISTRATION OR MISTAKEN REGISTRATION UNDER THE 1965 ACT

Section 22

Introductory

1

In this Schedule 'the 1965 Act' means the Commons Registration Act 1965 (c 64).

Non-registration of common land

2

(1)   If a commons registration authority is satisfied that any land not registered as common land or as a town or village green is land to which this paragraph applies, the authority shall, subject to this paragraph, register the land as common land in its register of common land.

(2)   This paragraph applies to any land which—

(a)   was not at any time finally registered as common land or as a town or village green under the 1965 Act;

(b)   is land which is—

(i)   regulated by an Act made under the Commons Act 1876 (c 56) confirming a provisional order of the Inclosure Commissioners;

(ii)   subject to a scheme under Metropolitan Commons Act 1866 (c 122) or the Commons Act 1899 (c 30);

(iii)   regulated as common land under a local or personal Act; or

(iv)   otherwise recognised or designated as common land by or under an enactment;

(c)   is land to which this Part applies; and

(d)   satisfies such other conditions as regulations may specify.

(3)   A commons registration authority may only register land under sub-paragraph (1) acting on—

(a)   the application of any person made before such date as regulations may specify; or

(b)   a proposal made and published by the authority before such date as regulations may specify.

Non-registration of town or village green

3

(1)   If a commons registration authority is satisfied that any land not registered as a town or village green or as common land is land to which this paragraph applies, the authority shall, subject to this paragraph, register the land as a town or village green in its register of town or village greens.

(2) This paragraph applies to any land which—

    (a)   on 31 July 1970 was land allotted by or under any Act for the exercise or recreation of the inhabitants of any locality;

    (b)   was not at any time finally registered as a town or village green or as common land under the 1965 Act;

    (c)   continues to be land allotted as specified in paragraph (a);

    (d)   is land to which this Part applies; and

    (e)   satisfies such other conditions as regulations may specify.

(3) A commons registration authority may only register land under sub-paragraph (1) acting on—

    (a)   the application of any person made before such date as regulations may specify; or

    (b)   a proposal made and published by the authority before such date as regulations may specify.

Waste land of a manor not registered as common land

4

(1) If a commons registration authority is satisfied that any land not registered as common land or as a town or village green is land to which this paragraph applies, the authority shall, subject to this paragraph, register the land as common land in its register of common land.

(2) This paragraph applies to land which at the time of the application under sub-paragraph (1) is waste land of a manor and where, before the commencement of this paragraph—

    (a)   the land was provisionally registered as common land under section 4 of the 1965 Act;

    (b)   an objection was made in relation to the provisional registration; and

    (c)   the provisional registration was cancelled in the circumstances specified in sub-paragraph (3), (4) or (5).

(3) The circumstances in this sub-paragraph are that—

    (a)   the provisional registration was referred to a Commons Commissioner under section 5 of the 1965 Act;

    (b)   the Commissioner determined that, although the land had been waste land of a manor at some earlier time, it was not such land at the time of the determination because it had ceased to be connected with the manor; and

    (c)   for that reason only the Commissioner refused to confirm the provisional registration.

(4) The circumstances in this sub-paragraph are that—

    (a)   the provisional registration was referred to a Commons Commissioner under section 5 of the 1965 Act;

    (b)   the Commissioner determined that the land was not subject to rights of common and for that reason refused to confirm the provisional registration; and

    (c)   the Commissioner did not consider whether the land was waste land of a manor.

(5) The circumstances in this sub-paragraph are that the person on whose application the provisional registration was made requested or agreed to its cancellation (whether before or after its referral to a Commons Commissioner).

(6) A commons registration authority may only register land under sub-paragraph (1) acting on—

(a) the application of any person made before such date as regulations may specify; or

(b) a proposal made and published by the authority before such date as regulations may specify.

Town or village green wrongly registered as common land

5

(1) If a commons registration authority is satisfied that any land registered as common land is land to which this paragraph applies, the authority shall, subject to this paragraph, remove the land from its register of common land and register it in its register of town or village greens.

(2) This paragraph applies to land where—

(a) the land was provisionally registered as common land under section 4 of the 1965 Act;

(b) the provisional registration became final; but

(c) immediately before its provisional registration, the land was a town or village green within the meaning of that Act as originally enacted.

(3) A commons registration authority may only remove and register land under sub-paragraph (1) acting on—

(a) the application of any person made before such date as regulations may specify; or

(b) a proposal made and published by the authority before such date as regulations may specify.

Buildings registered as common land

6

(1) If a commons registration authority is satisfied that any land registered as common land is land to which this paragraph applies, the authority shall, subject to this paragraph, remove that land from its register of common land.

(2) This paragraph applies to land where—

(a) the land was provisionally registered as common land under section 4 of the 1965 Act;

(b) on the date of the provisional registration the land was covered by a building or was within the curtilage of a building;

(c) the provisional registration became final; and

(d) since the date of the provisional registration the land has at all times been, and still is, covered by a building or within the curtilage of a building.

(3) A commons registration authority may only remove land under sub-paragraph (1) acting on—

(a) the application of any person made before such date as regulations may specify; or

(b) a proposal made and published by the authority before such date as regulations may specify.

Other land wrongly registered as common land

7

(1) If a commons registration authority is satisfied that any land registered as common land is land to which this paragraph applies, the authority shall, subject to this paragraph, remove the land from its register of common land.

(2) This paragraph applies to land where—
- (a) the land was provisionally registered as common land under section 4 of the 1965 Act;
- (b) the provisional registration of the land as common land was not referred to a Commons Commissioner under section 5 of the 1965 Act;
- (c) the provisional registration became final; and
- (d) immediately before its provisional registration the land was not any of the following—
  - (i) land subject to rights of common;
  - (ii) waste land of a manor;
  - (iii) a town or village green within the meaning of the 1965 Act as originally enacted; or
  - (iv) land of a description specified in section 11 of the Inclosure Act 1845 (c 118).

(3) A commons registration authority may only remove land under sub-paragraph (1) acting on—
- (a) the application of any person made before such date as regulations may specify; or
- (b) a proposal made and published by the authority before such date as regulations may specify.

Buildings registered as town or village green

8

(1) If a commons registration authority is satisfied that any land registered as a town or village green is land to which this paragraph applies, the authority shall, subject to this paragraph, remove that land from its register of town or village greens.

(2) This paragraph applies to land where—
- (a) the land was provisionally registered as a town or village green under section 4 of the 1965 Act;
- (b) on the date of the provisional registration the land was covered by a building or was within the curtilage of a building;
- (c) the provisional registration became final; and
- (d) since the date of the provisional registration the land has at all times been, and still is, covered by a building or within the curtilage of a building.

(3) A commons registration authority may only remove land under sub-paragraph (1) acting on—
- (a) the application of any person made before such date as regulations may specify; or
- (b) a proposal made and published by the authority before such date as regulations may specify.

Other land wrongly registered as town or village green

9

(1) If a commons registration authority is satisfied that any land registered as a town or village green is land to which this paragraph applies, the authority shall, subject to this paragraph, remove the land from its register of town or village greens.

(2) This paragraph applies to land where—
- (a) the land was provisionally registered as a town or village green under section 4 of the 1965 Act;

(b)   the provisional registration of the land as a town or village green was not referred to a Commons Commissioner under section 5 of the 1965 Act;

(c)   the provisional registration became final; and

(d)   immediately before its provisional registration the land was not—

    (i)   common land within the meaning of that Act; or

    (ii)   a town or village green.

(3) For the purposes of sub-paragraph (2)(d)(ii), land is to be taken not to have been a town or village green immediately before its provisional registration if (and only if)—

(a)   throughout the period of 20 years preceding the date of its provisional registration the land was, by reason of its physical nature, unusable by members of the public for the purposes of lawful sports and pastimes; and

(b)   immediately before its provisional registration the land was not, and at the time of the application under this paragraph still is not, allotted by or under any Act for the exercise or recreation of the inhabitants of any locality.

(4) A commons registration authority may only remove land under sub-paragraph (1) acting on—

(a)   the application of any person made before such date as regulations may specify; or

(b)   a proposal made and published by the authority before such date as regulations may specify.

Costs

10

(1) Regulations may make provision as to the payment of costs which pursuant to an application under this Schedule are incurred by the applicant, an objector or the person determining the application.

(2) That provision may in particular include provision—

(a)   for the payment of costs by the applicant, an objector or a commons registration authority;

(b)   for the person determining an application or the appropriate national authority to determine who is liable to pay costs and how much they are liable to pay.

SCHEDULE 3
REGISTRATION: TRANSITIONAL PROVISION

Section 23

Interpretation

1

In this Schedule 'the 1965 Act' means the Commons Registration Act 1965 (c 64).

Transitional period for updating registers

2

(1) Regulations may make provision for commons registration authorities, during a period specified in the regulations ('the transitional period'), to amend their registers of common land and town or village greens in consequence of qualifying events which were not registered under the 1965 Act.

(2) The following are qualifying events for the purposes of this Schedule—

(a) the creation of a right of common (by any means, including prescription), where occurring in relation to land to which this Part applies at any time—
    (i) after 2 January 1970; and
    (ii) before the commencement of this paragraph;

(b) any relevant disposition in relation to a right of common registered under the 1965 Act, or any extinguishment of such a right, where occurring at any time—
    (i) after the date of the registration of the right under that Act; and
    (ii) before the commencement of this paragraph;

(c) a disposition occurring before the commencement of this paragraph by virtue of any relevant instrument in relation to land which at the time of the disposition was registered as common land or a town or village green under the 1965 Act;

(d) the giving of land in exchange for any land subject to a disposition referred to in paragraph (c).

(3) In sub-paragraph (2)(b) 'relevant disposition' means—

(a) the surrender of a right of common;

(b) the variation of a right of common;

(c) in the case of a right of common attached to land, the apportionment or severance of the right;

(d) in the case of a right not attached to land, the transfer of the right.

(4) In sub-paragraph (2)(c) 'relevant instrument' means—

(a) any order, deed or other instrument made under or pursuant to the Acquisition of Land Act 1981 (c 67);

(b) a conveyance made for the purposes of section 13 of the New Parishes Measure 1943 (No 1);

(c) any other instrument made under or pursuant to any enactment.

(5) Regulations under this paragraph may include provision for commons registration authorities to amend their registers as specified in sub-paragraph (1)—

(a) on the application of a person specified in the regulations; or

(b) on their own initiative.

(6) Regulations under sub-paragraph (5)(b) may include provision requiring a commons registration authority to take steps to discover information relating to qualifying events, including in particular requiring an authority to—

(a) carry out a review of information already contained in a register of common land or town or village greens;

(b) publicise the review;

(c) invite persons to supply information for, or to apply for amendment of, the register.

3

At the end of the transitional period, any right of common which—

(a) is not registered in a register of common land or town or village greens, but

(b) was capable of being so registered under paragraph 2,

is by virtue of this paragraph at that time extinguished.

4

(1) Regulations may make provision for commons registration authorities to amend their registers of common land or town or village greens after the end of the transitional period, in circumstances specified in the regulations, in consequence of qualifying events.

(2)   Regulations under this paragraph may provide that paragraph 3 is to be treated as not having applied to any right of common which is registered pursuant to the regulations.

5

Regulations under paragraph 2 or 4 may in particular include provision as to what is or is not to be regarded as severance of a right of common for the purposes of those regulations.

Effect of repeals

6

The repeal by this Act of section 1(2)(b) of the 1965 Act does not affect the extinguishment of rights of common occurring by virtue of that provision.

7

The repeal by this Act of section 21(1) of the 1965 Act does not affect the application of section 193 of the Law of Property Act 1925 (c 20) in relation to any land.

Ownership of common land or town or village green

8

(1)   Where the ownership of any land is registered in any register under the 1965 Act immediately before the commencement of this Schedule the ownership shall, subject to this Part, continue to be registered in that register.

(2)   Where the ownership of land continues to be registered in a register of common land or town or village greens pursuant to sub-paragraph (1), if the commons registration authority is notified by the Chief Land Registrar that the land has been registered in the register of title, the authority shall—

  (a)   remove the registration of ownership; and

  (b)   indicate in the register in such manner as may be specified in regulations that the land has been registered in the register of title.

(3)   Regulations may require commons registration authorities—

  (a)   to remove registration of ownership of land from their registers of common land and town or village greens;

  (b)   to keep or otherwise deal with documents received by them in connection with the registration of ownership of land in such manner as the regulations may specify.

Vesting of unclaimed land

9

(1)   The repeal by this Act of section 8 of the 1965 Act does not affect the vesting of land in any local authority (within the meaning of that Act) occurring by virtue of that provision.

(2)   Unless land so vesting is regulated by a scheme under the Commons Act 1899 (c 30), sections 10 and 15 of the Open Spaces Act 1906 (c 25) (power to manage and make byelaws) shall continue to apply to it as if the local authority had acquired the ownership under that Act of 1906.

SCHEDULE 4
WORKS: SUPPLEMENTARY

Section 44

1–4

[*Amending only, and therefore not set out here.*]

New parishes

5

In section 15 of the New Parishes Measure 1943 (No 1) (land subject to rights of common), in subsection (1), for the words from 'without the consent' to the end substitute 'without the consent of the Secretary of State and sections 39 and 40 of the Commons Act 2006 apply in relation to an application for such consent as they apply in relation to an application for consent under section 38(1) of that Act.'

Transitional provision

6

In its application to any works carried out on or after 28 June 2005 but before the day on which section 38(1) above comes into force, section 194(2) of the Law of Property Act 1925 (c 20) shall have effect as if the words 'interested in the common' were omitted.

7

The prohibition in section 38(1) does not apply to works carried out in connection with the taking or working of minerals if—

    (a)   the works were granted planning permission under any enactment before the commencement of section 38;

    (b)   the works are carried out in accordance with that planning permission in the period allowed for the works to be carried out (subject to any extension of time granted before or after the commencement of that section).

LOCAL GOVERNMENT AND PUBLIC INVOLVEMENT IN HEALTH ACT 2007

PART 1

STRUCTURAL AND BOUNDARY CHANGE IN ENGLAND

CHAPTER 1

STRUCTURAL AND BOUNDARY CHANGE
Change from two tiers to single tier of local government

1 "Principal authority" and "single tier of local government"

(1) For the purposes of this Chapter, each of the following is a "principal authority"—

    (a)   a county council in England;

    (b)   a district council in England.

(2)   For the purposes of this Chapter there is "a single tier of local government" for an area if—

    (a)   there is a county council and no district councils for that area; or

    (b)   there is a district council and no county council for that area.

(3)   For the purposes of subsection (2)(b) there is a county council "for" an area which is a district if there is a county council which has in relation to that area the functions of a county council.

2 Invitations and directions for proposals for single tier of local government

(1)   The Secretary of State may invite or direct any principal authority to make one of the following proposals—

    (a)   a Type A proposal;

    (b)   a Type B proposal;

    (c)   a Type C proposal;

    (d)   a combined proposal.

(2)   A Type A proposal is a proposal that there should be a single tier of local government for the area which is the county concerned.

(3)   A Type B proposal is a proposal that there should be a single tier of local government for an area which—

    (a)   is currently a district, or two or more districts, in the county concerned; and

    (b)   is specified in the proposal.

(4)   A Type C proposal is a proposal that there should be a single tier of local government for an area specified in the proposal which currently consists of—

    (a)   the county concerned or one or more districts in the county concerned; and

    (b)   one or more relevant adjoining areas.

(5)   A combined proposal is a proposal that consists of—

    (a)   two or more Type B proposals,

    (b)   two or more Type C proposals, or

    (c)   one or more Type B proposals and one or more Type C proposals,

but a proposal is not a combined proposal if it includes any Type B or C proposals that are alternatives.

(6)   In this section "the county concerned" means—

    (a)   in relation to a principal authority which is the council for a county, that county;

    (b)   in relation to a principal authority which is the council for a district, the county in which the district is.

(7)   In this section a "relevant adjoining area" means an area which adjoins the county concerned and is currently a county in England, a district in England, or two or more such counties or districts.

(8)   An invitation or direction may either—

    (a)   be such that the authority may choose whether to make a Type A, Type B, Type C or combined proposal; or

    (b)   specify which one of those kinds of proposal is invited (or, in the case of a direction, required).

(9)   Subsection (1) is subject to section 3(1).

3 Invitations, directions and proposals: supplementary

(1)   A direction under section 2—

    (a)   may not be given after 25 January 2008; and

    (b)   may be given on or before that date only where the Secretary of State believes that giving the direction would be in the interests of effective and convenient local government.

(2)   A direction under section 2 may specify a date by which a proposal must be made.

(3)   An invitation under section 2 may specify a date by which a proposal may be made.

(4)   A proposal made by virtue of section 2 may not specify an area as one for which there should be a single tier of local government unless the whole or any part of that area is currently a two-tier area (as defined by section 23(2)).

(5)   In responding to an invitation under section 2, or complying with a direction under that section, an authority must have regard to any guidance from the Secretary of State as to—

(a)   what a proposal should seek to achieve;

(b)   matters that should be taken into account in formulating a proposal.

(6)   Where invitations or directions under section 2 are given to more than one authority, any authority that has received an invitation or direction may respond to the invitation, or comply with the direction, either by—

(a)   making its own proposal in accordance with the invitation or direction; or

(b)   making a proposal, in accordance with the invitation or direction, jointly with any of the other authorities.

(7)   An invitation or direction under section 2 may be varied or revoked.

(8)   But a direction under section 2 may not be varied after 25 January 2008 if—

(a)   the direction as originally given required the making of a Type A or Type B proposal; and

(b)   the direction as varied would require or permit the making of a Type C or combined proposal.

4   Request for [Local Government Boundary Commission's] advice

(1)   This section applies where the Secretary of State receives a proposal in response to an invitation or direction under section 2.

(2)   The   Secretary   of   State   may   request   the   [Local   Government Boundary Commission] to advise, no later than a date specified in the request, on any matter that—

(a)   relates to the proposal; and

(b)   is specified in the request.

(3)   The Secretary of State may at any time substitute a later date for the date specified in a request under subsection (2) (or for any date previously substituted under this subsection).

5   [Local Government Boundary Commission's] powers

(1)   This section applies where the [Local Government Boundary Commission] receive a request for advice under section 4.

(2)   The [Local Government Boundary Commission] may provide the advice requested.

(3)   Where they provide that advice, the [Local Government Boundary Commission] may also do any of the following that they think appropriate—

(a)   recommend that the Secretary of State implements the proposal without modification;

(b)   recommend that he does not implement it;

(c)   make an alternative proposal to him.

(4)   In subsection (3)(a) "the proposal" means the Type A, Type B, Type C or combined proposal to which the request for advice related.

(5)   In subsection (3)(c) "an alternative proposal" means—

(a)   a proposal that there should be a single tier of local government for an area that—

      (i)   is, or includes, the whole or part of the county concerned; and

      (ii)   is specified in the alternative proposal; or

  (b)   a proposal consisting of two or more proposals that are within paragraph (a) (and are not alternatives to one another).

(6) In this section "the county concerned" means—

  (a)   the county that, under section 2(6), is the county concerned in relation to the authority which made the proposal referred to in subsection (4) above; or

  (b)   where that proposal was made by more than one authority, any county that (under section 2(6)) is the county concerned in relation to any of the authorities which made that proposal.

(7) The area specified in an alternative proposal under this section may not extend into any area that is currently outside all local government areas.

6 [Local Government Boundary Commission's] procedure

(1) A local authority must if requested by the [Local Government Boundary Commission] to do so provide the [Commission], by such date as the [Commission] may specify, with any information that the [Commission] may reasonably require in connection with any of their functions under section 5.

(2) In making a recommendation or alternative proposal under section 5 the [Local Government Boundary Commission] must have regard to any guidance from the Secretary of State about the exercise of the [Commission's] functions under that section.

(3) Any recommendation or alternative proposal under section 5 must be made no later than the relevant date.

(4) Before making an alternative proposal under section 5(3)(c) the [Local Government Boundary Commission] must—

  (a)   publish a draft of the proposal; and

  (b)   take such steps as they consider sufficient to secure that persons who may be interested are informed of—

      (i)   the draft proposal; and

      (ii)   the period within which representations about it may be made to the [Commission].

(5) The [Local Government Boundary Commission]—

  (a)   must take into account any representations made to them within that period; and

  (b)   if they make any proposal to the Secretary of State, must inform any person who made such representations—

      (i)   of the proposal made; and

      (ii)   that representations about the proposal may be made to the Secretary of State until the end of the relevant period.

(6) In subsection (5)(b) "the relevant period" means four weeks beginning with the relevant date.

(7) In this section and section 7 "the relevant date" means the date specified in the request under section 4(2) (or, if a later date is substituted under section 4(3), the date substituted (or last substituted) under that provision).

7 Implementation of proposals by order

(1) Where the Secretary of State has received a proposal in response to an invitation or direction under section 2, he may—

  (a)   by order implement the proposal, with or without modification;

  (b)   if he has received an alternative proposal from the [Local Government Boundary Commission] under section 5, by order implement that alternative proposal with or without modification; or

(c)   decide to take no action.

(2) But where the Secretary of State has made a request under section 4 in relation to the proposal received in response to the invitation or direction, he may not make an order or decision under this section before the end of six weeks beginning with the relevant date (as defined by section 6(7)).

(3) The Secretary of State may not in any case make an order under subsection (1)(a) implementing a proposal unless he has consulted the following about the proposal—

> (a)   every authority affected by the proposal (except the authority or authorities which made it); and
>
> (b)   such other persons as he considers appropriate.

(4) For the purposes of this section an authority is "affected by" a proposal if it is a principal authority for an area which is, or any part of which is, in an area that the proposal suggests should have a single tier of local government.

(5) Subsection (3) does not apply if the proposal was made jointly by every authority affected by it, and in that case the Secretary of State may before making an order under subsection (1)(a) (or deciding not to) consult such other persons as he considers appropriate.

(6) In any case where he has received an alternative proposal from the [Local Government Boundary Commission] under section 5, the Secretary of State may request the [Commission] to provide him with information or advice on any matter relating to the proposal.

(7) Where they receive such a request the [Local Government Boundary Commission] may provide the information or advice requested.

Boundary change

8 Review by [Local Government Boundary Commission] of local government areas

(1) The [Local Government Boundary Commission] may, either on their own initiative or at the request of the Secretary of State or a local authority, conduct a review of one or more local government areas.

(2) Where they have conducted a review under this section the [Local Government Boundary Commission] may (subject to subsection (4)) recommend to the Secretary of State such boundary change as in consequence of the review seems to them desirable.

(3) For the purposes of this section "boundary change" means any of the following or any combination of the following—

> (a)   the alteration of a local government area boundary;
>
> (b)   the abolition of a local government area;
>
> (c)   the constitution of a new local government area.

(4) None of the following may be recommended under this section—

> (a)   a change consisting of the alteration of the boundary of a single-tier area and consequent abolition of an area that is currently two-tier;
>
> (b)   a change consisting of the alteration of the boundary of a two-tier area and consequent abolition of an area that is currently single-tier;
>
> (c)   a change consisting of the constitution of a new local government area and consequent abolition of an existing local government area, where the new local government area would include—
>
> > (i)   the whole or part of any area that is currently single-tier; and
> >
> > (ii)   the whole or part of any area that is currently two-tier;
>
> (d)   a change consisting of the alteration of a local government area, or constitution of a new local government area, where the altered or new area would extend into an area that is currently outside all local government areas;

(e)   a change whose effect would be that England (excluding the Isles of Scilly, the City of London, the Inner Temple and the Middle Temple) is no longer divided into areas each of which is—

(i)   a county divided into districts, or comprising one district; or

(ii)   a London borough.

(5)   Where the [Local Government Boundary Commission] have conducted a review under this section and consider that no boundary change is desirable, they may recommend to the Secretary of State that no boundary change should be made.

(6)   In considering whether (and, if so, what) boundary change is desirable, the [Local Government Boundary Commission] must have regard to—

(a)   the need to secure effective and convenient local government; and

(b)   the need to reflect the identities and interests of local communities.

[(6A)   Where under subsection (2) the Local Government Boundary Commission recommend that a boundary change should be made in relation to any local government area, the Commission must recommend to the Secretary of State whether, in consequence, a change should be made to—

(a)   the electoral arrangements of the area of a local authority;

(b)   the electoral arrangements of the area of a parish council.

(6B)   In subsection (6A)(a) "electoral arrangements", in relation to the area of a local authority means—

(a)   the total number of members of the local authority ("councillors");

(b)   the number and boundaries of electoral areas for the purposes of the election of councillors;

(c)   the number of councillors to be returned by any electoral area in that area; and

(d)   the name of any electoral area.

(6C)   In subsection (6A)(b) "electoral arrangements", in relation to the area of a parish council means—

(a)   the total number of members of the parish council ("parish councillors");

(b)   arrangements for the division of the parish or (in the case of a common parish council) any of the parishes into wards for the purposes of the election of parish councillors;

(c)   the number and boundaries of any wards;

(d)   the number of parish councillors to be returned by any ward or, in the case of a common parish council, by each parish; and

(e)   the name of any ward.

(6D)   Schedule 2 to the Local Democracy, Economic Development and Construction Act 2009 applies in relation to the making of recommendations under subsection (6A).

(6E)   Where under subsection (2) the Local Government Boundary Commission recommend that a boundary change should be made in relation to the area of a London borough council, the Commission must recommend to the Secretary of State whether, in consequence, a change should be made to the area of any constituency for the London Assembly in order to comply with the rules set out in paragraph 7 of Schedule 1 to the Greater London Authority Act 1999.]

(7)   In exercising a function under [this section], a local authority or the [Local Government Boundary Commission] must have regard to any guidance from the Secretary of State about the exercise of that function.

(8)   A local authority must if requested by the [Local Government Boundary Commission] to do so provide the [Commission], by such date as the [Commission] may specify, with any information that the [Commission] may reasonably require in connection with any of their functions under this section.

9 [Local Government Boundary Commission's] review: consultation etc

(1) This section applies where the Boundary Committee conduct a review under section 8.

(2) In conducting the review the [Local Government Boundary Commission] must consult—

    (a)   the council of any local government area to which the review relates; and

    (b)   such other local authorities, parish councils and other persons as appear to them to have an interest.

(3) Before making any recommendation to the Secretary of State the [Local Government Boundary Commission] must—

    (a)   publish a draft of the recommendation; and

    (b)   take such steps as they consider sufficient to secure that persons who may be interested are informed of—

        (i)   the draft recommendation; and

        (ii)   the period within which representations about it may be made to the [Commission].

(4) The [Local Government Boundary Commission]—

    (a)   must take into account any representations made to them within that period; and

    (b)   if they make any recommendation to the Secretary of State, must inform any person who made such representations—

        (i)   of the recommendation made; and

        (ii)   that representations about the recommendation may be made to the Secretary of State until the end of four weeks beginning with the recommendation date.

(5) In this section and section 10 "the recommendation date" means the date the recommendation was sent by the [Local Government Boundary Commission] to the Secretary of State.

10 Implementation of recommendations by order

(1) Where the [Local Government Boundary Commission] make a recommendation to the Secretary of State under section 8(2), the Secretary of State may do any of the following—

    (a)   by order implement the recommendation, with or without modification;

    (b)   decide to take no action with respect to the recommendation;

    (c)   make a request under section 8 for a further review.

(2) Where the [Local Government Boundary Commission] make a recommendation to the Secretary of State under section 8(5) the Secretary of State may—

    (a)   make a request under section 8 for a further review; or

    (b)   decide not to make such a request.

[(2A) Subsections (2B) to (2D) apply where the Local Government Boundary Commission make a recommendation to the Secretary of State under section 8(6A) or (6E) in consequence of a recommendation under section 8(2).

(2B) Where under subsection (1)(a) the Secretary of State implements the recommendation under section 8(2) without modification, the Secretary of State must by order implement the recommendation under section 8(6A) or (6E).

(2C) Where pursuant to subsection (1)(a) the Secretary of State proposes to implement the recommendation under section 8(2) with modification, the Secretary of State must request the Local Government Boundary Commission to recommend whether a modification is needed to their recommendation under section 8(6A) or (6E).

(2D) Where under section (1)(a) the Secretary of State implements a recommendation under section 8(2) with modification—

(a)   if the Local Government Boundary Commission have recommended under subsection (2C) that a modification is needed to their recommendation under section 8(6A) or (6E), the Secretary of State must by order implement the recommendation under section 8(6A) or (6E) with that modification;

(b)   if the Local Government Boundary Commission have recommended under subsection (2C) that no modification is needed to the recommendation under section 8(6A) or (6E), the Secretary of State must by order implement that recommendation.]

(3)   The Secretary of State may not do as mentioned in paragraph (a), (b) or (c) of subsection (1) or paragraph (a) or (b) of subsection (2) before the end of six weeks beginning with the recommendation date (as defined by section 9(5)).

(4)   Before doing as mentioned in any of those paragraphs the Secretary of State may request the [Local Government Boundary Commission] to provide him with information or advice on any matter relating to the recommendation.

(5)   Where they receive such a request the [Local Government Boundary Commission] may provide the information or advice requested.

Implementation of changes

11 Implementation orders: provision that may be included

(1)   An order under section 7 or 10 may in particular include provision, for the purpose of implementing a proposal or recommendation or in connection with the implementation of a proposal or recommendation, for or with respect to—

(a)   any of the matters mentioned in subsection (3);

(b)   any of the matters mentioned in subsection (4) (incidental, consequential etc matters).

(2)   In subsection (1) "implementing" includes implementing with modifications and "implementation" is to be read accordingly.

(3)   The matters referred to in subsection (1)(a) are—

(a)   the constitution of a new local government area;

(b)   the abolition of any existing local government area;

(c)   the boundary of any local government area;

(d)   whether a county or district is to be metropolitan or non-metropolitan;

(e)   the establishment, as a county council, district council or London borough council, of an authority for any local government area;

(f)   the winding up and dissolution of an existing local authority;

(g)   the transfer to a county council of the functions, in relation to an area, of district councils;

(h)   the transfer to a district council of the functions, in relation to an area, of a county council;

[(i)   electoral matters within the meaning of section 12].

(4)   The matters referred to in subsection (1)(b) are—

(a)   the name of any local government area;

(b)   the name of any local authority;

(c)   the boundary of any parish;

(d)   . . .

(e)   the establishment or membership of public bodies in any area affected by the order and the election of members of such bodies;

(f)   the abolition or establishment, or the restriction or extension, of the jurisdiction of any public body in or over any part of any area affected by the order;

(g)   the boundary of any police area in England.

(5)   For the purposes of subsection (3)(e)—

    (a)   the "establishment" of an authority as a council for a county includes an existing district council's becoming the county council for the county;

    (b)   the "establishment" of an authority as a council for a district includes an existing county council's becoming the district council for the district.

(6)   The power of the Secretary of State under section 7(1)(a) to implement a proposal with modifications includes power to make provision whose effect is that there will be a single tier of local government for an area ("the area concerned") that—

    (a)   includes all or part of an area specified in the proposal as one for which there should be a single tier of local government; but

    (b)   is not an area that could itself have been so specified.

(7)   But subsection (6) does not authorise the area concerned to extend into any area that is currently outside all local government areas.

12 Provision relating to membership etc of authorities

(1)   In [section 11(3)] "electoral matters" means any of the following—

    (a)   the total number of members of any local authority or parish council ("councillors");

    (b)   the number and boundaries of electoral areas for the purposes of the election of councillors;

    (c)   the number of councillors to be returned by any electoral area;

    (d)   the name of any electoral area;

    (e)   the election of councillors for any electoral areas;

    (f)   the order of retirement of councillors;

    (g)   the election of a mayor of a local authority;

    (h)   the election of an executive of a local authority;

    (i)   the appointment by the Secretary of State of members of an existing local authority to be members of a new local authority for a transitional period;

    (j)   the appointment for a transitional period of an executive of a new local authority;

    (k)   the functions of a new local authority, and the discharge of those functions, during a transitional period;

    [(l)   the ordinary year of election for a parish council].

(2)   In subsection (1)(i) to (k)—

    "a new local authority" means a local authority established by the order;

    "a transitional period" means a period before the coming into office of members of the authority elected at the first election after the establishment of the authority.

(3)   In subsection (2) "established" and "establishment" are to be read in accordance with section 11(5).

(4)   An order under section 7 or 10 may provide for an electoral division of a non-metropolitan county to return more than one councillor, and in such a case section 6(2)(a) of the Local Government Act 1972 (c 70) does not apply.

(5)   As soon as practicable after the making of an order under section 7 or 10, [the Local Government Boundary Commission must consider whether to exercise its power under section 56(2) of the Local Democracy, Economic Development and Construction Act 2009 (electoral reviews)].

(6)   . . .

13 Implementation orders: further provision

(1)   The power to make an order under section 7 or 10 includes (as well as power to make any provision authorised by section 11(1)(b)) power to make any other incidental, consequential, transitional or supplementary provision.

(2)   Subsection (1) is to be read with section 15.

(3) Any incidental, consequential, transitional or supplementary provision included in an order under section 7 or 10 may relate either to other provisions of the order or to a previous order under section 7 or 10 (and the reference in section 12(2) to "the order" accordingly includes a previous order under section 7 or 10).

(4) The Secretary of State must exercise his powers under section 11(4)(g) in such a way as to ensure that none of the following is divided between two or more police areas—

    (a)   a county in which there are no district councils;

    (b)   a district;

    (c)   a London borough.

14 Regulations for supplementing orders

(1) The Secretary of State may by regulations of general application make incidental, consequential, transitional or supplementary provision—

    (a)   for the purposes or in consequence of any orders under section 7 or 10; or

    (b)   for giving full effect to such orders.

(2) Subsection (1) is to be read with section 15.

(3) Regulations under this section have effect subject to any provision included in an order under section 7 or 10.

15 Incidental etc provision in orders or regulations

(1) In sections 13 and 14 references to incidental, consequential, transitional or supplementary provision include, in particular, provision—

    (a)   for the transfer of functions, property, rights or liabilities from a local authority or [local policing body] for any area to another local authority or [local policing body] whose area consists of or includes the whole or part of that area;

    (b)   for the transfer of property, rights or liabilities, and of related functions, from an authority which ceases to exist to a residuary body established under section 17;

    (c)   for legal proceedings commenced by or against any body to be continued by or against a body to whom functions, property, rights or liabilities are transferred;

    (d)   for the transfer of staff, compensation for loss of office, pensions and other staffing matters;

    (e)   for treating any body to whom a transfer is made for some or all purposes as the same person in law as the body from whom the transfer is made;

    (f)   with respect to the management or custody of transferred property (real or personal);

    [(fa)   as to who is to be a police and crime commissioner;]

    (g)   with respect to the functions, areas of jurisdiction and costs and expenses of any public body or of—

        (i)   any justice of the peace other than a District Judge (Magistrates' Courts);

        (ii)   any coroner or keeper of the rolls;

        (iii)   any lord-lieutenant, lieutenant or high sheriff; or

        (iv)   any other officers (including police officers) within the area of any local authority affected by an order under section 7 or 10;

    (h)   with respect to the functions of any District Judge (Magistrates' Courts);

    (i)   with respect to charter trustees;

    (j)   equivalent to any provision that could be contained in an agreement under section 16 (agreements about incidental matters).

[(1A) Provision falling within subsection (1)(fa) includes, in particular—

    (a)   provision for the police and crime commissioner for a police area affected by an order by virtue of provision made under section 11(4)(g) to become the police and crime commissioner for a police area resulting from the order;

    (b)   provision for the holding of an election for the police and crime commissioner for any police area resulting from the order.]

(2) Any order under section 7 or 10 or regulations under section 14 may for any incidental, consequential, transitional or supplementary purpose—

    (a)   modify, exclude or apply (with or without modifications) any enactment;

    (b)   repeal or revoke any enactment with or without savings.

(3) In subsection (2)—

    "enactment" includes—

        (a)   any enactment contained in this Act (other than a provision of this Part) or in an Act passed after this Act;

        (b)   any instrument made at any time under an enactment (including an enactment contained in this Act or in an Act passed after this Act);

        (c)   any charter, whenever granted;

    "modify" includes amend.

[(3A) Without prejudice to subsection (2), an order under section 7 or 10 which includes provision within subsection (1A)(b) may, in particular, require the election in question to be held before the alteration of police areas takes effect.]

16 Agreements about incidental matters

(1) Any public bodies affected by an order under section 7 or 10 may from time to time make agreements with respect to—

    (a)   any property, income, rights, liabilities and expenses (so far as affected by the order) of the parties to the agreement;

    (b)   any financial relations between the parties to the agreement.

(2) Such an agreement may in particular provide—

    (a)   for the transfer or retention of any property, rights and liabilities, with or without conditions, and for the joint use of any property;

    (b)   for the making of payments by any party to the agreement in respect of—

        (i)   property, rights and liabilities so transferred or retained;

        (ii)   such joint use; or

        (iii)   the remuneration or compensation payable to any person;

    (c)   for any such payment to be made by instalments or otherwise;

    (d)   for interest to be charged on any such instalments.

(3) In default of agreement about any disputed matter, the matter is to be referred to the arbitration of a single arbitrator—

    (a)   agreed on by the parties; or

    (b)   in default of agreement, appointed by the Secretary of State.

(4) The arbitrator's award may make any provision that could be contained in an agreement under this section.

(5) In subsection (3) "disputed matter" means any matter that—

    (a)   could be the subject of provision contained in an agreement under this section; and

    (b)   is the subject of a dispute between two or more public bodies that is not resolved by or under any order or regulations under this Chapter.

(6) In this section "public body" includes a parish council.

17 Residuary bodies

(1)   The Secretary of State may by order establish one or more bodies corporate ("residuary bodies") for the purpose of taking over any property, rights or liabilities, and any related functions, of local authorities which cease to exist by virtue of orders under section 7 or 10.

(2)   An order under subsection (1) may—

    (a)   make provision with respect to the constitution and membership of a residuary body;

    (b)   make provision with respect to the powers of a residuary body to make levies and to borrow and lend money and the treatment and distribution of capital and other money by such a body;

    (c)   make provision with respect to the keeping and auditing of accounts of a residuary body;

    (d)   make provision with respect to directions which may be given by the Secretary of State in relation to the carrying out by a residuary body of any of its functions;

    (e)   make provision enabling the Secretary of State to require a residuary body to submit to him a scheme for the winding up of the body and the disposal of its property, rights and liabilities and related functions.

(3)   The Secretary of State may by order provide—

    (a)   for the transfer to any other body or bodies (including any body or bodies corporate established under the order for the purpose) of any property, rights or liabilities, and any related functions, of a residuary body; and

    (b)   for giving effect (with or without modifications) to any scheme submitted to him under a provision made by virtue of subsection (2)(e) and for the dissolution of a residuary body.

(4)   An order under this section may include incidental, consequential, transitional or supplementary provision, including in particular provision of a kind mentioned in paragraphs (c) to (f) of section 15(1).

(5)   Section 15(2) and (3) (power to apply etc enactments) apply to an order under this section as to an order under section 7.

18 Staff commissions

(1)   The Secretary of State may by order establish one or more staff commissions for the purpose of—

    (a)   considering and keeping under review the arrangements for the recruitment of staff by relevant authorities affected by orders under this Chapter and for the transfer in consequence of any such order of staff employed by such authorities;

    (b)   considering such staffing problems arising in consequence of such an order, and such other matters relating to staff employed by any such authority, as may be referred to the staff commission by the Secretary of State; and

    (c)   advising the Secretary of State on the steps necessary to safeguard the interests of such staff.

(2)   Such a commission may be established for the whole or any part of England.

(3)   The Secretary of State may give directions to a staff commission with respect to their procedure.

(4)   The Secretary of State may give directions to any relevant authority affected by an order under this Chapter with respect to—

    (a)   the provision of any information requested and the implementation of any advice given by a staff commission;

    (b)   the payment by such an authority of any expenses incurred by a staff commission in doing anything requested by the authority.

(5) Any expenses incurred by a staff commission under this section and not recovered from a relevant authority shall be paid by the Secretary of State out of money provided by Parliament.

(6) The Secretary of State may by order provide for the winding up of any staff commission established under this section.

(7) A direction under this section may be varied or revoked by a subsequent direction.

(8) In this section "relevant authority" means—

    (a)   a local authority; or

    (b)   a residuary body established under section 17.

19 Certain county councils to be billing authorities

(1) Where an order under this Chapter transfers the functions of district councils in relation to any area to a council for a county consisting of that area, the county council—

    (a)   shall, for any financial year beginning at the same time as or after that transfer, be a billing authority for the purposes of Part 1 of the Local Government Finance Act 1992 (c 14) in relation to the area;

    (b)   shall not, for any such year, be a major precepting authority for those purposes.

(2) This section does not limit any power to make provision by order under this Chapter or any power to make incidental, consequential, transitional or supplementary provision in connection with the provisions of any such order.

(3) In this section "financial year" means 12 months beginning with 1 April.

Supplementary

20 Correction of orders

(1) Where—

    (a)   an order under any provision of this Chapter has been made by the Secretary of State, and

    (b)   the Secretary of State is satisfied that there is a mistake in the order which cannot be rectified by a subsequent order made under that provision by virtue of section 14 of the Interpretation Act 1978 (c 30) (power to amend),

the Secretary of State may rectify the mistake by order under this section.

(2) For the purposes of this section, a "mistake" in an order includes a provision contained in or omitted from the order in reliance on inaccurate or incomplete information supplied by any public body.

(3) In subsection (2) "public body" includes a parish council.

21 Pre-commencement invitations etc

(1) In this section a "pre-commencement invitation" means an invitation given by the Secretary of State before the commencement of this Chapter which, after that commencement, could have been given under the power in section 2.

(2) If before the commencement of this Chapter—

    (a)   a pre-commencement invitation was given,

    (b)   guidance as to what a proposal should seek to achieve, or as to matters that should be taken into account in formulating a proposal, was given by the Secretary of State in connection with such an invitation,

    (c)   a proposal was made in response to such an invitation, or

    (d)   consultation was carried out by the Secretary of State in relation to such a proposal, it is immaterial that the invitation or guidance was given, the proposal made, or the consultation carried out, before rather than after the commencement of this Chapter.

(3) Accordingly (and without prejudice to the generality of subsection (2))—

    (a)   any reference in this Chapter to an invitation under section 2 includes a pre-commencement invitation;

    (b)   any reference in this Chapter to a proposal made by virtue of section 2 includes a proposal (whenever made) made in response to a pre-commencement invitation;

    (c)   any reference in this Chapter to the Secretary of State's receiving a proposal in response to an invitation under section 2 includes his receiving before the commencement of this Chapter a proposal made in response to a pre-commencement invitation.

22 Consequential amendments

Schedule 1 (amendments consequential on this Chapter) has effect.

23 Definitions for purposes of Chapter 1

(1)   In this Chapter—

    . . .

"local authority" means a county council in England, a district council in England or a London borough council;

"local government area" means a county in England, a district in England or a London borough;

["the Local Government Boundary Commission" means the Local Government Boundary Commission for England;]

"principal authority" has the meaning given by section 1;

"public body" includes—

        (a)   a local authority;

        (b)   a police authority;

        (c)   a residuary body established under section 17;

        (d)   a joint board, or joint committee, on which a local authority is represented;

        (e)   a levying body within the meaning of section 74(1) of the Local Government Finance Act 1988 (c 41);

      [(f)   an economic prosperity board established under section 88 of the Local Democracy, Economic Development and Construction Act 2009;

        (g)   a combined authority established under section 103 of that Act;]

"single-tier" has the meaning given by subsection (2);

"staff" includes officers and employees;

"two-tier" has the meaning given by subsection (2);

"Type A", "Type B", "Type C" and "combined", in relation to a proposal, have the meanings given by section 2.

(2)   For the purposes of this Chapter an area is—

    (a)   "single-tier" if there is a single tier of local government for it (within the meaning of section 1) or it is a London borough; and

    (b)   "two-tier" if it is—

        (i)   a district for which there is a district council and in relation to which a county council has the functions of a county council; or

        (ii)   a county for which there is a county council and in which there are districts all of which have district councils.

(3)   Any reference in this Chapter to a proposal "in response to" an invitation or direction under section 2 is to a Type A, Type B, Type C or combined proposal which—

(a)   is in response to such an invitation or direction; and

(b)   is in accordance with the invitation or direction and section 3(4).

(4) Any reference in this Chapter, however framed, to a body affected by an order includes a body—

(a)   whose area or functions are affected by the order;

(b)   which is to cease to exist in pursuance of the order; or

(c)   which is established by or in consequence of the order.

CHAPTER 2

CONTROL OF DISPOSALS ETC

24 Authorities dissolved by orders: control of disposals, contracts and reserves

(1) The Secretary of State may direct that, with effect from a date specified in the direction, a relevant authority may not without the written consent of a person or persons so specified—

(a)   dispose of any land if the consideration for the disposal exceeds £100,000;

(b)   enter into any capital contract—

    (i)   under which the consideration payable by the relevant authority exceeds £1,000,000; or

    (ii)   which includes a term allowing the consideration payable by the relevant authority to be varied;

(c)   enter into any non-capital contract under which the consideration payable by the relevant authority exceeds £100,000, where—

    (i)   the period of the contract extends beyond a date specified in the direction; or

    (ii)   under the terms of the contract, that period may be extended beyond that date; or

(d)   include an amount of financial reserves in a calculation under section [31A(3) or 42A(3)] of the Local Government Finance Act 1992 (c 14).

(2) In this Chapter "relevant authority" means a local authority—

(a)   which by virtue of an order under section 7 or 10 is to be dissolved; and

(b)   which is specified, or of a description specified, in the direction.

(3) In this section—

"capital contract" means a contract as regards which the consideration payable by the relevant authority would be capital expenditure for the purposes of Chapter 1 of Part 1 of the Local Government Act 2003 (c 26) (capital finance);

"non-capital contract" means a contract which is not a capital contract.

(4) A person specified in the direction as a person whose consent is required may be the Secretary of State or such authority or other person as he thinks appropriate; and the direction may specify different persons—

(a)   in relation to different matters for which consent is required;

(b)   in relation to different relevant authorities or descriptions of relevant authority.

25 Directions: further provision about reserves

(1) A direction under section 24—

(a)   may provide that the consent of the person or persons specified in the direction is not required for the inclusion, in a calculation under section [31A(3) or 42A(3)] of the Local Government Finance Act 1992, of financial reserves of a description specified in the direction;

(b)   may, in relation to any authority or description of authority, provide that that consent is not required for the inclusion in such a calculation of an amount of financial reserves not exceeding an amount specified in or determined under the direction.

(2)   If a direction contains provision by virtue of subsection (1), the reference in section 24(1)(d) to an amount of financial reserves is to be read as a reference to an amount of financial reserves other than an amount permitted by the direction.

26 Directions: supplementary

(1)   In this section "direction" means a direction under section 24.

(2)   A consent for the purposes of a direction may be given—

(a)   in respect of a particular disposal or contract, or in respect of disposals or contracts of any description;

(b)   unconditionally or subject to conditions.

(3)   The following enactments have effect subject to any direction—

(a)   section 123 of the Local Government Act 1972 (c 70) (power to dispose of land);

(b)   any other enactment relating to the disposal of land by local authorities.

(4)   The consent required by a direction is in addition to any consent required by the enactments mentioned in subsection (3)(a) and (b).

(5)   Where the consideration or any of the consideration under a contract is not in money, the limits specified in a direction by virtue of section 24(1)(a) to (c) apply to the value of the consideration.

(6)   Where—

(a)   a question arises in relation to a direction as to the value of any consideration, and

(b)   the relevant authority concerned and the person or persons specified under section 24(1) fail to reach agreement,

the value is to be determined by the Secretary of State.

(7)   A direction may be varied or revoked by a subsequent direction.

27 Consideration to be taken into account for purposes of direction

(1)   In determining whether the limit specified in a direction by virtue of section 24(1)(a) is exceeded in the case of a disposal of land by a relevant authority, the consideration with respect to any other disposal of land made after 31 December 2006 by the relevant authority is to be taken into account.

(2)   In determining whether a limit specified in a direction by virtue of section 24(1)(b) or (c) is exceeded in the case of a contract entered into by a relevant authority ("the contract in question"), the consideration payable by the relevant authority under any other relevant contract shall be taken into account.

(3)   For the purposes of subsection (2) a "relevant contract" means a contract which is either or both—

(a)   a contract entered into after 31 December 2006 by the relevant authority and the person with whom the contract in question is entered into;

(b)   a contract entered into after that date by the relevant authority which relates to the same or a similar description of matter as that to which the contract in question relates.

28 Contraventions of direction

(1)   A disposal made in contravention of a direction under section 24 is void.

(2)   A contract entered into by an authority ("the old authority") in contravention of a direction under section 24 is not enforceable against a successor.

(3)   In subsection (2) a "successor" means a local authority (other than the old authority)—

(a)   which is established by an order under section 7 or 10; and

(b) whose area consists of or includes the whole or part of the area of the old authority.

(4) A contract which apart from this subsection would be a certified contract for the purposes of the Local Government (Contracts) Act 1997 (c 65) is not a certified contract for those purposes if it is entered into in contravention of a direction under section 24.

(5) If an authority includes financial reserves in a calculation under section [31A(3)] of the Local Government Finance Act 1992 (c 14) in contravention of a direction under section 24, the authority is to be treated for the purposes of section 30(8) of that Act as not having made the calculations required by Chapter 3 of Part 1 of that Act.

(6) If an authority includes financial reserves in a calculation under section [42A(3)] of that Act in contravention of a direction under section 24, the authority is to be treated for the purposes of section 40(7) of that Act as not having made the calculations required by Chapter 4 of Part 1 of that Act.

29 Power to amend

(1) The Secretary of State may by order—

(a) substitute another sum for any sum for the time being specified in section 24(1);

(b) substitute another date for the date for the time being specified in section 27(1) and (3).

(2) An order under this section may include transitional or saving provision.

30 Definitions for purposes of Chapter 2

(1) In this Chapter—

"local authority" means a county council in England, a district council in England or a London borough council;

"relevant authority" has the meaning given by section 24(2).

(2) References in this Chapter to disposing of land include references to—

(a) granting or disposing of any interest in land;

(b) entering into a contract to dispose of land or grant or dispose of any such interest;

(c) granting an option to acquire any land or any such interest.

PART 2

ELECTORAL ARRANGEMENTS

Power of district councils to alter years of ordinary elections of parish councillors

53 Power of council to alter years of ordinary elections of parish councillors

(1) This section applies if a council passes a resolution under this Chapter.

(2) The council may by order make provision that changes the years in which the ordinary elections of parish councillors for any parish situated in the council's area are to be held.

(3) The power may only be exercised so as to secure that those elections are to be held in years in which ordinary elections of district councillors for a ward in which any part of the parish is situated are to be held.

(4) The order may include transitional provision—

(a) for the retirement of existing parish councillors at times different from those otherwise applying;

(b) for the retirement of some parish councillors after their initial election after the order comes into force at times different from those otherwise applying.

PART 4

CHAPTER 3

REORGANISATION
Amendment of existing provisions about schemes for ordinary elections

79 Community governance reviews

(1)　A community governance review is a review of the whole or part of the principal council's area, for the purpose of making recommendations of the kinds set out in sections 87 to 92 (if, and so far as, those sections are applicable).

(2)　In undertaking a community governance review the principal council must comply with—

　　(a)　this Chapter, and

　　(b)　the terms of reference of the review.

(3)　A district council which is to undertake a community governance review must notify the county council for its area (if any)—

　　(a)　that the review is to be undertaken, and

　　(b)　of the terms of reference of the review (including any modification of those terms).

80 Community governance petitions

(1)　A community governance petition is a petition for a community governance review to be undertaken.

(2)　A petition is not a valid community governance petition unless the conditions in subsections (3) to (6) are met (so far as they are applicable).

(3)　The petition must be signed as follows—

　　(a)　if the petition area has fewer than 500 local government electors, the petition must be signed by at least 50% of the electors;

　　(b)　if the petition area has between 500 and 2,500 local government electors, the petition must be signed by at least 250 of the electors;

　　(c)　if the petition area has more than 2,500 local government electors, the petition must be signed by at least 10% of the electors.

(4)　The petition must—

　　(a)　define the area to which the review is to relate (whether on a map or otherwise), and

　　(b)　specify one or more recommendations which the petitioners wish a community governance review to consider making.

(5)　If the specified recommendations include the constitution of a new parish, the petition must define the area of the new parish (whether on a map or otherwise).

(6)　If the specified recommendations include the alteration of the area of an existing parish, the petition must define the area of the parish as it would be after alteration (whether on a map or otherwise).

(7)　If the specified recommendations include the constitution of a new parish, the petition is to be treated for the purposes of this Chapter as if the specified recommendations also include the recommendations in section 87(5) to (7).

(8)　If the specified recommendations include the establishment of a parish council or parish meeting for an area which does not exist as a parish, the petition is to be treated for the purposes of this Chapter as if the specified recommendations also include recommendations for such a parish to come into being (either by constitution of a new parish or alteration of the area of an existing parish).

81 Terms of reference of review

(1)　The terms of reference of a community governance review are the terms on which the review is to be undertaken.

(2) The terms of reference of a community governance review must specify the area under review.

(3) Sections 83 and 84 make further provision about the terms of reference of community governance reviews.

(4) Subject to subsection (2), and sections 83 and 84, it is for a principal council—

    (a)   to decide the terms of reference of any community governance review which the council is to undertake; and

    (b)   to decide what modifications (if any) to make to terms of reference.

(5) As soon as practicable after deciding terms of reference, the principal council must publish the terms.

(6) As soon as practicable after modifying terms of reference, the principal council must publish the modified terms.

Undertaking community governance reviews

82 Council's power to undertake review

A principal council may undertake a community governance review.

83 No review being undertaken: duty to respond to petition

(1) This section applies if these conditions are met—

    (a)   a principal council is not in the course of undertaking a community governance review;

    (b)   the council receives a community governance petition which relates to the whole or part of the council's area.

(2) The principal council must undertake a community governance review that has terms of reference that allow for the petition to be considered.

(3) But the duty in subsection (2) does not apply if—

    (a)   the principal council has concluded a previous community governance review within the relevant two-year period, and

    (b)   in the council's opinion the petition area covers the whole or a significant part of the area to which the previous review related.

For further provision about this case, see section 85.

84 Review being undertaken: duty to respond to petition

(1) This section applies if the following conditions are met—

    (a)   a principal council is in the course of undertaking a community governance review of part of the council's area ("the current review");

    (b)   the council receives a community governance petition which relates to part of the council's area;

    (c)   the petition area is wholly outside the area under review.

(2) The principal council must follow one of the options in subsection (4), (5) or (6).

(3) But the duty in subsection (2) does not apply if—

    (a)   the principal council has concluded a previous community governance review within the relevant two-year period, and

    (b)   in the council's opinion the petition area covers the whole or a significant part of the area to which the previous review related.

For further provision about this case, see section 85.

(4) The first option mentioned in subsection (2) is for the principal council to modify the terms of reference of the current review so that they allow for the petition to be considered.

(5) The second option is for the principal council to undertake a community governance review that—

    (a)   is separate from the current review, and

    (b)   has terms of reference that allow for the petition to be considered.

(6)   The third option is for the principal council to—

    (a)   modify the terms of reference of the current review,

    (b)   undertake a community governance review that is separate from the current review ("the new review"), and

    (c)   secure that (when taken together)—

        (i)   the terms of reference of the current review (as modified), and

        (ii)   the terms of reference of the new review,

allow for the petition to be considered.

85 Power to respond to petition

(1)   In any of the following cases where a principal council receive a community governance petition, it is for the council to decide what action (if any) to take under section 82 (power to undertake review) or 81(4)(b) (power to modify terms of review) in response to that petition.

(2)   The first case is where—

    (a)   section 83 applies (no review being undertaken when petition received), but

    (b)   the duty in section 83(2) does not apply because of section 83(3) (no duty to respond to petition because previous review concluded in relevant two-year period).

(3)   The second case is where—

    (a)   section 84 applies (review being undertaken when petition received: petition area wholly outside area under review), but

    (b)   the duty in section 84(2) does not apply because of section 84(3) (no duty to respond to petition because previous review concluded in relevant two-year period).

(4)   The third case is where these conditions are met—

    (a)   a principal council is in the course of undertaking a community governance review of part of the council's area;

    (b)   the council receives a community governance petition which relates to part of the council's area;

    (c)   the petition area is not wholly outside the area under review.

(5)   The fourth case is where these conditions are met—

    (a)   a principal council is in the course of undertaking a community governance review of part of the council's area;

    (b)   the council receives a community governance petition which relates to the whole of the council's area.

(6)   The fifth case is where these conditions are met—

    (a)   a principal council is in the course of undertaking a community governance review of the whole of the council's area;

    (b)   the council receives a community governance petition which relates to the whole or part of the council's area.

Reorganisation of community governance

86 Reorganisation of community governance

(1)   This section applies if a community governance review is undertaken.

(2)   The principal council may, by order, give effect to the recommendations made in the review (except recommendations made to the [Local Government Boundary Commission] in accordance with section 92).

(3)   But such an order may not include provision giving effect to any recommendations to change protected electoral arrangements, unless the [Local Government Boundary Commission] agrees to that provision.

(4) An order under this section must include a map showing in general outline the area affected by the order.

(5) An order under this section may vary or revoke a provision of an order previously made under—

    (a)   this section,

    (b)   Part 1 of this Act,

    [(ba)   section 59 of the Local Democracy, Economic Development and Construction Act 2009,]

    (c)   section 17 of the Local Government Act 1992 (c 19), or

    (d)   section 16 or 17 of the Local Government and Rating Act 1997 (c 29).

(6) For the purposes of this section electoral arrangements are "protected" if—

    (a)   the electoral arrangements relate to the council of an existing parish,

    (b)   the electoral arrangements were made, or altered, by or in pursuance of an order under [section 59 of the Local Democracy, Economic Development and Construction Act 2009,] section 17 of the Local Government Act 1992 (c 19) or section 14 of the Local Government and Rating Act 1997 (c 29), and

    (c)   that order was made during the period of five years ending with the day on which the community governance review starts.

Recommendations of review

87 Constitution of new parish

(1) A community governance review must make recommendations as to what new parish or parishes (if any) should be constituted in the area under review.

(2) A new parish is constituted in any one of the following ways—

    (a)   by establishing an unparished area as a parish;

    (b)   by aggregating one or more unparished areas with one or more parished areas;

    (c)   by aggregating parts of parishes;

    (d)   by amalgamating two or more parishes;

    (e)   by separating part of a parish;

but the aggregation of one or more unparished areas with a single parish is not the constitution of a new parish.

(3) For the purposes of subsection (2)—

    "parished area" means an area which—

        (a)   is a parish, or

        (b)   is part of a parish;

    "unparished area" means an area which—

        (a)   is not a parish, and

        (b)   is not part of a parish.

(4) The following subsections apply if the review recommends that a new parish should be constituted.

(5) The review must also make recommendations as to the name of the new parish.

(6) The review must also make recommendations as to whether or not the new parish should have a parish council.

(7) The review must also make recommendations as to whether or not the new parish should have one of the alternative styles.

88 Existing parishes under review

(1) A community governance review must make the following recommendations in relation to each of the existing parishes under review (if any).

(2) The review must make one of the following recommendations—

    (a)   recommendations that the parish should not be abolished and that its area should not be altered;

    (b)   recommendations that the area of the parish should be altered;

    (c)   recommendations that the parish should be abolished.

(3)   The review must make recommendations as to whether or not the name of the parish should be changed.

(4)   The review must make one of the following recommendations—

    (a)   if the parish does not have a council: recommendations as to whether or not the parish should have a council;

    (b)   if the parish has a council: recommendations as to whether or not the parish should continue to have a council.

(5)   But the review may not make any recommendations for the parish—

    (a)   to begin to have an alternative style (if it does not already have one), or

    (b)   to cease to have an alternative style, or to have a different alternative style, (if it already has one).

(6)   In this section—

    (a)   "existing parishes under review" means each of the parishes (if any) which are already in existence in the area under review;

    (b)   references to the alteration of an area of a parish are references to any alteration which is not the constitution of a new parish (within the meaning of section 87(2)).

89 New council: consequential recommendations

(1)   This section applies if, under a relevant provision, a community governance review makes recommendations that a parish should have a parish council.

(2)   The review must also make recommendations as to what electoral arrangements should apply to the council.

(3)   These are the relevant provisions for the purposes of this section—

    (a)   section 87 (new parishes);

    (b)   section 88 (existing parishes).

90 Council retained: consequential recommendations

(1)   This section applies if, under a section 88, a community governance review makes recommendations that a parish should continue to have a parish council.

(2)   The review must also make recommendations as to what changes (if any) should be made to the electoral arrangements that apply to the council.

91 Grouping or de-grouping parishes

(1)   A community governance review may make recommendations as to whether or not grouping or de-grouping provision should be made.

(2)   If the review recommends that grouping or de-grouping provision should be made, those recommendations must in particular include recommendations as to what changes (if any) should be made to the electoral arrangements that apply to any council affected by the provision.

(3)   The reference to grouping or de-grouping provision is a reference to provision equivalent to the provision of an order under section 11 of the Local Government Act 1972 (c 70).

92 County, district or London borough: consequential recommendations

(1)   This section applies if a community governance review makes recommendations under any other provision of this Chapter.

(2)   The review may make recommendations to the [Local Government Boundary Commission] as to what related alteration (if any) should be made to the boundaries of the electoral areas of any affected principal council.

(3) The [Local Government Boundary Commission] may by order give effect to recommendations made under subsection (2).

(4) The [Local Government Boundary Commission] must notify each relevant principal council of whether or not the Commission have given effect to recommendations made under subsection (2).

(5) If the [Local Government Boundary Commission] have given effect to the recommendations, they must also send each relevant principal council two copies of the order under this section.

(6) In this section—

"affected principal council" means any principal council whose area the community governance review relates to (including the council carrying out the review);

"related" means related to the other recommendations made under this Chapter.

"relevant principal council", in relation to recommendations under subsection (2), means—

(a)   the principal council that made the recommendations, and

(b)   if the recommendations are made by a district council for an area for which there is a county council, the county council.

Duties of council undertaking review

93 Duties when undertaking a review

(1) The principal council must comply with the duties in this section when undertaking a community governance review.

(2) But, subject to those duties, it is for the principal council to decide how to undertake the review.

(3) The principal council must consult the following—

(a)   the local government electors for the area under review;

(b)   any other person or body (including a local authority) which appears to the principal council to have an interest in the review.

(4) The principal council must have regard to the need to secure that community governance within the area under review—

(a)   reflects the identities and interests of the community in that area, and

(b)   is effective and convenient.

(5) In deciding what recommendations to make, the principal council must take into account any other arrangements (apart from those relating to parishes and their institutions)—

(a)   that have already been made, or

(b)   that could be made,

for the purposes of community representation or community engagement in respect of the area under review.

(6) The principal council must take into account any representations received in connection with the review.

(7) As soon as practicable after making any recommendations, the principal council must—

(a)   publish the recommendations; and

(b)   take such steps as it considers sufficient to secure that persons who may be interested in the review are informed of those recommendations.

(8) The principal council must conclude the review within the period of 12 months starting with the day on which the council begins the review.

94 Recommendations to create parish councils

(1) This section applies where a community governance review is required to make any of the following recommendations—

(a) recommendations under section 87(6) as to whether or not a new parish should have a parish council;

(b) recommendations under section 88(4)(a) as to whether or not an existing parish should have a parish council.

(2) If the parish has 1,000 or more local government electors, the review must recommend that the parish should have a council.

(3) If the parish has 150 or fewer local government electors, the review must recommend that the parish should not have a council.

(4) But subsection (3) does not apply if any part of the parish mentioned in subsection (1) is currently—

(a) a parish which has a council, or

(b) part of such a parish.

(5) If neither subsection (2) nor (3) applies, it is for the principal council to decide whether or not the parish should have a council.

95 Electoral recommendations: general considerations

(1) This section applies to the principal council when deciding a recommendation of a kind listed in the following table.

Recommendation	Made under
What electoral arrangements should apply to a new parish council	Section 89(2)
What changes (if any) should be made to the electoral arrangements which apply to a parish council	Section 90(2)

(2) The principal council must consider the questions in subsection (3) when deciding whether to recommend that a parish should, or should not, be or continue to be divided into wards for the purpose of electing councillors.

(3) Those questions are—

(a) whether the number, or distribution, of the local government electors for the parish would make a single election of councillors impracticable or inconvenient;

(b) whether it is desirable that any area or areas of the parish should be separately represented on the council.

(4) If the principal council decides to recommend that a parish should be divided into wards, the principal council must have regard to the factors in subsection (5) when considering—

(a) the size and boundaries of the wards, and

(b) the number of councillors to be elected for each ward.

(5) Those factors are—

(a) the number of local government electors for the parish;

(b) any change in the number, or distribution, of the local government electors which is likely to occur in the period of five years beginning with the day when the review starts;

(c) the desirability of fixing boundaries which are, and will remain, easily identifiable;

(d) any local ties which will be broken by the fixing of any particular boundaries.

(6)   If the principal council decides to recommend that a parish should not be divided into wards, the principal council must have regard to the factors in subsection (7) when considering the number of councillors to be elected for the parish.

(7)   Those factors are—

  (a)   the number of local government electors for the parish;

  (b)   any change in that number which is likely to occur in the period of five years beginning with the day when the review starts.

Publicising outcome of review

96 Publicising outcome

(1)   This section applies if a community governance review is undertaken.

(2)   As soon as practicable after a principal council has decided to what extent it will give effect to the recommendations made in a community governance review, the council must—

  (a)   publish—

   (i)   that decision, and

   (ii)   the council's reasons for making that decision; and

  (b)   take such steps as the council considers sufficient to secure that persons who may be interested in the review are informed of that decision and those reasons.

(3)   The following subsections apply if the council makes a reorganisation order.

(4)   As soon as practicable after making the order, the council must deposit at its principal office—

  (a)   a copy of the reorganisation order, and

  (b)   a map which shows the effects of the order in greater detail than the map included in the order.

(5)   The council must make the copy of the order and the map available for public inspection at all reasonable times.

(6)   The council must publicise that the order and map are available for public inspection in accordance with subsection (5).

(7)   As soon as practicable after making the order, the principal council must inform all of the following that the order has been made—

  (a)   the Secretary of State;

  (b)   the [Local Government Boundary Commission];

  (c)   the Office of National Statistics;

  (d)   the Director General of the Ordnance Survey;

  (e)   any other principal council whose area the order relates to.

Miscellaneous

97 Supplementary regulations

(1)   The Secretary of State may by regulations of general application make incidental, consequential, transitional or supplementary provision for the purposes of, or in consequence of, reorganisation orders.

(2)   Regulations under this section are to have effect subject to any provision made by a reorganisation order.

98 Orders and regulations under this Chapter

(1)   If a principal council makes a reorganisation order, the council must send—

  (a)   two copies of the order to the Secretary of State; and

  (b)   two copies of the order to the [Local Government Boundary Commission].

(2)   If the Secretary of State makes regulations under section 97, he must send two copies of the regulations to the [Local Government Boundary Commission].

(3)   A reorganisation order may include such incidental, consequential, transitional or supplementary provision as may appear to the principal council to be necessary or proper for the purposes of, or in consequence of, or for giving full effect to, the order.

(4)   A reorganisation order, or regulations under section 97, may include any of the following provision—

    (a)   provision with respect to the transfer and management or custody of property (whether real or personal);

    (b)   provision with respect to the transfer of functions, property, rights and liabilities.

(5)   Provision made under subsection (4)(b) may include any of the following—

    (a)   provision for legal proceedings commenced by or against any body to be continued by or against a body to whom functions, property, rights or liabilities are transferred;

    (b)   provision for the transfer of staff, compensation for loss of office, pensions and other staffing matters;

    (c)   provision for treating any body to whom a transfer is made for some or all purposes as the same person in law as the body from whom the transfer is made.

(6)   A reorganisation order, or regulations under section 97, may include provision for the exclusion or modification of the application of any of the following—

    (a)   section 16(3) or 90 of the Local Government Act 1972 (c 70), or

    (b)   rules under section 36 of the Representation of the People Act 1983 (c 2), whenever made.

(7)   An order under section 92 may include such incidental, consequential, transitional or supplementary provision as may appear to the [Local Government Boundary Commission] to be necessary or proper for the purposes of, or in consequence of, or for giving full effect to, the order.

99   Agreements about incidental matters

(1)   Any public bodies affected by a reorganisation of community governance may from time to time make agreements with respect to—

    (a)   any property, income, rights, liabilities and expenses (so far as affected by the order) of the parties to the agreement;

    (b)   any financial relations between the parties to the agreement.

(2)   Such an agreement may in particular provide—

    (a)   for the transfer or retention of any property, rights and liabilities, with or without conditions, and for the joint use of any property;

    (b)   for the making of payments by any party to the agreement in respect of—

        (i)   property, rights and liabilities so transferred or retained;

        (ii)   such joint use; or

        (iii)   the remuneration or compensation payable to any person;

    (c)   for any such payment to be made by instalments or otherwise;

    (d)   for interest to be charged on any such instalments.

(3)   In default of agreement about any disputed matter, the matter is to be referred to the arbitration of a single arbitrator—

    (a)   agreed on by the parties; or

    (b)   in default of agreement, appointed by the Secretary of State.

(4)   The arbitrator's award may make any provision that could be contained in an agreement under this section.

(5)   In this section—

    "disputed matter" means any matter that—

    (a)   could be the subject of provision contained in an agreement under this section; and

    (b)   is the subject of a dispute between two or more public bodies that is not resolved by or under any order or regulations under this Chapter;

"public body" has the same meaning as in section 16;

"reorganisation of community governance" means any changes made by giving effect to a community governance review.

100 Guidance

(1) The Secretary of State may issue guidance about undertaking community governance reviews.

(2) The [Local Government Boundary Commission] may issue guidance about the making of recommendations under sections 89(2) or 90(2) (electoral arrangements for parish councils) or 92 (consequential recommendations about county, district or London borough councils).

(3) The Secretary of State may issue guidance about giving effect to recommendations made in community governance reviews.

(4) A principal council must have regard to guidance issued under this section.

101 Consequential amendments

Schedule 5 (consequential amendments) has effect.

102 Interpretation

(1) This section applies for the purposes of this Chapter.

(2) The following expressions have the meanings given—

"alternative style" has the same meaning as in sections 9 to 16A of the Local Government Act 1972 (c 70) (see section 17A of that Act);

"area under review", in relation to a community governance review, means however much of the area of a principal council is subject to the review;

"community governance petition" has the meaning given by section 80;

"community governance review" has the meaning given by section 79;

"electoral arrangements", in relation to a parish council, means all of the following—

    (a)   the year in which ordinary elections of councillors are to be held;

    (b)   the number of councillors to be elected to the council, or (in the case of a common council) the number of councillors to be elected to the council by each parish;

    (c)   the division (or not) of the parish, or (in the case of a common council) any of the parishes, into wards for the purpose of electing councillors;

    (d)   the number and boundaries of any such wards;

    (e)   the number of councillors to be elected for any such ward;

    (f)   the name of any such ward;

"local government elector" has the same meaning as in the Local Government Act 1972 (see section 270);

["Local Government Boundary Commission" means the Local Government Boundary Commission for England;]

"petition area" means the area to which a community governance petition relates;

"principal council" means—

    (a)   a district council in England,

    (b)   a county council in England for an area in which there are no district councils, or

    (c)   a London borough council;

"reorganisation order" means an order under section 86;

"relevant two-year period", in relation to receipt of a community governance petition, means the period of two years ending with the day on which the petition is received by the principal council;

"specified recommendations", in relation to a community governance petition, means the recommendations—

    (a)   specified in the petition, or

    (b)   treated by section 80 as included in the recommendations specified in the petition;

"terms of reference" has the meaning given by section 81.

(3)   A principal council "begins" a community governance review when the council publishes the terms of reference of the review.

(4)   A principal council "concludes" a community governance review when the council publishes the recommendations made in the review.

(5)   A principal council is "in the course of undertaking" a community governance review in the period between—

    (a)   beginning the review, and

    (b)   concluding the review.

(6)   The terms of reference of a community governance review "allow for a community governance petition to be considered" if the terms of reference of the review are such that—

    (a)   the area under review includes the whole of the petition area; and

    (b)   the recommendations to be considered by the review include all of the petition's specified recommendations.

PART 6

BYELAWS

135 Further amendments relating to byelaws

Schedule 6 (further amendments of the law relating to byelaws) has effect.

PART 7

BEST VALUE

Best value authorities

136 Parish councils and community councils etc not to be best value authorities

(1)–(2)   [*These subsections are amending only and are not reproduced.*]

(3)   Schedule 7 (consequential amendments) has effect.

PART 10

ETHICAL STANDARDS

201 Supplementary and consequential provision

(1)   Subsection (2) applies in relation to any provision of Part 3 of the Local Government Act 2000 (c 22) which is applied (with or without modifications) by an order under section 70 of that Act made before the passing of this Act.

(2)   Any amendment of that provision by this Part does not extend to the provision as so applied.

(3)   Where a provision mentioned in section 70(2)(a) of that Act is amended by this Part, the power in section 70(2) of that Act to apply or reproduce that provision (with

or without modifications) is a power to apply or reproduce (with or without modifications) that provision either as amended by this Part or without the amendments made by this Part.

(4)–(6) [*These subsections are amending only and are not reproduced.*]

INCOME TAX ACT 2007

CHAPTER 4

838 Local authorities and local authority associations

(1) A local authority in the United Kingdom is not liable to income tax in respect of its income.

(2) A local authority association in the United Kingdom is not liable to income tax in respect of its income.

(3) Tax is repayable as a result of subsection (1) or (2) only if a claim for repayment is made.

CORPORATION TAX ACT 2010

984 Local authorities and local authority associations

(1) A local authority in the United Kingdom is not liable to corporation tax.

(2) A local authority association in the United Kingdom is not liable to corporation tax.

. . .

1130 "Local authority"

(1) In the Corporation Tax Acts "local authority", in relation to England and Wales, means—

    (a)   A local authority association in the United Kingdom is not liable to corporation tax.

    (b)   a billing authority as defined in section 1(2) of the Local Government Finance Act 1992,

    (c)   a precepting authority as defined in section 69(1) of that Act,

    (d)   a body with power to issue a levy (by virtue of regulations under section 74 of the Local Government Finance Act 1988),

    (e)   a fire and rescue authority in Wales constituted by a scheme under section 2 of the Fire and Rescue Services Act 2004 or a scheme to which section 4 of that Act applies,

    (f)   an authority with power to make or determine a rate, or

    (g)   a residuary body established by order under section 22(1) of the Local Government Act 1992.

CHARITIES ACT 2011

PART 1

MEANING OF "CHARITY" AND "CHARITABLE PURPOSE"

CHAPTER 1

GENERAL

Charity

1 Meaning of "charity"

(1) For the purposes of the law of England and Wales, "charity" means an institution which—

    (a)   is established for charitable purposes only, and

    (b)   falls to be subject to the control of the High Court in the exercise of its jurisdiction with respect to charities.

(2) The definition of "charity" in subsection (1) does not apply for the purposes of an enactment if a different definition of that term applies for those purposes by virtue of that or any other enactment.

2 Meaning of "charitable purpose"

(1) For the purposes of the law of England and Wales, a charitable purpose is a purpose which—

    (a)   falls within section 3(1), and

    (b)   is for the public benefit (see section 4).

(2) Any reference in any enactment or document (in whatever terms)—

    (a)   to charitable purposes, or

    (b)   to institutions having purposes that are charitable under the law relating to charities in England and Wales,

is to be read in accordance with subsection (1).

(3) Subsection (2) does not apply where the context otherwise requires.

(4) This section is subject to section 11 (which makes special provision for Chapter 2 of this Part onwards).

3 Descriptions of purposes

(1) A purpose falls within this subsection if it falls within any of the following descriptions of purposes—

    (a)   the prevention or relief of poverty;

    (b)   the advancement of education;

    (c)   the advancement of religion;

    (d)   the advancement of health or the saving of lives;

    (e)   the advancement of citizenship or community development;

    (f)   the advancement of the arts, culture, heritage or science;

    (g)   the advancement of amateur sport;

    (h)   the advancement of human rights, conflict resolution or reconciliation or the promotion of religious or racial harmony or equality and diversity;

    (i)   the advancement of environmental protection or improvement;

    (j)   the relief of those in need because of youth, age, ill-health, disability, financial hardship or other disadvantage;

    (k)   the advancement of animal welfare;

    (l)   the promotion of the efficiency of the armed forces of the Crown or of the efficiency of the police, fire and rescue services or ambulance services;

    (m)   any other purposes—

        (i)   that are not within paragraphs (a) to (l) but are recognised as charitable purposes by virtue of section 5 (recreational and similar trusts, etc) or under the old law,

        (ii)   that may reasonably be regarded as analogous to, or within the spirit of, any purposes falling within any of paragraphs (a) to (l) or sub-paragraph (i), or

        (iii)   that may reasonably be regarded as analogous to, or within the spirit of, any purposes which have been recognised, under the law relating to charities in England and Wales, as falling within sub-paragraph (ii) or this sub-paragraph.

(2) In subsection (1)—

    (a)   in paragraph (c), "religion" includes—

        (i)   a religion which involves belief in more than one god, and

        (ii)   a religion which does not involve belief in a god,

    (b)   in paragraph (d), "the advancement of health" includes the prevention or relief of sickness, disease or human suffering,

    (c)   paragraph (e) includes—

        (i)   rural or urban regeneration, and

        (ii)   the promotion of civic responsibility, volunteering, the voluntary sector or the effectiveness or efficiency of charities,

    (d)   in paragraph (g), "sport" means sports or games which promote health by involving physical or mental skill or exertion,

    (e)   paragraph (j) includes relief given by the provision of accommodation or care to the persons mentioned in that paragraph, and

    (f)   in paragraph (l), "fire and rescue services" means services provided by fire and rescue authorities under Part 2 of the Fire and Rescue Services Act 2004.

(3) Where any of the terms used in any of paragraphs (a) to (l) of subsection (1), or in subsection (2), has a particular meaning under the law relating to charities in England and Wales, the term is to be taken as having the same meaning where it appears in that provision.

(4) In subsection (1)(m)(i), "the old law" means the law relating to charities in England and Wales as in force immediately before 1 April 2008.

4 The public benefit requirement

(1) In this Act "the public benefit requirement" means the requirement in section 2(1)(b) that a purpose falling within section 3(1) must be for the public benefit if it is to be a charitable purpose.

(2) In determining whether the public benefit requirement is satisfied in relation to any purpose falling within section 3(1), it is not to be presumed that a purpose of a particular description is for the public benefit.

(3) In this Chapter any reference to the public benefit is a reference to the public benefit as that term is understood for the purposes of the law relating to charities in England and Wales.

(4) Subsection (3) is subject to subsection (2).

. . .

PART 4

REGISTRATION AND NAMES OF CHARITIES

The register

29 The register

(1)   There continues to be a register of charities, to be kept by the Commission in such manner as it thinks fit.

(2)   The register must contain—

    (a)   the name of every charity registered in accordance with section 30, and

    (b)   such other particulars of, and such other information relating to, every such charity as the Commission thinks fit.

(3)   In this Act, except in so far as the context otherwise requires, "the register" means the register of charities kept under this section and "registered" is to be read accordingly.

Charities required to be registered

30 Charities required to be registered: general

(1)   Every charity must be registered in the register unless subsection (2) applies to it.

(2)   The following are not required to be registered—

    (a)   an exempt charity (see section 22 and Schedule 3),

    (b)   a charity which for the time being—

        (i)   is permanently or temporarily excepted by order of the Commission, and

        (ii)   complies with any conditions of the exception,

    and whose gross income does not exceed £100,000,

    (c)   a charity which for the time being—

        (i)   is, or is of a description, permanently or temporarily excepted by regulations made by the Minister, and

        (ii)   complies with any conditions of the exception,

  and whose gross income does not exceed £100,000, and

    (d)   a charity whose gross income does not exceed £5,000.

(3)   A charity within—

    (a)   subsection (2)(b) or (c), or

    (b)   subsection (2)(d),

  must, if it so requests, be registered in the register.

(4)   In this section any reference to a charity's gross income is to be read, in relation to a particular time—

    (a)   as a reference to the charity's gross income in its financial year immediately preceding that time, or

    (b)   if the Commission so determines, as a reference to the amount which the Commission estimates to be the likely amount of the charity's gross income in such financial year of the charity as is specified in the determination.

31 Restrictions on extending the range of excepted charities etc

(1)   No order may be made under section 30(2)(b) so as to except any charity that was not excepted immediately before 31 January 2009.

(2)   Subject to subsection (3), no regulations may be made under section 30(2)(c) so as to except any charity or description of charities that was not excepted immediately before 31 January 2009.

(3) Such regulations must be made under section 30(2)(c) as are necessary to secure that any institution ceasing to be an exempt charity by virtue of an order made under section 23 is excepted under section 30(2)(c) (subject to compliance with any conditions of the exception and the financial limit mentioned in section 30(2)(c)).

(4) Subsection (1) does not prevent an order which—

    (a)   was in force immediately before 31 January 2009, and

    (b)   has effect (by virtue of paragraph 4 of Schedule 8) as if made under section 30(2)(b),

from being varied or revoked.

(5) Subsection (2) does not prevent regulations which—

    (a)   were in force immediately before 31 January 2009, and

    (b)   have effect (by virtue of paragraph 4 of Schedule 8) as if made under section 30(2)(c),

from being varied or revoked.

32 Power to alter sums specified in s 30(2)

(1) The Minister may by order amend—

    (a)   section 30(2)(b) and (c), or

    (b)   section 30(2)(d),

by substituting a different sum for the sum for the time being specified there.

(2) The Minister may only make an order under subsection (1)—

    (a)   so far as it amends section 30(2)(b) and (c), if the Minister considers it expedient to do so with a view to reducing the scope of the exceptions provided by section 30(2)(b) and (c);

    (b)   so far as it amends section 30(2)(d), if the Minister considers it expedient to do so—

        (i)   in consequence of changes in the value of money, or

        (ii)   with a view to extending the scope of the exception provided by section 30(2)(d).

(3) No order may be made by the Minister under subsection (1)(a) unless a copy of a report under section 73 of the Charities Act 2006 has been laid before Parliament in accordance with that section.

33 Power to repeal provisions relating to excepted charities

The following provisions—

    (a)   section 30(2)(b) and (c) and (3)(a),

    (b)   section 31,

    (c)   section 32(1)(a), (2)(a) and (3), and

    (d)   this section,

cease to have effect on such day as the Minister may by order appoint for the purposes of this section.

34 Removal of charities from register

(1) The Commission must remove from the register—

    (a)   any institution which it no longer considers is a charity, and

    (b)   any charity which has ceased to exist or does not operate.

(2) If the removal of an institution under subsection (1)(a) is due to any change in its trusts, the removal takes effect from the date of the change.

(3) A charity which is for the time being registered under section 30(3) (voluntary registration) must be removed from the register if it so requests.

35 Duties of trustees in connection with registration

(1) If a charity required to be registered by virtue of section 30(1) is not registered, the charity trustees must—

    (a)   apply to the Commission for the charity to be registered, and

    (b)   supply the Commission with the required documents and information.

(2)   The required documents and information are—

    (a)   copies of the charity's trusts or (if they are not set out in any extant document) particulars of them,

    (b)   such other documents or information as may be prescribed by regulations made by the Minister, and

    (c)   such other documents or information as the Commission may require for the purposes of the application.

(3)   If an institution is for the time being registered, the charity trustees (or the last charity trustees) must—

    (a)   notify the Commission if the institution ceases to exist, or if there is any change in its trusts or in the particulars of it entered in the register, and

    (b)   so far as appropriate, supply the Commission with particulars of any such change and copies of any new trusts or alterations of the trusts.

(4)   Nothing in subsection (3) requires a person—

    (a)   to supply the Commission with copies of schemes for the administration of a charity made otherwise than by the court,

    (b)   to notify the Commission of any change made with respect to a registered charity by such a scheme, or

    (c)   if the person refers the Commission to a document or copy already in the Commission's possession, to supply a further copy of the document.

36 Claims and objections to registration

(1)   A person who is or may be affected by the registration of an institution as a charity may, on the ground that it is not a charity—

    (a)   object to its being entered by the Commission in the register, or

    (b)   apply to the Commission for it to be removed from the register.

(2)   Provision may be made by regulations made by the Minister as to the manner in which any such objection or application is to be made, prosecuted or dealt with.

(3)   Subsection (4) applies if there is an appeal to the Tribunal against any decision of the Commission—

    (a)   to enter an institution in the register, or

    (b)   not to remove an institution from the register.

(4)   Until the Commission is satisfied whether the decision of the Commission is or is not to stand, the entry in the register—

    (a)   is to be maintained, but

    (b)   is in suspense and must be marked to indicate that it is in suspense.

(5)   Any question affecting the registration or removal from the register of an institution—

    (a)   may be considered afresh by the Commission, even though it has been determined by a decision on appeal under Chapter 2 of Part 17 (appeals and applications to Tribunal), and

    (b)   is not concluded by that decision, if it appears to the Commission that—

        (i)   there has been a change of circumstances, or

        (ii)   the decision is inconsistent with a later judicial decision.

37 Effect of registration

(1)   An institution is, for all purposes other than rectification of the register, conclusively presumed to be or to have been a charity at any time when it is or was on the register.

(2)   For the purposes of subsection (1) an institution is to be treated as not being on the register during any period when the entry relating to it is in suspense under section 36(4).

38 Right to inspect register

(1) The register (including the entries cancelled when institutions are removed from the register) must be open to public inspection at all reasonable times.

(2) If any information contained in the register is not in documentary form, subsection (1) is to be read as requiring the information to be available for public inspection in legible form at all reasonable times.

(3) If the Commission so determines, subsection (1) does not apply to any particular information contained in the register that is specified in the determination.

(4) Copies (or particulars) of the trusts of any registered charity as supplied to the Commission under section 35 (duties of trustees in connection with registration) must, so long as the charity remains on the register—

(a) be kept by the Commission, and

(b) be open to public inspection at all reasonable times.

(5) If a copy of a document relating to a registered charity—

(a) is not required to be supplied to the Commission as the result of section 35(4), but

(b) is in the Commission's possession,

a copy of the document must be open to inspection under subsection (4) as if supplied to the Commission under section 35.

39 Statement required to be made in official publications etc

(1) This section applies to a registered charity if its gross income in its last financial year exceeded £10,000.

(2) If this section applies to a registered charity, the fact that it is a registered charity must be stated in legible characters—

(a) in all notices, advertisements and other documents issued by or on behalf of the charity and soliciting money or other property for the benefit of the charity,

(b) in all bills of exchange, promissory notes, endorsements, cheques and orders for money or goods purporting to be signed on behalf of the charity, and

(c) in all bills rendered by it and in all its invoices, receipts and letters of credit.

(3) The statement required by subsection (2) must be in English, except that, in the case of a document which is otherwise wholly in Welsh, the statement may be in Welsh if it consists of or includes "elusen cofrestredig" (the Welsh equivalent of "registered charity").

(4) Subsection (2)(a) has effect—

(a) whether the solicitation is express or implied, and

(b) whether or not the money or other property is to be given for any consideration.

40 Power to alter sum specified in s 39(1)

The Minister may by order amend section 39(1) by substituting a different sum for the sum for the time being specified there.

41 Offences

(1) It is an offence for a person, in the case of a registered charity to which section 39 applies, to issue or authorise the issue of any document falling within section 39(2)(a) or (c) which does not contain the statement required by section 39(2).

(2) It is an offence for a person, in the case of a registered charity to which section 39 applies, to sign any document falling within section 39(2)(b) which does not contain the statement required by section 39(2).

(3) A person guilty of an offence under subsection (1) or (2) is liable on summary conviction to a fine not exceeding level 3 on the standard scale.

42 Power to require name to be changed

(1) If this subsection applies to a charity, the Commission may give a direction requiring the name of the charity to be changed, within such period as is specified in the direction, to such other name as the charity trustees may determine with the approval of the Commission.

(2) Subsection (1) applies to a charity if—

    (a)   it is a registered charity and its name ("the registered name")—

        (i)   is the same as, or

        (ii)   is in the opinion of the Commission too like,

the name, at the time when the registered name was entered in the register in respect of the charity, of any other charity (whether registered or not),

    (b)   the name of the charity is in the opinion of the Commission likely to mislead the public as to the true nature of—

        (i)   the purposes of the charity as set out in its trusts, or

        (ii)   the activities which the charity carries on under its trusts in pursuit of those purposes,

    (c)   the name of the charity includes any word or expression for the time being specified in regulations made by the Minister and the inclusion in its name of that word or expression is in the opinion of the Commission likely to mislead the public in any respect as to the status of the charity,

    (d)   the name of the charity is in the opinion of the Commission likely to give the impression that the charity is connected in some way with Her Majesty's Government or any local authority, or with any other body of persons or any individual, when it is not so connected, or

    (e)   the name of the charity is in the opinion of the Commission offensive.

(3) Any direction given by virtue of subsection (2)(a) must be given within 12 months of the time when the registered name was entered in the register in respect of the charity.

(4) In subsection (2) any reference to the name of a charity is, in relation to a registered charity, a reference to the name by which it is registered.

(5) Any direction given under this section with respect to a charity must be given to the charity trustees.

43 Duty of charity trustees on receiving direction under s 42

(1) On receiving a direction under section 42 the charity trustees must give effect to it regardless of anything in the trusts of the charity.

(2) If the name of any charity is changed by virtue of section 42, the charity trustees must without delay notify the Commission of—

    (a)   the charity's new name, and

    (b)   the date on which the change occurred.

(3) Subsection (2) does not affect section 35(3) (duty of charity trustees to notify changes in registered particulars).

44 Change of name not to affect existing rights and obligations etc

A change of name by a charity by virtue of section 42 does not affect any rights or obligations of the charity; and any legal proceedings that might have been continued or commenced by or against it in its former name may be continued or commenced by or against it in its new name.

45 Change of name where charity is a company

(1) In relation to a charitable company, any reference in section 42 or 43 to the charity trustees of a charity is to be read as a reference to the directors of the company.

(2) Subsections (3) to (5) apply if a direction is given under section 42 with respect to a charitable company.

(3)   The direction is to be treated as requiring the name of the company to be changed by resolution of the directors of the company.

(4)   Where a resolution of the directors is passed in accordance with subsection (3), the company must give notice of the change to the registrar of companies.

(5)   Where the name of the company is changed in compliance with the direction, the registrar of companies must—

(a)   if satisfied that the new name complies with the requirements of Part 5 of the Companies Act 2006, enter the new name on the register of companies in place of the former name, and

(b)   issue a certificate of incorporation altered to meet the circumstances of the case;

and the change of name has effect from the date on which the altered certificate is issued.

PART 5

INFORMATION POWERS

Inquiries instituted by Commission

46   General power to institute inquiries

(1)   The Commission may from time to time institute inquiries with regard to charities or a particular charity or class of charities, either generally or for particular purposes.

(2)   But no such inquiry is to extend to any exempt charity except where this has been requested by its principal regulator.

(3)   The Commission may—

(a)   conduct such an inquiry itself, or

(b)   appoint a person to conduct it and make a report to the Commission.

(4)   This section and sections 47 to 49 (obtaining evidence and search warrants) have effect in relation to a body entered in the Scottish Charity Register which is managed or controlled wholly or mainly in or from England or Wales as they have effect in relation to a charity.

47   Obtaining evidence etc for purposes of inquiry

(1)   In this section "inquiry" means an inquiry under section 46.

(2)   For the purposes of an inquiry, the Commission, or a person appointed by the Commission to conduct it, may direct any person—

(a)   if a matter in question at the inquiry is one on which the person has or can reasonably obtain information—

(i)   to provide accounts and statements in writing with respect to the matter, or to return answers in writing to any questions or inquiries addressed to the person on the matter, and

(ii)   to verify any such accounts, statements or answers by statutory declaration;

(b)   to provide copies of documents which are in the custody or under the control of the person and which relate to any matter in question at the inquiry, and to verify any such copies by statutory declaration;

(c)   to attend at a specified time and place and give evidence or produce any such documents.

But this is subject to the provisions of this section.

(3)   For the purposes of an inquiry—

(a)   evidence may be taken on oath, and the person conducting the inquiry may for that purpose administer oaths, or

(b)   the person conducting the inquiry may instead of administering an oath require the person examined to make and subscribe a declaration of the truth of the matters about which that person is examined.

(4)   The Commission may pay to any person attending to give evidence or produce documents for the purpose of an inquiry the necessary expenses of doing so.

(5)   A direction under subsection (2)(c) may not require a person to go more than 10 miles from the person's place of residence unless those expenses are paid or tendered to the person.

48 Power to obtain search warrant for purposes of inquiry

(1)   A justice of the peace may issue a warrant under this section if satisfied, on information given on oath by a member of the Commission's staff, that there are reasonable grounds for believing that each of the conditions in subsection (2) is satisfied.

(2)   The conditions are—

    (a)   that an inquiry has been instituted under section 46,

    (b)   that there is on the premises to be specified in the warrant any document or information relevant to that inquiry which the Commission could require to be produced or provided under section 52(1), and

    (c)   that, if the Commission were to make an order requiring the document or information to be so produced or provided—

        (i)   the order would not be complied with, or

        (ii)   the document or information would be removed, tampered with, concealed or destroyed.

(3)   A warrant under this section is a warrant authorising the member of the Commission's staff who is named in it ("P")—

    (a)   to enter and search the premises specified in it;

    (b)   to take such other persons with P as the Commission considers are needed to assist P in doing anything that P is authorised to do under the warrant;

    (c)   to take possession of any documents which appear to fall within subsection (2)(b), or to take any other steps which appear to be necessary for preserving, or preventing interference with, any such documents;

    (d)   to take possession of any computer disk or other electronic storage device which appears to contain information falling within subsection (2)(b), or information contained in a document so falling, or to take any other steps which appear to be necessary for preserving, or preventing interference with, any such information;

    (e)   to take copies of, or extracts from, any documents or information falling within paragraph (c) or (d);

    (f)   to require any person on the premises to provide an explanation of any such document or information or to state where any such documents or information may be found;

    (g)   to require any such person to give P such assistance as P may reasonably require for the taking of copies or extracts as mentioned in paragraph (e).

49 Execution of search warrant

(1)   Entry and search under a warrant under section 48 must be at a reasonable hour and within one month of the date of its issue.

(2)   The member of the Commission's staff who is authorised under such a warrant ("P") must, if required to do so, produce—

    (a)   the warrant, and

    (b)   documentary evidence that P is a member of the Commission's staff, for inspection by the occupier of the premises or anyone acting on the occupier's behalf.

(3) P must make a written record of—

    (a)   the date and time of P's entry on the premises,

    (b)   the number of persons (if any) who accompanied P on to the premises and the names of any such persons,

    (c)   the period for which P (and any such persons) remained on the premises,

    (d)   what P (and any such persons) did while on the premises, and

    (e)   any document or device of which P took possession while there.

(4) If required to do so, P must give a copy of the record to the occupier of the premises or someone acting on the occupier's behalf.

(5) Unless it is not reasonably practicable to do so, P must before leaving the premises comply with—

    (a)   the requirements of subsection (3), and

    (b)   any requirement made under subsection (4) before P leaves the premises.

(6) Where possession of any document or device is taken under section 48—

    (a)   the document may be retained for so long as the Commission considers that it is necessary to retain it (rather than a copy of it) for the purposes of the relevant inquiry under section 46, or

    (b)   the device may be retained for so long as the Commission considers that it is necessary to retain it for the purposes of that inquiry,

as the case may be.

(7) Once it appears to the Commission that the retention of any document or device has ceased to be so necessary, it must arrange for the document or device to be returned as soon as is reasonably practicable—

    (a)   to the person from whose possession it was taken, or

    (b)   to any of the charity trustees of the charity to which it belonged or related.

For the purposes of this subsection as it has effect by virtue of section 46(4), the reference in paragraph (b) to the charity trustees of the charity is to be read as a reference to the persons having the general control and management of the administration of the body entered in the Scottish Charity Register.

(8) It is an offence for a person intentionally to obstruct the exercise of any rights conferred by a warrant under section 48.

(9) A person guilty of an offence under subsection (8) is liable on summary conviction—

    (a)   to imprisonment for a term not exceeding 51 weeks, or

    (b)   to a fine not exceeding level 5 on the standard scale,

or to both.

50 Publication of results of inquiries

(1) This section applies where an inquiry has been held under section 46.

(2) The Commission may—

    (a)   cause the report of the person conducting the inquiry, or such other statement of the results of the inquiry as the Commission thinks fit, to be printed and published, or

    (b)   publish any such report or statement in some other way which is calculated in the Commission's opinion to bring it to the attention of persons who may wish to make representations to the Commission about the action to be taken.

51 Contributions by local authorities to inquiries into local charities

(1) A council may contribute to the expenses of the Commission in connection with inquiries under section 46 into local charities in the council's area.

(2)   In subsection (1) "council" means—
  (a)   a district council;
  (b)   a county council;
  (c)   a county borough council;
  (d)   a London borough council;
  (e)   the Common Council of the City of London.

52 Power to call for documents

(1)   The Commission may by order—
  (a)   require any person to provide the Commission with any information which is in that person's possession and which—
      (i)   relates to any charity, and
      (ii)   is relevant to the discharge of the functions of the Commission or of the official custodian;
  (b)   require any person who has custody or control of any document which relates to any charity and is relevant to the discharge of the functions of the Commission or of the official custodian—
      (i)   to provide the Commission with a copy of or extract from the document, or
      (ii)   to transmit the document itself to the Commission for its inspection (unless the document forms part of the records or other documents of a court or of a public or local authority).

(2)   The Commission is entitled without payment to keep any copy or extract provided to it under subsection (1).

(3)   If a document transmitted to the Commission under subsection (1) for it to inspect—
  (a)   relates only to one or more charities, and
  (b)   is not held by any person entitled as trustee or otherwise to the custody of it,
the Commission may keep it or may deliver it to the charity trustees or to any other person who may be so entitled.

(4)   This section has effect in relation to any body entered in the Scottish Charity Register which is managed or controlled wholly or mainly in or from England or Wales as it has effect in relation to a charity.

53 Power to search records

(1)   Any member of the staff of the Commission, if so authorised by it, is entitled without payment to inspect and take copies of or extracts from the records or other documents of—
  (a)   any court, or
  (b)   any public registry or office of records,
for any purpose connected with the discharge of the functions of the Commission or of the official custodian.

(2)   The reference in subsection (1) to a member of the staff of the Commission includes the official custodian even if not a member of the staff of the Commission.

(3)   The rights conferred by subsection (1), in relation to information recorded otherwise than in legible form, include the right to require the information to be made available in legible form—
  (a)   for inspection, or
  (b)   for a copy or extract to be made of or from it.

54 Disclosure to Commission: general

(1) A relevant public authority may disclose information to the Commission if the disclosure is made for the purpose of enabling or assisting the Commission to discharge any of its functions.

(2) Subsection (1) is subject to section 55.

(3) In this section "relevant public authority" means—

- (a) any government department (including a Northern Ireland department),
- (b) any local authority,
- (c) any constable, and
- (d) any other body or person discharging functions of a public nature (including a body or person discharging regulatory functions in relation to any description of activities).

55 Disclosure to Commission: Revenue and Customs information

(1) Revenue and Customs information may be disclosed under section 54(1) only if it relates to an institution, undertaking or body falling within one (or more) of the following paragraphs—

- (a) a charity;
- (b) an institution which is established for charitable, benevolent or philanthropic purposes;
- (c) an institution by or in respect of which a claim for tax exemption has at any time been made;
- (d) a subsidiary undertaking of a charity;
- (e) a body entered in the Scottish Charity Register which is managed or controlled wholly or mainly in or from England or Wales.

(2) In subsection (1)(d) "subsidiary undertaking of a charity" means an undertaking (as defined by section 1161(1) of the Companies Act 2006) in relation to which—

- (a) a charity is (or is to be treated as) a parent undertaking in accordance with the provisions of section 1162 of, and Schedule 7 to, the Companies Act 2006, or
- (b) two or more charities would, if they were a single charity, be (or be treated as) a parent undertaking in accordance with those provisions.

(3) For the purposes of the references to a parent undertaking—

- (a) in subsection (2), and
- (b) in section 1162 of, and Schedule 7 to, the Companies Act 2006 as they apply for the purposes of subsection (2),

"undertaking" includes a charity which is not an undertaking as defined by section 1161(1) of that Act.

(4) In this section "Revenue and Customs information" means information held as mentioned in section 18(1) of the Commissioners for Revenue and Customs Act 2005.

(5) For the purposes of subsection (1)(c), "claim for tax exemption" means—

- (a) a claim for exemption under section 505(1) of the Income and Corporation Taxes Act 1988,
- (b) a claim for exemption under Part 10 of the Income Tax Act 2007, or
- (c) a claim for exemption under Part 11 of the Corporation Tax Act 2010, if it is not—
    - (i) a claim for exemption under section 475, 476 or 477 (reliefs for eligible bodies and scientific research organisations), or
    - (ii) a claim made by virtue of section 490 or 491 (application of exemptions to eligible bodies and scientific research organisations).

56 Disclosure by Commission: general

(1)   The Commission may disclose to any relevant public authority any information received by the Commission in connection with any of the Commission's functions if—

    (a)   the disclosure is made for the purpose of enabling or assisting the relevant public authority to discharge any of its functions, or

    (b)   the information so disclosed is otherwise relevant to the discharge of any of the functions of the relevant public authority.

(2)   Subsection (1) is subject to subsection (3) and section 57(1) and (2).

(3)   In the case of information disclosed to the Commission under section 54(1), the Commission's power to disclose the information under subsection (1) is exercisable subject to any express restriction subject to which the information was disclosed to the Commission.

(4)   In this section "relevant public authority" has the same meaning as in section 54, except that it also includes any body or person within section 54(3)(d) in a country or territory outside the United Kingdom.

57 Disclosure by Commission: Revenue and Customs information

(1)   Section 56(3) does not apply in relation to Revenue and Customs information disclosed to the Commission under section 54(1).

(2)   But any such information may not be further disclosed (whether under section 56(1) or otherwise) except with the consent of the Commissioners for Her Majesty's Revenue and Customs.

(3)   It is an offence for a responsible person to disclose information in contravention of subsection (2).

(4)   A person guilty of an offence under subsection (3) is liable—

    (a)   on summary conviction, to imprisonment for a term not exceeding 12 months or to a fine not exceeding the statutory maximum, or both;

    (b)   on conviction on indictment, to imprisonment for a term not exceeding 2 years or to a fine, or both.

(5)   It is a defence, where a responsible person is charged with an offence under subsection (3) of disclosing information, to prove that that person reasonably believed—

    (a)   that the disclosure was lawful, or

    (b)   that the information had already and lawfully been made available to the public.

(6)   In the application of this section to Northern Ireland, the reference to 12 months in subsection (4) is to be read as a reference to 6 months.

(7)   In this section "Revenue and Customs information" means information held as mentioned in section 18(1) of the Commissioners for Revenue and Customs Act 2005.

(8)   In this section "responsible person" means a person who is or was—

    (a)   a member of the Commission,

    (b)   a member of the staff of the Commission,

    (c)   a person acting on behalf of—

        (i)   the Commission, or

        (ii)   a member of the staff of the Commission, or

    (d)   a member of a committee established by the Commission.

58 Disclosure to and by principal regulators of exempt charities

(1)   Sections 54 to 57 apply with the modifications in subsections (2) to (4) in relation to the disclosure of information to or by the principal regulator of an exempt charity.

(2)   References in those sections to the Commission or to any of its functions are to be read as references to the principal regulator of an exempt charity or to any of the functions of that body or person as principal regulator in relation to the charity.

(3)   Section 55 has effect as if for subsections (1) and (2) there were substituted—

"(1) Revenue and Customs information may be disclosed under section 54(1) only if it relates to—
  (a) the exempt charity in relation to which the principal regulator has functions as such, or
  (b) a subsidiary undertaking of the exempt charity.

(2) In subsection (1)(b) "subsidiary undertaking of the exempt charity" means an undertaking (as defined by section 1161(1) of the Companies Act 2006) in relation to which—
  (a) the exempt charity is (or is to be treated as) a parent undertaking in accordance with the provisions of section 1162 of, and Schedule 7 to, the Companies Act 2006, or
  (b) the exempt charity and one or more other charities would, if they were a single charity, be (or be treated as) a parent undertaking in accordance with those provisions."

(4) Section 57 has effect as if for the definition of "responsible person" in subsection (8) there were substituted a definition specified by regulations under section 25 (meaning of "principal regulator").

(5) Regulations under section 25 may also make such amendments or other modifications of any enactment as the Minister considers appropriate for securing that any disclosure provisions that would otherwise apply in relation to the principal regulator of an exempt charity do not apply in relation to that body or person as principal regulator.

(6) In subsection (5) "disclosure provisions" means provisions having effect for authorising, or otherwise in connection with, the disclosure of information by or to the principal regulator concerned.

(7) In subsection (5) "enactment" includes—
  (a) any provision of subordinate legislation (within the meaning of the Interpretation Act 1978), and
  (b) a provision of a Measure of the Church Assembly or of the General Synod of the Church of England,

and references to enactments include enactments whenever passed or made.

59 Disclosure: supplementary

Nothing in sections 54 to 57 (or in those sections as applied by section 58(1) to (4)) authorises the making of a disclosure which—
  (a) contravenes the Data Protection Act 1998, or
  (b) is prohibited by Part 1 of the Regulation of Investigatory Powers Act 2000.

. . .

PART 6

CY-PRÈS POWERS AND ASSISTANCE AND SUPERVISION OF CHARITIES
BY COURT AND COMMISSION

Cy-près powers and variation of charters

61 Duty of trustees in relation to application of property cy-près

It is hereby declared that a trust for charitable purposes places a trustee under a duty, where the case permits and requires the property or some part of it to be applied cy-près, to secure its effective use for charity by taking steps to enable it to be so applied.

62 Occasions for applying property cy-près

(1) Subject to subsection (3), the circumstances in which the original purposes of a charitable gift can be altered to allow the property given or part of it to be applied cy-près are—

    (a) where the original purposes, in whole or in part—

        (i) have been as far as may be fulfilled, or

        (ii) cannot be carried out, or not according to the directions given and to the spirit of the gift,

    (b) where the original purposes provide a use for part only of the property available by virtue of the gift,

    (c) where—

        (i) the property available by virtue of the gift, and

        (ii) other property applicable for similar purposes,

can be more effectively used in conjunction, and to that end can suitably, regard being had to the appropriate considerations, be made applicable to common purposes,

    (d) where the original purposes were laid down by reference to—

        (i) an area which then was but has since ceased to be a unit for some other purpose, or

        (ii) a class of persons or an area which has for any reason since ceased to be suitable, regard being had to the appropriate considerations, or to be practical in administering the gift, or

    (e) where the original purposes, in whole or in part, have, since they were laid down—

        (i) been adequately provided for by other means,

        (ii) ceased, as being useless or harmful to the community or for other reasons, to be in law charitable, or

        (iii) ceased in any other way to provide a suitable and effective method of using the property available by virtue of the gift, regard being had to the appropriate considerations.

(2) In subsection (1) "the appropriate considerations" means—

    (a) (on the one hand) the spirit of the gift concerned, and

    (b) (on the other) the social and economic circumstances prevailing at the time of the proposed alteration of the original purposes.

(3) Subsection (1) does not affect the conditions which must be satisfied in order that property given for charitable purposes may be applied cy-près except in so far as those conditions require a failure of the original purposes.

(4) References in subsections (1) to (3) to the original purposes of a gift are to be read, where the application of the property given has been altered or regulated by a scheme or otherwise, as referring to the purposes for which the property is for the time being applicable.

(5) The court may by scheme made under the court's jurisdiction with respect to charities, in any case where the purposes for which the property is held are laid down by reference to any such area as is mentioned in column 1 in Schedule 4, provide for enlarging the area to any such area as is mentioned in column 2 in the same entry in that Schedule.

(6) Subsection (5) does not affect the power to make schemes in circumstances falling within subsection (1).

63 Application cy-près: donor unknown or disclaiming

(1) Property given for specific charitable purposes which fail is applicable cy-près as if given for charitable purposes generally, if it belongs—

    (a) to a donor who after—

(i)   the prescribed advertisements and inquiries have been published and made, and

(ii)   the prescribed period beginning with the publication of those advertisements has ended,

cannot be identified or cannot be found, or

(b)   to a donor who has executed a disclaimer in the prescribed form of the right to have the property returned.

(2) Where the prescribed advertisements and inquiries have been published and made by or on behalf of trustees with respect to any such property, the trustees are not liable to any person in respect of the property if no claim by that person to be interested in it is received by them before the end of the period mentioned in subsection (1)(a)(ii).

(3) Where property is applied cy-près by virtue of this section, all the donor's interest in it is treated as having been relinquished when the gift was made.

(4) But where property is so applied as belonging to donors who cannot be identified or cannot be found, and is not so applied by virtue of section 64 (donors treated as unidentifiable)—

(a)   the scheme must specify the total amount of that property,

(b)   the donor of any part of that amount is entitled, on making a claim within the time limit, to recover from the charity for which the property is applied a sum equal to that part, less any expenses properly incurred by the charity trustees after the scheme's date in connection with claims relating to the donor's gift, and

(c)   the scheme may include directions as to the provision to be made for meeting any claims made in accordance with paragraph (b).

(5) For the purposes of subsection (4)(b)—

(a)   a claim is made within the time limit only if it is made no later than 6 months after the date on which the scheme is made, and

(b)   "the scheme's date" means the date on which the scheme is made.

(6) Subsection (7) applies if—

(a)   any sum is, in accordance with any directions included in the scheme under subsection (4)(c), set aside for meeting claims made in accordance with subsection (4)(b), but

(b)   the aggregate amount of any such claims actually made exceeds the relevant amount;

and for this purpose "the relevant amount" means the amount of the sum so set aside after deduction of any expenses properly incurred by the charity trustees in connection with claims relating to the donors' gifts.

(7) If the Commission so directs, each of the donors in question is entitled only to such proportion of the relevant amount as the amount of the donor's claim bears to the aggregate amount referred to in subsection (6)(b).

64 Donors treated as unidentifiable

(1) For the purposes of section 63 property is conclusively presumed (without any advertisement or inquiry) to belong to donors who cannot be identified, in so far as it consists of—

(a)   the proceeds of cash collections made—

(i)   by means of collecting boxes, or

(ii)   by other means not adapted for distinguishing one gift from another, or

(b)   the proceeds of any lottery, competition, entertainment, sale or similar money-raising activity, after allowing for property given to provide prizes or articles for sale or otherwise to enable the activity to be undertaken.

(2) The court or the Commission may by order direct that property not falling within subsection (1) is for the purposes of section 63 to be treated (without any

advertisement or inquiry) as belonging to donors who cannot be identified if it appears to the court or the Commission—

(a)   that it would be unreasonable, having regard to the amounts likely to be returned to the donors, to incur expense with a view to returning the property, or

(b)   that it would be unreasonable, having regard to the nature, circumstances and amounts of the gifts, and to the lapse of time since the gifts were made, for the donors to expect the property to be returned.

65   Donors treated as disclaiming

(1)   This section applies to property given—

(a)   for specific charitable purposes, and

(b)   in response to a solicitation within subsection (2).

(2)   A solicitation is within this subsection if—

(a)   it is made for specific charitable purposes, and

(b)   it is accompanied by a statement to the effect that property given in response to it will, in the event of those purposes failing, be applicable cy-près as if given for charitable purposes generally, unless the donor makes a relevant declaration at the time of making the gift.

(3)   A relevant declaration is a declaration in writing by the donor to the effect that, in the event of the specific charitable purposes failing, the donor wishes to be given the opportunity by the trustees holding the property to request the return of the property in question (or a sum equal to its value at the time of the making of the gift).

(4)   Subsections (5) and (6) apply if—

(a)   a person has given property as mentioned in subsection (1),

(b)   the specific charitable purposes fail, and

(c)   the donor has made a relevant declaration.

(5)   The trustees holding the property must take the prescribed steps for the purpose of—

(a)   informing the donor of the failure of the purposes,

(b)   enquiring whether the donor wishes to request the return of the property (or a sum equal to its value), and

(c)   if within the prescribed period the donor makes such a request, returning the property (or such a sum) to the donor.

(6)   If those trustees have taken all appropriate prescribed steps but—

(a)   they have failed to find the donor, or

(b)   the donor does not within the prescribed period request the return of the property (or a sum equal to its value),

section 63(1) applies to the property as if it belonged to a donor within section 63(1)(b) (application of property where donor has disclaimed right to return of property).

(7)   If—

(a)   a person has given property as mentioned in subsection (1),

(b)   the specific charitable purposes fail, and

(c)   the donor has not made a relevant declaration,

section 63(1) similarly applies to the property as if it belonged to a donor within section 63(1)(b).

(8)   For the purposes of this section—

(a)   "solicitation" means a solicitation made in any manner and however communicated to the persons to whom it is addressed,

(b)   it is irrelevant whether any consideration is or is to be given in return for the property in question, and

(c)   where any appeal consists of—

> > (i)   solicitations that are accompanied by statements within subsection (2)(b), and
> >
> > (ii)   solicitations that are not so accompanied,

a person giving property as a result of the appeal is to be presumed, unless the contrary is proved, to have responded to the former solicitations and not the latter.

66 Unknown and disclaiming donors: supplementary

(1)   For the purposes of sections 63 and 65, charitable purposes are to be treated as failing if any difficulty in applying property to those purposes makes that property or the part not applicable cy-près available to be returned to the donors.

(2)   In sections 63 to 65 and this section—

> (a)   references to a donor include persons claiming through or under the original donor, and
>
> (b)   references to property given include the property for the time being representing the property originally given or property derived from it.

(3)   Subsection (2) applies except in so far as the context otherwise requires.

(4)   In sections 63 and 65 "prescribed" means prescribed by regulations made by the Commission.

(5)   Any such regulations are to be published by the Commission in such manner as it thinks fit.

(6)   Any such regulations may, as respects the advertisements which are to be published for the purposes of section 63(1)(a), make provision as to the form and content of such advertisements as well as the manner in which they are to be published.

67 Cy-près schemes

(1)   The power of the court or the Commission to make schemes for the application of property cy-près must be exercised in accordance with this section.

(2)   Where any property given for charitable purposes is applicable cy-près, the court or the Commission may make a scheme providing for the property to be applied—

> (a)   for such charitable purposes, and
>
> (b)   (if the scheme provides for the property to be transferred to another charity) by or on trust for such other charity,

as it considers appropriate, having regard to the matters set out in subsection (3).

(3)   The matters are—

> (a)   the spirit of the original gift,
>
> (b)   the desirability of securing that the property is applied for charitable purposes which are close to the original purposes, and
>
> (c)   the need for the relevant charity to have purposes which are suitable and effective in the light of current social and economic circumstances.

The "relevant charity" means the charity by or on behalf of which the property is to be applied under the scheme.

(4)   If a scheme provides for the property to be transferred to another charity, the scheme may impose on the charity trustees of that charity a duty to secure that the property is applied for purposes which are, so far as is reasonably practicable, similar in character to the original purposes.

(5)   In this section references to property given include the property for the time being representing the property originally given or property derived from it.

(6)   In this section references to the transfer of property to a charity are references to its transfer—

> (a)   to the charity,
>
> (b)   to the charity trustees,
>
> (c)   to any trustee for the charity, or

  (d) to a person nominated by the charity trustees to hold it in trust for the charity,

as the scheme may provide.

(7) In this section references to the original purposes of a gift are to be read, where the application of the property given has been altered or regulated by a scheme or otherwise, as referring to the purposes for which the property is for the time being applicable.

68 Charities governed by charter, or by or under statute

(1) Subsection (2) applies where a Royal charter establishing or regulating a body corporate is amendable by the grant and acceptance of a further charter.

(2) A scheme relating to the body corporate or to the administration of property held by the body (including a scheme for the cy-près application of any such property)—

  (a) may be made by the court under the court's jurisdiction with respect to charities even though the scheme cannot take effect without the alteration of the charter, but

  (b) must be so framed that the scheme, or such part of it as cannot take effect without the alteration of the charter, does not purport to come into operation unless or until Her Majesty thinks fit to amend the charter in such manner as will permit the scheme or that part of it to have effect.

(3) Subsection (4) applies where, under—

  (a) the court's jurisdiction with respect to charities or the corresponding jurisdiction of a court in Northern Ireland, or

  (b) powers conferred by this Act or by any Northern Ireland legislation relating to charities,

a scheme is made with respect to a body corporate and it appears to Her Majesty expedient, having regard to the scheme, to amend any Royal charter relating to that body.

(4) Her Majesty may, on the application of the body corporate, amend the charter accordingly by Order in Council in any way in which the charter could be amended by the grant and acceptance of a further charter; and any such Order in Council may be revoked or varied in the same manner as the charter it amends.

(5) The jurisdiction of the court with respect to charities is not excluded or restricted in the case of a charity of a description mentioned in Schedule 5 by the operation of the enactments or instruments there mentioned in relation to that description.

(6) A scheme established for a charity of a description mentioned in Schedule 5—

  (a) may modify or supersede in relation to it the provision made by any such enactment or instrument as if made by a scheme of the court, and

  (b) may also make any such provision as is authorised by that Schedule.

Powers of Commission to make schemes etc

69 Commission's concurrent jurisdiction with High Court for certain purposes

(1) The Commission may by order exercise the same jurisdiction and powers as are exercisable by the High Court in charity proceedings for the following purposes—

  (a) establishing a scheme for the administration of a charity;

  (b) appointing, discharging or removing a charity trustee or trustee for a charity, or removing an officer or employee;

  (c) vesting or transferring property, or requiring or entitling any person to call for or make any transfer of property or any payment.

(2) Subsection (1) is subject to the provisions of this Act.

(3) If the court directs a scheme for the administration of a charity to be established—

(a)   the court may by order refer the matter to the Commission for it to prepare or settle a scheme in accordance with such directions (if any) as the court sees fit to give, and

(b)   any such order may provide for the scheme to be put into effect by order of the Commission as if prepared under subsection (1) and without any further order of the court.

. . .

76 Suspension of trustees etc and appointment of interim managers

(1)   Subsection (3) applies where, at any time after it has instituted an inquiry under section 46 with respect to any charity, the Commission is satisfied—

(a)   that there is or has been any misconduct or mismanagement in the administration of the charity, or

(b)   that it is necessary or desirable to act for the purpose of—

    (i)   protecting the property of the charity, or

    (ii)   securing a proper application for the purposes of the charity of that property or of property coming to the charity.

(2)   The reference in subsection (1) to misconduct or mismanagement extends (regardless of anything in the trusts of the charity) to the employment—

(a)   for the remuneration or reward of persons acting in the affairs of the charity, or

(b)   for other administrative purposes,

of sums which are excessive in relation to the property which is or is likely to be applied or applicable for the purposes of the charity.

(3)   The Commission may of its own motion do one or more of the following—

(a)   by order suspend any person who is a trustee, charity trustee, officer, agent or employee of the charity from office or employment pending consideration being given to the person's removal (whether under section 79 or 80 or otherwise);

(b)   by order appoint such number of additional charity trustees as it considers necessary for the proper administration of the charity;

(c)   by order—

    (i)   vest any property held by or in trust for the charity in the official custodian,

    (ii)   require the persons in whom any such property is vested to transfer it to the official custodian, or

    (iii) appoint any person to transfer any such property to the official custodian;

(d)   order any person who holds any property on behalf of the charity, or of any trustee for it, not to part with the property without the approval of the Commission;

(e)   order any debtor of the charity not to make any payment in or towards the discharge of the debtor's liability to the charity without the approval of the Commission;

(f)   by order restrict (regardless of anything in the trusts of the charity) the transactions which may be entered into, or the nature or amount of the payments which may be made, in the administration of the charity without the approval of the Commission;

(g)   by order appoint (in accordance with section 78) an interim manager, to act as receiver and manager in respect of the property and affairs of the charity.

(4)   The Commission may not make an order under subsection (3)(a) so as to suspend a person from office or employment for a period of more than 12 months.

(5)   But any order under subsection (3)(a) made in the case of any person ("P") may make provision, as respects the period of P's suspension for matters arising out of it, and in particular—

    (a)   for enabling any person to execute any instrument in P's name or otherwise act for P, and

    (b)   in the case of a charity trustee, for adjusting any rules governing the proceedings of the charity trustees to take account of the reduction in the number capable of acting.

This does not affect the generality of section 337(1) and (2).

(6)   The Commission—

    (a)   must, at such intervals as it thinks fit, review any order made by it under paragraph (a), or any of paragraphs (c) to (g), of subsection (3), and

    (b)   if on any such review it appears to the Commission that it would be appropriate to discharge the order in whole or in part, must so discharge it (whether subject to any savings or other transitional provisions or not).

. . .

84   Power to direct specified action to be taken

(1)   This section applies where, at any time after the Commission has instituted an inquiry under section 46 with respect to any charity, it is satisfied either as mentioned in section 76(1)(a) (misconduct or mismanagement etc) or as mentioned in section 76(1)(b) (need to protect property etc).

(2)   The Commission may by order direct—

    (a)   the charity trustees,

    (b)   any trustee for the charity,

    (c)   any officer or employee of the charity, or

    (d)   (if a body corporate) the charity itself,

to take any action specified in the order which the Commission considers to be expedient in the interests of the charity.

(3)   An order under this section—

    (a)   may require action to be taken whether or not it would otherwise be within the powers exercisable by the person or persons concerned, or by the charity, in relation to the administration of the charity or to its property, but

    (b)   may not require any action to be taken which is prohibited by any Act or expressly prohibited by the trusts of the charity or is inconsistent with its purposes.

(4)   Anything done by a person or body under the authority of an order under this section is to be treated as properly done in the exercise of the powers mentioned in subsection (3)(a).

(5)   Subsection (4) does not affect any contractual or other rights arising in connection with anything which has been done under the authority of such an order.

85   Power to direct application of charity property

(1)   This section applies where the Commission is satisfied—

    (a)   that a person or persons in possession or control of any property held by or on trust for a charity is or are unwilling to apply it properly for the purposes of the charity, and

    (b)   that it is necessary or desirable to make an order under this section for the purpose of securing a proper application of that property for the purposes of the charity.

(2)   The Commission may by order direct the person or persons concerned to apply the property in such manner as is specified in the order.

(3)   An order under this section—

    (a)   may require action to be taken whether or not it would otherwise be within the powers exercisable by the person or persons concerned in relation to the property, but

    (b)   may not require any action to be taken which is prohibited by any Act or expressly prohibited by the trusts of the charity.

(4) Anything done by a person under the authority of an order under this section is to be treated as properly done in the exercise of the powers mentioned in subsection (3)(a).

(5) Subsection (4) does not affect any contractual or other rights arising in connection with anything which has been done under the authority of such an order.

86 Copy of certain orders, and reasons, to be sent to charity

(1) Where the Commission makes an order under a provision mentioned in subsection (2) it must send the documents mentioned in subsection (3)—

    (a)   to the charity concerned (if a body corporate), or

    (b)   (if not) to each of the charity trustees.

(2) The provisions are—

section 76 (suspension of trustees etc and appointment of interim managers);

section 79 (removal of trustee or officer etc for protective etc purposes);

section 80 (other powers to remove or appoint charity trustees);

section 81 (removal or appointment of charity trustees etc: supplementary);

section 83 (power to suspend or remove trustees etc from membership of charity);

section 84 (power to direct specified action to be taken);

section 85 (power to direct application of charity property).

(3) The documents are—

    (a)   a copy of the order, and

    (b)   a statement of the Commission's reasons for making it.

(4) The documents must be sent to the charity or charity trustees as soon as practicable after the making of the order.

(5) The Commission need not comply with subsection (4) in relation to the documents, or (as the case may be) the statement of its reasons, if it considers that to do so—

    (a)   would prejudice any inquiry or investigation, or

    (b)   would not be in the interests of the charity;

but, once the Commission considers that this is no longer the case, it must send the documents, or (as the case may be) the statement, to the charity or charity trustees as soon as practicable.

(6) Nothing in this section requires any document to be sent to a person who—

    (a)   cannot be found, or

    (b)   has no known address in the United Kingdom.

(7) Any documents required to be sent to a person under this section may be sent to, or otherwise served on, the person in the same way as an order made by the Commission under this Act could be served on the person in accordance with section 339.

. . .

Publicity relating to schemes and orders

88 Publicity relating to schemes

(1) The Commission may not—

    (a)   make any order under this Act to establish a scheme for the administration of a charity, or

    (b)   submit such a scheme to the court or the Minister for an order giving it effect,

unless, before doing so, the Commission has complied with the publicity requirements in subsection (2).

This is subject to any disapplication of those requirements under subsection (4).

(2)   The publicity requirements are—

    (a)   that the Commission must give public notice of its proposals, inviting representations to be made to it within a period specified in the notice, and

    (b)   that, in the case of a scheme relating to a local charity (other than an ecclesiastical charity) in a parish, or in a community in Wales, the Commission must communicate a draft of the scheme to—

        (i)   the parish council or, if the parish has no council, the chairman of the parish meeting, or

        (ii)   the community council or, if the community has no council, the county council or county borough council.

(3)   The time when any such notice is given or any such communication takes place is to be decided by the Commission.

(4)   The Commission may determine that either or both of the publicity requirements is or are not to apply in relation to a particular scheme if it is satisfied that—

    (a)   because of the nature of the scheme, or

    (b)   for any other reason,

compliance with the requirement or requirements is unnecessary.

(5)   Where the Commission gives public notice of any proposals under this section—

    (a)   it must take into account any representations made to it within the period specified in the notice, and

    (b)   it may (without further notice) proceed with the proposals either without modifications or with such modifications as it thinks desirable.

(6)   Where the Commission makes an order under this Act to establish a scheme for the administration of a charity, a copy of the order must be available, for at least a month after the order is published, for public inspection at all reasonable times—

    (a)   at the Commission's office, and

    (b)   if the charity is a local charity, at some convenient place in the area of the charity.

(7)   Subsection (6)(b) does not apply if the Commission is satisfied that for any reason it is unnecessary for a copy of the scheme to be available locally.

(8)   Any public notice of any proposals which is to be given under this section—

    (a)   is to contain such particulars of the proposals, or such directions for obtaining information about them, as the Commission thinks sufficient and appropriate, and

    (b)   is to be given in such manner as the Commission thinks sufficient and appropriate.

89 Publicity for orders relating to trustees or other individuals

(1)   The Commission may not make any order under this Act to appoint, discharge or remove a charity trustee or trustee for a charity, other than—

    (a)   an order relating to the official custodian, or

    (b)   an order under section 76(3)(b) (appointment of additional charity trustees),

unless, before doing so, the Commission has complied with the publicity requirement in subsection (2).

This is subject to any disapplication of that requirement under subsection (4).

(2)   The publicity requirement is that the Commission must give public notice of its proposals, inviting representations to be made to it within a period specified in the notice.

(3)   The time when any such notice is given is to be decided by the Commission.

(4)   The Commission may determine that the publicity requirement is not to apply in relation to a particular order if it is satisfied that for any reason compliance with the requirement is unnecessary.

(5)   Before the Commission makes an order under this Act to remove a person who is—

    (a)   a charity trustee or trustee for a charity, or

    (b)   an officer, agent or employee of a charity,

without the person's consent, the Commission must give the person not less than one month's notice of its proposals, inviting representations to be made to it within a period specified in the notice.

This does not apply if the person cannot be found or has no known address in the United Kingdom.

(6)   Where the Commission gives notice of any proposals under this section—

    (a)   it must take into account any representations made to it within the period specified in the notice, and

    (b)   it may (without further notice) proceed with the proposals either without modifications or with such modifications as it thinks desirable.

(7)   Any notice of any proposals which is to be given under this section—

    (a)   is to contain such particulars of the proposals, or such directions for obtaining information about them, as the Commission thinks sufficient and appropriate, and

    (b)   (in the case of a public notice) is to be given in such manner as the Commission thinks sufficient and appropriate.

(8)   Any notice to be given under subsection (5)—

    (a)   may be given by post, and

    (b)   if given by post, may be addressed to the recipient's last known address in the United Kingdom.

Property vested in official custodian

90 Entrusting charity property to official custodian, and termination of trust

(1)   The court may by order—

    (a)   vest in the official custodian any land held by or in trust for a charity,

    (b)   authorise or require the persons in whom any such land is vested to transfer it to the official custodian, or

    (c)   appoint any person to transfer any such land to the official custodian.

(2)   But subsection (1) does not apply to any interest in land by way of mortgage or other security.

(3)   Where property is vested in the official custodian in trust for a charity, the court may make an order discharging the official custodian from the trusteeship as respects all or any of that property.

(4)   Where—

    (a)   the official custodian is discharged from the trusteeship of any property, or

    (b)   the trusts on which the official custodian holds any property come to an end,

the court may make such vesting orders and give such directions as may seem to the court to be necessary or expedient in consequence.

(5)   No person is liable for any loss occasioned by—

(a)   acting in conformity with an order under this section, or

(b)   giving effect to anything done in pursuance of such an order.

(6)   No person is excused from—

(a)   acting in conformity with an order under this section, or

(b)   giving effect to anything done in pursuance of such an order,

because the order has been in any respect improperly obtained.

91 Supplementary provisions as to property vested in official custodian

(1)   Subject to the provisions of this Act, where property is vested in the official custodian in trust for a charity, the official custodian—

(a)   must not exercise any powers of management, but

(b)   as trustee of any property—

(i)   has all the same powers, duties and liabilities,

(ii)   is entitled to the same rights and immunities, and

(iii)   is subject to the control and orders of the court in the same way,

as a corporation appointed custodian trustee under section 4 of the Public Trustee Act 1906.

(2)   Subsection (1) does not confer on the official custodian a power to charge fees.

(3)   Subject to subsection (4), where any land is vested in the official custodian in trust for a charity, the charity trustees may, in the name and on behalf of the official custodian, execute and do all assurances and things which they could properly execute or do in their own name and on their own behalf if the land were vested in them.

(4)   If any land is so vested in the official custodian by virtue of an order under section 76(3)(c), the power conferred on the charity trustees by subsection (3) is not exercisable by them in relation to any transaction affecting the land, unless the transaction is authorised by order of the court or of the Commission.

(5)   Where any land is vested in the official custodian in trust for a charity—

(a)   the charity trustees have the same power to make obligations entered into by them binding on the land as if it were vested in them, and

(b)   any covenant, agreement or condition which is enforceable by or against the official custodian because the land is vested in the official custodian is enforceable by or against the charity trustees as if the land were vested in them.

(6)   In relation to a corporate charity, subsections (3) to (5) apply with the substitution of references to the charity for references to the charity trustees.

(7)   Subsections (3) to (5) do not authorise any charity trustees or charity to impose any personal liability on the official custodian.

(8)   Where the official custodian is entitled as trustee for a charity to the custody of securities or documents of title relating to the trust property, the official custodian may permit them to be in the possession or under the control of the charity trustees without incurring any liability by doing so.

Official custodian and Reverter of Sites Act 1987

92 Divestment of official custodian where 1987 Act due to operate

(1)   Subsection (2) applies where—

(a)   any land is vested in the official custodian in trust for a charity, and

(b)   it appears to the Commission that section 1 of the 1987 Act (right of reverter replaced by trust) will, or is likely to, operate in relation to the land at a particular time or in particular circumstances.

(2)   The jurisdiction which, under section 69, is exercisable by the Commission for the purpose of discharging a trustee for a charity may, at any time before section 1 of the 1987 Act operates in relation to the land, be exercised by the Commission of its own motion for the purpose of—

(a)   making an order discharging the official custodian from the trusteeship of the land, and

(b)   making such vesting orders and giving such directions as appear to the Commission to be necessary or expedient in consequence.

(3) In this section and sections 93 to 95—

(a)   "the 1987 Act" means the Reverter of Sites Act 1987, and

(b)   any reference to section 1 of the 1987 Act operating in relation to any land is a reference to a trust arising in relation to the land under that section.

93 Divestment of official custodian where 1987 Act has operated

(1) Subsection (2) applies where—

(a)   section 1 of the 1987 Act has operated in relation to any land which, immediately before the time when that section so operated, was vested in the official custodian in trust for a charity, and

(b)   the land remains vested in the official custodian but on the trust arising under that section.

(2) The court or the Commission (of its own motion) may—

(a)   make an order discharging the official custodian from the trusteeship of the land, and

(b)   (subject to sections 94 and 95) make such vesting orders and give such directions as appear to it to be necessary or expedient in consequence.

94 Vesting of land in relevant charity trustees following divestment

(1) Subsection (2) applies where an order discharging the official custodian from the trusteeship of any land—

(a)   is made by—

(i)   the court under section 90(3), or

(ii)   the Commission under section 69,

on the ground that section 1 of the 1987 Act will, or is likely to, operate in relation to the land, or

(b)   is made by the court or the Commission under section 93.

(2) The persons in whom the land is to be vested on the discharge of the official custodian are the relevant charity trustees, unless the court or (as the case may be) the Commission is satisfied that it would be appropriate for it to be vested in some other persons.

(3) In subsection (2) "the relevant charity trustees" means—

(a)   in relation to an order made as mentioned in subsection (1)(a), the charity trustees of the charity in trust for which the land is vested in the official custodian immediately before the time when the order takes effect, or

(b)   in relation to an order made under section 93, the charity trustees of the charity in trust for which the land was vested in the official custodian immediately before the time when section 1 of the 1987 Act operated in relation to the land.

95 Supplementary provisions in connection with 1987 Act

(1) Subsection (2) applies where—

(a)   section 1 of the 1987 Act has operated in relation to any such land as is mentioned in section 93(1)(a), and

(b)   the land remains vested in the official custodian as mentioned in section 93(1)(b).

(2) Subject to subsection (3)—

(a)   all the powers, duties and liabilities that would, apart from this section, be those of the official custodian as trustee of the land are instead to be those of the charity trustees of the charity concerned, and

(b)   those trustees may, in the name and on behalf of the official custodian, execute and do all assurances and things which they could properly execute or do in their own name and on their own behalf if the land were vested in them.

(3)   Subsection (2) is not to be treated as requiring or authorising those trustees to sell the land at a time when it remains vested in the official custodian.

(4)   Where—

(a)   the official custodian has been discharged from the trusteeship of any land by an order under section 93, and

(b)   the land has, in accordance with section 94, been vested in the charity trustees concerned or (as the case may be) in any persons other than those trustees,

the land is to be held by those trustees, or (as the case may be) by those persons, as trustees on the terms of the trust arising under section 1 of the 1987 Act.

(5)   The official custodian is not liable to any person in respect of any loss or misapplication of any land vested in the official custodian in accordance with section 1 of the 1987 Act unless it is occasioned by or through any wilful neglect or default of—

(a)   the official custodian, or

(b)   any person acting for the official custodian.

(6)   But the Consolidated Fund is liable to make good to any person any sums for which the official custodian may be liable because of any such neglect or default.

Establishment of common investment or deposit funds

96 Power to make common investment schemes

(1)   The court or the Commission may by order make and bring into effect schemes for the establishment of common investment funds under trusts which provide—

(a)   for property transferred to the fund by or on behalf of a charity participating in the scheme to be invested under the control of trustees appointed to manage the fund, and

(b)   for the participating charities to be entitled (subject to the provisions of the scheme) to the capital and income of the fund in shares determined by reference to the amount or value of the property transferred to it by or on behalf of each of them and to the value of the fund at the time of the transfers.

(2)   In this section and sections 97 to 99 "common investment scheme" means a scheme under subsection (1).

(3)   The court or the Commission may make a common investment scheme on the application of any two or more charities.

. . .

104 Meaning of "Scottish recognised body" and "Northern Ireland charity"

(1)   In sections 97 and 101 "Scottish recognised body" means a body—

(a)   established under the law of Scotland, or

(b)   managed or controlled wholly or mainly in or from Scotland,

to which HMRC have given intimation, which has not subsequently been withdrawn, that tax relief is due in respect of income of the body which is applicable and applied to charitable purposes only.

(2)   In sections 97 and 101 "Northern Ireland charity" means an institution—

(a)   which is a charity under the law of Northern Ireland, and

(b) to which HMRC have given intimation, which has not subsequently been withdrawn, that tax relief is due in respect of income of the institution which is applicable and applied to charitable purposes only.

(3) For the purposes of this section—

"HMRC" means the Commissioners for Her Majesty's Revenue and Customs;

"tax relief" means relief under—

(a) Part 10 of the Income Tax Act 2007, or

(b) any provision of Part 11 of the Corporation Tax Act 2010 other than sections 480 (exemption for profits of small-scale trades) and 481 (exemption from charges under provisions to which section 1173 applies).

[104A Investment of endowment fund on total return basis]

[(1) This section applies to any available endowment fund of a charity.

(2) If the condition in subsection (3) is met in relation to the charity, the charity trustees may resolve that the fund, or a portion of it—

(a) should be invested without the need to maintain a balance between capital and income returns, and

(b) accordingly, should be freed from the restrictions with respect to expenditure of capital that apply to it.

(3) The condition is that the charity trustees are satisfied that it is in the interests of the charity that regulations under section 104B(1)(b) should apply in place of the restrictions mentioned in subsection (2)(b).

(4) While a resolution under subsection (2) has effect, the regulations apply in place of the restrictions.

(5) In this section "available endowment fund", in relation to a charity, means—

(a) the whole of the charity's permanent endowment if it is all subject to the same trusts, or

(b) any part of its permanent endowment which is subject to any particular trusts that are different from those to which any other part is subject.]

[104B Total return investment: regulations]

[(1) The Commission may by regulations make provision about—

(a) resolutions under section 104A(2),

(b) the investment of a relevant fund without the need to maintain a balance between capital and income returns, and expenditure from such a fund, and

(c) the steps that must be taken by charity trustees in respect of a fund, or portion of a fund, in the event of a resolution under section 104A(2) ceasing to have effect in respect of the fund or portion.

(2) Regulations under subsection (1)(a) may, in particular—

(a) specify steps that must be taken by charity trustees before passing a resolution under section 104A(2),

(b) make provision about the variation and revocation of such a resolution,

(c) require charity trustees to notify the Commission of the passing, variation or revocation of such a resolution, and

(d) specify circumstances in which such a resolution is to cease to have effect.

(3) Regulations under subsection (1)(b) may, in particular—

(a) make provision requiring a relevant fund to be invested, and the returns from that investment to be allocated, in such a way as to maintain (so far as practicable) the long-term capital value of the fund,

(b)   make provision about the taking of advice by charity trustees in connection with the investment of, and expenditure from, a relevant fund,

(c)   confer on the charity trustees of a relevant fund a power (subject to such restrictions as may be specified in the regulations) to accumulate income,

(d)   make provision about expenditure from a relevant fund (including by imposing limits on expenditure and specifying circumstances in which expenditure requires the Commission's consent), and

(e)   require charity trustees to report to the Commission on the investment of, and expenditure from, a relevant fund.

(4)   A power to accumulate income conferred by regulations under subsection (1)(b) or (c) is not subject to section 14(3) of the Perpetuities and Accumulations Act 2009 (which provides for certain powers to accumulate income to cease to have effect after 21 years).

(5)   Any regulations made by the Commission under this section must be published by the Commission in such manner as it thinks fit.

(6)   In this section "relevant fund" means a fund, or portion of a fund, in respect of which a resolution under section 104A(2) has effect, and includes the returns from the investment of the fund or portion.]

Power to authorise dealings with charity property, ex gratia payments etc

105 Power to authorise dealings with charity property etc

(1)   Subject to the provisions of this section, where it appears to the Commission that any action proposed or contemplated in the administration of a charity is expedient in the interests of the charity, the Commission may by order sanction that action, whether or not it would otherwise be within the powers exercisable by the charity trustees in the administration of the charity.

(2)   Anything done under the authority of an order under this section is to be treated as properly done in the exercise of those powers.

(3)   An order under this section—

(a)   may be made so as to authorise a particular transaction, compromise or the like, or a particular application of property, or so as to give a more general authority, and

(b)   may authorise a charity to use common premises, or employ a common staff, or otherwise combine for any purpose of administration, with any other charity.

Paragraph (b) does not affect the generality of subsection (1).

(4)   An order under this section may give directions—

(a)   as to the manner in which any expenditure is to be borne, and

(b)   as to other matters connected with or arising out of the action authorised by the order.

(5)   Where anything is done in pursuance of an authority given by an order under this section, any directions given in connection with that authority—

(a)   are binding on the charity trustees for the time being as if contained in the trusts of the charity, but

(b)   may on the application of the charity be modified or superseded by a further order.

(6)   The directions which may be given by an order under this section in particular include directions—

(a)   for meeting any expenditure out of a specified fund,

(b)   for charging any expenditure to capital or to income,

(c)   for requiring expenditure charged to capital to be recouped out of income within a specified period,

(d)   for restricting the costs to be incurred at the expense of the charity, or

(e)   for the investment of money arising from any transaction.

This does not affect the generality of subsection (4).

(7) An order under this section may authorise any act even though—

(a)   it is prohibited by the Ecclesiastical Leases Act 1836, or

(b)   the trusts of the charity provide for the act to be done by or under the authority of the court.

(8) But an order under this section may not—

(a)   authorise the doing of any act expressly prohibited by any Act other than the Ecclesiastical Leases Act 1836, or by the trusts of the charity, or

(b)   extend or alter the purposes of the charity.

(9) In the case of a charitable company, an order under this section may authorise an act even though it involves the breach of a duty imposed on a director of the company under Chapter 2 of Part 10 of the Companies Act 2006 (general duties of directors).

(10) An order under this section does not confer any authority in relation to a building which has been consecrated and of which the use or disposal is regulated, and can be further regulated, by a scheme having effect or treated as having effect under or by virtue of the Mission and Pastoral Measure 2011.

(11) The reference in subsection (10) to a building is to be treated as including—

(a)   part of a building, and

(b)   any land which under such a scheme is to be used or disposed of with a building to which the scheme applies.

106 Power to authorise ex gratia payments etc

(1) Subject to subsection (5), the Commission may by order exercise the same power as is exercisable by the Attorney General to authorise the charity trustees of a charity to take any action falling within subsection (2)(a) or (b) in a case where the charity trustees—

(a)   (apart from this section) have no power to take the action, but

(b)   in all the circumstances regard themselves as being under a moral obligation to take it.

(2) The actions are—

(a)   making any application of property of the charity, or

(b)   waiving to any extent, on behalf of the charity, its entitlement to receive any property.

(3) The power conferred on the Commission by subsection (1) is exercisable by the Commission under the supervision of, and in accordance with such directions as may be given by, the Attorney General.

(4) Any such directions may in particular require the Commission, in such circumstances as are specified in the directions—

(a)   to refrain from exercising the power conferred by subsection (1), or

(b)   to consult the Attorney General before exercising it.

(5) Where—

(a)   an application is made to the Commission for it to exercise the power conferred by subsection (1) in a case where it is not precluded from doing so by any such directions, but

(b)   the Commission considers that it would nevertheless be desirable for the application to be entertained by the Attorney General rather than by the Commission,

the Commission must refer the application to the Attorney General.

(6) It is hereby declared that where—

(a)   an application is made to the Commission as mentioned in subsection (5)(a), and

(b)   the Commission determines the application by refusing to authorise charity trustees to take any action falling within subsection (2)(a) or (b),

that refusal does not preclude the Attorney General, on an application subsequently made to the Attorney General by the charity trustees, from authorising them to take that action.

Power to give directions about dormant bank accounts of charities

107 Power to direct transfer of credits in dormant bank accounts

(1)   The Commission may give a direction under subsection (2) where—

(a)   it is informed by a relevant institution—

(i)   that it holds one or more accounts in the name of or on behalf of a particular charity ("the relevant charity"), and

(ii)   that the account, or (if it so holds two or more accounts) each of the accounts, is dormant, and

(b)   it is unable, after making reasonable inquiries, to locate that charity or any of its trustees.

(2)   A direction under this subsection is a direction which—

(a)   requires the institution concerned to transfer the amount, or (as the case may be) the aggregate amount, standing to the credit of the relevant charity in the account or accounts in question to such other charity as is specified in the direction in accordance with subsection (3), or

(b)   requires the institution concerned to transfer to each of two or more other charities so specified in the direction such part of that amount or aggregate amount as is there specified in relation to that charity.

(3)   The Commission—

(a)   may specify in a direction under subsection (2) such other charity or charities as it considers appropriate, having regard, in a case where the purposes of the relevant charity are known to the Commission, to those purposes and to the purposes of the other charity or charities, but

(b)   must not so specify any charity unless it has received from the charity trustees written confirmation that those trustees are willing to accept the amount proposed to be transferred to the charity.

(4)   Any amount received by a charity by virtue of this section is to be received by the charity on terms that—

(a)   it is to be held and applied by the charity for the purposes of the charity, but

(b)   as property of the charity, it is nevertheless subject to any restrictions on expenditure to which it was subject as property of the relevant charity.

(5)   The receipt of any charity trustees or trustee for a charity in respect of any amount received from a relevant institution by virtue of this section is a complete discharge of the institution in respect of that amount.

108 Accounts which cease to be dormant before transfer

(1)   This section applies where—

(a)   the Commission has been informed as mentioned in section 107(1)(a) by any relevant institution, and

(b)   before any transfer is made by the institution in pursuance of a direction under section 107(2), the institution has, by reason of any circumstances, cause to believe that the account, or (as the case may be) any of the accounts, held by it in the name of or on behalf of the relevant charity is no longer dormant.

(2)   The institution must without delay notify those circumstances in writing to the Commission.

(3)   If it appears to the Commission that the account or accounts in question is or are no longer dormant, it must revoke any direction under section 107(2) which has previously been given by it to the institution with respect to the relevant charity.

. . .

Additional powers of Commission

110 Power to give advice

(1)   The Commission may, on the written application of any charity trustee or trustee for a charity, give the applicant its opinion or advice in relation to any matter—

    (a)   relating to the performance of any duties of the applicant, as such a trustee, in relation to the charity concerned, or

    (b)   otherwise relating to the proper administration of the charity.

(2)   A person ("P") who—

    (a)   is a charity trustee or trustee for a charity, and

    (b)   acts in accordance with any opinion or advice given by the Commission under subsection (1) (whether to P or another trustee),

is to be treated, as regards P's responsibility for so acting, as having acted in accordance with P's trust.

(3)   But subsection (2) does not apply to P if, when so acting—

    (a)   P knows or has reasonable cause to suspect that the opinion or advice was given in ignorance of material facts, or

    (b)   a decision of the court or the Tribunal has been obtained on the matter or proceedings are pending to obtain one.

111 Power to determine membership of charity

(1)   The Commission may—

    (a)   on the application of a charity, or

    (b)   at any time after the institution of an inquiry under section 46 with respect to a charity,

determine who are the members of the charity.

(2)   The Commission's power under subsection (1) may also be exercised by a person appointed by the Commission for the purpose.

(3)   In a case within subsection (1)(b) the Commission may, if it thinks fit, so appoint the person appointed to conduct the inquiry.

. . .

PART 7

CHARITY LAND

Restrictions on dispositions of land in England and Wales

117 Restrictions on dispositions of land: general

(1)   No land held by or in trust for a charity is to be conveyed, transferred, leased or otherwise disposed of without an order of—

    (a)   the court, or

    (b)   the Commission.

But this is subject to the following provisions of this section, sections 119 to 121 (further provisions about restrictions on dispositions) and section 127 (release of charity rentcharges).

(2)   Subsection (1) does not apply to a disposition of such land if—

    (a)   the disposition is made to a person who is not—

        (i)   a connected person (as defined in section 118), or

    (ii) a trustee for, or nominee of, a connected person, and

  (b) the requirements of—

    (i) section 119(1) (dispositions other than certain leases), or

    (ii) section 120(2) (leases which are for 7 years or less etc),

have been complied with in relation to it.

(3) The restrictions on disposition imposed by this section and sections 119 to 121 apply regardless of anything in the trusts of a charity; but nothing in this section or sections 119 to 121 applies to—

  (a) any disposition for which general or special authority is expressly given (without the authority being made subject to the sanction of an order of the court) by—

    (i) any statutory provision contained in or having effect under an Act, or

    (ii) any scheme legally established,

  (b) any disposition for which the authorisation or consent of the Secretary of State is required under the Universities and College Estates Act 1925,

  (c) any disposition of land held by or in trust for a charity which—

    (i) is made to another charity otherwise than for the best price that can reasonably be obtained, and

    (ii) is authorised to be so made by the trusts of the first-mentioned charity, or

  (d) the granting, by or on behalf of a charity and in accordance with its trusts, of a lease to any beneficiary under those trusts where the lease—

    (i) is granted otherwise than for the best rent that can reasonably be obtained, and

    (ii) is intended to enable the demised premises to be occupied for the purposes, or any particular purposes, of the charity.

(4) Nothing in this section or sections 119 to 121 applies to—

  (a) any disposition of land held by or in trust for an exempt charity,

  (b) any disposition of land by way of mortgage or other security, or

  (c) any disposition of an advowson.

118 Meaning of "connected person" in s 117(2)

(1) In section 117(2) "connected person", in relation to a charity, means any person who falls within subsection (2)—

  (a) at the time of the disposition in question, or

  (b) at the time of any contract for the disposition in question.

(2) The persons are—

  (a) a charity trustee or trustee for the charity,

  (b) a person who is the donor of any land to the charity (whether the gift was made on or after the establishment of the charity),

  (c) a child, parent, grandchild, grandparent, brother or sister of any such trustee or donor,

  (d) an officer, agent or employee of the charity,

  (e) the spouse or civil partner of any person falling within any of paragraphs (a) to (d),

  (f) a person carrying on business in partnership with any person falling within any of paragraphs (a) to (e),

  (g) an institution which is controlled—

    (i) by any person falling within any of paragraphs (a) to (f), or

    (ii) by two or more such persons taken together, or

  (h) a body corporate in which—

> (i)   any connected person falling within any of paragraphs (a) to (g) has a substantial interest, or
>
> (ii)   two or more such persons, taken together, have a substantial interest.

(3) Sections 350 to 352 (meaning of child, spouse and civil partner, controlled institution and substantial interest) apply for the purposes of subsection (2).

119 Requirements for dispositions other than certain leases

(1) The requirements mentioned in section 117(2)(b) are that the charity trustees must, before entering into an agreement for the sale, or (as the case may be) for a lease or other disposition, of the land—

> (a)   obtain and consider a written report on the proposed disposition from a qualified surveyor instructed by the trustees and acting exclusively for the charity,
>
> (b)   advertise the proposed disposition for such period and in such manner as is advised in the surveyor's report (unless it advises that it would not be in the best interests of the charity to advertise the proposed disposition), and
>
> (c)   decide that they are satisfied, having considered the surveyor's report, that the terms on which the disposition is proposed to be made are the best that can reasonably be obtained for the charity.

(2) Subsection (1) does not apply where the proposed disposition is the granting of such a lease as is mentioned in section 120(1).

(3) For the purposes of subsection (1) a qualified surveyor is a person who—

> (a)   is a fellow or professional associate of the Royal Institution of Chartered Surveyors or satisfies such other requirement or requirements as may be prescribed by regulations made by the Minister, and
>
> (b)   is reasonably believed by the charity trustees to have ability in, and experience of, the valuation of land of the particular kind, and in the particular area, in question.

(4) Any report prepared for the purposes of subsection (1) must contain such information, and deal with such matters, as may be prescribed by regulations made by the Minister.

120 Requirements for leases which are for 7 years or less etc

(1) Subsection (2) applies where the proposed disposition is the granting of a lease for a term ending not more than 7 years after it is granted (other than one granted wholly or partly in consideration of a fine).

(2) The requirements mentioned in section 117(2)(b) are that the charity trustees must, before entering into an agreement for the lease—

> (a)   obtain and consider the advice on the proposed disposition of a person who is reasonably believed by the trustees to have the requisite ability and practical experience to provide them with competent advice on the proposed disposition, and
>
> (b)   decide that they are satisfied, having considered that person's advice, that the terms on which the disposition is proposed to be made are the best that can reasonably be obtained for the charity.

121 Additional restrictions where land held for stipulated purposes

(1) Subsection (2) applies where—

> (a)   any land is held by or in trust for a charity, and
>
> (b)   the trusts on which it is so held stipulate that it is to be used for the purposes, or any particular purposes, of the charity.

(2) The land must not be conveyed, transferred, leased or otherwise disposed of unless the charity trustees have before the relevant time—

(a)   given public notice of the proposed disposition, inviting representations to be made to them within a time specified in the notice, which must be not less than one month from the date of the notice, and

(b)   taken into consideration any representations made to them within that time about the proposed disposition.

(3)   Subsection (2)—

(a)   is subject to subsections (5) and (6), and

(b)   does not affect the operation of sections 117 to 120.

(4)   In subsection (2) "the relevant time" means—

(a)   where the charity trustees enter into an agreement for the sale, or (as the case may be) for the lease or other disposition, the time when they enter into that agreement, and

(b)   in any other case, the time of the disposition.

(5)   Subsection (2) does not apply to any such disposition of land as is there mentioned if—

(a)   the disposition is to be effected with a view to acquiring by way of replacement other property which is to be held on the trusts referred to in subsection (1)(b), or

(b)   the disposition is the granting of a lease for a term ending not more than 2 years after it is granted (other than one granted wholly or partly in consideration of a fine).

(6)   The Commission may, if the condition in subsection (7) is met, direct—

(a)   that subsection (2) is not to apply to dispositions of land held by or in trust for a charity or class of charities (whether generally or only in the case of a specified class of dispositions or land, or otherwise as may be provided in the direction), or

(b)   that subsection (2) is not to apply to a particular disposition of land held by or in trust for a charity.

(7)   The condition is that the Commission, on an application made to it in writing by or behalf of the charity or charities in question, is satisfied that it would be in the interests of the charity or charities for the Commission to give the direction.

122 Instruments concerning dispositions of land: required statements, etc

(1)   Subsection (2) applies to any of the following instruments—

(a)   a contract for the sale, or for a lease or other disposition, of land which is held by or in trust for a charity, and

(b)   a conveyance, transfer, lease or other instrument effecting a disposition of such land.

(2)   An instrument to which this subsection applies must state—

(a)   that the land is held by or in trust for a charity,

(b)   whether the charity is an exempt charity and whether the disposition is one falling within section 117(3)(a), (b), (c) or (d), and

(c)   if it is not an exempt charity and the disposition is not one falling within section 117(3)(a), (b), (c) or (d), that the land is land to which the restrictions on disposition imposed by sections 117 to 121 apply.

(3)   Where any land held by or in trust for a charity is conveyed, transferred, leased or otherwise disposed of by a disposition to which section 117(1) or (2) applies, the charity trustees must certify in the instrument by which the disposition is effected—

(a)   (where section 117(1) applies) that the disposition has been sanctioned by an order of the court or of the Commission (as the case may be), or

(b)   (where section 117(2) applies) that the charity trustees have power under the trusts of the charity to effect the disposition and have complied with sections 117 to 121 so far as applicable to it.

(4)   Where subsection (3) has been complied with in relation to any disposition of land, then in favour of a person who (whether under the disposition or afterwards) acquires an interest in the land for money or money's worth, it is conclusively presumed that the facts were as stated in the certificate.

(5)   Subsection (6) applies where—

(a)   any land held by or in trust for a charity is conveyed, transferred, leased or otherwise disposed of by a disposition to which section 117(1) or (2) applies, but

(b)   subsection (3) has not been complied with in relation to the disposition.

(6)   In favour of a person who (whether under the disposition or afterwards) in good faith acquires an interest in the land for money or money's worth, the disposition is valid whether or not—

(a)   the disposition has been sanctioned by an order of the court or of the Commission, or

(b)   the charity trustees have power under the trusts of the charity to effect the disposition and have complied with sections 117 to 121 so far as applicable to it.

(7)   Subsection (8) applies to any of the following instruments—

(a)   a contract for the sale, or for a lease or other disposition, of land which will, as a result of the disposition, be held by or in trust for a charity, and

(b)   a conveyance, transfer, lease or other instrument effecting a disposition of such land.

(8)   An instrument to which this subsection applies must state—

(a)   that the land will, as a result of the disposition, be held by or in trust for a charity,

(b)   whether the charity is an exempt charity, and

(c)   if it is not an exempt charity, that the restrictions on disposition imposed by sections 117 to 121 will apply to the land (subject to section 117(3)).

(9)   In this section and section 123 references to a disposition of land do not include references to—

(a)   a disposition of land by way of mortgage or other security,

(b)   any disposition of an advowson, or

(c)   any release of a rentcharge falling within section 127(1).

123 Charity land and land registration

(1)   Where the disposition to be effected by any such instrument as is mentioned in section 122(1)(b) or (7)(b) will be—

(a)   a registrable disposition, or

(b)   a disposition which triggers the requirement of registration,

the statement which, by virtue of section 122(2) or (8), is to be contained in the instrument must be in such form as may be prescribed by land registration rules.

(2)   Where the registrar approves an application for registration of—

(a)   a disposition of registered land, or

(b)   a person's title under a disposition of unregistered land,

and the instrument effecting the disposition contains a statement complying with section 122(8) and subsection (1), the registrar must enter in the register a restriction reflecting the limitation under sections 117 to 121 on subsequent disposal.

(3)   Where—

(a)   any such restriction is entered in the register in respect of any land, and

(b)   the charity by or in trust for which the land is held becomes an exempt charity,

the charity trustees must apply to the registrar for the removal of the entry.

(4)   On receiving any application duly made under subsection (3) the registrar must remove the entry.

(5)   Where—

(a)   any registered land is held by or in trust for an exempt charity and the charity ceases to be an exempt charity, or

(b)   any registered land becomes, as a result of a declaration of trust by the registered proprietor, land held in trust for a charity (other than an exempt charity),

the charity trustees must apply to the registrar for such a restriction as is mentioned in subsection (2) to be entered in the register in respect of the land.

(6)   On receiving any application duly made under subsection (5) the registrar must enter such a restriction in the register in respect of the land.

Restrictions on mortgages of land in England and Wales

124   Restrictions on mortgages

(1)   Subject to subsection (2), no mortgage of land held by or in trust for a charity is to be granted without an order of—

(a)   the court, or

(b)   the Commission.

(2)   Subsection (1) does not apply to a mortgage of any such land if the charity trustees have, before executing the mortgage, obtained and considered proper advice, given to them in writing, on the relevant matters or matter mentioned in subsection (3) or (4) (as the case may be).

(3)   In the case of a mortgage to secure the repayment of a proposed loan or grant, the relevant matters are—

(a)   whether the loan or grant is necessary in order for the charity trustees to be able to pursue the particular course of action in connection with which they are seeking the loan or grant,

(b)   whether the terms of the loan or grant are reasonable having regard to the status of the charity as the prospective recipient of the loan or grant, and

(c)   the ability of the charity to repay on those terms the sum proposed to be paid by way of loan or grant.

(4)   In the case of a mortgage to secure the discharge of any other proposed obligation, the relevant matter is whether it is reasonable for the charity trustees to undertake to discharge the obligation, having regard to the charity's purposes.

(5)   Subsection (3) or (as the case may be) subsection (4) applies in relation to such a mortgage as is mentioned in that subsection whether the mortgage—

(a)   would only have effect to secure the repayment of the proposed loan or grant or the discharge of the proposed obligation, or

(b)   would also have effect to secure the repayment of sums paid by way of loan or grant, or the discharge of other obligations undertaken, after the date of its execution.

(6)   Subsection (7) applies where—

(a)   the charity trustees of a charity have executed a mortgage of land held by or in trust for a charity in accordance with subsection (2), and

(b)   the mortgage has effect to secure the repayment of sums paid by way of loan or grant, or the discharge of other obligations undertaken, after the date of its execution.

(7)   In such a case, the charity trustees must not after that date enter into any transaction involving—

(a)   the payment of any such sums, or

(b)   the undertaking of any such obligations,

unless they have, before entering into the transaction, obtained and considered proper advice, given to them in writing, on the matters or matter mentioned in subsection (3)(a) to (c) or (4) (as the case may be).

(8)   For the purposes of this section proper advice is the advice of a person—

(a)   who is reasonably believed by the charity trustees to be qualified by ability in and practical experience of financial matters, and

(b)   who has no financial interest in relation to the loan, grant or other transaction in connection with which the advice is given;

and such advice may constitute proper advice for those purposes even though the person giving it does so in the course of employment as an officer or employee of the charity or of the charity trustees.

(9)   This section applies regardless of anything in the trusts of a charity; but nothing in this section applies to any mortgage—

(a)   for which general or special authority is given as mentioned in section 117(3)(a), or

(b)   for which the authorisation or consent of the Secretary of State is required as mentioned in section 117(3)(b).

(10)   Nothing in this section applies to an exempt charity.

125 Mortgages: required statements, etc

(1)   Any mortgage of land held by or in trust for a charity must state—

(a)   that the land is held by or in trust for a charity,

(b)   whether the charity is an exempt charity and whether the mortgage is one falling within section 124(9), and

(c)   if it is not an exempt charity and the mortgage is not one falling within section 124(9), that the mortgage is one to which the restrictions imposed by section 124 apply.

(2)   Where section 124(1) or (2) applies to any mortgage of land held by or in trust for a charity, the charity trustees must certify in the mortgage—

(a)   (where section 124(1) applies) that the mortgage has been sanctioned by an order of the court or of the Commission (as the case may be), or

(b)   (where section 124(2) applies) that the charity trustees have power under the trusts of the charity to grant the mortgage, and have obtained and considered such advice as is mentioned in section 124(2).

(3)   Where subsection (2) has been complied with in relation to any mortgage, then in favour of a person who (whether under the mortgage or afterwards) acquires an interest in the land in question for money or money's worth, it is conclusively presumed that the facts were as stated in the certificate.

(4)   Subsection (5) applies where—

(a)   section 124(1) or (2) applies to any mortgage of land held by or in trust for a charity, but

(b)   subsection (2) has not been complied with in relation to the mortgage.

(5)   In favour of a person who (whether under the mortgage or afterwards) in good faith acquires an interest in the land for money or money's worth, the mortgage is valid whether or not—

(a)   the mortgage has been sanctioned by an order of the court or of the Commission, or

(b)   the charity trustees have power under the trusts of the charity to grant the mortgage and have obtained and considered such advice as is mentioned in section 124(2).

(6)   Where section 124(7) applies to any mortgage of land held by or in trust for a charity, the charity trustees must certify in relation to any transaction falling within

section 124(7) that they have obtained and considered such advice as is mentioned in section 124(7).

(7)   Where subsection (6) has been complied with in relation to any transaction, then, in favour of a person who (whether under the mortgage or afterwards) has acquired or acquires an interest in the land for money or money's worth, it is conclusively presumed that the facts were as stated in the certificate.

126 Mortgages of charity land and land registration

(1)   Where the mortgage referred to in section 125(1) will be a registrable disposition, the statement required by section 125(1) must be in such form as may be prescribed by land registration rules.

(2)   Where any such mortgage will be one to which section 4(1)(g) of the Land Registration Act 2002 applies—

> (a)   the statement required by section 125(1) must be in such form as may be prescribed by land registration rules, and
>
> (b)   if the charity is not an exempt charity, the mortgage must also contain a statement, in such form as may be prescribed by land registration rules, that the restrictions on disposition imposed by sections 117 to 121 apply to the land (subject to section 117(3)).

(3)   Where—

> (a)   the registrar approves an application for registration of a person's title to land in connection with such a mortgage as is mentioned in subsection (2),
>
> (b)   the mortgage contains statements complying with section 125(1) and subsection (2), and
>
> (c)   the charity is not an exempt charity,

the registrar must enter in the register a restriction reflecting the limitation under sections 117 to 121 on subsequent disposal.

(4)   Subsections (3) and (4) of section 123 (removal of entry) apply in relation to any restriction entered under subsection (3) as they apply in relation to any restriction entered under section 123(2).

Release of charity rentcharges

127 Release of charity rentcharges

(1)   Section 117(1) does not apply to the release by a charity of a rentcharge which it is entitled to receive if the release is given in consideration of the payment of an amount which is not less than 10 times the annual amount of the rentcharge.

(2)   Where a charity which is entitled to receive a rentcharge releases it in consideration of the payment of an amount not exceeding £1,000, any costs incurred by the charity in connection with proving its title to the rentcharge are recoverable by the charity from the person or persons in whose favour the rentcharge is being released.

(3)   Neither section 117(1) nor subsection (2) of this section applies where a rentcharge which a charity is entitled to receive is redeemed under sections 8 to 10 of the Rentcharges Act 1977.

128 Power to alter sum specified in s 127(2)

The Minister may by order amend section 127(2) by substituting a different sum for the sum for the time being specified there.

Interpretation

129 Interpretation

(1) In sections 117 to 126 "land" means land in England and Wales.

(2) In sections 124 to 126 "mortgage" includes a charge.

(3) Sections 123 and 126 are to be construed as one with the Land Registration Act 2002.

PART 8

CHARITY ACCOUNTS, REPORTS AND RETURNS

CHAPTER 1

Individual Accounts

130 Accounting records

(1) The charity trustees of a charity must ensure that accounting records are kept in respect of the charity which are sufficient to show and explain all the charity's transactions, and which are such as to—

    (a)   disclose at any time, with reasonable accuracy, the financial position of the charity at that time, and

    (b)   enable the trustees to ensure that, where any statements of accounts are prepared by them under section 132(1), those statements of accounts comply with the requirements of regulations under section 132(1).

(2) The accounting records must in particular contain—

    (a)   entries showing from day to day all sums of money received and expended by the charity, and the matters in respect of which the receipt and expenditure takes place, and

    (b)   a record of the assets and liabilities of the charity.

131 Preservation of accounting records

(1) The charity trustees of a charity must preserve any accounting records made for the purposes of section 130 in respect of the charity for at least 6 years from the end of the financial year of the charity in which they are made.

(2) Subsection (3) applies if a charity ceases to exist within the period of 6 years mentioned in subsection (1) as it applies to any accounting records.

(3) The obligation to preserve the accounting records in accordance with subsection (1) must continue to be discharged by the last charity trustees of the charity, unless the Commission consents in writing to the records being destroyed or otherwise disposed of.

132 Preparation of statement of accounts

(1) The charity trustees of a charity must (subject to section 133) prepare in respect of each financial year of the charity a statement of accounts complying with such requirements as to its form and contents as may be prescribed by regulations made by the Minister.

(2) Regulations under subsection (1) may in particular make provision—

    (a)   for any such statement to be prepared in accordance with such methods and principles as are specified or referred to in the regulations;

    (b)   as to any information to be provided by way of notes to the accounts.

(3) Regulations under subsection (1) may also make provision for determining the financial years of a charity for the purposes of this Act and any regulations made under it.

(4)   But regulations under subsection (1) may not impose on the charity trustees of a charity that is a charitable trust created by any person ("the settlor") any requirement to disclose, in any statement of accounts prepared by them under subsection (1)—

   (a)   the identities of recipients of grants made out of the funds of the charity, or

   (b)   the amounts of any individual grants so made,

if the disclosure would fall to be made at a time when the settlor or any spouse or civil partner of the settlor was still alive.

133 Account and statement an option for lower-income charities

If a charity's gross income in any financial year does not exceed £250,000, the charity trustees may, in respect of that year, elect to prepare—

   (a)   a receipts and payments account, and

   (b)   a statement of assets and liabilities,

instead of a statement of accounts under section 132(1).

134 Preservation of statement of accounts or account and statement

(1)   The charity trustees of a charity must preserve—

   (a)   any statement of accounts prepared by them under section 132(1), or

   (b)   any account and statement prepared by them under section 133,

for at least 6 years from the end of the financial year to which any such statement relates or (as the case may be) to which any such account and statement relate.

(2)   Subsection (3) applies if a charity ceases to exist within the period of 6 years mentioned in subsection (1) as it applies to any statement of accounts or account and statement.

(3)   The obligation to preserve the statement or account and statement in accordance with subsection (1) must continue to be discharged by the last charity trustees of the charity, unless the Commission consents in writing to the statement or account and statement being destroyed or otherwise disposed of.

   . . .

CHAPTER 3

AUDIT OR EXAMINATION OF ACCOUNTS
Audit or examination of individual accounts

144 Audit of accounts of larger charities

(1)   Subsection (2) applies to a financial year of a charity if—

   (a)   the charity's gross income in that year exceeds £500,000, or

   (b)   the charity's gross income in that year exceeds the accounts threshold and at the end of the year the aggregate value of its assets (before deduction of liabilities) exceeds £3.26 million.

"The accounts threshold" means the sum for the time being specified in section 133 (account and statement an option for lower-income charities).

(2)   If this subsection applies to a financial year of a charity, the accounts of the charity for that year must be audited by a person who—

   (a)   is eligible for appointment as a statutory auditor under Part 42 of the Companies Act 2006, or

   (b)   is a member of a body for the time being specified in regulations under section 154 and is under the rules of that body eligible for appointment as auditor of the charity.

145 Examination of accounts an option for lower-income charities

(1) If section 144(2) does not apply to a financial year of a charity but its gross income in that year exceeds £25,000, the accounts of the charity for that year must, at the election of the charity trustees, be—

    (a)   examined by an independent examiner, that is, an independent person who is reasonably believed by the trustees to have the requisite ability and practical experience to carry out a competent examination of the accounts, or

    (b)   audited by a person within section 144(2)(a) or (b).

(2) Subsection (1) is subject to—

    (a)   subsection (3), and

    (b)   any order under section 146(1).

(3) If subsection (1) applies to the accounts of a charity for a year and the charity's gross income in that year exceeds £250,000, a person qualifies as an independent examiner for the purposes of subsection (1)(a) if (and only if) the person is independent and—

    (a)   a member of one of the bodies listed in subsection (4), or

    (b)   a Fellow of the Association of Charity Independent Examiners.

(4) The bodies referred to in subsection (3)(a) are—

    (a)   the Institute of Chartered Accountants in England and Wales;

    (b)   the Institute of Chartered Accountants of Scotland;

    (c)   the Institute of Chartered Accountants in Ireland;

    (d)   the Association of Chartered Certified Accountants;

    (e)   the Association of Authorised Public Accountants;

    (f)   the Association of Accounting Technicians;

    (g)   the Association of International Accountants;

    (h)   the Chartered Institute of Management Accountants;

    (i)   the Institute of Chartered Secretaries and Administrators;

    (j)   the Chartered Institute of Public Finance and Accountancy.

(5) The Commission may—

    (a)   give guidance to charity trustees in connection with the selection of a person for appointment as an independent examiner;

    (b)   give such directions as it thinks appropriate with respect to the carrying out of an examination in pursuance of subsection (1)(a);

and any such guidance or directions may either be of general application or apply to a particular charity only.

(6) The Minister may by order—

    (a)   amend subsection (3) by adding or removing a description of person to or from the list in that subsection or by varying any entry for the time being included in that list;

    (b)   amend subsection (4) by adding or removing a body to or from the list in that subsection or by varying any entry for the time being included in that list.

146 Commission's powers to order audit

(1) The Commission may by order require the accounts of a charity for a financial year to be audited by a person within section 144(2)(a) or (b) if it appears to the Commission that—

    (a)   section 144(2), or (as the case may be) section 145(1), has not been complied with in relation to that year within 10 months from the end of that year, or

(b)   although section 144(2) does not apply to that year, it would nevertheless be desirable for the accounts of the charity for that year to be audited by a person within section 144(2)(a) or (b).

(2)   If the Commission makes an order under subsection (1) with respect to a charity, the auditor must be a person appointed by the Commission unless—

(a)   the order is made by virtue of subsection (1)(b), and

(b)   the charity trustees themselves appoint an auditor in accordance with the order.

(3)   The expenses of any audit carried out by an auditor appointed by the Commission under subsection (2), including the auditor's remuneration, are recoverable by the Commission—

(a)   from the charity trustees of the charity concerned, who are personally liable, jointly and severally, for those expenses, or

(b)   to the extent that it appears to the Commission not to be practical to seek recovery of those expenses in accordance with paragraph (a), from the funds of the charity.

. . .

Duty of auditors etc to report matters to Commission

156 Duty of auditors etc to report matters to Commission

(1)   This section applies to a person ("P") who—

(a)   is acting as an auditor or independent examiner appointed by or in relation to a charity under sections 144 to 146 (audit or examination of individual accounts),

(b)   is acting as an auditor or examiner appointed under section 149(2) or (3) (audit or examination of English NHS charity accounts), or

(c)   is the Auditor General for Wales acting under section 150(2) or (3) (audit or examination of Welsh NHS charity accounts).

(2)   If, in the course of acting in the capacity mentioned in subsection (1), P becomes aware of a matter—

(a)   which relates to the activities or affairs of the charity or of any connected institution or body, and

(b)   which P has reasonable cause to believe is likely to be of material significance for the purposes of the exercise by the Commission of its functions under the provisions mentioned in subsection (3),

P must immediately make a written report on the matter to the Commission.

(3)   The provisions are—

(a)   sections 46, 47 and 50 (inquiries by Commission);

(b)   sections 76 and 79 to 82 (Commission's powers to act for protection of charities).

(4)   If, in the course of acting in the capacity mentioned in subsection (1), P becomes aware of any matter—

(a)   which does not appear to P to be one that P is required to report under subsection (2), but

(b)   which P has reasonable cause to believe is likely to be relevant for the purposes of the exercise by the Commission of any of its functions,

P may make a report on the matter to the Commission.

(5)   Where the duty or power under subsection (2) or (4) has arisen in relation to P when acting in the capacity mentioned in subsection (1), the duty or power is not affected by P's subsequently ceasing to act in that capacity.

(6) Where P makes a report as required or authorised by subsection (2) or (4), no duty to which P is subject is to be regarded as contravened merely because of any information or opinion contained in the report.

. . .

CHAPTER 4

ANNUAL REPORTS AND RETURNS AND PUBLIC ACCESS TO ACCOUNTS ETC
Annual reports etc

162 Charity trustees to prepare annual reports

(1) The charity trustees of a charity must prepare in respect of each financial year of the charity an annual report containing—
  (a) such a report by the trustees on the activities of the charity during that year, and
  (b) such other information relating to the charity or to its trustees or officers, as may be prescribed by regulations made by the Minister.
(2) Regulations under subsection (1) may in particular make provision—
  (a) for any such report as is mentioned in subsection (1)(a) to be prepared in accordance with such principles as are specified or referred to in the regulations;
  (b) enabling the Commission to dispense with any requirement prescribed by virtue of subsection (1)(b)—
    (i) in the case of a particular charity or a particular class of charities, or
    (ii) in the case of a particular financial year of a charity or of any class of charities.

. . .

Annual returns

169 Annual returns by registered charities

(1) Subject to subsection (2), every registered charity must prepare in respect of each of its financial years an annual return in such form, and containing such information, as may be prescribed by regulations made by the Commission.
(2) Subsection (1) does not apply in relation to any financial year of a charity in which the charity's gross income does not exceed £10,000 (but this subsection does not apply if the charity is constituted as a CIO).
(3) Any such return must be transmitted to the Commission by the date by which the charity trustees are, by virtue of section 163(1), required to transmit to the Commission the annual report required to be prepared in respect of the financial year in question.
(4) The Commission may dispense with the requirements of subsection (1)—
  (a) in the case of a particular charity or a particular class of charities, or
  (b) in the case of a particular financial year of a charity or of any class of charities.

Availability of documents to public

170 Public inspection of annual reports etc kept by Commission

Any document kept by the Commission in pursuance of section 165(1) (preservation of annual reports etc) must be open to public inspection at all reasonable times—
  (a) during the period for which it is so kept, or

(b)　if the Commission so determines, during such lesser period as it may specify.

171 Supply by charity trustees of copy of most recent annual report

(1)　This section applies if an annual report has been prepared in respect of any financial year of a charity in pursuance of section 162(1) or 168(3).

(2)　If the charity trustees of a charity—

(a)　are requested in writing by any person to provide that person with a copy of its most recent annual report, and

(b)　are paid by that person such reasonable fee (if any) as they may require in respect of the costs of complying with the request,

they must comply with the request within the period of 2 months beginning with the date on which it is made.

(3)　The reference in subsection (2) to a charity's most recent annual report is a reference to the annual report prepared in pursuance of section 162(1) or 168(3) in respect of the last financial year of the charity in respect of which an annual report has been so prepared.

172 Supply by charity trustees of copy of most recent accounts

(1)　If the charity trustees of a charity—

(a)　are requested in writing by any person to provide that person with a copy of the charity's most recent accounts, and

(b)　are paid by that person such reasonable fee (if any) as they may require in respect of the costs of complying with the request,

they must comply with the request within the period of 2 months beginning with the date on which it is made.

(2)　The reference in subsection (1) to a charity's most recent accounts is—

(a)　in the case of a charity other than one falling within paragraph (b) or (c), a reference to—

(i)　the statement of accounts prepared in pursuance of section 132(1), or

(ii)　the account and statement prepared in pursuance of section 133,

in respect of the last financial year of the charity in respect of which a statement of accounts or account and statement has or have been so prepared;

(b)　in the case of a charitable company, a reference to the most recent annual accounts of the company prepared under Part 16 of the Companies Act 2006 in relation to which any of the following conditions is satisfied—

(i)　they have been audited,

(ii)　they have been examined by an independent examiner under section 145(1)(a), or

(iii)　they relate to a year in respect of which the company is exempt from audit under Part 16 of the Companies Act 2006 and neither section 144(2) nor section 145(1) applied to them, and

(c)　in the case of an exempt charity, a reference to the accounts of the charity most recently audited in pursuance of any statutory or other requirement or, if its accounts are not required to be audited, the accounts most recently prepared in respect of the charity.

(3)　In subsection (1), the reference to a charity's most recent accounts includes, in relation to a charity whose charity trustees have prepared any group accounts under section 138(2), the group accounts most recently prepared by them.

Offences

173 Offences of failing to supply certain documents

(1) If any requirement within subsection (2) is not complied with, each person who immediately before the specified date for compliance was a charity trustee of the charity is guilty of an offence.

(2) A requirement is within this subsection if it is imposed—

    (a) by section 163 or by virtue of section 166(4) (requirements to transmit annual report to Commission), taken with sections 164, 166(5) and 168(7) (documents to be supplied with annual report), as applicable,

    (b) by section 169(3) (requirement to transmit annual return to Commission),

    (c) by section 171(2) (supply by charity trustees of copy of most recent annual report), or

    (d) by section 172(1) or by virtue of section 172(3) (supply by charity trustees of copy of most recent accounts);

and in subsection (1) "the specified date for compliance" means the date for compliance specified in the section in question.

(3) It is a defence, where a person is charged with an offence under subsection (1), to prove that the person took all reasonable steps for securing that the requirement in question would be complied with in time.

(4) A person guilty of an offence under subsection (1) is liable on summary conviction to—

    (a) a fine not exceeding level 4 on the standard scale, and

    (b) for continued contravention, a daily default fine not exceeding 10% of level 4 on the standard scale for so long as the person in question remains a charity trustee of the charity.

. . .

PART 9

CHARITY TRUSTEES, TRUSTEES AND AUDITORS ETC

Meaning of "charity trustees"

. . .

179 Disqualification: pre-commencement events etc

(1) Case A—

    (a) applies whether the conviction occurred before or after the commencement of section 178(1), but

    (b) does not apply in relation to any conviction which is a spent conviction for the purposes of the Rehabilitation of Offenders Act 1974.

(2) Case B applies whether the adjudication of bankruptcy or the sequestration or the making of a bankruptcy restrictions order or an interim order occurred before or after the commencement of section 178(1).

(3) Case C applies whether the composition or arrangement was made, or the trust deed was granted, before or after the commencement of section 178(1).

(4) Cases D to F apply in relation to orders made and removals effected before or after the commencement of section 178(1).

(5) In Case D—

    (a) "the Commissioners" means the Charity Commissioners for England and Wales, and

    (b) "relevant earlier enactment" means—

    (i)   section 18(2)(i) of the Charities Act 1993 (power to act for protection of charities),

    (ii)   section 20(1A)(i) of the Charities Act 1960, or

    (iii)   section 20(1)(i) of the 1960 Act (as in force before the commencement of section 8 of the Charities Act 1992).

(6)   In Case E, "the relevant earlier legislation" means section 7 of the Law Reform (Miscellaneous Provisions) (Scotland) Act 1990 (powers of Court of Session to deal with management of charities).

180 Disqualification: exceptions in relation to charitable companies

(1)   Where (apart from this subsection) a person ("P") is disqualified under Case B [or G] from being a charity trustee or trustee for a charitable company [or a CIO], P is not so disqualified if leave has been granted under section 11 of the Company Directors Disqualification Act 1986 (undischarged bankrupts) for P to act as director of the company [or charity trustee of the CIO (as the case may be)].

(2)   Similarly, a person ("P") is not disqualified under Case F from being a charity trustee or trustee for a charitable company [or a CIO] if, in a case set out in the first column of the table, leave has been granted as mentioned in the second column for P to act as director of the company [or charity trustee of the CIO (as the case may be)]—

P is subject to a disqualification order or disqualification undertaking under the Company Directors Disqualification Act 1986.	Leave has been granted for the purposes of section 1(1)(a) or 1A(1)(a) of the 1986 Act.
P is subject to a disqualification order or disqualification undertaking under the Company Directors Disqualification (Northern Ireland) Order 2002 (SI 2002/3150 (NI 4)).	Leave has been granted by the High Court in Northern Ireland.
P is subject to an order under section 429(2) of the Insolvency Act 1986.	Leave has been granted by the court which made the order.

181 Power to waive disqualification

(1)   This section applies where a person ("P') is disqualified under section 178(1).

(2)   The Commission may, if P makes an application under this subsection, waive P's disqualification—

    (a)   generally, or

    (b)   in relation to a particular charity or a particular class of charities.

(3)   If—

    (a)   P is disqualified under Case D or E and makes an application under subsection (2) 5 years or more after the date on which the disqualification took effect, and

    (b)   the Commission is not prevented from granting the application by subsection (5),

the Commission must grant the application unless satisfied that, because of any special circumstances, it should be refused.

(4)   Any waiver under subsection (2) must be notified in writing to P.

(5)   No waiver may be granted under subsection (2) in relation to any charitable company [or CIO] if—

    (a)   P is for the time being prohibited from acting as director of the company [or charity trustee of the CIO (as the case may be)], by virtue of—

        (i)   a disqualification order or disqualification undertaking under the Company Directors Disqualification Act 1986, or

    (ii) a provision of the 1986 Act mentioned in subsection (6), and

  (b) leave has not been granted for P to act as [director of any company or charity trustee of any CIO].

(6) The provisions of the 1986 Act are—

section 11(1) (undischarged bankrupts);

section 12(2) (failure to pay under county court administration order);

section 12A (Northern Irish disqualification orders);

section 12B (Northern Irish disqualification undertakings).

182 Records of persons removed from office

(1) For the purposes of sections 178 to 181 the Commission must keep, in such manner as it thinks fit, a register of all persons who have been removed from office as mentioned in Case D—

  (a) by an order of the Commission or the Commissioners made before or after the commencement of section 178(1), or

  (b) by an order of the High Court made after the commencement of section 45(1) of the Charities Act 1992;

and, where any person is so removed from office by an order of the High Court, the court must notify the Commission of the person's removal.

(2) The entries in the register kept under subsection (1) must be available for public inspection in legible form at all reasonable times.

(3) In this section "the Commissioners" means the Charity Commissioners for England and Wales.

183 Criminal consequences of acting while disqualified

(1) Subject to subsection (2), it is an offence for any person to act as a charity trustee or trustee for a charity while disqualified from being such a trustee by virtue of section 178.

(2) Subsection (1) does not apply if—

  (a) the charity concerned is a company [or a CIO], and

  (b) the disqualified person is disqualified by virtue only of Case B[, F or G].

(3) A person guilty of an offence under subsection (1) is liable—

  (a) on summary conviction, to imprisonment for a term not exceeding 12 months or to a fine not exceeding the statutory maximum, or both;

  (b) on conviction on indictment, to imprisonment for a term not exceeding 2 years or to a fine, or both.

184 Civil consequences of acting while disqualified

(1) Any acts done as charity trustee or trustee for a charity by a person disqualified from being such a trustee by virtue of section 178 are not invalid merely because of that disqualification.

(2) Subsection (3) applies if the Commission is satisfied that any person—

  (a) has acted as charity trustee or trustee for a charity while disqualified from being such a trustee by virtue of section 178, and

  (b) while so acting, has received from the charity any sums by way of remuneration or expenses, or any benefit in kind, in connection with acting as charity trustee or trustee for the charity.

(3) The Commission may by order direct the person—

  (a) to repay to the charity the whole or part of any such sums, or

  (b) (as the case may be) to pay to the charity the whole or part of the monetary value (as determined by the Commission) of any such benefit.

(4) Subsection (3) does not apply to any sums received by way of remuneration or expenses in respect of any time when the person concerned was not disqualified from being a charity trustee or trustee for the charity.

185 Remuneration of charity trustees or trustees etc providing services to charity

(1)   This section applies to remuneration for services provided by a person ("P") to or on behalf of a charity where—

(a)   P is a charity trustee or trustee for the charity, or

(b)   P is connected with a charity trustee or trustee for the charity and the remuneration might result in that trustee obtaining any benefit.

This is subject to subsection (3).

(2)   If Conditions A to D are met in relation to remuneration within subsection (1), P is entitled to receive the remuneration out of the funds of the charity.

Condition A

Condition A is that the amount or maximum amount of the remuneration—

(a)   is set out in an agreement in writing between the charity or its charity trustees (as the case may be) and P under which P is to provide the services in question to or on behalf of the charity, and

(b)   does not exceed what is reasonable in the circumstances for the provision by P of the services in question.

Condition B

Condition B is that, before entering into that agreement, the charity trustees decided that they were satisfied that it would be in the best interests of the charity for the services to be provided by P to or on behalf of the charity for the amount or maximum amount of remuneration set out in the agreement.

Condition C

Condition C is that if immediately after the agreement is entered into there is, in the case of the charity, more than one person who is a charity trustee and is—

(a)   a person in respect of whom an agreement within Condition A is in force,

(b   a person who is entitled to receive remuneration out of the funds of the charity otherwise than by virtue of such an agreement, or

(c)   a person connected with a person falling within paragraph (a) or (b),

the total number of them constitute a minority of the persons for the time being holding office as charity trustees of the charity.

Condition D

Condition D is that the trusts of the charity do not contain any express provision that prohibits P from receiving the remuneration.

(3)   Nothing in this section applies to—

(a)   any remuneration for services provided by a person in the person's capacity as a charity trustee or trustee for a charity or under a contract of employment, or

(b)   any remuneration not within paragraph (a) which a person is entitled to receive out of the funds of a charity by virtue of—

(i)   any provision contained in the trusts of the charity;

(ii)   any order of the court or the Commission;

(iii)   any statutory provision contained in or having effect under an Act other than this section.

(4)   Before entering into an agreement within Condition A the charity trustees must have regard to any guidance given by the Commission concerning the making of such agreements.

(5)   The duty of care in section 1(1) of the Trustee Act 2000 applies to a charity trustee when making such a decision as is mentioned in Condition B.

(6)   For the purposes of Condition C an agreement within Condition A is in force so long as any obligations under the agreement have not been fully discharged by a party to it.

(7)   Sections 187 and 188 (interpretation) apply for the purposes of this section.

186 Disqualification of charity trustee or trustee receiving remuneration under s 185

(1)   This section applies to any charity trustee or trustee for a charity—

    (a)   who is or would be entitled to remuneration under an agreement or proposed agreement within Condition A, or

    (b)   who is connected with a person who is or would be so entitled.

(2)   The charity trustee or trustee for a charity is disqualified from acting as such in relation to any decision or other matter connected with the agreement.

(3)   But if an act is done by a person who is disqualified from doing it by virtue of subsection (2), the act is not invalid merely because of that disqualification.

(4)   If the Commission is satisfied—

    (a)   that a person ("P") has done any act which P was disqualified from doing by virtue of subsection (2), and

    (b)   that P or a person connected with P has received or is to receive from the charity any remuneration under the agreement in question,

it may make an order under subsection (5) or (6) (as appropriate).

(5)   An order under this subsection is one requiring P—

    (a)   to reimburse to the charity the whole or part of the remuneration received as mentioned in subsection (4)(b);

    (b)   to the extent that the remuneration consists of a benefit in kind, to reimburse to the charity the whole or part of the monetary value (as determined by the Commission) of the benefit in kind.

(6)   An order under this subsection is one directing that P or (as the case may be) the connected person is not to be paid the whole or part of the remuneration mentioned in subsection (4)(b).

(7)   If the Commission makes an order under subsection (5) or (6), P or (as the case may be) the connected person accordingly ceases to have any entitlement under the agreement to so much of the remuneration (or its monetary value) as the order requires P to reimburse to the charity or (as the case may be) as it directs is not to be paid to P.

(8)   Sections 187 and 188 (interpretation) apply for the purposes of this section.

187 Meaning of "benefit", "remuneration", "services" etc

In sections 185 and 186—

    "benefit" means a direct or indirect benefit of any nature;

    "maximum amount", in relation to remuneration, means the maximum amount of the remuneration whether specified in or ascertainable under the terms of the agreement in question;

    "remuneration" includes any benefit in kind (and "amount" accordingly includes monetary value);

    "services", in the context of remuneration for services, includes goods that are supplied in connection with the provision of services.

188 Meaning of "connected person"

(1)   For the purposes of sections 185 and 186, the following persons are connected with a charity trustee or trustee for a charity—

    (a)   a child, parent, grandchild, grandparent, brother or sister of the trustee;

    (b)   the spouse or civil partner of the trustee or of any person falling within paragraph (a);

    (c)   a person carrying on business in partnership with the trustee or with any person falling within paragraph (a) or (b);

(d)   an institution which is controlled—

    (i)   by the trustee or by any person falling within paragraph (a), (b) or (c), or

    (ii)   by two or more persons falling within sub-paragraph (i), when taken together.

(e)   a body corporate in which—

    (i)   the trustee or any connected person falling within any of paragraphs (a) to (c) has a substantial interest, or

    (ii)   two or more persons falling within sub-paragraph (i), when taken together, have a substantial interest.

(2)   Sections 350 to 352 (meaning of child, spouse and civil partner, controlled institution and substantial interest) apply for the purposes of subsection (1).

Indemnity insurance for charity trustees and trustees

189 Indemnity insurance for charity trustees and trustees

(1)   The charity trustees of a charity may arrange for the purchase, out of the funds of the charity, of insurance designed to indemnify the charity trustees or any trustees for the charity against any personal liability in respect of—

(a)   any breach of trust or breach of duty committed by them in their capacity as charity trustees or trustees for the charity, or

(b)   any negligence, default, breach of duty or breach of trust committed by them in their capacity as directors or officers of—

    (i)   the charity (if it is a body corporate), or

    (ii)   any body corporate carrying on any activities on behalf of the charity.

(2)   But the terms of such insurance must be so framed as to exclude the provision of any indemnity for a person ("P") in respect of—

(a)   any liability incurred by P to pay—

    (i)   a fine imposed in criminal proceedings, or

    (ii)   a sum payable to a regulatory authority by way of a penalty in respect of non-compliance with any requirement of a regulatory nature (however arising),

(b)   any liability incurred by P in defending any criminal proceedings in which P is convicted of an offence arising out of any fraud or dishonesty, or wilful or reckless misconduct, by P, or

(c)   any liability incurred by P to the charity that arises out of any conduct—

    (i)   which P knew (or must reasonably be assumed to have known) was not in the interests of the charity, or

    (ii)   in the case of which P did not care whether it was in the best interests of the charity or not.

(3)   For the purposes of subsection (2)(b)—

(a)   the reference to any such conviction is a reference to one that has become final,

(b)   a conviction becomes final—

    (i)   if not appealed against, at the end of the period for bringing an appeal, or

    (ii)   if appealed against, at the time when the appeal (or any further appeal) is disposed of, and

(c)   an appeal is disposed of—

    (i)   if it is determined and the period for bringing any further appeal has ended, or

    (ii)   if it is abandoned or otherwise ceases to have effect.

(4) The charity trustees of a charity may not purchase insurance under this section unless they decide that they are satisfied that it is in the best interests of the charity for them to do so.

(5) The duty of care in section 1(1) of the Trustee Act 2000 applies to a charity trustee when making such a decision.

(6) This section—

    (a)   does not authorise the purchase of any insurance whose purchase is expressly prohibited by the trusts of the charity, but

    (b)   has effect despite any provision prohibiting the charity trustees or trustees for the charity receiving any personal benefit out of the funds of the charity.

190 Power to amend s 189

The Minister may by order make such amendments of section 189(2) and (3) as the Minister considers appropriate.

Powers to relieve trustees and auditors etc from liability

191 Commission's power to relieve trustees and auditors etc from liability

(1) This section applies to a person ("P") who is or has been—

    (a)   a charity trustee or trustee for a charity,

    (b)   a person appointed to audit a charity's accounts (whether appointed under an enactment or otherwise), or

    (c)   an independent examiner or other person appointed to examine or report on a charity's accounts (whether appointed under an enactment or otherwise).

(2) If the Commission considers—

    (a)   that P is or may be personally liable for a breach of trust or breach of duty committed in P's capacity as a person within subsection (1)(a), (b) or (c), but

    (b)   that P has acted honestly and reasonably and ought fairly to be excused for the breach of trust or duty,

the Commission may make an order relieving P wholly or partly from any such liability.

(3) An order under subsection (2) may grant the relief on such terms as the Commission thinks fit.

(4) Subsection (2) does not apply in relation to any personal contractual liability of a charity trustee or trustee for a charity.

(5) For the purposes of this section and section 192—

    (a)   subsection (1)(b) is to be read as including a reference to the Auditor General for Wales acting as auditor under Part 8, and

    (b)   subsection (1)(c) is to be read as including a reference to the Auditor General for Wales acting as examiner under Part 8;

and in subsection (1)(b) and (c) any reference to a charity's accounts is to be read as including any group accounts prepared by the charity trustees of a charity.

(6) This section does not affect the operation of—

    (a)   section 61 of the Trustee Act 1925 (power of court to grant relief to trustees),

    (b)   section 1157 of the Companies Act 2006 (power of court to grant relief to officers or auditors of companies), or

    (c)   section 192 (which extends section 1157 to auditors etc of charities which are not companies).

192 Court's power to grant relief to apply to all auditors etc of charities which are not companies

(1)   Section 1157 of the Companies Act 2006 (power of court to grant relief to officers or auditors of companies) has effect in relation to a person to whom this section applies as it has effect in relation to a person employed as an auditor by a company.

(2)   This section applies to—

    (a)   a person acting in a capacity within section 191(1)(b) or (c) in a case where, apart from this section, section 1157 of the 2006 Act would not apply in relation to that person as a person so acting, and

    (b)   a charity trustee of a CIO.

. . .

PART 13

UNINCORPORATED CHARITIES

Power to transfer all property of unincorporated charity

267 Introduction

(1)   Section 268 (resolution to transfer all property) applies to a charity if—

    (a)   (subject to subsection (2)) its gross income in its last financial year did not exceed £10,000,

    (b)   it does not hold any designated land, and

    (c)   it is not a company or other body corporate.

"Designated land" means land held on trusts which stipulate that it is to be used for the purposes, or any particular purposes, of the charity.

(2)   Subsection (1)(a) does not apply in relation to a resolution by the charity trustees of a charity—

    (a)   to transfer all its property to a CIO, or

    (b)   to divide its property between two or more CIOs.

(3)   Where a charity has a permanent endowment, sections 268 to 272 have effect in accordance with sections 273 and 274.

(4)   In sections 268 to 274 references to the transfer of property to a charity are references to its transfer—

    (a)   to the charity,

    (b)   to the charity trustees,

    (c)   to any trustee for the charity, or

    (d)   to a person nominated by the charity trustees to hold it in trust for the charity,

as the charity trustees may determine.

268 Resolution to transfer all property

(1)   The charity trustees of a charity to which this section applies (see section 267) may resolve for the purposes of this section—

    (a)   that all the property of the charity should be transferred to another charity specified in the resolution, or

    (b)   that all the property of the charity should be transferred to two or more charities specified in the resolution in accordance with such division of the property between them as is so specified.

(2)   Any charity so specified may be either a registered charity or a charity which is not required to be registered.

(3)   But the charity trustees of a charity ("the transferor charity") do not have power to pass a resolution under subsection (1) unless they are satisfied—

(a) that it is expedient in the interests of furthering the purposes for which the property is held by the transferor charity for the property to be transferred in accordance with the resolution, and

(b) that the purposes (or any of the purposes) of any charity to which property is to be transferred under the resolution are substantially similar to the purposes (or any of the purposes) of the transferor charity.

(4) Any resolution under subsection (1) must be passed by a majority of not less than two-thirds of the charity trustees who vote on the resolution.

(5) Where charity trustees have passed a resolution under subsection (1), they must send a copy of it to the Commission, together with a statement of their reasons for passing it.

269 Notice of, and information about, resolution to transfer property

(1) Having received the copy of the resolution under section 268(5), the Commission—

(a) may direct the charity trustees to give public notice of the resolution in such manner as is specified in the direction, and

(b) if it gives such a direction, must take into account any representations made to it—

(i) by persons appearing to it to be interested in the charity, and

(ii) within the period of 28 days beginning with the date when public notice of the resolution is given by the charity trustees.

(2) The Commission may also direct the charity trustees to provide the Commission with additional information or explanations relating to—

(a) the circumstances in and by reference to which they have decided to act under section 268, or

(b) their compliance with any obligation imposed on them by or under section 268 or this section in connection with the resolution.

270 General rule as to when s 268 resolution takes effect

Subject to section 271, a resolution under section 268(1) takes effect at the end of the period of 60 days beginning with the date on which the copy of it was received by the Commission.

271 S 268 resolution not to take effect or to take effect at later date

(1) A resolution does not take effect under section 270 if before the end of—

(a) the 60-day period, or

(b) that period as modified by subsection (4) or (5),

the Commission notifies the charity trustees in writing that it objects to the resolution, either on procedural grounds or on the merits of the proposals contained in the resolution.

(2) "The 60-day period" means the period of 60 days mentioned in section 270.

(3) "On procedural grounds" means on the grounds that any obligation imposed on the charity trustees by or under section 268 or 269 has not been complied with in connection with the resolution.

(4) If under section 269(1) the Commission directs the charity trustees to give public notice of a resolution, the running of the 60-day period is suspended by virtue of this subsection—

(a) as from the date on which the direction is given to the charity trustees, and

(b) until the end of the period of 42 days beginning with the date on which public notice of the resolution is given by the charity trustees.

(5) If under section 269(2) the Commission directs the charity trustees to provide any information or explanations, the running of the 60-day period is suspended by virtue of this subsection—

(a)   as from the date on which the direction is given to the charity trustees, and

(b)   until the date on which the information or explanations is or are provided to the Commission.

(6)   Subsection (7) applies once the period of time, or the total period of time, during which the 60-day period is suspended by virtue of either or both of subsections (4) and (5) exceeds 120 days.

(7)   At that point the resolution (if not previously objected to by the Commission) is to be treated as if it had never been passed.

272 Transfer of property in accordance with s 268 resolution

(1)   Subsection (2) applies where a resolution under section 268(1) has taken effect.

(2)   The charity trustees must arrange for all the property of the transferor charity to be transferred in accordance with the resolution, and on terms that any property so transferred—

(a)   is to be held by the charity to which it is transferred ("the transferee charity") in accordance with subsection (3), but

(b)   when so held is nevertheless to be subject to any restrictions on expenditure to which it was subject as property of the transferor charity;

and the charity trustees must arrange for the property to be so transferred by such date after the resolution takes effect as they agree with the charity trustees of the transferee charity or charities concerned.

(3)   The charity trustees of any charity to which property is transferred under this section must secure, so far as is reasonably practicable, that the property is applied for such of its purposes as are substantially similar to those of the transferor charity.

But this requirement does not apply if those charity trustees consider that complying with it would not result in a suitable and effective method of applying the property.

(4)   For the purpose of enabling any property to be transferred to a charity under this section, the Commission may, at the request of the charity trustees of that charity, make orders vesting any property of the transferor charity—

(a)   in the transferee charity, in its charity trustees or in any trustee for that charity, or

(b)   in any other person nominated by those charity trustees to hold property in trust for that charity.

273 Transfer where charity has permanent endowment: general

(1)   This section and section 274 provide for the operation of sections 268 to 272 where a charity within section 267(1) has a permanent endowment (whether or not the charity's trusts contain provision for the termination of the charity).

(2)   If the charity has both a permanent endowment and other property ("unrestricted property")—

(a)   a resolution under section 268(1) must relate to both its permanent endowment and its unrestricted property, and

(b)   sections 268 to 272 apply—

(i)   in relation to its unrestricted property, as if references in those sections to all or any of the property of the charity were references to all or any of its unrestricted property, and

(ii)   in relation to its permanent endowment, in accordance with section 274.

(3)   If all of the property of the charity is comprised in its permanent endowment, sections 268 to 272 apply in relation to its permanent endowment in accordance with section 274.

274 Requirements relating to permanent endowment

(1) Sections 268 to 272 apply in relation to the permanent endowment of the charity (as mentioned in section 273(2)(b)(ii) and (3)) with the following modifications.

(2) References in sections 268 to 272 to all or any of the property of the charity are references to all or any of the property comprised in its permanent endowment.

(3) If the property comprised in its permanent endowment is to be transferred to a single charity, the charity trustees must (instead of being satisfied as mentioned in section 268(3)(b)) be satisfied that the proposed transferee charity has purposes which are substantially similar to all of the purposes of the transferor charity.

(4) If the property comprised in its permanent endowment is to be transferred to two or more charities, the charity trustees must (instead of being satisfied as mentioned in section 268(3)(b)) be satisfied—

    (a)   that the proposed transferee charities, taken together, have purposes which are substantially similar to all of the purposes of the transferor charity, and

    (b)   that each of the proposed transferee charities has purposes which are substantially similar to one or more of the purposes of the transferor charity.

(5) In the case of a transfer to which subsection (4) applies, the resolution under section 268(1) must provide for the property comprised in the permanent endowment of the charity to be divided between the transferee charities in such a way as to take account of such guidance as may be given by the Commission for the purposes of this section.

(6) For the purposes of sections 268 to 272, the references in sections 269(2)(b) and 271(3) to any obligation imposed on the charity trustees by or under section 268 or 269 includes a reference to any obligation imposed on them by virtue of any of subsections (3) to (5).

(7) The requirement in section 272(3) applies in the case of every such transfer, and in complying with that requirement the charity trustees of a transferee charity must secure that the application of property transferred to the charity takes account of such guidance as may be given by the Commission for the purposes of this section.

(8) Any guidance given by the Commission for the purposes of this section may take such form and be given in such manner as the Commission considers appropriate.

Powers to alter purposes or powers etc of unincorporated charity

275 Resolution to replace purposes of unincorporated charity

(1) This section applies to a charity if—

    (a)   its gross income in its last financial year did not exceed £10,000,

    (b)   it does not hold any designated land, and

    (c)   it is not a company or other body corporate.

"Designated land" means land held on trusts which stipulate that it is to be used for the purposes, or any particular purposes, of the charity.

(2) The charity trustees of such a charity may resolve for the purposes of this section that the trusts of the charity should be modified by replacing all or any of the purposes of the charity with other purposes specified in the resolution.

(3) The other purposes so specified must be charitable purposes.

(4) But the charity trustees of a charity do not have power to pass a resolution under subsection (2) unless they are satisfied—

    (a)   that it is expedient in the interests of the charity for the purposes in question to be replaced, and

    (b)   that, so far as is reasonably practicable, the new purposes consist of or include purposes that are similar in character to those that are to be replaced.

(5)   Any resolution under subsection (2) must be passed by a majority of not less than two-thirds of the charity trustees who vote on the resolution.

(6)   Where charity trustees have passed a resolution under subsection (2), they must send a copy of it to the Commission, together with a statement of their reasons for passing it.

276 Notice of, and information about, s 275 resolution

(1)   Having received the copy of the resolution under section 275(6), the Commission—

    (a)   may direct the charity trustees to give public notice of the resolution in such manner as is specified in the direction, and

    (b)   if it gives such a direction, must take into account any representations made to it—

        (i)   by persons appearing to it to be interested in the charity, and

        (ii)   within the period of 28 days beginning with the date when public notice of the resolution is given by the charity trustees.

(2)   The Commission may also direct the charity trustees to provide the Commission with additional information or explanations relating to—

    (a)   the circumstances in and by reference to which they have decided to act under section 275, or

    (b)   their compliance with any obligation imposed on them by or under section 275 or this section in connection with the resolution.

277 General rule as to when s 275 resolution takes effect

Subject to section 278, a resolution under section 275(2) takes effect at the end of the period of 60 days beginning with the date on which the copy of it was received by the Commission.

278 S 275 resolution not to take effect or to take effect at a later date

(1)   A resolution does not take effect under section 277 if before the end of—

    (a)   the 60-day period, or

    (b)   that period as modified by subsection (4) or (5),

the Commission notifies the charity trustees in writing that it objects to the resolution, either on procedural grounds or on the merits of the proposals contained in the resolution.

(2)   "The 60-day period" means the period of 60 days mentioned in section 277.

(3)   "On procedural grounds" means on the grounds that any obligation imposed on the charity trustees by or under section 275 or 276 has not been complied with in connection with the resolution.

(4)   If under section 276(1) the Commission directs the charity trustees to give public notice of a resolution, the running of the 60-day period is suspended by virtue of this subsection—

    (a)   as from the date on which the direction is given to the charity trustees, and

    (b)   until the end of the period of 42 days beginning with the date on which public notice of the resolution is given by the charity trustees.

(5)   If under section 276(2) the Commission directs the charity trustees to provide any information or explanations, the running of the 60-day period is suspended by virtue of this subsection—

    (a)   as from the date on which the direction is given to the charity trustees, and

    (b)   until the date on which the information or explanations is or are provided to the Commission.

(6)   Subsection (7) applies once the period of time, or the total period of time, during which the 60-day period is suspended by virtue of either or both of subsections (4) and (5) exceeds 120 days.

(7)   At that point the resolution (if not previously objected to by the Commission) is to be treated as if it had never been passed.

279   Replacement of purposes in accordance with s 275

As from the time when a resolution takes effect under section 277, the trusts of the charity concerned are to be taken to have been modified in accordance with the terms of the resolution.

280   Power to modify powers or procedures of unincorporated charity

(1)   This section applies to any charity which is not a company or other body corporate.

(2)   The charity trustees of such a charity may resolve for the purposes of this section that any provision of the trusts of the charity—

   (a)   relating to any of the powers exercisable by the charity trustees in the administration of the charity, or

   (b)   regulating the procedure to be followed in any respect in connection with its administration,

should be modified in such manner as is specified in the resolution.

(3)   Subsection (4) applies if the charity is an unincorporated association with a body of members distinct from the charity trustees.

(4)   Any resolution of the charity trustees under subsection (2) must be approved by a further resolution which is passed at a general meeting of the body—

   (a)   by a majority of not less than two-thirds of the members entitled to attend and vote at the meeting who vote on the resolution, or

   (b)   by a decision taken without a vote and without any expression of dissent in response to the question put to the meeting.

(5)   Where—

   (a)   the charity trustees have passed a resolution under subsection (2), and

   (b)   (if subsection (4) applies) a further resolution has been passed under that subsection,

the trusts of the charity are to be taken to have been modified in accordance with the terms of the resolution.

(6)   The trusts are to be taken to have been so modified as from—

   (a)   such date as is specified for this purpose in the resolution under subsection (2), or

   (b)   (if later) the date when any such further resolution was passed under subsection (4).

Powers of unincorporated charities to spend capital

281   Power of unincorporated charities to spend capital: general

(1)   This section applies to any available endowment fund of a charity which is not a company or other body corporate.

(2)   But this section does not apply to a fund if sections 282 to 284 (power to spend larger fund given for particular purpose) apply to it.

(3)   If the condition in subsection (4) is met in relation to the charity, the charity trustees may resolve for the purposes of this section that the fund, or a portion of it, ought to be freed from the restrictions with respect to expenditure of capital that apply to it.

(4)   The condition is that the charity trustees are satisfied that the purposes set out in the trusts to which the fund is subject could be carried out more effectively if the

capital of the fund, or the relevant portion of the capital, could be expended as well as income accruing to it, rather than just such income.

(5)   Once the charity trustees have passed a resolution under subsection (3), the fund or portion may by virtue of this section be expended in carrying out the purposes set out in the trusts to which the fund is subject without regard to the restrictions mentioned in that subsection.

(6)   The fund or portion may be so expended as from such date as is specified for this purpose in the resolution.

(7)   In this section "available endowment fund", in relation to a charity, means—

    (a)   the whole of the charity's permanent endowment if it is all subject to the same trusts, or

    (b)   any part of its permanent endowment which is subject to any particular trusts that are different from those to which any other part is subject.

282   Resolution to spend larger fund given for particular purpose

(1)   This section applies to any available endowment fund of a charity which is not a company or other body corporate if—

    (a)   the capital of the fund consists entirely of property given—

        (i)   by a particular individual,

        (ii)   by a particular institution (by way of grant or otherwise), or

        (iii)   by two or more individuals or institutions in pursuit of a common purpose, and

    (b)   the charity's gross income in its last financial year exceeded £1,000 and the market value of the endowment fund exceeds £10,000.

(2)   If the condition in subsection (3) is met in relation to the charity, the charity trustees may resolve for the purposes of this section that the fund, or a portion of it, ought to be freed from the restrictions with respect to expenditure of capital that apply to it.

(3)   The condition is that the charity trustees are satisfied that the purposes set out in the trusts to which the fund is subject could be carried out more effectively if the capital of the fund, or the relevant portion of the capital, could be expended as well as income accruing to it, rather than just such income.

(4)   The charity trustees—

    (a)   must send a copy of any resolution under subsection (2) to the Commission, together with a statement of their reasons for passing it, and

    (b)   may not implement the resolution except in accordance with sections 283 and 284.

(5)   In this section—

    "available endowment fund" has the same meaning as in section 281;

    "market value", in relation to an endowment fund, means—

        (a)   the market value of the fund as recorded in the accounts for the last financial year of the relevant charity, or

        (b)   if no such value was so recorded, the current market value of the fund as determined on a valuation carried out for the purpose.

(6)   In subsection (1), the reference to the giving of property by an individual includes the individual's giving it by will.

283   Notice of, and information about, s 282 resolution

(1)   Having received the copy of the resolution under section 282(4), the Commission may—

    (a)   direct the charity trustees to give public notice of the resolution in such manner as is specified in the direction, and

    (b)   if it gives such a direction, must take into account any representations made to it—

        (i)   by persons appearing to it to be interested in the charity, and

        (ii)   within the period of 28 days beginning with the date when public notice of the resolution is given by the charity trustees.

(2)   The Commission may also direct the charity trustees to provide the Commission with additional information or explanations relating to—

    (a)   the circumstances in and by reference to which they have decided to act under section 282, or

    (b)   their compliance with any obligation imposed on them by or under section 282 or this section in connection with the resolution.

284 When and how s 282 resolution takes effect

(1)   When considering whether to concur with the resolution under section 282(2), the Commission must take into account—

    (a)   any evidence available to it as to the wishes of the donor or donors mentioned in section 282(1)(a), and

    (b)   any changes in the circumstances relating to the charity since the making of the gift or gifts (including, in particular, its financial position, the needs of its beneficiaries, and the social, economic and legal environment in which it operates).

(2)   The Commission must not concur with the resolution unless it is satisfied—

    (a)   that its implementation would accord with the spirit of the gift or gifts mentioned in section 282(1)(a) (even though it would be inconsistent with the restrictions mentioned in section 282(2)), and

    (b)   that the charity trustees have complied with the obligations imposed on them by or under section 282 or 283 in connection with the resolution.

(3)   Before the end of the period of 3 months beginning with the relevant date, the Commission must notify the charity trustees in writing—

    (a)   that the Commission concurs with the resolution, or

    (b)   that it does not concur with it.

(4)   In subsection (3) "the relevant date" means—

    (a)   if the Commission directs the charity trustees under section 283(1) to give public notice of the resolution, the date when that notice is given, and

    (b)   otherwise, the date on which the Commission receives the copy of the resolution in accordance with section 282(4).

(5)   Where—

    (a)   the charity trustees are notified by the Commission that it concurs with the resolution, or

    (b)   the period of 3 months mentioned in subsection (3) has elapsed without the Commission notifying them that it does not concur with the resolution,

the fund or portion may, by virtue of this section, be expended in carrying out the purposes set out in the trusts to which the fund is subject without regard to the restrictions mentioned in section 282(2).

Supplementary

285 Power to alter sums specified in this Part

(1)   The Minister may by order amend any provision listed in subsection (2)—

    (a)   by substituting a different sum for the sum for the time being specified in that provision, or

    (b)   if the provision specifies more than one sum, by substituting a different sum for any sum specified in that provision.

(2)   The provisions are—

section 267(1) (income level for purposes of resolution to transfer property of unincorporated charity);

section 275(1) (income level for purposes of resolution to replace purposes of unincorporated charity);

section 282(1) (income level and market value of fund for purposes of resolution to spend larger fund given for particular purpose).

286 Effect of provisions relating to vesting or transfer of property

No vesting or transfer of any property in pursuance of any provision of this Part operates as a breach of a covenant or condition against alienation or gives rise to a forfeiture.

. . .

PART 15

LOCAL CHARITIES

INDEXES AND REVIEWS ETC

293 Meaning of "local charity"

In this Act, except in so far as the context otherwise requires, "local charity" means, in relation to any area, a charity established for purposes which are—

(a)   by their nature, or

(b)   by the trusts of the charity,

directed wholly or mainly to the benefit of that area or of part of it.

294 Local authority's index of local charities

(1)   A council may maintain an index of local charities or of any class of local charities in the council's area, and may publish information contained in the index, or summaries or extracts taken from it.

(2)   A council proposing to establish or maintaining under this section an index of local charities or of any class of local charities must, on request, be supplied by the Commission free of charge—

(a)   with copies of such entries in the register of charities as are relevant to the index, or

(b)   with particulars of any changes in the entries of which copies have been supplied before;

and the Commission may arrange that it will without further request supply a council with particulars of any such changes.

(3)   An index maintained under this section must be open to public inspection at all reasonable times.

295 Reviews of local charities by local authority

(1)   A council may—

(a)   subject to the following provisions of this section, initiate, and carry out in co-operation with the charity trustees, a review of the working of any group of local charities with the same or similar purposes in the council's area, and

(b)   make to the Commission such report on the review and such recommendations arising from it as the council, after consultation with the trustees, think fit.

(2)   A council having power to initiate reviews under this section may—

(a)   co-operate with other persons in any review by them of the working of local charities in the council's area (with or without other charities), or

(b)   join with other persons in initiating and carrying out such a review.

(3)   No review initiated by a council under this section is to extend—
    (a)   to any charity without the consent of the charity trustees, or
    (b)   to any ecclesiastical charity.

(4)   No review initiated under this section by a district council is to extend to the working in any county of a local charity established for purposes similar or complementary to any services provided by county councils unless the review so extends with the consent of the council of that county.

(5)   Subsection (4) does not apply in relation to Wales.

296 S 294 and s 295: supplementary

(1)   In sections 294 and 295 and this section "council" means—
    (a)   a district council,
    (b)   a county council,
    (c)   a county borough council,
    (d)   a London borough council, or
    (e)   the Common Council of the City of London.

(2)   A council may employ any voluntary organisation as their agent for the purposes of sections 294 and 295, on such terms and within such limits (if any) or in such cases as they may agree.

(3)   In subsection (2), "voluntary organisation" means any body—
    (a)   whose activities are carried on otherwise than for profit, and
    (b)   which is not a public or local authority.

(4)   A joint board discharging any of a council's functions has the same powers under sections 294 and 295 and this section as the council as respects local charities in the council's area which are established for purposes similar or complementary to any services provided by the board.

297 Co-operation between charities, and between charities and local authorities

(1)   Any local council and any joint board discharging any functions of a local council—
    (a)   may make, with any charity established for purposes similar or complementary to services provided by the council or board, arrangements for co-ordinating—
        (i)   the activities of the council or board, and
        (ii)   those of the charity,
in the interests of persons who may benefit from those services or from the charity, and
    (b)   is at liberty to disclose to any such charity in the interests of those persons any information obtained in connection with the services provided by the council or board, whether or not arrangements have been made with the charity under this subsection.

(2)   In subsection (1), "local council" means—
    (a)   in relation to England—
        (i)   a district council,
        (ii)   a county council,
        (iii)   a London borough council,
        (iv)   a parish council,
        (v)   the Common Council of the City of London, or
        (vi)   the Council of the Isles of Scilly, and
    (b)   in relation to Wales—
        (i)   a county council,
        (ii)   a county borough council, or
        (iii)   a community council.

(3)   Charity trustees may, regardless of anything in the trusts of the charity, by virtue of this subsection do all or any of the following things, if it appears to them likely to promote or make more effective the work of the charity—

(a)   they may co-operate in any review undertaken under section 295 or otherwise of the working of charities or any class of charities;

(b)   they may make arrangements with an authority acting under subsection (1) or with another charity for co-ordinating their activities and those of the authority or of the other charity;

(c)   they may publish information of other charities with a view to bringing them to the notice of those for whose benefit they are intended.

(4)   Charity trustees may defray the expense of acting under subsection (3) out of any income or money applicable as income of the charity.

Parochial charities

298   Transfer of property to parish or community council or its appointees

(1)   This section applies where trustees hold any property—

(a)   for the purposes of a public recreation ground, or of allotments (whether under inclosure Acts or otherwise), for the benefit of inhabitants of a parish having a parish council or (in Wales) community having a community council, or

(b)   for other charitable purposes connected with such a parish or community;

and it applies to property held for any public purposes as it applies to property held for charitable purposes.

But it does not apply where trustees hold property for an ecclesiastical charity.

(2)   The trustees may, with the approval of the Commission and with the consent of the parish or community council, transfer the property to—

(a)   the parish or community council, or

(b)   persons appointed by the parish or community council;

and the council or their appointees must hold the property on the same trusts and subject to the same conditions as the trustees did.

299   Local authorities' power to appoint representative trustees

(1)   This section applies where a parochial charity in a parish or (in Wales) a community is not—

(a)   an ecclesiastical charity, or

(b)   a charity founded within the preceding 40 years.

(2)   If the charity trustees do not include persons—

(a)   elected by the local government electors or inhabitants of the parish or community, or

(b)   appointed by the parish council or parish meeting or (in Wales) by the community council or the county council or (as the case may be) county borough council,

the parish council or parish meeting or the community council or the county council or county borough council may appoint additional charity trustees, to such number as the Commission may allow.

(3)   If there is a sole charity trustee not elected or appointed as mentioned in subsection (2), the number of the charity trustees may, with the approval of the Commission, be increased to 3, of whom—

(a)   one may be nominated by the person holding the office of the sole trustee, and

(b)   one may be nominated by the parish council or parish meeting or by the community council or the county council or county borough council.

300 Powers of appointment deriving from pre-1894 powers

(1) Subsection (2) applies where, under the trusts of a charity other than an ecclesiastical charity—

(a)   the inhabitants of a rural parish (whether in vestry or not), or

(b)   a select vestry,

were formerly (in 1894) entitled to appoint charity trustees for, or trustees or beneficiaries of, the charity.

(2)   The appointment is to be made—

(a)   in a parish having a parish council or (in Wales) a community having a community council, by the parish or community council, or in the case of beneficiaries, by persons appointed by the parish or community council;

(b)   in a parish not having a parish council or (in Wales) a community not having a community council, by the parish meeting or by the county council or (as the case may be) county borough council.

(3)   Subsection (4) applies where—

(a)   overseers as such, or

(b)   except in the case of an ecclesiastical charity, churchwardens as such,

were formerly (in 1894) charity trustees of or trustees for a parochial charity in a rural parish, either alone or jointly with other persons.

(4)   Instead of the former overseer or church warden trustees there are to be trustees (to a number not greater than that of the former overseer or churchwarden trustees) appointed—

(a)   by the parish council or, if there is no parish council, by the parish meeting, or

(b)   by the community council or, if there is no community council, by the county council or (as the case may be) county borough council.

(5)   In this section "formerly (in 1894)" relates to the period immediately before the passing of the Local Government Act 1894 and "former" is to be read accordingly.

301 Powers of appointment deriving from pre-1927 powers

(1)   Subsection (2) applies where, outside Greater London (other than the outer London boroughs), overseers of a parish as such were formerly (in 1927) charity trustees of or trustees for any charity, either alone or jointly with other persons.

(2)   Instead of the former overseer trustees there are to be trustees (to a number not greater than that of the former overseer trustees) appointed—

(a)   by the parish council or, if there is no parish council, by the parish meeting, or

(b)   (in Wales) by the community council or, if there is no community council, by the county council or (as the case may be) county borough council.

(3)   In the case of an urban parish existing immediately before the passing of the Local Government Act 1972 which after 1st April 1974 is not comprised in a parish, the power of appointment under subsection (2) is exercisable by the district council.

(4)   In this section "formerly (in 1927)" relates to the period immediately before 1 April 1927 and "former" is to be read accordingly.

302 Term of office of trustees appointed under s 299 to s 301

(1)   Any appointment of a charity trustee or trustee for a charity which is made by virtue of sections 299 to 301 must be for a term of 4 years, and a retiring trustee is eligible for re-appointment.

But this is subject to subsections (2) and (3).

(2)   On an appointment under section 299, where—

(a)   no previous appointments have been made by virtue of—

(i)   section 299, or

>> (ii)   the corresponding provision of the Local Government Act 1894, the Charities Act 1960 or the Charities Act 1993, and
>
> (b)   more than one trustee is appointed,
>
> half of those appointed (or as nearly as may be) must be appointed for a term of 2 years.

(3)   An appointment made to fill a casual vacancy must be for the remainder of the term of the previous appointment.

303 S 298 to s 302: supplementary

(1)   In sections 299 and 300, "parochial charity" means, in relation to any parish or (in Wales) community, a charity the benefits of which are, or the separate distribution of the benefits of which is, confined to inhabitants of—

> (a)   the parish or community,
>
> (b)   a single ancient ecclesiastical parish which included that parish or community or part of it, or
>
> (c)   an area consisting of that parish or community with not more than 4 neighbouring parishes or communities.

(2)   Sections 298 to 302 do not affect the trusteeship, control or management of any foundation or voluntary school within the meaning of the School Standards and Framework Act 1998.

(3)   Sections 298 to 302—

> (a)   do not apply to the Isles of Scilly, and
>
> (b)   have effect subject to any order (including any future order) made under any enactment relating to local government with respect to local government areas or the powers of local authorities.

Supplementary

304 Effect of provisions relating to vesting or transfer of property

No vesting or transfer of any property in pursuance of any provision of this Part operates as a breach of a covenant or condition against alienation or gives rise to a forfeiture.

. . .

SCHEDULE 3
EXEMPT CHARITIES

Section 9

Institutions with an exemption from the Charitable Trusts Acts 1853 to 1939

1

(1)   Any institution which, if the Charities Act 1960 had not been passed, would be exempted from the powers and jurisdiction, under the Charitable Trusts Acts 1853 to 1939, of—

> (a)   the Charity Commissioners for England and Wales, or
>
> (b)   the Minister of Education,

(apart from any power of the Commissioners or Minister to apply those Acts in whole or in part to charities otherwise exempt) by the terms of any enactment not contained in the Charitable Trusts Acts 1853 to 1939 other than section 9 of the Places of Worship Registration Act 1855.

(2)   Sub-paragraph (1) does not include—

> (a)   any Investment Fund or Deposit Fund within the meaning of the Church Funds Investment Measure 1958,

    (b)   any investment fund or deposit fund within the meaning of the Methodist Church Funds Act 1960, or

    (c)   the representative body of the Welsh Church or property administered by it.

Educational institutions

2

The universities of Oxford, Cambridge, London, Durham, Newcastle and Manchester.

3

King's College London and Queen Mary and Westfield College in the University of London.

4

(1) Any of the following, if Her Majesty declares it by Order in Council to be an exempt charity for the purposes of this Act—

    (a)   a university in England,

    (b)   a university college in England, or

    (c)   an institution which is connected with a university in England or a university college in England.

(2) Sub-paragraph (1) does not include—

    (a)   any college in the university of Oxford;

    (b)   any college or hall in the university of Cambridge or Durham;

    (c)   any students' union.

(3) For the purposes of this paragraph—

    (a)   a university or university college is in England if its activities are carried on, or principally carried on, in England;

    (b)   the Open University is to be treated as a university in England.

5

(1) An English higher education corporation.

(2) For the purposes of this paragraph a higher education corporation is an English higher education corporation if the activities of the institution conducted by that corporation are carried on, or principally carried on, in England.

6

(1) A successor company to a higher education corporation at a time when the institution conducted by the company is eligible, by virtue of an order made under section 129 of the 1988 Act, to receive support from funds administered by the Higher Education Funding Council for England.

(2) In this paragraph "the 1988 Act" means the Education Reform Act 1988 and "successor company to a higher education corporation" has the meaning given by section 129(5) of the 1988 Act.

7

A further education corporation.

8

A qualifying Academy proprietor (as defined in section 12(2) of the Academies Act 2010).

9

The governing body of any foundation, voluntary or foundation special school.

10

Any foundation body established under section 21 of the School Standards and Framework Act 1998.

11

A sixth form college corporation (within the meaning of the Further and Higher Education Act 1992).

Museums, galleries etc

12

The Board of Trustees of the Victoria and Albert Museum.

13

The Board of Trustees of the Science Museum.

14

The Board of Trustees of the Armouries.

15

The Board of Trustees of the Royal Botanic Gardens, Kew.

16

The Board of Trustees of the National Museums and Galleries on Merseyside.

17

The trustees of the British Museum.

18

The trustees of the Natural History Museum.

19

The Board of Trustees of the National Gallery.

20

The Board of Trustees of the Tate Gallery.

21

The Board of Trustees of the National Portrait Gallery.

22

The Board of Trustees of the Wallace Collection.

23

The Trustees of the Imperial War Museum.

24

The Trustees of the National Maritime Museum.

25

The British Library Board.

Housing

26

Any registered society within the meaning of the Co-operative and Community Benefit Societies and Credit Unions Act 1965, if the society is also a non-profit registered provider of social housing.

27

Any registered society within the meaning of the Co-operative and Community Benefit Societies and Credit Unions Act 1965, if the society is also registered in the register of social landlords under Part 1 of the Housing Act 1996.

Connected institutions

28

(1) Any institution which—

    (a)   is administered by or on behalf of an institution included in any of paragraphs 1 to 8 and 11 to 25, and

    (b)   is established for the general purposes of, or for any special purpose of or in connection with, the institution mentioned in paragraph (a).

(2) Sub-paragraph (1) does not include—

    (a)   any college in the university of Oxford which is administered by or on behalf of that university;

    (b)   any college or hall in the university of Cambridge or Durham which is administered by or on behalf of that university;

    (c)   any student's union.

(3) Any institution which—

    (a)   is administered by or on behalf of a body included in paragraph 9 or 10, and

    (b)   is established for the general purposes of, or for any special purpose of or in connection with, that body or any foundation, voluntary or foundation special school or schools.

. . .

SCHEDULE 11
INDEX OF DEFINED EXPRESSIONS

Section 357

Institutions with an exemption from the Charitable Trusts Acts 1853 to 1939

aggregate gross income (in Part 8)	section 175
the appropriate registrar (in sections 230 to 233)	section 230(2)
application for amalgamation (in sections 237 to 239)	section 237(7)
application for conversion (in sections 230 to 233)	section 230(3)
available endowment fund (in Parts 13 and 14)	section 281(7) (and see also sections 282(5) and 288(7))
benefit (in sections 185 and 186, 198 and various provisions in Part 11)	sections 187, 199 and 248
charitable company	section 193
charitable purpose or purposes	sections 2(1) and 11
charitable purposes, failure of (in sections 63 and 65)	section 66(1)
charity	sections 1 and 10 (and see also section 12)
charity law (in Chapter 3 of Part 17)	section 331(1)

charity trustees	section 177
child (in sections 118(2)(c), 188(1)(a), 200(1)(a) and 249(2)(a))	section 350(1)
CIO	section 204
CIO regulations (in Part 11)	section 247
civil partner (in sections 118(2)(e), 188(1)(b), 200(1)(b) and 249(2)(b))	section 350(2)
the Commission	section 13(1)
common deposit scheme (in sections 100 to 103)	section 100(2)
common investment scheme (in sections 96 to 99)	section 96(2)
company	section 353(1)
connected institution or body (in section 156(2))	section 157
connected person, in relation to a charity (in section 117(2))	section 118
connected person—person connected with: a charity trustee or trustee (in sections 185 and 186); a director or member of a charitable company (in section 198(2)(c)); or a charity trustee or member of a CIO (in various provisions in Part 11)	sections: 188; 200; and 249
constitutional capacity, lack of (in sections 218 and 219)	section 218(7)(a)
constitutional limitations (in sections 218 and 219)	section 218(7)(b)
constitutional powers (in sections 218 and 219)	section 218(7)(b)
control of institution (in sections 118(2)(g), 157(1)(a), 188(1)(d), 200(1)(d) and 249(2)(d))	section 351
the court	section 353(1)
document	section 353(2)
donor (in sections 63 to 66)	section 66(2)
dormant account (in sections 107 to 109)	section 109(2)
ecclesiastical charity	section 353(1)
enactment (extended meanings)	sections 9(1), 23(4) and 27(2), 58(7), 245(4), 246(5) and 331(1); Schedule 7, paragraph 2(2) and Schedule 8, paragraph 15(2)
exempt charity	section 22 and Schedule 3
financial year	section 353(1)
gross income (generally and in section 30)	sections 353(1) and 30(4)
the group (in Part 8)	section 141(5)
group accounts (in Part 8)	section 142
incorporated body (in Part 12)	section 265
independent examiner	section 353(1)
institution	section 9(3)

land (in sections 117 to 126)	section 129(1)
maximum amount, in relation to remuneration (in sections 185 and 186)	section 187
members, in relation to a charity with a body of members distinct from the charity trustees	section 353(1)
members, in relation to a group (in Part 8)	section 141(5)
the Minister	section 353(1)
mortgage (in sections 124 to 126)	section 129(2)
Northern Ireland charity (in sections 97 and 101)	section 104(2)
the official custodian	section 21(1)
parent charity (in Part 8)	section 141(2)
parochial charity (in sections 299 and 300)	section 303(1)
permanent endowment	section 353(3)
the principal regulator	section 25
prescribed (in sections 63 and 65)	section 66(4)
the public benefit requirement	section 4(1)
the register	section 29(3)
registered	section 29(3)
the relevant charity, in relation to an incorporated body (in Part 12)	section 265
the relevant charity, in relation to power to spend capital subject to special trust (in Part 14)	section 288(1)
relevant charity merger (in Part 16)	section 306(1)
the relevant commencement date (in Schedule 9)	Schedule 9, paragraph 29
relevant institution (in sections 107 to 109)	section 109(3)
remit (in column 3 of Schedule 6)	section 323
remuneration (in sections 185 and 186)	section 187
reviewable matter (in Chapter 2 of Part 17)	section 322
Scottish recognised body (in sections 97 and 101)	section 104(1)
services (in sections 185 and 186)	section 187
special trust	section 287
spouse (in sections 118(2)(e), 188(1)(b), 200(1)(b) and 249(2)(b))	section 350(2)
subsidiary undertaking, in relation to a parent charity (in Part 8)	section 141(3) and (4)
substantial interest in a body corporate (in sections 118(2)(h), 157(1)(b), 188(1)(e), 200(1)(e) and 249(2)(e))	section 352
transfer of property (in sections 268 to 274)	section 267(4)
transfer of property (in sections 306 to 308)	section 306(4)(a)

transferee and transferor (in Part 16)	sections 306(1) and 312
transferor's property, all of (in Part 16)	sections 306(3)(a) and 312(1)(b)
the Tribunal	section 315(1)
trusts, in relation to a charity and other institutions	section 353(1)
undertaking (for certain specified purposes)	sections 55(3) and 141(6)
vesting declaration (in sections 306 to 308)	section 306(4)(b)
the 1958 Act (in Part 2 of Schedule 8)	Schedule 8, paragraph 9
the 1987 Act, and references to section 1 of the 1987 Act operating (in sections 92 to 95)	section 92(3)
the 1993 Act (in Schedule 9)	Schedule 9, paragraph 30
the 2006 Act (in Schedule 9)	Schedule 9, paragraph 30

LOCALISM ACT 2011

PART 1

LOCAL GOVERNMENT

CHAPTER 1

GENERAL POWERS OF AUTHORITIES

1 Local authority's general power of competence

(1)   A local authority has power to do anything that individuals generally may do.

(2)   Subsection (1) applies to things that an individual may do even though they are in nature, extent or otherwise—

     (a)   unlike anything the authority may do apart from subsection (1), or

     (b)   unlike anything that other public bodies may do.

(3)   In this section "individual" means an individual with full capacity.

(4)   Where subsection (1) confers power on the authority to do something, it confers power (subject to sections 2 to 4) to do it in any way whatever, including—

     (a)   power to do it anywhere in the United Kingdom or elsewhere,

     (b)   power to do it for a commercial purpose or otherwise for a charge, or without charge, and

     (c)   power to do it for, or otherwise than for, the benefit of the authority, its area or persons resident or present in its area.

(5)   The generality of the power conferred by subsection (1) ("the general power") is not limited by the existence of any other power of the authority which (to any extent) overlaps the general power.

(6)   Any such other power is not limited by the existence of the general power (but see section 5(2)).

(7)   Schedule 1 (consequential amendments) has effect.

2 Boundaries of the general power

(1)   If exercise of a pre-commencement power of a local authority is subject to restrictions, those restrictions apply also to exercise of the general power so far as it is overlapped by the pre-commencement power.

(2)   The general power does not enable a local authority to do—

    (a)   anything which the authority is unable to do by virtue of a pre-commencement limitation, or

    (b)   anything which the authority is unable to do by virtue of a post-commencement limitation which is expressed to apply—

        (i)   to the general power,

        (ii)   to all of the authority's powers, or

        (iii)   to all of the authority's powers but with exceptions that do not include the general power.

(3)   The general power does not confer power to—

    (a)   make or alter arrangements of a kind which may be made under Part 6 of the Local Government Act 1972 (arrangements for discharge of authority's functions by committees, joint committees, officers etc);

    (b)   make or alter arrangements of a kind which are made, or may be made, by or under Part 1A of the Local Government Act 2000 (arrangements for local authority governance in England);

    (c)   make or alter any contracting-out arrangements, or other arrangements within neither of paragraphs (a) and (b), that authorise a person to exercise a function of a local authority.

(4)   In this section—

"post-commencement limitation" means a prohibition, restriction or other limitation expressly imposed by a statutory provision that—

    (a)   is contained in an Act passed after the end of the Session in which this Act is passed, or

    (b)   is contained in an instrument made under an Act and comes into force on or after the commencement of section 1;

"pre-commencement limitation" means a prohibition, restriction or other limitation expressly imposed by a statutory provision that—

    (a)   is contained in this Act, or in any other Act passed no later than the end of the Session in which this Act is passed, or

    (b)   is contained in an instrument made under an Act and comes into force before the commencement of section 1;

"pre-commencement power" means power conferred by a statutory provision that—

    (a)   is contained in this Act, or in any other Act passed no later than the end of the Session in which this Act is passed, or

    (b)   is contained in an instrument made under an Act and comes into force before the commencement of section 1.

3 Limits on charging in exercise of general power

(1)   Subsection (2) applies where—

    (a)   a local authority provides a service to a person otherwise than for a commercial purpose, and

    (b)   its providing the service to the person is done, or could be done, in exercise of the general power.

(2)   The general power confers power to charge the person for providing the service to the person only if—

    (a)   the service is not one that a statutory provision requires the authority to provide to the person,

    (b)   the person has agreed to its being provided, and

    (c)   ignoring this section and section 93 of the Local Government Act 2003, the authority does not have power to charge for providing the service.

(3)   The general power is subject to a duty to secure that, taking one financial year with another, the income from charges allowed by subsection (2) does not exceed the costs of provision.

(4)   The duty under subsection (3) applies separately in relation to each kind of service.

4 Limits on doing things for commercial purpose in exercise of general power

(1)   The general power confers power on a local authority to do things for a commercial purpose only if they are things which the authority may, in exercise of the general power, do otherwise than for a commercial purpose.

(2)   Where, in exercise of the general power, a local authority does things for a commercial purpose, the authority must do them through a company.

(3)   A local authority may not, in exercise of the general power, do things for a commercial purpose in relation to a person if a statutory provision requires the authority to do those things in relation to the person.

(4)   In this section "company" means—

    (a)   a company within the meaning given by section 1(1) of the Companies Act 2006, or

    (b)   a society registered or deemed to be registered under the Co-operative and Community Benefit Societies and Credit Unions Act 1965 or the Industrial and Provident Societies Act (Northern Ireland) 1969.

5 Powers to make supplemental provision

(1)   If the Secretary of State thinks that a statutory provision (whenever passed or made) prevents or restricts local authorities from exercising the general power, the Secretary of State may by order amend, repeal, revoke or disapply that provision.

(2)   If the Secretary of State thinks that the general power is overlapped (to any extent) by another power then, for the purpose of removing or reducing that overlap, the Secretary of State may by order amend, repeal, revoke or disapply any statutory provision (whenever passed or made).

(3)   The Secretary of State may by order make provision preventing local authorities from doing, in exercise of the general power, anything which is specified, or is of a description specified, in the order.

(4)   The Secretary of State may by order provide for the exercise of the general power by local authorities to be subject to conditions, whether generally or in relation to doing anything specified, or of a description specified, in the order.

(5)   The power under subsection (1), (2), (3) or (4) may be exercised in relation to—

    (a)   all local authorities,

    (b)   particular local authorities, or

    (c)   particular descriptions of local authority.

(6)   The power under subsection (1) or (2) to amend or disapply a statutory provision includes power to amend or disapply a statutory provision for a particular period.

(7)   Before making an order under subsection (1), (2), (3) or (4) the Secretary of State must consult—

    (a)   such local authorities,

    (b)   such representatives of local government, and

    (c)   such other persons (if any),

as the Secretary of State considers appropriate.

(8)   Before making an order under subsection (1) that has effect in relation to Wales, the Secretary of State must consult the Welsh Ministers.

6 Limits on power under section 5(1)

(1)   The Secretary of State may not make provision under section 5(1) unless the Secretary of State considers that the conditions in subsection (2), where relevant, are satisfied in relation to that provision.

(2) Those conditions are that—

    (a)   the effect of the provision is proportionate to the policy objective intended to be secured by the provision;

    (b)   the provision, taken as a whole, strikes a fair balance between the public interest and the interests of any person adversely affected by it;

    (c)   the provision does not remove any necessary protection;

    (d)   the provision does not prevent any person from continuing to exercise any right or freedom which that person might reasonably expect to continue to exercise;

    (e)   the provision is not of constitutional significance.

(3) An order under section 5(1) may not make provision for the delegation or transfer of any function of legislating.

(4) For the purposes of subsection (3) a "function of legislating" is a function of legislating by order, rules, regulations or other subordinate instrument.

(5) An order under section 5(1) may not make provision to abolish or vary any tax.

7 Procedure for orders under section 5

(1) If, as a result of any consultation required by section 5(7) and (8) with respect to a proposed order under section 5(1), it appears to the Secretary of State that it is appropriate to change the whole or any part of the Secretary of State's proposals, the Secretary of State must undertake such further consultation with respect to the changes as the Secretary of State considers appropriate.

(2) If, after the conclusion of the consultation required by section 5(7) and (8) and subsection (1), the Secretary of State considers it appropriate to proceed with the making of an order under section 5(1), the Secretary of State must lay before Parliament—

    (a)   a draft of the order, and

    (b)   an explanatory document explaining the proposals and giving details of—

        (i)   the Secretary of State's reasons for considering that the conditions in section 6(2), where relevant, are satisfied in relation to the proposals,

        (ii)   any consultation undertaken under section 5(7) and (8) and subsection (1),

        (iii)   any representations received as a result of the consultation, and

        (iv)   the changes (if any) made as a result of those representations.

(3) Sections 15 to 19 of the Legislative and Regulatory Reform Act 2006 (choosing between negative, affirmative and super-affirmative parliamentary procedure) are to apply in relation to an explanatory document and draft order laid under subsection (2) but as if—

    (a)   section 18(11) of that Act were omitted,

    (b)   references to section 14 of that Act were references to subsection (2), and

    (c)   references to the Minister were references to the Secretary of State.

(4) Provision under section 5(2) may be included in a draft order laid under subsection (2) and, if it is, the explanatory document laid with the draft order must also explain the proposals under section 5(2) and give details of any consultation undertaken under section 5(7) with respect to those proposals.

(5) Section 5(7) does not apply to an order under section 5(3) or (4) which is made only for the purpose of amending an earlier such order—

    (a)   so as to extend the earlier order, or any provision of the earlier order, to a particular authority or to authorities of a particular description, or

    (b)   so that the earlier order, or any provision of the earlier order, ceases to apply to a particular authority or to authorities of a particular description.

8 Interpretation of Chapter

(1) In this Chapter—

"the general power" means the power conferred by section 1(1);

"local authority" means—

(a) a county council in England,

(b) a district council,

(c) a London borough council,

(d) the Common Council of the City of London in its capacity as a local authority,

(e) the Council of the Isles of Scilly, or

(f) an eligible parish council;

"statutory provision" means a provision of an Act or of an instrument made under an Act.

(2) A parish council is "eligible" for the purposes of this Chapter if the council meets the conditions prescribed by the Secretary of State by order for the purposes of this section.

. . .

CHAPTER 7

STANDARDS

26 Amendments of existing provisions

Schedule 4 (which amends the existing provisions relating to the conduct of local government members and employees in England and makes related provision) has effect.

27 Duty to promote and maintain high standards of conduct

(1) A relevant authority must promote and maintain high standards of conduct by members and co-opted members of the authority.

(2) In discharging its duty under subsection (1), a relevant authority must, in particular, adopt a code dealing with the conduct that is expected of members and co-opted members of the authority when they are acting in that capacity.

(3) A relevant authority that is a parish council—

(a) may comply with subsection (2) by adopting the code adopted under that subsection by its principal authority, where relevant on the basis that references in that code to its principal authority's register are to its register, and

(b) may for that purpose assume that its principal authority has complied with section 28(1) and (2).

(4) In this Chapter "co-opted member", in relation to a relevant authority, means a person who is not a member of the authority but who—

(a) is a member of any committee or sub-committee of the authority, or

(b) is a member of, and represents the authority on, any joint committee or joint sub-committee of the authority,

and who is entitled to vote on any question that falls to be decided at any meeting of that committee or sub-committee.

(5) A reference in this Chapter to a joint committee or joint sub-committee of a relevant authority is a reference to a joint committee on which the authority is represented or a sub-committee of such a committee.

(6) In this Chapter "relevant authority" means—

(a) a county council in England,

(b) a district council,

(c) a London borough council,

(d)   a parish council,

(e)   the Greater London Authority,

(f)   . . .

(g)   the London Fire and Emergency Planning Authority,

(h)   the Common Council of the City of London in its capacity as a local authority or police authority,

(i)   the Council of the Isles of Scilly,

(j)   a fire and rescue authority in England constituted by a scheme under section 2 of the Fire and Rescue Services Act 2004 or a scheme to which section 4 of that Act applies,

(k)   . . .

(l)   a joint authority established by Part 4 of the Local Government Act 1985,

(m)   an economic prosperity board established under section 88 of the Local Democracy, Economic Development and Construction Act 2009,

(n)   a combined authority established under section 103 of that Act,

(o)   the Broads Authority, or

(p)   a National Park authority in England established under section 63 of the Environment Act 1995.

(7)   Any reference in this Chapter to a member of a relevant authority—

(a)   in the case of a relevant authority to which Part 1A of the Local Government Act 2000 applies, includes a reference to an elected mayor;

(b)   in the case of the Greater London Authority, is a reference to the Mayor of London or a London Assembly member.

(8)   Functions that are conferred by this Chapter on a relevant authority to which Part 1A of the Local Government Act 2000 applies are not to be the responsibility of an executive of the authority under executive arrangements.

(9)   Functions that are conferred by this Chapter on the Greater London Authority are to be exercisable by the Mayor of London and the London Assembly acting jointly on behalf of the Authority.

(10)   In this Chapter except section 35—

(a)   a reference to a committee or sub-committee of a relevant authority is, where the relevant authority is the Greater London Authority, a reference to—

(i)   a committee or sub-committee of the London Assembly, or

(ii)   the standards committee, or a sub-committee of that committee, established under that section,

(b)   a reference to a joint committee on which a relevant authority is represented is, where the relevant authority is the Greater London Authority, a reference to a joint committee on which the Authority, the London Assembly or the Mayor of London is represented,

(c)   a reference to becoming a member of a relevant authority is, where the relevant authority is the Greater London Authority, a reference to becoming the Mayor of London or a member of the London Assembly, and

(d)   a reference to a meeting of a relevant authority is, where the relevant authority is the Greater London Authority, a reference to a meeting of the London Assembly;

and in subsection (4)(b) the reference to representing the relevant authority is, where the relevant authority is the Greater London Authority, a reference to representing the Authority, the London Assembly or the Mayor of London.

28 Codes of conduct

(1) A relevant authority must secure that a code adopted by it under section 27(2) (a "code of conduct") is, when viewed as a whole, consistent with the following principles—

    (a)   selflessness;

    (b)   integrity;

    (c)   objectivity;

    (d)   accountability;

    (e)   openness;

    (f)   honesty;

    (g)   leadership.

(2) A relevant authority must secure that its code of conduct includes the provision the authority considers appropriate in respect of the registration in its register, and disclosure, of—

    (a)   pecuniary interests, and

    (b)   interests other than pecuniary interests.

(3) Sections 29 to 34 do not limit what may be included in a relevant authority's code of conduct, but nothing in a relevant authority's code of conduct prejudices the operation of those sections.

(4) A failure to comply with a relevant authority's code of conduct is not to be dealt with otherwise than in accordance with arrangements made under subsection (6); in particular, a decision is not invalidated just because something that occurred in the process of making the decision involved a failure to comply with the code.

(5) A relevant authority may—

    (a)   revise its existing code of conduct, or

    (b)   adopt a code of conduct to replace its existing code of conduct.

(6) A relevant authority other than a parish council must have in place—

    (a)   arrangements under which allegations can be investigated, and

    (b)   arrangements under which decisions on allegations can be made.

(7) Arrangements put in place under subsection (6)(b) by a relevant authority must include provision for the appointment by the authority of at least one independent person—

    (a)   whose views are to be sought, and taken into account, by the authority before it makes its decision on an allegation that it has decided to investigate, and

    (b)   whose views may be sought—

        (i)   by the authority in relation to an allegation in circumstances not within paragraph (a),

        (ii)   by a member, or co-opted member, of the authority if that person's behaviour is the subject of an allegation, and

        (iii)   by a member, or co-opted member, of a parish council if that person's behaviour is the subject of an allegation and the authority is the parish council's principal authority.

(8) For the purposes of subsection (7)—

    (a)   a person is not independent if the person is—

        (i)   a member, co-opted member or officer of the authority,

        (ii)   a member, co-opted member or officer of a parish council of which the authority is the principal authority, or

        (iii)   a relative, or close friend, of a person within sub-paragraph (i) or (ii);

    (b)   a person may not be appointed under the provision required by subsection (7) if at any time during the 5 years ending with the appointment the person was—

> > > (i)   a member, co-opted member or officer of the authority, or
> > >
> > > (ii)   a member, co-opted member or officer of a parish council of which the authority is the principal authority;
> >
> > (c)   a person may not be appointed under the provision required by subsection (7) unless—
> >
> > > (i)   the vacancy for an independent person has been advertised in such manner as the authority considers is likely to bring it to the attention of the public,
> > >
> > > (ii)   the person has submitted an application to fill the vacancy to the authority, and
> > >
> > > (iii) the person's appointment has been approved by a majority of the members of the authority;
> >
> > (d)   a person appointed under the provision required by subsection (7) does not cease to be independent as a result of being paid any amounts by way of allowances or expenses in connection with performing the duties of the appointment.

(9)   In subsections (6) and (7) "allegation", in relation to a relevant authority, means a written allegation—

> (a)   that a member or co-opted member of the authority has failed to comply with the authority's code of conduct, or
>
> (b)   that a member or co-opted member of a parish council for which the authority is the principal authority has failed to comply with the parish council's code of conduct.

(10)   For the purposes of subsection (8) a person ("R") is a relative of another person if R is—

> (a)   the other person's spouse or civil partner,
>
> (b)   living with the other person as husband and wife or as if they were civil partners,
>
> (c)   a grandparent of the other person,
>
> (d)   a lineal descendant of a grandparent of the other person,
>
> (e)   a parent, sibling or child of a person within paragraph (a) or (b),
>
> (f)   the spouse or civil partner of a person within paragraph (c), (d) or (e), or
>
> (g)   living with a person within paragraph (c), (d) or (e) as husband and wife or as if they were civil partners.

(11)   If a relevant authority finds that a member or co-opted member of the authority has failed to comply with its code of conduct (whether or not the finding is made following an investigation under arrangements put in place under subsection (6)) it may have regard to the failure in deciding—

> (a)   whether to take action in relation to the member or co-opted member, and
>
> (b)   what action to take.

(12)   A relevant authority must publicise its adoption, revision or replacement of a code of conduct in such manner as it considers is likely to bring the adoption, revision or replacement of the code of conduct to the attention of persons who live in its area.

(13)   A relevant authority's function of adopting, revising or replacing a code of conduct may be discharged only by the authority.

(14)   Accordingly—

> (a)   in the case of an authority to whom section 101 of the Local Government Act 1972 (arrangements for discharge of functions) applies, the function is not a function to which that section applies;
>
> (b)   in the case of the Greater London Authority, the function is not a function to which section 35 (delegation of functions by the Greater London Authority) applies.

26 Register of interests

(1) The monitoring officer of a relevant authority must establish and maintain a register of interests of members and co-opted members of the authority.

(2) Subject to the provisions of this Chapter, it is for a relevant authority to determine what is to be entered in the authority's register.

(3) Nothing in this Chapter requires an entry to be retained in a relevant authority's register once the person concerned—

  (a)   no longer has the interest, or

  (b)   is (otherwise than transitorily on re-election or re-appointment) neither a member nor a co-opted member of the authority.

(4) In the case of a relevant authority that is a parish council, references in this Chapter to the authority's monitoring officer are to the monitoring officer of the parish council's principal authority.

(5) The monitoring officer of a relevant authority other than a parish council must secure—

  (a)   that a copy of the authority's register is available for inspection at a place in the authority's area at all reasonable hours, and

  (b)   that the register is published on the authority's website.

  (6)   The monitoring officer of a relevant authority that is a parish council must—

  (a)   secure that a copy of the parish council's register is available for inspection at a place in the principal authority's area at all reasonable hours,

  (b)   secure that the register is published on the principal authority's website, and

  (c)   provide the parish council with any data it needs to comply with subsection (7).

(7) A parish council must, if it has a website, secure that its register is published on its website.

(8) Subsections (5) to (7) are subject to section 32(2).

(9) In this Chapter "principal authority", in relation to a parish council, means—

  (a)   in the case of a parish council for an area in a district that has a district council, that district council,

  (b)   in the case of a parish council for an area in a London borough, the council of that London borough, and

  (c)   in the case of a parish council for any other area, the county council for the county that includes that area.

(10)   In this Chapter "register", in relation to a relevant authority, means its register under subsection (1).

30 Disclosure of pecuniary interests on taking office

(1) A member or co-opted member of a relevant authority must, before the end of 28 days beginning with the day on which the person becomes a member or co-opted member of the authority, notify the authority's monitoring officer of any disclosable pecuniary interests which the person has at the time when the notification is given.

(2) Where a person becomes a member or co-opted member of a relevant authority as a result of re-election or re-appointment, subsection (1) applies only as regards disclosable pecuniary interests not entered in the authority's register when the notification is given.

(3) For the purposes of this Chapter, a pecuniary interest is a "disclosable pecuniary interest" in relation to a person ("M") if it is of a description specified in regulations made by the Secretary of State and either—

  (a)   it is an interest of M's, or

  (b)   it is an interest of—

(i)   M's spouse or civil partner,

(ii)   a person with whom M is living as husband and wife, or

(iii)   a person with whom M is living as if they were civil partners,

and M is aware that that other person has the interest.

(4) Where a member or co-opted member of a relevant authority gives a notification for the purposes of subsection (1), the authority's monitoring officer is to cause the interests notified to be entered in the authority's register (whether or not they are disclosable pecuniary interests).

31 Pecuniary interests in matters considered at meetings or by a single member

(1) Subsections (2) to (4) apply if a member or co-opted member of a relevant authority—

(a)   is present at a meeting of the authority or of any committee, sub-committee, joint committee or joint sub-committee of the authority,

(b)   has a disclosable pecuniary interest in any matter to be considered, or being considered, at the meeting, and

(c)   is aware that the condition in paragraph (b) is met.

(2) If the interest is not entered in the authority's register, the member or co-opted member must disclose the interest to the meeting, but this is subject to section 32(3).

(3) If the interest is not entered in the authority's register and is not the subject of a pending notification, the member or co-opted member must notify the authority's monitoring officer of the interest before the end of 28 days beginning with the date of the disclosure.

(4) The member or co-opted member may not—

(a)   participate, or participate further, in any discussion of the matter at the meeting, or

(b)   participate in any vote, or further vote, taken on the matter at the meeting,

but this is subject to section 33.

(5) In the case of a relevant authority to which Part 1A of the Local Government Act 2000 applies and which is operating executive arrangements, the reference in subsection (1)(a) to a committee of the authority includes a reference to the authority's executive and a reference to a committee of the executive.

(6) Subsections (7) and (8) apply if—

(a)   a function of a relevant authority may be discharged by a member of the authority acting alone,

(b)   the member has a disclosable pecuniary interest in any matter to be dealt with, or being dealt with, by the member in the course of discharging that function, and

(c)   the member is aware that the condition in paragraph (b) is met.

(7) If the interest is not entered in the authority's register and is not the subject of a pending notification, the member must notify the authority's monitoring officer of the interest before the end of 28 days beginning with the date when the member becomes aware that the condition in subsection (6)(b) is met in relation to the matter.

(8) The member must not take any steps, or any further steps, in relation to the matter (except for the purpose of enabling the matter to be dealt with otherwise than by the member).

(9) Where a member or co-opted member of a relevant authority gives a notification for the purposes of subsection (3) or (7), the authority's monitoring officer is to cause the interest notified to be entered in the authority's register (whether or not it is a disclosable pecuniary interest).

(10) Standing orders of a relevant authority may provide for the exclusion of a member or co-opted member of the authority from a meeting while any discussion or

vote takes place in which, as a result of the operation of subsection (4), the member or co-opted member may not participate.

(11)   For the purpose of this section, an interest is "subject to a pending notification" if—

(a)   under this section or section 30, the interest has been notified to a relevant authority's monitoring officer, but

(b)   has not been entered in the authority's register in consequence of that notification.

32 Sensitive interests

(1)   Subsections (2) and (3) apply where—

(a)   a member or co-opted member of a relevant authority has an interest (whether or not a disclosable pecuniary interest), and

(b)   the nature of the interest is such that the member or co-opted member, and the authority's monitoring officer, consider that disclosure of the details of the interest could lead to the member or co-opted member, or a person connected with the member or co-opted member, being subject to violence or intimidation.

(2)   If the interest is entered in the authority's register, copies of the register that are made available for inspection, and any published version of the register, must not include details of the interest (but may state that the member or co-opted member has an interest the details of which are withheld under this subsection).

(3)   If section 31(2) applies in relation to the interest, that provision is to be read as requiring the member or co-opted member to disclose not the interest but merely the fact that the member or co-opted member has a disclosable pecuniary interest in the matter concerned.

33 Dispensations from section 31(4)

(1)   A relevant authority may, on a written request made to the proper officer of the authority by a member or co-opted member of the authority, grant a dispensation relieving the member or co-opted member from either or both of the restrictions in section 31(4) in cases described in the dispensation.

(2)   A relevant authority may grant a dispensation under this section only if, after having had regard to all relevant circumstances, the authority—

(a)   considers that without the dispensation the number of persons prohibited by section 31(4) from participating in any particular business would be so great a proportion of the body transacting the business as to impede the transaction of the business,

(b)   considers that without the dispensation the representation of different political groups on the body transacting any particular business would be so upset as to alter the likely outcome of any vote relating to the business,

(c)   considers that granting the dispensation is in the interests of persons living in the authority's area,

(d)   if it is an authority to which Part 1A of the Local Government Act 2000 applies and is operating executive arrangements, considers that without the dispensation each member of the authority's executive would be prohibited by section 31(4) from participating in any particular business to be transacted by the authority's executive, or

(e)   considers that it is otherwise appropriate to grant a dispensation.

(3)   A dispensation under this section must specify the period for which it has effect, and the period specified may not exceed four years.

(4)   Section 31(4) does not apply in relation to anything done for the purpose of deciding whether to grant a dispensation under this section.

34 Offences

(1) A person commits an offence if, without reasonable excuse, the person—

    (a)   fails to comply with an obligation imposed on the person by section 30(1) or 31(2), (3) or (7),

    (b)   participates in any discussion or vote in contravention of section 31(4), or

    (c)   takes any steps in contravention of section 31(8).

(2) A person commits an offence if under section 30(1) or 31(2), (3) or (7) the person provides information that is false or misleading and the person—

    (a)   knows that the information is false or misleading, or

    (b)   is reckless as to whether the information is true and not misleading.

(3) A person who is guilty of an offence under this section is liable on summary conviction to a fine not exceeding level 5 on the standard scale.

(4) A court dealing with a person for an offence under this section may (in addition to any other power exercisable in the person's case) by order disqualify the person, for a period not exceeding five years, for being or becoming (by election or otherwise) a member or co-opted member of the relevant authority in question or any other relevant authority.

(5) A prosecution for an offence under this section is not to be instituted except by or on behalf of the Director of Public Prosecutions.

(6) Proceedings for an offence under this section may be brought within a period of 12 months beginning with the date on which evidence sufficient in the opinion of the prosecutor to warrant the proceedings came to the prosecutor's knowledge.

(7) But no such proceedings may be brought more than three years—

    (a)   after the commission of the offence, or

    (b)   in the case of a continuous contravention, after the last date on which the offence was committed.

(8) A certificate signed by the prosecutor and stating the date on which such evidence came to the prosecutor's knowledge is conclusive evidence of that fact; and a certificate to that effect and purporting to be so signed is to be treated as being so signed unless the contrary is proved.

(9) The Local Government Act 1972 is amended as follows.

(10) In section 86(1)(b) (authority to declare vacancy where member becomes disqualified otherwise than in certain cases) after "2000" insert "or section 34 of the Localism Act 2011".

(11) In section 87(1)(ee) (date of casual vacancies)—

    (a)   after "2000" insert "or section 34 of the Localism Act 2011 or", and

    (b)   after "decision" insert "or order".

(12) The Greater London Authority Act 1999 is amended as follows.

(13) In each of sections 7(b) and 14(b) (Authority to declare vacancy where Assembly member or Mayor becomes disqualified otherwise than in certain cases) after sub-paragraph (i) insert—

    "(ia)   under section 34 of the Localism Act 2011,".

(14) In section 9(1)(f) (date of casual vacancies)—

    (a)   before "or by virtue of" insert "or section 34 of the Localism Act 2011", and

    (b)   after "that Act" insert "of 1998 or that section".

35 Delegation of functions by Greater London Authority

(1) The Mayor of London and the London Assembly, acting jointly, may arrange for any of the functions conferred on them by or under this Chapter to be exercised on their behalf by—

    (a)   a member of staff of the Greater London Authority, or

(b)   a committee appointed in accordance with provision made by virtue of this section.

(2)   Standing orders of the Greater London Authority may make provision regulating the exercise of functions by any member of staff of the Authority pursuant to arrangements under subsection (1).

(3)   Standing orders of the Greater London Authority may make provision for the appointment of a committee ("the standards committee") to exercise functions conferred on the Mayor of London and the London Assembly by or under this Chapter in accordance with arrangements under subsection (1).

(4)   Standing orders of the Greater London Authority may make provision about the membership and procedure of the standards committee.

(5)   The provision that may be made under subsection (4) includes—

(a)   provision for the standards committee to arrange for the discharge of its functions by a sub-committee of that committee;

(b)   provision about the membership and procedure of such a sub-committee.

(6)   Subject to subsection (7), the standards committee and any sub-committee of that committee—

(a)   is not to be treated as a committee or (as the case may be) sub-committee of the London Assembly for the purposes of the Greater London Authority Act 1999, but

(b)   is a committee or (as the case may be) sub-committee of the Greater London Authority for the purposes of Part 3 of the Local Government Act 1974 (investigations by Commission for Local Administration in England).

(7)   Sections 6(3)(a) (failure to attend meetings) and 73(6) (functions of monitoring officer) of the Greater London Authority Act 1999 apply to the standards committee or any sub-committee of that committee as they apply to a committee of the London Assembly or any sub-committee of such a committee.

(8)   Part 5A of the Local Government Act 1972 (access to meetings and documents) applies to the standards committee or any sub-committee of that committee as if—

(a)   it were a committee or (as the case may be) a sub-committee of a principal council within the meaning of that Part, and

(b)   the Greater London Authority were a principal council in relation to that committee or sub-committee.

(9)   Arrangements under this section for the exercise of any function by—

(a)   a member of staff of the Greater London Authority, or

(b)   the standards committee,

do not prevent the Mayor of London and the London Assembly from exercising those functions.

(10)   References in this section to the functions of the Mayor of London and the London Assembly conferred by or under this Chapter do not include their functions under this section.

(11)   In this section "member of staff of the Greater London Authority" has the same meaning as in the Greater London Authority Act 1999 (see section 424(1) of that Act).

36 Amendment of section 27 following abolition of police authorities

In section 27(6) (which defines "relevant authority" for the purposes of this Chapter) omit—

(a)   paragraph (f) (the Metropolitan Police Authority), and

(b)   paragraph (k) (police authorities).

. . .

PART 5

COMMUNITY EMPOWERMENT

. . .

CHAPTER 2

COMMUNITY RIGHT TO CHALLENGE

81 Duty to consider expression of interest

(1) A relevant authority must consider an expression of interest in accordance with this Chapter if—

(a)   it is submitted to the authority by a relevant body, and

(b)   it is made in writing and complies with such other requirements for expressions of interest as the Secretary of State may specify by regulations.

This is subject to section 82 (timing of expressions of interest).

(2) In this Chapter "relevant authority" means—

(a)   a county council in England,

(b)   a district council,

(c)   a London borough council, or

(d)   such other person or body carrying on functions of a public nature as the Secretary of State may specify by regulations.

(3) The persons or bodies who may be specified by regulations under subsection (2)(d) include a Minister of the Crown or a government department.

(4) In this Chapter "expression of interest", in relation to a relevant authority, means an expression of interest in providing or assisting in providing a relevant service on behalf of the authority.

(5) In this Chapter "relevant service", in relation to a relevant authority, means a service provided by or on behalf of that authority in the exercise of any of its functions in relation to England, other than a service of a kind specified in regulations made by the Secretary of State.

(6) In this Chapter "relevant body" means—

(a)   a voluntary or community body,

(b)   a body of persons or a trust which is established for charitable purposes only,

(c)   a parish council,

(d)   in relation to a relevant authority, two or more employees of that authority, or

(e)   such other person or body as may be specified by the Secretary of State by regulations.

(7) For the purposes of subsection (6) "voluntary body" means a body, other than a public or local authority, the activities of which are not carried on for profit.

(8) The fact that a body's activities generate a surplus does not prevent it from being a voluntary body for the purposes of subsection (6) so long as that surplus is used for the purposes of those activities or invested in the community.

(9) For the purposes of subsection (6) "community body" means a body, other than a public or local authority, that carries on activities primarily for the benefit of the community.

(10) The Secretary of State may by regulations—

(a)   amend or repeal any of paragraphs (a) to (d) of subsection (6);

(b)   amend or repeal any of subsections (7) to (9);

(c)   make other amendments to this Chapter (including amendments to any power to make regulations) in consequence of provision made under subsection (2)(d) or (6)(e) or paragraph (a) or (b) of this subsection.

82 Timing of expressions of interest

(1)   Subject as follows, a relevant body may submit an expression of interest to a relevant authority at any time.

(2)   A relevant authority may specify periods during which expressions of interest, or expressions of interest in respect of a particular relevant service, may be submitted to the authority.

(3)   The relevant authority must publish details of each specification under subsection (2) in such manner as it thinks fit (which must include publication on the authority's website).

(4)   The relevant authority may refuse to consider an expression of interest submitted outside a period specified under subsection (2).

83 Consideration of expression of interest

(1)   The relevant authority must—

(a)   accept the expression of interest, or

(b)   reject the expression of interest.

This is subject to section 84(1) (modification of expression of interest).

(2)   If the relevant authority accepts the expression of interest it must carry out a procurement exercise relating to the provision on behalf of the authority of the relevant service to which the expression of interest relates.

(3)   The exercise required by subsection (2) must be such as is appropriate having regard to the value and nature of the contract that may be awarded as a result of the exercise.

(4)   A relevant authority must specify—

(a)   the minimum period that will elapse between—

(i)   the date of the relevant authority's decision to accept an expression of interest, and

(ii)   the date on which it will begin the procurement exercise required by subsection (2) as a result of that acceptance, and

(b)   the maximum period that will elapse between those dates.

(5)   The relevant authority may specify different periods for different cases.

(6)   The relevant authority must publish details of a specification under subsection (4) in such manner as it thinks fit (which must include publication on the authority's website).

(7)   The relevant authority must comply with a specification under subsection (4).

(8)   A relevant authority must, in considering an expression of interest, consider whether acceptance of the expression of interest would promote or improve the social, economic or environmental well-being of the authority's area.

(9)   A relevant authority must, in carrying out the exercise referred to in subsection (2), consider how it might promote or improve the social, economic or environmental well-being of the authority's area by means of that exercise.

(10)   Subsection (9) applies only so far as is consistent with the law applying to the awarding of contracts for the provision on behalf of the authority of the relevant service in question.

(11)   The relevant authority may reject the expression of interest only on one or more grounds specified by the Secretary of State by regulations.

84 Consideration of expression of interest: further provisions

(1)   A relevant authority that is considering an expression of interest from a relevant body may modify the expression of interest.

(2)   A relevant authority may exercise the power in subsection (1) only if—

    (a)   the authority thinks that the expression of interest would not otherwise be capable of acceptance, and

    (b)   the relevant body agrees to the modification.

(3) A relevant authority must specify the maximum period that will elapse between—

    (a)   the date on which it receives an expression of interest submitted by a relevant body, and

    (b)   the date on which it notifies the relevant body of its decision in respect of the expression of interest.

(4) The relevant authority may specify different periods for different cases.

(5) The relevant authority must publish details of a specification under subsection (3) in such manner as it thinks fit (which must include publication on the authority's website).

(6) A relevant authority that receives an expression of interest from a relevant body in accordance with this Chapter must notify the relevant body in writing of the period within which it expects to notify the relevant body of its decision in respect of the expression of interest.

(7) The relevant authority must give the notification under subsection (6)—

    (a)   where the expression of interest is one to which a specification under section 82(2) relates and is made within a period so specified, within the period of 30 days beginning immediately after the end of the period so specified, or

    (b)   otherwise, within the period of 30 days beginning with the day on which the relevant authority receives the expression of interest.

(8) The relevant authority must—

    (a)   notify the relevant body in writing of its decision in respect of the expression of interest within the period specified by it under subsection (3), and

    (b)   if the authority's decision is to modify or reject the expression of interest, give reasons for that decision in the notification.

(9) The relevant authority must publish the notification in such manner as it thinks fit (which must include publication on the authority's website).

(10) A relevant body may withdraw an expression of interest after submitting it to a relevant authority (whether before or after a decision has been made by the authority in respect of the expression of interest).

(11) The withdrawal of an expression of interest, or the refusal of a relevant body to agree to modification of an expression of interest, does not prevent the relevant authority from proceeding as described in section 83(2) if the relevant authority thinks that it is appropriate to do so.

85 Supplementary

(1) The Secretary of State may by regulations make further provision about the consideration by a relevant authority of an expression of interest submitted by a relevant body.

(2) A relevant authority must, in exercising its functions under or by virtue of this Chapter, have regard to guidance issued by the Secretary of State.

86 Provision of advice and assistance

(1) The Secretary of State may do anything that the Secretary of State considers appropriate for the purpose of giving advice or assistance to a relevant body in relation to—

    (a)   the preparation of an expression of interest for submission to a relevant authority and its submission to a relevant authority,

    (b)   participation in a procurement exercise carried out by a relevant authority in response to an expression of interest, or

(c)   the provision of a relevant service on behalf of a relevant authority following such a procurement exercise.

(2)   The Secretary of State may do anything that the Secretary of State considers appropriate for the purpose of giving advice or assistance about the operation of this Chapter to a body or person other than a relevant body.

(3)   The things that the Secretary of State may do under this section include, in particular—

(a)   the provision of financial assistance to a relevant body;

(b)   the making of arrangements with a body or person (whether or not a relevant body), including arrangements for things that may be done by the Secretary of State under this section to be done by that body or person;

(c)   the provision of financial assistance to a body or person other than a relevant body in connection with arrangements under paragraph (b).

(4)   In this section references to a relevant body include a body that the Secretary of State considers was formed wholly or partly by employees or former employees of the relevant authority for the purposes of, or for purposes including—

(a)   participating in a procurement exercise carried out by the authority, or

(b)   providing a relevant service on the authority's behalf.

(5)   In this section—

(a)   the reference to giving advice or assistance includes providing training or education, and

(b)   any reference to the provision of financial assistance is to the provision of financial assistance by any means (including the making of a loan and the giving of a guarantee or indemnity).

CHAPTER 3

Assets of Community Value
List of assets of community value

87 List of assets of community value

(1)   A local authority must maintain a list of land in its area that is land of community value.

(2)   The list maintained under subsection (1) by a local authority is to be known as its list of assets of community value.

(3)   Where land is included in a local authority's list of assets of community value, the entry for that land is to be removed from the list with effect from the end of the period of 5 years beginning with the date of that entry (unless the entry has been removed with effect from some earlier time in accordance with provision in regulations under subsection (5)).

(4)   The appropriate authority may by order amend subsection (3) for the purpose of substituting, for the period specified in that subsection for the time being, some other period.

(5)   The appropriate authority may by regulations make further provision in relation to a local authority's list of assets of community value, including (in particular) provision about—

(a)   the form in which the list is to be kept;

(b)   contents of an entry in the list (including matters not to be included in an entry);

(c)   modification of an entry in the list;

(d)   removal of an entry from the list;

(e)   cases where land is to be included in the list and—

        (i)   different parts of the land are in different ownership or occupation, or

        (ii)   there are multiple estates or interests in the land or any part or parts of it;

    (f)   combination of the list with the local authority's list of land nominated by unsuccessful community nominations.

(6)   Subject to any provision made by or under this Chapter, it is for a local authority to decide the form and contents of its list of assets of community value.

88 Land of community value

(1)   For the purposes of this Chapter but subject to regulations under subsection (3), a building or other land in a local authority's area is land of community value if in the opinion of the authority—

    (a)   an actual current use of the building or other land that is not an ancillary use furthers the social wellbeing or social interests of the local community, and

    (b)   it is realistic to think that there can continue to be non-ancillary use of the building or other land which will further (whether or not in the same way) the social wellbeing or social interests of the local community.

(2)   For the purposes of this Chapter but subject to regulations under subsection (3), a building or other land in a local authority's area that is not land of community value as a result of subsection (1) is land of community value if in the opinion of the local authority—

    (a)   there is a time in the recent past when an actual use of the building or other land that was not an ancillary use furthered the social wellbeing or interests of the local community, and

    (b)   it is realistic to think that there is a time in the next five years when there could be non-ancillary use of the building or other land that would further (whether or not in the same way as before) the social wellbeing or social interests of the local community.

(3)   The appropriate authority may by regulations—

    (a)   provide that a building or other land is not land of community value if the building or other land is specified in the regulations or is of a description specified in the regulations;

    (b)   provide that a building or other land in a local authority's area is not land of community value if the local authority or some other person specified in the regulations considers that the building or other land is of a description specified in the regulations.

(4)   A description specified under subsection (3) may be framed by reference to such matters as the appropriate authority considers appropriate.

(5)   In relation to any land, those matters include (in particular)—

    (a)   the owner of any estate or interest in any of the land or in other land;

    (b)   any occupier of any of the land or of other land;

    (c)   the nature of any estate or interest in any of the land or in other land;

    (d)   any use to which any of the land or other land has been, is being or could be put;

    (e)   statutory provisions, or things done under statutory provisions, that have effect (or do not have effect) in relation to—

        (i)   any of the land or other land, or

        (ii)   any of the matters within paragraphs (a) to (d);

    (f)   any price, or value for any purpose, of any of the land or other land.

(6)   In this section—

        "legislation" means—

        (a)   an Act, or

(b)   a Measure or Act of the National Assembly for Wales;

"social interests" includes (in particular) each of the following—

(a)   cultural interests;

(b)   recreational interests;

(c)   sporting interests;

"statutory provision" means a provision of—

(a)   legislation, or

(b)   an instrument made under legislation.

89 Procedure for including land in list

(1)   Land in a local authority's area which is of community value may be included by a local authority in its list of assets of community value only—

(a)   in response to a community nomination, or

(b)   where permitted by regulations made by the appropriate authority.

(2)   For the purposes of this Chapter "community nomination", in relation to a local authority, means a nomination which—

(a)   nominates land in the local authority's area for inclusion in the local authority's list of assets of community value, and

(b)   is made—

(i)   by a parish council in respect of land in England in the parish council's area,

(ii)   by a community council in respect of land in Wales in the community council's area, or

(iii) by a person that is a voluntary or community body with a local connection.

(3)   Regulations under subsection (1)(b) may (in particular) permit land to be included in a local authority's list of assets of community value in response to a nomination other than a community nomination.

(4)   The appropriate authority may by regulations make provision as to—

(a)   the meaning in subsection (2)(b)(iii) of "voluntary or community body";

(b)   the conditions that have to be met for a person to have a local connection for the purposes of subsection (2)(b)(iii);

(c)   the contents of community nominations;

(d)   the contents of any other nominations which, as a result of regulations under subsection (1)(b), may give rise to land being included in a local authority's list of assets of community value.

(5)   The appropriate authority may by regulations make provision for, or in connection with, the procedure to be followed where a local authority is considering whether land should be included in its list of assets of community value.

90 Procedure on community nominations

(1)   This section applies if a local authority receives a community nomination.

(2)   The authority must consider the nomination.

(3)   The authority must accept the nomination if the land nominated—

(a)   is in the authority's area, and

(b)   is of community value.

(4)   If the authority is required by subsection (3) to accept the nomination, the authority must cause the land to be included in the authority's list of assets of community value.

(5)   The nomination is unsuccessful if subsection (3) does not require the authority to accept the nomination.

(6)   If the nomination is unsuccessful, the authority must give, to the person who made the nomination, the authority's written reasons for its decision that the land could not be included in its list of assets of community value.

91 Notice of inclusion or removal

(1) Subsection (2) applies where land—

   (a)   is included in, or

   (b)   removed from,

a local authority's list of assets of community value.

(2) The authority must give written notice of the inclusion or removal to the following persons—

   (a)   the owner of the land,

   (b)   the occupier of the land if the occupier is not also the owner,

   (c)   if the land was included in the list in response to a community nomination, the person who made the nomination, and

   (d)   any person specified, or of a description specified, in regulations made by the appropriate authority,

but where it appears to the authority that it is not reasonably practicable to give a notice under this subsection to a person to whom it is required to be given, the authority must instead take reasonable alternative steps for the purpose of bringing the notice to the person's attention.

(3) A notice under subsection (2) of inclusion of land in the list must describe the provision made by and under this Chapter, drawing particular attention to—

   (a)   the consequences for the land and its owner of the land's inclusion in the list, and

   (b)   the right to ask for review under section 92.

(4) A notice under subsection (2) of removal of land from the list must state the reasons for the removal.

92 Review of decision to include land in list

(1) The owner of land included in a local authority's list of assets of community value may ask the authority to review the authority's decision to include the land in the list.

(2) If a request is made—

   (a)   under subsection (1), and

   (b)   in accordance with the time limits (if any) provided for in regulations under subsection (5),

the authority concerned must review its decision.

(3) Where under subsection (2) an authority reviews a decision, the authority must notify the person who asked for the review—

   (a)   of the decision on the review, and

   (b)   of the reasons for the decision.

(4) If the decision on a review under subsection (2) is that the land concerned should not have been included in the authority's list of assets of community value—

   (a)   the authority must remove the entry for the land from the list, and

   (b)   where the land was included in the list in response to a community nomination—

      (i)   the nomination becomes unsuccessful, and

      (ii)   the authority must give a written copy of the reasons mentioned in subsection (3)(b) to the person who made the nomination.

(5) The appropriate authority may by regulations make provision as to the procedure to be followed in connection with a review under this section.

(6) Regulations under subsection (5) may (in particular) include—

   (a)   provision as to time limits;

   (b)   provision requiring the decision on the review to be made by a person of appropriate seniority who was not involved in the original decision;

(c)   provision as to the circumstances in which the person asking for the review is entitled to an oral hearing, and whether and by whom that person may be represented at the hearing;

(d)   provision for appeals against the decision on the review.

List of land nominated by unsuccessful community nominations

93 List of land nominated by unsuccessful community nominations

(1)   A local authority must maintain a list of land in its area that has been nominated by an unsuccessful community nomination (see sections 90(5) and 92(4)(b)(i)).

(2)   The list maintained under subsection (1) by a local authority is to be known as its list of land nominated by unsuccessful community nominations.

(3)   Where land is included in a local authority's list of land nominated by unsuccessful community nominations, the entry in the list for the land—

(a)   may (but need not) be removed from the list by the authority after it has been in the list for 5 years, and

(b)   while it is in the list, is to include the reasons given under section 90(6) or 92(3)(b) for not including the land in the authority's list of assets of community value.

(4)   Subject to any provision made by or under this Chapter, it is for a local authority to decide the form and contents of its list of land nominated by unsuccessful community nominations.

Provisions common to both lists

94 Publication and inspection of lists

(1)   A local authority must publish—

(a)   its list of assets of community value, and

(b)   its list of land nominated by unsuccessful community nominations.

(2)   A local authority must at a place in its area make available, for free inspection by any person, both—

(a)   a copy of its list of assets of community value, and

(b)   a copy of its list of land nominated by unsuccessful community nominations.

(3)   A local authority must provide a free copy of its list of assets of community value to any person who asks it for a copy, but is not required to provide to any particular person more than one free copy of the same version of the list.

(4)   A local authority must provide a free copy of its list of land nominated by unsuccessful community nominations to any person who asks it for a copy, but is not required to provide to any particular person more than one free copy of the same version of the list.

(5)   In this section "free" means free of charge.

Moratorium on disposing of listed land

95 Moratorium

(1)   A person who is an owner of land included in a local authority's list of assets of community value must not enter into a relevant disposal of the land unless each of conditions A to C is met.

(2)   Condition A is that that particular person has notified the local authority in writing of that person's wish to enter into a relevant disposal of the land.

(3)   Condition B is that either—

(a)   the interim moratorium period has ended without the local authority having received during that period, from any community interest group, a written request (however expressed) for the group to be treated as a potential bidder in relation to the land, or

(b)   the full moratorium period has ended.

(4)   Condition C is that the protected period has not ended.

(5)   Subsection (1) does not apply in relation to a relevant disposal of land—

    (a)   if the disposal is by way of gift (including a gift to trustees of any trusts by way of settlement upon the trusts),

    (b)   if the disposal is by personal representatives of a deceased person in satisfaction of an entitlement under the will, or on the intestacy, of the deceased person,

    (c)   if the disposal is by personal representatives of a deceased person in order to raise money to—

        (i)   pay debts of the deceased person,

        (ii)   pay taxes,

        (iii)   pay costs of administering the deceased person's estate, or

        (iv)   pay pecuniary legacies or satisfy some other entitlement under the will, or on the intestacy, of the deceased person,

    (d)   if the person, or one of the persons, making the disposal is a member of the family of the person, or one of the persons, to whom the disposal is made,

    (e)   if the disposal is a part-listed disposal of a description specified in regulations made by the appropriate authority, and for this purpose "part-listed disposal" means a disposal of an estate in land—

        (i)   part of which is land included in a local authority's list of assets of community value, and

        (ii)   part of which is land not included in any local authority's list of assets of community value,

    (f)   if the disposal is of an estate in land on which a business is carried on and is at the same time, and to the same person, as a disposal of that business as a going concern,

    (g)   if the disposal is occasioned by a person ceasing to be, or becoming, a trustee,

    (h)   if the disposal is by trustees of any trusts—

        (i)   in satisfaction of an entitlement under the trusts, or

        (ii)   in exercise of a power conferred by the trusts to re-settle trust property on other trusts,

    (i)   if the disposal is occasioned by a person ceasing to be, or becoming, a partner in a partnership, or

    (j)   in cases of a description specified in regulations made by the appropriate authority.

(6)   In subsections (3) and (4)—

"community interest group" means a person specified, or of a description specified, in regulations made by the appropriate authority,

"the full moratorium period", in relation to a relevant disposal, means the six months beginning with the date on which the local authority receives notification under subsection (2) in relation to the disposal,

"the interim moratorium period", in relation to a relevant disposal, means the six weeks beginning with the date on which the local authority receives notification under subsection (2) in relation to the disposal, and "the protected period", in relation to a relevant disposal, means the eighteen months beginning with the date on which the local authority receives notification under subsection (2) in relation to the disposal.

(7)   For the purposes of subsection (5)(d), a person ("M") is a member of the family of another person if M is—

(a)   that other person's spouse or civil partner, or

(b)   a lineal descendant of a grandparent of that other person.

(8)   For the purposes of subsection (7)(b) a relationship by marriage or civil partnership is to be treated as a relationship by blood.

(9)   For the meaning of "relevant disposal", and for when a relevant disposal is entered into, see section 96.

96   Meaning of "relevant disposal" etc in section 95

(1)   This section applies for the purposes of section 95.

(2)   A disposal of the freehold estate in land is a relevant disposal of the land if it is a disposal with vacant possession.

(3)   A grant or assignment of a qualifying leasehold estate in land is a relevant disposal of the land if it is a grant or assignment with vacant possession.

(4)   If a relevant disposal within subsection (2) or (3) is made in pursuance of a binding agreement to make it, the disposal is entered into when the agreement becomes binding.

(5)   Subject to subsection (4), a relevant disposal within subsection (2) or (3) is entered into when it takes place.

(6)   In this section "qualifying leasehold estate", in relation to any land, means an estate by virtue of a lease of the land for a term which, when granted, had at least 25 years to run.

(7)   The appropriate authority may by order amend this section.

97   Publicising receipt of notice under section 95(2)

(1)   This section applies if a local authority receives notice under section 95(2) in respect of land included in the authority's list of assets of community value.

(2)   The authority must cause the entry in the list for the land to reveal—

(a)   that notice under section 95(2) has been received in respect of the land,

(b)   the date when the authority received the notice, and

(c)   the ends of the initial moratorium period, the full moratorium period and the protected period that apply under section 95 as a result of the notice.

(3)   If the land is included in the list in response to a community nomination, the authority must give written notice, to the person who made the nomination, of the matters mentioned in subsection (2)(a), (b) and (c).

(4)   The authority must make arrangements for those matters to be publicised in the area where the land is situated.

98   Informing owner of request to be treated as bidder

(1)   Subsection (2) applies if—

(a)   after a local authority has received notice under section 95(2) in respect of land included in the authority's list of assets of community value, and

(b)   before the end of the interim moratorium period that applies under section 95 as a result of the notice,

the authority receives from a community interest group a written request (however expressed) for the group to be treated as a potential bidder in relation to the land.

(2)   The authority must, as soon after receiving the request as is practicable, either pass on the request to the owner of the land or inform the owner of the details of the request.

(3)   In this section "community interest group" means a person who is a community interest group for the purposes of section 95(3) as a result of regulations made under section 95(6) by the appropriate authority.

99 Compensation

(1)   The appropriate authority may by regulations make provision for the payment of compensation in connection with the operation of this Chapter.

(2)   Regulations under subsection (1) may (in particular)—

   (a)   provide for any entitlement conferred by the regulations to apply only in cases specified in the regulations;

   (b)   provide for any entitlement conferred by the regulations to be subject to conditions, including conditions as to time limits;

   (c)   make provision about—

      (i)   who is to pay compensation payable under the regulations;

      (ii)   who is to be entitled to compensation under the regulations;

      (iii)   what compensation under the regulations is to be paid in respect of;

      (iv)   the amount, or calculation, of compensation under the regulations;

      (v)   the procedure to be followed in connection with claiming compensation under the regulations;

      (vi)   the review of decisions made under the regulations;

      (vii)   appeals against decisions made under the regulations.

. . .

PART 6

PLANNING

. . .

CHAPTER 3

Neighbourhood Planning

116 Neighbourhood planning

(1)   Schedule 9 (which makes provision about neighbourhood development orders and neighbourhood development plans) has effect.

(2)   After Schedule 4A to the Town and Country Planning Act 1990 insert the Schedule 4B set out in Schedule 10 to this Act.

(3)   After the inserted Schedule 4B to that Act insert the Schedule 4C set out in Schedule 11 to this Act.

117 Charges for meeting costs relating to neighbourhood planning

(1)   The Secretary of State may with the consent of the Treasury make regulations providing for the imposition of charges for the purpose of meeting expenses incurred (or expected to be incurred) by local planning authorities in, or in connection with, the exercise of their neighbourhood planning functions.

(2)   A local planning authority's "neighbourhood planning functions" are any of their functions exercisable under any provision made by or under—

   (a)   any of sections 61E to 61Q of, or Schedule 4B or 4C to, the Town and Country Planning Act 1990 (neighbourhood development orders),

   (b)   any of sections 38A to 38C of the Planning and Compulsory Purchase Act 2004 (neighbourhood development plans), or

   (c)   this section.

(3)   The regulations must secure—

(a) that the charges are payable in relation to development for which planning permission is granted by a neighbourhood development order made under section 61E of the Town and Country Planning Act 1990,

(b) that the charges become payable when the development is commenced (determined in accordance with the regulations), and

(c) that the charges are payable to local planning authorities.

(4) The regulations may authorise local planning authorities to set the amount of charges imposed by the regulations; and, if so, the regulations may—

(a) provide for the charges not to be payable at any time unless at that time a document (a "charging document") has been published by the authority setting out the amounts chargeable under the regulations in relation to development in their area,

(b) make provision about the approval and publication of a charging document,

(c) prescribe matters to which the authorities must have regard in setting the charges,

(d) require the authorities, in setting the charges, to disregard such expenditure expected to be incurred as mentioned in subsection (1) as falls within a description prescribed by the regulations,

(e) authorise the authorities to set different charges for different cases, circumstances or areas (either generally or only to the extent specified in the regulations), and

(f) authorise the authorities to make exceptions (either generally or only to the extent specified in the regulations).

(5) The regulations must make provision about liability to pay a charge imposed by the regulations.

(6) The regulations may make provision—

(a) enabling any person to assume (in accordance with any procedural provision made by the regulations) the liability to pay a charge imposed by the regulations before it becomes payable,

(b) about assumption of partial liability,

(c) about the withdrawal of assumption of liability,

(d) about the cancellation by a local planning authority of assumption of liability,

(e) for the owner or developer of land to be liable to pay the charge in cases prescribed by the regulations,

(f) about joint liability (with or without several liability),

(g) about liability of partnerships,

(h) about apportionment of liability, including provision for referral to a specified body or other person for determination and provision for appeals, and

(i) about transfer of liability (whether before or after the charge becomes due and whether or not liability has been assumed).

(7) In subsection (6)(e)—

(a) "owner" of land means a person who owns an interest in land, and

(b) "developer" means a person who is wholly or partly responsible for carrying out a development.

(8) The provision for appeals that may be made as a result of subsection (6)(h) includes provision about—

(a) the period within which the right of appeal may be exercised,

(b) the procedure on appeals, and

(c)   the payment of fees, and award of costs, in relation to appeals (including provision requiring local planning authorities to bear expenses incurred in connection with appeals).

118 Regulations under section 117: collection and enforcement

(1) Regulations under section 117 must include provision about the collection of charges imposed by the regulations.

(2) The regulations may make provision—

(a)   for payment on account or by instalments,

(b)   about repayment (with or without interest) in cases of overpayment, and

(c)   about the source of payments in respect of a Crown interest or Duchy interest (within the meaning of section 227(3) or (4) of the Planning Act 2008).

(3) Regulations under section 117 must include provision about enforcement of charges imposed by the regulations; and that provision must include provision—

(a)   for a charge (or other amount payable under the regulations) to be treated as a civil debt due to a local planning authority, and

(b)   for the debt to be recoverable summarily.

(4) The regulations may make provision—

(a)   about the consequences of failure to assume liability, to give a notice or to comply with another procedure under the regulations,

(b)   for the payment of interest (at a rate specified in, or determined in accordance with, the regulations),

(c)   for the imposition of a penalty or surcharge (of an amount specified in, or determined in accordance with, the regulations),

(d)   replicating or applying (with or without modifications) any provision made by any of sections 324 to 325A of the Town and Country Planning Act 1990 (rights of entry), and

(e)   for enforcement in the case of death or insolvency of a person liable for the charge.

119 Regulations under section 117: supplementary

(1) Regulations under section 117 may make provision about procedures to be followed in connection with charges imposed by the regulations.

(2) The regulations may make provision about—

(a)   procedures to be followed by a local planning authority proposing to start or stop imposing a charge,

(b)   procedures to be followed by a local planning authority in relation to the imposition of a charge,

(c)   the arrangements of a local planning authority for the making of any decision prescribed by the regulations,

(d)   consultation,

(e)   the publication or other treatment of reports,

(f)   timing and methods of publication,

(g)   making documents available for inspection,

(h)   providing copies of documents (with or without charge),

(i)   the form and content of documents,

(j)   giving notice,

(k)   serving notices or other documents, and

(l)   procedures to be followed in connection with actual or potential liability for a charge.

(3) Provision made by the regulations as a result of subsection (2)(c) is to have effect despite provision made by any enactment as to the arrangements of a local planning

authority for the exercise of their functions (such as section 101 of the Local Government Act 1972 or section 13 of the Local Government Act 2000).

(4) Regulations under section 117 may make provision binding the Crown.

(5) Regulations under section 117 may make—

 (a) provision applying any enactment (with or without modifications), and

 (b) provision for exceptions.

(6) A local planning authority must have regard to any guidance issued by the Secretary of State in the exercise of any of their functions under regulations under section 117.

(7) For the purposes of sections 117 and 118 and this section "local planning authority" means an authority that have made or have power to make—

 (a) a neighbourhood development order under section 61E of the Town and Country Planning Act 1990, or

 (b) a neighbourhood development plan under section 38A of the Planning and Compulsory Purchase Act 2004.

(8) Nothing in section 117, 118 or this section that authorises the inclusion of any particular kind of provision in regulations under section 117 is to be read as restricting the generality of the provision that may be included in the regulations.

120 Financial assistance in relation to neighbourhood planning

(1) The Secretary of State may do anything that the Secretary of State considers appropriate—

 (a) for the purpose of publicising or promoting the making of neighbourhood development orders or neighbourhood development plans and the benefits expected to arise from their making, or

 (b) for the purpose of giving advice or assistance to anyone in relation to the making of proposals for such orders or plans or the doing of anything else for the purposes of, or in connection with, such proposals or such orders or plans.

(2) The things that the Secretary of State may do under this section include, in particular—

 (a) the provision of financial assistance (or the making of arrangements for its provision) to any body or other person, and

 (b) the making of agreements or other arrangements with any body or other person (under which payments may be made to the person).

(3) In this section—

 (a) the reference to giving advice or assistance includes providing training or education,

 (b) any reference to the provision of financial assistance is to the provision of financial assistance by any means (including the making of a loan and the giving of a guarantee or indemnity),

 (c) any reference to a neighbourhood development order is to a neighbourhood development order under section 61E of the Town and Country Planning Act 1990, and

 (d) any reference to a neighbourhood development plan is to a neighbourhood development plan under section 38A of the Planning and Compulsory Purchase Act 2004.

121 Consequential amendments

Schedule 12 (neighbourhood planning: consequential amendments) has effect.

MEASURES OF THE WELSH ASSEMBLY

LOCAL GOVERNMENT (WALES) MEASURE 2011

. . .

PART 7

COMMUNITIES AND COMMUNITY COUNCILS

. . .

CHAPTER 6

COMMUNITY COUNCILS' POWERS OO PROMOTE WELL-BEING

126 Community councils' powers to promote well-being

(1) In section 1 of the Local Government Act 2000 (meaning of "local authority" in Part 1 of that Act), at the end of subsection (1)(b) insert "or a community council".

(2) In section 2 of that Act (promotion of well-being), insert the following after subsection (3B)—

> "(3C) The community strategy for the area of a community council is the strategy referred to in subsection (3B) that is published by the county council or county borough council in whose area lies the community or communities for which the community council is established.".

(3) In section 5 of that Act (power to amend or repeal enactments), insert the following after subsection (6)—

> "(7) The reference to local authorities in subsection (1) does not include community councils.".

127 Modifications of enactments preventing or obstructing a community council from exercising their well-being power

(1) The Welsh Ministers may by order make modifications of any enactment if they consider that the enactment prevents or obstructs community councils from exercising their power under section 2(1) of the Local Government Act 2000 (promotion of well-being).

(2) The power under subsection (1) may be exercised in relation to—

> (a)   all community councils,
>
> (b)   particular community councils, or
>
> (c)   particular descriptions of community council.

(3) The power under subsection (1) includes a power to make modifications of an enactment for a particular period.

128 Transitional provision

(1) This section applies to a community council for so long as the local authority in whose area it lies has not published a community strategy under section 39(4) of the Local Government (Wales) Measure 2009.

(2) Where this section applies to a community council, the reference in section 2(3C) of the Local Government Act 2000 to the community strategy for the area of the community council is to be read as a reference to the community strategy of the county council or county borough council under section 4 of that Act.

CHAPTER 7

GRANTS TO COMMUNITY COUNCILS

129 Welsh Ministers' power to pay grant to community councils

(1) The Welsh Ministers may pay a grant to a community council towards expenditure incurred or to be incurred by it.

(2) The amount of a grant under this section and the manner of its payment are to be such as the Welsh Ministers may determine.

(3) A grant under this section may be paid on such conditions as the person paying it may determine.

(4) Conditions under subsection (3) may include (but are not limited to)—

    (a) provision as to the use of the grant;

    (b) provision as to circumstances in which the whole or part of the grant must be repaid.

CHAPTER 8

MODEL CHARTER AGREEMENTS BETWEEN LOCAL AUTHORITIES AND COMMUNITY COUNCILS

130 Power to set out model charter agreement

(1) The Welsh Ministers may by order make provision setting out a model charter agreement between a local authority and a community council for a community or communities within its area.

(2) In subsection (1), "model charter agreement between a local authority and a community council" means a description of the way in which their functions can be exercised for the purpose of maintaining and improving cooperation between them.

(3) The provision that may be made by an order under subsection (1) includes (but is not limited to) provision—

    (a) setting out the way in which specified functions, or aspects of such functions, are to be exercised;

    (b) setting out specified functions, or aspects of such functions, in respect of which the local authority and the community council are to seek agreement as to how they are to be exercised;

    (c) setting out specified functions which are to be exercised by reference to specified principles.

(4) In this section and section 131, a reference to the exercise of functions includes a reference to the doing of anything which is calculated to facilitate, or is conducive or incidental to, the exercise of the functions.

131 Directions requiring the adoption of model charter agreements

(1) The Welsh Ministers may by direction require a local authority and a community council for a community or communities within the authority's area to adopt a model charter agreement set out in an order under section 130(1).

(2) In subsection (1), "adopt" means resolve, in accordance with any procedure specified in the direction, to exercise functions, or to seek agreement as to how to exercise functions, in accordance with—

    (a) all the provisions of the model charter agreement, or

    (b) those provisions specified in the direction.

(3) A direction under subsection (1) may—

    (a) relate to all, or any one or more, of the community councils for communities within the area of the local authority, and

    (b) if the direction relates to more than one community council, make different provision in relation to different councils.

(4) A direction under subsection (1) is enforceable by mandatory order on the application of the Welsh Ministers.

132 Guidance about model charter agreements
A local authority and a community council must, in acting under a direction under section 131(1), have regard to guidance given by the Welsh Ministers.

133 Consultation
(1) The Welsh Ministers must, before making an order under section 130(1), consult—

    (a)   such bodies representative of local authorities and community councils as the Welsh Ministers consider it appropriate to consult, and

    (b)   such other persons as the Welsh Ministers consider it appropriate to consult.

(2) The Welsh Ministers must, before giving a direction under section 131(1), consult the authority and council to which the direction relates.

CHAPTER 9

SCHEMES FOR THE ACCREDITATION OF QUALITY IN COMMUNITY GOVERNMENT

134 Schemes for the accreditation of quality in community government
(1) The Welsh Ministers may by regulations provide for a scheme under which the Welsh Ministers may or, if the regulations so require, must grant accreditation to a community council if—

    (a)   the Welsh Ministers are satisfied that the criteria set in the regulations are satisfied in relation to a council (see section 135),

    (b)   the Welsh Ministers are satisfied that a council has made a valid application for accreditation (see section 136), and

    (c)   the required fee (if any) has been paid to the Welsh Ministers (see section 137).

(2) An accreditation under subsection (1) is referred to in this Chapter as an accreditation of quality in community government.

135 Accreditation of quality in community government: criteria
(1) If the Welsh Ministers make regulations under section 134(1), the regulations must set criteria to be met on an application for accreditation of quality in community government.

(2) The criteria that may be set include (but are not limited to) criteria about the following matters—

    (a)   the percentage of the members of the council who hold office by virtue of having been elected as described in section 35(1) of the Local Government Act 1972 (election of community councillors);

    (b)   qualifications of and training for officers of the council;

    (c)   training for members of the council and community youth representatives;

    (d)   the frequency with which meetings of the council are held and the publicity given to meetings (both before and after they are held);

    (e)   involving persons in the work of the community council;

    (f)   encouraging persons to improve the well-being of the community or communities for which the council is established;

    (g)   annual reports;

    (h)   accounts.

136 Accreditation of quality in community government: applications
If the Welsh Ministers make regulations under section 134(1), the regulations must set requirements to be met in order for a valid application for accreditation of quality in community government to be made.

137 Accreditation of quality in community government: fees
If the Welsh Ministers make regulations under section 134(1), the regulations may prescribe a fee that an applicant for accreditation of quality in community government is required to pay.

138 Accreditation of quality in community government: removal of accreditation
If the Welsh Ministers make regulations under section 134(1), the regulations must provide for—
    (a)   review of accreditations of quality in community government, and
    (b)   the grounds on which an accreditation of quality in community government may be removed and the removal process.

139 Applications for accreditation of quality in community government: delegation of functions
(1)   The Welsh Ministers may make arrangements with any person under which that person is to exercise, in accordance with the terms of the arrangements, the functions of the Welsh Ministers under regulations made under section 134(1).
(2)   If such arrangements are made, section 134(1)(c) is to have effect so that any required fee is to be paid to the person with whom the arrangements are made.

140 Accreditation of quality in community government: consequences
(1)   The Welsh Ministers may by regulations make modifications of any enactment which imposes any obligation upon or in respect of a community council so that, in the case of a council in respect of which an accreditation of quality in community government is in force, the obligation is—
    (a)   disapplied, or
    (b)   altered so as to make it easier to comply with.
(2)   The Welsh Ministers may by regulations make modifications of any enactment which confers a power upon or in respect of a community council so that, in the case of a council in respect of which an accreditation of quality in community government is not in force, the power—
    (a)   may not be exercised, or
    (b)   may only be exercised if prescribed conditions are satisfied.

WELSH LANGUAGE (WALES) MEASURE 2011

PART 1

OFFICIAL STATUS OF THE WELSH LANGUAGE

1 Official status of the Welsh language
(1)   The Welsh language has official status in Wales.
(2)   Without prejudice to the general principle of subsection (1), the official status of the Welsh language is given legal effect by the enactments about—
    (a)   duties on bodies to use the Welsh language, and the rights which arise from the enforceability of those duties, which enable Welsh speakers to use the language in dealings with those bodies (such as the provision of services by those bodies);

    (b)   the treatment of the Welsh language no less favourably than the English language;

    (c)   the validity of the use of the Welsh language;

    (d)   the promotion and facilitation of the use of the Welsh language;

    (e)   the freedom of persons wishing to use the Welsh language to do so with one another;

    (f)   the creation of the Welsh Language Commissioner; and

    (g)   other matters relating to the Welsh language.

(3)   Those enactments include (but are not limited to) the enactments which—

    (a)   require the Welsh and English languages to be treated on the basis of equality in the conduct of the proceedings of the National Assembly for Wales;

    (b)   confer a right to speak the Welsh language in legal proceedings in Wales;

    (c)   give equal standing to the Welsh and English texts of—

        (i)   Measures and Acts of the National Assembly for Wales, and

        (ii)   subordinate legislation;

    (d)   impose a duty on the Welsh Ministers to adopt a strategy setting out how they propose to promote and facilitate the use of the Welsh language;

    (e)   create standards of conduct that relate to the use of the Welsh language, or the treatment of the Welsh language no less favourably than the English language, in connection with—

        (i)   delivering services,

        (ii)   making policy, and

        (iii) exercising functions or conducting businesses and other undertakings;

    (f)   create standards of conduct in promoting and facilitating the use of the Welsh language;

    (g)   create standards of conduct for keeping records in connection with the Welsh language;

    (h)   impose a duty to comply with those standards of conduct that are created, and create remedies for failures to comply with them; and

    (i)   create the Welsh Language Commissioner with functions that include—

        (i)   promoting the use of the Welsh language,

        (ii)   facilitating the use of the Welsh language,

        (iii) working towards ensuring that the Welsh language is treated no less favourably than the English language,

        (iv) conducting inquiries into matters relating to the Commissioner's functions, and

        (v)   investigating interference with the freedom to use the Welsh language.

(4)   This Measure does not affect the status of the English language in Wales.

PART 2

THE WELSH LANGUAGE COMMISSIONER
The Commissioner

2 The Welsh Language Commissioner

(1)   There is to be a Welsh Language Commissioner (referred to in this Measure as "the Commissioner").

(2)   The First Minister must appoint the Commissioner.

(3)   Schedule 1 makes further provision about the Commissioner.

(4)   For provision about the integrity of the Commissioner, see Chapter 1 of Part 8.

General duty

3 The Commissioner's principal aim

(1)   The principal aim of the Commissioner in exercising his or her functions is to promote and facilitate the use of the Welsh language.

(2)   The actions which the Commissioner must undertake in exercising functions in accordance with subsection (1) include (but are not limited to) working towards increasing—

  (a)   the use of the Welsh language in the provision of services, and

  (b)   other opportunities for persons to use the Welsh language.

(3)   In exercising functions in accordance with subsection (1), the Commissioner must have regard to—

  (a)   the official status which the Welsh language has in Wales,

  (b)   the duties to use Welsh which are (or may be) imposed by law, and the rights which arise from the enforceability of those duties,

  (c)   the principle that, in Wales, the Welsh language should be treated no less favourably than the English language, and

  (d)   the principle that persons in Wales should be able to live their lives through the medium of the Welsh language if they choose to do so.

. . .

PART 4

STANDARDS

CHAPTER 1

DUTY TO COMPLY WITH STANDARDS

25 Duty to comply with a standard

(1)   A person (P) must comply with a standard of conduct specified by the Welsh Ministers in accordance with Chapter 2 if, and for as long as, the following conditions are met.

(2)   Condition 1 is that P is liable to be required to comply with standards (see Chapter 3).

(3)   Condition 2 is that the standard is potentially applicable to P (see Chapter 4).

(4)   Condition 3 is that the standard is specifically applicable to P (see Chapter 5).

(5)   Condition 4 is that the Commissioner has given a compliance notice to P (see Chapter 6).

(6)   Condition 5 is that the compliance notice requires P to comply with the standard (see Chapter 6).

(7)   Condition 6 is that the compliance notice is in force (see Chapter 6).

(8)   Subsection (1) is subject to the provisions of the compliance notice given to P.

(9)   For provision about—

  (a)   rights of challenge in respect of the duty to comply with standards, see Chapter 7;

  (b)   standards investigations and reports, see Chapter 8;

  (c)   general matters, see Chapter 9.

CHAPTER 2

STANDARDS AND THEIR SPECIFICATION

. . .

28 Service delivery standards

(1) In this Measure "service delivery standard" means a standard that—

    (a)   relates to a service delivery activity, and

    (b)   is intended to promote or facilitate the use of the Welsh language, or to work towards ensuring that the Welsh language is treated no less favourably than the English language, when that activity is carried out.

(2) In this section "service delivery activity" means a person—

    (a)   delivering services to another person, or

    (b)   dealing with any other person in connection with delivering services—

        (i)   to that other person, or

        (ii)   to a third person.

Appendix II

STATUTORY INSTRUMENTS

Contents

Notes

(1)   In this appendix the words of a statutory instrument are printed, with certain exceptions, only if they are necessary for a local council's work. In some cases knowledge only of the existence of an instrument is necessary; such instruments have been briefly summarised.

(2)   Texts are printed as amended by later instruments. The author's notes or summaries are printed in italics within square brackets.

(3)   The exceptions mentioned in (1) above are cases where a precedent may be useful.

The Symbol T

(4)   For the meaning of the symbol T used in the first part of this book, see the note on p x. The symbol is not used in this appendix, but the user should bear in mind that references in the statutory instruments to counties, districts and their councils may have to be read in England as references either to counties or to districts and their council, and in Wales to counties, county boroughs and their councils.

Interpretation Act

(5)   All these instruments contain a paragraph in the following (or a very similar) form—
'The Interpretation Act 1889 [or '1978'] applies for the interpretation of this order as it applies for the interpretation of an Act of Parliament'.
The Interpretation Act 1889 is wholly superseded by the Act of 1978 which re-enacts it with additions and takes its place.

PUBLIC TRUSTEE RULES 1912

(SR&O 1912/348)

30
(1)   The following corporations shall be entitled to act as custodian trustees:—

. . .

(h)   any of the following, namely:—

. . .

(iii)   a county council, district council, parish council or community council

. . .

WALKWAYS REGULATIONS 1973

(SI 1973/686)

3 Modification of statutory provisions

(1) The enactments specified in Schedule 3 to these Regulations and any local statutory provision affecting highways which is similar in effect to an enactment so specified, shall in their application to a walkway or to anything done on or in

connection with a walkway be modified so that the power thereby conferred on the highway authority or the local authority to execute works, or to place or do anything, on or in relation to the walkway, or to authorise some other person to execute works, or to place or do anything, on or in relation to the walkway, shall not be exercisable by such authority without the consent of the building owner, except insofar as the walkway agreement provides for such exercise without that consent.

. . .

LOCAL AUTHORITIES (ENGLAND) (PROPERTY ETC) ORDER 1973

(SI 1973/1861)

4 Interpretation

. . .

(2)   In this order—

'the Act' means the Local Government Act 1972;

'buildings', except in article 22, means buildings not within the meaning of the term 'land';

'corporate land' means corporate land within the meaning of the Local Government Act 1933;

. . .

'historic and ceremonial property' does not include any property held (or under article 19, 20, 22 or 39 deemed to be held) for the purposes of any statutory functions;

'land' includes land covered by water and any interest or right in, to or over land;

. . .

. . .

5 Other express provision

This order shall have effect subject to the express provision of—

(a)   any other order made (whether before or after this order) under section 254 of the Act;

(b)   any regulations made under section 7 or 8 of the Superannuation Act 1972, or,

(c)   section 16, 25 or 54(2) of the National Health Service Reorganisation Act 1973 or any order made under those sections.

9 Transfer of specified classes of property, etc

(1)   Nothing in this article applies to—

(a)   any property held as sole trustee, exclusively for charitable purposes, by an existing local authority for an area outside Greater London, other than the parish council, parish meeting or representative body of a parish . . . transferred by section 210 of the Act;

(b)   any property so held by the parish council, parish meeting or representative body of an existing parish mentioned in paragraph 1 of Part IV of Schedule 1 to the Act or in paragraph (2) of article 3 of the New Parishes Order 1973 transferred by article 9(1) of that order;

(c)   any other property held for the purposes of any charitable trust;

. . .

(e)   any property vested in a county council by virtue of section 226 of the Highways Act 1959;

. . .

(g)   any matter provided for in article 11(1) in so far as it applies to rights ensured by article 23 in its application to any property transferred by article 6, 7 or 8;

(h)   any matter provided for in article 11(2) or (3) in their application to any matter provided for in articles 7 and 8;

(i)   any matter provided for in article 18 in its application to any matter described in the preceding items of this paragraph.

(2)   Nothing in paragraphs (4) to (6) of this article applies to matters provided for in paragraphs (2) to (4) of article 18 in their application to any matters provided for in paragraph (3) of this article, and nothing in paragraphs (5) and (6) of this article applies to any matters provided for in paragraphs (3) and (4) of article 18 in their application to any liabilities provided for in paragraph (4) of this article.

(3)–(4)   [*Distribution of property owned by particular dissolved authorities among country, district and parish authorities which were designated to administer the area of the dissolved authorities.*]

. . .

(7)   Save in so far as express provision is made in item No 13 of the table in Schedule 2, this article does not extend to the historic and ceremonial property other than land and buildings, and in particular to the charters, insignia and plate, of any area.

10 Provision supplementary to article 9

(1)   The provision made in this article applies in the application of article 9.

. . .

(3)   Any question whether any property is historic or ceremonial property shall, subject to the provision of paragraph (6), be determined by the transferor authority.

. . .

(8)   The provision of off-street parking places for vehicles shall be treated as a function exercisable on and after 1st April 1974 by both county and district councils.

11 Fittings, furniture, equipment and stores

(1)   Where by paragraph (1) of article 23 any right to the use of any accommodation is ensured for any authority other than the authority in whom the accommodation is vested on and after 1st April 1974, the fittings, furniture, equipment and stores in such accommodation which have been provided exclusively for the purposes of the functions described in (i) or (ii) of the said paragraph shall, except in so far as the first-mentioned authority shall otherwise agree, by virtue of this order be transferred to and vest in such authority.

(2)   Subject to paragraph (1), where by article 7, 8 or 9 or by any provision of any order by which this article is applied any building is transferred to and vested in any authority, the fittings, furniture and equipment of such building, and the stores therein which have been provided for the discharge of functions therein, shall, except in so far as such authority shall otherwise agree, by virtue of this order be transferred to and vest in such authority.

If the value of any stores transferred by this paragraph is included in any revenue balance, the necessary adjustment shall be made in such balance.

(3)   Subject to paragraph (1), where by article 7, 8 or 9 or by any provision of any order by which this article is applied any land to which paragraph (2) does not apply is transferred to and vested in any authority, the equipment of such land shall, except in so far as such authority shall otherwise agree, by virtue of this order be transferred to and vest in such authority.

(4)   For the purposes of this article—

(a)   'equipment' includes records; and

(b)   any vehicles or other mobile equipment used wholly or mainly in the performance of the functions carried out in any accommodation or building or on any land shall be deemed to be equipment thereof.

16 Residual transfer of property, etc

(1)   Save as provided in paragraph (2) of this article, paragraph (1) of article 9 applies to this article as it applies to article 9.

(2)   The following entry in Schedule 4, namely—

'The representative body of any parish not included in the preceding items'

shall extend to property held by any such representative body for the purposes of charitable trusts.

(2A)   The following entry in the said Schedule 4, namely

'The Water Supply Industry Training Board' shall extend to property held by the Board for the purposes of charitable trusts.

shall extend to property held by the Board for the purposes of charitable trusts.

(3)   Subject to the provisions of articles 9 to 15 or of articles 11(2) and (3) and 18 in their application to any matters provided for in articles 9 to 15—

(a)   all property and liabilities vested in or attaching to an authority described in column (1) of Part I or II of Schedule 4 (or of any extension thereof effected by any further order under section 254 of the Act made before 1st April 1974) shall by virtue of this order be transferred to and vest in or attach to the authority specified in respect of such authority in column (2);

(b)   all contracts, deeds, bonds, agreements and other instruments subsisting in favour of, or against, and all notices in force which were given (or have effect as if they had been given) by, or to, an authority described in column (1) of Part I or II of Schedule 4 (or of any extension thereof as aforesaid) shall be of full force and effect in favour of, or against, the authority specified in respect of such authority in column (2);

(d)   any power to appoint any person to any body belonging to an authority described in column (1) of Part I or II of Schedule 4 (or of any extension thereof as aforesaid) in respect of any matter provided for in (a) or (b) shall be transferred to the authority specified in respect of such authority in column (2).

17 General saving for agreements

(1)   The authority to whom any account or fund is transferred, or any amount of any fund is payable, by virtue of any provision of this order, may agree that any particular amount in the account or fund shall be payable to any other authority.

(2)   The authority to whom any other property other than land is transferred by the preceding articles of this order other than article 7 may by resolution agree that the property shall be transferred to any other authority specified in the resolution, and paragraphs (2) to (5) of article 18 shall apply accordingly.

(3)   The transferee authority in respect of any matter other than property, provided for in paragraph (4), (5) or (6) of article 9 or in (a), (b) or (c) of paragraph (3) of article 16, and any other authority, may agree that that other authority shall be substituted for the transferee authority in the application of any such provision.

(4)   The provision made by the preceding articles of this order, other than articles 12, 14, 15 and 16A or by any provision of any order by which this article is applied, for the transfer of any matter is without prejudice to any agreement which may be made for payment in respect of such matter.

18 Liabilities, contracts etc, notices and proceedings in respect of transferred property, etc

(1)   This article applies to the following matters, namely—

    (a)   any property described in (a), (b) or (e) of article 9(1); and

    (b)   any property transferred by this order.

(2) Subject to paragraph (6), all liabilities attaching to any authority in respect of any property to which this article applies shall by virtue of this order be transferred to and attach to the authority to whom such property is transferred.

(3) All contracts, deeds, bonds, agreements and other instruments subsisting in favour of, or against, and all notices in force which were given (or have effect as if they had been given) by, or to, the authority first mentioned in paragraph (2) in respect of any property to which this article applies, or in respect of liabilities transferred by paragraph (2), shall be of full force and effect in favour of, or against, the authority to whom such property and liabilities are transferred.

. . .

(5) Any power to appoint any person to any body belonging to the authority first mentioned in paragraph (2) in respect of any property (other than that described in (a) and (b) of article 9(1)) to which this article applies or any matter provided for in paragraphs (2) and (3) shall be transferred to the authority to whom such property or matter is transferred.

. . .

23 User rights

(1) This paragraph applies to—

    (a)   accommodation in any property transferred to and vested in any authority by virtue of this order (hereinafter referred to as 'case (a)');

    (b)   accommodation in any property held by a parish authority and not transferred by virtue of this order (hereinafter referred to as 'case (b)');

immediately before 1st April 1974 used (or in the case of accommodation not yet in occupation proposed to be used) otherwise than temporarily—

    (i)   in case (a) for the purposes of any functions which on and after 1st April 1974 are not exercisable (or not exercisable as regards any part of the area served from the accommodation) by the authority to whom the property is transferred;

    (ii)   in case (b) for the purposes of any functions which on and after 1st April 1974 are not exercisable (or not exercisable as regards any part of the area served from the accommodation) by a parish authority.

In the case of any accommodation to which this paragraph applies the authority exercising the functions described in (i) or (ii) in the area served by the accommodation or, as the case may be, the part thereof shall be entitled to the use of such accommodation, whether for the purposes of such functions or for the purposes of any other functions exercisable by them.

In the preceding sub-paragraph the reference to the authority exercising the functions described in (i) or (ii) extends to an authority established by the National Health Service Reorganisation Act 1973 exercising the functions so described.

(2) Where—

    (a)   any property is immediately before 1st April 1974 used (or in the case of property not yet in use proposed to be used) otherwise than temporarily for the purposes of functions exercisable by one authority in relation to any area;

    (b)   the functions become exercisable on and after that day by two or more authorities; and

    (c)   the property is by virtue of this order transferred to and vested in one of the authorities described in (b),

(hereinafter referred to as 'case (c)') any other of the authorities described in (b) shall be entitled to the use of such property, whether for the purposes of such functions or for the purposes of any other functions exercisable by them.

(3) [*This subsection covers transfers of property from county, county borough or county district councils to new principal authorities.*]

(4) Where—

    (a)   any property is immediately before 1st April 1974 used (or in the case of property not yet in use proposed to be used) otherwise than temporarily for the purposes of functions exercisable by two or more authorities;

    (b)   the property is by virtue of this order transferred to and vested in one authority;

(hereinafter referred to as 'case (e)') any other authority exercising any of the functions described in (a) shall be entitled to the use of such property whether for the purposes of such functions or for the purposes of other functions exercisable by them.

In the preceding sub-paragraph the reference to any other authority exercising any of the functions described in (a) extends to an authority established by the National Health Service Reorganisation Act 1973 exercising the functions so described.

(4A)   The parish council of any parish constituted under Part V of Schedule 1 to the Act in the area of any borough or urban district or the parish council of Alston with Garrigill, Disley or Tintwistle, constituted by section 9(4) of the Act for an area coextensive with a rural district (hereinafter referred to as 'case (f)') shall be entitled, for the proper discharge of their functions, to the use of accommodation in property which immediately before 1st April 1974 is held by the council of the borough, urban district or rural district under section 125 of the Local Government Act 1933.

(5)   Any question—

    (a)   whether any accommodation in any property to which paragraph (1) applies is used (or proposed to be used) for the purposes described in (i) or (ii) of that paragraph;

    (b)   whether any property to which paragraph (2) applies is used (or proposed to be used) as described in (a) thereof;

    (c)   whether any property to which paragraph (4) applies is used (or proposed to be used) as described in (a) thereof; or

    (d)   without prejudice to (c) whether any use (or proposed use) is temporary,

shall, subject to the following provision of this paragraph, be determined by the authority in whom the property is, before 1st April 1974, vested.

If, before 1st April 1976, notice is given by any authority that they are dissatisfied with any such determination (or, no determination having been made, that a question exists) the question shall be determined by agreement between the authorities concerned or failing such agreement by the decision of a person agreed on by such authorities or in default of agreement appointed by the Secretary of State.

(6)   The use of any accommodation or property by virtue of this article shall be for such period and on such terms as may be determined by agreement between the authority entitled under this article to use the accommodation or property and, in case (a), (c), (d), (e) or (f) the authority to whom the property is transferred and in case (b) the parish authority, or failing such agreement by the decision of a person agreed on by such authorities or in default of agreement appointed by the Secretary of State.

(7)   In this article 'exercisable' means exercisable otherwise than by virtue of section 101, 110 or 187(2) or (3) of the Act.

(8)   An authority shall not sell, exchange, lease or otherwise dispose of property in respect of which user rights are ensured by this article, or develop the land on which such property is situated, unless they have consulted all authorities entitled to such user rights and made such arrangements as may be determined by agreement between the authorities concerned or failing such agreement by the decision of a person agreed on by such authorities or in default of agreement appointed by the Secretary of State.

24 Charter trustees

(1)   It shall be the duty of the council of a district in which a city or town for which there are charter trustees is situated to provide accommodation for the proper discharge of the functions of the charter trustees.

(2)   The accommodation to be provided and the terms on which it is provided shall be determined by agreement between the district council and the charter trustees, or failing such agreement by the decision of a person agreed on by them or in default of agreement appointed by the Secretary of State.

25 Corporate land

(1)   Any question whether any land vested in the corporation of a borough is corporate land shall, subject to the following provision of this paragraph, be determined by the council of the borough . . .

(2)   Any corporate land to which article 20(2) does not apply and which is transferred by this order to any authority shall be held by that authority as if it had been acquired by that authority under section 120(1)(b) or 124(1)(b), as the case may be, of the Act.

28 Property and liabilities to attach to whole areas

(1)   Subject to paragraph (2), any interest in any property or any liability transferred by the preceding articles of this order or by any provision of any order by which this article is applied to the authority for any county, district or parish shall be held or discharged by them in respect of the whole of such area.

(2)   Paragraph (1)—

    (a)   shall not apply to any property or liability transferred by article 16 as extended by paragraph (2) thereof;

    (b)   shall not apply in respect of any interest in any property or any liability which by reason of agreements made by authorities abolished by the Act falls to be held or discharged in respect of any specific area; and

    (c)   shall have effect subject to the provision of subsections (4) and (5) of section 248 of the Act (freemen and inhabitants of existing boroughs).

29 Byelaws, etc

(1)   Any byelaws in force for the regulation of any property described in (a) or (b) of article 9(1) or transferred by preceding articles of this order or by any provision of any order by which this article is applied shall have effect as if they had been made by the authority to whom such property is transferred.

If such authority has no power, apart from this sub-paragraph, to amend or revoke byelaws, any byelaws to which the preceding sub-paragraph applies may be amended by a byelaw made under this sub-paragraph. Section 236(3) to (10) of the Act shall apply to any such byelaw and the Secretary of State or any appropriate Minister shall be the confirming authority in relation thereto. In this sub-paragraph 'the appropriate Minister', in relation to any byelaw, means the Minister in charge of any Government department concerned with the subject matter of the byelaw; but the validity of the confirmation of any byelaw shall not be affected by any question as to whether or not any Minister so confirming was the appropriate Minister for the purpose.

(2)   Any provision of any local Act or of any order made under or confirmed by any Act which applies to any property described in (a) or (b) of article 9(1) or transferred by the preceding articles of this order or by any provision of any order by which this article is applied shall have effect with the substitution for any references to (or having effect as references to) the authority from whom such property is transferred of references to the authority to whom the property is transferred.

33 Security for loans

Where under this order any liability or part of a liability charged indifferently on all the revenues of a public body or on any particular revenues or fund of such body is transferred to another public body, the liability or part of the liability shall be charged indifferently on all the revenues of the public body to whom it is transferred and shall cease to be a charge on any revenues or fund of the public body from whom it is transferred.

34 Capital and renewal and repairs funds

(1) A local authority may transfer the balance on any capital fund or renewal and repairs fund transferred to them under article 16 or the amount of any such fund received by them under article 14 or 15 to the credit of a capital fund or a renewal and repairs fund, as the case may be, established by them under Schedule 13 to the Act.

(2) Where any matter in respect of which a repayable advance which has not been fully repaid has been made from a capital fund or a renewal and repairs fund is transferred by the Act or this order to any authority, that authority may treat the outstanding amount of the advance as an advance from a capital fund or a renewal and repairs fund established by them under Schedule 13 to the Act and make such payments to such fund as the authority consider appropriate, but otherwise any liability to make repayments in respect of the advance shall cease.

SCHEDULE 1
TRANSFER OF PARTICULAR PROPERTIES

Paragraph (3) of article 10, and paragraph (6) in so far as it applies thereto, shall apply to any question whether any property is historic or ceremonial property.

(1) Transferor authority	(2) Property	(3) Transferee authority
The corporation of any borough for the whole of the area of which charter trustees are constituted	Historical and ceremonial property, and in particular the charters insignia and plate, of the borough	The charter trustees
. . .		

SCHEDULE 4
RESIDUAL TRANSFER OF PROPERTY, ETC

PART II

(1) Transferor authority	(2) Transferee authority
. . .	
The corporation or council of any borough included in a rural district	The parish council of the parish replacing the borough
The representative body of any parish not included in the preceding items	The parish trustees of the parish
Any burial board, joint burial board or joint committee which ceases to exist by virtue of section 214(1)(b) of the Act	The authority or authorities exercising the functions specified in paragraph 1 of Schedule 26 of the Act in relation to the cemeteries and crematoria of the board or committee, or where such authority is a parish meeting the parish trustees of the parish
. . .	

LOCAL AUTHORITIES (WALES) (PROPERTY ETC) ORDER 1973

(SI 1973/1863)

4 Interpretation

(2) In this order—

'the Act' means the Local Government Act 1972;

'buildings', except in article 22, means buildings not within the meaning of the term 'land';

'corporate land' means corporate land within the meaning of the Local Government Act 1933;

'historic and ceremonial property' does not include any property held (or under article 19, 20, 22 or 38 deemed to be held) for the purposes of any statutory functions;

'land' includes land covered by water and any interest or right in, to or over land;

. . .

5 Other express provision

[*The wording is the same as that of art 5 of Local Authority (England) (Property etc) Order 1973 (above).*]

7 Particular matters

(1) Any property described in column (2) of Schedule 1 (or of any extension thereof effected by any further order under section 254 of the Act made before 1st April 1974) of an authority named in column (1) shall by virtue of this order be transferred to and vest in the authority specified in respect of such property in column (3).

. . .

9 Transfer of specified classes of property, etc

(1) Nothing in this article applies to—

(a) any property held as sole trustee, exclusively for charitable purposes, by an existing local authority (being property transferred by section 210 of the Act);

(b) any property vested in the council of an existing county or county borough which is required to be applied in accordance with a scheme under section 19 of the Welsh Church Act 1914 (being property which is vested in the council of a new county by section 211 of the Act);

(c) any other property held for the purposes of any charitable trust;

. . .

(e) any property vested in a county council by virtue of section 226 of the Highways Act 1959;

(f) any matter provided for in article . . . 7 . . . ;

(g) any matter provided for in article 11(1) in so far it applies to rights ensured by article 23 in its application to any property transferred by article . . . 7 . . . ;

(h) any matter provided for in article 11(2) or (3) in their application to any matter provided for in articles 7 . . . ;

(i) any matter provided for in article 18 in its application to any matter described in the preceding items of this paragraph.

(2) Nothing in paragraphs (4) to (6) of this article applies to matters provided for in paragraphs (2) to (4) of article 18 in their application to any matters provided for in

paragraph (3) of this article, and nothing in paragraphs (5) and (6) of this article applies to any matters provided for in paragraphs (3) and (4) of article 18 in their application to any liabilities provided for in paragraph (4) of this article.

(3) All property vested in an authority described in column (2) of the table in Schedule 2 . . . and within any description of matters specified in respect of such authority in column (3) shall by virtue of this order be transferred to and vest in the authority specified in respect of such description of matters in column (4).

(4) All liabilities attaching to an authority described in the said column (2) and within any description of matters specified in respect of such authority in column (3) shall by virtue of this order be transferred to and attach to the authority specified in respect of such description of matters in column (4).

. . .

(7) Save in so far as express provision is made in item No 10 of the table in Schedule 2, this article does not extend to the historic and ceremonial property other than land and buildings, and in particular to the charters, insignia and plate, of any area.

10 Provision supplementary to article 9
[The wording is identical to that of art 10 of SI 1973/1861 above.]

11 Fittings, furniture, equipment and stores
(1) Where by paragraph (1) of article 23 any right to the use of any accommodation is ensured for any authority other than the authority in whom the accommodation is vested on and after 1st April 1974, the fittings, furniture, equipment and stores in such accommodation which have been provided exclusively for the purposes of the functions first described in the said paragraph shall, except in so far as the first-mentioned authority shall otherwise agree, by virtue of this order be transferred to and vest in such authority.

(2)–(4) *[The wording of these paragraphs is identical to that of art 11(2)–(4) of SI 1973/1861 above.]*

16 Residual transfer of property, etc
(1) Paragraph (1) of article 9 applies to this article as it applies to article 9.

(2) Subject to the provisions of articles 9 to 15 or of articles 11(2) and (3) and 18 in their application to any matters provided for in articles 9 to 15—

  (a) all property and liabilities vested in or attaching to an authority described in column (1) of Part . . . II of Schedule 4 (or of any extension thereof effected by any further order under section 254 of the Act made before 1st April 1974) shall by virtue of this order be transferred to and vest in or attach to the authority specified in respect of such authority in column (2);

  (b) all contracts, deeds, bonds, agreements and other instruments subsisting in favour of, or against, and all notices in force which were given (or have effect as if they had been given) by, or to, an authority described in column (1) of Part . . . II of Schedule 4 (or of any extension thereof as aforesaid) shall be of full force and effect in favour of, or against, the authority specified in respect of such authority in column (2);

  (c) any action or proceeding or any cause of action or proceeding, pending or existing at 1st April 1974, by, or against, an authority described in column (1) of Part . . . II of Schedule 4 (or of any extension thereof as aforesaid) shall not be prejudicially affected by reason of the Act . . . and may be continued, prosecuted, and enforced by, or against, the authority specified in respect of such authority in column (2); and

  (d) any power to appoint any person to any body belonging to an authority described in column (1) of Part I or II of Schedule 4 (or of any extension thereof as aforesaid) in respect of any matter provided for in (a) or (b) shall be transferred to the authority specified in respect of such authority in column (2).

17 General saving for agreements

(1)   The authority to whom any account or fund is transferred, or any amount of any fund is payable, by virtue of any provision of this order, may agree that any particular amount in the account or fund shall be payable to any other authority.

(2)   The authority to whom any other property other than land is transferred by the preceding articles of this order other than article 7 may by resolution agree that the property shall be transferred to any other authority specified in the resolution, and paragraphs (2) to (5) of article 18 shall apply accordingly.

(3)   The transferee authority in respect of any matter other than property, provided for in paragraph (4), (5) or (6) of article 9 or in (a), (b) or (c) of paragraph (2) of article 16, and any other authority, may agree that that other authority shall be substituted for the transferee authority in the application of any such provision.

(4)   The provision made by the preceding articles of this order, other than articles 12, 14, 15 and 16A or by any provision of any order by which this article is applied for the transfer of any matter is without prejudice to any agreement which may be made for payment in respect of such matter.

18 Liabilities, contracts etc, notices and proceedings in respect of transferred property, etc

(1)–(4)   [*The wording of these paragraphs is identical to art 18(1)–(4) of SI 1973/1861 above.*]

(5)   Any power to appoint any person to any body belonging to the authority first mentioned in paragraph (2) in respect of any property (other than that described in (a) of article 9(1)) to which this article applies or any matter provided for in paragraphs (2) and (3) shall be transferred to the authority to whom such property or matter is transferred.

  . . .

23 User rights

(1)   Where, immediately before 1st April 1974, accommodation in any property transferred to and vested in any authority by virtue of this order is used (or in the case of accommodation not yet in occupation proposed to be used) otherwise than temporarily for the purposes of any functions which, on and after that date, are not exercisable (or not exercisable as regards any part of the area served from the accommodation) by the authority to whom the property is transferred, the authority exercising those functions in the area served by the accommodation or, as the case may be, the part thereof shall be entitled to the use of such accommodation, whether for the purposes of such functions or for the purposes of any other functions exercisable by them.

   In the preceding sub-paragraph the reference to the authority exercising those functions extends to an authority established by the National Health Service Reorganisation Act 1973 exercising such functions.

(2)   Where—
  (a)   any property is immediately before 1st April 1974 used (or in the case of property not yet in use proposed to be used) otherwise than temporarily for the purposes of functions exercisable by one authority in relation to any area;
  (b)   the functions become exercisable on and after that day by two or more authorities; and
  (c)   the property is by virtue of this order transferred to and vested in one of the authorities described in (b),

any other of the authorities described in (b) shall be entitled to the use of such property, whether for the purposes of such functions or for the purposes of any other functions exercisable by them.

(3) Where—

> (a) any property to which paragraph (2) does not apply is immediately before 1st April 1974 held by the council of a county, county borough or county district under section 125 of the Local Government Act 1933; and
>
> (b) the property is by virtue of this order transferred to and vested in the council of any relevant area,

the council of any other relevant area shall be entitled to the use of the property.

In this paragraph, 'relevant areas' means—

> in relation to a county, new counties;
>
> in relation to a county borough or county district, new counties and districts,

being areas in which the area of the county, county borough or county district is comprised.

(4) Where—

> (a) any property is immediately before 1st April 1974 used (or in the case of property not yet in use proposed to be used) otherwise than temporarily for the purposes of functions exercisable by two or more authorities;
>
> (b) the property is by virtue of this order transferred to and vested in one authority;

any other authority exercising any of the functions described in (a) shall be entitled to the use of such property whether for the purposes of such functions or for the purposes of other functions exercisable by them.

In the preceding sub-paragraph the reference to any other authority exercising any of the functions described in (a) extends to an authority established by the National Health Service Reorganisation Act 1973 exercising the functions so described.

(4A) Any community council established under section 27(3) or (4) of the Act in the area of any borough or urban district shall be entitled, for the proper discharge of their functions, to the use of accommodation in property which immediately before 1st April 1974 is held by the council of the borough or urban district under section 125 of the Local Government Act 1933.

(5) Any question

> (a) whether any accommodation in any property to which paragraph (1) applies is used (or proposed to be used) for the purposes described in that paragraph;
>
> (b) whether any property to which paragraph (2) applies is used (or proposed to be used) as described in (a) thereof;
>
> (c) whether any property to which paragraph (4) applies is used (or proposed to be used) as described in (a) thereof; or
>
> (d) without prejudice to (c), whether any use (or proposed use) is temporary,

shall, subject to the following provision of this paragraph, be determined by the authority in whom the property is, before 1st April 1974, vested.

[*Spent*]

(6) The use of any accommodation or property by virtue of this article shall be for such period and on such terms as may be determined by agreement between the authority entitled under this article to use the accommodation or property and the authority to whom the property is transferred or failing such agreement by the decision of a person agreed on by such authorities or in default of agreement appointed by the Secretary of State.

(7) In this article 'exercisable' means exercisable otherwise than by virtue of section 101, 110 or 187(2) or (3) of the Act.

(8) An authority shall not sell, exchange, lease or otherwise dispose of property in respect of which user rights are ensured by this article, or develop the land on which

such property is situated, unless they have consulted all authorities entitled to such user rights and made such arrangements as may be determined by agreement between the authorities concerned or failing such agreement by the decision of a person agreed on by such authorities or in default of agreement appointed by the Secretary of State.

24 Charter trustees
[*The wording of this article is identical to that of art 24 of SI 1973/1861 above.*]

27 Property and liabilities to attach to whole areas
(1) Subject to paragraph (2), any interest in any property or any liability transferred by the preceding articles of this order or by any provision of any order by which this article is applied to the authority for any county, district or community shall be held or discharged by them in respect of the whole of such area.

(2) Paragraph (1)—
    (a)   shall not apply in respect of any interest in any property or any liability which by reason of agreements made by authorities abolished by the Act falls to be held or discharged in respect of any specific area; and
    (b)   shall have effect subject to the provision of subsections (4) and (5) of section 248 of the Act (freemen and inhabitants of existing boroughs).

28 Byelaws, etc
[*The wording of this article is identical to that of art 19 of SI 1973/1861 above.*]

31 Loan sanctions
Any authorisation of the borrowing of money in force in respect of any property or liability described in (a), (b) or (e) of article 9(1) or transferred by the preceding articles of this order or by any provision of any order by which this article is applied to the council of any county, district or community may, subject to the terms applicable thereto, be acted on by such council.

32 Security for loans
[*The wording is of this article is identical to that of art 33 of SI 1973/1861 above.*]

33 Capital and renewal and repairs funds
[*The wording is of this article is identical to that of art 34 of SI 1973/1861 above.*]

SCHEDULE 1

TRANSFER OF PARTICULAR PROPERTIES

Paragraph (3) of article 10, and paragraph (6) in so far as it applies thereto, shall apply to any question whether any property is historic or ceremonial property.

(1) Transferor authority	(2) Property	(3) Transferee authority
The corporation of any borough for the whole of the area of which charter trustees are constituted	Historical and ceremonial property other than land buildings, and in particular the charters, insignia and plate, of the borough	The charter trustees
. . .		

SCHEDULE 2
TRANSFER OF SPECIFIED CLASSES OF PROPERTY, ETC

1

In the following table—

(a) 'county matters' and 'district matters', in relation to any transferor authority, mean—

    (i) in the case of property, property (not being excepted property) held for the purposes of functions not exercisable on and after 1st April 1974 by an authority of the relevant class in relation to the transferor authority but so exercisable by the authority specified in respect of the matters transferred in column (4) of the table in this Schedule;

    (ii) in the case of liabilities, liabilities incurred in relation to such functions;

    (iii) in the case of contracts, deeds, bonds, agreements and other instruments, and notices, such instruments subsisting and notices given in relation to such functions;

    (iv) in the case of actions and proceedings and causes of action or proceeding, such actions and proceedings pending or causes existing in relation to such functions;

but if specified as such matters in relation to any area include only such matters being local matters in respect of such area;

(b) 'community matters', in relation to any transferor authority, means—

    (i) in the case of property—

        (a) property held for the purposes of functions not exercisable on and after 1st April 1974 by county or district councils; and

        (b) parish property within the meaning of the Local Government Act 1933, the proceeds of sale of such property and any securities in which such proceeds have been invested;

    (ii) in the case of liabilities, liabilities incurred in relation to such functions or parish property;

    (iii) in the case of contracts, deeds, bonds, agreements and other instruments, and notices, such instruments subsisting and notices given in relation to such functions or parish property;

    (iv) in the case of actions and proceedings and causes of action or proceeding, such actions and proceedings pending or causes existing in relation to such functions or parish property;

but if specified as such matters in relation to any area includes only such matters being local matters in respect of such area . . . ;

(d) 'local matters', in relation to any area, means—

    (i) in the case of property—

        (a) subject to the provision of paragraph 3, sited property situated in; and

        (b) other property held exclusively in respect of,

    the area;

    (ii) in the case of liabilities, liabilities incurred exclusively in respect of the area;

    (iii) in the case of contracts, deeds, bonds, agreements and other instruments, and notices, such instruments subsisting and notices given exclusively in respect of the area;

885

(iv)   in the case of actions and proceedings and causes of action or proceeding, such actions and proceedings pending or causes existing exclusively in respect of the area.

2

In paragraph 1, 'excepted property' means any property within article 20(1) which is not covered by the provision of article 20(2) and 'exercisable' means exercisable otherwise than by virtue of section 101 or 110 of the Act.

3

(a)   In this Schedule 'sited property' means—
(i)   land;
(ii)   buildings;

. . .

(iv)   subject to the provision of article 6, lamps, lamp posts and other apparatus for public lighting.

(b)   The transferor authority may determine that any sited property shall, by reason of the fact that it is used wholly or mainly for an area other than the one in which it is situated, constitute local matters in respect of such other area.

(c)   If notice is given by any authority concerned that they are dissatisfied with any determination under sub-paragraph (b) or that a determination should have been made thereunder, the question of the area which is to be the relevant area in relation to any sited property in the application of this Schedule shall be determined by agreement between the authorities concerned or failing such agreement by the decision of a person agreed on by such authorities or in default of agreement appointed by the Secretary of State.

4

Article 12 has effect, within the meaning of items 2, 7, 8, 9, 11 and 12 in the table in this Schedule, in relation to any property, where before 1st April 1974, in respect of such property—

an agreement has been entered into under paragraph (3), (4) or (5) of that article;

a determination has been given under paragraph (7) of that article;

notice has been given under paragraph (3) of article 38

and in relation to any liabilities incurred, contracts, deeds, bonds, agreements and other instruments subsisting, notices given, actions and proceedings pending and causes of action or proceeding existing in relation to such property.

(2) Transferor authority	(3) Matters transferred	(4) Transferee authority
The corporation or council of any non-county borough or the council of any urban district not included in items 7, 8 and 9	County matters Where a community council is established for the area of the borough or urban district under section 27(3) or (4) of the Act community matters and the historic and ceremonial property, and in particular the charters, insignia and plate, of the borough or district	The community council

SCHEDULE 4
RESIDUAL TRANSFER OF PROPERTY, ETC
PART II

(1) Transferor authority	(2) Transferee authority
. . .	
Any separate parish council	The community council which replaces the parish council
In any group of parishes, the common parish council and the parish meeting and representative body of every parish in the group	The community council which replaces the parish council
The parish meeting and representative body of any parish not included in the last preceding item	The council of the district in which the area of the parish is comprised
Any burial board, joint burial board or joint committee which ceases to exist by virtue of section 214(1) of the Act	The authority or authorities exercising the functions specified in paragraph 1 of Schedule 26 to the Act in relation to the cemeteries and crematoria of the board or committee
Any joint board which ceases to exist by virtue of section 263(2)(b) of the Act	The authority in whom the functions of the board are vested by section 263(2)(a) of the Act
Any joint board which ceases to exist by virtue of section 263(3) of the Act	The local authority which becomes the port health authority for the district of the board under the said section 263(3)
. . .	

CHARTER TRUSTEES ORDER 1974

(SI 1974/176)

2 Application

This order shall not apply to the area consisting of the counties established by section 20 of the Act (new local government areas in Wales)

3 Interpretation

(2) In this order—

'the Act' means the Local Government Act 1972;

'city or town' means an area for which charter trustees act under section 246(4) to (8) of the Act;

'the district council', in relation to any city or town, means the council of the district in which the city or town is comprised; and

references to a city or town mayor or a deputy city or town mayor shall be construed, where no city or town mayor or deputy city or town mayor is elected, as references to a chairman or vice-chairman.

4 Appointment of local government electors as trustees

(1) The provisions of this article shall have effect where a local government elector, or two local government electors, for a city or town fall to be appointed by the district council as charter trustees under section 246(4)(a) of the Act.

(2) One local government elector, or two local government electors, as the case may be, shall be appointed . . . at the annual meeting of the district council in . . . 1979 and every fourth year thereafter.

(3) Any local government elector appointed as charter trustee for a city or town shall (subject to the provisions of the Act and this order) hold office until the time fixed for the meeting of the next annual meeting of the district council at which under paragraph (2) above appointments fall to be made.

(4) Where the number of district councillors for the wards wholly or partly comprising the city or town is increased to two, such one of the local government electors appointed as aforesaid as may be determined by the district council shall forthwith cease to hold office as a charter trustee.

(5) Where the number of district councillors for the said wards is increased to three or more, any local government elector appointed as aforesaid shall forthwith cease to hold office as a charter trustee.

(6) Sections 80(1)(b), (c), (d) and (e), 80(5), 81(1) and (2) and 92 of the Act shall apply to a local government elector being appointed, or holding office as, a charter trustee as they apply to a person being elected to, or being a member of, a local authority subject to any necessary modifications and in particular to the modification that for section 80(1)(e) there shall be substituted—

'(e) is disqualified for being a member of the council of the district in which the city or town is comprised under Part III of the Representation of the People Act 1949 or for being a charter trustee under Part VIII below.'.

(7) A local government elector appointed as a charter trustee may at any time resign his office by written notice delivered to the proper officer of the district council and his resignation shall take effect upon receipt of the notice by the proper officer.

(8) The district council may remove from office a local government elector appointed as a charter trustee under this article if, in their opinion, he has, without sufficient cause, failed to attend two or more consecutive meetings of the charter trustees.

(9) A casual vacancy in the office of charter trustee shall arise at any time when—

(a)   a local government elector appointed as a charter trustee ceases to be a local government elector for the city or town, becomes disqualified, resigns, is removed by the district council under paragraph (8) above or dies; or

(b)   under electoral arrangements for the time being in force, the number of district councillors for the wards wholly or partly comprising the city or town is reduced to two or one, as the case may be.

(10)   When any such casual vacancy as aforesaid arises, the district council shall, as soon as practicable, appoint a local government elector for the city or town to fill the vacancy.

(11)   A local government elector appointed under paragraph (10) above shall (subject to the provisions of the Act and this order) hold office until the time specified in paragraph (3) above and he shall then retire.

(12)   Where there are so many vacancies in the office of district councillor for the wards wholly or partly comprising a city or town that the charter trustees for the city or town are unable to act, the district council may appoint local government electors for the city or town to fill all or any of the vacancies until other district councillors for these wards are elected and take up office.

(13)   The acts and proceedings of any person appointed and acting as charter trustee shall, notwithstanding his disqualification or want of qualification, be as valid and effectual as if he had been qualified.

(14)   If the register of local government electors is not so framed as to show the local government electors for the city or town, the registration officer shall make such alteration thereof as may be proper for that purpose.

5 Meetings of charter trustees

(1)   Charter trustees for any city or town shall in every year hold an annual meeting.
    . . . The annual meeting   . . . shall be held within the 21 days following the annual meeting of the district council . . . .

(2)   The election of a city or town mayor and a deputy city or town mayor shall be the first business transacted at the annual meeting of the charter trustees for any city or town.

    . . .

(4)   . . . meetings of charter trustees may be held as they may determine.

(5)   Charter trustees shall be bodies to which the Public Bodies (Admission to Meetings) Act 1960 applies.

(6)   Paragraph 10 of Schedule 12 to the Act shall apply in relation to meetings of charter trustees as it applies in relation to meetings of parish councils.

(7)   No business shall be transacted at a meeting of charter trustees unless at least one-third of the whole number of trustees are present at the meeting: but in no case shall the quorum be less than two.

(8)   At a meeting of charter trustees the city or town mayor, if present, shall preside.

(9)   If the city or town mayor is absent from a meeting of charter trustees the deputy city or town mayor, if present, shall preside.

(10)   If both the city or town mayor and deputy city or town mayor are absent from a meeting of charter trustees, such trustee as the trustees present shall choose shall preside.

(11)   Paragraphs 39 to 44 of Schedule 12 to the Act shall apply to charter trustees as they apply to parish councils.

6 Mayor and deputy mayor

(1)   A city or town mayor or a deputy city or town mayor shall (unless he ceases to be a charter trustee) hold office until immediately after the election of a city or town mayor at the next annual meeting.

(2)   On a casual vacancy occurring in the office of city or town mayor or deputy city or town mayor the charter trustees shall, as soon as practicable, meet for the election of one of their number to such office and any trustee so elected shall (subject to the provisions of the Act or this order) hold office until the time specified in paragraph (1) above and shall then retire.

7 Disability for voting on account of interests in contracts, etc

Sections 94 to 98 of the Act shall apply to charter trustees as they apply to parish councillors, subject to any necessary modifications and in particular to the modification that in section 94(5)(a), for 'chairman, vice-chairman or deputy chairman of a principal council' there shall be substituted 'city or town mayor or deputy city or town mayor'.

8 Acquisition of property

Charter trustees for any city or town may acquire, or accept gifts of, and hold historic or ceremonial property other than land and buildings, and in particular charters, insignia and plate, of the city or town, and may execute any work (including works of maintenance or improvement) incidental to or consequential on the acquisition, acceptance or holding.

9 Arrangements for discharge of functions

(1)   Charter trustees may arrange for the discharge of any of their functions other than—

> the appointment of a city or town mayor or a deputy city or town mayor or of any local officers of dignity; and
> functions with respect to issuing a precept for a rate or borrowing money

by a committee thereof or by an officer of theirs or of the district council.

(2)   Where by virtue of paragraph (1) above any functions of charter trustees may be discharged by a committee thereof, unless the charter trustees otherwise direct, the committee may arrange for the discharge of any of those functions by an officer of the charter trustees or of the district council.

(3)   Any arrangements made by charter trustees or a committee under paragraph (1) or (2) above for the discharge of functions by a committee or officer shall not prevent the trustees or committee from exercising those functions.

(4)   Section 106 of the Act shall apply as respects any committee appointed by charter trustees as it applies as respects a committee of a local authority.

10 Subsidiary powers in relation to functions

Sections 111 and 140 of the Act shall apply in relation to charter trustees as they apply to parish councils.

11 Officers

(1)   Charter trustees may appoint such officers as they think necessary for the proper discharge of their functions.

(2)   Sections 112(2) and (5) and 114 to 119 of the Act shall apply in relation to officers appointed by charter trustees as they apply in relation to officers appointed by parish councils, subject to any necessary modifications.

12 Use of schoolroom etc in city or town

Section 134 of the Act shall apply to charter trustees as it applies to parish councils subject to any necessary modifications.

LOCAL AUTHORITIES ETC (WALES) (PROPERTY ETC: FURTHER PROVISION) ORDER 1974

(SI 1974/404)

1 Citation and commencement

. . .

(2)   The principal order and this order may be cited together as the Local Authorities etc (Wales) (Property etc) Orders 1973 and 1974.

. . .

2 Interpretation

. . .

(2)   In this order—

'the Act' means the Local Government Act 1972;

'the principal order' means the Local Authorities (Wales) (Property etc) Order 1973;

. . .

3 Other express provision

This order shall have effect subject to the express provision of—

(a)   any other order (other than the principal order) made (whether before or after this order) under section 254 of the Act;

(b)   any regulations made under section 7 or 8 of the Superannuation Act 1972; or

(c)   section 16, 25 or 54(2) of the National Health Service Reorganisation Act 1973 or any order made under those sections.

6 Easements and rights over land

(1)   Where parts of any land are in consequence of the principal order vested in two different authorities, and any easement or other right over one part is required to enable the other part to be used, the authority in whom the said other part is vested may serve notice on the authority in whom the said one part is vested specifying such easement or other right and requiring the authority in whom the said one part is vested to grant the same to them on terms specified in the notice.

(2)   Any question—

(a)   whether any easement or other right is required to enable the said other part to be used; or

(b)   as to the terms on which any easement or other right shall be conferred,

shall be determined by the decision of a person agreed on by the authorities concerned or in default of agreement appointed by the Secretary of State.

(3)   Paragraphs (4) and (5) of article 38 of the principal order (which make provision in relation to the decision of questions) shall apply as if the provision of this article were contained in the principal order.

7 Sale, etc, and development of land

(1)   This article shall cease to have effect on 1st April 1979 except that a certificate given under paragraph (4)(d) or (e) shall continue to have effect as a document of title.

. . .

(4)

(a)   This paragraph applies where an authority to whom this article applies are proposing—

to sell or to exchange,

to lease, or otherwise to dispose of, for a term exceeding 21 years, land transferred to them by any provision of the principal order other than land transferred by article 7 thereof.

(b) Save as provided in sub-paragraph (e), the authority shall give notice of their proposal to the other relevant authorities.

(c) Any notice required by sub-paragraph (b) shall—

be given by recorded delivery;

indicate the purpose for which the land was held immediately before 1st April 1974;

indicate whether the land is registered;

if it is registered, indicate the title number;

if it is not registered, indicate the name and address of the purchaser, lessee or other disponee or of such persons as have been nominated by him or, if that is the case, that the proposal is to sell the land by auction or tender.

(d) At the expiration of 30 days from the giving of the notice under sub-paragraph (b) the authority first mentioned in that sub-paragraph shall give to the purchaser, lessee or other disponee, or to such persons as have been nominated by him, a certificate that they gave the notice and where the land is not registered, if that is the case, that no notices under sub-paragraph (f)(ii) were received by them within the period there specified.

(e) Sub-paragraphs (b), (c) and (d)—

(i) shall not apply where an authority have on an earlier proposal to sell, exchange, lease or otherwise dispose of the land in question taken action under sub-paragraph (b) and no relevant authority or other water or area health authority have lodged a caution with the Chief Land Registrar in respect of the land or given notice by recorded delivery to the first-mentioned authority that they dispute the transfer to such authority;

. . .

(iii) shall not apply where notice has been given by an authority under paragraph (7) in respect of the land in question, and no relevant authority or other water or area health authority have given such notice as is described in (i),

but on any proposed sale, exchange, lease or other disposition in relation to which, apart from this sub-paragraph, the said sub-paragraphs would have applied such a certificate as is described in sub-paragraph (*d*) shall be given to the purchaser, lessee or other disponee, or to such persons as have been nominated by him.

. . .

LOCAL AUTHORITIES ETC (ENGLAND) (PROPERTY ETC: FURTHER PROVISION) ORDER 1974

(SI 1974/406)

1 Citation and commencement

. . .

(2) The principal order and this order may be cited together as the Local Authorities etc (England) (Property etc) Orders 1973 and 1974.

. . .

2 Interpretation

. . .

(2)   In this order—

'the Act' means the Local Government Act 1972;

'the principal order' means the Local Authorities (England) (Property etc) Order 1973;

. . .

3 Other express provision

This order shall have effect subject to the express provision of—

(a)   any other order (other than the principal order) made (whether before or after this order) under section 254 of the Act;

(b)   any regulations made under section 7 or 8 of the Superannuation Act 1972, or,

(c)   section 16, 25 or 54(2) of the National Health Service Reorganisation Act 1973 or any order made under those sections.

8 Easements and rights over land

(1)   Where parts of any land are in consequence of the principal order vested in two different authorities, and any easement or other right over one part is required to enable the other part to be used, the authority in whom the said other part is vested may serve notice on the authority in whom the said one part is vested specifying such easement or other right and requiring the authority in whom the said one part is vested to grant the same to them on terms specified in the notice.

(2)   Any question—

(a)   whether any easement or other right is required to enable the said other part to be used; or

(b)   as to the terms on which any easement or other right shall be conferred,

shall be determined by the decision of a person agreed on by the authorities concerned or in default of agreement appointed by the Secretary of State.

(3)   Paragraphs (4) and (5) of article 39 of the principal order (which make provision in relation to the decision of questions) shall apply as if the provision of this article were contained in the principal order.

9 Sale, etc, and development of land

(1)   This article shall cease to have effect on 1st April 1979 except that a certificate given under paragraph (4)(d) or (e) shall continue to have effect as a document of title.

. . .

(4)   [*The relevant words of this paragraph are identical with those of paragraph (4) of art 7 of SI 1974/404 (above).*]

LOCAL AUTHORITIES ETC (MISCELLANEOUS PROVISION) ORDER 1974

(SI 1974/482)

5 Reference to repealed enactments in local Acts, etc

Where by or under the Act—

(a)   a provision of an enactment or instrument has been repealed or revoked in respect of any area; and

(b)   a corresponding provision has been applied to that area or to any part thereof, any reference in any local Act or in any instrument made under any Act to the provision mentioned in (a) shall, in the application of such Act or instrument to the area or such part, as the case may be, unless the contrary intention appears, be construed as a reference to the provision mentioned in (b).

In this article, 'local Act' includes an Act confirming a provisional order.

6 Enforcement, and amendment, etc of instruments notwithstanding repeal of enactments, etc

(1)   Any provision of any enactment which imposes fines on persons offending against any instrument which by virtue of paragraph (a) of section 262(1) of the Act or this order or any other order made under section 254 or 262 of the Act applies to any area, things or persons shall continue to have effect in relation to offences against the instrument notwithstanding the repeal (whether by the Act or by such an order) of the enactment.

(2)   Any instrument constituting local statutory provision within the meaning of section 270(1) of the Act (not being byelaws in relation to which article 29(1) of the Local Authorities (England) (Property etc) Order 1973 or article 28(1) of the Local Authorities (Wales) (Property etc) Order 1973 makes provision) which by virtue of paragraph (a) of section 262(1) of the Act or an order made under section 254 or 262 of the Act applies, notwithstanding the changes of administrative areas and local authorities effected by or under the Act and notwithstanding the repeal of the enactment under which it was made, to any area, things or persons may be amended or revoked—

(a)   in the case of an instrument made by a Minister, by any appropriate Minister;

(b)   in the case of byelaws for good rule and government and the prevention and suppression of nuisances, as regards any area within a district, by the council of the district;

(c)   in any other case, as respects any county council, district council or community council substituted in references by section 262(3), (4) or (5) or an order made under section 262(6) of the Act, by the county council, district council or community council, as the case may be.

Section 236(3) to (10) of the Act shall apply to byelaws for such amendment or revocation, and the Secretary of State or any appropriate Minister shall be the confirming authority for the purposes of such subsections.

. . .

7 Protective provision, and requirements for consent, in local Acts, orders, etc

(1)   Any protective provision in any local Act or in any order made under or confirmed by any Act for the benefit of an authority abolished by section 1(10) or 20(6) of the Act or their predecessors shall enure—

(a)   if the protection relates to a highway, for the benefit of the highway authority for the highway;

(b)   if the protection relates to any other matter transferred by or under the Act to any authority, for the benefit of that authority;

(c)   in any other case, for the benefit of the council of the district in which the matter to which the protection relates is situated,

and shall be construed as if a reference to the authority specified in (a), (b) or (c) were substituted for any reference to the authority named in the protective provision.

(2)   Any provision in any local Act or in any order made under or confirmed by any Act which requires the consent (whether it empowers the requirement of conditions or otherwise) of an authority abolished by section 1(10) or 20(6) of the Act or their predecessors shall have effect as if it had required the consent of (and in that event empowered the requirement of conditions by) the following authority, namely—

(a)   where the matter in respect of which the consent is required is a highway, the highway authority for the highway;

(b)   where the matter in respect of which the consent is required is any other matter transferred by or under the Act to any authority, that authority;

(c)   in any other case, the council of the district in which the matter in respect of which the consent is required is situated.

(3)   Paragraphs (1) and (2) shall not apply to any provision in any local Act or in any order made under or confirmed by any Act in respect of which provision is made under section 254, as extended by section 262(8), or under section 262(8), of the Act.

8 References to specified officers in local statutory provisions

(1)   Subject to paragraphs (2) and (3), in any local statutory provision (within the meaning of section 270(1) of the Act) which remains in force after 1st April 1974 in any area—

. . .

(c)   any reference to a specified officer of a rural parish which so ceases to exist shall be construed as a reference to the proper officer of the council of the parish or community in which the area is comprised.

(2)   The council of the . . . parish or community in which any area is comprised may, with the agreement of any other local authority, by resolution provide that that authority shall be substituted for such council in item . . . (c), as the case may be, of paragraph (1).

15 Places of burial

(1)   In paragraphs (2) to (4) 'burial ground' means a burial ground maintained under the Burial Acts 1852 to 1906.

(2)

(a)   In relation to a burial ground or crematorium maintained immediately before 1st April 1974 by the parish council of Birtley, Blagdon, Brafield-on-the Green, Burrington, Great Houghton, Harworth, Milton Malsor, Rothersthorpe, Shifnal or Sopley, the functions conferred by section 214 of and Schedule 26 to the Act shall be exercised by the parish councils of the parishes, or where there is no parish the council of the district, in which parts of the area of the parish are comprised.

(b)   Where by virtue of sub-paragraph (a) the functions therein described become exercisable by two or more councils, then, unless a joint board is established under section 6 of the Public Health Act 1936 to exercise those functions, it shall be the duty of the said councils to make arrangements under Part VI of the Act for the discharge of those functions by a joint committee of those councils, and paragraph 4 of Schedule 26 to the Act shall apply to any such arrangements as they apply to arrangements made in pursuance of paragraph 2 of such Schedule.

(3)   . . .

(4)

(a)   Any burial ground transferred by the Local Authorities (England) (Property etc) Order 1973 or the Local Authorities (Wales) (Property etc) Order 1973 to any authority shall be held by them as a cemetery within the meaning of section 214 of the Act.

(b)   Any other burial ground maintained by the parish council or parish meeting of a parish in England shall be held by them as such a cemetery.

(5)   Nothing in the Act, in the orders referred to in paragraph (4) or in this order shall affect any right of burial or of constructing a place of burial which any person may have acquired prior to 1st April 1974 or prejudicially affect the amount of any fee, payment or sum in respect of interment in, or the right of erecting or placing any

monument, gravestone, tablet or monumental inscription on, any grave or place of burial in respect of which any such right has been so acquired.

16 Maintenance of closed churchyards

Where, outside the area in which the Church of England was disestablished by the Welsh Church Act 1914 the functions and liabilities of the parochial church council of a parish with respect to the maintenance and repair of a churchyard have under section 269(2) of the Local Government Act 1933 before 1st April 1974 been transferred to the council of the borough or urban district, or to the parish council, the authority on whom a request under section 215(2) of the Act would fall to be served shall maintain the churchyard by keeping it in decent order and its walls and fences in good repair.

17 Franchise and prescriptive rights

(1) This article applies to the following matters, namely—
- (a) any powers to appoint local officers other than—
  - (i) local officers of dignity within the meaning of section 246 of the Act; and
  - (ii) mayors and deputy mayors;
- (b) any powers to hold courts other than courts abolished by section 221 of the Act;
- (c) any powers to maintain markets;
- (d) any powers to hold fairs;
- (e) any other powers to maintain any undertakings or events;
- (f) any rights to take tolls; and
- (g) any other rights or liabilities,

exercisable by or attaching to the corporation or council of a city or borough (including a borough included in a rural district) or the council of an urban or rural district immediately before 1st April 1974 under any franchise or by virtue of prescription.

(2) Subject to paragraph (3) and to the provisions of any other order made under section 254 of the Act, any such matter shall be exercisable by or attach to—
- (a) in the case of a borough included in a rural district, the parish council of the parish replacing the borough:
- (b) in the case of any other area wholly comprised in a district, the council of the district; and
- (c) in the case of any other area, the council of the district specified in respect of the area in column (2) of Part I or II of Schedule 4 (Residual transfer of Property etc) to the Local Authorities (England) (Property etc) Order 1973 or the Local Authorities (Wales) (Property etc) Order 1973.

(3) The power to maintain the Richmond market shall be exercisable by the Parish Council of Richmond.

(4) Any council to whom any matter is transferred by paragraph (2) or (3) shall have the same powers in relation thereto as were exercisable immediately before 1st April 1974 by the corporation or council from whom the matter is transferred.

18 Honorary freedoms

(1) [*This article provides that honorary freedoms existing before 1 April 1974 not to be affected by the Act, subject to special arrangements at Whitley Bay and the former Teesside.*]

27 Security for loans

Where under any agreement made under section 68 of the Act as applied by section 254(6) thereof any liability or part of a liability charged indifferently on all the revenues of a public body or on any particular revenues or fund of such body is transferred to another public body, the liability or part of the liability shall be charged indifferently on all the revenues of the public body to whom it is transferred and shall cease to be a charge on any revenues or fund of the public body from whom it is transferred.

LOCAL AUTHORITY (STOCKS AND BONDS) REGULATIONS 1974

(SI 1974/519)

[*These regulations were printed in previous editions of this work (except the 7th edn) but it seems that local councils have never, between 1974 and 2013, sought to issue stocks or bonds, and they are accordingly omitted here. They deal with the issue of stocks and bonds, the conversion of other securities, registration and certificates, transfers and transmission, trustees, payment of interest and redemption, rectification of the register and receivership. It remains open to a local council to operate these regulations.*]

LOCAL AUTHORITIES ETC (MISCELLANEOUS PROVISION) (NO 2) ORDER 1974

(SI 1974/595)

2 Interpretation

. . .

(2) In this order—
'the Act' means the Local Government Act 1972; and
'Wales' means the area consisting of the counties established by section 20 of the Act (new local government areas in Wales), and 'England' does not include any area included in any of those counties.

. . .

3 Miscellaneous amendments of public general and other Acts

. . .

(19) In the Act, paragraph 6(2)(b) and (4) of Schedule 29 (provision for the construction of references to parishes and rural parishes) shall apply to the areas constituting parishes by virtue of article 3(2) of the New Parishes Order 1973 and article 3 of the New Parishes (Amendment) Order 1973 as they apply to the areas mentioned in paragraph 3 of Part IV of Schedule 1 to the Act.

. . .

14 Confederation of the Cinque Ports
The district council, town council or charter trustees for any area being a port, antient town or corporate limb of the Confederation of the Cinque Ports shall exercise the functions in relation to such Confederation which were immediately before 1st April 1974 exercised by the corporation for such area.

In this article 'town council' means the council of a parish having the status of a town by virtue of a resolution under section 245(6) of the Act.

LOCAL AUTHORITIES (ARMORIAL BEARINGS) ORDER 1974

(SI 1974/869)

[*This Order in Council conferred on thirty-seven parish and community councils the right to assume the armorial bearings of their predecessors in the area, subject however to the following article.*]

4

Any armorial bearings the bearing and use of which is authorised by Article 3 of this Order shall be first exemplified according to the laws of arms and recorded in the College of Arms, otherwise such authority shall be void and of no effect.

LOCAL AUTHORITIES ETC (MISCELLANEOUS PROVISION) (NO 3) ORDER 1974

(SI 1974/968)

2 Interpretation

. . .

(2)   In this order 'the Act' means the Local Government Act 1972.

(3)   In this order—

   (a)   references to any enactment shall be construed as references to that enactment as amended, extended or applied by or under any other enactment;

   (b)   references to any instrument shall be construed as references to that instrument as amended, extended or applied by any other instrument.

4 Dissolution of charter trustees on grants of charters

(1)   The provisions of this article shall have effect where charter trustees constituted under subsection (4) of section 246 of the Act for any city or town (other than Deal, Dover, Folkestone, Margate and Ramsgate are dissolved under subsection (7) of that section on the grant of a charter under section 245 of the Act to the council of the district in which the city or town is comprised (hereinafter referred to as 'the district council').

(2)   Any mayor or deputy mayor of the city or town shall cease to hold office as such.

(3)   Any local officer of dignity appointed under paragraph (c) of the said subsection (4) shall hold office as if he had been appointed by the district council.

(4)   All property and liabilities vested in or attaching to the charter trustees shall by virtue of this order be transferred to and vest in or attach to the district council.

   All contracts, deeds, bonds, agreements and other instruments subsisting in favour of, or against, and all notices in force which were given (or have effect as if they had been given) by, or to, the charter trustees shall be of full force and effect in favour of, or against, the district council.

   Any action or proceeding or any cause of action or proceeding, pending or existing at the dissolution of the charter trustees, by, or against, the charter trustees shall not be prejudicially affected by reason of the dissolution, and may be continued, prosecuted and enforced by, or against, the district council.

(5)   The accounts of the charter trustees and of the committees and officers thereof shall be made up to the dissolution of the charter trustees and shall be audited in like

manner and subject to the same incidents and consequences as if the charter trustees had not been dissolved:

Provided that any sum certified by a district auditor as due from any person shall be paid to the district council.

(6)   Any officer of the charter trustees shall be transferred to the employment of the district council, and paragraphs (1), (6), (8) and (13) of article 13 of the Local Authorities etc (Staff Transfer and Protection) Order 1974 shall apply to such officer as they apply to officers transferred by an article, scheme or determination mentioned in the said paragraph (1).

(7)   In this article 'city or town' means an area for which charter trustees act under section 246(4) to (8) of the Act.

(8)   This article applies only to England.

7 Grant of burial rights and rights to erect memorials, and agreements for maintenance of graves and memorials

(1)   This article applies to any such grant as is described in paragraph (1) of article 9 of the Local Authorities' Cemeteries Order 1974 or any such agreement as is described in paragraph (5) of that article made or entered into between 31st March 1974 and the coming into operation of this order.

(2)   Subject to paragraph (3) below, any such grant or agreement shall be of full force and effect notwithstanding—

     (a)   in the case of a grant, that the right is to subsist in perpetuity, or for a period exceeding 100 years; and

     (b)   in the case of an agreement, that it is to extend over a period exceeding 100 years,

and if the grant or agreement is expressed to have been made under any provision other than the said or order, notwithstanding that circumstance.

(3)   The provision of Part III of Schedule 2 to the said order (determination of rights and agreements for periods exceeding 100 years) shall apply to rights and agreements to which this article applies as they apply to rights granted or agreements entered into before 1st April 1974.

LOCAL AUTHORITIES ETC (MISCELLANEOUS PROVISION) (NO 4) ORDER 1974

(SI 1974/1351)

2 Territorial extent of exercise of powers

(1)   Article 10(1), in so far as it relates to Part II of Schedule 2, and article 10(2), are made by the Secretary of State for the Environment.

(2)   Article 10(1), in so far as it relates to Part III of Schedule 2, and article 10(3), are made by the Secretary of State for Wales.

(3)   Subject to paragraphs (1) and (2), this order is made by the Secretary of State for the Environment in relation to England and by the Secretary of State for Wales in relation to Wales.

3 Interpretation

(2)   In this order 'the Act' means the Local Government Act 1972.

(3)   In this order—

     (a)   references to any enactment shall be construed as references to that enactment as amended, extended or applied by or under any other enactment;

(b)   references to any instrument shall be construed as references to that instrument as amended, extended or applied by any other instrument.

(4) Any reference in this order to a numbered article or schedule shall, unless the reference is to an article or schedule of a specified order, be construed as a reference to the article or schedule bearing that number in this order.

9 Franchise and prescriptive rights

(1) The powers to maintain markets in streets and to hold fairs exercisable immediately before 1st April 1974 by the corporation or council of the borough of Helston shall be exercisable by the Town Council of Helston.

(2) The right of wreck enjoyed immediately before 1st April 1974 by the corporation or council of the borough of Southwold shall be exercisable by the Parish Council of Southwold.

(3) Any parish council to whom any matter is transferred by paragraph (1) or (2) above shall have the same powers in relation thereto as were exercisable immediately before 1st April 1974 by the corporation or council from whom the matter is transferred.

10 Property, liability, contracts, etc, notices and proceedings

(1) Any property described in column (2) of Part . . . II or III of Schedule 2 of an authority named in column (1) and all liabilities attaching to the said authority in respect of any such property shall by virtue of this order be transferred to and vest in or attach to the authority specified in respect of such property in column (3), and—

(a)   all contracts, deeds, bonds, agreements and other instruments subsisting in favour of, or against, and all notices in force which were given (or have effect as if they had been given) by, or to, the authority named in the said column (1) in respect of such property and liabilities shall be of full force and effect in favour of, or against, the authority specified in column (3); and

(b)   any action or proceeding or any cause of action or proceeding, pending or existing at the coming into operation of this order, by, or against, the authority named in the said column (1) in respect of such property and liabilities shall not be prejudicially affected by reason of this article, and may be continued, prosecuted and enforced by, or against, the authority specified in column (3).

(2) Articles 11, 17, 23, 28, 29, 32, 33, 34(2), 35, 38 and 39 of the Local Authorities (England) (Property etc) Order 1973 and articles 7 and 8 of the Local Authorities etc (England) (Property etc: Further Provision) Order 1974 shall apply as if paragraph (1) above and Parts I and II of Schedule 2 were contained in the said order of 1973.

(3) Articles 11, 17, 23, 27, 28, 31, 32, 33(2), 34, 37 and 38 of the Local Authorities (Wales) (Property etc) Order 1973 and articles 6 and 8 of the Local Authorities etc (Wales) (Property etc: Further Provision) Order 1974 shall apply as if paragraph (1) above and Parts I and III of Schedule 2 were contained in the said order of 1973.

. . .

SCHEDULE 2
TRANSFER OF PARTICULAR PROPERTIES

PART II
[*This part specifies properties transferred by article 10 between councils.*]

PART II
[*This part specifies properties transferred by article 10 from (amongst others) Welsh district councils to three communities.*]

LOCAL AUTHORITIES ETC (MISCELLANEOUS PROVISION) (NO 2) ORDER 1975

(SI 1975/944)

11 Subscriptions to Association of Charter Trustees

The following bodies namely—

> charter trustees for any area; and

> any cinque port trustees or corporate trustees which may be constituted by the operation of article 6 of the Local Authorities (Miscellaneous Provision) Order 1975,

may pay reasonable subscriptions, whether annually or otherwise, to the funds of the Association of Charter Trustees.

LOCAL GOVERNMENT AREA CHANGES REGULATIONS 1976

(SI 1976/246)

2 Application: extent of exercise of powers

These regulations make incidental, consequential, transitional or supplementary provision for the purposes or in consequence of orders made under Part IV of the Local Government Act 1972 by the Secretary of State for the Environment or the Secretary of State for Wales, or both, or under paragraph 7 of Schedule 10 to the said Act by the Secretary of State for Wales, . . .

3 Interpretation

 . . .

(2)   In these regulations—

> 'the appointed day' means the day on which the order comes into operation otherwise than for any purposes set out in regulation 4(1);

> 'as altered' means as altered by any orders under Part IV of the Local Government Act 1972, or paragraph 7 of Schedule 10 thereto, coming into operation on the appointed day;

> 'byelaws' includes any regulation, scale of charges, list of tolls or table of fees and payments;

> 'charity', 'charity trustees', 'court' and 'trust' have the same meanings as in the Charities Act 1960; . . .

> 'dissolved authority' means an authority dissolved by the order;

> 'exercisable', in relation to functions, means exercisable otherwise than by virtue of section 101, 110 or 187(2) or (3) of the Local Government Act 1972, section 15 of the Water Act 1973 or article 19 of the Local Authorities etc. (Miscellaneous Provision) Order 1974;

> 'local Act' includes an Act confirming a provisional order;

> 'officer', in relation to any authority, includes the holder of any office or employment under that authority;

> 'the order' means the order under Part IV of the Local Government Act 1972, or paragraph 7 of Schedule 10 thereto, for the purposes or in consequence of which the provisions in these regulations become applicable;

'parish authority' means in the case of a parish having a separate parish council that council, and in any other case the parish meeting or the parish trustees of the parish, as may be appropriate;

. . .

'the proper officer', in relation to any purpose and any body, means the officer appointed for that purpose by that body;

'residuary successor', in relation to any dissolved authority, means the authority specified as such in the order;

except in paragraph 6 of Schedule 3 'the Secretary of State', without more, means the Secretary of State or the Secretaries of State by whom the order is made; . . .

(3)   These regulations have effect subject to the provisions of the order.

(4)   For the purposes of these regulations and of the order—

    (a)   an area shall be treated as transferred from any relevant area wherever it ceases on the appointed day to be comprised in that relevant area, whether that area continues to exist or not, and if it does not whether the first-mentioned area constitutes only part of it or the whole;

    (b)   an area shall be treated as transferred to any relevant area wherever it first comes on the appointed day to be comprised in that relevant area, whether that area previously existed or not, and if it did not whether the first-mentioned area constitutes only part of it or the whole.

In this paragraph, 'relevant area' means a county, district, London borough, parish, community, local justice area, police area or the area of a health authority or Primary Care Trust.

(5)   In these regulations and in the order, unless the context otherwise requires—

    (a)   references to any enactment shall be construed as references to that enactment as amended, extended or applied by or under any other enactment;

    (b)   references to any instrument shall be construed as references to that instrument as amended, extended or applied by any other instrument.

(6)–(8)   [*Any reference in these regulations to a numbered regulation, sub-paragraph or Schedule shall, unless the reference is to a regulation paragraph, sub-paragraph or Schedule of a specified instrument, be construed as a reference to the regulation paragraph, sub-paragraph or Schedule bearing that number in these regulations.*]

5 Maps

(1)   A print of any map referred to in the order shall be deposited in the offices of the Secretary of State.

(2)   A print of any such map shall be deposited—

with the council of any district or London borough affected by the changes of areas made by the order; . . .

A print deposited under this paragraph shall at all reasonable times be open to inspection by any person affected by the changes of areas made by the order, and on payment of a reasonable fee (to be determined by the body with whom the print is deposited) any such person shall be entitled to a copy of or an extract from it, certified by the proper officer of such body to be a true copy or extract, which shall be received in all courts of justice and elsewhere as prima facie evidence of the contents of the map as regards the changes of areas made by the order.

(3)   In addition— . . .

    (b)   if the map is relevant to any change in the boundaries of a parish, a print thereof, or an extract therefrom, shall be supplied to the parish authority;

    (c)   if the map is relevant to any change in the boundaries of a community having a community council, a print thereof, or an extract therefrom, shall be supplied to that council.

(4)   Any print or extract supplied under (b) or (c) of paragraph (3) shall be deposited with the records of the parish or community.

6 Mereing of boundaries

The boundaries established by the order shall be mered by Ordnance Survey. Any boundary defined on any map referred to in the order by reference to proposed works shall, if such works have not been executed at the time of the completion of the first survey including such boundary made after the coming into operation of the order for a new edition of Ordnance Survey large scale plans, be mered as if the boundary had not been so defined.

7 General continuance of matters

Subject to the other provisions of these regulations, any of the following things done or treated by virtue of any enactment as having been done by, or to, or in relation to, any authority from whom any area is transferred by the order in connection with the discharge of any of their functions in relation to such area, that is to say—

any written agreement or other instrument in writing or any determination or declaration made or treated as made by such an authority;

any notice or direction given or treated as given by, or to, such an authority;

any licence, permission, consent, approval, exemption, dispensation or relaxation granted or treated as granted by, or to, such an authority;

any application, proposal or objection made or treated as made by, or to, such an authority;

any condition or requirement imposed or treated as imposed by, or on, such an authority; or

any appeal allowed by, or in favour of, or against, such an authority,

shall, as from the appointed day, be treated as having been done by, to, or in relation to, the authority by whom the functions become exercisable in the area on and after that day by virtue of the order, and any such thing shall as from that day have effect as if any reference therein to the first-mentioned authority were a reference to the authority secondly mentioned.

8 Councillors

(1)   Any person in office at the appointed day as councillor for any electoral area which is altered by the order shall represent the area as altered until the date on which he would have retired if the order had not been made. Any casual vacancy which exists at the coming into operation of the order or occurs before the appointed day in the office of councillor for any such area shall (except where notice of the election has at the coming into operation of the order already been given) be deemed to have arisen in the representation of the area as altered. Where notice of the election has at the coming into operation of the order already been given the person elected shall represent the area as altered until the date on which he would have retired if the order had not been made.

(2)   In relation to the qualification of any person to be elected and to be a member of any . . . parish council or community council . . . or of any committee, joint board or joint committee, the order shall be deemed, for the purposes of section 79 of the Local Government Act 1972, to have been in operation during the whole of the twelve months preceding the relevant day within the meaning of that section.

(3)   No person who remains in office after the appointed day as a member of any . . . parish council or community council . . . or of any committee, joint board or joint committee, shall, during the term for which he remains in office, lose his qualification for being a member by reason of the changes of areas made by the order.

9 Local government electors

If in relation to any election, parish meeting or community meeting for any area consisting of or comprising any area established or altered by the order the register of local government electors has not been prepared and published on the basis that the changes of areas made by the order had become operative, the registration officer shall make such alteration of the register as may be proper for the purpose of such election or meeting.

10 Grouped parishes

(1)   The provisions of this regulation shall have effect where parishes are grouped.

(2)   There shall be a separate parish meeting for each parish.

(3)   Where under the provisions of any enactment or instrument the consent of the parish meeting for a parish is required in respect of any act done, or proposed to be done, by a parish council, the consent of the parish meeting of each parish affected by the act shall be necessary in respect of such act done, or proposed to be done, by the common parish council.

(4)   For the purposes of the application to the parishes of all or any of the provisions of section 37 of the Charities Act 1960 and of any of the provisions of the Local Government Act 1972 with respect to the custody of parish documents, so as to preserve the separate rights of each parish, the common parish council shall be deemed to be the separate parish council for each parish:

Provided that the consent of the parish meeting for any parish shall be required to any act of the common parish council under the said provisions which relates only to the affairs of that parish.

11 Grouped communities

(1)   The provisions of this regulation shall have effect where communities are grouped.

(2)   For the purposes of the application to the communities of all or any of the provisions of section 37 of the Charities Act 1960 and of any of the provisions of the Local Government Act 1972 with respect to the custody of community documents, so as to preserve the separate rights of each community, the common community council shall be deemed to be the separate community council for each community.

12 Dissolution of charter trustees

(1)   The provisions of this regulation shall have effect where the city or town for which charter trustees have been constituted under subsection (4) of section 246 of the Local Government Act 1972—

  (a)   becomes a parish;

  (b)   becomes wholly comprised in a parish; or

  (c)   becomes wholly comprised in two or more parishes,

and the said subsection (4) therefore, in accordance with subsection (8) of the said section 246, ceases to apply to the city or town.

(2)   Any reference in this regulation to 'the parish council' shall be construed—

  (a)   in the cases described in (a) and (b) in paragraph (1), as a reference to the parish council for the parish so described;

  (b)   in the case described in (c) in paragraph (1), as a reference to the parish council specified in relation to this paragraph in respect of the city or town in the order.

(3)   The charter trustees shall be dissolved.

(4)   Any mayor or deputy mayor of the city or town shall cease to hold office as such.

(5)   Any local officer of dignity appointed under paragraph (c) of the said subsection (4) shall hold office as if he had been appointed by the parish council.

(6)   All property and liabilities vested in or attaching to the charter trustees shall by virtue of the order be transferred to and vest in or attach to the parish council.

All contracts, deeds, bonds, agreements and other instruments subsisting in favour of, or against, and all notices in force which were given (or have effect as if they had been given) by, or to, the charter trustees shall be of full force and effect in favour of, or against, the parish council.

Any action or proceeding or any cause of action or proceeding, pending or existing at the dissolution of the charter trustees, by, or against, the charter trustees shall not be prejudicially affected by reason of the dissolution, and may be continued, prosecuted and enforced by, or against, the parish council.

(7)   The accounts of the charter trustees and of the committees and officers thereof shall be made up to the dissolution of the charter trustees and shall be audited in like manner and subject to the same incidents and consequences as if the charter trustees had not been dissolved:

Provided that where the audit is carried out by a district auditor the expression

'the body in question' in section 161(2)(a) (orders for repayment of expenditure declared unlawful) and (4) (certification of sums not brought into account or losses) of the Local Government Act 1972 shall include the parish council.

(8)   Any officer of the charter trustees shall be transferred to the employment of the parish council, and regulation 71 shall apply to such officer as it applies to officers transferred by regulation 70.

(9)   In this regulation, 'city or town' means an area for which charter trustees act under section 246(4) to (8) of the Local Government Act 1972.

(10)   This regulation applies only to England.

13 Honorary freedoms

Nothing in the order shall affect the status of any person who is immediately before the appointed day an honorary freeman of any place being a London borough or a district having the status of a city, borough or royal borough or of any body which at such time enjoys privileges of a similar nature to honorary freedom of any such place.

16 Appointments to bodies

(1)   Any power to appoint any person to any body belonging to an authority in respect of any property or liability transferred by regulation 12 or 62 shall be transferred to the authority to whom such property or liability is transferred.

(2)   Any other power to appoint any person to any body belonging to a dissolved authority shall be transferred to the residuary successor of that authority.

(3)   In this regulation any reference to a power to appoint includes references to powers to elect or to nominate any persons for appointment.

18 Agency arrangements

(1)   Any arrangements made under section 101 or 110 of the Local Government Act 1972 for the discharge of functions of one authority by another authority which would apart from the changes of areas effected by the order be in force on and after the appointed day throughout any relevant area altered by the order shall be in force throughout the area as altered.

In this paragraph, 'relevant area' means a district, London borough, parish or community . . . .

23 Education

(1)   The managers or governors of any school in any area transferred by the order shall (unless a new instrument of management instrument of government is made for the school) remain in office until the date on which they would have retired if the order had not been made.

(2)

(a)   This paragraph shall apply where an area is transferred from the area of one local education authority to the area of another such authority and in this paragraph—

'the specified enactments' means sections 50, 61(2) and 81 of the Education Act 1944, section 6 of the Education (Miscellaneous Provisions) Act 1953 and sections 1 and 2 of the Education Act 1962;

'the transferor authority' means the local education authority from whose area the area is transferred; and

'the transferee authority' means the local education authority to whose area the area is transferred.

In the application of this paragraph to a county, district or London borough regulation 3(4) shall apply.

(b) Any instrument made by the transferor authority in connection with the discharge of any of their functions, and any other thing done by, to or in relation to such authority in connection therewith, shall in relation to the area transferred be treated as having been made by, or done by, to or in relation to, the transferee authority, and any instrument relating to the exercise of those functions, or to things done in their exercise, or to property held or maintained for the purposes of those functions, shall so far as it relates to such area have effect as if any reference to the transferor authority or their area were a reference to the transferee authority or their area.

This sub-paragraph does not extend to any byelaws or order to which paragraph (6) or (7) of regulation 62 applies.

. . .

24 Charities

(1)

(a) The provisions of this paragraph shall have effect in relation to property held, immediately before the appointed day, as sole trustee, exclusively for charitable purposes, by any authority described in column (1) of the following table affected by the order.

(b) Where such property is held for the benefit of, or of the inhabitants of, or of any particular class or body of persons in, a specified area the whole or the greater part of which is transferred from the authority so described to an authority specified in respect thereof in column (2), that property shall by virtue of this paragraph be transferred to and vest (on the same trusts) in the authority so specified.

(c) Where the authority so described is dissolved any other property to which this paragraph applies shall by virtue of this paragraph be transferred to and vest (on the same trusts) in the authority specified in respect of such authority in column (2) to whom the whole or the greater part of the area of the first-mentioned authority is transferred.

(1)	(2)
The parish council of a parish, or the community council of a community	The corporation or council of a London borough, the parish council (or where there is no parish council the parish meeting or parish trustees) of a parish, the community council of a community or where there is in a district in England no parish or in Wales no community council the council of the district

The parish meeting or parish trustees of a parish	The corporation or council of a London borough, the parish meeting or parish trustees of a parish not having a separate parish council, the parish meeting or in the case of real property the parish council of a parish having a separate parish council, the community council of a community or where there is in a district in England no parish or in Wales no community council the council of the district

(d) All liabilities attaching to any authority in respect of any property transferred by sub-paragraph (b) or (c) shall by virtue of this paragraph be transferred to and attach to the authority to whom such property is transferred.

(e) All contracts, deeds, bonds, agreements and other instruments subsisting in favour of, or against, and all notices in force which were given (or have effect as if they had been given) by, or to, the authority first mentioned in sub-paragraph (d) in respect of any property transferred by sub-paragraph (b) or (c), or in respect of liabilities transferred by sub-paragraph (d), shall be of full force and effect in favour of, or against, the authority to whom such property and liabilities are transferred.

(f) Any action or proceeding or any cause of action or proceeding, pending or existing at the appointed day, by, or against, the authority first mentioned in sub-paragraph (d) in respect of any property transferred by sub-paragraph (b) or (c), or in respect of liabilities transferred by sub-paragraph (d), shall not be prejudicially affected by reason of this paragraph, and may be continued, prosecuted and enforced by, or against, the authority to whom such property and liabilities are transferred.

(2)

(a) Where, immediately before the appointed day, any power with respect to a charity, not being a charity incorporated under the Companies Acts or by charter, is under the trusts of the charity or by virtue of any enactment vested in, or in the holder of an office connected with, an authority to whom paragraph (1)(b) or (c) applies, that power shall vest in, or in the holder of the corresponding office connected with, the authority in whom, had property of the charity been vested in the first-mentioned authority, that property would have been transferred by paragraph (1).

(b) If there is no corresponding office the power shall vest in the authority described in sub-paragraph (a).

(3)

(a) References in paragraph (2) to a power with respect to a charity do not include references to a power of any person by virtue of being a charity trustee thereof, but where under the trusts of any charity, not being a charity incorporated under the Companies Acts or by charter, the charity trustees immediately before the appointed day include either an authority to whom paragraph (1)(b) or (c) applies or the holder of an office connected with such an authority, those trustees shall instead include the authority specified in paragraph 2(a) or, as the case may require, the holder of the corresponding office connected with that authority.

(b) If there is no corresponding office, the charity trustees shall include the person appointed for that purpose by the authority.

(4)

(a) Where, immediately before the appointed day, any power with respect to a charity to which paragraphs (1) to (3) do not apply, not being a charity incorporated under the Companies Acts or by charter, is under the trusts

907

of the charity or by virtue of any enactment vested in, or in the holder of an office connected with, the local authority of any area affected by the order, that power shall be exercisable, if the Charity Commissioners so direct, by such other authority or persons as may be specified in the direction.

(b)   In this paragraph, 'local authority' includes a parish meeting, the Common Council, the Honourable Society of the Inner Temple or the Honourable Society of the Middle Temple.

(5)   Nothing in this regulation shall affect any power of Her Majesty, the court or any other person to alter the trusts of any charity.

25 Commons

(1)   Any agreement under section 2(2) of the Commons Registration Act 1965 (one council to be registration authority for land which spans the boundaries of counties or Greater London) which is in force immediately before the appointed day in relation to any common affected by the changes of areas effected by the order shall cease to have effect, without prejudice to the making of a new agreement under the said subsection.

(2)   Where any common regulated by a scheme under the Commons Act 1899 is transferred from one district or London borough to another such area, any functions under the scheme of the council of the district or London borough from which the common is transferred shall be exercised by the council of the district or London borough to which the common is transferred.

(3)   Where any common so regulated—

(a)   is immediately before the appointed day comprised in a single district or London borough; and

(b)   comes on the appointed day to be comprised in two or more districts or London boroughs,

any functions under the scheme of the council of the area described in (a) shall be exercised by the council of the area described in (b) in which the greater part of the common is situated unless all such councils agree that they shall be exercised by the council of any other such area.

35 Cemeteries

(1)   Nothing in the order shall affect any right of burial, to construct a walled grave or vault or to place and maintain, or to put any additional inscription on, a tombstone or other memorial which any person may have acquired before the appointed day or affect the amount of any fee payable by him in respect of any such right.

(2)   This paragraph shall have effect where an area (hereinafter referred to as 'the transferred area') is transferred by the order from an area for which a cemetery to which the Local Authorities' Cemeteries Order 1974 applies has been provided (hereinafter referred to as 'the cemetery area').

In the period of 25 years beginning on the appointed day—

(a)   any inhabitant or parishioner of the transferred area shall be entitled to the same rights of burial as the inhabitants or parishioners of the cemetery area as altered;

(b)   any provisions in relation to inhabitants or parishioners in any table of fees in force in respect of the cemetery shall apply to the inhabitants or parishioners of the transferred area as they apply to the inhabitants or parishioners of the cemetery area as altered;

(c)   no differential charges shall be imposed on the inhabitants or parishioners of the transferred area.

(3)   Subject to paragraph (2), any provisions in relation to inhabitants or parishioners of any area which is altered by the order in any table of fees in force in respect of any cemetery to which the Local Authorities' Cemeteries Order 1974 applies shall apply to the inhabitants or parishioners of the area as altered.

(4)   In the area in which the Church of England was disestablished by the Welsh Church Act 1914 the references in this regulation to inhabitants and parishioners shall be read as references to inhabitants.

36 Maintenance of highways
Where the council of a district altered by the order have, under section 187(2)(a) of the Local Government Act 1972, undertaken the maintenance of all the footpaths, bridleways and urban roads which are neither trunk roads nor classified roads in the district, the undertaking shall extend to all such highways in the district as altered.

40 Statutory definitions of areas
(1)
    (a)   This paragraph applies to any provision of any Act or of any order, rules or regulations made by a Minister under any Act defining an area for any purpose wholly by reference to entire relevant areas.

In this sub-paragraph, 'relevant areas' means—
        (i)   counties, districts, London boroughs, parishes and communities;
        (ii)   areas common to parishes or communities;
        (iii)   Greater London, the City, the Inner Temple and the Middle Temple;
        (iv)   electoral divisions of counties or of Greater London and wards of districts, London boroughs, parishes, communities and the City;
        (v)   the areas of former counties, boroughs, urban districts and rural districts;
        (vi)   any area described in (i) to (v) other than another such area;
        (vii) any area described in (i) or (iii) other than an area expressly defined;
        (viii) any part of an area described in (i) or (iv) defined wholly by reference to circumstances existing immediately before 1st April 1974;
        (ix)   any [local justice area].
    (b)   In any provision to which this paragraph applies, subject to sub-paragraph (c)—
        (i)   any reference to any relevant area altered by the order shall be construed as a reference to such area as altered,
        (ii)   any reference to any relevant area abolished by the order shall cease to have effect, and
        (iii)   there shall be deemed to be included a reference to any county, district, London borough, parish or community formed by the order and wholly comprised in the area.

(2)   Any provision of any Act or of any order, rules or regulations made under any Act defining an area for any purpose to which paragraph (1) does not apply shall not be affected by the order except by express provision therein.

(3)   If the order alters any of the counties of Buckinghamshire, Essex, Hertfordshire and Kent the references to those counties in Schedule 1 to the Home Counties (Music and Dancing) Licensing Act 1926 as amended by section 204(7) of the Local Government Act 1972 shall be construed as a reference to those counties as altered.

40A Construction of pre-1967 references to parishes
(1)   The provisions of this regulation—
    (a)   apply in relation to England outside Greater London;
    (b)   so apply for the construction of any enactment passed before 22nd March 1967; and
    (c)   shall have effect subject to any contrary intention which may appear in any such enactment.

(2)   Where any part of a parish ceases to form part of any parish, any reference in any such enactment to a parish or an urban parish shall be construed as including a reference to such part of a parish.

(3)   Where any part of an area to which paragraph (2), (3) or (4) of paragraph 6 of Schedule 29 to the Local Government Act 1972, as enacted or as extended by article 3(19) of the Local Authorities etc. (Miscellaneous Provision) (No 2) Order 1974, applies becomes a parish or part of a parish, such paragraph shall cease to apply to the first-mentioned part.

41 Local Acts, orders and byelaws—General
(1)   This regulation shall apply to—
    (a)   any provision of any local Act,
    any order made under any Act, or
    any byelaws,
which would apart from the changes of areas effected by the order be in force on the appointed day throughout a relevant area;
    (b)   any provision of any Act other than a local Act which would be in force as aforesaid by reason of any application thereof by any Act, instrument or resolution,
    other than—
        (i)   a provision relating to any railway, light railway, tramway, road transport, water transport, canal, inland navigation, ferry, dock, harbour, pier or lighthouse undertaking, any telephone undertaking, any market undertaking or any undertaking for the supply of electricity, gas, hydraulic power or district heating;
        . . .
        (iv)   a provision contained in the Green Belt (London and Home Counties) Act 1938.

(2)   In this regulation, 'relevant area' means a county, district, London borough, parish or community, Greater London, ...

(3)   Any provision to which this regulation applies in force immediately before the appointed day throughout a relevant area which is altered by the order shall be in force throughout the area as altered.

(4)   Any provision to which this regulation applies in force throughout such relevant areas as may be specified in relation to this paragraph in the order shall be in force throughout the area so specified in relation to the areas specified.

(5)   Subject to paragraphs (3) and (4), any provision to which this regulation applies shall cease to have effect in relation to any area transferred by the order.

(6)   In any provision in relation to which paragraph (3) or (4) has effect any reference to a relevant area shall have effect as a reference to the area as altered or the area specified in accordance with paragraph (4), as the case may be.

(7)   Nothing in this regulation shall apply to any provision applying to property held on a charitable trust.

44 Compulsory purchase orders and other instruments
(1)   Any order authorising the compulsory acquisition of land (hereinafter referred to as a 'compulsory purchase order'), whether confirmed before the coming into operation of the order for the purposes mentioned in regulation 4(1) or submitted for confirmation before or after such coming into operation, may be amended by the Minister by whom it was confirmed, or by whom it falls to be confirmed, by the substitution, as the authority to be authorised to acquire the land comprised therein, or any part thereof, of such authority as seems to him to be appropriate, and thereafter the order shall have effect, or be considered and if confirmed have effect, accordingly.

(2)   Any compulsory purchase order which has not been submitted to a Minister for confirmation before the appointed day may be so submitted by any authority, and any

action which requires to be taken prior to the submission of the order which has not already been taken shall be taken by such authority.

(3) Any instrument other than a compulsory purchase order which has been submitted to a Minister for confirmation before the appointed day may be amended by such Minister by the substitution of references to the whole or parts of one or more specified areas or of references to one or more specified authorities, and thereafter the instrument may be considered and if confirmed have effect accordingly.

(4) Any instrument which has not been submitted to a Minister for confirmation before the appointed day may be so submitted by a specified authority, and—

    (a)   any action which requires to be taken prior to the submission of the instrument which has not already been taken shall be taken by such authority; and

    (b)   paragraph (3) shall apply to such instrument as it applies to the instruments therein described.

(5) In paragraphs (3) and (4)— . . .

    'specified area' means a . . . district, . . . ; and

    'specified authority' means a . . . district council, London borough council, ...

45 Instruments made by Ministers

Any instrument which has been made by a Minister before the appointed day may be amended by the appropriate Minister by the substitution of references to—

    the whole or parts of one or more specified areas (as defined in regulation 44); or

    one or more specified authorities (as so defined);

and thereafter the instrument shall have effect, or be proceeded with, accordingly.

In this regulation, 'the appropriate Minister', in relation to any instrument, means the Minister in charge of any government department concerned with the subject matter of the instrument, but the validity of any action shall not be affected by any question as to whether or not any Minister was the appropriate Minister for the purpose.

46 Instruments subject to special parliamentary procedure

(1) Regulations 44 and 45 shall not apply to any instrument which at the appointed day is subject to the procedure regulated in the Statutory Orders (Special Procedure) Acts 1945 and 1965 until the completion of such procedure.

(2) In any such procedure—

    (a)   any notice given by a Minister that he desires that rights and functions conferred on him shall be exercisable by any authority shall have effect; but

    (b)   otherwise, the instrument subject to the procedure shall be dealt with as if the order had not been made.

47 Inspection of parish and community books, etc

Any person shall at all times be entitled to the rights to which he would have been entitled if the order had not been made of inspecting and making extracts from the public books, writings and papers of a parish or community (including any photographic copies thereof) and all documents directed by law to be kept therewith.

48 Registration—General

(1) Subject to paragraph (2), in this regulation—

    'register' means any register under any enactment, rule, order or regulation and includes any index of local charities maintained under section 10 of the Charities Act 1960;

    'registration' means inclusion in any register; and

    'exemption' means exemption from any obligation in respect of registration.

(2) This regulation does not extend to—

(a) any register of parliamentary and local government electors;

(b) any register of births, marriages or deaths;

(c) any register maintained under the Local Authorities' Cemeteries Order 1974;

(d) any register to which regulation 49 applies.

(3) Immediately before the appointed day the proper officer of any dissolved authority shall deliver any register of the authority to the proper officer of the following authority, namely—

(a) if the register is not appropriate for the residuary successor of the dissolved authority and is appropriate for one other authority only, to that authority;

(b) in any other case, to the residuary successor of the dissolved authority.

(4) As soon as may be after the appointed day the proper officer of any authority shall—

(a) send to the proper officer of any other authority a copy of every entry in any register of the authority by whom he is employed or received by him under paragraph (3)(b) which is appropriate for the register of that other authority; and

(b) incorporate or include in the appropriate register of the authority by whom he is employed, with any necessary modifications—

(i) the entries in the registers delivered to him under paragraph (3)(b) of which copies have not been sent, under (a), to the proper officer of any other authority; and

(ii) the particulars of every entry furnished to him under (a) in its application to the proper officer of any other authority,

and every entry so incorporated or included shall continue in force as fully and effectively as if it had originally been made in the register in which it is incorporated or included.

Where any register is kept in such manner that the entries therein are separable, (a) may be complied with, as regards any entry, by sending the entry to the proper officer specified therein, and if the entry is so sent (b)(ii) may be complied with, as regards that entry, by the inclusion of the entry in the appropriate register.

(5) Any application made before the appointed day for registration in any register, or for exemption from any obligation in respect of inclusion in such register, which concerns or has effect in relation to any area transferred from the authority to whom the application is made or to any person, property, matter or thing therein, shall be treated as having been made to the authority for whose register the application is appropriate.

(6) Any order, decision, notice or certificate made, taken, given or issued before the appointed day by any authority in relation to—

any entry in any register of the authority; or

any application for registration or exemption,

which concerns or has effect in relation to any area transferred from such authority shall have effect as if it had been made, taken, given or issued by the authority in whose register the entry falls to be incorporated or included or in relation to whose register the application is appropriate.

(7) Paragraphs (5) and (6) shall have effect in relation to any area transferred within a county, . . . in relation to matters which on and after the appointed day are appropriate for the register of an authority other than the county council . . . as if the area had been transferred from the county, or from Greater London.

62 Property, liabilities, contracts, etc, notices and proceedings

(1) Nothing in this regulation shall apply to—

(a) property held for the purposes of, and liabilities incurred, contracts, deeds, bonds, agreements and other instruments subsisting, notices given, actions and proceedings pending, and causes of action or proceeding existing in relation to, any charitable trust;

(b) any property specified in relation to this sub-paragraph in the order, and liabilities incurred, contracts, deeds, bonds, agreements and other instruments subsisting, notices given, actions and proceedings pending, and causes of action or proceeding existing in relation thereto, . . .

(2) Subject to the provision of paragraph (1)—

(a) all property vested in an authority described in column (1) of the table in Part I of Schedule 6 or in any extension thereof made in the order for the purposes of this paragraph and specified in respect of such authority in column (2) (whether by reason of its inclusion in any description of matters or particularly), and all liabilities attaching to the said authority in respect of any such property, shall by virtue of this paragraph be transferred to and vest in or attach to the authority specified in respect of such property in column (3);

(b) all other liabilities attaching to an authority described in the said column (1) and within any description of matters specified in respect of such authority in column (2) shall by virtue of this paragraph be transferred to and attach to the authority specified in respect of such description of matters in column (3);

(c) all contracts, deeds, bonds, agreements and other instruments subsisting in favour of, or against, and all notices in force which were given (or have effect as if they had been given) by, or to, an authority described in the said column (1) in respect of any property or liability transferred by sub-paragraph (*a*) or (*b*) shall be of full force and effect in favour of, or against, the authority to whom such property or liability is transferred;

(d) all other contracts, deeds, bonds, agreements and other instruments subsisting in favour of, or against, and all notices in force which were given (or have effect as if they had been given) by, or to, an authority described in the said column (1) and within any description of matters specified in respect of such authority in column (2) shall be of full force and effect in favour of, or against, the authority specified in respect of such description of matters in column (3);

(e) any action or proceeding or any cause of action or proceeding, pending or existing at the appointed day, by, or against, an authority described in the said column (1) in respect of any property or liability transferred by sub-paragraph (a) or (b) shall not be prejudicially affected by reason of the order, and may be continued, prosecuted and enforced by, or against, the authority to whom such property or liability is transferred;

(f) any other action or proceeding or any other cause of action or proceeding, pending or existing at the appointed day, by, or against, an authority described in the said column (1) and within any description of matters specified in respect of such authority in column (2) shall not be prejudicially affected by reason of the order, and may be continued, prosecuted and enforced by, or against, the authority specified in respect of such description of matters in column (3).

Paragraphs 1 to 7 in Part I of Schedule 6 shall have effect in relation to the table in that Part.

Part II of Schedule 6 shall have effect in the application of this paragraph.

(3) Subject to the provisions of paragraphs (1) and (2)—

(a) all property and liabilities vested in or attaching to a dissolved authority shall by virtue of this paragraph be transferred to and vest in or attach to the residuary successor of that authority;

(b)   all contracts, deeds, bonds, agreements and other instruments subsisting in favour of, or against, and all notices in force which were given, or have effect as if they had been given, by, or to, a dissolved authority shall be of full force and effect in favour of, or against, the residuary successor of that authority;

(c)   any action or proceeding or any cause of action or proceeding, pending or existing at the appointed day, by, or against, a dissolved authority shall not be prejudicially affected by reason of the order, and may be continued, prosecuted and enforced by, or against, the residuary successor of that authority.

(4) The authority to whom any property other than land is transferred by paragraph (2) or (3) (otherwise than by its particular inclusion in an extension of the table in Part I of Schedule 6 made in the order for the purposes of paragraph (2)) may by resolution agree—

(a)   that the property shall not be transferred; or

(b)   that it shall be transferred to any other authority named in the resolution, and in the case of (b) sub-paragraph (a) of paragraph (2) in so far as it relates to liabilities, and sub-paragraphs (c) and (e) thereof, shall apply accordingly.

(5)

(a)   Subject to sub-paragraph (b), any interest in any property or any liability transferred by paragraph (2) or (3) to the authority for any . . . district, London borough, parish or community, . . . shall be held or discharged by them in respect of such area as existing on and after the appointed day.

(b)   Sub-paragraph (a)—

(i)   shall not apply in respect of any interest in any property or any liability which by reason of agreements made (or having effect as if made) by the transferor authority falls to be held or discharged in respect of any specified area; . . .

(6) Any byelaws in force for the regulation of any property transferred by paragraph (2) or (3) shall have effect as if they had been made by the authority to whom such property is transferred (but in the case of property transferred to a parish meeting or parish trustees only if such byelaws could have been made by the parish meeting).

(7) Any provision of any local Act or of any order made under any Act which applies to any property transferred by paragraph (2) or (3) to any authority shall have effect with the substitution of references to that authority for any references to (or having effect as references to) the authority from whom the property is transferred.

(8) Any authorisation of the borrowing of money in force in respect of any property or liability transferred by paragraph (2) or (3) to any authority may, subject to the terms applicable thereto, be acted on by such authority.

(9) Any excise licence, operators' licence, public service vehicle licence, road service licence, plating certificate or other document issued in respect of any vehicle transferred by paragraph (2) or (3) to any authority shall have effect as if it had been issued to such authority, and any reference to the authority from whom the vehicle is transferred in any such licence or certificate or in any registration book or other document issued in respect of such vehicle shall have effect as a reference to the authority to whom the vehicle is transferred.

(11) Where parts of any land are in consequence of paragraph (2) or (3), or of both such paragraphs, vested in two different authorities, and any easement or other right over one part is required to enable the other part to be used, the authority in whom the said other part is vested may within the 6 months following the appointed day serve notice on the authority in whom the said one part is vested specifying such easement or other right and requiring the authority in whom the said one part is vested to grant the same to them on terms specified in the notice.

Any question—

    (a)   whether any easement or other right is required to enable the said other part to be used; or

    (b)   as to the terms on which any easement or other right shall be conferred,

shall be determined by the decision of a person agreed on by the authorities or in default of agreement appointed by the Secretary of State.

(12)   The provision made by this regulation is without prejudice to—

    (a)   any agreement which may be made for payment in respect of any property transferred by paragraph (2) or (3);

    (b)   any agreement which may be made under section 68 of the Local Government Act 1972, or arbitration in default of such agreement—

        (i)   as to the use of any property transferred as aforesaid;

        (ii)   in relation to any matter not so transferred.

63 Audit of accounts

(1)   Sections 2 to 27 of the Audit Commission Act 1998 shall apply in relation to the accounts of any county or district council established by the order, and of the committees and officers thereof, . . .

(2)   The said sections shall apply in relation to the accounts of the parish councils, parish meetings or community councils of each of the parishes or communities in a district established by the order and of every joint committee of the councils of two or more parishes or communities, both or all of which are situated in that district, and of the committees and officers of any such body, . . .

(3)   The accounts of any dissolved authority (other than charter trustees) and of the committees and officers thereof shall be made up to the appointed day and shall be audited in like manner and subject to the same incidents and consequences as if the order had not been made: . . .

64 Security for loans

Where under these regulations, the order or any agreement made under section 68 of the Local Government Act 1972 any liability or part of a liability charged indifferently on all the revenues of a public body or on any particular revenues of such body is transferred to another public body, the liability or part of the liability shall be charged indifferently to all the revenues of the public body to whom it is transferred and shall cease to be a charge on any revenues or fund of the public body from whom it is transferred.

65 Legal proceedings

All legal proceedings pending at the appointed day shall be amended in such manner as may be necessary or proper in consequence of these regulations and the order.

66 Liabilities of certain funds

(1)   Where by virtue of these regulations or of the order any matter for the purposes of which in pursuance of paragraph 19 of Schedule 13 to the Local Government Act 1972 moneys forming part of a fund to which that paragraph applies have been used is transferred to an authority other than the authority by whom such fund is maintained on and after the appointed day, the provisions of sub-paragraph (2) of that paragraph, and sub-paragraph (3) thereof in so far as it relates to the debiting of accounts, shall be applicable to the first-mentioned authority.

   . . .

(3)   Where by virtue of these regulations or of the order any matter in respect of which any advance from a fund established or deemed to be established under paragraph 16 of Schedule 13 to the Local Government Act 1972, as set out in section 28(1) of the Local Government (Miscellaneous Provisions) Act 1976, is not fully repaid is transferred to an authority other than the authority by whom such fund is maintained on and after the appointed day, the first-mentioned authority may treat

the outstanding amount of the advance as an advance to any similar fund so established or deemed to be established by them and make such payments to the fund as they consider appropriate, but otherwise any liability to make repayments in respect of the advance shall cease.

. . .

67 Schemes for the allocation of officers for transfer—Local authorities

(1)   Schemes for the allocation of officers for transfer shall be made by the councils of counties, districts, London boroughs, parishes and communities,   . . .   and the Common Council in accordance with the provisions of this regulation and regulation 69.

(2)

(a)   Where the area of any authority to be dissolved by the order is not transferred as a whole to the area of one relevant authority a scheme for the allocation of all their officers for transfer shall be made by the first-mentioned authority unless the relevant authorities other than one notify the first-mentioned authority that no officers need be allocated for transfer to them.

(b)   In sub-paragraph (a), 'relevant authorities' means, in relation to any authority described in column (1) of the following table, the authorities specified in respect thereof in column (2).

(1)	(2)
The parish authority of any parish or the community council of any community	The parish authorities of the parishes, and the community councils of communities with such councils, in which the area of the parish or community is to be comprised

. . .

(c)   In sub-paragraph (a), the reference to all the officers of the authority does not include—

(i)   any person who will by virtue of any agreement entered into between him and any authority enter into the employment of that authority before or on the appointed day; and

(ii)   any person as regards any employment which, otherwise than by virtue of the dissolution of the authority, is to be terminated before or on the appointed day.

. . .

(6)   A scheme for the allocation of officers for transfer may be made by any council described in paragraph (1) in any other circumstances in which they consider it appropriate to make a scheme and shall be made by such a council if they are notified by any other such council that they require a scheme to be made.

. . .

(8)   Subject to paragraphs (2)(c)   . . .   paragraph (2)(a), in its application to any authority, applies to any officer who, immediately before the appointed day, will be in the employment of the authority.

69 Provision as to schemes

(1)   Any scheme made under regulation 67   . . .   or under any provision of the order shall allocate the officers covered by it on the basis of the likely needs of the services to be provided on and after the appointed day.

(2)   In any scheme made under regulation 67 any arrangements made under section 101 or 110 of the Local Government Act 1972, or any direction given under the said section 110, shall be taken into account.

(3)   In preparing any scheme under regulation 67 or 68 or under any provision of the order an authority shall—

(a)   consult the authorities and bodies representatives of officers appearing to them to be concerned; and—

(b)

(i)   notify any officer likely to be allocated for transfer otherwise than to the residuary successor of the authority of such likelihood and supply to him a copy of regulations 67 to 79; and

(ii)   take into consideration any representations made by such officer.

(4)   Upon making any such scheme an authority shall—

(a)   transmit copies thereof to the authorities and bodies representative of officers appearing to them to be concerned; and

(b)   notify every officer allocated of such allocation and (unless such copy has already been supplied) supply to him a copy of regulations 67 to 79.

(5)   Any such scheme may be amended by the authority by whom it was made, but—

no substantive amendment shall be made in a matter in respect of which there has been no consultation under paragraph (3) with any authority or body representative of staff appearing to the first-mentioned authority to be concerned without such consultation; and

no officer shall be allocated for transfer unless the action described in paragraph (3)(b) has been taken in relation to him.

Upon making any amendment an authority shall—

(a)   transmit copies of the scheme as amended or of the amendments to the authorities and bodies representative of officers appearing to them to be concerned; and

(b)   notify every officer affected by the amendments of his allocation and (unless such copy has already been supplied) supply him with a copy of regulations 67 to 79.

(6)   If notice is given by any authority that they are dissatisfied with the provisions of any such scheme as made or amended the question shall be determined by agreement between the authorities concerned or failing such agreement by the decision of a person agreed on by such authorities or in default of agreement appointed by the Secretary of State.

Upon any determination which involves a variation of the scheme the authority by whom the scheme was made shall vary it in accordance with the determination and—

(a)   transmit copies of the scheme as amended or of the amendments to the authorities and bodies representative of staff appearing to them to be concerned; and

(b)   notify every officer affected by the variation of his allocation and (unless such copy has already been supplied) supply him with a copy of regulations 67 to 79.

(7)   In the application of paragraph (2)(a), (3), (4), (5) or (6) of regulation 67, regulation 68 or any provision of the order to any authority, any allocation of a person not in the whole-time employment of the authority shall be limited to the extent of his employment with the authority.

(8)   Any question by an officer of any authority in relation to the application of a scheme to him may be determined in accordance with the arrangements applicable to the determination of disputes as to employment and terms and conditions thereof between the officer and the authority, and on the determination of such question by any body, any necessary amendment of the scheme shall be made by that body.

(9)   No scheme made under any provision of the order shall extend to the officers specified in regulation 67(7).

70 Transfer of officers

(1) Every officer allocated by any scheme made under regulation 67 or 68 or under any provision of the order for transfer to any authority shall, to the extent of the allocation, be transferred to the employment of that authority.

. . .

(3) Any other officer of a dissolved authority (other than charter trustees) shall be transferred to the employment of the residuary successor of that authority.

(4) Nothing in paragraph . . . (3) applies to any person described in (i) or (ii) of sub-paragraph (2)(c) of regulation 67 or in paragraph (7) of that regulation.

(5) Subject to paragraph (4), paragraph (2) or (3), in its application to any authority, applies to any officer who immediately before the appointed day is in the employment of the authority, but in the case of a person not in the whole-time employment of the authority the transfer effected by such paragraph in such application is limited to the extent of his employment with the authority.

(6) Any officer who will be transferred by paragraph (2) or (3) shall be notified by the authority employing him of such transfer not later than one month before the appointed day, and (unless such copy has already been supplied) shall be supplied with a copy of regulations 67 to 79.

(7)

(a)   The following questions by an officer of any authority, namely—

(i)   any question of hardship; and

(ii)   any question whether he is or is not employed in any manner specified in paragraph (2)(a);

may be determined in accordance with the arrangements applicable to the determination of disputes as to employment and terms and conditions thereof between the officer and the authority.

(b)   Any question described in item (ii) of sub-paragraph (a) shall be raised as soon as may be and in any case not later than the expiration of 2 months (or such longer period as may be agreed by the authority) from the notification under paragraph (6).

(c)   Where any question described in sub-paragraph (a) has been determined before the appointed day in such manner that no transfer of the officer is appropriate the officer shall not be transferred by this regulation.

(d)   Where any such question is so determined in such manner that a transfer of the officer otherwise than in accordance with the provisions of paragraphs (1) to (3) is appropriate the officer shall be transferred on the appointed day in accordance with the determination.

(e)   Where any such question is determined on or after the appointed day in such manner that a transfer or further transfer of the officer is appropriate the officer shall be transferred in accordance with the determination at the expiration of 28 days from the date thereof or such other date as may be agreed by the authorities concerned and the officer.

(f)   Where it is determined that an officer will sustain or has sustained hardship in consequence of his transfer (and sub-paragraph (c), (d) or (e) is not applicable) the authority to whom he will be or has been transferred shall in consultation with the officer and representatives of their employees seek a remedy and, not later than the expiration of one month (or such longer period as may be agreed by the officer) following the notification of the determination, notify the officer of any remedy which they are able to offer him or that they are unable to offer him any remedy but that an allowance would be paid to him in respect of the hardship.

(g) In either event, the officer shall be informed that he may, subject to sub-paragraph (j), request that his employment be terminated and of his entitlements if it is so terminated.

(h) Any remedy offered under sub-paragraph (f) may be accepted by the officer within the 2 months following the notification thereof, or within such longer period as may be agreed by the authority.

(i) An allowance in respect of hardship shall be by periodic payments of such amount as may be determined by agreement between the officer and the authority or failing such agreement in accordance with the arrangements applicable to the determination of disputes as to employment and terms and conditions thereof between them.

(j) No such request as is described in sub-paragraph (g) shall be made after the expiration of 2 months from the determination of the amount of the periodic payments of the allowance.

(k) Regulation 77 shall not apply to any officer to whom an allowance is payable under this paragraph.

(l) If the remedy offered is, with the agreement of the authority from whose employment the officer was transferred, transfer back to the employment of that authority, and that remedy is accepted by the officer and he is so transferred, paragraph (12) of regulation 71, and regulations 72 to 78, shall cease to apply to him. Otherwise, such provisions shall apply to any officer transferred under sub-paragraph (f) as they apply to officers transferred by this regulation.

71 Protection of officers transferred

(1) Every officer transferred by or under regulation 70 to the employment of any body (other than an officer transferred under paragraph (7)(f) of that regulation back to the employment of the authority from whose employment he was transferred) shall, so long as he continues in that employment by virtue of the transfer and until he is served with a statement in writing referring to these regulations and specifying new terms and conditions of employment, enjoy terms and conditions of employment not less favourable than those which he enjoyed immediately before the appointed day.

(2) A statement of new terms and conditions of employment shall not be served on any officer in relation to whom a question has been referred under regulation 70(7) until the determination of the question has been notified.

A statement of new terms and conditions of employment shall not be served on any officer to whom sub-paragraphs (f) to (l) of regulation 70(7) apply until the remedy offered under the said sub-paragraph (f) or the allowance there referred to has been accepted by the officer.

(3) Subject to paragraph (2), a statement of new terms and conditions of employment may be served before the appointed day.

(4) Subject to paragraph (2), a statement of new terms and conditions of employment shall be served before the expiry of 12 months after the appointed day.

(5) If after service of a statement of new terms and conditions of employment upon any officer (whether before the appointed day or otherwise) a question is referred under regulation 70(7), the statement shall cease to have effect and paragraphs (1) and (2) shall have effect as if the statement had not been served.

(6) The new terms and conditions of employment shall be such that—

(a) so long as the officer is engaged in duties reasonably comparable to those in which he was engaged immediately before the appointed day, the scale of his salary or remuneration is not less favourable than that which he enjoyed immediately before the appointed day; and

(b) the other terms and conditions of his employment are not less favourable than those which he enjoyed immediately before the appointed day.

(7)   Where between the appointed day and the service of the statement of new terms and conditions of employment upon any officer the scale of the salary or remuneration which such officer enjoyed immediately before the appointed day is improved, paragraph (6)(a) shall have effect as if the scale as improved has been so enjoyed.

(8)   Where the new terms and conditions of employment involve any diminution of the scale of the salary or remuneration of an officer they shall not come into effect until the date, not earlier than the expiration of 3 months from the service of the statement thereof, specified in that statement.

(9)   Any question by an officer of any authority—

whether duties are reasonably comparable within the meaning of paragraph (6);

whether the scale of his salary or remuneration is such as is required by paragraphs (6) and (7); or

whether the other terms and conditions of his employment are not less favourable than those which he enjoyed immediately before the appointed day,

shall be determined in accordance with the arrangements applicable to the determination of disputes as to employment and terms and conditions thereof between the officer and the authority.

(10)   In this regulation, 'terms and conditions of employment' includes any restriction arising under any Act or any instrument made under any Act on the termination of the employment of any officer.

(11)   A written statement given in accordance with section 4(1) of the Contracts of Employment Act 1972 shall not be regarded as a statement of new terms and conditions of employment for the purposes of this regulation unless the statement so indicates.

(12)   A notice to terminate the contract of employment of any officer transferred by regulation 70, given by reason of the fact that the officer to whom it is given has become redundant in consequence of the order, shall, unless such officer otherwise agrees, not come into operation earlier than the expiration of 3 months from the service thereof.

72 Secondary transfers

Any officer transferred by regulation 70 to the employment of any authority may, within the 2 years following the appointed day, be transferred by the said authority, with the agreement of any other authority, and of the officer, to the employment of that other authority, and regulation 71 shall thereupon apply to such officer as it applies to officers transferred by regulation 70.

74 Saving for training arrangements

Where any officer transferred by regulation 70 or under regulation 72 is undergoing training under arrangements which have not been discharged before the appointed day, those arrangements shall continue to apply with the substitution, for the authority in whose employment the officer was prior to the commencement of the training, of the authority to whose employment he has been transferred as aforesaid.

75 Saving for dispensations

Any dispensation from the requirements of any Act or of any instrument made under any Act granted to the authority from whom any officer is transferred by regulation 70 or under regulation 72 shall have effect, in relation to such officer, as if it had been granted to the authority to whose employment he has been transferred as aforesaid.

76 Saving for extensions of service

Any extension of service under regulation L.15 of the Local Government Superannuation Regulations 1974 effective on the appointed day in relation to an officer transferred by regulation 70 or under regulation 72 shall continue to have effect as if it had been made by the authority to whose employment he has been transferred as aforesaid.

77 Travelling and removal expenses

Any additional travelling expenses, and any removal or incidental expenses, reasonably incurred by any officer in consequence of the order shall be reimbursed by the authority to whose employment he is transferred by regulation 70 or under regulation 72.

78 Commencing points on scales

Where in relation to any officer—

(a)   on the scale of salary or remuneration applicable to him immediately before the appointed day he would have become entitled to an increment on that day; and

(b)   by reason of any appointment effective as from the appointed day made by the authority to whose employment he is transferred by regulation 70 or under regulation 72, any other scale of salary or remuneration becomes applicable to him as from that day,

any term of his employment as to his commencing point on such other scale shall be applicable as if his employment before, and on and after, the said day were one continuous employment under one authority.

79 Continuity of employment

Where, apart from this regulation, a person's continuity of employment would be broken by any transfer referred to in (a) or (b) then nevertheless, for the purposes of the Redundancy Payments Act 1965, section 28 of the Industrial Relations Act 1971 as re-enacted in paragraph 10 of Schedule 1 to the Trade Union and Labour Relations Act 1974 (qualifying period for protection from unfair dismissal), sections 1 and 2 of the Contracts of Employment Act 1972 (minimum periods of notice) and section 61 of the Employment Protection Act 1975—

(a)   the period of his employment in the employment from which he is transferred by paragraph (1), (2), (3) or (7)(d) or (e) of regulation 70 and the period of his employment in the employment to which he is transferred by such provision shall in the case of an officer further transferred by or under paragraph (7)(e) or (f) of the said regulation or under regulation 72 count as a period of employment in the employment to which he is so further transferred;

(b)   the period of his employment in the employment from which he is transferred by paragraph (1), (2), (3) or (7)(d) or (e) of regulation 70 shall in the case of any other officer so transferred count as a period of employment in the employment to which he is so transferred; and

(c)   no change of employment covered by (a) or (b) shall break the continuity of the period of employment.

80 Appointment of officers before appointed day

(1)   Where before the appointed day the local authority for any area established or altered by the order appoint to hold any office or employment before or as from that day any person (hereinafter referred to as 'the officer') who is in the employment of the local authority for any area so altered or abolished, the appointment shall be on such terms and conditions that—

(a)   so long as the officer is engaged in duties reasonably comparable to those in which he was engaged immediately before the appointment, the scale of his salary or remuneration; and

(b)   the other terms and conditions of his employment,

are not less favourable than those he enjoyed immediately before the appointment.
Any question by the officer—

whether duties are reasonably comparable as aforesaid; or

whether the scale of his salary or remuneration or the other terms and conditions of his employment are not less favourable than those which he enjoyed immediately before the appointment,

shall be determined in accordance with the arrangements applicable to the determination of disputes as to employment and terms and conditions thereof between the officer and the first-mentioned authority.

In this paragraph, 'terms and conditions of employment' includes any restriction arising under any Act or any instrument made under any Act on the termination of the employment of any officer.

(2) This paragraph may be applied by the order in respect of any authority (hereinafter referred to as 'the new employing authority') and of any authority specified in relation thereto (hereinafter referred to as 'the existing employing authority') and in this paragraph 'the officer' means a person appointed as mentioned in paragraph (1).

The appointment of an officer to hold any office or employment before the appointed day shall not result in his employment by the new employing authority until that day, and his employment by the existing employing authority shall continue to that day, unless determined otherwise than by reason of the said appointment; and—

(a)   the existing employing authority shall place the services of the officer at the disposal of the new employing authority to such extent as may be agreed between the said authorities;

(b)   the salary or remuneration payable by the existing employing authority to the officer at any time shall be the aggregate of the following amounts, namely—

(i)   the amount of the salary or remuneration which would have been payable by the existing employing authority apart from their action under (a) hereof which is for the time being agreed between the existing employing authority and the officer to be appropriate having regard to such action; and

(ii)   the amount for the time being agreed between the new employing authority and the officer in respect of the office or employment; and

(c)   the new employing authority shall reimburse to the existing employing authority—

(i)   the amounts described in (b)(ii) hereof paid by the existing employing authority; and

(ii)   such proportion of all other payments to or in respect of the officer as may be agreed between the said authorities or, failing such agreement, as may be determined by a person agreed on by them or in default of agreement appointed by the Secretary of State:

Provided that the said authorities may, in any particular case, agree that no reimbursement shall be made.

(3) Paragraphs (1) and (2) shall apply, where an officer appointed by the new employing authority is in the employment of two or more existing employing authorities, and paragraph (1) shall apply, where the officer is in two or more employments of one such authority, as if he were only in the employment in respect of which there is paid to him the highest salary or remuneration, or if two or more salaries or remunerations are equal such employment as the new employing authority shall determine.

(4) Where an adjustment of superannuation funds is required to be made in respect of any person to whom paragraphs (1) to (3) apply and in consequence of action taken under those paragraphs his remuneration is higher or lower than it would have been if those paragraphs had not applied to him, no account shall be taken of that increase or decrease in determining his remuneration for the purposes of calculating the amount

payable by way of adjustment but the said amount shall be increased or decreased as the case may be by a sum equivalent to the aggregate of the contributions payable or which would have been payable by the employing authority and the employee in respect of the amount by which his remuneration was increased or decreased during the period for which the said paragraphs apply to him.

81 Gratuities and pensions

(1) Where at any time before the appointed day a gratuity or allowance, by way of periodical payment or an annuity—

(a)   has been granted to any person by any authority on his ceasing to be employed by them; or

(b)   has been granted to the widow or other dependant of a person who died while in or after leaving the employment of any authority,

and, if payment in respect of the gratuity or allowance had continued in accordance with the terms of the grant or any subsequent increase, one or more payments would have been made on or after the appointed day (whether under legal obligation or otherwise) by a dissolved authority, those payments shall be made by the specified authority.

(2) Without prejudice to paragraph (1), where, if the order had not been made, any dissolved authority would for the purposes of any statutory provision relating to pensions have been the employing authority or former employing authority in relation to a person who died before the appointed day while in the employment of, or otherwise ceased to be employed by, any authority, or the widow or other dependant of such a person, the specified authority shall be treated as being at that time the employing authority or former employing authority for those purposes in relation to that person, his widow or other dependant.

(3) In paragraphs (1) and (2), 'the specified authority' means—

(a)   if the person described in (a) or (b) of paragraph (1) or in paragraph (2) was—

(i)   in the case of a person who died while in the employment of the authority, last employed before he died; or

(ii)   otherwise, last employed before he ceased to hold the employment referred to,

exclusively in the discharge of functions in relation to any area transferred by the order and those functions are, on and after the appointed day, exercisable in relation to that area by an authority other than the residuary successor of the dissolved authority, that other authority; and

(b)   otherwise, the residuary successor of the dissolved authority.

82 Inspection of documents

(1) This regulation shall apply in the circumstances set out in the entries in column (1) of the following table and in this regulation 'transferred area' means an area described in any such entry, and—

'transferor authority,' in relation to any transferred area, means an authority specified in respect of the area in column (2) in whose area the transferred area is comprised before the appointed day; and

'transferee authority', in relation to any transferred area, means an authority specified in respect of the transferor authority in column (3) in whose area the transferred area is comprised on and after the appointed day.

(1)	(2)	(3)
. . .		

Where an area is transferred from a parish or community to another such area	The parish authority or community council or where in Wales there is no community council	The parish authority or community council or where in Wales there is no community council
Where an area in England becomes or becomes part of a parish	The district council	The parish authority
Where an area in England ceases to be part of any parish	The parish authority	The district council

(2)   As from the coming into operation of the order any officer of a transferee authority, duly authorised in that behalf, shall for the purposes of the functions of the authority by whom he is employed, be entitled during ordinary office hours to inspect and take copies of or extracts from any books or documents of a transferor authority relating to the transferred area not in the custody of the transferee authority, and a transferor authority shall supply such information and afford such assistance in relation to such books and documents as a transferee authority may reasonably require.

(3)   In relation to any highways in an area transferred from a district to another district in the same county—

(a)   if such highways are immediately before the appointed day being maintained by the district council by virtue of section 187(2)(a) of the Local Government Act 1972 but will on and after that day be maintained by the county council, paragraph (2) shall apply as if the county council were a transferee authority; and

(b)   if such highways are immediately before the appointed day being maintained by the county council but will on and after that day be maintained by the district council by virtue of the said section 187(2)(a), paragraph (2) shall apply as if the county council were a transferor authority.

83 Minutes of last meetings

(1)   This regulation shall apply to any dissolved authority other than parish trustees and to the committees and sub-committees thereof.

(2)   The minutes of the last meeting of any body to whom this regulation applies shall if practicable be signed at such meeting.

(3)   If it is not practicable for the minutes to be so signed they may be signed by the person who presided at the meeting in accordance with paragraph (4), (5) or (6), and—

(a)   any minute purporting to be so signed shall be received in evidence without further proof; and

(b)   until the contrary is proved, the meeting in respect of the proceedings whereof a minute has been made and so signed shall be deemed to have been duly convened and held, and all the members present at the meeting shall be deemed to have been duly qualified, and where the proceedings are the proceedings of a committee or sub-committee the committee or sub-committee shall be deemed to have been duly constituted and to have had power to deal with the matters referred to in the minutes.

(4)   Minutes of the proceedings of the last meeting of any body to whom this regulation applies other than a committee or sub-committee or a parish meeting may be signed as aforesaid on or after the 7th day following the transmission to every member of the body of a copy of the minutes and of a notification of the purport of paragraph (3) and this paragraph. The person who presided at the meeting shall take into consideration any representations made by any such member.

(5) Minutes of the proceedings of the last meeting of a committee or sub-committee may be signed as aforesaid on or after the 7th day following the transmission to every member of the committee or sub-committee of a notification of the purport of paragraph (3) and this paragraph, with a copy of the minutes or information as to the availability of a copy for inspection. The person who presided at the meeting shall take into consideration any representations made by any such member.

(6) Minutes of the proceedings of the last meeting of a parish meeting may be signed as aforesaid after such consultation as the person presiding at the meeting shall think appropriate.

(7) If the person who presided at the meeting is not able to sign the minutes in accordance with paragraph (4), (5) or (6), paragraph (3) and such paragraph shall have effect with the substitution for any reference to the person who presided at the meeting of a reference to such person as the Secretary of State may direct.

84 General provision as to disputes

(1) Any question as to the interpretation of these regulations (other than regulation 24) or of the order may be determined by the decision of a person agreed on by the authorities concerned or in default of agreement appointed by the Secretary of State.

(2) Where a determination required by any provision in Part II of Schedule 6 has not been made by the transferor authority before the appointed day notice that a question exists may be given within the 12 months following the appointed day by any authority concerned.

(3) Where—

    (a)   at the appointed day—

        (i)   notice has been given by any authority under any provision in Part II of Schedule 6; or

        (ii)   notice has been given by any authority that the interpretation of any provision made by paragraphs (2) or (3) of regulation 62 is in dispute;

and the question has not been determined; or

    (b)   thereafter, but within the 12 months following the appointed day—

        (i)   notice is given by any authority under any provision in Part II of Schedule 6;

        (ii)   notice is so given under paragraph (2); or

        (iii)   notice is so given that the interpretation of any provision made by paragraphs (2) or (3) of regulation 62 is in dispute,

then from the appointed day or from the later day on which the notice is given, as the case may be—

    (k)   paragraph (2) of regulation 62 shall cease to have effect in relation to the property;

    (l)   where the transferor authority is dissolved by the order, paragraph (3) of that regulation shall apply to the property and to any liabilities incurred, contracts, deeds, bonds, agreements and other instruments subsisting, notices given, actions and proceedings pending and causes of action or proceeding existing in relation thereto, as temporary provision pending the determination of the question:

Provided that the authorities concerned may by instrument in writing agree that any authority may in such application be substituted for the residuary successor of the dissolved authority;

        (m)   where notice has been given under paragraph (2), the question shall be determined by agreement between the authorities concerned or failing such agreement by the decision of a person agreed on by such authorities or in default of agreement appointed by the Secretary of State; and

(n)   on the determination of the question whether under (m) or otherwise—

    (x)   the determination shall specify the authority to whom the property is to be transferred; and

    (y)   if paragraph (3) of regulation 62 has been applied by (l) it shall cease to have effect; and

    (z)   the property shall by virtue of the determination be transferred to and vest in the authority specified in the determination, and the provisions of these regulations which would have applied to the property if the transfer had been effected by paragraph (2) of regulation 62 shall apply to it.

(4) Any reference in any provision of these regulations for the decision of any question by a person shall be construed as including a reference to three persons.

(5) Section 31 of the Arbitration Act 1950 shall have effect for the purposes of the determination of any question by any person or persons under any provision of these regulations as if such determination were an arbitration under any other Act within the meaning of that section.

85 General savings

(1) Nothing in these regulations or the order shall affect—

   . . .

    (b)   any ecclesiastical parish or district;

   . . .

    (f)   the functions of the conservators of any common;

   . . .

    (i)   any right or interest under any inclosure award.

(2) Save as provided in the order, nothing in these regulations or the order shall affect—

    (a)   any electoral area;

   . . .

    (c)   the trusts of any charity.

SCHEDULE 6

TRANSFER OF SPECIFIED CLASSES OF PROPERTY, ETC

PART I

1

'Local matters', in relation to any area, means—

    (a)   in the case of property—

        (i)   sited property situated in the area;

        (ii)   specified property in relation to buildings or other land constituting local matters in relation to the area, except in so far as such property is excluded by the agreement of the transferee authority; and

        (iii)   other property held exclusively in respect of the area;

    (b)   in the case of liabilities, liabilities incurred exclusively in respect of the area;

    (c)   in the case of contracts, deeds, bonds, agreements and other instruments, and notices, such instruments subsisting and notices given exclusively in respect of the area;

    (d)   in the case of actions and proceedings and causes of action or proceeding, such actions and proceedings pending or causes existing exclusively in respect of the area.

In this paragraph—

    'sited property' means—

        land, including any interest in land and any easement [or right] in, to or over land;

        buildings not within the meaning of the term 'land';

        fittings, furniture, equipment and stores supplied in respect of a voluntary school or a controlled community home;

        lamps, lamp posts and other apparatus forming part of a system not constituting highway matters under paragraph 3;

    'specified property', in relation to any building, means—

        the fittings, furniture, equipment and records of the building;

        any stores in the building which have been provided for the discharge of functions therein;

        any vehicle or other mobile equipment used wholly or mainly in the performance of the functions carried out in the building;

and in the case of any other land means any vehicle or other mobile equipment used wholly or mainly in the performance of the functions carried out on the land.

2

'County matters', 'district matters', 'parish matters', 'community matters', 'Greater London matters' and 'borough matters', in relation to any area, mean the following classes of local matters—

    (a)   in the case of property, property held for the purposes of functions not exercisable in the area on and after the appointed day by the transferor authority or the authority of the relevant class in relation to the transferor authority but so exercisable by the authority specified in respect of the matters transferred in column (3) of the table;

    (b)   in the case of liabilities, liabilities incurred in relation to such functions;

    (c)   in the case of contracts, deeds, bonds, agreements and other instruments, and notices, such instruments subsisting and notices given in relation to such functions;

    (d)   in the case of actions and proceedings and causes of action or proceeding, such actions and proceedings pending or causes existing in relation to such functions.

In this paragraph, the relevant class of authorities, in relation to any transferor authority described in column (1) below, means the class specified in respect thereof in column (2).

(1)	(2)
. . .	
A parish authority or a community council	Parish authorities and community councils
. . .	

6

No entry in column (2) of the table in this Part of this Schedule shall extend to any property included in any extension of the table effected by the order.

7

No entry other than the first in the said table shall extend to any property described in such first entry.

(1) Transferor authority	(2) Matters transferred	(3) Transferee authority
. . .		
The council of a district from which any area is transferred to a county and district or to another district in the same county	County matters in relation to the area	The council of the county in which the area is comprised on and after the appointed day
	If the area is transferred to a parish, parish matters in relation to the area	The parish authority for the parish
	If the area is transferred to a community with a community council, community matters in relation to the area	The community council
	Other local matters in relation to the area	The council of the district to which the area is transferred
The council of a district within which any area is transferred from one parish or community to a parish or a community with a community council	Parish or community matters in relation to the area	The parish authority for the parish or the community council for the community
The council of a district in England	Parish matters in relation to any area which becomes or becomes part of a parish	The parish authority for the parish
The council of a district or the parish authority of a parish from which any area is transferred to Greater London and a London borough	Greater London matters in relation to the area	The Greater London Council
	Other local matters in relation to the area	The corporation or council of the London borough to which the area is transferred
The parish authority for a parish, or the community council for a community, from which any area is transferred otherwise than to Greater London and a London borough	District matters in relation to the area	The council of the district in which the area is comprised on and after the appointed day
	Other local matters in relation to the area	In England, the parish authority for the parish, or if the area is not transferred to a parish, the council of the district, to which the area is transferred

(1) Transferor authority	(2) Matters transferred	(3) Transferee authority
		In Wales, the community council for the community, or if there is no community council the council of the district, to which the area is transferred
The corporation or council of any London borough from which any area is transferred to a county and district	County matters in relation to such area	The council of the county to which the area is transferred
	If the area is transferred to a parish, parish matters in relation to the area	The parish authority for the parish
	Other local matters in relation to such area	The council of the district to which the area is transferred

. . .

PART II

1

(a)   Any question as to the functions for the purposes of which any property is held, any liabilities have been incurred, any contract, deed, bond, agreement or other instrument subsists, any notice has been given or any action or proceeding or cause of action or proceeding relates shall, subject to the provision of sub-paragraph (b), be determined by the transferor authority.

(b)   If notice is given by any authority that they are dissatisfied with any determination under sub-paragraph (a), the question shall be determined by agreement between the authorities concerned or failing such agreement by the decision of a person agreed on by such authorities or in default of agreement appointed by the Secretary of State.

2

The provisions of section 187(2) and (3) of the Local Government Act 1972 shall be disregarded.

3

(a)   This paragraph applies to—

    (i)   any property held for the purposes of section 132 or 133 of the Local Government Act 1972;

    (ii)   any land acquired under section 112, 114 or 119(1)(a) of the Town and Country Planning Act 1971 or any earlier provision corresponding to any such enactment;

    (iii)   any land acquired under section 120(1)(b) of the said Act of 1972, section 124(1)(b) thereof or any other provision empowering the acquisition of land for the benefit, improvement or development of any area and not allocated or appropriated for any statutory purpose; and

    (iv)   any property acquired by a local authority as a gift otherwise than for charitable purposes;

(b)   Where any property to which this paragraph applies is, immediately before the appointed day—

929

(i)   in the case of property referred to in sub-paragraph (a)(i), used wholly or substantially so for the purposes of a particular function being purposes authorised by enactments other than the said sections 132 and 133;

(ii)   in the case of property referred to in sub-paragraph (a)(ii), used wholly or mainly for the purposes of a statutory function other than those exercised under the Town and Country Planning Acts 1971 and 1972; or

(iii)   in the case of property referred to in sub-paragraph (a)(iii) or (iv), used wholly or mainly for the purpose of any statutory function,

it shall for the purposes of paragraph (2) of regulation 62 be deemed to be held for the purposes of the function for which it is so used.

(c)   In the application of sub-paragraph (b) any temporary use of the property shall be disregarded.

(d)   Two (but not more) functions shall be treated as a single function in the application of sub-paragraph (b).

(e)   Any property to which sub-paragraph (b) applies shall be held by the authority to whom it is transferred for the purposes of the function described in (i), (ii) or (iii) of that sub-paragraph or where two functions have been treated as a single function for the purposes of such one of those functions as is determined by the authority to whom the property is transferred.

(f)   Any question whether any property to which this paragraph applies is, immediately before the appointed day, used as described in (i), (ii) or (iii) of sub-paragraph (b) shall, subject to the provision of sub-paragraph (g), be determined by the authority in whom the property is, before the appointed day, vested.

(g)   If notice is given by any authority that they are dissatisfied with any such determination the question shall be determined by agreement between the authorities concerned or failing such agreement by the decision of a person agreed on by such authorities or in default of agreement appointed by the Secretary of State, and sub-paragraph (e) shall apply accordingly. Sub-paragraphs (c) and (d) shall apply in the application of this sub-paragraph.

4

(a)   The provisions of this paragraph shall apply where—

(i)   at the appointed day any building or part of a building is to be wholly or substantially so replaced by another building which is completed or in the course of erection or for the erection of which a contract has been entered into, or by part of such building;

(ii)   it has been resolved by the transferor authority before the coming into operation of the order that the first-mentioned building or part of a building or the site thereof is to be used for some function other than the one for which it is held; and

(iii)   the nature of the building or the location of its site is such as to make it peculiarly suited for use for the purposes of such function rather than for other local government purposes,

and apart from the provisions of this paragraph the two buildings or parts of buildings would be transferred to the same authority.

(b)   The transferor authority may determine that for the purposes of paragraph (2) of regulation 62 the land on which the building or part of a building first mentioned in sub-paragraph (a) is erected shall be deemed to be held for the purposes for which by the resolution described in (ii) thereof it is to be used.

(c)   If notice is given by any authority concerned that they question whether (i), (ii) or (iii) in sub-paragraph (a) is satisfied, the determination shall be of no effect and the question of the purpose for which the land is to be deemed to be held shall be determined by agreement between the authorities concerned or failing such agreement by the decision of a person agreed on by such authorities or in default of agreement appointed by the Secretary of State.

5

(a) The provisions of this paragraph shall have effect in relation to any land appropriated within the 12 months preceding the appointed day and to any financial adjustment made on the appropriation.

(b) Any such land shall for the purposes of paragraph (2) of regulation 62 be treated as held for the purposes for which it has been appropriated, and any financial adjustment made on the appropriation shall be of full effect, unless an authority give notice that the land falls to be treated for the purposes of the said paragraph as being held for the purpose for which it was held before the appropriation, or that the financial adjustment falls to be varied. If such notice is given the question of the purpose for which the land is held, or as the case may be the adjustment to be made, shall be determined by agreement between the authorities concerned or failing such agreement by the decision of a person agreed on by such authorities or in default of agreement appointed by the Secretary of State.

LOCAL AUTHORITIES' CEMETERIES ORDER 1977

(SI 1977/204)

2 Interpretation

(1) The Interpretation Act 1889 shall apply for the interpretation of this order as it applies for the interpretation of an Act of Parliament.

(2) In this order, unless the context otherwise requires—

'the Act' means the Local Government Act 1972;

'bishop' means, in relation to any ecclesiastical district or place not subject to the jurisdiction of a bishop, the authority known to the law of the Church of England as 'the ordinary';

'burial' includes—

(a)   the interment of cremated human remains;

(b)   the interment of the bodies of still-born children or of the cremated remains thereof; and

(c)   the placing in a vault of human remains, cremated human remains, or the bodies of still-born children or the cremated remains thereof;

'burial authority' means the council of a district, London borough, parish or community, the Common Council of the City of London, the parish meeting of a parish having no parish council, whether separate or common, or a joint board established under section 6 of the Public Health Act 1936 or by or under any local Act for the provision and maintenance of cemeteries;

'cemetery' means a cemetery provided and maintained by a burial authority;

'computer' means any device for storing and processing information;

'consecration' means consecration according to the rites of the Church of England, and cognate expressions shall be construed accordingly;

'grave' includes a walled grave, but subject to the provision of article 16(2) does not include a vault;

'the order of 1974' means the Local Authorities' Cemeteries Order 1974;

'the specified circumstances', in respect of any owner or person, are where—

any communication addressed to him at his last recorded address has been returned to the burial authority (whether as such or otherwise) as undeliverable; or

his last recorded address is that of premises which no longer exist;
'tombstone' includes kerbs;
'vault' means a chamber provided for the reception of human remains or
cremated human remains, together with the access thereto;
'walled grave' means a grave the sides of which are lined with walls; and
'the Welsh Church Act' means the Welsh Church Act 1914, and 'the area
subject to the Welsh Church Act' means the area in which the Church of
England was disestablished by that Act.

(3)   Any reference in this order to a chapel provided as mentioned in article 6(1)(b)
includes a reference to any chapel provided under section 2(2) or (3) of the Burial Act
1900 or article 6(1)(b) of the order of 1974.

(4)   For the purposes of this order, subject to the provisions thereof, any power or
right to provide anything includes a power or right to maintain it.

(5)   Any reference in this order to a right to place and maintain a tombstone or other
memorial includes a reference to a right to place a tombstone or other memorial.

(6)   Any reference in any provision of this order other than paragraph 5, 11 or 14 of
Schedule 3 (as to which provision is made in paragraph 19 of that Schedule) to a right
described in article 10(1)(a)(i) or (ii) includes a reference to any right granted under
sub-paragraph (a) of article 9(1) of the order of 1974 or any enactment replaced by
that sub-paragraph, and the reference in article 10(1)(c) to a right described in (a)(i)
includes a reference to any similar right so granted.

(7)   For the purposes of this order any railings surrounding a grave, vault, tombstone
or other memorial shall be treated as forming part thereof.

(8)   In this order, unless the context otherwise requires, references to any enactment
shall be construed as references to that enactment as amended, extended or applied by
or under any other enactment or by this order.

(9)   Any reference in this order to a numbered article or Schedule shall, unless the
reference is to an article or Schedule of a specified order, be construed as a reference to
the article or Schedule bearing that number in this order.

. . .

3 General powers of management

(1)   Subject to the provisions of this order, a burial authority may do all such things as
they consider necessary or desirable for the proper management, regulation and
control of a cemetery.

(2)   Nothing in paragraph (1) shall be construed as authorising—

(a)   any action in relation to any chapel provided as mentioned in
article 6(1)(b); or

(b)   any action in relation to any vault, or any tombstone or other memorial,
other than action which is necessary to remove a danger which arises by
reason of the condition of the vault, or the tombstone or other memorial,
itself.

(3)   Where in the exercise of the powers conferred by paragraph (1) a burial authority
enter into any agreement with the rural dean or the representatives of a particular
denomination or religious body in relation to the management of any part of a
cemetery, or where any such agreement has been entered into under paragraph (1) of
article 3 of the order of 1974 or enactments replaced by that paragraph—

(a)   the first-mentioned paragraph shall have effect subject to the provisions
of the agreement; and

(b)   article 16 shall not be construed as empowering any departure from such
provisions.

4 Layout, repair and access

(1)   A burial authority may enclose, lay out and embellish a cemetery in such manner
as they think fit, and from time to time improve it, and shall keep the cemetery in good

order and repair, together with all buildings, walls and fences thereon and other buildings provided for use therewith.

Nothing in this paragraph shall be construed as requiring any action in relation to any chapel provided as mentioned in article 6(1)(b).

(2) Schedule 1 shall have effect with respect to the provision of access to cemeteries.

5 Consecration, and setting apart for particular denominations

(1) Subject to paragraphs (2) and (3), a burial authority may if they think fit—

    (a) apply to the bishop of the diocese in which a cemetery is situated for the consecration of any part thereof;

    (b) set apart for the use of a particular denomination or religious body any part of a cemetery which has not been consecrated.

(2) A burial authority in exercising the powers conferred by paragraph (1) shall satisfy themselves that a sufficient part of the cemetery remains unconsecrated and not set apart for the use of particular denominations or religious bodies.

(3) Paragraph (1)(a) does not apply to cemeteries within the area subject to the Welsh Church Act, and any part of such a cemetery which was consecrated before the end of March 1920, or in respect of which a ceremony of consecration was performed between that time and 1st April 1974 in accordance with the rites of the Church in Wales, shall be treated for the purposes of this order as having been set apart for the use of that Church (and as not having been consecrated).

(4) A burial authority shall mark off any consecrated part of a cemetery in such manner as they consider suitable.

(5) Notwithstanding the consecration or the setting apart for the use of a particular Christian denomination of the part of a cemetery in which any burial is to be effected, the burial may take place without any religious service or with such Christian and orderly religious service at the grave, conducted by such person or persons, as the person having the charge of or being responsible for the burial may think fit.

(6) A burial authority may at the request of a particular denomination or religious body prohibit the interring or scattering of cremated human remains in or over a part of the cemetery set apart for their use.

6 Provision of chapels

(1) A burial authority may provide chapels as follows—

    (a) on any part of a cemetery which is not consecrated or set apart for the use of a particular denomination or religious body, they may provide any chapel which they consider necessary for the due performance of funeral services, and

    (b) on any part of a cemetery which is consecrated or so set apart, they may, subject to paragraph (3), provide a chapel for the performance of funeral services according to the rites of the Church of England or other particular denomination or religious body.

(2) A chapel provided on any part of a cemetery which is neither consecrated nor set apart for the use of a particular denomination or religious body shall not itself be consecrated or reserved for such a use.

(3) A burial authority may provide a chapel as mentioned in paragraph (1)(b) only at the request of members of the Church of England or other particular denomination or religious body, and out of funds provided for the purpose otherwise than by the authority; and the authority shall not be required to maintain any chapel so provided except so far as funds provided otherwise than by them are available for that purpose.

(4) At the request of persons appearing to them to be representative of the members of the Church of England or other particular denomination or religious body at whose request a chapel was provided as mentioned in paragraph (1)(b), a burial authority may make such chapel available for funeral services according to the rites of any other such body or for the due performance of any funeral services.

(5)   Where the cemeteries of any two authorities adjoin each other, the authorities may agree to exercise their powers under paragraph (1) by providing jointly, on either cemetery or partly on one and partly on the other, one chapel to be used in connection with both cemeteries in accordance with the terms of the agreement.

(6)   A burial authority may furnish and equip their chapels in such manner as they think proper, but, in the case of one provided as mentioned in paragraph (1)(b), only out of funds provided for the purpose otherwise than by the authority.

(7)   Where a chapel provided as mentioned in paragraph (1)(b) becomes dangerous, a burial authority may take such action, including removal, in relation thereto as they consider proper.

7 Provision of mortuaries and biers

(1)   A burial authority may if they think fit provide a mortuary for use in connection with a cemetery, and may furnish and equip any mortuary so provided in such manner as they think proper.

(2)   A burial authority may provide biers, and such other things as they consider necessary or desirable, for use in connection with burials taking place in a cemetery.

8 Arrangements for sharing of facilities

(1)   A burial authority may enter into such agreements as they think fit for—

 (a) the use in connection with burials taking place in a cemetery of chapels, mortuaries, biers and other things provided by persons other than the authority, or

 (b) the use in connection with burials taking place in other places of burial, or in connection with cremations, of any chapel, mortuary, bier or other thing provided for use in connection with burials taking place in the cemetery.

Nothing in this paragraph shall be construed as authorising any action in relation to any chapel provided as mentioned in article 6(1)(b).

(2)   An agreement under this article may include terms as to the services of any staff employed in connection with the subject matter of the agreement.

9 Plan and record of cemetery

(1)   A burial authority shall maintain a plan showing and allocating distinctive numbers to—

 (a) all graves or vaults in which burials are made after the coming into operation of this order or are known to have been made before that event; and

 (b) the grave spaces subject to the specified rights.

(2)   A burial authority shall also maintain records, by reference to the numbers in the plan, of—

 (a) the burials made after the coming into operation of this order in any graves or vaults; and

 (b) the specified rights existing in any graves or vaults, or grave spaces, and the names of the grantees thereof as recorded in the register maintained under Part II of Schedule 2 or in the registers described in paragraph 2(b) of that Part.

(3)   In this article 'the specified rights' means—

 (a) the rights granted by the burial authority or any predecessors of theirs under article 10(1) or under article 9(1) of the order of 1974; and

 (b) the rights granted under section 33 of the Burial Act 1852, section 40 of the Cemeteries Clauses Act 1847 or a corresponding provision in any local Act.

10 Grant of burial rights and rights to erect memorials, and agreements for maintenance of graves and memorials

(1) A burial authority may grant, on such terms and subject to such conditions as they think proper—

    (a)   to any person—

        (i)   the exclusive right of burial in any grave space or grave, or the right to construct a walled grave or vault together with the exclusive right of burial therein; or

        (ii)   the right to one or more burials in any grave space or grave which is not subject to any exclusive right of burial;

    (b)   to the owner of a right described in (a)(i) or (ii) (or to any person who satisfies them that he is a relative of a person buried in the grave or vault, or is acting at the request of such a relative and that it is impractical for him, or such relative, to trace the owner of the right so described), the right to place and maintain, or to put any additional inscription on, a tombstone or other memorial on the grave space, grave or vault in respect of which the right so described subsists;

    (c)   to any person, the right to place and maintain a memorial in a cemetery otherwise than on a grave space, grave or vault in respect of which a right described in (a)(i) has been granted, but—

        (i)   in the case of a memorial to be placed in a chapel provided as mentioned in article 6(1)(b), only at the request of persons appearing to the burial authority to be representative of the Church of England or other particular denomination or religious body at whose request the chapel was provided; and

        (ii)   in the case of any other memorial being an additional inscription on an existing memorial, only with the consent of the owner of the right to place and maintain such existing memorial.

(2) Subject to paragraph (3), a right under paragraph (1), other than a right described in (a)(ii), shall subsist for the period specified in the grant, being a period beginning with the date of the grant and not exceeding 100 years.

(3) Where—

    any exclusive right of burial in any grave space; or

    any right to construct a walled grave or vault together with the exclusive right of burial therein,

granted under paragraph (1) or under article 9(1) of the order of 1974 for a period exceeding 75 years has not been exercised before the expiration of 75 years from the date of the grant, the burial authority may serve notice on the owner of the right of its liability to determination under this paragraph, and the right shall determine by virtue of the notice unless, within 6 months of the date of service, the owner of the right notifies the authority in writing of his intention to retain it.

    Where the burial authority are entitled to serve a notice under this paragraph in respect of any right, but the specified circumstances exist in respect of the owner of the right, they may instead—

    (a)   display the notice in conspicuous positions at the entrances to the cemetery; and

    (b)   publish the notice in two successive weeks in the newspaper or newspapers which in their opinion would secure the best publicity in the area served by the cemetery,

and this paragraph shall then have effect as if the notice had been duly served on the date on which it was first published pursuant to item (b).

(4) A burial authority may from time to time extend the period of any grant under paragraph (1) or under paragraph (1) of article 9 of the order of 1974 or any

enactment replaced by that provision (subject, if they think fit, to any modification of its terms or conditions) for up to 100 years from the date on which the extension is granted.

(5) The burial authority may, at the expiration of the period of any grant under (b) or (c) of paragraph (1) or under (b) or (c) of paragraph (1) of article 9 of the order of 1974 or any enactment replaced by those provisions, or of any extension of such period—

    (a)   move to another place in the cemetery; or

    (b)   remove from the cemetery, for preservation elsewhere or for destruction,

any tombstone or other memorial which has not been removed from the cemetery by the owner of the right to place and maintain it in the cemetery.

(6) No body shall be buried, or cremated human remains interred or scattered, in or over any grave or vault in which an exclusive right of burial for the time being subsists except by, or with the consent in writing of, the owner of the right.

This paragraph shall not extend to the body, or remains, of—

the person who immediately before his death was the owner of the right;

or any other person specified in the deed of grant or in an indorsement thereon made at the request of the owner for the time being of the right by the officer appointed for that purpose by the burial authority.

(7) A burial authority shall also have power to agree with any person, on such terms and subject to such conditions as they think proper, to maintain any grave, vault, tombstone or other memorial in a cemetery for a period not exceeding 100 years from the date of the agreement.

Any agreement under section 1(1)(a) of the Parish Councils and Burial Authorities (Miscellaneous Provisions) Act 1970 shall have effect as if it had been entered into under this paragraph.

(8) Rights granted under paragraph (1) or under paragraph (1) of article 9 of the order of 1974 or enactments replaced by that paragraph shall be exercisable subject to and in accordance with the provisions of Part I of Schedule 2.

The provisions of Part II of that Schedule shall have effect with respect to grants under paragraph (1), the extension of the period of such grants and grants made under paragraph (1) of article 9 of the order of 1974 or any enactment replaced by that paragraph and the registration of, and other matters concerning rights granted under any such paragraph or enactment.

The provisions of Part III of the said Schedule shall have effect for the purpose of enabling a burial authority to terminate the rights and agreements described in paragraph 1 thereof.

11 Registration of burials and disinterments

(1) A burial authority shall maintain a register of all burials in a cemetery in a book or books provided for the purpose, or in a computer.

(2) Where the register of burials is maintained in a book—

    (a)   the book shall be of good and durable paper and be strongly bound and if it is the second or any subsequent book to be provided it shall be numbered accordingly; and

    (b)   the pages in which entries are to be made in any book provided after the coming into operation of this order shall be numbered and shall be printed in columns, including columns headed—

Number/Date of burial/Names in full/Age/Address/Grave or vault number/Other particulars/Signature of person directing or making entry,

and in entry spaces of such uniform depth as the burial authority shall consider sufficient: provided that in a book provided within the 12 months following the coming into operation of this order—

     (i)   the headings of any column of a page may be altered in manuscript so as to comply with this sub-paragraph; and

     (ii)   the column headed 'Other particulars' may be omitted.

(3)   As soon as is reasonably practical after any burial in the cemetery the officer of the burial authority appointed for that purpose shall, in durable black ink, number an entry space in the book and enter the burial therein.

(4)   Where the burial is that of the body of a still-born child or of the cremated remains thereof the words 'Still-born child of' and the name of at least one of the parents shall be written in the column headed 'Names in full', the column headed 'Age' shall be left blank and the address of the parents or parent shall be written in the column headed 'Address'.

(5)   Where the burial is the interment of cremated remains the entry shall record that it is such.

(6)   Where the burial is the re-interment of disinterred remains the entry shall record that it is such and the previous place of burial.

(7)   Subject to paragraphs (4) to (6), the burial shall be entered in accordance with the headings to the columns in the book.

(8)   Where the register of burials is maintained in a computer the burial shall be entered in the computer so as to ensure that any document produced by the computer in relation to that burial contains the same information as would have been recorded if the burial had been entered in a book.

(9)   A burial authority shall maintain a record of any disinterments in a cemetery made after the coming into operation of this order, showing—

     (a)   the date of disinterment;

     (b)   the number of the grave or vault;

     (c)   the names, in full, of the person whose remains are disinterred;

     (d)   the book, page and entry number of the entry of burial or, where the burial was entered in a computer, the number of the entry;

     (e)   particulars of the authority for disinterment; and

     (f)   if the remains are re-interred in the same cemetery, the number of the grave and the date of re-interment; or

     (g)   if the remains are to be re-interred elsewhere or cremated, the place and date of proposed re-interment or cremation.

(10)   As soon as is reasonably practical after any disinterment, the officer of the burial authority appointed for the purpose shall complete the record as regards items (a) to (e) and (g) in paragraph (9) and, where the burial was entered in a book, add to the entry in the register of burials, in durable ink of a colour readily distinguishable from black, a reference to such record. As soon as is reasonably practical after a re-interment in the same cemetery, the said officer shall complete the record as regards item (f) in paragraph (9).

(11)   The register of burials and record of disinterments shall at all reasonable times be available for consultation by any person free of charge.

11A

(1)   A burial authority may charge such fees as they think proper for the making by them of searches in, and the provision of certified copies of entries in, the register of burials or the record of disinterments.

(2)   For the purposes of paragraph (1), a document produced by a computer shall be deemed to be a certified copy of an entry in the register or record if it is accompanied by a certificate signed by a person occupying a responsible position in relation to the operation of the computer—

     (a)   identifying the document and describing the manner in which it was produced;

(b)   giving such particulars of any device involved in the production of that document as may be appropriate for the purpose of showing that the document was produced by a computer; and

(c)   stating that—

    (i)   the document was produced by the computer during a period in which the computer was used regularly to store or process information for the purpose of maintaining burial records;

    (ii)   during that period there was regularly supplied to the computer information of the kind contained in the document or of the kind from which the information so contained was derived;

    (iii)   throughout the material part of that period the computer was operating properly or, if not, that any respect in which it was not operating properly or was out of operation during that part of the period was not such as to affect the production of the document or the accuracy of its contents; and

    (iv)   the information contained in the document reproduces or is derived from information supplied to the computer in the ordinary course of activities.

12 Storage of records

The following, namely—

the plan maintained under article 9(1);

the records maintained under article 9(2);

the register of burials maintained under article 11(1);

any register of burials in the cemetery maintained before the coming into operation of this order;

the record of disinterments maintained under article 11(9);

the register maintained under Part II of Schedule 2;

the registers described in paragraph 2(b) of the said Part II; and

the records of memorials made and kept under paragraph 16 of Schedule 3,

shall be stored so as to preserve them from loss or damage and be in the charge of the officer of the burial authority appointed for that purpose.

13 Right of bishop to object to inscriptions in consecrated parts

A bishop of the Church of England shall, as respects the consecrated part of any cemetery (including any chapel thereon), have the same rights of objecting to, and procuring the removal of, any inscription on a tombstone or other memorial placed, or intended to be placed, therein as he has in the case of churches of the Church of England and the churchyards belonging thereto.

14 Cost of removal of unauthorised memorials

If a burial authority remove from a cemetery any tombstone or other memorial placed therein otherwise than in the exercise of a right granted by, or otherwise with the approval of, the burial authority or any predecessor of theirs, the burial authority may recover the cost thereby incurred by them—

(a)   from the person to whose order the tombstone or memorial was placed;

(b)   within two years from the placing of the tombstone or memorial, from the personal representative of such person,

as a simple contract debt in any court of competent jurisdiction.

15 Fees and other charges

(1) Subject to the provisions of this article a burial authority may charge such fees as they think proper—

(a)   for or in connection with burials in a cemetery;

(b)   for any grant of a right to place and maintain a tombstone or other memorial in a cemetery otherwise than in a chapel provided as mentioned in article 6(1)(b); or

(c)   for any grant of a right to put an additional inscription on such a tombstone or other 147(3 memorial.

In determining the fees to be charged the burial authority shall take into account the effect of any resolution under section) of, or under paragraph 6 of Schedule 26 to, the Act.

(2)   Fees collected by a burial authority in respect of services rendered by any minister of religion or sexton acting at the request of the authority shall be paid by the authority to the minister of religion or sexton, except that, in the case of fees collected for services rendered by a minister of the Church of England, the fees shall be paid to the diocesan board of finance to which fees are payable under section 1 of the Ecclesiastical Fees Measure 1986.

(3)   A burial authority shall keep a table showing the matters in respect of which fees or other charges are payable to them, and the amount of each such fee or charge, and the table shall be available for inspection by the public at all reasonable times.

(4)   ....

16 Maintenance of graves, etc: removal of memorials and levelling, etc

(1)   A burial authority may—

(a)   put and keep in order any grave or vault, or any tombstone or other memorial, in a cemetery; and

(b)   level the surface of any grave, consisting wholly or substantially so of earth or grass, to the level of the adjoining ground.

In respect of any grave levelled by them in exercise of the powers set out in (b), the burial authority may, and shall if so requested in writing by—

the owner of a right described in article 10(1)(a)(i) or (ii) in respect of the grave; or

a relative of any person buried in the grave,

provide at their own expense such identification mark as they consider adequate.

(2)   A burial authority may, subject to and in accordance with the provisions of Schedule 3—

(a)   remove from the cemetery and destroy—

(i)   any tombstone or other memorial on a grave of which all material particulars are illegible or which is dilapidate by reasons of long neglect;

(ii)   any kerbs surrounding a grave (whether containing any commemorative inscription or not) together with the foundation slabs of such kerbs;

(iii)   any tombstone or other memorial, not falling within (i) or (ii), on a grave, except where the owner of the right to place and maintain it in the cemetery has, before the date specified in the notice under paragraph 3 of Schedule 3 as the date before which the carrying out of the proposals will not be commenced, requested that it shall be re-erected in the cemetery or elsewhere;

(iv)   any surface fittings not falling within (i), (ii) or (iii), or any flowering or other plants, on a grave; and

(v)   any railings surrounding a grave, a tombstone or other memorial on a grave or a grave space;

(b)   alter the position on a grave of, or re-erect at another place in the cemetery or elsewhere, any tombstone or other memorial on a grave;

(c)   level the surface of any grave, other than a grave described in paragraph (1)(b), to the level of the adjoining ground;

(d) alter the position of any railings surrounding a grave or vault, a tombstone or other memorial or a grave space;

(e) re-erect at another place in the cemetery a memorial other than one on a grave or vault or in a chapel provided as mentioned in article 6(1)(b).

Any reference to a grave in (a), (b) or (c) or in Schedule 3 other than paragraph 1 thereof includes a reference to a vault constructed wholly or substantially so below the level of the ground adjoining the vault.

17 Rites of Church of England

(1) The incumbent or priest in charge of an ecclesiastical parish situated wholly or partly in an area chargeable with the expenses of a cemetery shall, with respect to members of the Church of England who are his own parishioners or who die in his parish, where he is requested to do so, be under the same obligation to perform funeral services in the consecrated part, if any, of the cemetery as he has to perform funeral services in any churchyard of the ecclesiastical parish and section 1 of the Ecclesiastical Fees Measure 1986 (1986 No 2) shall have effect where any funeral service is conducted by a person mentioned in subsection (1) of that section.

(2) This article does not apply to a cemetery in the area subject to the Welsh Church Act.

18 Offences in cemeteries

(1) No person shall—

(a) wilfully create any disturbance in a cemetery;

(b) commit any nuisance in a cemetery;

(c) wilfully interfere with any burial taking place in a cemetery;

(d) wilfully interfere with any grave or vault, any tombstone or other memorial, or any flowers or plants on any such matter; or

(e) play at any game or sport in a cemetery.

(2) No person not being an officer or servant of the burial authority or another person so authorised by or on behalf of the burial authority shall enter or remain in a cemetery at any hour when it is closed to the public.

19 Penalties

Every person who contravenes—

(a) any prohibition under article 5(6);

(b) article 10(6);

(c) article 18;

(d) Part I of Schedule 2

shall be liable on summary conviction to a fine not exceeding £100 and in the case of a continuing offence to a fine not exceeding £10 for each day during which the offence continues after conviction therefor.

20 Commonwealth War Graves Commission

(1) In this article—

'the Commission' means the Commonwealth War Graves Commission; and 'Commonwealth war burial' means a burial of any member of the forces of His Majesty fallen in the war of 1914–1921 or the war of 1939–1947.

(2) A burial authority may grant to the Commission the right to provide any structure or any tree, plant, path or other feature.

(3) Nothing in article 3 shall be construed as authorising any action in relation to any tombstone or other memorial, any structure or any tree, plant, path or other feature provided by the Commission, except with the consent of the Commission.

(4) Any right described in article 10(1) may also be granted to the Commission and in relation to any such right—

the words 'Subject to paragraph (3),' and 'and not exceeding 100 years' in article 10(2);

article 10(3);

the words 'for up to 100 years from the date on which the extension is granted' in article 10(4);

article 10(5); and

the words 'for a period not exceeding 100 years from the date of the agreement' in article 10(7),

shall not have effect.

(5)   Before their first exercise of the powers conferred by article 10(5) or 16(2) in relation to any particular cemetery, the burial authority shall notify the Commission.

(6)   The powers described in article 10(5) or 16(2) shall not be exercisable in respect of—

any grave, vault, tombstone or other memorial provided or maintained by or on behalf of the Commission; or

any other grave or vault containing a Commonwealth war burial,

except with the consent in writing of the Commission.

(7)   Part III of Schedule 2 shall not apply to the Commission.

22 Repeals etc

. . .

(2)   Except in its application to operations commenced before the coming into operation of this order, any enactment which makes provision for the matters described in article 16 is hereby repealed in so far as it makes such provision in respect of cemeteries.

. . .

(4)   The order of 1974 is hereby revoked. Its revocation shall have the like effect as if it and this order were Acts of Parliament to which section 38(2) of the Interpretation Act 1889 applied.

23 General saving

Nothing in this order shall be construed as authorising the disturbance of human remains.

SCHEDULE 1

ACCESS TO CEMETERIES

1

A burial authority may construct such roads to a cemetery as they think fit and, subject to paragraph 2, may widen or otherwise improve any road leading to a cemetery or giving access to such a road.

2

A burial authority shall not widen or otherwise improve any road which is not vested in them except with the consent of the highway authority or other person in whom it is vested.

3

A burial authority shall be responsible as such for maintaining in a proper state of repair any road constructed by them or any predecessor of theirs, not being a highway which is for the time being maintainable at the public expense.

SCHEDULE 2
BURIAL RIGHTS, RIGHTS TO ERECT MEMORIALS, AND AGREEMENTS
FOR MAINTENANCE OF GRAVES AND MEMORIALS

PART I

EXERCISE OF RIGHTS

1

No burial shall take place, no cremated human remains shall be scattered and no tombstone or other memorial shall be placed in a cemetery, and no additional inscription shall be made on a tombstone or other memorial, without the permission of the officer appointed for that purpose by the burial authority.

2

No body shall be buried in a grave in such a manner that any part of the coffin is less than three feet below the level of any ground adjoining the grave:

Provided that the burial authority may, where they consider the soil to be of suitable character, permit a coffin made of perishable materials to be placed not less than two feet below the level of any ground adjoining the grave.

3

No body shall be buried in a grave unless the coffin is effectively separated from any coffin interred in the grave on a previous occasion by means of a layer of earth not less than six inches thick.

4

When any grave is reopened for the purpose of making another burial therein, no person shall disturb any human remains interred therein or remove therefrom any soil which is offensive.

5

Every walled grave or vault shall be properly constructed of suitable materials.

6

Within 24 hours of any burial in a walled grave or vault, the coffin shall be—

(a) embedded in concrete, and covered with a layer of concrete not less than six inches thick; or

(b) enclosed in a separate cell or compartment of brick, slate, stone flagging or precast concrete slabs of a 1:2:4 mix, in any case not less than two inches thick, in such a manner as to prevent, as far as may be practicable, the escape of any noxious gas from the interior of the cell or compartment.

7

Any person to whose order a body is buried in a grave in respect of which an exclusive right of burial has been granted shall, as soon as conveniently may be after the subsidence of the earth has been completed, cause the surface of the grave to be covered with any tombstone or other memorial in respect of which a right has been granted by the burial authority or any predecessor of theirs, or with fresh turf, or, where the burial authority permit, with such flowering or other plants, or in such other manner, as may be permitted.

8

Where the burial authority permit uncoffined burials, any reference in this Part to a coffin includes a reference to the wrappings of an uncoffined body.

PART II

PROVISION AS TO GRANTS, EXTENSION OF THE PERIODS THEREOF AND MATTERS CONCERNING RIGHTS

1

(1)   A grant under article 10 shall be in writing signed by the officer appointed for that purpose by the burial authority.

(2)   Any extension of the period of such a grant or of a grant made under article 9(1) of the order of 1974 or any enactment replaced by that provision shall also be in writing signed by such an officer.

2

A burial authority shall—

   (a)   maintain a register of all rights granted by them or any predecessor of theirs under article 10(1) or under article 9(1) of the order of 1974, which shall show as respects each such right the date on which it was granted, the name and address of the grantee, the consideration for the grant, the place in which it is exercisable and its duration; and

   (b)   subject to the provision of section 229 of the Act, preserve registers of the rights granted under section 33 of the Burial Act 1852, section 40 of the Cemeteries Clauses Act 1847, or a corresponding provision in any local Act, maintained by them before 1st April 1974 or transferred to them by any order made under section 254 of the Local Government Act 1972.

3

Rights to which paragraph 2 applies may be assigned by deed or bequeathed by will.

4

A burial authority shall, subject to such investigation as they think proper, record particulars of any assignment or transmission of any such right notified to them in the register maintained or preserved under paragraph 2.

5

A register under paragraph 2 shall at all reasonable times be available for inspection by any person free of charge.

6

A burial authority may charge such fees as they think proper for the making by them of searches in, and the provision of certified copies of entries in, a register under paragraph 2.

PART III

DETERMINATION OF CERTAIN RIGHTS AND AGREEMENTS

1

(1)   This paragraph applies to the following rights and agreements granted or entered into by a burial authority or any predecessor of theirs at a time before 1st April 1974 and to the rights and agreements made or entered into between 31st March 1974 and 28th June 1974 which were validated by article 7 of the Local Authorities etc. (Miscellaneous Provision) (No. 3) Order 1974—

   (a)   all rights in respect of any grave space granted under a provision falling within paragraph (b) of Part II in perpetuity, or for a period exceeding 75 years from the date of the grant;

   (b)   any other right to place and maintain a tombstone or other memorial so granted; and

943

(c)   any agreement to maintain a grave, vault, tombstone or other memorial in a cemetery either in perpetuity or for a period ending more than 100 years after the date of the agreement.

(2)   Where any rights described in paragraph 1(1)(a) or (b) have not been exercised, the burial authority may, at any time after the expiration of 75 years beginning with the first day on which any such rights were granted, serve notice on the owner of the rights of their liability to determination under this paragraph, and the rights shall determine by virtue of the notice unless, within 6 months of the date of service, the owner notifies the authority in writing of his intention to retain them.

(3)   In the case of any agreement described in paragraph 1(1)(c), the burial authority may at any time after the period of 100 years beginning with the date of the agreement serve a like notice on the person entitled to its benefit, and the agreement shall determine by virtue of the notice unless, within 6 months of the date of service, that person notifies the authority in writing of his intention that the agreement should continue in force.

2

Where a burial authority are entitled to serve a notice under sub-paragraph (2) or (3) of paragraph 1 in respect of any rights or agreement, but the specified circumstances exist in respect of the owner of the rights or, as the case may be, the person entitled to the benefit of the agreement, they may instead—

(a)   display the notice in conspicuous positions at the entrances to the cemetery; and

(b)   publish the notice in two successive weeks in the newspaper or newspapers which in their opinion would secure the best publicity in the area served by the cemetery,

and the sub-paragraph in question shall then have effect as if the notice had been duly served thereunder on the date on which it was first published pursuant to item (b) of this paragraph.

SCHEDULE 3
REMOVAL OF MEMORIALS AND LEVELLING, ETC

Restrictions on exercise of powers

1

The powers described in article 16(2) shall not be exercisable—

(a)   contrary to the terms of the agreement, in respect of any grave, vault, tombstone or other memorial which the burial authority are bound by agreement to maintain;

(b)   within the period of the grant or of any extension thereof, in respect of any tombstone or other memorial placed in the cemetery in pursuance of a grant made after the coming into operation of this order;

(c)   within the period of the grant or of any extension thereof, except where a reservation as to the exercise of powers under any local enactment was made on the making of the grant, in respect of any tombstone or other memorial placed in the cemetery in pursuance of a grant made under the order of 1974;

(d)   in respect of any other tombstone or other memorial placed in the cemetery (otherwise than under a permission expressed to be revocable) within the 20 years preceding the first publication of the notice required by paragraph 3,

except with the consent in writing of the person entitled to the benefit of the agreement to maintain, the owner of the right to place and maintain the tombstone or other memorial or the person granted permission to place the tombstone or other memorial.

2

The said powers shall not be exercisable in relation to any building of special architectural or historic interest included in a list compiled or approved under section 54 of the Town and Country Planning Act 1971 unless the works have been authorised under section 55(2) of that Act.

Notification of exercise of powers

3

Before exercising the powers described in article 16(2) the burial authority shall—

(a) display a notice of their intention to do so in conspicuous positions at the entrances to the cemetery and if the powers are to be exercised only in any area of the cemetery in conspicuous positions in or adjoining such area;

(b) publish the notice in two successive weeks in the newspaper or newspapers which in their opinion would secure the best publicity in the area served by the cemetery;

(c) where the area of the cemetery in which the powers are to be exercised, or any part thereof, has been consecrated or set apart for the use of a particular denomination or religious body, notify the rural dean or persons representative of the particular denomination or religious body, and where such dean or persons within the 3 months following the notification make any representations to them, consider such representations with them; and

(d) if they have not already done so, comply with article 20(5).

4

Before exercising the said powers in respect of any grave on which there is a tombstone or other memorial the burial authority shall, in the circumstances in which this paragraph applies, subject to paragraph 6, serve copies of the said notice and of paragraphs 9, 10, 12, 15, 17 and 18 on the owner of the right to place and maintain it or (if they have a record of his name and address) on the person granted permission to place it.

The circumstances in which this paragraph applies are where—

a burial in the grave has taken place;

the right to place and maintain, or the permission to place, the tombstone or other memorial has been granted or renewed;

the right, or permission, to place any additional inscription on the tombstone or other memorial has been granted; or

notification of any assignment or transmission of the right to place and maintain the tombstone or other memorial, or of the address of the owner of such right or of the person granted permission to place it, has been given,

within the 30 years preceding the first display of the notice under paragraph 3.

5

Before exercising the powers described in article 16(2)(c) in respect of any other grave the burial authority shall, in the circumstances in which this paragraph applies, subject to paragraph 6, serve copies of the said notice and of paragraphs 11, 14, 17 and 19 on the owner of the right described in article 10(1)(a)(i) or (ii) in respect of the grave.

The circumstances in which this paragraph applies are where—

a burial in the grave has been made in exercise of the right described in article 10(1)(a)(i) or (ii); or

notification of any assignment or transmission of such right, or of the address of the owner thereof, has been given,

within the 30 years preceding the first display of the notice under paragraph 3.

6

Paragraph 4 or 5 shall not apply in relation to any owner or person where the specified circumstances exist in respect of him.

7

The said notice shall—

(a) contain brief particulars of the proposals and unless the proposals are incapable of further statement specify an address at which further particulars are obtainable free of charge;

(b) specify a date before which the carrying out of the proposals will not be commenced, being a date not less than 3 months following the completion of the action required by paragraph 3; and

(c) indicate that particulars as to—

(i) the objections which can be made to the proposals;

(ii) requests for the re-erection of tombstones or other memorials; and

(iii) the removal of tombstones and other memorials,

are obtainable free of charge from a specified address.

Objections

8

The burial authority shall consider all objections made to the proposals.

9

If notice of objection, and of the grounds thereof, to the proposals in respect of any tombstone or other memorial placed and maintained on a grave in pursuance of a right is given—

by the owner of such right; or

by a relative of any person buried in the grave,

to the burial authority before the date specified in the notice under paragraph 3, the proposals shall not be carried out in respect of that tombstone or other memorial unless the objection is withdrawn:

Provided that if the burial authority consider that the grave has been long neglected they may make representations to the Secretary of State, and, if the Secretary of State approves, the proposals may be carried out in respect of the tombstone or other memorial after the expiration of two months after notification of the Secretary of State's approval by the burial authority to the objector.

10

If notice of objection, and of the grounds thereof, to the proposals in respect of any tombstone or other memorial placed on a grave in the exercise of a permission not expressed to be revocable is given—

by the person to whom permission was granted; or

by a relative of any person commemorated by the memorial,

to the burial authority before the date specified in the notice under paragraph 3, the proposals shall not be carried out in respect of that tombstone or other memorial unless the objection is withdrawn:

Provided that the burial authority may make representations to the Secretary of State, and, if the Secretary of State approves, the proposals may be carried out in respect of the tombstone or other memorial after the expiration of two months after notification of the Secretary of State's approval by the burial authority to the objector.

11

If notice of objection, and of the grounds thereof, to the levelling of any grave not included in paragraph 9 or 10 in exercise of the powers set out in article 16(2)(c) is given—

> by the owner of a right described in article 10(1)(a)(i) or (ii) in respect of the grave; or
>
> by a relative of any person buried in the grave,

to the burial authority before the date specified in the notice under paragraph 3, the grave shall not be levelled unless the objection is withdrawn:

Provided that the burial authority may make representations to the Secretary of State, and, if the Secretary of State approves, the grave may be levelled after the expiration of two months after notification of the Secretary of State's approval by the burial authority to the objector.

Removal of tombstones

12

Where the burial authority propose to re-erect at another place in the cemetery or elsewhere, or to remove from the cemetery and destroy, any tombstone or other memorial, not being a tombstone or other memorial provided by the Commonwealth War Graves Commission, the owner of the right to place and maintain, or the person granted permission to place, the tombstone or other memorial may, whether or not he gives notice of objection under paragraph 9 or 10, claim the tombstone or other memorial. A claim under this paragraph shall be made before the date specified in the notice under paragraph 3 or, where the tombstone or other memorial is to be removed with the approval of the Secretary of State, within the period of two months after the notification required by paragraph 9 or 10.

The tombstone or other memorial shall be removed by the person claiming it at such date as may be arranged between such person and the burial authority or if the burial authority give notice to such person that it has been removed from the ground or dismantled, and is available for removal from the cemetery, within one month of such notice.

Identification of graves

13

Before levelling the surface of any grave or removing any tombstone or other memorial or other identification from a grave, the burial authority shall ensure that the situation of the grave is shown in the plan required by article 9.

Identification marks and substitute memorials

14

In respect of any grave levelled by them in exercise of the powers set out in article 16(2)(c), the burial authority may, and shall if so requested in writing by—

> the owner of a right described in article 10(1)(a)(i) or (ii) in respect of the grave, or
>
> a relative of any person buried in the grave,

within a year of the date specified in the notice under paragraph 3 (whether such owner or relative made objection under paragraph 11 or not), provide at their own expense such identification mark as they consider adequate.

15

Where the burial authority remove from a grave either the whole of an existing tombstone or other memorial or the part thereof containing any material particulars they may, and shall if so requested by—

the owner of the right to place and maintain, or the person granted permission (not expressed to be revocable) to place, the tombstone or other memorial, or

a relative of any person buried in the grave,

within a year of the date specified in the notice under paragraph 3 (whether such owner or relative made objection under paragraph 9 or 10 or not), place on the grave at their own expense such memorial stone or tablet as they consider suitable.

Records of memorials

16

The burial authority shall make and keep—

(a)   a record of the tombstones and other memorials removed from graves, showing whether they have been destroyed or re-erected by them in the cemetery or elsewhere and if so re-erected of the positions in which they have been re-erected; and

(b)   a photographic or other record of all legible inscriptions on the tombstones and other memorials destroyed.

Interpretation

17

In this Schedule, 'relative' means, in relation to any person buried in a grave—

a spouse or a civil partner;

a child or grandchild;

a grandparent;

a parent or step-parent;

a brother or sister or half-brother or half-sister;

an uncle or aunt or a child thereof.

In the application of this paragraph, an adopted person to whom sub-paragraphs (1) and (2) of paragraph 3 of Schedule 1 to the Children Act 1975 did not apply shall be treated as if the said paragraphs had applied to him.

18

In this Schedule, any reference to a permission to place a memorial includes a permission granted by the burial authority or any predecessors of theirs, and any reference to the person granted such a permission includes a reference to his personal representatives.

19

In paragraphs 5, 11 and 14, any reference to a right described in article 10(1) (a)(i) or (ii) includes a reference to any right granted under sub-paragraph (a) of article 9(1) of the order of 1974 or any enactment replaced by that sub-paragraph.

General saving

20

Nothing in article 16(2) or this Schedule shall affect any right described in article 10(1)(a)(i) or (ii).

PARISH AND COMMUNITY COUNCILS (COMMITTEES) REGULATIONS 1990

(SI 1990/2476)

2

In these Regulations—
　　　'the 1972 Act' means the Local Government Act 1972;
　　　'the 1989 Act' means the Local Government and Housing Act 1989;
　　　'financial year' means a period of twelve months ending on 31st March.

3

(1)　The following functions when performed by a committee of a parish or community council are prescribed for the purposes of section 13(4)(g) of the 1989 Act—

　　(a)　the management of land owned or occupied by the council;
　　(b)　where the council are a harbour authority as defined in section 57(1) of the Harbours Act 1964, their functions as such;
　　(c)　any function under section 144 of the 1972 Act relating to the promotion of tourism;
　　(d)　any function under section 145 of the 1972 Act relating to the management of a festival.

(2)　For the purposes of paragraph (1)(a) and (d), 'management' does not include the determination of the total amount of money which may be expended in any financial year by the council in respect of the land or festival.

4

A sub-committee of a parish or community council appointed exclusively to discharge any of the functions mentioned in regulation 3(1) is prescribed for the purposes of section 13(4)(h) of the 1989 Act; and the case of a member of such a sub-committee is prescribed for the purposes of section 13(3)(b) of that Act.

LOCAL GOVERNMENT (PARISHES AND PARISH COUNCILS) REGULATIONS 1999

(SI 1999/545)

PART I

GENERAL

1 Citation and commencement

These Regulations may be cited as the Local Government (Parishes and Parish Councils) Regulations 1999 and shall come into force on 1st April 1999.

2 Interpretation

In these Regulations—
　　　'the Act' means the Local Government and Rating Act 1997;
　　　'the 1992 Act' means the Local Government Act 1992;
　　　'the 1972 Act' means the Local Government Act 1972;

'abolished authority' means a parish council which is wound up and dissolved by an order;

'enactment' includes a local and personal Act, a private Act and any subordinate legislation within the meaning of the Interpretation Act 1978;

'existing', in relation to an area affected by an order, means that area as it exists on the date the order is made;

'order' means an order under section 14 (implementation by Secretary of State) of the Act;

'order date' means the date (being 1st April in any year) which is specified as such in the order;

'proper officer', in relation to any purpose and any body, means the person appointed for that purpose by that body;

'transferor authority' means a parish council which, in consequence of an order, ceases to exercise functions in relation to an area ('transferred area') on the order date; and

'transferee authority' means—

    (a)   a parish council by which, in consequence of an order, functions in relation to a transferred area are exercisable on and after the order date;

    (b)   where there is no such council, the district council or unitary county council in whose area the transferred area is situated.

3 Application of Regulations

These Regulations (which make incidental, consequential, transitional and supplementary provision for the purposes and in consequence of orders, and for giving full effect to them) apply to every order, but have effect, in each case, subject to any relevant agreement under section 20 (agreements as to incidental matters) of the 1992 Act (as well as having effect subject to the provisions of the order, as provided by section 15(2) of the Act).

4 Matters not affected

Nothing in these Regulations shall affect—

    (a)   the status of any city;

    (b)   the status of any person who is an honorary freeman of any parish having the status of a city or entitled to be called or styled a royal town;

    (c)   any person's status, or the right of any person to be admitted, as a freeman of any place;

    (d)   any right—

        (i)   of burial; or

        (ii)   to construct a grave or vault; or

        (iii)   to place, maintain or inscribe a tombstone or memorial.

5 Continuity of matters

(1) Any thing which, at the order date, is in the process of being done by or in relation to a transferor authority in the exercise of, or in connection with, any of its functions in relation to a transferred area may be continued by or in relation to the transferee authority.

(2) Any thing done before the order date by or in relation to a transferor authority in the exercise of, or in connection with, any of its functions in relation to a transferred area shall, so far as is required for continuing its effect on and after that date, have effect as if done by or in relation to the transferee authority.

(3) References in paragraphs (1) and (2) to things done by or in relation to a transferor authority include references to things which, by virtue of any enactment, are treated as having been done by or in relation to that authority.

(4)   So far as is required for giving effect to paragraphs (1) and (2), any reference in any document to a transferor authority shall be construed as a reference to the transferee authority.

6 Maps

(1)   A print of any map referred to in an order shall be deposited in—

  (a)   the office a London office of the Secretary of State; and

  (b)   the offices of the district council or unitary county council in whose area a parish affected by the order is situated.

(2)   The prints deposited in accordance with paragraph (1) shall be available for inspection by any person at any reasonable time.

(3)   Prints of any such map shall also be supplied to—

  (a)   Ordnance Survey;

  (b)   the Registrar General;

  (c)   the Land Registry;

  (d)   the Valuation Office;

  (e)   the Boundary Commission for England; and

  (f)   the Local Government Commission for England.

7 Mereing of boundaries

(1)   The boundaries of any area established by an order shall be mered by Ordnance Survey.

(2)   Where—

  (a)   a boundary of any area is defined on a map referred to in the order by reference to proposed works; and

  (b)   those works have not been executed at the time the boundary is mered, the boundary shall be mered as if it had not been so defined.

PART II

PROPERTY, RIGHTS AND LIABILITIES

8 Transfer of property, rights and liabilities

(1)   Nothing in this regulation shall apply to—

  (a)   any property held by an authority, as sole trustee, exclusively for charitable purposes;

  (b)   any rights or liabilities of an authority in respect of such property, but see regulation 9.

(2)   Subject to paragraph (5), all property vested in, and all rights and liabilities acquired, accrued or incurred by, an authority described in column (1) of the Table below and specified in relation to that authority in column (2) shall transfer to and vest in or, as the case may be, become rights and liabilities of, the authority specified in column (3).

(1) Transferor authority	(2) Specified property, rights and liabilities	(3) Transferee authority
An abolished authority	Property, rights and liabilities of the abolished authority which relate to the transferred area	The transferee authority to which the transferred area transfers

(1) Transferor authority	(2) Specified property, rights and liabilities	(3) Transferee authority
The council of a parish which is subject to an alteration in its administrative area consisting of the loss of a transferred area	Property, rights and liabilities of that council which relate to the transferred area	The council of the transferee parish or, if there is no such parish, or the parish has no council, the council of the district or, where there is no council for the district, the county council within whose area the transferred area lies

(3) All contracts, deeds, bonds, agreements, licences and other instruments subsisting immediately before the order date in favour of, or against, and all notices in force immediately before that date which were given, or have effect as if given, by or to a transferor authority in respect of any transferred area shall be of full force and effect in favour of, or against, the transferee authority.

(4) Any action or proceeding, or any cause of action or proceeding, pending or existing at the order date by or against a transferor authority in respect of any transferred property may be continued, prosecuted or enforced, as the case may be, by or against the authority to which such property is transferred.

(5) Where, in relation to an abolished authority, there is more than one transferee authority an amount equal to the appropriate proportion of the balances of the abolished authority as shown immediately before the order date in the authority's capital and revenue accounts shall be transferred to the capital and revenue accounts, respectively, of each of the transferee authorities.

(6) In paragraph (5), 'the appropriate proportion', in relation to a transferee authority, means the same proportion as the population of the area transferred to that authority bears to the population of the area of the abolished authority; and the population of an area shall be taken to be the number estimated by the proper officer of the district in which the area of the abolished authority is situated by reference to the day immediately before the order date.

(7) For the purposes of this regulation, property, rights and liabilities of an authority are to be treated as property, rights and liabilities in relation to a transferred area if—

    (a)   in the case of land, it is situated in, or held exclusively for the purposes of, or in connection with, the exercise of functions in, or in relation to, the area;

    (b)   in the case of liabilities, they are liabilities incurred exclusively in respect of the area;

    (c)   in the case of contracts, deeds, bonds, agreements and other instruments, and notices, they relate exclusively to the area;

    (d)   in the case of actions and proceedings and causes of action or proceedings, they relate exclusively to the area.

(8) In this regulation 'transferred property' means any property, rights or liabilities transferred by virtue of this regulation.

9 Charitable property, etc

(1) In this regulation—

    'charity', 'charity trustees', 'company', 'the court' and 'trusts' have the same meanings as in the Charities Act 1993;

    'charitable property' means property (of whatever description) which, immediately before the order date, is held as sole trustee—

    (a)   by an abolished authority; or

    (b)   by a transferor authority other than an abolished authority, exclusively for charitable purposes; and

'relevant charity' means a charity other than a charity incorporated by charter of a company.

(2) Charitable property held by an abolished authority for the benefit of—

(a) a specified area, or

(b) the inhabitants of that area, or

(c) any particular class or body of persons in that area,

shall, on the order date, vest (on the same trusts) in the transferee authority within whose area the whole or the greater part of that specified area is situated immediately before that date.

(3) Other charitable property held by an abolished authority shall, on the order date, vest (on the same trusts)—

(a) in the transferee authority within whose area the whole or the greater part of the area of the abolished authority is situated immediately before that date; or

(b) if sub-paragraph (a) does not apply, in such one of the transferee authorities as may be agreed between them not later than three months before the order date or, in default of such agreement, in such transferee authority as the Charity Commissioners may determine.

(4) Where—

(a) charitable property is held by a transferor authority which is not an abolished authority for any such benefit as is mentioned in paragraph (2); and

(b) the whole or the greater part of the specified area so mentioned is situated within the transferred area,

that property shall, on the order date, vest (on the same trusts) in the transferee authority.

(5) Charitable property held as mentioned in paragraph (1)(b) which is not vested in accordance with paragraph (4) shall continue to be held by the transferor authority.

(6) Any rights and liabilities in respect of charitable property which vests in accordance with any of paragraphs (2) to (4) shall on the order date become rights and liabilities of the transferee authority in which that property vests.

(7) Where, immediately before the order date, any power with respect to a relevant charity is, under the trusts of the charity or by virtue of any enactment, exercisable by a transferor authority in relation to a transferred area or by the holder of an office connected with such an authority, that power shall, on and after the order date, be exercisable by the authority in which property of the charity would have vested if it had been charitable property or, as the case may be, by the holder of the corresponding office connected with that authority or, if there is no such office, by the proper officer of that authority.

(8) References in paragraph (7) to a power with respect to a relevant charity do not include references to the powers of any person by virtue of being a charity trustee of the charity.

(9) Where, under the trusts of a relevant charity, the charity trustees immediately before the order date include—

(a) an abolished authority;

(b) the transferor authority in relation to a transferred area; or

(c) the holder of an office connected with an authority mentioned in subparagraph (a) or (b),

on and after the order date those trustees shall include the authority in which property of the charity would have vested as mentioned in paragraph (7) or, as the case may be, the holder of the corresponding office connected with that authority or, if there is no such office, the proper officer of that authority.

(10) Nothing in this regulation shall affect any power of Her Majesty, the court or any other person to alter the trusts of any charity.

10 Land held or used for purposes of the Allotments Acts 1908 to 1950

Where immediately before the order date land in an area constituted as a parish by an order—

    (a)   is held by a district council for any purpose of the Allotments Acts 1908 to 1950; or

    (b)   is vested in a district council and used for those purposes,

it shall on the order date transfer to and be vested in the parish council for that parish or, if there is no such council, the parish meeting for that parish.

PART III

OTHER CONSEQUENTIAL AND TRANSITIONAL PROVISIONS

11 Councillors

(1) Any person in office immediately before the order date as a parish councillor for an area which is altered by the order ('an altered area') shall, unless he resigns his office or it otherwise becomes vacant, continue as parish councillor for the area as so altered until the date on which he would ordinarily have retired had the order not been made.

(2) Where any casual vacancy for the office of parish councillor arises in an altered area on or before the order date, that vacancy shall be treated as a vacancy for a parish councillor of the altered area.

(3) Notwithstanding subsection (3) of section 16 (parish councillors) of the 1972 Act, any persons in office as parish councillors of an abolished authority immediately before the order date shall retire on that date.

12 Electoral registers

Each registration officer shall make such rearrangement or adaptation of the register of local government electors as may be necessary for the purposes or in consequence of any order.

13 Staff: continuity of employment

(1) This regulation applies to any person who ceases to be employed by an abolished authority or a transferor authority ('the authority') where—

    (a)   the termination of his employment is attributable to the winding-up and dissolution of the authority;

    (b)   within four weeks of the date of the termination of that employment he is employed by another parish council ('the new employer'); and

    (c)   by virtue of section 138 (no dismissal in cases of renewal of contract or re-engagement) of the Employment Rights Act 1996 ('the 1996 Act') that subsequent employment precludes his receiving any redundancy payment under Part XI of that Act with respect to his terminated employment.

(2) The period during which a person to whom this regulation applies was employed by the authority shall count as a period of employment with the new employer for the purposes of computing his period of continuous service for the purposes of the 1996 Act and the change of employer shall not break the continuity of his employment.

(3) A person to whom this regulation applies shall be entitled to count the period of his employment with the authority as a period of employment with his new employer for the purposes of any provision of his contract which depends on his length of service.

14 Minutes of last meetings

(1) This regulation applies to the minutes of the last meeting of—

    (a)   an abolished authority;

    (b)   a committee or sub-committee of such an authority; and

    (c)   a joint committee which ceases to exist by reason of the winding-up and dissolution of such an authority.

(2) Where practicable, the minutes shall be signed at the conclusion of the last meeting by the person who chaired that meeting ('the chairman').

(3) In every other case, as soon as practicable after the last meeting, the minutes shall be circulated to the chairman and every other member present at the meeting; and

    (a)   the chairman may sign the minutes after taking into consideration any representations made by any such member within seven days of the date on which those minutes were sent to him; or

    (b)   if the chairman is unable to sign the minutes, the proper officer of the district council or unitary county council in whose area the area of the abolished authority is situated may nominate another person who was present at the meeting to sign the minutes.

(4) Any minutes purporting to be signed in accordance with paragraph (2) or (3) shall be received in evidence without further proof and, until the contrary is proved—

    (a)   the meeting shall be deemed to have been duly convened and held;

    (b)   those present at the meeting shall be deemed to have been qualified to attend and vote; and

    (c)   where the meeting was of a committee, a sub-committee or a joint committee, it shall be deemed to have been duly constituted and to have had power to deal with the matters referred to in the minutes.

15 Audit

(1) Any functions under Part II (accounts and audit of public bodies) of the Audit Commission Act 1998 ('the 1998 Act') exercisable by or in relation to an abolished authority in respect of any financial year ending before the order date shall be exercisable on or after that date by or in relation to the transferee authority or, if there is more than one transferee authority, such one of them as is specified for the purposes of this paragraph in the order.

(2) In the following paragraphs 'the relevant authority' means the transferee authority by which functions under Part II are exercisable on or after the order date.

(3) Without prejudice to the generality of paragraph (1), the relevant authority—

    (a)   shall ensure that the accounts of the abolished authority are made up, balanced and audited; and

    (b)   may recover any sum or amount which, but for the order, would have been recoverable for the benefit of the abolished authority in accordance with section 18(2) of the 1998 Act.

(4) For the purposes of paragraph (1), anything done before the order date by or in relation to an abolished authority in the exercise of its functions under Part II of the 1998 Act shall be treated on and after that date as if it had been done by or in relation to the relevant authority.

(5) A transferee authority which is not a relevant authority shall provide the designated authority with such information as it may reasonably require to enable it to discharge its functions under paragraph (1); and shall, if so requested, provide copies of, or otherwise afford access to, such documents or other material in their possession or under their control as the relevant authority may specify.

16 Charter trustees

(1) The following provisions of this regulation apply in any case where, in consequence of an order, a city or town for which charter trustees have been

constituted by or under any enactment becomes wholly comprised in a parish or in two or more parishes.

(2)   On the date on which the first parish councillors for the parish or, as the case may be, the parishes, come into office—

    (a)   the charter trustees shall be dissolved;

    (b)   the mayor and deputy mayor (if any) shall cease to hold office as such;

    (c)   the appointment of any local officer of dignity shall be treated as if it had been made by the parish council;

    (d)   all property, rights and liabilities (of whatever description) of the charter trustees shall become property, rights and liabilities of the parish council;

    (e)   any legal proceedings to which the charter trustees are party may, subject to rules of court, be prosecuted or defended (as the case may be) by the parish council.

(3)   Without prejudice to paragraph (2), regulation 5 (continuity of matters) shall apply in a case to which this regulation applies as if the charter trustees were a transferor authority and the parish council were a transferee authority.

(4)   In paragraphs (2) and (3) 'the parish council'—

    (a)   in relation to a city or town which becomes comprised in the area of a single parish, means the council of that parish;

    (b)   in relation to a city or town which becomes comprised in the area of more than one parish, means the council of such one of those parishes as is specified in the order.

(5)   The accounts of the charter trustees and of its committees and officers shall be made up to the date referred to in paragraph (2), and shall be audited in the same manner, and subject to the same procedures and penalties, as if the charter trustees had not been dissolved.

LOCAL AUTHORITIES (MEMBERS' ALLOWANCES) (ENGLAND) REGULATIONS 2003

(SI 2003/1021)

PART 5

PARISH COUNCILS

24 Application of this Part

Any reference in this Part—

    (a)   to an authority is, unless otherwise specified, a reference to a parish council;

    (b)   to a member is, unless otherwise specified or the context otherwise requires, a reference to a member of a parish council, whether or not elected to such office;

    (c)   to a responsible authority is, in relation to a parish council, a reference to the district council or unitary county council—

        (i)   where the parish council is the council for one parish, in whose area the parish council is situated; or

        (ii)   where the parish council is the council for a group of parishes, in whose area all the parishes in the group are situated or, where that is not the case, in whose area the greatest number of local government electors for the parishes in the group is situated; and

(d)   to an establishing authority is, in relation to a parish remuneration panel, a reference to the responsible authority that established that parish remuneration panel.

25 Parish basic allowance

(1)   An authority may pay an allowance for each year ('parish basic allowance')—

    (a)   to its chairman only; or

    (b)   to each of its members,

and the amount of that allowance payable to its chairman may differ from that payable to each other member of the authority, but otherwise that amount shall be the same for each such member.

(2)   Where an authority proposes to pay parish basic allowance, whether to its chairman only or to each of its members, it must have regard, in setting the level or levels of such allowances, to the recommendations which have been made in respect of it by a parish remuneration panel in accordance with regulation 28.

(3)   Subject to paragraph (4), where an authority proposes to pay parish basic allowance in any year to its members and the term of office of any member begins or ends otherwise than at the beginning or end of a year, that member's entitlement shall be to payment of such part of the parish basic allowance as bears to the whole the same proportion as the number of days during which his term of office subsists bears to the number of days in that year.

(4)   Where an authority proposes to pay parish basic allowance in any year—

    (a)   to its chairman only; or

    (b)   to all its members but at a higher level to the chairman,

and the term of office of the chairman as chairman begins or ends otherwise than at the beginning or end of a year, his entitlement for the period during which he holds the office of chairman shall be to payment of such part of the parish basic allowance to which he is entitled as chairman as bears to the whole the same proportion as the number of days during which his term of office as chairman subsists bears to the number of days in that year.

(5)   Where a member is suspended or partially suspended from his responsibilities or duties as a member of an authority in accordance with Part III of the Local Government Act 2000 or regulations made under that Part, the part of the parish basic allowance payable to him in respect of the period for which he is suspended or partially suspended may be withheld by the authority.

(6)   An authority shall, as soon as reasonably practical after setting the levels at which any parish basic allowance is to be paid and to whom, arrange for the publication in a conspicuous place or places in the area of the authority, for a period of at least 14 days, of a notice or notices containing the following information—

    (a)   any recommendation in respect of parish basic allowance made by the parish remuneration panel;

    (b)   the level or levels at which the authority has decided to pay parish basic allowance and to which members it is to be paid; and

    (c)   a statement that in reaching the decision on the matters referred to in sub-paragraph (b) the authority has had regard to the recommendation of the parish remuneration panel.

(7)   An authority shall ensure that it keeps a copy of the information referred to in paragraph (6) available for inspection by members of the public on reasonable notice.

(8)   An authority may require that where payment of parish basic allowance has already been made in respect of any period during which the member concerned is—

    (a)   suspended or partially suspended from his responsibilities or duties as a member of the authority in accordance with Part III of the Local Government Act 2000 or regulations made under that Part;

    (b)   ceases to be a member of the authority; or

(c)   is in any other way not entitled to receive the allowance in respect of that period,

such part of the allowance as relates to any such period shall be repaid to the authority.

(9) An authority may not make any payment, and a member is not entitled to receive any payment, under the provisions of this regulation in respect of any period prior to 31st December 2003 if payment is made, in respect of any duties carried out by the member during that same period, under any of the provisions referred to in regulation 34(1).

(10) For the purposes of this Regulation any reference to a member is a reference to an elected member of a parish council.

26 Parish travelling and subsistence allowance

(1) An authority may pay to its members allowances in respect of travelling and subsistence ('parish travelling and subsistence allowance'), including an allowance in respect of travel by bicycle or by any other non-motorised form of transport, undertaken or incurred in connection with the performance of any duty within one or more of the following categories—

(a)   the attendance at a meeting of the authority or of any committee or sub-committee of the authority, or of any other body to which the authority makes appointments or nominations, or of any committee or sub-committee of such a body;

(b)   the attendance at a meeting of any association of authorities of which the authority is a member;

(c)   the performance of any duty in pursuance of any standing order made under section 135 of the Local Government Act 1972 requiring a member or members to be present while tender documents are opened;

(d)   the performance of any duty in connection with the discharge of any function of the authority conferred by or under any enactment and empowering or requiring the authority to inspect or authorise the inspection of premises; and

(e)   the carrying out of any other duty approved by the authority, or any duty of a class so approved, for the purpose of, or in connection with, the discharge of the functions of the authority or of any of its committees or sub-committees.

(2) Where a member is suspended or partially suspended from his responsibilities or duties as a member of an authority in accordance with Part III of the Local Government Act 2000 or regulations made under that Part, any parish travelling and subsistence allowance payable to him in respect of the responsibilities or duties from which he is suspended or partially suspended may be withheld by the authority.

(3) An authority may require that where payment of travelling and subsistence allowance has already been made in respect of any period during which the member concerned is—

(a)   suspended or partially suspended from his responsibilities or duties as a member of the authority in accordance with Part III of the Local Government Act 2000 or regulations made under that Part;

(b)   ceases to be a member of the authority; or

(c)   is in any other way not entitled to receive the allowance in respect of that period,

such part of the allowance as relates to any such period shall be repaid to the authority.

(4) An authority may not make any payment, and a member is not entitled to receive any payment, under the provisions of this regulation in respect of any period prior to 31st December 2003 if payment is made, in respect of any travelling and subsistence expenses incurred by the member during that same period, under any of the provisions referred to in regulation 34(1).

26A Reimbursement of expenses

(1)   An authority may reimburse to a member any monies expended by that member in respect of travelling or subsistence expenses, including any expenses in respect of travel by bicycle or by any other non-motorised form of transport, incurred in connection with the performance by that member of any duty falling within one or more of the categories set out in regulation 26(1)(a) to (e) during the period beginning with 31st December 2003 and ending on 2nd November 2004.

(2)   Any reference to a member in paragraph (1) of this Regulation is a reference to a member of a parish council other than an elected member.

27 Parish remuneration panels

(1)   A parish remuneration panel may be established—

    (a)   by a responsible authority and shall make recommendations in respect of the authorities for which the establishing authority is the responsible authority; or

    (b)   jointly by any responsible authorities and shall make recommendations in respect of the authorities for which the establishing authorities are the responsible authorities.

(2)   Subject to paragraph (3), a parish remuneration panel shall consist of those persons who are also members of the independent remuneration panel which exercises functions in respect of the establishing authority or authorities.

(3)   A parish remuneration panel shall not include any member who is also a member of an authority in respect of which it makes recommendations or is a member of a committee or sub-committee of such an authority.

(4)   The authorities in respect of which a parish remuneration panel established under paragraph (1) makes recommendations shall each pay to the parish remuneration panel an equal share of the amount of the expenses incurred by that panel in carrying out that panel's functions.

28 Recommendations of parish remuneration panels

(1)   A parish remuneration panel shall produce a report in relation to the members of the authorities in respect of which it was established, making recommendations, in accordance with the provisions of regulation 29, as to—

    (a)   the amount of parish basic allowance payable to members of such authorities;

    (b)   the amount of travelling and subsistence allowance payable to members of such authorities;

    (c)   whether parish basic allowance should be payable only to the chairman of any such authority or to all of its members;

    (d)   whether, if parish basic allowance should be payable to both the chairman and the other members of any such authority, the allowance payable to the chairman should be set at a level higher than that payable to the other members and, if so, the higher amount so payable; and

    (c)   the responsibilities or duties in respect of which members should receive parish travelling and subsistence allowance.

(2)   A copy of a report made under paragraph (1) shall be sent to each authority in respect of which recommendations have been made.

(3)   For the purposes of this Regulation any reference to a member in relation to payments of parish basic allowance is a reference to an elected member of a parish council.

29 Levels of allowances

(1)   A parish remuneration panel may, in making its recommendations in accordance with regulations 27 and 28, either—

(a) apply the same recommended levels of parish basic allowance and parish travelling and subsistence allowance to all the authorities in respect of which it was established; or

(b) make different recommendations for different authorities.

(2) A parish remuneration panel shall express its recommendation as to the level of parish basic allowance, in respect of a parish or parishes, as a percentage of the sum that an independent remuneration panel has recommended as the level of basic allowance for the establishing authority which is the responsible authority for that parish or parishes.

(3) The percentage referred to in paragraph (2) may be one hundred per cent.

(4) A parish remuneration panel shall also express its recommendation as to the level of parish basic allowance as a monetary sum being a monetary sum equivalent to the percentage expressed in accordance with paragraphs (2) and (3).

30 Publicity in respect of reports of parish remuneration panels

(1) Once an authority receives a copy of a report made to it by a parish remuneration panel in accordance with regulation 28, it shall, as soon as reasonably practicable—

(a) ensure that copies of that report are available for inspection by members of the public on reasonable notice; and

(b) arrange for the publication in a conspicuous place or places in the area of the authority, for a period of at least 14 days, of a notice which—

(i) states that it has received recommendations from a parish remuneration panel in respect of allowances;

(ii) describes the main features of that panel's recommendations and specifies the recommended amounts of each allowance mentioned in the report in respect of that authority; and

(iii) states that copies of the panel's report are available for inspection on reasonable notice and gives details of the manner in which notice should be given of an intention to inspect the report.

(2) An authority shall supply a copy of a report made by a parish remuneration panel in accordance with regulation 28 to any person who requests a copy and who pays to the authority such reasonable fee as the authority may determine.

31 Records of parish allowances

(1) An authority shall keep a record of the payments made by it in respect of—

(a) parish basic allowance; and

(b) parish travelling and subsistence allowance.

(2) Such a record shall—

(a) specify the name of the recipient and the amount and nature of each payment;

(b) be available for inspection on reasonable notice and at no charge, by any local government elector for the area of that authority; and

(c) be supplied in copy to any person who is entitled to inspect a record under paragraph (b) and who requests a copy and pays to the authority such reasonable fee as it may determine.

(3) As soon as reasonably practicable after the end of a year, an authority shall arrange for the publication, for a period of at least 14 days, of a notice in a conspicuous place or places in the area of the authority stating the total sum paid by it in the year to each member in respect of each of the following—

(a) parish basic allowance; and

(b) parish travelling and subsistence allowance.

32 Elections to forgo parish allowances

A member may, by notice in writing given to the proper officer of the authority, elect to forgo his entitlement or any part of his entitlement to allowances.

ACCOUNTS AND AUDIT (WALES) REGULATIONS 2005

(SI 2005/368)

[*These regulations make effectively the same provision for the preparation and audit of the accounts of Welsh local authorities as the Accounts and Audit (England) Regulations 2011 do for English local authorities.*]

LOCAL GOVERNMENT (PARISHES AND PARISH COUNCILS) (ENGLAND) REGULATIONS 2008

(SI 2008/625)

PART 1

GENERAL

1 Citation and commencement and application

(1) These Regulations may be cited as the Local Government (Parishes and Parish Councils) (England) Regulations 2008 and shall come into force on 8th April 2008.

(2) These Regulations apply in relation to England.

2 Interpretation

In these Regulations—

'the Act' means the Local Government and Public Involvement in Health Act 2007;

'the 1992 Act' means the Local Government Act 1992;

'the 1972 Act' means the Local Government Act 1972;

'abolished authority' means a parish council which is wound up and dissolved by a reorganisation order;

'enactment' includes a local and personal Act, a private Act and any subordinate legislation within the meaning of the Interpretation Act 1978;

'existing', in relation to an area affected by a reorganisation order, means the area as it exists on the date the order is made;

'order date' means the date (being 1st April in any year) which is specified as such in the reorganisation order;

'proper officer', in relation to any purpose and any body, means the person appointed for that purpose by that body;

'transferor authority' means a parish council which, in consequence of a reorganisation order, ceases to exercise functions in relation to an area ('transferred area') on the order date; and

'transferee authority' means—

    (a)   a parish council by which, in consequence of a reorganisation order, functions in relation to a transferred area are exercisable on and after the order date;

    (b)   where there is no such council, the principal council in whose area the transferred area is situated.

3 Application of Regulations

These Regulations (which make incidental, consequential, transitional and supplementary provision for the purposes and in consequence of reorganisation orders) apply in relation to every reorganisation order.

4 Matters not affected

Nothing in these Regulations shall affect—

    (a)   the status of any city;

    (b)   the status of any person who is an honorary freeman of any parish having the status of a city or entitled to be called or styled a royal town;

    (c)   any person's status, or the right of any person to be admitted, as a freeman of any place;

    (d)   any right—

        (i)   of burial; or

        (ii)   to construct a grave or vault; or

        (iii)   to place maintain or inscribe a tombstone or memorial.

5 Continuity of matters

(1) Any thing which, at the order date, is in the process of being done by or in relation to a transferor authority in the exercise of, or in connection with, any of its functions in relation to a transferred area may be continued by or in relation to the transferee authority.

(2) Any thing done before the order date by or in relation to a transferor authority in the exercise of, or in connection with, any of its functions in relation to a transferred area shall, so far as is required for continuing its effect on and after that date, have effect as if done by or in relation to the transferee authority.

(3) References in paragraphs (1) and (2) to things done by or in relation to a transferor authority include references to things which, by virtue or any enactment, are treated as having been done by or in relation to that authority.

(4) So far as is required for giving effect to paragraphs (1) and (2), any reference in any document to a transferor authority shall be construed as a reference to the transferee authority.

6 Maps

(1) A print of any map referred to in a reorganisation order shall be deposited in—

    (a)   the office of the Secretary of State;

    (b)   the principal office of the principal council in whose area a parish affected by the order is situated.

(2) The prints deposited in accordance with paragraph (1) shall be available for inspection by any person at any reasonable time.

(3) Prints of any such map shall also be supplied to—

    (a)   Ordnance Survey;

    (b)   the Registrar General;

    (c)   the Land Registry;

    (d)   the Valuation Office Agency;

    (e)   the Boundary Commission for England; and

    (f)   the Electoral Commission.

PART 2

PROPERTY, RIGHTS AND LIABILITIES

7 Transfer of property, rights and liabilities

(1) Nothing in this regulation shall apply to—

(a)   any property held by an authority, as sole trustee, exclusively for charitable purposes;

(b)   any rights or liabilities of an authority in respect of such property.

(2)   Subject to paragraph (5), all property vested in, and all rights and liabilities acquired, accrued or incurred by, an authority described in column (1) of the Table below and specified in relation to that authority in column (2) shall transfer to and vest in or, as the case may be, become rights and liabilities of, the authority specified in column (3).

Table

(1) Transferor authority	(2) Specified property, rights and liabilities	(3) Transferee authority
An abolished authority	Property, rights and liabilities of the abolished authority which related to the transferred area	The transferee authority to which the transferred area transfers
The council of a parish which is subject to an alteration in its administrative area consisting of the loss of a transferred area	Property, rights and liabilities of that council which relate to the transferred area	The council of the transferee parish or, if there is no such parish, or the parish has no council, the principal council within whose area the transferred area lies

(3)   All contracts, deeds, bonds, agreements, licences and other instruments subsisting immediately before the order date in favour of, or against, and all notices in force immediately before that date which were given, or have effect as if given, by or to a transferor authority in respect of any transferred area shall be of full force and effect in favour of, or against, the transferee authority.

(4)   Any action or proceeding, or any cause of action or proceeding, pending or existing at the order date by or against a transferor authority in respect of any transferred property may be continued, prosecuted or enforced, as the case may be, by or against the authority to which such property is transferred.

(5)   Where, in relation to an abolished authority, there is more than one transferee authority an amount equal to the appropriate proportion of the balances of the abolished authority as shown immediately before the order date in the authority's capital and revenue accounts shall be transferred to the capital and revenue accounts, respectively, of each of the transferee authorities.

(6)   In paragraph (5), the 'appropriate proportion', in relation to a transferee authority, means the same proportion as the population of the area transferred to that authority bears to the population of the area of the abolished authority; and the population of an area shall be taken to be the number estimated by the proper officer of the principal council within whose area of the abolished authority is situated by reference to the day immediately before the order date.

(7)   For the purposes of this regulation, property, rights and liabilities of an authority are to be treated as property, rights and liabilities in relation to a transferred area if—

(a)   in the case of land, it is situated in, or held exclusively for the purposes of, or in connection with, the exercise of functions in, or in relation to, the area;

(b)   in the case of liabilities, they are liabilities incurred exclusively in respect of the area;

(c)   in the case of contracts, deeds, bonds, agreements and other instruments, and notices, they relate exclusively to the area;

(d)   in the case of actions and proceedings and causes of action or proceedings, they relate exclusively to the area.

(8)   In this regulation 'transferred property' means any property, rights or liabilities transferred by virtue of this regulation.

8 Charitable property, etc

(1)   In this regulation—

'charity', 'charity trustees', 'company', 'the court' and 'trusts' have the same meanings as in the Charities Act 1993;

'charitable property' means property (of whatever description) which, immediately before the order date is held as sole trustee—

(a)   by an abolished authority; or

(b)   by a transferor authority other than an abolished authority,

exclusively for charitable purposes; and

'relevant charity' means a charity other than a charity incorporated by charter of a company.

(2)   Charitable property held by an abolished authority for the benefit of—

(a)   a specified area, or

(b)   the inhabitants of that area, or

(c)   any particular class or body of persons in that area,

shall, on the order date, vest (on the same trusts) in the transferee authority within whose area the whole or the greater part of that specified area is situated immediately before that date.

(3)   Other charitable property held by an abolished authority shall, on the order date, vest (on the same trusts)—

(a)   in the transferee authority within whose area the whole or the greater part of the area of the abolished authority is situated immediately before that date; or

(b)   if sub-paragraph (a) does not apply, in such one of the transferee authorities as may be agreed between them not later than three months before the order date or, in default of such agreement, in such transferee authority as the Charity Commission may determine.

(4)   Where—

(a)   charitable property is held by a transferor authority which is not an abolished authority for any such benefit as is mentioned in paragraph (2); and

(b)   the whole or the greater part of the specified area so mentioned is situated within the transferred area,

that property shall, on the order date, vest (on the same trusts) in the transferee authority.

(5)   Charitable property held as mentioned in paragraph (1)(b) which is not vested in accordance with paragraph (4) shall continue to be held by the transferor authority.

(6)   Any rights and liabilities in respect of charitable property which vests in accordance with any of paragraphs (2) to (4) shall on the order date become rights and liabilities of the transferee authority in which that property vests.

(7)   Where, immediately before the order date, any power with respect to a relevant charity is, under the trusts of the charity, or by virtue of any enactment, exercisable by a transferor authority in relation to a transferred area or by the holder of an office connected with such an authority, that power shall, on and after the order date, be exercisable by the authority in which property of the charity would have vested if it had been charitable property or, as the case may be, by the holder of the corresponding office connected with that authority or, if there is no such office, by the proper officer of that authority.

(8)   References in paragraph (7) to a power with respect to a relevant charity do not include references to the powers of any person by virtue of being a charity trustee of the charity.

(9)   Where, under the trusts of a relevant charity, the charity trustees immediately before the order date include—

> (a)   an abolished authority;
> (b)   the transferor authority in relation to a transferred area; or
> (c)   the holder of an office connected with an authority mentioned in subparagraph (a) or (b),

on and after the order date those trustees shall include the authority in which property of the charity would have vested as mentioned in paragraph (7) or, as the case may be, the holder of the corresponding office connected with that authority or, if there is no such office, the proper officer of that authority.

(10)   Nothing in this regulation shall affect any power of Her Majesty, the court of any other person to alter the trusts of any charity.

9 Land held or used for purposes of the Allotments Acts 1908 to 1950

Where immediately before the order date land in an area constituted as a parish by a reorganisation order—

> (a)   is held by a principal council for any purpose of the Allotments Acts 1908 to 1950; or
> (b)   is vested in a principal council and used for those purposes,

it shall on the order date transfer to and be vested in the parish council for that parish or, if there is no such council, the parish meeting for that parish.

PART 3

OTHER CONSEQUENTIAL AND TRANSITIONAL PROVISIONS

10

(1)   Any person in office immediately before the order date as a parish councillor for an area which is altered by the order ('an altered area') shall, unless he resigns his office or it otherwise becomes vacant, continue as parish councillor for the area as so altered until the date on which he would ordinarily have retired had the order not been made.

(2)   Where any casual vacancy for the office of parish councillor arises in an altered area on or before the order date, that vacancy shall be treated as a vacancy for a parish councillor of the altered area.

(3)   Notwithstanding subsection (3) of section 16 of the 1972 Act (parish councillors), any persons in office as parish councillors of an abolished authority immediately before the order date shall retire on that date.

11 Electoral registers

Each registration officer shall make such rearrangement or adaptation of the register of local government electors as may be necessary for the purposes or in consequence of any reorganisation order.

12 Staff: continuity of employment

(1)   This regulation applies to any person who ceases to be employed by an abolished authority or a transferor authority ('the authority') where—

> (a)   the termination of his employment is attributable to the winding-up and dissolution of the authority;
> (b)   within four weeks of the date of the termination of that employment he is employed by another parish council ('the new employer'); and
> (c)   by virtue of section 138 of the Employment Rights Act 1996 (no dismissal in cases of renewal of contract or re-engagement) ('the

1996 Act') that subsequent employment precludes his receiving any redundancy payment under Part 11of that Act with respect to his terminated employment.

(2)   The period during which a person to whom this regulation applies was employed by the authority shall count as a period of employment with the new employer for the purposes of computing his period of continuous service for the purposes of the 1996 Act and the change of employer shall not break the continuity of his employment.

(3)   A person to whom this regulation applies shall be entitled to count the period of his employment with the authority as a period of employment with his new employer for the purposes of any provision of his contract which depends on his length of service.

13 Minutes of last meeting

(1)   This regulation applies to the minutes of the last meeting of—
- (a)   an abolished authority;
- (b)   a committee or sub-committee of such an authority; and
- (c)   a joint committee which ceases to exist by reason of the winding-up and dissolution of such an authority.

(2)   Where practicable, the minutes shall be signed at the conclusion of the last meeting by the person who chaired that meeting ('the chairman').

(3)   In every other case, as soon as practicable after the last meeting, the minutes shall be circulated to the chairman and every other member present at the meeting; and
- (a)   the chairman may sign the minutes after taking into consideration any representations made by any such member within seven days of the date on which those minutes were sent to him; or
- (b)   if the chairman is unable to sign the minutes, the proper officer of the principal council in whose area the area of the abolished authority is situated may nominate another person who was present at the meeting to sign the minutes.

(4)   Any minutes purporting to be signed in accordance with paragraph (2) or (3) shall be received in evidence without further proof and, unless the contrary is proved—
- (a)   the meeting shall be deemed to have been duly convened and held;
- (b)   those present at the meeting shall be deemed to have been qualified to attend and vote; and
- (c)   where the meeting was of a committee, a sub-committee or a joint committee, it shall be deemed to have been duly constituted and to have had power to deal with the matters referred to in the minutes.

14 Audit

(1)   Any functions under Part 2 (accounts and audit of public bodies) of the Audit Commission Act 1998 ('the 1998 Act') exercisable by or in relation to an abolished authority in respect of any financial year ending before the order date shall be exercisable on or after that date by or in relation to the transferee authority or, if there is more than one transferee authority, such one of them as is specified for the purposes of this paragraph in the reorganisation order.

(2)   In the following paragraphs 'the relevant authority' means the transferee authority by which functions under Part 2 of the 1998 Act are exercisable on or after the order date.

(3)   Without prejudice to the generality of paragraph (1), the relevant authority—
- (a)   shall ensure that the accounts of the abolished authority are made up, balanced and audited; and
- (b)   may recover any sum or amount which, but for the reorganisation order, would have been recoverable for the benefit of the abolished authority in accordance with section 18(2) of the 1998 Act.

(4)   For the purposes of paragraph (1), anything done before the order date by or in relation to an abolished authority in the exercise of its functions under Part 2 of the 1998 Act shall be treated on and after that date as if it had been done by or in relation to the relevant authority.

(5)   A transferee authority which is not a relevant authority shall provide the relevant authority with such information as it may reasonably require to enable it to discharge its functions under paragraph (1); and shall, if so requested, provide copies of, or otherwise afford access to, such documents or other material in their possession or under their control as the relevant authority may specify.

15 Charter trustees

(1)   The following provisions of this regulation apply in any case where, in consequence of a reorganistion order, a city or town for which charter trustees have been constituted by or under any enactment becomes wholly comprised in a parish or in two or more parishes.

(2)   On the date on which the first parish councillors for the parish or parishes (as the case may be) come into office—

(a)   the charter trustees shall be dissolved;

(b)   the mayor and deputy mayor (if any) shall cease to hold office as such;

(c)   the appointment of any local officer of dignity shall be treated as if it had been made by the parish council;

(d)   all property, rights and liabilities (of whatever description) of the charter trustees shall become property, rights and liabilities of the parish council; and

(e)   any legal proceedings to which the charter trustees are party may, subject to rules of court, be prosecuted or defended (as the case may be) by the parish council.

(3)   Without prejudice to paragraph (2), regulation 5 (continuity of matters) shall apply in a case to which this regulation applies as if the charter trustees were a transferor authority and the parish council were a transferee authority.

(4)   In paragraphs (2) and (3) 'the parish council'—

(a)   in relation to a city or town which becomes comprised in the area of a single parish, means the council of that parish;

(b)   in relation to a city or town which becomes comprised in the area of more than one parish, means the council of such one of those parishes as is specified in the reorganisation order.

(5)   The accounts of the charter trustees and of its committees and officers shall be made up to the date referred to in paragraph (2), and shall be audited in the same manner, and subject to the same procedures and penalties, as if the charter trustees had not been dissolved.

LOCAL GOVERNMENT FINANCE (NEW PARISHES) (ENGLAND) REGULATIONS 2008

(SI 2008/626)

1 Citation, commencement and application

(1)   These Regulations may be cited as the Local Government Finance (New Parishes) (England) Regulations 2008 and shall come into force on 8th April 2008.

(2)   These Regulations apply in relation to England.

2 Interpretation

In these Regulations—

'the 1992 Act' means the Local Government Finance Act 1992;

'the 2007 Act' means the Local Government and Public Involvement in Health Act 2007;

'billing authority' means a district council or London borough council, the Common Council or the Council of the Isles of Scilly;

'establishment order', as respects a relevant parish council or relevant chairman, means the order under section 86 of the 2007 Act (reorganisation of community governance) which constituted the new parish for which it is the council, or in relation to which he is the chairman;

'new parish' means a parish constituted by an order under section 86 of the 2007 Act;

'prospective billing authority', in relation to a new parish, means the billing authority within whose area the new parish is or will be situated;

'relevant parish council' means a parish council established by an order under section 86 of the 2007 Act; and

'relevant year', in relation to a new parish, means the financial year in which the parish is constituted, or, if a separate parish council is established for the parish, the financial year in which that council is first established.

3 Calculation of council tax requirement

(1)   This regulation applies—

    (a)   in relation to a new parish, the prospective billing authority, the relevant year, the relevant chairman and the relevant parish council (if any); and

    (b)   as respects the period beginning on the day after that on which the establishment order is made and ending immediately before the day on which a precept for the relevant year is issued by the relevant parish council or the relevant chairman (as the case may be).

(2)   Subject to paragraph (3), in making calculations in accordance with section 31A of the 1992 Act (calculation of council tax requirement), originally or by way of substitute, the prospective billing authority shall anticipate a precept by taking into account for the purposes of its estimate under subsection (2)(a) of that section an amount equal to that specified in the establishment order, in relation to the relevant parish council or the relevant chairman (as the case may be), for the purposes of these Regulations.

(3)   For the purposes of paragraph (2), section 31A of the 1992 Act shall have effect as if subsection (6)(b) were omitted.

(4)   The relevant parish council or the relevant chairman (as the case may be), shall make the calculations required by section 49A of the 1992 Act (calculation of council tax requirement by authorities in England) for the relevant year so as to secure that the amount calculated as its council tax requirement for that year does not exceed the amount specified in relation to the council or the chairman in the establishment order.

4 Special items

In relation to an amount taken into account for the purposes of section 32(2)(a) of the 1992 Act by virtue of regulation 3(2), Chapter 3 of Part 1 of the 1992 Act (setting of council tax) shall have effect as if the amount were an item mentioned in section 35(1) of the 1992 Act (special items for purposes of section 34) which related to a part of the area of the prospective billing authority.

5 Issue of precepts

(1)   This regulation applies in relation to a relevant parish council or a relevant chairman (as the case may be), and the relevant year.

(2)   Section 41(4) of the 1992 Act (issue of precepts by local precepting authorities) shall have effect as if for 'March in the financial year preceding that for which it is issued' there were substituted 'October in the financial year for which it is issued'.

(3)   The reference in section 42(2) to section 41 shall have effect as if it were a reference to section 41 as modified by paragraph (2).

(4)   Regulation 3 of the Billing Authorities (Anticipation of Precepts) (Amendment) Regulations 1995 shall have effect as if the amount to be paid by the prospective billing authority to the relevant parish council or the relevant chairman which issued the precept were a sum equal to the amount of the precept issued (or last issued) by it.

6 Limitation of council tax and precepts

In relation to a prospective billing authority, a new parish and the relevant year, the references in sections 52X(1) (calculations to be net of precepts) and 52Y(2) (information for purposes of Chapter 4A) of the 1992 Act to the aggregate amount of precepts anticipated by a billing authority in pursuance of regulations under section 41 shall have effect as if the aggregate amount included the amount specified in the establishment order in relation to the relevant parish council or the relevant chairman (as the case may be).

LOCAL AUTHORITIES (MODEL CODE OF CONDUCT) (WALES) ORDER 2008

(SI 2008/788; W82)

1 Title, commencement and application

(1)   The title of this Order is the Local Authorities (Model Code of Conduct) (Wales) Order 2008 and it comes into force on 18 April 2008.

(2)   This Order applies to each relevant authority in Wales.

2 Interpretation

In this Order—

> 'the Act' ('*y Ddeddf*') means the Local Government Act 2000;
>
> 'co-opted member' ('*aelod cyfetholedig*') has the meaning set out in Part 1 of the model code in the Schedule to this Order;
>
> 'member' ('*aelod*') has the meaning set out in Part 1 of the model code in the Schedule to this Order; and
>
> 'relevant authority' ('*awdurdod perthnasol*') has the meaning set out in Part 1 of the model code in the Schedule to this Order.

3 Model Code of Conduct

(1)   A model code as regards the conduct which is expected of members of a relevant authority is set out in the Schedule to this Order.

(2)   For the purposes of section 50(4) of the Act, the provisions of the model code are to be regarded as mandatory.

4 Provisions to be disapplied

(1)   Where a relevant authority which is a county, county borough or community council or fire and rescue authority has adopted a code of conduct or such a code applies to it, the following will, where applicable to the relevant authority, be disapplied as respects that authority—

> (a)   sections 94 to 98 and 105 of the Local Government Act 1972; and
>
> (b)   any regulations made or code issued under sections 19 and 31 of the Local Government and Housing Act 1989.

(2)   Where a relevant authority which is a National Park authority has adopted a code of conduct or such a code applies to it, the following will, where applicable to the relevant authority, be disapplied as respects that authority—

    (a)   paragraphs 9 and 10 of Schedule 7 to the Environment Act 1995; and

    (b)   any regulations made or code issued under sections 19 and 31 of the Local Government and Housing Act 1989.

(3)   Section 16(1) of the Interpretation Act 1978 will apply to a disapplication under paragraph (1) or (2) above as if it were a repeal, by an Act, of an enactment.

5 Revocation

The following orders are revoked:

    (a)   the Conduct of Members (Model Code of Conduct) (Wales) Order 2001;

    (b)   the Conduct of Members (Model Code of Conduct) (Amendment) (Wales) Order 2004; and

    (c)   the Conduct of Members (Model Code of Conduct) (Wales) (Amendment) (No 2) Order 2004.

6 Transitional Provisions and Savings

The orders referred to in article 5 continue to have effect for the purposes of and for purposes connected with—

    (a)   the investigation of any written allegation under Part 3 of the Act, where that allegation relates to conduct that occurred before the date when, pursuant to section 51 of the Act—

        (i)   the relevant authority adopts a code of conduct incorporating the mandatory provisions of the model code of conduct in the Schedule to this Order in place of its existing code of conduct;

        (ii)   the relevant authority revises its existing code of conduct to incorporate the mandatory provisions of the model code of conduct in the Schedule to this Order; or

        (iii)   the mandatory provisions of the model code of conduct in the Schedule to this Order apply to members or co-opted members of the relevant authority under section 51(5)(b) of that Act;

    (b)   the adjudication (or determination) of a matter raised in such an allegation; and

    (c)   an appeal against the decision of a standards committee, an interim case tribunal or case tribunal in relation to such an allegation.

SCHEDULE

The Model Code of Conduct

Part 1

Interpretation

1

(1) In this code—

'co-opted member' ('*aelod cyfetholedig*'), in relation to a relevant authority, means a person who is not a member of the authority but who—

(a) is a member of any committee or sub-committee of the authority, or

(b) is a member of, and represents the authority on, any joint committee or joint sub-committee of the authority,

and who is entitled to vote on any question which falls to be decided at any meeting of that committee or sub-committee;

'meeting' ('*cyfarfod*') means any meeting—

(a) of the relevant authority,

(b) of any executive or board of the relevant authority,

(c) of any committee, sub-committee, joint committee or joint sub-committee of the relevant authority or of any such committee, sub-committee, joint committee or joint sub-committee of any executive or board of the authority, or

(d) where members or officers of the relevant authority are present other than a meeting of a political group constituted in accordance with regulation 8 of the Local Government (Committees and Political Groups) Regulations 1990,

and includes circumstances in which a member of an executive or board or an officer acting alone exercises a function of an authority;

'member' ('*aelod*') includes, unless the context requires otherwise, a co-opted member;

'relevant authority' ('*awdurdod perthnasol*') means—

(a) a county council,

(b) a county borough council,

(c) a community council,

(d) a fire and rescue authority constituted by a scheme under section 2 of the Fire and Rescue Services Act 2004 or a scheme to which section 4 of that Act applies,

(e) a National Park authority established under section 63 of the Environment Act 1995;

'you' ('*chi*') means you as a member or co-opted member of a relevant authority; and

'your authority' ('*eich awdurdod*') means the relevant authority of which you are a member or co-opted member.

(2) In relation to a community council, references to an authority's monitoring officer and an authority's standards committee are to be read, respectively, as references to the monitoring officer and the standards committee of the county or county borough council which has functions in relation to the community council for which it is responsible under section 56(2) of the Local Government Act 2000.

Part 2

General Provisions

2

(1) Save where paragraph 3(a) applies, you must observe this code of conduct—

(a) whenever you conduct the business, or are present at a meeting, of your authority;

(b) whenever you act, claim to act or give the impression you are acting in the role of member to which you were elected or appointed;

(c) whenever you act, claim to act or give the impression you are acting as a representative of your authority; or

(d) at all times and in any capacity, in respect of conduct identified in paragraphs 6(1)(a) and 7.

(2) You should read this code together with the general principles prescribed under section 49(2) of the Local Government Act 2000 in relation to Wales.

3

Where you are elected, appointed or nominated by your authority to serve—

(a) on another relevant authority, or any other body, which includes a police authority or Local Health Board you must, when acting for that other authority or body, comply with the code of conduct of that other authority or body; or

(b) on any other body which does not have a code relating to the conduct of its members, you must, when acting for that other body, comply with this code of conduct, except and insofar as it conflicts with any other lawful obligations to which that other body may be subject.

4

You must—

(a) carry out your duties and responsibilities with due regard to the principle that there should be equality of opportunity for all people, regardless of their gender, race, disability, sexual orientation, age or religion;

(b) show respect and consideration for others;

(c) not use bullying behaviour or harass any person; and

(d) not do anything which compromises, or which is likely to compromise, the impartiality of those who work for, or on behalf of, your authority.

5

You must not—

(a) disclose confidential information or information which should reasonably be regarded as being of a confidential nature, without the express consent of a person authorised to give such consent, or unless required by law to do so;

(b) prevent any person from gaining access to information to which that person is entitled by law.

6

(1) You must—

(a) not conduct yourself in a manner which could reasonably be regarded as bringing your office or authority into disrepute;

(b) report, whether through your authority's confidential reporting procedure or direct to the proper authority, any conduct by another member or anyone who works for, or on behalf of, your authority which you reasonably believe involves or is likely to involve criminal behaviour (which for the purposes of this paragraph does not include offences or behaviour capable of punishment by way of a fixed penalty);

(c) report to the Public Services Ombudsman for Wales and to your authority's monitoring officer any conduct by another member which you reasonably believe breaches this code of conduct;

(d) not make vexatious, malicious or frivolous complaints against other members or anyone who works for, or on behalf of, your authority.

(2) You must comply with any request of your authority's monitoring officer, or the Public Services Ombudsman for Wales, in connection with an investigation conducted in accordance with their respective statutory powers.

7

You must not—

(a) in your official capacity or otherwise, use or attempt to use your position improperly to confer on or secure for yourself, or any other person, an advantage or create or avoid for yourself, or any other person, a disadvantage;

(b) use, or authorise others to use, the resources of your authority—

(i) imprudently;

(ii) in breach of your authority's requirements;

(iii) unlawfully;

(iv) other than in a manner which is calculated to facilitate, or to be conducive to, the discharge of the functions of the authority or of the office to which you have been elected or appointed;

(v) improperly for political purposes; or

(vi) improperly for private purposes.

8

You must—

(a) when participating in meetings or reaching decisions regarding the business of your authority, do so on the basis of the merits of the circumstances involved and in the public interest having regard to any relevant advice provided by your authority's officers, in particular by—

(i) the authority's head of paid service;

(ii) the authority's chief finance officer;

(iii) the authority's monitoring officer;

(iv) the authority's chief legal officer (who should be consulted when there is any doubt as to the authority's power to act, as to whether the action proposed lies within the policy framework agreed by the authority or where the legal consequences of action or failure to act by the authority might have important repercussions);

(b) give reasons for all decisions in accordance with any statutory requirements and any reasonable additional requirements imposed by your authority.

9

You must—

(a) observe the law and your authority's rules governing the claiming of expenses and allowances in connection with your duties as a member;

(b) avoid accepting from anyone gifts, hospitality (other than official hospitality, such as a civic reception or a working lunch duly authorised by your authority), material benefits or services for yourself or any person which might place you, or reasonably appear to place you, under an improper obligation.

Part 3

Interests

Personal Interests

10

(1) You must in all matters consider whether you have a personal interest, and whether this code of conduct requires you to disclose that interest.

(2) You must regard yourself as having a personal interest in any business of your authority if—

(a) it relates to, or is likely to affect—

(i) any employment or business carried on by you;

(ii) any person who employs or has appointed you, any firm in which you are a partner or any company for which you are a remunerated director;

(iii) any person, other than your authority, who has made a payment to you in respect of your election or any expenses incurred by you in carrying out your duties as a member;

(iv) any corporate body which has a place of business or land in your authority's area, and in which you have a beneficial interest in a class of securities of that body that exceeds the nominal value of £25,000 or one hundredth of the total issued share capital of that body;

(v) any contract for goods, services or works made between your authority and you or a firm in which you are a partner, a company of which you are a remunerated director, or a body of the description specified in sub-paragraph (iv) above;

(vi) any land in which you have a beneficial interest and which is in the area of your authority;

(vii) any land where the landlord is your authority and the tenant is a firm in which you are a partner, a company of which you are a remunerated director, or a body of the description specified in sub-paragraph (iv) above;

(viii) any body to which you have been elected, appointed or nominated by your authority;

(ix) any—

(aa) public authority or body exercising functions of a public nature;

(bb) company, industrial and provident society, charity, or body directed to charitable purposes;

(cc) body whose principal purposes include the influence of public opinion or policy;

(dd) trade union or professional association; or

(ee) private club, society or association operating within your authority's area,

in which you have membership or hold a position of general control or management;

(x) any land in your authority's area in which you have a licence (alone or jointly with others) to occupy for 28 days or longer;

(b) a member of the public might reasonably perceive a conflict between your role in taking a decision, upon that business, on behalf of your authority as a whole and your role in representing the interests of constituents in your ward or electoral division; or

(c) a decision upon it might reasonably be regarded as affecting—

(i) your well-being or financial position, or that of a person with whom you live, or any person with whom you have a close personal association;

(ii) any employment or business carried on by persons as described in 10(2)(c)(i);

(iii) any person who employs or has appointed such persons described in 10(2)(c)(i), any firm in which they are a partner, or any company of which they are directors;

(iv) any corporate body in which persons as described in 10(2)(c)(i) have a beneficial interest in a class of securities exceeding the nominal value of £5,000; or

(v) any body listed in paragraphs 10(2)(a)(ix)(aa) to (ee) in which persons described in 10(2)(c)(i) hold a position of general control or management,

to a greater extent than the majority of—

(aa) in the case of an authority with electoral divisions or wards, other council tax payers, rate payers or inhabitants of the electoral division or ward, as the case may be, affected by the decision; or

(bb) in all other cases, other council tax payers, ratepayers or inhabitants of the authority's area.

Disclosure of Personal Interests

11

(1) Where you have a personal interest in any business of your authority and you attend a meeting at which that business is considered, you must disclose orally to that meeting the existence and nature of that interest before or at the commencement of that consideration, or when the interest becomes apparent.

(2) Where you have a personal interest in any business of your authority and you make—

(a) written representations (whether by letter, facsimile or some other form of electronic communication) to a member or officer of your authority regarding that business, you should include details of that interest in the written communication; or

(b) oral representations (whether in person or some form of electronic communication) to a member or officer of your authority you should disclose the interest at the commencement of such representations, or when it becomes apparent to you that you have such an interest, and confirm the representation and interest in writing within 14 days of the representation.

(3) Subject to paragraph 14(1)(b) below, where you have a personal interest in any business of your authority and you have made a decision in exercising a function of an executive or board, you must in relation to that business ensure that any written statement of that decision records the existence and nature of your interest.

(4) You must, in respect of a personal interest not previously disclosed, before or immediately after the close of a meeting where the disclosure is made pursuant to sub-paragraph 11(1), give written notification to your authority in accordance with any requirements identified by your authority's monitoring officer from time to time but, as a minimum containing—

(a) details of the personal interest;

(b) details of the business to which the personal interest relates; and

(c) your signature.

(5) Where you have agreement from your monitoring officer that the information relating to your personal interest is sensitive information, pursuant to paragraph 16(1), your obligations under this paragraph 11 to disclose such information, whether orally or in writing, are to be replaced with an obligation to disclose the existence of a personal interest and to confirm that your monitoring officer has agreed that the nature of such personal interest is sensitive information.

(6) For the purposes of sub-paragraph (4), a personal interest will only be deemed to have been previously disclosed if written notification has been provided in accordance with this code since the last date on which you were elected, appointed or nominated as a member of your authority.

(7) For the purposes of sub-paragraph (3), where no written notice is provided in accordance with that paragraph you will be deemed as not to have declared a personal interest in accordance with this code.

Prejudicial Interests

12

(1) Subject to sub-paragraph (2) below, where you have a personal interest in any business of your authority you also have a prejudicial interest in that business if the interest is one which a member of the public with knowledge of the relevant facts would reasonably regard as so significant that it is likely to prejudice your judgement of the public interest.

(2) Subject to sub-paragraph (3), you will not be regarded as having a prejudicial interest in any business where that business—

(a) relates to—

(i) another relevant authority of which you are also a member;

(ii) another public authority or body exercising functions of a public nature in which you hold a position of general control or management;

(iii) a body to which you have been elected, appointed or nominated by your authority;

(iv) your role as a school governor (where not appointed or nominated by your authority) unless it relates particularly to the school of which you are a governor;

(v) your role as a member of a Local Health Board where you have not been appointed or nominated by your authority;

(b) relates to—

(i) the housing functions of your authority where you hold a tenancy or lease with your authority, provided that you do not have arrears of rent with your authority of more than two months, and provided that those functions do not relate particularly to your tenancy or lease;

(ii) the functions of your authority in respect of school meals, transport and travelling expenses, where you are a guardian, parent, grandparent or have parental responsibility (as defined in section 3 of the Children Act 1989) of a child in full time education, unless it relates particularly to the school which that child attends;

(iii) the functions of your authority in respect of statutory sick pay under Part XI of the Social Security Contributions and Benefits Act 1992, where you are in receipt of, or are entitled to the receipt of such pay from your authority;

(iv) the functions of your authority in respect of an allowance or payment made under sections 22(5), 24(4) and 173 to 176 of the Local Government Act 1972, an allowance or pension under section 18 of the Local Government and Housing Act 1989 or an allowance or payment under section 100 of the Local Government Act 2000;

(c) your role as a community councillor in relation to a grant, loan or other form of financial assistance made by your community council to community or voluntary organisations up to a maximum of £500.

(3) The exemptions in subparagraph (2)(a) do not apply where the business relates to the determination of any approval, consent, licence, permission or registration.

Overview and Scrutiny Committees

13

You also have a prejudicial interest in any business before an overview and scrutiny committee of your authority (or of a sub-committee of such a committee) where—

(a) that business relates to a decision made (whether implemented or not) or action taken by your authority's executive, board or another of your authority's committees, sub-committees, joint committees or joint sub-committees; and

(b) at the time the decision was made or action was taken, you were a member of the executive, board, committee, sub-committee, joint-committee or joint sub-committee mentioned in sub-paragraph (a) and you were present when that decision was made or action was taken.

Participation in Relation to Disclosed Interests

14

(1) Subject to sub-paragraphs (2), (3) and (4), where you have a prejudicial interest in any business of your authority you must, unless you have obtained a dispensation from your authority's standards committee—

(a) withdraw from the room, chamber or place where a meeting considering the business is being held—

(i) where sub-paragraph (2) applies, immediately after the period for making representations, answering questions or giving evidence relating to the business has ended and in any event before further consideration of the business begins, whether or not the public are allowed to remain in attendance for such consideration; or

(ii) in any other case, whenever it becomes apparent that that business is being considered at that meeting;

(b) not exercise executive or board functions in relation to that business;

(c) not seek to influence a decision about that business;

(d) not make any written representations (whether by letter, facsimile or some other form of electronic communication) in relation to that business; and

(e) not make any oral representations (whether in person or some form of electronic communication) in respect of that business or immediately cease to make such oral representations when the prejudicial interest becomes apparent.

(2) Where you have a prejudicial interest in any business of your authority you may attend a meeting but only for the purpose of making representations, answering questions or giving evidence relating to the business, provided that the public are also allowed to attend the meeting for the same purpose, whether under a statutory right or otherwise.

(3) Sub-paragraph (1) does not prevent you attending and participating in a meeting if—

(a) you are required to attend a meeting of an overview or scrutiny committee, by such committee exercising its statutory powers; or

(b) you have the benefit of a dispensation provided that you—

(i) state at the meeting that you are relying on the dispensation; and

(ii) before or immediately after the close of the meeting give written notification to your authority containing—

(aa) details of the prejudicial interest;

(bb) details of the business to which the prejudicial interest relates;

(cc) details of, and the date on which, the dispensation was granted; and

(dd) your signature.

(4) Where you have a prejudicial interest and are making written or oral representations to your authority in reliance upon a dispensation, you must provide details of the dispensation within any such written or oral representation and, in the latter case, provide written notification to your authority within 14 days of making the representation.

Part 4

The Register of Members' Interests

Registration of Financial and Other Interests and Memberships and Management Positions

15

(1) Subject to sub-paragraph (3), you must, within 28 days of—

(a) your authority's code of conduct being adopted or the mandatory provisions of this model code being applied to your authority; or

(b) your election or appointment to office (if that is later),

register your financial interests and other interests, where they fall within a category mentioned in paragraph 10(2)(a) in your authority's register maintained under section 81(1) of the Local Government Act 2000 by providing written notification to your authority's monitoring officer.

(2) You must, within 28 days of becoming aware of any new personal interest or change to any personal interest registered under sub-paragraph (1), register that new personal interest or change by providing written notification to your authority's monitoring officer.

(3) Sub-paragraphs (1) and (2) do not apply to sensitive information determined in accordance with paragraph 16(1).

(4) Sub-paragraph (1) will not apply if you are a member of a relevant authority which is a community council when you act in your capacity as a member of such an authority.

Sensitive Information

16

(1) Where you consider that the information relating to any of your personal interests is sensitive information, and your authority's monitoring officer agrees, you need not include that information when registering that interest, or, as the case may be, a change to the interest under paragraph 15.

(2) You must, within 28 days of becoming aware of any change of circumstances which means that information excluded under sub-paragraph (1) is no longer sensitive information, notify your authority's monitoring officer asking that the information be included in your authority's register of members' interests.

(3) In this code, 'sensitive information' ('*gwybodaeth sensitif*') means information whose availability for inspection by the public creates, or is likely to create, a serious risk that you or a person who lives with you may be subjected to violence or intimidation.

Registration of Gifts and Hospitality

17

You must, within 28 days of receiving any gift, hospitality, material benefit or advantage above a value specified in a resolution of your authority, provide written notification to your authority's monitoring officer of the existence and nature of that gift, hospitality, material benefit or advantage.

ACCOUNTS AND AUDIT (ENGLAND) REGULATIONS 2011

(SI 2011/817)

PART 1

INTRODUCTORY

1 Citation, commencement and application

(1) These Regulations may be cited as the Accounts and Audit (England) Regulations 2011 and come into force on 31st March 2011.

(2) These Regulations apply in relation to England only.

(3) These Regulations apply as follows—

- (a) Regulations 2, 4 to 6(2), and 21 to 28 apply to all relevant bodies;
- (b) Regulations 6(3) to 11 apply to larger relevant bodies;
- (c) Regulations 12 to 16 apply to smaller relevant bodies;
- (d) Regulations 17 to 20 apply to the particular relevant bodies mentioned in Part 5; and
- (e) Regulations 4 to 28 apply, with all necessary modifications, to the accounts of an officer whose accounts are required to be audited by section 26 (audit of accounts of officers) of the 1998 Act.

2 Interpretation

(1) In these Regulations—

"the 1972 Act" means the Local Government Act 1972;

"the 1989 Act" means the Local Government and Housing Act 1989;

"the 1998 Act" means the Audit Commission Act 1998;

"notice by advertisement" means a notice published in one or more local newspapers circulating in the area of the relevant body;

"parish meeting" means a parish meeting of a parish not having a separate parish council;

"relevant body" means a body whose accounts are required to be audited in accordance with section 2 (required audit of accounts) of the 1998 Act other than a NHS body as defined in paragraph 1 of Schedule 15 to the National Health Service Act 2006 or a local probation board;

"larger relevant body" means a relevant body which is not a smaller relevant body;

"smaller relevant body" means a relevant body which is not a local authority for the purposes of Part 1 (capital finance etc and accounts) of the Local Government Act 2003, which—

- (a) for an established body, meets the qualifying condition for the year concerned, or for either of the two immediately preceding years,
- (b) for a newly established body, meets the qualifying condition for its first or second year,

the qualifying condition being that the body's gross income or gross expenditure (whichever is higher) is not more than £6.5 million;

"working day" means any day other than a Saturday, a Sunday, Christmas Day, Good Friday or a day which is a bank holiday in England under the Banking and Financial Dealings Act 1971; and

"year" means the period of 12 months ending with 31st March.

(2) Any reference in these Regulations to the "responsible financial officer" means—

(a)   the person who, by virtue of—
   (i)   section 151 (financial administration) of the 1972 Act;
   (ii)   section 17(1) (accounts) of the Norfolk and Suffolk Broads Act 1988;
   (iii) section 112(1) (financial administration as to certain authorities) of the Local Government Finance Act 1988;
   (iv)   section 6(1) (officer responsible for financial administration of certain authorities) of the 1989 Act;
   (v)   paragraph 13(6) of Schedule 7 (National Park Authorities) to the Environment Act 1995; or
   (vi)   section 127(2) (proper financial administration and chief finance officer) of the Greater London Authority Act 1999;

as the case may be, is responsible for the administration of the financial affairs of a relevant body or, if no person is so responsible, the person who is responsible for keeping the accounts of such a body, or

(b)   if the person referred to in sub-paragraph (a) is unable to act owing to absence or illness, such member of that person's staff as is nominated by that person for the purposes of section 114 (functions of responsible officer as regards reports) of the Local Government Finance Act 1988 or, if no nomination is made under that section, such member of staff nominated by the person referred to in sub-paragraph (a) for the purposes of these Regulations.

(3)   Any reference in regulations 4 to 28 to a relevant body must, in the case of a parish meeting, be construed as a reference to the chairman of that meeting.

3 Revocations

The instruments listed in the Schedule to these Regulations are revoked.

PART 2

FINANCIAL MANAGEMENT AND INTERNAL CONTROL

4 Responsibility for financial management

(1)   The relevant body is responsible for ensuring that the financial management of the body is adequate and effective and that the body has a sound system of internal control which facilitates the effective exercise of that body's functions and which includes arrangements for the management of risk.

(2)   The relevant body must conduct a review at least once in a year of the effectiveness of its system of internal control.

(3)   The findings of the review referred to in paragraph (2) must be considered—
   (a)   in the case of a larger relevant body, by the members of the body meeting as a whole or by a committee, and
   (b)   in the case of a smaller relevant body, by the members of the body meeting as a whole, and

following the review, the body or committee must approve an annual governance statement, prepared in accordance with proper practices in relation to internal control.

(4)   The relevant body must ensure that the statement referred to in paragraph (3) accompanies—
   (a)   any statement of accounts it is obliged to prepare in accordance with regulation 7, or
   (b)   any accounting statement it is obliged to prepare in accordance with regulation 12.

5 Accounting records and control systems

(1) Subject to paragraphs (2) and (4), and, in so far as they are not in conflict with this paragraph, to any instructions given by a relevant body to its responsible financial officer, that officer must determine, on behalf of the body, its—

    (a)   accounting records, including the form of accounts and supporting accounting records; and

    (b)   accounting control systems,

and such an officer must ensure that the accounting control systems determined by that officer are observed and that the accounting records of the body are kept up to date.

(2) The accounting records determined in accordance with paragraph (1)(a) must be sufficient to show and explain a relevant body's transactions and to enable the responsible financial officer to ensure that any statement of accounts or accounting statement which are prepared under these Regulations, comply with these Regulations.

(3) The accounting records determined in accordance with paragraph (1)(a) must in particular contain—

    (a)   entries from day to day of all sums of money received and expended by the body and the matters to which the income and expenditure or receipts and payments account relate;

    (b)   a record of the assets and liabilities of the body;

    (c)   a record of income and expenditure of the body in relation to claims made, or to be made, by them for contribution, grant or subsidy from any Minister of the Crown, a body to whom such a Minister may pay sums out of moneys provided by Parliament or an EU institution; and

    (d)   a record of any approval given for the purposes of paragraph (4)(c).

(4) The accounting control systems determined in accordance with paragraph (1)(b) must include—

    (a)   measures—

        (i)   to ensure that the financial transactions of the body are recorded as soon as, and as accurately as, reasonably practicable;

        (ii)   to enable the prevention and detection of inaccuracies and fraud, and the reconstitution of any lost records; and

        (iii)   to ensure that risk is appropriately managed;

    (b)   identification of the duties of officers dealing with financial transactions and division of responsibilities of those officers in relation to significant transactions; and

    (c)   procedures to ensure that uncollectable amounts, including bad debts, are not written off except with the approval of the responsible financial officer, or such member of that officer's staff as is nominated by that officer for this purpose.

6 Internal audit

(1) A relevant body must undertake an adequate and effective internal audit of its accounting records and of its system of internal control in accordance with the proper practices in relation to internal control.

(2) Any officer or member of a relevant body must, if the body requires—

    (a)   make available such documents and records as appear to that body to be necessary for the purposes of the audit; and

    (b)   supply the body with such information and explanation as that body considers necessary for that purpose.

(3) A larger relevant body must, at least once in each year, conduct a review of the effectiveness of its internal audit.

(4) The findings of the review referred to in paragraph (3) must be considered, as part of the consideration of the system of internal control referred to in regulation 4(3), by the committee or body referred to in that paragraph.

PART 3

PUBLISHED ACCOUNTS AND AUDIT—LARGER RELEVANT BODIES

7 Statement of accounts

(1) A larger relevant body must prepare, in accordance with proper practices in relation to accounts, a statement of accounts for each year, which must include such of the following accounting statements as are relevant to the functions of the relevant body—

(a)   housing revenue account;

(b)   collection fund;

(c)   firefighters' pension fund;

(d)   any other statements relating to each and every other fund in relation to which the body is required by any statutory provision to keep a separate account.

(2) The statement required by paragraph (1) must include a note—

(a)   demonstrating whether the Dedicated Schools Grant (made under section 14 (power of Secretary of State to give financial assistance for purposes related to education or children etc) of the Education Act 2002) has been deployed in accordance with regulations made under sections 45A (determination of specified budgets of local authority), 45AA (power to require local authorities to make initial determination of schools budget), 47 (determination of schools' budget share), 48(1) and (2) (local authorities' financial schemes) and 138(7) (orders and regulations) of, and paragraph 1(7)(b) of Schedule 14 to, the School Standards and Framework Act 1998;

(b)   except in relation to persons to whom paragraph (c) applies, of the number of employees or senior police officers in the year to which the accounts relate whose remuneration fell in each bracket of a scale in multiples of £5,000 starting with £50,000;

(c)   of the remuneration, set out according to the categories listed in paragraph (3), and the relevant body's contribution to the person's pension, by the relevant body during the relevant year of—

(i)   senior employees, or

(ii)   relevant police officers,

in respect of their employment by the relevant body or in their capacity as a police officer, whether on a permanent or temporary basis, to be listed individually in relation to such persons who must nevertheless be identified by way of job title only (except for persons whose salary is £150,000 or more per year, who must also be identified by name).

(3) The categories are:

(i)   the total amount of salary, fees or allowances paid to or receivable by the person in the current and previous year;

(ii)   the total amount of bonuses so paid or receivable in the current and previous year;

(iii)   the total amount of sums paid by way of expenses allowance that are chargeable to United Kingdom income tax, and were paid to or receivable by the person;

(iv)   the total amount of any compensation for loss of employment paid to or receivable by the person, and any other payments made to or receivable by the person in connection with the termination of their employment by the relevant body, or, in the case of a relevant police officer, the total amount of any payment made to a relevant police officer who ceases to hold office before the end of a fixed term appointment;

(v)   the total estimated value of any benefits received by the person otherwise than in cash that do not fall within (i) to (iv) above, are emoluments of the person, and are received by the person in respect of their employment by the relevant body or in their capacity as a police officer; and

(vi)   in relation to relevant police officers, any payments, whether made under the Police Regulations 2003 or otherwise, which do not fall within (i) to (v) above.

(4) In this regulation—

"contribution to the person's pension" means an amount to be calculated as follows—

(a)   in relation to contributions to the local government pension scheme established under section 7 of the Superannuation Act 1972, the sum of—

(i)   the common rate of employer's contribution specified in a rates and adjustments certificate prepared under regulation 36 (actuarial valuations and certificates) of the Local Government Pension Scheme (Administration) Regulations 2008, being the amount appropriate for that body calculated in accordance with the certificate and regulation 39(4) (employer's contributions) of those Regulations, multiplied by the person's pensionable pay; and

(ii)   if applicable, the appropriate sum within the meaning of regulation 40 (employer's payment following resolution to increase membership or award additional pension) of those Regulations;

(b)   in relation to contributions to the firefighters' pension scheme established under the Fire Services Acts 1947 and 1959, the percentage of the aggregate of the pensionable pay calculated for the purposes of paragraph G2(3) and (4) of Schedule 2 to the Firemen's Pension Scheme Order 1992, multiplied by the person's pensionable pay;

(c)   in relation to contributions to the firefighters' pension scheme established under the Fire and Rescue Services Act 2004, the percentage of the aggregate of the pensionable pay calculated for the purposes of paragraphs (2) and (3) of Rule 2 of Part 13 of Schedule 1 to the Firefighters' Pension Scheme (England) Order 2006, multiplied by the person's pensionable pay;

(d)   in relation to contributions to police pension schemes established under the Police Pensions Regulations 1987 or the Police Pensions Regulations 2006, the percentage of pensionable pay specified in regulation 5(1) (police pension authority contributions) of the Police Pension Fund Regulations 2007, multiplied by the person's pensionable pay;

"employee" includes a member of the relevant body, and a holder of an office under the relevant body, but does not include a person who is an elected councillor, and "employment" is to be construed accordingly;

"relevant police officer" means—

(e)   in relation to a police force maintained under section 2 (maintenance of police forces) of the Police Act 1996, the chief constable,

(f)   in relation to the metropolitan police force, the Commissioner of Police of the Metropolis,

(g)   in relation to the City of London police force, the Commissioner of Police for the City of London, and

(h)   any other senior police officer whose salary is £150,000 per year or more;

"remuneration" means all amounts paid to or receivable by a person, and includes sums due by way of expenses allowance (so far as those sums are chargeable to United Kingdom income tax), and the estimated money value of any other benefits received by an employee otherwise than in cash;

"senior employee" means an employee whose salary is £150,000 or more per year, or an employee whose salary is £50,000 or more per year (to be calculated pro rata for an employee employed for fewer than the usual full time hours for the relevant body concerned) who falls within at least one of the following categories—

    (i)   a person employed by a relevant body to which section 2 (politically restricted posts) of the 1989 Act applies who—

        (i)   has been designated as head of paid service under section 4(1)(a);

        (ii)   is a statutory chief officer within the meaning of section 2(6) of that Act; or

        (iii)   is a non-statutory chief officer within the meaning of section 2(7) of that Act;

    (j)   a person who is the head of staff for any relevant body to which section 4 of the 1989 Act does not apply; or

    (k)   a person who has responsibility for the management of the relevant body to the extent that the person has power to direct or control the major activities of the body (in particular activities involving the expenditure of money), whether solely or collectively with other persons; and

"senior police officer" means a member of a police force holding a rank above that of superintendent.

(5)   In the case of a local authority which is required by section 74 of the 1989 Act to keep a housing revenue account, the statement of accounts required by paragraph (1) must include also an account in respect of a reserve for major repairs to property of the authority to which section 74(1) of the 1989 Act for the time being applies (to be called a major repairs reserve), showing in particular—

    (a)   a credit of an amount in respect of any charge for depreciation included in the housing revenue account for that year under item 8 of Part 2 of Schedule 4 to the 1989 Act;

    (b)   a debit in respect of any capital expenditure, within the meaning of section 16 ("capital expenditure") of the Local Government Act 2003, which was—

        (i)   incurred in that year,

        (ii)   met by payments out of the major repairs reserve, and

        (iii)   in respect of any land, houses or other property to which section 74(1) of the 1989 Act for the time being applies, other than capital expenditure for the purpose of demolition of any such property;

    (c)   a debit in respect of any repayment, made in that year, of the principal of any amount borrowed where the repayment was met by payments out of the major repairs reserve; and

    (d)   a debit in respect of the meeting of any liability, in that year, in respect of credit arrangements, other than any liability which, in accordance with proper practices in relation to accounts, must be charged to a revenue account, where the meeting of that liability was met by payments out of the major repairs reserve.

(6) The Common Council of the City of London must in relation to the accounts referred to in paragraph 2 of Schedule 2 (accounts subject to audit) to the 1998 Act prepare for each year, in accordance with proper practices in relation to accounts, a statement of accounts including—

(a)   a summarised statement of capital expenditure in relation to each of the funds mentioned in that paragraph, differentiated in respect of different services and showing the sources of finance of the year's total capital expenditure incurred in the period;

(b)   a summarised statement of the income and expenditure of each of those funds; and

(c)   a balance sheet in respect of each of those funds,

and in relation to amounts shown in pursuance of sub-paragraphs (b) and (c) must show any corresponding amounts for the immediately preceding period.

8 Signing, approval and publication of statement of accounts

(1) A larger relevant body must ensure that the statement of accounts required by paragraphs (1) or (6) of regulation 7, as the case may be, is prepared in accordance with these Regulations.

(2) Before the approval referred to in paragraph (3) is given, the responsible financial officer of a larger relevant body must, no later than 30th June immediately following the end of a year, sign and date the statement of accounts, and certify that it presents a true and fair view of the financial position of the body at the end of the year to which it relates and of that body's income and expenditure for that year.

(3) Subject to paragraph (4), a larger relevant body must, no later than 30th September in the year immediately following the end of the year to which the statement relates—

(a)   consider either by way of a committee or by the members meeting as a whole the statement of accounts;

(b)   following that consideration, approve the statement of accounts by a resolution of that committee or meeting;

(c)   following approval, ensure that the statement of accounts is signed and dated by the person presiding at the committee or meeting at which that approval was given; and

(d)   publish (which must include publication on the body's website), the statement of accounts together with any certificate, opinion, or report issued, given or made by the auditor under section 9 (general report) of the 1998 Act.

(4) The responsible financial officer must re-certify the presentation of the statement of accounts before the relevant body approves it.

(5) A larger relevant body must keep copies of the documents mentioned in paragraph (3)(d) for purchase by any person on payment of a reasonable sum.

9 Procedure for public inspection of accounts

The procedure for public inspection of accounts for a larger relevant body, mentioned in regulation 22, is that it must make the documents mentioned in that regulation available for public inspection for 20 working days before the date appointed by the auditor under regulation 21.

10 Notice of public rights

(1) The procedure for a larger relevant body to give notice of public rights, mentioned in regulation 24, is that, not later than 14 days before the commencement of the period during which the accounts and other documents are made available in pursuance of regulation 9, the body must give notice by advertisement and on its website of the matters set out in paragraph (2).

(2) The matters referred to in paragraph (1) are—

(a)   the period during which the accounts and other documents referred to in paragraph (1) will be available for inspection in accordance with regulation 9;

(b)   the place at which, and the hours during which, they will be so available;

(c)   the name and address of the auditor;

(d)   the provisions contained in section 15 (inspection of documents and questions at audit) and section 16 (right to make objections at audit) of the 1998 Act; and

(e)   the date appointed under regulation 21 for the exercise of rights of electors.

11 Notice of conclusion of audit

As soon as reasonably possible after conclusion of an audit, a larger relevant body must give notice by advertisement and on its website stating that the audit has been concluded and that the statement of accounts is available for inspection by local government electors and including—

(a)   a statement of the rights conferred on local government electors by section 14 (inspection of statements of accounts and auditors' reports) of the 1998 Act;

(b)   the address at which and the hours during which those rights may be exercised; and

(c)   details of where the statement of accounts can be found on the body's website.

PART 4

PUBLISHED ACCOUNTS AND AUDIT—SMALLER RELEVANT BODIES

12 Accounting statements

(1) Subject to paragraph (2), a smaller relevant body must prepare for each year either—

(a)   an income and expenditure account and a statement of balances in accordance with, and in the form specified in any Annual Return required by, proper practices in relation to accounts; or

(b)   a statement of accounts prepared in accordance with regulation 7, as if that regulation applied to smaller relevant bodies.

(2) Where in relation to a smaller relevant body, the gross income or expenditure (whichever is the higher) was not more than £200,000 for the year or for either of the two immediately preceding years, the body may, instead of complying with paragraph (1), prepare in accordance with, and in the form specified in any Annual Return required by, proper practices in relation to accounts, a record of receipts and payments of the body in relation to that year.

13 Signing, approval and publication of accounting statements

(1) A smaller relevant body must ensure that the accounting statements required by regulation 12 are prepared in accordance with these Regulations.

(2) Before the approval referred to in paragraph (3) is given, the responsible financial officer of a relevant body must—

(a)   in a case where the body has prepared a statement of accounts, sign and date the statement of accounts, and certify that it presents a true and fair view of the financial position of the body at the end of the year to which it relates and of that body's income and expenditure for that year;

(b)   in a case where the body has prepared a record of receipts and payments, sign and date that record, and certify that it properly presents that body's receipts and payments for the year to which the record relates; or

(c)   in any other case, sign and date the income and expenditure account and statement of balances, and certify that they present fairly the financial position of the body at the end of the year to which they relate and that body's income and expenditure for that year.

(3)   A smaller relevant body must, no later than 30th June—

(a)   consider the accounting statements by the members meeting as a whole;

(b)   following that consideration, approve the accounting statements for submission to the auditor by a resolution of the body; and

(c)   following approval, ensure that the accounting statements are signed and dated by the person presiding at the meeting at which that approval was given.

(4)   A smaller relevant body must, no later than 30th September in the year immediately following the end of the year to which the statement relates, either—

(a)   publish the accounting statements by means other than solely by reference in the minutes of meetings, together with any certificate, opinion, or report issued, given or made by the auditor under section 9 (general report) of the 1998 Act; or

(b)   display a notice containing the documents mentioned in sub-paragraph (a) in a conspicuous place or places in the area of the body for a period of at least 14 days.

(5)   A smaller relevant body must keep copies of the documents mentioned in paragraph (4)(a) for purchase by any person on payment of a reasonable sum.

14 Procedure for public inspection of accounts

The procedure for public inspection of accounts for a smaller relevant body, mentioned in regulation 22, is that the body must make the documents mentioned in that regulation available for public inspection on reasonable notice, during a period of 20 working days before the date appointed by the auditor under regulation 21.

15 Notice of public rights

(1)   The procedure for a smaller relevant body to give notice of public rights, mentioned in regulation 24, is that it must display, in a conspicuous place or places in the area of the body for a period of at least 14 days immediately prior to the period during which the accounts and other documents are made available under regulation 14, a notice containing the matters set out in paragraph (2).

(2)   The matters referred to in paragraph (1) are—

(a)   the period during which the accounts and other documents referred to in paragraph (1) will be available for inspection in accordance with regulation 14;

(b)   details of the manner in which notice should be given of an intention to inspect the accounts and other documents;

(c)   the name and address of the auditor;

(d)   the provisions contained in section 15 (inspection of documents and questions at audit) and section 16 (right to make objections at audit) of the 1998 Act; and

(e)   the date appointed under regulation 21 for the exercise of rights of electors.

16 Notice of conclusion of audit

As soon as reasonably possible after conclusion of an audit, a smaller relevant body must display a notice in a conspicuous place or places in the area of the body for a period of at least 14 days stating that the audit has been completed and that the relevant accounting statements required by these Regulations are available for inspection by local government electors on reasonable notice and including—

(a)   a statement of the rights conferred on local government electors by section 14 (inspection of statements of accounts and auditors' reports) of the 1998 Act; and

(b)   details of the manner in which notice should be given of an intention to exercise the right of inspection.

PART 5

PARTICULAR AUTHORITIES

17 Passenger Transport Executives

A statement of accounts of a Passenger Transport Executive must be prepared as if the proper practices in relation to accounts applicable to a local authority were, so far as appropriate, applicable to an Executive.

18 Internal drainage boards

An internal drainage board must charge to a revenue account an amount equal to the payments and contributions statutorily payable for that year under an arrangement accounted for as a defined benefit pension plan or as other long-term employee benefits (as defined in accordance with proper practices in relation to accounts).

19 Summary statement of accounts—Greater London Authority

The summary statement of accounts which the Greater London Authority ("the Authority") is required to prepare by section 134 (summary of statement of accounts of Authority) of the Greater London Authority Act 1999 must be prepared in accordance with proper practices in relation to accounts and must include—

(a)   a summary of the income and expenditure of the Authority;

(b)   a summary of the income and expenditure of each of the functional bodies and the London Pensions Fund Authority;

(c)   a summary of the capital expenditure of the Authority;

(d)   a summary of the capital expenditure of each of the functional bodies and the London Pensions Fund Authority.

20 Joint committees etc

(1)   Any joint committee, joint board, combined authority or National Park authority to which these regulations apply must deposit with each constituent authority—

(a)   where the committee, board or authority is a smaller relevant body, within the period of fourteen days specified by regulation 16, a copy of the auditor's report and accounting statements, and

(b)   where the committee, board or authority is a larger relevant body, on giving notice under regulation 11, a copy of the auditor's report and statement of accounts.

(2)   In this regulation, "constituent authority" means any county, district, London borough or parish council for the time being entitled to appoint members of the committee, board or authority in question; and in relation to a National Park authority includes—

(a)   the Secretary of State; and

(b)   Natural England.

PART 6

AUDIT PROCEDURE

21 Appointment of date for the exercise of rights of electors

The auditor must, for the purpose of the exercise of rights under section 15 (right of local government elector to request an opportunity to question the auditor about the accounts) and 16 (right of local government elector to make objections to the auditor) of the 1998 Act, appoint a date on or after which those rights may be exercised, and must notify the relevant body concerned of that date.

22 Public inspection of accounts

A relevant body notified under regulation 21 must make the accounts and other documents mentioned in section 15 (inspection of documents and questions at audit) of the 1998 Act available in accordance with the procedure specified for larger relevant bodies in regulation 9, or for smaller relevant bodies in regulation 14, as appropriate.

23 Alteration of accounts

Except with the consent of the auditor, accounts and other documents must not be altered after the date on which they are first made available for inspection in pursuance of either regulations 9 or 14.

24 Notice of public rights

A relevant body must give notice of public rights in accordance with the procedure specified for larger relevant bodies in regulation 10, or for smaller relevant bodies in regulation 15.

25 Written notice of objection

(1) Any written notice of an objection given in pursuance of section 16 of the 1998 Act must state the facts on which the local government elector relies, and contain, so far as possible—

(a) particulars of any item of account which is alleged to be contrary to law, and

(b) particulars of any matter in respect of which it is proposed that the auditor could make a report under section 8 (immediate and other reports in public interest) of that Act.

(2) In relation to relevant bodies to which Part 3 of the Local Government Act 2000 (conduct of local government members and employees) applies, paragraph (1) applies in respect of matters occurring before such a body first adopted a code of conduct under that Act or such a code was first applied to it, with the addition of particulars of any person from whom it is alleged that the auditor should certify under section 18 (recovery of amount not accounted for etc) of the 1998 Act that a sum or amount of loss or deficiency is due and the sum of that amount.

26 Notice of conclusion of audit

A relevant body must give notice of conclusion of audit in accordance with the procedure specified for larger relevant bodies in regulation 11, or for smaller relevant bodies in regulation 16, as appropriate.

27 Publication of annual audit letter

As soon as reasonably possible after receipt of the annual letter from the auditor, the members of the relevant body meeting as a whole or, in the case of a larger relevant body only, a committee of that body, must meet to consider it and following that consideration must—

(a) publish the annual audit letter received from the auditor; and

(b) make copies available for purchase by any person on payment of such sum as the relevant body may reasonably require.

28 Extraordinary audit

Where, under section 25 (extraordinary audit) of the 1998 Act, the Commission directs an auditor to hold an extraordinary audit of accounts of a relevant body, the body must—

(a) in the case of a larger relevant body, give notice by advertisement, and

(b) in the case of a smaller relevant body, display a notice in a conspicuous place or places in the area of the body, concerning the right of any local government elector for the area to which the accounts relate to make objections to any of those accounts.

SCHEDULE

Regulation 3

(1) Instruments revoked	(2) References	(3) Extent of revocation
The Accounts and Audit Regulations 2003	SI 2003/533	The whole Regulations
The Accounts and Audit (Amendment) Regulations 2004	SI 2004/556	The whole Regulations
The Fire and Rescue Services Act 2004 (Consequential Amendments) (England) Order 2004	SI 2004/3168	Regulation 67
The Accounts and Audit (Amendment) (England) Regulations 2006	SI 2006/564	The whole Regulations
The Local Government (Early Termination of Employment) (Discretionary Compensation) (England and Wales) Regulations 2006	SI 2006/2914	Paragraph 4 of Schedule 1 to the Regulations
The Offender Management Act 2007 (Consequential Amendments) Order 2008	SI 2008/912	Paragraph 5 of Schedule 2 to the Regulations
The Accounts and Audit (Amendment) (England) Regulations 2009	SI 2009/473	The whole Regulations
The Accounts and Audit (Amendment No 2) (England) Regulations 2009	SI 2009/3322	The whole Regulations

PARISH COUNCILS (GENERAL POWER OF COMPETENCE) (PRESCRIBED CONDITIONS) ORDER 2012

(SI 2012/965)

1 Citation, commencement and interpretation

(1) This Order may be cited as the Parish Councils (General Power of Competence) (Prescribed Conditions) Order 2012 and comes into force on the day after the day on which it is made.

(2) In this Order—

"annual meeting" means a meeting of a parish council held in pursuance of paragraph 7(1) of Schedule 12 to the Local Government Act 1972;

"relevant annual meeting" means an annual meeting that takes place in a year of ordinary elections of parish councillors.

2 Prescribed conditions

The conditions prescribed for the purposes of section 8(2) of the Localism Act 2011 are those specified in the Schedule to this Order.

3 Transitional provision

(1) This article applies to a parish council in the circumstances described in paragraph (2).

(2) The circumstances are that—

- (a) the parish council has passed a resolution under paragraph 1 of the Schedule; and
- (b) at the next relevant annual meeting to be held after the meeting at which that resolution is passed, the parish council does not pass another resolution under that paragraph.

(3) The council shall continue to be an eligible parish council for the purpose of completing any activity—

- (a) undertaken in the exercise of the general power, but
- (b) not completed before the day of the meeting referred to in paragraph (2)(b).

SCHEDULE
CONDITIONS OF ELIGIBILITY

Article 2

1

The council has resolved at a meeting of the council and each subsequent relevant annual meeting that it meets the conditions in paragraph 2 below.

2

(1) At the time a resolution under paragraph 1 is passed—

- (a) the number of members of the council that have been declared to be elected, whether at ordinary elections or at a by-election, is equal to or greater than two-thirds of the total number of members of the council;
- (b) the clerk to the parish council holds—
  - (i) the Certificate in Local Council Administration;
  - (ii) the Certificate of Higher Education in Local Policy;
  - (iii) the Certificate of Higher Education in Local Council Administration; or
  - (iv) the first level of the foundation degree in Community Engagement and Governance awarded by the University of Gloucestershire or its successor qualifications; and
- (c) the clerk to the parish council has completed the relevant training, unless such training was required for the purpose of obtaining a qualification of a description mentioned in paragraph (b).

(2) For the purposes of this paragraph "relevant training" means training—

- (a) in the exercise of the general power;
- (b) provided in accordance with the national training strategy for parish councils adopted by the National Association of Local Councils, as revised from time to time.

RELEVANT AUTHORITIES (DISCLOSABLE PECUNIARY INTERESTS) REGULATIONS 2012

(SI 2012/1464)

1 Citation, commencement and interpretation

(1) These Regulations may be cited as the Relevant Authorities (Disclosable Pecuniary Interests) Regulations 2012 and shall come into force on 1st July 2012.

(2) In these regulations—

"the Act" means the Localism Act 2011;

"body in which the relevant person has a beneficial interest" means a firm in which the relevant person is a partner or a body corporate of which the relevant person is a director, or in the securities of which the relevant person has a beneficial interest;

"director" includes a member of the committee of management of an industrial and provident society;

"land" excludes an easement, servitude, interest or right in or over land which does not carry with it a right for the relevant person (alone or jointly with another) to occupy the land or to receive income;

"M" means a member of a relevant authority;

"member" includes a co-opted member;

"relevant authority" means the authority of which M is a member;

"relevant period" means the period of 12 months ending with the day on which M gives a notification for the purposes of section 30(1) or section 31(7), as the case may be, of the Act;

"relevant person" means M or any other person referred to in section 30(3)(b) of the Act;

"securities" means shares, debentures, debenture stock, loan stock, bonds, units of a collective investment scheme within the meaning of the Financial Services and Markets Act 2000 and other securities of any description, other than money deposited with a building society.

2 Specified pecuniary interests

The pecuniary interests which are specified for the purposes of Chapter 7 of Part 1 of the Act are the interests specified in the second column of the Schedule to these Regulations.

SCHEDULE

Regulation 2

Subject	Prescribed description
Employment, office, trade, profession or vocation	Any employment, office, trade, profession or vocation carried on for profit or gain.

Subject	Prescribed description
Sponsorship	Any payment or provision of any other financial benefit (other than from the relevant authority) made or provided within the relevant period in respect of any expenses incurred by M in carrying out duties as a member, or towards the election expenses of M. This includes any payment or financial benefit from a trade union within the meaning of the Trade Union and Labour Relations (Consolidation) Act 1992.
Contracts	Any contract which is made between the relevant person (or a body in which the relevant person has a beneficial interest) and the relevant authority— (a) under which goods or services are to be provided or works are to be executed; and (b) which has not been fully discharged.
Land	Any beneficial interest in land which is within the area of the relevant authority.
Licences	Any licence (alone or jointly with others) to occupy land in the area of the relevant authority for a month or longer.
Corporate tenancies	Any tenancy where (to M's knowledge)— (a) the landlord is the relevant authority; and (b) the tenant is a body in which the relevant person has a beneficial interest.
Securities	Any beneficial interest in securities of a body where— (a) that body (to M's knowledge) has a place of business or land in the area of the relevant authority; and (b) either— (i) the total nominal value of the securities exceeds £25,000 or one hundredth of the total issued share capital of that body; or (ii) if the share capital of that body is of more than one class, the total nominal value of the shares of any one class in which the relevant person has a beneficial interest exceeds one hundredth of the total issued share capital of that class.

Appendix III

USEFUL CONTACTS

Action with Communities in Rural England (ACRE) Somerford Court Somerford Road Cirencester, Glos GL7 1TW	Tel: 01285 653477 Fax: 01285 654537 Email: acre@acre.org.uk Website: www.acre.org.uk
Age UK Tavis House 1-6 Tavistock Square London WC1H 9NA	Tel: 0800 169 6565 Website: www.ageuk.org.uk
Arboricultural Association The Malthouse Stroud Green Standish Stonehouse Glos GL10 3DL	Tel: 01242 522152 Fax 01242 577766 Email: admin@trees.org.uk Website: www.trees.org.uk
Arts Council of England 14 Great Peter Street London SW1P 3NQ	Tel: 0845 300 6200 Fax: 0161 934 4426 Textphone: 020 7793 6564 Email: enquiries@artscouncil.org.uk Website: www.artscouncil.org.uk
Arts Council of Wales Bute Place Cardiff CF10 5AL	Tel: 0845 8734 900 Fax: 029 2044 1400 Minicom: 029 20 390027 Email: info@artscouncilofwales.org.uk Website: www.artswales.org.uk
Association for Neighbourhood Democracy Room G43 Baskerville House Broad Street Birmingham B1 2ND	Tel: 0121 200 1027
Audit Commission 1st Floor, Millbank Tower Millbank	Tel: 020 7828 1212 Email: public-enquiries@audit-commission.gov.uk

London SW1P 1HQ	Website: www.audit-commission.gov.uk
Auditor General for Wales	see Wales Audit Office
Big Lottery Fund 2 St. James' Gate	Tel: 020 7211 1888
	Email: customer.services@biglotteryfund.otg.uk
Newcastle NE1 4BE	Website: www.biglotteryfund.org.uk
British Telecommunications (BT) BT Group plc BT Centre 81 Newgate Street London EC1A 7AJ	Tel: 0800 800 150 Website: www.btplc.com
Campaign to Protect Rural England 5-11 Lavington Street London SE1 0NZ	Tel: 020 7981 2800 Fax: 020 7981 2899 Email: info@cpre.org.uk Website: www.cpre.org.uk
Campaign for the Protection of Rural Wales Ty Gwyn 31 High Street Welshpool Powys SY21 7YD	Tel: 01938 552525 / 556212 Fax: 01938 871552 Email: info@cprwmail.org.uk Website: www.cprw.org.uk
Canal & River Trust First Floor North Station House, 500 Elder Gate, Milton Keynes MK9 1BB	Tel: 0303 040 4040 Email: customer.services@canalrivertrust.org.uk Website: canalrivertrust.org.uk
Charities Official Investment Fund CCLA Management Ltd Senator House 85 Queen Victoria Street London EC4V 4ET	Tel: 0800 022 3505 Fax: 0844 561 5126 Email: clientservice@ccla.co.uk Website: www.ccla.co.uk
Charity Commission 30 Millbank London SW1P 4DU	Tel: 0845 300 0218 Website: www.charitycommission.gov.uk/
Civic Voice Unit 101 82 Wood Street, The Tea Factory, Liverpool L1 4DQ	Tel: 0151 708 9920 Email: info@civicvoice.org.uk Website: www.civicvoice.org.uk

Commission for Local Administration in England (Local Government Ombudsman)	Tel: 0300 061 0614
PO Box 4771	Fax: 024 7682 0001
Coventry CV4 0EH	Website: www.lgo.org.uk
Communities and Local Government, Department for	Tel: 030 3444 0000
Eland House	Email: contactus@communities.gsi.gov.uk
Bressenden Place	Website: www.gov.uk/government/organisations/department-for-communities-and-local-government
London SW1E 5DU	
Community Engagement & Governance	Tel: 01242 714551
University of Gloucestershire	
Francis Close Hall	Website: www.glos.ac.uk
Swindon Road	
Cheltenham	
Gloucestershire GL50 4AZ	
Copyright Licensing Agency	Tel: 020 7400 3100
Saffron House	Fax: 020 7400 3101
6-10 Kirby Street	Email: cla@cla.co.uk
London EC1N 8TS	Website: www.cla.co.uk
Country Land and Business Association	Tel: 020 7235 0511
16 Belgrave Square	Fax: 020 7235 4696
London SW1X 8PQ	Email: mail@cla.org.uk
	Website: www.cla.org.uk
Culture, Media and Sport, Department for	Tel: 020 7211 6000
2-4 Cockspur Street	Email: enquiries@culture.gov.uk
London SW1Y 5DH	Website: www.culture.gov.uk
Electoral Commission	Tel: 020 7271 0500
3 Bunhill Row	Fax: 020 7271 0505
London EC1Y 8YZ	Email info@electoralcommission.org.uk
	Website: www.electoralcommission.gov.uk
Environment, Food & Rural Affairs, Department for (DEFRA)	Tel: 08459 33 55 77
Headquarters:	
Nobel House	Email: defra.helpline@defra.gsi.gov.uk
17 Smith Square	Website: www.defra.gov.uk
London SW1P 3JR	

Fields in Trust 2nd Floor	Tel: 020 7427 2110
15 Crinan Street	Email: info@fieldsintrust.co.uk
London N1 9SQ	Website: www.fieldsintrust.org
Forestry Commission	Tel: 0117 906 6000
620 Bristol Business Park	Fax: 0117 931 2859
Coldharbour Lane	E-mail: fe.england@forestry.gsi.gov.uk
Bristol BS16 1EJ	Website: www.forestry.gov.uk
Gambling Commission	Tel: 0121 230 6666
Victoria Square House	Fax: 0121 230 6720
Victoria Square	Email: info@gamblingcommission.gov.uk
Birmingham B2 4BP	Website: www.gamblingcommission.gov.uk
Health, Department of	Tel: 0207 210 4850 Fax: 0207 210 5952
Richmond House 79 Whitehall London SW1A 2NS	Website: www.dh.gov.uk
Heritage Lottery Fund	Tel: 020 7591 6000
7 Holbein Place	Fax: 020 7591 6001
London SW1W 8NR	Email: enquire@hlf.org.uk
	Website: www.hlf.org.uk
Home Office	Tel: 020 7035 4848
Direct Communication Unit 2 Marsham Street	Fax: 020 7035 4745
London SW1P 4DF	Email: public.enquiries@homeoffice.gsi.gov.uk
	Website: www.homeoffice.gov.uk
Homes & Communities Agency	Tel: 0300 1234 500
149 Tottenham Court Road	Email: mail@homesandcommunities.co.uk
London W1T 7BN	Website: www.homesandcommunities.co.uk
Institute of Local Government Studies (INLOGOV)	Tel: 0121 414 5008
School of Public Policy	Email: c.e.rance@bham.ac.uk
University of Birmingham	Website: www.birmingham.ac.uk
Edgbaston, Birmingham B15 2TT	
Institution of Lighting Engineers	Tel: 01788 576492
Regent House	Fax: 01788 540145
Regent Street	Email: info@ile.org.uk
Rugby CV21 2DT	Website: www.ile.org.uk
Land Registry, HM	Tel: 020 7917 8888

32 Lincoln's Inn Fields	Fax: 020 7955 0110
London WC2A 3PH	Website: www.landregistry.gov.uk
Law Society	Tel: 020 7242 1222
113 Chancery Lane	Fax: 020 7831 0344
London WC2A 1PL	Email: contact@lawsociety.org.uk
	Website: www.lawsociety.org.uk
Local Authorities Mutual Investment Trust (LAMIT)	Tel: 0800 022 3503
CCLA Management Ltd	Fax: 0844 561 5126
Senator House	Email: clientservices@ccla.co.uk
85 Queen Victoria Street	Website: www.ccla.co.uk
London EC4V 4ET	
Local Government Association	Tel: 020 7664 3000
Local Government House	Fax: 020 7664 3030
Smith Square	Email: info@lga.gov.uk
London SW1P 3HZ	Website: www.local.gov.uk
Local Government Boundary Commission for Wales	Tel: 029 2046 4819
Ground Floor, Hastings House	Fax: 029 2046 4823
Fitzalan Court	Email: lgbc@wales.gsi.gov.uk
Cardiff CF10 3BE	Website: www.lgbc-wales.gov.uk
National Archives	Tel: 020 8876 3444
Kew, Richmond	Website: www.nationalarchives.gov.uk
Surrey TW9 4DU	
National Assembly for Wales	Tel: 0845 010 5500
Cardiff Bay	Email: assembly.info@wales.gov.uk/online form
Cardiff CF99 1NA	Website: www.assemblywales.gov.uk
National Association of Councillors	Tel: 0191 378 9947
Council Offices	Email: generalsecretary@nationalassociationof councillors.org
8 Goatbeck Terrace	Website: www.nationalassociationofcouncillors.org
Langley Moor	
Co. Durham DH7 8JJ	
National Association of Local Councils	Tel: 020 7637 1865
109 Great Russell Street	Fax: 020 7436 7451
London WC1B 3LD	Email: nalc@nalc.gov.uk
	Website: www.nalc.gov.uk
National Council of Voluntary Organisations (NCVO)	Tel: 020 7713 6161
Society Building	Fax: 020 7713 6300
8 All Saints Street	Textphone: 0800 01 88 111

London N1 9RL	Helpdesk: 0800 279 8798
	Email: ncvo@ncvo-vol.org.uk
	Website: www.ncvo-vol.org.uk
Natural Resources Wales	Tel: 0300 066 3000
Ty Cambria	Email: enquiries@naturalresourceswa les.gov.uk
Newport Road	Website: www.naturalresourceswales. gov.uk
Cardiff	
CF24 0TP	
National Trust	Tel: 0844 800 1895
Heelis	Fax: 0844 800 4642
Kemble Drive	Textphone: 0844 800 4410
Swindon SN2 2AA	Email: enquiries@thenationaltrust.or g.uk
	Website: www.nationaltrust.org.uk
Natural England	Tel: 0845 600 3078
Foundry House	
3 Millsands	Email: enquiries@naturalengland.org. uk
Riverside Exchange	Website: www.naturalengland.org.uk
Sheffield S3 8NH	
Noise Abatement Society	Tel: 01273 682 223
The Courtyard	Email: info@noise-abatement.org
Shoreham Road	Website: www.noiseabatementsociet y.com
Upper Beeding	
Steyning	
West Sussex BN44 3TN	
One Voice Wales	Tel: 01269 595400
24 College Street	Fax: 01269 598510
Ammanford SA18 2ET	Website: www.onevoicewales.org.uk
Open Spaces Society	Tel: 01491 573535
25a Bell Street	Fax: 01491 573051
Henley-on-Thames	Email: hg@oss.org.uk
Oxfordshire RG9 2BA	Website: www.oss.org.uk
Performing Right Society	Tel: 020 7580 5544
29-33 Berners Street	Fax: 020 7306 4455
London W1T 3AB	Website: www.prsformusic.co.uk
Public Services Ombudsman for Wales	Tel: 0845 601 0987
I Fford yr Hen Gae	Fax: 01656 641199
Pencoed	Website: www.ombudsman-wales.or g.uk
CF35 5LJ	

Public Works Loan Board (PWLB) UK Debt Management Office Eastcheap Court 11 Philpot Lane London EC3M 8UD	Tel: 0845 357 6610 Fax:0845 357 6509 Email: pwlb@dmo.gov.uk Website: www.dmo.gov.uk
Ramblers' Association 2nd Floor Camelford House 87-90 Albert Embankment London SE1 7TW	Tel: 020 7339 8500 Fax: 020 7339 8501 Email: ramblers@ ramblers.org.uk Website: www.ramblers.org.uk
Society for the Protection of Ancient Buildings 37 Spital Square London E1 6DY	Tel: 020 7377 1644 Fax: 020 7247 5296 Email: info@spab.org.uk Website: www.spab.org.uk
Society of Local Council Clerks 8 The Crescent Taunton Somerset TA1 4EA	Tel: 01823 253646 Fax: 01823 253681 Email: admin@slcc.co.uk Website: www.slcc.co.uk
Sport England 3rd Floor Victoria House Bloomsbury Square London WC1B 4SE	Tel: 0845 850 850 Fax: 020 7383 5740 Email: info@sportengland.org Website: www.sportengland.org
Sport Wales Sophia Gardens Cardiff CF11 9SW	Tel: 0845 045 0904 Email: info@sportwales.org.uk Website: www.sportwales.co.uk
Town and Country Planning Association (TCPA) 17 Carlton House Terrace London SW1Y 5AS	Tel: 020 7930 8903 Fax: 020 7930 3280 Email: tcpa@tcpa.org.uk Website: www.tcpa.org.uk
Transport, Department for Great Minster House 33 Horseferry Road London SW1P 4DR	Tel: 0300 330 3000 Contact form: www.dft.gov.uk Website: www. gov.uk/government/or ganisations/depart-for-transport
UK Sport 40 Bernard Street London SW1W 8NB	Tel: 0207 211 5100 Fax: 0207 211 5246 Email: info@uksport.gov.uk Website: www.uksport.gov.uk
UNISON 130 Euston Road London NW1 2AY	Tel: 0845 355 0845 Website: www.unison.org.uk

Wales Audit Office 24 Cathedral Road Cardiff CF11 9LJ	Tel: 029 2032 0500 Fax: 029 2032 0600 Email: info@wao.gov.uk Website: www.wao.gov.uk
Wales Council for Voluntary Action Baltic House Mount Stuart Square Cardiff Bay Cardiff CF10 5FH	Tel: 0800 2888 329 Email: help@wcva.org.uk Website: www.wcva.org.uk
Welsh Assembly Government Cathays Park Cardiff CF10 3NQ	Tel: 0300 060 3300 Email: wag-en@mail.uk.custhelp.com Website: www.wales.gov.uk
Work and Pensions, Department for Caxton House Tothill Street London SW1H 9DA	Website: www.dwp.gov.uk
Women's Institutes, National Federation of 104 New Kings Road London SW6 4LY	Tel: 020 7371 9300 Email: hq@thewi.org.uk Website: www.thewi.co.uk

Index

Index

Index

Index

Index